International Business
Third Edition

D0166132

The third edition of *International Business* offers an action-focused, practical approach to international business, helping students understand the global business environment and its repercussions for executives. The book provides thorough coverage of the field, delving into fundamental concepts and theory; the cultural, political, and economic environment; international business strategies; and even functional management areas.

More comprehensive than competing books, *International Business* includes:

- Strengthened, expanded global cases, examples, and "industry" and "country" mini-cases that give students practical insight into the ways that domestic, foreign, and global companies actually behave within a competitive, global environment
- Updated coverage of key trends that impact how international business functions, including the drivers of globalization, e-commerce and the impact of the Internet, and international entrepreneurship
- New material on international issues, such as technology issues, the impact of the financial crisis, and problems in the EU
- Expanded discussion of the relevant skills and strategies students need to succeed in today's international business environment, including dynamic capabilities, foreign direct investment, and market entry strategies

Also featuring a companion website with a test bank, PowerPoint slides, and instructor's manual, this book is ideal for undergraduate and graduate students and instructors of any international business course. *International Business* combines broad and insightful coverage with practical application and global examples, providing students with a solid understanding of the field, and the tools to succeed within it.

Oded Shenkar is the Ford Motor Company Chair in Global Business Management and Professor of Management and Human Resources at Ohio State University. A Fellow and past Vice President of the Academy of International Business, he has authored numerous books and over a hundred articles.

Yadong Luo is the Emery M. Findley Jr. Distinguished Chair of Graduate Business Studies and Professor of Management at the University of Miami, USA. He is an author of over a dozen books and over a hundred journal articles, and is a Fellow of the Academy of International Business.

Tailan Chi is Professor of International Business and Carl. A. Scupin Faculty Fellow at the University of Kansas, USA. He has published in leading journals of international business and management, including *Journal of International Business Studies, Strategic Management Journal,* and *Management Science.*

International Business

Third Edition

Oded Shenkar, Yadong Luo, and Tailan Chi

Routledge
Taylor & Francis Group

NEW YORK AND LONDON

This edition published 2015
by Routledge
711 Third Avenue, New York, NY 10017

and by Routledge
2 Park Square, Milton Park, Abingdon, Oxon OX14 4RN

Routledge is an imprint of the Taylor & Francis Group, an informa business

© 2015 Taylor & Francis

The right of Oded Shenkar, Yadong Luo, and Tailan Chi to be identified as authors of this work has been asserted by them in accordance with sections 77 and 78 of the Copyright, Designs and Patents Act 1988.

All rights reserved. No part of this book may be reprinted or reproduced or utilised in any form or by any electronic, mechanical, or other means, now known or hereafter invented, including photocopying and recording, or in any information storage or retrieval system, without permission in writing from the publishers.

Trademark notice: Product or corporate names may be trademarks or registered trademarks, and are used only for identification and explanation without intent to infringe.

First edition published by Wiley 2004
Second edition published by Sage 2008

Library of Congress Cataloging-in-Publication Data

CIP data has been applied for

ISBN: 978-0-415-81712-7 (hbk)
ISBN: 978-0-415-81713-4 (pbk)
ISBN: 978-0-203-58486-6 (ebk)

Typeset in Sabon
by Apex CoVantage, LLC

Printed in Canada by Transcontinental Printing Inc.

FSC
www.fsc.org

MIX
Paper from
responsible sources
FSC® C011825

Brief Contents

1   International Business in an Age of Globalization   1

Part 1
Concepts and Theories in International Business   19

2   International Trade Theory and Application   21

3   Foreign Direct Investment Theory and Application   71

4   The Multinational Enterprise   115

Part 2
Endowments and Environments of International Business   153

5   Country Competitiveness   155

6   The Cultural Environment   187

7   The Political and Legal Environment   219

Part 3
Global Markets and Institutions   251

8   International Economic Integration and Institutions   253

9   The International Monetary System and Financial Markets   289

Part 4
International Business Strategies 331

    10 International Entry Strategies 333

    11 MNE Organization Structure and Design 377

    12 Building and Managing Global Strategic Alliances (GSAs) 405

    13 Managing Global Research and Development (R&D) 433

Part 5
Functional International Business Areas 457

    14 Financial Management for Global Operations 459

    15 International Accounting for Global Operations 495

    16 Global Marketing and Supply Chain 523

    17 Global Human Resource Management 563

Part 6
Emerging Issues in International Business 593

    18 Internet and Global E-commerce 595

    19 Social Responsibility and Corruption in the Global Marketplace 615

    20 International Entrepreneurship 639

Detailed Contents

1 International Business in an Age of Globalization   1

OPENING CASE: THE COCA-COLA COMPANY   2

An Age of Globalization   3

    What Does Globalization Mean to You? 4

The Face of Globalization   5

    Who Benefits from Globalization? 6

    The Impact of Globalization 8

Globalization and International Business   10

    What is International Business? 10

    International versus Domestic Business 11

INDUSTRY/COUNTRY BOX: SINOSTONE COMES TO ELBERTON   13

    Why Expand Internationally? 13

The Structure of this Book   15

    Pedagogical Thrust 17

Part 1
Concepts and Theories in International Business   19

2 International Trade Theory and Application   21

OPENING CASE: BANANA WARS   22

International Trade Theories   23

    The Mercantilist Doctrine 23

    Absolute Advantage Theory 24

    Comparative Advantage Theory 25

    Heckscher-Ohlin Theorem 26

    The Leontief Paradox 28

Human Skills and Technology-Based Views   29
The Product Life-Cycle Model   31
Linder's Income-Preference Similarity Theory   34
The New Trade Theory   35
INDUSTRY BOX: THE GLOBAL AUTOMOTIVE INDUSTRY   37
Theory Assessment   37
International Trade Patterns   40
International Trade Volume and Growth   40
Service Trade   44
Trade Measurement   45
Major Exporters and Importers   45
US Trade Partners   46
Trade Balance   50
Arguments for Trade Restrictions   53
The Sovereignty Argument   54
The Lowest Common Denominator Argument   54
Trade Reciprocity   54
Optimal Tariff Theory   55
Infant Industry Argument   55
Types of Trade Barriers   57
Tariff Barriers   57
Non-Tariff Barriers   59
COUNTRY BOX: THE UNITED STATES AND STEEL IMPORTS   60

3   Foreign Direct Investment Theory and Application   71
OPENING CASE: JAPAN CHANGES ITS MIND ABOUT FDI   72
Definition and Types of Foreign Direct Investment   73
FDI versus Foreign Portfolio Investment   74
Types of FDI   74
Entry Mode   75
The Strategic Logic of FDI   76
How the MNE Benefits from Foreign Direct Investment   77
Enhancing Efficiency from Location Advantages   77
Improving Performance from Structural Discrepancies   77
Increasing Return from Ownership Advantages   77
Ensuring Growth from Organizational Learning   78
The Impact of FDI on the Host (Destination) and
   Home (Origin) Countries   79
Employment   79
FDI Impact on Domestic Enterprises in the Host Country   80
Current Theories on FDI   82
Product Life-Cycle Theory   82

Monopolistic Advantage Theory 83
Internalization Theory and other Transaction Cost-Based Theories 84
The Eclectic Paradigm 86
New Perspectives on FDI   88
The Dynamic Capability Perspective 88
The Evolutionary Perspective 90
INDUSTRY BOX: MNEs AND FDI IN THE AUTOMOTIVE INDUSTRY   91
The Real Option Perspective 92
The Integration-Responsiveness Perspective 94
Patterns of FDI   95
FDI Inflows   101
Transnationality and FDI Performance of Individual Economies 103
FDI Entry Forms 106
The Investment Environment   108
FDI Decision Criteria 109
COUNTRY BOX: FDI IN ISRAEL   110

4   The Multinational Enterprise   115

OPENING CASE: JOHNSON & JOHNSON   116
What is a Multinational Enterprise?   117
The Degree of Internationalization 118
History of the MNE 119
The World's Largest MNEs   120
The Growth of Service MNEs 122
The Image of the MNE   125
The MNE in the Public Eye 125
The Borderless Corporation: Myth or Reality? 126
The Competitive Advantage of the MNE   127
Capabilities and Competitive Advantage 128
The MNE from Emerging/Developing Economies (DMNE)   131
The Largest Developing Country MNEs 131
Obstacles Facing MNEs from Developing Economies 134
DMNE Advantage in Global Markets 134
Typical Features of DMNEs 135
COUNTRY BOX: AN ISRAELI FIRM BECOMES
    THE WORLD'S LARGEST GENERIC DRUG MAKER   138
The Small and Medium-Size International Enterprise (SMIE)   139
What is an SMIE? 139
Obstacles to SMIE Internationalization 140
SMIE Advantages in Internationalization 143
SMIE Internationalization Features 143
INDUSTRY BOX: INVESTMENT MANAGEMENT AND THE SMIE   148

Part 2
Endowments and Environments of International Business   **153**

   5   Country Competitiveness   **155**

      OPENING CASE: SINGAPORE'S CHANGING COMPETITIVE
        ADVANTAGE IN THE HARD DISK DRIVE INDUSTRY   156
      Defining Country Competitiveness   157
        Country Competitiveness and MNEs   159
      Country-Level Determinants   160
        Institutional System   161
        Infrastructure   163
        Macroeconomic Soundness   164
        Science, Education, and Innovation   167
        Internationalization   170
      Industry-Level Determinants   171
      INDUSTRY BOX: E-COMMERCE AS AN ELEMENT OF COUNTRY COMPETITIVENESS   175
      Firm-Level Determinants   176
      Individual-Level Determinants   178
      COUNTRY BOX: ITALY: OWNER SNEAKS FACTORY TO POLAND   180
        Interplay of the Four-Level Determinants   181
      Government Role   181

   6   The Cultural Environment   **187**

      OPENING CASE: RENAULT-NISSAN ALLIANCE   188
      What is Culture?   189
      Culture and International Business   189
        Culture Does Not Explain Everything   190
        Correlates of Culture   191
      National Culture Classifications   197
        Hofstede's Dimensions of Culture   197
      COUNTRY BOX: TOYOTA: A SHIFT IN TOYOTA'S CORPORATE CULTURE   198
        Schwartz's Classification   203
        The GLOBE Classification   205
        Trompenaars and Hampden-Turner's Classification   205
        Other Dimensions of Culture   206
        National Culture Clustering   207
        Measuring Cultural Differences   207
      Corporate Culture   210
      Other Layers of Culture   210
        Ethnicity   210
        Industry   210
        Demographics   211
        Ideology   211

Key Cultural Issues   211
   Cultural Etiquette 211
   Cultural Stereotypes 212
   Convergence and Divergence 214
INDUSTRY BOX: ISLAMIC FINANCE   214

7   The Political and Legal Environment   219

OPENING CASE: BOLIVIA NATIONALIZES NATURAL GAS   220
The Political Environment   221
   Political System 222
   The Institutional Context 226
The MNE–Government Relationship   227
   The MNE Relationship with the Host Government 227
   The MNE and its Home Government 230
   Coalition Building and Influence Tactics 231
INDUSTRY BOX: MANAGING POLITICS IN THE AUTOMOTIVE INDUSTRY   232
   Economic Freedom 233
   Political Risk 233
   Regional-Level Politics 237
   Micro-Region Political Processes 238
The Legal Environment   239
   The Institutional Context 239
COUNTRY BOX: INDONESIA: MANUFACTURERS LIFE
  WEATHERS THE STORM IN INDONESIA   240
   Legal Jurisdiction 242
   Legal Issues of Interest to the MNE 243

Part 3
Global Markets and Institutions   251

8   International Economic Integration and Institutions   253

OPENING CASE: 3M'S RESPONSE TO EUROPEAN MARKET INTEGRATION   254
International Economic Integration   255
Global-Level Cooperation Among Nations   257
   The World Trade Organization (WTO) 258
COUNTRY BOX: RUSSIA: RUSSIA JOINS THE WTO   262
   The International Monetary Fund (IMF) 263
   The World Bank Group 264
   Other International Economic Organizations 265
Regional-Level Cooperation Among Nations   267
   Postwar Regional Integration 267
   North America: The North American Free Trade Agreement (NAFTA) 269
   Europe: The European Union (EU) 271

INDUSTRY BOX: SIEMENS SHARPENS ITS FOCUS TO
   RESPOND TO THE SINGLE MARKET   273
   Asia Pacific 274
   Latin America 277
   Africa and the Middle East 279
   Regionalization vs. Globalization 279
Commodity-Level Cooperation Among Nations   281
   Organization of Petroleum Exporting Countries (OPEC) 282
   Other Commodity Agreements 284
Strategic Responses of MNEs   284

9   The International Monetary System and Financial Markets   289

OPENING CASE: FOREIGN EXCHANGE CRISIS IN MEXICO   290
History of the International Monetary System   291
   The Gold Standard Period (1876–1914) 292
   The Inter-War Years and World War II (1914–1944) 292
   The Bretton Woods System (1944–1973) 293
   The Post-Bretton Woods System: 1973–Present 294
Contemporary Exchange Rate Systems   297
   Fixed-Rate System 297
   Crawling Peg System 298
COUNTRY BOX: HONG KONG: SHOULD THE HONG KONG
   DOLLAR RETAIN THE FIXED PEG TO THE US DOLLAR?   299
   Target-Zone Arrangement 300
   Managed Float System 301
   Independent Float System 301
   Advantages and Disadvantages of the Floating System 302
Determination of Foreign Exchange Rates   303
   Foreign Exchange Rate Quotations 303
   Gold Standard 305
   Purchasing Power Parity (PPP) 306
   Interest Rate Parity (IRP) 307
   Foreign Exchange Rate Overshooting 308
   Implications for MNEs: Foreign Exchange Forecasting 310
The Balance of Payments   311
   Current Account 313
   Capital Account 313
   Official Reserves Account 313
International Foreign Exchange Markets   314
   Landscape of the International Foreign Exchange Market 314
   Market Participants and Functions 315
   Transaction Forms 316
   Foreign Exchange Arbitrage 317

Black Market and Parallel Market 318
International Capital Markets   319
International Money Markets 319
International Bond Markets 320
INDUSTRY BOX: US FIRMS FIND CHEAPER FINANCING FROM FOREIGN SOURCES   321
International Stock Markets 321
International Loan Markets 322
Major International Financial Crises in Recent Times   324
The Asian Financial Crisis 324
The Global Financial Crisis 327

Part 4
International Business Strategies   **331**

10 International Entry Strategies   **333**

OPENING CASE: DUPONT'S ENTRY STRATEGIES INTO CHINA   334
Dimensions of a Market Entry Strategy   335
International Location Selection (*Where*)   336
Locational Determinants 337
COUNTRY BOX: FEDERAL EXPRESS SHIFTS ITS HUB FROM
SUBIC BAY TO GUANGZHOU, CHINA   344
Decision Framework 345
Timing Of Entry (*When*)   347
Uncertainty and Potential for Learning 347
Competitive Preemption and Pioneering Costs 349
Decision Framework 352
Entry Mode Selection (*How*)   355
Entry Mode Choices 355
Trade-Centered Entry Modes 355
Transfer-Centered Entry Modes 359
FDI-Centered Entry Modes 362
Decision Framework 368
Greenfield Investment, Acquisition, and Merger 370
INDUSTRY BOX: UNILEVER'S ACQUISITIONS IN LATIN AMERICA   371
The Evolutionary Path 371

11 MNE Organization Structure and Design   **377**

OPENING CASE: PROCTER & GAMBLE: WORLDWIDE STRUCTURE   378
International Strategy and Organization Design   378
Global Integration and Local Responsiveness 379
MNE Strategy and Design 380
Subsidiary Roles and Imperatives 381

MNE Organizational Structures   383
   The National Subsidiary Structure 383
   The International Division Structure 384
   The Global Functional Structure 384
   The Global Geographic Structure 385
COUNTRY BOX: INTERNATIONALIZING THE BOARD OF DIRECTORS   388
   The Global Product Structure 389
INDUSTRY BOX: "FORD 2000"   391
   The Global Matrix Structure 393
Integrating Global Operations   398
   Tools for Global Integration 398
   The Transition Challenge 400
   The Corporate Headquarters 400

12 Building and Managing Global Strategic Alliances (GSAs)   405

OPENING CASE: ALLIANCES BETWEEN INFINEON TECHNOLOGIES
   AG AND MOTOROLA, INC.   406
Defining Global Strategic Alliances   407
   Types of GSAs 407
   Rationales for Building GSAs 409
   Challenges Facing GSAs 411
Building Global Strategic Alliances   413
   Selecting Local Partners 413
   Negotiating Alliance Contracts 417
   Structuring Global Strategic Alliances 418
COUNTRY BOX: SPAIN: FUJITSU IN SPAIN: BARRIERS TO ALLIANCE MANAGEMENT   420
Managing Global Strategic Alliances   421
   Managing Inter-Partner Learning 421
   Exercising Managerial Control 423
   Heightening Cooperation 426
   Thinking Ahead of Exit 428
INDUSTRY BOX: WISDOM GAINED FROM EXPERIENCE IN BUILDING GSAs   429

13 Managing Global Research and Development (R&D)   433

OPENING CASE: INTEL'S R&D NETWORK IN DEVELOPING COUNTRIES   434
Why Globalize R&D?   435
   Benefits and Challenges of Global R&D 437
COUNTRY BOX: INDIA: R&D CENTERS OF GLOBAL COMPANIES IN INDIA   440
Designing and Structuring Global R&D   441
   Types of Foreign R&D Units 441
   Selecting R&D Location 442
INDUSTRY BOX: FORD LOCATES ITS R&D CENTER IN AACHEN, GERMANY   444
   Structuring Global R&D Activities 445

Managing and Operating Global R&D 448
Human Resource Management 448
Autonomy Setting 448
Global Planning 449
Communication Improvement 450
Technology Transfer Across Borders 452

Part 5
Functional International Business Areas **457**

14 Financial Management for Global Operations **459**

OPENING CASE: MINIMIZING EXPOSURE IN RTZ 460
Why Learn Financial Management? 461
International Trade Finance 462
International Trade Payment 462
Export Financing 467
Financing for Global Business 471
Intercompany Financing 471
Equity Financing 472
Debt Financing 473
Local Currency Financing 474
Financing Decisions 475
Managing Foreign Exchange Risk and Exposure 476
Foreign Exchange Risk and Exposure 476
Transaction and Economic Exposures 477
Managing Transaction Exposure 480
Managing Economic (Operating) Exposure 483
INDUSTRY BOX: NETTING IN PHILIPS 486
Global Coordination of Exposure Management 487
COUNTRY BOX: INDIA: INDIA FACES DILEMMA ON FOREIGN EXCHANGE HEDGING 488
Working Capital Management 489
Cash Management 489
Foreign Receivable Management 491

15 International Accounting for Global Operations **495**

OPENING CASE: GLAXO TO SETTLE TAX DISPUTE WITH IRS FOR $3.4 BILLION 496
Country Differences in Accounting 497
Why Accounting Systems Differ Among Countries 497
INDUSTRY BOX: ACCOUNTING DIVERSITY IN SIEMENS 502
National Accounting Zones 502
International Accounting Harmonization 504
International Accounting Standards 505

COUNTRY BOX: AUSTRALIA: ACCOUNTING IN AUSTRALIA 507
Foreign Currency Translation 508
   Commonly Used Translation Methods 509
   Harmonization of Translation Methods 511
   International Accounting Information Systems 512
Transfer Pricing and Taxation Strategies 514
   Why Transfer Pricing? 514
   Transfer Pricing Techniques 515
   Transfer Pricing Regulations and Penalties 516
Tax Havens, Treaties, and Strategies 517
   Tax Havens 517
   Tax Treaties 518
   Other Tax Strategies for MNEs 519

16 Global Marketing and Supply Chain **523**

OPENING CASE: DOMINO'S PIZZA 524
The International Marketing Challenge 525
   Assessing Market Potential 526
Globalization and Localization in International Markets 528
   Globalization Forces 529
   Localization Forces 530
   Product Adaptation 531
COUNTRY BOX: KIMCHI WARS 534
   Country-of-Origin Effect 535
   Branding 537
   Channel Decisions 540
   Promotion 542
   Marketing Alliances 543
The Global Supply Chain 544
   The Globalization of Supply Chains 545
   Global Sourcing 546
   Customizing the Supply Chain 546
   Packaging 547
   Transportation Modes 548
   Crossing National Borders 554
INDUSTRY BOX: GLOBAL LOGISTICS AT WAL-MART 554

17 Global Human Resource Management **563**

OPENING CASE: MANAGING GLOBAL HUMAN RESOURCES AT HSBC 564
Strategic IHRM 565
Staffing the MNE 567
   The Globalization of Boards of Directors 567
INDUSTRY BOX: AIRLINE PILOTS GO GLOBAL 569

COUNTRY BOX: KOREAN COMPANIES SEEK GLOBAL TALENT   570
    Staffing the MNE Ranks   570
    Country-Specific Issues   572
The Expatriate Workforce   573
    Types and Distribution of Expatriates   573
    Using Expatriates: Pros and Cons   574
    Expatriate Failure   574
    Expatriate Selection   575
    Preparing for a Foreign Assignment   576
    Compensation   578
    Culture and Compensation   583
    Repatriation   585
HRM in International Affiliates   586
    Human Resource Problems in Foreign Affiliates   587

Part 6
Emerging Issues in International Business   **593**

  18 Internet and Global E-commerce   **595**

    OPENING CASE: EBAY IN CHINA   596
    Internet and E-commerce Infrastructure   597
      Internet Diffusion   597
    COUNTRY BOX: THE UNITED STATES LAGS BEHIND IN
      HIGH-SPEED INTERNET ACCESS   598
      E-Readiness   599
    Cross-border E-commerce   603
      The Impact of E-commerce on International Business   603
    INDUSTRY BOX: THE ONLINE BROKERAGE INDUSTRY GOES GLOBAL   605
    Global E-commerce Challenges   607
      Standardization Forces   607
      Localization Challenges   608
      Taxation Issues   611

  19 Social Responsibility and Corruption in the Global Marketplace   **615**

    OPENING CASE: SHELL'S BRENT SPAR PROJECT   616
    Corporate Social Responsibility in International Business   617
      MNE Social Responsibilities   618
    INDUSTRY BOX: SOCIAL IMPACT ASSESSMENT STEPS AT SHELL   620
      Global Guidelines and Mandates   621
      A Culture of Social Responsibility   622
      Auditing and Assessing MNE Social Responsibility   623
    Corruption in International Business   624

Definition and Magnitude of Corruption 624
The Origins of Corruption 625
Drawbacks of Corruption 626
Corruption Rankings 626
Types of Corrupt Practices   628
Smuggling 628
Money Laundering 629
Piracy and Counterfeiting 629
Bribe Paying 630
The Foreign Corrupt Practices Act (FCPA) 630
The Globalization of the Fight Against Corruption 632
COUNTRY BOX: DRUG COMPANIES FACE BRIBERY PROBE ON PAYMENTS
TO OFFICIALS OF FOREIGN EMERGING MARKETS   634

20 International Entrepreneurship   639

OPENING CASE: WILL ENTREPRENEURSHIP
HELP JAPAN REGAIN ITS LOST DECADES?   640
Defining International Entrepreneurship   641
Comparative Entrepreneurship   642
Culture and Entrepreneurship 645
Funding New Ventures 646
Cross-Border Entrepreneurship   652
Internationalizing the Born Global Enterprise 652
INDUSTRY BOX: ISRAELI START-UPS IN THE GLOBAL MARKETPLACE   654

Index   657

chapter 1

international business in an age of globalization

AN AGE OF GLOBALIZATION	3
THE FACE OF GLOBALIZATION	5
GLOBALIZATION AND INTERNATIONAL BUSINESS	10
THE STRUCTURE OF THIS BOOK	15

Do You Know?

1. What is globalization? Why is globalization important even to firms that do not have any international involvement at present? How does globalization affect the consumer and the employee?
2. What are the benefits of globalization, and what are its threats, both real and perceived?
3. What do the terms "international business," "international transaction," "international trade," and "international investment" mean? Can you distinguish between the multinational enterprise (MNE) and the international firm?
4. What are the differences between international business and domestic business? What is the source of these differences?
5. Why do firms expand globally? What do they hope to gain and what hazards do they face? Does every firm seek identical goals or face the same obstacles and opportunities when expanding into international markets?

OPENING CASE   The Coca-Cola Company

Atlanta-based Coca-Cola Company, a manufacturer, distributor, and marketer of non-alcoholic beverages, is one of the first examples that comes to mind when people think of a global company. With almost 500 beverage brands, and sales in more than 200 countries, few other companies can match Coca-Cola's worldwide presence or the visibility of its products, particularly its flagship Coke, which has become the symbol of a global product. Studies show that the brand enjoys the highest name recognition in the world. The Coca-Cola Company ranked 59th on the Fortune 500 list for 2012 (up 11 slots from 2011), with roughly $46.54 billion in revenue and $8.57 billion in profit. The company, which first sold trademark-registered Coke in the United States in 1886, relied on international markets for 78 percent of its gallon volume in 2011. At 44.2 percent of the total, net operating revenue was highest for North America in the same year, followed by the Pacific with 11.7 percent, and 10.3 percent for Europe.

Coca-Cola normally sells concentrate, based on the recipe that Dr. John Pemberton invented over a hundred years ago and that has been kept secret ever since, to local bottlers that prepare the beverage and distribute it in their respective markets. However, in some countries it does not grant bottlers full manufacturing rights. Unlike its domestic contracts, its international agreements are limited in time, allowing for termination at the company's discretion, and marketing support, while common, is not provided in all markets. True to the now famous slogan, "think global, act local," the company preserves a coherent marketing theme, yet also adapts product taste and operations to local markets. The "think global, act local" slogan embodies what may be the central dilemma in international business: the need to maintain global strategic focus and leverage scale advantages, while allowing for adaptation to local circumstances in everything from product specifications to packaging and distribution. The company's most global function—advertising—avoids themes that would be controversial in local markets. This is in contrast to its rival Pepsi, which, for example, irked religious circles in Israel with ads showing monkeys as human ancestors. Both its secret concentrate recipe and its marketing know-how are considered key factors in its global success. In addition, the company also achieves cost savings by purchasing certain raw materials centrally in large quantities for its global operations and by siting bottling plants locally (thus reducing shipping costs), particularly in locations where labor and land costs are lower.

Coca-Cola's global success has ruffled some feathers. A few years ago, the European Commission rejected its bid to acquire a French beverage maker, pointing out that it already had a majority share in European Union (EU) markets. More recently, the Chinese Ministry of Commerce blocked its attempt to acquire a privately owned beverage company in China, also on anti-monopoly grounds. The company's argument that it has a tiny share of the total market—defined as all liquids consumed, including water— has fallen on deaf ears. Efforts to promote a global image did not prevent the company from being identified and labeled an American icon, making it a lightning rod for criticism and attacks by anti-US and anti-globalization activists. In 2001, Coca-Cola's facilities were bombed by Muslim rebels in India and by Maoist guerrillas in Nepal. In the years that followed, Coca-Cola has been the target of protests against US policies in Serbia, Europe, and the Arab world, among others.

Source: Coca Cola Annual Report 2011; *Fortune Magazine* 500 list 2012; media reports.

An Age of Globalization

"Globalization" has become one of the buzzwords of modern times. People see its manifestations all around them, from the Coke can in a small village store in Africa, to McDonald's golden arches in a Chinese city, to an article in the local newspaper about the outsourcing of software maintenance to India or the shifting of a call center to Canada. Opinions regarding the impact of globalization vary widely, ranging from praise for its association with rising living standards, to condemnation of its ill effects such as industrial pollution. On the evening news you may hear praise for globalization from a farmer who has just concluded a contract for a large shipment of soybeans to China, only to see it followed by coverage of an anti-globalization demonstration outside a trade conference. So, what is globalization, and why does it generate such diverse and often emotional reactions?

In line with the diversity of opinion, globalization has been defined in numerous ways. In this book, we define **globalization** as the acceleration and extension of the interdependence of economic and business activities across national boundaries. Simply put, this means that a development on one side of the globe will have consequences on another. It is easy to see the impact within a particular industry, for instance, the automotive industry. US-based makers of auto parts such as Delphi and Visteon have been pushed to restructure by pressure from low-cost producers in Asia, Mexico, and Eastern Europe, who can make the same automotive components for less. Volkswagen has demanded concessions from its German workforce as a condition for keeping production locally. Closer to home, the price you pay at the pump is partially determined by energy demand in other countries, with soaring consumption in China and India accounting for much of the doubling of oil prices between 2004 and 2006. This interdependence will not go away. So, both the ongoing process and outcome of globalization have profound implications for not only the economic policies of governments, but also for the strategies of firms around the world. The US National Intelligence Council notes in its 2020 Project Report that "certain aspects of globalization, such as the growing global connectedness, are not likely to go away," and that this will have far reaching consequences for the expansion of international business:

> Interdependence has widened the reach of multinational business, enabling smaller firms as well as large multinationals to market across borders and bringing heretofore non-traded services into the international arena.[1]

What Does Globalization Mean to You?

To the consumer, globalization means more choices, generally lower prices (but not always, as the example of gas prices shows), and an increasingly blurred national identity for products and services. Send a package from New York to London via DHL, and you have contributed to the revenue of the German Postal Service. Buy a Swedish Volvo, and you have increased the revenue of its Chinese owner, Geely Automobile Holdings Limited. Buy a Jaguar, and you have contributed to the bottom line of its Indian owner, Tata Motors. Buy a Dodge, and you have purchased a product of Italian-based Fiat. Buy a foreign brand, and you may find out that it is manufactured in the United States: Honda Civics in Ohio, Mercedes M class in Alabama, Nissan pickup trucks in Tennessee. If you prefer to buy Canadian, you can choose between a GM or a Ford vehicle manufactured in Canada; or you can settle for the Mercedes M class, made in the United States, but advertised in Canada as "made by a Canadian"—alluding to the manager of a US plant. If you are an Australian consumer who wants to buy a locally produced vehicle, you can select between three locally produced foreign brands: Holden (a GM brand whose design is influenced by its German subsidiary Opel), a Ford, or a Toyota. These Australian operations also export to other countries while facing more competition from imports as local tariffs are reduced.

Similar trends can be observed in the service sector. The mortgage on your US property might be underwritten by Swiss bank UBS, your life insurance by French insurer AXA. Your retirement funds might be invested in the stock of Swiss food giant Nestlé and Japanese electronics maker Sony, or managed by German-based Deutsche Bank. The advertisement enticing you to buy Cincinnati-based P&G's Pampers may have been conceived by the UK's Saatchi & Saatchi, but the graphic work may have been done in India. If you buy at your local Wal-Mart, chances are that much of the products on the shelves are made outside the country; Wal-Mart's imports from China, for instance, exceed those of the United Kingdom. Even the student sitting next to you may well be a foreign national, as might be the patient waiting next to you in the hospital clinic. You may take your next vacation in Mexico, rather than in Florida; just remember to take your Chinese-manufactured iPod along for the ride.

In addition to offering a dizzying array of consumer products and services, globalization affects your career prospects. At times, it will also limit your opportunities, as when the transcription of medical records is outsourced to India; at other times, especially if you are better educated, globalization will greatly expand your career choices and opportunities. It is increasingly possible that you will join one of the many foreign firms in the United States upon graduation, or that you will be assigned to work in another country by a US-, local-, or a third-country foreign firm. If you are considering employment with a foreign firm, you may want to know whether the recruiting company tends to open its senior-most ranks to other than its own nationals. If in doubt, look for foreign names on the list of members of the board of directors, which provide a good indication of how open the company is to non-natives. Whether you work for a domestic or a foreign corporation, you will not only have to consider a foreign assignment, but will spend time negotiating, entertaining, coaching, and learning from foreign executives and employees. How well you perform these tasks will determine the rest of your career, as companies are increasingly on the lookout for individuals who can successfully operate globally.

Interim Summary

1. Globalization is the accelerated interdependence of economic and business activities across national boundaries.
2. Globalization influences the availability and pricing of products and services around the world, while often blurring their source and identity.
3. Globalization affects your career opportunities and the skills you will need to be successful.

The Face of Globalization

Countries differ greatly in their globalization levels. Exhibit 1.1 ranks the 15 most global countries according to their overall globalization level, as well as according to the three components which make up the Globalization Index developed by KOF Swiss Economic Institute, an economic think tank: economic integration, social integration, and political integration. Economic integration scores are based on a country's trade and foreign investment, discussed later in Chapters 2 and 3 of this book. Social integration scores are composed of such indicators as the number of Internet users, international travel and tourism, international telephone and mail traffic, and foreign population. Finally, political engagement scores are composed as a combination of membership in international organizations, participation in UN Security Council missions, the number of international treaties ratified, and the number of embassies in the country.

Exhibit 1.2 provides the top 30 countries in each component: economic, social, political, and overall, ranked by their 2011 scores. Belgium is in first place overall. The United States is in 27th place, with its high levels of global integration along the social and political dimensions counterbalanced by its relatively low level of economic integration (typical of countries with large domestic markets), where the US does not even place in the top 30. Indeed one could argue that, in a global environment, being large is sometimes a liability in the sense that it allows firms to neglect international markets for too long. A well-known study of globalization was published in *Foreign Policy* magazine in 2005.[2] The study did not find a strong relation between globalization and the propensity to suffer terrorist attacks on one's soil, discounting speculation that opening up to the outside world invites

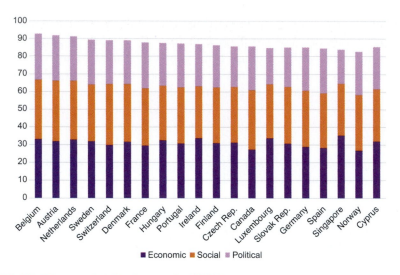

Exhibit 1.1 The World's 20 most globalized countries (2001)

Source: KOF Index of Globalization 2013. The methodology is based on Axel Dreher, "Does globalization affect growth? Evidence from a new Index of Globalization," *Applied Economics*, 38, 10, 2006, 1091–1110.

security risks. However, the study did find a relation between globalization and public education spending, especially in the developing world. In other words, success in a global, knowledge-based economy depends on having an educated workforce. Elsewhere, a New York Times Op-Ed noted that countries that ranked high on the Globalization Index had higher economic and political stability (see Chapter 7), more flexible labor markets, better regulation, and less corruption (see Chapter 19).[3]

Who Benefits from Globalization?

One of the main arguments against globalization is that it confers benefits on rich nations at the expense of poor ones. Before we discuss this argument, let us take a look at the relationship between development level and globalization. It is evident from Exhibit 1.2 that some developed nations (e.g., Japan) obtain only moderate globalization scores, while some developing and emerging economies (e.g., the Czech Republic and Malaysia) obtain respectable scores. Still, the overall relationship is quite clear: The 14 nations that score highest on globalization are all developed economies, while the bottom half is occupied by developing and emerging economies. This does not mean that globalization brings no value to the developing world; on the contrary, integration into the global economy may well pave the route to economic growth and prosperity, as the case of China, one of the world's fastest growing economies, shows clearly. In contrast, countries that fail to integrate into the global economy face the prospect of falling further behind. Two related factors tend to limit the extent of benefit that poor countries can gain from globalization. One is the presence of serious deficiencies in domestic economic and politico-legal governance (e.g., civil conflict, macroeconomic mismanagement, lack of property rights protection, and corruption) that prevent the country from exploiting its advantages in international trade and that deter foreign investment. The other is the

	Globalization (Overall)		Economic Globalization			Social Globalization			Political Globalization		
Rank	Country	Score	Rank	Country	Score	Rank	Country	Score	Rank	Country	Score
1	Belgium	92.6	1	Singapore	96.8	1	Switzerland	92.36	1	France	98.43
2	Austria	91.67	2	Luxembourg	93.11	2	Austria	91.74	2	Italy	98.37
3	Netherlands	91.17	3	Ireland	92.93	3	Belgium	90.43	3	Belgium	98.13
4	Sweden	89.26	4	Malta	91.98	4	Canada	89.46	4	Austria	97.37
5	Switzerland	88.98	5	Belgium	90.95	5	Netherlands	88.91	5	Spain	96.62
6	Denmark	88.96	6	Netherlands	90.72	6	Denmark	87.72	6	Sweden	96.3
7	France	87.65	7	Hungary	89.82	7	UK	87.16	7	Netherlands	95.11
8	Hungary	87.62	8	Estonia	89.2	8	France	86.3	8	Portugal	95.08
9	Portugal	87.28	9	Bahrain	88.49	9	Sweden	85.8	9	Poland	94.9
10	Ireland	86.45	10	Sweden	87.9	10	Slovak Rep.	85.41	10	Canada	94.64
11	Finland	86.43	11	Cyprus	87.62	11	Portugal	84.89	11	Greece	94.11
12	Czech Rep.	86.33	12	Austria	87.58	12	Germany	84.59	12	Denmark	93.95
13	Canada	85.81	13	Denmark	86.73	13	Norway	84.27	13	Switzerland	93.81
14	Luxembourg	85.62	14	Czech Rep.	86.56	14	Finland	83.96	14	Turkey	93.68
15	Slovak Rep.	85.3	15	Finland	85.77	15	Czech Rep.	83.94	15	US	93.6
16	Germany	85.1	16	Chile	85.71	16	Australia	82.48	16	Egypt	93.56
17	Spain	84.71	17	UAE	85.62	17	Spain	82.44	17	Brazil	93.5
18	Singapore	84.39	18	Montenegro	84.89	18	Hungary	81.94	18	Germany	93.35
19	Norway	83.23	19	Slovak Rep.	84.77	19	Luxembourg	81.13	19	Argentina	93.28
20	Cyprus	82.81	20	Portugal	84.26	20	Liechtenstein	79.76	20	Romania	92.89
21	UK	81.68	21	New Zealand	83.08	21	Cyprus	79.63	21	Hungary	92.87
22	Australia	81.41	22	UK	82.98	22	Singapore	78.81	22	India	92.46
23	Italy	81.13	23	Slovenia	82.43	23	Andorra	78.76	23	Norway	92.41
24	Estonia	80.22	24	Switzerland	82.04	24	Ireland	78.44	24	Australia	91.71
25	New Zealand	80.08	25	France	81.45	25	US	78.36	25	Nigeria	91.16
26	Slovenia	79.87	26	Panama	80.38	26	Malta	77.51	26	Finland	91.02
27	US	79.84	27	Israel	79.98	27	Italy	77.28	27	Chile	90.18
28	Poland	79.67	28	Germany	79.81	28	Aruba	76.76	28	Bulgaria	90.14
29	Greece	76.98	29	Latvia	79.29	29	Poland	76.37	29	Pakistan	90.14
30	Malta	76.63	30	Bulgaria	78.67	30	New Zealand	75.75	30	Morocco	89.76

Exhibit 1.2 Globalization index rankings, 2011

Source: KOF Index of Globalization, Axel Dreher, "Does globalization affect growth? Evidence from a new Index of Globalization," Applied Economics, 38, 10, 2006, 1091–1110.

lack of trained personnel for effective participation in international economic institutions such as the International Monetary Fund, the World Trade Organization, and the World Bank.

The good news as we begin the 21st century is that the share of developing countries in world merchandise trade is rising to its highest level in more than 50 years, and the trade growth of the 49 least developed countries (LDCs) exceeds the global average. It is also important to realize that many of the manifestations of globalization in wealthy nations end up helping poorer economies. For instance, when a Singaporean tourist is visiting Laos, he is in effect increasing the export sales of Laos by purchasing such services as hotel stays and tours. And while wages in developing country factories are low by developed nation standards, employees of foreign affiliates in developing economies are paid, on average, far more than those employed by domestic firms. While some local firms are unable to compete with large foreign corporations and exit the market, others take advantage of the learning opportunities associated with multinational presence and upgrade their capabilities, thus positioning themselves as future global players. If large multinational firms seem an exclusive club of rich nations, they are now joined by multinationals from developing economies. In 2000, for the first time ever, multinational firms from developing nations made it into the ranks of the top 100 global multinationals.[4] According to a more recent UN report from 2012, firms from Mexico, China, Brazil, and other developing nations continue to break into the top multinational ranks, with new contenders like China-based Lenovo growing rapidly.[5]

The Impact of Globalization

A common lamentation against globalization is that it deprives nations of their sovereignty. This will supposedly occur because of the growing power of international institutions such as the World Trade Organization (WTO) or the International Monetary Fund (IMF), whose officials are not elected by popular vote (see Chapter 8). Yet, while the WTO has assumed a conflict resolution role that was previously the domain of bilateral negotiations, its resolutions are based on consensus, meaning that the vote of the smallest nation counts as much as that of the largest. The most important decisions regarding international trade are still made by governments, and trade relations are governed by bilateral agreements negotiated and monitored by sovereign governments. And, while mega-multinational corporations abound, small firms remain viable players that have a role in the global economy. As you will see in Chapter 4, small firms in the United States and in many other countries have actually increased their share of national exports over the last decade.

Another complaint against globalization is that it comes at the expense of the environment. Environmentalists accuse firms of relocating their operations abroad solely for reasons of escaping tough pollution rules in their home country, an argument often titled "a race to the bottom" in search of "the lowest common denominator." While there is no question that globalization increases pollution levels in rapidly industrializing economies such as Vietnam and China, rising living standards in those nations, in particular the purchase of automobiles, are at least partially to blame. And, although some firms shed their environmental responsibilities in their quest for larger profits, others adhere to strict codes of environmental protection and make a positive contribution by introducing sophisticated environmental technologies in the developing world. For instance, Dow Chemicals has been credited with environmental cleanup in Eastern Europe and the former East Germany. Further, the reality is that, for most firms, environmental standards are only one of many criteria used in determining their investment and location decision, meaning that the concept of "a race to the bottom" does not always apply. Still, globalization poses huge environmental challenges, and firms and governments must remain vigilant. You will find further discussion of foreign direct investment in Chapter 3.

Throughout this book, we will take the position that globalization is a complex phenomenon whose repercussions are often less than crystal clear. Globalization carries both promises and threats, and produces winners as well as losers. Whether you view globalization as a blessing or a curse will often depend on your perspective and vantage point. For instance, while globalization is correlated with higher overall economic growth, this will probably be of little consolation to an employee who loses his job as a result of foreign competition. Keep in mind, however, that globalization is not the only factor influencing job loss and wage levels. Research shows that it is technology, rather than globalization, that puts the bulk of downward pressures on the wages of unskilled labor.[6] The challenge of globalization involves enhancing its benefits and mitigating its negative impact, maintaining a balance between the public and the individual interest.

Globalization can yield negatives at the national level as well. Global capital flow makes less regulated emerging economies such as Mexico, Thailand, and Argentina vulnerable to volatilities of international capital movements and foreign exchange markets, and may contribute to a financial or currency crisis in these countries. Globalization exposes national economies to the uncertainties of the global economy, and, ironically, the most open economies are also the most at risk of a global slowdown. When prices of commodities, especially raw materials and natural resources, are undervalued due to market control, influence by transnational cartels, or barriers imposed by importing nations, developing countries that export these commodities to developed countries lose many of the economic gains that would otherwise accrue. While asking for market access into developing countries, some developed nations themselves erect new barriers against developing country imports, in particular against farm products, which are heavily subsidized in the European Union and, to a somewhat lesser extent, the United States.

To reap most of its benefits and mitigate some of the drawbacks, it helps to have a developed infrastructure for globalization. **Globalization infrastructure** is the institutional framework (e.g., multilateral agreements in trade, investment, and services) and market efficiency (e.g., efficiency of international capital markets or foreign exchange markets) that support fair and transparent transactions of products and services and streamline flows of commodities, capital, labor, knowledge, and information. As discussed in Chapter 8, international economic organizations, such as the International Monetary Fund (IMF), World Bank, and World Trade Organization (WTO), play a vital role in facilitating such flows, as do firms, governments, and regional blocs, among others.

Interim Summary

1. It is useful to develop a balanced view on globalization, recognizing its positive and negative aspects, so as to focus attention on constructive solutions to the negatives while leveraging opportunities created by the positives.
2. International economic organizations such as the International Monetary Fund, World Bank, and World Trade Organization provide the infrastructure necessary to facilitate globalization.

Globalization and International Business

It is sometimes suggested that globalization means the advance of a homogeneous civilization and a uniform business system that would no longer require adjustment to different business environments. Nothing could be further from the truth. While globalization marches on, pressures to maintain national identity and solidarity are not subsiding. On the contrary, the growing interaction between different systems makes people more, rather than less, aware of the differences among them, often leading them to suspect foreign inputs as potentially threatening to their group identity. Unfortunately, the erroneous assumption regarding homogeneity might lead firms to believe that their strategies, practices, and products or services have universal applicability, with no need to distinguish between domestic and international business. Instead, company executives should strive to learn the intricacies of the foreign environments in which they operate because this is the only way to leverage their firms' global reach and scale. Globalization and localization may seem contradictory, but they are two sides of the same coin and are bound to live side by side into the future.

Throughout this book, you will be made aware of this simultaneous existence of global and local forces and their interaction in international business. Examples include: how to leverage the global resources of the multinational enterprise yet compensate for its unfamiliarity with the foreign environments in which it operates; how to extract economies of scale by selling a product in multiple locations, while making product adjustments and adaptations to reflect different tastes and selling methods; or how to maintain a globally unified compensation system for employees, while taking into account the vast differences in practices, values, standards of living, and taxation across the globe. Please note that we use the terms "country" and "nation" in this book to denote the boundaries of economic and political units that are not necessarily sovereign states. For example, Hong Kong is part of China but is a separate entity for foreign trade and investment purposes.

What is International Business?

International business refers to business activities that involve the transfer of resources, goods, services, knowledge, skills, or information across national boundaries. The resources that make up this flow are raw materials, capital, goods, services, and people. Goods may be semi-finished or finished assemblies and products. Services include accounting, legal counsel, banking, insurance, management consulting, trade service, education, health care, and tourism, among others. Knowledge and skills include technology and innovation, organizational and managerial skills, and intellectual property rights such as copyrights, trademarks, and brand names. Information flows include databases and their channels and information networks, among others. The parties involved may be individuals (e.g., tourists and individual investors buying foreign stocks or bonds), companies (private or public), company clusters (e.g., alliances), government bodies (e.g., central banks), and international institutions (e.g., World Bank, International Monetary Fund). Of these, companies are the dominant player. The firm is the primary economic agent facilitating and gaining (or suffering) from globalization. Firm activities and exchanges that involve the crossing of national boundaries are called international transactions. **International transactions** are manifested mainly in **international trade and investment**. International trade occurs when a company exports goods or services to buyers (importers) in another country. International investment occurs when the company invests resources in business activities outside its home country.

Any firm, regardless of its size, that is engaged in international business is defined in this book as an **international firm**. A firm that has directly invested abroad and has at least one working affiliate in a foreign country (e.g., a factory or a branch office) over which it maintains effective control is defined in this book as a **multinational enterprise**, or **MNE**. Please note that there are multiple definitions of MNE out there, most of which are rather arbitrary (for instance, one definition requires presence in at least six foreign locations, another that the firm has a presence in all major regions—North America, Europe, and Asia). For the sake of clarity, however, we use the standard working definition noted above.

International companies are the beneficiaries of, as well as the reason for, the growing interdependence among nations. Nokia has development, design, manufacturing, and sales facilities in multiple countries, and derives most of its revenues from foreign operations. Companies like Nokia can be listed and raise capital in financial markets around the world, including New York, London, Paris, Zurich, Singapore, Tokyo, and Hong Kong. Both large and small firms can benefit from competitively priced labor, cheap resources, and enormous market opportunities by shifting their production facilities to emerging economies such as Vietnam, China, and India, while benefiting from the high skill level available in places such as Ireland and Israel to do development and design work. Levi Strauss jeans and other apparel are made by subcontractors in Bangladesh, China, and other locations, and are then sold in markets throughout the world. IBM and Microsoft employ Indian software developers based in India and the United States, and both firms have development centers in Israel and other foreign nations. Among service providers, US architectural firms design buildings across Asia, while US airlines compete for passengers on international routes with both foreign and third-party carriers. Such activities involve the movement of capital, people, knowledge, and products from one country to another. They are a consequence of globalization, as much as a generator of it.

Just how global are different industries? The international business field offers ways to measure that level. One measure involves the industry's international linkages, which gauges the extent to which a particular activity is concentrated in one country (low globalization) or in many countries (high globalization). Another measure is the integration of value-added activities, that is, whether most activities leading to a final product or service are done in one versus many countries. Together, these two measures tell us how global an industry is.[7] Other ways to measure industry globalization, such as the "transnationalization index," are mentioned in Chapters 2 and 3.

International versus Domestic Business

Traditionally, international business has been the outgrowth of domestic business. In fact, most major corporations that are active in today's international scene started their operations in the domestic market. Leading Japanese auto makers, such as Toyota and Honda, started their operations in their domestic market before beginning to export to other countries. As the magnitude of their operations grew, they found it profitable or otherwise necessary to build plants and facilities in other countries, most notably, the United States. While many firms still follow the traditional route of domestic growth first, international expansion second, we increasingly see firms that target international markets when launching their operations. These firms are called **born global, global startups,** or **international new ventures** (INV) and are discussed in Chapters 4 and 20. NASDAQ-traded Israeli firm Checkpoint, a leader in the software security segment, is one such company. In addition, some companies engage in international activities without having a home base in the traditional sense. An example is the mainland operations of many Hong Kong investors whose "suitcase companies" do not have a presence in their home base.

Although international business is often an extension of domestic business, it is significantly different from the latter in **environmental dynamics** and **operational nature**. Environmentally, the diversity that exists between countries with regard to cultures, social customs, business practices, laws, government regulations, and political stability is among the many reasons for the complexity of international business. Therefore, international business is usually riskier than domestic business, though, as a whole, presence in multiple international markets provides a measure of diversification, which mitigates risk. Variations in inflation, currency, taxation, and interest rates among different nations have a significant impact on the profitability of an international firm. For a firm that is borrowing and investing in a foreign country, higher interest rates, tax rates, and inflation rates mean higher cost of operation and lower profitability. At the same time, for a firm that is depositing money in a foreign bank, higher interest rates mean a higher return. Similarly, when the euro goes down in value against the US dollar, US exporters to the EU will receive (unless they are hedging their currency exposure) fewer dollars for their euro-denominated transactions, while US importers of EU goods will be able to either lower the cost of the imports or increase their profitability.

The Coca-Cola Company, described in the opening case, needs not only to hedge its currency risk, but also navigate financial environments with different accounting and tax systems. It also needs to attend to different cultures and social systems, different regulations, and different consumption patterns, among other factors. The competitive landscape can also be dramatically different. For instance, in some markets, Coca-Cola faces strong local competition, like Wahaha in China, while in others it must adjust to different rules, for instance, a ban on comparative advertising. Competition can spring from nowhere (e.g., the emergence of Mecca Cola in the Middle East partially to take advantage of anti-American sentiment). The complexity entailed in operating in numerous markets that are different from each other, and the uncertainty involved in the potential for a sudden change in any of those environments, together define the essence of international business. They create opportunities—for instance, the opening of a new market such as Vietnam—but also pose risks and uncertainties. Broadly, **risk** refers to the unpredictability of operational and financial outcomes. **Uncertainty** refers to the unpredictability of environmental or organizational conditions that affect firm performance. Uncertainty about environmental or organizational conditions increases the unpredictability of corporate performance, and therefore increases risk. However, as noted earlier, being in multiple markets also mitigates risk: for instance, General Motors lost billions of dollars in North America in 2005, but its profits in China helped to somewhat narrow its overall loss.

Operationally, international business tends to be more difficult and costly to manage than business activities confined to a single country. Whatever benefits might be available from international operations, they will not be realized if the firm cannot run a complex business effectively. Local employees and expatriates (i.e., people who were sent to a foreign location from the home headquarters, as discussed in Chapter 17) may have trouble getting along because of cultural, language, and managerial style differences. The cultural diversity encountered when operating in several countries may create problems of communication, coordination, and motivation. Organizational principles and managerial philosophies may differ widely, increasing the cost and difficulty of operation.

Industry/Country Box

Sinostone Comes to Elberton

With 150 outfits turning out 250,000 gravestones every year, Elberton, Georgia, produced more granite monuments than any other place in the United States. Twenty percent of the local inhabitants are engaged in the granite business, carving gravestones from local quarries and from imported colored stone, unavailable locally. With the US population aging and mortality rates on the rise, the industry was expecting robust sales. Then, in the mid-1990s, a new company opened up shop in town. Unlike its local competitors, Sinostone, owned by China-based Wanli Stone Group, imported finished gravestones from China, offering them at half the going price. The relatively young Wanli, established in 1996, already exported its products to Japan and Europe, and it was now targeting the US market. It decided to locate in Elberton because of the large number of buyers who come there every year and the location's ready transportation lines to dealers across the United States. Assigned to oversee the new operation was Su Xian, a physician and the wife of a Wanli co-owner.

The local business community was not sure how to react. Some competitors spread the word that Sinostone's products were inferior and that the color on their gravestone would soon fade, an accusation the Chinese company strongly denied. The Elberton Granite Association organized a "buy American" campaign from which Sinostone was excluded. Others suggested to Mrs. Su that she should raise her prices. Still others traveled to Tianjin to examine the Wanli site that is dedicated to US exports. They noted that the operation, located next door to operations of Boeing, was "ten years ahead" in 2002 compared to other Chinese competitors (some of whom were "thirty years behind" their US counterparts.) Sinostone's US competitors have now started to import finished gravestones from China, more than tripling China imports to the United States in this category in the early 2000s. Today China is the second largest exporter to the US of worked and slab granite, shipping 371,471 metric tons in 2012.

Source: Adapted from Neil King, "Grave reservations: Why Dr. Su's arrival rocks Georgia town," *Wall Street Journal*, July 23, 2002, A1, & "US granite imports up in 2012," Stone Update, February 11, 2013.

Why Expand Internationally?

It is useful to distinguish the immediate motivations for conducting international business from the factors that must be present for the international business undertakings to be successful (i.e., profitable). The immediate motivations include **market motives, economic motives,** and **strategic motives.**

The motives vary from one business activity to another, producing multiple motivations for the international firm with a broad scope of activities in different parts of the globe.

Market motives can be **offensive** or **defensive**. An offensive motive is to seize market opportunities in foreign countries through trade or investment. Amway, Avon, and Mary Kay all entered China in the early 1990s in search of opportunities in the country's direct-marketing business. Besides having the largest population and one of the fastest-growing economies in the world, China's strong culture of personal connections, and the pervasiveness of close-knit families and friends, helped make the country the world's biggest direct-selling market. That the Chinese government later outlawed direct selling altogether exemplifies the inherent risk in doing business abroad, though the companies have found ways to adjust (for instance, Mary Kay has opened up customer "learning centers" as a substitute for direct door-to-door marketing and sales) until the ban was lifted years later.

A defensive motive is to protect and hold a firm's market power or competitive position in the face of threats from domestic rivalry or changes in government policies. Lenovo, now the world's leading maker of personal computers, entered international markets via purchase of IBM's personal computers division partially to defend itself from growing encroachment into its domestic market by Dell and Hewlett-Packard. Similarly, many North American and Asian companies in the computer and electronics industries invested heavily in European countries in order to bypass various barriers against imports from non-European Union members. Foreign auto makers, such as the French Peugeot-Citroen, have established operations in China partially to offset inroads by their global competitors into this important market.

Economic motives apply when firms go internationally to increase their return through higher revenues and/or lower costs. International trade and investment are vehicles enabling a firm to benefit from inter-country differences in costs of labor, natural resources, and capital, as well as differences in regulatory treatments, such as taxation. For example, more than 2,000 plants have sprung up near the US–Mexico border to take advantage of low-wage Mexican labor to assemble American-made components for re-export to the United States. Some of the investors later relocated their plants to still cheaper China, Vietnam, and India. Fossil, a leading producer of wristwatches, opted to locate its overseas manufacturing headquarters in East Asia, rather than in its home country, the United States. Firms such as Boeing, Microsoft, Alcatel-Lucent, Intel, Otis, and Coca-Cola established production facilities in China's special economic zones or open coastal cities in order to attain a significantly lower taxation rate than is applicable in the United States.

Strategic motives lead firms to participate in international business when they seek, for instance, to capitalize on distinctive resources or capabilities developed at home (e.g., technologies and economy of scale). By deploying these resources or capabilities abroad or increasing production through international trade, firms may be able to increase their cash inflows. Firms may also go international to be the first-mover in the target foreign market before a major competitor gets in, gaining strategic benefits such as technological leadership, brand image, customer loyalty, and competitive position. Volkswagen was the second auto maker to enter China and the first to locate in the all-important Shanghai market, gaining a virtual monopoly in that market for years. Additionally, firms may benefit from vertical integration involving different countries. For example, a company in the oil exploration and drilling business may integrate "downstream" by acquiring or building an oil refinery in a foreign country that has a market for its refined products. Conversely, a company that has strong distribution channels (e.g., gas stations) in a country but needs a steady supply of gasoline at a predictable price may integrate "upstream" and acquire an oil producer and refiner in another country.

Yet another strategic motive is to follow the company's major customers abroad (often termed "piggybacking"). Japanese tire maker Bridgestone found itself in the US market when its customers—Japanese car makers—exported their cars, with Bridgestone tires mounted on them, to the United States, and their buyers needed replacement tires. Other suppliers of Honda, Nissan, and Toyota followed suit, many eventually locating manufacturing operations in the United States. Bridgestone, for instance, took over US tire manufacturer Firestone to become one of the leading global tire makers. Since responsiveness and product adaptation are becoming increasingly critical for business success, proximity to foreign customers is an important driver of overseas investment.

Not all attempts to expand internationally turn out to be profitable, of course. What factors then underlie a firm's success in international business? Richard Caves gives a succinct summary of such factors: **economies of location, economies of scale,** and **economies of scope.**[8] **Economies of location** refer to cost efficiencies that a firm can achieve by locating some of its activities overseas. Such cost efficiencies can result from lower labor or raw material costs, superior labor skills, or elimination of transport or tariff costs. **Economies of scale** refer to the reduction of average production costs due to the expansion of sales in additional markets when fixed costs (e.g., plant and equipment expenditures or R&D expenses) are amortized onto a larger quantity of units sold, thus lowering the production cost per unit. **Economies of scope** refer to the realization of additional profit from the exploitation of certain valuable assets in additional foreign markets because those assets can be utilized to yield substantial incremental revenues while incurring only limited incremental costs. Assets that exhibit such properties typically include technology, marketing know-how, or management expertise.

Interim Summary

1. International business is the conducting of business activities that involve the transfer of resources, goods, services, knowledge, skills, or information across national boundaries.
2. International business is typically more complex and uncertain than domestic business due to differences in environments and operational requirements.
3. If an international business is not run effectively, the benefit of doing business internationally may turn into a drawback because of the costs and difficulties associated with managing activities in multiple locations.

The Structure of this Book

This book is not about globalization per se, but about conducting international business in a global and rapidly changing world environment. The book will help you learn the basic concepts, principles, procedures, and practices in international business, and provide you with an understanding of the environments in which it is conducted and the institutions that oversee or otherwise play a role in international business activities. This should prepare you for a future where you will conduct international business effectively, responsibly, and ethically, whether in your home country or in another county.

The structure of this book is based on a vision of international business as a proactive managerial undertaking. Thus, the sequence consists of a description of the major international activities and the players that pursue them, the environments in which they operate, the institutions governing their transactions, their strategies and design, the various functional areas that conduct specialized international business activities, and the issues that currently top the agenda of international business practice and scholarship. A more detailed outline follows.

Part 1 introduces three core topics in international business: international trade in Chapter 2 (imports/exports); foreign direct investment in Chapter 3 (e.g., establishing foreign subsidiaries); and the major "players" in international business in Chapter 4 (the more traditional multinational enterprise hailing from a developed country, the rising multinationals from developing economies, and the small- and medium-sized international company).

Part 2 discusses the environment of international business. Understanding the environment is essential if we are to understand the motivations and nature of home and host country firms, as well as explain the features that draw or inhibit trade and investment in a host country. We start in Chapter 5 with country competitiveness, a key determinant of trade, foreign investment, and the operation and performance of the multinational firm; such competitiveness is also a product of the endowments described in this part and the strategies undertaken by nations, industries, and firms. We proceed with culture in Chapter 6, a somewhat intangible yet crucial facet of international business that is too often underestimated. In Chapter 7, we also discuss the political and legal environments that establish the ground rules within which international business operates.

Part 3 focuses on global markets and institutions. It covers international economic integration and organizations (Chapter 8), the international monetary system, and financial markets (Chapter 9). These global institutions are key elements of the infrastructure of globalization. They affect either regulatory frameworks or market efficiency for cross-border transactions. Global institutions are part of the environments in which they operate, but they also participate in shaping the international business environment within which transactions take place.

Part 4 deals with international business strategies, the starting point for a firm's operations in international markets. This part begins with Chapter 10 on international entry strategies, followed by Chapter 11 on the organization design of the multinational firm, explaining how this firm organizes its operations in order to execute its set strategy. Chapter 12 focuses on building and managing global strategic alliances, an increasingly popular yet problematic type of organization. Finally, Chapter 13 focuses on global research and development (R&D), an increasingly crucial element in an increasingly knowledge-based economy.

Part 5 deals with the separate international business functions. The aim is to illustrate the main challenges international business poses to each of the functional business areas and the knowledge base necessary for effective performance in each of those areas. In this part, we include chapters on finance (e.g., raising capital) (Chapter 14), accounting (e.g., transfer pricing issues) (Chapter 15), marketing (e.g., advertising and pricing) and supply chain (logistic issues such as distribution modes) (Chapter 16), and human resource management (e.g., staffing subsidiaries) (Chapter 17).

Part 6 highlights emerging issues in international business. One is global e-commerce (Chapter 18). After a much-hyped false start in the late 1990s, e-commerce has been growing rapidly. The nature of e-commerce challenges some key ways of doing business internationally, as well as the regulatory systems that govern them; it also exposes firms that have hitherto engaged only in domestic business to the vagaries of international commerce. The second emerging topic, ethics and corruption (Chapter 19), has long been associated with international business, especially in developing economies. In recent years, this once taboo subject has become the subject of much debate in developing and developed markets alike. For instance, technological advances and increased globalization have opened the door to piracy, counterfeiting, and similar phenomena on an unprecedented scale. This assault on property rights is having a major influence on firms' global strategy and operational performance. The third emerging topic, addressed in the concluding Chapter 20 of this book, is international entrepreneurship, a subject of great importance in an increasingly knowledge-based, innovation economy. The chapter covers both comparative (e.g., the motives of entrepreneurial activity in different countries) and international (e.g., European startups raising money in the US) aspects of entrepreneurship.

Pedagogical Thrust

While providing an in-depth discussion of individual topics as described above, the emphasis in this book is on the integration of topical areas. For instance, although culture is discussed in a separate chapter, its impact on environments, institutions, and firms is apparent throughout the book. Thus, when we discuss accounting, we note that certain features of accounting and auditing systems tend to correlate with cultural patterns, and when we discuss human resource management, we examine the role of cultural differences in expatriate adjustment. The manager's challenge, after all, is about integration across functions and regions, and this book reflects this responsibility. In addition to offering topical cross-references across chapters, we utilize special integration mechanisms, the **country box** and the **industry box**, in each of the subsequent chapters. These boxes provide a zoom-in into a particular national market, in the case of the country box, and into a particular sector, in the case of an industry box. Readers should use these boxes not only to learn about the country or industry being highlighted, but also to ask, and attempt to answer, what would have been different in another country or industry.

To sum up, this book is based on an appreciation for the diversity of business systems around the globe, and a belief that awareness of the changing and intensifying nature of globalization and global competition should be high on the agenda of the international manager. Whereas some observers see globalization as leading to a more homogeneous world, we view it as a continually changing mosaic whose diverse pieces come into more frequent contact with each other, affecting each and every piece in a unique manner. The role of management is to monitor, understand, and respond to this changing environment with sensitivity and respect for those differences, while realizing that international business decisions influence a great variety of constituencies in multiple locations and, ultimately, the future and quality of life on the planet. This book is a reflection of this philosophy.

Chapter Summary

1. Globalization enhances economic interdependence but does not necessarily make nations more similar; it is a complex phenomenon that carries both negative and positive consequences and produces both winners and losers.
2. Globalization intensifies the ongoing tension between forces for standardization and consolidation on the one hand, and those pushing for localization and adaptation on the other. This tension represents one of the main challenges of doing business internationally.
3. International business consists of business activities and resources transferred across national boundaries. Firms that have directly invested in at least one foreign market are considered multinational enterprises (MNEs) in this book.
4. International business is more complex and unpredictable than domestic business, and often requires different types and scales of resources and capabilities.

Notes

1 National Intelligence Council, *The Contradictions of Globalization*, 2005.
2 "Measuring globalization," *Foreign Policy*, May/June 2005, 52–60.
3 Richard W. Fisher and W. Michael Cox, "Globalizing good government," *The New York Times*, April 10, 2006, A25.
4 World Investment Report 2000 (UNCTAD).
5 The world's top 100 non-financial TNCs, ranked by foreign assets, UNCTAD, 2012.
6 W.R. Cline, Institute of International Economics, cited in *The Economist*, September 29, 2001.
7 Mona V. Makhija, Kim Kwangsoo, and Sandra D. Williamson, "Measuring globalization of industries using a national industry approach: Empirical evidence across five countries and over time," *Journal of International Business Studies*, 28, 4, 1997, 679–710.
8 R.E. Caves, *Multinational Enterprise and Economic Analysis* (3rd ed), Cambridge: Cambridge University Press, 2007.

part 1

concepts and theories in international business

2   INTERNATIONAL TRADE THEORY AND APPLICATION   21

3   FOREIGN DIRECT INVESTMENT THEORY AND APPLICATION   71

4   THE MULTINATIONAL ENTERPRISE   115

chapter 2

international trade theory and application

INTERNATIONAL TRADE THEORIES   23

INTERNATIONAL TRADE PATTERNS   40

ARGUMENTS FOR TRADE RESTRICTIONS   53

TYPES OF TRADE BARRIERS   57

Do You Know?

1. What are the major theories of international trade?
2. How applicable are those theories in today's environment?
3. How do governments limit trade with other countries, and what are their reasons for doing so?
4. How does level of development influence a country's trade relationships?
5. What is your country's balance of trade with its trade partners and how might it affect you?

OPENING CASE   Banana Wars

In April of 1999, the World Trade Organization (WTO) ruled that the European Union (EU) violated international trade law by establishing quotas and tariffs on bananas imported from Latin America by US-based Chiquita Brands International, Dole Foods, and Fresh Del Monte Produce. At the same time, the EU allowed licensed access for bananas from former colonies in Africa, Asia, and the Caribbean. According to the WTO ruling, the arrangement cost the United States $191 million in trade opportunities.

The banana business is hardly lucrative. Retail prices and sales of bananas have been falling for years, margins are narrow, the crop is susceptible to disease, and transportation is tricky. At 800 to 900 euros per ton, European banana prices are double those in the United States, but the growers hardly benefit. The Center for International Economics in Canberra, Australia estimates that only $150 million of the $2 billion this arrangement costs European consumers finds its way to the banana growers. The main beneficiaries are the firms that hold the banana import licenses. Still, bananas represent a major export for many developing nations. In the small Caribbean nation of St. Lucia, bananas brought in over 40 percent of export revenues in 2011. Such nations find it difficult to substitute bananas' high output with other crops. Bananas are also labor intensive, providing a crucial source of employment.

The Latin American nations whose banana exports have been restricted in Europe have been hopeful that another, more recent WTO ruling will bear more fruit. In late 2009, ambassadors from Latin America and the EU met at the WTO in Geneva and finally agreed to end the 15-year dispute over EU banana imports. As part of the deal, which was finally ratified in early 2011, the EU will gradually reduce its import tariffs on bananas from Latin America from 176 to 114 euros per ton by the year 2017. In an attempt to help the main African and Caribbean banana-exporting countries, the EU will also set aside nearly 200 million euros to aid them in adjusting to the now stiffer competition from Latin America. In the years to come, this will have numerous effects on both the price of bananas in the EU and around the world, as well as the export destinations and futures of Latin American, African, and Caribbean banana producers.

Sources: G. Fairclough and D. McDermott, "The banana business is rotten, so why do people fight over it?," *Wall Street Journal* August 9, 1999; N. Dunne, "US lists sanctions over bananas," *Financial Times,* April 10, 1999, 4; A. DePalma, "US and Europeans agree on deal to end banana trade war," *The New York Times,* April 12, 2001, C1; H. Cooper and G. Winestock, "Tough talkers," *Wall Street Journal,* November 15, 2001, A1; United Nations Conference on Trade and Development, "Banana split: How EU politics divide global producers," Policy Series Issues #31, 2005; CIA Library, "Saint Lucia: Economy," *The World Factbook,* 2013; R. Peters, "Banana wars: Who are the real winners?," *Guardian,* February 4, 2011.

International Trade Theories

International (or foreign) trade is the exchange of goods and services across borders. Bananas, the subject of the opening case, are a major export commodity for some developing African, Caribbean, Pacific, and Latin American countries, whose economies are susceptible to international market conditions on bananas and other agricultural commodities. Industrialized countries, such as EU members and the United States, have a markedly different export structure. Their primary exports are technology-intensive (e.g., machine tools), knowledge-intensive (e.g., software), capital-intensive (e.g., construction machinery and equipment), or a combination of all of the above (e.g., telecom products, pharmaceuticals, airplanes, and motor vehicles). You may wonder why export structures vary across countries, why nations do not mimic each other, and why they have different vulnerabilities to trade conditions and disruptions. The answers can be found in the international trade theories that are described below. Following their introduction, we will comment on the merits and limitations of each theory.

The Mercantilist Doctrine

Emerging in England in the mid-sixteenth century, **mercantilism** is the first (or pre-classical) theory of international trade. The doctrine placed great faith in the ability of a government to improve the well-being of its residents using a system of centralized controls. Under mercantilism, the primary goal of the government in foreign economic policy is to increase the wealth of the nation by acquiring gold. Mercantilists identified national wealth with the size of a nation's reserves of precious metals (which could then be used to hire mercenary armies). Apart from directly mining gold around the world, the primary means for achieving this policy goal was to extract trade gains from foreigners through regulations and controls so as to achieve a surplus in the balance of trade by increasing exports (e.g., by subsidies) and decreasing imports (e.g., by tariffs and quotas) because trade balances among countries at the time were settled via the transfer of gold.

In the modern economy, however, gold reserves are merely potential claims on foreigners against real goods. In addition, as demonstrated by David Hume in 1752, an influx of gold in the country running a large trade surplus would increase the domestic price level and boost the price of exports.[1] Hence, the country holding the gold would lose the competitive edge in price that had enabled it to acquire the gold earlier by exporting more than it imported. In contrast, the loss of gold in the foreign nation running a large trade deficit would reduce prices there and reinforce its exports. Furthermore, even in the absence of this natural equilibrating process, no country can truly run large trade surpluses on a sustained basis if all countries find this policy attractive and adopt measures to reduce imports and raise exports, resulting in smaller international trade for all countries. Today, gold reserves represent a minor portion of national foreign exchange reserves. Governments use such reserves to intervene in foreign exchange markets (e.g., selling some of these reserves in exchange for local currencies) so as to influence foreign exchange rates.

Despite the apparent obsolescence of the theory due to the relatively minor role that gold plays in a nation's trade and money supply, some still advocate a policy called "neo-mercantilism." This policy also aims at running a trade surplus for the purpose of keeping domestic production and hence domestic employment at a higher level than possible under balanced trade with foreign countries. This policy, however, encounters the same problems as the traditional mercantilist policy because a large and persistent trade surplus will cause the country to increase money supply due to the inflow of foreign exchange earnings, which will in turn lead to higher inflation in the country than in its trading partners and a dent in the competitiveness of its exports.

Mercantilism also overlooked other sources of a country's wealth accumulation, such as the quantity of its capital, the skill of its workforce, and the strength of other production inputs like land and natural resources. The absolute and comparative advantage theories to be discussed below address some of these logical holes in the mercantilist theory. In Chapter 5, we explain in detail that a country's wealth today is accumulated mainly through superior competitiveness, which is in turn determined not only by the abundance of resources but also by national policies, industrial structure, firm efficiency, and individual productivity.

Absolute Advantage Theory

In his 1776 landmark treatise, *An Inquiry into the Nature and Causes of the Wealth of Nations*, Adam Smith from the United Kingdom introduced the doctrine of **laissez-faire** to international trade.[2] Laissez-faire means, literally, "let make freely" or, more generally, "freedom of enterprise and freedom of commerce." Elimination of ubiquitous regulations was the touchstone of nineteenth-century liberalism. Smith argued that all nations would benefit from unregulated, free trade that would permit individual countries to specialize in goods they were best suited to produce because of natural and acquired advantages. Smith's theory of trade has come to be known as the theory of absolute advantage. This theory stated that a nation's imports should consist of goods made more efficiently abroad, while exports should consist of goods made more efficiently at home. According to this theory, Caribbean countries should export bananas (which have absolute advantage at home) and import apples from the state of Washington (which have absolute advantage in the United States).

The absolute advantage theory holds that the market would reach an efficient end by itself. Government intervention in the economic life of a nation and in trade relations among nations (e.g., in the form of tariffs) is counterproductive. A nation would benefit from free trade simply because imports would cost less than domestic products it otherwise had to produce. Unlike the mercantilist doctrine that a nation could only gain from trade if the trading partner lost (i.e., that trade was a zero-sum game), the absolute advantage theory argued that both countries would gain from the efficient allocation of national resources globally.

Exhibit 2.1 provides a simple illustration of how a country gains from free trade. It shows that the United States has an absolute advantage in producing wheat, whereas Colombia has an absolute advantage in producing coffee. It takes two labor-hours to produce a unit of wheat in the United States, whereas it takes ten labor-hours to produce a unit of wheat in Colombia. Therefore, the

	Wheat (1 unit)	Coffee (1 unit)
United States	2	8
Columbia	10	2

Exhibit 2.1 Labor-hours required to produce one unit of a good

United States should specialize in the production of wheat. Similarly it takes eight labor-hours to produce a unit of coffee in the United States, and two labor-hours to produce a unit of coffee in Colombia. Therefore, Colombia should specialize in the production of coffee. Smith argued that, in a situation like this, both countries benefit from specialization and trade. World production would increase if both countries specialized in the production of the good in which they have an absolute advantage and then traded to obtain the other goods in which they have an absolute disadvantage.

An obvious gap in this theory is its inability to explain a situation where, for example, one country has an absolute advantage in producing *all* goods. Would it still benefit both countries to trade if one country were more efficient than the other in producing both goods? This question is resolved by the comparative advantage theory discussed below.

Comparative Advantage Theory

David Ricardo, a nineteenth-century English economist, explained in his landmark 1817 book, *On the Principles of Political Economy and Taxation*, that both countries would still gain from trade even if one had an absolute advantage in producing all goods.[3] Thus, it was the **comparative advantage** of a nation in producing a good relative to the other nation that determined international trade flows. To illustrate this, Ricardo used the example in Exhibit 2.2. In England, a gallon of wine costs 120 hours of work and a yard of cloth 100 hours of work, while in Portugal, the real cost (labor cost) of wine and cloth amounts to 80 and 90 hours of work, respectively. Portugal thus has an absolute advantage over England in the production of wine, as well as in the production of cloth, because the labor cost of production for each unit of the two commodities is less in Portugal than in England.

To demonstrate that trade between England and Portugal will, even in this case, lead to gains for both countries, it is useful to introduce the concept of **opportunity cost**. The opportunity cost for a good X is the amount of other goods which have to be given up in order to produce one unit of X. Exhibit 2.3 shows the opportunity costs for producing wine and cloth in Portugal and England, based on the information given in Exhibit 2.2.

A country has a comparative advantage in producing a good if the opportunity cost for producing the good is lower at home than in the other country. Exhibit 2.3 shows that Portugal has the lower opportunity cost of the two countries in producing wine, while England has the lower opportunity cost in producing cloth. Thus Portugal has a comparative advantage in the production of wine and England has a comparative advantage in the production of cloth. Once trade between the two countries is launched, England will export cloth and import wine. As long as the opportunity costs for the same commodities differ between countries, open trade will result in gains for each country through specialization in producing a commodity (or commodities) in which a country has comparative advantage vis-à-vis its trading partner(s).

	Wine (1 gallon)	Cloth (1 yard)
England	120	100
Portugal	80	90

Exhibit 2.2 Labor-hours required to produce one unit of a good

	Opportunity Cost for Wine	Opportunity Cost for Cloth
England	120/100 = 12/10	100/120 = 10/12
Portugal	80/90 = 8/9	90/80 = 9/8

Exhibit 2.3 Opportunity costs for producing wine and cloth

It is important to understand the *sources* of comparative advantage. The immediate source of trade is a difference in the price of the same commodity between different countries, thus the difference in opportunity costs. But why does such a difference arise? Price is essentially determined by the interaction of supply and demand. Therefore, a price differential derives from differences in demand conditions, supply conditions, or both. On the demand side, differences in tastes and incomes will cause differences in patterns of demand, and hence, prices. When two countries share similar income levels and consumer tastes, however, income is unlikely to be a major source of demand differences. Similarly, differences in tastes are unlikely to account for significant demand differences—and thus for trade—between countries belonging to the same social-cultural matrix. On the supply side, we know that differences in supply patterns result from differences in the patterns of production costs.

Thus, in today's world economy, comparative advantage must be explained by reference to differences in **comparative production cost,** which further depends on the commodity's production process (especially the state of technology) and on the prices of **production factors** such as labor, land, capital, and natural resources. Production factor prices, in turn, are related to the availability of those factors in the national economy. Economists refer to inputs to the production process as production factors. They then refer to conditions (availability and cost) of production factors as the country's factor endowment. In today's global economy, quality levels of production factors (e.g., the knowledge and productivity of workers or service and the efficiency of a banking sector) become even more important for improving a country's exports or attracting foreign investments. In today's international business environment, therefore, factor endowment should also include the quality of production factors. However, because inter-country differences in technology were relatively minor in the nineteenth century, international variations in comparative advantage were attributed primarily to different national endowments in terms of availability and cost. This was the theoretical root of the **Heckscher-Ohlin theorem.**

Heckscher-Ohlin Theorem

The Heckscher-Ohlin (or H-O) theorem is named for its authors, Eli Heckscher and Bertil Ohlin, both Swedish economists. It explained the link between national factor endowments and the comparative advantage of nations.[4] The theorem states that a country has a comparative advantage in commodities whose production is intensive in its relatively abundant factor, and hence it will export those commodities. Meanwhile, a country would import commodities whose production is intensive in the country's relatively scarce factor of production. Thus, differences in comparative advantage are attributed to the differences in the structure of the economy. A country is relatively more efficient in those activities that are better suited to its economic structure, and it does best with what it has most of.

If, for example, the United States is more abundant in capital relative to labor than other countries, it will export commodities whose production requires a greater use of capital than other products do (e.g., motor vehicles), and it will import labor-intensive commodities (e.g., clothing).

Several assumptions underlie the Heckscher-Ohlin theorem. First, it is assumed that countries vary in the availability of various factors of production. Second, while each commodity is assumed to have its own specific production function, the production function is assumed to be identical anywhere in the world. **Production function** shows the amount of output that can be produced by using a given quantity of capital and labor. In other words, this theorem assumes that the same level of input combination (e.g., the combination of five units of labor and three units of capital) will produce the same output in any country. Third, the theorem holds that technology is constant in all trading countries and that the same technology is used in all those countries. Finally, it assumes that the conditions of demand for production factors are the same in all countries. With identical demand conditions, differences in the relative supply of a factor of production will lead to differences in the relative price of that factor between the two countries.

The H-O theorem also implied international equalization of the prices of production factors under free trade. This implication was articulated by Wolfgang Stolper and Paul Samuelson through an extension of the theory known as the **Stolper-Samuelson theorem of factor-price equalization.**[5] It argued that the exchange of goods between agricultural and industrial countries would result in an increase in the previously relatively low levels of land rents, and a drop in the high level of industrial wages in the agricultural country. In the industrial country, however, the opposite change in factor prices occurs: an increase in industrial wages and a decrease in land rents. In addition to identical production factors across different countries, the theorem assumed other conditions under which free commodity trade equalizes factor prices: (1) free competition in all markets; (2) absence of transportation costs; and (3) all commodities continue to be produced in both countries after free trade has begun.

The factor-price equalization theorem has an important implication for the political economies of trade: any change in trade policy, such as a decrease or increase in trade barriers to a product, will always create both winners and losers in the economy and in at least one of its trading partners. Consider the policy of the EU that protects farmers from foreign competition. The production of such agricultural products as wheat requires intensive use of land. In comparison with the land-rich countries like the US, the EU as a whole is relatively scarcely endowed with agricultural land. This makes the cost of land use more expensive, which in turn keeps the cost of wheat production high in the EU relative to the US. If the EU decided to eliminate all barriers to wheat imports, such a policy change would result in the following outcomes in the EU and the US:

	EU	US
• Trade in wheat	Rise in imports	Rise in exports
• Wheat production	Down	Up
• Demand for land use	Down	Up
• Price of land use	Down	Up
• Welfare of land owners	Down	Up
• Welfare of land users	Up	Down

This example illustrates that a policy change in the EU not only affects trade and production in both the EU and the US, but also creates both winners and losers in each of these economies. So, even though trade in general creates a bigger pie for everyone to share, the actual distribution of the gain is likely uneven and can easily cause some socioeconomic groups to suffer substantial losses of income. It is no wonder that most changes in trade policies encounter vehement oppositions from some groups. In order for an economically beneficial policy change to be adopted, the government of the country may need to take some of gain from the winners to compensate the losers. Most developed countries do have programs to help their citizens deal with negative impact of trade on their lives, such as unemployment compensation and job-training subsidies tied to new trade initiatives (e.g., during the implementation of NAFTA in the US). Such programs can enable a country to exploit its comparative advantage more fully and accelerate economic growth.

The main implications of the H-O theorem for world trade are highlighted below:

1. Trade, as well as trade gains, should be greatest between countries with the greatest differences in economic structure.
2. Countries should export goods that make intensive use of their relatively abundant factors.
3. Free trade should equalize factor prices between countries, especially those with fairly similar relative factor endowments and with more liberal mutual trade.

A phenomenon that has caused considerable debate both in policy circles and in the public media is the shift of production in labor-intensive industries such as textiles from developed to developing countries. The process visibly intensified as some large developing countries such as China opened their economies to international trade, taking up an increasing share of world production in these industries. As these economies develop, however, wage rates start to rise, making the production of some labor-intensive goods less and less profitable. More recently, it is widely reported that China has been outsourcing the production of low value-added and unskilled labor-intensive goods to even less developed economies such as Vietnam and Cambodia, and some companies have also moved production from China back to the United States and Europe—a trend known as re-shoring. These developments are apparently consistent with the implications of the H-O theorem highlighted above.[6]

The Leontief Paradox

The central notion of the H-O theorem is that a country exports goods that make intensive use of the country's abundant factor and imports goods that make intensive use of the country's scarce factor. Wassily Leontief, the 1973 winner of the Nobel Prize in Economics, attempted in 1953 to test this proposition for the United States. Using input-output tables covering 200 industries and 1947 trade figures, he found that US exports were apparently labor-intensive and its imports capital-intensive, even though the US was relatively better endowed with capital. Since this result contradicted the predictions of the H-O theorem, it has become known as the **Leontief paradox**. The Leontief study motivated further empirical research. The empirical evidence accumulated since then shows many paradoxical results and contains serious challenges to the general applicability of a factor-endowments explanation in other countries such as Germany, India, Canada, and Japan.

	Exports	Import Replacements
Capital (in 1947 $)	2,550,780	3,091,339
Labor (worker-years)	182	170
Capital per worker-year ($)	14,015	18,184

Exhibit 2.4 Capital position in US exports and imports

Source: W. Leontief, "Domestic production and foreign trade: The American capital position reexamined," *Proceedings of the American Philosophical Society*, 97, November 1953, 332–349.

Exhibit 2.4 shows the principal findings of Leontief's study in 1953. Since the ratio of imports to exports in terms of capital per worker-year (18,184/14,015) was about 1.30, US exports were less capital-intensive (or more labor-intensive) than US import replacements. Instead of capital-intensive exports and labor-intensive import replacements, Leontief showed that a representative bundle of US import replacements required 30 percent more capital per worker-year to produce than a representative bundle of US exports.

The Leontief paradox stimulated a search for explanations, among them:[7]

- *Demand bias for capital-intensive goods.* The US demand for capital-intensive goods is so strong that it reverses the US comparative cost advantage in such goods.
- *Existence of trade barriers.* US labor-intensive imports were reduced by trade barriers (e.g., tariffs and quotas) imposed to protect and save American jobs.
- *Importance of natural resources.* Leontief considered only capital and labor inputs, leaving out natural resource inputs. Because natural resources and capital are often used together in production, a country that imports capital-intensive goods may be actually importing natural resource-intensive goods. For example, the United States imports crude oil, which is capital-intensive.
- *Prevalence of factor-intensity reversals.* A **factor-intensity reversal** occurs when the relative prices of labor and capital change over time, which changes the relative mix of capital and labor in the production process of a commodity from being capital-intensive to labor-intensive (or vice versa).

One condition that was overlooked in Leontief's initial study and many subsequent studies, however, is that there exist different types of labor (e.g., skilled vs. unskilled) and that skilled labor requires substantial investment in education and training to develop and can actually contain a high level of capital content. This idea was later advanced in the human skill and technology-based views of trade that offer a justifiable resolution of the Leontief paradox.

Human Skills and Technology–Based Views

The aforementioned explanations were subsequently found to have offered only a partial explanation of the Leontief paradox.[8] Searching for better explanations of the sources of comparative advantage, several scholars challenged the conventional theory of trade which assumed technology and human skills equivalence among different nations.[9] Rather than a separate theory, the human skills and technology-based view is regarded as a refinement of the conventional theory of trade.

It added two new factors of production, namely **human skills** and **technology gaps,** to the explanation of comparative advantage sources.

Human skill theorists explained the source of comparative advantage in terms of the comparative abundance of professional skills and other high-level human skills. According to Donald B. Keesing, these include: (1) scientists and engineers; (2) technicians and draftsmen; (3) managers; (4) other professionals; and (5) skilled manual workers. Keesing argued that US export industries employ higher proportions of highly skilled labor than do import-competing industries. Thus, the US exports more skill-intensive manufactures than do other countries. Studies treating professional and skilled human resources as capital-intensive reversed the Leontief paradox and found that US exports were actually capital-intensive.[10] The relative abundance of professional and other highly skilled labor in the United States is thus a major source of its comparative advantage in manufacturing products.

Technology theorists argued that certain countries have special advantage as innovators of new products. They also postulated that there was an **imitation lag** that prevents other countries from immediately duplicating the new products of the innovating country. These two conditions gave rise to **technology gaps** in those products that afford the innovating country an export monopoly during the period of imitation lag.[11] In other words, for the duration of the imitation gap, the innovator is the only exporter on world markets. Similarly, when a firm discovers a different and more advanced production technique, it will enjoy a cost advantage and dominate the world market for a while (especially if its innovation is legally protected from imitators by the international patent system). For example, it was found that transportation, electrical machinery, instruments, chemicals, and non-electrical machinery were the five strongest industries in the United States in terms of R&D, accounting for 89.4 percent of US total R&D in 1962. These five industries accounted for 72 percent of US exports of manufactures in the same year.[12] As long as technological progress is made, the technology gap would serve as a major source of comparative advantage. As such, technology, like human skills, is a separate factor of production whose relative abundance or scarcity in a country determines comparative advantage or disadvantage in technology-intensive products. This notion, despite being more than four decades old, still has strong implications for country competitiveness (as discussed in Chapter 5), competitive advantage of MNEs (Chapter 4), and global R&D management (Chapter 13).

Once we bring human skills and technology into the picture, we must consider some special features of these production factors because they can disseminate across borders much more rapidly through education and training than such factors of productions as land and generic labor (with labor migration restricted). This consideration suggests that comparative advantage is dynamic and changeable if some countries are able to invest in education and training more successfully than others, calling for the development of more dynamic perspectives on trade. The **product life-cycle model** discussed below is in essence a dynamic perspective, and the **infant industry argument** to be examined later in this chapter is another.

Some proponents of the human skills and technology-based views on trade went even further and asked the question: Why have some countries developed sophisticated human skills in their labor forces, and advanced technologies in their industries, earlier and faster than other countries?[13] Their search for answers to this question focused on the variation across countries in the "advanced factors" of production: education system, transportation and communication infrastructure, and economic, socio-political, and legal institutions. The key insight of this institutions-based view is that a country's success in developing human skills and technology requires not only sustained and efficient investment in education and training but also a set of economic, political, social, and legal institutions that are conducive to innovation and entrepreneurship. We will take a closer look at the institutional requirements for country competitiveness in Chapter 5. Suffice it here to say that a country's comparative advantage in high-technology industries is likely more dependent on the institutional factors than on such traditional factors of production as land and generic labor.

The Product Life–Cycle Model

Closely related to the technology gap view is the **product life-cycle model,** proposed by Raymond Vernon in the mid-1960s.[14] Vernon's theory further developed the imitation-gap approach by suggesting that changes occur in the input requirements of a new product as it becomes established in a market and standardized in production. As the product cycle develops, the cost advantage will change accordingly, and a comparative advantage in innovative capacity may be offset by a cost disadvantage. To explain the patterns of US trade in manufactured goods after World War II, Vernon developed a four-stage model which assumes that the export effects of product innovation are undermined by technological diffusion and lower costs abroad. This life-cycle model includes the following four stages:

1. The United States has an export monopoly in a new product.
2. Foreign production of this product begins.
3. Foreign production of this product becomes competitive in export markets.
4. The United States becomes an importer of this no-longer-new product.

Vernon postulated that US producers are likely to be the first to exploit market opportunities for a technology-intensive new product. They will first produce this new product in the United States regardless of the costs of production inputs in other countries because of close proximity to customers and suppliers. In this first stage, US producers have a monopoly in export markets and they proceed to build up sales with no concern for foreign competition. During the second stage, producers in other industrial countries start to manufacture the product whose design and production is now standardized. Consequently, the overall growth rate of US exports declines. During the third stage, foreign producers displace US exports in the remaining export markets. Finally, foreign producers achieve sufficient competitive strength arising from economies of scale and lower labor costs to export to the US market.

Exhibit 2.5 graphically presents the product cycle model of international trade for the innovating country (e.g., the United States) and an imitating country (e.g., Germany or Mexico), respectively. As Exhibit 2.5 shows, the innovating country starts production of the new product at time *0*, but it does not export that product until time *A* when production exceeds domestic consumption. At time *B,* foreign production begins to compete against the innovating country's exports which, in turn, begin to fall. Exports come to an end at time *C* as the innovating country becomes an importer of this no-longer-new product.

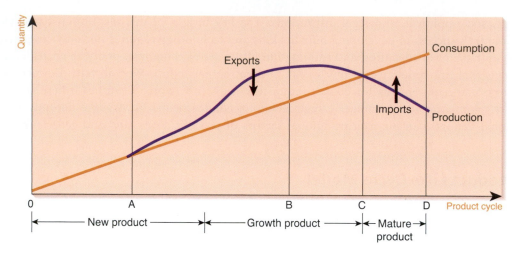

Exhibit 2.5 Product cycle model of international trade—innovating country

Exhibit 2.6 shows that an imitating country starts to import the new product from the innovating country at time A'. If this imitating country is a high-income, advanced country (e.g., Germany), then time A' most likely coincides with time A in Exhibit 2.5. If, however, it is a low-income, developing country (e.g., Mexico), then time A' will come after time A. Local production begins at time B' when the local market grows to sufficient size and cost conditions favor production against imports. If the imitating country is an advanced country, then B' will coincide with B in Exhibit 2.5. If it is a developing country, B' will come after time B. At time C', when production begins to exceed consumption, the imitating country begins to export, and may export first to third countries and later to the innovating country.

Vernon's theory also suggests that the product cycle model of international trade is associated with the life-cycle stage of the product itself. As the product moves through its life cycle, the life cycle of international trade will change. The *new-product stage* is associated with the first production of the product in the innovating country (time 0–A) and the early portion of the export monopoly stage (time A–B). During this stage, production functions are unstable and techniques used in production are rapidly changing. No economy of scale is reached. This phase is also characterized by a small number of firms and no close substitute products. The *growth-product stage* is associated with the later portion of the export monopoly (time A–B) and the start of foreign production (time C). During this stage, mass-production methods are used to exploit expanding markets, and therefore high returns are achieved from economy of scale and market growth. Finally, the *mature-product stage* is associated with the third and fourth stages of the product cycle model of international trade (time C–D). This last stage is characterized by production of standardized products with stable techniques and intense price competition.

The product life-cycle theory helps to explain changes in production and trade in new product lines. It is generally true that the United States has been the principal innovator, and production has spread rapidly to other countries that have been technically competent (e.g., Germany)

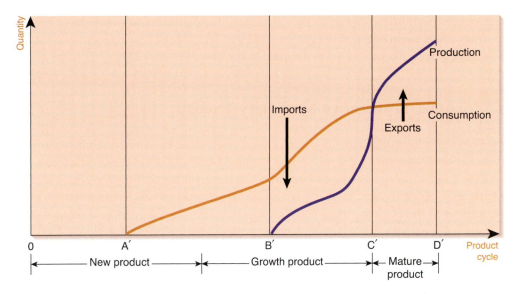

Exhibit 2.6 Product cycle model of international trade—imitating country

and to those which have had a comparative advantage in terms of cheap labor (e.g., Mexico). It is also useful to remember that since the development of the model in the 1960s, the share of the United States in global GDP declined substantially, with other countries, such as Germany and Japan, emerging as innovators. Also, some countries (e.g., the United Kingdom) were innovators of major products such as the passenger jet but failed to dominate the market for those products.

Several facts emerged in connection with product cycles:

1. The export performance of the mature, principal innovating country is better for new products than it is for products approaching maturity.
2. Technology is simplified as the maturing process continues, and products that are initially produced with skilled labor can later be produced by an increased use of automation, combined with the use of unskilled labor.
3. The relationship between innovating and imitating countries changes over time. Countries that were once the principal innovators might fall into relative decline. Britain, for example, was the first country to build railways, at the time with a narrow gauge and small goods wagons. Later, this investment proved to be a drag on progress, and subsequent imitators like Germany and the United States adapted their railways more successfully to new technological and economic conditions.
4. International trade may increase in the later stages of the product cycle. As a consumer good matures and income rises, products once seen as luxury (e.g., cell phones) become a necessity. General growth of *per capita* incomes broadens the market for mass production.

Finally, it is important to remember that elements of the product life cycle have changed since Vernon proposed this theory in the 1960s. For example, the iPhone, conceived and designed in the United States, has been manufactured only outside the country from Day One (time *0*).

Linder's Income-Preference Similarity Theory

When you observe the actual pattern of international trade since the 1970s (described in the second part of this chapter), you will find a prominent feature: Developed countries trade more with other developed countries. Overall, developed countries generate among themselves about three-quarters of total world exports. This fact, by itself, is an indictment of Heckscher-Ohlin's factor-endowment theory. According to the H-O theorem, the incentive to trade is greatest among nations of radically different factor endowments. This means that trade would take place in larger part between developed manufacturing countries and developing countries producing primary products (i.e., natural resource commodities such as oil and petroleum) and labor-intensive goods.

Staffan B. Linder, a Swedish economist, divided international trade into two different categories: primary products (natural resource products) and manufactures.[15] Linder asserts that differences in factor endowments explain trade in natural resource-intensive products but not in manufactures. He argues that the range of a country's manufactured exports is determined by *internal demand*. International trade in manufactures takes place largely among developed nations because nations will only export those goods they manufacture at home and will only manufacture at home those goods for which there is a strong domestic demand. Note, however, that Chapter 4 on the MNE will introduce "born global" enterprises whose very first products are destined for foreign markets, and that China became "factory to the world" long before its consumers could afford many of the goods that it produced.

Linder also contends that the more similar the demand preferences for manufactured goods in two countries (e.g., the United States and the United Kingdom), the more intensive is the potential trade in manufactures between them. If two countries have the same or similar demand structures, then their consumers and investors will demand the same goods with similar degrees of quality and sophistication, a phenomenon known as **preference similarity.** This similarity boosts trade between the two industrialized countries. To explain the determinants of the demand structure, Linder argues that average *per capita* income is the most important one. Countries with high *per capita* income will demand high-quality, "luxury" consumer goods (e.g., motor vehicles) and sophisticated capital goods (e.g., telecommunications equipment and machinery), while low *per capita* income countries will demand low-quality, "necessity" consumer goods (e.g., bicycles) and less sophisticated capital goods (e.g., food-processing machinery). Consequently, a rich country that has a comparative advantage in the production of high-quality, advanced manufactures will find its big export markets in other affluent countries where people demand such products. Similarly, manufactured exports of the poor countries should find their best markets in other poor countries with similar demand structures. Linder also acknowledged that the effect of *per capita* income levels on trade in manufactures may be constrained or distorted by entrepreneurial ignorance, cultural and political differences, transportation costs, and legislative obstacles such as tariffs.

The New Trade Theory

A basic assumption that underlies the classical trade theories, including the comparative advantage theory and the Heckscher-Olin theorem, is that production is subject to constant returns to scale, meaning that an increase in the inputs results in a proportional increase in the output (e.g., doubling inputs causes the output also to double). This assumption seems reasonable for such traditional industries as textiles, but becomes quite unrealistic for more modern industries where fixed investment on capital equipment or R&D constitutes a major portion of the production cost. If production requires a significant amount of fixed investment, the industry exhibits increasing returns to scale or **economies of scale,** meaning that the average production cost falls as the scale of production is increased. The reason is that a larger scale of production allows the fixed cost to be amortized onto more units, lowering the fixed portion of the cost that must be borne by each unit. By relaxing the assumption of constant returns to scale, a number of economists, including Dixit and Norman, Lancaster, Krugman, Helpman, and Ethier, are able to show that economies of scale can provide firms in a country with an advantage in international trade even if the country possesses neither an advantage nor a disadvantage in terms of technology or factor endowment compared to other countries.[16] The theory developed by these economists is known as the **new trade theory.** Although this theory is not totally "new," it makes several contributions to the understanding of international trade.

First, the new trade theorists introduce an industrial organization view into trade theory, and include real-life imperfect competition in international trade. They show that, in the presence of economies of scale, there are increasing returns to specialization in many industries, ranging from automobiles to commercial aircrafts to pharmaceuticals. In particular, when scale economies are large, world demand may be able to support only a very small number of firms in an industry (e.g., only Boeing and Airbus remain as makers of large passenger jets).

Second, the new trade theory suggests that *inter-industry trade* (international trade between different industries in different nations) continues to be determined by the Heckscher-Ohlin theory. In contrast, *intra-industry trade* (international trade involving the same industry) is largely driven by increasing returns resulting from specialization within the industry. This suggests that comparative advantage from factor endowment differences and increasing returns from economy of scale can coexist because they differ in the application of inter- versus intra-industry trade.

Finally, the new trade theory realizes the importance of externality in international specialization and trade. **Externality** occurs when the actions of one agent directly affect the environment of another. For example, firms that cause pollution or noise would have an adverse impact on local residents. In international trade, externalities include government policies, political relations between two countries, history of the importing or exporting country, consumption differences between different cultures, accident and luck (e.g., first entrant of the industry), among others. The new trade theorists contend that these externalities could be the alternatives to comparative advantage as the factors influencing actual patterns of international trade.

One especially noteworthy type of externality is the trade policy of a country's government. Specifically, when an industry exhibits a sufficiently large economy of scale, it is possible that (1) the world demand can support only one firm earning monopoly profit, and (2) the presence of two competitors will force both or at least one of them to operate at a loss. The question then arises: Which country of the world will have the good fortune of hosting such a profitable firm in the industry that not only pays good wages but also may provide technology spillovers for other industries? Apart from luck and entrepreneurial foresight, the decision of a country's government to offer a domestic entrant a subsidy that is high enough for the entrant to avoid losses even if a foreign firm also enters the industry, can also make the difference. Can you imagine that a foreign firm would still enter an industry when it seems destined to lose money because of an entrant whose foray is guaranteed and subsidized by its home government? No rational foreign firm will do so, of course, unless it also receives a subsidy from its own government. This line of reasoning suggests the potential for a country's government to influence international competition and help its firms dominate highly profitable new industries. In such a case, shouldn't all governments adopt such a policy?

The full implications of this analysis, however, are not as straightforward as it may seem at first glance. The same economists who demonstrated the potential for a country to gain through government intervention in international trade at the expense of other countries also showed that such a beggar-thy-neighbor policy can easily backfire and hurt every country in the world. Consider the following:

- In order for such a policy to have the desired effect, the government must select promising industries under a high level of uncertainty before their true attributes are revealed (i.e., with regard to their economies of scale). The government can easily choose an industry that has either (a) such small economies of scale that many firms are able to survive at a breakeven point without earning any real profit, or (b) such large economies of scale that world demand cannot even support a single firm operating at breakeven.

- If a government takes it upon itself to select future champions, it will undoubtedly be subject to heavy lobbying from profit-seeking firms in the country, and those who are most influential and eventually successful in getting their projects supported are more likely to be large established firms than small startups that tend to be the sources of breakthrough innovation. Such lobbying or rent-seeking behavior can easily cause the government to tax industries that have a proven record of economic efficiency and subsidize shaky "new" industries, many of which end up in failure.

- Even if the aforementioned problems of uncertainty and political lobbying could be resolved, one country's success in following such a policy would induce other countries to imitate and adopt similar policies. When many or all countries of the world subsidize the same "promising" industries, no country will enjoy any advantage because the measures of trade intervention by the different countries cancel one another out. The end result, similar to the result from all countries pursuing a mercantilist policy, will be a shrinkage of world trade to the detriment of all.

In brief, even though the new trade theory points to the possibility for government trade interventions to help a country to gain at the expense of other countries, it ultimately also raises serious concerns about the efficacy of such interventions and their possibly grave consequences for the world trading system.

It is worth noting that this theory helps explain intra-firm trade, which occurs when import and export activities take place between the subsidiaries of the same MNE. Driven by the prospect of increasing returns, MNEs see intra-firm trade as a facilitator of global integration of upstream and downstream activities. Chapter 4 discusses the MNE in more detail.

Industry Box

The Global Automotive Industry

Global trade in the automotive industry is a century old. Almost as soon as the first products appeared, some of the manufacturers (e.g., the Ford Motor Company) began to export their cars. Today, the major exporters of automotive products are also the major importers (e.g., the European Union, Japan, the United States, South Korea, Mexico, Canada, China), supporting Linder's income-preference similarity theory (see Exhibit 2.7). The largest volume of trade in automotive products involves trade among the countries of the European Union. The numbers are not necessarily balanced, however. For example, as noted earlier in this chapter, Japan exports (and manufactures) many more cars in the United States than the United States exports to and manufactures in Japan, suggesting a pattern of specialization consistent with the new trade theory and possibly reflecting the impact of non-tariff barriers.

Although Mexico's increasing role as a car exporter seems to challenge the view of developed nations exporting to other developed nations, it is in line with the new trade theory, which suggests that intra-industry trade is driven mainly by increasing returns resulting from specialization within the industry. Mexican car exports to the United States contain a substantial content of components imported from the United States. The result, according to Lucinda Vargas of the Federal Reserve Bank of Dallas, is that "in some respects, each country is sending the other essentially the same product but at a different stage of production." China, which also imports sophisticated vehicle components, is currently a minor exporter of motor vehicles, but this is likely to change dramatically as the country producers (many of them Foreign Invested Enterprises) rapidly enhance their capabilities.

Theory Assessment

Although none of the theories is capable of explaining the entire range of motives for international trade, they collectively provide invaluable insights into why international trade occurs. With reference to the sources of comparative advantage, differences in factor endowments (i.e., the Heckscher-Ohlin theorem) survive as the most general explanation of the pattern of "old" trade (e.g., labor-intensive products). The comparative advantage theory, despite its diminishing power in explaining today's international trade, is still capable of explaining international trade in natural resource products such as bananas (see opening case). When we extend the factor endowments by including skilled labors and technologies, the Heckscher-Ohlin theorem applies to current import and export activities between developed and developing countries. As an example, let us look at trade between Europe and Southeast Asia. Major exports from Europe are technology-intensive, including power-generation equipment, petroleum-processing machinery, medical equipment, and transportation equipment, whereas exports from Southeast Asia are mostly labor- or skill-labor-intensive, such as garments, furniture, shoes, rubber products, arts and crafts, and standardized electric and electronics products.

	Value	Share % in World Exports/Imports				Annual Percentage Change			
	2011	1980	1990	2000	2011	2005–11	2009	2010	2011
Exporters									
European Union (27)	659	–	–	49.8	51.2	5	–30	18	21
Extra–EU (27) exports	226	–	–	12.3	17.6	10	–35	45	28
Japan	151	19.8	20.8	15.3	11.7	3	–40	45	1
United States	119	11.9	10.2	11.7	9.3	6	–35	37	20
Korea, Republic of	69	0.1	0.7	2.6	5.4	11	–24	47	27
Mexico [a]	68	0.3	1.4	5.3	5.3	11	–21	54	22
Canada	54	6.9	8.9	10.5	4.2	–4	–34	47	8
China [a]	37	0.0	0.1	0.3	2.9	25	–31	41	34
Thailand	18	0.0	0.0	0.4	1.4	15	–28	60	–2
Turkey	16	0.0	0.0	0.3	1.2	9	–33	15	14
Brazil	14	1.1	0.6	0.8	1.1	3	–42	47	14
Argentina	10	0.1	0.1	0.4	0.8	22	–18	47	24
India	9	–	0.1	0.1	0.7	24	–2	65	20
South Africa	7	0.1	0.1	0.3	0.6	9	–34	32	9
United Arab Emirates [b]	6	–	0.0	0.1	0.5	13	–10	3	8
Taipei, Chinese	6	–	0.3	0.4	0.4	7	–13	33	18
Above 15	**1244**	–	–	**98.2**	**96.7**	–	–	–	–
Importers									
European Union (27)	501	–	–	42.9	38.2	3	–29	9	17
Extra–EU (27) imports	68	–	–	5.6	5.2	4	–33	10	17
United States	212	20.3	24.7	29.4	16.2	0	–33	42	12
China [a]	70	0.6	0.6	0.7	5.3	31	6	72	31
Canada [c]	64	8.7	7.7	8.0	4.9	2	–29	37	8
Russian Federation [c, d]	39	–	–	0.2	3.0	23	–70	63	67
Mexico [a, c]	35	1.8	0.3	3.5	2.7	6	–30	37	18
Australia [c]	25	1.3	1.2	1.5	1.9	9	–30	52	9
Brazil [c]	23	0.3	0.2	0.7	1.7	30	–11	45	34
Turkey	19	–	0.4	1.0	1.5	8	–31	47	26
Japan	17	0.5	2.3	1.7	1.3	4	–37	41	20
Saudi Arabia, Kingdom of [d]	17	2.7	0.9	0.7	1.3	9	–18	53	6
Switzerland	15	1.8	1.9	1.1	1.1	10	–16	21	28
Argentina	14	0.6	0.1	0.5	1.0	21	–37	76	27
United Arab Emirates	12	0.4	0.3	0.4	0.9	10	–49	24	9
Korea, Republic of	10	–	0.3	0.3	0.7	16	–26	49	22
Above 15	**1071**	–	–	**92.5**	**81.8**	–	–	–	–

[a] Includes significant shipments through processing zones.
[b] Mainly re–exports.
[c] Imports are valued f.o.b.
[d] Includes Secretariat estimates.

Exhibit 2.7 Leading exporters and importers of automotive products (billion dollars and percentage) top 15 exporters

Source: WTO International Trade Statistics, 2013.

Meanwhile, the technological gap (i.e., human skills and technology-based views) and the product life-cycle theories emerge as powerful explanations of trade in "new" products (i.e., manufactures made by skilled workforce using technologies). These skills and technologies are the key stimulus to improving a country's terms of trade, the major concern of both developed and developing countries today. The **terms of trade** is the relative price of exports, that is, the unit price of exports divided by the unit price of imports. The terms of trade improve if the country exports more goods that are associated with advanced human skills and technologies. In this case, the contribution of foreign trade to the nation's economic growth will be stronger. Although the product life-cycle model is less applicable today than at the time of its inception, it still explains key patterns in the evolution of international trade. A nation's import and export structures change over time. Similarly, every new product has its life stages in the global marketplace.

The Leontief paradox and Linder's income-preference similarity theory provide insights on the triggers of international trade for sophisticated manufacturing products and on trade between regions with similar income levels and consumption preferences. These theories view market demand (income levels and demand structure) as important parameters of international trade. Indeed, international trade today is driven not only by national differences in factor endowments but also by national differences in market demand. Intra-regional trade still accounts for a high proportion of world trade because of similarities in income levels and demand structures, as well as efficiencies arising from reduced uncertainty and transaction costs. The limitation of these theories is that they did not illuminate how trade activities would take place between two nations sharing similar income levels, but with different consumption preferences. Because of this weakness, they seem unable to explain the increasing trade between developed countries and newly industrialized (e.g., Singapore, South Korea, Taiwan, and Hong Kong) or emerging markets (e.g., China, Brazil, India, Russia, and Mexico). These countries are not in the same region, nor do they share similar consumption preference with the Western world. Increasing income and elevated purchasing power seem to be the key driver of this trade phenomenon.

Finally, the new trade theory enriches our understanding of intra-industry and intra-firm trade. It links national factor endowments with firm behavior and government incentives in explaining international trade. As Chapter 4 shows, this link is important because firms, rather than countries, conduct international trade and investment. The efficiency of international trade is maximized if both national factor endowment differences and economies-of-scale advantages of firms are combined and realized simultaneously. Since the MNE's role in international trade and investment is highly visible, the new trade theory has attracted more attention in recent years. The limitation of this theory, however, is that it overlooks other incentives beyond increasing returns from economy of scale. MNEs seek geographical diversification and accumulate knowledge about the target market from international trade. Chapter 4 articulates these issues in more detail.

Can we expect new theoretical development about international trade in the future? We believe so. As the following sections of this chapter demonstrate, the patterns and characteristics of today's international trade are quite different from those of trade activities in the last century and even those of two decades ago, a period when the last trade theory emerged. The most important thrust for a new line of theoretical development will be a shift from the analysis of country comparative advantages to the assessment of country capabilities (or competitiveness). Factor endowment conditions (including human resources, technology, and information) are a critical aspect of country competitiveness, and factor endowment differences between two nations remain an important foundation for international trade. However, other aspects of country capabilities also shape international trade. For example, an importing country's macroeconomic soundness, demand conditions, local competition, government policies, support of related industries (e.g., banking service and foreign exchange hedging systems) as well as culture are expected to affect trade activities. At the same time, an exporting country's infrastructure, business rivalry, openness, and innovation are important factors influencing the volume of, and gains from, export activities. Chapter 5 focuses on country competitiveness. A nation generally gains more from international trade if its competitiveness in the world market is higher than that of other countries. Japan, for instance, is not rich in factor endowments, but its competitiveness in innovation, adaptability, and business management made it a major player in international trade.

Interim Summary

1. Many theorists have created models to show the reasons, rationale, gains, or complexities of international trade. Some older theories such as the mercantilist doctrine and the absolute advantage theory, while accurate for their time, are inaccurate in today's world, due to drastic changes in technological diffusion, information exchange, and capital flow as well as the enhanced role of MNEs.
2. The Heckscher-Ohlin theorem, the most general explanation of "old" trade, is not entirely obsolete. By integrating advanced technology and a skilled workforce into systems of comparative advantage between countries, modern international trade can be modeled relatively accurately by the theorem.
3. When a new technology is created, the innovating country enjoys a trade advantage until the imitation gap is closed.
4. The new trade theory explains intra-industry and intra-firm trade. Theories of international trade must be continually revised as new technology and new political and economic realities create a different global climate.

International Trade Patterns

International Trade Volume and Growth

International trade continues to grow briskly, outpacing the growth in economic output. In 2012, global merchandise exports reached $18.4 trillion, boosted by both volume and price changes, and global exports of commercial services reached $4.35 trillion. Between 2003 and 2012, both global merchandise and commercial services exports rose at an average annual rate of about 10 percent. From a historical perspective, however, it is useful to recall that rapidly growing trade growth was

Log. scale

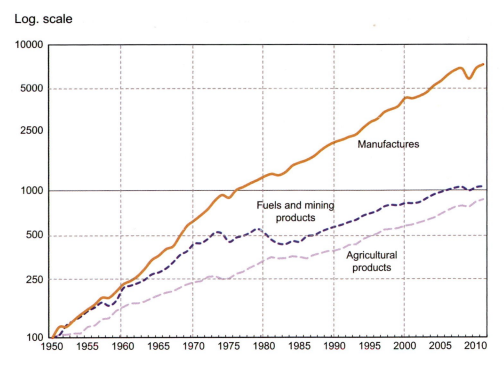

Exhibit 2.8 World merchandise trade volume by major product group, 1950–2011
Source: WTO International Trade Statistics, 2012.

reversed a century ago by high tariff regimes raised in the name of domestic interests. This is a reminder of how trade is intertwined with other realities, such as domestic and global political interests, which will be explored later in this book.

Exhibit 2.8 shows the growth in international merchandise trade volume between 1950 and 2011. The exhibit shows that the increase in merchandise trade has been more pronounced in manufacturing (especially exports of scientific and controlling instruments) than in agricultural products, a pattern partially explained by the shift of relative production costs in the world, and by the presence of trade barriers discussed later in this chapter. While overall trade has been growing steadily, there has been, over time, a considerable change in the share of various world regions (see Exhibit 2.9, parts 1 & 2). In exports, the Americas went from about 39.4 percent of the total in 1948 to 17.4 percent in 2012, while Africa lost more than half of its share. In contrast, Asia's share more than doubled, and Western Europe's share showed an increasing trend until the start of the 21st century when many of the European countries faced stiff competition from emerging economies in Asia. In imports, Asia and the Middle East have dramatically increased their intake, while other regions had either stayed relatively constant (North America) or shown substantial declines (Africa and South and Central America). A noteworthy feature in the last decade is that the two most populous countries in the world—China and India—recorded outstanding economic growth (averaging 10.5 percent and 7.5 percent, respectively, in the last decade) and trade expansion. For many commodities, China has become the largest importer and the largest supplier in the world for a number of manufactured goods.

41

	1948	1953	1963	1973	1983	1993	2003	2012
				Value				
World	59	84	157	579	1838	3677	7380	17930
	Share							
World	100.0	100.0	100.0	100.0	100.0	100.0	100.0	100.0
North America	**28.1**	**24.8**	**19.9**	**17.3**	**16.8**	**18.0**	**15.8**	**13.2**
United States	21.7	18.8	14.9	12.3	11.2	12.6	9.8	8.6
Canada	5.5	5.2	4.3	4.6	4.2	3.9	3.7	2.5
Mexico	0.9	0.7	0.6	0.4	1.4	1.4	2.2	2.1
South and Central America	**11.3**	**9.7**	**6.4**	**4.3**	**4.4**	**3.0**	**3.0**	**4.2**
Brazil	2.0	1.8	0.9	1.1	1.2	1.0	1.0	1.4
Argentina	2.8	1.3	0.9	0.6	0.4	0.4	0.4	0.5
Europe	**35.1**	**39.4**	**47.8**	**50.9**	**43.5**	**45.3**	**45.9**	**35.6**
Germany[a]	1.4	5.3	9.3	11.7	9.2	10.3	10.2	7.8
France	3.4	4.8	5.2	6.3	5.2	6.0	5.3	3.2
Italy	1.8	1.8	3.2	3.8	4.0	4.6	4.1	2.8
United Kingdom	11.3	9.0	7.8	5.1	5.0	4.9	4.1	2.6
Commonwealth of Independent States (CIS)[b]	**–**	**–**	**–**	**–**	**–**	**1.5**	**2.6**	**4.5**
Africa	**7.3**	**6.5**	**5.7**	**4.8**	**4.5**	**2.5**	**2.4**	**3.5**
South Africa[c]	2.0	1.6	1.5	1.0	1.0	0.7	0.5	0.5
Middle East	**2.0**	**2.7**	**3.2**	**4.1**	**6.8**	**3.5**	**4.1**	**7.5**
Asia	**14.0**	**13.4**	**12.5**	**14.9**	**19.1**	**26.1**	**26.1**	**31.5**
China	0.9	1.2	1.3	1.0	1.2	2.5	5.9	11.4
Japan	0.4	1.5	3.5	6.4	8.0	9.9	6.4	4.5
India	2.2	1.3	1.0	0.5	0.5	0.6	0.8	1.6
Australia and New Zealand	3.7	3.2	2.4	2.1	1.4	1.4	1.2	1.6
Six East Asian Traders	3.4	3.0	2.5	3.6	5.8	9.7	9.6	9.7
Memorandum item:								
EU[d]	–	–	24.5	37.0	31.3	37.4	42.3	32.4
USSR, Former	2.2	3.5	4.6	3.7	5.0	–	–	–
GATT/WTO Members[e]	63.4	69.6	75.0	84.1	78.4	89.3	94.3	96.6

[a] Figures refer to the Fed. Rep. of Germany from 1948 through 1983.
[b] Figures are significantly affected by including the mutual trade flows of the Baltic States and the CIS between 1993 and 2003.
[c] Beginning with 1998, figures refer to South Africa only and no longer to the Southern African Customs Union.
[d] Figures refer to the EEC(6) in 1963, EC(9) in 1973, EC(10) in 1983, EU(12) in 1993, EU(25) in 2003 and EU(27) in 2012.
[e] Membership as of the year stated.

Exhibit 2.9 Part 1 World merchandise exports by region and selected economy, 1948, 1953, 1963, 1973, 1983, 1993, 2003 and 2012 (billion dollars and percentage)

Source: WTO International Trade Statistics, 2013.

Note: Between 1973 and 1983 and between 1993 and 2003 export shares were significantly influenced by oil price developments.

	1948	1953	1963	1973	1983	1993	2003	2012
	Value							
World	62	85	164	594	1882	3787	7696	18188
	Share							
World	100.0	100.0	100.0	100.0	100.0	100.0	100.0	100.0
North America	**18.5**	**20.5**	**16.1**	**17.2**	**18.5**	**21.4**	**22.4**	**17.6**
United States	13.0	13.9	11.4	12.3	14.3	15.9	16.9	12.8
Canada	4.4	5.5	3.9	4.2	3.4	3.7	3.2	2.6
Mexico	1.0	0.9	0.8	0.6	0.7	1.8	2.3	2.1
South and Central America	**10.4**	**8.3**	**6.0**	**4.4**	**3.8**	**3.3**	**2.5**	**4.1**
Brazil	1.8	1.6	0.9	1.2	0.9	0.7	0.7	1.3
Argentina	2.5	0.9	0.6	0.4	0.2	0.4	0.2	0.4
Europe	**45.3**	**43.7**	**52.0**	**53.3**	**44.2**	**44.6**	**45.0**	**35.9**
Germany[a]	2.2	4.5	8.0	9.2	8.1	9.0	7.9	6.4
France	5.5	4.9	5.3	6.4	5.6	5.7	5.2	3.7
Italy	2.5	2.8	4.6	4.7	4.2	3.9	3.9	2.7
United Kingdom	13.4	11.0	8.5	6.5	5.3	5.5	5.2	3.8
Commonwealth of Independent States (CIS)[b]	–	–	–	–	–	1.2	1.7	3.1
Africa	**8.1**	**7.0**	**5.2**	**3.9**	**4.6**	**2.6**	**2.2**	**3.4**
South Africa[c]	2.5	1.5	1.1	0.9	0.8	0.5	0.5	0.7
Middle East	1.8	2.1	2.3	2.7	6.2	3.3	2.8	4.1
Asia	**13.9**	**15.1**	**14.1**	**14.9**	**18.5**	**23.6**	**23.5**	**31.8**
China	0.6	1.6	0.9	0.9	1.1	2.7	5.4	10.0
Japan	1.1	2.8	4.1	6.5	6.7	6.4	5.0	4.9
India	2.3	1.4	1.5	0.5	0.7	0.6	0.9	2.7
Australia and New Zealand	2.9	2.3	2.2	1.6	1.4	1.5	1.4	1.6
Six East Asian Traders	3.5	3.7	3.2	3.9	6.1	10.3	8.6	9.6
Memorandum item:								
EU[d]	–	–	–	–	–	–	41.8	32.6
USSR, Former	1.9	3.3	4.3	3.6	4.3	–	–	–
GATT/WTO Members[e]	58.6	66.9	75.3	85.5	81.3	88.7	94.8	97.6

[a] Figures refer to the Fed. Rep. of Germany from 1948 through 1983.
[b] Figures are significantly affected by including the mutual trade flows of the Baltic States and the CIS between 1993 and 2003.
[c] Beginning with 1998, figures refer to South Africa only and no longer to the Southern African Customs Union.
[d] Figures refer to the EEC(6) in 1963, EC(9) in 1973, EC(10) in 1983, EU(12) in 1993, EU(25) in 2003 and EU(27) in 2012.
[e] Membership as of the year stated.

Exhibit 2.9 Part 2 World merchandise imports by region and selected economy, 1948, 1953, 1963, 1973, 1983, 1993, 2003 and 2012 (billion dollars and percentage)

Source: WTO International Trade Statistics, 2013.

Service Trade

Trade in services currently accounts for about one-quarter of global trade, but as developed countries move towards service-based economies, its share is rapidly growing. **Service trade** encompasses the import and export of transportation services, travel, and other commercial services such as financial services, information services, the provision of education and training, health care, consulting and advisory services, and so on. Because of their advantage in services, developed countries tend to push much more aggressively for a removal of barriers to trade in services. In 2012, exports of transportation services, travel services, and other commercial services reached $890 billion, $1,110 billion, and $2,345 billion, respectively. While developed countries, such as those in the European Union and the United States, enjoy competitive advantages in exporting financial services, insurance services, computer, and information services, as well as education, training, and advisory services, some emerging economies, notably India and China, are establishing a competitive edge in exporting communications services (e.g., call centers) and technical support services.

Exhibit 2.10 shows US service exports and imports for 2008 and 2012. For 2012, US service exports exceeded imports by more than $210 billion. Its service exports were mainly contributed

	Export				Import			
	Value (million USD)		Share %		Value (million USD)		Share %	
	2008	2012	2008	2012	2008	2012	2008	2012
Commercial services (services excl. government services)	522,231	621,218	100%	100%	373,890	411,110	100%	100%
♦ Transportation	74,671	82,827	14%	13%	87,944	89,830	24%	22%
♦ Travel	139,123	162,793	27%	26%	86,904	91,825	23%	22%
♦ Other commercial services (commercial services—travel and transport)	308,437	375,598	59%	60%	199,042	229,455	53%	56%
• Communications services	10,301	14,047	2%	2%	8,353	8,280	2%	2%
▪ Telecommunication services	9,999	13,790	2%	2%	7,761	7,903	2%	2%
• Construction	3,885		1%	0%	3,451		1%	0%
• Insurance services	13,403	16,626	3%	3%	58,913	53,340	16%	13%
• Financial services	63,027	72,328	12%	12%	17,218	15,641	5%	4%
• Computer and information services	13,120		3%	0%	16,895		5%	0%
▪ Computer services	8,502		2%	0%	15,925		4%	0%
• Royalties and license fees	102,125	124,303	20%	20%	29,623	41,992	8%	10%
• Other business services	101,829	127,248	19%	20%	64,295	81,622	12%	13%
• Personal, cultural, and recreational services	747		0%	0%	294		0%	0%

Exhibit 2.10 Trade in commercial services of the United States, 2008 and 2012 (million dollars and percentage)
Source: WTO Statistics Database, Time Series, 2013.

by travel, transportation, royalties and license fees, and financial services. Imports are divided roughly equally between transportation, travel, insurance, and other services.

Trade Measurement

The United States has systematically recorded its imports and exports since 1821. Since 1989, it has used a harmonized system for classifying trade that facilitates comparability of data with the country's major trade partners. With the exception of Canada (where the United States substitutes Canadian import figures for US exports), export data are compiled from Shipper's Export Declarations filed by exporters, forwarders, and carriers. Import data are compiled from US customs forms. Trade data are used not only by governments, but also by firms and research institutions to gauge such measures as market penetration and share.

While most trade statistics in this chapter appear in the aggregate, it is useful to remember that they are available for different categories: for example, domestic exports (produced or materially transformed in the United States) versus re-exports (commodities of foreign origin that have not been materially changed in the United States); or foreign imports (of foreign origin or those returned to the United States in their original form) versus American Goods Returned to the United States after Processing and/or Assembly. Additional data, for example, on transportation mode (see Chapter 16 on Global Marketing and Supply Chain) are also available.[17]

Major Exporters and Importers

Exhibits 2.11a and 2.11b show the largest exporters and importers of merchandise trade and commercial services, respectively. Not surprisingly, developed countries dominate imports and exports in both

Rank	Exporters	Value	Share	Annual Percentage Change	Rank	Importers	Value	Share	Annual Percentage Change
1	China	2,049	11.1	8	1	United States	2,336	12.6	3
2	United States	1,546	8.4	4	2	China	1,818	9.8	4
3	Germany	1,407	7.6	−5	3	Germany	1,167	6.3	−7
4	Japan	799	4.3	−3	4	Japan	886	4.8	4
5	Netherlands	656	3.6	−2	5	United Kingdom	690	3.7	2
6	France	569	3.1	−5	6	France	674	3.6	−6
7	Korea, Republic of	548	3.0	−1	7	Netherlands	591	3.2	−1
8	Russian Federation	529	2.9	1	8	Hong Kong, China	553	3.0	8
9	Italy	501	2.7	−4		retained imports	140	0.8	6
10	Hong Kong, China	493	2.7	8					
	domestic exports	22	0.1	33	9	Korea, Republic of	520	2.8	−1
	re-exports	471	2.6	7	10	India	490	2.6	5
	World	**18,401**	**100.0**	**0**		**World**	**18,601**	**100.0**	**1**

Exhibit 2.11a Top ten leading exporters and importers in world merchandise trade, 2012 (billion dollars and percentage)

Source: WTO International Trade Statistics, 2013.

Rank	Exporters	Value	Share	Annual Percentage Change	Rank	Importers	Value	Share	Annual Percentage Change
1	United States	621	14.3	6	1	United States	411	9.9	4
2	United Kingdom	280	6.4	−3	2	Germany	293	7.1	−1
3	Germany	257	5.9	−1	3	China	280	6.7	18
4	France	211	4.8	−6	4	Japan	175	4.2	5
5	China	190	4.4	8	5	United Kingdom	174	4.2	0
6	Japan	142	3.3	0	6	France	172	4.1	−9
7	India	141	3.2	3	7	India	127	3.1	3
8	Spain	136	3.1	−4	8	Netherlands	119	2.9	−1
9	Netherlands	131	3.0	−3	9	Singapore	118	2.8	3
10	Hong Kong, China	123	2.8	5	10	Ireland	112	2.7	−3
	World	**4,350**	**100.0**	**2**		**World**	**4,150**	**100.0**	**3**

Exhibit 2.11b Top ten leading exporters and importers in world trade in commercial services, 2012 (billion dollars and percentage)

Source: WTO International Trade Statistics, 2013.

merchandise trade and commercial services. In merchandise trade, the top ten exporters and importers are developed countries, with the notable exception of China that recently became the world's largest exporter and second largest importer (after the United States) of merchandise trade. It is worth noting, however, that some developing economies, such as Republic of Korea, Mexico, Russia, Singapore, Hong Kong (China), Taiwan, and Malaysia are also emerging as important merchandise trade partners in both imports and exports (among the top 20). In commercial services, the top ten importers and exporters are also mostly developed economies, with China, India, and Singapore being the exceptions. One reason for the gap between developed and developing economies in the trade of services is that many commercial services such as financial services, global transportation, consulting, and health care are knowledge intensive and hence less likely to be either produced or consumed in a developing economy. Nevertheless, some newly industrialized and emerging economies, such as Hong Kong (China), Republic of Korea, Russia, and Brazil are rapidly advancing as important participants in commercial services trade (among the top 20).

US Trade Partners

Exhibit 2.12 shows US merchandise trade with various regions and countries. The EU, Canada, China, Mexico, and Japan are the United States' top five trade partners. How can these patterns be explained? With the exception of Mexico and China, three of the United States' five major trading partners are developed economies, which is consistent with Linder's income-preference similarity theory. Canada, the major partner of the United States, has additional advantages in

	Exports						Imports				
Destination	Value	Share		Annual Percentage Change		Origin	Value	Share		Annual Percentage Change	
	2012	2005	2012	2011	2012		2012	2005	2012	2011	2012
Region						Region					
World	**1,545,709**	**100.0**	**100.0**	**16**	**4**	**World**	**2,335,537**	**100.0**	**100.0**	**15**	**3**
North America	509,044	36.9	32.9	16	6	Asia	896,416	36.8	38.4	10	6
Asia	422,283	26.6	27.3	13	2	North America	608,137	26.8	26.0	14	4
Europe	313,803	22.6	20.3	14	−1	Europe	430,332	20.0	18.4	16	3
South and Central America	180,046	7.9	11.6	21	8	South and Central America	177,606	7.5	7.6	31	−1
Middle East	69,602	3.5	4.5	20	19	Middle East	119,609	3.8	5.1	38	13
Africa	33,144	1.7	2.1	16	0	Africa	68,484	3.9	2.9	8	−28
CIS	15,333	0.7	1.0	40	19	CIS	34,953	0.1	1.5	30	−17
Economy						Economy					
Canada	291,675	23.5	18.9	13	4	China	444,407	15.0	19.0	9	6
European Union (27)	265,743	20.8	17.2	12	−1	European Union (27)	389,061	18.4	16.7	15	4
Mexico	216,331	13.3	14.0	21	10	Canada	327,482	16.8	14.0	14	3
China	110,590	4.6	7.2	13	6	Mexico	280,017	10.0	12.0	14	6
Japan	70,043	6.1	4.5	9	6	Japan	150,401	8.2	6.4	7	14
Above 5	**1,480,697**	**68.4**	**61.7**			**Above 5**	**2,269,643**	**68.4**	**68.1**		

Exhibit 2.12 Merchandise trade of the United States by region and economy, 2012 (billion dollars and percentage)
Source: WTO International Trade Statistics, 2013.

terms of trade with the United States: geographic proximity, relative cultural similarity, and NAFTA membership. More than 100,000 US companies export to Canada, more than double the number that exports to Mexico, the second-ranked destination. Mexico also benefits from its proximity to the United States and from NAFTA membership. Since NAFTA's establishment in 1994, Mexico's exports have grown threefold, with the United States and Canada accounting for much of the growth.

The trade relationships that the US has with China and Mexico are consistent with the comparative advantage theory and factor endowment model. China clearly enjoys a comparative advantage in the production of many manufactured goods over the US, which is attributable to its abundant endowment of semi-skilled labor. From the perspective of the Heckscher-Ohlin theorem, it is easy to see why US eateries import agricultural products and processed foods from Mexico, where expenses are low and wages start at about $50 a week;[18] or why pencil imports, mostly from China, increased five-fold from 1996 to 2011, with US producers now making up just 14 percent of the market.[19] Similarly, it is clear why Africa exports mostly mining products to North America, but very few manufacturing products.[20] The overall trade picture, however, is more complex.

Let's start with the numbers. With increased globalization, more and more exported products contain a myriad of inputs from other countries, including those that end up importing the final product. The IBM plant in El Salto, Mexico incorporates US components in products that are then exported to the United States or sold in other export markets. They are registered as Mexican exports. Between 1995 and 1998 alone, exports to countries other than the United States by the Mexican affiliates of US corporations tripled.[21] The same is true for information technology exports out of the Philippines, Malaysia, and Thailand that represent a probable value added of no more than 20 percent, given the importation of semiconductors and other manufacturing inputs that go into the exported products.[22] Exports from China to the United States include manufacturing goods; however, many incorporate foreign inputs and are made by firms from developed economies, including the United States, Japan, and the EU, which use China as an export platform. In 2012, 52 percent of China's exports came from Foreign Invested Enterprises, a category that includes all enterprises with an element of foreign equity. Vietnam stood to benefit only modestly from the abolition of US tariffs on its textile exports because those are made with imported raw material.

Exhibit 2.13a and 2.13b present the trade flow, by product, between the United States and Japan, a flow that is one of the world's most important bilateral flows, both politically and economically. Some components of the flow are easily explained; for example, the flow of foodstuff from the United States to Japan can be explained by factor endowments. Other components of the flow, however, are not easily explained. For example, Japanese vehicle exports to the United States are more than ten times larger than US vehicle exports to Japan. Since the United States has the

Rank	Description	Million USD			% Share			% Change
		2010	2011	2012	2010	2011	2012	2012 / 2011
	TOTAL	**60,472**	**65,686**	**69,955**				**6.50%**
1	(22090) Civilian aircraft, engines, equipment, and parts	4,308	4,154	7,168	7%	6%	10%	72.56%
2	(40100) Pharmaceutical preparations	3,234	3,056	4,229	5%	5%	6%	38.39%
3	(21610) Medicinal equipment	3,285	3,637	4,126	5%	6%	6%	13.44%
4	(00300) Meat, poultry, etc.	2,461	3,030	3,187	4%	5%	5%	5.16%
5	(00200) Corn	3,028	3,838	3,006	5%	6%	4%	−21.67%
6	(21400) Telecommunications equipment	1,527	1,789	2,331	3%	3%	3%	30.29%
7	(12540) Chemicals—organic	2,069	2,066	2,067	3%	3%	3%	0.03%
8	(41050) Other household goods	2,020	1,956	2,006	3%	3%	3%	2.55%
9	(21180) Industrial machines, other	1,887	1,919	1,710	3%	3%	2%	−10.87%
10	(11120) Petroleum products, other	951	1,232	1,496	2%	2%	2%	21.41%

Exhibit 2.13a US exports to Japan (top ten commodities)
Source: US Dept. of Commerce, Bureau of the Census, 2013.

Rank	End-Use Code	Million USD			% Share			% Change
		2010	2011	2012	2010	2011	2012	2012 / 2011
	TOTAL	**120,552**	**128,928**	**146,392**				**13.55%**
1	(30000) Passenger cars, new and used	32,028	29,908	37,666	27%	23%	26%	25.94%
2	(30230) Other parts and accessories	8,626	9,576	12,238	7%	7%	8%	27.80%
3	(21180) Other industrial machinery	7,203	9,275	9,517	6%	7%	7%	2.60%
4	(21301) Computer accessories, peripherals and parts	5,359	5,314	4,815	4%	4%	3%	−9.39%
5	(30200) Engines and engine parts	3,209	3,849	4,689	3%	3%	3%	21.81%
6	(20005) Electric apparatus and parts, n.e.c.	3,839	3,860	4,485	3%	3%	3%	16.17%
7	(21030) Excavating, paving, and construction machinery	1,360	2,657	3,953	1%	2%	3%	48.78%
8	(21120) Machine tools, metalworking, molding and rolling	1,864	3,190	3,716	2%	2%	3%	16.49%
9	(22010) Parts for civilian aircraft	2,136	2,676	3,389	2%	2%	2%	26.66%
10	(21100) Industrial engines, pumps, compressors and generators	2,158	2,700	3,167	2%	2%	2%	17.29%

Exhibit 2.13b US imports from Japan (top ten commodities)
Source: US Dept. of Commerce, Bureau of the Census, 2013.

largest motor vehicle industry in the world and has (through its subsidiaries) a substantial share of a competitive market, such as the EU, it is difficult to explain the large gap via comparative advantage or scale economy. Other factors must be at play, among them: trade barriers (described in the next section) that limit the access of US firms to the Japanese market; currency exchange rates that have made US vehicles expensive in Japan; and externalities, such as rising fuel prices, that made Japanese vehicles more attractive in the United States.

Recall that the new trade theory suggests that, while inter-industry trade is governed by the Heckscher-Ohlin theorem (trade between countries with different factor endowments), intra-industry trade is not. US textile imports, for example, come mostly from the developing world, with China, India, Vietnam, Bangladesh, Indonesia, Pakistan, and Mexico in top places, as one might expect from a labor-intensive product. Still, Canada and Italy remain other important sources, but the products they export to the US are different, generally being of a higher price and quality. In the case of Mexico, proximity and re-exports account for much of the exports to the United States, but their importance has markedly declined once tariff barriers started to come down.[23]

The Leontief paradox asks why the United States exports labor-intensive products when it had no advantage in labor rates. Labor migration is one reason. In this case, it is labor moving in the pursuit of capital rather than the other way around. Rather than moving south of the border, US carpet manufacturers rely on Mexican migration to northwest Georgia to lower labor costs and remain competitive. While labor costs are still higher relatively to Mexican plants, transportation costs to US customers are much lower, making domestic production cost effective.[24] With the wages of US trading partners rising as a percentage of US wages (about doubling from 1960 to 1992, and slowing in growth in the 2000s with the increased trade from China, Mexico, and other developing nations), wage differentials are not the only factor determining the location of production, although they remain a vitally important criterion.[25]

Trade Balance

The **balance of trade** is calculated as exports minus imports of goods and services. As will be discussed further in Chapter 9, trade surplus (deficit) is fundamentally due to the excess (shortfall) of a country's savings relative to consumption, so countries that run large trade surpluses (deficits) tend to have high (low) savings rates (e.g., China, Germany, Japan, and Singapore). The United States has by far the largest trade deficit of any country (Exhibit 2.14a), though as a percentage of GDP its deficit is much lower than that of many other nations (Exhibit 2.14b). The US deficit in merchandise trade persisted since the early 1980s, and has been especially pronounced in trade with Japan during the 1980s and early 1990s and with China since the late 1990s. In both cases, considerable anxiety arose surrounding the possible repercussions of the deficit to US competitiveness, income distribution, and national security. The trade surplus of China, which grew very large in the 2000s and was widely criticized as the result of the deliberately low value of its currency, has been falling in recent years due to the Chinese government's effort in promoting domestic consumption in conjunction with the appreciation of its currency. As China's trade surplus fell below that of Germany (Exhibit 2.14a), the US government shifted the focus of its criticism, in the 2013 US Treasury Department report on international economic and exchange rate policies, from China to Germany for insufficient domestic consumption.[26]

In contrast to its deficit in merchandise trade, the United States enjoys substantial surplus in services. In 2012, the US deficit in merchandise trade approached $790 billion, roughly double the 1999 figure, but its service trade was in the plus column to the tune of more than $210 billion. This discrepancy explains why the United States is at the forefront of those fighting to reduce barriers in service trade. For instance, the United States has been a major proponent of "open skies" agreements that liberalize the markets for commercial aviation and has fought hard for the opening of hitherto closed markets (e.g., China) for financial services. India, a country that has been dramatically increasing its service exports, has become a center for software export. This success played a role in the Indian government's decision to open up its own market to realize the benefits of free trade, though many barriers still remain.

Knowledge is often the most valuable contribution toward a competitive advantage in services. This can be seen clearly in the distribution of US service exports. The US exports intellectual property (paid as royalties and license fees) and legal services to Europe, while it sells mostly education and engineering services in the Asia-Pacific region. US freight services are sold mainly in the Asia-Pacific and Africa/Middle East regions, while Latin America absorbs US exports in advertising, insurance, communications, and travel services.[27]

Current account balance ($bn)

US $ billions (minus sign = deficit)

#	Country	2012
1	Germany	238.33
2	China Mainland	201.71 [1]
3	Switzerland	84.72
4	Russia	81.30
5	Netherlands	76.91
6	Norway	71.13
7	Japan	58.94
8	Qatar	55.04
9	Singapore	51.44
10	Taiwan	49.55
11	Korea	43.14
12	Sweden	37.56
13	UAE	29.40
14	Malaysia	19.49
15	Denmark	16.46
16	Venezuela	11.02
17	Austria	8.16
18	Kazakhstan	7.72
19	Philippines	7.13
20	Ireland	3.71
21	Luxembourg	3.18
22	Hong Kong	2.94
23	Thailand	2.73
24	Hungary	2.12
25	Slovak Republic	2.07
26	Slovenia	1.12
27	Argentina	0.48
28	Croatia	0.05
29	Israel	-0.20
30	Lithuania	-0.22
31	Estonia	-0.30
32	Latvia	-0.47
33	Iceland	-0.66
34	Bulgaria	-0.68
35	Finland	-3.89
36	Jordan	-5.62
37	Portugal	-6.05
38	Czech Republic	-6.18 [1]
39	New Zealand	-6.52 [1]
40	Belgium	-6.65
41	Peru	-7.14
42	Greece	-7.18
43	Romania	-7.91 [1]
44	Mexico	-9.25
45	Chile	-9.50
46	Spain	-10.62
47	Colombia	-11.42
48	Italy	-12.21
49	Ukraine	-14.76
50	Poland	-17.36
51	South Africa	-24.07
52	Indonesia	-24.18
53	Turkey	-47.48
54	Brazil	-54.25
55	Australia	-56.69
56	France	-62.85
57	Canada	-67.00
58	United Kingdom	-85.53
59	India	-92.80
60	USA	-474.98

Exhibit 2.14a Economic performance—international trade

Source: World Competitiveness Yearbook, Copyright © 2013, IMD, Switzerland, www.imd.org/wcc.

Balance of trade (%)

Percentage of GDP

		2012
1	Qatar	53.86
2	UAE	32.10
3	Ireland	25.91
4	Kazakhstan	23.56
5	Norway	14.72
6	Singapore	10.37
7	Malaysia	10.14
8	Venezuela	9.68
9	Russia	9.44
10	Netherlands	8.33
11	Czech Republic	8.07
12	Germany	7.06
13	Hungary	6.86
14	Taiwan	6.48
15	Switzerland	4.45
16	Denmark	4.35
17	Slovak Republic	3.58
18	China Mainland	2.80
19	Argentina	2.60
20	Korea	2.50
21	Iceland	2.13
22	Belgium	1.92
23	Sweden	1.89
24	Peru	1.55
25	Italy	0.70
26	Brazil	0.41
27	Slovenia	0.36
28	Colombia	0.31
29	Indonesia	-0.21
30	Australia	-0.27
31	Chile	-0.44
32	New Zealand	-0.57
33	Mexico	-0.82
34	Canada	-1.11
35	Finland	-1.29
36	Japan	-1.46
37	Poland	-2.57
38	Austria	-3.01
39	Spain	-3.02
40	France	-4.02
41	Thailand	-4.94
42	USA	-5.04
43	Israel	-5.09
44	Philippines	-5.34
45	Lithuania	-6.11
46	Portugal	-6.54
47	Estonia	-7.13
48	Romania	-7.30
49	United Kingdom	-8.85
50	Ukraine	-9.14
51	South Africa	-9.62
52	India	-10.53
53	Turkey	-10.63
54	Latvia	-10.94
55	Greece	-11.12
56	Bulgaria	-11.81
57	Luxembourg	-14.20
58	Croatia	-14.91
59	Hong Kong	-23.03
60	Jordan	-41.39

Exhibit 2.14b Economic performance—international trade

Source: World Competitiveness Yearbook, Copyright © 2013, IMD, Switzerland, www.imd.org/wcc.

> **Interim Summary**
>
> 1. World trade levels have shifted dramatically in the last 50 years, with merchandise trade more pronounced in manufacturing than in mining and agricultural products. Also, the balance of trade between countries and regions has altered significantly.
> 2. Highly developed countries often have services as a major export. The United States is a prominent example.
> 3. The considerable US surplus in service trade is outweighed by its much bigger deficit in merchandise trade, producing an overall deficit that has persisted for a quarter of a century.

Arguments for Trade Restrictions

Generally speaking, trade theories show the benefits to be derived from international trade, but dwell less on its potential drawbacks. This is particularly true for the theories of absolute and comparative advantage, which point out that trade allows for the efficient deployment of national resources from which everyone benefits. At the same time, opponents of free trade have been wrangling for years, most recently in their strong opposition to "globalization." Most countries have taken the position that trade needs first and foremost to protect the interests of their citizens. For example, the US Foreign Trade Anti-Trust Improvement Act permits price-fixing agreements among exporters if neither US consumers, nor US competitors, are harmed.[28]

Opinion surveys (see also Chapter 7 on the political and legal environment) show that the American public is divided on the benefits of free trade. Specifically, the American public tends to view trade with other developed economies (e.g., Canada, Europe, and Japan) positively, but shows ambivalence and skepticism toward trade with newly industrialized countries (e.g., China and South Korea) and believes free trade agreements to be bad for the US by a significant margin (44 to 35 percent, according to a Pew Research Center survey in 2010).[29] How can we reconcile the two views? One answer rests with the gap between the macro and micro views. Although trade may be good for the overall national economy, its impact varies across regional, occupational, and other lines. A survey by the Institute of International Economics shows that unskilled workers are much less likely to support free trade, because they are threatened by a shift of their jobs to lower cost locales. In contrast, skilled and highly educated people are more likely to benefit from trade at least in the short term, and hence tend to support free trade. Other studies confirm that people with lower incomes tend to be more negatively disposed toward trade. This is ironic because, as the head of the WTO once noted, poor people are more adversely affected by protectionism because it increases the price of consumer goods.[30] Union membership may not have much impact on attitudes toward trade, though it is often assumed to do so.[31] The schism between social groups regarding trade may in itself trigger opposition to trade on the part of governments that are worried about its economic, social, and political impact.

To deal with the uneven impact of trade, the US government provides trade adjustment assistance under the Trade Act of 1974 (amended and extended in 2002 and 2009) in the form of extended unemployment benefits, job relocation assistance, a refundable health care tax credit, and retraining funds for workers who lose their jobs to overseas competition. In 2010, 280,000 people were certified as eligible for this assistance program, which was a 40 percent increase from 2009 and nearly double the number eligible in 2007. It is estimated that an employee who loses his/her job in a high import-competing industry will receive a 13 percent pay cut once reemployed.[32]

The Sovereignty Argument

Another source of opposition to trade is the supposed threat it represents to national sovereignty. According to this argument, the shift in production to the most efficient location deprives a country of the base it needs to be a viable economic entity. In turn, this will make a country too dependent on nations that may challenge its national interests. This argument is particularly salient in industries considered key to national security, either directly (e.g., the arms industry), or indirectly (e.g., airlines). The United States, like many other countries, prohibits non-US firms from acquiring a majority stake in a US airline on the pretext that the aircraft need to be mobilized should an emergency occur. For similar reasons, countries sometimes curb the exports of certain products to designated countries.

Free trade is sometimes opposed as a threat to national culture and institutions. You will be reminded of that when you read about cultural industries in Chapter 6. Some countries, notably France and Canada, impose restrictions on the introduction of foreign media under the pretext that open importation would endanger their culture and language. As we will see in our discussion of tariffs below, countries may establish particularly high tariffs on products that they see as essential to their way of life (e.g., rice in Japan).

The Lowest Common Denominator Argument

Still another source of opposition to free trade has to do with its potentially adverse consequences for the environment, safety, and such. This is the "lowest common denominator" argument, according to which production will shift to nations with the least protection since they will offer the lowest cost base, but eventually, everyone else will end up paying for the adverse impact in the form of pollution, environmental degradation, and global warming. As you may recall from Chapter 1, the lowest common denominator argument has been one of the main complaints lodged by the anti-globalization movement.

Trade Reciprocity

Although trade theories assume benefits even when a country opens its borders to free trade unilaterally, additional benefits can be gained from reciprocity. Those additional benefits are not only economic (e.g., the ability to export the goods and services in which it has a comparative advantage), but also political and social, in that it is difficult to build domestic support for unilateral opening. For instance, if the US government were to permit all Chinese imports unilaterally, it might be supported by some consumer groups, but opposed by almost everyone else. In contrast, the pressure it applied to China to open its borders to US exports brought it the support of US exporters. Reciprocity also appeals to our sense of fairness (itself a key US value). In a *Business Week* survey from 2000, only 10 percent of respondents identified themselves as "free traders"; 37 percent identified themselves as "protectionists," while the rest identified as "fair traders."[33] In a more recent NBC News/Wall Street Journal poll, the percentage of Americans who think trade agreements are generally bad for the country rose from 30 percent in 1999 to 53 percent in 2010, with those with a favorable opinion of trade agreements falling from 39 percent to 17 percent during that period.[34]

Trebilcock and Howse distinguish between two kinds of reciprocity: passive and active. **Passive reciprocity** is a position taken by a country where it refuses to lower or eliminate its barriers to trade until the other party does the same. **Active or aggressive reciprocity** may be conducted through the threat of retaliation. For example, the withdrawal of previous commitments and concessions, or the undertaking of other retaliatory measures until the other party fulfills its obligations. An example is "super 301" which may be invoked by the United States in the case of "unreasonable and discriminatory" trade behavior by a foreign country.[35] Adam Smith suggested that retaliation should be considered a possible response to protectionism, although he was concerned that this could harm the retaliating nation as well.

Indeed, reciprocity and retaliation are an integral part of the international trade scene. Countervailing duties and subsidies are commonly used by nations to retaliate or compensate for the value produced by preferences provided for foreign manufacturers or service providers.

Optimal Tariff Theory

The **optimal tariff theory** assumes that by imposing a tariff, governments can capture a significant portion of the manufacturer's profit margin. In other words, assuming that the exporter cannot raise prices at will, domestic customers will not have to pay higher prices while their government manages to obtain part of the proceeds that would otherwise have been obtained by the exporter. The optimal tariff theory assumes, however, that the exporter can absorb the lower prices and will not simply shift its efforts into other markets. The theory also does not take into account the fact that high tariffs are likely to trigger smuggling (see Chapter 19 on Ethics and Corruption) that eventually reduce government revenue. An example is the importation of cigarettes, traditionally a high-tariff item, where even the manufacturers themselves have been accused of rampant smuggling to circumvent tariffs.

Infant Industry Argument

The **infant industry argument** for trade protection is that an industry new to a country, especially a developing one, needs to be protected by tariff walls or risk being squashed by established global players before it is given a chance to grow and develop. The proponents of this idea are not inherently averse to free trade and favor only *temporary* protection of new industries in countries that face stiff competition from producers based in more developed countries. The argument is rooted in the notion of **experience curve** or **learning effect** that people tend to become more proficient in performing a task (e.g., manufacturing a new product) as they accumulate more experience. So, when a country is starting a new industry that has already grown strong in a more developed country, its producers are likely less proficient for a period of time until they catch up with those in the more developed country through experience (e.g., as indicated by cumulative production volume).

The argument was vigorously raised by the United States throughout the nineteenth century, by Japan after World War II, and by Korea in the 1960s. These countries wanted to encourage the development of their domestic industry while generating revenues for the state, at the expense of foreign manufacturers. The interest of consumers, amply demonstrated by theories of international trade, was not considered. When US motor vehicles were kept out of both Japan and Korea through high tariffs and other barriers, the result was higher local prices. The same was true for the "voluntary export restraints" set in the US during the mid-1970s, which limited the number of Japanese cars sold in the US and cost the US consumer more than $1,000 per car. Here the argument was not one of infant industry (US car manufacturers have been in business since early in the twentieth century), but rather that the industry needed time to recuperate from the Japanese onslaught and restructure to produce more fuel-efficient cars. Although critics refer to the premise for such protection sarcastically as the acquisition of a "second childhood," this type of protective measure against "import surge" has since become an acceptable policy under WTO.

Apart from the damage to consumers, policies adopted under the infant industry argument can also have other harmful effects. First, there is no guarantee that the producers in the country will learn sufficiently fast to catch up with the more efficient producers overseas. The domestic producers may lack the educational background to learn at a reasonable pace, or the foreign producers may improve their efficiency even faster than the domestic producers can. Second, the protection in the form of a tariff or quota can actually remove or reduce the incentive for the domestic producers to improve their efficiency, particularly if the protection helps the domestic producers to grow into economically and politically powerful forces that can effectively lobby the government to perpetuate the protection. In fact, the proponents of the argument also recognize these potential harms and suggest that any protection should have a predetermined expiration point (e.g., based on the length of time or cumulative volume of domestic production), to stop the waste in case the domestic producers fail to catch up, and to give them a strong incentive to improve efficiency.

Finally, in the presence of an efficient capital market, if a new industry is perceived to have a bright future in the country, private capital can be expected to flow into the industry, treating any initial loss as an investment in a promising industry. It is true that many developing countries also suffer from an inefficient capital market and an underdeveloped public education system that make it difficult for entrepreneurs to take advantage of good opportunities. Even though the protection of infant industries may be justified in the presence of such institutional weaknesses, the country should still make serious efforts in strengthening its financial and educational institutions so as to reduce future needs for protecting new industries.

> **Interim Summary**
>
> 1. Free trade and globalization are hot-button issues. Some constituencies believe that protectionism is the best stance, whereas most economists assert that free trade is the only path to a healthy economy in the long term.
> 2. There are many reasons for a nation to be cautious when entering into free trade with other nations. For example, a country must balance protection of its workforce, national security, and national culture and identity with the benefits brought about by free trade.
> 3. A major concern with free trade and globalization is the potential for environmental damage from firms operating in poorly regulated markets.
> 4. Trade reciprocity can bring about additional benefits to countries engaged in free trade.

Types of Trade Barriers

Barriers to trade are typically divided into tariff and non-tariff barriers. **Tariff barriers** are official constraints on the importation of certain goods and services in the form of a special levy. **Non-tariff barriers** are indirect measures that discriminate against foreign manufacturers in the domestic market or otherwise distort and constrain trade. While tariff barriers have been significantly reduced during the several decades of the General Agreement on Tariffs & Trade (GATT) regime, debate continues on whether similar progress has been made vis-à-vis non-tariff barriers that are by definition much more difficult to measure.

Although some non-tariff barriers (e.g., subsidies) have been targeted and reduced, others have emerged in their place. Sometimes, both tariff and non-tariff barriers are applied in tandem. India, which was once one of the most protective markets in the world, called the combination "swadeshi" or "nationalist policies."[36] This meant, for instance, prohibiting foreign firms from bidding on strategic defense projects (a tariff barrier), while preventing those firms from winning less sensitive bids by failing to disclose essential requirements or by publicizing the bids in obscure local outlets unlikely to be scrutinized by foreign firms (a non-tariff barrier).

Together, tariff and non-tariff barriers pose a serious obstacle to international trade. In a survey of Minnesota businesses, regulations and tariffs were considered the most serious barriers to entry into international trade, ahead of lack of information, cost and financing, qualified employees, language, and culture.[37]

Tariff Barriers

Tariffs are surcharges that an importer must pay above and beyond taxes levied on domestic goods and services. Tariffs are transparent (listed in the Harmonized Tariff Schedule) and are typically set *ad valorem*, that is, based on the value of the product or service. Tariffs were used widely in the nineteenth century but were incrementally reduced over time. The Smoot-Hawley Act in 1930 reversed this trend, pushing tariffs to a level of almost 60 percent of import value. Predictably, they brought on retaliatory measures by major trade partners of the United States.

In the decades that followed, tariffs in the United States and later in other nations declined substantially, reaching single digits for most products. Nevertheless, US tariffs on some products (e.g., sugar) remain very high. Examples of particularly high tariffs include a 300 percent tariff on butter in Canada, a 179 percent tariff on sweet powdered milk in the United States, a 215 percent tariff on frozen beef in the EU, and a 550 percent tariff on rice in Japan.[38] The Japanese tariff on rice is particularly interesting, since the Japanese government maintains that its rationale is to uphold a social and cultural way of life that is linked with rice cultivation. The more prosaic reason is the political strength of the farm lobby within Japan's ruling Liberal Democratic Party (LDP). The result, as trade theories would predict, is that the Japanese consumer pays much more for rice than do consumers in the United States and in most other countries.

Not surprisingly, tariffs have been on the agenda of virtually all rounds of trade negotiations through GATT (the predecessor of WTO), and remarkable progress has been made toward their elimination or reduction. Nevertheless, a hike in tariff is not unheard of. The United States and other nations often use punitive tariffs as a way to retaliate or obtain reciprocity. India, while generally reducing tariffs, has increased tariffs on such goods as whiskey from an already high level of 104 percent to 220 and 550 percent.[39] Companies, on their part, have been investing efforts in circumventing tariffs. Heartland By-Products, a small Michigan firm, circumvents the high US tariff on sugar by buying sugar-molasses from its Canadian sister company, which makes it from sugar bought at world prices, and then reversing the process, turning the molasses into sugar syrup that it sells to US makers of ice cream, cereals, and candy.[40]

With overall tariffs low, governments often attempt to shift a product into a higher tariff category while firms develop strategies to benefit from the lower tariff category. The EU imposes a 288 percent tariff on imported vegetables, which is geared toward protecting the farm lobby in the Union, but only a 20 percent tariff on sauces. The EU decided to apply the very high tariff to imported sauces containing more than 20 percent of "lumps of fruits and vegetables," but now faces the ire of European firms such as Nestlé whose own sauces have faced retaliatory tariffs in other countries.[41] Similarly, the United States imposes 12.5 percent (if water packed) and 35 percent (if oil packed) tariffs on imported tuna in cans or pouches, but only 1.5 percent on cooked non-canned fish. Bumble Bee, a unit of Conagra Foods, takes advantage of the gap by importing cooked tuna to automated processing plants in California and Puerto Rico, thereby qualifying for the lower tariff. Its rival Starkist, a unit of Heinz, which imports canned tuna from Ecuador, is fighting to reduce the tariff.[42]

Dumping and Anti-Dumping

Dumping is defined by the WTO as selling a product at an unfairly low price, with the "fair price" defined as the domestic price, the price charged by an exporter in another market, or a calculation of production costs. Because it distorts pricing, dumping interferes with free trade flow. Dumping undermines the principle of comparative advantage because it may cause the exporting country to specialize in a product or service in which it has no advantage over the importing country.

Because of its adverse impact on trade, the WTO allows remedies against dumping, but only where "material injury" to the domestic industry has been demonstrated. In theory, the extra duties that can add up to 40 percent of product price will bring the price back to a realistic level, restoring a level playing field and permitting the more efficient producers to sell their goods. The problem is that the retaliation, in the form of anti-dumping duties, is often used to protect inefficient domestic producers, thereby producing the opposite impact.

Whereas anti-dumping measures were once almost exclusively applied by developed nations fearing competition from developing and especially emerging economies, they are now taken by developed and developing nations alike. For example, India, which had no anti-dumping cases in 1993, became the number one user of anti-dumping measures in 1999, with 68 cases, and its number one target for anti-dumping measures was China, with 310 cases brought against it in the ensuing decade.[43] It is easy to see why: China has abundant low-cost labor and is a world leader in labor-intensive exports such as toys and apparel. The case of China also shows how anti-dumping can distort trade. Before signing NAFTA in 1992, Mexico imposed anti-dumping duties on 4,000 Chinese products, basically covering all Chinese-made goods, even some not produced in Mexico. For 2002, the Mexican textiles and apparel industries extended anti-dumping tariffs of 557 percent on Chinese-made clothing and 1,100 percent on Chinese-made shoes, effectively keeping them off the retail shelf.[44]

With the recent growth of Chinese exports, a critical issue in anti-dumping complaints against Chinese manufacturers has been whether China has a market economy (in which case producers' cited pricing of anything from raw material to labor would be accepted at face value as an indication of cost) or not (in which case comparable data from other, market economies, will be used as a base). In general, the United States does not certify China as a market economy, though some other countries (e.g., South Korea) do. However, the US International Trade Commission ruled in 2005 that certain sectors of the Chinese economy were market-based, and thus assigned only a 10 percent tariff on Chinese household furniture imports, rather than the 60 percent demanded by domestic competitors.

Non-Tariff Barriers

By definition, **non-tariff barriers** are any obstacles to trade that are not in the form of a tariff. They can take many different forms and are often not anchored in laws and official regulations, and therefore are not transparent. It is difficult to fight non-tariff barriers because often the offending party will not admit that a barrier is in place and therefore will not enter into negotiations for its removal. Some barriers are especially difficult to detect and monitor. For instance, a change in domestic product standards will typically be publicized only in that country with the result that foreign manufacturers may not be aware of it and may take a long time to make adjustment so that their products comply with the new standards. When a developing country limits the importation of used cars, the stated argument is safety, even though the imports may be safer than the vehicles currently on the road. The idea is to protect local manufacturers and/or obtain the higher duties obtained from selling new vehicles, or to reduce imports altogether, since most consumers cannot afford a new import.

There is great variety of non-tariff barriers, and their combined effect can be substantial. For instance, Brazil's foreign minister, Celso Lafer, estimated that 60 percent of Brazil's exports to the United States face non-tariff barriers.[45] The following section outlines some of the key barriers.

Quotas

Quotas are quantitative limitations on the importation of goods typically spelled in terms of units (e.g., 10,000 shirts) or value (ad valorem). Some quotas allow for a preset increase, for example, an annual increase of 3 percent. Some quotas allow for a preset decrease, as contained in the NAFTA agreement and most recently in China's admission into the WTO that will trigger stepwise tariff reductions. Quotas may also be established in terms of a market share beyond which either tariff or cessation of imports is triggered.

Unlike tariffs, quotas hold the promise of definitive, quantifiable protection of domestic producers. They may, however, yield unintended consequences. The "voluntary" quotas capping Japanese auto imports at roughly 1.8 million units (set in terms of units rather than value) encouraged Japanese manufacturers to move beyond the entry-level cars they were exporting at the time into more expensive models so as to increase their dollar volume without violating the quotas. In contrast to tariffs, quotas do not have the potential to trigger the efficiencies that arise from the need to remain competitive with domestic producers. The unmet demand for Japanese cars was simply translated into higher margins for the dealers that sold them.

A good example of the impact of quotas is the Multifiber agreement (MFA) that governed trade in garments for decades. Once the quota regime expired on January 1, 2005, the composition of garment imports into the United States, the EU, and other markets changed dramatically. China had quickly overtaken Mexico as the largest source of garment imports into the United States, with the share of some developing nations, such as Lesotho, declining precipitously. Proponents of the regime's expiration pointed out that the change has shifted production and exports toward the most efficient distributors, in the process lowering cost for domestic consumers, while opponents pointed to the change as a vindication of their argument that many producers in least developed nations would be wiped out.

Country Box

The United States and Steel Imports

The United States, once the world's leading producer of steel, now trails both China and Japan in steel production. The United States imports steel from many countries, including Japan, Russia, Ukraine, South Korea, and Brazil. The US steel industry has consistently blamed low-priced imports for its decline since the late 1970s. During the Administration of President Jimmy Carter, the US steel industry successfully lobbied the US government to institute a "Trigger Price Mechanism," whereby any imports sold under the price of the Japanese producers (who were deemed the most efficient steel makers at the time) were subjected to anti-dumping duties. In 1984, President Ronald Reagan imposed import quotas to slow down the import of cheap foreign steel. In 1999–2000, President Bill Clinton guaranteed $1 billion in loans to struggling steel producers and imposed punitive tariffs on some imports. These protective measures were insufficient to reverse the fortune of the industry, however. In the late 1990s, there was another round of increases in steel imports that brought several major US steel makers to bankruptcy in the early 2000s, including Wheeling-Pittsburgh, LTV Corporation, National Steel Corporation, and Bethlehem Steel.

To protect itself from further shrinkage, the industry waged an all-out campaign to restrict steel imports. To appeal to the sensitivity of Americans to national security shortly after the 2001 terrorist attack, the industry argued that steel was a vital input in armaments and that the US could ill-afford to become dependent on other nations for its supply. The industry also tried to appeal to the concern of some about economic security by arguing that steel was a vital input in such industries as motor vehicles, so its price and availability would have a ripple effect in the economy. To further justify their argument for government protection, the industry also asserted that the US steel industry was competitive and would not be in trouble, if not for dumping by and subsidies for foreign producers.

The US International Trade Commission (ITC) recommended in December 2001 to levy additional tariffs, ranging from 5 to 40 percent, on key steel products. In the meantime, the top economic advisors of then-President George W. Bush weren't so sure about the efficacy of high tariffs. They were concerned that the steel makers would again hide behind tariff walls and fail to improve their efficiency. Another concern they had was the likely retaliations by some major trading partners of the US that were also major exporters of steel into the US, including the EU and Japan. A key factor that President Bush needed to consider was the implications of the tariffs for domestic politics. Some of the main steel-producing regions, particularly Ohio, Pennsylvania, and West Virginia, were potential swing states in presidential elections. Rejecting the recommendation of the US ITC could adversely affect the reelection of the sitting president. After considerable debate among his economic and political advisors, President Bush decided to impose tariffs up to 30 percent on imported steel as a temporary protective measure on the ground that a sudden surge in imports threatened the US steel industry.

The imposition of the tariffs immediately provoked a strong reaction from the EU and other trading partners of the US. With the EU in the lead, these countries jointly launched a complaint before the WTO, blaming the rising imports on the US steel industry and its outdated management and labor practices. In the meantime, many US manufacturers that rely on steel as their key inputs (such as makers of air-conditioning ducts and heavy equipment) started losing markets to their foreign competitors due to the resultant higher steel prices in the US and complained loudly about the adverse effects of the steel tariffs on downstream industries. After a lengthy investigation, the WTO ruled in November 2003 that the US tariffs were illegal because there was insufficient evidence to prove that the US industry had been harmed by a sudden surge of cheap imports. The EU immediately threatened to impose retaliatory tariffs on US exports. Given the dual pressures from the trading partners of the US and from the domestic users of steel, the Bush Administration decided to comply with the WTO ruling and terminated the temporary steel tariffs.

Even though the steel tariffs were short lived, the reorganized steel mills that emerged from bankruptcy revamped their management practices and labor rules and significantly improved efficiency. Ironically, what remained of the US steel industry stopped shrinking and became profitable again partly due to a surge in China's imports of steel to feed its construction boom in the latter half of the 2000s.

Source: R.G. Matthews "A big stick: The US won't take 'no' for an answer at Paris steel summit," *Wall Street Journal*, December 14, 2001, A1; N. King, S. Miller, C. Tejada, and D. Streitfeld, "US steel tariffs ruled illegal, sparking potential trade war," *Wall Street Journal*, November 11, 2003; "Is steel's revival a model for Detroit?," *New York Times*, November 22, 2008.

SIMILARITIES AND DIFFERENCES BETWEEN A TARIFF AND A QUOTA Since quotas and tariffs both restrict imports, they both drive up the domestic price and hurt consumers. In addition, under a given set of supply and demand conditions, the government can limit the quantity of imports to the same level and thus afford domestic producers the same extent of protection using either a quota or a tariff. In the meantime, if domestic demand grows, or if foreign producers become more efficient over time, imports will increase to meet the higher domestic demand or to take advantage of lower production cost overseas under a tariff, but not under a quota. So, a tariff is less restrictive than a quota under dynamic demand or supply conditions. Finally, a tariff enables the government to collect additional revenues, but a quota provides foreign producers and/or domestic importers with opportunities to earn higher margins from the increased domestic price without contributing to the government treasury. So, even though the country that imposes the trade restriction receives less benefit from a quota than from a tariff, a quota seems more palatable to foreign producers and their governments than a tariff.

RULE OF ORIGIN Both tariffs and quotas are administered on the basis of their country of origin, for which the default is the first exporting country. For example, a product that was manufactured in Belgium and exported to France and from there to the United States will be considered a Belgian product unless the product has undergone material change in France. It is also important to remember that **rule of origin** terms may differ between different types of tariffs and supports. For instance, under GSP (Generalized System of Preferences), only 35 percent of a product's value needs to be from a developing nation to be granted duty-free treatment, whereas under the Buy American Act, a product needs to be made in the United States from at least half US content.

Rule of origin is often an issue of contention, however, because the value added to the product in the transient country may be debatable. For instance, the French government once returned a shipment of US-made Honda cars, arguing that the cars were in fact Japanese and hence fell under the quota for Japanese car imports into the country, which had already been exceeded. Before the expiration of the MFA, the US government suspected that many garments imported from Hong Kong were in fact manufactured in Mainland China, but had their origin concealed to circumvent the quota regime. The United States demanded that it be allowed to post inspectors at the Mainland–Hong Kong border, something the Hong Kong authorities saw as a threat to their sovereignty.

To remedy the problem, the WTO issued a first-ever agreement on rules of origin. It requires that the rules be transparent, that they be applied in a consistent and impartial manner, that they be based on a positive, rather than a negative, standard (i.e., state what confers origin rather than what does not), and that they will not restrict, distort, or disrupt trade.

Production Subsidies

Subsidies are payments provided by a government or its agencies to domestic companies in order to make them more competitive vis-à-vis foreign competitors at home and/or abroad. A case in point is Airbus Industries, which receives subsidies from the EU and national governments to support the development of its aircraft. It has also been alleged that national airlines such as Air France receive government support with the understanding that they will utilize Airbus products. Airbus countered that Boeing received subsidies as well, through military procurement by the US government. Airbus also accused Boeing of signing "exclusive supplier" agreements with some airlines (e.g., Continental) that were designed to keep Airbus out of the market. In 2005, the two companies submitted formal complaints against each other to the WTO via their respective governments, with the WTO subsequently ruling that both companies received unfair favor and financing from their local governments. The companies and their attendant governments continue to adapt to, as well as dispute, their charges.

Subsidies introduce an artificial incentive into the production equation of domestic manufacturers, funneling resources away from their optimal deployment. Again, under a given set of demand and supply conditions, the government can afford domestic producers the same extent of protection via a subsidy as via a tariff or quota. In contrast to tariffs and quotas, however, subsidies do not distort consumer decisions because they do not raise prices beyond their global level.[46] Under WTO rules, a country may impose **countervailing duties** on foreign imports when a foreign country is demonstrably providing certain types of subsidies for its producers. The WTO distinguishes three types of subsidies: prohibited, actionable, and non-actionable. Prohibited subsidies require the recipient to meet export targets or to use domestic rather than foreign goods. Actionable subsidies are disallowed only when damage to national interests (of the complaining country) is demonstrated. Non-actionable subsidies include support for disenfranchised regions (e.g., China's western provinces), to help companies comply with more stringent environmental laws (up to one-fifth the cost) and R&D assistance not exceeding one-half (for basic research) or one-quarter (for applied research) of total R&D cost. Countervailing duties cannot be imposed on non-actionable subsidies.

Countervailing duties, designed to protect against the distortion of dumping and other forms of subsidies, often result in a barrier of their own. Such duties are set to counter the impact of the subsidies, thus leveling the playing field, but this can result in a recurring retaliatory game that is likely to dampen trade.

Emergency Import Protection

The WTO recognizes remedies against a **surge in imports,** defined as a sudden and dramatic increase in imports or in market share that can cause material damage to the domestic industry. Although the remedies cannot be targeted at a particular country, they can establish a quota formula to allocate supply among different exporting countries. In general, developing countries are held to a lower standard in the application of remedies. A variation of emergency restrictions can be seen in the setting of "voluntary quotas." These quotas, such as those imposed by the US government to stem the rising tide of Japanese auto imports, are often anything but voluntary, since the importing country threatens other measures if the quotas are not heeded. Although emergency import protection can be seen to disrupt the flow of free trade, it may be justified in that it can safeguard competition by preventing existing players from exiting the market because of a one-time surge, allowing them to regroup and remain viable competitors.

In the garment sector, import surges have been used in the United States (in 2005) and the EU (in 2006) as the ground for protecting local producers from a flood of Chinese imports that followed the expiration of the Multifiber agreement on January 1, 2005. In the EU, the surge quotas were set so swiftly that dozens of boats carrying Chinese imports were stranded in European ports, unable to unload their merchandise. Intensive negotiations between the EU, European retailers, and the Chinese government enabled the release of the merchandise. It should be noted, however, that under the rules of China's accession to the WTO, anti-surge quotas in this sector expired in 2008.

Foreign Sales Corporations

In February 2000, the WTO ruled in response to an EU complaint that US use of "foreign sales corporations" (FSCs) represented a subsidy to exports, and that the United States had to remedy the situation or face sanctions. Such sanctions would take the form of retaliatory tariffs on US products, producing an additional trade barrier in the opposite part of the trade flow. **Foreign sales corporations** are offshore corporations that market the products and/or services of firms in foreign countries. The benefit to the firms is that part of the income generated by the foreign sales corporation is excluded from US taxes. The US Treasury estimates that the arrangement saves US firms more than $4 billion a year. Between 1991 and 1998, Cisco Systems saved $203.4 million. Boeing alone saved $230 million in 1999. That reactions to the FSC issue are mixed is a testament to the complex reality of global business. For instance, British jet engine manufacturer Rolls-Royce was hurt by the use of FSCs because they benefited its archrival Pratt & Whitney, but it also benefited from a FSC through sales from its Illinois plant. Rolls-Royce was also worried by the specter of a global trade war that would severely harm its business.[47]

Attempts in the US House of Representatives to replace the Extraterritorial Income Exclusion with other tax breaks encountered stiff opposition on the part of large US exporters such as Boeing, whose benefits from the break amounted to more than $1.2 billion between 1991 and 2000, and General Electric, whose benefits for the same period are estimated at more than $1.15 billion.[48] Still, after a long delay, and after the WTO had authorized the EU to undertake a number of retaliatory steps against imports from the United States, the US Congress changed the tax law in 2005, replacing the tax break with changes in the corporate tax and a broad-based exemption for foreign-source income whether generated by exports or by foreign plants, comparable to exemptions granted by EU countries such as France and the Netherlands.

Export Controls

Many countries limit the type of products that can be exported to other countries, particularly those that are considered enemy nations or a security risk. **Export controls** are typically activated against products with a national security potential (e.g., armaments), but also for so-called "dual-use" products, such as computers and trucks, that can have both security and civilian uses. An example is the sale of aerospace equipment to China by McDonnell Douglas Corporation (which has since been acquired by Boeing). The company was fined $2.1 million by the Commerce Department because some of the machining tools it sold for use in a joint venture to manufacture commercial aircraft parts were later found in a facility that was to manufacture military aircraft. More recently, a number of US companies have been prosecuted by the government for breaking rules on exports to Iran, a country high on the export control list because of its support for global terrorism and suspicions that it is developing a nuclear bomb.

In emergency situations, export controls can be used to prevent the export of goods that are vital to domestic industry and armed forces—for example, oil. Export controls are different from most other trade barriers in that they are placed by the exporting country, rather than by the importing one. Exporting companies often pressure their government to ease export controls, arguing that the importing country will get the products from a competitor whose country does not apply strict controls. Finally, export controls affect not only manufacturers in the home country, but also those in a third country. This is especially relevant in the case of countries with a substantial surplus in technology balance of payments such as the United States. For instance, the United States has often warned Israel to make sure that it does not use sensitive US technologies incorporated into Israeli equipment when the equipment is exported to China.

Embargoes and Boycotts

Embargoes and boycotts interfere with the free flow of trade by halting trade that would otherwise take place. Both seek to damage a country by withdrawing the benefits of international trade. **An embargo** is the prohibition on exportation to a designated country. In recent years, the United States has applied an embargo primarily to rogue states such as Iraq and Iran. In contrast to export controls, most embargoes are applied across the board. **A boycott** is the blank prohibition on importation of all or some goods and services from a designated country. The United States has anti-boycott legislation that is seldom found in other countries. In one publicized case, Baxter, a US medical equipment company, was fined for supporting the Arab boycott against Israel. Boycotts often constitute non-tariff barriers. For instance, with the exception of Fuji Heavy Industries (manufacturer of Subaru cars), Japanese car makers refused to sell their cars in Israel, but argued that the decision was made for economic reasons (e.g., too small a market). As soon as one other major manufacturer entered Israel without triggering Arab retaliation, however, other manufacturers jumped into the market.

Boycotts are usually initiated by national governments. Examples are the US embargo on Cuba, or France's embargo on Israel after the 1967 war. They are sometimes also initiated by Non-Government Organizations (NGOs), such as business associations and consumer groups in the importing country. Supported by domestic growers, Japanese consumers organized protests against US agricultural imports, at one time suggesting that US oranges were sprayed with Agent Orange, a herbicide used during the Vietnam War that got its name from its coloring and had nothing to do with oranges.

Finally, **buy local campaigns** are efforts to curb all imports, regardless of the country of origin. Korean consumer groups held frequent demonstrations suggesting that buyers of imported products were undermining the national interest. This was especially true during economic hard times and, whether organized by the producers or at a genuine grass-roots level, had a chilling effect on imports. In the United States, "Buy American" campaigns are often held, sometimes pointing out that the purchase of foreign products might put one's neighbors out of work. In all those cases, the campaigns constitute a non-tariff barrier in that the free flow of trade is being interfered with, resulting in discrimination against foreign producers. Such campaigns should be distinguished from the Buy American Act that obliges federal agencies and the recipients of certain federal support to purchase US products and services unless no US products are available (e.g., a flight to a destination not served by a US carrier) and, in certain instances, unless the US product is substantially more expensive. The Act creates a tariff barrier in the sense that it establishes a transparent and formal constraint on the free trade in goods and services.

Administrative Barriers

Many administrative requirements result in the erection of barriers to trade. Often a government will use an administrative measure to block the entry of products, while continuing to argue that no barrier exists. In one case, the French government tried to protect its domestic VCR manufacturer against Japanese competition by channeling those imports through a tiny custom station. This caused enormous delays and increased the cost of the Japanese exports without the French government having to accept responsibility for a policy violating trade agreements.

Labeling is one example of an administrative barrier. Most countries require product labels in the local language, which is a reasonable requirement, but one that puts an additional burden on the small exporter who may not find it economically feasible to do so. A US requirement to list the nutritional value of a food product may seem simple and reasonable, but may represent a substantial burden to a small exporter from a developing country where the requisite analysis is not easily obtained. Even for a large exporter, the need to make substantial adjustment in a small market may not make economic sense.

Another example of an administrative barrier described in Chapter 16 is the United States barring Mexican trucks from entering the United States on safety grounds. This alleged violation of the NAFTA agreement hurts not only Mexican truck companies that are unable to export their services into the United States, but also increases the cost to Mexican manufacturers (including the Mexican affiliates of US firms) that export to the United States.

An interesting case of an administrative barrier involves the dispute resolution mechanisms themselves. The Canadian government complained to the WTO that the United States was dragging its feet in appointing representatives to the WTO panel that is supposed to investigate US sanctions against soft wood imports from Canada.

Technical Standards

Technical standards are provisions made by government agencies in various countries that pertain to a large array of areas, for example, safety, pollution, technical performance, and the like. Companies that wish to sell in that country are then required to demonstrate that their products meet those standards. Whether an intentional by-product or not, the existence of domestic standards that are at variance with those of other countries represents a trade barrier. A group appointed by the US National Research Council and headed by Gary Hufbauer concluded:

(1) Standards that differ from international norms are employed as a means to protect domestic producers; (2) restrictive standards are written to match the design features of domestic products, rather than essential performance criteria; there remains unequal access to testing and certification systems between domestic producers and exporters in most nations; (3) there continues to be a failure to accept test results and certifications performed between domestic producers and exporters in most nations; (4) there continues to be a failure to accept test results and certifications performed by competent foreign organizations in multiple markets; and (5) there is significant lack of transparency in the systems for developing technical regulations and assessing conformity in most countries.[49]

An example of regulations that represent non-tariff barriers are the EU's bans on the importation of hormone-treated beef and genetically modified corn and soybeans, which adversely affects US producers. In both cases, the official reason was a potential health risk, although there is little in the form of scientific evidence to support it. On the contrary, the spread of mad cow and foot-and-mouth disease in Europe has made US beef probably less risky than the domestic European variety. More recently, the EU banned the import of certain Chinese foods, arguing that they contained traces of a banned antibiotic. The Chinese, on their part, now require special safety permits for the import of genetically modified foods.[50]

We should note that the WTO agreement "encourages" countries to use international standards where appropriate, but does not obligate them to do so. The organization does however enforce import licensing procedures that require import licenses to be "simple, transparent, and predictable." The goal is to ensure that the administrative process will not in itself restrict or distort imports.

Corruption

Corruption, discussed separately in Chapter 19 of this book, is another barrier to trade. For instance, firms from countries with anti-bribing legislation, such as the United States, may refrain from doing business in a country where bribes are expected. Exporters may also refrain from selling in markets where intellectual property is not respected. For example, many US publishers avoid selling books to Chinese customers, fearing that the books will be copied and then sold in bootlegged editions. Trebilcock and Howse argue that intellectual property is a case where the interests of developed and developing countries do not coincide, challenging a key assumption in international trade theories that trade benefits all participants. They suggest that intellectual property protection serves the interests of innovating countries such as the United States, but not the interests of economies like Korea and Taiwan, which tend to be "imitators" of new knowledge developed elsewhere.[51]

Ironically, the efforts to fight corruption can also represent trade barriers. An example is "pre-shipment inspection," a practice in many developing countries presumably aimed at preventing capital flight, tax evasion, and fraud by subjecting imports to rigorous inspection by contracted private companies. In many instances, such inspections are used to delay or block imports in order to protect domestic producers that may be associated with the inspectors.

Barriers to Service Trade

Barriers to trade in services are quite different from those affecting merchandise trade. Because knowledge plays such a key role in a service economy, any limitations on the free flow of information, including constraints on individual mobility (e.g., immigration controls), represent barriers to service trade. Some barriers to trade in services are similar in nature to tariff barriers. For example, the regulation of landing rights for airlines constitutes a tariff barrier governed mostly by bilateral treaties. Progress toward "open skies" has been made, especially within the EU, but elsewhere this remains a relatively distant goal. Some restrictions on service trade that are often popular with the general public can easily harm a country's economic growth and development. For example, immigration controls hinder the flow of technical and managerial expertise into the country, slowing down the development of more skill- or technology-intensive industries in the country.

Trebilcock and Howse note that in the absence of global standards and regulation, free trade in services may actually result in a reduction in global welfare. A case in point is lax regulation in the banking industry of one country that is damaging to depositors from another country, resulting in a net reduction in global welfare.[52] Opponents of globalization will argue that a similar situation exists in merchandise trade, where manufacturers transfer production to countries with lax environmental standards, resulting in global warming and other adverse consequences, with a net reduction in global welfare.

Interim Summary

1. Tariff barriers and some non-tariff barriers are an obvious and transparent means of controlling trade, including tariffs, quotas, and their derivatives, as well as export controls. Using these transparent barriers, countries must account for the fact that the imposition of the barriers will likely trigger retaliation.

2. Quotas and tariffs are applied to goods based on their country of origin. However, what defines a country of origin can change based on individual bodies of law. A clear definition of country of origin is difficult because a product may pass through many countries and contain inputs from many others.

3. Some non-tariff barriers, such as certain forms of subsidies and technical standards, are highly opaque and thus much more difficult to respond to and offer an advantage to domestic businesses.

4. Barriers to service trade are different than those to merchandise trade. Because service is based on individuals, rather than goods, any limitation on individual movement is a non-tariff barrier.

Chapter Summary

1. International trade is the exchange of goods and services across borders. Theories explaining trade flows include the mercantilist doctrine, the absolute advantage theory, the comparative advantage theory, the Heckscher-Ohlin theorem, the product life-cycle model, Linder's income-preference similarity theory, and the new trade theory.

2. Although none of the theories is capable of explaining the entire range of motives for international trade, they collectively provide insights into why international trade occurs. Differences in factor endowments as explained by the Heckscher-Ohlin theorem are still largely valid in explaining trade in labor-intensive or natural resource products, whereas theories of technological gap and product life cycle are more useful in explaining trade of technology-intensive products. The new trade theory documents intra-industry and intra-firm trade.

3. Further theoretical development for international trade is needed because many new factors that affect trade today have not been taken into account in extant theories. Examples of these factors include fast-paced flows of human, capital, information, and technological resources across nations, and the importance of country capabilities such as openness and innovation.

4. International trade has grown dramatically in recent decades; global trade in services is growing especially rapidly among the most developed nations and is likely to become more important as time passes.

5. International trade is becoming more difficult to measure and analyze as more and more products and services contain inputs that originate in a variety of nations. Consequently, it is difficult to pinpoint the origin of a product or a service and the rules under which it is to be traded.

6. There are two types of trade barriers, tariff and non-tariff. Tariff barriers include tariffs, quotas, export controls, and dumping regulations. Non-tariff barriers are less transparent and include administrative barriers, technical standards, foreign sales corporations, and corrupt practices, among others. Because of their nature, non-tariff barriers are more difficult to argue and negotiate.

Notes

1   D. Hume, "Of the balance of trade" In *Essays, Moral, Political and Literary*, vol. 1, Oxford: Oxford University Press, 1973.

2   A. Smith, *An Inquiry into the Nature and Causes of the Wealth of Nations*, Book IV, Oxford: Clarendon Press, 1869, pp. 29–31.

3   D. Ricardo, *On the Principles of Political Economy and Taxation*, New York: Dutton, 1948.

4   E. Heckscher, "The effects of foreign trade on the distribution of income." Reprinted in H. Ellis and L. Metzler (eds), *Readings in the Theory of International Trade*, Homewood, IL: Irwin, 1949; B. Ohlin, *International and Interregional Trade*, Cambridge, MA: Harvard Economic Studies, 1933; revised edition, 1967.

5   W. Stolper and P. A. Samuelson, "Protection and real wages," *Review of Economic Studies*, 9, November 1941, 58–73.

6   R. Sharma, "China slows down, and grows up," *The New York Times*, April 25, 2012.

7   R. E. Baldwin, "Determinants of the commodity structure of US trade," *The American Economic Review*, March 1971, 126–146; J. Vanek, "The natural resource content of foreign trade, 1870–1955, and the relative abundance of natural resources in the United States," *Review of Economics and Statistics*, May 1959, 146–153.

8   P. B. Kenen, "Nature, capital, and trade," *Journal of Political Economy*, October 1965, 437–460; I. B. Kravis, "Wages and foreign trade," *Review of Economics and Statistics*, February 1956, 14–30.

9   D. B. Keesing, "Labor skills and comparative advantage," *American Economic Review*, May 1966, 249–258; R. E. Baldwin, "Determinants of the commodity structure of US trade," *The American Economic Review*, March 1971, 126–146; W. H. Gruber, D. Metha, and R. Vernon, "The R&D factor in international trade and international investment of United States industries," *Journal of Political Economy*, February 1967, 20–37; M. Posner, "International trade and technical change," *Oxford Economic Papers*, 13, October 1961, 323–341.

10 P. B. Kenen, "Nature, capital and trade," *Journal of Political Economy*, October 1965, 437–460; R. E. Baldwin, "Determinants of the commodity structure of US trade," *American Economic Review*, March 1971, 126–146; J. Romalis, "Factor proportions and the stracture of commodity trade," *American Economic Review*, 2004, 67–97.

11 G. C. Hufbauer, *Synthetic Materials and the Theory of International Trade*, Cambridge, MA: Harvard University Press, 1966; M. Posner, "International trade and technical change." *Oxford Economic Papers*, 13, October 1961, 323–341.

12 W. H. Gruber, D. Metha, and R. Vernon, "The R&D factor in international trade and international investment of United States industries," *Journal of Political Economy*, February 1967, 20–37.

13 M. E. Porter, *Competitive Advantage of Nations*, New York: Free Press, 1990.

14 R. Vernon, "International investments and international trade in the product life cycle," *Quarterly Journal of Economics*, May 1966, 190–207.

15 S. B. Linder, *An Essay on Trade and Transformation*, New York: Wiley, 1961.

16 A. Dixit and V. Norman, *Theory of International Trade*, Cambridge: Cambridge University Press, 1980; K. Lancaster, "Intra-industry trade under perfect monopolistic competition." *Journal of International Economics*, 10, 1980, 151–175; P. Krugman, "Increasing returns, monopolistic competition, and international trade," *Journal of International Economics*, 9, 1980, 469–479; P. Krugman, "Scale economies, product differentiation, and the pattern of trade," *American Economic Review*, 70, 1980, 950–959; P. Krugman, "Intraindustry specialization and the gains from trade," *Journal of Political Economy*, 89, 1981, 959–973; E. Helpman, "International trade in the presence of product differentiation, economies of scale, and monopolistic competition—A Chamberlinian-Heckscher-Ohlin approach," *Journal of International Economics*, 11, 1981, 305–340; W. Ethier, "National and international returns to scale in the modern theory of international trade," *American Economic Review*, 72, 1982, 389–405.

17 US Commerce Department, US Trade Online, Guide to Foreign Trade Statistics.

18 J. Millman, "Mexico's newest export: your meal," *Wall Street Journal*, January 19, 2000, B1.

19 C. Berolzheimer, "Chinese pencil anti-dumping duties revisited," *Studio 602*, June 29, 2011.

20 WTO, *International Trade Statistics, 2001* p. 78.

21 "This trade deficit was made in the USA," *Wall Street Journal*, August 7, 2000, A1.

22 P. Bowring, "Pessimism unwarranted," *International Herald Tribune*, April 6, 2001, p. 17.

23 WTO, *International Trade Statistics 2001*, p. 145; O. Shenkar, *The Chinese Century*. Philadelphia, PA: Wharton School Publishing, 2006.

24 J. Millman and W. Pinkston, "Mexicans transform a town in Georgia—and an entire industry," *Wall Street Journal*, August 30, 2001, A1.

25 International Labor Office, *Yearbook of Labor Statistics*, Geneva, Switzerland, 2000.

26 US Department of the Treasury Office of International Affairs, *Report to Congress on International Economic and Exchange Rate Policies*, US Government Printing Office, October 30, 2013.

27 International Trade Administration, US services trade highlights, December 1999.

28 For a broader discussion, see M. J. Trebilcock and R. Howse, *The Regulation of International Trade*. London: Routledge, 2000.

29 D. S. Broder, "US opinion on free trade is divided," *International Herald Tribune*, March 17–18, 2001, 10; S. Murray and D. Belkin, "Americans sour on trade," *Wall Street Journal*, October 2, 2010; Pew Research Center, *Americans Are of Two Minds on Trade*, November 9, 2010.

30 "The human face of globalization," *The Economist*, 2000.

31 "Protests: Face of future or just a blast from the past," *Wall Street Journal*, December 2, 1999, A8.

32 The Chairman's Staff of the Economic Committee, "The Importance of trade adjustment assistance for America's workers," Joint Economic Committee of the US Senate, September 19, 2011, 2.

33 "Globalization: what Americans are worried about," *Business Week*, April 24, 2000, 44.

34 J. Harwood, "53% in US say free trade hurts nation: NBC/WSJ poll," *CNBC*, September 28, 2010.

35 M. J. Trebilcock and R. Howse, *The Regulation of International Trade*, Routledge, London: 2000, 2nd edn.

36 P. Constable and R. Lakshmi, "India braces for flood of imports," *International Herald Tribune*, April 6, 2001.

37 "What business thinks," *Twin Cities Business Monthly*, August 24–27 Survey, 2000.

38 *The Economist*, October 3, 1998.

39 P. Constable and R. Lakshmi, "India braces for flood of imports," *International Herald Tribune*, April 6, 2001, 13.

40 "Sugar solution," *The Economist*, April 22, 2000, 58.

41 "One lump or two?," *The Economist*, January 5, 2002, 61.

42 N. King, Jr. "Tale of the tuna: Grocery rivalry fuels tariff spat," *Wall Street Journal*, April 20, 2002, B1.

43 S. Sakuma, "What's unfair?—The WTO rules on dumping," Japan Economic Currents, Keizai Koho Center, No. 9, June 2001.

44 T. Beal, "A Mexican standoff with China, the Asian," *Wall Street Journal*, June 1–3, 2001, 6.

45 J. Karp, "Brazil to be vocal in America's trade talks," *Wall Street Journal*, April 19, 2001, A13.

46 Trebilcock and Howse, *The Regulation of International Trade*, pp. 113–114.

47 G. Winestock, "US, EU risk trade war over export tax shelters," *Wall Street Journal*, September 5, 2000, A26; (no author), "US export subsidy has some fans in Europe," *Wall Street Journal*, September 29, 2000, A17.

48 J. D. McKinnon, "Exporters attack tax proposal," *Wall Street Journal*, May 1, 2002, A2.

49 "Standards, Conformity Assessment and Trade," cited in Trebilcock and Howse, *The Regulation of International Trade*, p. 132.

50 "Is EU's vision of free trade blurred by protectionism?," *Wall Street Journal*, March 29, 2002, A10.

51 Trebilcock and Howse, *The Regulation of International Trade*, p. 311.

52 Trebilcock and Howse, *The Regulation of International Trade*, p. 274.

chapter 3

foreign direct investment theory and application

DEFINITION AND TYPES OF FOREIGN DIRECT INVESTMENT 73

HOW THE MNE BENEFITS FROM FOREIGN DIRECT INVESTMENT 77

THE IMPACT OF FDI ON THE HOST (DESTINATION) AND
    HOME (ORIGIN) COUNTRIES 79

CURRENT THEORIES ON FDI 82

NEW PERSPECTIVES ON FDI 88

PATTERNS OF FDI 95

FDI INFLOWS 101

THE INVESTMENT ENVIRONMENT 108

Do You Know?

1. What are the various types of foreign direct investment (FDI)?
2. What are the strategic goals of multinational enterprises (MNEs) undertaking FDI? Do they vary by market and industry?
3. If you were the head of the investment authority of India, what benefits would you cite to MNE executives to attract them to establish operations in your country?
4. What drives FDI distribution and patterns? For instance, why was Africa left out of the FDI mix for many years?
5. Do you believe the liberalization of FDI regimes will continue in the coming years?

OPENING CASE   Japan Changes its Mind about FDI

Among the industrialized nations, Japan has attracted the lowest level of FDI by far. By the end of 2010, its inward FDI stock amounted to just 3.9 percent of GDP, compared to 23.5 percent in the United States and 48.4 percent in the United Kingdom. Historical suspicion of foreigners (the country was closed to foreigners for 200 years until the mid-nineteenth century), restrictive regulation (for instance, from 1962 to 1974, foreign investors had to settle for a joint venture with a Japanese firm), high cost of doing business, and multiple entry barriers ranging from a fragmented retail system to nepotistic relations between domestic producers, suppliers, and distributors, combined to limit FDI in the country despite the allure of access to one of the largest markets in the world and the availability of a highly qualified workforce. Shinzo Abe, Japan's Prime Minister, wanted to change that. Building on the initiative of his predecessor, Junichiro Koizumi, he announced, in the fall of 2006, the "third opening" of the country (the first two followed the Meiji restoration in 1968 and World War II). The Japanese government has recently placed full-page advertisements in global newspapers calling on firms to invest in Japan not only via the establishment of new operations, but also through mergers and acquisitions—the first time a Japanese government has done so.

Japan's change of heart regarding FDI was triggered by a number of factors, ranging from demographics (because of low birth rates, Japan is projected to suffer a declining population and labor shortage) to a growing realization that global competition from both emerging (e.g., China) and developed economies (e.g., the European Union) necessitates enhanced openness and the pooling of resources and talent from around the world. To create a more conducive investment environment, the government has identified 74 policy measures, covering: (a) increased publicity of investment opportunities; (b) facilitating mergers and acquisitions; (c) improved administrative procedures; (d) better living arrangements for foreign workers; and (e) assigning a larger role in FDI to local governments, who now compete with each other in attracting FDI. A goal of FDI reaching 5 percent of GDP by 2010 was set, and additional measures, including the establishment of Special Economic Zones, increased flexibility regarding cross-border mergers and acquisitions, and the availability of subsidies for international companies to encourage research and development activities in Japan, have begun. To increase transparency, 180 laws pertaining to FDI have also been translated into English. However, the attractiveness of Japan for foreign direct investment remains an issue, with inward FDI rising from 2.5 percent of GDP in 2006 to a high of 4.2 percent in 2008, and fluctuating back down to 3.9 percent in 2011.

Source: S. Moffett, S., "Abe has remedy to spur Japan: Open up more; population decline creates hurdles for the economy; A foreign investment drive," *Wall Street Journal*, November 2, 2006.

Definition and Types Of Foreign Direct Investment

As the opening case shows, increasing globalization has captured the attention not only of entrepreneurs and businesspeople, but also of government officials who are searching for international business advantages in an ever-changing world. The active pursuit of FDI for the first time in Japanese history is a signal that the rules of the game have changed under globalization. The message is clear: markets are moving toward international competition and, to prosper, nations need to tap the resources and opportunities available beyond their borders. To this end, they need to not only attract FDI to their shores but also to engage in outward investment in foreign markets. However, as we will see in this chapter, as well as in Chapters 4, 6, 7, and 10, among others, investment in foreign markets is full of potential pitfalls. The complexities involved in controlling and coordinating foreign affiliates that are situated far from headquarters and from each other, and the uncertainty of operating in unfamiliar environments that differ from each other and from the home environment culturally, legally, and politically, represent major challenges to firms. Failed international expansions such as Swissair (which collapsed as a result) and Gateway Computers (which retreated to its domestic US market) serve as reminders of the difficulty of investing and operating abroad.

Companies can enter a foreign market either through exporting or FDI. Exporting is a relatively low-risk and simple vehicle with which to enter a foreign market because it does not involve actual presence in the target market. While relatively low in risk, exporting does not enable the firm to maintain control over foreign production and operations nor benefit from opportunities available only through actual presence in a foreign market. **Foreign direct investment** (FDI) occurs when a firm invests directly in production or other facilities in a foreign country over which it has effective control. Manufacturing FDI requires an establishment of production facilities abroad (e.g., Coca-Cola had built bottling facilities in about 200 countries), whereas service FDI requires either the building of service facilities (e.g., Disneyland Hong Kong) or the establishing of an investment foothold via capital contribution and building office facilities (e.g., Citigroup's acquisition of private banking and financial services firm Confia). Overseas units or entities are broadly called **foreign subsidiaries** or **affiliates.** The country in which a foreign subsidiary operates is termed the **host country.**

One needs to distinguish between the flow of FDI and the stock of FDI. The **flow of FDI** refers to the amount of FDI undertaken over a given time period (e.g., a year). The **stock of FDI** refers to the total accumulated value of foreign-owned assets at a given time (which takes into account possible divestment along the way). With regard to the flow of FDI, it is important to differentiate between outflow and inflow of FDI. **Outflow of FDI** means the flow of FDI out of a country, that is, firms undertaking direct investment in foreign countries. **Inflow of FDI** means the flow of FDI into a country, that is, foreign firms undertaking direct investment in the host country. We will later present the patterns and characteristics of FDI flows and stocks involving major world nations.

FDI versus Foreign Portfolio Investment

Foreign portfolio investment is investment by individuals, firms, or public organs (e.g., governments or nonprofit organizations) in foreign financial instruments such as government bonds, corporate bonds, mutual funds, and foreign stocks. In other words, portfolio investment is the investment in **financial assets** comprising stocks, bonds, and other forms of debt denominated in terms of a foreign country's national currency, whereas FDI is the investment in real or **physical assets** such as factories and distribution facilities. As such, FDI involves control over foreign production or operations undertaken by the MNE, but portfolio investment does not. To understand foreign portfolio investment, one needs to be familiar with portfolio theory. **Portfolio theory** describes the behavior of individuals or firms administering large amounts of financial assets in search of the highest possible risk-adjusted net return. Fundamental to this theory is the idea that a guaranteed rate of return (say, 9 percent per year fixed over the next five years) is preferable to a rate of return which is higher on average but fluctuates over time (e.g., average 9.5 percent per year but with high volatility during this five-year period). The variability of the rate of return over time is referred to as the **financial risk** in portfolio investment. The key task of portfolio management is to reduce the variability (or risk) of a group of stocks so that the variability of the whole set is less than that of its component parts. If it is possible to identify some stocks whose yields will increase when the yields of others decrease, then, by including both types of securities in the portfolio, the portfolio's overall variability will be reduced. This is why some people interpret this theory as "putting eggs in different baskets, rather than in one basket." This logic also applies to the establishment of a conglomerate that diversifies into many product lines rather than specializing in a single line of products. A more detailed discussion of portfolio investment can be found in Chapters 9 and 14.

Types of FDI

We distinguish between horizontal and vertical FDI. **Horizontal FDI** occurs when the MNE enters a foreign country to produce the same product(s) produced at home (or offer the same service that it sells at home). It represents, therefore, a geographical diversification of the MNE's domestic product line. Most Japanese MNEs, for instance, begin their international expansion with horizontal investment because they believe that this approach enables them to share experiences, resources, and knowledge already developed at home, thus reducing risk. If FDI abroad is to manufacture products not manufactured by the parent company at home, it is called **conglomerate FDI**. For example, Hong Kong MNEs often set up foreign subsidiaries or acquire local firms in Mainland China to manufacture goods that are unrelated to the parent company's portfolio of products. The main purpose is to seize emerging market opportunities and capitalize on their established business and personal networks with the Mainland that western MNEs do not have. **Vertical FDI** occurs when the MNE enters a foreign country to produce intermediate goods that are intended for use as inputs in its home country (or in other subsidiaries) production process (this is called "backward vertical FDI"), or to market its homemade products overseas or produce final outputs in a host country using its home-supplied intermediate goods or materials (this is called "forward vertical FDI"). An example of backward vertical FDI is offshore extra-active investments in petroleum and minerals. An example of forward vertical integration is the establishment of an assembly plant or a sales outlet overseas.

The **liability of foreignness** represents the costs of doing business abroad that result in a competitive disadvantage vis-à-vis indigenous firms. An example of this liability is the lack of adaptation to European customs, from transportation models to food, by the Walt Disney Company when establishing its first park in Europe, Eurodisney (renamed Disneyland Europe since then). Utilizing established competencies abroad in the same product or business as that at home helps the firm overcome the liability of foreignness, and thus reduces the risks inherent in foreign production and operations. Horizontal FDI enables the MNE to quickly establish its competitive advantage in the host country because the company's key competencies, whether technological or organizational, are generally more transferable. Conglomerate FDI involves more difficulties in establishing market power and competitive position in the host country. These difficulties arise from the firm's inability to share distinctive competencies developed at home. Finally, vertical FDI, whether backward or forward, can create financial and operational benefits (e.g., transfer pricing, high profit margin, market power, and quality control), but also requires global coordination by the headquarters.

Entry Mode

The manner in which a firm chooses to enter a foreign market through FDI is referred to as **entry mode**. Entry mode examples include international franchising, branches, contractual alliances, equity joint ventures, and wholly foreign-owned subsidiaries. While Damon's restaurants, for example, used franchising to enter the Panama market, Lucent Technologies (now merged with French firm Alcatel) preferred a contractual alliance (i.e., co-production) to minimize investment risks when it entered this market. While US-based General Electric (GE) and French company SNECMA formed a joint venture to produce civilian jet engines, Germany-based DaimlerChrysler (a merger later dissolved) chose to establish a wholly owned subsidiary in Alabama to manufacture sports utility vehicles. Once the entry mode is selected, firms determine the specific approach they will use to establish or realize the chosen mode. Specific investment approaches include: (a) greenfield investment (i.e., building a brand-new facility); (b) cross-border mergers; (c) cross-border acquisitions; and (d) sharing or utilizing existing facilities. Entry modes and investment approaches are further detailed in Chapter 10.

The Strategic Logic of FDI

Different MNEs might have different strategic logic underlying FDI. **Resource-seeking FDI** attempts to acquire particular resources at a lower real cost than could be obtained in the home country. Resource seekers can be further classified into three groups: those seeking physical resources; those seeking cheap and/or skilled labor; and those seeking technological, organizational, and managerial skills. **Market-seeking FDI** attempts to secure market share and sales growth in the target foreign market. Apart from market size and the prospects for market growth, the reasons for market-seeking FDI include situations where: (1) the firm's main suppliers or customers have set up foreign producing facilities abroad, and the firm needs to follow them overseas; (2) the firm's products need to be adapted to local tastes or needs, and to indigenous resources and capabilities; and (3) the firm considers it necessary, as part of its global production and marketing strategy, to maintain a physical presence in the leading markets served by its competitors. **Efficiency-seeking FDI** attempts to rationalize the structure of established resource-based or marketing-seeking investment in such a way that the firm can gain from the common governance of geographically dispersed activities. MNEs with this motive generally aim to take advantage of different factor endowments, cultures, economic systems and policies, and market structures by concentrating production in a limited number of locations to supply multiple markets. Finally, **strategic asset-seeking FDI** attempts to acquire the assets of foreign firms so as to promote their long-term strategic objectives, especially advancing their international competitiveness. MNEs with this intention often establish global strategic alliances or acquire local firms. Many MNEs today pursue pluralistic goals and engage in FDI that combines characteristics of several of the preceding categories. Procter & Gamble, for instance, has sales in over 140 countries and on-the-ground operations in over 70 countries. Its strategic aims behind product and geographical diversifications include better resources, larger markets, and higher efficiency.

Interim Summary

1. Although FDI involves a higher risk than exportation, it allows a company greater control over its products or services in foreign markets as well as access to specialized opportunities not available to exporters.
2. In addition to FDI in the form of subsidiaries and physical plants, many MNEs engage in foreign portfolio investment whereby they purchase foreign stocks, bonds, or other foreign financial instruments.
3. The strategic logic of FDI includes resource-seeking, market-seeking, efficiency-seeking, and strategic asset-seeking.
4. Horizontal FDI is a safe way to enter a foreign market because it produces the same product as the parent company, so experience and infrastructure are easily shared. If the investment produces a product unrelated to the parent's, it is a conglomerate FDI. Vertical FDI acts as an intermediary or finishing stage in the production process, offering either inputs to the parent or access to a foreign market.

How the MNE Benefits from Foreign Direct Investment

Enhancing Efficiency from Location Advantages

In Chapter 2 we introduced the concept of comparative advantage of nations. Firms can realize these advantages not only through international trade but also through FDI. In fact, FDI is potentially a better vehicle than trade for firms in terms of leveraging factor endowment differences between home and host countries. This is because through FDI the firm owns and controls actual operations overseas, and can consequently capture the entire profit margin that otherwise must be shared between an importer and an exporter. **Location advantages** are defined as the benefits arising from a host country's comparative advantages accrued to foreign direct investors. Firms are prompted to invest abroad to acquire particular and specific resources at lower real costs than could be obtained in their home country. The motivation for FDI is to make the investing firm more profitable and competitive in the markets it serves or intends to serve. In addition to natural endowments, location-specific advantages include created endowments such as economic systems and investment incentives. PepsiCo Inc., for example, invested heavily in Brazil, Argentina, and Mexico to seek out benefits resulting from economic liberalization in these economies. Generally, MNEs that use cost-leadership strategies will choose the location that minimizes total costs. Labor cost differentials, transportation costs, tariff and non-tariff barriers, as well as governmental policies (e.g., taxes affecting investment in a host country) are important determinants of location choice. MNEs use their knowledge and information-scanning ability to locate manufacturing activities in countries that are the most advantageous from the standpoint of cost or other strategic considerations.

Improving Performance from Structural Discrepancies

Structural discrepancies are the differences in industry structure attributes (e.g., profitability, growth potential, and competition) between home and host countries. Through FDI, MNEs are likely to achieve higher performance than firms operating domestically because they benefit from such structural discrepancies by investing those distinct resources that can enhance competitive advantages vis-à-vis their rivals in indigenous markets. Because national markets vary in industry life-cycle stages and in consumer purchasing power, market demand and sophistication are heterogeneous across borders. For instance, many emerging economies present vast market opportunities for MNEs to attain above-average returns from pent-up demand long stifled by government intervention.

Increasing Return from Ownership Advantages

Ownership advantages are benefits derived from the proprietary knowledge, resources, or assets possessed only by the owner (the MNE). The possession of intangible assets (e.g., reputation, brand image, and unique distribution channels) or proprietary knowledge (e.g., technological expertise, organizational skills, and international experience) confers competitive advantages on their foreign owners. FDI serves as an instrument that allows firms to transfer capital, technology, and organizational skills from one country to another. FDI expands the market domain from which the MNE can deploy, exploit, and utilize its core competence developed at home. **Core competence** is skill(s) within the firm that competitors cannot easily match or imitate. These skills may exist in any of the firm's value-creation activities, such as production, marketing, R&D, human resources, and the like. Such skills are typically expressed in product or service offerings that other firms find difficult to imitate; the core competencies are thus the bedrock of a firm's competitive advantage. They enable an MNE to reduce the cost of value creation and/or create value in such a way that premium pricing is possible from product or service differentiation. FDI is hence a way of further exploiting the value-creation potential of skills and product offerings by applying them to new markets. IBM, for example, generates significant income from its voice recognition software used by many Chinese. This software, first developed in the United States, did not generate sizable income until a Chinese version was developed by the company's subsidiary in Beijing.

Ensuring Growth from Organizational Learning

FDI creates the diversity of environments in which the MNE operates. This diversity exposes the MNE to multiple stimuli, allows it to develop diverse capabilities, and provides it with broader learning opportunities than those available to a domestic firm. Organizational learning has long been a key building block and major source of competitive advantage. Sustainable competitive advantages are only possible when firms continuously reinvest in building new resources or upgrading existing resources. FDI provides learning opportunities through exposure to new markets, new practices, new ideas, new cultures, and even new competition. These opportunities result in the development of new capabilities that may be applicable to operations in similar markets. For example, many early movers entering China, such as Motorola, Kodak, Philips, Sony, and Occidental Petroleum, realized that the relationship-building (personal ties with local business community) skills they learned in China apply in their business in Vietnam, Egypt, Southeast Asia, and Latin America. Moreover, host country environments are often characterized by both market opportunities and tremendous uncertainties. This forces MNEs to learn how to respond to local settings. Further, through global alliances, FDI offers opportunities to acquire distinctive skills from foreign businesses or rivals. A global alliance can provide a firm with low-cost, fast access to new markets by "borrowing" a partner's existing core competencies, innovative skills, and country-specific knowledge. Chapter 12 discusses global alliances in detail.

The benefits suggested above are not guaranteed, however, since FDI is undertaken in a highly uncertain environment. Additional costs arise from unfamiliarity with the cultural, political, and economic dimensions of a new environment. The impact of a host country's regulatory and industrial environment on FDI is substantial. In an uncertain foreign environment, regulatory factors (e.g., FDI policies, taxation and financing regulations, foreign exchange administration rules, threat of nationalization, earnings repatriation, and price controls) are especially important. The effect of uncertainty is particularly significant in formerly centrally planned economies undergoing transition and emerging markets undergoing drastic privatization, despite their promising potentials.

Interim Summary

1. The location advantages of a host country are its comparative advantages for FDI in relation to other countries. Those include cheaper and/or quality resources such as labor, capital, and natural resources (factor endowments) as well as investment incentives (created endowments) that affect cost.
2. National markets vary in their industry life-cycle stage, market growth potential, competition intensity, consumer purchasing power, and other factors. These variations can be used to the advantage of the MNE.
3. FDI expands the market domain in which an MNE capitalizes on its core competencies, generating more income from existing resources, capabilities, or knowledge.
4. FDI is also a vehicle for organizational learning. Being actively involved in FDI grants the MNE more learning opportunities that would not have been available otherwise.

The Impact of FDI on the Host (Destination) and Home (Origin) Countries

The impact of FDI on national welfare is best assessed from the perspective of the home and host countries, although those too vary internally by region and constituency. While nationals of the Netherlands, Finland, and the United States find FDI and globalization the least threatening, those from Colombia, the Philippines, and Venezuela perceive it as a threat.[1] In Venezuela, the attitude toward inward FDI has turned much more negative in recent years. At the same time, many of the factors that may make FDI attractive to a host country may make it look detrimental to the home country. For instance, although FDI benefits employment in the host country, this is often accompanied by job losses in the home country. A case in point would be any labor-intensive industry in the United States (e.g., garment, furniture) that moved much of their operations first to Mexico and, more recently, to China.

Employment

When US firms such as Xerox, Staples, and Cendant establish a customer-service call center in Canada, they do so to capitalize on an abundant and less expensive workforce vis-à-vis the United States.[2] While this enhances employment in Canada, the emphasis of most host governments today is placed on jobs requiring knowledge and high added value. Host governments are especially keen on attracting firms that will augment high-end employment, and home governments are especially worried about losing such jobs. One consequence of the increased diversity of functional areas for FDI is frequent criticism of FDI as a deployment of the less desirable segments of the production process abroad, while retaining the most attractive portions, especially R&D, at home. Still, developed countries like the United States are concerned about the loss of those jobs and the resulting downward pressure on domestic wages. As noted in Chapter 2, when a job moves abroad, the displaced workers are unlikely to find a higher paying job than the one they lost. Recently, the

79

more sophisticated parts of the value chain, including R&D, are also performed abroad, putting higher-end jobs on the line in the home country.

FDI in many instances involves the relocation of production from the origin country to the destination country and is thus widely seen as having an adverse effect on employment in the origin country. The full effect of FDI on employment in the origin country, however, is not as straightforward. Even though an MNE's decision to move some of its lower-end production from a developed country to a developing country reduces some employment in the origin country, the move can also lower the cost of its products and expand its sales worldwide, which may in turn enable the MNE to expand the scale of higher-end production in the origin country. Hence, the overall effect can be a rise in employment in the origin country, with the number of new hires in the higher-end operations exceeding the number of layoffs in the lower-end operations. Nevertheless, even with a positive overall effect on employment, the move can still adversely affect income distribution in the origin country by raising the demand for higher-skilled and higher-paid workers and suppressing the demand for lower-skilled and lower-paid workers.

FDI Impact on Domestic Enterprises in the Host Country

Thanks to their resource endowment, foreign-invested enterprises are likely to be more productive than their local counterparts. The contribution of foreign affiliates to exports tends to be much higher than their proportional share in a national economy would suggest. For instance, firms with foreign equity (both wholly and partially owned) accounted in 2010 for over 50 percent of China's exports.[3] FDI could adversely affect domestic enterprises. Its superiority is sometimes rooted in favorable treatment (e.g., lower taxation rate or tax break) offered by host governments, but not accorded to local firms. Thus local firms may be institutionally discriminated against, resulting in lesser competition in the industry. Heightened competition contributed by FDI could hurt individual local firms who lose market share, resulting in layoffs, profit reduction, and/or the closure of facilities and factories. Such negative effects were felt in Nigeria when the oil MNEs of Shell (Anglo-Dutch), Chevron (US), and Texaco (US) started operations there. Local firms such as the Nigerian National Petroleum Corporation (NNPC) have yielded the market leader position to those MNEs.

In response to the pressures of FDI, local enterprises seek to improve productivity and strengthen competitiveness on their own or through allying with other local firms or with MNEs. Since the establishment of NAFTA, the number of Mexican firms undertaking outbound FDI has grown manifold. Mexican food firm Bimbo used its supplier relationship with McDonald's to piggyback on the US firm and establish supply bases throughout Latin America. Chinese manufacturers like appliance maker Haier are now exporting to both developing and developed markets and have established manufacturing plants abroad, a step that was inconceivable before a massive FDI flow into China changed work practices and standards there. As discussed in Chapter 4, FDI tends to create innovation and knowledge, which are eventually dispersed throughout the many levels of the local economy. The extent to which local firms can take advantage of this depends on a host of other factors (e.g., local infrastructure and government policies).

The United Nations Conference for Trade and Development (UNCTAD) documented the various relationships between MNEs and domestic firms, ranging from purchasing to joint ventures to various contractual relationships (Exhibit 3.1). The key point is that the spillover from FDI is substantial.

| Form | Relationship of Foreign Affiliate to Local Enterprise | | | Relationship of foreign affiliate to non-business institutions |
	Backward (sourcing)	Forward (distribution)	Horizontal (cooperation in production)	
Spot market transaction	• Off-the-shelf purchases	• Off-the-shelf sales		
Short-term linkage	• Once-for-all or intermittent purchases (on contract)	• Once-for-all or intermittent sales (on contract)		
Longer-term linkage	• Longer-term (contractual) arrangement for the procurement of inputs for further processing • Subcontracting of the production of final or intermediate products	• Longer-term (contractual) relationship with local distributor or end-customer • Outsourcing from domestic firms to foreign affiliates	• Joint projects with competing domestic firm	• R&D contracts with local institutions such as universities and research centers • Training programs for firms by universities • Traineeships for students in firms
Equity relationship	• Joint venture with supplier • Establishment of new supplier affiliate (by existing foreign affiliate)	• Joint venture with distributor or end-customer • Establishment of new distribution affiliate (by existing foreign affiliate)	• Horizontal joint venture • Establishment of new affiliate (by existing foreign affiliate) for the production of same goods and services as it produces	• Joint public-private R&D centers/training centers/universities

Spillover	• Demonstration effects in unrelated firms
	  - Spillover on processes (incl. technology)
	  - Spillover on product design
	  - Spillover on format and on tacit skills (shop floor and managerial)
	• Effects due to mobility of trained human resources
	• Enterprise spin-offs
	• Competition effects			

Exhibit 3.1 Backward linkages between foreign affiliates and local enterprises and organizations
Source: UNCTAD, 2001.

In typical developed economies, for example, MNE affiliates realize between 10 to 20 percent of their input locally and there is some evidence that local procurement increases over time.

Interim Summary

1. Job shift to the host country is one of the benefits of FDI to that country. Desirable jobs such as product design and research and development are usually retained in the home country, but this is starting to change.
2. MNEs are powerful competitors to local businesses. However, depending on the business environment of the host country, local companies may be able to learn from the MNE and become globally competitive.

Current Theories on FDI

Product Life-Cycle Theory

International product life-cycle theory (first introduced in Chapter 2) provides theoretical explanations for both trade and FDI. The theory, developed by Raymond Vernon, explains why US manufacturers shift from exporting to FDI. The manufacturers initially gain a monopolistic export advantage from product innovations developed for the US market. In the new product stage, production continues to be concentrated in the United States even though production costs in some foreign countries may be lower. When the product becomes standardized in its growth product stage, the US manufacturer has an incentive to invest abroad to exploit lower manufacturing costs and to prevent the loss of the export market to local producers. The US manufacturer's first investment will be made in another industrial country where export sales are large enough to support economies of scale in local production. In the mature product stage, cost competition among all producers, including imitating foreign firms, intensifies. At this stage, the US manufacturer may also shift production from the country of the initial FDI to a lower-cost country, sustaining the old subsidiary with new products.[4]

Vernon's theory is more relevant to manufacturers' initial entries into foreign markets than to MNEs that have FDI already in place. Many MNEs are able to develop new products abroad for subsequent sale in the United States, thus standing the product life-cycle model on its head. For example, Procter & Gamble employed more than 8,000 scientists and researchers in 2000 in 18 technical centers in nine countries and had 72 percent of its 127,000 workers stationed outside the US in 2011.[5] Many new products in the health care and beauty care segments were developed in these offshore research centers and subsequently marketed in the United States and other foreign countries. MNEs can also transfer new products from the United States directly to their existing foreign subsidiaries, thereby skipping the export stage. Otis Elevator, a wholly owned subsidiary of United Technologies Corp., offers its products in more than 200 countries and maintains major manufacturing facilities in Europe, Asia, and the Americas. Despite being headquartered in the United States, 83 percent of Otis's 2011 revenues of $12.4 billion are generated elsewhere. Most of Otis's new elevators, escalators, moving walkways, and shuttle systems were first developed in the United States and then transferred to, and manufactured by, its foreign subsidiaries in the target overseas markets, though the company increasingly engages in development work abroad.

Even though the product life-cycle theory explains why the innovating firm may find it advantageous to move production from its home country to foreign countries as the life cycle of the product progresses, it does not explain why the firm needs to own the foreign production operations. Since the firm can have its products made by a foreign licensee without bearing the cost and risk of investing in and managing production operations in unfamiliar foreign countries, a complete theory of FDI must explain why it is advantageous for the innovating firm to own and manage the production operations itself. This question is addressed by the internalization theory and its extensions that will be discussed later in the chapter.

Monopolistic Advantage Theory

The monopolistic advantage theory suggests that the MNE possesses monopolistic advantages enabling it to operate subsidiaries abroad more profitably than local competing firms can.[6] **Monopolistic advantage** is the benefit incurred to a firm that maintains a monopolistic power in the market. Such advantages are specific to the investing firm rather than to the location of its production. Stephen H. Hymer found that FDI takes place because powerful MNEs choose industries or markets in which they have greater competitive advantages, such as technological knowledge not available to other firms operating in that country. These competitive advantages are also referred to as firm-specific or ownership-specific advantages.

According to this theory, monopolistic advantages come from two sources: superior knowledge and economies of scale. The term "knowledge" includes production technologies, managerial skills, industrial organization, and knowledge of product. Although the MNE could possibly exploit its already developed superior knowledge through licensing to foreign markets, many types of knowledge cannot be directly sold. This is because it is impossible to package technological knowledge in a license, as is true for managerial expertise, industrial organization, knowledge of markets, and such. Even when the knowledge can be embodied in a license, the local producer may be unwilling to pay its full value because of uncertainties about its utilization. Given these reasons, the MNE realizes that it can obtain a higher return by producing directly through a subsidiary than by selling the license.

Besides superior knowledge, another determinant of FDI is the opportunity to achieve economies of scale. Economies of scale occur through either horizontal or vertical FDI. An increase in production through horizontal investment permits a reduction in unit cost of services such as financing, marketing, or technological research. Because each overseas plant produces the same product in its entirety, horizontal investment may also have the advantage of allowing the firm to even out the effects of business cycles in various markets by rearranging sales destinations across nations. Through vertical investment in which each affiliate produces those parts of the final product for which local production costs are lower, the MNE may benefit from local advantages in production costs while achieving maximum economies of scale in the production of single components. Such an international integration of production would be much more difficult through trade because of the need for close coordination of different producers and production phases.

The proponents of the monopolistic advantage theory seem to be of two minds about the effects of MNEs on the welfare of the society. On the one hand, they view the monopoly powers of MNEs as likely damaging to social welfare. On the other hand, they also recognize that monopoly powers can be rooted in innovation, which the governments of most countries try to promote by granting such monopoly protection as patent and trademark rights for at least a period of time. This question was taken up again by the proponents of the internalization theory discussed below, which highlights the role of technological, marketing, and managerial innovation in fostering the growth of the MNE, and thus holds an overall more positive view of MNE expansion and its social welfare implications.

Internalization Theory and other Transaction Cost–Based Theories

Focusing on the potentially serious difficulties in using the external market to transfer such proprietary knowledge as technology, marketing know-how, and management expertise, the internalization theory proposes that FDI tends to be an economically more efficient way for firms to exploit their knowledge-based assets internationally. According to the scholars who initially developed and further extended the internalization theory, the transfer of knowledge via an arm's-length deal on the market can engender the following difficulties:[7]

■ When the true value of the knowledge to be transferred is presumably known to the seller but uncertain to the buyer, the buyer is likely to suspect the seller of overstating the value and thus bargain hard to get a lower price, possibly causing the negotiation to fail.

■ When the knowledge contains many tacit elements that require person-to-person training and learning-by-doing to transfer, the buyer will not know exactly what needs to be taught and how the teaching is to be done. This makes it difficult for the buyer to monitor the effort of the seller and also tempts the seller to shirk its transfer effort, likely resulting in a rather incomplete transfer. The buyer's awareness of this risk, in turn, can easily cause it again to bargain hard for a heavily discounted price in the initial negotiation.

■ Given the uncertainty about the payoff from the knowledge from the buyer's perspective, the typical contract between the buyer and seller of proprietary knowledge such as technology generally allows the buyer to pay the seller a licensing fee in installments or a periodic royalty based on net sales (i.e., gross sales minus taxes). Once the buyer acquires the knowledge, however, it may lose the incentive to pay the later installment(s) or the periodic royalty and renege on its contractual obligations. The buyer may demand a renegotiation by claiming that the initial terms of the contract were unfair or simply make the product in an unlicensed facility to avoid the payment of the licensing fee or royalty. In the international arena, it is often difficult for the seller of proprietary knowledge to enforce its contractual rights due to differences in legal traditions and weaknesses in the country's protection of contracts and property rights.

■ To protect its intellectual property rights, the seller may want to restrict the buyer's use of the licensed technology and know-how to a narrow scope of applications and the sales of the output from the buyer's licensed facility to a defined territory (e.g., only the buyer's country or region of the world). In addition, the seller may want to retain the rights to inspect the quality of the product or set the price in order to respond flexibly to a global competitor's price cutting elsewhere. Even though the seller could put these restrictions in the contract, such restrictive contractual clauses can also be difficult to enforce.

Internalization theorists suggest that, in the face of the above difficulties, the firm is likely to find it more efficient to utilize its proprietary knowledge by engaging in FDI overseas because the **internalization** of the market within the firm largely circumvents these difficulties. This kind of international expansion via FDI turns the firm into an MNE consisting of multiple geographically dispersed units that include its headquarters and different national subsidiaries. The MNE is considered a more efficient way to organize knowledge transfer across countries because the internalization of the market within the MNE saves on the **transaction costs** that result from the various difficulties in contract negotiation and enforcement mentioned above.

In addition to the aforementioned difficulties in the exploitation of proprietary knowledge via the market, the application of the transaction-cost framework that underlies internalization theory has uncovered other conditions that can also make it advantageous for firms to undertake FDI.[8] Specifically, it is sometimes more cost-efficient for two adjacent stages of production to be located in two different parts of the world due to differing labor, energy, and transportation costs, but the equipment used in the two stages must be adapted to each other to minimize production costs. An example is the aluminum industry that mines bauxite, refines it for alumina, smelts alumina to yield aluminum, and fabricates aluminum into desired shapes. The chemical attributes of the bauxite determine how the equipment in each subsequent stage of production should be specified so as to achieve efficient production, and a piece of equipment designed for a particular type of bauxite cannot be used efficiently for a different type. Under these conditions, if the two adjacent stages of production (e.g., refinery and smelting) are controlled by two independent firms, they may have frequent disputes on the pricing of the refined alumina when world market prices fluctuate, possibly causing repeated breakdowns of production. The specialization of the assets used in each stage of production to those of other stages then makes it advantageous to have a single firm owning and managing both stages located in different countries. Unified ownership and control under such conditions again saves on the transaction costs resulting from coordination breakdowns. The advantage of unified ownership and control exists whenever an intermediate production input must be transferred between two specialized production facilities located in different countries. For instance, Falk, a global power transmission manufacturer, must use intermediate goods such as couplings and backstops produced by its Brazilian subsidiary, owing to their unavailability from any outside source. Similarly, IBM's speech recognition technology is "transacted" internally among different units, and Rubbermaid's subsidiary in China uses materials supplied by its sister subsidiary in Thailand and then ships products to the United States, Europe, and Japan. In many industries, MNEs are no longer able to compete as a collection of nationally independent subsidiaries. Rather, competition is based in part on the ability to link or integrate subsidiary activities across geographic locations. To summarize, internalization has the following objectives:

1. To avoid search and negotiating costs;
2. To avoid costs of moral hazard. **Moral hazard** refers to hidden detrimental action by external partners such as suppliers, buyers, and joint venture partners;
3. To avoid cost of violated contracts and ensuing litigation;

4. To capture economies of interdependent activities;
5. To avoid government intervention (e.g., quotas, tariffs, price controls);
6. To control supplies and conditions of sale of inputs (including technology);
7. To control market outlets;
8. To better apply cross-subsidization, predatory pricing, and transfer pricing.

Through internalization, global competitive advantages are developed by forming international economies of scale and scope and by triggering organizational learning across national markets. Operational flexibility can leverage the degree of integration. The allocation and dispersal of resources (both tangible and intangible) serve as a primary device for maintaining operational flexibility in global business activities. Essentially, by directing resource flows, an MNE may shift its activities in response to changes in tax structures, labor rates, exchange rates, governmental policy, competitor moves, or other uncertainties. Thus, resource flows are a necessary condition for achieving either location-specific or competitive advantages in global business. Resource flow requires internalization within an MNE network because it involves interdependence among subsidiaries. Internalization, in turn, requires centralized decision-making responsibility and authority. Nevertheless, control should be segmented by product line, geographies, and the like, and distributed among different subsidiaries, depending on particular capabilities and environmental conditions.

The Eclectic Paradigm

The eclectic paradigm offers a general framework for explaining international production.[9] This paradigm includes three sets of variables: Ownership-specific (O), Location-specific (L), and Internalization (I), all identified in earlier theories of trade and FDI. The paradigm is also called **OLI framework**. It stands at the intersection between the theory of international trade (L) and the theory of the firm (O and I). It is an exercise in resource allocation and organizational economics. The key assertion is that all three factors (OLI) are important in determining the extent and pattern of FDI. Ownership-specific variables include tangible assets such as natural endowments, manpower, and capital, but also intangible assets such as technology and information, managerial, marketing, and entrepreneurial skills, and organizational systems. Many of these variables have also been considered in the **monopolistic advantage theory**. Location-specific (or country-specific) variables refer to factor endowments introduced in the preceding chapter, as well as market structure, government legislation and policies, and the political, legal, and cultural environments in which FDI is undertaken. These are closely related to the factors that motivate firms to expand internationally, as per the **product life-cycle theory**. Finally, internalization refers to the firm's inherent flexibility and capacity to produce and market through its own internal subsidiaries. It is the inability of the market to produce a satisfactory deal between potential buyers and sellers of intermediate products that explains why MNEs often choose internalization over the market route for exploiting differences in comparative advantages between countries. The internalization variables are basically the same as those that make it advantageous for a firm to internalize the market via FDI as per the **internalization theory**.

The eclectic paradigm distinguishes between structural and transactional market failure. Structural market failure is an external condition that gives rise to monopoly advantages as a result of entry barriers erected or increased by incumbent firms or governments. Structural market failure thus discriminates between firms in terms of their ability to gain and sustain control over property rights or to govern geographically dispersed valued-added activities. Transactional market failure is the failure of intermediate product markets to transact goods and services at a lower cost than that incurred via internalization.

Overall, the eclectic paradigm provides a more comprehensive view explaining FDI than does the product life-cycle theory, the monopolistic advantage theory, or the internalization theory. It combines and integrates country-specific, ownership-specific, and internalization factors in articulating the logic and benefits of international production. Although today's international business environment and MNE behavior differ markedly from that of two decades ago when the theory first emerged, the OLI advantages are still vital to explaining why FDI takes place and where MNEs' superior returns come from. The eclectic paradigm, like other theories of FDI, has some limitations, however. First, it does not adequately address how an MNE's ownership-specific advantages, such as distinctive resources and capabilities, should be deployed and exploited in international production. Possessing these resources is indeed important, but it will not yield high returns for the MNE unless they are efficiently deployed, allocated, and utilized in foreign production and operations. Second, the paradigm does not explicitly delineate the ongoing, evolving process of international production. FDI itself is a dynamic process in which resource commitment, production scale, and investment approaches are changing over time. The product life-cycle theory also falls short on explaining adequately the dynamics of the FDI process. Third, the conventional wisdom seems inadequate in illuminating how geographically dispersed international production should be appropriately coordinated and integrated. The internalization perspective addresses how an MNE could circumvent or exploit market failure for intermediate products and services, but does not discuss how a firm could integrate a multitude of sophisticated international production and balance global integration with local adaptation. To redress these deficiencies, several new theoretical perspectives have emerged in recent years. We introduce these perspectives next.

Interim Summary

1. The product life-cycle theory adequately describes how a new MNE develops a new product and then engages in FDI; however, it fails to describe the actions of existing MNEs with substantial FDI which may skip steps in the model or even reverse the process.
2. Monopolization theory suggests that the core competencies of an MNE are products over which it holds a monopoly. FDI occurs when it is more cost-effective to directly exploit and market these monopolies rather than license them to a local company.
3. Internalization theory states that one of the major reasons for MNEs to engage in FDI is to internalize most parts of the production process. This significantly reduces normal business risks and gives the MNE economy-of-scale advantages. The eclectic paradigm restates this concept and integrates it with corporate monopolization and national comparative advantage.

New Perspectives on FDI

The Dynamic Capability Perspective

This perspective argues that ownership-specific resources or knowledge are necessary but insufficient for the success of international investment and production. This success depends not only on whether the MNE possesses distinctive resources, but also on how and whether it deploys and uses these resources in an efficient manner.[10] For example, IBM's breakthrough development in voice recognition systems did not generate much income until this system was deployed and adapted to such markets as Singapore, Hong Kong, Taiwan, China, and Korea through its subsidiaries there. FDI itself is not a single transaction, nor a one-step activity. Rather it is a dynamic process involving continued resource commitment. The ability of an MNE to thrive in today's turbulent international environment depends on its dynamic capabilities during international investment, production, and operations. **Dynamic capabilities** refer to a firm's ability to diffuse, deploy, utilize, and rebuild firm-specific resources in order to attain a sustained competitive advantage. Dynamic capability requires a capacity to extract economic returns from current resources (i.e., **capability exploitation**), as well as a capacity to learn and develop new capabilities (**capability building**). In other words, dynamic capabilities take MNE resources beyond their role as static sources of inimitable advantage toward aspects of sustainable, evolving advantage.

Resource deployment is the first step in efficient capability exploitation. Capability deployment involves both quantity- and quality-based resource commitment and allocation. **Quantity-based** deployment refers to the amount of key resources deployed in a target foreign market. **Quality-based** deployment involves the distinctiveness of resources allocated to a target market. To optimally deploy distinctive resources, MNEs need to know what factors affect the efficiency of deployment. Resources will generate stronger competitive advantages when they are applied through an appropriate configuration with external and internal dynamics in a competitive environment. Chapter 4 explains how this configuration should be made, and how capability deployment may lead to competitive advantages for international expansion.

Resource deployment requires an MNE to transfer critical resources within a globally coordinated network. This transfer is the process whereby the MNE draws on some or all of its distinctive resources or capabilities from its home base or integrated network to give its operations in a foreign country a competitive advantage. **Transferability** is the extent to which MNE resources or knowledge developed at home can be transferred to a foreign sub-unit to result in competitive advantage or contribute to business success in the target foreign setting (industry, segmented market, or host country). Although foreign subsidiaries could rely on local resources or self-developed capabilities as needed in a local setting, this is usually inefficient because indigenous firms are already more effective at developing such capabilities. In other words, a foreign business can only gain an advantage if it is able to transfer critical capabilities unavailable to local players. For instance, McDonald's overseas success has been built on the firm's ability to rapidly transfer the capacity to operate its entire business system to foreign entrepreneurs. Similarly, KFC's superior knowledge in organizing and managing fast-food restaurants is transferable to its operations in foreign markets such as Australia and Russia.

Transferability may vary for different resources or capabilities. While Toyota's quality control system applies well to all its global sub-units, the Just-in-Time (JIT) system is problematic in locations where supply disruptions are common due to such factors as inclement weather and labor strife. Technological capabilities are generally more transferable than organizational skills. For instance, in globalizing its research and development (R&D) activities, Sony did not encounter difficulties transferring core technologies to overseas R&D units, but it was uncertain about which R&D management approach to use. Sony later realized that the top-down management approach used at home did not apply abroad and changed to a bottom-up approach. Furthermore, financial capabilities are more transferable than operational capabilities. Capital or cash flow management skills may be more mobile than workforce-related capabilities. Home country experience and reputation are also not easily transferred abroad, but international experience and global reputation are transferable across borders. Possession or control of a superior distribution network in the home market is another resource that cannot be shifted overseas. Knowing how to establish and manage a distribution network is, however, a critical capability that can be transferred to a foreign country. Finally, because environmental conditions differ across nations, transferability of the same resource or capability may also vary across nations. For example, Avon's direct selling skills have been effective in Japan and Europe, but encountered serious obstacles in China, whose government banned direct selling from the late 1990s until 2006.

The dynamic capability perspective holds that FDI requires resource commitment but also creates opportunities for acquiring new capabilities. Through FDI, an MNE becomes a social community that specializes in the creation and internal dissemination of knowledge. It uses relational structures and shared coding schemes to enhance the transfer and communication of new skills and capabilities within this community. FDI, especially by forming foreign alliances, also helps the MNE acquire external knowledge. Through alliances, the MNE increases its store of knowledge by internalizing knowledge not previously available within the organization. Within the MNE network or community, a firm may establish several centers of excellence with job rotation in and out of the center so as to transfer expertise among major regional headquarters. Centers of excellence are foreign units equipped with the best practices of managing knowledge. At the heart of each center of excellence is the leading-edge knowledge of a small number of individuals responsible for the continual maintenance and upgrading of the knowledge base in question. Other managerial actions to facilitate knowledge transfer within the community may include building more flexible and up-to-date information systems, encouraging external benchmarking and communications, and sharing information and success stories.

It is increasingly common to find FDI in a range of functions, from back-office activities (e.g., bookkeeping and cash management) to R&D. For example, many financial service MNEs use Ireland and India as a place for conducting certain back-office operations, whereas high-tech firms such as Intel are locating R&D operations in Israel (though increasingly also in India and China). This enables MNEs to effectively use location advantages across the spectrum of corporate operations. Indeed, one of the main criticisms of the global corporation is that it places its activities wherever it is more economical to do so. One by-product of this trend is a phenomenon also discussed in other chapters (e.g., Chapters 2, 4, and 16), namely, the increasing difficulty in determining company domicile and product country of origin.

The dynamic capability perspective highlights that an MNE's continued profitability entails not only the types of ownership advantages identified by the eclectic paradigm but also the capabilities of recombining its advantages to create new ones and deploying them in the right place, at the right time, and with the appropriate organizational mechanisms. In other words, it holds a broader and more dynamic view of what sustains an MNE in the global marketplace and views the ability to exploit its ownership, location, and internalization advantages effectively over time as a key driver.

The Evolutionary Perspective

The evolutionary perspective of FDI views international investment as an ongoing, evolutionary process shaped by an MNE's international experience, organizational capabilities, strategic objectives, and environmental dynamics. At the core of the evolutionary perspective is the **Uppsala (or Scandinavian) model,** named after a group of scholars at Uppsala University in Sweden who published a series of articles about the international expansion process.[11] This perspective views international expansion as a process involving a series of incremental decisions through which firms develop international operations in small steps. The basic assumptions of the model are that lack of knowledge is an important obstacle to international operations, and that the necessary knowledge can be acquired through time-based experience with operations abroad. Accumulated knowledge about country-specific markets, practices, and environments helps firms increase local commitment, reduces operational uncertainty, and enhances economic efficiency. The internationalization process evolves around the interplay between the development of knowledge about foreign markets and operations on the one hand, and an increasing commitment of resources to foreign markets on the other.

Two kinds of knowledge are distinguished in the model: objective, which can be taught, and experiential, which can only be acquired through personal experience. A critical assumption is that market knowledge, including perceptions of market opportunities and problems, is acquired primarily through experience in current business activities in the market. Experiential market knowledge can bring in more business opportunities and is a driving force in the internationalization process. Experiential knowledge is also assumed to be the primary way to reduce market uncertainty. Thus, the firm is expected to make stronger resource commitments incrementally as it gains experience from current activities in a given market. This experience is to a large extent country-specific and may not be applicable to other markets.

The internationalization process model explains two patterns of internationalization of the firm. The first pattern is that the firm progressively engages in a target market. During the first stage, export starts to take place via independent representatives (trading companies). During the second stage, sales subsidiaries are set up in the foreign market, specializing in marketing and promotion. During the third stage, manufacturing facilities are established overseas, involving a multitude of activities such as production, R&D, marketing, outsourcing, and reinvestment. This sequence of stages indicates an increasing commitment of resources to the market, as well as market experience accumulation. While the first stage provides almost no market experience, the second allows the firm to receive fairly regular but superficial information about market conditions. The subsequent business activities lead to more differentiated market experience.

Kenich Ohmae extends this three-stage process by including a fourth (insiderization) and fifth stage (complete globalization). In the insiderization stage, MNEs shift major functions such as engineering, R&D, customer financing, personnel, and finance from headquarters to local subsidiaries, which then become virtual microcosms in managing and running overseas activities. In the fifth and final stage of internationalization, MNEs coordinate common functions such as global branding, information systems, corporate finance, and R&D, while foreign subsidiaries share common purposes, corporate missions, and corporate philosophies. This coordination substantially reduces fixed costs in research, development, and administration, and fosters knowledge sharing among subsidiaries in different locations or businesses. At the same time, local activities and operations are fully decentralized and local subsidiaries are totally autonomous in dealing with local markets and customers. The Industry Box shows some evolutionary experience of global auto makers such as Ford and Toyota.

Another pattern stemming from the internationalization process model is that a firm tends to enter psychically more distant markets as it deepens its international involvement over time. **Psychic distance** is defined as differences in language, culture, political systems, and the like, which disturb the flow of information between the firm and the market. Thus firms start internationalization in those markets where they can easily understand the environment, spot opportunities, and control operational risks. Overall, the model has gained some empirical support. This second pattern is an extension of **familiarity theory**, a theory which held that firms would rather invest in host countries that are relatively close to it culturally (see Chapter 6), and that they were likely to be more successful in such relatively familiar environments.

Some internalization theorists criticized the evolutionary perspective for predicting a rigid pattern of expansion from export to licensing to FDI.[12] Recall that the internalization theory predicts that firms will undertake FDI without going through the intermediate step of licensing when the market for knowledge transfer is subject to serious inefficiencies. There are indeed many high-technology firms that refuse to license their core technologies to any other firm. Well-known examples include IBM, Intel, and Microsoft. So, the pattern of international expansion predicted by the evolutionary perspective should be viewed as only illustrative and probabilistic, rather than deterministic. Despite this weakness, the theory does provide the insight that a firm should limit its resource commitment in the face of high uncertainty about the target market and try to increase its resource commitment in a gradual manner as it learns more about the market and its participants. This insight is also embodied in and articulated with greater precision and nuance by the real option perspective, which we will examine next.

Industry Box

MNEs and FDI in the Automotive Industry

The automotive industry was at the forefront of FDI early in the twentieth century. Initially, FDI in automotives was mainly the result of high tariff barriers that prevented exportation into the host market. When the Ford Motor Company was founded in Detroit in 1903, it was aware of the promise of the neighboring Canadian market, but it was a 35 percent tariff that launched its joint venture with a Canadian firm to assemble cars in Windsor, Ontario, just across the water from Ford's US base in Michigan. Today, Ford Motor has 77 office and plant locations worldwide and sells automobiles in over 130 markets around the world.

Because of its visibility, automotive FDI has always triggered strong emotions. The investments made by Japanese auto makers, starting with Honda and then continued by Nissan, Toyota, Mazda (then a Ford affiliate), and others have prompted an initial outcry in the United States. Japanese car makers were accused of bringing low-added-value jobs to the United States, while maintaining the production of sophisticated components, such as computer-controlled fuel injection systems, at home. On their part, Japanese manufacturers have worked to convey the impression that they are local players contributing to the US economy and trade balance and especially to the economies of the locals in which they have invested. Eager to expand employment, state governments from all around the United States have competed in recent years for automotive investment not only from Japan (e.g., Indiana won a new Honda plant in 2006), but also from Germany (Daimler's Mercedes division and BMW) and South Korea (Hyundai), and have started to encourage the location of Chinese-owned part makers in their state.

If automotive FDI was initially prompted by tariff walls, today's investments seek to realize advantages of economies of scale and host country competitive advantage, whether in labor costs, component availability, or proximity to market. As auto makers can export their products from Mexico to the US tariff-free under NAFTA, Mexico has in recent years attracted investments from Volkswagen, Nissan, Mazda, and General Motors in large amounts (over $400 million each) because manufacturing costs there are 25 percent lower than in the US. As part of this evolution, R&D, finance, and other high-knowledge functions have now started to migrate to foreign locations. A number of Japanese car producers have major design studios in the United States. For instance, Toyota has design studios in Newport Beach, California and Ann Arbor, Michigan. It also has research and development centers in Michigan, California, Arizona, North Carolina, and Timmins, Ontario. At the same time, General Motors opened a technical research center in China in 2011 and continues to develop the industrious and forward-looking Advanced Technical Center in order to benefit GM as a whole.

Sources: Ford company website, 2013; Toyota company website, 2013; GM company website, 2013.

The Real Option Perspective

As explained earlier, a firm can choose from among a number of methods for entering a new foreign market, including export, licensing, and FDI. The real option perspective views the choice among these alternatives as dynamic in the sense that the firm can switch from one to another as it gathers new information that may change its assessment as to which is the best.[13] For the purpose of discussion, let us consider three basic alternatives:

- **Option 0** (Invest Immediately): Setting up a wholly owned subsidiary immediately that involves substantial investment in a manufacturing facility.
- **Option 1** (Delay Investment): Postpone the decision until after more information has been gathered, particularly when the level of uncertainty is currently high but is likely to fall as the true state of nature reveals itself (e.g., after a highly contested national election in the target country).
- **Option 2** (Invest Incrementally): Enter the market without making any substantial investment that cannot be fully recovered in the case of failure and withdrawal from the market, and expand the

resource commitment when the market looks profitable. In general, export entails less resource commitment than licensing, which entails less resource commitment than a joint venture, which entails less resource commitment than setting a wholly owned manufacturing subsidiary.

The real option perspective considers four key factors to be important to the decision: (1) the nature and level of uncertainty; (2) the extent of irreversibility of the requisite investment (e.g., to set up a manufacturing plant); (3) the likelihood of competitive preemption; and (4) expected rate of return from the investment.

Uncertainty is defined in terms of the unpredictable volatility in the outcome (e.g., the return on the investment). The volatility can be exogenous or endogenous. Under **exogenous** uncertainty, there is little that the decision maker can do to gather additional information other than waiting and following the uncertain and evolving event, such as a tight electoral contest between two political parties with highly divergent economic ideologies. Under **endogenous** uncertainty, the decision maker can gather significant new information by taking some actions that require a series of relatively small investments, such as in the case of high uncertainty about how well the target market will receive the firm's new product. Because the results of market research are generally far from being fully reliable, the firm may need to conduct a real test of the market by exporting its product there or having the product assembled by a local firm without any substantial investment in manufacturing. The **level** of uncertainty can be thought of in statistical terms as the variance of the outcome (e.g., the return on investment).

Irreversibility or **sunk cost** refers to the extent of the investment that cannot be recovered if the investment decision is reversed. For instance, if the MNE has to abandon the market due to serious political instability or poor customer reception, it may have to sell its plant and equipment at a deeply discounted price and let most of the past managerial and engineering invested in the market go to waste.

In many circumstances, an MNE that is the first to enter a new market can enjoy **first-mover advantage** due to early establishment of reputation with customers, relationship with suppliers, or a chance to shape the country's regulatory system in its own favor. If the expected first-mover advantage is large, MNEs will be concerned about competitive **preemption** because late entrants are likely to be put in a much weaker competitive position.

The **expected rate of return** from the investment means what it normally does, reflecting how profitable the investment is likely to be based on current information.

The real option perspective makes the following predictions about the choice among the three alternatives based on the four factors discussed above:

- **Option 0** (Invest Immediately) is likely the optimal choice when exogenous uncertainty or irreversibility is low, the risk of competitive preemption is high, or the expected return from the investment is high.
- **Option 1** (Delay Investment) is likely the optimal choice when exogenous uncertainty and irreversibility are both high, the risk of competitive preemption is low, and the expected return from the investment is not extremely high.
- **Option 2** (Invest Incrementally) is likely the optimal choice when endogenous uncertainty is high and it is economically feasible to enter the market initially using a low-commitment method such export or licensing.

One may notice that the course of action that the real option perspective suggests under Option 2 above is similar to the prediction of the evolutionary perspective. In the meantime, its consideration of not only uncertainty and learning, but also irreversibility and competitive preemption, and its distinction between exogenous and endogenous uncertainty, make the real option perspective a broader theoretical framework with greater analytical precision.

The Integration–Responsiveness Perspective

For a large MNE, FDI is a complex process requiring coordinating subsidiary activities across national boundaries. Business people often talk about "thinking globally, but acting locally." Prahalad and Doz offer a theoretical framework on how such balance can be achieved.[14] The framework, known as the global integration (I) and local responsiveness (R) paradigm (or the **I-R paradigm**), suggests that participants in global industries develop competitive postures across two dimensions. These dimensions represent two imperatives that simultaneously confront a business competing internationally. The first dimension, **global integration**, refers to the coordination of activities across countries in an attempt to build efficient operations networks and maximize the advantage of similarities across locations. The second, **local responsiveness**, concerns response to specific host country needs. MNEs choose to emphasize one dimension over another or compete in both dimensions, resulting in three basic strategies: integrated, multifocal, or locally responsive. Integrated strategy requires strong worldwide coordination, whereas locally responsive strategy necessitates strong national adaptation. The required degree of internalization is highest for integrated strategy, followed by multifocal strategy, and finally by locally responsive strategy (for details, see Chapter 11).

Rugman and Verbeke suggested a way to link the I-R perspective to the internalization theory and the eclectic paradigm.[15] Specifically, if the knowledge-based assets of the MNE are applicable in most countries without any significant adaptation (e.g., technology for computer chip design and manufacturing), then the most efficient strategy for exploiting the assets around the world is likely to be one that emphasizes global integration. However, if most of the MNE's knowledge-based assets must be adapted to local conditions (e.g., know-how for retail banking) before they can be effectively applied, then the most efficient strategy for exploiting the assets around the world is likely to be one that emphasizes local responsiveness.

Bruce Kogut enriched the I-R paradigm by incorporating the strategic flexibility view.[16] The view is composed of two related, complementary concepts: *operational flexibility* and *strategic options*. The key notion in operational flexibility is that the balance of global integration and local responsiveness lies less in designing long-term strategic plans than in instilling flexibility. Flexibility permits a firm to exploit future changes in competition, government policies, and market dynamics. This flexibility is gained by decreasing the firm's dependence on assets already in place. This suggests that managers will alter their decisions when such changes are justified by emerging conditions in an uncertain and dynamic environment. If a decision made now has a chance of being altered later in response to new information, then the economic consequences of such change should be properly accounted for when evaluating the current decision. For example, if the establishment of a joint venture with a local partner may lead to acquisition of the partner's stake in the future, the evaluation of the joint venture *ex ante* should take into account the economic impact of the possible acquisition. The basic idea of strategic flexibility is rooted in the real option perspective discussed earlier. Kogut summarizes the five opportunities arising from strategic flexibility as follows:

1. *Production movement.* This permits the firm to respond to shifts in market and cost factors, especially exchange rates.
2. *Tax avoidance.* An MNE can adjust its markup on intra-company sales of goods in order to realize profits in a low tax jurisdiction.
3. *Financial arbitrage.* MNEs can circumvent many host government-instituted restrictions on finance, remittance, and foreign exchange balance with some innovative financial products.
4. *Information transfer.* Strategic flexibility enables MNEs to benefit from identifying more opportunities, scanning world markets to match sellers and buyers, and avoiding tariff and non-tariff barriers to trade.
5. *Competitive power.* This flexibility enables MNEs to differentiate prices according to their world competitive posture. Different links in the international value-added chain also provide leverage on enforcing equity claims or contracts in national markets.

Interim Summary

1. According to the dynamic capability perspective, FDI is not a one-time occurrence, but rather a dynamic attribute of adaptability that an MNE possesses in conjunction with an understanding of its own capabilities.
2. The evolutionary perspective suggests that, as the company accumulates experience and know-how about foreign expansion, its pattern of FDI will change.
3. The real option perspective argues that it is beneficial to delay FDI under high exogenous uncertainty, higher investment irreversibility, and low risk of competitive preemption, and to test the market using export or licensing first to gather more accurate information, if there is high endogenous uncertainty about the market.
4. Global integration and local responsiveness are important in FDI so as to leverage both scale and ownership advantages on the one hand while permitting for local adaptation on the other.

Patterns of FDI

In this section, we describe the patterns of FDI throughout the world. Our focus is on FDI rather than on portfolio investment. Exhibit 3.2 shows that, of all capital flows to developing nations, FDI has often constituted the largest component. In 2011, FDI inflows accounted for more than 50 percent of all resource flows to developing countries and were slightly higher than bank loans and significantly higher than portfolio flows.

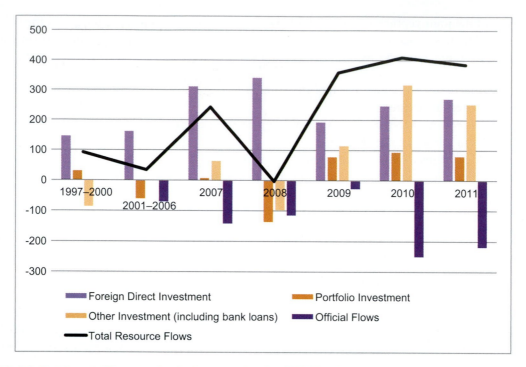

Exhibit 3.2 Net financial flows to developing countries (in US$ billions) 1997–2011

Sources: IMF, World Economic Outlook Database, October 2010; Institute of International Finance, "Capital flows to emerging market economies," IIF Research Note, October 4, 2010; UNCTAD; and UN/DESA.

Note: Net financial flows here are defined as net financial inflows less net financial outflows, and the values for 2010 are partially estimated and the values for 2011 are forecasted.

FDI continues to register dramatic growth. In 1990, the global FDI stock was about 10 percent of global GDP; in 2012, it grew to over 30 percent. At the end of 2012, FDI outward stock stood at $23.59 trillion, compared to 2.09 trillion in 1990. In 2010 and 2011, FDI inflows had increased 9.3 and 16.4 percent, respectively, primarily due to the growth of emerging economies; but the inflows experienced a significant decrease in 2012, partly due to a slowdown in emerging economies.[17] In 2012, FDI inflows amounted to $1,351 billion. Between 1990 and 2007 (the year before the start of the worldwide financial crisis), the growths of FDI inflows and outflows had averaged 13 to 14 percent per year. This growth rate had declined since 2008 due to the worldwide economic downturn. The data in Exhibit 3.3 can also be used to calculate the growth of the selected FDI indicators from 1990 to 2012. Note, for instance, that between 1990 and 2012, FDI outward stock grew about ten-fold. The value-added product and total assets of foreign affiliates grew seven-fold and nearly 17-fold, respectively.

The composition of FDI also continues to change. Increasingly, service investment in the form of financial services, tourism establishments, retail operations, health care centers, and the like is becoming more pronounced. Wal-Mart, the world's leading retailer, has a Mexican subsidiary with 2,247 stores and annual sales approaching $30 billion. Mexican operations bring in about one-third of the $1.1 billion annual operating profit Wal-Mart earns abroad.[18] The University of

Item	Value at Current Prices (Billions of Dollars)				
	1990	2005–2007 pre-crisis average	2010	2011	2012
FDI inflows	207	1 491	1 409	1 652	1 351
FDI outflows	241	1 534	1 505	1 678	1 391
FDI inward stock	2 078	14 706	20 380	20 873	22 813
FDI outward stock	2 091	15 895	21 130	21 442	23 593
Income on inward FDI	75	1 076	1 377	1 500	1 507
Rate of return on inward FDI (percent)	4	7	6.8	7.2	6.6
Income on outward FDI	122	1 148	1 387	1 548	1 461
Rate of return on outward FDI (percent)	6	7	6.6	7.2	6.2
Cross-border M&As	99	703	344	555	308
Sales of foreign affiliates	5 102	19 579	22 574	24 198	25 980
Value added (product) of foreign affiliates	1 018	4 124	5 735	6 260	6 607
Total assets of foreign affiliates	4 599	43 836	78 631	83 043	86 574
Exports of foreign affiliates	1 498	5 003	6 320	7 436	7 479
Employment by foreign affiliates (thousands)	21458	51 795	63 043	67 852	71 695
Memorandum:					
GDP	22 206	50 319	63 468	70 221	71 707
Gross fixed capital formation	5 109	11 208	13 940	15 770	16 278
Royalties and license fee receipts	27	161	215	240	235
Exports of goods and services	4 382	15 008	18 956	22 303	22 432

Exhibit 3.3 Selected indicators of FDI and international production, 1990–2012

Source: UNCTAD, World Investment Report, 2013 (page xvi).

Note: The net differences between FDI inflows and outflows, and between FDI inward stock and outward stock figures, on the worldwide basis are not zero due to differences in measurement and recording by various countries (e.g., a recipient nation may record reinvestment from a foreign investor's retained earnings as FDI inflow, but the firm's home country may not record it as FDI outflow).

Pittsburgh invested in a joint venture transplant center in Sicily, Italy. Citibank has opened a representative office in Israel and is looking forward to expanding its operations there when regulatory changes and political circumstances permit. In 2006, the bank, which is part of Citigroup, also bought a stake in a Chinese bank, with Citibank China fully incorporated locally in April 2007. Today, Citibank China is the leading international bank in China, with 13 corporate branches and 48 consumer bank outlets.[19]

From the FDI theories described earlier in this chapter, it should come as no surprise that developed countries account for most of the outflow of FDI. MNEs from developed countries are more likely to possess ownership or monopolistic advantages, more likely to be innovators (and hence at the beginning of the product life cycle), more likely to be able to extract advantages from internalization, and more likely to have the dynamic capabilities necessary for successful venturing abroad. Indeed, in 2005 and 2012, respectively, the Triad countries (United States, Europe, and Japan) accounted for 82 percent and 74 percent of FDI outward stock, with much of their FDI outflow going to other Triad countries. There has been, nevertheless, a decline from 2005 to 2012 in the percentage of FDI outflow stock that the Triad countries account for, due to the increases of FDI outflows from emerging economies such China, India, Russia, and Brazil. FDI outflows in 2012 were $1,391 billion ($23,593 billion in FDI outward stock), of which $909 billion were from developed countries. These countries remain significant net capital exporters through FDI: outflows exceeded inflows of developed countries by nearly $348 billion. In 2012, FDI outflows from the United States fell slightly to $339 billion from its peak of $397 billion in 2011, which exceeded the pre-crisis peak in 2007.

Exhibit 3.4 shows FDI outward stock for 2005 and 2012. The United States remains first in terms of FDI outward stock, with $3,638 billion of outstanding FDI in 2005 and $5,191 billion in 2012. Other leading countries in FDI outward stock include the United Kingdom ($1,808 billion), Germany ($1,547 billion), France ($1,497 billion), Japan ($1,055 billion), and the Netherlands ($976 billion). The EU, as a whole, had by far the highest FDI outflow, but this included FDI by member countries in each other.

The theory of familiarity suggests that MNEs prefer investments in countries and regions that are relatively similar to their own. In line with the theory, we can see that most FDI from Spanish firms targets Latin America, most outward FDI from Hong Kong targets Mainland China, and so forth. The first wave of FDI in many eastern and central European nations following the collapse of the Soviet Union was by Americans and European citizens of Hungarian, Polish, and Czech ancestry, who quickly spotted the opportunities available. These individuals and their small businesses had a competitive advantage in having acquired free market knowledge while being familiar with the investment target culture and language.

As you will recall from the theoretical discussion, the Scandinavian school suggests that FDI occurs incrementally, with firms gradually moving away from familiar to less familiar markets. P&G is a good example. The company's first foreign operation, and for 15 years its only one, was established in Canada, a destination especially close, given P&G's location in Cincinnati, Ohio. The company's second foreign operation was established in 1930, in the United Kingdom, whose "psychic distance" from the United States is relatively small. The third investment, in 1935, was in the Philippines, then under US control, followed by Puerto Rico (1947), and Mexico (1948).

Developing countries remain a secondary, yet increasingly important, source of FDI. From 2005 to 2012, the share of developing countries in outflow FDI grew from 15 to 31 percent. Similarly, FDI outward stock from developing countries reached about 11.5 percent in 2005, and 18.9 percent in 2012 of the world's total outstanding FDI. Contributing to this outflow were mostly Asian firms, although Latin American firms also increased their FDI outflow.[20] In terms of outward FDI stock in 2012, top developing country investors are Hong Kong, China, Russia, Brazil, Taiwan, South Korea, Mexico, and India. Many emerging economy enterprises recently started to expand internationally in some aggressive manner (e.g., foreign acquisitions), which spurred the wave of FDI outflows from these economies.[21] Chapter 4 discusses in detail the investment rationale and strategy of MNEs from developing countries. It notes that such MNEs rely on a different kind of competitive advantage and are often motivated by a search for knowledge, rather than by a desire to leverage existing knowledge resources.

Year	2005	2012
World	12,575,883	23,592,739
Developing economies	1,447,274	4,459,356
Developing economies: Africa	48,236	144,735
Eastern Africa	813	4,425
Middle Africa	730	12,579
Northern Africa	4,661	30,402
Southern Africa	38,658	83,099
South Africa	37,706	82,367
Western Africa	3,376	14,230
Developing economies: America	404,917	1,150,092
Caribbean	170,937	551,943
Central America	88,721	177,696
Mexico	64,205	137,684
South America	145,259	420,453
Argentina	23,340	32,914
Brazil	79,259	232,848
Chile	22,589	97,141
Developing economies: Asia	993,373	3,159,803
Eastern Asia	750,715	2,243,384
China	57,206	509,001
China, Hong Kong SAR	551,009	1,309,849
China, Taiwan Province of	103,332	226,093
Korea, Republic of	38,680	196,410
Southern Asia	11,660	123,715
India	9,741	118,167
South-Eastern Asia	189,580	596,075
Singapore	159,869	401,426
Western Asia	41,417	196,628
Developing economies: Oceania	748	4,727
Transition economies	152,193	460,760
Russian Federation	146,679	413,159
Developed economies	10,976,416	18,672,623
Developed economies: America	4,026,554	5,906,953
United States	3,637,996	5,191,116
Developed economies: Asia	409,695	1,129,674
Japan	386,581	1,054,928
Developed economies: Europe	6,319,458	11,192,494
Belgium	478,170	1,037,782
France	1,232,249	1,496,795
Germany	927,489	1,547,185
Netherlands	643,913	975,552
Portugal	41,965	71,261
Spain	305,427	627,212
Sweden	207,836	406,851
United Kingdom	1,215,513	1,808,167
Developed economies: Oceania	220,709	443,502

Exhibit 3.4 Outward foreign direct investment stock, annual, 2005 and 2012 (US dollars at current prices and current exchange rates in millions)

Source: UNCTAD, UNCTADstat, 2013.

Year	1970	1980	1990	2000	2010	2012	Inward Stock as of 2012
World	13,346	54,069	207,362	1,413,169	1,408,537	1,350,926	22,812,680
Developing economies	3,854	7,469	34,762	264,543	637,063	702,826	7,744,523
Developing economies: Africa	1,266	400	2,846	9,621	43,582	50,041	629,632
Eastern Africa	81	197	389	1,468	7,513	13,297	70,322
Middle Africa	31	353	-345	1,503	6,119	2,941	55,610
Northern Africa	436	152	1,155	3,250	15,709	11,502	227,186
Southern Africa	334	132	93	1,269	2,265	5,484	145,570
South Africa	334	-10	-78	887	1,228	4,572	138,964
Western Africa	385	-434	1,553	2,131	11,977	16,817	130,945
Developing economies: America	1,599	6,416	8,925	98,048	189,855	243,861	2,310,630
Caribbean	409	390	827	20,521	70,021	77,725	623,245
Central America	570	2,505	3,056	20,472	27,700	21,733	397,292
Mexico	312	2,099	2,633	18,282	21,372	12,659	314,968
South America	619	3,521	5,042	57,056	92,134	144,402	1,290,092
Argentina	90	678	1,836	10,418	7,848	12,551	110,704
Brazil	392	1,910	989	32,779	48,506	65,272	702,208
Chile	12	213	661	4,860	15,373	30,323	206,594
Developing economies: Asia	854	532	22,658	156,581	400,687	406,770	4,779,316
Eastern Asia	178	939	8,820	125,490	214,604	214,804	2,492,960
China	0	57	3,487	40,715	114,734	121,080	832,882
China, Hong Kong SAR	50	710	3,275	70,508	82,708	74,584	1,422,375
China, Taiwan Province of	62	166	1,330	4,928	2,492	3,205	59,359
Korea, Republic of	66	6	789	9,283	10,110	9,904	147,230
Southern Asia	96	284	213	4,864	28,726	33,511	306,660
India	45	79	237	3,588	21,125	25,543	226,345
South-Eastern Asia	460	2,636	12,821	22,641	97,898	111,336	1,319,479
Singapore	93	1,236	5,575	15,515	53,623	56,651	682,396
Western Asia	119	-3,328	804	3,586	59,459	47,119	660,217
Developing economies: Oceania			333	292	2,939	2,154	24,945
Transition economies	0	24	75	7,038	75,056	87,382	847,854
Russian Federation				2,714	43,168	51,416	508,890
Developed economies	9,491	46,576	172,525	1,141,588	696,418	560,718	14,220,303
Developed economies: America				380,869	227,240	213,123	4,570,442
United States	1,260	16,918	48,422	314,007	197,905	167,620	3,931,976
Developed economies: Asia	143	287	1,943	15,280	4,259	12,145	281,305
Japan	94	278	1,806	8,323	-1,251	1,731	205,361
Developed economies: Europe	5,226	21,363	104,414	728,480	429,230	275,580	8,676,610
Belgium	314	1,545	8,047	88,739	85,676	-1,614	1,010,967
France	621	3,328	15,629	43,252	33,627	25,093	1,094,961
Germany			2,962	198,277	57,428	6,565	716,344
Netherlands	633	2,005	10,514	63,855	-7,366	-244	572,986
Portugal	29	165	2,902	6,635	2,646	8,916	117,161
Spain	222	1,493	13,294	39,575	39,873	27,750	634,539
Sweden	108	251	1,971	23,433	-64	13,711	376,181
United Kingdom	1,488	10,123	30,461	121,898	50,604	62,351	1,321,352
Developed economies: Oceania	1,039	2,200	10,164	16,959	35,689	59,870	691,946

Exhibit 3.5 Inward foreign direct investment flows, annual, 1970–2012 (US dollars at current prices and current exchange rates in millions)

Source: UNCTAD, UNCTADstat, 2013.

FDI Inflows

Similar to FDI outflow patterns, FDI inflows had been steadily growing in most years over the past three decades, and reached their peak in 2007 ($2 trillion). Developed countries dominated FDI inflows for these decades, but this dominance has been gradually weakening since 2001. For instance, this group accounted for more than 80 percent of the world's total FDI inflows each year prior to the end of 2000, but this percentage has reduced to slightly above 40 percent in 2012. By contrast, FDI inflows into developing countries, especially major emerging economies, such as China, Brazil, Mexico, and India, have markedly increased, and accounted for 52 percent of the world's total in 2012. This is congruent with the market-seeking logic we previously noted, in that foreign emerging markets provide more market opportunities for developed country multinationals to explore and exploit. Their monopolistic advantages may enable them to reap the benefits from these opportunities. Exhibit 3.5 shows FDI inflows and stocks in selected years. Notice the significant growth in overall FDI before 2000, and even more so in such regions as Asia, and Latin America. As of the end of 2012, world stock of FDI inflows amounted to $22.81 trillion.

FDI inflows are generally correlated with economic growth. Most of the countries and regions with high economic growth rates over the past decades also recorded an increase in FDI inflows during the same period. A number of developing countries in Asia and Latin America, for instance, experienced a generally strong economic growth after 1990s and, partly as a result, received significantly higher FDI inflows. In contrast, some EU countries that grew at slower rates saw declining or stagnating FDI inflows. In addition to economic growth, increases in FDI inflows may also be contributed by weakening host country currencies, meaning less cost for foreign investors, as evidenced by the wave of FDI inflows into the United States in the 1980s. The declining currency also improved the price competitiveness of companies located in these countries, therefore attaching efficiency-seeking FDI. The currency's depreciation boosts exports, which further stimulates FDI inflows. Rising exports are often accompanied by increasing FDI for improving distribution and marketing facilities for exports and for meeting the specific needs of exporters. Some institutional factors, such as reduced country risk, governmental support, regulatory transparency, increased market access, and business privatization also drive up FDI inflows. Interestingly, the above exhibits show that the curve for FDI inflows into developing countries increasingly tracks the curve for FDI outflows for those countries, suggesting that the general environment of those countries has an important impact on their FDI involvement as both home and host countries.

Exhibit 3.6 documents the composition of FDI inflows from 2007 to 2012. FDI is in general financed by equity capital, reinvested earnings, and other capital (primarily intra-company loans). Equity capital is often the largest component of FDI financing (35 to 60 percent during the period 2007 to 2012), followed by reinvested earnings (25 to 60 percent) and other capital (around 10 percent). Intra-company loans are particularly preferred when a host country's corporate income tax is high. For example, foreign investors may react to the high tax rate in Germany by preferring intra-company loans to equity financing for their investments in Germany. This practice allows the investors to record interest expense and thus pay less income tax. Although still accounting for a lower percentage, reinvested earnings have been rising substantially as a means of FDI financing (i.e., foreign affiliates' earnings not distributed as dividends to the parent company). For instance,

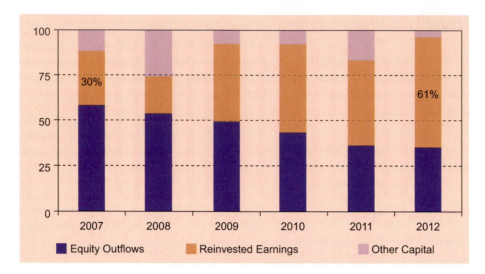

Exhibit 3.6 FDI outflows by components for 37 selected developed countries, 2007 to 2012 (billions of dollars)

Source: UNCTAD FDI-TNC-GVC Information System, FDI database (www.unctad.org/fdistatistics).

Countries included are Australia, Austria, Belgium, Bermuda, Bulgaria, Canada, Cyprus, the Czech Republic, Denmark, Estonia, Finland, France, Germany, Greece, Hungary, Iceland, Ireland, Israel, Italy, Japan, Latvia, Lithuania, Luxembourg, Malta, the Netherlands, New Zealand, Norway, Poland, Portugal, Romania, Slovakia, Slovenia, Spain, Sweden, Switzerland, the United Kingdom, and the United States.

Note: Data for reinvested earnings may be underestimated as they are reported together with equity in some countries.

many MNEs investing in emerging economies use their retained earnings to reinvest in their FDI projects and increase economies of scale and scope in host markets.

It is also worth noting that the growing share of services in developed economies makes them ripe for investment in services, a sector representing a growing portion of total FDI. More than half of the outflow from major investor countries is in the service sector, whether by retailers such as Wal-Mart and Home Depot, airlines such as British Airways (which holds a 25 percent stake in Qantas, the Australian airline), Houston-based construction firm Hines, or financial institutions such as Deutsche Bank (which purchased US Bankers Trust). Second, the decline in the value of labor and commodities in overall product price somehow erodes the competitive advantage of some developing economies that offer cheap labor pools. Meanwhile, as the global demand for fuels and other mineral resources has been drastically increasing, FDI inflows into these sectors in developing countries increase. Third, FDI flows into developing countries are concentrated in a relatively small number of countries, such as China and India in Asia, and Brazil, Mexico, and Chile in Latin America. In contrast, the entire continent of Africa received only 6 percent of global FDI inflows, although investment in some countries (e.g., Nigeria) was high in relation to gross domestic capital formation.

MNEs play an important part in FDI flows. Exhibit 3.7 shows that foreign assets, sales, and employment already account for more or less 60 percent in each category's total for the world's 100 largest MNEs. General Electric is the leading MNE, with foreign assets of $338 billion; the next largest non-financial and non-petroleum MNE is Toyota, with foreign assets of $233 billion. Although more service companies have joined the top rankings, some MNEs in traditional industries

102

Variable	100 Largest TNCs Worldwide					100 Largest TNCs from Developing and Transition Economies		
	2010	2011[a]	2010–2011 % change	2012[b]	2011–2012 % change	2010	2011	% change
Assets (billions of dollars)								
Foreign	7 285	7 634	4.8	7 698	0.8	1 104	1 321	19.7
Domestic	4 654	4 897	5.2	5 143	5.0	3 207	3 561	11.0
Total	11 939	12 531	5.0	12 842	2.5	4 311	4 882	13.2
Foreign as % of total	61	61	–0.1	60	–1.0[c]	26	27	1.5[c]
Sales (billions of dollars)								
Foreign	4 883	5 783	18.4	5 662	–2.1	1 220	1 650	35.3
Domestic	2 841	3 045	7.2	3 065	0.7	1 699	1 831	7.8
Total	7 723	8 827	14.3	8 727	–1.1	2 918	3 481	19.3
Foreign as % of total	63	66	2.3[c]	65	–0.6[c]	42	47	5.6[c]
Employment (thousands)								
Foreign	9 392	9 911	5.5	9 845	–0.7	3 561	3 979	11.7
Domestic	6 742	6 585	–2.3	7 030	6.8	5 483	6 218	13.4
Total	16 134	16 496	2.2	16 875	2.3	9 044	10 197	12.7
Foreign as % of total	58	60	1.9[c]	58	–1.7[c]	39	39	–0.3[c]

[a] Revised results.
[b] Preliminary results.
[c] In percentage points.

Exhibit 3.7 Internationalization statistics of 100 largest non-financial TNCs, worldwide and from developing and transition economies, 2010–2012

Source: UNCTAD.

Note: From 2009 onwards, data refer to fiscal year results reported between April 1 of the base year to March 31 of the following year. Complete 2012 data for the 100 largest TNCs from developing and transition economies were not available at press time.

have remained in the highest rankings in terms of foreign assets, foreign sales, and foreign employment. In the petroleum industry, for instance, Shell, BP, Total, and ExxonMobil are still among the top 10 MNEs in the world. Motor vehicle companies based in the US, such as Ford and General Motors that used to be among the top 10, have now fallen to below the top 30. The largest MNEs remain geographically concentrated in a few home countries, such as the United States, France, Germany, Japan, and the United Kingdom.

Transnationality and FDI Performance of Individual Economies

When we account for the size of the economy in terms of output, employment, and the like, the impact of FDI looks quite different. The United Nations Conference for Trade and Development (UNCTAD) calculated a **Host Economy Transnationality Index** as the average of four shares: FDI inflows as a percentage of gross capital formation, FDI inward stock as a percentage of GDP, value added of foreign affiliates as a percentage of GDP, and employment of foreign affiliates as a percentage of total employment. The results, presented in Exhibit 3.8, show the United States—the largest nominal recipient of FDI—near the bottom of the index, with only Japan below it. When size of

Developed Economies	Transnationality Index 2005
Weighted average of group	11.8
Simple average of group	24.4
Belgium	65.9
Luxembourg	64.8
Estonia	49.5
Bulgaria	39.6
Slovakia	37.1
Hungary	33.5
Czech Republic	33.0
Netherlands	31.9
Ireland	29.7
New Zealand	28.5
Sweden	28.1
Denmark	26.8
Norway	23.9
Romania	22.8
United Kingdom	21.9
Latvia	21.4
Poland	21.0
Lithuania	20.6
France	19.5
Switzerland	18.4
Portugal	17.5
Finland	17.2
Israel	16.8
Austria	16.2
Spain	16.2
Australia	16.0
Canada	15.5
Slovenia	13.6
Germany	10.4
Greece	9.6
Italy	9.2
United States	6.4
Japan	1.1

Developing Economies	Transnationality Index 2005
Weighted average of group	14.0
Simple average of group	21.8
Hong Kong, China	103.7
Singapore	65.2
Trinidad and Tobago	48.6
Chile	32.5
Jamaica	31.5
Honduras	29.0
Panama	27.7
South Africa	24.9
Thailand	22.4
Bahamas	20.8
Costa Rica	20.5
Colombia	20.2
Malaysia	19.2
Ecuador	18.6
United Arab Emirates	17.6
Argentina	17.5
Guatemala	17.2
Egypt	16.3
Dominican Republic	15.6
Venezuela, Bolivarian Rep. Of	15.0
Mexico	15.0
Peru	14.2
Turkey	13.7
Brazil	13.5
China	12.0
Indonesia	8.8
Philippines	7.9
Taiwan Province of China	7.8
Barbados	6.3
Saudi Arabia	6.0
Korea, Republic of	4.5
India	4.1

Transition Economies	Transnationality Index 2005
Weighted average of group	13.5
Simple average of group	19.6
TFY Rep. of Macedonia	38.6
Bosnia and Herzegovina	29.2
Croatia	26.9
Ukraine	22.3
Moldova, Republic of	17.8
Serbia and Montenegro	16.4
Russian Federation	11.8
Albania	10.0
Belarus	3.3

Exhibit 3.8 Transnationality Index of Host Economies, 2005 (percentage)
Source: UNCTAD, World Investment Report, 2008 (p.12).

the economy is accounted for, Belgium, Luxembourg, Estonia, Bulgaria, and Slovakia are the top five developed economies in terms of national-level inward openness or internationalization. Among developing economies, Hong Kong ranks first, reaching 103.7 percent (highest among all nations in the world), followed by Singapore and Trinidad and Tobago.

The Inward FDI Performance and Potential indices, as well as the Outward FDI Performance Index, were also introduced by UNCTAD to assess FDI performance of individual countries. The **Inward FDI Performance Index** is a measure of the extent to which a host economy receives inward FDI relative to its economic size. It is calculated as the ratio of a country's share in global FDI inflows to its share in global GDP. This compares FDI inflow levels across different countries when the GDP size is controlled for. According to this index, Azerbaijan, Belgium, Luxembourg, Angola, and Ireland are among the best-performing countries, while Cameroon, Indonesia, Iran, Japan, Kuwait, Nepal, and Saudi Arabia are among the most poorly performing in this regard. The Inward **FDI Potential Index** is based on several economic variables indicating a country's investment infrastructure and growth potential for foreign businesses. It is an average of scores (ranging from 0 to 1) on such economic conditions as GDP per capita, GDP growth rate, share of exports in GDP, telecoms infrastructure, commercial energy use per capita, share of R&D expenditures in gross national income, and country risk, among others. The United States, Norway, the United Kingdom, Canada, and Singapore are among the best locations concerning FDI potential. By comparing the Inward FDI Potential index with that of the Performance Index, one can get an indication of how each country performs against its potential. Finally, the **Outward FDI Performance Index** is defined as the ratio of a country's share in global FDI outflows to its share in world GDP. Top outward FDI performers include Belgium, Luxembourg, Panama, Hong Kong, Azerbaijan, Iceland, and Singapore.

FDI flows and performance differ not only among countries but also across regions (states or provinces) within a large country. In most diversified host countries, the distribution of FDI is uneven, triggering criticism that only a few benefit from the investment, and that the beneficiaries are concentrated in areas that are already relatively affluent. For example, in the United States, FDI projects are generally concentrated in a small number of states. California, Michigan, New Jersey, and Massachusetts have about a quarter of manufacturing employment of Japanese affiliates in the United States and two-thirds (157 of 251) of these foreign investors' R&D facilities.[22] Thus, these states enjoyed the benefits of high-wage, knowledge-based employment of FDI much more than other states. FDI in services is even more skewed toward investment on the East Coast (primarily), followed by California and, to a lesser extent, Texas.[23] This reality explains some of the political undercurrents of trade and investment discussed in Chapter 7, on the Political and Legal Environment.

In China, FDI was initially confined to special economic zones and remains concentrated along coastal areas and in a small number of other regions. This pattern is beginning to change, however. The Chinese government, like many others, is offering special incentives to firms willing to invest in less developed regions. Such incentives to disadvantaged regions are allowable under WTO rules. In Israel, the government offers extra incentives for foreign investors willing to locate in rural towns, as it recently did for Intel. In the United States, state governments have been competing with each other in offering FDI incentives in the hope of attracting investors into their state. Ohio provided such incentives to Honda, Tennessee to Nissan, and Alabama to BMW.

The location pattern of FDI is often correlated with the investor country of origin, which again may be predicted by the theory of familiarity. In China, much of the initial investment from Hong

105

Year	Gross M&As				Net M&As			
	Number of deals		Value		Number of deals		Value	
	Number	Share in total (%)	$ billion	Share in total (%)	Number	Share in total (%)	$ billion	Share in total (%)
1996	932	16	42	16	464	13	19	14
1997	925	14	54	15	443	11	18	10
1998	1 089	14	79	11	528	11	38	9
1999	1 285	14	89	10	538	10	40	6
2000	1 340	13	92	7	525	8	45	5
2001	1 248	15	88	12	373	9	42	10
2002	1 248	19	85	18	413	13	28	11
2003	1 488	22	109	27	592	20	53	29
2004	1 622	22	157	28	622	17	76	33
2005	1 737	20	221	24	795	16	121	26
2006	1 698	18	271	24	786	14	128	20
2007	1 918	18	555	33	1 066	15	288	28
2008	1 785	18	322	25	1 080	17	204	29
2009	1 993	25	107	19	1 065	25	58	23
2010	2 103	22	131	18	1 147	21	65	19
2011	2 020	19	153	14	902	15	77	14
2012	2 229	23	182	22	1 104	20	51	16

Exhibit 3.9 Cross-border M&As by private equity firms, 1996–2012 (number of deals and value)

Source: UNCTAD FDI-TNC-GVC Information System, cross-border M&A database (www.unctad.org/fdistatistics).

Note: Value on a net basis takes into account divestments by private equity funds. Thus it is calculated as follows: Purchases of companies abroad by private equity funds (-) Sales of foreign affiliates owned by private equity funds. The table includes M&As by hedge and other funds (but not sovereign wealth funds). Private equity firms and hedge funds refer to acquirers as "investors not elsewhere classified." This classification is based on the Thomson Finance database on M&As.

Kong (now a Special Administrative Region of China, but a separate entity for investment purposes) was concentrated in Guangdong province, which is adjacent to Hong Kong and shares regional culture and dialect; Taiwanese investment was proportionally higher in Fujian province, which shares culture, language, and ethnicity with many Taiwan residents; and South Koreans were more likely to invest in areas of China with a large Korean minority. As familiarity theory predicts, such investment gradually expanded into other regions.

FDI Entry Forms

Firms may enter host economies through greenfield investments or mergers and acquisitions (M&As). A **greenfield investment** occurs when a firm single-handedly (i.e., wholly owned), or jointly with another firm (i.e., joint venture), builds brand-new facilities from scratch in a host country. An **acquisition** occurs when a firm buys out some proportion (i.e., partial acquisition) or the entire ownership (i.e., complete acquisition) of a target firm in a host country. The choice of entry form is influenced by industry-specific factors. For example, greenfield investment is more likely to be used as a form of entry in industries in which technological skills and production technology are key. The choice may also be influenced by institutional, cultural, and transaction cost factors, in particular the attitude toward takeovers, conditions in capital markets, policies, privatization, regional integration, currency risks, and the role played by intermediaries (e.g., investment banks) actively seeking acquisition opportunities and taking initiatives in making deals. Chapter 10 explains these issues in greater detail.

In recent years, the proportion of M&As in total FDI has been growing at the expense of greenfield investments. Completed cross-border M&As rose in value from a little over $42 billion in 1996 to more than $182 billion in 2012. Moreover, as shown in Exhibit 3.9, the number of cross-border deals has more than doubled from 1996 to 2012. The trend has been criticized by FDI opponents who say that M&As do not add to the capital stock and may stifle competition.[24] Proponents of FDI respond that acquisitions bring new technologies and better management that enable the acquired firm to survive and prosper under stiff global competition. They point out that, at least in transition economies, greenfield and acquisition investments do not substitute for each other but rather play a different role, the former providing new facilities and capacities, the latter contributing to the restructuring and improvement of existing facilities and capacities.[25]

Although the acquisition of major local firms in developing nations draws frequent media attention, the most common form of M&A is one originating in and targeting developed country firms. Many large firms have embarked on multiple acquisitions. Examples are Ford Motor's acquisition of UK-based Jaguar and more recently of Swedish company Volvo and of the Land Rover division of the UK-based Rover group, formerly owned by German auto maker BMW; Daimler's acquisition and partial acquisition, respectively, of Chrysler and Mitsubishi; and the controlling interest taken in Nissan by French auto maker Renault. This wave is not limited to the car industry. Swedish paper manufacturer Svenska Cellulosa acquired both Pennsylvania-based Tuscarora and an Atlanta-based unit of Georgia Pacific.[26] British utility National Grid completed three international acquisitions in 2000. In 2004, M&As between companies within EU increased value to almost $100 billion, accounting for 57 percent of the value of all cross-border deals in that region. Low interest rates and strategic needs for global expansion via M&As are among the major factors contributing to the rise in cross-border M&As, which resumed in 2006. In 2006, Japan's Toshiba acquired US-based Westinghouse, while French telecommunications maker Alcatel has merged with US-based Lucent.

Developing countries have attracted a larger number of greenfield investments than developed countries. This illustrates the tendency for developing countries to receive more FDI through greenfield projects than through M&As. Although acquisitions by developing country MNEs are much less numerous than those by developed country MNEs, they are increasing. Mumbai-based Silverline Technologies acquired New Jersey-based SeraNova in 2000 for $99 million. Like other Indian high-tech firms with recent US acquisitions, the company sought to gain an understanding of the US market, which increasingly sources software in India.[27] There was also a significant rise in cross-border M&A purchases in China and India in 2004, with a doubling of value in both countries, to record highs of $6.8 billion and $1.8 billion, respectively. In 2012, China was the largest target country for cross-border M&As in developing countries, followed by Russia, Brazil, and India.[28] As in the case of M&As, China and India also attracted significant numbers of greenfield investments, together accounting for nearly half of the total number in developing countries. Recent liberalization measures in India and strong economic growth in China, combined with its WTO access (see Chapter 8), contributed to this trend.

Interim Summary

1. FDI levels continue to increase while the companies engaging in FDI are becoming more diverse. However, FDI outflow is overwhelmingly from the Triad countries, mostly into other Triad countries.
2. The bulk of FDI entering into developing countries goes to a small number of nations with exceptionally attractive investment environments.
3. Recently, M&As outpaced greenfield investments given their advantages such as quick access to local markets or better use of local firms' established supply or distribution channels. FDI tends to concentrate in limited areas within host countries, generating uneven benefits.

The Investment Environment

With most nations keen on attracting FDI, market liberalization and openness to FDI have been on the increase. For instance, between 1991 and 2000, there were a total of 1,185 regulatory changes pertaining to FDI across the globe, of which 1,121 favored investors. In 1999 alone, 150 regulatory changes were made in 69 nations, and 147 of those were positive to FDI.[29] Many of the recently signed bilateral investment and double taxation treaties contain supportive FDI provisions.[30] The nations with the most liberal FDI environment in terms of freedom to control domestic firms are Luxembourg, Ireland, Argentina, and Hong Kong. The nations with the least open environment in this respect are China, Russia, Malaysia, and Slovenia. Russia offers by far the least protection for the foreign investor.[31] Still, recent data suggests a slowdown in the liberalization of FDI regimes: While in 2000, of 150 regulatory changes only three were unfavorable, by 2006, 37 of 184 were reported unfavorable by the United Nations Conference on Trade and Development.[32] Typically justified on the basis of economic security, national interest, or the safeguarding of so-called strategic industries, the more recent reaction to the globalization of business and the general economic environment may not necessarily be a permanent trend, but it is a reminder that the continued liberalization in the FDI environment should not be taken for granted.

Increased liberalization should also not be confused with the uncertainty that continues to characterize international operations in developing and in transition economies (Country Box: FDI in Israel shows an example). Weak property rights, political upheaval, wild currency shifts, and the like make the international environment an uncertain terrain. However, liberalization means that FDI is less often made with the sole purpose of circumventing tariff barriers, but rather for more fundamental economic and strategic reasons. With rapid globalization, product life-cycle assumptions have also been increasingly questioned. If in the past an MNE could simply utilize its older products in another, especially developing market, it is now often demanded, or necessary (owing to internal efficiencies or competitive pressures), to transfer more technology to foreign affiliates at an early stage.

Global competition to attract FDI leads many countries to offer not only a liberalized investment market but also an array of incentives to the foreign investor. Such incentives include tax holidays, tariff concessions, direct and indirect financial subsidies, training support, infrastructure improvement, capital repatriation rights, and a host of other incentives. Countries offering the most attractive incentives to foreign investors include Ireland, Singapore, Luxembourg, and the Netherlands. Russia, Slovenia, New Zealand, and Venezuela offer the fewest investment incentives.

High-tech investment that involves substantial employment is particularly in demand, enhancing the bargaining power of the MNE. Intel was thus able to extract substantial concessions from governments in various parts of the world. In Costa Rica, Intel received an eight-year tax holiday (and several more years at a reduced rate), unlimited fund repatriation rights, and infrastructure support in the form of a power station supplying power to the Intel plant at a reduced rate. Advanced Micro Devices (AMD) was similarly able to extract an array of incentives from the German government, especially since it agreed to locate its plant in the depressed eastern part of the country.[33]

FDI Decision Criteria

In the theory section, we discussed the location advantages of host countries as a major drive for FDI. We have noted that such advantages include natural endowments (e.g., mineral resources) and creative endowments (e.g., consumer purchasing power, skilled workforce), and government incentives. We have also noted that these endowments vary by region and by industry, and that they tend to shift over time. For example, many foreign firms that were enticed to invest in the United Kingdom as their EU base (the United Kingdom is the preferred EU entry point for Japanese firms, for example) have been rethinking their investment in the aftermath of the United Kingdom not joining the euro mechanism. With the British pound appreciating vis-à-vis the euro, UK-made products sold in the EU have either become more expensive for consumers or less profitable for their producers.

The location factors may change in importance according to the industries involved. For instance, in industries based on monopolistic advantage, concentration of multiple competitors in one location is negative, despite potential agglomeration benefits such as the availability of trained workers and established supply networks. Low-tech labor-intensive industries (e.g., most garment manufacturers) typically regard wages as a critical location factor. Similarly, tire manufacturers are much more concerned with transportation costs than electronic chip producers for whom the value-to-weight ratio is much higher.

Nor is the relationship between cost of production and location simple. As you may recall from Chapter 2, the Leontief paradox showed that the United States, a country with high capital endowment, was also exporting many labor-intensive products. The United States is also domestically manufacturing low-tech products despite wages that are often more than ten times higher vis-à-vis alternative locations. For example, most light bulbs sold in the United States are made locally, sometimes by foreign firms such as German-based Siemens. The reasons are transportation costs, capital intensity (i.e., automation), the importance of quick delivery and on-site service, local tastes, trade barriers, skills that are not easily transferable, and the ability to quickly implement innovation.[34]

Similarly, Conference Board data show that US manufacturers are more likely to choose a high- rather than a low-wage country for investment, and that this holds in North America, Asia, and Europe. For instance, Motorola chose to invest in Germany despite its having the highest labor costs and one of the highest tax regimes in the EU. Quality and productivity supplemented by local incentives have turned the decision in Germany's favor.[35]

National boundaries do not always provide a good indication of key criteria for the location decision. As an example, wage costs can vary substantially across regions of the same country due to varying levels of development (e.g., it is much more expensive to do business in Shanghai than in the Chinese inland), or due to special arrangement in free trade zones or territorially contiguous areas. For instance, Ohio-based firm R.G. Barry opened a footwear plant in Laredo, Texas, thanks to the Twin Plant plan that allowed it to employ Mexican workers at a fraction of its US domestic cost. The plant was, however, moved to Mexico in 2002 when the further wage savings were no longer offset by tariffs, thanks to the NAFTA agreement, and then to China in 2004, to keep up with cheaper outsourcing costs.[36] Chapter 10 provides a detailed framework with which to analyze location decisions.

Country Box

FDI in Israel

In 1994, foreign investment in Israel stood at roughly $500 million. By 2000, it grew ten-fold, reaching one of the highest per capita figures for any economy. How this transformation has come about reveals a lot about the factors that motivate FDI. Israel is a country that lacks natural resources, has a tiny land area, and has a relatively small population of about 7.8 million. However, Israel has a highly skilled workforce and one of the highest ratios of scientists and engineers in the world (almost double that of the United States), further boosted by the immigration of thousands of scientists from the former Soviet Union. Israel ranks third, after the United States and Japan, in the number of patents per capita. MNEs flocked to Israel to take advantage of this knowledge resource as well as Israel's sophisticated infrastructure and a supportive tax and investment environment.

Despite the worldwide economic slowdown, FDI in Israel grew to $4.4 billion and $5.1 billion in 2009 and 2010, respectively. A long list of major MNEs have set up R&D centers and production facilities in the country, including Intel, Microsoft, Motorola, Google, Applied Materials, HP, Deutsche Telecom, and Samsung. Apple also announced its intention to open its first overseas R&D center in Israel. FDI in the country often involves the acquisitions of Israeli companies that have developed innovative technologies. The following table lists some recent acquisitions of this type, illustrating the attractiveness of Israeli companies to MNEs in the hi-tech sector.

MNE Acquirer	Israeli Target	Amount
Facebook	Face.com	$60 million
EMC	XtremIO	$450 million
Akamai	Cotendo	268 million
DG FastChannel	MediaMind Technologies	$517 million
CSR	Zoran	$679 million
Intel	Telmap Ltd	$300 million
Broadcom	Provigent	$313 million

Interim Summary

1. Global competition to attract FDI promotes liberalization of global markets and opening of the world economic environment. Many countries offer a host of incentives to foreign investors.
2. For high-tech investors, FDI concerns are less related to natural endowments and more to creative endowments such as knowledge infrastructure, access to capital, consumer purchasing power, and government incentives.

Chapter Summary

1. Foreign direct investment (FDI) involves investment in a manufacturing facility, service provision facility, or other assets in a foreign market over which the firm maintains control.
2. FDI can be horizontal (same product or service as the one produced or rendered in the home country) or vertical (investment in inputs preceding or following in the firm's value chain).
3. MNEs benefit from FDI by generating efficiencies from location advantages, leveraging structural discrepancies, getting returns from ownership advantages, and learning and leveraging their capabilities.
4. Among conventional perspectives, the monopolistic advantage approach suggests that MNEs possess monopolistic power, enabling them to operate subsidiaries abroad more profitably than local competitors. The internalization perspective suggests that it is more efficient for MNEs to internalize (e.g., vertical integration) overseas operations through a unified governance structure than otherwise to trade through open markets (if they exist). The OLI paradigm integrates these perspectives with country-specific comparative advantages.
5. Among emerging perspectives, the dynamic capability view suggests that global success depends not only on a firm's distinctive resources but also on how it deploys, uses, and upgrades these resources. The evolutionary perspective holds that internationalization is an evolutionary process, shifting from export, to building foreign branches, to relocating facilities overseas, to insiderization, and finally to globalization. The I-R paradigm addresses the balance between global integration and local responsiveness.
6. The United States has the highest stock of both outflows and inflows of FDI in the world. However, its share of the fast-growing pie of global FDI is shrinking, and today it is no longer the biggest investor.
7. In recent years, more FDI has been done via mergers and acquisitions rather than via "greenfield" investment.
8. The global investment environment continues to liberalize, reflecting increasing competition for investment dollars and a belief that FDI benefits outweigh its disadvantages; however, the rate of liberalization has slowed in recent years.

Notes

1   A.T. Kearney, Globalization Ledger, Global Business Policy Council, April 2000; "Measuring globalization," *Foreign Policy,* January/February 2001.
2   L.M. Greenberg, "Canada answers the call for US firms," *Wall Street Journal,* October 1, 1999, A13.
3   The World Bank, "Foreign investment dominates China's export industry," *World Bank News*, July 16, 2010.
4   R. Vernon, "International investments and international trade in the product life cycle," *Quarterly Journal of Economics*, May 1966, 190–207.
5   J.L. Yang, "Corporations pushing for job-creation tax breaks shield US-vs.-abroad hiring data," *The Washington Post*, August 12, 2011.
6   The first systematic presentation of this theory was made by S.H. Hymer in his doctoral dissertation in 1960. See S.H. Hymer, *The International Operations of National Firms*, Cambridge, MA: The MIT Press, 1976. Follow-up efforts to reiterate this theory include C.P. Kindleberger, *American Business Abroad*, New Haven: Yale University Press, 1969; R.Z. Aliber, "A theory of direct foreign investment." In *The International Corporation: A Symposium*, edited by C.P. Kindleberger, Cambridge, MA: The MIT Press, 1970; and R.E. Caves, "International corporations: The industrial economics of foreign investment," *Economica*, February 1971, 1–27; D.J. Teece, "The multinational enterprise: Market failure and market power considerations," *American Economic Review*, 1981, 233–238.
7   P.J. Buckley and M. Casson, *The Future of the Multinational Enterprise*, New York: Holmes and Meier, 1976; A.M. Rugman, *In-side the Multinationals*, New York: Columbia University Press, 1981; J.-F. Hennart, *A Theory of Multinational Enerprise*, Ann Arbor, MI: University of Michigan Press, 1982; D.J. Teece, "Multinational enterprise, internal governance, and industrial organization," *Sloan Management Review*, 1985, 3–17.
8   J. Stuckey, *Vertical Integration and Joint Ventures in the Aluminum Industry*, Cambridge, MA: Harvard University Press, 1983; D.J. Teece, "Profiting from technological innovation: Implications for integration, collaboration, licensing and public policy," *Research Policy*, 1986, 285–305.
9   J.H. Dunning, "Toward an eclectic theory of international production: Some empirical tests," *Journal of International Business Studies*, 11, 1, 1980, 9–31; J.H. Dunning, *International Production and the Multinational Enterprise*, London: Allen and Unwin, 1981; J.H. Dunning, *Explaining International Production*, London: Unwin Hyman, 1988.
10 D.J. Collis, "A resource-based analysis of global competition: The case of the bearings industry," *Strategic Management Journal*, 12, 1991, 49–68; Y. Luo, "Dynamic capabilities in international expansion," *Journal of World Business*, 35, 4, 2000, 355–378; S. Tallman, "Strategic management models and resource-based strategies among MNEs in a host market," *Strategic Management Journal*, 12, 1991, 69–82; U. Zander and B. Kogut, "Knowledge and the speed of the transfer and imitation of organizational capabilities," *Organization Science*, 6, 1, 1995, 76–92; D.J. Teece, G. Pisano, and A. Shuen, "Dynamic capabilities and strategic management," *Strategic Management Journal*, 18, 7, 1997, 509–533.
11 See J. Johanson and J. Vahlne, "The internationalization process of the firm: A model of knowledge development and increasing foreign market commitment," *Journal of International Business Studies*, 8, 1977, 23, 32; R. Luostarinen, *Internationalization of the Firm*, Helsinki, Finland: Helsinki School of Economics, 1980. Follow-up efforts include W. Davidson, "The location of foreign direct investment activity: Country characteristics and experience effects," *Journal of International Business Studies*, 11, 1980, 9–22; B. Kogut, "Foreign direct investment as a sequential process." In C.P. Kindleberger and D. Audretsch (eds), *The Multinational Corporation in the 1980s*, pp. 35–56, Cambridge, MA: MIT Press, 1983. O. Andersen,"On the internationalization process of firms: A critical analysis," *Journal of International Business Studies*, 24, 2, 1993, 209–231; S.J. Chang, "International expansion strategy of Japanese firms: Capability building through sequential entry," *Academy of Management Journal*, 38, 1995, 383, 407; Y. Luo and M.W. Peng, "Learning to compete in a transition economy: Experience, environment, and performance," *Journal of International Business Studies*, 30, 2, 1999, 269–296, among others.

12 E. Fina and A.M. Rugman, "A test of internalization theory and internationalization theory: The Upjohn Company," *Management International Review*, 1996, 199–213.

13 B. Kogut, "Joint ventures and the option to expand and acquire," *Management Science*, 1991, 19–33; T. Chi and D.J. McGuire, "Collaborative ventures and value of learning: Integrating the transaction cost and strategic option perspectives on the choice of market entry modes," *Journal of International Business Studies*, 1996, 285–307; P. Rivoli and E. Salorio, "Foreign direct investment and investment under uncertainty," *Journal of International Business Studies*, 1996, 335–357; T. Chi and A. Seth, "Joint ventures through a real options lens." In F.J. Contractor and P. Lorange (eds), *Cooperative Strategies and Alliances*, The Netherlands: Elsevier Science, pp. 71–87; T. Chi and A. Seth, "A dynamic model of the choice of mode for exploiting complementary capabilities," *Journal of International Business Studies*, 2009, 365–387.

14 See C.K. Prahalad and Y. Doz, *The Multinational Mission: Balancing Local Demands and Global Vision*, New York: The Free Press, 1987. Contributions to this perspective also come from C.A. Bartlett and S. Ghoshal, *Managing across Borders*, Boston, MA: Harvard Business School Press, 1989; K. Roth and A.J. Morrison, "An empirical analysis of the integration-responsiveness framework in global industries," *Journal of International Business Studies*, 21, 4, 1991, 541–564; S.J. Kobrin, "An empirical analysis of the determinants of global integration," *Strategic Management Journal*, 12 summer, 1991, 17–32; G.S. Yip, *Total Global Strategy*, Englewood Cliffs, NJ: Prentice-Hall, 1995.

15 A. Rugman and A. Verbeke, "A note on the transnational solution and the transaction cost theory of multinational strategic management," *Journal of International Business Studies*, 1992, 761–771.

16 See B. Kogut, "Designing global strategies: Comparative and competitive value-added chains," *Sloan Management Review*, summer, 1985a, 15–27; B. Kogut, "Designing global strategies: Profiting from operational flexibility," *Sloan Management Review*, fall, 1985b, 27–38; B. Kogut, "Joint ventures and the option to expand and acquire," *Management Science*, 37, 1, 1990, 19–33; B. Kogut, "Options thinking and platform investments: Investing in opportunity," *California Management Review*, winter, 1994, 52–71.

17 *World Investment Report—2010 & 2011*, UNCTAD.

18 WalMart, "Walmart Mexico posts 8.9% increase in revenues for November 2012," Company Website, 2012, www.retail-insight-network.com/news/newswalmart-mexico-posts-89-increase-in-revenues-for-november-2012.

19 Citigroup Inc., Citibank (China) Co. Ltd.: "About Citi," 2013.

20 *World Investment Report—2013*.

21 *The World Competitiveness Yearbook* 2000, 388.

22 *World Investment Report—2008*, 82.

23 L. Nachum, "Economic geography and the location of TNCs: Financial and professional service FDI to the US," *Journal of International Business Studies*, 31, 3, 2000, 367–385.

24 *World Investment Report—2009*.

25 *Transnational Corporations*, 10, 3, UNCTAD 2002.

26 C. Terhune, "Swedish concern to expand in the U.S. through two deals," *Wall Street Journal*, January 23, 2001.

27 J. Pesta, "Indian companies buy passage to U.S.," *Wall Street Journal*, January 22, 2001, A16.

28 Mergermarket, "2012 m&a roundup," January 14, 2013, 10.

29 *World Investment Report—2001*, 6.

30 *World Investment Report—2000*.

31 *The World Competitiveness Yearbook—2000*, 390.

32 C. Barfield, "Beware of investment protectionism," *The American*, December 17, 2008.

33 C.M. Yee, "Let's make a deal," *Wall Street Journal*, September 25, 2000, R10.

34 "The strange life of low-tech America," *The Economist*, October 17, 1998, 73.

35 C. Rhoades, "A contrarian Motorola picks Germany," *Wall Street Journal*, October 10, 1997, A18.

36 J. Millman, "Mexican workers suffer as plants relocate South of the border," *Wall Street Journal*, March 26, 2002, A20.

113

chapter 4

the multinational enterprise

WHAT IS A MULTINATIONAL ENTERPRISE?   117

THE WORLD'S LARGEST MNES   120

THE IMAGE OF THE MNE   125

THE COMPETITIVE ADVANTAGE OF THE MNE   127

THE MNE FROM EMERGING/DEVELOPING ECONOMIES (DMNE)   131

THE SMALL AND MEDIUM-SIZE INTERNATIONAL ENTERPRISE (SMIE)   139

Do You Know?

1. Who are the players in the international business arena?
2. How can you tell the degree of a firm's internationalization?
3. What advantages and disadvantages do MNEs have when they operate overseas compared to local firms, and what are the essential capabilities with which a successful MNE must be equipped?
4. What are the typical features of developing country MNEs and how do they differ from those of developed country MNEs?
5. What would you advise a small international firm seeking to compete with an established MNE?

OPENING CASE   Johnson & Johnson

Incorporated in 1886, Johnson & Johnson is the world's most comprehensive manufacturer of health care products, as well as a provider of related services, for the consumer, pharmaceutical, and medical devices and diagnostics markets. Consisting of more than 275 operating companies located in 60 countries, the company sells its products throughout the world. Just over half of its $67.2 billion in sales in 2012 were derived from international sales. Johnson & Johnson has been conducting international operations for decades. The company established its first affiliate in Canada in 1919, followed by the United Kingdom in 1924. Affiliates were established in Australia in 1931, India in 1947, Sweden in 1956, Japan in 1961, South Korea in 1981, and Egypt in 1985. In 1990, Shanghai Johnson & Johnson Limited, a joint venture, was opened in China, followed the next year by Johnson & Johnson China Ltd. By 1995, the Company already had five companies in China. The year 1990 also saw the establishment of the first offices in Hungary, Poland, and the former Yugoslavia, and in the Czech Republic the following year. Johnson & Johnson used both greenfield investment and acquisitions to expand its global reach. It acquired Belgian pharmaceutical firm Janssen Pharmaceutica in 1961, German sanitary protection manufacturer Dr. Carl Hahn in 1974, German baby toiletries maker Penaten in 1986, and French skin care firm RoC, S.A. in 1993. In 1998, the Company consolidated its manufacturing, until then done purely on a local basis, along regional lines. In 2001, it acquired the 40 percent it did not previously own in its Japanese joint venture, and in 2002 it bought Belgina firm Tibotec-Virca, and Pfizer's Consumer Healthcare unit in 2006. In 2008 Johnson & Johnson was an official partner in the Beijing Olympics. In 2012, Johnson & Johnson made the largest acquisition in its 126-year history when it purchased Synthes, Inc., a Swedish company that makes medical devices, for $20 billion.

The company has made significant strides in its efforts to leverage its global reach. In Europe, for example, it has moved to establish "global platforms" consolidating production facilities in one country from which neighboring countries are served. It also embarked on a global human resources strategy, ranging from international recruitment to global management development. Many challenges remain, however, including how to expand in emerging markets while sustaining growth in established locations, how to coordinate the global network of member companies with different national and corporate cultures, and how to respond to changes such as health care regulatory reforms in the multiple environments in which it operates. For a number of years, a strong dollar weighed heavily on the profitability of Johnson & Johnson's overseas operations by depressing its earnings when converted from foreign currencies into US dollars; however, the US currency has reversed direction since the early 2000s, boosting the company's profits from international operations.

Source: 2012 Annual Report and company website, Johnson and Johnson.

What is a Multinational Enterprise?

When reading about international business, you will encounter many terms describing a company with significant international operations and presence. These include:

- The **internationally committed company** is a firm with at least one majority-owned plant or a joint venture abroad, but which is not represented in every major region of the world, e.g., Asia, Europe, and the Americas.[1]
- The **internationally leaning** firm is one with foreign sales and possibly a representative office and/or a licensing agreement, but no ownership of foreign production sites.[2]
- The **multidomestic** firm is an enterprise with multiple international subsidiaries that are relatively independent from headquarters.
- The **global** firm consists of closely integrated international subsidiaries controlled and coordinated from central headquarters.
- The **transnational** firm consists of subsidiaries that fulfill varying roles, with some subsidiaries playing a strategic role that in the global firm is reserved for headquarters.[3] Some scholars as well as the United Nations Conference on Trade and Development (UNCTAD) use this term to refer to the most global of companies; however, in this book we prefer to use the more commonly used term "multinational."
- The **multinational** firm, or MNE, according to the OECD, is "an enterprise that engages in FDI and owns or controls value-adding activities in more than one country." An MNE typically:
    - (a) Has "multiple" facilities around the globe. According to the Conference Board, to merit the title of an MNE, a firm needs to own a majority stake in plants in the three key regions of North America, Europe, and the Pacific Rim.
    - (b) Derives a "substantial" portion of revenues from foreign operations.
    - (c) Runs subsidiaries that possess a common strategic vision and draw from a common pool of resources.
    - (d) Places foreign nationals or expatriates at the board level and/or in senior management posts.

Firms such as Johnson & Johnson, Ford Motor, and Nestlé meet all of those criteria. Others may meet some, or most, or do so only partially, but are still commonly referred to as MNEs. For instance, French dairy producer Danone has only two foreign nationals on its board; however, it has vast global presence, a common vision, and revenues from foreign operations make up a substantial portion of its overall revenues.

Throughout this textbook, we use the term **Multinational Enterprise (MNE)** to denote a firm with foreign direct investment (FDI), whether in manufacturing or in services, over which it maintains effective control. A firm might have investment in only one foreign market, but if this investment is controlled by it, we will classify it as an MNE. A firm engaged in trade activities, but without an FDI component, will be called an **international firm**. For example, a US-based company that specializes in import and export management services, such as export logistics, or an Italian firm that is exclusively an importer or exporter of, say, handbags, is referred to in this book as an international firm. A firm that has a small (less than 10 percent) equity stake in a single foreign investment and has no control over its operation and management is also an international firm, rather than a multinational enterprise.

In this chapter, we first discuss "traditional" MNEs, that is, large firms based in developed nations, e.g., the European Union (EU), that have activities in most parts of the world. Johnson & Johnson belongs to this group. The second group consists of MNEs from developing and emerging economies (DMNEs), such as China and South Korea. The third group includes small and midsize enterprises engaged in international business. Most of these firms do not have FDI, and hence do not qualify as MNEs under our definition. In this book, they will be called **Small and Midsize International Enterprises,** or SMIEs.

The Degree of Internationalization

The level of MNE internationalization can be gauged by the **Transnationality Index (TNI)** used by UNCTAD. This index is calculated as the average of three ratios: (a) foreign assets to total assets, (b) foreign sales to total sales; and (c) foreign employment to total employment.[4] Exhibit 4.1 shows

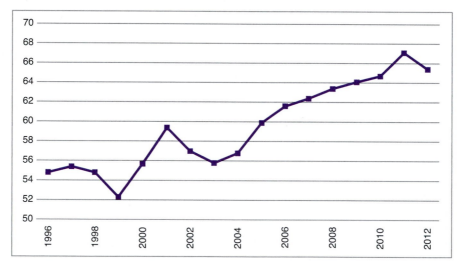

Note: TNI is a percentage. The simple average TNI is the sum of the TNI values of all the companies, divided by the total number of companies.

Exhibit 4.1 Average TNI of the top 100 largest TNCs worldwide, 1996–2012
Source: UNCTAD, World Investment Report, 1996–2012.

the average TNI for the world's largest MNEs. While the average has been rising over the years (especially for the top 50 firms), it remains under 70 percent, indicating that even the largest of multinationals are still dependent on their home country for a relatively significant amount of their sales, assets, and human resources. Empirical evidence has been inconclusive regarding the possible link between TNI level and corporate performance. This may be because, despite their obvious prowess, even the most global firms face daunting challenges in such realms as coordination and oversight of far-flung operations, establishment of a complex global supply chain, and the management of a diverse workforce. Also, as we will discuss elsewhere in the book, TNI is not the only measure of firm internationalization. For instance, in Chapter 11 we will mention that truly global companies do not retain all of their high-value-added activities in the home country, while in Chapter 17 we will point to the presence of foreign nationals on the board of directors as an indicator of how global a firm truly is.

History of the MNE

The MNE is not a new phenomenon. In their book *The Birth of the Multinational*, Moore and Lewis trace the origin and evolution of the MNE during the Phoenician, Carthaginean, Greek, and Roman empires. Formed as stock ownership companies, these firms appeared in Assyria shortly after 2000 BC. They deployed their resources from the capital Ashur into foreign markets using both domestic and foreign employees engaged in value-adding activities. These early firms had to overcome many of the same obstacles facing current MNEs, such as tariffs and nationalist opposition to foreign trade and investment, but used their competitive advantage and market power to prevail.[5] MNEs continued to flourish and expand their reach in modern times. In the eighteenth and nineteenth centuries, the British-based East India Company took advantage of England's colonial rule and control of shipping lanes to become a formidable force in Asia. When the company lost its monopoly on trading with China in the 1830s, competitors quickly emerged. Jardine-Matheson, formed in Canton (today's Guangzhou), China, opened an office at that time in the newly established colony of Hong Kong. A decade later it became the first foreign trading firm to open an office in Japan. Jardines is now a diversified MNE listed in Bermuda, but conducting most of its business in Asia from its Hong Kong base.

In recent decades, the number of MNEs has expanded dramatically. The same 15 developed countries that had 7,276 MNEs at the end of 1960 were home to 39,650 multinationals by the second half of the 1990s. Today, the MNE is a key player in the global economy. Consider this:

- US-based MNEs alone employed over 34 million workers in 2011 and made capital expenditures totaling $706 worldwide.[6]
- One percent of all MNEs own 50 percent of the total stock of all foreign direct investment.[7]
- The world's largest 500 industrial firms, most of which are MNEs, account for roughly 70 percent of world trade.
- In a Conference Board survey of 1,250 publicly listed large firms, MNEs represented only 13 percent of the sample, but had 53 percent of total sales.[8]
- Roughly 40 to 50 percent of world trade is conducted between MNEs and their affiliates. One-third of US trade consists of internal transfers among units of the same MNE.
- At the beginning of the twenty-first century, the annual sales of each of the ten largest industrial MNEs exceeded the tax revenues of Australia.[9] In Ireland, foreign firms account for two-thirds of national output and roughly 50 percent of employment.

> **Interim Summary**
>
> 1. There are many different types of international companies and multiple definitions of a multinational firm. In this book, we use the term multinational enterprise (MNE) to refer to any company that has control over a foreign investment.
> 2. One indicator of the degree of an MNE's internationality is its TNI score.
> 3. While the MNE is not a new phenomenon, recent decades have seen a significant growth in the number and reach of such firms.

The World's Largest MNEs

Exhibit 4.2 shows the top 50 non-financial MNE list for 2011 ranked by foreign assets. As the Exhibit shows, the top ten on the list are a diverse group led by General Electric (which is a diversified firm, although it is classified as an electronics firm under the UNCTAD classification) and dominated by energy, utilities, telecommunications, motor vehicles, and pharmaceuticals companies. With the exceptions of Hong Kong-based Hutchison, Mainland China-based CITIC Group, and Taiwan-based Hon Hai Precision Industries, all of the top 50 hail from developed economies in North America, Western Europe, or Japan.

Ranked by[a]

Foreign Assets	TNI[b]	Corporation	Home Economy	Industry[c]
1	79	General Electric Co	United States	Electrical & electronic equipment
2	32	Royal Dutch Shell plc	United Kingdom	Petroleum expl./ref./distr.
3	22	BP plc	United Kingdom	Petroleum expl./ref./distr.
4	77	Toyota Motor Corporation	Japan	Motor vehicles
5	28	Total SA	France	Petroleum expl./ref./distr.
6	45	Exxon Mobil Corporation	United States	Petroleum expl./ref./distr.
7	8	Vodafone Group plc	United Kingdom	Telecommunications
8	62	GDF Suez	France	Utilities (electricity, gas and water)
9	61	Chevron Corporation	United States	Petroleum expl./ref./distr.
10	64	Volkswagen Group	Germany	Motor vehicles
11	51	Eni SpA	Italy	Petroleum expl./ref./distr.
12	1	Nestlé SA	Switzerland	Food, beverages and tobacco
13	71	Enel SpA	Italy	Electricity, gas and water
14	48	E.ON AG	Germany	Utilities (electricity, gas and water)
15	4	Anheuser-Busch InBev NV	Belgium	Food, beverages and tobacco
16	6	ArcelorMittal	Luxembourg	Metal and metal products

Exhibit 4.2 The world's top 50 non-financial TNCs, ranked by foreign assets, 2012 (millions of dollars and number of employees)

120

17	29	Siemens AG	Germany	Electrical & electronic equipment
18	36	Honda Motor Co Ltd	Japan	Motor vehicles
19	92	Mitsubishi Corporation	Japan	Wholesale trade
20	98	EDF SA	France	Utilities (Electricity, gas and water)
21	73	Daimler AG	Germany	Motor vehicles
22	67	Deutsche Telekom AG	Germany	Telecommunications
23	66	Pfizer Inc	United States	Pharmaceuticals
24	40	BMW AG	Germany	Motor vehicles
25	42	Telefonica SA	Spain	Telecommunications
26	25	Hutchison Whampoa Limited	Hong Kong, China	Diversified
27	95	Wal-Mart Stores Inc	United States	Retail & trade
28	60	Iberdrola SA	Spain	Utilities (electricity, gas and water)
29	46	Nissan Motor Co Ltd	Japan	Motor vehicles
30	27	Fiat SpA	Italy	Motor vehicles
31	52	Sanofi	France	Pharmaceuticals
32	3	Xstrata plc	Switzerland	Mining & quarrying
33	88	Ford Motor Company	United States	Motor vehicles
34	2	Anglo American plc	United Kingdom	Mining & quarrying
35	86	ConocoPhillips	United States	Petroleum expl./ref./distr.
36	100	CITIC Group	China	Diversified
37	99	Statoil ASA	Norway	Petroleum expl./ref./distr.
38	39	Novartis AG	Switzerland	Pharmaceuticals
39	85	General Motors Co	United States	Motor vehicles
40	20	Hon Hai Precision Industries	Taiwan Province of China	Electrical & electronic equipment
41	43	Rio Tinto plc	United Kingdom	Mining & quarrying
42	55	Procter & Gamble Co	United States	Diversified
43	44	BHP Billiton Group Ltd	Australia	Mining & quarrying
44	87	RWE AG	Germany	Utilities (electricity, gas and water)
45	53	International Business Machines Corporation	United States	Electrical & electronic equipment
46	19	BG Group plc	United Kingdom	Electricity, gas and water
47	78	Johnson & Johnson	United States	Pharmaceuticals
48	13	SABMiller plc	United Kingdom	Food, beverages and tobacco
49	56	Hewlett-Packard Co	United States	Electrical & electronic equipment
50	16	Unilever plc	United Kingdom	Diversified

[a] Preliminary results based on data from the companies' financial reporting; corresponds to the financial year from April 1, 2012 to March 31, 2013.

[b] TNI, the Transnationality Index, is calculated as the average of the following three ratios: foreign assets to total assets, foreign sales to total sales and foreign employment to total employment.

[c] Industry classification for companies follows the United States Standard Industrial Classification as used by the United States Securities and Exchange Commission (SEC).

Exhibit 4.2 (*Continued*)

Source: UNCTAD World Development Report 2013.

Rank	Company	Sales	Profits	Assets	Market Value
1	JPMorgan Chase	$108.2 B	$21.3 B	$2,359.1 B	$191.4 B
2	General Electric	$147.4 B	$13.6 B	$685.3 B	$243.7 B
3	Exxon Mobil	$420.7 B	$44.9 B	$333.8 B	$400.4 B
4	Berkshire Hathaway	$162.5 B	$14.8 B	$427.5 B	$252.8 B
5	Wells Fargo	$91.2 B	$18.9 B	$1,423 B	$201.3 B
6	Chevron	$222.6 B	$26.2 B	$233 B	$232.5 B
7	Apple	$164.7 B	$41.7 B	$196.1 B	$416.6 B
8	Wal-Mart Stores	$469.2 B	$17 B	$203.1 B	$242.5 B
9	Citigroup	$90.7 B	$7.5 B	$1,864.7 B	$143.6 B
10	AT&T	$127.4 B	$7.3 B	$272.3 B	$200.1 B

Note: Forbes' ranking of public companies is based on a composite measure that includes sales, profits, assets, and market value.

Exhibit 4.3 Ten largest US MNEs in 2013

Source: Forbes 2013, www.forbes.com/global2000/list/.

Exhibit 4.3 provides information on the top US-based MNEs. Unlike the UNCTAD list of the world's multinationals, this list includes financial services firms, which populate nearly half of the top ten firms.

The Growth of Service MNEs

Recent years saw a significant growth of MNEs in media, education, transportation, information services, travel, tourism, health care, and professional services. There are several reasons for the growth, as follows:

- *Economic transformation.* As developed nations have shifted into service economies, their service firms have sought to leverage their scale and resources toward new growth venues in foreign markets. For instance, large US airlines such as United, Delta, and Continental expanded their international route network to serve the increasingly global destinations of their customers and to capture the better profit margins as compared with domestic routes.
- *Globalization and liberalization of regulatory systems.* Because many service MNEs are "location-bound," that is, production and consumption must take place in the same location, they are especially dependent on global regulatory regimes, as well as on the domestic regulations in each market in which they operate. New "open skies" aviation agreements allowed carriers to serve more foreign markets and opened domestic markets to foreign competition. The globalization of accounting standards made it possible for large US-based accounting firms to operate abroad. The relaxation of the "Big Store" law in Japan permitted Toys 'R' Us to operate the large-scale retail operations it has come to master in the United States.

■ *Communications advances.* Progress in communications and computer technologies enable service MNEs to coordinate knowledge-intensive operations across borders. As an example, consulting firms can now exchange information and transfer knowledge quickly and efficiently among far-flung subsidiaries, making coordination easier and better.

The growth of service MNEs has been especially pronounced in the United States, which is regarded as having the most competitive service sector, as a result of relative openness and intense domestic competition, in comparison with the European and Japanese service industries. As noted in Chapter 2, the United States runs a substantial trade surplus in services vis-à-vis a chronic deficit in its merchandise trade. US firms do not dominate all service sectors, however. Exhibit 4.4 shows the list of the world's 20 largest banks by assets in 2013. Only two US banks (JP Morgan Chase and Bank of America) are among the top 20, with the top ten dominated by Asian and European banks. Although this is partly the result of US limitations on interstate banking, it does provide a

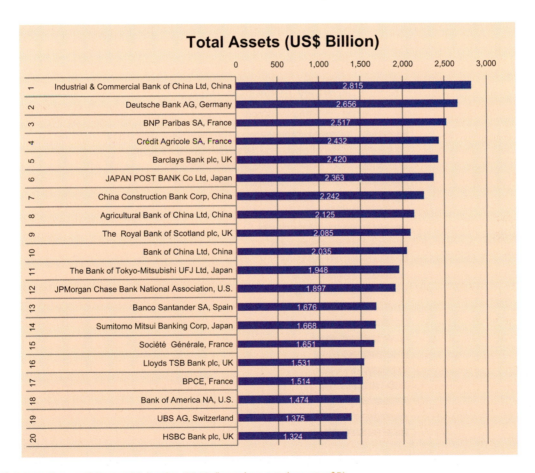

Total Assets (US$ Billion)

Rank	Bank	Total Assets
1	Industrial & Commercial Bank of China Ltd, China	2,815
2	Deutsche Bank AG, Germany	2,656
3	BNP Paribas SA, France	2,517
4	Crédit Agricole SA, France	2,432
5	Barclays Bank plc, UK	2,420
6	JAPAN POST BANK Co Ltd, Japan	2,363
7	China Construction Bank Corp, China	2,242
8	Agricultural Bank of China Ltd, China	2,125
9	The Royal Bank of Scotland plc, UK	2,085
10	Bank of China Ltd, China	2,035
11	The Bank of Tokyo-Mitsubishi UFJ Ltd, Japan	1,948
12	JPMorgan Chase Bank National Association, U.S.	1,897
13	Banco Santander SA, Spain	1,676
14	Sumitomo Mitsui Banking Corp, Japan	1,668
15	Société Générale, France	1,651
16	Lloyds TSB Bank plc, UK	1,531
17	BPCE, France	1,514
18	Bank of America NA, U.S.	1,474
19	UBS AG, Switzerland	1,375
20	HSBC Bank plc, UK	1,324

Exhibit 4.4 The world's top 20 banks, 2013 (based on total assets, $B)
Source: Adapted from Bankers Almanac, August 2013.

sense of how competitive this sector is globally. The four Chinese banks, all still state-owned, ascended into the top ten rank only in the last two years after they each had their initial public offerings and subsequently expanded significantly due to the rapid growth of the Chinese economy. Although their international footprints are still quite small, the four state-owned banks have all formulated ambitious plans to expand internationally.

In advertising, US and European agencies are the leaders, whereas the Japanese lag behind. Dentsu—Japan's dominant advertising agency—still generated only a modest portion of its revenue from foreign sources. This is not for lack of trying. Dentsu opened a New York office in 1959, and in 1999 it took a 20 percent stake in US-based Bcom3 Group, a merger of Leo Burnett and D'arcy Masius Benton & Bowles. In many service sectors, however, US firms face tough competition. As you can see in Exhibit 4.5, US-based carriers are among the largest airlines in terms of passenger traffic, but this is mostly the result of the size of the US domestic aviation market. When it comes to service reputation, US firms lag behind foreign carriers, in particular Singapore Airlines and Hong Kong-based Cathay Pacific that have been occupying the top spots in global surveys.

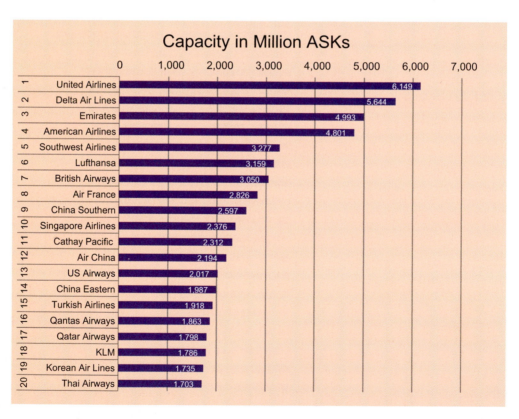

Exhibit 4.5 The world's largest airlines by available seat kilometers (ASKs)
Source: Adapted from Innovata, December 2012.

> **Interim Summary**
>
> 1. With a few exceptions, the largest MNEs are based in the Triad countries of Western Europe, the United States, and Japan.
> 2. The annual revenues of the largest MNEs are higher than the tax incomes of some countries.
> 3. Service MNEs are growing rapidly, the result of a shift toward service economies in developed nations, changes in regulatory regimes, and the availability of modern means of communication.
> 4. US MNEs are competitive in many areas, but they face intense competition in sectors such as banking from other global players.

The Image of the MNE

The MNE in the Public Eye

Over the years, the MNE has been both lauded and vilified for its impact on its host (especially) and home countries. If the MNE was criticized as a monopolistic player representing a threat to national sovereignty in the 1970s, in the 1980s it was labeled a cumbersome dinosaur unable to adapt to change and hence doomed. In the 1990s, the MNE emerged as a relatively benevolent provider of knowledge and capital, whose technology and expertise contribute to national productivity and export performance.[10] For instance, in 2010, foreign invested enterprises (FIEs) accounted for 76 percent of China's top 200 export-oriented enterprises. MNEs were also positively cited for being an agent of change, introducing new ways of doing business that would eventually be adopted by local firms. For example, the first industrial robots were introduced to Singapore by MNEs, with local firms adopting the technology later. Finally, MNEs have been noted for creating jobs. In Turkey, MNEs increased their staffing at a double-digit level in an otherwise stagnant labor market, and those jobs have been paying more than double the average wage.[11]

At the dawn of the twenty-first century, MNEs are once again seen in some circles as a threat to national sovereignty. The Economist suggests that this is because the MNE is the most visible symbol of globalization. Developing nations expect the MNE to bring in capital and technology but refrain from bringing in foreign ideas. The MNE is accused of having an unfair advantage, exploiting incentives granted exclusively to foreign firms to shift production to ever lower-cost locations. It is also criticized for limiting knowledge transfer to "intermediate" technologies, constraining the host country's ability to become a global competitor. For instance, Motorola has been criticized for limiting its R&D efforts in Brazil to the adaptation of its existing technology to Latin American markets, rather than creating new technologies.[12] A related criticism is that MNEs generate low-paying, low-tech jobs in the host country while keeping high value-added jobs at home. In China, there are now many voices calling on the government to curb the rising influence of foreign MNEs.

The image of the MNE varies, among other factors, by country, industry, market orientation, and the constituency affected. The impact of the MNE in developed countries is assessed using different yardsticks than in developing countries. MNEs in extraction industries (e.g., oil, mining) are scrutinized more closely than those engaged in manufacturing, and those that bring advanced technology are often treated differently from those that provide mere assembly ("screwdriver plants").[13] In the public eye, MNEs and host country governments involve both cooperation and bargaining elements in their interdependent relationships. The two cooperate by contributing complementary resources. An MNE's technological resources, capital investment, global distribution, and managerial expertise add critical value to local economies, especially to developing countries. MNEs need support from local governments in developing investment infrastructure, creating a better environment for fair competition, and improving the quality of production factors such as labor (through training and education), information (through advancing the information technology industry), and capital (through improving the banking sector). When a particular MNE's strategic goals are not compatible with those of the host country government, bargaining ensues. The government may want to control critical natural resources demanded by the MNE or safeguard an infant local industry by posing many entry or operational barriers against the MNE. We further discuss MNE–government relations in Chapter 7.

The image of the MNE in its home country is also often ambivalent. On the one hand, it is often recognized that the MNE brings resources that are unavailable in the home country, lowering prices for domestic consumers and helping a nation sustain its global competitiveness. Another plus is that the MNE's successes in foreign markets allow suppliers and other host country firms to "piggyback" on the MNE, thus increasing national output and job creation at home. At the same time, MNEs are criticized for shifting production and investment from their home base to foreign locations, undermining employment and "hollowing-out" the production and knowledge base of the home country.

The Borderless Corporation: Myth or Reality?

The rise of a borderless, transnational corporation, which owes allegiance to no one, has been a major theme in the popular media. According to this view, the MNE establishes its headquarters anywhere it sees fit, shifts its operations at will to wherever it can garner the highest return, and adopts the form of governance and management that it finds most suitable in terms of profitability, rather than in terms of social responsibility or other broader considerations. Proponents of this thesis point out that it is increasingly difficult to pinpoint country-of-origin for firms engaged in international business. Chrysler, an auto company founded in the US in 1925, was acquired by German auto maker Daimler Benz in 1998, returned to majority US ownership in 2007, and became an Italian-owned company in 2012 after Fiat purchased a majority stake in it. Rhombic Corp. was founded in Nevada, but is based in Vancouver, Canada, while the highest turnover of its shares is in Hamburg, Germany.

Opponents of this thesis argue that the borderless corporation is a myth; that most MNEs maintain a clear national base and that enduring national and political realities shape their governance, financing, R&D, FDI, and intra-firm trading strategies.[14] MNEs based in different countries utilize various competitive advantages developed in response to factor and product market circumstances in their home countries.[15] Most MNEs still produce more than two-thirds of their output and employ two-thirds of their workforce in their home countries.[16] For instance, a recent study suggests that there remain significant differences among Triad firms in product strategy. While US firms compete on "economy" (lower price, lower quality), Japanese MNEs highlight the superior value of their products (a combination of higher quality and lower prices), whereas Europeans emphasize the premium nature of their product (higher quality, higher price). Companies that aligned their global strategy with the national stereotype performed better than those that did not.[17]

Interim Summary

1. The image of MNEs varies by time, country, and industry.
2. The level of MNEs' contribution to the local economy is affected by whether or not MNEs and the local government share goals and contribute complementary resources; MNEs and the government both cooperate and bargain with each other.
3. Despite a heightened tendency toward borderless activities and a growing contribution from foreign production and sales, most MNEs retain their home country roots and characteristics.

The Competitive Advantage of the MNE

When McDonald's opened its first restaurant in Moscow, the MNE increased the number of customers served there more than 20-fold over the number served in the Soviet-era cafeteria which occupied the site before. Thanks to its global scale and experience, the MNE has a large capital, human, brand, and technological resource base that it can effectively leverage in multiple countries. As the chairman and CEO of Toronto-based Four Seasons Hotels justified its drive for foreign expansion, "we can double the size of the company, and then can double it again, without changing the product or brand." Procter & Gamble's operations in some 180 countries allow it to spread development, manufacturing, and marketing costs. With almost five billion customers worldwide, the company can monitor the performance of each of its 100 brands and apply lessons from one market to another. Global spread also permits the MNE an effective response to trade and investment barriers. PepsiCo was able to profitably sell its cola in the Soviet Union despite the lack of a convertible currency by taking Russian vodka as payment and then using its US distribution channels to market it. Similarly, KFC used its China revenues to commission uniforms for its branches in other Asian countries.

Global spread also provides MNEs with diversification, allowing them to compensate for low performance or uncertainties such as currency fluctuations in certain markets. This allows them to overcome entry barriers in the form of high start-up costs and be early entrants in emerging markets where return is often not realized for many years. One of the most successful MNEs in China, Procter & Gamble, entered the country in the 1980s, but it did not turn a profit until the mid-1990s.

Automotive MNEs did not make money in China during many years of operation, but most of them now enjoy high profitability in this market. Although the performance of MNEs varies by company and markets, as a group they have been consistently more profitable than local counterparts. However, this higher rate of return must be considered against the higher risk associated with foreign investment.[18] In contrast, the returns for internationally committed and internationally leaning firms were found to be quite comparable with those of domestic companies. Despite the reputation of developing markets as being a difficult place to do business, profitability was higher for firms operating in those markets than for those in developed markets, a spread especially pronounced for internationally leaning firms.[19] One reason is that monopoly profits are often easier to obtain in developing markets that are less regulated and have lesser competition.

Capabilities and Competitive Advantage

In Chapter 3, we introduced the dynamic capability theory. It suggests that, to prosper in today's turbulent international environment, the MNE cannot merely rely on its existing resources; it must develop "dynamic capabilities" to create, deploy, and upgrade resources in pursuit of sustained competitive advantage. It must instill its capabilities within its global operating units. If superior knowledge is the main source of its competitive advantage, the MNE must have an organization that extends and exploits its knowledge throughout its global operations.

Types of Capabilities

Firm capabilities include familiarity with national culture, industrial structure, and government requirements, as well as relationships with customers, suppliers, and regulators. These and various other aspects of doing business locally give a domestic business a potential edge over a foreign competitor. The MNE must have strategic and organizational capabilities to mitigate this disadvantage. Such capabilities include resources that are unique to the firm, difficult to imitate, and can generate economic returns and competitive advantage. Such unique and hard-to-imitate resources can be either static or dynamic. In the case of Coca-Cola, for instance, the vast number of bottling facilities it controls worldwide are advantageous but not nearly as critical as its secret recipes for syrups and concentrates (a unique but basically static asset) and skills in marketing beverages to divergent consumers worldwide (a more dynamic capability).

Strategic capabilities include technological assets such as patents, trade secrets, proprietary designs, product development, and process innovation. IBM's Chinese speech recognition system ViaVoice has dominated the greater China market for years. The system uses IBM's most advanced voice recognition technology and can be adapted to standard Mandarin and a number of special dialects. The Body Shop's franchising skills with international retail operations, Merrill Lynch's relationships with Japanese financial institutions, and Kodak's extensive networking with Chinese government agencies have significantly contributed to each firm's success.

Managerial skills are an important component of MNE capabilities. Such skills are manifested in global human resource management as well as in information, organization design, and control systems. Kodak's skills in recruiting, evaluating, motivating, and training its overseas employees provide a distinct advantage. Coca-Cola's ability to propagate a common human resources philosophy and develop a group of internationally minded mid-level executives also constitutes an advantage. Colgate's system of recruiting MBAs who speak at least one foreign language and have lived outside the United States is another example. Colgate does not assign foreign-born trainees to their native countries for initial postings, but rather to a third country.

International experience is essential to strategic and organizational capabilities. Gillette's 20-plus years of experience in emerging markets and a century of experience in its industry helped the company become a global leader. This experience allows Gillette (now part of Procter & Gamble) to select and enter foreign markets successfully. The same is true for Starbuck's Coffee, which leveraged its first experience in foreign forays into Tokyo in 1996 to expand into other foreign markets. Starbuck's is now present in 36 foreign markets, from Bahrain to the Philippines.

Capability Deployment

To be successful, the MNE must transfer critical capabilities unavailable to local players. McDonald's and KFC's overseas success has been built on their ability to rapidly transfer the capacity to operate their entire complex business system to foreign entrepreneurs. Leveraging capabilities across markets is difficult, however. As market conditions in other countries vary, so does the effectiveness of those skills. Toyota's "Just in Time" (JIT) system yields benefits globally, but the risks associated with reduced inventory levels are greater in countries where change and disruptions—from weather conditions to strikes—are common.

Technological and financial capabilities (e.g., cash flow management) are generally more transferable than organizational skills. Among strategic capabilities, both a superior market position and an oligopolistic market power are competitive edges that are not immediately transferable. The same is true for home country experience and reputation, although some firms and brands (e.g., the Four Seasons Hotel Chain) possess a global reputation that can be leveraged. A superior distribution network cannot be easily replicated overseas; however, knowing how to establish and manage a distribution network is transferable. Nestlé's experience with promotion and distribution in China was helpful in other emerging markets such as Vietnam and Russia.

Capability Upgrading

Learning capability is the capacity to generate ideas and acquire new knowledge. It is generally more transferable than firm resources. Firms with the capacity to learn can gain more from experience and apply it to other relevant situations. This capacity helps mitigate the "liabilities of foreignness" during international expansion. To translate learning into competence, the MNE must convert it into firm-specific resources. This involves acquisition, sharing, and utilization. Knowledge acquisition accrues through internal development or external learning. Some MNEs offer seminars in which senior managers regularly share their best practices and knowledge about foreign markets across functional, divisional, and geographical boundaries. Measuring, benchmarking, tracking, and rewards for knowledge enhancement may also increase learning. Centers of excellence that represent the best practice of managing knowledge are another learning mechanism. An MNE can put together a list of best practices in core marketing activities; for example, the best database marketing is done in London, the best distribution logistics can be found in Singapore, and the best account management is in New York. Many MNEs have gained ideas and experience from foreign businesses that were early movers in a host country market. Next, firms must be able to generate innovative ideas useful in international expansion through competency acquisition, experimentation, and spanning boundaries. When learning through competency acquisition is coupled with a high capacity for change, MNEs tend to be more innovative, proactive, and willing to take risks. They react to market changes in different countries more quickly.

External knowledge acquisition through alliances is also an important vehicle for upgrading capabilities. Starbuck's takes a 20 percent stake in many of its overseas stores with the hope of learning about the local market and eventually increasing its stake.[20] Alliances enable firms to run product development programs in conjunction with their own internal development efforts or to broaden their access to new skills and insights. Motorola licensed some of its microprocessor technology to Toshiba, and in return Toshiba licensed some of its memory chip technology to Motorola. The alliance experience can trigger learning but can also expose the MNE to technology loss. In the alliance between GE and SNECMA to build commercial aircraft engines, GE tried to reduce the risk of excess transfer by walling off certain sections of the production process. This modularization was supposed to cut off transfer of what GE felt was key competitive technology, but complete separation was found to be impractical and detrimental to the effectiveness of the venture. Chapter 12 is focused on the opportunities and challenges associated with global strategic alliances.

Sharing and disseminating newly acquired knowledge among different subunits of an MNE will determine the efficiency of capability upgrading. Once new knowledge is acquired, firms integrate it with their existing skills. The integration depends on having an effective information transfer system, an incentive structure promoting external learning and experimentation, and an organizational implementing mechanism. Sharing experiences and mindsets through training programs, efficient communications systems, and clear information transfer is crucial, as is a governance structure that facilitates learning diffusion.

Interim Summary

1. MNEs have many advantages over local firms. They can draw on larger financial, knowledge, and human resources, have broader experience than most local firms, and can afford to operate at a loss in unfavorable markets for a longer time before turning a profit. However, local firms enjoy superior knowledge of their home market and are often supported by their government.

2. It is relatively easy to transfer capital and equipment to a new operation but much more difficult to transfer knowledge, skill, and experience. It is crucial for the MNE to be able to disseminate knowledge to new operations and to integrate information acquired from those operations into already existing procedures. Effective knowledge transfer is the most important capability for an MNE to develop.

The MNE from Emerging/Developing Economies (DMNE)

For years, the term MNE was synonymous with the likes of General Motors, Coca-Cola, Siemens, and Matsushita—large firms from developed nations, mostly from the United States, Europe, and Japan. Firms from emerging and developing nations were rarely in a position to amass the resources and knowledge necessary for extensive forays into foreign markets. Although MNEs from developed nations still dominate global business, **developing nations' MNEs** (DMNEs), especially those from emerging economies, have become global competitors and sometimes leaders in their field. Taiwan-based Acer is a leader in notebook computers. Thai conglomerate Charoen Pokphand is a major force in food production and processing in Asia.[21] Philippines' brewer San Miguel and Singapore Telecom are also global players.

The rise of DMNEs is intertwined with the increase in outward FDI from developing countries. In 1960, the stock of FDI from developing countries amounted to a mere 0.8 percent of the global FDI stock, whereas it reached 1.2 percent in 1975, remained in the single digit in the 1980s and 1990s, and shot up to 17.5 percent in 2011, with growth rate about double that from developed nations.[22] In Asia and Eastern Europe, DMNEs represent a considerable proportion of FDI. Hong Kong and Taiwan are the largest foreign investors in Mainland China, while Singapore and South Korea are major investors there.

The Largest Developing Country MNEs

Exhibit 4.6 lists the top 50 DMNEs in 2011, led by Hutchison Whampoa, a diversified Hong Kong-based conglomerate with interests ranging from shipping to mobile phone networks. While these firms come from many countries, the list is dominated by Asian-based companies, a reflection of the rapid economic growth in this part of the world. The industry base of those DMNEs is also

Ranked by[a]				
Foreign Assets	TNI[b]	Corporation	Home Economy	Industry[c]
1	18	Hutchison Whampoa Limited	Hong Kong, China	Diversified
2	90	CITIC Group	China	Diversified
3	13	Hon Hai Precision Industries	Taiwan Province of China	Electrical and electronic equipment
4	63	Vale SA	Brazil	Mining and quarrying
5	61	China Ocean Shipping (Group) Company	China	Transport and storage
6	77	Petronas—Petroliam NasionalBhd	Malaysia	Petroleum expl./ref./distr.
7	20	Cemex SAB de CV	Mexico	Non-metalic mineral products
8	47	AméricaMóvil SAB de CV	Mexico	Telecommunications
9	53	VimpelCom Ltd	Russian Federation	Telecommunications
10	89	China National Offshore Oil Corp	China	Petroleum expl./ref./distr.
11	67	Lukoil OAO	Russian Federation	Petroleum and natural gas
12	37	Singapore Telecommunications Ltd	Singapore	Telecommunications

Exhibit 4.6 The top 50 non-financial TNCs from developing and transition economies, ranked by foreign assets, 2011 (millions of dollars and number of employees)

Foreign Assets	TNI[b]	Corporation	Home Economy	Industry[c]
13	87	Petróleos de Venezuela SA	Venezuela, Bolivarian Republic of	Petroleum expl./ref./distr.
14	57	Samsung Electronics Co Ltd	Korea, Republic of	Electrical & electronic equipment
15	82	Hyundai Motor Company	Korea, Republic of	Motor vehicles
16	22	Wilmar International Limited	Singapore	Food, beverages and tobacco
17	45	Jardine-Matheson Holdings Ltd	Hong Kong, China	Diversified
18	97	PetroleoBrasileiro SA	Brazil	Petroleum expl./ref./distr.
19	19	Qatar Telecom	Qatar	Telecommunications
20	86	Formosa Plastics Group	Taiwan Province of China	Chemicals
21	5	Noble Group Ltd	Hong Kong, China	Wholesale trade
22	43	Tata Steel Ltd	India	Metal and metal products
23	54	Tata Motors Ltd	India	Automobile
24	100	China National Petroleum Corporation	China	Petroleum expl./ref./distr.
25	21	Quanta Computer Inc	Taiwan Province of China	Electrical & electronic equipment
26	27	CapitaLand Ltd	Singapore	Construction and real estate
27	35	Abu Dhabi National Energy Co PJSC	United Arab Emirates	Utilities (electricity, gas and water)
28	85	Gazprom JSC	Russian Federation	Petroleum and natural gas
29	55	Gerdau SA	Brazil	Metal and metal products
30	29	MTN Group Ltd	South Africa	Telecommunications
31	68	Bharti Airtel Ltd	India	Telecommunications
32	60	CLP Holdings Ltd	Hong Kong, China	Utilities (electricity, gas and water)
33	26	GentingBhd	Malaysia	Other consumer services
34	70	Sinochem Group	China	Petroleum expl./ref./distr.
35	56	DP World Limited	United Arab Emirates	Transport and storage
36	2	First Pacific Company Ltd	Hong Kong, China	Electrical & electronic equipment
37	71	New World Development Ltd	Hong Kong, China	Diversified
38	91	Oil and Natural Gas Corp Ltd	India	Petroleum expl./ref./distr.
39	24	Steinhoff International Holdings Ltd	South Africa	Other consumer goods
40	14	China Resources Enterprises Ltd	Hong Kong, China	Petroleum expl./ref./distr.
41	93	Sun Hung Kai Properties Ltd	Hong Kong, China	Other services
42	23	YTL Corporation Bhd	Malaysia	Utilities (electricity, gas and water)
43	15	Zain	Kuwait	Telecommunications
44	4	Flextronics International Ltd	Singapore	Electrical & electronic equipment
45	40	Hindalco Industries Ltd	India	Diversified
46	11	Li & Fung Ltd	Hong Kong, China	Wholesale trade
47	92	POSCO	Korea, Republic of	Metal and metal products
48	8	Shangri-La Asia Ltd	Hong Kong, China	Other consumer services
49	79	Sasol Limited	South Africa	Chemicals
50	75	FomentoEconomicoMexicano SAB	Mexico	Food, beverages and tobacco

[a] All data are based on the companies' annual reports unless otherwise stated; corresponds to the financial year from April 1, 2011 to March 31, 2012.

[b] TNI, the Transnationality Index, is calculated as the average of the following three ratios: foreign assets to total assets, foreign sales to total sales, and foreign employment to total employment.

[c] Industry classification for companies follows the United States Standard Industrial Classification as used by the United States Securities and Exchange Commission (SEC).

Exhibit 4.6 (Continued)

Source: UNCTAD World Development Report, 2013.

quite diverse, ranging from energy to shipping to telecommunications, and including a number of highly diversified conglomerates.

Exhibit 4.7 shows the country and industry distribution of the 100 largest DMNEs. The list is dominated by Chinese economies, including China, Hong Kong (a Special Administrative Region of China), and Taiwan (which China views as a renegade province), and Singapore. Together, these economies, which are sometimes labeled as "Greater China," hold more than 60 percent of the top DMNEs. In terms of industry composition, the most common are telecommunications, electrical/electronic, petroleum, and diversified companies, the last of which are a unique feature of DMNEs, particularly in Asia.

Home Country	Number of MNEs in Top 100
Hong Kong, China	20
China	12
Singapore	9
Taiwan Province of China	9
India	8
South Africa	8
Russia	8
Malaysia	6
Korea, Republic of	5
Brazil	4
Mexico	4
United Arab Emirates	3
Industry	
Telecommunications	12
Electrical/electronics	11
Petroleum	11
Diversified	10
Metal and metal products	10
Other consumer services	8
Food and beverages	6
Other consumer goods	5
Transport and storage	3
Chemicals	3
Utilities (electricity, gas and water)	3
Wholesale trade	3
Average TNI	**53.7**

Exhibit 4.7 Country/industry composition of the 100 largest MNEs from developing economies, 2011
Source: UNCTAD, 2011.

Obstacles Facing MNEs from Developing Economies

DMNEs face a number of obstacles in entering foreign markets, including:

- *Resource Constraints.* Israeli drug maker Teva (see Country Box) focused initially on generic drugs, partly because it could ill-afford the huge capital investment involved in the development of new drugs. Lack of reputation and brand recognition are other obstacles faced by DMNEs.
- *Lack of Knowledge.*[23] For Teva, the complex process involved in obtaining FDA approval in the United States—a prerequisite for selling pharmaceutical products in many markets—was a major hurdle. DMNEs lack experience in foreign operations and may lack the production, marketing, and management skills that are necessary in competitive international markets.
- *A Sheltered Environment.* Teva was initially protected by duties on the foreign drugs with which it competed. Many DMNEs have been sheltered in their domestic market for a long time. They often benefited from a domestic monopoly or enjoyed a cost advantage thanks to protectionist measures. International activities (if any) were mediated by specialized government or quasi-government agencies (e.g., China's foreign trade corporations), which prevented those firms from developing the knowledge and expertise that result from conducting international business directly (e.g., feedback from international clients).

DMNE Advantage in Global Markets

Obstacles notwithstanding, DMNEs develop some unique advantages that position them well in the competition with established MNEs. These include:

- *Home Government Support.* DMNEs enjoy the backing of their home government to an extent that may compensate for their ownership and location disadvantages.[24] A major reason for the support is the impact of the DMNE on the national economy. One form of indirect support and subsidy is local government procurement: Embraer accounts for 50 percent of the Brazilian Air Force fleet. In Thailand, government support for commercial chicken farming assists the animal feed business of Charoen Pokphand. Many DMNEs benefit from monopolized access to a natural resource, such as oil. They have access to low-cost capital, subsidies, and incentives as well as to competitively priced labor, although their wage advantage tends to erode as their home economies develop. When that happens, exchange rates become less favorable, and DMNEs move production to other low-cost locations. This is what is happening today in China where a number of garment makers have been shifting some production to Laos and Cambodia.

    Government support, which is often justified on the basis of the infant-industry argument, is a double-edged sword. It shields the firm from the marketplace, thereby acting as a damper on its capability development. The price for the support is often government interference in such key decisions as the domain and location of investment, limiting the strategic leeway of the firm. One reason for the development of "bogus blue-eyed" ventures in Mainland China—ventures that are funded by the Chinese firms themselves through a foreign registered entity—is to circumvent government control and involvement.

■ *Flexibility.* While reducing scale advantages, the lower production scale of the DMNE permits flexibility and adaptation that are critical in international markets. DMNEs tend to have less investment sunk in older plants and technologies and can leapfrog into cutting-edge technologies. They develop a competitive advantage in their ability to "mediate" technologies for use in developing markets by downscaling, simplifying and substituting local inputs, and by increasing the labor intensity of production.[25] DMNEs also have experience in customizing technologies and products, capabilities that serve them well, especially in other developing markets.[26]

Typical Features of DMNEs

DMNEs differ along national lines. For example, Li found that, compared to their Taiwanese counterparts, South Korean MNEs put more emphasis on market share or revenue growth than on profit margins (although the Asian crisis has probably narrowed the differences) and focused more on cost reduction than on value maintenance and enhancement. While Korean MNEs favored mass and domestic markets, Taiwanese MNEs favored niche and international markets, relied more on core competencies, and were less centralized than their Korean counterparts.[27] Because many of these differences can be attributed to cultural and institutional factors, it is reasonable to assume that as DMNEs mature, they will follow a different path.

At the same time, some generalities seem to hold for most DMNEs, as follows:

■ *Internationalization Patterns.* Some of the motivations of DMNEs are similar to those of MNEs from developed economies. Both groups seek to exploit their firm-specific advantages, overcome obstacles to exports in the form of tariff and non-tariff barriers, escape stringent environmental limitations at home, and obtain lower cost production bases. Although both groups seek to enter new and promising markets, DMNEs have a number of unique reasons to pursue foreign trade and investment:

1. *To develop ownership advantages.* Although traditional MNEs move abroad to exploit their ownership and skill advantages, DMNEs often do so to develop and gain such advantages.[28] A survey of outward FDI by Chinese enterprises found that learning manufacturing and marketing techniques was a key reason for internationalization.[29] DMNEs also seek to exploit their advantage in intermediate technologies. These DMNEs are not devoid of any ownership advantages, however. The fact that some of them acquire technologically more advanced firms in developed countries to boost their competitiveness and eventually become formidable global players (e.g., Samsung of South Korea and Lenovo of China) suggests that they possess some ownership advantages that the technologically more advanced firms from developed countries cannot easily imitate. These advantages probably reside in the ability to attain superior manufacturing efficiency and reasonable quality by optimally combining the resources from their home countries with resources acquired from overseas and to leverage such efficiency for global competitiveness. This type of capability may be not only culturally embedded and thus difficult for established MNEs from developed countries to imitate, but also rare and hard for the indigenous firms in their home countries to replicate.

2. *To serve as intermediaries.* DMNEs mediate the flow of technologies from industrialized to developing countries.[30] For instance, Korean VCR makers relied on Japanese technology

to develop low-cost VCRs which they then exported to developing (and also developed) markets.

3. *To overcome import quotas in developed markets.*[31] By locating FDI in developed markets, or in a developing market that has a trade agreement with a developed country, quota barriers can be overcome.

4. *To reduce risk via diversification.*[32] By shifting assets abroad, DMNEs based in regions characterized by political risk and volatility can reduce risk exposure and protect some of their capital base. FDI in this case serves as a substitute for portfolio investment that is limited owing to foreign exchange controls in many developing countries.

■ *Focus on Other Developing Markets.* DMNEs are more likely to have a greater share of FDI in other developing markets where their combination of intermediary technology and low cost provides a competitive advantage. For instance, Brazilian companies sell arms to other developing countries. However, DMNEs often find it necessary to eventually enter developed markets to increase scale and improve learning.

■ *Reliance on Third Parties.* To compensate for their limited resource base, DMNEs tend to rely on other entities in their international activities, whether alliance partners, export intermediaries, government organizations, and the like.

■ *Governance.* DMNEs are less likely to be publicly traded and are often tightly controlled by a founding family or the government. For instance, Hong Kong-listed Lippo is controlled by the founding Riady family, Indonesians with overseas Chinese roots. Some DMNEs eventually evolve into market entities, however. Embraer (Empresa Brasiliera de Aeronáutica) was founded in 1969 as a government company with the purpose of developing a local aircraft industry. Privatized in 1994, it was purchased by Bozano Simonsen, one of Brazil's biggest investment firms and by the country's two largest pension funds, PREVI and SISTEL. In 1999, Embraer formed a strategic alliance with a group of French aerospace companies—Aerospatiale-Matra, Dassault Aviation, Snecma, and Thomson-CSF—which jointly acquired 20 percent of Embraer's voting shares.

■ *Industry Domain.* When not diversified, DMNEs are likely to be in manufacturing, starting with labor-intensive production and gradually moving into technological and marketing-intensive products often based on imported technology.[33] Some emerging market MNEs can be found in services (e.g., Singapore Airlines, consistently ranked at the top of the industry in terms of service and profitability).

■ *Bargaining Power.* DMNEs are less likely to export from their foreign affiliates, and when they do are less likely to target their home markets.[34] DMNEs lack bargaining power in the host country. Although their home governments are very supportive, they usually cannot offer much assistance in the form of pressuring the host government to purchase the DMNE's products or to accord it favorable investment terms. DMNEs sometimes have bargaining power intra-regionally (e.g., a Brazilian firm investing in Venezuela). A DMNE advantage is that it is often perceived in other developing economies to be less intimidating than developed country MNEs.

■ *Strategy.* DMNEs are more likely to compete on price than on product differentiation initially and move into more differentiated product segments as they catch up with established MNEs.[35] Activity often begins with manufacturing for private brands and continues with low-end branded products.

DMNEs also tend to pursue niche strategies. Having already entered other developing markets, China-based Haier has entered the US market for small office refrigerators, a product line abandoned by most domestic manufacturers such as GE and Amana because of its low profitability. Embraer specializes in regional aircraft ranging from 30 to 108 seats, one of the fastest-growing segments in the industry, but one in which Boeing and Airbus currently do not compete. DMNEs are less likely to be the innovator, but rather quickly offer a lower priced version of an original product introduced in a developed market. With the entry of competitors from less developed markets, however, DMNEs seek to go up the value chain. This is what happened to Taiwanese TV and computer makers with the advance of Mainland Chinese firms. Taiwanese computer maker Acer started by selling components that were used in computers sold by such firms as Hitachi and Siemens, but then proceeded to also sell them under its own name. Korean electronics maker LG (then Lucky Goldstar) started by selling under private label, but it eventually developed its own brand name and now sells most of its products under it. When Korean firms first began selling TV sets in the United States, they focused on the low-end, offering limited-feature sets priced substantially below their Japanese and US competitors. However, rises in wages and the currency exchange rate in their home country put pressure on costs and forced Korean firms to move up market.

DMNEs are also less likely to be vertically integrated than MNEs from developed economies.[36] This strategy has been viewed as an advantage in changing global markets and has been adopted to a considerable extent by established MNEs. DMNEs are more likely to establish alliances and to take a minority stake both for lack of resources and because of a lesser need to protect proprietary technology.

Craig and Douglas outline six strategies that DMNEs can pursue: (1) Low-cost commodity, where a firm competes only on price and exports out of its domestic base; (2) manufacture for private label, where a company manufactures a product, but sells it under a retailer's brand name; (3) component manufacturing, where a company manufactures inputs to be assembled and marketed by the developed country firm; (4) low-cost leader, where the emerging market MNE sells an assembled product but competes mostly on cost; (5) first-generation or market-specific technology, where the emerging market firm focuses on a market with characteristics similar to its domestic market; and (6) a specialized niche, whether in a given country or region or worldwide.[37] Some DMNEs continue with the same strategy for a long period. For example, Taiwanese Foxconn has maintained its focus as the premier OEM manufacturer of electronics and IT products, whereas others move through those strategies as they mature.

For the DMNE, the shift away from cost leadership implies developing its own technological base, emphasizing profitability, expanding foreign sales, locating production abroad, and moving toward a product-based organization structure.[38] In the wake of the Asian financial crisis, Samsung and LG divested entire subsidiaries and product lines at home and abroad to reduce their debt load and sharpen their competitive advantage. Both companies have now achieved a leadership position in newer technologies such as HD plasma TVs. DMNEs must also contend with the threats to competitiveness that accompany development and liberalization. Higher wages erode their competitive advantage at home, with lower-priced competitors from "new tigers" such as Malaysia and Indonesia and especially China threatening their lower-end products. Greater openness at home means that the home market is not as well protected as it was and cannot serve as an assured base from which to launch foreign expansion. Rapid changes in technology require capital investment that is more difficult to obtain as home base creditors have become more careful in scrutinizing investment projects. Other erstwhile powerful South

Korean conglomerates such as Daewoo, however, were broken up and sold off by pieces because they were unable to adapt fast enough to changes in their domestic institutional system and global competitive environment (e.g., removal of import protection and entry of new competitors from abroad).

Country Box

An Israeli Firm Becomes the World's Largest Generic Drug Maker

Israel-based Teva was established in Jerusalem in 1901 as a drug distribution agency and started its pharmaceutical operations in the 1930s as a small-scale producer competing with foreign imports. Taking advantage of the immigration-driven growth in its domestic market, as well as of the cessation of imports during wartimes, the company grew rapidly, then merged with its domestic competitors Asia and Zori, and embarked on exports as a major thrust. Teva solidified its entry into the US market via a joint venture with W.R. Grace in 1985 and the acquisition of Lemmon in 1986. In the 1990s, Teva embarked on an aggressive acquisition strategy in the United States and Europe, eventually gaining a berth among the world's 50 largest pharmaceutical companies. By 2001, the company became the world's largest maker of generic drugs. It has also emerged as a developer of new drugs in a number of areas. The company shares are trading on the NASDAQ, the Tel-Aviv Stock Exchange, the Seaq International in London, and the Frankfurt Stock Exchange.[39] Today, Teva continues to grow through joint ventures, acquisitions, and innovation and is active in 60 countries and ranks among the top ten pharmaceutical companies in the world.[40]

Like Teva, many DMNEs start by competing on price, using "intermediary" technology that is not cutting edge, but still represents sufficient improvement over local standards in developing markets. South Korean firms such as Samsung and Daewoo (which eventually collapsed) expanded in Southeast Asia, Eastern Europe, and the (former) Soviet republics, where their products were superior to those available locally, yet competitively priced. Today, South Korean conglomerates LG and Samsung sell their consumer electronics in the United States and the EU, while China-based Haier dominates the small refrigerator market in the United States. Brazilian regional jet manufacturer Embraer has been holding its own in this very competitive market contested by developed market players such as Canadian-based Bombardier. In the wake of the US presidential election impasse in 2000, Brazilian Procomp (acquired by Ohio-based Diebold) offered electronic voting machines superior to those currently in use.[41]

Interim Summary

1. DMNEs are increasingly competitive with developed country MNEs and many enhance their competitive position over time.
2. Compared to traditional MNEs, DMNEs are smaller and more diversified.
3. DMNEs tend to lack the capital resources of other MNEs as well as experience in dealing with foreign institutions and the rigors of international competition; however, they have some unique advantages, for instance, flexibility in taking advantage of new products, technologies, and market opportunities.

The Small and Medium-Size International Enterprise (SMIE)

Small and medium-size enterprises (SMEs) have been major participants in international business since at least the 1920s. According to the US Department of Commerce, a total of 295,594 SMEs exported from the United States in 2011, accounting for nearly 98 percent of all US exporters. The SME share of US merchandise exports has recently hovered around 30 percent. SMEs were responsible for 33 percent of merchandise exports in 2011, up from 27.2 percent in 2003, 28.8 percent in 1999, and 29.5 percent in 1992.[42]

What is an SMIE?

There are numerous definitions of a small and medium-size enterprise. A common definition of "small" business in the United States is a firm with fewer than 100 employees and less than $5 million in annual revenues. Midsize firms, according to the Conference Board, are firms with annual revenues in the range of $100 to $500 million. Although this may sound like a lot, keep in mind that large MNEs are in a different league. IBM, for instance, has annual revenues in excess of $100 billion. As of 2009, the 24 million US-based SMEs represented 99.7 percent of all employers in the country and employed 49.4 percent of the private workforce in both manufacturing and services. Between 1993 and 2009, US SMEs were responsible for 65 percent of the 15 million net new jobs created.[43] They account for approximately 50 percent of US GDP and, remarkably, 55 percent of technological innovations, producing 16.5 times more patents per employee than large patenting firms.[44] The SBA notes that every $1 billion in exports of manufactured goods creates an estimated 15,000 new jobs; two to three times that number of additional jobs emerge to support the new products and personnel (e.g., restaurants, housing).[45] In Minnesota alone, SMIE exporters pay 18 percent higher wages and increase employment four times faster than their counterparts that do not export.[46] In general, American exporting SMEs across the board increase employment faster and pay higher wages than non-exporting SME firms. They are also more skill- and capital- intensive, more productive and more competitive than those SMEs that do not export.[47]

The importance of the SME sector varies by country. For example, they are a formidable force in Luxembourg and Cyprus, where they accounted for 72.8 and 76 percent of economic value added in 2011.[48] In contrast, in New Zealand and Malaysia, SMEs account for 36 and 47 percent of economic value added, respectively.[49] The contribution of SMIEs to national exports also varies. In France and Italy, the export contribution of SMIEs approaches that of large MNEs. In Italy, 70 percent of exports were attributed to SMIEs in 2012.[50] In Korea, they accounted for 30.8 percent of total merchandise export in 2008.[51] In contrast, Canadian SMEs contributed just 25 percent of the country's merchandise exports in 2010.[52]

SME involvement in international business is likely to grow rapidly in the coming years, especially in services and technology-related areas, the fastest growing sectors in the economy, where SMEs tend to be concentrated.[53] Their potential is still largely untapped. In 2011, just 295,000 of the over 27 million US SMEs were currently exporting.[54] SMEs account for 99.47 percent of total US firms but only 33 percent of total exports. Nearly three-fifths of SMIEs send their products to just one country, while more than half of large firms export to five or more foreign countries.[55]

139

A study by PricewaterhouseCoopers found that access to international markets was viewed as an important benefit by SMEs from many nations.[56] The Internet may lower entry barriers into international markets (see also Chapter 18 on Internet and Global E-commerce). Technological developments such as Flexible Manufacturing Systems are also making it possible for a small firm to profitably produce relatively small batches of goods. Developments in financial services have had a similar effect.

Size and Internationalization

In one study, only a quarter of SMIEs considered their size a constraint.[57] Indeed, the fastest export growth occurred among very small businesses—those with fewer than 20 employees. These firms made up 65 percent of all US exporting firms in 1997, up from 59 percent in 1992. Even among firms with sales of $1,000 to $99,000, almost half were exporting.[58] Other studies, however, suggest that size matters. Even among small international firms, the larger the firm, the more likely it was to engage in international business and to have an international strategy. Size was significantly correlated with exports; 82 percent of larger (more than $50 million in sales) firms were exporters versus 48 percent of the small firms.[59]

Midsize firms ($100 million to $500 million annual sales) seem to have an especially appropriate balance of size and agility for international operations. The Conference Board found that such firms reported a significant percentage of foreign sales and early manufacturing presence overseas. Foreign sales accounted for 22 percent of total annual turnover for firms in the midsize category. Small international firms grew three times as fast as companies their size that did not internationalize and twice as fast as the large MNEs. Those with sales below $100 million grew at an annual rate of 67 percent with a 35 percent annual return in the 1986 to 1991 time period.

Obstacles to SMIE Internationalization

Exhibits 4.8a and 4.8b presents the results of two recent surveys of SMEs on barriers to internalization and foreign investment. Exhibit 4.8a lists ten main barriers as perceived by SMEs in OECD member countries, which consist mostly of developed economies in Europe and North America. Exhibit 4.8b lists seven main challenges faced by SMEs that are based in China—a developing country—and already have investment overseas. The respondents in the two surveys share some common concerns such as cultural barriers and lack of internationally experienced managerial personnel, but also show differences in their assessment of the challenges. Specifically, while the main barriers faced by SMEs in developed countries tend to be rooted in the lack of information and experience, SMEs in developing countries often face stiff competition from technologically more sophisticated rivals in foreign markets. Note that some of the obstacles noted in the exhibit (e.g., lack of familiarity with foreign business practices and cultural differences) are not different, in principle, from those encountered by established MNEs, although they are likely more pronounced for SMEs. However, much of the challenge presented by SME entry into international markets involves the unique character of the smaller enterprise.[60] A study examining the concerns of US-based SMIEs expanding into Europe found that their concerns differed considerably from those of large MNEs. For example, managing foreign exchange risk was ranked the most minor concern of the large MNE, but is a concern for the SMIE, which lacks the resources to effectively manage risk or geographical diversity. Similarly, international communications was an important concern for smaller firms but not for the larger ones. In contrast, developing a manufacturing strategy was a concern for large MNEs, but not for the SMIEs, possibly because of lack of awareness of the need for formal planning on the SMIEs' part.[61]

A UN report states that internationalizing SMEs face problems relating to management, training, and quality control as well as market and infrastructure problems, such as the lack of capital and intense competition. However, it considers the greatest obstacle to be the barriers created or permitted by governments, such as regulatory impediments or corruption. Some of the main obstacles for the internationalizing SME are listed below.

Rank-Weighted Factor	Description of Barrier
1	Inadequate quantity of and/or untrained personnel for internationalization
2	Shortage of working capital to finance exports
3	Limited information to locate/analyze markets
4	Difficulty in identifying foreign business opportunities
5	Lack of managerial time to deal with internationalization
6	Inability to contact potential overseas customers
7	Difficulty in developing new products for foreign markets
8	Unfamiliar foreign business practices
9	Meeting export product quality/standard/specifications
10	Unfamiliar exporting procedures/paperwork

Exhibit 4.8a Top ten barriers to SME internationalization as reported by OECD member economies
Source: OECD, 2008.

Challenges	Percentage (%) of Respondents Selecting Each Answer				
	Critical	Important	Unimportant	Irrelevant	Total
Lack of brand recognition to local consumers	11	43	35	11	100
Local consumers' concern over the quality of Chinese brands	8	44	36	11	100
Difficulty in financing investment	11	53	25	9	100
Lack of internationally experienced managerial personnel	11	54	27	8	100
Lack of understanding about international law and market risk	6	59	27	8	100
Uncompetitive product and technology	11	40	39	10	100
Cultural differences	8	44	37	11	100

Exhibit 4.8b Top seven challenges to Chinese SMEs in investing overseas
Source: China Council for the Promotion of International Trade, 2011.

Scale and Transaction Constraints

The small scale and limited reach of the SMIE constrain its production and service delivery options and costs. The transaction costs of the SMIE are substantially higher than those of the large MNE, which internalizes much of its operations. While large MNEs conduct much of their trade via internal networks, SMIEs have to go through the complex process of cross-border trade flow that can add as much as 10 percent to the final value of goods.[62] Relying on export intermediaries is an option, but it is costly and implies distance from the customer.

Access to Capital

An important roadblock on the internationalization route for the SME is shortage of capital[63] and its correlates (e.g., inability to obtain reliable market information and lack of training for traders and expatriates). Public institutions judged financial strength the single most important problem for internationalizing SMIEs.[64] Much of the problem has to do with lack of access. The SBA reports that only 150 to 200 of the 9,000 banks operating in the United States offer significant financing for SMIEs.[65] At the same time, the globalization of financial services is rapidly changing the patterns of access to capital and opening new opportunities for raising capital. This is true not only in the United States, where venture capital has created many opportunities for SMIEs (especially in high tech), but also in countries like Japan where in the past banks would rarely extend loans to SMIEs.

Lack of Knowledge

A critical resource for SMEs entering foreign markets is knowledge.[66] Lacking a track record in exporting and experience in foreign investment, such firms usually do not possess the relevant knowledge ranging from how to conduct market research in foreign locations to how to address currency fluctuations. Tiny Hatteras Yachts was hard hit when the euro declined in value against the US dollar (it has strongly rebounded since) because it did not employ sophisticated hedging techniques and lacked the ability to source globally.[67] SMEs also face problems when having to transfer their knowledge to foreign recipients. More than in large MNEs, the knowledge possessed by SMIEs tends to be less codified and more tacit and embedded. Combined with weak information processing, SMIEs find it hard to "level the playing field" with larger players.[68]

To compensate for its knowledge deficiency, the SMIE is often compelled to look to others for assistance. UNCTAD recommends that governments assist SMIEs with information on market conditions, opportunities, and government regulations and requirements. Channels include commercial attachés and embassies, trade missions, trade shows, networking systems, chambers of commerce, international agencies, technology-exchange programs, international forums and conferences, websites, market-research consultants, and national trade promotions. A US Chamber of Commerce survey shows that 66 percent of SMIEs utilized at least one form of government export assistance, while 50 percent used two or more agencies.

Another way to compensate for knowledge deficiency is by learning from the experience of others in a similar situation in the industry.[69] An important source is the knowledge shared by executives with experience in foreign markets. SMIEs with internationally experienced management teams obtained foreign sales more quickly than those without such teams.[70]

Lack of Market Power

Lack of market power is another key deficiency for smaller firms, which often find themselves powerless against trade barriers. They are too small to bargain with local governments and cannot produce the large quantities that would trigger local suppliers to manufacture to their specifications.[71] They are also vulnerable to trade barriers. The SBA is required to promote the interests of US small business in international trade under the Small Business Export Promotion Act of 1980.

Vulnerability to Intellectual Property Violations

US SMIEs are very concerned with intellectual property rights such as patents, copyrights, and trademarks. This issue is particularly important to SMIEs because they are overrepresented in high-tech areas, but lack the resources to pursue violators across the globe or the political muscle to pressure host governments to protect their rights. A number of US-based SMIEs had to withdraw from the Chinese market because their product designs had been copied and they lacked the contacts and resources to fight the violators.

SMIE Advantages in Internationalization

The many obstacles noted previously notwithstanding, SMIEs have been successful in the global marketplace owing to a number of distinct advantages. Innovativeness, creativity, entrepreneurial spirit, lower overhead costs, and the ability to move fast to take advantage of new opportunities are all important factors in the global marketplace, and are relatively common at SMIEs. Some of the advantages noted for DMNEs, such as lack of investment in outdated technologies, and hence the ability to "leapfrog" technologically, also apply to SMIEs.

SMIE Internationalization Features

Internationalization Motivation

An UNCTAD survey identified a number of drivers of SME internationalization, including "push" factors, "pull" factors, management factors, and chance. The push factors are competitive pressures in its domestic market, which "push" the SME to increase the scale of its operations via exports so as to reduce unit cost, or to reduce its labor costs by moving operations to low-cost countries. Another push factor is decline in domestic demand. For instance, facing an economic downturn in the 1990s, architectural firms in Hawaii doubled their efforts to penetrate Asian markets. Pull factors make foreign locations more attractive (e.g., rapidly expanding markets, growth potential, or lower production costs). Management factors include managerial commitment and resources devoted to international activity. Finally, chance factors are unforeseen circumstances that create internationalization opportunities. According to the survey findings, when SMIEs invest in other small firms, management and chance factors are the most important, followed by push factors. For larger enterprises investing in foreign SMEs, management and pull factors are the most important, whereas push factors are relatively less important.[72]

143

Brush[73] found that the manager's personal knowledge of markets, personal contacts, and expertise were important factors influencing the export decision of young firms. However, these factors were linked to the perceived market opportunity in terms of demand and growth potential, an opportunity often expressed in the form of unsolicited orders from foreign customers. Personal contacts, owner/manager's expertise and competencies (often acquired earlier in another venture or another firm), product innovation, and foreign market information were key factors behind internationalization. For established SMIEs, perceived market demands and managerial factors were less instrumental than the desire for expansion and growth. Host country transportation and distribution were also more important for established firms than for newer firms. Established firms were also more likely to use export intermediaries or piggyback on large exporters and investors. They tended to sell more products to a wider array of countries and to derive more overall revenues from export than the younger firms. Exhibits 4.9a and 4.9b present the results of two recent surveys of SMEs on their motives to invest abroad. Exhibit 4.9a lists seven main motives of EU-based SMEs to invest overseas, and Exhibit 4.9b lists 13 factors that tend to drive China-based SMEs to invest overseas. Even though lower production cost and proximity to customers can motivate SMEs in both the EU and China to undertake FDI, China-based SMEs often invest in developed economies to acquire new technology and name brands and to integrate such resources with their own to enhance their competitiveness both in the domestic market and in international markets.

Internationalization Patterns

Controlling for industry, significant differences have been found between the foreign expansion strategies of large and small firms.[74] SMIE internationalization is often not incremental. Newer, high-tech, small firms in particular tend to "leapfrog" into international markets before gaining a foothold in their domestic markets. This has been found to be the case for small software firms.[75] Other SMIEs go through a number of stages, but follow a different route than that of large MNEs, often starting with inward investment before moving to outward investment.

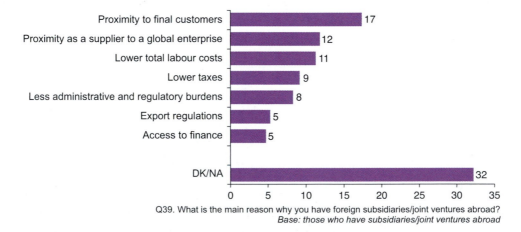

Q39. What is the main reason why you have foreign subsidiaries/joint ventures abroad?
Base: those who have subsidiaries/joint ventures abroad

Exhibit 4.9a Main reasons for EU SMEs to have foreign subsidiaries/joint ventures abroad
Source: European Commission, 2007.

Reasons	Percentage (%) of Respondents Selecting Each Answer				
	Critical	Important	Unimportant	Irrelevant	Total
Favorable policies and assistance from home government	25	67	5	3	100
Depressed or slow-growing market at home	7	50	45	8	100
Availability of capital for foreign investment	17	63	18	2	100
Rising labor cost at home	7	44	37	12	100
Reduction of transportation cost	12	48	28	12	100
Host country's market potential	37	49	12	2	100
Host country's natural resources	21	7	34	38	100
Host country's skilled labor	4	40	46	10	100
Host country's low labor cost	8	37	40	15	100
Host country's advanced technology	11	37	40	12	100
Acquisition of name brand	10	28	46	16	100
Favorable policies of host country	15	55	22	8	100
Avoidance of trade barriers	9	57	25	9	100

Exhibit 4.9b Reasons for Chinese SMEs to invest abroad
Source: China Council for the Promotion of International Trade, 2011.

More than large MNEs, SMIEs rely on exports rather than on FDI. This is understandable in light of the SMIEs' resource constraints, as well as the fact that SMIEs are often in an early phase of the internationalization process. SMIEs are also more likely to rely on export intermediaries such as export agents, export merchants, export management firms, and export trading firms. Like their larger counterparts, SMIEs often use foreign markets as an export platform to third countries.[76] This is probably more accurate for Japan and other high labor cost countries faced with a decline in their export competitiveness at home. Indeed, manufacturing SMIEs are more likely to internationalize in the more labor-intensive areas of textiles, clothing, and mechanical equipment.

SMIE Exporter Profile

Non-manufacturing companies dominate exporting by SMEs. In 2011, wholesalers and other non-manufacturing firms made up 76 percent of all SME exporters and generated 66 percent of total SME exports. Because many exports consist of intra-company transfers within subsidiaries of the same MNE, the proportion of SMIEs in inter-company exports is considerably larger. According to the US Central Budget Office, small exporters were more likely to export 50 percent or more of their product than were large exporters. Some 22.8 percent of self-employed exporters (i.e., with no hired employees) exported half or more of their product, compared with 3.7 percent of the exporters with 100 or more employees. Canada is by far the most popular export destination for SMEs. In 2003, some 87,596 SME exporting companies registered sales to Canada—an increase of 94 percent over 1992. Mexico ranked second, receiving merchandise exports from 33,408 US SMEs. Other popular markets for SME exporters were the United Kingdom, Japan, and Germany.

The position of Canada and the United Kingdom shows that as in the case of traditional MNEs, cultural familiarity is a major factor in determining where SMIEs choose to invest. In the same vein, many French firms entering the North American market start with Quebec, the French-speaking province of Canada. This reality may be changing, however. Smaller major markets are among the fastest-growing customers for SMEs. From 1992 to 2003, SME exports to China surged by 416 percent, while exports to Malaysia increased 259 percent, sales to Ireland increased 227 percent, and sales to Brazil rose 152 percent. This record is especially impressive, since China has been one of the most difficult markets for foreign investors to crack.

Foreign investment by SMIEs is at present relatively small (which is why, as you may recall, most of these firms do not qualify as MNEs). In Japan, it accounts for more than half of the cases, but only about 10 percent of the value of outward FDI. In the United States, SMIEs account for 6 percent of the number and 3 percent of the assets of foreign affiliates.[77] Still, as far back as 1988, American SMIEs controlled $15 billion in FDI stock, with Western Europe being the largest target for foreign investment. In Singapore, Taiwan, and Vietnam, SMEs are the recipients of FDI by large foreign MNEs. "Small-package FDI" (less that $1 million) accounts for 5 to 20 percent by value in Myanmar and less than half a percent in Vietnam. In the Philippines, it accounts for more than 60 percent of projects, but only about 2 to 10 percent by value. In recent years, FDI by SMIEs has been growing, often at a more rapid pace than FDI overall. A UN survey of Asian SMIEs found that factors considered important for their internationalization include improving the quality of products/services, local management and staff training, and government relations. SMIEs were found to be three times more likely than MNEs to regard training unskilled staff as very important to strategic success, more than twice as likely to regard the introduction or improvement of products or services as very important, and more than 50 percent more likely to regard local managers' training an increase in foreign earnings as very important.

SMIEs' exports and FDI are often not a systematically planned strategic move but rather a response to an incidental opportunity. In a survey of 100 US entrepreneurial technology firms commissioned by the US firm Protégé, 82 percent of CEOs acknowledged that their foreign expansion was not part of a broader strategy, but rather an opportunistic pursuit of clients and an inexpensive way to achieve internationalization.[78] Chances for internationalization include, for example, a customer expanding into a foreign location ("piggybacking"). The piggybacking may occur at the initiative of an MNE that needs supply, components, and such for its international operations. For example, Japanese automotive suppliers followed Japanese auto manufacturers to the United States.[79] Pico Rivera, a shelving company that once sold only in the United States and Canada, followed its customer Disney to Eastern Europe and other countries where Disney wanted to install the same shelves that it has in the United States.[80]

Nature of FDI by SMIEs

■ *Emphasis on Developed Markets.* When engaging in FDI, SMIEs are more likely to invest in developed rather than developing markets. In one study, 80 percent of SMIEs located in developed countries. Host country red tape, economic instability, hard currency restrictions, procurement difficulties, and lack of domestic bank support were among the reasons why SMIEs avoided investment in developing markets. Japanese, Australian, and Hong Kong firms are an exception, probably because most markets in their area are developing.[81] The trend is also true for medium-size firms. Conference Board data show that firms with more than 20 overseas plants were much more likely to invest in developing countries than firms with fewer than ten foreign plants.[82] SMIEs are also more likely to establish new operations (greenfield investments) than to acquire existing operations. This is largely a product of their resource limitations.

■ *Selective Globalization.* SMIEs tend to focus on one link in the supply chain (e.g., manufacturing) as well as on a selected market.[83] In one study, 17 percent of the large firms exported to more than 50 countries versus none among the small and medium-size firms.[84] In a Conference Board study, very large firms ($5 billion and over) had an average of 36 plants in 14 foreign countries, compared with 13 plants in six countries for firms with $1 to $5 billion in annual sales. Companies with sales of less than $100 million had one to three overseas plants.

■ *Strategy.* SMIEs often adopt niche strategies, pursuing areas that are not covered by large firms because of neglect, lack of expertise, or high cost structure.[85] In making investment decisions, SMIEs are unlikely to be motivated by host country incentives,[86] which is not surprising given their lack of market power. However, SMIE investment is less likely to trigger the visibility and the resentment that sometimes accompanies FDI.

SMIEs rely more on cooperative strategies, often as a result of the local partner initiative to compensate for a resource shortfall. This is particularly true for those with experienced management.[87] In the UN survey, SMIEs are shown to engage a local partner in a joint venture in more than half of the cases. When Canadian Sleeman Brewing entered the highly competitive US market, it teamed up with the Boston Beer Company, whose beer was already being sold in Canada, to launch a US brand.[88]

Namiki lists effective export strategies for small firms as follows: competitive pricing and brand identification; specialty product manufacturing; technological advantage; and superior customer service. Exploiting niche markets is also very important.[89] Smaller firms often went abroad to avoid direct competition with large MNEs. This led them to develop in-depth narrow expertise that may be useful in developing "deep niche" strategies.[90]

A recent UNCTAD report recommends that governments should encourage cross-border alliances between SMIEs. Governments can create a pool of suitable partners, initiate introductions, and resolve conflicts. They can encourage investment and trade missions, conferences, and investment/trade shows designed to encourage business matching, electronic business-matching services, chambers of commerce and other facilitators, and clustering programs.

BORN INTERNATIONAL Some firms develop an international orientation very early. Those include "international market makers," namely, multinational traders or import/export start-ups, and "geographically focused start-ups," which utilize their knowledge of a particular world area. The most advanced form is the "global start-up," or **born international,** a "business organization that from inception seeks to derive significant competitive advantages from the use of resources and sale of output in multiple countries."[91] While "born international" firms have existed for many years (e.g., the East India Company, established in 1600), the phenomenon is associated mainly

Industry Box

Investment Management and the SMIE

Recent surveys of client satisfaction with service placed Geneva (Switzerland)-based Pictet & Cie at the top of the league in providing financial custodian services. The bank, which calls itself "a Swiss bank with an international presence," has substantial presence in Europe (Switzerland, Italy, Germany, England, Spain, and Luxembourg) and Asia (Singapore, Japan, and Hong Kong), as well as one subsidiary in North America (Montreal). Pictet & Cie offers personalized service to high net-worth individuals around the globe. The two-century-old bank actually views its size as an advantage. "We offer the size and breadth of experience to offer a quality service. But we are still small enough to offer a service tailored to each client's specific needs," says Judith Webster, a client relationship manager. Pictet & Cie is taking advantage of the consolidation in the financial service industry to expand its reach by appealing to smaller clients who seek the personal service they feel is unavailable from the increasingly large and diversified providers.

Pictet & Cie is a niche player that builds on its strengths. The firm is active mostly in the pension fund market where it feels it has a competitive advantage. It also tries to minimize administration and coordination costs by staying closer to its home base in Geneva and using a network of contracted providers in their home countries. As of 2013, only nine of its 24 subsidiaries are outside Europe.

Source: "Small business proves worthy challenger," *Financial Times*, July 14, 2000, III; company website 2007, 2013.

with the last two decades, particularly in the high-tech sector. Examples of "born international" are European and Israeli high-tech start-ups that generate most, and sometimes all, of their revenues abroad from the very start.[92] Oviatt and McDougall (p. 46) provide this interview with a United Kingdom executive:

> We did not succeed because we tried to sell the product by starting up in England and then selling in the US, and by that time it was too late. We should have developed our products first of all for the US market and then sold it back into England.

In his subsequent venture, this executive targeted the United States and Japan before turning his attention to the United Kingdom and continental Europe. According to the authors, successful global start-ups have global vision from inception; internationally experienced management; strong international business networks; use of preemptive technology or marketing, building on a unique intangible asset; incremental, closely linked extensions in product/service; and tight worldwide coordination. You will find a broader discussion of born-international firms in Chapter 20 which focuses on international entrepreneurship.

Interim Summary

1. Although each SMIE is small, collectively they are a force to be reckoned with in international business.
2. SMIEs face many of the same difficulties that DMNEs experience in internationalization, and make up for their disadvantages with adaptability, innovation, and partnering with other firms.
3. SMIEs usually develop niche market strategies when going international, often "piggybacking" on an established client base.
4. "Born international" firms plan on exporting from the very beginning, without developing a local market until after they have found success abroad.

Chapter Summary

1. The "players" in the international business scene include a great variety of companies, but only those with foreign direct investment over which the company maintains effective control are called, in this book, multinational enterprises (MNEs).
2. MNEs, whether in manufacturing or service sectors, need strong competitive advantages to compete with established local firms. They need to effectively and efficiently build, deploy, exploit, and upgrade distinctive capabilities (technological, organizational, operational, and financial) if they want to prosper.
3. MNEs from developing and emerging economies (DMNEs) and small and medium-size international companies (SMIEs, which include "born international" firms) play an important role in global business. The MNE, DMNE, and SMIE differ significantly in their internationalization patterns, resources, and obstacles to international expansion.
4. DMNEs suffer from resource constraints, lack of knowledge, and a sheltered environment. However, they enjoy unique advantages such as flexibility and home government support.
5. SMIEs emphasize export rather than FDI due to their resource limitations. They either export directly to a foreign market or sell through export intermediaries.

Notes

1 *US manufacturers in the global market place.* The Conference Board, *Report # 1058-94-RR, 1994.*
2 *US manufacturers in the global market place.* The Conference Board, *Report # 1058-94-RR, 1994.*
3 C. A. Bartlett and S. Ghoshal, *Managing Across Borders:* The Transnational *Solution,* Cambridge, MA: Harvard Business School Press, 1989.

4 World Investment Report 2000, United Nations Conference on Trade and Development (UNCTAD).

5 K. Moore and D. Lewis, *Birth of the Multinational,* Copenhagen: Business School Press, 2000.

6 US Department of Commerce, "Summary estimates for multinational companies: Employment, sales and capital expenditures for 2011."

7 Share the World's Resources, "Multinational Corporations" webpage.

8 *US manufacturers in the global market place.* The Conference Board, *Report #1058-94-RR, 1994.*

9 "The world view of multinationals," *The Economist,* January 29, 2000, 21.

10 R.E. Caves, *Multinational Enterprise and Economic Analysis,* Cambridge: Cambridge University Press, 1996.

11 "The world view of multinationals," *The Economist,* January 29, 2000.

12 P. Druckerman, "The foreign invasion," *Wall Street Journal,* September. 25, 2000, R21.

13 L.T. Wells, "Multinationals and the developing countries," *Journal of International Business Studies,* 29, 1, 1998, 101–114.

14 P.N. Doremus, W.W. Keller, L.W. Pauly, and S. Reich, *The Myth of the Global Corporation,* Princeton, NJ: Princeton University Press.

15 D.J. Lecraw, "Performance of transnational corporations in less developed countries," *Journal of International Business Studies,* spring/summer, 1983, 15–33.

16 "The world view of multinationals," *The Economist,* January 29, 2000, 21.

17 M.S. Roth and J.B. Romeo, "Matching product category and country image perceptions: A framework for managing country-of-origin effects," *Journal of International Business Studies,* 3, 1992, 477–497.

18 D.J. Lecraw, "Performance of transnational corporations in less developed countries," *Journal of International Business Studies,* spring/summer, 1983, 15–33.

19 "US manufacturers in the global marketplace," The Conference Board, *Report #1058-94-RR, 1994.*

20 J. Ordonez, "Starbuck's to start major expansion in overseas markets," *Wall Street Journal,* October 27, 2000.

21 P. Pananond and C.P. Zeithaml, "The international expansion of MNEs from developing countries: A case study of Thailand's CP group," *Asia Pacific Journal of Management,* 15, 1998, 163–184.

22 H.W.C. Yeung, "Transnational corporations from Asian developing countries: Their characteristics and competitive edge," *Journal of Asian Business,* 10, 4, 1994, 17–58; World Investment Report, 2001–2011.

23 D.J. Lecraw, "Performance of transnational corporations in less developed countries," *Journal of International Business Studies,* spring/summer, 1983, 15–33.

24 R. Aggarwal and T. Agmon, "The international success of developing country firms: Role of government directed comparative advantage," *Management International Review,* 30, 2, 1990, 163–180.

25 L.T. Wells, *Third World Multinationals: The Rise of Foreign Investment from Developing Countries,* Cambridge, MA: MIT Press, 1983.

26 H. Vernon-Wortzel and L.H. Wortzel, "Globalizing strategies for multinationals from developing countries," *Columbia Journal of World Business,* spring 1988.

27 P.P. Li, "Strategy profiles of indigenous MNEs from the NIEs: The case of South Korea and Taiwan," *The International Executive,* 36, 2, 1994, 147–170.

28 D.J. Lecraw, "Outward direct investment by Indonesian firms: Motivation and effects," *Journal of International Business Studies,* 3rd quarter, 1993, 589–600.

29 H. Zhang and D. Ven den Bulcke, *International Management Strategies of Chinese Multinational Firms,* University of Antwerp, E/17, 1994.

30 S. Tallman and O. Shenkar, "International cooperative venture strategies: Outward investment and small firms from NICs," *Management International Review,* 34, 1994, 75–91.

31 D.J. Lecraw, "Direct investment by firms from less developed countries," *Oxford Economic Papers,* 29, 3, 1977, 442–457.

32 Ibid.

33 Ibid.

34 Ibid.

35 Ibid.

36 H. Vernon-Wortzel and L.H. Wortzel, "Globalizing strategies for multinationals from developing countries," *Columbia Journal of International Business,* spring 1988, 27–35.

37 C.S. Craig and S.P. Douglas, "Managing the transnational value chain—strategies for firms from emerging markets," *Journal of International Marketing,* 3, 1997, 71–84.

38 Y.H. Kim and N. Campbell, "Strategic control in Korean MNCs," *Management International Review,* 1, 1995, 95–108.

39 Company publications.

40 TEVA Pharmaceutical Industry Ltd., "Company Profile," 2013.

41 J. Karp, "Procomp hopes to bring Brazilian efficiency to Floridian chaos," *Wall Street Journal,* November 13, 2000, A27.

42 International Trade Administration, "US exporters in 2011."

43 Small Business and Entrepreneurship Council, "Small business facts & data," 2009.

44 US Small Business Administration, Office of International Trade: A report, November 1999.

45 US Small Business Administration, Office of International Trade: A report, November 1999.

46 Business Roundtable, "Trade creates jobs for Minnesota," January 2010.

47 Office of the United States Trade Representative, "Kirk welcomes report on small- and medium-sized exporter," January 2010.

48 European Commission Memo, "Small and medium sized enterprises in 2011: Situations per EU member state," October 15, 2012.

49 Magazines Today, "The New Zealand SME business network: One voice"; N.M. Aris, "SMEs: Building blocks for economic growth," 2007.

50 Jeddah: Arab News, "Italian SMEs key drivers of eco-innovation," Arab News website, June 2, 2013.

51 Small & Medium Business Corporation, "Export performance," 2009.

52 Industry Canada, "Key small business statistics," July 2012.

53 US Department of Commerce News, August 17, 2001.

54 B. Morris, "Small business stats for small business week 2011," *Get Busy Media,* May 18, 2011.

55 International Trade Administration, "US exporting companies," 2011.

56 Pricewaterhousecoopers. *Transforming a Business,* 2000.

57 M. Fujita, *The Transnational Activities of Small and Medium-Size Enterprises,* Dordrecht: Kluwer, 1998.

58 *US manufacturers in the global market place.* The Conference Board, *Report #1058-94-RR, 1994.*

59 J.L. Calof, "The relationship between firm size and export behavior revisited," *Journal of International Business Studies,* 25, 2, 1994, 367–387, S. Baird, M.A. Lyles, and J.B. Orris, "The choice of international strategies by small business," *Journal of Small Business Management,* January 1994, 48–59.

60 J.C. Shuman and J.A. Seeger, "The theory and practice of strategic management in smaller rapid growth companies," *American Journal of Small Business,* 11, 1, 1996, 7–18; N.E. Coviello and A. McAuley, "Internationalization and the smaller firm," *Management International Review,* 3, 1999, 223–256.

61 R. Klassen and C. Whyback, "Barriers to the management of international operations," *Journal of Operations Management,* 11, 1994, 385–397.

62 UNCTAD, World Investment Report, 1993.

63 G. Fairclough and M. Murray, "Small banks expand their trade financing for exports," *Wall Street Journal,* February 24, 1998, B2.

64 Fujita, *The Transnational Activities of Small and Medium-Size Enterprises.*

65 G. Fairclough and M. Murray, "Small banks expand their trade financing for exports," *Wall Street Journal,* February 24, 1998, B2.

66 P. Liesch and G.A. Knight, "Information internalization and hurdle rates in small and medium enterprise internationalization," *Journal of International Business Studies,* 30, 1, 383–394.

67 C. Cooper, "Euro drop is hardest for the smallest," *Wall Street Journal,* October 2, 2000.

151

68 E. Prater and S. Gosh, "The globalization process of US small and medium-sized firms: A comparative analysis." Working paper #97-005, DuPree School of Management, Georgia Institute of Technology.

69 Prater and Gosh, "The globalization process of US small and medium-sized firms: A comparative analysis."

70 A.R. Reuber and E. Fischer, "The influence of the management team's international experience on the internationalization behaviors of SMEs," *Journal of International Business Studies*, 28, 4, 1997, 807–825.

71 Fujita, *The Transnational Activities of Small and Medium-Size Enterprises*.

72 UNCTAD, World Investment Report, 1999.

73 C.A. Brush, *International Entrepreneurship: The Effect of Firm Age on Motives for Internationalization*, New York: Garland, 1995.

74 J.W. Ballantine, F.W. Cleveland, and C.T. Koeller, "Characterizing profitable and unprofitable strategies in small and large businesses," *Journal of Small Business Management*, April 1992, 13–24.

75 H. Boter and C. Holmquist, "Industry characteristics and internationalization processes in small firms," *Journal of Business Venturing*, 11, 1996, 471–487; B.M. Oviatt and P.P. McDougal, "Toward a theory of international new ventures," *Journal of International Business Studies*, 25, 1, 1994, 45–64; J. Bell, "The internationalization of small computer software firms—a further challenge to stage theories," *European Journal of Marketing*, 29, 8, 1995, 60–75.

76 Fujita, *The Transnational Activities of Small and Medium-Size Enterprises*.

77 Fujita, *The Transnational Activities of Small and Medium-Size Enterprises*.

78 C. Fleming, "US tech firms press on with global expansion," *Toronto Globe and Mail* (by agreement with the *Wall Street Journal*), August 17, 2001, B7.

79 K. Banejri and R. Sambharya, "Vertical Keiretsu and international market entry: The case of the Japanese automobile ancillary industry," *Journal of International Business Studies*, 27, 1, 1996, 89–113.

80 S. Doggett and A. Haddad, "Global savvy," *Los Angeles Times*, February 21, 2000.

81 Fujita, *The Transnational Activities of Small and Medium-Size Enterprises*.

82 *US manufacturers in the global market place*. Conference Board, *Report #1058-96-RR*, 1994.

83 K. Roth, "International configuration and coordination archetypes for medium-sized firms in global industries," *Journal of International Business Studies*, 3, 1992, 533–549; P.W. Beamish, A. Goerzen, and H. Munro, "The export characteristics of Canadian manufacturers: A profile by firm size." Working paper # 824, School of Business and Economics, Wilfred Laurier University, 1984.

84 J.L. Calof, "The relationship between firm size and export behavior revisited," *Journal of International Business Studies*, 25, 2, 1994, 367–387.

85 D.L. Balcome, "Choosing their own paths: Profiles of the export strategies of Canadian manufacturers." International Business Research Center Report 06–86, Conference Board of Canada, 1986.

86 Fujita, *The Transnational Activities of Small and Medium-Size Enterprises*.

87 B. Gomes-Casseres, "Alliance strategies of small firms." In Z.J. Acs and B. Yeung, *Small and Medium-Sized Enterprises in the Global Economies*, Ann Arbor: The University of Michigan Press, 1999.

88 E. Cherney, "Canadian brewery seeks export success to US market," *Wall Street Journal*, July 24, 2001, B2.

89 N. Namiki, "Export strategy for small business," *Journal of Small Business Management*, 26, April 1988, 32–37.

90 Namiki, "Export strategy for small business," 32–37; B. Gomes-Casseres and T. Kohn, "Small firms in international competition: A challenge to traditional theory?" In P. Buckley et al., *International Technology Transfer by Small and Medium-Size Enterprises: Country Studies*, pp. 280–296, New York: St. Martin's Press, 1997.

91 B.M. Oviatt and P.P. McDougal, "Toward a theory of international new ventures," *Journal of International Business Studies*, 25, 1, 1994, 45–64.

92 T. Almor, "Ownership structure of small high tech global companies: The case of Israel." Discussion paper #99.8, The College of Management, Tel-Aviv, Israel, 1999.

part 2

endowments and environments of international business

5   COUNTRY COMPETITIVENESS   155

6   THE CULTURAL ENVIRONMENT   187

7   THE POLITICAL AND LEGAL ENVIRONMENT   219

chapter 5

country competitiveness

DEFINING COUNTRY COMPETITIVENESS   157

COUNTRY-LEVEL DETERMINANTS   160

INDUSTRY-LEVEL DETERMINANTS   171

FIRM-LEVEL DETERMINANTS   176

INDIVIDUAL-LEVEL DETERMINANTS   178

GOVERNMENT ROLE   181

Do You Know?

1. Why do countries differ in their overall competitiveness in the global marketplace?
2. Why is a country's competitiveness more salient in some industries? For example, why do Swiss watches or pharmaceuticals dominate the world market, as do German upscale cars or Italian gold and silver jewelry?
3. What roles should firms and individuals play in shaping country competitiveness? For example, can Japanese firms' total quality management improve their country's competitiveness?
4. How does a foreign country's competitiveness influence the strategies and decisions of MNEs?

OPENING CASE   Singapore's Changing Competitive Advantage in the Hard Disk Drive Industry

Singapore is known as one of the most competitive nations in the world. Between 1995 and 2012, the country ranked second in the national competitiveness scoreboard released by the Swiss-based International Institute for Management Development (IMD). Hard disk drive (HDD) production in Singapore reached about $10 billion and accounted for approximately 70 percent of the world's production of HDDs in 1999. In 2012, however, with the growing technology production sector in greater Asia, Singapore shifted toward more knowledge-intensive hard disk drive media production, accounting for 40 percent of global hard disk drive media. Though much lower-skilled technology manufacturing has exited the country, Singapore is still home to the world's top three hard disk drive manufacturers.

HDDs are highly standardized and easily transportable. Demand is primarily driven by their technical and operating characteristics. This allows manufacturing to be located in distant locations away from consumers. Many world MNEs and domestic companies once used Singapore as the platform of HDD manufacturing and as the gateway to international markets, particularly to other Asian countries. Seagate, a world leader in the industry and once the largest industrial employer in Singapore, built a $130 million facility there for assembling disk drives and making printed circuit boards. Recently however, Seagate and other technology manufacturers have begun shifting lower-end production out of Singapore to other Asian hubs, like Thailand, Malaysia, and China.

Singapore's workforce was rated the best in the world by the Business Environment Risk Intelligence (BERI), based on such factors as relative productivity, worker attitude, technical skills, and legal framework. Although not rich in natural resources, Singapore is situated in a strategic location on a major trading route across continents, and it is a focal point for Southeast Asian shipping routes. Singapore is also a thriving financial center served by 149 commercial banks, 77 merchant banks, and eight international money brokers, and was rated the fourth top global financial center in 2012. Additionally, Singapore has first-class infrastructure in telecommunications and communications. The National Science and Technology Board (NSTB) was established in Singapore in 1991 in order to promote R&D through a financial assistance

156

program, coordinating with several research institutions such as the Institute of Microelectronics (IME) and the Institute of Manufacturing Technology (IMT).

To promote growth and productivity in the electronics industry, the Singaporean government also established several major agencies. Apart from the NSTB, the Economic Development Board (EDB) devises incentives to attract competitive companies into the nation's electronics sector. In addition, the National Computer Board (NCB) was created to drive Singapore to excel in the information age and to exploit the information technology (IT) niche. The NCB spearheads the implementation of Singapore's national IT master plan—IT2000. The government also initiated eight large-scale industrial parks in China, Indonesia, India, and Vietnam. These flagship projects, each of which is geographically concentrated in the same area, are positioned as premier investment locations not only for Singaporean investors, but also for other foreign firms and local enterprises. Singapore is increasingly dependent on the value-added edge that a highly skilled workforce brings. Therefore, through research aid and program development, the government assists higher educational institutions in providing a skilled workforce.

Today, Singapore has transitioned into production of hard disk drive media and more intensive R&D activities, which require a highly skilled labor force, allowing it to sustain its edge against other low-cost Asian countries. As Seagate's Senior Vice President, Doug Dehaan said in 2009, "although it [is] difficult for Singapore to compete on labor cost, Seagate [considers] the high level of education in Singapore a strong advantage for product development and [expects] to continue to keep its high value-added production in Singapore for the long term." A highly important industry for Singapore, it remains to be seen whether this focus will be enough to retain Singapore's once great technological foothold in hard disk drives.

Sources: World Economic Forum, "Global Competitiveness Report," 2012; Singapore Economic Development Board, "Electronics," Future Ready Singapore, 2012; Global Financial Centres Index 13, 2012; Shields, "Seagate closes Singapore HDD plant; Continuing electronics decline," August 5, 2009.

Defining Country Competitiveness

The preceding chapters explained that MNEs are a dominant force in today's international business activities (Chapter 4), and that activities such as trade and FDI are largely determined by comparative advantages of nations (Chapters 2 and 3). So how are MNEs and comparative advantages of nations linked? How do national advantages in a foreign country influence MNE strategies? If these advantages are important to national wealth, social welfare, and business operations, then how are these advantages determined, established, and maintained? We explain these issues from a country competitiveness perspective.

Competitiveness is the relative strength that one needs in order to win in competition against rivals. **Country competitiveness** is the extent to which a country is capable of generating more wealth than its competitors do in world markets. It measures and compares the effectiveness of countries in providing firms with an environment that sustains the domestic and international competitiveness of those firms. In the opening case, the Singaporean government created several institutions and offshore zones to help local businesses excel in international competition in the information industry. The core of country competitiveness centers on productivity. **Productivity** is the value of the output produced by a unit of labor or capital. It is the prime determinant of a nation's long-term standard of living and is the root source of national per capita income. The level of productivity depends on both the quality and features of products and services, and the efficiency with which they are produced or provided. As such, increasing productivity is key to enhancing country competitiveness. Many factors (such as a nation's educational and scientific strengths) influence productivity, which in turn determines a country's capabilities.

Country competitiveness is associated with, but different from, country comparative advantages. As introduced in Chapter 2, conventional wisdom suggests that comparative advantages of nations are based on factor endowment conditions (abundance and costs of production factors such as labor, land, natural resources, and capital). The resultant conclusion is that a nation's competitiveness is high if it possesses an abundance of labor, capital, and/or natural resources at low prices.[1] This theory falls short of explaining the reality that we see today: there are many countries with abundant resources that are characterized by poor economies, and vice versa. Germany, Switzerland, and Sweden have prospered, despite having high wages and labor shortages. Similarly, Japan, South Korea, and Singapore have limited natural resources, but are very successful in maintaining their high competitiveness. In today's world, where raw materials, capital, and even labor move across national borders, endowed resources can influence, but in and of themselves do not fully determine, a nation's competitiveness. Country comparative advantages (e.g., cheap land and labor in developing countries) may influence the level of competitiveness in industries that are labor-intensive or cost-sensitive. However, a nation's comparative advantage in production factors alone is far from sufficient in determining its international competitiveness, that is, its competitive advantage in the global marketplace.

International trade and investment can both improve a nation's competitiveness and threaten it. They increase national productivity by allowing a nation to specialize in industries where its companies are more productive, and to import where its companies are less productive. No nation can be competitive in everything. The ideal is to deploy the nation's limited human and other resources into their most productive use. Yet, international trade and FDI can also threaten productivity growth as they expose a nation's industries to the test of international productivity standards, especially if the country abruptly removes protective barriers in a wide range of industries, as some of the Central and Eastern European countries did after they decided to shift from a centrally planned system to a market-oriented one. The country's industries will suffer if their productivity is not as high as the productivity of their foreign rivals. If a nation loses the ability to compete in a range of high-productivity industries, its standard of living may be lowered for at least a period of time, until its existing industries catch up or newer and more competitive ones form and develop. In several industrialized countries, the rapid development of information technology has led to increased productivity and higher economic growth. Meanwhile, large disparities in the global economy continue to exist. Of major concern to international managers is why such national disparities exist and how companies should respond to them.

> **Interim Summary**
>
> 1. Country competitiveness measures and compares how effective countries are in providing firms with an environment that sustains the domestic and international competitiveness of those firms. Productivity is the core of country competitiveness.
> 2. Country competitiveness is associated with, but different from, country comparative advantages. Germany, Switzerland, and Sweden have all prospered, despite having high wages and labor shortages.

Country Competitiveness and MNEs

In a world of increasing global competition, nations have become more, rather than less, influential in international business operations. Differences in national values, culture, economic structures, institutions, and histories all contribute to competitive success. The national environment influences national competitiveness through the development of particular profiles of resources and capabilities (e.g., Italian footwear and textiles or Japanese semiconductors and electronics). The national environment also influences national competitiveness through its impact on the conditions for innovation. For example, as concern for product safety has grown in many industrialized countries, Swedish companies such as Volvo and Atlas Copco have succeeded by anticipating the market opportunities in this area. The impacts of country competitiveness on MNEs are fourfold.

First, *country competitiveness affects an MNE's selection of its global operations location.* Nike, for example, utilizes China as one of its major offshore production centers in order to benefit from cheap labor, abundant materials, and large market demand.

Second, *country competitiveness affects an MNE's industry selection.* For diversified MNEs, it is important to choose a foreign industry that will fit with the firm's global product portfolio and benefit from industry structure differences between home and host countries. A country's competitiveness is industry-specific, meaning that no nation can, nor should, maintain high competitiveness in every industry. Japan, for example, while very competitive in motor vehicles, has large sectors of its economy (i.e., aircraft, chemicals, and banking) that lag far behind the world's leading competitors. Thus, a more important question that concerns international managers is which industry of the target country is superior in terms of environment and competitiveness.

Third, *country competitiveness affects an MNE's innovation and capability building.* Trade and FDI patterns often reflect the sectors favored by a country's organizing and technological strengths (e.g., Japan's VCRs and Singapore's hard disk drives), and these patterns promote further expansion and investment in these capabilities. The variations in country competitiveness pertain to differences in organizational and institutional capabilities. By investing and operating in a country with superior organizing and technological strengths, MNEs can learn more from local partners and the business community.

Finally, *country competitiveness affects an MNE's global strategy.* A country's competitiveness is reflected in different elements, including rich resources, strong market demand, efficient governmental administration, and superior infrastructure for innovation. This diversity enables MNEs to globally differentiate their dispersed functions and businesses so as to leverage the advantages of various countries' competitiveness. Several Taiwanese companies (e.g., Acer) have greatly benefited from this differentiated process in which R&D is located in Taiwan and the United States, products are manufactured in Mainland China, financing is obtained in Hong Kong, and worldwide distribution is channeled through Singapore or Hong Kong.

Interim Summary

1. Country competitiveness affects an MNE's location selection and industry selection. For example, Nike chose China because it benefits from cheap labor and abundant resources needed for its production.
2. Country competitiveness affects an MNE's capability building and global strategy. For example, India has lured many software MNEs because it offers a favorable environment for developing software, which is then marketed globally.

Country-Level Determinants

Country competitiveness improves via increased productivity, which is driven by a large array of *country-level, industry-level, firm-level,* and *individual-level* factors. Sustained productivity growth requires that an economy continuously upgrade itself. International managers search for those decisive characteristics of a nation that allow its companies to create and sustain competitive advantage in particular fields (industries or sectors). Country competitiveness necessitates competitive strength across all these four levels (see Exhibit 5.1).

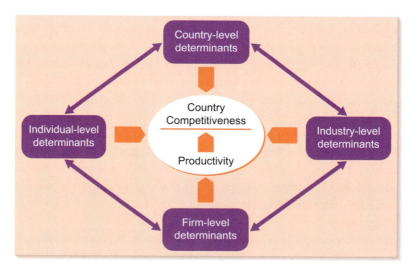

Exhibit 5.1 Determinants of country competitiveness

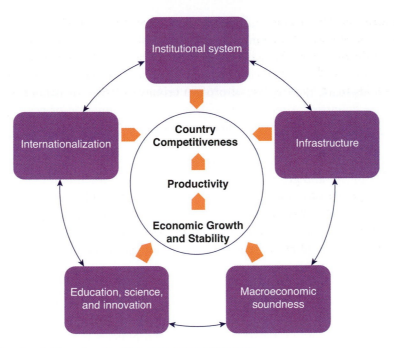

Exhibit 5.2 Country-level determinants of country competitiveness

Economic growth and stability cannot be sustained without political/social stability, a well-constructed and -enforced legal system, and sound macroeconomic conditions. This chapter presents an overview of the important conditions for country competitiveness and leaves the detailed discussions of the social/cultural and political/legal environments to the next two chapters. As summarized in Exhibit 5.2, these country-level fundamentals include: (1) institutional system; (2) infrastructure; (3) macroeconomic soundness; (4) education, science, and innovation; and (5) internationalization.[2]

Institutional System

A country's institutional system consists of its politico-legal, economic, and socio-cultural institutions, under which all economic players (e.g., producers, consumers, and government regulators) in the country must operate. The nature and quality of institutions are arguably the most important determinants of the country's ability to generate economic growth and improve the welfare of its citizens in the long term. Serious flaws in any of the system's key components can impair the country's competitiveness, and the different components must be compatible with and complement one another in order to make the system work effectively and efficiently.

1. **Political stability** is perhaps the most basic requirement. Countries embroiled in civil wars or other serious forms of anarchy and lawlessness due to ethnic or civil conflicts inevitably see their economies regress, with few willing to risk their investment in productive activities. There are sadly too many countries that had such experience in recent times, including Afghanistan, Somalia, and the Democratic Republic of Congo.

2. Efficiency in a country's productive activities requires a political and economic system that allows its citizens to retain at least a significant portion of the wealth they create. The systems of the countries that followed Soviet-style socialism, such as the former Soviet Union and China before the start of economic reforms, failed to reward efficient and innovative producers and even in some time periods made the earning of profit a criminal offense. It is no wonder that the vast majority of these countries, after experiencing prolonged stagnation or near economic collapse, decided to shift to a more **market-oriented system** that in general rewards more efficient and more innovative producers.

3. Not all countries that supposedly have a market-oriented system are able to achieve respectable economic development and growth because of serious institutional flaws. A particularly damaging type of systemic flaw is official abuse and corruption that dampen the gains from entrepreneurial and innovative activities and citizens' incentive to engage in such activities. Excessive government red tape, albeit not as morally reprehensible as corruption, has a similar effect, as it also reduces the gains from entrepreneurship and innovation. So, a **functioning administrative system** that guards against rampant official abuse and corruption and excessive red tape is also critical to a country's competitiveness.

4. The mere existence of a market does not necessarily ensure that people are willing to engage in economic exchanges. A high level of fraud by some market participants can severely discourage trade. Serious risks of fraud by buyers make efficient producers reluctant to expand production and sales beyond what they can sell to a small number of buyers they can trust. Serious risks of fraud by sellers make buyers reluctant to make their purchases. To overcome such problems, the government needs to establish a regulatory regime that can effectively catch and punish fraudsters. A case in point is the collapse of the Chinese dairy product market in 2008, after some milk collectors were found to be "spiking" their milk with a toxic chemical (melamine) in an attempt to enhance the milk's protein reading at inspection by milk processors.[3] So, effective **protection of contractual and consumer rights** against fraud is also needed to ensure the normal functioning of the market.

5. Most countries of the world have enacted laws guarding against official abuse and corruption and protecting contractual and consumer rights, but these laws are often inadequately enforced due to flaws in their political and legal systems. Some countries (e.g., China and Vietnam) do not allow their courts to operate independently, making it difficult for judges to rule on cases of official corruption and contractual abuse. Even in countries that allow the judicial branch to be independent of the executive branch, poorly paid and inadequately supervised judges can be tempted to abuse their powers and fail to enforce laws as they are supposed to. So, effective **rule of law** is another critical component in a country's institutional system.

The different components of a country's institutional system inevitably interact with and influence one another. For historical and practical reasons, they are not always compatible with or complement one another. When a country is in the process of major institutional reforms, such as in the case of China or Vietnam, newly enacted laws may be quite incompatible with the court system that is supposed to enforce the laws. Furthermore, the government can more easily change laws than the beliefs of its citizens about what is right and wrong, which is rooted in the cultural values and norms of a society and tends to evolve more slowly. For instance, the establishment of laws protecting such intellectual property as books and films does not immediately change the beliefs and behaviors of those who are used to reading books and watching films that are duplicated without proper copyright permission. The lack of conviction among many citizens about such intellectual property rights also makes the officials in the country's legal and regulatory system reluctant to impose strong penalties on violators. In the meantime, gradual strengthening of enforcement can also serve to change people's beliefs over time about what is right and wrong, influencing their cultural values and norms. Because of its complexity and historical embeddedness, it tends to take a long time to build up a country's institutional system. That is the main reason that developing countries and transition economies (e.g., the former Soviet republics), especially those with lower levels of per capital income and literacy, suffer from more serious imperfections in their institutional system.

Infrastructure

The infrastructure of a country is also multilayered and includes not only the more tangible transport, communications, and public utility networks but also the less tangible health care and education and job training systems.

1. Well-developed and efficient **transport networks** (roads, railways, airports, and seaports) move goods and people to their intended destinations in a speedy fashion without undue delays, and they lower the costs of finished goods and services to consumers and the costs of raw materials and intermediate inputs to producers.

2. Well-developed and efficient **communications networks** (mail, telephone, Internet, radio, and TV broadcast) provide the means for information to flow freely, so that both businesses and individuals can exchange information fully, and they also lower the costs of goods and services to consumers and the costs of intermediate inputs to producers.

3. Well-developed and efficient **public utility networks** (electricity, gas, water, and garbage disposal) enable businesses to operate and individuals to work and live without undue interruptions and excessive costs.

4. A broadly accessible, high-quality **health care system** maintains the health of the labor force both for the present and the future and reduces the risks of disruptions to the economy arising from public health threats such as diseases and natural disasters. A healthier force also keeps the costs of absences low to businesses and the overall health care costs low to the economy.

5. A broadly accessible, high-quality **education and training system** (from daycare, through various levels of schools, to adult job training) keeps the knowledge and skills of the labor force up to date not only for routine productive activities, but also for more advanced innovative activities. A more educated force is, in general, more flexible because individuals with broader sets of skills can shift to new fields more easily and acquire new skills more quickly.

The buildup of a country's infrastructure entails continual public and private investment, and the role of the government is often critical because the benefits of good infrastructure tend to be difficult for private investors to capture fully because of externality effects. For instance, it may be unprofitable to build roads to, or hospitals in, impoverished areas, but such infrastructure projects can be quite effective in alleviating poverty and preventing the area from being stuck in a vicious circle of underdevelopment. The high growth rate of the Chinese economy in last two to three decades, for example, has been supported by its rapid infrastructure improvement. Foreign investors in China previously complained about an inadequacy of electric supply and freight transportation, but today these infrastructure elements have expanded to a point where they can compare with, or even exceed, those in the most developed countries, making China one of the most attractive investment destinations in the world. The comparative robustness of the German economy among the EU countries is often attributed partly to the country's well-established vocation training system for both young people and adults (retraining or skill upgrading for job change).[4]

A country's infrastructure is both dependent on, and intertwined with, its institutions. First, effective political, economic, and social institutions are needed to invest in the development, management, and upgrading of infrastructure. Given the indispensable role that public funds play in such investment, political instability, corruption, and ineffective tax appropriation can all be serious impediments. Moreover, the less tangible parts of a country's infrastructure, such as the agencies responsible for the management and coordination of electricity networks, and the overarching systems for ensuring the coverage and quality of health care, are also parts of a country's economic and social institutions.

Macroeconomic Soundness

Economic soundness can be defined as the extent to which an economy has been equipped with the economic prerequisites for sustained development and growth. **Macroeconomic soundness** concerns both economic stability and economic growth, which are two distinct but interrelated fundamentals of the macroeconomic environment. An economy may be stable, but the policies that are in place may not be conducive to growth. Long-term growth and sustained competitiveness can be accomplished, however, only if economic stability is maintained. Generally, economic stability is reflected in a low rate of **inflation**. In high-inflation situations, the loss of competitiveness and the emergence of balance-of-payments difficulties may interrupt economic growth. Rising public expenditures without accompanying tax increases and the resultant budget deficits are often a principal cause of inflation. Expansionary public policies may initially stimulate economic growth, but as capacity limits are reached, output fails to keep up with rising expenditures, which eventually results in increased difficulty in financing the deficits. High inflation in the US and some European countries in the 1970s, in a number of Latin American countries in the 1980s, and in Russia in the 1990s dried up investment and resulted in economic stagnation or even serious contraction.

The world financial crisis of 2008–2012 that originated in the US and Europe has highlighted the risks associated with inflation in the asset markets (i.e., real estate and equity stock), in addition to inflation in the markets for goods and services. Both historical experience and experimental research in economics have shown that it is easy to build asset bubbles that eventually burst and cause serious economic dislocations.[5] In the absence of perfect information, market participants, including some highly trained financial professionals, use past price movements to predict future prices and also assume (correctly) that some other market participants may have better information than they do, and so they exhibit a herd mentality in their investment decisions. In addition, even when certain assets (e.g., stocks or real estate assets) look grossly overvalued, some market participants (presumably because of greed or overconfidence in their ability to beat the market) are often unwilling to unload those assets lest they miss the chance to make more money if the prices continue to rise for a bit longer. Such herd or bandwagon behavior leads to economically unjustified high prices that eventually fall precipitously as the asset bubbles burst when enough people recognize the economic reality. One of the best-known historical asset bubbles is the tulip mania in the Netherlands in 1637, when a single tulip bulb cost more than ten times the annual income of a skilled craftsman. More recently, the buildup and eventual burst of the real estate bubbles in the US, Ireland, and Spain was one of the main causes for the financial crises that these countries experienced in the 2008–2012 period. Hence, given the severity of the consequences from asset bubbles, macroeconomic soundness must involve shrewd management of asset inflation and of the buildup of asset bubbles. China was widely believed to have been threatened by potentially serious risks of stock and real estate bubbles in the late 2000s and early 2010s, although the Chinese government was successful in controlling the growth of the bubbles and letting the air out gradually via taxes on stock trading and curbs on real estate purchases, as well as repeated official warnings to the public about the dangers of bubbles growing and bursting.

Important conditions for macroeconomic soundness include *stability and efficiency of the financial system, effective taxation and stable government finance, balanced growth of investment and consumption, and sustainable pattern of trade and capital flows.* First, as explained in the discussion of inflation in the goods and asset markets and its importance to macroeconomic soundness, a country's financial system is the front line in the fight against economic instability. At the apex of the financial system are the central bank and other agencies in charge of regulating banks and other financial institutions and of ensuring the public's confidence in the system. The central bank controls money supply that is directly tied to price stability. It is considered critical that the decisions of the central bank are not unduly influenced by politicians who may at times prefer short-term economic gains over long-term stability. Money supply and other activities of the central bank affect the valuation of the country's currency in terms of other currencies. A currency is considered overvalued or undervalued if its value in terms of other currencies exceeds or falls below its intrinsic economic value, as determined by the general price level in the domestic economy relative to the general price levels in its trading partners (see Chapter 9 for details). High overvaluation or undervaluation can be a source of instability and is unhealthy for long-term economic growth. One of the factors leading to the collapse of the Thai baht and the Korean won in 1997 involved overvaluation of their currencies. A weak banking system can be a source of instability as well. The nature of banking itself—borrowing short and lending long—always leaves banks vulnerable to abrupt and unanticipated losses on deposits. This can happen internationally, just as it can happen domestically. If the creditors of the bank happen to be foreign, then perceptions of exchange rate vulnerability can interact with perceived banking vulnerability to produce a particularly volatile mixture. While the Netherlands, Luxembourg, and Australia are considered to have the most solvent banks, banks in Indonesia and Thailand are considered the most vulnerable, which is one of the major causes of the banking crisis that began in the region in 1997.[6] One of the key tasks of banking regulation is to ensure that banks have sufficient cash to withstand unexpected large withdrawals. This requires that banks have adequate reserves and match the terms of its liabilities (deposits) with the terms of its assets (loans). A major cause for the financial crisis that emerged in the US in 2007–2008 was the mismatch between the terms of liabilities and assets at several very large financial institutions, such as Bear Stearns and Merrill Lynch. The catastrophic failures of these previously highly reputable banks exposed a glaring weakness in the financial regulatory system of the US, which until then was viewed as one of the most advanced and most secure.

Second, to be able to provide its residents with appropriate levels of public services, the government of any modern economy needs corresponding levels of funding. Countries that are unable to establish an effective taxation system suffer from rampant tax evasion and inadequate funding for essential government services, and so they often turn to excessive deficit spending and inflationary monetization of government deficits through their central banks. Many Latin American countries fell into such untenable situations in the 1980s and 1990s, including Argentina, Brazil, Mexico, and Peru. To rectify this problem, the Peruvian government even called in troops to surround businesses in downtown Lima while tax inspectors checked their books. The more recent default of the Greek economy is also partly attributed to the country's inability to curb tax evasion. Other countries with effective taxation systems, such as the US, are sometimes unable to balance their government budgets due to divergent political ideologies among politicians and the electorate, and so they resort to excessive deficit spending and risk economic stability in the long run.[7]

Third, investment by domestic firms and foreign businesses plays an important role in stimulating economic growth. Investment does not just augment a factor of production; it is also the means by which new technologies are put into practice. In addition, investment in one sector stimulates investment in others and encourages technological progress. When an economy slows down, investments from public or private sectors are important forces driving economic growth. After the world financial crisis hit in 2008, for example, a number of countries, particularly the US and China, introduced "stimulus packages" to arrest their economies from a likely "free fall" and are now considered to have prevented a more severe economic downturn.[8] For economic growth to be sustainable, however, investment alone is not sufficient. An overemphasis on investment at the expense of consumption, such as in the case of China in the later 2000s and early 2010s, can create manufacturing overcapacity, price information and asset bubbles, risking a potentially severe economic contraction down the road. Furthermore, economies that appropriate excessive amounts of money via taxation for investment in public projects also curb per capita consumption, which is important because an economy's sustained growth depends partly on its citizens' final consumption.

Finally, even though it is not always necessary or even desirable for a country to have balanced flows of trade and capital with other countries, the patterns of such external flows have to be sustainable in the long run. When a country is developing and in need of substantial infusion of capital and imported technology, it is reasonable for the country to run substantial trade deficits and also receive corresponding capital inflows to finance those deficits. In the meantime, another country that is experiencing an export boom due to either rapid productivity increases in recent times or high demand for its resources (e.g., petroleum) may run substantial trade surpluses and net outflows of capital to the importing countries for a period of time. Because persistent trade deficits and reliance on foreign capital inflows to finance the deficits will eventually cause a country's trade partners to lose confidence in the country's ability to pay, no country can sustain large trade deficits indefinitely; as a result, neither can any country sustain large trade surpluses indefinitely. As will be discussed in Chapter 9, countries need to adjust their economic policies, particularly exchange rates and economic levers that affect exchange rates (e.g., government finance and money supply) to keep its external trade and capital flows sustainable. An almost absurd situation arose in the economic relation between the US and China in the mid-to late 2000s. On the one hand, the US, an economically advanced country, ran large trade deficits with China and many other countries and used capital inflows to finance these deficits. On the other hand, China, a still developing country with per capita income less than one-seventh of the US level, ran large surpluses with the US and some other countries and saw large amounts of capital flowing to the US. Although some attribute it primarily to the undervalued Chinese currency during this time, the fundamental cause for this situation was the imbalances between consumption and savings in each of the two countries. On the one hand, the excessively low interests and asset bubbles in the US made consumers feel rich and spend more than their income levels could justify. On the other hand, the rudimentary welfare system and low per capita income level, combined with high costs of real estate, health care, and education, caused Chinese consumers to feel nervous about the future and save a large percentage of their incomes (30–40 percent). Such a situation is clearly unsustainable, and both countries have struggled to address the imbalances within their respective economies.[9]

As can be seen in the above discussion, macroeconomic soundness must be rooted in sound economic institutions for the supervision and regulation of banks; management of money supply, inflation, interest rates, and foreign exchange rates; and taxation and government finance. The World Economic Forum (WEF) based in Geneva, Switzerland, and The International Institute for Management Development (IMD) based in Lausanne, Switzerland, both publish reports that rank countries in terms of economic soundness. Exhibit 5.3 shows the rankings of countries by these two institutions. The WEF ranking focuses on macroeconomic stability while the IMD ranking focuses on various factors considered to be drivers of economic growth such as investment, consumption, real income level, economic sectors' performance, and infrastructure development. It is interesting to note that the US is ranked #1 in the IMD list, but it is not even among the top 50 in the WEF list because the WEF looks at only macroeconomic stability and gives the US a low ranking due to a high level of government indebtedness.

Science, Education, and Innovation

Technological innovation has long been seen in all economies as central to the process of raising productivity and thereby improving country competitiveness. By increasing the range of choices with respect to new products and production processes, technological progress raises the potential for economic expansion and, in general, fosters human and economic development. Conversely, technological deficiencies are one of the major reasons for low incomes in some developing countries. To build and maintain a strong record of innovation, a country has to develop and promote science and education. Technological innovation and diffusion is a complex process, requiring support from a set of institutions. The United States, for example, has developed a rich set of institutions in both the public and private sectors to support a high level of technological innovation.

Rank	WEF: Macroeconomic Environment 2013-2014	IMD: Macroeconomic Strength 2013
1	Brunei Darussalam	United States
2	Norway	Qatar
3	Kuwait	China
4	Saudi Arabia	Norway
5	Oman	Japan
6	Qatar	Australia
7	United Arab Emirates	Germany
8	Azerbaijan	United Arab Emirates
9	Korea, Rep.	Canada
10	China	Switzerland
11	Switzerland	Chile
12	Hong Kong	India
13	Gabon	Indonesia
14	Sweden	Thailand
15	Luxembourg	Mexico
16	Libya	France
17	Chile	Sweden
18	Singapore	Malaysia
19	Russia	Korea, Rep.
20	Peru	Singapore
21	Bahrain	United Kingdom
22	Estonia	Austria
23	Kazakhstan	Russia
24	Botswana	Taiwan
25	Australia	Luxembourg
26	Indonesia	Poland
27	Germany	Israel
28	Bolivia	Netherlands
29	Latvia	Hong Kong
30	Bulgaria	Turkey
31	Thailand	Brazil
32	Taiwan	Philippines
33	Colombia	Peru
34	Algeria	Belgium
35	Timor-Leste	Denmark
36	Finland	Colombia
37	Austria	Kazakhstan
38	Malaysia	Italy
39	Lesotho	Venezuela
40	Philippines	New Zealand
41	Nepal	Ireland
42	Denmark	Finland
43	New Zealand	Lithuania
44	Ecuador	Spain
45	Netherlands	Latvia
46	Nigeria	South Africa
47	Romania	Argentina
48	Puerto Rico	Estonia
49	Mexico	Slovak Republic
50	Canada	Czech Republic

Exhibit 5.3 Macroeconomic conditions of countries (top 50 ranking)

Sources: World Economic Forum (WEF), *The Global Competitiveness Reports 2013–2014*, Geneva, Switzerland, 2013; The International Institute for Management Development (IMD), *The World Competitiveness Yearbook*, Copyright © 2013, IMD, Switzerland, www.imd.org/wcc.

Innovation depends on a complex interplay between basic science and new technologies and on commercialization of those technologies in new products and production processes. Basic science is not exclusively a market-driven activity, because it is difficult to ensure payoff. Thus, non-market institutions usually carry out most projects in basic science. Examples include government laboratories (such as the National Institutes of Health in the US) and academic centers (such as universities). Some corporations sponsor basic scientific research in their laboratories as well.

The level of technological innovation depends largely on the commercialization of new products and processes. Several developing countries, most notably Russia, China, and India, have a large number of world-class scientists in basic science. However, because they lack a developed commercialization system, the competitiveness of these countries remains low. An effective commercialization process requires several ingredients:

1. There must be a close interface between basic scientists and R&D managers in the corporate world. In the United States, the education system has allowed scientific faculty to participate in private-sector R&D undertakings, and has allowed universities to own patents for products developed by their faculty. This pattern of close business–university linkage is quite distinct from the situation in Poland or Ukraine, for instance, in which universities belong to state institutions and have minimal contact with industry sectors.
2. There must be strong support for developing intellectual property rights in order to encourage enterprises to make large outlays in R&D activities before a product is introduced to market. About 1 percent of the US GDP is provided as seed money for basic science in many crucial areas such as information technology, biotechnology, and material sciences.
3. The economy must be flexible enough to support the rapid adoption and diffusion of new technologies. For example, venture capital funds should be available to innovative firms to commercialize new technologies.

Apart from commercialization, technological innovation can also be improved by adopting and assimilating technology from foreign countries. There are several channels through which this can be done. First, a country can attract investments from MNEs, thereby bringing advanced technological innovation into its economy. For example, Mexico has dramatically upgraded its production technology through the rapid inflow of US investments in such key sectors as automotive, electronics, textiles, and pharmaceuticals. International joint ventures with MNEs (discussed in Chapter 12) are a quick and effective means for the host country to acquire foreign technologies and innovation expertise. Second, technology (e.g., robots) can be bought from a foreign country, or licensed from a foreign patent holder for use in the borrowing country. In fact, international trade in technology via licensing, franchising, export, or lease has been growing since the early 1990s. Finally, the technology can be engineered by an adopting country and suitably modified by local engineers for domestic production and use. Generally, knowledge acquisition from foreign firms is a better strategy for relatively small but newly industrialized countries, since they usually lack the scientific and technological base to innovate on their own, yet still have the ability to absorb technologies introduced in advanced countries. The competitiveness growth of the four mini-dragons—namely, Singapore, South Korea, Taiwan, and Hong Kong—is largely attributable to this strategy.

169

It is difficult to think about competitiveness and technological innovation without considering education. Education has become the prerequisite for entry into the knowledge-based economy, while technology has become the prerequisite for bringing education to society. The excellence in basic skills required in a good primary and secondary school system is important, but by itself it is not very helpful in pushing countries up the ladder of country competitiveness, if it is not matched by superior higher education in technology and management. Vietnam, for example, is one of the top-ranking countries with regard to the math skills exhibited by its elementary and high school students. Its weakness in higher education, however, hampers the nation's competitiveness. The executives of the twenty-first century require not only business savvy, but also strong technical, communication, project management, and human resource management skills. This is the new formula for grooming leaders who can handle the business world's increasingly complex problems.

Internationalization

Internationalization associated with country competitiveness refers to the extent to which the country participates in international trade and investment. (As you may recall from Chapter 1, this participation is one of the key indicators on the Globalization Index.) This internationalization is influenced by a nation's strength in the following areas: (1) exports (both goods and services) and related current account balance (see Chapter 9); (2) exchange rate systems; (3) foreign investment (both FDI and portfolio investment); (4) foreign exchange reserves; and (5) openness of the economy. A high degree of competitiveness requires a high degree of internationalization of that economy, because competitiveness measures a nation's competitive advantage in an international marketplace compared to other countries. A large and growing domestic economy may or may not translate into a strong international competitiveness; it depends on the economy's openness and strength of foreign trade and investment as reflected in its current account and foreign exchange reserves. This openness is in turn dependent upon a nation's economic soundness, as well as on the government's policies pertaining to foreign trade, investment, and exchange rate. A country's **openness** refers to the extent to which its national economy is linked to world economies through the flow of resources, goods, services, people, technologies, information, and capital. In a competitive nation, this flow means both inflow and outflow. The inflow of goods, capital, services, and the like is determined not only by an economy's attractiveness but also by the extent of its national protectionism. **National protectionism** reflects the level of barriers that foreign goods, capital, services, and other inputs of production are confronted with when moving into the focal country. As introduced in Chapter 2, examples of these barriers include import tariffs, quotas, voluntary export restraints, and commodity inspection standards, among others. For developing countries in which economic foundations and systems are underdeveloped, a certain degree of protectionism during an early stage of economic development may be necessary for ensuring trade balance and economic stability. For this reason, the World Trade Organization (WTO) permits a few developing country members, such as Poland, Hungary, and the Czech Republic, to have a higher bar against foreign imports.

170

> **Interim Summary**
>
> 1. Country competitiveness is determined by four levels of factors: country-level, industry-level, firm-level, and individual-level. They affect competitiveness individually as well as jointly.
> 2. Country-level determinants include: (a) institutional system; (b) infrastructure; (c) macroeconomic soundness; (d) education, science, and innovation; and (e) internationalization.
> 3. Macroeconomic soundness is determined by the stability and efficiency of the financial system, effective taxation and stable government finance, balanced growth of investment and consumption, and sustainable pattern of trade and capital flows.

Industry-Level Determinants

Sound country-level foundations such as macroeconomic fundamentals and science and innovation are necessary for enhancing country competitiveness. However, they are not sufficient to ensure a prosperous economy. Although country-level determinants influence overall competitiveness of a nation and are important to improving national productivity, no country can build and maintain high competitiveness in every industry. Within a country, different industries are not the same in terms of comparative advantages. Economically, it is neither necessary nor realistic to expect high competitiveness in every industry of the economy. This industry-specific perspective is especially important for international managers because it is often a target country's *industrial*, rather than national, environment that directly impacts firm decisions and operations. Of course, for a nation's government, the more industries with high international competitiveness, the greater the overall country competitiveness. Governments should devote more resources to improving infrastructures of those industries (or sub-industries) in which their nations are potentially already competitive.

When you look closely at any national economy, you will see enormous differences among a nation's industries in the area of competitive success. International advantage is often concentrated in particular industry sectors or segments within a given economy. For example, US commercial aircraft and defense industries have dominated the world market, while Japanese semiconductors and VCRs have led as well. In the automobile industry, German exports are heavily skewed toward high-performance cars, whereas Korean exports were clustered at the low end of the market until the 2010s. The assessment of country competitiveness is therefore about competitive advantage of a nation in particular industries or industry segments. To help assess this competitiveness, classical theory explains the successes of nations in certain industries based on production factors (or inputs) such as land, labor, and natural resources. A nation gains comparative advantages in industries that make intensive use of the factors it possesses in abundance. This classical view, however, has been overshadowed in advanced industries and economies by the globalization of competition and the power of technology.

171

A new perspective called the "diamond framework," developed by Michael E. Porter, offers an analytical tool for international managers to appraise a country's competitive advantage in particular fields.[10]

According to Porter's diamond framework, there are four broad attributes which individually and collectively constitute the diamond of national advantage in particular fields:

1. *Factor Conditions.* This concerns the nation's position in factors of production, including basic factors such as labor, capital, land, and natural resources, and sophisticated factors such as skilled workforce, scientific base, infrastructure, and information. Each country may be abundant in certain factors while lacking in others. For example, Hungary's optical instrument industry is abundant in skilled workers but lacks a well-developed supplier infrastructure. The same is true for China's copy-machine industry. Low design costs and growing market demand for copier machines are also major considerations luring foreign companies such as Xerox to invest there. Country competitiveness is likely to be higher in industries in which the country has superior factors of production. Basic factors are generally important in obtaining competitive advantage in labor-intensive industries but do not constitute an advantage in knowledge-intensive industries that require sophisticated factors of production. The contribution of factor conditions to country competitiveness changes over time. The stock of factors that a nation enjoys at a particular time is less important than the rate and efficiency with which it creates, upgrades, and deploys them in particular industries.

2. *Demand Conditions.* This involves the nature of market demand for the industry's product or service. International companies often enter a foreign market because of promising opportunities arising from strong market demand. Strong market demand drives an economy's gross domestic product (GDP) upward and facilitates the improvement of productivity in a competitive environment. In addition to the size of market demand, the character of demand is also critical. Nations can gain competitive advantage in industries where the market demand gives their companies a clearer or earlier picture of emerging buyer needs, as well as where demanding buyers pressure companies to innovate faster and achieve more sophisticated competitive advantages than their foreign rivals. If domestic buyers in a particular sector are the world's most sophisticated and demanding buyers, then a nation's companies in this sector are more likely to gain competitive advantage through constantly improving and upgrading their products or services. As an example, Japanese firms have pioneered compact, quiet air-conditioning units powered by energy-saving rotary compressors. This is largely because the firms have responded to the needs of Japanese consumers, most of whom live in small, crowded homes in a country where humid summers are the norm.

3. *Related and Supporting Industries.* This refers to the presence and support level of a nation's suppliers or other related industries. For foreign investors, the availability and supportiveness of local suppliers, as well as other related industries such as banking, foreign exchange services, and infrastructure services, are fundamental to their routine operations. For the country itself, the competitiveness of related industries provides benefits of information flow and technical interchange among related industries, which in turn speeds up the rate of innovation and upgrading. For example, Switzerland's success in pharmaceuticals evolved from previous international success in the dye industry. Having home-based suppliers that are internationally

competitive can create advantages in downstream industries. Italian gold and silver jewelry companies lead the world in part because other Italian companies supply two-thirds of the world's jewelry-making and precious-metal recycling machinery. In addition, suppliers and end-users located near each other can take advantage of short lines of communication, quick and constant flow of information, and an ongoing exchange of ideas and innovations. Through close working relationships, companies have the opportunity to influence their suppliers' technical efforts and can serve as test sites for R&D work, accelerating the pace of innovation. When suppliers, manufacturers, and even distributors are located near each other or concentrated in the same area (a city or part of the city), we call this geographical concentration a **cluster.** Examples include: Silicon Valley in California for the semiconductor and software industry; Milan in Italy for fashion garments; Hamamatsu in Japan for motorcycles and musical instruments; Pusan in South Korea for footwear products; and Zhongguanchun in Beijing for electronics.

4. *Rivalry and Business Practice.* This involves the nature of domestic rivalry, in addition to the conditions governing how businesses are organized, managed, and operated in a nation. International investors may select a country in which local rivalry is low. However, in terms of competitiveness, the presence of strong local rivals is a powerful stimulus to the creation and persistence of national competitive advantage. This is especially true for small countries such as Switzerland, where the rivalries among its pharmaceutical companies—Ciba-Geigy, Sandoz, and Hoffman-La Roche—contribute to global leadership. Domestic rivalries exert pressure on companies to innovate and improve. Local rivals force each other to lower costs, improve quality and service, and create new products and processes. Domestic rivals compete not only for market share, but also for people, for technical excellence, and more importantly, for product quality, customer responsiveness, and innovation. Business and management practice is relevant to country competitiveness because competitiveness in a specific industry results from convergence of management and business policy with the sources of competitive advantage in the industry. In industries where Italian companies are among the world's leaders (e.g., lighting, furniture, footwear, woolen fabrics, and packaging machines), a company strategy that emphasizes customized products, niche marketing, rapid adaptation, and great flexibility fits well, both with the dynamics of the industry and with the character of the Italian management system. Successful Italian international competitors also tend to be small or medium-size companies (SMEs) that are privately owned and operated like extended families. In Germany, companies tend to be hierarchical in organization and management practices, and top managers usually have technical backgrounds. This system works well in technical or engineering-oriented industries (e.g., optics, chemicals) where complex products demand precision manufacturing as well as a highly disciplined management. Germany's success, however, is quite limited in consumer goods and services, where image marketing and product innovation are important to competition. In the greater China region, including the People's Republic of China (PRC), Taiwan, Hong Kong, Macao, and Singapore, successful companies are technologically innovative as well as skillful in cultivating and developing personal ties with government officials and with top managers of other firms. Personal relations (or *guanxi* in Mandarin) may be conducive to improving competitiveness in such industries where the regulatory environment is highly unpredictable.

173

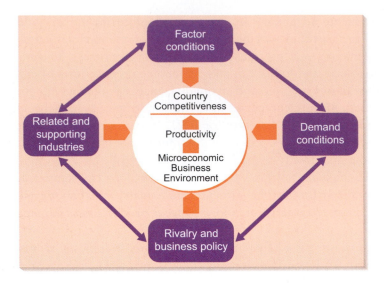

Exhibit 5.4 Industry-level determinants of country competitiveness
Source: Adapted from M. E. Porter, "The competitive advantage of nations," *Harvard Business Review*, March–April 1990, 73–93.

Exhibit 5.4 highlights the diamond framework of national competitive advantage. The four determinants in this framework create the national environment into which companies are born and in which they learn to compete. Each point on the diamond—as well as the diamond itself as a system—produces essential ingredients for achieving international competitive success. In general, companies gain a competitive advantage when a national environment (1) permits and supports the most rapid accumulation of specialized assets and skills, (2) affords better ongoing information and insight into product and process needs, and (3) pressures companies to innovate and invest. It is also important to note that the diamond factors create an environment that may promote competitiveness of other related industries. Japan's strength in consumer electronics, for example, drove its success in semiconductors toward the memory chips and integrated circuits these products use.

The four diamond attributes together serve as the microeconomic business environment that affects country competitiveness. Unless there is appropriate improvement at the microeconomic environment, the country-level determinants (i.e., macroeconomic business environment) discussed earlier will not bear full fruit.[11] National productivity is ultimately set by the productivity of a nation's companies. Companies need appropriate conditions for rapid and sustained productivity growth. The country-level determinants create the potential for improving national prosperity, but wealth is actually created at the microeconomic (industrial) level—in the ability of firms to create valuable goods and services productively. A country's economy cannot be competitive unless the companies operating within it are competitive, whether they are domestic or foreign company subsidiaries. To conclude, the improvement of country competitiveness is a process of successive upgrading, in which a nation's business environment evolves to support and encourage increasingly sophisticated and productive ways of competing and innovating. This chapter's Industry Box illustrates how e-business may shape country competitiveness in the future. Chapter 18 provides more detailed information on global e-commerce.

Interim Summary

1. It is neither possible nor necessary to expect *every* industry in a country to be competitive. Industry-level fundamentals determine a country's microeconomic business environment.
2. The "diamond framework" is often used to assess country competitiveness in particular industries or fields. This framework consists of four factors—factor conditions, demand conditions, related and supporting industries, and rivalry and business practice.
3. A cluster is a geographical concentration in which suppliers, manufacturers, and even distributors are located near each other. Cluster can help improve country competitiveness.

Industry Box

E-commerce as an Element of Country Competitiveness

E-commerce capabilities can help boost a country's competitiveness in many ways. First, the Internet is a global network, enabling people and businesses to connect to the rest of the world. Second, the Internet provides easy access to the global market, matching buyers and sellers across national boundaries. Third, the Internet is an efficient distribution tool, saving transaction costs. Fourth, the Internet lets small businesses play in the big business arena. Finally, the Internet shortens a company's time to market.

However, many countries lag behind in the e-business race, and in many cases the e-business laggards are at the bottom of the competitive rankings. The reasons are threefold: language, education, and technical infrastructure. But many governments are taking steps to address these issues because they understand that the Internet presents developing nations the opportunity to bolster their competitiveness and economy. Asia-Pacific Economic Cooperation (APEC) leaders, for instance, acknowledged during their meetings in Vancouver as long ago as 1997 that there existed a need for Asian economies to construct and utilize a global information infrastructure. Today, while still lagging behind the global average in Internet penetration, Asia has some of the top countries in number of Internet users. For example, in 2000, China had less than a quarter as many Internet users as the United States. However, by 2012, China had more than twice as many. For governments, adequate regulations and supervision also need to be in place to ensure that private enterprises are playing their part in innovating and implementing the global systems and needed infrastructure. International companies such as GE Capital and Infotech Global have also made investments in emerging markets, with both companies expanding their services in India.

As a growing and developing aspect of today's business world, e-commerce continues to play an ever more important role in global business, projected to bring in $1.2 trillion worldwide in 2013. With North America currently the largest e-commerce driver, bringing in over $373 billion in 2012, the Asia-Pacific region is growing much more rapidly (along with the newer Middle East and African e-commerce markets) and is expected to surpass North America to become the largest e-commerce market in the world by 2014.

Source: Adapted from E. Sprano and A. Zakak, "E-Commerce capable: Competitive advantage for countries in the new world e-economy," *Competitiveness Review,* 10, 2, 2000, 114–131; "Top 20 Internet Countries," Internet World Stats: Usage and Population Statistics, 2012; L. Indvik, "Study: Global economic commerce to hit $1.2 trillion this year, led by Asia," *Mashable Business News*, June 27, 2013.

Firm-Level Determinants

An economy's product competitiveness stems from companies within that nation. It is firms that produce products and provide services. Thus, country competitiveness is also associated with firm-level factors that can characterize country-unique organizational, innovational, and operational strategies employed by most firms of that nation. These strategies, principles, or approaches should differentiate one country's firms from those of other countries, and more importantly, create competitive advantages for both the nation and firms to which they belong. For example, most Japanese firms have obtained their competitive advantages vis-à-vis American and European companies through superior process innovations, quality control systems, and unique manager–employee relationships. These firm-level policies have become Japan's national standards and have been widely applied by most Japanese firms. Country competitiveness can thus be partly explained by differences in country capabilities in terms of technologies and organizing principles. These technologies and organizing principles diffuse more slowly across borders than within a nation. In other words, these unique firm-level factors are virtually embedded in Japanese firms. This embeddedness helps Japan maintain strong country competitiveness.

Organizing principles of technological innovation and production are particularly important because they are not easily diffused across nations. National economic leadership of a country is not driven by technological investments alone, but also by the efficiency of a country's dominant organizing principles.[12] The superiority of US competitiveness in relation to that of European countries is attributable not only to the country's creation of technologies (as measured by patents) but also to its adoption of new methods of management. Although the basic research skills of Japanese firms are generally inferior to those of US firms, organizing principles such as lean flexible production, total quality management, just-in-time manufacturing, and the multi-sourcing strategy used by Japanese firms add substantial value to the international competitiveness of Japanese products.

The contribution of technologies and organizing principles to creating competitive advantages for both firms and the country cannot last forever. Technology, and even organizing principles, are inevitably diffused across nations, and eventually imitated by foreign rivals. Through technology transfer, foreign direct investment, and global strategic alliances, one nation's firms can learn both technologies and organizing principles that were developed and employed by counterparts in another nation. This suggests that firms need to continuously upgrade their technological skills and organizing approaches if they wish to sustain competitive advantages that help maintain their country's competitiveness in the long run. Constant and rapid technological progress, rather than one single innovation, is the secret to retaining competitive advantage.

Firms can also influence the environment that impacts country competitiveness. Companies do not simply accept the status quo of factor development in the nation, but instead seek to upgrade it. For example, Italian industry associations invest in marketing information, process technology, and common infrastructure in such industries as woolens, ceramic tiles, and lighting equipment. Swiss and German firms participate widely in apprenticeship programs. In Britain, successful industries such as chemicals and pharmaceuticals are characterized by close ties with universities and government research institutes. Firms can, and probably need to, invest directly in factor creation through their own training, research, and infrastructure building. Internal efforts at factor creation lead to the most specialized, and often most important, factors. Competitive firms often have well-developed internal training programs and, compared to their rivals, set aside higher amounts of resources for R&D. Leading US and Japanese companies usually have their own universities or schools. Yamaha, for example, faced a shortage of skilled piano technicians in Japan, so it founded its own educational program for acoustics training that is now highly regarded internationally. The benefits flow to Yamaha as well as to the entire Japanese industry.

Firms can also join with, or participate in, the efforts of government entities, educational institutions, and the local communities, in order to influence factor creation or improvement. Nestlé, for example, founded and supports Switzerland-based IMD, which has become a leading European business school. Nestlé has benefited from a steady flow of talented management as well as ongoing management training. German chemical companies have established relationships with all of the major German universities and also sponsor institutes devoted to chemical research, contributing to advancements in the industry. In addition, they sponsor students or their staff to study at the universities. They also play an active role in helping institutions identify the needs of the industry by assisting with planning curriculum, placing graduates, and providing financial support for facilities and scholarships. Exhibit 5.5 outlines the firm-level determinants of country competitiveness.

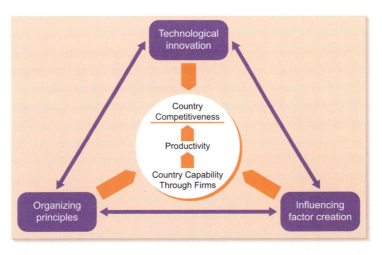

Exhibit 5.5 Firm-level determinants of country competitiveness

> **Interim Summary**
>
> 1. It is firms that directly create national wealth, and thus the productivity of firms is central to country competitiveness.
> 2. Technologies and organizing principles (e.g., process innovation and quality control systems) are two firm-level fundamentals. When unique and productive organizing principles and technological skills become national standards or are permeated throughout the nation, they will substantially heighten country competitiveness.

Individual-Level Determinants

Individual-level determinants are people or human resources associated with country competitiveness. They include workers, entrepreneurs, professional managers, designers and engineers, educators and intellectuals, and politicians and government officials (see Exhibit 5.6). Human resources affect productivity (the core of country competitiveness) by shaping the environment for developing competitiveness and by combining and arranging the preceding physical competitiveness determinants at both the country and industry levels.

Workers: Workers' productivity affects country productivity. For example, skillful and diligent workers in Singapore are an important force in improving its country-level productivity. In addition to the wage level and the size of labor pool, other important factors associated with worker productivity include educational level, loyalty to organizations, passion for work, self-motivation, learning skills, and discipline. In Denmark, Finland, and Sweden, superior education and passion for work is an important reason for the superior productivity of workers. In Japan, workers' loyalty to organizations and learning skills are partly responsible for its competitiveness.

Entrepreneurs: Entrepreneurs venture into new businesses despite a high degree of risks arising from uncertainty about the future. They are a special group of businesspeople taking risks in the development of new products, new markets, or new technologies. They create new businesses, stimulating a nation's economic development. A nation's competitiveness is strengthened in the course of their efforts and commitments to take high risks and maximize returns. Singapore's high level of competitiveness can in large part be attributed to the high percentage of entrepreneurs in its total population.

Managers: Experienced and skillful managers in various enterprises, whether public, private, or state-owned, play an important role in increasing country competitiveness. Production and operation processes are becoming increasingly complex and interrelated among different value chain activities (e.g., from inbound logistics and operations to outbound logistics, marketing, and service; or from human resource management to technological development and procurement). As a result, a country with a large pool of educated and experienced managers who are well versed in production, operation, and organization will have a much better chance of creating and sustaining high competitiveness. Several newly industrialized economies such as South Korea and Taiwan have successfully secured

178

and retained a large number of Western-educated and experienced managers who were educated abroad. This greatly helps raise the level of national competitiveness in these countries.

Engineers: Engineers and designers stand at the forefront of country competitiveness. They are key players in improving a nation's productivity because they create value through production innovation and process innovation. A country's expertise in these two types of innovations is a crucial element for elevating its competitiveness. Because international competitiveness involves worldwide consumers, it is important for engineers and designers to have a global vision. Engineers in Switzerland and the Netherlands have a strong educational background, industrial experience, and global vision, which in turn helps stimulate the competitiveness of these nations.

Educators: Educators and intellectuals represent a prime force for strengthening education and science. High competitiveness of an economy requires the creation and dissemination of knowledge needed for improving productivity. Although intellectuals are the major source of knowledge creation, educators at various levels (from elementary to higher education) are a prominent source for knowledge dissemination. For countries moving to knowledge-based economies, growth depends heavily on the contributions of educators and intellectuals. A country's productivity and competitiveness are generally positively correlated with the salary level, or more broadly, living standards, of educators and intellectuals.

Politicians: The role of politicians and government officials in supporting competitiveness cannot be underestimated simply because government policies and administrative efficiency exert a significant effect on other determinants of country competitiveness. Nations with politicians who make economic development their personal ambition, and do not let their desires for power and wealth override this ambition, tend to create competitiveness. South Korea in the 1970s is a manifestation of how a national economy can benefit from political leaders with a strong commitment to economic growth even under a non-democratic regime. Government officials apply policies to the economy. Their role can be compared to that of an automobile's transmission: the most efficient transmission would convey the power with minimum loss of power. Officials who can implement politicians' policies in the most efficient way can enhance their nation's competitiveness.[13]

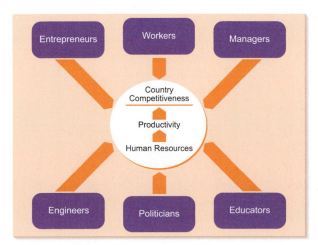

Exhibit 5.6 Individual-level determinants of country competitiveness

Country Box

Italy

Owner Sneaks Factory to Poland

On August 2, 2013, Fabrizio Pedroni, proprietor of an electric component factory in northern Italy, wished his employees a happy summer holiday and told them to return to work in three weeks. That night, he began dismantling his factory and moving its machinery off to Poland. Eleven days after he initiated his plan, some of his employees became suspicious of the movements around the factory and went to check what was happening. But their surprise finding came too late: They could stop only the last of the 20 trucks packed with machinery leaving the factory.

"Had I told them earlier about any plans to shift the production abroad, they would have occupied my factory and seized all my stuff," Pedroni said from Poland in a telephone interview. "The plain truth is that I wanted my business to survive and there weren't the right conditions for me to operate in Italy any longer." The unfavorable conditions, according to Pedroni and other entrepreneurs like him, are numerous and severe in totality. First, wage rates in Italy are high compared with central European or Asian countries, but labor productivity cannot match that of more competitive northern European countries such as Germany and Denmark. Second, rigid labor market regulations make it difficult to lay off unproductive workers. To skirt the rigid regulations, many firms keep the number of employees under 15, making themselves unable to afford the costs of the R&D effort needed to keep themselves technologically competitive. Third, the tax burden is high because the expansion of the country's social welfare system significantly exceeded the rate of productivity increases over the years. Fourth, budget shortfalls have prevented the country from making the necessary infrastructure investments to maintain itself, which has become a great obstacle to growth. Finally, there has been a serious deterioration in the quality of education at every level. Successive governments in the country have attempted institutional reforms aimed at addressing these problems, but political gridlock has made their efforts half-hearted and ineffectual.

After months of stalemate following Italy's inconclusive national election in February 2013, a new "grand coalition" government between the center-left Democratic Party (PD) and the center-right People of Liberty Party (PDL) finally emerged. The head of the new government is Prime Minister Enrico Letta of the PD, with the Deputy Prime Minister being Angelino Alfano of the PDL. Such a coalition government had not existed in Italy since 1946. Both of the political parties in the government claim that their top priority is to stimulate Italy's ailing economy. The question is how: Can the new political experiment of governing by a grand coalition succeed in undertaking deeper institutional reforms where successive governments have failed? Will Fabrizio Pedroni (now hiding in Poland in the face of death threats) and his fellow entrepreneurs who have moved their factories abroad be able to find a sufficiently attractive environment in the future to move at least some of their operations back to Italy?

Source: C. Emsden, "Italy takes first steps in reviving economy," *Wall Street Journal*, May 17, 2013; L. Totaro, "Italian job sneaks factory to Poland under cover," *Bloomberg*, August 23, 2013.

Interplay of the Four-Level Determinants

The preceding four levels of determinants are not exclusive of each other. Country-level determinants provide an overall national foundation for developing country competitiveness. This foundation provides a general economic and technological environment, which can directly or indirectly influence industrial, organizational, and individual determinants of competitiveness. For example, a nation's education system (a country-level determinant) affects the qualifications of workers, managers, and engineers (individual-level determinants). Conversely, politicians and officials (individual-level determinants) have the power to change country-level determinants such as economic policies and financial systems. Industry-level determinants jointly create a microeconomic business environment that impacts companies' productivity. They are a central force linking a nation's comparative advantage with firms' competitive advantages in wealth creation. While country-level and industry-level determinants together provide a context for improving country competitiveness, firm-level and individual-level determinants are direct "hands" in creating and improving this competitiveness. These "hands" can be stronger or weaker, depending on both country-level and industry-level conditions. This chapter's Country Box provides an illustrative case in which Italy's country competitiveness is jointly influenced by various determinants at the individual-level (e.g., politicians, entrepreneurs, workers), firm-level (e.g., flexibility, cluster, small size) industry-level (competition, factor conditions, related industries), and country-level (infrastructure, education, legal system, economic soundness).

Interim Summary

1. Individual-level determinants are people or human resources that affect country competitiveness. They include workers, entrepreneurs, managers, engineers and designers, educators and intellectuals, and politicians and government officials.
2. Human resources affect country competitiveness in such a way that they determine a country's expertise, creativity, and efficiency.
3. Multilevel fundamentals also interactively affect country competitiveness. Country- and industry-level determinants provide an important context in which firms and individuals directly create national wealth. Firms and individuals are also able to reshape this context so that macro- and microeconomic business environments become more favorable for productivity.

Government Role

Government plays an important role in shaping country competitiveness. It can affect all four levels of determinants outlined previously. Through policy making and intervention, government can impact investment, savings, and trade. Through a combination of trade liberalization and exchange rate adjustment, government can strengthen the balance of payments and improve international competitiveness. The experiences of several newly industrialized nations (NIEs) in the early 1980s suggest that a certain amount of governmental control over macroeconomic problems is necessary. In that particular instance, when macroeconomic fundamentals grew seriously out of line, governments acted promptly to bring the situation under control. They were also committed to export expansion, rather than import substitution, as a means of relieving balance-of-payment constraints.

Governments can also exert influence on the microeconomic business environment and on human resource development. Such influence is normally exerted through a set of industrial policies. **Industrial policies** can be defined as all forms of conscious and coordinated government interventions to promote industrial development. Such forms include, but are not limited to: import protection, financial subsidies, regulatory changes, and interventions in capital, labor, technology, and natural resource markets. For example, a government can shape factor conditions through its training and infrastructure policies. Factor conditions are also affected through subsidies and policies aimed at the development of capital markets. Furthermore, market demand conditions are influenced by regulatory standards and processes, government purchasing, and openness to imports. Governments are often a major buyer of many products, including defense goods, telecommunications equipment, aircraft for a national airline, and so on. Governments can shape the circumstances of related and supporting industries through control of advertising media and also regulation of supporting services such as banking and foreign exchange. Finally, government policy also influences competition and business practices through such means as capital market regulation, tax policy, and antitrust laws.

The effect of government policies on country competitiveness can be positive (stimulating competitiveness) or negative (obstructing competitiveness). Too much dependence on direct help or interference from the government may hurt companies in the long run and only lead to them becoming more dependent. On the other hand, a government that has a hands-off policy may miss out on the benefits of shaping the macro- and microeconomic business environment and institutional structure that can stimulate companies to gain competitive advantage. Thus, the appropriate role that a government should play is one of a catalyst and challenger—it should encourage, or even push, companies to aspire to higher levels of competitive performance, even though this process may be difficult. Governments cannot directly create competitive industries; only companies can do that. Government policies that succeed are those that create an environment in which companies can gain competitive advantage.

There are several principles that governments should embrace in order to play a supporting role in national competitiveness:

1. *They should emphasize competitiveness infrastructure.* Governments have critical responsibilities for developing and improving infrastructure such as education, science, research, transportation, and information technology.

2. *They should enforce strict product, safety, and environmental standards.* Stringent standards for product performance, product safety, and environmental control pressure companies to improve quality, upgrade technology, and provide features that respond to consumer and social demands.

3. *They should deregulate competition.* Regulation through maintaining a state monopoly, controlling entry to industry, or fixing prices hampers rivalry and innovation.

4. *They should adopt strong domestic antitrust policies.* These policies, especially when applied to horizontal mergers, alliances, and collusive behavior, are fundamental to innovation. Government policy should generally favor new entry over acquisition.

5. *They should boost goal-setting that leads to sustained investment.* Governments can indirectly affect the goals of investors, managers, and employees through various policies. For instance, the tax rate for long-term capital gains is a powerful tool for adjusting the rate of sustained investment in industry as it affects the level of new investment in corporate equity.

This chapter concludes with two summary measures of country competitiveness by the World Economic Forum (WEF) and the International Institute for Management Development (IMD), respectively (see Exhibit 5.7). The WEF's *Global Competitive Reports* evaluates "12 pillars" of competitiveness (institutions, infrastructure, macroeconomic environment, health and primary education, higher education and training, goods market efficiency, labor market efficiency, financial market development, technological readiness, market size, business sophistication, and innovation) and summarizes the 12 measures in a Global Competitiveness Index for each country. The IMD's *World Competitiveness Yearbook* groups eight competitiveness input factors (domestic economy, science and technology, people, firm management, internationalization, infrastructure, finance, and government) into four main categories (economic performance, government efficiency, business efficiency, and infrastructure) and summarizes these measures in a World Competitive Score for each country.

Interim Summary

1. Government is a critical force impacting country competitiveness and can influence virtually all determinants discussed previously.

2. In order to improve country competitiveness, governments should be committed to upgrading competitiveness infrastructures, encouraging competition, enforcing strict product, safety, and environmental standards, and motivating firms and individuals for better innovation and creativity.

Rank	WEF: The Global Competitiveness Index 2013–2014	IMD: The World Competitiveness Scoreboard 2013
1	Switzerland	United States
2	Singapore	Switzerland
3	Finland	Hong Kong
4	Germany	Sweden
5	United States	Singapore
6	Sweden	Norway
7	Hong Kong	Canada
8	Netherlands	United Arab Emirates
9	Japan	Germany
10	United Kingdom	Qatar
11	Norway	Taiwan
12	Taiwan	Denmark
13	Qatar	Luxembourg
14	Canada	Netherlands
15	Denmark	Malaysia
16	Austria	Australia
17	Belgium	Ireland
18	New Zealand	United Kingdom
19	United Arab Emirates	Israel
20	Saudi Arabia	Finland
21	Australia	China
22	Luxembourg	Korea, Rep.
23	France	Austria
24	Malaysia	Japan
25	Korea, Rep.	New Zealand
26	Brunei Darussalam	Belgium
27	Israel	Thailand
28	Ireland	France
29	China	Iceland
30	Puerto Rico	Chile
31	Iceland	Lithuania
32	Estonia	Mexico
33	Oman	Poland
34	Chile	Kazakhstan
35	Spain	Czech Republic
36	Kuwait	Estonia
37	Thailand	Turkey
38	Indonesia	Philippines
39	Azerbaijan	Indonesia
40	Panama	India
41	Malta	Latvia
42	Poland	Russia
43	Bahrain	Peru
44	Turkey	Italy
45	Mauritius	Spain
46	Czech Republic	Portugal
47	Barbados	Slovak Republic
48	Lithuania	Colombia
49	Italy	Ukraine
50	Kazakhstan	Hungary

Exhibit 5.7 Top 50 countries ranked by their global competitiveness

Sources: World Economic Forum (WEF), *The Global Competiveness Reports 2013–2014,* Geneva, Switzerland, 2013; The International Institute for Management Development (IMD), *The World Competitiveness Yearbook,* Copyright © 2013, IMD, Switzerland, www.imd.org/wcc.

Chapter Summary

1. Country competitiveness is the extent to which a country is capable of generating more wealth than its competitors in world markets. The central force for improving country competitiveness is productivity. There are four levels of specific determinants of country competitiveness: country-level, industry-level, firm-level, and individual-level.

2. Country competitiveness can be analyzed by governments for consummating competitiveness infrastructures, by local firms for selecting a more favorable environment in which sustained competitive advantages can be developed, or by MNEs for electing optimal foreign locations and industries.

3. Country-level determinants of competitiveness comprise: (a) science, education, and innovation; (b) economic soundness; (c) finance; and (d) internationalization. These fundamentals are the cornerstone for economic development and the building blocks of macroeconomic business environment for country competitiveness.

4. Industry-level determinants of competitiveness comprise: (a) factor conditions; (b) demand conditions; (c) related and supporting industries; and (d) rivalry and business practice. They affect country competitiveness individually as well as collectively. MNEs operating in foreign countries are often impacted more directly by these industry-level determinants than by country-level determinants.

5. Firm-level determinants are country-unique organizational, technological, or operational strategies, policies, and practices employed by most firms in that nation. Country competitiveness can be partly explained by differences in national capabilities in terms of technologies and organizing principles (e.g., lean flexible production, total quality management, just-in-time manufacturing, and multi-sourcing strategy used by Japanese firms).

6. Individual-level determinants are human resources that shape the environment for developing competitiveness. Major players include workers, entrepreneurs, managers, engineers, educators, politicians, and government officials. Country competitiveness is positively correlated with the productivity or creativity of these individuals.

7. Governments significantly shape country competitiveness through industrial policies and the development of a competitiveness infrastructure. Governments should serve as catalysts in providing a stimulating environment for companies to gain a competitive advantage in international markets.

Notes

1 B. Ohlin, *Interregional and International Trade*, Cambridge, MA: Harvard University Press 1952; W. W. Leontief, "Domestic production and foreign trade: The American capital position reexamined," *Proceedings of the American Philosophical Society*, 1953.

2 X. Sala-i-Martin, *Global Competitiveness Report*, Geneva, Switzerland: World Economic Forum, 2011.

3 T. Branigan, "Chinese figures show fivefold rise in babies sick from contaminated milk," *Guardian*, December 2, 2008.

4 Economist, "Germany's economic model: What Germany offers the world," *The Economist*, April 14, 2012.

5 R.J. Shiller, *Irrational Exuberance* (2nd edn.), Princeton, NJ: Princeton University Press, 2005; P. Krugman, "Don't cry for me, America," *New York Times*, January 18, 2008; G. Tett, *Dumb Money: How Our Greatest Financial Minds Bankrupted the Nation*, New York: Free Press, 2009; S. Palan, *Bubbles and Crashes in Experimental Asset Markets*, New York: Springer, 2010; S. Hong and E. Fung, "China's central bank calls property market 'turning point'," *Wall Street Journal*, December 2, 2011.

6 *The Global Competitiveness Report 1999*, Geneva, Switzerland: World Economic Forum, 1999, 14–27.

7 T. Kamm, "Peru's top tax collector goes Rambo," *Wall Street Journal*, January 8, 1992; A. Granitsas and A. Ferliel, "Greece seeks ways to cut this year's budget deficit," *Wall Street Journal*, June 26, 2009; C. Crook, "To the intransigent go the spoils," *Financial Times*, July 31, 2011.

8 International Monetary Fund, World Economic Outlook, International Monetary Fund, April, 2012.

9 N. King Jr. and J.T. Areddy, "US urges Chinese to save less, buy more," *Wall Street Journal*, October 14, 2005.

10 M.E. Porter, *The Competitive Advantage of Nations*, New York: The Free Press, 1990; also see M.E. Porter, "The competitive advantage of nations," *Harvard Business Review,* March–April 1990, 73–93.

11 M.E. Porter, "The current competitiveness index: Measuring the microeconomic foundations of prosperity," *The Global Competitiveness Report 1999,* Geneva, Switzerland: World Economic Forum, 1999.

12 B. Kogut, "Country capabilities and the permeability of borders," *Strategic Management Journal,* 12 (summer special), 1991, 33–47.

13 D.S. Cho, "From national competitiveness to bloc and global competitiveness," *Competitiveness Review,* 8, 1, 1998, 11–23.

chapter 6

the cultural environment

WHAT IS CULTURE?	189
CULTURE AND INTERNATIONAL BUSINESS	189
NATIONAL CULTURE CLASSIFICATIONS	197
CORPORATE CULTURE	210
OTHER LAYERS OF CULTURE	210
KEY CULTURAL ISSUES	211

Do You Know?

1. Is it possible to define and measure culture?
2. What are the similarities and differences between "national culture," "industry culture," and "corporate culture"?
3. Does culture influence international investment and trade?
4. How does culture influence strategy? Does it have an impact on marketing, human resource management, and other functional areas?
5. Is it possible to measure differences between cultures? How and what are the potential pitfalls?

OPENING CASE Renault-Nissan Alliance

Founded in 1999, the Renault-Nissan Alliance is considered one of the most successful cross-border alliances among major car makers. This Franco-Japanese partnership achieved record sales of over seven million units as of 2013, and remains one of the leading auto groups in the world. Though first labeled "a marriage of desperation," the Renault-Nissan alliance fared much better than most other cross-border alliances in that sector, such as the one between Daimler and Mitsubishi.

Overall, research shows that well over 50 percent of cross-border alliances fail. The failures are caused, among other factors, by cross-cultural miscommunication, a lack of unified leadership and integration, and unfulfilled expectations. So why was the Renault-Nissan alliance successful? One reason was the cultural sensitivity that Renault's CEO Carlos Ghosn put into place. Ghosn, a Brazilian assigned by Renault to take over the top job at Nissan and now CEO of both companies, entered the Japanese workplace void of stereotypes and cultural chauvinism. His open-mindedness, coupled with his careful selection of key executives to work with the existing Japanese leadership team, was the first step in developing a cultural competency and composing a relationship that was mindful of the cultures of the two companies yet agile enough to address difficult business issues.

Source: "Renault Nissan Alliance facts and figures 2012-2013," Nissan Global; "THE RENAULT-NISSAN ALLIANCE," Renault; "International joint ventures in emerging economies: Past drivers and emerging trends," P. Morosini; "Nurturing successful alliances across boundaries," in O. Shenkar and J.J. Reuer, *Handbook of strategic alliances*, Thousand Oaks, CA: Sage, 2006.

As the opening case illustrates, cultural awareness is vital to the success of strategic alliances. Neither of the alliance partners was a particularly strong industrial competitor. Nissan was virtually bankrupt at the beginning of the union. Many observers feared a cultural clash between Renault and Nissan given their different national and corporate values and norms, but the two firms were able to turn this diversity into strength. Ghosn's ability to craft a culturally sensitive team has led to one of the most successful turnarounds in history. "It is important how you handle small frustrations. And when you have taken time to understand and accept that people don't think or act the same way in France or Japan, then the cultural differences can become seeds for innovation as opposed to seeds for dissention."[1]

What is Culture?

The *Oxford Encyclopedic English Dictionary* defines **culture** as *the art and other manifestations of human intellectual achievement regarded collectively; the customs, civilization, and achievement of a particular time or people; the way of life of a particular society or group.* Culture has been defined, however, in literally hundreds of ways[2]—a testament both to its importance and to its elusive and intangible nature. For example, anthropologists Melville Herskovits and Marvin Harris define culture as "the man-made part of the environment" and "the learned patterns of thought and behavior characteristic of a population or society," respectively. Samuel P. Huntington, a political scientist, distinguishes "culture" from "civilization"—both civilization and culture refer to a people's way of life, values, norms, and modes of thinking; however, a civilization is the broadest cultural entity.[3] Among modern management scholars, Geert Hofstede defines culture as "the collective programming of the human mind that distinguishes the members of one group or category of people from another."[4] Fons Trompenaars and Charles Hampden-Turner define culture as "the way in which people solve problems and recognize dilemmas."

Whitely and England synthesized more than 100 definitions of culture to arrive at this working definition, which we use in this book:[5] *The knowledge, beliefs, art, law, morals, customs and other capabilities of one group distinguishing it from other groups.*

Different definitions notwithstanding, there is a broad consensus regarding the main features of culture:

- *Culture is shared.* It is not an individual but rather a group property. Multiple group affiliations (e.g., with a nation, a firm) create multiple cultural memberships. Individuals vary, however, in the extent to which they adhere to cultural prescriptions.
- *Culture is intangible.* Culture is not only about "things," like products or customs, but about meanings, which are not very visible; thus, many aspects of culture must be inferred.[6]
- *Culture is confirmed by others.* To understand a culture, you need to step back and observe it from the outside. This is why the most astute observers of a given culture are often members of another.

Culture and International Business

The importance of culture to international business cannot be overstated. For instance, cultural differences are a key ingredient in the "liability of foreignness," a set of obstacles interfering with a MNE's success abroad. The impact of culture at the firm level ranges from strategy formulation, to FDI and organization design.[7] Culture not only influences how strategic moves are presented, but it can also impact the decisions themselves. Organization behavior processes such as perception, motivation, communication, and leadership, as well as human resource management, are all influenced by culture, as are management styles, decision making, and negotiations. Not surprisingly, a majority of the articles on international organization behavior and international human resource management include culture as a relevant variable.[8] As you will discover throughout this book, the impact of culture is not limited to management. Marketing, supply chain management (see Chapter 16), accounting, finance, taxation (see Chapter 15), and virtually all other business functions are influenced by culture. Culture also plays a key role in international alliances and mergers, and has been found to correlate with corruption and entrepreneurial behavior (see Chapters 12, 19, and 20), among many other business phenomena.

According to Huntington, the role of culture will not be reduced in the global era; on the contrary:[9]

> In this new world the most pervasive, important and dangerous conflicts will not be between social classes, rich and poor, or other economically defined groups, but between people belonging to different cultural entities.

Culture, says Huntington, "is both a divisive and a unifying force." It is a force of cohesion among members, but a source of friction between them and others. Culture can also be a source of internal friction, where strict adherents struggle with others whom they see as betraying or straying from the cultural heritage. Often, cultural imports such as movies and TV programs are a subject of contention in such disputes.

Culture Does Not Explain Everything

Although we should not ignore the important role culture plays in the business world, we should not commit the opposite error of treating culture as a "residual variable," namely as the explanation for everything that is different. For instance, uncertainty of what drives the strategy of a foreign competitor makes it tempting to conclude that culture is behind it. But the strategy could well be the result of other factors, be they economic, political, social, or firm-level variables. The ascent of Japan and eventually China, as well as the rise of the "four tigers" of Taiwan, Korea, Hong Kong, and Singapore, was attributed by many to Confucian values of frugality and discipline. However, the best-sellers that drove this explanation have failed to note that Confucianism also contains elements that can be considered negative to progress, such as support for the status quo and low regard for economic activity. As for the Japanese, many of them overplayed the role of culture in their economic success and as a result failed to make the governance and structural changes that could have salvaged Japan from decades of stagnation.

A useful strategy with which to isolate the impact of culture, as opposed to other environmental variables, is to compare native and bicultural groupings. Kelley and his associates compared Japanese-Americans with Anglo-Americans and Japanese managers, to gauge whether differences in management styles and the like were the result of national origin or the current national environment. The authors also compared Japanese, Chinese, and Mexican managers with their ethnic American counterparts (Japanese-Americans, Chinese-Americans, and Mexican-Americans).[10] Another strategy has been used by Shenkar and Ronen, who compared managerial values in Mainland China,

Hong Kong, Taiwan, and Singapore, so as to isolate the role of culture from that of political, economic, and social variables.[11]

Correlates of Culture

Culture is correlated with other variables that vary cross-nationally (e.g., language and religion). It is useful to remember, however, that culture often cuts across linguistic and religious boundaries, and that the latter cut across national borders. For example, Switzerland, Belgium, Singapore, Israel, and Nigeria are all countries with multiple official languages. South Korea has a large Christian minority (although this does not necessarily imply that this minority has developed a meaningful subculture), while upward of 8 percent of French citizens are Muslims. Lebanon has a large Christian minority, while Northern Ireland has both Protestant and Catholic communities.

Language

Webster's Dictionary definition of **language** is "a systematic means of communicating ideas or feelings by the use of conventionalized signs, gestures, marks, or especially articulate vocal sounds." Language is one of the defining expressions of culture. It instills basic socialization themes and determines how values and norms are expressed and communicated. Just as culture is both a unifying and dividing force, so is language. Exhibits 6.1 and 6.2 show the major families of languages and the number of speakers in the most commonly spoken languages.

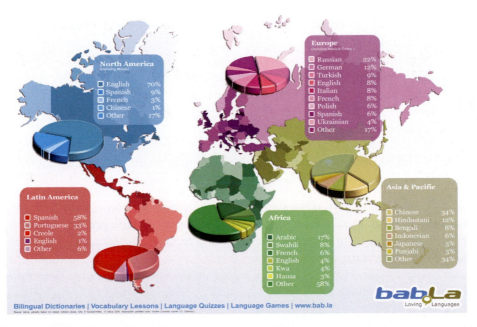

Exhibit 6.1 Languages of the world
Source: bab.la primarily based on various census data and Eurobarometer. @bab.la. Reproduction permitted under Creative Commons License 3.0 (Germany).

Language Family	Living Languages		Number of Speakers			
	Count	Percent	Total	Percent	Mean	Median
Afro-Asiatic	366	5.15	362,281,758	5.81	989,841	23,000
Austronesian	1,221	17.19	345,818,471	5.55	283,226	3,640
Indo-European	436	6.14	2,916,732,355	46.77	6,689,753	139,000
Niger-Congo	1,524	21.45	430,784,205	6.91	282,667	28,000
Sino-Tibetan	456	6.42	1,268,209,279	20.34	2,781,161	15,000
Trans-New Guinea	475	6.69	3,536,267	0.06	7,445	1,500
Totals	4,478	63.03	5,327,362,335	85.42		

Exhibit 6.2 Major language families of the world

Source: Adapted from M. Paul Lewis, Gary F. Simons, and Charles D. Fennig (eds), 2013. *Ethnologue: Languages of the World*, 17th edn, Dallas, Texas: SIL International. Online version: http://www.ethnologue.com.

Because of fundamental differences between languages in structure, grammar, and in the usage of slang and dialects, language blunders are common. Such mistakes as launching a hair product by the name of "Mist Stick" in Germany, where "mist" is slang for *manure*, are humorous, but the consequences for the manufacturer may be dire. Coca-Cola was originally translated into Chinese as "bite the wax tadpole," only to be outdone by Pepsi, whose jingle "(Pepsi) comes alive" was translated into "brings your ancestors from their burial place" (especially insulting in a country where ancestors are often worshipped). Name evaluation, where native speakers get an opportunity to comment on the proposed product or service name prior to its launch, is a simple way to mitigate the problem.

Differences in grammatical and structural format produce radically different types of discourse between languages. For instance, in contrast to the preference for subject-predicate format in English and other European languages, most Chinese utterances are of the topic-comment type. This means that the topic precedes the comment. Young's recording of a budget meeting illustrates the point (literal translation from the Chinese original):[12]

Chairman: So by purchasing the new machine, do you think we need to recruit additional workers or our existing workforce will cope with our requirement?

Subordinate: I think that with this new machine, the production time will be shortened or will become more efficient. And the number of staff required, I think we can utilize the existing staff for the time being, and no more new staff is necessary. So that we can solve the problem in recruiting the new staff.

And, again in the following example:

One thing I would like to ask. Because most of our raw materials are coming from Japan and this year is going up and up and uh it's not really I think an increase in price but uh we lose a lot in exchange rate and secondly I understand we've spent a lot of money in TV ad last year. So, in that case I would like to suggest here: chop half of the budget in TV ads and spend a little money on Mad Magazine.

Note that the "punch line" does not appear until the end, which is typical of Chinese discourse. This is contrary to Western discourse that tends to start with a preview statement providing tone and direction for the rest of the conversation. Young notes that the main points were often lost on native English speakers listening to these examples. This explains why patience and listening skills are promoted as key communications and negotiation skills with Chinese. Listening patiently is especially critical because the most important points will come at the end rather than at the beginning of a conversation.

Finally, non-verbal language is an important means of communication that varies across languages and cultures and is more important in some cultures than in others. Variations in the meaning of non-verbal cues may lead to embarrassing gaffes. For instance, in Chinese culture, it is customary for an individual to point to something using their lips or their chin. In a Western setting, this could be taken humorously, resulting in an unfortunate mishap. Likewise, in Korea, the Western gesture of signaling someone to come close is reserved for pets, and may therefore be deemed insulting.

THE EMERGENCE OF ENGLISH AS "LINGUA FRANCA" The term **lingua franca** comes from the Franks, people originating in southern France who traded with other people in the Mediterranean who spoke a variety of languages—Arabic, Italian, Greek, Spanish, and Portuguese. The Franks developed a language that was a mixture of the preceding languages and which became the language of commerce in the Mediterranean. Today, the term *lingua franca* denotes any language shared by people of different national and linguistic origins.

English has become the business world's *lingua franca*, the number-one foreign language taught in non-English-speaking countries. Germans and French speakers are more likely to converse with each other in English than they are in each other's language. Only 20 percent or so of Germans learn French as a foreign language, whereas roughly 60 percent choose English. This is resented in some countries as "cultural imperialism." France is an example. In 1975, the country banned the use of foreign words in commercials, as well as in TV and radio broadcasts. In 1992, the constitution was amended to declare French the official language, and in 1994, the use of foreign words was banned. In Quebec, a province of Canada with a French majority, these laws are still in force. In 2013, a nightclub was cited by a language inspector for using the word "pasta" on its otherwise French menu.[13]

The dominance of English does not imply that knowledge of other languages is not necessary. On the contrary, knowledge of foreign languages is often viewed as a distinct advantage. Much has been said of the advantage enjoyed by Europeans who typically master at least one foreign language, as compared to the limited foreign language knowledge of Americans. Yet, some parts of the United States are different thanks to a diverse population or other factors. Utah has become attractive to international firms because of the abundance of residents who have learned foreign languages on missionary trips abroad. Moncton in New Brunswick, Canada has become the call center of choice in Canada because it enjoys bilingual (English and French) fluency, while Canada's Maritime Provinces attract US firms with the "neutral accent of their residents."[14] However, multilingualism also has its drawbacks. Multilingual states such as Belgium (which has a Flemish population who speak a Dutch dialect, and a Walloon population who speak French) and Canada are often ripe for tension and conflict. Indeed, there tends to be a correlation between multilingualism and political risk.

While English is a *lingua franca*, its adoption might have a symbolic and even a strategic meaning. When Korean car manufacturer Daewoo Motor was acquired by General Motors, the Korean executives quickly embarked on the study of English, figuring that this will now be the enterprise's working language.[15] The adoption of English as a working language in an Italian-British joint venture helped the British executives gain the upper hand because it meant adopting their working routines.[16] And English is not the only language vying for international acceptance: recently, the Chinese government has embarked on an effort to expand the study of Chinese as a foreign language, joining France and Germany, among others, who have already established cultural centers around the world devised, among other roles, to spread their native language around the globe.

Religion

Religion embeds key values and norms that are reflected in an adherent's way of life. Its impact extends to the secular segment of the population, albeit to a lesser extent. Globally, Christianity claims the most adherents, while Islam is the fastest growing. De Blij and Murphy call both, together with Buddhism, "global religions," whereas religions that dominate a single nation are labeled "cultural religions" (see Exhibit 6.3).

Religion influences international business in multiple ways. National government and business firms seek to adopt practices that will satisfy religious decrees and expectations without undermining modern business practice. For instance, because bank interest is generally prohibited under Islamic law, banks in Muslim countries issue shares to depositors and charge borrowers fees and commissions to maintain profitability without charging interest. Increasingly, products consistent with Islamic practice are also offered by non-Islamic banks. Religion and its associated customs also influence marketing. In China, birth rates tend to rise during the Year of the Dragon in the Chinese 12-year calendar, creating opportunities for manufacturers of children's clothes and toys. In Muslim countries from Saudi Arabia to Indonesia, believers do not eat during daylight hours during the month of Ramadan, curtailing lunch business at restaurants, but creating opportunities for traditional buffet dinners after dark.

Interim Summary

1. Culture plays an important role in international business. Culture affects not only how employees behave and interact, but also the strategy that firms and business units develop and employ.
2. Language and religion often create communication and coordination challenges within the MNE, but cultural diversity is also a source of strength because it brings about different and new opinions and perspectives that the firm can benefit from.

	Judaism	Christianity	Islam	Hinduism	Buddhism	Daoism (Taoism)	Atheism and Agnosticism
Founder	The Hebrew leader Abraham founded Judaism around 2000 BCE. Moses gave the Jews the Torah around 1250 BCE.	Jesus Christ, who was born shortly before the start of the common era and crucified around 30 CE in Jerusalem.	Muhammad, who was born in 570 CE at Mecca, in Saudi Arabia.	Hinduism has no founder. It is the oldest religion still practiced today, possibly started in prehistoric times.	Siddhartha Gautama (born a high-cast Hindu), called the Buddha, in the 4th or 5th century BCE in India.	Loazi (Lao Tzu), who may have lived around 500 BCE, is traditionally regarded as the founder.	No specific founder.
Number of Gods	One	One	One	Many gods and goddesses that are all considered different forms of one Supreme Being.	None, but there are enlightened beings (Buddhas) that are worshiped as deities.	Many mythical and historical figures, such as the Jade Emperor and Laozi, are deified as objects of worship.	None
Sacred Writings	The most important are the Torah. Others include Judaism's oral tradition, the written form of which is known as the Talmud.	The main sacred text is the Bible, which consists of the Old Testament (with Judaism's Torah as its first five books) and New Testament.	The Koran is the sacred book of Islam, which has references both the Torah and the New Testament of the Bible.	The most ancient are the four Vedas: Rigveda, Sāmaveda, Yajurveda, and Atharvaveda.	The most important are the Tripitaka, the Mahayana Sutras, Tantra, and Zen texts.	Daodejing (Laozi or Lao-tzu), Zhuangzi (Chuang-tzu), and Yijing (I Ching) and the most important texts.	None
Main Beliefs	Jews believe in the laws of God and the words of the prophets. In Judaism, however, actions are more important than beliefs.	Jesus Christ is the Messiah promised in the Old Testament and the Son of God, sent to Earth by God to save humanity. The Christian belief in one God involves three elements: God the Father, God the Son, and the Holy Spirit.	The Five Pillars, or main duties, are: (1) profession of faith; (2) prayer; (3) charitable giving; (4) fasting during the month of Ramadan; and (5) pilgrimage to Mecca at least once.	Reincarnation states that all living things are caught in a cycle of death and rebirth. Life is ruled by the laws of karma, in which rebirth depends on moral behavior.	The Four Noble Truths: (1) all beings suffer; (2) desire—for possessions, power, and so on—causes suffering; (3) desire can be overcome; and (4) the path that leads away from desire is the Eightfold Path (the Middle Way). Similar to Hinduism, Buddhism also believes in reincarnation.	Key concepts include Dao or Tao (the path or the way), Yin and Yang (opposite but interdependent forces) and Wu Wei (inaction or refrain from action). Emphasis is on acting in harmony with Dao or the law of nature, which is done by behaving morally or ethically.	Lack of belief in any deity. Such a worldview has existed since the Verdic era (1700–1100 BCE) in India but spread more widely since the Renaissance era (14th to 17th century) in Europe.

Exhibit 6.3 Major religions of the world

Source: Adapted from *Major religions of the world* by Pearson Education (2007) and *World of Religion* by National Post (2012).

	Judaism	Christianity	Islam	Hinduism	Buddhism	Daoism (Taoism)	Atheism and Agnosticism
Types or Sects	The three main types are Orthodox, Conservative, and Reform. Conservative Jews follow most traditional practices, but less strictly than the Orthodox. Reform Jews are the least traditional.	In 1054 Christians separated into the Eastern Orthodox Church and the Roman Catholic Church. In the early 1500s the major Protestant groups (Lutheran, Presbyterian, and Episcopalian) came into being. A variety of other groups have since developed.	Almost 90% of Muslims are Sunnis. Shiites are the second-largest group. The Shiites split from the Sunnis in 632 when Muhammad died.	No single belief system unites Hindus. A Hindu can believe in only one god, in many, or in none. The oldest sect—the Shaivites—considers the deity Shiva as the supreme being. The largest sect—the Vaishnavites—considers Lord Vishnu as the supreme deity.	Theravada (Way of the Elders) and Mahayana (Greater Vehicle) are the two main sects. Lamaism (Tibetan Buddhism) is derived from Mahayana and the ancient Tibetan religion of Bönism.	Major sects are Quanzhen (Completely Real) and Zhengyi (Orthodox Unity). Daoist concepts are integrated into Neo-Confucianism and also influenced other religious of East Asia (e.g., Japanese Shinto and Vietnamese folk religions).	Atheism rejects belief in any kind of deity. Agnosticism believes that it is impossible to know the truth of religious and metaphysical claims, particularly those of the existence of a deity.
Number of Adherents	14,900,000	1,957,100,000	1,070,450,000	832,000,000	329,000,000	500,000,000	1,100,000,000
Geographic Spread	There are large Jewish populations in Israel and the US.	Through its missionary activity, Christianity has spread to most parts of the globe.	Islam is the main religion of the Middle East, North Africa, and parts of Central, South, and Southeast Asia.	Hinduism is practiced by more than 80% of India's population.	Buddhism is a dominant religion in many countries in East, Southeast, and South Asia.	Predominantly in East and Southeast Asia, but also spread to Western countries.	Present in all regions of the world, but more concentrated in East Asia and Central and Western Europe.

Exhibit 6.3 (Continued)

National Culture Classifications

To international business scholars and practitioners, nation is the most visible layer of culture. This is not to say that culture and nation are synonymous—cultural and national boundaries overlap only partially—but the national unit represents a convenient way of assessing culture together with other environmental sectors such as the economic and the political. Nations also diffuse and reinforce what they see, or aspire to see, as the national culture.

National cultures have been viewed and measured via a number of classifications, each of which identifies a set of distinct dimensions. The following are the key classifications of national culture.

Hofstede's Dimensions of Culture

By far the most used (and, some would say, abused) work on culture is that of Geert Hofstede, who studied more than 100,000 IBM employees in the company's subsidiaries around the world.[17] The study, controlling for employee function and level, was also noteworthy for its attempt to correlate its findings with a host of other political predictors (e.g., climate). Hofstede's survey yielded four underlying dimensions: power distance, uncertainty avoidance, individualism/collectivism, and masculinity/femininity. A fifth dimension, long-term orientation, has been added later.

Power Distance (PD)

Power Distance (PD) is the extent to which the less powerful members of institutions and organizations within a country expect and accept that power is distributed unequally.[18] PD should not be confused with the actual distribution of wealth and power in a nation. For instance, Israel is very low on the power distance scale, although its income inequality is among the highest in the developed world. In contrast, Japan is relatively egalitarian in terms of wealth and income distribution (though this is changing, and some Japanese already describe Japan's "middle-class society" as a myth) yet scores relatively high on power distance. Exhibit 6.4 shows countries that are high or low on power distance, and some of the organizational ramifications of this cultural dimension.

Uncertainty Avoidance (UA)

Uncertainty Avoidance (UA) refers to the extent to which uncertainty and ambiguity are tolerated. Exhibit 6.5 includes country examples and organizational implications of uncertainty avoidance. Japan's high score on uncertainty avoidance (seventh highest on Hofstede's list) is reflected in the attempt to standardize behavior and rules, as in the following example:

> *The design and construction of Japanese parks is highly regulated. The rules cover not only how many trees each park must contain, but how many of them must be small, medium-sized and large, and at what density they should be planted.*[19]

197

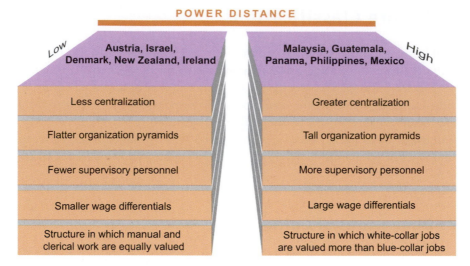

POWER DISTANCE

Low — Austria, Israel, Denmark, New Zealand, Ireland	High — Malaysia, Guatemala, Panama, Philippines, Mexico
Less centralization	Greater centralization
Flatter organization pyramids	Tall organization pyramids
Fewer supervisory personnel	More supervisory personnel
Smaller wage differentials	Large wage differentials
Structure in which manual and clerical work are equally valued	Structure in which white-collar jobs are valued more than blue-collar jobs

Exhibit 6.4 Power distance: Country examples and organizational implications
Source: Adapted from G. Hofstede, *Culture's Consequences*, 1980 and 2001.

Country Box

Toyota

A Shift in Toyota's Corporate Culture

In 2010, the Japanese automotive giant made ¥18,950,973 million in net revenues, but this did not come without several setbacks. In 2005, the auto maker recalled roughly 900,000 vehicles regarding a steering issue. In 2009, it recalled 3.8 million vehicles in the United States due to a safety issue regarding the floor mats and sticking accelerator pedals. In 2010, Toyota announced another recall of 2.3 million automobiles. The enormous number of recalls was an issue that Toyota president Akio Toyoda did not take lightly. He appeared in Washington before a House committee to assure the public that the corporation was putting most of its efforts into quality control.

Toyota then ventured on a journey to comprehensive cultural reform. First, the organization appointed key executives in each world region to monitor quality. In the US, Toyota broadly enhanced its lines of communication between Japanese engineers and North American executives. This restored collaboration and fostered greater accountability within the company, leading to similar recalls in Japan, where transparency was previously less valued. In addition, the company made significant changes to its organizational practices surrounding decision making, combining the Japanese cultural custom of consensus decision making with Western-style individual accountability, seeking to become the world's leading auto maker. Combining the best of world cultures with its Japanese heritage is one of Toyota's primary challenges.

Sources: M. Maynard, "At Toyota, a cultural shift," *New York Times*, June 2, 2010; Toyota Motor Company, 2012 Annual Report, consolidated performance highlights; "Toyota recall 2010: More than 2 million cars recalled due to gas pedals issue," *Huffington Post*, March 23, 2010; K. Thomas, "Toyota, Lexus mat recall: 3.8 million vehicles recalled over floor mats," *Huffington Post*, September 29, 2009.

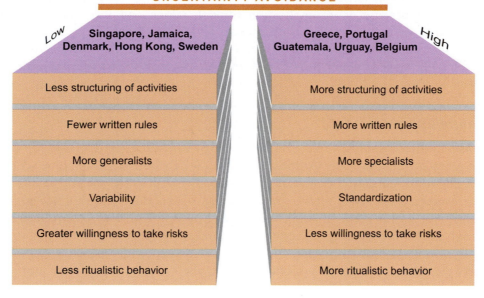

Exhibit 6.5 Uncertainty avoidance: Country examples and organizational implications
Source: Adapted from G. Hofstede, *Culture's Consequences*, 1980 and 2001.

Recognizing the Highest Ranked

- His business card will generally be presented by a subordinate. Sometimes he will not even carry a card.
- He drinks his tea first.
- He speaks last.
- He sits the farthest to the rear.
- He speaks the least.
- No one minds if he nods off.
- Climbing stairs, the highest ranked walks last.
- Coming down, he walks first.

Recognizing Rank by Car Manners

- The highest ranked sits deepest in the back seat.
- When the owner is driving, the highest ranked sits in the passenger's seat.
- More recently, he rides where it is easiest to get in and out.
- If the owner's wife is along, she sits in the passenger's seat.

Exhibit 6.6 Rank distinctions among the Japanese
Source: Japan External Trade Organization.

Hofstede believes that uncertainty avoidance is probably the most critical dimension for foreign investment because of its implication for risk taking and investment. For instance, MNEs from cultures high on uncertainty avoidance are likely to take a more incremental approach to internationalization (e.g., be late entrants: Japanese car manufacturers such as Nissan and Mazda lagged behind their European and US counterparts in establishing production facilities in China).

Individualism/Collectivism (I/C)

Individualism/Collectivism (I/C) refers to the extent to which the self or the group constitutes the center point of identification for the individual (See Exhibit 6.7). To some scholars, this is the most important dimension of culture. High collectivism does not mean that individuals do not seek self-interest. Rather, it means that the pursuit is conducted within acceptable group frameworks, with group norms guiding individual behavior and with group harmony being an important endeavor. In highly collectivistic cultures, preference is given to group members (e.g., family members, friends), whereas outsiders are treated with suspicion. Gannon distinguishes between different types of collectivism (e.g., the Chinese family altar and the Israeli kibbutz).[20]

McClelland used children's literature to study national cultures. He assumed that such literature can help us learn about the patterns of acculturation—the process by which the basic values of culture are instilled into its members. The following illustration, taken from a Chinese children's book, shows how collectivism is woven into a story:

"What are you looking for, Mom?"
"A sweater for you to take to kindergarten. It may be windy today."
"Two new friends have come to our class . . . They won't know about the wind."
Mom nods and smiles. She puts three sweaters in Qin's satchel.
"Good child," says the teacher. "So little, but you already know about helping others."[21]

Exhibit 6.7 Individualism/collectivism: Country examples and organizational implications
Source: Adapted from G. Hofstede, *Culture's Consequences*, 1980 and 2001.

MNEs from highly collectivistic cultures (e.g., Taiwan's Acer) tend to be more paternalistic. For instance, they are less likely to lay off employees during a downturn. However, such protection does not always extend to overseas subsidiaries.

Masculinity/Femininity (M/F)

Masculinity/Femininity (M/F) describes the extent to which traditional masculine values such as aggressiveness and assertiveness are emphasized. MNEs from feministic cultures (e.g., a car maker such as Volvo (now owned by China's Geely Automobile Holdings)) tend to emphasize social rewards and benefits in the workplace that are sometimes viewed as excessive by parent firms who hail from high masculinity countries. As with other dimensions of culture, this dimension has implications in various functional domains (See Exhibit 6.8). De Mooij found that masculinity/femininity explained differences in consumer behavior. For example, consumers in feminine European cultures preferred coupé cars in 1990 and hatchbacks in 1996.[22]

Long-Term Orientation (LTO)

Originally termed "**Confucian Dynamism,**" this dimension was renamed "**long-term orientation (LTO)**" to connote its underlying meaning and business ramifications. The LTO dimension represents such values as thrift and persistence, as well as traditional respect for social obligations. In high LTO cultures, organizations are more likely to adopt a longer planning horizon, with individuals ready to delay gratification. MNEs that hail from such cultures are more likely to defer return on investment for the sake of long-term return. This tendency, however, has often led to a

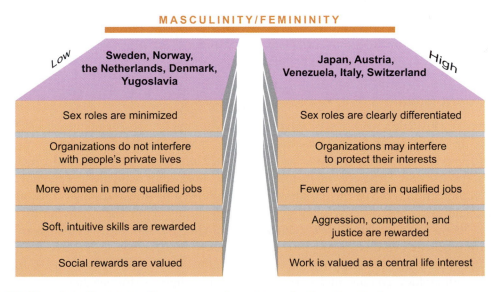

Exhibit 6.8 Masculinity/femininity: Country examples and organizational implications
Source: Adapted from G. Hofstede, *Culture's Consequences*, 1980 and 2001.

Exhibit 6.9 Long-term orientation (LTO): Country examples and organizational implications
Source: Adapted from G. Hofstede, *Culture's Consequences*, 2001.

disregard for basic principles of economic cost/benefit, as in the case of Korean conglomerates prior to the Asian financial crisis. Firms from high LTO cultures may also find it difficult to operate in a way that challenges deeply rooted traditions and practices.

The LTO is *not* one of the original dimensions unveiled in Hofstede's 1980 book. Rather, it is the result of his cooperation with Michael Bond and his associates (known as The Chinese Cultural Connection) who developed the **Chinese Values Survey (CVS)**. The dimension was identified via an innovative technique: A group of Chinese social scientists was asked to name at least ten "fundamental and basic values for Chinese people." Supplemented by readings of Chinese philosophy and social science, this produced a list of 40 values that made up the survey. The survey was then distributed to students in 22 countries. Countries like China, Taiwan, Japan, and South Korea had high LTO scores, while Nigeria, Canada, and Pakistan had very low scores. Exhibit 6.9 shows countries high or low on long-term orientation, and some of its organizational ramifications. A full list of rankings may be found in Exhibit 6.10.

Criticism of Hofstede

Over the years, Hofstede's work has received considerable support. Hofstede himself has replicated his original IBM surveys in other firms and expanded it with information from more countries. Sondergrad[23] reviewed the empirical studies which used Hofstede's framework and concluded that Hofstede's results were generally confirmed and the dimensions validated. The individualism/collectivism dimension received the broadest support, followed by power distance, then uncertainty avoidance, and lastly masculinity/femininity. Hoppe replicated Hofstede's masculinity/femininity dimension among business elites in 19 countries, and obtained a rank order that was strongly correlated with Hofstede's results.[24]

Still, in recent years, Hofstede's work has come under growing criticism, with his measures, data, and methodology coming under attack for lacking rigor or for misdirected analysis. For instance, Michael Bond suggested that a rigorous analysis would not have shown the United States and Japan being on the opposite side of the individualism/collectivism dimension.[25]

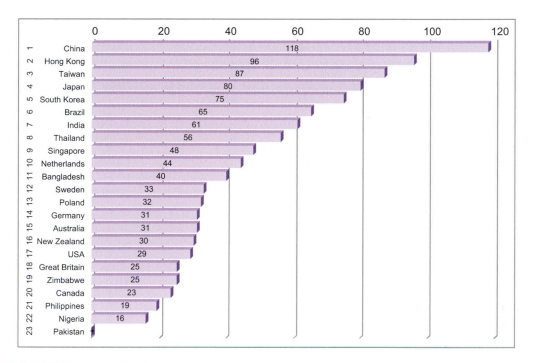

Exhibit 6.10 LTO score ranking by country

Source: Geert Hofstede, Gert Jan Hofstede, and Michael Minkov, *Cultures and Organizations: Software of the Mind* (revised and expanded 3rd edn), New York: McGraw-Hill, 2010.

Schwartz's Classification

Originating in psychology, this framework has been used to a limited extent in the business literature, but it is now becoming more popular. Schwartz arrived at his classification by a conceptualization of values prior to their sampling and measurement. His data is more recent than Hofstede's, having been collected in the 1980s and 1990s, though it has also been updated since. Schwartz and his colleagues have collected data on a fairly large number of countries (including sub-regions).[26]

Schwartz and his associates identify three polar dimensions of culture, producing the following dimensions:

I. *Embeddedness versus Autonomy*
    (1) Embeddedness (conservatism) implies emphasis on social relationships and tradition.
    (2) Autonomy implies finding meaning in one's own uniqueness and being encouraged to express one's own attributes. There are two kinds of autonomy:
    (a) Intellectual autonomy—self-direction, creativity
    (b) Affective autonomy—the pursuit of stimulation and hedonism.

II. *Hierarchy versus Egalitarianism*

    (3) Hierarchy means legitimacy of hierarchical role and resource allocation

    (4) Egalitarianism means transcendence of self-interests and promoting others' welfare.

III. *Mastery versus Harmony*

    (5) Mastery implies mastering the social environment via self-assertion (success, ambition)

    (6) Harmony implies being "at peace" with nature and society. Organizations are viewed as part of the broader social system.

Exhibit 6.11 presents some examples of countries that are very high or very low on Schwartz's dimensions in comparison to Hofstede's. Individualism (IDV) and Power Distance (PDI) are attributed

Table 1 Scores for the 20 countries in the Hofstede and Schwartz dimensions

	MODELS			
	Hofstede		**Schwartz**	
Country	**IDV**	**DPO**	**AUT**	**CON**
Germany	67 (8)	35 (15)	4.31 (4)	3.50 (16)
Australia	90 (2)	36 (14)	3.81 (13)	4.06 (5)
Brazil	38 (13)	69 (3)	3.72 (16)	3.97 (8)
Denmark	74 (5)	18 (19)	4.30 (5)	3.64 (15)
Spain	51 (11)	57 (10)	4.44 (3)	3.42 (17)
United States	91 (1)	40 (13)	3.93 (10)	3.90 (9)
Finland	63 (9)	33 (17)	4.06 (8)	3.84 (11)
France	71 (6)	68 (5)	4.78 (2)	3.35 (19)
Greece	35 (15)	60 (9)	4.03 (9)	3.68 (14)
Hong Kong	25 (18)	68 (4)	3.60 (19)	4.04 (6)
Israel	54 (10)	13 (20)	3.75 (15)	4.36 (2)
Italy	76 (4)	50 (12)	3. 78 (14)	3.82 (12)
Japan	46 (12)	54 (II)	4.11 (7)	3.87 (10)
Mexico	30 (16)	81 (1)	3.72 (17)	4.03 (7)
New Zealand	79 (3)	22 (18)	4.17 (6)	3.73 (13)
Portugal	27 (17)	63 (8)	3.83 (12)	3.36 (18)
Singapore	20 (20)	74 (2)	3.36 (20)	4.38 (1)
Switzerland	68 (7)	34 (16)	4.79 (1)	3.25 (20)
Thailand	20 (19)	64 (7)	3.8-(II)	4.22 (4)
Turkey	37 (14)	66 (6)	3.69 (18)	4.27 (3)
Mean	53.1	50.2	4.0	3.8
Standard deviation	23.32	19.96	.38	.34

Exhibit 6.11 Hofstede and Schwartz dimension comparisons

Source: Adapted from V.V. Gouveia and M. Ros, "Hofstede and Schwartz's models for classifying individualism at the cultural level: their relation to macro-social and macro-economic variables," *Psicothema* 12.Suplemento (2000), 28.

to Hofstede, while Autonomy (Affective and Intellectual) (AUT) and Conservation (CON) are attributed to Schwartz.[27]

You will notice that there is a partial overlap between Schwartz's classification and that of Hofstede. For instance, autonomy in Schwartz's model is close to Hofstede's individualism/collectivism dimension, whereas hierarchy is similar to Hofstede's power distance. Mastery is close to masculinity in that both emphasize goal achievement. Harmony is relatively similar to uncertainty avoidance; Schwartz found positive correlation between them. Egalitarian commitment overlaps with femininity; a positive correlation was found between the two.

The GLOBE Classification

The GLOBE classification was originally devised to measure perceptions and attitudes vis-à-vis organizational leadership, but later become a way to broadly conceptualize and measure cross-national differences in culture. Data were collected by a large group of researchers between 1994 and 1997. GLOBE has classified cultures according to their scores on nine cultural dimensions: future orientation, gender equality, assertiveness, humane orientation, in-group collectivism, performance orientation, power distance, and uncertainty avoidance. Here too you will note the partial overlap with Hofstede's dimensions. Leadership behavior was classified separately, according to six dimensions: charismatic value based, team oriented, participative, humane oriented, autonomous, and self-protective.[28] The GLOBE framework has been used in a number of subsequent studies, most often in the "micro" area (i.e., motivation, leadership, and the like).

Trompenaars and Hampden–Turner's Classification

This classification found followers especially in the practitioner community, but it has not been often applied in scholarly studies. The classification consists of seven dimensions drawn largely from previous literature, in particular work by the eminent sociologist Talcott Parsons, but validated, according to the authors, by large-scale practitioner surveys.

- *Universalism versus particularism* (rules versus relationships): In universal cultures, rules are assumed to apply in all situations and legal solutions are prominent. Countries high on universalism include the United States, Canada, the United Kingdom, the Netherlands, Germany, and the Scandinavian countries. Cultures high on particularism (e.g., Arab) typically provide more benefits to employees in return for commitment.
- *Communitarianism versus individualism* (the group versus the individual): In individualistic cultures, people see themselves primarily as individuals, whereas in communal cultures they see themselves as members of a group. Among the countries high on individualism are Israel, Canada, Nigeria, Romania, the United States, the Czech Republic, and Denmark. Countries high on communitarianism include Egypt, Nepal, Mexico, India, and Japan.
- *Neutral versus emotional*: In neutral cultures, interactions are impersonal and objective; in emotional cultures, they are laden with emotions. Countries high on neutral expression include Ethiopia, Japan, Poland, and New Zealand; they prefer indirect, non-confrontational response, and

205

emphasize control. Countries high on emotional expression include Kuwait, Egypt, Oman, and Spain; they prefer direct, emotional response, and avoid social distance.

■ *Diffuse versus specific*: Countries high on diffuse involvement include Japan, Mexico, and France; such cultures make no clear separation between different life domains. Response is situational, depending on the person and other circumstances. In specific cultures, interaction is confined to a narrow domain, and private life is kept separate from work. Countries high on specific involvement— the United States and Germany—allow outspoken expression and encourage transparency.

■ *Achievement versus ascription*: In achievement cultures, status is based on achievement and people are evaluated by performance. In ascriptive cultures, status is bestowed by birth, kinship, and age. Countries high on achievement—the United States and Canada—permit individuals to make commitments in the name of their company, and make use of detailed technical data to support their position. Countries high on ascription—Kuwait and Saudi Arabia—make ample use of titles and show respect for superiors.

■ *Attitudes to time*: Countries emphasizing the short term—the United States, Ireland, and Brazil— plan for a shorter time horizon than countries with long time horizons (e.g., Portugal and Pakistan). Countries with orientation toward the past—Hong Kong, Israel, and China—emphasize heritage and reputation more than the present or future. Countries with sequential time perception, such as the United States, adhere to planning more than those with synchronic culture, such as Italy and Spain.

■ *Attitudes toward the environment*: Countries geared toward controlling the environment, such as the United States, Israel, and Spain, appreciate control and dominance, whereas countries not geared toward that control (e.g., Venezuela, Nepal, and Russia) accept that many life events cannot be controlled.

Trompenaars and Hampden-Turner's classification also bears partial resemblance to Hofstede's model. The long- versus short-term orientation is similar to the fifth dimension (LTO) in Hofstede's model. The communitarianism versus individualism dimension is similar to Hofstede's collectivism versus individualism. There is no equivalent in Hofstede's scheme to the specific/diffuse dimension; however, in individualistic cultures interpersonal relationships tend to be more specific, whereas in collectivist cultures they tend to be diffuse. Achievement versus ascription has no direct match in Hofstede's model; however, people with achievement orientation are likely to emphasize success and goal attainment, whereas high-power-distance cultures are more likely to contain ascriptive assumptions.

Other Dimensions of Culture

The classifications presented here do not cover all aspects of culture. For instance, Hall distinguishes between "high-context" and "low-context" cultures. High-context cultures such as Japan underplay verbal communications, prefer a strong leader, and have a polychromatic perception of time (i.e., they will handle various issues and groups at the same time). In contrast, low-context cultures, such as the United States, have a monochronic time perspective (i.e., they usually attend to various issues sequentially).[29] Overall, it remains difficult, if not impossible, to capture all aspects of culture via a single lens.

National Culture Clustering

Culture clustering is the grouping of cultures based on their relative similarity. Based on historical and political observations (although not quantitative empirical research), Huntington distinguishes seven civilizations: Sinic, Japanese, Hindu, Islamic, Western, Latin American, and African[30] (see Exhibit 6.13); there, Sinic includes Orthodox, Confucian, and Buddhist civilizations. Huntington's grouping has received considerable attention since September 11, 2001, partly because of the probable clash he sees between Western and Islamic civilizations. Most of the studies mentioned earlier have also produced country clusters, but those, while empirically assisted, have usually been formed on the basis of historical and political assumptions and have not been statistically validated.

The Ronen and Shenkar Clustering

The Ronen and Shenkar classification is based on a statistical synthesis of all earlier clustering studies. The updated clustering map is presented in Exhibit 6.12. Please note that the degree of similarity between countries is relative; that is, countries are more similar in their culture to countries that are members of the same cluster than to countries that are found in other clusters. Note also that language, religion, and geography are all correlated with cluster affiliation, albeit to a limited extent. For instance, note that the Anglo cluster includes countries from three continents, namely North America, Europe, and Australia/New Zealand. Like Hofstede's classification, the Ronen and Shenkar scheme was utilized to predict MNE strategies (e.g., entry mode, as in Chapter 10) and organization design (see Chapter 11). It is interesting to note that the 2013 clustering is remarkably similar to clustering published by the authors in 1985, suggesting considerable continuity and stability in culture clustering,[31] something we discuss later in this chapter in the convergence/divergence section.

Measuring Cultural Differences

Researchers and practitioners of international business face the need to evaluate just how different certain cultures are. For instance, you may want to know whether the difference between the cultures of the United States and the United Kingdom is smaller than the difference between, say, the cultures of the United States and France; this would imply, for instance, that the liability of foreignness of an American company when doing business in the UK would be lower than when doing business in France. Currently, this is assessed by a popular index called **"cultural distance,"** a measure of the extent to which one culture differs from another. Devised by Kogut and Singh, the index sums up the differences on Hofstede's original four cultural dimensions, producing a number that presumably reflects the extent to which two cultures are different.[32]

$$CD_j = \sum_{i=1}^{4} \{(I_{ij} - I_{iu})^2 / V_i\}/4$$

The Kogut and Singh index came under serious criticism in recent years. Hofstede himself suggested that some of his dimensions were more important than others for certain purposes. For instance, as mentioned earlier, he forecast uncertainty avoidance to be the most important dimension for FDI

207

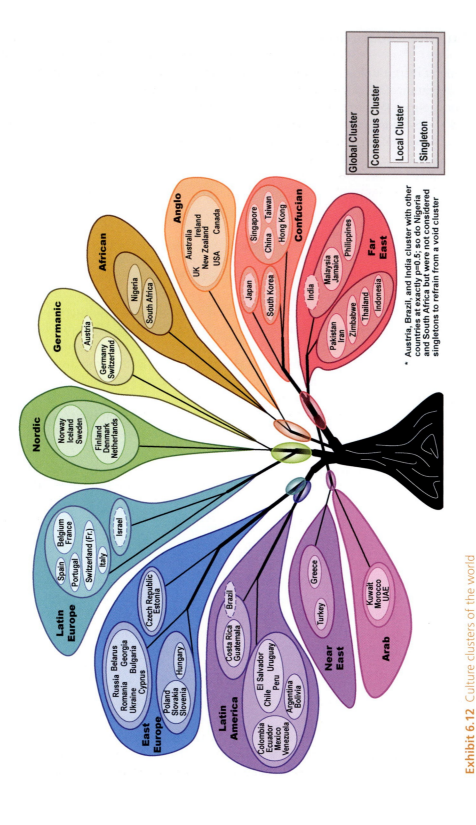

Exhibit 6.12 Culture clusters of the world

Source: Adapted from S. Ronen and O. Shenkar, "Mapping world cultures: Cluster formation, sources and implications," *Journal of International Business Studies,* 2013.

Legend within figure:

Global Cluster

Consensus Cluster

Local Cluster

Singleton

* Austria, Brazil, and India cluster with other countries at exactly p=0.5; so do Nigeria and South Africa but were not considered singletons to refrain from a void cluster

Cluster labels and members:

Nordic: Norway, Iceland, Sweden; Finland, Denmark, Netherlands

Germanic: Austria; Germany, Switzerland

African: Nigeria, South Africa

Anglo: UK, Australia, Ireland, New Zealand, USA, Canada

Confucian: Singapore, China, Taiwan, Hong Kong; Japan, South Korea

Far East: India; Malaysia, Jamaica, Philippines; Pakistan, Iran; Zimbabwe, Thailand, Indonesia

Latin Europe: Spain, Belgium, France, Portugal, Switzerland (Fr.), Italy; Israel

East Europe: Russia, Belarus, Romania, Georgia, Ukraine, Bulgaria, Cyprus; Czech Republic, Estonia; Poland, Slovakia, Slovenia; Hungary

Latin America: Costa Rica, Guatemala; Colombia, Ecuador, Mexico, Venezuela; El Salvador, Chile, Peru, Uruguay; Argentina, Bolivia; Brazil

Near East: Turkey, Greece

Arab: Kuwait, Morocco, UAE

because it involved different perceptions of risk.[33] Other studies confirmed the variability in the impact of various dimensions.[34] Trompenaars and Hampden-Turner elaborated on the encounters of different cultures and the problems likely to arise from such encounters.[35] Shenkar observed that most of the assumptions underlying the cultural index measure are questionable; for instance, the measure assumes symmetry (meaning, say, a US firm entering France faces the same cultural distance as a French company entering the United States), an assumption that goes against empirical evidence.[36] He noted that there are various ways in which "cultural distance" can be measured accurately and rigorously:

- Add the fifth dimension of long-term orientation.
- Measure differences on individual dimensions rather than the aggregate index.
- Use multiple measures (e.g., Schwartz, GLOBE).
- Consider culture as dependent/quasi-moderator.
- Control for industry and corporate cultures.
- Control for closing distance mechanisms.
- Control for cultural and strategic synergies.
- Control for strategic intent.
- Add emic methodologies.
- Add cognitive measures (e.g., stereotypes).
- Use general similarity measures (e.g., clustering).

To improve the measurement of cultural differences, it is highly recommended to use multiple measures (e.g., use both the GLOBE and Schwartz's measure described earlier). To avoid attributing all differences to culture, it is important to control for differences in economic and technological development, among others. It is also advisable to add another measure, "institutional distance," which gauges the difference between the institutional environments of countries, thus going beyond culture in comparing the national environments in which firms operate in diverse countries.[37]

Despite measurement issues, cultural differences are an important factor in MNE strategies and foreign investment. Recall, for instance, familiarity theory (discussed in Chapter 3), which suggests that firms prefer investment in culturally similar locations. In addition, the internationalization theory hypothesizes that firms will incrementally invest in culturally distant locations and that doing so will improve the probability of success. Cultural distance also affects entry mode (see Chapter 10) and alliance performance (see Chapter 12), among others.

Interim Summary

1. There are multiple classifications of national cultures, including Hofstede, Schwartz, GLOBE, and Trompenaars/Hampden-Turner.
2. The most widely applied, but also the most criticized, framework has been the one produced by Hofstede.
3. Culture clustering enables a comparison of cultures based on their relative similarity.
4. Measuring the difference, or "distance" between national cultures is a complex endeavor, and the usefulness of measurement tools is limited. The cultural distance measure produced by Kogut and Singh (1988), while popular, should be avoided when possible, due to fundamental conceptual and methodological flaws.

209

Corporate Culture

Corporate Culture is the culture adopted, developed, and disseminated by a company. It is of vital importance, for instance, for an MNE that adopts a global strategy and uses corporate culture as an integrator of its various units. Corporate culture can deviate from the "national norm." For example, Honda is often described as being different from the "typical" Japanese firm in that it is less immersed in tradition and more open to change. Hofstede points out that corporate culture is more superficial than national culture, because the latter reflects more deeply embedded values. While national culture forms values through early socialization, corporate culture involves the subsequent acquisition of organizational practices and symbols in the firm.

Hofstede and his colleagues studied corporate cultures in two countries, the Netherlands and Denmark, and found differences in values, but they found more considerable differences in practices among the firms they studied. They proposed that national and corporate cultures are distinctive— if related—constructs.[38] Laurent proposes that corporate culture can modify (a) behavior and artifacts, and (b) beliefs and values, but the deeper level of underlying assumptions is derived from national culture.[39] Laurent found that national differences in beliefs regarding firm practices were considerably greater in a single MNE than in multi-firm samples, leading Schneider to suggest "a paradox that national culture may play a stronger role in the face of a strong corporate culture. The pressures to conform may create the need to reassert autonomy and identity, creating a national mosaic rather than a melting pot."[40]

Other Layers of Culture

Ethnicity

Significant ethnic communities exist in many countries. In the United States, Hispanic and various Asian communities have been growing rapidly, creating subcultures. In Asia, Chinese have long constituted much of the business elite in countries such as Thailand, Malaysia, and Indonesia. Such variations must be recognized by the MNE, as they are likely to affect a myriad of issues, from consumption patterns to employee relations.

Industry

Although little research has been done, industry is an important layer of culture. For instance, the high-tech industry is considered flexible, informal, and innovative. It is also probably the most "global" industry in the sense of people having shared values and interaction. Profession also provides an important source of cultural affiliation. Common values and norms shared by, say, marketers across the markets in which the MNE operates can facilitate global integration.

Demographics

Hofstede et al. found that education, age, seniority, and hierarchical level strongly affected differences in values, although not differences in practices.[41] For instance, Ralston et al.[42] found the new generation of Chinese managers to be considerably more individualistic and to adhere less to Confucianism than the previous generation. These subcultures also vary geographically, making the country unit less homogeneous and making the MNE's integration challenge more complex.

Ideology

An important, although less stable, layer of culture is ideology. In China, for example, Maoist ideology provided many of the beliefs and values in the country from the mid-1950s to the mid-1970s. Ideologies are not always consistent with cultures (for instance, Mao endorsed low power distance) and can vary along time and across regions.

McClelland, the motivational theorist, studied the strength of achievement, affiliation, and power motivations during different periods and locations in Chinese history: Republican (or Nationalist) China, which existed between 1911 and 1949; Taiwan, which has been ruled by the Nationalist regime since 1949; and Mainland Communist China.[43] The differences could be attributed, among other factors, to changes in the prevailing ideologies—for example, between relatively free-market Taiwan and the Communist Mainland. Ideological, as well as political and legal, differences between the Chinese Mainland and Taiwan imply that countries with a similar culture may still require the MNE to adopt different operational modes and practices.

Interim Summary

1. Corporate culture is embedded in national culture, but is also notably different. Corporate culture is less deeply imprinted than national culture.
2. Culture is composed of many layers. These layers, such as ethnicity and demographic background of employee, are all modifiers of the base national culture.
3. The various layers of culture affect MNE strategy and operations in both the home and host country.

Key Cultural Issues

Cultural Etiquette

Each culture has values, beliefs, and norms that distinguish it from other cultures. **Cultural or business etiquette** is the manner and behavior expected in a given situation, be it business negotiations, a supervisor–subordinate discussion of a raise, or the behavior expected outside the workplace and after business hours. Violations of business culture are often considered offensive, especially in cultures with high uncertainty avoidance and which emphasize ritualistic behavior.

Cultural Stereotypes

Our view of other people's culture is a function of our perceptions and stereotypes. To an extent, we are all **ethnocentric**, that is, we look at the world from a perspective shaped by our own culture and upbringing. Ethnocentrism, in turn, shapes our **mental maps**, namely our perceptions of the world around us and even our perceptions of geographic realities. Note the following interview with a Japanese executive on how his firm made its site location selection in the United States:

> *In picking a site . . . companies like Mazda or Nissan look for areas in which the population is relatively well educated, and where there is not a lot of competition for labor. Asked which part of America the Japanese were eyeing now, he replied, "the Northeast."—The Northeast? Where land is expensive and the demand for skilled labor particularly intense? "No, no," he replied, "I mean up around Washington, Oregon, around there . . ." The Northeast, that is, viewed from Tokyo, Beijing, and Seoul.*[44]

Although we may not always believe our culture is superior, we use it as an anchor when looking at ourselves as well as when interacting with others. **Stereotypes** are our beliefs about others, their attitudes and behavior. **Auto-stereotypes** are how we see ourselves as a group distinguished from others. The following are the auto-stereotypes of Americans according to Adler and Jelinek:[45]

1. Distrust of others, combined with a belief that individual change is possible.
2. Man mastering a predictable environment. Situations are problems to be resolved.
3. The individual above all else—hence, impermanence of relationships.
4. Emphasis on doing rather than on being.
5. A present to slightly future orientation; immediate gratification, but change is constant.

According to Graham and Sano, Americans are:[46]

Informal—not bound by rules
Materialistic
Non-deterministic
Egalitarian
Individualistic
Achievement/action oriented
Open/direct
Practical/efficient
Litigious
Culturally ignorant/monolingual.

Hetero-stereotypes are how we are seen by others. In Exhibit 6.13, Americans were described by Chinese observers who visited the United States for the first time. Note that the Chinese noticed precisely those elements that are different in their culture. For instance, the "me-first" attitude is salient to someone who comes from a collectivistic culture. Stereotypes are important because they affect how MNE staff at headquarters and in various locations perceive other MNE employees. For instance, if headquarters staff believe that employees in a given country are not self-motivating, they may be reluctant to delegate authority to that subsidiary.

Exhibit 6.13 displays the dominant categories of American cultural patterns. These configurations most frequently become associated with white middle-class Americans, but numerous subcultural variations exist between race, ethnicity, and social clusters.

A	Americans are Westerners.
B	Busy folks, whether blue or brown eyed.
C	Competition in business.
D	Dollars are an uncommonly common goal.
E	Enter and exit human relations quickly.
F	Friendly to good friends.
G	"Go for it" is a motto.
H	Hypertension goes with high income and high living.
I	Impatience is a trait.
J	Jamboree may jeopardize your health.
K	Kiss and ride, a sign in a subway.
M	"Me-first" attitude.
N	Nosiness is tabooed.
O	"Oops" is an exclamation or interjection.
P	Penny wise and pound foolish in value judgments.
Q	Quest for influence.
R	Risk is the foundation of the firm.
S	Salesmanship is a benign tumor.
T	Teasing is a sign of being liked.
U	Unemployment breeds foreclosures.
V	Vulnerable to temptations.
W	Woo fame and fortune.
X	A movie classification for sex and violence.
Y	Yen for yen, the Japanese currency.
Z	Zest for fun and pleasure.

Exhibit 6.13 Americans from A to Z

Source: S. Wang, *Westerners Through Chinese Eyes,* Beijing: Foreign Languages Press, 1990.

Convergence and Divergence

The debate surrounding "convergence" versus "divergence" presents two competing theses. The **convergence hypothesis** assumes that technology and globalization are making countries more alike, and that with market integration and the diffusion of MNC practices, convergence will accelerate. The **divergence hypothesis** argues that nations will maintain their distinctive characteristics, and that differences may even be accentuated over time. The case for convergence is often made in the proliferation of "global products" recognized throughout the world and sold with little or no adaptation; examples are McDonald's and Coca-Cola, though, as you will see in Chapter 16, even those products are tinkered with in different markets. Trompenaars and Hampden-Turner suggest that even "global goods" are subject to cultural variations. This is because these products and services have different meanings to the people in each culture. Nor do global products imply harmony among diverse cultures and civilizations. John Bolton has pointed out in the *Washington Times* that the Kosovo conflict punctured the myth that "no two countries which both have a McDonald's will ever go to war with each other."[47] As noted earlier, the Ronen-Shenkar comparison of their 1985 and 2013 data shows very little change over time, suggesting strong support for the convergence hypothesis.

Industry Box

Islamic Finance

In accordance with Sharia law, the moral and religious code of Islam, Islamic banks develop their banking methods according to a number of principles. Some of these include a reliance on Muslim versus foreign investors, an obligation for profit-and-loss sharing, and a prohibition on charging interest. Islamic banking makes room for a myriad of depositors to also function as investors. Banks are stand-in supervisors over their customers' funds, and the depositors gain a percentage of the profits. The increase in the Muslim population, and the rising economic clout of some Muslim nations, has led non-Islamic banks to consider offering Islamic finance as a broader option to customers.

In 2001, a Japanese bank, Nomura, studied Sharia-compliant banks in Turkey at the time of the nation's financial crisis, but concluded that "Islamic finance has no systemic advantage over the conventional banking model." "Islamic banking has not been affected in the same way during the financial crisis as conventional banks, but they have been affected," says Khalid Hamad, executive director of bank supervision at the Central Bank of Bahrain. The Vatican lately argued that banks should look to adopt the principles of Islamic finance in order to restore confidence, and lower the danger of excessive credit, since Islamic financial transactions are backed by a physical asset, rather than on debt financing.

Sources: Adapted from R. Wigglesworth, "Credit crunch may test industry beliefs," *Financial Times: Islamic Finance*, May 6, 2009; L. Hardy, "The evolution of participation banking in Turkey," *Online Journal on Southwest Asia and Islamic Civilization*, 2012.

Interim Summary

1. Cultural stereotypes are an important force in international business. For instance, they influence how headquarters and subsidiary staff perceive each other.
2. The issue of convergence versus divergence is vital for firms as they try to forecast the business challenges they will face in the future and prepare accordingly.

Chapter Summary

1. Culture is a very important force in international business. However, culture does not explain everything, and we should not attribute all differences observed across nations to culture.
2. When interacting with other cultures, individuals and firms use their own culture as an anchor.
3. Language and religion are correlates of culture that also exert direct influence on international business strategies and operations.
4. There are various classifications of national culture, including those of Hofstede, Schwartz, GLOBE, and Trompenaars-Hampden-Turner, among others. Using the Ronen and Shenkar framework, it is possible to cluster countries according to the relative similarity of their cultures.
5. While it is possible to calculate the "cultural distance" among countries, this requires more sophistication than that provided by most current approaches.
6. In addition to the national level, we should be aware of corporate culture as well as of differences in culture by industry, ethnicity, and ideology, among other factors.
7. Key cultural issues include stereotypes (e.g., how we see others) and convergence/divergence.
8. The difference between cultures is not as important in an international business context as is the question of what happens when those cultures interact.

Notes

1   Z. Miller and T. Zaun, "Nissan intends to return favor to a French ally," *Asian Wall Street Journal*, April 5, 2002, A1; E. Thorton, "Remaking Nissan," *Business Week*, November 15, 1999, 70–74.
2   R.S. Bhagat and S.J. McQuaid, "The role of subjective culture in organizations: A review and direction for future research," *Journal of Applied Psychology Monograph*, 67, 5, 1982, 635–685.
3   S.P. Huntington, *The Clash of Civilizations and the Remaking of World Order*, New York: Simon & Schuster, 1996.
4   G.H. Hofstede. "Values and culture." In *Culture's Consequences: Comparing Values, Behaviors, Institutions, and Organizations across Nations*, 2nd edn, Thousand Oaks, CA: Sage Publications, 2001.
5   W. Whitely and G.W. England, "Managerial values as a reflection of culture and the process of industrialization," *Academy of Management Journal*, 20, 3, 1977, 439–453.

6   C. Geertz, "Thick description: Towards an interpretative theory of culture." In *The Interpretation of Culture*, New York: Basic Books, 1973.

7   S. Ronen, *Comparative and Multinational Management*. NY: Wiley, 1986.

8   N.J. Adler and S. Bartholomew, "Academic and professional communities of discourse: Generating knowledge on transnational human resource management," *Journal of International Business Studies*, 23, 3, 1992, 551–569.

9   P. Huntington, *The Clash of Civilizations and the Remaking of World Order*, New York: Simon & Schuster, 1996.

10 L. Kelley and R. Worthley, "The role of culture in comparative management: A cross-cultural perspective," *Academy of Management Journal*, 24, 1, March 1981, 164–173; L. Kelley, A. Whately, and R. Worthley, "Assessing the effects of culture on managerial attitudes: A three-culture test," *Journal of International Business Studies*, 28, 2, summer 1987, 17–31.

11 O. Shenkar and S. Ronen, "Structure and importance of work goals among managers in the People's Republic of China," *Academy of Management Journal*, 30, 3, 1987, 564–576.

12 L.W. Young, "Inscrutability revisited," In J.J. Gumperz (ed.), *Language and Social Identity*, New York: Cambridge University Press, 1982.

13 H. Brenhouse, "Quebec's war on English: Language politics intensify in Canadian province," In *World Quebecs War on English Language Politics Intensify in Canadian Province Comments*, Time World, April 8, 2013.

14   M. Greenberg, "Canada answers the call for US firms," *Wall Street Journal*, October 1, 1999, A13.

15 Ki-tae Kim, "Daewoo Motor staff engrossed in English learning," *Korea Times* on-line, September 29, 2001.

16 J. Salk and O. Shenkar, "Social identities in an international joint venture: An exploratory case study," *Organization Science*, 12, 2, 2001, 161–178.

17 G.H. Hofstede, *Culture's Consequences: Comparing Values, Behaviors, Institutions, and Organizations across Nations*, Thousand Oaks, CA: Sage, 2001.

18 Hofstede, *Culture's Consequences: Comparing Values, Behaviors, Institutions, and Organizations across Nations*.

19 "A land fit for consumers," *The Economist*, November 27, 1999, 16.

20 M.J. Gannon et al., *Understanding Global Cultures: Metaphorical Journeys Through 17 Countries*, Thousand Oaks, CA: Sage, 1994.

21 S. Wang, *Three Sweaters*, Beijing: Foreign Languages Press, 1976.

22 M. De Mooj, "Masculinity/femininity and consumer behavior." In G. Hofstede with W.A. Arrindell, *Masculinity and Femininity The Taboo Dimension of National Cultures*, Thousand Oaks, CA: Sage, 1998.

23 M. Sondergraad, "Hofstede's consequences: A study of reviews, citations and replications," *Organization Studies*, 15, 3, 1994, 447–456.

24 M.H. Hoppe, "Validating the masculinity/femininity dimension on elites from 19 countries." In G. Hofstede, with W. Arrindell, *Masculinity and Femininity: The Taboo Dimension of National Cultures*, Thousand Oaks, CA: Sage, 1998.

25 M. Bond, "Reclaiming the individual from Hofstede's ecological analysis—a 20-year odyssey: Comment on Oyserman et al. (2002)," *Psychological Bulletin*, 128, 1, 2002, 73–77.

26 S.H. Schwartz, "A theory of cultural values and some implications for work," *Applied Psychology: An International Review*, 1999, 48–1, 23–47.

27 V.V. Gouveia and M. Ros, "Hofstede and Schwartz's models for classifying individualism at the cultural level: Their relation to macro-social and macro-economic variables," *Psicothema*, 12, 2000, 25–33.

28 R.J. House and M. Javidan, "Overview of GLOBE." In R.J. House, R.J. Hanges, P.J. Javidan, P.W. Dorfman, and V. Gupta (eds), *Leadership, Culture, and Organizations: The GLOBE Study of 62 Societies*, Thousand Oaks, CA: Sage.

29 T. Hall, *Beyond Culture*, New York: Doubleday, 1976; *The Silent Language*, Greenwich, CT: Fawcett, 1959.

30 S.P. Huntington, *The Clash of Civilizations and the Remaking of World Order*, New York: Simon & Schuster, 1996.

31 S. Ronen and O. Shenkar, "Clustering countries on attitudinal dimensions: A review and synthesis," *Academy of Management Review*, Working Paper, 2013.

32 B. Kogut and H. Singh, "The effect of national culture on the choice of entry mode," *Journal of International Business Studies*, 19, 3, 1988, 411–432.

33 G. Hofstede, "Organizing for cultural diversity," *European Management Journal*, 7, 1989, 390–397.

34 O. Shenkar and Y. Zeira, "Role conflict and role ambiguity of chief executive officers in international joint ventures," *Journal of International Business Studies*, 23, 1992, 55–75.

35 F. Trompenaars and C. Hampden-Turner, *Riding the Waves of Culture: Understanding Diversity in Global Business*, New York: McGraw-Hill, 1998.

36 O. Shenkar, "Cultural distance revisited: Towards a more rigorous conceptualization and measurement of cultural differences," *Journal of International Business Studies*, 32, 3, 2001, 519–535.

37 T. Kostova, "Country institutional profile: Concept and measurement," *Academy of Management Best Papers Proceedings*, 1997, 180–184.

38 G. Hofstede, B. Neujen, D.D. Ohayv, and G. Sanders, "Measuring organizational cultures: A qualitative and quantitative study across twenty cases," *Administrative Science Quarterly*, 35, 1990, 286–316.

39 A. Laurent, "The cross-cultural puzzle of international human resource management," *Human Resource Management*, 25, 1, 1986, 91–102.

40 S. Schneider, "National vs. corporate culture: Implications for human resource management," *Human Resource Management*, 27, 2, 1988, 231–246.

41 G. Hofstede, B. Neujen, D.D. Ohayv, and G. Sanders, "Measuring organizational cultures: A qualitative and quantitative study across twenty cases," *Administrative Science Quarterly*, 35, 1990, 286–316.

42 D.A. Ralston, C.P. Egri, S. Stewart, R.H. Terpstra, and Y. Kaicheng, "Doing business in the 21st century with the new generation of Chinese managers. A study of generational shifts in work values in China," *Journal of International Business Studies*, 30, 2, 1999, 415–428.

43 D.C. McClelland, "Motivational patterns in Southeast Asia with special reference to the Chinese case," *Social Issues*, 19, 1963, 6–19.

44 *Newsweek*, February 22, 1988, 14.

45 N.J. Adler and M. Jelinek, "Is 'organization culture' culture bound?," *Human Resource Management*, 25, 1, 1986, 73–90.

46 J.L. Graham and Y. Sano, *Smart Bargaining: Doing Business with the Japanese*, Cambridge, MA: Ballinger, 1984.

47 Cited in *The Economist*, July 31, 1999, 8, "That thing that won't go away."

chapter 7

the political and legal environment

THE POLITICAL ENVIRONMENT   221

THE MNE–GOVERNMENT RELATIONSHIP   227

THE LEGAL ENVIRONMENT   239

Do You Know?

1. How do geopolitical factors and internal politics affect international trade and foreign investment? Can you distinguish between different types of political risk?
2. How can an MNE constructively engage the political organizations and constituencies that most affect its operations and performance?
3. What are the challenges of working in countries whose legal systems are different from that of the MNE's home country?
4. How do different national laws regarding competition, product liability, and the like affect an MNE's operations?

OPENING CASE   Bolivia Nationalizes Natural Gas

Just a few months into his election as President in December 2005, Bolivia's Evo Morales announced that, in line with his campaign's promise, he was nationalizing the country's natural gas industry. Declaring that "the time has come" for Bolivia to retake "absolute control" of its natural resources, the Bolivian leader decreed that natural gas becomes the property of the state as soon as it is extracted. The foreign MNEs that previously owned and continue to operate the fields, mainly Brazil's Petrobras and Spain's Repsol, will receive, from now on, 18 percent of the natural gas the fields produce.

The move by the Bolivian President was not entirely unexpected; prior to his election he led a rebellion against a $6 billion pipeline project that would pump natural gas to Chile, a country hated in Bolivia since their nineteenth-century war. The nationalization act also mimicked earlier moves by Mr. Morales' then Venezuelan counterpart, Hugo Chavez, to assert control over his country's oil industry. Mr. Chavez forced foreign multinationals to accept a minority stake in oilfields they had previously controlled outright while paying higher royalties and taxes to the Venezuelan government. Multinational executives have been worried that the nationalization drive will rapidly expand throughout the region. Just prior to the Bolivian decision, Ecuador enacted a law limiting the profits of foreign crude oil producers, and its newly elected leader suggested he might follow in the footsteps of Venezuela and Bolivia; however, close wins by the right in Peru and Mexico have made the prospect of similar measures in those countries more distant.

In the name of "equitable service," Morales has since nationalized telecoms, much of electricity generation, and zinc and tin mining, as well. So far, the nationalization efforts have seemed fruitful, with Bolivia earning over $16 billion in hydrocarbons revenues from 2006 to 2012, versus only $2 billion from 1999 to 2005. The rapid urbanization and a commodities-driven economic boom have been able to shelter the new government-subsidized businesses thus far, but it remains to be seen whether these new government-run industries can survive once the economy slows. In Venezuela, in the meantime, state-owned companies failed to maintain the output of the experienced multinationals.

Source: Adapted from D. Luchnow and J. De Cordoba, "Bolivia's President Morales orders nationalization of natural gas," *Wall Street Journal*, May 2, 2006, A1; E. Achtenberg and R. Currents, "Industrializing Bolivia's gas in Bolivia, not Brazil," North American Congress on Latin America, May 23, 2013; *The Economist*, "From tap to socket: Can the government do a better job than the private sector?," January 19, 2013.

The political and legal environment provides a critical context for the MNE at home and abroad. As the opening case illustrates, political factors, including political risk, are part and parcel of conducting business across national boundaries. Such factors are geopolitical, in that they are concerned with the relations among nations and their relative bargaining power in the world, as well as internal, in that they are related to domestic constituencies and their position regarding trade, investment, and other international business issues. As the opening case illustrates, these two sets of factors are interrelated. For instance, the ideological affinity between the current leaders is a major reason behind the mimicking of Venezuela's approach to FDI by Bolivia. Historical factors, such as the animosity between Bolivia and Chile, are shown to retain their importance in current affairs more than a century later. The MNE, on its part, must not only respond to the pressures exerted by political factors, but also be proactive in anticipating their repercussions, responding to multiple constituencies, and continuously reassess its options in a changing environment.

If the political environment identifies key constituencies and determines the sensitivity and vulnerability of MNE operations, the legal environment sets the "rules of the game," as well as the range within which legitimate business activity is conducted. Since, at least in democratic systems, laws are enacted by elected legislative bodies, political processes both determine legal issues and are guided by them. While the MNEs caught up in the Bolivian nationalization have few legal options at present, they may still undertake legal action at some point, especially if they decide to pull out of the country altogether. For instance, they may attempt to seize Bolivian funds held in other countries on the argument that those funds represent revenues from gas fields the MNEs claim ownership for.

The Political Environment

Political behavior is defined as "the acquisition, development, securing, and use of power in relation to other entities, where power is viewed as the capacity of social actors to overcome the resistance of other actors."[1] While not unique to international operations, the political processes faced by the MNE—compliance, evasion, negotiation, cooperation, coalition building, and co-optation[2]—are more complex and problematic than is typically the case for domestic operations. The number of political constituencies—governments, political parties' interest groups, unions, and public opinion—is multiplied in the international business environment, where the MNE is often viewed as a foreign implant, prompting coalitions of domestic forces that unite against the "foreign

221

invasion." Geopolitics also play an important role in the international context; for instance, Venezuela's repeated efforts to build a counterweight to US influence in the hemisphere is also behind its encouragement of and support for the Bolivian nationalization drive, even though the main companies impacted are not American. As part of this effort, Venezuela has been subsidizing oil exports to Cuba and Bolivia, and has negotiated deals with Chinese energy companies. Similarly, the US government resists efforts by South Korea to include exports from its Kaesong special zone in North Korea in the free trade agreement the two countries signed in 2012, though the two countries were scheduled to discuss it once more in late 2013.[3]

Political processes can naturally change the incentives and constraints that economic players face. All legislations and regulations that set the rules of the game for businesses come out of political processes. The outcomes can, however, be sometimes specific governmental actions that interfere with the flow of production factors or intermediary and final goods, distorting supply and demand. Either a change in regulations or a specific action by the government can substantially alter the benefits and costs from the alternative courses of action that a firm faces. For instance, high import tariffs imposed by a government may lead an MNE to launch foreign investment that it would not have otherwise pursued. At other times, a host government may protect a foreign firm by limiting the access of other foreign players into its market. Being politically astute—having superior political intelligence and influence skills[4]—is a key capability for MNEs, many of which have placed "government liaison" executives in senior positions.

The nature of international business activity influences the political constraints and the political agenda. For instance, while importers are typically concerned with achieving such goals as tariff reduction, exporters may seek to reduce limitations on high-technology exportation. Foreign investors, on their part, seek a more favorable investment climate in a host country. Domestic firms utilize political pressure to keep foreign competitors out of their home turf or to create obstacles to their operation. Certain industries are more sensitive to political pressures than others; for instance, industries that are viewed as having a national strategy role, in particular national security, are especially susceptible to political interference, as is the case for firms regarded as "national champions." However, the ability to garner domestic political support by the firm's constituencies (e.g., owners, employees, unions) in the home and host country is no less important in determining the outcome of a political process.

Political System

The political environment facing an MNE is inherently multifaceted, involving at the minimum the political conditions of its home country, those of each of its host countries, and the political relations between its home and host countries. In addition, developments in the political sphere of a country where the MNE currently has no presence can also have significant bearing on its global operations. For instance, the shift toward a more open political and economic system in Myanmar in 2010 opened up new opportunities for MNEs, and the Arab Spring that started in Tunisia in 2011 spread to and eventually toppled the regimes of several Arab countries (e.g., oil-rich Libya) where many MNEs do business. The overall political environment in which an MNE finds itself is inevitably complex, but an understanding must start somewhere, perhaps with the political system of each relevant country. **Political system** can be defined as the institutions that constitute the government, the prescribed behaviors of its components, and the informal and informal socio-political processes in which they interact with the broader society.[5] Given the complexity of contemporary political systems in the world and their historical paths of evolution, it is impossible to classify them neatly. There are, however, some important dimensions along which political systems vary.

Discussions in the popular media tend to put a country's political system in either of two categories: democratic or authoritarian. Despite the importance of this distinction, it is perhaps as important to recognize the complexity of and variation within each type of system across countries. The original meaning of "democracy" in Greek (*dēmokratiā*) is *rule by the people*, with decisions made by an assembly of all those eligible to be members of it. The system in modern times generally takes the form of **representative democracy**, with decisions made by a governing body that is set up and sustained on the basis of "free and fair" elections. Any political system that concentrates powers in the hands of individuals who may have gained powers initially in an election, instead of a coup or inheritance, but who cannot be removed from their positions, falls into the category of **authoritarianism**. Elected leaders can still turn authoritarian if they use their powers successfully to remove any effective constraints on their behaviors. Such a slide back to authoritarianism is more likely in a society that has not yet established the institutions required for a democratic system to sustain itself, as happened in many countries in the recent past (e.g., Belarus, Uzbekistan, and Zimbabwe). Observers point out that elections alone are not sufficient to establish a democracy, and that it is the gradual buildup of democratic institutions (e.g., rule of law and control of corruption) over time that can sustain the system.[6] Such institutions can develop prior to the holding of the first free and fair election, as happened in a number of societies (e.g., South Korea and Taiwan).

Both democratic and authoritarian governments can vary in the extent to which they represent the long-term interests of the citizens. A political party viewed as an alternative to the current government that is failing in some major aspect (e.g., ethnic conflict, economic stagnation, or acute income inequality) can get elected and adopt policies that seriously harm the stability or economic development of the country in the long term. For instance, as economic difficulties and ethnic tensions intensified in the leadup to the breakup of the former Yugoslavia in 1992, elections in several of the republics put in power highly nationalistic leaders who got the Yugosphere embroiled in a bloody war that lasted for over three years. As discussed in the opening case, the policies of the governments in Bolivia and Venezuela may lessen the severe income inequality in the short term, but may also slow down economic development in the long term. As one may expect, the extent to which the policies of an authoritarian regime represent the long-term interests of the country's citizens is subject to even greater variation. It is easy to find examples of authoritarian leaders who, in their pursuit of personal power and wealth, exhibit little care for the well-being of the country's citizens. Mobutu Sese Seko, who ruled Zaire (the Democratic Republic of Congo today) from 1960 to 1997, amassed a fortune of over $45 billion but left the country's per capita income 65 percent below the level prevailing at the time he seized power.[7] In roughly the same time period, the dictators of South Korea and Chile, despite grave human rights abuses against their political opponents, adopted policies that put their respective nations on a firm footing for economic growth. It is also useful to distinguish between totalitarianism and authoritarianism. A **totalitarian** regime is typically guided by a strong ideology and pushes for the ideological end at the expense of almost everything else, with no tolerance of any debate or dissent. A merely **authoritarian** regime, however, tolerates some pluralism, exercises power within relatively predictable limits, and tends to be more responsive to the desires of the country's citizens, while limiting the freedom to form opposition parties to challenge its power.[8] In short, even though a democracy, in principle and on average, represents the long-term interests of a country's citizens better than an authoritarian regime, there is wide variation across countries that follow each type of political system.

The effectiveness of governance also varies across countries with democratic governments and across countries with authoritarian governments. *The Economist* develops a Democracy Index for 165 independent states and two territories based on five indicators (electoral process and pluralism, civil liberties, the functioning of government, political participation, and political culture) and classifies them into four types of regimes (full democracies, flawed democracies, hybrid regimes, and authoritarian regimes). The World Bank publishes indices that measure the quality of governance in each member country based on six factors: (1) citizen voice and government accountability; (2) political stability; (3) government effectiveness; (4) regulatory quality; (5) rule of law; and (6) control of corruption. As can be seen, this set of indicators are quite similar to the set of indicators that the World Economic Forum uses to measures institutional quality, which we discussed in Chapter 4. Exhibit 7.1 lists selected countries by their 2012 Democracy Index and also shows their 2012 indices of Government Effectiveness and Control of Corruption. As can be expected, more developed countries tend to perform better on each of the two dimensions of government effectiveness. It is also interesting to note that, among the developing countries listed, those with more democratic systems (e.g., India and Indonesia) do not always perform better on these two dimensions than those with more authoritarian systems (e.g., Singapore and China). There are at least two reasons for this apparent enigma. First, the ability of an authoritarian government to deliver government services and control corruption critically depends on the ambition and competence of the ruling group. As noted in Chapter 5, the personal ambitions of a country's leaders can make a major difference in the development of the country. Since the quality of governance is important to the economic development, a group of individuals with the ambition to develop the country's economy may be able to implement the requisite policies and measures more effectively without the constraints of checks and balances. Second, even though a democratically elected government is subject to media monitoring and held responsible by the electorate, the ruling party may lack the majority needed to stay in power without relying on coalition partners. A downside is that the leaders of the ruling party are sometimes held hostage by the coalition partner, unable to take decisive actions in reforming the government and fighting corruption.

Finally, countries also vary in their levels of success in developing their economies no matter whether they have a democratic or authoritarian system. Interestingly, most of the economies that experienced rapid growth in the last few decades, and made substantial progress in catching up with the developed ones, did so at least initially under authoritarian regimes, including Chile, Hong Kong, Mainland China, Malaysia, South Korea, Singapore, and Taiwan. One plausible explanation is the likely difference between democratic and authoritarian regimes in susceptibility to the influence of interest groups. As discussed in Chapter 5, economic development often entails major institutional overhauls, such as switching to a market-oriented system and opening up the economy to foreign competition. Such changes inevitably cause some to lose and others to gain economically,

Category of Political System	Country Name	Democracy Index	Government Effectiveness	Control of Corruption
Full democracies	Sweden	9.73	1.94	2.31
	Ireland	8.56	1.53	1.45
	Germany	8.34	1.57	1.78
	Korea, Rep.	8.13	1.20	0.47
	United States	8.11	1.51	1.38
	Japan	8.08	1.40	1.61
	Spain	8.02	1.11	1.05
Flawed democracies	Portugal	7.92	1.03	0.93
	France	7.88	1.33	1.42
	Italy	7.74	0.41	−0.03
	Greece	7.65	0.31	−0.25
	India	7.52	−0.18	−0.57
	Brazil	7.12	−0.12	−0.07
	Poland	7.12	0.66	0.59
	Indonesia	6.76	−0.29	−0.66
	Malaysia	6.41	1.01	0.30
	Ghana	6.02	−0.07	−0.09
Hybrid regimes	Singapore	5.88	2.15	2.15
	Bangladesh	5.86	−0.83	−0.87
	Bolivia	5.84	−0.37	−0.70
	Georgia	5.53	0.57	0.25
Authoritarian regimes	Nigeria	3.77	−1.00	−1.13
	Russian Federation	3.74	−0.43	−1.01
	China	3.00	0.01	−0.48
	Vietnam	2.89	−0.29	−0.56

Exhibit 7.1 Government Effectiveness and Control of Corruption of selected countries, listed by Democracy Index (high to low)

Source: The Category of Political System and Democracy Index are based on *Democracy index 2012: Democracy at a Standstill* by the Economist Intelligence Unit (2012), and the estimates of Government Effectiveness and Control of Corruption are based on the World Bank Governance Indicators (2012).

Note: The Democracy Index ranges from (most authoritarian) 0 to 1 (most democratic), and estimates of Government Effectiveness and Control of Corruption range from approximately -2.5 (weak) to 2.5 (strong).

and the losers can form powerful interest groups that fight hard to block the needed changes. In addition, the benefits of such reforms are often spread across a large number of people with small gains per person, while the costs are born by a much smaller number of people, making it easier to organize the losers in political activities designed to influence elections and government policies. This condition, therefore, can make it harder for countries with a democratic system to undertake the needed but controversial reforms than those with an authoritarian system.[9] It should be noted, however, that rapid economic development also yields some negative outcomes. All of the countries that experienced rapid economic growth in recent decades also went through a period of environmental degradation and rising income inequality, with associated social problems. Some argue that a slower rate of growth with markedly less environmental damage and more equitable income distribution could have made the citizens happier and left a more livable environment to future generations.[10] By the mid- to late 2000s, the largest developing countries of the world, including Brazil, China, and India, started reorienting their economic policies to promote more balanced, inclusive, and sustainable growth, emphasizing the quality of life, instead of a single-minded pursuit of higher GDP.[11] However, due to the incredibly rapid growth of these developing countries, and despite their good intentions, Brazil's income disparity is still one of the highest in the world, and China has some of the worst air pollution problems of any country in the world (contributing to 1.2 million deaths in the country in 2010 alone).[12]

The Institutional Context

The historical landscape of political institutions and relations both between and within countries constitute a crucial layer of the political environment. Some 40 years after the end of French colonial rule, former colonies in western Africa still import most of their needs from France. Air France enjoys a virtual monopoly on many West African routes, which as a result have been very lucrative for the French state-owned airline. In Latin America, Spanish banks dominate foreign investment in the financial industry. In addition to linguistic, cultural affinity, personal relationships, and knowledge of the local market (hence lower "liability of foreignness"), the trade and investment dominance of former colonial powers is the result of political pressure, often in the form of economic aid packages tied to spending by the donor. The endurance of political ties is also evident in the "banana war" in which European governments devised a tariff regime to protect former colonies and present allies in Africa and the Caribbean. This triggered a backlash on the part of the United States whose firms dominate Latin American banana plantations, and who is more closely aligned with Latin American nations (see opening case in Chapter 2).

Affinity or **animosity** between nations, reflecting how closely aligned, or estranged, nations are based on history and political reality, is an important determinant of international business relations.[13] Nations that share a historical bond and political affinity, such as the United States and the United Kingdom, tend to have high levels of mutual trade and investment. In contrast, trade and investment among hostile countries are often prohibited. US firms are not allowed to invest in Cuba, and Syrian citizens are prohibited from doing business with Israel. Even where trade and investment are not legally banned, animosity can still have a serious effect. Trade and investment flows between Turkey and Greece are much smaller than they would be, if not for the historical hostility between the two nations. However, animosity—and trade barriers in general—also create opportunities for those that act as middlemen between the foes or that have special access to one of the trading partners. Prior to the opening of the Chinese Mainland, Hong Kong benefited from its position as gateway to China. Jordan benefits from transferring Israeli goods to and from countries, such as Indonesia, that do not permit direct trade with Israel.

Political considerations also influence third countries. The US administration successfully lobbied the Israeli government to cancel the sale of airborne aircraft warning systems to China, threatening to withhold economic aid to Israel if it were to consummate the deal. The pressure reflected geopolitical considerations—the United States feared the equipment could tempt China to mount an attack on Taiwan. Israel argued that the intervention was aimed at protecting US firms from competition and that another foreign supplier would emerge in the event it withdrew from the deal. Israel finally caved in to US pressure, and had to face an angry Chinese government that became less enthusiastic about promoting Israeli trade and investment. Trade is also used to influence political outcomes. Such is the effort by some EU members to deny duty-free access to Israeli products made in the territories held by Israel since 1967.[14]

Political relations among nations not only influence trade and investment but are also influenced by them. According to John Bolton of the American Enterprise Institute, the myth that no two countries that both have a McDonald's will go to war with each other has been exploded with the Kosovo crisis[15] (and, more recently, with the Israel-Lebanon conflict). Still, a study showed that countries belonging to the same preferential trade agreement (PTA) were 30 to 45 percent less likely to become involved in military disputes than countries that did not have such agreements. When PTA members did have military disputes, they were less likely to go to war over them. Only 2 percent of such disputes led to war among signatories of PTA agreements vis-à-vis 11 percent for non-signatories. When not accompanied by a PTA, trade flows did not contribute to reduced hostilities, however.[16]

The MNE–Government Relationship

The relationship with governments in its host and home countries is probably the most important political challenge facing the MNE. Governments affect the economic and legal environment in which the MNE operates, for example, by setting monetary and tax policies, setting price controls, enacting, endorsing, and enforcing intellectual property legislation, and influencing labor relations. Governments are also responsible for trade and investment policies, capital and exchange controls, and transfer-pricing regulations.[17] In some countries, they have a broader role than in a parliamentary democracy.[18] For instance, in Vietnam, the government is a regulator, a competitor, a customer, and a potential partner. With no clear separation of the executive and the judiciary, the Vietnamese government also influences legal procedures and plays the key role in enforcement decisions.

The MNE Relationship with the Host Government

Three models have been used to describe the government–MNE relationship: *Sovereignty at Bay*, *Dependency*, and *Neo-Mercantilism*. All three assume a powerful MNE at odds with the government of a weaker, developing nation over market access or broader sovereignty issues. The *Sovereignty at Bay* model goes the furthest by viewing the MNE as a threat to the national sovereignty of the host country. The *Dependency* model also sees a cooperative relationship, but only between the MNE and its home government.[19]

At the beginning of the twenty-first century, the nature of the relationship between MNEs and host governments can perhaps be best described as **coopetition**, that is, a combination of cooperation and competition. Cooperation reflects mutual accommodation and collaboration, with the government and the MNE seeking joint payoffs and goal accomplishment from their inter-dependent activities or resources. Competition reflects bargaining or control and related conflicts with the government and the MNE, each seeking private gains at the expense of the other's interests. From a government's viewpoint, increasing pressure for global integration, heightened competition for inbound FDI, decelerated economic growth, and a stronger need for upgrading economic structure all encourage cooperation with MNEs. From an MNE's viewpoint, foreign operations increasingly depend on the educational, technological, industrial, and financial infra-structure built by host governments. Whether a host government provides a stable set of rules for business players to act accordingly, and whether the rules can be adapted to changing conditions, has become increasingly crucial for firm growth and international expansion. However, despite the liberalization of foreign investment regimes (see Chapter 3), the MNE and the government are often at odds and end up bargaining over control of resources and/or market access.

MNE Political Objectives in the Host Country

Typically, the key political goal of the MNE in the host country is the establishment of a favorable trade and investment environment. This means nondiscrimination, i.e., equal (if not preferential) treat-ment of the foreign firm. Except where it seeks to block the entry of other MNEs, the MNE strives to remove limits on foreign ownership, to open access to local markets (i.e., to face few or no tariff and non-tariff barriers), and to have as few regulatory hurdles as possible. In short, it wishes to remove any obstacles that interfere with its freedom to locate, manufacture, and sell where it can deploy its resources most effectively and obtain the highest return. MNEs also wish to reduce mandatory requirements for product or service adaptation, especially where they judge adaptation to be unnecessary in terms of competitive advantage or customer preferences.

Another important goal for the MNE in the host environment is to obtain **legitimacy**. Legitimacy is the acceptance of the MNE as a natural organ in the local environment. Legitimacy is not trans-ferable across borders, and acceptance in one market may even constitute a liability in another.[20] The MNE will often try to convince political constituencies that it operates as a domestic company, contributes to the local economy, and takes social responsibility seriously. Airbus often buys full-page advertisements in US newspapers to highlight its use of US suppliers, as do Toyota, Honda, and Nissan. When McDonald's opened its first Russian restaurant, children from a local orphanage were invited to head the customer line. In Saipan, part of the Northern Marianas (a US common-wealth), MNEs improved roads and local schools. Research shows that such positive corporate citizenship is a good investment that improves the MNE's bargaining power.[21]

Pressure for good citizenship can also come from outside the host country, and is particularly strong when the MNE operates under regimes with poor political records. Canadian oil firm Talisman has been confronted with the fact that its operations in Sudan bring the host government revenues that are then being used to fund a civil war with the southern part of the country. To pacify the critics, Talisman funded community programs in Sudanese villages, builds hospitals, and digs watering ponds for cattle.[22] Similarly, Apple had been criticized for the conditions under which its iPod devices are manufactured in China, though the company argued its review has found only marginal violations of labor standards.

Host Government Objectives

Host governments are primarily interested in protecting national interests, especially where "vital interests" such as national security are concerned. In Venezuela, the dependence on oil as the major foreign exchange earner meant considerable government intervention in the form of taxation, government participation in the industry, and the protection of external markets and prices; and, eventually, nationalization of the industry.[23] Host governments have been found to discriminate against MNEs, especially during the later stages of industry competition.[24] Today, when competition for FDI is keen, host government efforts are directed at technology transfer and exports, and there are often instances where foreign investors receive terms that are more favorable than those of domestic players (e.g., a lower tax rate).

Increasingly, local governments are also concerned with protecting their environment from pollution, unsustainable logging, and the like. Host nations, especially (but not only) developing economies, are also concerned with MNE interference with the political process either directly (e.g., via lobbying) or by way of introducing foreign values and lifestyles that erode the standing of current political actors. MNEs are often criticized for aligning with elite segments of society that do not necessarily express the interest of the vast majority of the people.

The Bargaining Power of the MNE and the Host Government

When the political objectives of the MNE and the host nation diverge, their relative bargaining power will, to a significant extent, determine the outcome. When a nation offers an attractive environment that is unmatched by other locations, its bargaining power is high, especially when competition among investors is intense.[25] For instance, when the price of oil tripled on world markets, competition for investment in Russia heated up, and the government offered less generous terms than initially contemplated. In contrast, some 15 years earlier, when investment opportunities emerged in Eastern and Central Europe following the collapse of the Soviet Union, the Chinese government relaxed its investment requirements in order to remain an attractive investment target. When the country later became the location of choice among emerging markets, it withdrew some of the special incentives. In the end, however, the outcome of the bargaining also depends on the success of the parties in building political coalitions that will enlist support for their cause in both the host and the home country.

The bargaining power of the MNE tends to be greater when it offers a differentiated, technologically advanced product that others cannot or are unwilling to provide, but that is vital to the host economy (for instance, it constitutes a nation's major source of foreign currency). Extractive industries usually provide the foreign investor with considerable leverage with both the home and host governments, but this advantage fast erodes once the investment has been consummated because the investment is by and large irreversible. The MNE also has a stronger bargaining position when the subsidiary is complex to operate and manage, when its volume of exports is large, and when the ratio of expatriates is high.[26]

While "traditional" MNEs operating in developing markets command substantial marketing power vis-à-vis their host governments, developing country MNEs (DMNEs) typically do not. DMNEs are usually not in a position to pressure host governments for concessions and favorable investment terms, although they can insist on reciprocity in host countries that are substantial investors in their home market. For small and mid-sized international enterprises (SMIEs), the probability of pressuring host governments is even lower, though they may build alliances and coalitions to exert such pressure. Some of the liabilities of SMIEs and DMNEs can be seen as advantages, however. Both types of firms are considered less of a menace to national sovereignty than traditional MNEs and are less likely to arouse nationalist sentiments in the host country; as a result, such firms are more likely to be granted access to a market where local sensitivities run high.

Government Investment Support

In an era of keen competition for FDI, governments compete with each other and are willing to bargain with the MNE over the provision of investment incentives. These incentives typically are administered by a designated investment agency whose main roles are to solicit potential investors, weigh project feasibility, and contribute to national goals, and assure compliance with investment requirements. Incentives range from outright grants and investment allowances to subsidies for infrastructure development, preferential tax treatment (tax holidays, reduced rates, and accelerated depreciation), import duties exemption, loans and loan guarantees, and interest subsidies.[27] For example, it is estimated that, to entice Mercedes-Benz to invest in Alabama, the state offered the auto maker $253 million—$169,000 for every job the company promised to create.[28] More recently, Indiana won over Ohio as a location for a new Honda plant by offering, among other reasons, a more generous incentive package.

Special support is often provided to MNEs willing to invest in troubled areas, such as Northern Ireland, or in disadvantaged regions, such as former East Germany, China's Western provinces, and inner city neighborhoods in the United States. Such preferences are permitted under the World Trade Organization (WTO) rules. The WTO also makes sure that foreign MNEs are not discriminated against, though domestic firms sometimes complain that they are being shortchanged by not being offered the support and incentives available to the foreign investor. To counter, domestic firms build political coalitions to counterbalance incentives granted to foreign firms or decide to invest in their home country via a foreign entity. An example is "bogus blue-eyed" ventures, domestic Chinese firms disguised as foreign investors by registering a Hong Kong entity.

Investment incentives are more likely to be offered when competition among potential sites is intense, when the investment at stake is considered vital, and when a country perceives itself to be at a disadvantage owing to worsening economic conditions or political and social turmoil. Research conducted in the Caribbean shows that the attractiveness of various FDI incentives offered by host governments varies with market orientation and the type, size and location of the investment, its timing, and the type of product involved. Import duty concessions were seen as the most desirable by exporters in that region because of the high ratio of imported components in the exported product.[29]

The MNE and its Home Government

Globalization notwithstanding, the MNE remains firmly grounded in its home environment.[30] The state continues to charter and steer the MNE, shape its operating environment, and is the only entity to conduct international affairs, including international trade and investment policies. For example, the long-simmering dispute between US aircraft maker Boeing and its European competitor Airbus is arbitrated and negotiated in the WTO on behalf of the government of the United States and those of the European Union, respectively. Nor is the government role in international business diminishing. In developed nations, the ratio of government expenditure as percentage of GDP now stands at five times the level during World War I. MNEs are engaged in lobbying their home governments in support of their cause, as US MNEs did in the 1990s when they sought to end the trade embargo on Vietnam and lift the restrictions on investment there.

The home government plays an important role in facilitating the MNE political objectives. When Saudi Arabia had to choose between buying aircraft from Boeing or Airbus, then-President Clinton personally called the Saudi king on behalf of Boeing. Years later, China has used the occasion of a visit by President Bush to announce a large airplane purchase from Boeing, while ordering Airbus planes on the occasion of a visit by the president of France. In November 2012, Boeing announced the largest order in its history (230 planes, worth $20.1 billion at list prices), from Lion Air of Indonesia, on the occasion of President Obama's visit to the country. Understandably, not every deal is accorded such high-level treatment. The larger the magnitude and visibility, and the bigger the perceived importance to the country's MNE, the more likely are political leaders to intervene. The stated rationale for the intervention is usually to protect the national interest and preserve jobs, goals that have broad political appeal at home. In contrast, when French cheeses were included on the list of US retaliatory measures in the "banana war," the president of the French Cheese Association lamented, "We represent the flower of French gastronomy, but we have no political clout."[31]

While political pressure is often applied in the opening of foreign markets, it can also be exercised to obtain the closure of the home market to foreign competition. In the late 1970s and 1980s, US car manufacturers sought to limit Japanese imports to the United States. The media decried the "buying up of America," suggesting that the United States was becoming a low-tech platform for Japanese firms, which were keeping high-value-added production at home. As a result, the US government was persuaded to set "voluntary" quotas on Japanese car imports. In South Korea, activist groups pressured their government not to open its market to foreign goods, stalling international efforts to open the country's economy.

Coalition Building and Influence Tactics

Nations and governments are not unitary entities but rather collections of individuals, political parties, interest groups, and agencies that negotiate internally as much as externally to define and achieve their agendas. Singapore, Finland, and Ireland are examples of governments with more policy consensus than the United States; Slovenia, the Philippines, and Russia have a much lower policy consensus.[32] In the United States, elite groups are more favorably disposed toward trade, whereas lower income groups tend to support mercantilism.[33] Political interests influence not only the general approach toward trade but also the treatment of specific goods and services. In the aftermath of September 11, the United States abolished tariffs on the importation of cotton yarn from Pakistan and eased restrictions on the importation of bed linen from that country. The US government refused, however, to do the same for textiles, fearful of angering the then-chairman of the House Ways and Means Committee, whose congressional district included a large textile manufacturer.[34] US political activities—constituency building, political action committee contributions, advocacy advertising, lobbying, and coalition building[35]—have all been used at one time or another in the service of international business objectives. For example, dozens of foreign countries have registered lobbyists in the United States representing their interests.

The appointment of executives with political experience and contacts is evidence of the importance of political activities. For example, Boeing appointed Thomas Pickering, former Undersecretary of State for Political Affairs, as Senior Vice President for Political Affairs. To build political goodwill, firms channel investment into regions and industries supported by a political party or an influential constituency. Political contributions are made with a similar purpose even though they are prohibited or restricted in many nations. Coalition building also involves bringing on board local constituencies, sometimes in the form of alliance partners. For instance, Italian company Finmeccanica aligned with Boeing in the hope of winning a Pentagon bid for a new cargo aircraft, and sought to win points with the US administration by criticizing its European competitor, EADS, for selling planes to Venezuela.[36]

Industry Box

Managing Politics in the Automotive Industry

The automotive industry, which includes the manufacturing, service, and sale of vehicles and their component parts, is one of the most important to both developed and developing nations, from the United States and Germany to Thailand and Malaysia. For instance, in China, automotive is classified as a "pillar industry," which means that it gets priority in resource allocation, whether it is steel or access to low-cost capital. Many other industries are dependent on automotives in one way or another, for instance, the industry is the largest buyer of research and development.

US auto makers, in particular the "big three" (General Motors (GM), Ford, and Chrysler), have been under considerable pressure in their domestic market, in some world markets (e.g., the EU). The big three have often sought the help of the US government, which bailed out Chrysler in 1980 and both GM and Chrysler in 2008, seeking support ranging from import quotas on Japanese cars (in the 1980s) to the establishment of fuel economy standards that were conducive to their interest. They also negotiated with states where their plants are located over various support and concessions, though foreign car makers, from BMW to Hyundai, seem to achieve more significant concessions.

At the same time, GM and Ford have been successful in some emerging markets, in particular China. GM, which now competes for the number one spot in that growing market, manufactures Buicks in Shanghai via a joint venture with Shanghai Automotive Industry Corporation (SAIC), a state-owned enterprise, among other joint ventures. GM has sought the help of both the Chinese and US governments in a dispute over the alleged copying of one of its models by a Chinese competitor, and the case was eventually settled out of court after apparent intervention from Chinese government officials.

Sources: J. Mackintosh and G. Dyer, "GM and Chery settle legal action," *Financial Times*, November 19, 2005; J. Meiners, "Ford and GM battle for sales in China," *Car and Driver*, September 2010.

Economic Freedom

A major factor of variation among political environments as they relate to business is economic freedom, or the degree to which the government interferes with free enterprise in a variety of ways, from selecting winners and losers, to the ability of firms to engage in various lines of business. Exhibit 7.2 provides the 2013 rankings on economic freedom. Note that first-place Hong Kong is not a country but a Special Administrative Region of a non-democratic country, China, a reminder that economic and political freedom need not go hand in hand.

Political Risk

Political risk is the probability of disruption to an MNE's operations from political forces and events and their correlates. The risk may come from the actions of government, as the opening case illustrates, or from other sources. For instance, Shell has seen its pipelines sabotaged and

List of Top 20 Countries				List of Bottom 20 Countries			
Country Name	World Rank	2013 Score	Change in Yearly Score from 2012	Country Name	World Rank	2013 Score	Change in Yearly Score from 2012
Hong Kong	1	89.3	−0.6	Angola	158	47.3	0.6
Singapore	2	88.0	0.5	Ecuador	159	46.9	−1.4
Australia	3	82.6	−0.5	Argentina	160	46.7	−1.3
New Zealand	4	81.4	−0.7	Ukraine	161	46.3	0.2
Switzerland	5	81.0	−0.1	Uzbekistan	162	46.0	0.2
Canada	6	79.4	−0.5	Kiribati	163	45.9	−1.0
Chile	7	79.0	0.7	Chad	164	45.2	0.4
Mauritius	8	76.9	−0.1	Solomon Islands	165	45.0	−1.2
Denmark	9	76.1	−0.1	Timor-Leste	166	43.7	0.4
United States	10	76.0	−0.3	Congo, Rep.	167	43.5	−0.3
Ireland	11	75.7	−1.2	Iran	168	43.2	0.9
Bahrain	12	75.5	0.3	Turkmenistan	169	42.6	−1.2
Estonia	13	75.3	2.1	Equatorial Guinea	170	42.3	−0.5
United Kingdom	14	74.8	0.7	Congo, Dem. Rep.	171	39.6	−1.5
Luxembourg	15	74.2	−0.3	Burma	172	39.2	0.5
Finland	16	74.0	1.7	Eritrea	173	36.3	0.1
Netherlands	17	73.5	0.2	Venezuela	174	36.1	−2.0
Sweden	18	72.9	1.2	Zimbabwe	175	28.6	2.3
Germany	19	72.8	1.8	Cuba	176	28.5	0.2
Taiwan	20	72.7	0.8	Korea, North	177	1.5	0.5

Exhibit 7.2 Index of Economic Freedom (2013)
Source: www.heritage.org.

233

workers kidnapped in the Niger Delta area of Nigeria, where local militant groups are fighting with the government over the share of proceeds from the region's oil resources. Political risk is not only about political stability, it is also about a steady society, a stable economic and regulatory climate, policy continuity, and the likelihood of unforeseen problems for the trader and investor. An arbitrary change in investment conditions (e.g., retroactive change in investment rules) and the undermining of property rights by the court system are also examples of political risk.

Political risk is a problem for the foreign trader and investor, since they like to have a predictable environment in which to plan and operate. Firms undertaking FDI are more vulnerable to political risk, since foreign investors commit more resources to the host country and are much more likely to place staff on the ground. Political risk narrows the decision-making span of the foreign investor, in effect transferring power to the host government or other entities. A high political risk ranking, or even the perception of political risk, may lead the MNE to refrain from investing in a country, or in a particular region in that country, or to seek a high premium to compensate for the extra risk, for instance, in the form of extra incentives. A country does not need to be democratic to rank low on political risk. Nor is political risk the exclusive realm of developing countries. Prospects for the breakup of Canada triggered by Quebec's possible secession represent a political risk for investors who may find their investment located in a different political entity than the one they initially targeted for investment.

The events of September 11, 2001 drew attention to the risk of terrorism, which is now becoming a more acute concern for companies. Terrorism not only puts a company's own workforce at risk, it also endangers its business prospects. Understandably, some industries are more vulnerable than others, for instance, tourism is much more sensitive than high tech to terrorist attacks, as the cases of Israel and India clearly show. At the same time, firms in countries that are vulnerable to terrorism learn early on how to deal with the phenomenon and are therefore also more open to invest in world regions that are considered risky by other investors.

The Measurement of Political Risk

The inherent problem in the measurement of political risk is that the political landscape is notoriously difficult to forecast. Change may come as a result of election, as in the opening case, but it can also come with a decision by an autocratic ruler, such as Saddam Hussein's invasion of Kuwait, or may be a political misstep by an MNE; for instance, Credit Suisse First Boston Corp. was removed from a foreign underwriting team for a lucrative share offering in China after company executives hosted conferences attended by senior Taiwanese officials.[37] Political risk can also occur as a result of a shifting power or balance. Coca-Cola partnered with the son-in-law of the president of Uzbekistan, who became the president of its local bottling company. When the son-in-law separated from the president's daughter, the company found itself harassed by the authorities, with its operations shut for a period of 18 months.[38] In the opening case, we described how regime change in Latin America has dramatically altered the treatment of FDI in Bolivia and Venezuela. The violent uprisings that occurred in Libya and Syria after the start of the Arab Spring in the early 2010s also created a high level of uncertainty to MNEs operating in that part of the world.

The importance of political risk creates demand for its assessment. The various ways to measure the risk can be roughly classified into five categories: (1) qualitative approaches; (2) aggregates of expert opinions; (3) scenario approaches; (4) decision-tree methods; and (5) quantitative techniques that result in political risk indices. Many MNEs use their own customized instruments to gauge political risk; others rely on independent assessments (e.g., by the Economist Intelligence Unit, Business International, and Eurasia).

Exhibit 7.3 shows the risk of political instability according to the *World Competitiveness Yearbook*.

Types of Political Risk

The three types of political risk include ownership risk, operational risk, and transfer risk. **Ownership risk** represents a threat to the current ownership structure, or to the ability of the MNE to select or shift to a given governance structure. Its extreme form is outright expropriation, namely the forced divestment of assets as a result of a host government decision to nationalize or otherwise transfer ownership. Such divestment may or may not carry compensation, but even when it does, this rarely compensates the MNE for actual damages, especially in opportunity cost. Expropriation risk has been traditionally higher in extractive industries such as oil, natural gas, and mining. Milder forms of ownership risk include pressure toward, or a formal change in, investment rules that forces firms to reduce their stake (e.g., sharing ownership with the government or a local firm). In the early 1970s, the Indian government established such rules that resulted in a strategic shift toward unrelated diversification and eventually to the exodus of many foreign MNEs.[39] Ownership risk has lessened in recent years because of competition for investment dollars and because of the development of institutions such as the WTO that make such unilateral steps prohibitively difficult. Still, as the opening case shows, ownership risk exists and is unlikely to disappear in the foreseeable future.

Operational risk includes any change to the "rules of the game" under which the foreign firm operates (e.g., new and arbitrary taxation), especially when foreign firms are singled out. Operational risk is less tangible than ownership risk but may be equally damaging should it limit strategic freedom and autonomy. For example, Amway faced an effort on the part of the Japanese and the Chinese authorities to curb the direct selling practices which are at the core of its business model. Finally, **transfer risk** involves impediments to the transfer of production factors (e.g., newly imposed capital controls). The three risk types are interrelated. For instance, if a government prohibits the placement of expatriates in key positions, this may present an operational risk compromising efficient operation and technology protection.

While host governments have been moving away from a confrontational stance, to a partnership where bargaining is focused on the value-added activities of the MNE,[40] the level of risk in many nations remains substantial. Furthermore, due to increased global integration, problems in one location can adversely influence operations in another: If a strike shuts down your Polish operations, for instance, you may be unable to complete product assembly in the UK. MNE operations in one market can be used as leverage by political groups at home or in third countries. For instance, US-based Apple has been targeted by European protest groups over the employment practices of its Chinese suppliers. Political risk also affects outward investment. Firms and individuals in high-political-risk nations often seek "safe haven" investment locations, such as the United States, as a way of protecting capital.[41] This trend is more apparent for portfolio

Risk of political instability

The risk of political instability is very low

		2013
1	Denmark	9.47
2	Norway	9.42
3	Switzerland	9.37
4	Sweden	9.05
5	Luxembourg	8.86
6	Canada	8.84
7	Finland	8.77
8	New Zealand	8.60
9	Germany	8.52
10	United Kingdom	8.50
11	Austria	8.45
12	Singapore	8.41
13	Chile	8.40
14	Qatar	8.25
15	USA	8.17
16	UAE	8.15
17	Ireland	8.00
18	Mexico	8.00
19	Netherlands	7.82
20	France	7.72
21	Australia	7.49
22	Brazil	7.35
23	Hong Kong	7.29
24	China Mainland	7.03
25	Taiwan	6.92
26	Philippines	6.65
27	Turkey	6.64
28	Malaysia	6.57
29	Estonia	6.49
30	Slovak Republic	6.30
31	Japan	6.19
32	Lithuania	6.00
33	Colombia	5.98
34	Poland	5.92
35	Kazakhstan	5.90
36	Spain	5.89
37	Belgium	5.80
38	Israel	5.74
39	Peru	5.74
40	Czech Republic	5.64
41	Croatia	5.52
42	Russia	5.29
43	Latvia	5.24
44	Indonesia	5.19
45	India	5.19
46	Korea	5.16
47	Portugal	5.08
48	South Africa	4.84
49	Jordan	4.80
50	Romania	4.37
51	Hungary	4.12
52	Greece	3.71
53	Argentina	3.58
54	Thailand	3.28
55	Iceland	3.26
56	Italy	2.93
57	Bulgaria	2.55
58	Slovenia	2.04
59	Ukraine	1.88
60	Venezuela	0.86

Exhibit 7.3 Risk of political instability

Source: IMD WCY Executive Opinion Survey based on an index from 0 to 10
© IMD World Competitiveness Online 1995–2013 (updated: May 2013).

investment than for FDI, because it is much easier to shift capital than to start actual operations in a foreign location.

Finally, as in other facets of business, risk can be associated with opportunities. US-based AES is fueling much of its growth-acquiring utilities in global hot spots, many of them in Latin America, where its competitors are reluctant to tread. AES relies on cultivating close relationships with host governments and their leaders, as it did in Venezuela, where it bought the leading utility.[42] A similar strategy has been adopted by Taiwan-based Grace T.H.W. Group when seeking a semiconductor venture in mainland China, whose investors included the son of then President Jiang Zemin.[43] Obviously such strategies entail their own risk (e.g., a change in government which renders a past relationship obsolete (or even especially vulnerable when a new regime does not look kindly on its predecessor)).

Strategies for Managing Political Risk

Despite the decline in expropriation, political risk remains a vital concern for the MNE. The successful MNE is not only educated about political risk, but it also knows how to proactively manage it. To manage political risk, the MNE can:

- Minimize outright investment, leasing rather than buying, and relying on government incentives, where available.
- Sign bilateral or multilateral treaties that protect foreign investment.
- Identify or create reciprocal settings where investment from the host country can be seized in case of expropriation.
- Avoid high-visibility acquisitions, especially if a firm or its key assets are viewed as national icons.
- Reduce capital exposure by utilizing host country financing.
- Accelerate profit repatriation.
- Develop a staggered technology transfer policy.
- Source locally, reducing the host country incentive to harm the foreign firm.
- Opt for strategic alliances with a local partner, reducing the foreign investor outlays, and pacifying nationalist sentiment.
- Utilize agencies such as the Overseas Private Investment Corporation (OPIC) which insure companies against political risk.
- Build political support at home and in the host nation through lobbying, public relations, and a proactive social responsibility.
- Monitor political and economic development so as to prepare, avoid, or counter intervention.

Regional-Level Politics

Although the national government is typically the most influential in the political arena, it is not the only one to exert power over incoming foreign investment. Above the state level, regional and federated organizations are partners to the dialogue with the MNE. This is especially apparent where economic integration is accompanied by political integration, as is the case in the European Union (see Chapter 8). Global industry organizations such as airline association IATA also play a role in this dialogue, for instance, by negotiating over industry standards.

237

Below the national level there are also relevant political entities with whom the MNE interacts. For instance, Hong Kong has its own trade and investment agreements with foreign countries that are separate from those of its national sovereign, China. We have already mentioned the incentives offered by various American states to lure foreign car manufacturers such as Mercedes-Benz, Toyota, Nissan, BMW, and Hyundai. Most American states maintain trade and investment offices in foreign countries and often compete with each other on attracting FDI. In Canada, provincial governments play a substantial role in trade and investment regulation. In China, provincial governments often act as quasi-independent fiefdoms, with powers often beyond the reach of the central government. In India, US power producers in Tamil Nadu found out that the state government could not pay for the electricity their multi-million-dollar investment has produced. In Indonesia, Freeport-McMoran Copper & Gold has a land-rights agreement with the Amungme and Kamoro tribes in its Indonesian West Papua province, which exists side by side with its contract with the Indonesian government.[44] Finally, Non-Government Organizations (NGOs) are increasingly involved in dialogue and negotiations with MNEs, for instance, over environmental and employment standards. In the United States, student groups (e.g., at the University of Michigan) have sought to boycott Coca-Cola because of the alleged use of pesticides in its beverages sold in India (something the company has strenuously denied).

Micro-Region Political Processes

Entities smaller than the state or province (e.g., municipalities) are also part of the political landscape for international business. A conference of mayors from France, Germany, and the United States convened in Lyons, France to discuss the problems and opportunities stemming from globalization. They concluded that, like nations and firms, cities were now in a global competition for investment and skilled employees. According to Alain Juppe, the mayor of Bordeaux and a former French prime minister, "governments are too small to deal with the big problems and too big to deal with the small problems. Cities are now competing with each other to attract people who can choose to live where they wish, but also cooperate and establish alliances with each other."[45]

Interim Summary

1. The political environment for international business includes both geopolitics (country-to-country relations) and internal political processes.
2. The MNE's main political relationship is with the host government; its bargaining power will vary by location, time, and industry.
3. Among the three types of political risk, ownership risk, including possible nationalization, is more severe than operational and transfer risk.
4. Entities below the state level are important players in the political environment of the MNE.

The Legal Environment

The Institutional Context

History, colonization, migration, and related phenomena combine to define the nature of the legal system used in a country. The United States and other former British colonies, such as Australia and New Zealand, rely on a **common law** system, which originated in England. Common law is associated with an independent judiciary relying on case precedents. Some US politicians are decrying the use of foreign court precedents by US courts, who are thus basing their decisions "on the fads, the cultural environment, the laws, the constitutions and the biases of foreigners," as argued by Representative Tom Feeney,[46] a reminder that legal systems too are correlated with variations in culture and institutions, as well as subject to political processes.

In contrast to the Anglo system of precedents, most of continental Europe and Latin America use a **civil law** system that originated in the Roman Empire. Civil law relies almost exclusively on the legal code and is applied universally. It is therefore considered less flexible than the common law system. The implications of those differences are substantial. For instance, in common law, ownership rights are affected by actual use and are generally better protected. Common law limits the range of events that justify noncompliance to "acts of God," such as a natural disaster, and, common law is generally less receptive to government intervention than civil law. An additional type of legal system is **theocratic law,** which relies on religious code. Among the countries using theocratic law are Iran and Saudi Arabia, which rely on Islamic law as the basis of their legal system. Countries such as Indonesia and Malaysia use limited elements of Islamic law, for example, in family-related matters.

Another fundamental difference between legal systems is the status of the judiciary versus the executive and legislative branches. Even in civil law systems, where the law is administered by public officials, there is clear separation of powers. In contrast, in China and Vietnam, "rule by man and not by law" has been a longtime tradition, and although these nations have now developed the contours of a modern legal system, much of that tradition lives with the judiciary lacking real independence. A judiciary that lacks independence will often act not on the merits of the case but in accordance with the desire of the political echelon. Canadian insurer, Manufacturers Life Insurance, has had great difficulty enforcing its ownership rights after its bankrupt Indonesian partner protested the sale of its stake. Furthermore, it was targeted by Indonesian police and was prevented from obtaining effective recourse from the Indonesian justice system[47] (See Country Box). In Ukraine, a small investor in a pharmaceutical factory won a legal battle to recover assets pillaged by his joint venture partner, only to have the ruling overturned following pressure by the country's president, who, in a televised visit to the factory, said:

> I often say . . . we must obey the law. But there is something slightly higher than the law: The country's national interest. And this means the interests of our people, not someone else's.[48]
> "This is no longer a legal case, this is a political case," said the exasperated investor.

Judiciary systems that lack independence also tend to have an enforcement problem, meaning that even if a company were to obtain a favorable ruling, there is no certainty that the ruling will

239

actually be acted upon. Plaintiffs in such countries as China, Vietnam, Nigeria, and Russia are often unable to collect won damages or to force a violator of intellectual property rights (IPR), say, a Starbuck's look-alike, to cease operations.

Finally, legal environments differ in the tendency to rely on the court as the primary conflict resolution mechanism. In the United States, which is considered one of the most litigious societies in the world, it is taken for granted that disputes are mostly settled via the court system. Japan, in contrast, is a "non-contractual" society, relying more on such mechanisms as third-party mediation, to resolve conflicts. Unlike the United States, in Japan a signed contract reflects mostly general understanding that is subject to change should circumstances so demand.

Exhibit 7.4 shows country rankings on the fair administration of justice, based on survey results, according to the World Competitiveness Yearbook. At the bottom of the list you will find mostly developing and emerging economies.

Country Box

Indonesia

Manufacturers Life Weathers the Storm in Indonesia

First entering the Indonesian market in 1985, Canadian insurer Manufacturers Life Insurance Company (Manulife) established a joint venture in Indonesia in 1995. By the end of 1999, the joint venture, the largest in Indonesia, accounted for 7 percent of the life insurance market there, with over 70 branches in more than 30 cities in the country. When its local partner became insolvent, Manulife offered to buy its 40 percent stake in a bankruptcy auction. During the auction, the local partner presented documentation that a company registered in the British Virgin Islands had already bought the same shares from a western Samoan firm. The judge ruled that the Virgin Island company had no title to the shares and approved Manulife's bid. This did not resolve Manulife's problems, however. The Indonesian partner launched criminal complaints with the Jakarta police, leading to the arrest of senior Manulife executives. Although they were never charged, some executives were held in custody for weeks, while others received harassing phone calls. In February 2002, the company was cleared from any wrongdoing and it urged the Indonesian authorities to take action against those responsible for the share scam.

Having weathered the crisis, and with Indonesia moving toward democracy and a stable and less corrupt government, the business of Manulife has thrived. In 2012, after nearly 30 years doing business in the country, Manulife Indonesia serves 1.7 million customers, with a staff of over 10,000 employees and full-time agents from over 20 cities across the country. It has become the country's top mutual fund firm, second pension provider, and third in life insurance.

Sources: T. Mapes, "Manufacturers Life learns Indonesian hardball," *Wall Street Journal*, December 11, 2000, A32; Company press releases 2000–2006; Company website 2013.

Justice

Justice is fairly administered

		2013
1	Denmark	9.29
2	Norway	8.88
3	Sweden	8.88
4	Finland	8.74
5	Singapore	8.51
6	Canada	8.45
7	United Kingdom	8.43
8	Switzerland	8.37
9	Australia	8.36
10	Hong Kong	8.26
11	Netherlands	8.21
12	Germany	8.13
13	Ireland	7.96
14	New Zealand	7.92
15	UAE	7.89
16	Luxembourg	7.71
17	France	7.62
18	Japan	7.57
19	USA	7.45
20	Israel	7.40
21	Qatar	7.32
22	Iceland	7.14
23	Belgium	7.12
24	Austria	6.77
25	Malaysia	6.77
26	Thailand	6.05
27	South Africa	5.95
28	Chile	5.88
29	Taiwan	5.76
30	Estonia	5.66
31	Poland	5.53
32	India	5.36
33	Korea	5.26
34	Jordan	5.05
35	Latvia	4.86
36	Lithuania	4.58
37	Hungary	4.54
38	Brazil	4.47
39	Czech Republic	4.46
40	Greece	4.44
41	Romania	4.30
42	Philippines	4.22
43	Kazakhstan	4.21
44	Indonesia	4.16
45	Croatia	4.12
46	Turkey	3.75
47	China Mainland	3.52
48	Mexico	3.42
49	Spain	3.28
50	Slovenia	3.04
51	Italy	3.03
52	Argentina	2.91
53	Colombia	2.80
54	Russia	2.51
55	Portugal	2.10
56	Peru	1.74
57	Slovak Republic	1.64
58	Bulgaria	1.49
59	Ukraine	0.98
60	Venezuela	0.63

Exhibit 7.4 Fair administration of justice

Source: IMD WCY Executive Opinion Survey based on an index from 0 to 10
© IMD World Competitiveness Online 1995–2013 (updated: May 2013).

Legal Jurisdiction

When a supersonic Concorde crashed outside Paris, victims' families filed suit in the United States because the plane, which was manufactured in France and the United Kingdom and flown by national carrier Air France with mostly German passengers on board, was bound for New York, and because a Continental Airlines jet was implicated in the investigation. The more generous awards meted out by US courts were an additional incentive to file suit in New York, but it is the nature of the service that provided the opportunity to argue for American jurisdiction in an otherwise French and German affair.

Legal jurisdiction is the legal authority under which a case can be adjudicated. It is often difficult to determine legal jurisdiction in international business. The MNE is subject to the laws of both its home and host countries and, less often, to the laws of a third country. These laws may be in conflict—compliance with one legal jurisdiction could invoke noncompliance or violation of the other. As an example, the 2002 corporate governance law known as the Sarbanes-Oxley Act requires US companies to establish hotlines for potential whistle blowers; however, doing this in their French subsidiaries will most likely violate French privacy laws.[49] As Chapter 18 illustrates, jurisdictional issues come to the fore even more prominently in electronic trade, where it is especially difficult to determine the origin of manufacturing, distribution, and consumption.

Jurisdictional Levels

At the international level, a firm is subject to international law and to a rapidly internationalizing regulatory system often run by global organizations. The WTO, for one, has become more proactive in deciding matters of jurisdiction and contradictory laws. For instance, it has ruled that a US law denying protection to trademarks held by businesses confiscated in Cuba contradicted WTO trade rules, thereby allowing Pernod Ricard, a French company producing distilled beverages, to sue a US firm over the rights to Havana Club rum.[50] A firm may also be subject to the laws and regulations of a regional entity, such as the EU, or of a trade framework (e.g., ASEAN). Generally speaking, the more integrated the region, the more important are the laws enacted at that level (see Chapter 8). Still, the national level, whether in its home, host country, and sometimes third country, remains the most important and relevant for the MNE.

International Jurisdiction

Because international law relies on customs and treaties, but has no government behind it, it is rarely enforced. The International Court of Justice in The Hague (Netherlands) is a UN institution that has no jurisdiction in most cases unless the governments involved agree to submit the matter to the court (this is beginning to change, however, in regard to war-related violations). Parties to international business contracts often agree in advance to an arbitration authority, such as the International Court of Arbitration, the Inter-American Commercial Arbitration Commission, or the Canadian-American Commercial Arbitration Commission, each specializing in arbitrating between firms from their region and US companies. Parties can also choose a

242

body such as the International Center for Settlement of Investment Disputes, which specializes in FDI.

Recent years saw a rapid globalization in international business regulation, evolving around a number of key principles, chief among them transparency.[51] The United States and the EU have been the most active supporters of the globalization of regulation, while other countries and firms have been active in niche areas. For instance, Lloyd's of London has been a major driving force behind the globalization of marine insurance. International organizations also play a major role in the globalization of regulation. Much of the global regulatory work takes place in technical committees of such organizations as the WTO (see Chapter 8).

In the aircraft and airline industries, the United States has often taken the regulatory lead. National regulators typically await certification by the US Federal Aviation Administration (FAA) before sending in their teams to Boeing's facilities, largely to rubber-stamp that decision. Similarly, although inspection orders issued by the FAA are binding only for US carriers and, in some instances, for aircraft flying to the United States, they are often followed by other carriers wishing to uphold safety and sustain their reputation. Similarly, while approval by the Federal Drug Administration (FDA) is required for any drug sold in the United States, authorities in many other countries require such approval as an indication of product safety and effectiveness.[52]

Regional Jurisdiction

Increasingly, regional bodies are taking responsibility for the enactment and enforcement of laws. At times, considerable uncertainty prevails as to whether regional jurisdiction supersedes national jurisdiction. For example, the European Court of Justice ruled that no EU country could limit trade in a product imported into the EU. In this case, the court found that French rules prohibiting such trade were incompatible with European laws.[53]

National Jurisdiction

While the MNE must comply with domestic jurisdiction at home and foreign jurisdiction abroad, many of its foreign operations fall under domestic jurisdiction as well. One example is the Foreign Corrupt Practices Act that holds US MNEs responsible for bribery and related activities in their foreign operations (see Chapter 19). Recently, activist groups in the United States resurrected a 1789 law enacted to protect foreigners from sea pirates to prosecute US-based MNEs accused of unethical business practices. In one case, 18 US-based retailers and garment manufacturers were sued on behalf of 50,000 garment workers in Saipan.[54] Such alien-tort precedents may mean that in the future, MNEs will become more vulnerable to suits filed at home concerning their foreign operations.

Legal Issues of Interest to the MNE

Legal issues that are of particular concern to the MNE include the protection of corporate and individual property, contract law (the United Nations Convention on Contracts for the International Sale of Goods sets standards for the formulation and enforcement of contracts among its signatories),

243

as well as restriction on foreign asset ownership. For instance, the United States does not permit foreign entities to own a majority share in a US airline, in case its aircraft are needed for emergency deployment of American troops. This rule was used to block British Airways' attempt to acquire a controlling stake in US Air, a US carrier. In a related case, the United States ordered an immediate halt to the operations of Discovery Airlines, a Hawaii-based inter-island carrier, when it was discovered that the airline owner, while US-registered, was a Japanese corporation. Limitations on foreign ownership together with historical and regulatory factors explain why the global airline industry has not consolidated like many other industries (e.g., automotive). Also on national security grounds, the United States does not permit foreigners to own television and radio stations. Rupert Murdoch, an Australian citizen and owner of News Corporation (which operates the Fox television network), has overcome the restriction by becoming a naturalized American citizen.

Rule of Origin Laws

Knowing **product origin** is important for determining duties or for measuring local content, a frequent requirement in trade and FDI. Local content is an especially important issue in developing economies. For instance, Brazil and India, among others, require substantial local content for cars produced domestically by foreign manufacturers. Determining product origin is increasingly complex however. The US Federal Trade Commission determined that for a product to be labeled "Made in the USA," it must be "all or virtually all" made in the United States and should contain "no— or negligible—foreign content"; however, it is unclear what "negligible" means. The EU, on its part, uses 60 percent local value as a threshold.

Competition Laws

(A) ANTITRUST LEGISLATION AND ENFORCEMENT Antitrust and takeovers are one area where legal provisions vary significantly, even within the EU. Take the case of France Telecom, which purchased a 54 percent stake in Equant NV. Because Equant was incorporated in the Netherlands, France Telecom did not have to make the same or better offer to all shareholders, as it would have to do if the acquired firm was located in the United Kingdom or Germany.[55] US antitrust legislation is among the most advanced and a model emulated by several countries. For example, Japan's antitrust legislation dates back to its occupation by US forces, and its American heritage is evident. In contrast to the United States, however, antitrust laws are seldom enforced in Japan. The United States poses the most stringent transparency requirements and is willing to enforce its authority abroad. For instance, the Securities and Exchange Commission filed a suit alleging fraud on the part of German-based, US-traded E.ON for failing to disclose merger intentions.[56] Chrysler's biggest shareholder sued DaimlerChrysler for allegedly concealing its takeover of Chrysler as a "merger of equals" (Daimler has since divested Chrysler, which is now controlled by Fiat). Nevertheless, when asked whether competition laws prevented unfair competition in their country, respondents from Finland, the Netherlands, Germany, and Norway gave their legal systems a better grade than the United States, as did respondents in 15 other countries. Indonesia, Argentina, and Russia ranked lowest.[57]

In recent years, the European Commission has become an aggressive enforcer of antitrust legislation. The Commission derailed the purchase of a French beverage company by Coca-Cola on the grounds that it would give the Atlanta-based company a monopoly position in the European market. The Commission has also investigated Coca-Cola's sales and distribution practices following allegations by its US archrival PepsiCo that Coca-Cola is paying retail outlets to refrain from stocking Pepsi's products. The Commission also derailed the acquisition of Honeywell by General Electric, both US companies, arguing that it would lower competition in the European aviation market. The United States has undertaken a major effort to adopt a global approach to antitrust regulation and enforcement. It proposed the establishment of an independent international agency to oversee mergers and acquisitions, whose increasingly global scope involves multiple jurisdictions. The EU endorses the idea, but would like to see such an agency operate within the WTO.[58]

(B) SUBSIDIES EU rules prohibit government subsidies that give an unfair edge to a firm from one country over another. The Commission tried (but failed) to prevent the French government from providing a hefty subsidy to Air France, the then-ailing national French carrier. The commission seems less concerned, however, with infringements detrimental to non-EU firms. Boeing contends that Airbus, a European consortium, holds an unfair advantage because it has been receiving subsidies from the German, French, Spanish, and British governments of its partner firms. Airbus counters that the award of military contracts to Boeing by the US government amounts to a subsidy because it permits the company to use research and development and manufacturing techniques developed for the military in their civilian aircraft production. The case's outcome before the WTO has been thus far inconclusive.

Marketing and Distribution Laws

National laws determine allowable practices in distribution, advertising, and promotion. For instance, TV cigarette advertising is prohibited in many countries. Norway does not permit two-for-one promotions. In France, a manufacturer cannot offer a product it does not manufacture as an inducement to buy one of its products. In Germany, comparative advertising (arguing that product A is superior to product B) is prohibited; in China, it is prohibited if the comparison reflects negatively on the other product (e.g., suggesting that the competing product is unsafe). Of special interest to MNEs, especially in the EU, is a ruling by the European court in favor of San Francisco-based Levi Strauss & Co. The court ruled against British retailer Tesco, which imported Levi's jeans from outside the EU, where they are cheaper, and undercut the prices charged by Levi Strauss in the EU (see also Chapter 16).[59] The decision is important to the strategy of MNEs, which often position their brands differently in different locations.

Product Liability Laws

Product liability laws are stringent in the United States and the EU and many other developed countries, but are they lax or not enforceable in some economies. In Japan, product liability cases are rarely brought to court, partly because it is more difficult to prove negligence. When a case is brought to court outside the United States, restitution rarely includes the punitive damages that are common in the United States and that can increase an award manifold. The Bridgestone/Firestone tire controversy revealed just how much the United States and Japan differed on product liability enforcement. Where the United States had 47 people in the National Highway Traffic Safety administration working on tire issues, Japan had only two, and they lacked authority to investigate and press for recalls.[60]

Since US laws are considered among the most stringent, numerous countries accept US certification of product safety as a substitute for their own, making it easier for US firms to export their products into those markets. Some countries (e.g., Japan) often do not accept US or EU product certification however, making it necessary for foreign firms to go through costly testing and product adaptation and at times abandon the export idea altogether. At the same time, the lesser rigor and enforcement of product liability legislation in developing country markers sometimes presents firms with a temptation to sell lower-standard products in those markets, an instance of unethical behavior in the case of safety standards, such as in the use of fire-retardant material.

Patent Laws

Patent registration is nation-based, meaning that a patent issued in the United States does not provide automatic protection from infringement in other countries. Separate patent applications must be made in each country, a costly and time-consuming investment, though global applications are now feasible (see section on Treaties, below). Some countries, notably Japan, require such detailed disclosure as part of the application process that the technology may be compromised. Finally, patents are granted for a limited number of years, which varies from one country to another, providing "arbitrage" opportunities.

Treaties

Treaties are agreements signed by two (bilateral) or more (multilateral) nations. In the United States, treaties require Senate approval, but **executive agreements** do not. A multilateral treaty that is ratified by many countries with a joint interest in the issue at hand is called a **law-making treaty**. Some of the international institutions described in Chapters 8, 17, and elsewhere, such as the International Labor Office (ILO), have their origins in multilateral treaties. **Treaties of Friendship, Commerce, and Navigation (FCN)** grant firms from signatory countries rights and privileges enjoyed by domestic businesses. Many of those treaties contain a **Most Favored Nation (MFN)** clause that entitles the signatory nation to a treatment as favorable as that provided to any other country (see Chapter 8). The UN Convention on the Recognition and Enforcement of Foreign Arbitration Awards facilitates the enforcement of arbitration rulings. When a judgment is issued and not performed, the plaintiff can pursue a court judgment in a foreign or domestic court, although an award by the latter may have little impact unless the company in question has substantial assets in the home country that can be seized.

Two international treaties govern patent protection. The first is the Paris Convention for the Protection of Industrial Property, which has been ratified by many countries but not by some Newly Industrialized Economies (NIEs), which are among the main violators of such rights. The Convention guarantees equal treatment of applicants from member countries. It sets a one-year grace period from the time of application in one country, during which the filer enjoys priority in registering the patent in other signatory countries. It also prevents automatic expiry of patent in all member countries when a patent has expired in one. The second international treaty governing patent protection is the Patent Cooperation Treaty, which permits a one-stop application for patents in all signatory countries.

Other treaties of importance include those involving the protection of intellectual property rights, for example, the Paris Convention for the Protection of Intellectual Property, the Berne Convention, the Madrid Trademark Convention, the Universal Copyright Convention, and the Geneva Phonograph Convention. The Berne Convention for the Protection of Literary and Artistic Work automatically extends protection of a copyright holder in one signatory country to all others, so that the copyright needs to be registered in only one office of a signatory country. For work done on or after January 1, 1987, protection is typically extended for up to 50 years after the death of the author (may be extended to 70 years). The Paris Convention for the Protection of Industrial Property recognizes the use of a trademark in one signatory country as a substitute for its use in another signatory country. For instance, because both the United States and Canada are signatories to the Convention, a Canadian firm that has used a trademark in Canada will be granted the use of the same trademark in the United States without having to show prior use of this trademark in the US. One of the obstacles for a smaller firm, especially one that lacks substantial resources, is that trademark information is often available only in the native language.

Interim Summary

1. Legal systems in different countries vary in their underlying principle (common, civil, or theocratic) as well as in judiciary independence, transparency, and enforcement.
2. The nation remains the most potent level for legal jurisdiction, although regional and international entities have become important in recent years.
3. MNEs study, adapt, and leverage national variations in competition, product liability, marketing, and rule-of-origin laws, among others, to further their competitive advantage.

Chapter Summary

1. The political environment in the home and host countries greatly influences international trade and investment.
2. The institutional context is an imprint of history and political relations that represents both a constraint and an advantage for MNE operations in a given market.
3. Managing the relationship with the home and host governments is probably the most important political challenge for the MNE.
4. Political risk is the probability of disruption to MNE operations; however, the MNE has numerous strategies at its disposal with which to mitigate its effects.
5. The type of legal system used in a country (i.e., common, civil, or theocratic), determines, for instance, the protections available to MNE's assets.
6. Jurisdictional issues are more complex in international compared to domestic business. MNEs face conflicting demands from overlapping jurisdictions but can also vary jurisdiction to further their interests.
7. Among the main legal issues in international business are rule of origin, competition, marketing and distribution, product liability, treaties, and patent laws.

Notes

1 W.G. Astley and P.S. Sachdeva, "Structural sources of interorganizational power: A theoretical synthesis," *Academy of Management Review*, 9, 1984, 104–113.
2 J.J. Boddewyn and T.L. Brewer, "International business political behavior: New theoretical directions," *Academy of Management Review*, 19, 1994, 119–143.
3 "S. Korea, US to discuss whether to include products from Kaesong in FTA," *The Philippine Star*, October 6, 2013.
4 J.J. Boddewyn, "Political aspects of MNE theory," *Journal of International Business Studies*, fall 1988, 341–363.
5 Britannica Online, 2013.
6 M.-R. Galloy and M-E. Gruénais, "Growing pains in African democratization: Electing dictators," *Le Monde Diplomatique*, November 1997.
7 H. French, "Mobutu, Zaire's 'Guide,' leads nation into chaos," *New York Times*, June 10, 1995.
8 Britannica Online, 2013.
9 J.N. Bhagwati and R.C. Feenstra, *Essays in International Economic Theory: The Theory of Commercial Policy*, Cambridge, MA: The MIT Press, 1987.
10 J. Dreze and A. Sen, "Putting growth in its place," *Outlook*, November 4, 2011.
11 R.C. Morais, "Interview with Brazilian President Lula," *Forbes*, July 5, 2005; A. Batson and N. Prusty, "China premier proposes economic adjustments," *Wall Street Journal*, March 6, 2008; S. Gupta and B. Majumdar, "India's Singh vows inclusive growth and reforms," *Reuters*, May 19, 2009.
12 C.I.A. World Factbook, 2012; P. Bump, "China's deadly air pollution is already up 30 percent this year," *The Atlantic Wire*, April 3, 2013.
13 S.B. Tallman, "Home country political risk and foreign direct investment in the United States," *Journal of International Business Studies*, summer 1988.

14 H. Keinon, "Israel fighting EU on duty-free products," *The Jerusalem Post Internet Edition,* November 14, 2001.

15 American Enterprise Institute. 2001 (press release).

16 E.D. Mansfield, J.C. Pevehouse, and D.H. Bearce, "Preferential trading arrangements and military disputes," *Security Studies,* 9, January 2, 2000.

17 T.L. Brewer, "Government policies, market imperfections, and foreign direct investment," *Journal of International Business Studies,* 1, 1993, 101–120.

18 A. Hillman and G. Keim, "International variation in the business–government interface," *Academy of Management Review,* January 1995.

19 T.L. Brewer, "An issue area approach to the analysis of MNE–government relations," *Journal of International Business Studies,* 2, 1998, 295–309.

20 J.N. Behrman, J.J. Boddewyn, and A. Kapoor, *International Business—Government Communications,* Lexington, MA: Lexington Books, 1975.

21 W.C. Kim, "The effects of competition and corporate social responsiveness on multinational bargaining power," *Strategic Management Journal,* 9, 1988, 289–295.

22 T. Carlisle, "For Canadian firm, an African albatross," *Wall Street Journal,* August 17, 2000, A19.

23 M.V. Makhija, "Government intervention in the Venezuelan petroleum industry: An empirical investigation of political risk," *Journal of International Business Studies,* 3, 1993, 531–555.

24 K.W. Chan, "Industry competition, corporate variables, and host government," *Management International Review,* 1988.

25 W.C. Kim, "Industry competition, corporate variables, and host government intervention in developing nations," *Management International Review,* 28, 2, 1988.

26 N. Fagre and L.T. Wells, "Bargaining power of multinationals and host governments," *Journal of International Business Studies,* fall 1982, 9–23; T.A. Poynter, "Government intervention in less developed countries: The experience of multinational companies," *Journal of International Business* Studies, spring/summer 1982, 9–25.

27 R. Mudambi, "Multinational investment attraction: Principal-agent considerations," *International Journal of Economics and Business,* February 1999.

28 R. Brooks, "How big incentives won Alabama a piece of the auto industry," *Wall Street Journal,* April 3, 2002, A1.

29 R.J. Rolfe, D.A. Ricks, M.M. Pointer, and M. McCarthy, "Determinants of FDI incentive preferences of MNEs," *Journal of International Business Studies,* 3, 1993, 335–355.

30 P.N. Doremus, W.W. Keller, L.W. Pauly, and S. Reich, *The Myth of the Global Corporation,* Princeton, NJ: Princeton University Press, 1998.

31 G. Winestock, "Why US trade sanctions don't faze Europe," *Wall Street Journal,* September 8, 2000, A15.

32 *The World Competitiveness Yearbook 2000,* Lausanne, Switzerland: International Institute of Management Development (IMD).

33 R.K. Herrmann, P.E. Tetlock, and M.N. Diascro, "How Americans think about trade: Combining ideas about politics and economics," Working paper, The Mershon Center, Ohio State University.

34 H. Cooperm and G. Winestock, "Domestic interests limit US, EU bargaining at WTO," *Wall Street Journal,* November 12, 2001, A24.

35 G.D. Keim and C.P. Zeithaml, "Corporate political strategy and legislative decision making: A review and contingency approach," *Academy of Management Review,* 11, 4, 1986, 828–843.

36 J. Karp, "Boeing joins team competing for US military plane contract," *Wall Street Journal,* April 28, 2006, B4.

37 "CSFB pays a steep price for offending Beijing," *Wall Street Journal,* August 31, 2001, A4.

38 S. LeVine and B. McKay, "Coke finds mixing marriage and business is tricky in Tashkent," *Wall Street Journal,* August 21, 2001, A1; E. Alden, "Bottled up: Why Coke stands accused of being too cozy with the Karimovs," *Financial Times,* June 14, 2006, 11.

39 Y.L. Doz, "How MNEs cope with host government intervention," *Harvard Business Review,* March–April 1980, 149–157.

40 J.H. Dunning, "An overview of relations with national governments," *New Political Economy*, 2, 3, 1998.

41 S.B. Tallman, "Home country political risk and foreign direct investment in the United States," *Journal of International Business Studies,* summer 1988.

42 P. Druckerman, "How to project power around the world," *Wall Street Journal,* November 13, 2000, A23.

43 R. Flannery, "Chip plant venture discussed by firms in China, Taiwan," *Wall Street Journal,* August 21, 2000, A13.

44 C. Cummins, "Freeport signs accord with Indonesian tribes," *Wall Street Journal,* August 21, 2000, A10.

45 "Mayors not stopping at city limits," *International Herald Tribune,* April 8–9, 2000, 1.

46 J. Bravin, "Congress may fight court on global front," *Wall Street Journal,* March 21, 2005, A4.

47 T. Mapes, "Manufacturers Life learns Indonesian hardball," *Wall Street Journal,* December 11, 2000, A32, company press releases.

48 T. Warner, "Lessons for foreign investors in Ukraine," *Wall Street Journal,* August 16, 2000, A18.

49 D. Reilly and S. Nassauer, "Tip-line bind: Follow the law in US or EU?," *The Wall Street Journal,* September 9, 2005, C1.

50 "WTO panel says US trademark law violates trade rules," *Wall Street Journal,* August 7, 2001, A11.

51 J. Braithwaite and P. Drahos, *Global Business Regulation,* Cambridge: Cambridge University Press, 2000.

52 J. Braithwaite and P. Drahos, *Global Business Regulation.*

53 "Trade ban fails trademark test," *Financial Times,* March 25, 1997.

54 "Go global, sue local," *The Economist,* August 14, 1999, 54.

55 A. Raghavan, "Netherlands remains cool to investors' concerns," *Wall Street Journal,* December 22, 2000, C1.

56 V. Fuhrmans, "Foreign firms trading in US get a warning on deception," *Wall Street Journal,* September 29, 2000, A12.

57 *The World Competitiveness Yearbook 2000,* Lausanne, Switzerland: International Institute of Management Development (IMD), p. 418.

58 B. Mitchener, "US endorses a global approach to antitrust," *Wall Street Journal,* September 15, 2000, A15.

59 *The Plain Dealer,* November 21, 2001, C1.

60 P. Dvorak and T. Zaun, "To grasp the tire case, pay a visit to Mr. Seki, a very mild regulator," *Wall Street Journal,* September 8, 2000, A1.

part 3

global markets and institutions

8 INTERNATIONAL ECONOMIC
   INTEGRATION AND INSTITUTIONS   253

9 THE INTERNATIONAL MONETARY SYSTEM
   AND FINANCIAL MARKETS   289

chapter 8

---

international economic integration and institutions

INTERNATIONAL ECONOMIC INTEGRATION   255

GLOBAL-LEVEL COOPERATION AMONG NATIONS   257

REGIONAL-LEVEL COOPERATION AMONG NATIONS   267

COMMODITY-LEVEL COOPERATION AMONG NATIONS   281

STRATEGIC RESPONSES OF MNES   284

Do You Know?

1. Why have world markets become more integrated today? How has this integration taken place? Why, for example, did the US government push hard to form NAFTA with Canada and Mexico?

2. What roles do the WTO, the World Bank, and the IMF play in the world economy? Are they "clubs" of rich nations? If not, why did thousands of people in Seattle protest against the WTO meeting?

3. Why do people debate whether regional blocs (e.g., the European Union or MERCOSUR) are compatible with globalization? If you are an export manager in an Australian company, would you like to see the advent of more blocs in other regions?

4. How should MNEs strategically respond to regional integration? Why, for example, have Siemens and Nokia proactively diversified their geographical presence throughout Europe since 1992, while Hitachi and Toshiba have substituted FDI in Europe for export to Europe?

OPENING CASE   3M's Response to European Market Integration

3M, a US supplier of branded industrial and consumer products, derives about one-fifth of its total revenues from its European operations. 3M integrated its Europe-wide production network in the early 1980s, specializing each plant to manufacture certain products for the entire European market. Even before the European Union was announced, the company had already integrated its upstream activities (e.g., outsourcing, supply base, and inbound logistics) to attain economies of production scale on a regional level. However, its downstream activities—marketing, sales, distribution, and after-sale service service—remained fragmented, with local sales forces and advertising geared toward a national, rather than a regional (European), market. By removing many costly barriers to cross-border flows of goods, information, capital, and services (such as advertising and after-sale support), the harmonized market program in Europe makes it possible for 3M to achieve scale economies not just in production but in customer-related activities as well. 3M took advantage of this development by consolidating the company's downstream activities within Europe. The manager of marketing communications at 3M Europe called the company's new marketing approach "Pan-European communication," in which marketing and selling expenses are spread over a regional customer base, creating economies of scale in advertising and distribution. Part of the strategy involves creating Euro-brands and uniform products and services whose brand image, packaging, attributes, and advertising are standardized throughout Europe. The reason why 3M is able to pursue such a strategy is that it sells relatively standardized products. Moreover, many of 3M's products enjoy high brand-name recognition. Substantial competitive advantages can accrue to the market leaders in this type of market segment—through significant economies of scale—after a large share of the market has been captured. 3M is in a good position to take advantage of globalizing operations—selling a single, standardized product to global markets—thereby maximizing profitability through worldwide economies of scale.

Source: Company Website and Annual Report, 2012.

International Economic Integration

The preceding case suggests that MNEs are facing a new landscape in the international market: increasing economic integration among countries. International managers must understand the influence of such integration on their worldwide operations and, more importantly, strategically respond to this integration as 3M did. International economic relations are governed by a variety of institutions and a complex web of principles, most of which have been established by treaties and agreements signed since World War II. These institutions (e.g., the International Monetary Fund and the World Bank), treaties or agreements (e.g., the General Agreement on Tariff and Trade, or GATT, and Agreement on Trade Related Investment Measures, or TRIMs) have helped boost global economic integration and erase barriers to free trade, investment, and services among nations. Meanwhile, many regions or sub-regions, from Europe and North America to Latin America and the Caribbean, have established harmonized blocs within their respective territories. Intra-regional trade and investments significantly increase as a result of reduction or elimination of various trade barriers. While MNEs have to realign international expansion strategies with increasingly integrated environments, they themselves are also a critical force steering international economic integration. MNEs are more committed today to intra-organizational trade and global vertical integration. This intra-MNE activity heightens cross-border and inter-regional flows of products, services, capital, technology, and human resources. Consequently, the world is entering a new era of economic integration which is simultaneously altering global political and social systems, although new obstacles have also arisen such as the stalled Doha Round of world trade negotiations and the Eurozone crisis of the early 2010s. This integration is characterized by high levels of both globalization and regionalization.

Economic integration is concerned with the removal of barriers to the flows of trade and production factors such as capital and labor between at least two participating nations and the establishment of cooperation and coordination between them. Economic integration helps steer the world toward globalization. As explained in Chapter 1, **globalization** refers to the growing economic interdependencies of countries worldwide through the increasing volume and variety of cross-border transactions in goods and services and of international capital flows, as well as through the rapid and widespread diffusion of technology and information. The following forms of economic integration are often implemented:

1. **Free trade area** involves country combination, where the member nations remove all trade impediments among themselves but retain their freedom concerning their policy-making vis-à-vis non-member countries. The Latin American Free Trade Area, or LAFTA, and the North American Free Trade Agreement, or NAFTA, are examples of this form.
2. **Customs union** is a more deeply integrated free trade area in which member nations must conduct and pursue common external commercial relations such as common tariff policies on imports from non-member nations. The Central American Common Market (CACM) and the Caribbean Community and Common Market (CARICOM) are examples of this form.
3. **Common market** is a more deeply integrated customs union that allows not only free trade of products and services, but also free mobility of production factors (capital, labor, technology) across national member borders. The Southern Common Market Treaty (MERCOSUR) is an example of this form.

4. **Economic union** is a more deeply integrated common market that involves the harmonization of certain economic and social institutions such as monetary and fiscal policies and banking and labor regulations. Participants introduce a central authority to exercise control over these matters so that member nations virtually become an enlarged single "country" in an economic sense. The European Union is perhaps the best example of such an entity today.

5. **Political union** requires the participating nations to become literally one nation in both an economic and political sense. This union involves the establishment of a common parliament and other political institutions. A political union most commonly takes the form of a federal or confederal system. Examples include India (a federation) and Switzerland (a confederation).

Along the above sequence from 1 to 5, the degree of economic integration increases. One form may shift to another over time if all the participating nations agree. For example, the European Union, or EU, started as a common market and shifted over the years to an economic union and now to a partial political union (e.g., citizens vote for both national and European parliaments).

The above forms reflect economic integration between or among nations within a region. Global economic integration also occurs through **multilateral cooperation,** in which participating nations are bound by rules, principles, or responsibilities stipulated in commonly agreed agreements. Unlike the preceding five forms that all lead to regional economic integration, multilateral agreements are largely used to promote worldwide economic exchanges. They may be designed to govern either general trade, service, and investments (e.g., the World Trade Organization), capital flows and financial market stability (e.g., the World Bank and the International Monetary Fund), or specific areas of trade such as dealing with particular commodities (e.g., the International Coffee Agreement).

Economic integration has the potential to generate economic gains for participating nations. We may distinguish between two types of gains: (1) efficiency gains from lower barriers to trade and other economic flows within the region of economic integration; and (2) distributional gains for member nations in a cartel-like organization for the sale or purchase of certain commodities. Efficiency in production may be enhanced by increased specialization in accordance with the law of comparative advantage.[1] The increased size of the market improves economies of scale, which in turn elevates production levels. Further, the collective bargaining power of member nations is increased vis-à-vis non-participating nations. This power may lead to better terms of trade, that is, lower prices on imports from the non-participating countries and higher prices on products exported to those countries.[2] It should be noted, however, that these gains are not guaranteed, nor will each member country benefit equally from integration. The unification of monetary and fiscal policies, for instance, may exert a different impact on participating countries that experience different macroeconomic conditions and varying levels of economic growth. Free mobility of production factors such as labor and capital may create different pressures on employment levels, inflation rates, income distribution, or trade balance for nations that are in different economic stages or have a varying dependence on the goods and services of other nations. Although there are legitimate reasons for possible economic gains from integration, integration in and of itself is not a panacea to cure all economic ills.

International economic integration is propelled by three levels of cooperation: *global, regional,* and *commodity.* Global-level cooperation occurs mainly through international economic agreements or organizations (e.g., WTO); regional-level cooperation proceeds through common markets or unions (e.g., NAFTA); and commodity-level cooperation proceeds through multilateral commodity

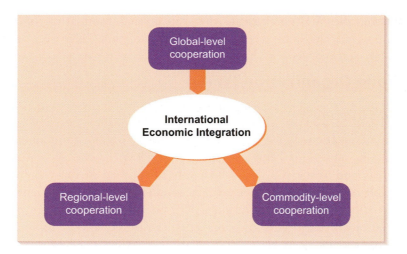

Exhibit 8.1 Forces stimulating international economic integration

cartels or agreements (e.g., OPEC). To international managers, it is important not only to understand how economic integration impacts their international expansion but, more importantly, to realign their resources and strategies to cope with increasingly borderless regions. Exhibit 8.1 lists these issues which are described in detail in the following sections.

Interim Summary

1. World markets are more integrated today because of (a) the formation of regional blocs such as the European Union and NAFTA; (b) the contribution of international economic organizations such as the WTO, the IMF, and the World Bank; and (c) increased intra-organizational investments, trade, and production undertaken by MNEs.
2. International economic integration takes several forms, including free trade area, customs union, common market, economic union, political union, and multilateral cooperation. Economic integration occurs at three levels including global, regional, and commodity.
3. Economic integration is likely to generate economic gains for participating nations. However, these gains are not necessarily equally distributed to all participating nations, nor will every individual or organization within a participating nation be equally impacted by integration.

Global-Level Cooperation Among Nations

The World Trade Organization (WTO), the World Bank, and the International Monetary Fund (IMF) are the three fundamental institutions affecting the global-level cooperation of nations. While the World Bank and IMF serve as the institutional foundation of the international monetary and financial system, the WTO represents the institutional foundation of the international trade system.

The World Trade Organization (WTO)

Background and Structure

The **World Trade Organization** (WTO) is a multilateral trade organization aimed at international trade liberalization. It came into being on January 1, 1995, as the successor to the General Agreement on Tariffs and Trade (GATT), which was established in the wake of World War II. GATT was the result of the first round of tariff negotiations at the 1947 Geneva conference on the proposed International Trade Organization (ITO). GATT evolved through periodic rounds of multilateral negotiations on tariff cuts and non-tariff barrier reductions. Exhibit 8.2 summarizes these negotiations.

Prior to the **Kennedy Round**, early negotiations dealt primarily with reducing tariffs. These tariff cuts facilitated postwar trade liberalization, pushing average trade growth to 8.1 percent per year. By the end of the **Tokyo Round** in 1979, the need to confront the increasing use of non-tariff barriers, particularly by developed countries, led to the adoption of a number of codes dealing with specific practices. The **Uruguay Round** sought to broaden the scope of GATT and reintroduced the idea of a comprehensive international trade organization to coordinate international economic activities, including those involving a large number of developing countries. The Uruguay Round led to the WTO's creation.

Taking effect in 1995, the Uruguay Round agreement specified several liberalization measures that affected the opportunities and threats for international companies. First, members agreed to slash domestic agricultural price supports by 20 percent and export subsidies by 36 percent. These subsidy reductions have benefited major food exporters such as Australia, Canada, New Zealand, Thailand, and the United States. Second, the Uruguay Round instituted several principles concerning trade in services. For instance, government controls on services trade should be administered

Round	Year	Number of Members	Average Tariff Cut (%)
Geneva Round	1947	23	35
Annecy Round	1949	13	n/a
Torquay Round	1950–51	38	25
Geneva Round	1955–56	26	n/a
Dillon Round	1961–62	45	n/a
Kennedy Round	1963–67	62	35
Tokyo Round	1973–79	99	33
Uruguay Round	1986–94	117	36
Doha Round	2001–	149	n/a

Exhibit 8.2 Multilateral negotiations under GATT/WTO

in a non-discriminatory manner. Third, the Uruguay Round agreement substantially strengthened the protection of intellectual property rights, which include patents, copyrights, trademarks, brand names, and expertise.

Negotiations continued after the end of the Uruguay Round. In February 1997, agreement was reached on telecommunications services, with 69 governments agreeing to wide-ranging liberalization measures that went beyond those agreed in the Uruguay Round. Also in this year, 40 governments successfully concluded negotiations for tariff-free trade in information technology products, and 70 members concluded a financial services deal covering more than 95 percent of trade in banking, insurance, securities, and financial information. From 2000 on, new talks started on agriculture and services. These have now been incorporated into a broader agenda launched at the fourth WTO Ministerial Conference in Doha, Qatar in November 2001. The Doha Development Agenda (DDA) adds negotiations and other work on non-agricultural tariffs, trade and environment, WTO rules such as anti-dumping and subsidies, investment, competition policy, trade facilitation, transparency in government procurement, intellectual property, and a range of issues raised by developing countries as difficulties they face in implementing the present WTO agreements. The positions of developing and developed countries diverged widely on most of these very complex issues, and the negotiations were stalled and restored multiple times. After more than 12 years, the major countries of the WTO were still unable to reach an agreement on these issues at the end of 2013.

As the successor to GATT, the WTO's main objective is the establishment of trade policy rules that help expand international trade and raise living standards. These rules foster non-discrimination, transparency, and predictability in the conduct of trade policy. The WTO pursues these objectives by:

- Administering trade agreements;
- Acting as a forum for trade negotiations;
- Settling trade disputes;
- Reviewing national trade policies;
- Assisting developing countries on trade policy issues through technical assistance and training programs;
- Cooperating with other international organizations.

The WTO had 149 members as of December 2005, accounting for about 95 percent of world trade. About 30 applicants are negotiating to become members. In November 2001, China's membership was officially approved, ending 15 years of marathon negotiations with WTO members (most notably the United States). China must slash import tariffs to 8 percent from 21 percent and reduce subsidies for farmers and state-owned enterprises. Decisions on admission into the WTO are made by the entire membership, not by the WTO itself.

The WTO's top-level decision-making body is the Ministerial Conference, which meets at least once every two years. In the intervals between sessions, the highest-level WTO decision-making body is the General Council where member nations are usually represented by ambassadors or the heads of delegations. The General Council also meets as the Trade Policy Review Body and the Dispute Settlement Body. Reporting to the General Council are the Goods Council, Services Council, and Trade-Related Aspects of Intellectual Property Council. In addition, numerous specialized working groups or committees deal with individual agreements and other important areas such as the environment, development, membership applications, regional trade agreements, trade and investment, trade and competition policy, and transparency in government procurement. Electronic commerce is also being studied by various councils and committees.

Functions and Measures

In addition to reduction in import duties, which is the dominant function of the WTO, the organization has several other functions. The first function is the *elimination of discrimination*. The two main principles designed to eliminate discrimination are the *most-favored-nation* treatment and *national treatment*. The **most-favored-nation (MFN) treatment** means that any advantage, favor, or privilege granted to one country must be extended to all other member countries. For example, if Canada reduces its tariff on imports of German cars to 20 percent, it must cut its tariffs on cars imported from all other member nations to 20 percent. **National treatment** means that once they have cleared customs, foreign goods in a member country should be treated the same as domestic goods.

Several exceptions to the MFN principle should be noted. First, the WTO allows members to establish bilateral or regional *customs unions* or free trade areas. For example, following China's admission into the WTO, the Association of Southeast Asian Nations (ASEAN) and China embarked on a plan to form the world's largest free trade area (total population of 1.7 billion) within a decade. Members in such unions or areas may enjoy more preferential treatment than those outside the group. Second, the WTO allows members to *lower tariffs to developing countries* without lowering them to developed countries. For example, the United States offers such treatment to developing countries (they must be GATT members) through what is called the *Generalized System of Preferences (GSP)*. Because of this system, US companies that are more vulnerable to import competition from developing countries face greater pressure on cost reduction. If a developing country is not a GATT member, it cannot enjoy such preferences. The third exception are the *escape clauses* permitted by the WTO. **Escape clauses** are special allowances permitted by the WTO to safeguard infant industries or nourish economic growth in newly admitted developing countries. Under escape clauses, developing countries may: (1) withdraw or modify concessions on customs duties if this is required for the establishment of a new industry that will improve standards of living; (2) restrict imports in order to keep the balance of payments in equilibrium and to obtain the necessary exchange for the purchase of goods for the implementation of development plans; and (3) grant governmental assistance if this appears necessary to promote the establishment of enterprises. The purpose of escape clauses is to help developing country members safeguard their economies. The term "safeguard" is used to denote government actions in response to imports that are believed to cause serious "harm" to the importing country's economic or domestic competing industries.

The second function of the WTO is to *combat various forms of protection and trade barriers*. In addition to the reduction of import duties as shown in Exhibit 8.2, the WTO is devoted to the elimination of quantitative restrictions (i.e., quotas) maintained for agricultural products or for balancing foreign exchange reserve by a member government. Quantitative restrictions are also levied on industrial products by slapping an anti-dumping duty on them. **Dumping** is the sale of imported goods either at prices below what a company charges in its home market, or at prices below cost. Other forms of protection include import deposit without interest, customs valuation, excise duties, subsidies, and countervailing duty (see Chapter 2 for more details). The Uruguay Round was particularly effective in combating non-tariff barriers. The WTO's Trade Policy Review Body regularly monitors the trade policies of its members. These efforts significantly enhance the degree of market access to members' markets.

The third function of the WTO is to *provide a forum for dealing with various emerging issues* concerning the world trade system such as intellectual property, the environment, economic development, regional agreements, unfair trade practices, government procurement, and special sectors such as agriculture, telecommunications, financial services, and maritime service. Many new rules have been derived from such forum discussions. For example, the Trade-Related Intellectual Property Agreement (TRIP) brings new discipline to the protection of patents, copyrights, trade secrets, and similar intellectual property components.

Finally, the WTO functions as *a united dispute settlement system for members* through its *Dispute Settlement Body (DSB)* consisting of representatives from every WTO member. The DSB has the sole authority to establish dispute settlement panels for cases, to adopt panel reports, to monitor the implementation of its rulings, and to authorize suspension of rights if its rulings are not acted upon by the member(s) in a timely fashion. Since the WTO's obligations extend only to member governments, non-members may neither take advantage of the WTO, nor are they subject to its requirements. In this regard, the WTO's judicial reach differs from that of the International Court of Justice, in which non-members of the United Nations may be parties as applicant, respondent, and perhaps intervenor. For example, the DSB established a panel to examine the European Union's complaint against Section 304 of the US Trade Act of 1994. Section 304 is often used by the United States to redress trade policies not covered by the WTO. The EU claimed that Section 304 violates WTO principles because it allows the US Trade Representative Office to unilaterally decide whether another WTO member has violated WTO rules *before* the DSB has ruled on the matter. Instead of ruling on the legality of Section 304, the DSB obtained US commitment to not use the authority in violation of any WTO rules, such as the dispute settlement procedure.

The WTO and its predecessor, GATT, have been viewed as the "club of rich nations" by some developing countries. While beneficial to world trade as a whole, benefits depend in large part on the bargaining power of a member nation or a group of nations. Developing countries often believe they are victims of unfair trade policies and practices adopted by rich nations. Developing countries have long been asking affluent nations to honor commitments to open more markets or remove unfair treatments. At WTO's ministerial meeting in Doha, the capital of Qatar, in November 2001, several developing countries such as Malaysia and India voiced the opinion that rich nations have no right to call for a new round of talks until they have honored past commitments. In subsequent negotiations, a number of developing countries banded together to form a negotiating block and took strong positions against those of developed countries on most of the key issues. This block, led by Brazil, China, India, and South Africa, became known as the G20 or G20+ developing nations, and substantially changed the dynamics of rule-making at the WTO.

Country Box

Russia

Russia Joins the WTO

Russia finally became a member of the WTO in August 2012 after 18 years of off-and-on negotiations, beating the previous record of 15 years that China set in the pursuit of its WTO membership. The road was so arduous that some people even called the WTO the "World Torture Organization" for the process that applicants must go through. Russia is the last major world economy to join the WTO. Among the thorny issues that dragged out the negotiations were Russia's reluctance to subject such inefficient domestic industries as agriculture and automobiles to international competition and the US insistence on Russia's adoption of stringent intellectual property protection measures well above and beyond the WTO Agreements on Trade-Related Aspects of Intellectual Property Rights (TRIPS). Even though Russia appears to have given in to US demands on both issues, there is still a question whether Russia will fully implement its agreements by incorporating them into its domestic laws and regulations and enforcing them effectively.

The terms of the accession accord require Russia to lower its tariffs from about 15 percent to 7 percent in a broad range of economic sectors. These would clearly benefit consumers who had to pay significantly higher prices for imported goods than consumers elsewhere or else buy domestically made ones of inferior quality. The increased Russian imports of such products as consumer electronics, automobiles, and apparel will boost the sales and profits of MNEs in these industries such as Volkswagen, Toyota, GE, Samsung, Nike, and Levi Strauss. The weak domestic competitors of these MNEs, however, are bound to suffer falling sales and profits or even risk bankruptcy unless they can restructure and catch up quickly. The towns and communities in which these Russian companies are based will likely see increased unemployment and decreased taxes until they can attract new investors that soak up the unemployed resources. The Gorky Automobile Plant (GAZ) in Nizhny Novgorod, for instance, has decided to shift more resources to the commercial vehicle sector (e.g., ambulances, rescue trucks, and buses) where its competitive position vis-à-vis its foreign counterparts is stronger, and it has also started assembling cars and vans for such MNEs as Skoda and Mercedes.

Russia's entry into the WTO is expected to raise the country's GDP growth by 3.3 percentage points a year in the next three years, according to World Bank estimates. The Russian economy, even with the added impetus of WTO entry, is still considered to be underperforming given its potential based on its highly educated workers and abundant natural resources, and may further accelerate its growth if the country undertakes deeper economic reforms that are in line with changes required by its WTO accession agreement. China, for instance, attained an average rate of GDP growth at over 10 percent in the decade after its WTO entry in 2001.

The International Monetary Fund (IMF)

The IMF and the World Bank together are often called the *Bretton Woods Institutions,* because they were both established at Bretton Woods, New Hampshire in July 1944. The overall objectives of the IMF are to promote international monetary cooperation and expansion of international trade and to reduce the disequilibrium in members' balances of payments. To accomplish these goals, the IMF seeks to promote exchange stability, maintain orderly exchange arrangements, avoid competitive exchange depreciation, and provide confidence to member states by placing the general resources of the Fund at the disposal of nations facing an economic crisis, subject to adequate safeguards. As the key institution in the international monetary system, the IMF was established to render temporary assistance to member countries trying to defend their currencies against cyclical, seasonal, or random fluctuations. It also assists countries having structural trade problems if they take adequate steps to correct their problems. If persistent deficits occur, however, the IMF cannot save a country from eventual devaluation.

The IMF is headed by a Board of Governors, composed of representatives from all member countries (187 as of the end of 2012). In order to facilitate the exchange of goods, services, and capital, and to provide conditions necessary for financial and economic stability, the IMF requires all members to collaborate with the Fund in promoting a stable system of exchange rates. Each member should avoid manipulating exchange rates for the purpose of preventing effective balance-of-payments adjustments or as an attempt to gain an unfair competitive advantage. Although members may apply the exchange arrangements of their choice, they must follow exchange policies compatible with these undertakings. While the financing role played by the IMF has diminished for industrial countries, this role remains significant for the vast majority of developing countries.

The world community has been increasingly using the IMF as an important forum for multilateral surveillance and coordination of national fiscal and monetary policies. Developing countries have a particularly strong stake in this process: it is only in a multilateral forum that major countries' policies are likely to be coordinated in a manner that accords due weight to the impact on and implications of these policies for the rest of the world community. The IMF played a major role in tackling the East Asian financial crisis of 1997 and the Eurozone crisis of 2008–2012, providing policy advice, financing, and international coordination. The policies that the IMF adopted during the East Asian crisis emphasized rapid restoration of government budgetary balances and balances in trade and capital flows (including drastic cuts in government spending and rapid currency devaluations) and were criticized as excessively harsh by many in the countries that were compelled to adopt those measures as conditions for financial assistance. After reevaluating the effects of those measures, the IMF significantly revised its approach when it assisted the Eurozone countries in dealing with their financial crisis, emphasizing instead the restoration of stability, avoidance of excessive adjustment pain, and long-term institutional reform. Because many of the developed countries experienced both large budget deficits and large balance-of-payments deficits during the world economic downturn of 2008–2012, some developing countries, notably China and to a lesser extent Brazil, become major sources of surplus capital in the world. The IMF increased the quotas (shares) of China and Brazil in this period by 72 percent and 66 percent, respectively, so as to gain additional capital for financing countries in difficulty, such as Greece, Portugal, and Spain. These quota changes also substantially boosted the voting powers of these two countries, making China the third largest quota holder (slightly below Japan) in the institution.

The growing integration of the world's money and capital markets, and the inevitable increased role of private capital, can at times greatly complicate the task of orderly economic management, particularly in developing countries with limited policy instruments at their disposal. As demonstrated by the Asian financial crisis of 1997 and the worldwide financial crisis of 2008–2012, weaknesses in the financial regulations of a few countries, combined with the volatility and unpredictability of portfolio capital flows, can cause the financial systems of multiple countries and even of the entire world to collapse, resulting in a severe regional or worldwide economic downturn. The world needs credible international safety nets, while preserving the freedom of capital markets, to protect the integrity of their development programs in the face of sudden outflows of private capital. In a rapidly changing and uncertain world, the IMF has already begun, and should continue, to develop greater flexibility to respond purposefully and quickly to constantly changing economic conditions.

In order to carry out the tasks of monitoring the international monetary system and supplementing foreign exchange reserves, the IMF created the **Special Drawing Right** *(SDR)*. As an international reserve asset, SDR serves as a unit of account for the IMF and other international and regional organizations, and is also the base against which some countries peg the rate of exchange for their currencies. Defined initially in terms of a fixed quantity of gold, the SDR was later the weighted value of currencies of the five IMF members that had the largest exports of goods and services at the time: US dollar, German mark, Japanese yen, French franc, and British pound sterling, with the mark and franc later replaced by the euro after Germany and France adopted it as their currency.

SDRs are not circulated internationally. Individual countries hold SDRs in the form of deposits in the IMF. These holdings are part of each country's international monetary reserves, along with each country's official holdings of gold, foreign exchange, and reserve position at the IMF. Members may settle transactions among themselves by transferring SDRs.

The World Bank Group

The World Bank refers to the *International Bank for Reconstruction and Development (IBRD)*. The World Bank and its three affiliates, the *International Development Association (IDA)*, the *International Finance Corporation (IFC)*, and the *Multilateral Investment Guarantee Agency (MIGA)*, are sometimes referred to as the **World Bank Group.** The common objective of these institutions is to help raise the standards of living in developing countries by channeling financial resources to them from developed countries, even though the IBRD was initially set up to help the Western European countries recover from the ruins of World War II.

Established in 1945, the World Bank is owned by the governments of 184 countries as of the end of 2005. Its capital is funded from the subscription of its member countries. The World Bank finances its lending operations primarily through its own borrowing in the world capital markets. A substantial contribution to the World Bank's capital resource also comes from its retained earnings and the flow of repayments on its loans. World Bank loans generally have a grace period of five years and are repayable over 15 to 20 years. Loans are geared toward developing countries that are in relatively more advanced stages of economic and social growth. The interest rates on these loans are calculated based on the cost of their borrowing, which makes them lower than market interest rates.

The World Bank's charter spells out basic rules that govern its operations. It must lend only for productive purposes and must stimulate economic growth in the recipient developing countries. It must pay due regard to the prospects of repayment. Each loan is made to a government or must be guaranteed by the government concerned. The use of loans cannot be restricted to purchases in any particular member country.

While the World Bank has traditionally financed all kinds of capital infrastructure (such as roads and railways, telecommunications, and port and power facilities), the centerpiece of its development strategy emphasizes investment that can directly affect the well-being of the masses of impoverished people in developing countries by making them more productive and by integrating them as active partners in the development process.

The International Development Association, or IDA, established in 1960, concentrates on assisting the least developed nations. The terms of IDA credits, which are traditionally made only to governments, are 10-year grace periods, 35- or 40-year maturities, and no interest. The International Finance Corporation, or IFC, was established in 1956 for the purpose of assisting the economic development of developing countries by promoting growth in the private sector of their economies and helping to mobilize domestic and foreign capital for this purpose. Finally, the Multilateral Investment Guarantee Agency, or MIGA, established in 1988, specializes in encouraging equity investment and other direct investment flows to the developing countries through the mitigation of non-commercial investment barriers. To carry out this mandate, MIGA offers investors guarantees against non-commercial risks, advises developing country governments on the design and implementation of policies concerning foreign investments, and sponsors a dialogue between the international business community and host governments on investment issues.

Since the late 1990s, cooperation between the WTO, the IMF, and the World Bank has increased significantly. This includes participation at meetings, information sharing, contacts at staff level, and the creation of a *High Level Working Group on Coherence* that oversees the process and prepares an annual joint statement on Coherence. In 1998, the WTO Secretariat cooperated with the staff of the IMF and the World Bank to assist developing countries in stimulating their foreign trade and their participation in the multilateral trading system. Such cooperation was also addressed in a Joint Statement by the director-general of the WTO, the managing director of the IMF, and the president of the World Bank, which was issued at the time of the *Seattle Ministerial Conference*. The Joint Statement calls upon ministers to make substantial progress on all three fronts, noting that such efforts represent the essence of adopting a more coherent approach to global economic policy making.

Other International Economic Organizations

The Organization for Economic Cooperation and Development (OECD)

The OECD was established in December 1960, replacing the former OEEC (the Organization for European Economic Cooperation) and includes non-European countries such as the United States, Canada, Japan, Australia, New Zealand, and Mexico. The OECD groups 30 member countries (as of September 1, 2006) sharing a commitment to democratic government and the market economy. With active relationships with some 70 other countries, non-governmental organizations, and civil society, it has a global reach. Its mission is to aid in the achievement of the highest and soundest possible growth in economies of member countries and also in non-member states. It emphasizes economic development, employment expansion, living standards improvement, financial stability, and extension of world trade on a multilateral and non-discriminatory basis. Best known for its publications and its statistics, its work covers economic and social issues from macroeconomics to trade, education, development, and science and innovation. The Council is the highest authority in the OECD. In the past, the OECD has made efforts to lower barriers to the exchange of goods, services and capital, stabilize financial fluctuations that may endanger economies of members or those of other countries, and promote scientific research and vocational training. The OECD, however, does not have specific provisions on the liberalization of goods, invisible transactions, and capital. Thus, the OECD has not made many concrete decisions, though it has issued many publications on international business. Coordination of economic policies of all developed countries became the principal aim of the OECD after the European Union was formed.

The United Nations Conference on Trade and Development (UNCTAD)

Prior to the first UNCTAD held in Geneva in June 1964, most international economic organizations concerned the economic interests of developed countries. UNCTAD is in many ways a forum for an examination of economic problems plaguing developing countries, as well as for formulating, negotiating, and implementing measures to improve the development process for these countries. This forum is essential to achieve the demand for "a new international economic order" involving more trade and capital concessions on the part of developed countries, which have generally benefited more

Special Area	Name of Organization	Major Function/Objective
Food	Food and Agriculture Organization (FAO) of the United Nations, founded in 1945	Collect, analyze, interpret, and disseminate information on nutrition, food, and agriculture
Health	World Health Organization (WHO), founded in 1946	Assist all people in achieving the highest level of health
Labor training Standardization	International Labor Organization (ILO), founded in 1919 International Organization for Standardization (ISO), founded in 1947	Promote employment, living standards, improve working conditions, social security Promote the development of standardization to facilitate exchange of goods and services throughout the world
Intellectual property	World Intellectual Property Organization (WIPO), founded in 1967	Promote the protection of intellectual property through cooperation among nations and intellectual property unions
Tourism	World Tourism Organization (WTO), founded in 1970	Promote and develop tourism to contribute to economic growth, international understanding, and peace
Environment	United Nations Environment Program (UNEP), founded in 1972	Preserve the environment and natural resources through international cooperation

Exhibit 8.3 Summary of specialized international economic organizations

266

from global trade and investment. As discussed in previous chapters, domestic institutional weaknesses and shortage of trained personnel for effective participation in international economic organizations are also factors limiting the benefits of trade and FDI for developing countries, especially the least developed ones. Specifically, developing countries hope to solve three problems via the UNCTAD:

1. Their share in world trade is decreasing and their terms of trade with developed countries are deteriorating.
2. Markets of developed countries are not sufficiently open to manufactured products of developing countries.
3. Although the aid given by developed countries has increased, it remains inadequate. In fact, many developing countries are still struggling with huge burdens of foreign debts.

The United Nations has a number of agencies with responsibilities for coordinating various aspects of international economic activities in the world, such as intellectual property protection and tourism. A list of these organizations is provided in Exhibit 8.3.

Interim Summary

1. The WTO, IMF, and the World Bank are the three major international economic organizations affecting global-level cooperation of nations. The WTO aims to facilitate trade through reducing trade barriers and eliminating discrimination, whereas the IMF and the World Bank focus on the monetary (currency stability) and fiscal (financial funding) system, respectively.
2. Although these organizations are supposed to help raise standards of living in member countries, developing countries often find their voice weak in these organizations, especially the WTO, and they ask affluent nations to remove unfair trade policies or honor commitments for further opening their markets.

Regional-Level Cooperation Among Nations

Multilateral trade liberalization after World War II has been paralleled by a process of integration through regional agreements.[3] The vast majority of WTO members are party to one or more regional trade agreements. A total of 546 agreements were reported to GATT/WTO from 1947 through the end of 2012, of which over 354 regional trade agreements are currently in force. These agreements have, for the most part, involved countries in the same geographic region (see Exhibit 8.4).

Postwar Regional Integration

Three features characterize postwar regional integration. First, postwar regional integration initially centered primarily in Western Europe but expanded to the Americas and the Asian Pacific more recently. The creation of the *European Economic Community (EEC)* in 1958 and of the *European*

Region	Regional Integration Agreements	Participating Countries
EUROPE	European Union (EU)	Austria, Belgium, Bulgaria, Croatia, Cyprus, Czech Rep., Denmark, Estonia, Finland, France, Germany, Greece, Hungary, Ireland, Italy, Latvia, Lithuania, Luxembourg, Malta, Netherlands, Poland, Portugal, Romania, Slovakia, Slovenia, Spain, Sweden, United Kingdom
	EC (predecessor of EU) Free Trade Agreements with	Norway, Iceland, Liechtenstein, Switzerland, Israel
	EC (predecessor of EU) Customs Union with	Andorra, Monaco, San Marino, Turkey
NORTH AMERICA	Canada–United States Free Trade Agreement (CUFTA), Superseded by NAFTA	
	North American Free Trade Agreement (NAFTA)	
LATIN AMERICA AND THE CARIBBEAN	Caribbean Community and Common Market (CARICOM)	
	Central American Common Market (CACM)	
	Latin American Integration Association (LAIA)	
	Southern Common Market (MERCOSUR)	
	Andean Community	
	Union of South American Nations (UNASUR)	
MIDDLE EAST	Economic Cooperation Market (ECO)	
	Gulf Cooperation Council (GCC)	
ASIAN PACIFIC	Association of South East Asian Nations (ASEAN)	Brunei, Cambodia, Indonesia, Laos, Malaysia, Myanmar, Philippines, Singapore, Thailand, Vietnam
	ASEAN Free Trade Agreements with	China, Korea, Rep., Japan, Australia, New Zealand, India
	Australia–New Zealand Closer Economic Relations Trade Agreement (CER)	
	Regional Comprehensive Economic Partnership (RCEP), being negotiated among	ASEAN members plus the six countries that ASEAN has Free Trade Agreements with (ASEAN + 6)
OTHER	Central America–US Free Trade Agreement (CAFTA)	
	Trans-Pacific Partnership, being negotiated among	Twelve countries in the Asian Pacific and the Americas
	U.S. Free Trade Agreements with	Australia, Bahrain, Chile, Colombia, Costa Rica, Dominican Rep., El Salvador, Guatemala, Honduras, Israel, Jordan, Korea, Rep., Morocco, Nicaragua, Oman, Panama, Peru, Singapore

Exhibit 8.4 Selected regional integration agreements (as of July 2013)

Free Trade Association (EFTA) in 1960 initiated a process of enlarging the scope of regional integration among European countries and with other countries. The European Union that superseded the EEC is still the regional arrangement with by far the widest and deepest integration, and it has concluded free trade agreements with additional countries in Europe, Africa, the Middle East, and other parts of the world. The advent of the North American Free Trade Agreement (NAFTA) in 1994 created the second largest free trade bloc in the world at the time, and efforts have been made to integrate NAFTA with other free trade blocs in Central and Latin America. Since the late 2000s, the Association of Southeast Asian Nations (ASEAN) has emerged as the crux of another cluster of free trade agreements in the Asian Pacific region and announced in November 2012 that it would negotiate a Regional Comprehensive Economic Partnership among the current ASEAN members and the six countries associated with it via free trade agreements (ASEAN+6). So, there are currently three major clusters of regional economic integration in Europe, the Americas, and the Asian Pacific, respectively. Even though there are also a number of economic integration arrangements in Africa, their weight and impact on the world are more limited. However, many African countries are still enthusiastic about joining other blocs of economic integration, particularly the EU, despite the rising skepticism about such arrangements within EU and elsewhere.[4]

Second, many developing countries, particularly in Latin America and Asia, have renewed their interest in regional integration since the Uruguay Round began. As part of their adoption of outward-oriented policies, regional integration can help broaden the openness and internationalization of developing economies while avoiding overdependence on world markets. Moreover, continued economic reforms, especially more developed macroeconomic and exchange rate policies, suggest that the overall policy environment has become more conducive to regional integration objectives.[5] This is evidenced by the proliferation of free trade agreements among developing countries (e.g., ASEAN+6) and free trade agreements linking developing countries with one of the other major blocks of regional economic integration, such as the EU and NAFTA countries.

Third, the level of economic integration varies widely among different agreements. Most regional integration agreements involve free trade areas, and the number of customs union agreements is small. Among free trade agreements, it is useful to distinguish between *reciprocal agreements* and *non-reciprocal agreements*. In a reciprocal agreement, each member agrees to reduce or eliminate barriers to trade. In a non-reciprocal agreement, some developed countries may reduce trade barriers, allowing more exports from some developing countries, without requesting reciprocity from the latter. The EU certainly has the deepest level of integration, followed by NAFTA. The ASEAN, however, is more flexible in its requirements for new free trade agreements with other countries such as China and India.

North America: The North American Free Trade Agreement (NAFTA)

On December 17, 1992, the leaders of Canada, Mexico, and the United States signed a historic trade accord, the North American Free Trade Agreement (NAFTA), creating a tri-national market area of more than 360 million people with a combined purchasing power of approximately $6.5 trillion. NAFTA is the first ever reciprocal free trade accord between industrial countries and a developing nation (Mexico), which explains why this pact is of special interest to developing countries, particularly those located in Latin America. NAFTA helps enhance the ability of North American producers (especially US companies) to compete globally. By improving the investment climate in North America and by providing companies with a larger market, NAFTA also helps increase economic growth despite the fact that this increase is not equal among the three members.

NAFTA went into effect on January 1, 1994, uniting the United States with its largest (Canada) and third-largest (Mexico) trading partners. Based on the earlier US-Canada Free Trade Agreement, NAFTA dismantled trade barriers for industrial goods and included agreements on services, investments, intellectual property rights, and agriculture.

NAFTA also includes side agreements on labor adjustment, environmental protection, and import surges. The side agreement on labor adjustment came in response to American workers' concerns that jobs in the United States would be exported to Mexico because of Mexico's lower labor wages, weak child labor laws, and other conditions that afford Mexican labor an economic advantage over its American counterpart. The side agreement is an attempt to manage the terms of the potential change in labor markets. The agreement involves such issues as restrictions on child labor, health and safety standards, and minimum wages. In addition to signing the labor side agreement, the Mexican government has pledged to link increases in the Mexican minimum wage to productivity increases.

The side agreement on environmental cooperation explicitly ensures the rights of the United States to safeguard the environment. NAFTA upholds all existing US health, safety, and environmental standards. It allows states and cities to enact even tougher standards, while providing mechanisms to encourage all parties to raise their standards. The side agreement on import surges creates an early warning mechanism to identify those sectors where a sudden, explosive trade growth may do significant harm to the domestic industry. It also establishes that in the future, a working group can provide for revisions in the treaty text based on the experiences with the existing safeguard mechanisms. During the transition period, safeguard relief is available in the form of a temporary retreat to pre-NAFTA duties if an import surge threatens to seriously damage a domestic industry. These three side agreements were negotiated to alleviate the fears of US labor and industry groups that felt threatened by the possible immediate adverse impact on their members.

With the integration of the Canadian, US, and Mexican markets, many companies have changed their business strategies and plans in order to serve the integrated North American market more efficiently. Many companies in Mexico, the United States, and Canada closed inefficient plants and concentrated production where it could generate the highest possible returns. Whether it is the Mexican company Cemex, the Canadian company Alcan Aluminum, or the American company Ford, each can take advantage of cheaper labor or resources for certain components and products. In the foreseeable future, assuming that Mexican worker productivity is equal or close to that of US or Canadian workers, one would expect that labor-intensive production would be performed in Mexico where workers' hourly wages are less than half of those in the United States.

Shortly after NAFTA took effect, an initiative was started to expand NAFTA to essentially all the countries in the Western Hemisphere (except Cuba) under a Free Trade Area of the Americas (FTAA), with negotiations expected to complete by 2005. The negotiations, however, were repeatedly bogged down by the same disagreements between developed and developing countries that stalled the Doha Round of world trade negotiations. The main points of contention were the Argentine and Brazilian demand for the US to eliminate agricultural subsidies, and the US demand for all the countries to adopt measures for strict enforcement of patents and copyrights. Despite a strong push by the US, the leaders of the Western Hemisphere failed to reach an agreement at their summit in Mar Del Plata, Argentina in November 2005. It was expected that those countries that do not want to see this initiative completely lost would negotiate a series of bilateral agreements to accomplish at least some of the original goals for FTAA.[6]

Europe: The European Union (EU)

The postwar efforts to establish the European Union have been a long process, beginning with the formation of the *European Economic Community (EEC)* in 1957. After three enlargement efforts ended on January 1, 1995, the *European Community (EC)* was formed, consisting of 15 member states: Belgium, the Netherlands, Luxembourg, France, Germany, Italy, Denmark, Ireland, the United Kingdom, Greece, Spain, Portugal, Finland, Sweden, and Austria. These EC member states constitute the core, as well as the deepest level, of European economic integration. The outer tier of trade and economic liberalization within the European Union is composed of countries in Central and Eastern Europe (e.g., Czech Republic, Hungary, Poland), as well as Mediterranean countries (e.g., Slovenia, Malta). There are currently 28 member states in the EU (see Exhibit 8.4), including Croatia, the newest member that joined on July 1, 2013. The EU has over 500 million people—surpassed only by China and India (see Exhibit 8.5).

The most fundamental step in strengthening economic and political ties among EC member states occurred with the *Treaty on European Union* (or the "Maastricht" Treaty). Signed in February 1992, the treaty was enforced beginning in November 1993. This treaty not only promotes economic and trade expansion within a common market, but also embraces the formation of a monetary union, the establishment of a common foreign and security policy, common citizenship, and the development of cooperation on justice and social affairs. Its significance was marked by the adoption of the new name: "European Union" (EU). The Maastricht Treaty contains several high-impact provisions, such as:

1. It creates a common European currency, known as the *euro*.
2. Every citizen in each member state in the EU is eligible to obtain a European passport, which bestows the right to move freely from one country to another within the Union.
3. It contains provisions on cooperation in the fields of justice and domestic affairs.
4. It empowers the Union to play a more active role in areas such as trans-European transport and environmental protection.
5. It increases the power of the European Parliament to enact legislation.
6. It removes all restrictions on capital movements between member states.
7. Finally, it establishes a European Central Bank responsible for monetary policy, and transforms the European Union into the European Economic and Monetary Union (EMU), under which the currencies of the member states are tied irrevocably to one another at the same exchange rate.

Exhibit 8.5 Map of the EU

The EU is run by five institutions, each playing a specific role:

- European Parliament (elected by the people of the member states).
- Council of the Union (governments of the member states).
- European Commission (executive body).
- Court of Justice (compliance with the law).
- Court of Auditors (lawful management of the EU budget).

272

Seventeen of the member countries have adopted the euro as their common currency and sole legal tender, including Austria, Belgium, Cyprus, Estonia, Finland, France, Germany, Greece, Ireland, Italy, Luxembourg, Malta, the Netherlands, Portugal, Slovakia, Slovenia, and Spain. These countries form the EMU, and the area consisting of these countries is known as the Eurozone. The rest of the member countries have either opted out of the EMU (i.e., Denmark and the UK), or have not yet joined it. To be eligible for joining the EMU, a member country must fulfill a set of monetary and fiscal conditions for stability (concerning inflation, government budget deficit, ration of government debt to GDP, exchange rate, and long-term interest rate), but the enforcement of these conditions appears to have been flawed, as some of the countries were reported to have fudged their economic statistics to meet the conditions.[7]

The EU's decision to set up a monetary union without effective coordination of fiscal policies or rigorous enforcement of the required stability conditions among the member countries was controversial from the beginning. The Eurozone crisis of the early 2010s, however, reveals that these institutional flaws have made the monetary union unsustainable. Even though some member countries maintained largely responsible fiscal policies, others ran large and persistent government budget deficits either to keep up their overly generous welfare systems (e.g., Greece and Portugal) or to bail out their collapsing private banks under the weight of burst real estate bubbles (e.g., Ireland and Spain). As international investors started to lose confidence in the abilities of the countries in crisis to finance their debt obligations, these countries saw the costs of financing soar to unsustainable levels (7 percent per annum or higher) and needed increasingly large infusions of capital from outside sources (e.g., other EU countries and the IMF). After rounds of heated negotiations under

Industry Box

Siemens Sharpens its Focus to Respond to the Single Market

Siemens, Germany's largest electronics firm, is an example of an MNE from the European Community that was forced to reorganize and expand geographically in the region. Before the single market was formed, Siemens was highly dependent on government purchases and concentrated in regulated markets such as telecommunications equipment, nuclear power and energy, and defense-related equipment. After 1992, Siemens and other former "national champions" in Europe faced deregulated markets in which they competed with MNEs such as AT&T, GE, and IBM. In response, Siemens diversified its geographical presence in Europe and refocused its product lines on those that had competitive advantages. It chose the United Kingdom and France as locations for major new markets in the Community. It integrated vertically to produce end products that share a common core in advanced semiconductor technology in high-growth sectors. Siemens decentralized from seven product-based divisions to 15 smaller independent units, making the company more flexible in a fast-changing environment. It acquired Plessey in the United Kingdom, which gave it a foothold in the UK and a 10 percent world market share for public branch exchange products. Siemens also entered into alliances with BASF in mainframes, Bendix in automotive electronics, and Westinghouse in factory automation and controls. All of these efforts helped Siemens to become a premier MNE in Europe in the electronics, semiconductor, computer, and software industries.

the threat of a Greek default and exit from the Eurozone, the EU members finally endorsed a new agreement at the end of 2011 that would give the EU the authority to monitor closely and intervene in the budgets of national governments and regulate the banking activities in the entire region. The institutional reforms outlined in the agreement, however, still needed to be fleshed out and incorporated in the EU charter and other EU regulations.[8]

Asia Pacific

The Association of Southeast Asian Nations (ASEAN) was founded in Bangkok, Thailand on August 8, 1967, consisting of only five members at the time: Indonesia, Malaysia, the Philippines, Singapore, and Thailand. The initial motivation was as much political as economic, since all of the five nations took a strong anti-communist stand, but faced domestic unrests or insurgencies from leftist political groups and the expansion of Soviet-style socialism in the region, namely in China and Vietnam. But as both China and Vietnam embarked on the course of reforms in the last decades of the twentieth century, the primary aim of the organization turned toward the promotion of economic development among member countries through the liberalization of trade and investment, expansion of the regional markets, and coordination of economic policies. ASEAN also expanded as an organization to include ten countries in Southeast Asia and concluded free trade agreements with six other countries in the Asia Pacific: namely China, Korea, Japan, Australia, New Zealand, and India. These six countries also participate regularly in ASEAN meetings as observers. They, together with the ten ASEAN members, are now referred to as ASEAN+6; a map of these countries is presented in Exhibit 8.6. At the conclusion of the ASEAN summit in Phnom Penh, Cambodia, on November 21, 2012, the 16 nations (i.e., ASEAN+6) announced that they would start negotiation on a Regional Comprehensive Economic Partnership (RCEP) and expected the new partnership to take effect in 2015.[9] If the 16 nations are able to complete the negotiation and implement the RCEP, the new group will be the world's largest, covering nearly half of the world's population.

An often-noted distinction between ASEAN and the EU and NAFTA is that ASEAN is more flexible toward the conditions for a country to join or form a free trade partnership with the group. Partly reflecting the culture of the region, ASEAN prefers to manage differences in a non-confrontational manner and is more willing to accommodate the other party in negotiations. As a result, the agreements that ASEAN have concluded among the member countries and with its free trade partners tend to have more exceptions or exclusions than the agreements negotiated with EU and NAFTA countries. Some critics argue that the ASEAN agreements leave too many trade barriers in place and are thus less effective in promoting efficiency and fairness in international trade.[10]

The Asia-Pacific Economic Cooperation Forum (APEC), founded in 1989, consists of 21 economies (as of January 2012), including Australia, New Zealand, Canada, Mexico, the United States, Chile, China, Hong Kong, Japan, South Korea, Papua New Guinea, Chinese Taipei (Taiwan), Indonesia, Malaysia, Peru, the Philippines, Russia, Singapore, Thailand, Brunei, and Vietnam. APEC member economies work together to sustain economic growth through a commitment to open trade, investment, and economic reform. In the 1994 summit declaration, members agreed to build on the commitments they made in the Uruguay Round of GATT, by accelerating their implementation, and broadening and deepening these commitments. By progressively reducing tariffs and other

Six Free Trade Partners of ASEAN   **Ten ASEAN Countries**

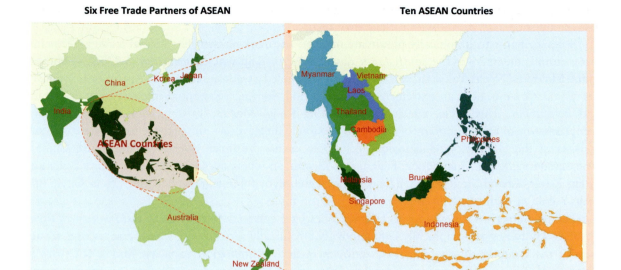

Exhibit 8.6 ASEAN+6

barriers to trade, imports and exports between member economies have expanded dramatically. Compared to other regional unions or areas, APEC is cross-regional, spanning Asia, North and South America, and the Pacific. Moreover, APEC is unique in terms of the mix of members involved, encompassing large and small, rich and poor, as well as politically divergent nations. APEC member economies generate nearly 70 percent of global economic growth, and the APEC region consistently outperformed the rest of the world, even during the Asian financial crisis.

APEC operates as a cooperative, multilateral economic and trade forum. It is unique in that it represents the only inter-governmental grouping in the world committed to reducing trade barriers and increasing investments without requiring its members to enter into legally binding obligations. The forum aims to promote dialogue and equal respect for the views of all participants and making decisions based on consensus to achieve its free and open trade and investment goals. APEC members take both individual and collective actions to open their markets and promote economic growth. Each year, one member economy plays host to APEC meetings and serves as the APEC chair. The APEC host economy is responsible for chairing the annual Government Leaders' Meeting, selected Ministerial Meetings, Senior Officials' Meetings, the APEC Business Advisory Council, and also fills the Executive Director position at the APEC Secretariat. The Forum has several special committees, including Committee on Trade and Investment, Economic Committee, Special Task Groups, and Budget and Management Committee, working for the above meetings.

Accounting for one-fifth of the world trade, Asia is distinctive in several ways. First, many countries in the region have accelerated their trade liberalization at the subnational level by authorizing export processing zones or special investment areas within each country. In China, for instance, the Standing Committee of the National People's Congress approved in August 1980 the establishment of four special economic zones: namely Shenzhen, Zhuhai, Shantou, and Xiamen.

Thailand, Vietnam, Indonesia, Malaysia, India, Bangladesh, and the Philippines, to name a few, also established such zones within their own territories.

Second, many geographically proximate neighbors in Asia reached less formal trade agreements. For example, members of the *South Asian Association for Regional Cooperation (SAARC)*—Bhutan, India, Maldives, Nepal, Pakistan, and Sri Lanka—concluded a trade agreement in April 1993. Similarly, the *China Circle* is now an extremely dynamic region exerting substantial impacts on world trade and investment. This circle, which includes Hong Kong, Macau, Taiwan, and Mainland China, comprises—from the standpoint of degree of economic integration—three concentric layers: the core consists of the Hong Kong–Guangdong economic nexus; the inner layer, "Greater South China," embraces Hong Kong, Guangdong, Fujian, and Taiwan; and the outer layer, "Greater China," includes Hong Kong, Taiwan, and China. Hong Kong is the pivot for integration of the China Circle and plays a role in each of its three layers.

Finally, numerous sub-regional economic zones have emerged. Intense trade and investment flows have grown among geographically contiguous, but politically separated, border areas, taking advantage of the complementarity in factor endowment and technological capacity among countries at different stages of economic development. These zones are alternately called *transnational export processing zones, natural economic territories,* or *growth triangles*. They include the *Tumen River Area Development Project* in northeast Asia, composed of the Russian Far East, Mongolia, northeast China, the Korean peninsula, and Japan; the *Baht Economic Zone,* encompassing Thailand and the contiguous border areas of southwest China, Myanmar, Laos, Cambodia, and Vietnam; the *Mekong River Basin Project,* involving the riparian countries of Thailand, Myanmar, Vietnam, Laos, Cambodia, and southwest China; and three growth triangles in ASEAN—the *Southern Growth Triangle* (Singapore, the Johor state in Malaysia, and Batam island in Indonesia), *Northern Growth Triangle* (western Indonesia, northern Malaysia, and southern Thailand), and the *Eastern Growth Triangle* (Brunei, eastern Indonesia, southern Philippines, and Sabah and Sarawak in eastern Malaysia).

The Trans-Pacific Partnership (TPP) is another free trade initiative involving countries across the Pacific. Initially in 2005, Brunei, Chile, New Zealand, and Singapore concluded a free trade agreement called the Trans-Pacific Strategic Economic Partnership (TPSEP). In 2008, the US joined a proposal to negotiate a new TPP agreement intended to include many more countries and to have a much broader scope. As of May 2014, the TPP was being negotiated among 12 countries: Australia, Brunei Darussalam, Canada, Chile, Japan, Malaysia, Mexico, New Zealand, Peru, Singapore, US, and Vietnam. A number of other economies in the region (Colombia, Indonesia, Laos, the Philippines, South Korea, Taiwan, and Thailand) have announced formally or indicated informally an interest in joining the negotiations. The proposed agreement is also very comprehensive in scope. It covers not only trade in goods, but also trade in services (e.g., financial services and e-commerce), as well as such trade-related issues as competition policies, customs procedures, government procurement rules, labor and environmental standards, intellectual property, and foreign direct investment.

Furthermore, the agreement is expected to include a "docking" mechanism for additional countries to join by simply acceding to its terms without having to negotiate with every existing member bilaterally. The negotiating countries imposed on themselves a deadline of October 2013 for the conclusion of the negotiations and aim at the elimination of all tariffs by 2017. The US insistence on "deep" integration that entails substantial changes in the domestic institutions of member countries in such areas as financial market regulation and intellectual property rights

276

protection has, however, encountered clear and at times nearly unanimous objections from other negotiating countries. It appears that an agreement will require significant concessions by the US.[11]

Latin America

Attempts to form free trade blocs in Latin America were made as early as 1960 when the *Latin American Free Trade Association (LAFTA)* (involving Argentina, Bolivia, Brazil, Chile, Colombia, Ecuador, Mexico, Paraguay, Peru, Uruguay, and Venezuela) and the *Central American Common Market (CACM)* (consisting of Costa Rica, El Salvador, Guatemala, Honduras, and Nicaragua) were initiated. Both failed to achieve their objectives because of different economic conditions and economic policies among member countries that worked against regional economic integration.

LAFTA was superseded in 1980 by the Montevideo Treaty, which established the *Latin American Integration Association (LAIA)*. Its goal was to increase bilateral trade among the member countries, carried out on a sectoral basis. In 1991, Argentina, Brazil, Paraguay, and Uruguay signed the *Southern Common Market Treaty (MERCOSUR)*, which called for a common market among the four countries with free circulation of goods, services, capital, and labor. The member countries also aimed to coordinate macroeconomic policy and to harmonize legislation to strengthen the integration process. Since January 1, 1995, MERCOSUR members have used a common tariff structure and common external tariff rates and further expanded to include an additional member (Venezuela), an accessing member (Bolivia), and six associate members (Chile, Colombia, Ecuador, Guyana, Peru, and Suriname).

Other LAFTA members, including Bolivia, Colombia, Ecuador, Peru, and Venezuela, formed the *Andean Community* in 1992 with a common external tariff. In 1995, these members adopted a four-tier external tariff structure of 5, 10, 15, and 20 percent, respectively, when trading with other members of this agreement. The *Central American Common Market (CACM)* reactivated its objectives and established a customs union on January 1, 1993. Countries in the Caribbean region started the *Caribbean Community and Common Market (CARICOM)* in 1973. The major objective of this treaty is to achieve economies of scale in the regional production of services, such as transportation, education, and health, and to pool financial resources for investment in a regional development bank. This treaty also targets the coordination of economic policies and development planning.

A more ambitious endeavor was undertaken in 2004 when 12 South American leaders signed the Cuzco Declaration in the city of Cuzco, Peru to form the South American Community of Nations (CSN), uniting two trade groups: the Andean Community and MERCOSUR. The leaders of the 12 countries renamed the organization the Union of South American Nations (UNASUR) in 2007 and signed the Constitutive Treaty of the South American Union of Nations in Brasilia, Brazil in 2008. The treaty established a general secretariat in Quito, Ecuador, a parliament in Cochabamba, Bolivia, and a bank, Bank of the South, in Caracas, Venezuela. Among the long-term goals of the alliance are to create a continental free trade zone, a single currency, and an interoceanic highway. The 12 member countries currently include Argentina, Bolivia, Brazil, Chile, Colombia, Ecuador, Guyana, Paraguay, Peru, Suriname, Uruguay, and Venezuela (see Exhibit 8.7), with two other countries, Panama and Mexico, holding observer status.

GUYANA
752,940

VENEZUELA
26,814,843

SURINAME
481,267

FRENCH GUIANA

COLOMBIA
45,586,233

ECUADOR
14,790,608

PERU
29,496,000

BRAZIL
191,796,000

BOLIVIA
10,907,778

PARAGUAY
6,349,000

CHILE
17,094,270

ARGENTINA
40,134,425

URUGUAY
3,494,382

UNASUR

Union of South American Nations

- Member of Unasur and Mercosur
- Member of Unasur and the Andean Community
- Member of Unasur
- Overseas region (not a member)
- ◉ Largest cities
- ★ Current President Pro Tempore of Unasur
- —— Pan American Highway
- —— International Highway
- CHILE
  17,094,270 Population (2010 estimates)

Exhibit 8.7 Regional integration in Latin America
Source: Camilo Sanchez, Wikipedia.

Africa and the Middle East

The Economic Community of West African States (ECOWAS), established in 1975, is composed of Benin, Burkina Faso, Cote d'Ivoire, Mali, Mauritania, Niger, Senegal, Guinea, Liberia, Sierra Leone, Cape Verde, Gambia, Ghana, Guinea-Bissau, Nigeria, and Togo. ECOWAS eliminated duties on unprocessed agricultural products and handicrafts in 1981, and implemented free trade for all unprocessed products in 1990. Other activities of the community have included progressive liberalization of industrial products, steps to avoid the use of hard currencies in intra-member trade through a regional payments-clearing system, and cooperation on industrial and agricultural investment projects.

Established in 1966 in former French Africa, the *Central African Economic and Customs Union (UDEAC)* consists of Congo, Gabon, Chad, the Central African Republic, Equatorial Guinea, and Cameroon. EDEAC provides a framework for the free movement of capital throughout the area and for the harmonization of fiscal incentives, as well as the coordination of industrial development. A common external tariff was introduced in 1990 by four members of the community—Cameroon, Congo, Gabon, and the Central African Republic.

In former British East Africa, the establishment of the *East African Economic Community (EAEC)* in 1967 by Kenya, Tanzania, and Uganda formalized the common market. The EAEC was dissolved in 1979 and the three members later joined with other states (Angola, Burundi, Comoros, Djibouti, Ethiopia, Lesotho, Malawi, Mauritius, Mozambique, Namibia, Rwanda, Somalia, Sudan, Swaziland, Zambia, and Zimbabwe) to establish the Preferential Trade Area for eastern and southern African states (PTA) in 1981. Its goals include the establishment of a common market and the promotion of trade and economic cooperation among its members.

In the Middle East, Kuwait, Saudi Arabia, Bahrain, Oman, Qatar, and the United Arab Emirates established the *Gulf Cooperation Council (GCC)* in 1981. A free trade area covering industrial and agricultural products (excluding petroleum products) was established. In 1989, the *Arab Maghreb Union* was also established by Algeria, Libya, Mauritania, Morocco, and Tunisia to lay the foundations for a Maghreb Economic Area.

Regionalization vs. Globalization

Does regionalization work? Let us look at how the preceding regional blocs or agreements have actually contributed to the increased share of intra-regional trade. Indeed, intra-regional trade increased in Western Europe (e.g., from 53 percent in 1958 to 70 percent in 1999), as it has done in North America. For example, Canada expanded its exports to the United States by 18 percent between 1997 and 1999 and Mexico's exports and imports, heavily linked to the US market, grew by 20 percent between 1997 and 1999. This seems to support a view that regionalization can increase the share of regional trade. However, the uniqueness of the European Union and NAFTA—in terms of the structure and commitment to integration—differs markedly from what has been envisaged in other regional integration agreements. Caution is required in generalizing the unique experiences of NAFTA and the European Union to other regional agreements (e.g., MERCOSUR experienced a contraction of its intra-trade by about one quarter during 1997–1999). In fact, many developing

279

countries encountered problems when implementing these agreements. Moreover, as Asia's experience indicates (e.g., despite the absence of any bilateral trade agreements, China's trade with Japan and Korea steadily increased in the late 1990s), regional integration agreements are not a prerequisite for a rising share of intra-regional trade. Economic growth, commodity structure, and demand-supply situations seem to be more profound factors affecting the level of intra-regional exchanges.[12]

Many people, from government officials and corporate executives to labor union leaders and business instructors, ask whether regionalization is compatible with globalization. To answer this question, we first need to examine the two opposing effects of regionalization and the conditions for one to outweigh the other. The two effects are trade creation and trade diversion. *Trade creation* refers to any new trade that is generated within the region and did not exist with any country outside the region prior to the implementation of the new economic integration arrangement. Take the recent US-Colombia free trade agreement, for example. Colombia is an efficient producer of Christmas trees. If US consumers find Colombian-produced Christmas trees to be less expensive than US-produced ones and thus import more of them from Colombia due to the reduced trade barriers, the additional trade in Christmas trees between the two countries constitutes trade creation. *Trade diversion* refers to the shift of trade from a more efficient producer outside the region to a less efficient producer inside the region of the new economic integration arrangement. To see this clearly, consider a hypothetical example. Suppose that a particular type of Christmas toy costs $10 to produce in Thailand and $12 to produce in Colombia, including shipping, and that the US tariff on the type of toy is $3 per unit. US consumers would obviously prefer to purchase it from Thailand if the US tariff applies to imports from both countries. However, if the tariff was eliminated for the Colombian-made toy but remained on the Thai-made toy after the new trade agreement took effect, then US consumers would find it economical to shift their purchase from Thailand (a more efficient producer) to Colombia (a less efficient producer). Such a shift of trade constitutes trade diversion. Obviously, trade creation promotes, and trade diversion hurts, the welfare of the world. In order for regional integration to have a net positive effect, its trade creation effect must outweigh its trade diversion effect. WTO rules regulating regionalization are intended to make sure that regional integration generates a net positive effect on the economic welfare of the world.

Both regional integration agreements (regionalization) and multilateral trading systems (globalization) share the general objective of achieving, within their respective spheres, substantial reduction of tariffs and other barriers to trade. The WTO requires that: (1) under the MFN (Most Favored Nations) rule, any privilege promised to another regional member as specified in a regional agreement must extend unconditionally to all other WTO members (bilateral or regional obligations thus transform into multilateral or global obligations); (2) members of a regional integration agreement must have a common trade policy with respect to third countries (outsiders), and this policy should not be more restrictive than policies of individual members prior to the agreement; and (3) WTO's dispute settlement mechanisms provide a platform to solve disputes between members concerning discrepancies between regional agreements and global trading rules. For WTO members, these rules make it possible for regional integration and global trading systems to mutually support (rather than conflict with) each other in reducing tariffs and other trade barriers.

The complementarity between regionalization and globalization in dismantling trade barriers is also manifested in other areas. With the exception of the EU, few regional agreements have specified the rules of non-tariff barrier reduction, intellectual property protection, and service trade. Multilateral trading systems such as the WTO, however, serve as an important framework for them to follow in these areas. In other words, members of regional agreements still benefit from the enhanced transparency and procedural guarantees for dealing with these issues in intra-regional trade, as well as in trade with third countries as covered under the WTO agreements in which they participate. On the other hand, implemented policies or measures taken by certain regional integration agreements (e.g., environmental rules, competition regulations, and investment policies enacted by the EU) help lay the foundation for progress in multilateral trading systems. Finally, the WTO has been provided with a strengthened dispute settlement system and a monitoring function, which together bring increased transparency and predictability to trade and economic policies. As a result, parties to regional integration have ensured—by virtue of being members of the WTO—the adoption of an enhanced set of policies and procedures for their trade and economic relations.

The preceding complementarity, however, holds true for WTO members only under the assumption that the multilateral trading rules will be fully enforced. For non-WTO members, regionalization of foreign markets may increase the barriers to their foreign trade, thus conflicting with their efforts toward global integration. Rules and procedures for trade-related policies are the essence of the world trading system. If these rules are not completely and strictly implemented by all members, the compatibility between regionalization and globalization will be obstructed.

Interim Summary

1. Regionalization, such as the formation of NAFTA and the European Union, is a prominent feature of the world economy today. In the near future, all WTO members will simultaneously be insiders of at least one regional bloc or agreement and outsiders of others.

2. Regional integration takes several different forms, including common markets (e.g., European Union and MERCOSUR), free trade areas (e.g., NAFTA and LAFTA), customs unions (e.g., CACM and CARICOM), economic cooperation forums (e.g., APEC and GCC), and economic and political associations (e.g., ASEAN).

3. Regionalization is generally compatible with globalization. However, insiders gain many more benefits than outsiders from economic integration, and the net effect can be negative if the trade creation effect is more than offset by the trade diversion effect.

Commodity-Level Cooperation Among Nations

The emergence of many international commodity agreements or organizations is a natural development in international economic relations. Countries may also cooperate with one another to control the production, pricing, and sale of goods that are traded internationally. A **commodity cartel** is a group of producing countries that wish to protect themselves from the wild fluctuations that often occur in the prices of certain commodities traded internationally (e.g., crude oil, coffee, rubber, or cocoa). Cartel members may also seek higher, as well as more stable, prices for their goods. By assigning production quotas to individual countries and limiting overall output, a commodity cartel can raise the price of its good in international markets. The most important commodity cartel influencing the world economy is OPEC.

Organization of Petroleum Exporting Countries (OPEC)

The most notable and critical commodity cartel today is the *Organization of Petroleum Exporting Countries (OPEC)*. OPEC is not a commercial entity, but an intergovernmental organization. Its members are Algeria, Angola, Ecuador, Iran, Iraq, Kuwait, Libya, Nigeria, Qatar, Saudi Arabia, United Arab Emirates, and Venezuela. OPEC is the strongest collective force impacting prices in the international oil market. OPEC controls the price of oil in world markets by assigning to its members production quotas that limit the overall amount of crude oil supplied internationally. This organization successfully augmented oil prices for the benefit of its members in the 1970s and successfully overcame crises facing it in the 1980s. Currently, OPEC members control more than 40 percent of the world's oil production and nearly 80 percent of the world crude oil reserves (see Exhibit 8.8).

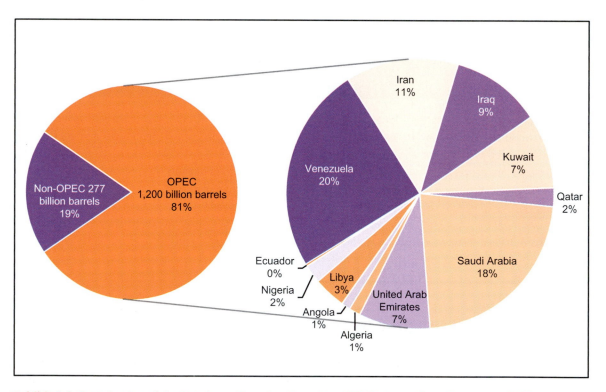

Exhibit 8.8 Organization of the Petroleum Exporting Countries (OPEC) share of world reserves, 2012
Source: OPEC Annual Statistical Bulletin 2013.

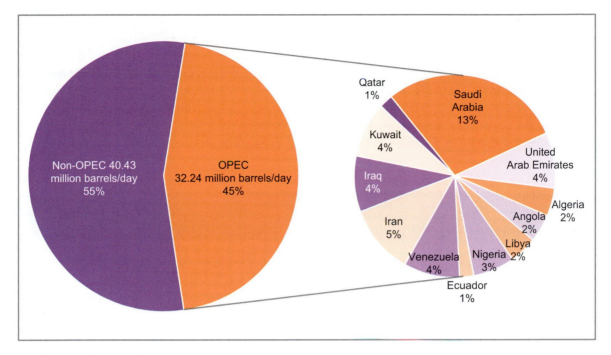

Exhibit 8.8 *(Continued)*

The world lives on oil. The bulk of OPEC oil reserves is located in the Middle East, with Saudi Arabia, Iran, and Iraq contributing 57 percent to the OPEC total. Total world oil demand in 2000 was about 76 million barrels per day. But as world economic growth continues, crude oil demand will rise to more than 90 million barrels per day in 2010 and more than 100 million barrels per day in 2020, according to the OPEC prediction. On the price side, crude oil prices react to the balance of demand and supply in the short run, and the rate of investment in the longer term. Sentiment is also an important factor: if traders in the oil market believe there will be a shortage of oil suppliers, they may raise prices before a shortage actually occurs. Other factors influencing the price of crude oil include accidents, bad weather, increasing demand, halting transport of oil from producers, labor disputes as well as other disruptions to production including war and natural disasters. The price of oil is reflected in most of the things we do. It impacts the price of transport, the cost of goods and services, and the availability of many products, including food, water, and shelter. If oil prices are too high, then these goods and services become more expensive and economies experience inflation.

OPEC became a catalyst for action by developing countries to ensure remunerative export earnings from their raw materials and tropical products. For instance, the *International Bauxite Association (IBA)* and the *Intergovernmental Council of Copper Exporting Countries (CIPEC)* were formed in the 1970s by the major developing countries producing these commodities, both following the model of OPEC.

Other Commodity Agreements

Other multilateral commodity agreements include *The Wheat Trade Convention (WTC), The International Sugar Agreement (ISA), The International Coffee Agreement (ICA), The International Cocoa Agreement (ICCA), The International Tin Agreement (ITA)*, and *The International Natural Rubber Agreement (INRA)*. These agreements, however, are far less impactful because the member countries are either unwilling or unable to affect world market prices due to competition from non-members and ease in finding substitutes for the commodity in question.

Interim Summary

1. International economic integration also occurs at the commodity level via the establishment of commodity cartels (e.g., OPEC and CIPEC) or multilateral arrangements (e.g., WTC and ISA).
2. OPEC is an intergovernmental organization and the strongest collective force impacting supply and price in the international oil market.

Strategic Responses of MNEs

International economic integration profoundly affects the operations of MNEs. So how should MNEs properly respond to, and further benefit from, increasing integration? As a result of heightened integration of the world economy, national boundaries have become increasingly irrelevant in the definition of market and production spaces, while at the same time regions, rather than countries, are emerging as the key economic policy arenas.

Economic integration triggers MNE activities, which then increase FDI in the integrated region. This is not surprising because MNEs quickly make adjustments to the new environment in which intra-regional trade barriers have been eliminated.[13] Three strategies can be identified in response to regional economic integration. The *defensive export-substituting investment* is a strategy by which MNEs defend their pre-existing market share achieved through exports by switching to direct production inside the region. Many Japanese MNEs such as Sony and Nissan employed this strategy in response to the European market integration in the early 1990s, in part to protect themselves against the possibility of future barriers to Japanese exports. In comparison to US MNEs, Japanese MNEs were latecomers to the European market and had a trade-based, rather than an investment-based, commercial relationship with the European community. As a result of defensive export-substituting investment, Japanese MNEs are now in a strong position to compete in the EU. As another example, both Du Pont and Dow Chemicals increased investments in their Canadian export-oriented operations in reaction to NAFTA.

The *offensive export-substituting investment* is a strategy by which MNEs choose to ensure market penetration by investing directly in the region before the region is officially integrated. This strategy is intended to gain an early position in the market, which is anticipated to grow rapidly as a result of an integration program. In order to gain an early foothold in the European market, Coca-Cola, which has an 80 percent share of the European cola market, used this strategy and invested more than $100 million in new European plants. Similarly, Campbell Soup and Quaker Oats have used this strategy to expand their operations in Canada. Aggressive acquisitions activities by these US MNEs in the Canadian market occurred in response to the passage of NAFTA.

The *rationalized foreign direct investment* is a strategy by which MNEs increase investment in, and heighten resource commitment to, the integrated region in pursuit of greater economic efficiency through scale economies and market expansion. IBM, for example, has been operating in Europe for about eight decades and is the industry leader in the European data-processing market. It used a rationalized FDI strategy in response to the European market integration by establishing 12 new manufacturing plants, nine R&D facilities, seven scientific centers, and a network of local sales and support offices. To benefit from NAFTA, IBM also invested more than $1 billion to upgrade its Canadian facilities, and it now exports all high-technology components and software manufactured in Canada to overseas markets, while importing computers for sale in the Canadian market.

Finally, the *reorganization investment* is a strategy by which MNEs realign their organizational structures and value-added activities to reflect a regional market. Firms realign investment capital among members of the trading bloc once protective barriers have been removed altogether. Under this strategy, an MNE's cross-border investment activity within the region increases, while the aggregate level of investment stock may not necessarily increase. Several European MNEs, for example, used this strategy to respond to European market integration. Philips, one of Europe's largest MNEs in the electronics industry, was reorganized as a collection of autonomous national subsidiaries. It restructured to create an integrated set of Europe-wide, product-based companies. To prepare for a single European market, Siemens launched a radical corporate reorganization in 1987, with plans to concentrate on high-growth segments of its core electronics/electrical businesses, while expanding geographically in the European Community through a series of acquisitions (see the Industry Box for details). In North America, Gillette and Whirlpool closed some of their Canadian facilities as a response to free trade in the region. They committed more production to their home markets and then exported to Canada from the United States.

As shown in the preceding examples, strategic choice depends on a company's current position in the regional market, the length of time it has had presence in the region, and the industry to which it belongs. In response to economic integration, MNEs, including those from developing economies such as South Korea, Taiwan, Singapore, and Brazil, have been actively employing cross-border strategic alliances. These alliances allow them to enter a new market far more rapidly than do mergers and acquisitions. Brazil, for example, is now one of the largest investors in the Portuguese economy, mostly with joint ventures in industries such as construction, textiles, and shoes.

285

Interim Summary

1. MNEs need to strategically respond to economic integration, whether at the regional or global level, if they want to survive in an increasingly competitive environment.
2. MNEs can emphasize one of the three strategies to cope with economic integration: defensive export-substituting investment, offensive export-substituting investment, and rationalized FDI. The selection of this strategy depends on an MNE's goals, experience, and capabilities.
3. MNEs, whether insiders or outsiders, can expand their presence within a regional bloc through acquisitions, alliances, or the building of new facilities.

Chapter Summary

1. International economic integration involves the preferential removal of all trade impediments, as well as the establishment of some elements of cooperation among several nations. This integration fosters globalization.
2. Economic integration takes several forms, including free trade areas, customs unions, common markets, economic unions, political unions, and multilateral cooperation, and occurs at three levels—global, regional, and commodity.
3. Global-level cooperation among nations proceeds through international economic organizations such as the WTO, the IMF, and the World Bank. While the WTO sets the institutional foundation for the global trading system, the IMF and the World Bank serve as the foundation of the global monetary and financial systems.
4. The WTO attempts to not only reduce tariff and non-tariff barriers in trade (commodity and service) but also to help solve problems associated with economic development, intellectual property, environmental protection, unfair practices, and dispute settlement.
5. Regional integration has become a prominent characteristic of the world economy. From the EU to NAFTA, from APEC to LAFTA, or from GCC to ECOWAS, most countries already belong to at least one regional bloc or agreement. Within a regional bloc, sub-regional integration such as a free trade area or a common market becomes increasingly pervasive.
6. From the perspective of the world economy, regionalization is an integral part of globalization. From the firm perspective, regionalization substantially benefits insiders, but not outsiders. Outsiders may shift exports to FDI because an actual investment within the region bypasses trade barriers against outsiders' exports and enables these firms to gain from free flows of products, capital, service, or human resources within the integrated region.
7. Commodity-level cooperation is reflected in commodity cartels or arrangements. The most important cartel is OPEC, which controls more than 40 percent of the world's oil production.

Notes

1   M.A.G. Van Meerhaeghe, *International Economic Institutions*, Boston, MA: Martinus Nijhoff Publishers, 1985; A.M. El-Agraa, *Economic Integration Worldwide*, New York: St. Martin's Press, 1997.

2   B. Hoekman and M. Kostechi, *The Political Economy of the World Trading Systems: From GATT and the WTO*, Oxford: Oxford University Press, 1995; J. Groome, *Reshaping the World Trading System: A History of the Uruguay Round*, Geneva: World Trade Organization, 1996.

3   *Regionalism and the World Trading System*, Geneva: World Trade Organization, 1995.

4   P. McGroarty, "Africa's goal: Europe without the currency," *Wall Street Journal*, November 21, 2011.

5   J.H. Jackson, *The World Trading System*, Cambridge, MA: MIT Press, 1997; B. Hettne, A. Inotai, and O. Sunkel, *Globalism and the New Regionalism*, New York: St. Martin's Press, 1999.

6   M. Moffett and J.D. Mckinnon, "Failed summit casts shadow on global trade talks," *Wall Street Journal*, November 7, 2005.

7   M. Stevis, "EU lets its members fudge statistics," *Guardian*, November 16, 2009.

8   A. Rinke, "Angela Merkel wants to reform EU charter by 2012," Reuters, November 13, 2011; S. Erlanger and S. Castle, "German vision prevails as European leaders agree on fiscal treaty," *The New York Times*, December 10, 2011.

9   E. Curran, "Asia leaders push regional trade pact," *Wall Street Journal*, November 19, 2012.

10 J. Perlez, "Asian nations plan trade bloc that, unlike US's, invites China," *The New York Times*, November 21, 2012.

11 M. Stoller, "Trans-Pacific Partnership: The biggest trade deal you've never heard of," *Salon*, October 23, 2012; A. Kahn, "The TPP has the potential to usher in a new peak for Pacific trade, but it could be a flop if negotiators don't get their act together," *The Santiago Times*, February 1, 2013.

12 *Regionalism and Its Place in the Multilateral Trading System*, France: OECD, 1996; R. Gibb and W. Michalak (eds), *Continental Trading Blocs: The Growth of Regionalism in the World Economy*, Chichester, UK: Wiley, 1994.

13 N.A. Phelps, *Multinationals and European Integration: Trade Investment and Regional Development*, London: Jessica Kingsley Publishers, 1997; H. Mirza, *Global Competitive Strategies in the New World Economy*, Cheltenham, UK: Edward Elgar, 1998.

chapter 9

the international monetary system and financial markets

HISTORY OF THE INTERNATIONAL MONETARY SYSTEM   291

CONTEMPORARY EXCHANGE RATE SYSTEMS   297

DETERMINATION OF FOREIGN EXCHANGE RATES   303

THE BALANCE OF PAYMENTS   311

INTERNATIONAL FOREIGN EXCHANGE MARKETS   314

INTERNATIONAL CAPITAL MARKETS   319

MAJOR INTERNATIONAL FINANCIAL CRISES IN RECENT TIMES   324

Do You Know?

1. What exchange rate systems are available today? Why don't nations use the same exchange rate system? For example, why does Cameroon peg its currency (CFA franc) to the French franc, whereas Romania allows its currency (leu) to independently float?
2. Why do some currencies fluctuate more than others? Why do some currencies depreciate while others appreciate? How do you determine and predict the foreign exchange rate?
3. What constitutes international financial markets? How do speculators earn profits from international foreign exchange markets? Is this speculation one of the reasons leading to the Asian financial crisis? How do MNEs finance global operations via international capital markets?

OPENING CASE Foreign Exchange Crisis in Mexico

Mexico experienced a financial crisis during 1994–1995. Mexico's exchange rate regime was modified a number of times, but it was consistently aimed at price stabilization. It started as a strict peg to the US dollar in 1988 and shifted to a crawl policy in early 1989. Beginning in 1992, an asymmetrical band was adopted, allowing for gradual depreciation, but placing a ceiling on the peso in relation to the dollar. Though steady from mid-1992 to early 1994, the Mexican peso became overvalued. The real effective exchange rate appreciated steadily as inflation exceeded the rate of the peso's depreciation. Between 1990 and December 1993, the peso depreciated by about 17 percent in nominal terms. However, consumer price inflation amounted to 56 percent from 1990 to 1993. Thus, the real effective exchange rate rose by nearly 35 percent over that period. The result was an increase in the current-account deficit from $7.5 billion in 1990 to $29.4 billion in 1994, which amounted to 7 percent of Mexico's GDP.

The year 1994 was an election year and a period of political upheaval in Mexico. Both the presidential candidate and the secretary-general of the majority party were assassinated. These and other events led to a slowdown in capital inflow and withdrawals of capital that had been invested in short-term government securities *(cetes)*. Reserves decreased by $11 billion in April 1994. The government then issued short-term peso obligations *(tesobonos)* with interest and principal linked to the dollar. The interest rate on these securities was considerably lower than on peso securities without a dollar link. Many Mexican residents shifted out of pesos into dollars, further escalating the peso devaluation. This crisis differs slightly from the one that occurred during the 1980s. In the previous crisis, Mexico fought to keep the peso fixed to the US dollar. In order to discourage investors from withdrawing funds from Mexico to avoid losses when the devaluation eventually occurred, the Mexican government had to maintain high interest rates. These high rates were the indirect consequence of fixed exchange rates, and they consequently stifled investment and job creation. The problem of high interest rates due to delayed devaluation with fixed exchange rates became known as "the peso problem."

Since this severe turbulence in the late 1990s, the peso has fallen in relation to the US dollar (from around eight pesos per US dollar in 1997 to around 13 in mid-2013) but Mexico's inflation rate has also fallen substantially (from 26 percent in 1997 to around 4 percent in 2013). Still, the issues faced by Mexico in the 1990s provide a timeless example of the many decisions and pitfalls surrounding currency valuation and use in a global economy.

Sources: Trading Economics, "Mexico inflation rate," 1974–2013; OANDA, "Historical exchange rates," 1990–2013.

History of the International Monetary System

The preceding case shows that a country's currency value is not always stable, and therefore, its exchange rate with other countries' currencies can change. International businesses operate in an uncertain environment in which exchange rates have been increasingly volatile over the past quarter century. Volatile exchange rates increase risk for international companies. To manage foreign exchange risk, management must first understand how the international monetary system works. As the opening case demonstrates, there are many new terms associated with this system (e.g., peg or crawl policies, nominal or real exchange rate). This chapter is designed to explain these concepts and related monetary system and financial markets.

The **international monetary system** refers primarily to the set of policies, institutions, practices, regulations, and mechanisms that determine foreign exchange rates. This system comprises currencies from individual countries and monetary unions (e.g., the Eurozone and CFA franc zone in Africa), as well as composite currency units such as the *Special Drawing Right (SDR)* as illustrated in Chapter 8. **Foreign exchange** refers to the money of a foreign country, such as foreign currency bank balances, banknotes, checks, and drafts. A **foreign exchange rate** (or simply, exchange rate) is the price of one currency expressed in terms of another currency (or gold). If the government of a country (e.g., India) regulates the rate at which the local currency (e.g., Indian rupee) is exchanged for other currencies, the system is classified as a **fixed, pegged, or management exchange rate system.** When a country's currency (e.g., Costa Rican colón) is tied or fixed to another country's currency (e.g., US dollar), this is called a **fixed or pegged exchange rate system.** The rate at which the currency is fixed is often referred to as its **par value.** If the government does not interfere in the valuation of its currency, it is classified as a **floating or flexible exchange rate system** (e.g., US dollar). The exchange rate that is directly observed as the price of a currency in terms of another is referred to as the **nominal exchange rate,** which does not necessarily reflect the true value of the currency due to differential rates of inflation across currencies. The **real exchange rate** is the exchange rate derived from removing the effect of differential inflation rates from the nominal exchange rate.

Changes in exchange rates may move in one of two directions. Associated with the fixed or managed exchange rate system, **devaluation** of a currency refers to a reduction in the foreign exchange value of a currency that is pegged to another currency or gold. In other words, the par value is reduced. The opposite of devaluation is **revaluation.** For instance, the Hong Kong dollar has been pegged to the US dollar around US$0.128/HK$ since 1983, and it has been allowed to fluctuate only within a narrow band. If the Hong Kong Monetary Authority makes the rate to go significantly below or above this target rate, we say that the Hong Kong dollar is devalued or revalued. Associated with the floating exchange rate system, **depreciation** (or weakening, deterioration) means a drop in the foreign exchange value of a floating currency. The opposite of depreciation is **appreciation** (or strengthening), which means a gain in the exchange value of a floating currency. For instance, the values of both the euro and US dollar float on the foreign exchange market and were traded around US$1.32/€1 on December 31, 2012. If the rate goes up or down significantly, we say that the euro has appreciated or depreciated. The media often use the terms devaluation and depreciation (or revaluation and appreciation) interchangeably, without distinction, which is incorrect.

The choice of foreign currencies used by international companies affects their cash flows and even their income levels. For example, firms in countries with soft currencies often use hard foreign currencies in export businesses. A **soft or weak currency** is one that is anticipated to devaluate or depreciate relative to major trading currencies. Conversely, a currency is considered **hard or strong** if it is expected to revalue or appreciate relative to major currencies. In daily life, the term "hard currency" is also used to denote the fully convertible currency of a major developed country (e.g., the US dollar, the UK pound, or the Japanese yen).

A brief review of the history of the international monetary system can help us better understand the present monetary system and also appraise the strengths and weaknesses of different foreign exchange systems.

The Gold Standard Period (1876–1914)

Since the days of the pharaohs (about 3000 BC), gold was used as a medium of exchange and a store of value. The gold standard gained acceptance as an international monetary system in the 1870s. Under this system, each country pegged its money to gold. For example, if the German Bank fixed the price of gold at 50 Deutsche mark (DM) per ounce of gold, it effectively stood ready to buy and sell gold at this rate. The same applied to the United States if the US Federal Reserve (the Fed) fixed the price of gold at $20 per ounce. The exchange rate, then, is simply the ratio of the two prices: DM50/$20 means an exchange rate of DM2.5 per US dollar.

The government of each country using the gold standard agreed to buy or sell gold on demand at its own fixed parity rate. Thus, the value of each individual currency in gold terms and the fixed parities between currencies remained stable. Under this system, it was very important for a country to maintain adequate gold reserves with which to back its currency's value. The gold standard worked adequately until the outbreak of World War I interrupted trade flows and the free movement of gold. As a result, the major trading nations suspended the gold standard.

The Inter-War Years and World War II (1914–1944)

During World War I and the early 1920s, currencies were allowed to fluctuate over fairly wide ranges in terms of both gold and another currency. This created arbitrage opportunities for international speculators. Such fluctuations hampered world trade in the 1920s, thereby contributing to the Great Depression in the 1930s.

The United States returned to a modified gold standard in 1934, when the US dollar was devalued to $35/ounce of gold from the $20.67/ounce price in effect prior to World War I. Although the United States returned to the gold standard, gold was traded only with foreign central banks, not with individual citizens. From 1934 to the end of World War II, exchange rates were determined, in theory, by each currency's value in terms of gold. During World War II and its immediate aftermath, however, many of the main trading currencies lost their convertibility into other currencies. The dollar was the only major trading currency that continued to be convertible.

The Bretton Woods System (1944–1973)

This period, commencing a year prior to the end of World War II, was characterized by a fixed exchange system. Under the provisions of the *Bretton Woods Agreement* signed in 1944, the government of each member country pledged to maintain a fixed, or pegged, exchange rate for its currency vis-à-vis the dollar or gold. Because one ounce of gold was set equal to $35, fixing a currency's gold price was equivalent to setting its exchange rate relative to the dollar. For example, the Deutsche mark was set equal to 1/140 of an ounce of gold, meaning it was worth $0.25 ($35/DM140). Participating countries agreed to try to maintain the value of their currencies within a 1 percent band by buying or selling foreign exchange or gold as needed. Devaluation was not to be used as a competitive trade policy, but if a currency became too weak to defend, a devaluation of up to 10 percent was allowed without formal approval by the IMF.

During this period, the US dollar was the main reserve currency held by central banks and was the key to the web of exchange rate values. Unfortunately, the United States ran persistent and growing deficits on its balance of payments. A heavy capital outflow of dollars was required to finance these deficits and to meet the growing demand for dollars from investors and businesses. Eventually the heavy overhang of dollars held abroad resulted in a lack of confidence in the ability of the United States to meet its commitment to convert dollars to gold. On August 15, 1971, the United States responded to a huge trade deficit by making the dollar inconvertible into gold. A 10 percent surcharge was placed on imports, and a program of wage and price controls was introduced. Many of the major currencies were allowed to float against the dollar. The dollar then began a decade of decline.

Under the *Smithsonian Agreement*, which was reached among the world's leading trading nations in Washington, DC in December 1971, the United States agreed to devalue the dollar to $38 per ounce of gold. In return, the other countries present agreed to revalue their own currencies upward in relation to the dollar by specified amounts. Actual revaluation ranged from 7.4 percent by Canada to 16.9 percent by Japan. Furthermore, the allowed floating band around par value was expanded from ±1 percent to ±2.25 percent.

Because of high inflation in the United States, the dollar devaluation remained insufficient to restore stability to the system. By 1973, the dollar was under heavy selling pressure even at its devalued rates. By late February 1973, a fixed-rate system appeared no longer feasible given the speculative flows of currencies. The major foreign exchange markets were actually closed for several weeks in March 1973. When they reopened, most currencies were allowed to float to levels determined by market forces.

The Post-Bretton Woods System: 1973–Present

This period is characterized by a floating exchange rate system. Since March 1973, exchange rates have become much more volatile and less predictable than they were during the "fixed" exchange rate period. The system became increasingly volatile as it approached the oil crisis in the fall of 1973. As mentioned in the preceding chapter, October 1973 marked the beginning of successful efforts by the *Organization of Petroleum Exporting Countries (OPEC)* to raise the price of oil. By 1974, oil prices had quadrupled. Several nations, most notably the United States, tried to offset the effect of higher energy bills by boosting spending. The results were high inflation and vast deficits in the balance of payments, which eventually caused the dollar crisis of 1977–1978.

The US dollar strengthened substantially in 1981–1985 due to a combination of factors. First, the Reagan Administration increased government expenditures and cut taxes substantially at the same time. This policy combination required heavy government borrowing to finance the budget deficits and raised the US interest rates substantially in the face of a tight monetary policy that the Federal Reserve System maintained. The high interest rates in the US, combined with a rapid recovery of the US economy, attracted large capital inflows and drove up the value of the dollar in terms of other currencies. Even though most analysts considered the high value of the US dollar unsustainable because it was causing severe difficulties to US exporters and large US trade deficits, the value of the dollar stayed high until 1985 when the US intervened in the foreign exchange market jointly with other major industrialized nations by selling large qualities of the dollar. The resumption of a downward slide in the value of the dollar at the time was due not only to government intervention, but more importantly to changes in US government policies with more serious efforts to reduce budget deficits and a slowdown in the US economy. Believing that the dollar had declined enough, the United States, Japan, West Germany, France, Britain, Canada, and Italy—also known as the **Group of Seven** (or G7)—met in February 1987 and agreed to slow the dollar's fall. This agreement, also known as the **Louvre Accords,** called for the G7 nations to support the falling dollar by pegging exchange rates within a narrow, undisclosed range. They agreed that exchange rates had been sufficiently realigned and pledged to support stability of exchange rates at or near their current levels. Although the dollar declined further during 1987, it rallied in early 1988, thereby ending for the moment its dramatic volatility during the period 1980–1987. The US dollar fell again in 1990 but then stayed basically flat during 1991–1992. It began falling again in 1993, especially against the Japanese yen and German mark.

The turmoil that has rocked Asian foreign exchange markets since June 1997 was the third major crisis of the 1990s. Its two predecessors were the crisis in the European Monetary System (EMS) of 1992–1993 and the Mexican peso crisis of 1994–1995 (see opening case). The collapse of the Thai currency, the baht, started the Asian crisis in June 1997. In one month, the baht lost 20 percent of its value against the dollar. The currencies of the Philippines, Malaysia, and Indonesia all weakened as well. Malaysian Prime Minister Mahathir Mohamad blasted "rogue speculators." Later he called billionaire hedge-fund manager George Soros a "moron" for betting against Asian currencies. In August 1997, Indonesian authorities were forced to allow the national currency, the rupiah, to move freely against other currencies. In December 1997, the IMF put together a $58.4 billion international bailout for Korea, the largest ever. The Koreans decided to let the won float. Faced with rapidly deteriorating foreign currency reserves, the Russian authorities devalued the ruble in August 1998.

The US Federal Reserve responded to fear of a US credit crunch by lowering interest rates three times in quick succession during the course of the fall, including a rare unilateral move by former Fed Chairman Alan Greenspan. Other industrialized countries such as Canada, Japan, and most of the European nations also eased monetary policies in September 1998. In October 1998, the world's rich nations, the G7, endorsed a US plan to allow the IMF to lend to countries before they get into financial difficulties. More recently, the global economic crisis that started in 2008 and the Eurozone crisis that started in 2009 have caused a weakening in the value of the US dollar and high viability in the value of the euro. China has also faced criticism, especially surrounding its entrance and membership in the WTO, for its currency valuations and has thus changed its exchange rate policies several times in recent years. Exhibit 9.1 lists major events related to the international monetary system during 1973–2011.

Date	Event	Impact
February 1973	US dollar devalued	Devaluation pressure increases on US$, forcing devaluation to $42.22/oz of gold.
February–March 1973	Currency markets in crisis	Fixed exchange rates no longer considered defensible; speculative pressures force closure of international foreign exchange markets for nearly two weeks; markets reopen with floating rates for major industrial currencies.
June 1973	US dollar depreciation	Floating rates continue to drive the new free-floating US$ down by about 10 percent by June.
Fall 1973–1974	OPEC oil embargo	Organization of Petroleum Exporting Countries (OPEC) imposes oil embargo, eventually quadrupling world price of oil; because oil prices are stated in US$, the US$ recovers some of its former strength.
January 1976	Jamaica Agreement	IMF meeting in Jamaica results in the "legalization" of the floating exchange rate system already in effect; gold is demonetized as a reserve asset; IMF quotas are increased.
1977–1978 **March 1979**	US inflation rate rises EMS created	Rising US inflation causes continued depreciation of the US$. European Monetary System (EMS) is created, establishing a cooperative exchange rate system for participating members of the EEC.
Summer 1979	OPEC raises prices	OPEC nations raise oil prices once again.
Fall 1979	Iranian assets frozen	President Carter responds to Iranian hostage crisis by freezing all Iranian assets held in US financial institutions.
Spring 1980	US dollar begins to rise	Worldwide inflation and early signs of recession coupled with real interest differential advantages for dollar-denominated assets contribute to rising demand for dollars.
August 1982	Latin American debt crisis	Mexico informs US Treasury that it will be unable to make debt service payments; Brazil and Argentina follow suit; the debt crisis begins.
February 1985	US dollar peaks	US dollar peaks against most major industrial currencies, hitting record highs against the Deutsche mark and other European currencies.

Exhibit 9.1 World currency events, 1973–2013

Date	Event	Impact
September 1985	Plaza Agreement	Group of Five members, meeting at the Plaza Hotel in New York, sign an international cooperative agreement to control the volatility of world currency markets and establish currency target zones.
February 1987	Louvre Accords	Group of Seven members state they will "intensify" economic policy coordination to promote growth and reduce external imbalances.
September 1992	EMS crisis	High German interest rates induce massive capital flows into Germany and Deutsche mark-denominated assets, eventually causing the withdrawal of the Italian lira and British pound from the EMS's Exchange Rate Mechanism (ERM).
July 31, 1993	EMS realignment	EMS adjusts allowable deviation band to +/–15 percent for all member currencies (except the Dutch guilder); US dollar continues to weaken against other major currencies; Japanese yen reaches ¥100.25/$ in August 1993.
1994	EMI founded	European Monetary Institute, the predecessor to the European Central Bank, is founded in Frankfurt, Germany.
December 1994	Peso collapses	Mexican peso suffers major devaluation as a result of increasing pressure on the managed devaluation policy; peso falls from Ps3.46/$ to Ps5.50/$ within days. The peso's collapse results in a fall in most major Latin American exchanges (tequila effect).
August 1995	Yen peaks	Japanese yen reaches an all-time high versus the US dollar of ¥79/$; yen slowly depreciates over the following two-year period, rising to over ¥130/$.
June 1997	Asian financial crisis	First afflicting Thailand in June 1997, then quickly spreading to South Korea, Indonesia, Malaysia, the Philippines, and other Southeast and East Asian countries.
August 1998	Financial turmoil in Russia and Latin America	Influenced by the Asian crisis, Russia devaluates the ruble and unilaterally restructures its debts. The situation worsens following the devaluation in Brazil in January 1999.
January 1, 1999	Euro launched	Official launch date for the single European currency, the euro. Participating states' exchange rates will be irrevocably locked; European Monetary Institute will be succeeded by the European Central Bank, establishing a single monetary policy for Europe.
January 1, 2002	Euro coinage	Euro coins and notes are introduced in parallel with home currencies; transition period to last no more than six months.
July 2005	RMB revaluation and shift to a crawling peg	The Chinese government increased the value of the country's currency, renminbi (RMB), by 2.1 percent and has continued to do so since then. China's main trading partners, especially the US, pressured the Chinese government for a change, saying that RMB was undervalued and made the country's exports artificially cheap.
March–October 2008	Global financial crisis	The collapse of major US banks threatened the world financial system, triggering the collapses of major banks in several European countries, particularly Iceland and Ireland. Investors rushed to move their money from risky currencies to safer currencies such as the Japanese yen and Swiss franc.

Exhibit 9.1 (*Continued*)

September 2008	RMB re-pegging to the US dollar	The Chinese government stopped the revaluation of the RMB and re-pegged it to the US dollar around RMB0.1464/US$ in response to weakening exports due to the worldwide economic downturn.
July 2010	RMB resumption of crawling peg	The Chinese government started increasing the value of the RMB again in the face of accelerating domestic inflation and criticism from trading partners (particularly the US) for undervaluing its currency.
Early 2010– Mid-2011	Eurozone crisis	The inability of several EU countries, particularly Greece and Portugal, threatened the breakup of the Eurozone and viability of the euro.
Early 2013	RMB appreciation reaching 25 percent	The RMB had appreciated by over 25 percent since July 2005, and the criticism of the Chinese government's currency policy was muted.
December 2013	Eurozone fiscal integration	The European Commission started to review the budgets of member states as a first step toward fiscal integration to reduce the chance of future financial crisis.

Exhibit 9.1 (*Continued*)

Interim Summary

1. The international monetary system has undergone several phases, including the gold standard period (1876–1914), the interwar years and World War II (1914–1944), the Bretton Woods system (1944–1973), and the post-Bretton Woods system (1973–present).
2. The fixed exchange rate system was a staple of the international monetary system prior to March 1973, and the floating exchange rate system was dominant after March 1973.

Contemporary Exchange Rate Systems

Fixed–Rate System

Under a **fixed-rate system,** governments (through their central banks) buy or sell their currencies in the foreign exchange market whenever exchange rates deviate from their stated par values. A purely fixed-rate system is employed currently by only a few centrally planned economies such as Cuba and North Korea. In these economies, it is generally mandatory that a local firm's foreign exchange earnings be surrendered to the central bank, which in return pays the firm a corresponding amount in local currency. The central bank often allocates these foreign exchange incomes to state-owned users on the basis of governmental priorities. Exhibit 9.2 presents typical foreign exchange control measures used by governments under fixed or managed foreign exchange systems.

Despite drawbacks such as resource misallocation, distortion of foreign exchange demand and supply, and a drag on company performance, the fixed-rate system may help economies stabilize

1. Import restrictions such as license or quota systems
2. Restrictions on remittance of foreign exchange such as profit, dividends, or royalty
3. Surrender of hard-currency export earnings to the central bank
4. Mandatory government approval for using a firm's retained foreign exchange earnings
5. Pre-deposit of foreign exchange expenditure for import business in interest-free accounts with the central bank for a certain period
6. Credit ceilings for foreign firms
7. Restriction or prohibition on offshore deposit or investment of hard currencies
8. Use of multiple exchange rates simultaneously for different items of the balance of payment

Exhibit 9.2 Frequently used foreign exchange control measures

their economic environment, emphasize priority projects that need foreign exchange, and control foreign exchange reserves. In a broader, international context, fixed rates provide stability in international prices for the conduct of trade, which in turn lessens risks for international companies.

Crawling Peg System

The peg system is situated between the fixed-rate and float-rate systems. The **crawling peg** is an automatic system for revising the exchange rate, establishing a par value around which the rate can vary up to a given percentage point. The par value is revised regularly according to a formula determined by the authorities. Once the par value is set, the central bank intervenes whenever the market value approaches a limit point. Suppose, for example, that the par value of the Mexican peso is 13,000 pesos for one dollar, and that it can vary ±2 percent around this rate, i.e., between 13,260 pesos and 12,740 pesos to the dollar. If the dollar approaches the rate of 13,260 pesos, the central bank intervenes by buying pesos and selling dollars. If the dollar approaches 12,740 pesos, the central bank intervenes by selling pesos and buying dollars. If it hovers around a limit point for too long, causing frequent central bank intervention, a new par value closer to this point is established. Suppose the dollar was hovering around 13,260 pesos. The government might then establish the new par value at 13,260 pesos with new limit points at 13,525 and 12,995.

A government can peg its currency to either another single currency (see the Country Box for illustration) or to a "basket" of foreign currencies. Today, 104 of the 182 members of the IMF peg their currency to some other currency. The US dollar is the base for 66 other currencies (e.g., Angola, Argentina, Dominica, Hong Kong, Iraq, Jordan, Mongolia, and Vietnam). The euro is the base for 27 currencies (e.g., Benin, Cameroon, Denmark, Gabon, Macedonia, Niger, Senegal, and Togo).

Other countries peg their currency to a composite basket of currencies, where the basket consists of a portfolio of currencies of their major trading partners. The base value of such a basket is more stable than any single currency. Under this regime, a country can peg its currency to the standard basket such as the Special Drawing Rights, or SDR (e.g., Libya and Myanmar until 2011), or to its own basket, designed to fit the country's unique trading and investing needs (e.g., Botswana, Costa Rica, Kuwait, Iran, Iraq, Morocco, Russia, and Tunisia). In the latter approach, the basket normally contains currencies of major trading partners, weighted according to trading relations with the focal country.

The peg system is not a panacea. When pegged rates become overvalued, countries are forced to deplete their foreign exchange reserves to defend the currency peg. With reserves depleted, countries try to manipulate interest rates but are often eventually forced to devalue, re-pegging at a lower rate or giving up the peg altogether. With a floating rate system, countries can maintain their foreign reserves and thereby maintain a defense against financial panic, which often plagues pegged exchange regimes. Foreign creditors understand that the central bank has sufficient reserves to repay short-term debts, thereby eliminating the possibility of a self-fulfilling creditor panic. Also, governments are not forced to break their word when international or domestic events force change in market exchange rates. For example, in April 2002, undergoing economic meltdown and five changes of president in two weeks, Argentina (under the floating regime) declared the world's largest debt default and devalued its peso by more than 70 percent.

Country Box

Hong Kong

Should the Hong Kong Dollar Retain the Fixed Peg to the US Dollar?

Many analysts over the last 30 years have questioned whether Hong Kong should retain the fixed peg to the US dollar. Several factors are in Hong Kong's favor. First, in addition to Hong Kong's foreign exchange reserves of some $303 billion, the Chinese government is also prepared to use its $3.5 trillion of reserves to defend the HK dollar. China has a vested economic and political interest in preserving Hong Kong's exchange rate and financial stability. Second, the overall economy of Hong Kong remains strong, as reflected in recurring fiscal and balance-of-payments surpluses, an extremely low foreign-debt service ratio (0.7 percent), and an efficiently regulated and supervised banking system. The peg system was established back in 1984 to counter the uncertainty following the UK—PRC declaration of the 1997 handover. A rather small economy like Hong Kong, which serves as a regional and global financial and trading center, needs stability and certainty, which the peg has continued to provide.

There has, however, been some debate on whether to reexamine the currency peg in recent years due to the appreciation of the Chinese currency and other Asian currencies against the US dollar. Because of the peg, the depreciation of the US dollar causes the Hong Kong dollar also to fall in value, thus giving Hong Kong producers an "unfair" competitive advantage and provoking negative reactions from producers in other Asian economies. In 2012, Joseph Yam, a former Hong Kong Monetary Authority (HKMA) chief who helped introduce the peg and defended it against speculators during the Asian crisis of the 1990s, called for a review of the currency policy. Many of the city's problems, such as inflation and lower living standards, can be attributed to the exchange rate policy, argues Chairman David Li, of the Bank of East Asia Ltd. Many analysts suggest pegging to a basket of currencies or to the Chinese yuan. China ended its US dollar peg in 2005, and has since seen a 36 percent strengthening of the yuan. Despite these critiques, the government of Hong Kong appears determined to maintain the current US peg policy for the sake of currency stability.

Source: Adapted from *Accountancy (International Edition)*, First Quarter 1998, anonymous, pp. 27–29; F. Li, "Hong Kong peg turning 30 as another decade forecast: Currencies," Bloomberg, October 17, 2013; "Foreign Exchange Reserves Hong Kong," *Trading Economics*, 2013; "Foreign Exchange Reserves China," *Trading Economics*, 2013.

Target-Zone Arrangement

Target-zone arrangement is virtually a joint float system cooperatively arranged by a group of nations sharing some common interests and goals. Under a target-zone arrangement, countries adjust their national economic policies to maintain their exchange rates within a specific margin around agreed-upon, fixed central exchange rates. Such an arrangement existed for the major European currencies participating in the European Monetary System (EMS) until May 1998 when those EU members participating in the Economic and Monetary Union (EMU) adopted the euro as their currency. Members of the EU had a cooperative agreement to maintain their currencies within a set range against other members of their group. The EMS was, in essence, a peg of each country's currency to all the others, as well as a joint float of all member currencies together against non-EMS currencies. The target-zone arrangement helps minimize exchange rate instability and enhance economic stability in the group (zone).

Let us use the EMS to illustrate this type of arrangement. As part of the EMS, the members established the European Currency Unit (ECU), which plays a central role in the functioning of the EMS. At the heart of the EMS was an exchange rate mechanism (ERM), which allowed each member to determine a mutually agreed central exchange rate for its currency; each rate was denominated in currency units per ECU (e.g., DM2.05853 per ECU). Central rates establish a grid of cross-exchange rates between currencies. For example, 2.05853 Deutsche marks per ECU, divided by 6.90403 French francs per euro, equals 0.29816 DM per French franc. Member nations pledged to keep their currencies within a ±2.25 percent margin around their central cross-exchange rates (Spain had a 6 percent margin).

Taking effect on January 1, 1999, the ECU transitioned to the **euro** when those EU countries participating in the EMU switched to the euro from their own currencies, which had already been pegged to the ECU. Denmark, the United Kingdom, and Sweden did not adopt the euro at the time and still have no plans to do so. The new member states (e.g., the Czech Republic, Estonia, Cyprus, Latvia, Lithuania, Hungary, Malta, Poland, Slovakia, and Slovenia) were expected to adopt the euro only when they fulfill certain economic criteria, namely a high degree of price stability, a sound fiscal situation, stable exchange rates, and converged long-term interest rates. In the transition stage (described as a "waiting room"), these countries follow essentially the same form of target-zone arrangement as the ERM, known as ERM-2.

The **European Central Bank** (ECB), based in Frankfurt and established in June 1998, is the central bank in the euro zone. It is as powerful in Europe as the Federal Reserve is in the United States. This central bank sets interest rates for the euro zone. However, the ECB is not a duplicate of the US Fed. One of the most important differences between the two is their respective mandates. The Fed's goal is to balance the objectives of price stability with those of employment and economic growth. The ECB, on the other hand, has a narrower focus patterned on the Bundesbank (Germany's former central bank). It is only responsible for keeping prices stable. In addition, the Fed deals with only one government, whereas the ECB is faced with all member governments, each with their own fiscal policies. Finance ministers from the currency-union members hold informal meetings regularly to coordinate fiscal policies.

The target-zone arrangement is not without problems. Owing to the divergence of national policies, the level of economic development, and the trade structure, it is difficult for every member to maintain the central exchange rate for a long period of time. Moreover, when currency speculators attack one of the zone currencies, defense is more costly. In fact, the euro's exchange rate mechanism had to be realigned in 1992, as a result of successive attacks by speculators against the Nordic currencies (Finland, Sweden, and Norway) as well as the French franc, British pound, and Italian lira.

Managed Float System

The **managed float,** also known as a *dirty float,* is employed by governments to preserve an orderly pattern of exchange rate changes and is designed to eliminate excess volatility. Each central bank sets the nation's exchange rate against a predetermined goal, but allows the rate to vary. In other words, rate change is not automatic but is based on the government's view of an appropriate rate in the context of the country's balance-of-payments position, foreign exchange reserves, and rates quoted outside the official market. Rather than resist the underlying market forces, the authorities occasionally intervene by buying or selling domestic currency to smooth the transition from one rate to another. At other times they intervene to moderate or counteract self-correcting cyclical or seasonal market forces. The rationale for the managed float is to improve the economic and financial environment by reducing uncertainty. For instance, government intervention may reduce exporters' uncertainty caused by disruptive exchange rate changes. Currently, about 44 countries (e.g., Afghanistan, Algeria, Cambodia, Georgia, Jamaica, Kenya, Singapore, and Ukraine) maintain a managed float system. The challenge behind this approach is to define just what is meant by "excess volatility." It is also questionable if governments are more capable than markets in determining what is fundamental, and what is temporary and self-correcting.[1]

Independent Float System

Approximately 40 countries currently allow full flexibility through an **independent float,** also known as a *clean float.* Under this system, an exchange rate is allowed to adjust freely to the supply and demand of this currency for another. Consequently, there is usually no need for an economy to undergo the painful adjustment process set in motion by a decrease or increase in the money supply. This category contains currencies of both developed (e.g., Switzerland and US) and developing (e.g., Brazil and Turkey) countries. Central banks of these countries allow exchange rates to be determined by market forces alone. Although some central banks may intervene in the market from time to time, such intervening usually attempts to alleviate speculative pressures on their currency. Further, central banks intervene only as one of many anonymous participants in the free market in an occasional, non-continuous manner. Exhibit 9.3 shows sample countries and their exchange rate systems.

Independent Float	Managed Float	Target Zone	Crawling Peg	Fixed
Albania	Afghanistan	Bulgaria	Argentina	Cuba
Brazil	Colombia	Bosnia Herzegovina	Bolivia	Panama
Canada	Egypt	Lithuania	Botswana	
Chile	Ghana	Tonga	China	
Eurozone countries	India		Costa Rica	
Indonesia	Malaysia		Dominican Rep.	
Israel	Nigeria		Ethiopia	
Japan	Peru		Honduras	
Korea	Singapore		Jamaica	
South Africa	Tanzania		Kazakhstan	
Switzerland	Thailand		Nicaragua	
United Kingdom	Uganda		Russia	
United States	Uruguay		Uzbekistan	

Exhibit 9.3 Sample countries using different exchange rate systems
Source: International Monetary Fund, *IMF Annual Report 2012.*

Advantages and Disadvantages of the Floating System

The float-rate system, whether managed or independent, is the dominant system in the beginning of the twenty-first century, utilized by about 100 countries. The flexible exchange rate system provides a less painful adjustment mechanism to trade imbalances than do fixed exchange rates, and it prevents a country from having large persistent deficits. Unlike the fixed-rate system, which requires a recession to reduce real (inflation-adjusted) income or prices when trade deficits arise, flexible exchange rates will only lower the foreign exchange value of the currency. In a fixed-rate system, reducing local currency income (wages) is likely to be painful for political and social reasons even though this reduction (and thus the decline in the value of this nation's currency) can improve trade balance.[2]

Moreover, flexible exchange rates do not require central banks to hold foreign exchange reserves because there is no need to intervene in the foreign exchange market. This means that the problem of insufficient liquidity (foreign exchange reserves) does not exist with truly flexible rates. Further, flexible exchange rates avoid the need for strict import and export regulations such as tariffs, foreign exchange control, and import restrictions. These regulations are not only costly to enforce but also prone to criticism and even retaliation from trade partner countries.

Finally, floating exchange rates can help ensure the independence of trade policies. For example, if the United States allows rapid growth in the money supply, this will tend to raise US prices and lower interest rates (in the short run), the former causing a deficit or deterioration in the current account, and the latter causing a deficit or deterioration in the capital account. If, for example, the Canadian dollar were fixed to the US dollar, the deficit in the United States would most likely mean a surplus in Canada. This would put upward pressure on the Canadian dollar, forcing the Bank of

Canada to sell Canadian dollars and hence increase the Canadian money supply. In this case an increase in the US money supply would cause an increase in the Canadian money supply. However, if exchange rates were flexible, the US dollar would simply depreciate against the Canadian dollar.

The role of flexible rates, however, is limited in balancing trade after a certain period of time. A depreciation or devaluation of currency will help the balance of trade if it reduces the relative prices of locally produced goods and services. However, after a short period of time, domestic prices of tradable goods will rise following depreciation or devaluation. This will increase the cost of living, which puts upward pressure on wages.[3] For example, if 1 percent depreciation raises production costs by the same percentage point, and if real wages are maintained, then nominal wages must rise by the amount of depreciation or devaluation. If wages rise 1 percent when the currency falls by 1 percent, the effects are offsetting, and changes in exchange rates will be ineffective. In addition, flexible rates could make it more difficult for governments to control inflation and also create less motivation for governments to combat it.[4] Finally, free-float rates may cause more uncertainty, which may in turn hamper the growth and stability of economies vulnerable to international financial and export markets. Under the floating system, international speculators can cause wide swings in the values of different currencies. These swings are the result of the movement of "hot money chasing better returns and the enormous speed of capital flows whose scale dwarfs that of trade flows."[5]

Interim Summary

1. Countries utilize the crawling peg system, target-zone arrangement, managed float system, or independent float system in a rising sequence of flexibility and volatility.
2. Countries select different exchange rate systems because they have different goals, different levels of internationalization, and different capabilities of managing foreign exchange volatility.

Determination of Foreign Exchange Rates

The determination of a national currency's exchange rate should answer two basic questions: (1) *How is the base rate between this nation's currency and foreign currencies determined?* That is, what is the underlying criterion used to determine the base level *(stocks)* of exchange rate of a currency *vis-à-vis* others?; and (2) *How does a nation's exchange rate change over time (flows)?* That is, what are the conditions under which the exchange rate should change, and how?

Foreign Exchange Rate Quotations

A foreign exchange quotation is the expression of willingness to buy or sell at a set rate. There are several pairs of quotations being used in foreign exchange businesses. Correctly interpreting the meanings of these quotations is important to our discussion of the principles for foreign exchange rate determination, as the different quotations are easy to confuse.

Direct and Indirect

A **direct quote** is a home currency price of a foreign currency unit (e.g., C$1.0048/US$1 in Canada), whereas an **indirect quote** is a foreign currency price of a home currency unit (US$0.9952/C$1 in Canada). In other words, the direct quote puts the domestic currency in the numerator, and the indirect quote puts the foreign currency in the numerator. Under a direct quote, an increase of the exchange rate (e.g., from C$1.0048 to C$1.0065 per dollar) means a depreciation of the home currency (C$) or appreciation of the foreign currency (US$). Conversely, under an indirect quote, an increase of the exchange rate (e.g., from US$0.9952 to US$0.9985 per Canadian dollar) means an appreciation of the home currency (C$) or depreciation of the foreign currency (US$). In most countries, banks use a direct quote. To avoid confusion, we will use the direct quote in our discussion below unless otherwise noted.

Bid and Offer

A **bid** is the exchange rate in one currency at which a dealer (usually a bank) will buy another currency. An **offer** (also referred to as an *ask*) is the exchange rate at which a dealer (usually a bank) will sell the other currency. The difference between the bid and offer prices, also known as the **bid-ask spread,** is the compensation for transaction cost for the dealer. For example, a Canadian bank's quotation for the US dollar (US$/C$) may be: 0.9932 (bid) and 0.9972 (offer). For widely traded currencies such as the US dollar, euro, yen, or pound, the spread ranges from 0.05 to 0.08 percent.

Spot and Forward

This pair of quotes is more commonly used for foreign exchange transactions between dealers in the interbank market. A **spot rate** is the exchange rate for a transaction that requires almost immediate delivery of foreign exchange (normally before the end of the second business day). A **forward rate** is the exchange rate for a transaction that requires delivery of foreign exchange at a specified future date (e.g., one month, three months, six months, or one year). See Exhibit 9.4 for some examples.

	Bid	Offer
Spot	1.3575	1.3583
1-Month Forward	1.3577	1.3586
3-Month Forward	1.3582	1.3591
6-Month Forward	1.3588	1.3597
1-Year Forward	1.3598	1.3608

Exhibit 9.4 Spot and forward quotations between the US dollar and euro

Forward Premium and Discount

This pair of definitions concern the deviations of the forward rate from the spot rate. A foreign currency is said to be selling at a forward **premium** or forward **discount** depending on whether its forward rate is higher or lower than its spot rate. To express them precisely, let S denote the spot rate and F denote the forward rate. The fractional deviation of the forward rate from the spot rate is $D = (F - S)/S$. The forward rate of the foreign currency is at a premium if $D > 0$ and at a discount if $D < 0$. For example, assuming away bid-offer spread for the purpose of illustration, if the spot rate of the US dollar in terms of the Canadian dollar is US$1.0048/US$1 and the 180-day forward rate is C$1.0071/US$1, the US dollar is selling at an annualized premium of $[(1.0071 - 1.0048)/1.0048] \times 360/180 = 0.46$ percent.

Cross Rates

The **cross rate** is the exchange rate between two infrequently traded currencies, calculated through a widely traded third currency. For example, an Argentine importer needs Hong Kong dollars to pay for a purchase in Hong Kong. The Argentinean peso is not quoted against the Hong Kong dollar. However, both currencies are quoted against the US dollar. Assuming:

Argentinean peso:	Arg$4.911/US$1
Hong Kong dollar:	HK$7.7715/US$1
Cross rates between Arg$ and HK$:	Arg$4.911/HK$7.7715 = Arg$0.6336/HK$
	or HK$7.7715/Arg$4.911 = HK$1.5784/Arg$

Gold Standard

Under the gold standard regime (1876–1914), the base level of a currency's exchange rate was determined by the stated value of gold per unit of the currency. Assuming, for example, that one Deutsche mark (the German currency before the adoption of the euro) is worth 0.02 ounce of gold, and that one US dollar is worth 0.048 ounce of gold, the gold equivalent then becomes the underlying criterion used in determining the base rate of the Deutsche mark against the US dollar (DM2.4/$1 in this case).

Under other foreign exchange regimes, however, there is no direct way to value one currency against others in terms of both levels and changes. Moreover, the present international monetary system is characterized by a mix of free floating, managed floating, pegged or target zone, and fixed exchange rates. No single general theory is available to forecast exchange rates under all conditions. Nevertheless, it is widely agreed that the purchasing power parity principle helps explain both the levels of and the relative changes in exchange rates in the long run. Other principles or approaches to analyze foreign exchange movements include interest rate parity and international Fisher parity. The **purchasing power parity** (PPP) approach emphasizes the role of prices of goods and services in determining exchange rates, whereas the **interest rate parity** focuses on the role of capital movements. Although these two perspectives are insufficient to explain exchange rate changes, they are useful building blocks of foreign exchange determination.

Purchasing Power Parity (PPP)

The purchasing power parity principle suggests that the exchange rate between two currencies should, in the long run, reflect purchasing power differences; that is, the exchange rate should equalize the price of an identical basket of goods and services in the two countries. This principle has absolute and relative perspectives toward purchasing power parity. **Absolute PPP** states that the exchange rate is determined by the relative prices of similar baskets of goods or services. In other words, the ratio of one currency's price of a bundle of goods and services to another currency's price of the same bundle should be the exchange rate between the two. For example, if the identical basket of goods cost ¥1,000 in Japan and $10 in the United States, the PPP-based exchange rate would be ¥100/$1.

The PPP principle in the absolute, or static, form offers a simple explanation for exchange rate determination. However, it is difficult in practice to compute the price indices. Different baskets of goods are used in different countries, given the different demand structures and consumption behaviors. To avoid this deficiency, **relative PPP** focuses on the relationship between the change in prices of two countries and the change in the exchange rate over the same period. The relative **PPP** suggests that if the exchange rate between two countries starts in equilibrium, any change in the differential rate of inflation between them tends to be offset over the long run by an equal but opposite change in the exchange rate. If the domestic inflation level is rising faster than the foreign inflation level, the exchange rate will change to effect a proportional depreciation of the domestic currency. If the foreign inflation level is rising faster than the domestic inflation level, the exchange rate will change to effectuate a proportional appreciation of the domestic currency. If the exchange rate does not change in this situation, the country's exports of goods and services will become less competitive with comparable products produced elsewhere. Imports from abroad will also become more price-competitive than higher-priced domestic products.

The PPP principle offers an economic foundation for determining and adjusting the exchange rates. In the real business world, however, PPP conditions may not hold at a given point in time and often do not hold in the short run because the principle does not take into account the effects of capital flows on exchange rates. The exchange rates are thus not always determined by the purchasing power parity. Reasons for departures from PPP include:

1. The PPP principle assumes that goods or services can move freely across borders. In practice, however, we see many restrictions on movement of goods and services (e.g., tariff and non-tariff barriers). These barriers affect both the price and quantity of exports and imports.
2. Many of the items that are often included in the commonly used price indexes do not enter into international trade (e.g., land and buildings). These non-traded items can allow departures from PPP to persist.
3. The PPP principle fails to consider cross-border transportation costs which enlarge the PPP deviations.
4. The PPP principle fails to consider the reality that different items have different weights in various nations' price indexes.
5. The PPP principle fails to consider the effect of capital flows on exchange rates.

Interest Rate Parity (IRP)

The PPP principle focuses only on goods and services and omits the importance of capital flows in the determination of exchange rates. To redress this limitation, the **interest rate parity** *(IRP)* principle provides an understanding of the way in which interest rates are linked between different countries through capital flows. The IRP principle suggests that the difference in national interest rates for securities of similar risk and maturity should be equal to, but opposite in sign of, the forward rate discount or premium for the foreign currency. The underlying rationale for the principle is that a particular form of investment in the foreign exchange market—covered interest arbitrage—will make an infinite amount of money (a logical impossibility) if the IRP is indefinitely violated.

To see the rationale, we need to understand how covered interest arbitrage works. For ease of discussion, we adopt the following notations: R_d = the domestic interest rate; R_f = the foreign interest rate; S = the spot rate; and F = the forward rate. Remember from our earlier discussion in this chapter that $D = (F - S)/S$ represents the forward premium or discount depending on whether $D > 0$ or $D < 0$. Suppose that a US investor has $1 million to invest in either the domestic market (i.e., the US), or the foreign market. If she invests the money in the US for a year, she will get back $1·$(1 + R_d) million. If she wants to invest in the foreign market, she will have to convert the $1 million to the foreign currency now. Given that the exchange rates are expressed in direct quotes (i.e., units of the domestic currency per unit of the foreign currency), the $1 million can be exchanged for 1/S million units of the foreign currency, assuming away any transaction costs. By the end of the year, she will get back (1 + R_f)/S million units in the foreign currency. There would be a risk, however, if the spot exchange rate in a year substantially differs from the current spot rate. To eliminate this risk, the investor can purchase a forward contract to sell the expected proceeds from the investment for US dollars. At the forward exchange rate F, the proceeds in the foreign currency can be exchanged for $F·$(1 + R_f)/S million in dollars. The IRP principle basically says that an investor must be able to get the same return from investing in each market: $1 + R_d = F·(1 + R_f)/S$. This equation can be rearranged to show the relationship more clearly:

$$(1 + R_d)/(1 + R_f) = F/S$$

or

$$(R_d - R_f)/(1 + R_f) = (F - S)/S$$

Note that $D = (F - S)/S$ is simply the forward premium or discount. In addition, if the foreign interest rate is relatively low (e.g., 5% or less), then the IRP principle is approximately $R_d - R_f \approx D$. The IRP means that the interest rate differential between two countries will be matched by the forward premium or discount of the exchange rate. If this principle is violated indefinitely, as in a case of $1 + R_d < F·(1 + R_f)/S$, someone will be able to make an infinite amount of money by borrowing in the domestic currency and investing the money in the foreign currency. In reality, any deviation from the equilibrium condition of IRP will be quickly eliminated if covered interest arbitrage can be carried out without serious restrictions. For instance, a situation of $1 + R_d < F·(1 + R_f)/S$ will trigger a capital outflow, which will decrease domestic supply of deposits, increase supply of deposits in the foreign economy, raise the demand of domestic currency holders for the foreign currency on the spot market, and reduce the demand of foreign currency holders for the domestic currency. These changes in demand and supply will, in turn, put pressure for the domestic interest rate R_d to rise, the foreign interest rate R_f to fall, the spot rate S to rise and the forward rate F to fall, restoring the equilibrium based on the IRP principle.

Consider, for example, the case in which the one-year interest rate in New York is 8.75 percent, and in London 11.75 percent. This seems to suggest that investors will earn an excess return of 3 percent if the funds are invested in the London bond market (or that borrowers will acquire funds more inexpensively in New York). However, if the prevailing current spot rate is \$1.6375/£1 and the one-year forward rate is \$1.5883/£1, then investors who convert their proceeds back to US dollars will have to pay a 3 percent forward discount on the pound sterling in the forward market. We see that the interest rate advantage is offset by the forward discount on the pound. If the investors did not use the forward market, they may suffer a loss greater than 3 percent, because the actual spot rate between dollar and pound a year later may drop more than 3 percent.

Like PPP, IRP also faces deviations due to transaction costs and tax factors in financial markets. Political risks can also cause deviations from interest parity between countries because investors expect to be compensated for the greater risk of investing in a foreign country. The forward market and related terms will be discussed in detail later in this chapter.

The IRP is generally applicable to securities with maturities of one year or less, since forward contracts are not routinely available for periods longer than one year. Similar to the IRP principle, but involving securities with maturity that could be longer than one year, the **international Fisher effect** addresses the relationship between the percentage change in the spot exchange rate over time and the differential between comparable interest rates in different national capital markets. Specifically, the international Fisher effect states that the spot exchange rate should change in an equal amount but in the opposite direction to the difference in interest rates between two countries. For example, if a dollar-based investor buys a ten-year yen bond earning 4 percent annual interest, compared with 6 percent interest available on dollars, the investor must be anticipating the yen to appreciate vis-à-vis the dollar by at least 2 percent per year during the ten years.

Foreign Exchange Rate Overshooting

At this point, you may wonder whether the equilibriums exchange rate derived from the PPP principle is always the same as the equilibriums exchange rate derived from the IRP principle. The answer is: No. As explained earlier, the PPP reflects the condition of equilibrium in the market for goods and services, while the IRP reflects the condition of equilibrium in the market for capital or financial assets. It turns out that, after an economic shock (e.g., a government decision to increase or decrease money supply), the goods market tends to adjust from one equilibrium point to another gradually, while the assets market adjusts almost instantaneously in the highly liquid global financial market of today. The slower adjustment in the goods market is due to the constraints of contracts and the higher costs of changing decisions on purchases and sales and on hiring and compensation: buyers and sellers often have long-term contracts and employers normally have wage agreements with unions. This means that the IRP typically dominates in the determination of exchanges in the short run and that the PPP generally works only in the long run. The difference in the paces of adjustment between the markets for goods and assets has a profound implication for exchange rate volatility and exchange rate forecast. Specifically, it makes the foreign exchange market more volatile and exchange rate forecast more difficult.

Let us consider a hypothetical example. Suppose that the Federal Reserve System decides to increase money supply in the US in order to speed up the recovery of the economy from a recession. Exhibit 9.5 shows the likely paths of adjustments in the various economic quantities. On the one hand, the rise in money supply can be expected to lower the US interest rates for at least a period of time and cause capital to flow from the US to foreign markets seeking higher interest rates. The capital outflows will in turn increase the demand of US dollar holders for foreign currencies and thus depress the value of the US dollar. Because the assets market adjusts quickly, all these can be expected to happen almost instantaneously. However, because at least some of the investors who take their money out of the US now will eventually bring the money back, their future movements of capital will increase the demand of foreign currency holders for the US dollar and thus increase the value of the US dollar over time. On the other hand, the rise in money supply can also be expected to raise the US inflation rate over time (as the economy recovers and reaches capacity), making US-made goods less competitive than foreign-made goods at the current exchange rates and thus resulting in fewer US exports and more US imports. According to the PPP, the expected rise in inflation will cause the value of the US dollar to fall over time. Because the goods market tends to adjust gradually, these changes take time to materialize. Now, there is a contradiction between what the IRP dictates and what the PPP requires: according to the IPR, the value of the US dollar is supposed to fall instantaneously and then *rise* over time; but according to the PPP, the value of the US dollar is supposed to *fall* over time without rising first. In order for both the IRP and the PPP to hold in the long run, the value of the US dollar must initially rise more than required by the PPP and then fall to a level consistent with the PPP, as illustrated in Exhibit 9.5. This is called foreign exchange rate overshooting.

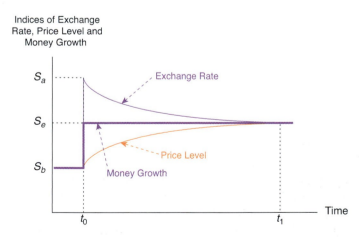

Exhibit 9.5 Foreign exchange rate overshooting

The overshooting of foreign exchange rates in response to an economic shock implies that an unexpected change in the economy of a country (e.g., a government decision to change economic policies) is likely to cause the exchange rates to jump up or down by more than is needed to satisfy the long-run equilibrium condition of the PPP. This not only creates a high level of volatility in the foreign exchange market but also causes sometimes prolonged violation of the PPP, making producers in the country more or less competitive in the world market than their actual production efficiency warrants. The years-long strengthening of the US dollar in the early 1980s is a case in point. The "schizophrenic" reactions of the assets market also make exchange rate forecast more difficult.

Implications for MNEs: Foreign Exchange Forecasting

Because future exchange rates are uncertain, participants in international financial markets can never know for sure what the exchange rate will be one month or one year ahead. As a result, forecasts must be made. Some forecasters believe that for the major floating currencies, foreign exchange markets are "efficient" and forward exchange rates are unbiased predictors of future spot exchange rates. However, empirical studies rejected this hypothesis.[6] Although referencing to the forward rate (see next section) is still necessary and useful, and can be viewed as a baseline in forecasting a foreign exchange rate, international managers should take into account many economic and non-economic factors in predicting foreign exchange rates, especially long-term rates (over one year).

Economic fundamentals that influence long-term exchange rates include balance of payments, foreign exchange reserves, relative inflation rates, relative interest rates, and the long-run properties of purchasing power parity. The strength of a focal country's economy, which is often reflected in its GDP (gross domestic product), GNP (gross national product), national income, investment growth, and export growth, among others, also influences the country's long-term exchange rates. Because governments differ in the extent to which they exert influence on foreign exchange rates, even under the floating system, managers should be aware of government declarations and agreements regarding exchange rate goals. Non-economic fundamentals that may affect exchange rates include political or social events, bilateral relations between the two countries, market speculations against the currency, the confidence of market participants, and natural disasters. As explained above, these unexpected events, together with unanticipated changes in government economic policies, can cause sudden and large capital flows that dominate exchange rate movements in the short run. So, any forecast of foreign exchange rates in the short run must take into account such capital flows.

In emerging markets with foreign exchange control set by the government, there often exists foreign exchange black (or parallel) markets in which buyers and sellers transact foreign currencies using the market rate, which is generally different from the official rate. Because this "market" rate is often a "shadow" price that reflects the demand and supply equilibrium in the foreign exchange market, it is often used as the reference rate in predicting managerial floating exchange rates. In predicting exchange rates, international managers also look at the country's foreign exchange rate system. If, for example, a country pegs its currency to that of another major trade partner, then the exchange rate prediction will emphasize the partner country's currency. To predict a long-term fixed rate, managers also need to see if the government is capable of controlling domestic inflation, in order to generate hard currency reserves to use for intervention, and to run trade surpluses. To predict a long-term floating rate, managers must focus on inflationary fundamentals and PPP as well as indicators for economic health such as growth and stability.

Time-series analysis of prior years, together with anticipated new factors about future changes, is a widely applied technique for predicting foreign exchange rates, particularly short-term trends. The accuracy of these forecasts depends on whether the foreign exchange market is efficient. The more efficient the market, the more likely it is that exchange rates are "random walks" (e.g., with past price behavior providing no clues to the future). The less efficient the foreign exchange market, the higher the probability that forecasters will find a key pattern that holds, at least in the short run. If the pattern is truly consistent, however, others will soon discover it, and the market will become efficient again with respect to that information.

Interim Summary

1. The purchasing power parity (PPP) principle holds that the exchange rate between two currencies is determined in the long run by the price of an identical basket of goods and services. The interest rate parity (IRP) principle holds that the interest rate differential between two countries will be matched by the premium of their forward exchange rate.
2. To predict or forecast foreign exchange rates, international managers analyze both economic and non-economic fundamentals, while making reference to forward or black market exchange rates.

The Balance of Payments

The exchange rate system is a necessary tool for international transactions involving different currencies. The national goal of these transactions is to accomplish gains from trade and investment activities, which are recorded in the balance-of-payments account. The **balance of payments** is an accounting statement that summarizes all the economic transactions between residents (individuals, companies, and other organizations) of the home country and those of all other countries. That is, it reports the country's international performance in trading with other nations and the volume of capital flowing in and out of the country. Balance-of-payments accounting uses the system of **double-entry bookkeeping,** which means that every debit or credit in the account is also represented as a credit or debit somewhere else. In a balance-of-payments sheet, currency inflows are recorded as *credits* (plus sign), whereas outflows are recorded as *debits* (minus sign).

A standard balance of payments includes *current account, capital account,* and *official reserves account.* Each category is made up of several subcategories. To maintain the balance of the total credit and total debit, the statistical discrepancy is also included in a balance of payments. Statistical discrepancy reflects net *errors and omissions* in collecting data on international transactions. Exhibit 9.6 illustrates the United States' balance-of-payments sheet for 2005 and 2011.

CURRENT ACCOUNT

Goods		
Exports	911.69	1,497.41
Imports	−1,692.42	−2,235.82
Balance merchandise trade	−780.73	−738.41
Services		
Exports	375.76	605.96
Imports	−303.65	−427.43
Balance service trade	72.11	178.53
Investment income		
Received	532.54	738.81
Paid	−453.80	−503.80
Balance of investment income	78.74	235.01
Compensation of employees		
Received	4.80	5.81
Paid	−14.95	−13.82
Balance of employee compensation	−10.15	−8.01
Unilateral transfers (net)	−105.74	−133.05
Balance on current account	**−745.78**	**−465.93**
CAPITAL ACCOUNT		
Private portfolio investment		
New investment/lending in US from abroad	875.44	555.18
New US investment/lending abroad	−530.03	55.22
Foreign direct investment		
New FDI in US from abroad	112.64	233.99
New US FDI abroad	−36.24	−419.33
Government assets, other than official reserve assets		
Foreign official assets in US	259.27	211.83
US government assets abroad	5.54	−103.67
Capital transfers	13.12	−1.21
Financial derivatives, net	0.00	39.01
Balance on capital account	**699.74**	**571.01**
OFFICIAL RESERVE ACCOUNT	**14.10**	**−15.88**
Gold	0.00	0.00
Special drawing rights	4.51	0.00
Reserve position in the International Monetary Fund	10.20	−18.08
Foreign currencies	−0.62	0.45
ERRORS AND OMISSIONS	**31.94**	**−89.21**
NET BALANCE	**0.00**	**0.00**

Exhibit 9.6 The US balance of payments, 2005 and 2011 (in billions of dollars)

Source: Bureau of Economic Analysis, US Department of Commerce, Washington, DC (www.bea.gov).

Current Account

The **current account** records flows of goods, services, and unilateral transfers (gifts). It includes exports and imports of merchandise (trade balance) and service transactions (also known as invisible items). The service account includes various service income and fees (e.g., interest, dividends, and royalty). Tourism income, financial charges (i.e., banking and insurance), and transportation charges (i.e., shipping and air travel) are part of service income. The investment income account separates investment income from service income, and it records income receipts on the country-owned assets abroad and income payments on foreign-owned assets within the country. Unilateral transfers include pensions, remittances, and other transfers for which no specific services are furnished.

Capital Account

The **capital account** records private and public investment or lending activities and is divided into portfolio (short- and long-term) and foreign direct investment. Foreign branches, wholly owned subsidiaries, and joint ventures are typical forms of direct investments. Foreign bonds, notes, or mutual funds are examples of portfolio investments, insofar as they confer no management or voting rights on their owners. The portfolio account includes both short-term (e.g., cash, deposits, and bills) and long-term investments or lending (e.g., securities with a maturity longer than one year, bank loans, and mortgages). Government borrowing and lending are also included in the capital account.

Official Reserves Account

The **official reserves account** records net holdings of the official reserves held by a national government. Reserves include gold, special drawing rights (SDRs), reserve positions in the IMF, and convertible foreign currencies. To most countries, foreign currency is by far the largest component of total international liquidity. Each government normally keeps foreign exchange reserves in the form of foreign treasury bills, short-term and long-term government securities, euros, and the like.

Note that the implications of the balance of payments, especially trade deficits or surplus under current account, may change over time and is subject to interpretation. Today many imports are actually "exported" by the country's own companies operating in a trading partner country. But, statistically, they are still "imports" recorded in the balance of payments. The United States had, for example, a $295.38 billion merchandise trade deficit with China, followed by $68.63 billion with Mexico, $64.63 billion with Japan, $49.8 billion with Germany and $38.26 billion with Canada in 2011. However, a sizable percentage of imports entering the United States were in fact "exported" by American companies (e.g., HP, Pepsi, GE, Xerox, and Rubbermaid) investing and operating in these partner countries. Over half of China's total exports and imports ($1,899 billion and $1,743 billion, respectively, in 2011), for instance, are undertaken by foreign investors in the country. From a wealth creation perspective, these "imports" may be viewed as a plus, rather than minus, sign in the balance of payments.

Interim Summary

1. The balance of payments records economic transactions between one country and the rest of the world. It contains current account, capital account, and official reserves balance.
2. A nation's trade deficits (such as those in the United States) may be reinterpreted if a large number of MNEs from this nation invest abroad and export back their products.

International Foreign Exchange Markets

The international monetary systems introduced earlier set up the institutional framework for the operations of the world financial markets, but it is the international financial markets where currency exchanges take place. International monetary systems and international financial markets are inherently linked such that the former impacts company decisions or firm operations through the latter. International firms face many opportunities as well as threats arising from the international financial markets, which are determined at least partly by the monetary systems. International financial markets are composed of *international foreign exchange markets* and *international capital markets*. International capital markets further include: (a) international money markets; (b) international stock markets; (c) international bond markets; and (d) international loan markets (see Exhibit 9.7).

Landscape of the International Foreign Exchange Market

The **foreign exchange market** is where foreign currencies are bought and sold. It is the physical as well as institutional structure through which currencies are exchanged, exchange rates determined, and foreign exchange transactions completed. A **foreign exchange transaction** is an agreement between a buyer and seller for the delivery of a certain amount of one currency at a specified rate in exchange for some other currency. The 2010 survey of foreign exchange markets conducted by the BIS (Bank of International Settlements) illustrated that average daily turnover in the international foreign exchange market was about $4 trillion. The US dollar was the most actively traded currency, reflecting its liquidity, its use as a settlement currency, and its predominance in trade-related transactions. The dollar was involved in nearly 80 percent of all foreign exchange transactions in 2010. The second, third, and fourth most traded currencies were the euro, Japanese yen, and pound sterling, respectively.

International Foreign Exchange Market	International Capital Markets			
	International Money Market	International Stock Market	International Bond Market	International Loan Market

Exhibit 9.7 International financial markets

The global foreign exchange business is concentrated in four centers, which together account for about two-thirds of total reported turnover. These four centers are London, New York, Tokyo, and Singapore. Other important exchange markets are located in Zurich, Hong Kong, Paris, Frankfurt, Amsterdam, Milan, Toronto, Brussels, and Bahrain. A larger share of US dollar turnover and euro turnover is conducted in London than in either New York or Frankfurt. The foreign exchange market is dominated by dealers, and is becoming increasingly automated and concentrated.

Market Participants and Functions

A market for foreign exchange consists of *individuals, corporations, banks,* and *brokers* who buy or sell currencies. Currency trading in each country is conducted through the intermediation of foreign exchange brokers, who match currency bids and offers of banks and also trade directly among themselves internationally. Banks in each country and throughout the world are linked together by telephone, Internet, telex, and a satellite communications network called the **Society for Worldwide International Financial Telecommunications (SWIFT)** based in Brussels, Belgium. Despite the long distance separating market participants, this computer-based communication system ensures that all significant events virtually and instantaneously impact the entire financial world. This in turn contributes to a worldwide market with narrower spreads for participants.

Although the market is global, the exchange market in each country has its own identity and institutional and regulatory framework. An efficient communication system can substitute for participants' needs to convene in a specific location *(bourse)*. Indeed, the UK–US type of market is based on communication networks, whereas the European approach remains traditional, based on the physical meeting of the participants, usually at the bourse. Daily meetings take place in some markets, such as those in Frankfurt and Paris, where representatives of commercial banks and central banks meet and determine a rate, known as the fixing rate. In those countries, the posted fixing rates serve as a guide for pricing small to medium-sized transactions between banks and their customers. Among major industrial countries, Japan, Germany, France, Italy, and the Scandinavian and Benelux countries have a daily fixing. The United Kingdom, Switzerland, Canada, and the United States do not.

Foreign exchange is traded in a 24-hour market. As the market in the Far East closes, trading in the Middle Eastern financial centers has been going on for a couple of hours, and trading in Europe is just beginning. As the London market closes, the one in New York opens. A few hours later, the market in San Francisco opens and trades with the East Coast of the United States and the Far East as well. Banks dominate the foreign exchange market, with about 90 percent of foreign exchange trading constituting interbank trading. Non-bank participants in foreign exchange trading include commodities dealers, multinational corporations, and non-bank financial institutions.

The foreign exchange market performs three major functions:

1. It is part of the international payments system and provides a mechanism for exchange or transfer of the national currency of one country into the currency of another country, thereby facilitating international business.
2. It assists in supplying short-term credits through the Eurocurrency market (see next section) and swap arrangements.

315

3. It provides foreign exchange instruments for hedging against exchange risk. Although most commercial banks handle actions for their clients, many banks also act as market-makers, with each prepared to deal with other banks at any time. This activity constitutes interbank market, where portfolio positions are adjusted and exchange rates determined.

Foreign exchange trading expanded sharply under the floating exchange rate system, and the number of banks participating in the market increased significantly as they entered the market to service their corporate clients. Increased hedging by companies of their cash flows and balance sheets was accompanied by the entry of new corporate participants into the market.

Transaction Forms

Spot Transactions

Spot transactions include bank notes transactions for individuals and spot transactions between banks. Bank notes transactions such as currency changes for individuals are exchanged for each other instantaneously over the counter. Spot transactions between banks, however, are normally settled on the second working day after the date on which the transaction is concluded. The interbank foreign exchange market is by far the world's largest financial market. On the *settlement date* (also referred to as value date), most dollar transactions in the world are settled through the computerized **Clearing House Interbank Payments Systems (CHIPS)** in New York, which provides for the calculation of new balances owed by any one bank to another and for payment by 6:00 P.M. the same day in Federal Reserve Bank of New York funds. This system, owned by large New York clearing banks, has more than 150 members, including the US agencies and subsidiaries of many foreign banks. It handles over 150,000 transactions a day, together worth hundreds of billions of dollars. Similar systems also exist in other major foreign exchange centers where currencies other than the US dollar are settled.

When a company (or individual) needs foreign exchange to be paid to a foreign company, it can use either customer drafts or international wire transfers through a bank. The bank sells this company a foreign exchange draft payable to the stated foreign company. For example, if a US business needs to make a Japanese yen payment to a Japanese company, it can buy a yen draft from a US bank, where this draft is drawn against the US bank's yen account at a Japanese bank. A wire transfer is the fastest settlement for international companies, paying foreign exchange to their foreign creditors. Under a wire transfer, the payment instructions are sent via SWIFT or similar electronic means.

Forward Transactions

A **forward transaction** occurs between a bank and a customer (company, broker, or another bank), calling for delivery at a fixed future date, of a specified amount of foreign exchange at the fixed forward exchange rate. This exchange rate is established at the time of agreement, but payment and delivery are not required until maturity. Customers such as international companies may either buy a foreign currency forward from a bank (e.g., in an import business) or sell a foreign currency forward to a bank (e.g., in an export bank). If the initial transaction represents an asset or future ownership claim to foreign currency, this position is described as a **long position.** If the cash market position represents a liability or a future obligation to deliver foreign currency, this position is described as a **short position.** Chapter 14 will describe forward transactions to avoid foreign exchange risks for MNEs.

Swap Transactions

A **swap** is an agreement to buy and sell foreign exchange at pre-specified exchange rates where the buying and selling are separated in time. In other words, a **swap transaction** involves the simultaneous purchase and sale of a given amount for two different settlement dates. Both purchase and sale are carried out by the same counter-party. Two common types of swap transactions are spot-forward swaps and forward-forward swaps.

In a **spot-forward swap,** an investor sells forward the foreign currency maturity value of the bill, and simultaneously buys the spot foreign exchange to pay for the bill. Since a known amount of the investor's home currency will be received according to the forward component of the swap, no uncertainty from exchange rates exists. Similarly, those who borrow in foreign currency can buy forward the foreign currency needed for repayment of the foreign currency loan at the same time that they convert the borrowed foreign funds on the spot market.

A **forward-forward swap** involves two forward transactions. For example, a dealer sells €1,000,000 forward for dollars for delivery in three months at US$0.94/euro, and simultaneously buys €1,000,000 forward for delivery in six months at US$0.94/euro. The difference between the buying price and the selling price is equivalent to the three-month interest rate differential between the euro and the US dollar.

The two preceding types of swaps are particularly popular with banks, because it is difficult for them to avoid risk when making a market for many future dates and currencies. For some dates and currencies, a bank may be in a long position, which means that it has agreed to purchase more of the foreign currency than it has agreed to sell. For other dates and currencies, the bank may be in a short position, which means that it has agreed to sell more of these currencies than it has agreed to buy. Swaps help the bank to balance its position and reduce financial risk.

Foreign Exchange Arbitrage

In the foreign exchange market, price information is readily available through computer networks, which makes it easy to compare prices in different markets. As such, exchange rates tend to be equal worldwide but temporary discrepancies do exist. These temporary discrepancies provide profit opportunities for simultaneously buying a currency in one market (at lower price) while selling it in another (at higher price). This activity is known as **arbitrage.** Arbitrage will continue until the exchange rates in different locales are so close that it is not worth the costs incurred in further buying and selling.[7]

For example, suppose Citibank is quoting the euro/US dollar exchange rate as 0.7545-55 and Dresdner Bank in Frankfurt is quoting 0.7525-35. This means that Citibank will buy dollars for

0.7545 euro and will sell dollars for 0.7555 euro. Dresdner will buy dollars for 0.7525 euro and will sell dollars for 0.7535 euro. This presents an arbitrage opportunity. We could buy $10 million at Dresdner's ask price of 0.7535 and simultaneously sell $10 million to Citibank at their bid price of 0.7545 euro. This would earn a profit of 0.0010 euro per dollar traded, so €10,000 would be the total arbitrage profit. If such a profit opportunity exists, the demand to buy dollars from Dresdner will cause it to raise its ask price above 0.7535, while the increased interest in selling dollars to Citibank at its bid price of 0.7545 euro will cause it to lower its bid. In this way, arbitrage activity pushes the prices of different traders to levels where no arbitrage profits are earned.

Arbitrage could also involve three or more currencies (e.g., the British pound, Swiss franc (CHF) and US dollar). Let us temporarily ignore the bid-ask spread and associated transaction costs. Suppose that CHF/£ = 3.00 in London, US$/CHF = 0.50 in Zurich, and US$/£ = 1.50 in New York. If we observe a market where one of the three exchange rates—CHF/£, $/CHF, £/US$—is out of line with the other two, there is an arbitrage opportunity. Suppose that the following three quotations are made: CHF/£ = 3.00 in London, US$/CHF = 0.50 in Zurich, and US$/£ = 1.4925 or £/US$ = 0.67 in New York. A trader could start with £1 million and buy CHF3 million in London, then use the Swiss francs to buy US$1.5 million in Zurich, and then use the dollars to buy £1.005 million in New York (1.5 × 0.67 = 1.005), earning a profit of £5,000.

Black Market and Parallel Market

As a result of government restrictions or legal prohibitions on foreign exchange transactions, illegal markets in foreign exchange exist in many developing countries in response to business or private demand for foreign exchange. These illegal markets are known as **black markets.** Such illegal markets exist openly in some countries (e.g., Myanmar and Venezuela), with little government interference. In some other countries however, foreign exchange laws are strictly enforced and lawbreakers receive harsh sentences when caught (e.g., North Korea).

Often, governments set an official exchange rate that deviates widely from that which the free market would establish. If a government will purchase foreign exchange only at the official rate, but private citizens are willing to pay the market-determined rate, there will be a steady supply of foreign exchange to the black market. Obviously, government policy creates the black market. The demand arises because of legal restrictions on buying foreign exchange, and the supply exists because government-mandated official exchange rates offer less than the free market rate. Ironically, governments defend the need for foreign exchange restrictions based on conserving scarce foreign exchange for high-priority uses. But such restrictions work to reduce the amount of foreign exchange that flows to the government as traders turn to the black market instead.

When the black market is legalized by the government, this market is referred to as the **parallel market** and operates as an alternative to the official exchange market. In many countries facing economic hardship, the parallel markets allow normal economic activities to continue through a steady supply of foreign exchange. For instance, Guatemala had an artificially low official exchange rate of one quetzale per dollar for more than three decades; however, a black market where the exchange rate fluctuated daily with market conditions was allowed to operate openly in front of the country's main post office. In Mexico, this parallel market thrived during times of crisis when

318

the official peso/dollar exchange rate varied greatly from the market rate. For instance, in August 1982, the Mexican government banned the sale of dollars by Mexican banks. Immediately, the parallel market responded. The official exchange rate was 69.5 pesos per dollar, but the rate on the street ranged from 120 to 150 as the parallel market demand increased with the ban on bank sales. Private currency trades between individuals were legal, so trading flourished at the Mexico City airport and other public places.

Interim Summary

1. A foreign exchange market consists of individuals, corporations, banks, and brokers who buy or sell currencies. Major foreign exchange markets in the world include London, New York, Tokyo, and Singapore. International foreign exchange markets offer spot transactions, forward transactions, and swap transactions.
2. It is possible to earn profits from foreign exchange arbitrage—simultaneously buying a currency in one market at a lower price while selling it in another market at a higher price. This type of activity escalates volatility in international foreign exchange markets.

International Capital Markets

International Money Markets

International money markets are the markets in which foreign monies are financed or invested (e.g., Hitachi and Matsushita borrow US dollars from several US banks in Tokyo to finance their worldwide operations). MNEs use international money markets to finance global operations at a lower cost than is possible domestically. They borrow currencies that have low interest rates and are expected to depreciate against their own currency. They incur the risk that the currencies borrowed may appreciate, however, which will increase their cost of financing. Investors, on the other hand, may achieve substantially higher returns in foreign markets than in their domestic markets when investing in currencies that appreciate against their home currency. However, if these currencies depreciate, the effective yield on the foreign investments will likely be lower than the domestic yield, and may even be negative. Investors attempt to capitalize on potentially high effective yields on foreign money market securities, while reducing the exchange rate risk by diversifying the investments across currencies.

Often, transactions in international money markets are conducted via the Eurocurrency market. The **Eurocurrency market** consists of commercial banks that accept large deposits and provide large loans in foreign currencies (e.g., banks in Zurich lend US dollars, or banks in Frankfurt provide loans in Japanese yen). Those banks offering Eurocurrency services are either local banks or foreign bank subsidiaries in a host country. Growing international trade and capital flows as well as cross-border differences in interest rates are the primary reasons for the growth of the Eurocurrency market. In this market, Eurodollar deposits are intensively transacted.

Eurodollars represent US dollar deposits in non-US banks. When interest rate ceilings were imposed on dollar deposits in US banks, corporations with large dollar balances often deposited their funds overseas to receive a higher yield. These deposits were used by local banks to provide loans to other corporations that needed US dollars. Eurodollar deposits are not subject to reserve requirements, so banks can lend out 100 percent of the deposits. For these reasons, the spread between the interest rate paid on large Eurodollar deposits and charged on Eurodollar loans is relatively small. Deposits and loan transactions in Eurodollars are typically $1 million or more per transaction.

Two popular Eurodollar deposits are *Eurodollar fixed-rate certificate of deposits (CD)* and *Eurodollar floating-rate certificate of deposits*. Investors in fixed-rate Eurodollar CDs receive guaranteed interest but are adversely affected by rising market interest rates. To neutralize this problem, floating-rate Eurodollar CDs provide the rate that is adjusted periodically to the *London Interbank Offer Rate (LIBOR)*—the rate charged on interbank dollar loans. The floating-rate CDs allow the borrower's cost and investor's return to reflect prevailing market interest rates.[8]

International Bond Markets

International bond markets are the markets where government bonds or corporate bonds are issued, bought, or sold in foreign countries (e.g., China International Trust and Investment Corporation, or CITIC, issued its corporate bonds in Japan, Europe, and the United States during the 1980s and 1990s). The growth of international bond markets is attributed to some unique features offered by international bonds that are not offered by domestic bonds (see the Industry Box). The development of international bond markets is partially attributed to tax law differentials across countries. Until 1984, foreign investors who purchased bonds that were placed in the United States paid a 30 percent withholding tax on interest payments. However, various tax treaties between the United States and other countries reduced the withholding tax. Interest payments to non-US investors were exempt from the withholding tax, triggering lower interest rates and allowing US firms to issue bonds at a higher price. The withholding tax on US-placed bonds was eliminated in 1984, causing an even larger increase in the foreign demand for US-placed bonds.

Bonds placed in international bond markets are typically underwritten by a syndicate of investment banking firms. Many underwriters in the *Eurobond* market (i.e., bonds in one foreign currency are issued in the country that uses this currency) are subsidiaries of US banks that have focused their growth on non-US countries, since they were historically banned by the Glass-Steagall Act from underwriting corporate bonds in the United States.[9] Some recent issuers of bonds in the Eurobond market include Daimler Financial, Citicorp, General Motors Acceptance Corp., and the World Bank. DaimlerChrysler Financial Corp. now obtains about a quarter of its funds from the Eurobond market. Its bonds have been denominated not only in dollars but also in Swiss francs, euros, and Australian dollars. Citicorp now borrows about half of its funds overseas.

Industry Box

US Firms Find Cheaper Financing from Foreign Sources

The turbulence in the US and European financial markets since the onset of the Global Financial Crisis has made foreign financing particularly compelling to MNEs that have easy access to bond markets on both sides of the Atlantic. Because the advent and resolution of crisis situations are not synchronized on the two continents, US and European interest rates often diverge significantly even though the international financial markets are considered highly integrated. As the EU weathered acute crises in a number of its member countries, such as Greece, Portugal, and Ireland, relative calm has been restored in the euro- and sterling-denominated bond markets, while the US is struggling with political gridlock on the debt ceiling for government borrowing.

US-based MNEs have increasingly found borrowing in euro and sterling attractive, taking advantage of the relative calm in Europe. Their sales of bonds denominated in the two currencies increased by over 60 percent in 2012, according to data provider Dealogic. US companies borrowing in Europe is part of a global trend to issue debt overseas. Borrowers find it beneficial to avoid competing issuers in their home markets. Non-US companies have also sold an increasing amount of dollar-denominated debt—known as "Yankee" bonds—in the US in recent years.

Many of these companies issued bonds in euros or sterling and convert the money back into dollars to finance their operations in the US at a cheaper rate than they could get if they issued their bonds in dollars. Some of them have factories and other assets in the foreign country where they are issuing debt and use foreign currency to pay bills there. Two recent examples are the biotechnology firm Amgen Inc. and the Satellite-TV provider DirecTV (which just sold bonds in the sterling market for the first time), both to fund their investment projects in the US. Other US firms that also took advantage of the present relative calm in Europe include Procter & Gamble Co., J.P. Morgan Chase & Co., Cargill Inc., and Wells Fargo & Co.

Source: Adapted from Katy Burne, "US firms have taste for foreign borrowing," *Wall Street Journal,* September 14, 2012.

International Stock Markets

International stock (or equity) markets are where company stocks are listed and traded on foreign stock exchanges (e.g., Nokia of Finland issues stock on the New York Stock Exchange, or NYSE). Firms in need of financing use foreign stock markets as additional sources of funds. Investors use foreign stock markets to enhance their portfolio performance. This financing source allows MNEs to attract more funds without flooding their home stock market, avoiding a decline in share price. A large number of MNEs also issue stock in foreign markets in order to circumvent regulations, since regulatory provisions differ among markets. Firms may also believe that they can achieve worldwide recognition among consumers if they issue stock in various foreign markets. Further, listing stock on a foreign stock exchange not only enhances the stock's liquidity but also increases the firm's perceived financial standing when the exchange approves the listing application. It can also protect a firm against hostile takeovers because it disperses ownership and makes it more difficult for other firms to gain a controlling interest. For instance, when Daimler-Benz AG announced its listing on the New York Stock Exchange, its share price quickly increased by 30 percent.

The *Euroequity market* (e.g., issuing US dollar-denominated stocks on non-US exchanges) has developed and grown at a rapid pace since the 1980s. The stocks issued in the Euroequity market are specifically designed for distribution among foreign markets. They are underwritten by a group of investment banks and purchased primarily by institutional investors in several countries. Many of the underwriters are US-based investment banks, such as First Boston (now part of Credit Suisse First Boston, or CSFB), Goldman Sachs, and Salomon Brothers.

The ability of firms to place new shares in foreign markets depends partially on the stock's perceived liquidity in that market. A secondary market for the stock must be established in foreign markets to enhance liquidity, and makes newly issued stocks more attractive. There are some costs of listing on a foreign exchange, such as translating a company's annual financial report from the local currency into the foreign currency, and making financial statements compatible with the accounting standards used in that country.

International Loan Markets

International loan markets involve large commercial banks and other lending institutions providing loans to foreign companies. Unlike international money markets that deal only with foreign money, loan markets are not restricted to foreign currency transactions. As regulations across Europe, Japan, and the United States are standardized, the markets for loans and other financial services are becoming more globalized. As a result, some financial institutions are attempting to achieve greater economies of scale on the services they offer. Even financial institutions that are not planning global expansion are experiencing increased foreign competition in their home markets. US banks have been particularly interested in foreign markets because US regulations used to restrain banks from spreading across state lines until recently.

Banks from all countries perceive *international lending* as a means of diversification. A portfolio of loans to borrowers across various countries is less susceptible to a recession in the bank's home country. International lending also allows banks to develop relationships with foreign firms, which create a demand for the banks' other services. In addition, a large portion of international lending is to support *international acquisitions*. Commercial banks and investment banks serve not only as advisers but also as financial intermediaries by placing stocks and bonds or by providing loans. One common form of participation has been to provide direct loans for financing acquisitions, especially for *leveraged buyouts (LBOs)* by management or some other group of investors. Since LBOs are financed mostly with debt, they result in a large demand for loanable funds. Many LBOs are supported by debt from an international syndicate of banks. In this way, each bank limits its exposure to any particular borrower. Because the firms engaged in LBOs are often in diversified industries, a problem in any given industry does not create a new lending crisis. In addition, the debt of each individual firm is relatively small, so that most borrowers would not have sufficient bargaining power to reschedule debt payments. For this reason, international bank financing of LBOs is perceived to be less risky than providing loans to governments of developing countries, another group of major borrowers in international loan markets.

Lending to developing countries often requires credit checking. International commercial banks and other lending institutions do so based on analysis by *credit rating agencies* such as *Standard & Poor's* and *Moody's*. Notably, political risk and overall pressures on the balance of payments and macroeconomic conditions are the focus of analysis (see also Chapter 7). Exhibit 9.8 provides an illustrative example.

Issuer Credit Ratings (or ICR) are offered by credit-rating agencies based on the preceding analysis. ICR apply to both *Corporate Credit Service* (company-level) and *Sovereign Credit Ratings* (country-level). Under the Standard & Poor's system, the long-term issuer credit ratings are classified into the following:

AAA   An obligor (debtor) has extremely strong capacity to meet its financial commitments.

AA   An obligor has very strong capacity to meet its financial commitments. It differs from the highest-rated obligor (AAA) only in small degree.

A   An obligor has strong capacity to meet its financial commitments but is somewhat more susceptible to the adverse effects of changes in circumstances and economic conditions.

BBB   An obligor has adequate capacity to meet its financial commitments. However, adverse economic conditions are more likely to weaken this capacity.

Political Risk

1. Form of government and adaptability of political institutions
2. Extent of popular participation
3. Orderliness of leadership succession
4. Degree of consensus on economic policy objectives
5. Integration into global trade and financial system
6. Internal and external security risks

Economic Factors

1. Income and economic structure
2. Economic growth prospects
3. Fiscal flexibility
4. Public debt burden
5. Price stability
6. Balance-of-payments flexibility
7. External debt and liquidity

Exhibit 9.8 Factors used in sovereign rating by Standard & Poor's

BB   An obligor is less vulnerable in the near term than other lower-rated obligors. However, it faces major ongoing uncertainties and exposure to adverse business, financial, or economic conditions which could lead to the obligor's inadequate capacity to meet its financial commitments.

B   An obligor is more vulnerable than in the case of BB, but currently has the capacity to meet its financial commitments. Adverse business, financial, or economic conditions will likely impair the obligor's capacity or willingness to meet its financial commitments.

CCC   An obligor is currently vulnerable, and is dependent upon favorable business, financial, and economic conditions to meet its financial commitments.

CC   An obligor is currently highly vulnerable.

The preceding ratings may be modified by the addition of a plus or minus sign to show relative standing within each rating category.

Interim Summary

1. MNEs can finance their global operations from international money markets, bond markets, equity markets, and loan markets. They can borrow money from money markets or loan markets, or issue corporate bonds (bond markets) or stocks (equity markets).
2. Banks and corporations actively participate in Eurocurrency markets (e.g., banks in Amsterdam lend US dollars), Eurobond markets (e.g., issue US dollar bonds in Brussels), and Euroequity markets (e.g., issue US dollar stocks on the Singapore Stock Exchange) to benefit interest rate differentials or regulatory differences.

Major International Financial Crises in Recent Times

The Asian Financial Crisis

The Asian financial crisis shows how a crisis could occur in international financial markets (foreign exchange market, stock market, money market, and loan market) and how this crisis relates to businesses (domestic and foreign), governments, financial institutions, and international financial markets. First afflicting Thailand in June 1997, the Asian financial crisis quickly spread to South Korea, Indonesia, Malaysia, the Philippines, and other Southeast and East Asian countries. The crisis initially took the form of a financial meltdown, with currencies, stock markets, and property prices tumbling across the region. Economic aftershocks ensued. The crisis was soon to affect markets and economies across the world from Europe to Latin America. The nations of East and Southeast Asia, accustomed to high single- or double-digit growth rates, shifted to slow or negative growth. These poor economic conditions prevailed in most of these nations until early 1999. Explanations concerning the causes of the crisis fall into three broad perspectives,[10] namely: (1) financial; (2) political/institutional; and (3) managerial.

The Financial Perspective

The financial perspective views the Asian financial crisis as resulting primarily from financial-sector weakness and market failure. From a financial perspective, two interrelated factors stand out as having contributed to financial sector weakness and market failure. The first is the maintenance of pegged exchange rates, which came to be viewed as implicit guarantees of exchange, constraining monetary remedies. The second is excessive private sector short-term and dollar-denominated borrowing. For example, Thailand pegged its currency to the US dollar, prompting dollar-denominated borrowing underpinned by higher interest rates for baht-denominated loans. From 1988 to 1994, international bank loans to Thai borrowers more than doubled. By the end of 1997, Thai foreign debt had reached $89 billion, of which $81.6 billion was owed by private corporations. About half of the debt carried a maturity date of under a year. In 1997, the value of private sector foreign liabilities was estimated at 25 percent of GDP. Thailand's weakening exports, growing current account deficit, and exploding dollar-denominated short-term private company debt began to weigh on foreign investors and lenders in late 1996. Attacks by currency speculators in the first half of 1997 were followed by loan defaults by several property companies, a downgrade of Thailand's long-term debt, and the unraveling of the Thai stock market. The situation quickly deteriorated and, on June 27, 1997, the government floated the baht.[11]

The financial perspective additionally emphasizes the effects of contagion on the crisis. Contagion fueled the crisis through the dynamics of competitive devaluation and the so-called *wake-up call* effect. The former pertains to the pressures faced by Asian countries to devalue their currency to match devaluation by neighboring Asian countries. The latter explains the tendency of most foreign investors to treat all Asian countries as one and pull out investments from a country regardless of its economic or market fundamentals. Undoubtedly, contagion played a major role in accelerating the pace by which the crisis spread from Thailand to South Korea, Indonesia, Malaysia, and throughout Southeast and East Asia.

The Political/Institutional Perspective

Political/institutional-based explanations contend that the causes of the Asian crisis extend much deeper than financial sector weaknesses and market failure, the latter often seen as symptoms rather than causes. The political and institutional perspective points to crony capitalism, irresponsible domestic governance, weak national and political institutions, corruption in the public and private sectors, a misguided and poorly enforced regulatory environment, and other political and institutional-related factors as the principal forces behind the crisis.

The crisis exposed key weaknesses in the political/economic systems and institutions of several Asian countries. The widespread practice of crony capitalism and the incestuous relationship between government, banking, and business in such countries as Indonesia, Malaysia, and Thailand led to an overextension of credit to undeserving companies with close ties to the political and military leadership. In addition, politicians and government bureaucrats have been largely ineffective in responding to the crisis due to conflicting business interests. In the case of Indonesia, for example, the Suharto government backpedaled in implementing the IMF reforms because of their possible adverse impact on the business interests of the ruler's extended family and cronies.

325

The IMF noted three political and institutional-related considerations as contributing forces to the Asian financial crisis:[12]

1. In financial systems, weak management and poor control of risks, lax enforcement of providential rules and inadequate supervision, and government direct lending practices led to a sharp deterioration in the quality of banks' loan portfolios.
2. Problems of data availability and lack of transparency hindered market participants from maintaining a realistic view of economic fundamentals, and at the same time added to uncertainty.
3. Problems of governance and political uncertainties exacerbated the crisis of confidence, the reluctance of foreign creditors to roll over short-term loans, and the downward pressure on currencies and stock markets.

The Managerial Perspective

The third group of explanations maintains that micro-mismanagement was at the heart of the crisis. Encouraged by a booming economy in the 1990s, many industrial companies in East and Southeast Asia pursued risky over-diversification. To fund their expansion, these companies relied heavily on short-term debt financing. In 1996, the five largest South Korean conglomerates or "chaebols" (i.e., Samsung, Hyundai, Lucky Goldstar, Daewoo, and Sunkyong) controlled over 250 subsidiaries in more than four dozen (mostly unrelated) lines of business. The combined liabilities of the five amounted to about 70 percent of South Korea's gross domestic product in 1996.

Over-diversification and extended leveraging created a vicious cycle for many companies. Firms pursued risky ventures in order to earn larger returns on their investments and service their expensive, short-term debt. When these risky projects failed, they turned to more borrowing to keep their operations afloat. These companies were able to maintain this practice for as long as banks were willing and able to extend credit. When the financial crisis hit, and banks refused or were unable to roll over their loans, many of these industrial companies, particularly the undercapitalized firms, were forced into bankruptcy.

Rising labor costs, falling commodity prices, contracting export markets, and other external pressures compounded the problems faced by industrial companies during the months preceding the financial crisis. Instead of addressing these external pressures by improving productivity, cutting costs, and focusing on the bottom line, the large majority of companies opted for growth and diversification into unrelated businesses. This strategy proved costly when the financial crisis hit and funds dried up. In contrast, firms that remained focused on their core competencies—enhanced productivity, cut costs, and focused on profitability—were able to weather the storm. Most notable among them are South Korea's Pohang Steel Company (POSCO) and Ayala Land Corporation in the Philippines.

Banks and financial institutions extended credit to undeserving companies. When those companies were unable to repay, the banks agreed to roll over the loans and extend them new credit. The financial perspective views the process as a market failure, but hardly explains its roots. The political/institutional perspective blames the decision to overextend credit on such factors as direct government lending, crony capitalism, close relationships between banks and industrial companies, and lack of transparency in financial reporting. The management perspective attributes such overextension of credit to the lack of management sophistication, as well as the absence of the administrative apparatus to conduct proper analysis and oversight. In addition, the management perspective sees a behavioral process of escalation, with banks increasing credit to justify earlier credit decisions.

The Global Financial Crisis

If the Asian financial crisis revealed financial, institutional, and managerial deficiencies in developing countries, the global financial crisis that started in 2008 revealed similar types of deficiencies in the most developed countries of the world, namely the US and EU. Similar to the Asian financial crisis, the causes for the more recent global financial crisis are also multifaceted. The direct cause was the buildup and burst of a real estate bubble primarily in the US, but the causes for the buildup of the bubble can be traced to missteps in macroeconomic management, agency problems in the governance of financial companies, and ultimately institutional flaws in the financial system of the countries involved.

As discussed in Chapter 5, any asset bubble is built on a questionable belief that the price of an asset will just go up, at least for a considerable time. US real estate prices had experienced a steady rise since the mid-1990s before a dangerous bubble started to form in the 2000s. The US Federal Reserve System (Fed) kept interest rates at very low levels to promote economic growth even after the US economy had recovered from the recession of the early 2000s. The low interest rates made investments in housing attractive in the face of rising real estate prices. Even though many policy analysts had raised concerns about the impact of Fed policies on the buildup of a real estate bubble, the Fed leaders dismissed such concerns based on the belief that the market is sufficiently efficient to correct itself before any serious damage occurs. A blind belief in the self-correcting capacity of the market without a careful look at the agency problems in financial companies and the loopholes in the US system of financial regulation was probably a significant contributor to the Fed's missteps in policy making, as Fed Chairman Alan Greenspan recognized later.

Tempted by the apparently ever-rising real estate prices, many individuals bought houses that were too expensive for them to afford. What enabled them to buy those houses was the availability of mortgage loans that required little down payment (e.g., only 5%) and allowed them to pay only interest in the first five years or so. The spread of such mortgage loans could be traced to skewed incentives systems that were commonly used at mortgage banks and investment banks at the time. Ostensibly to promote initiative and innovation, these financial companies gave large bonuses to their executives and managers without requiring them to bear the full consequences from taking excessive risks. One of the arguably most important contributors to the buildup of the bubble is a financial "innovation" that packaged highly risky mortgage loans into financial instruments and sold them to investors as securities with ordinary risk levels. Built into the formulae that the large investment banks (e.g., Bear Stearns and Lehman Brothers) used to repackage those assets, however, were unrealistic assumptions about the growth potential and risk profile of the assets. The executives and managers at most of the investment banks, however, failed to scrutinize and question the dubious assumptions underlying the repackaging of the assets. So, the skewed incentive systems at mortgage banks and investment banks that emphasized profit growth and downplayed risk control were arguably critical to the continued buildup of the real estate bubble that eventually reached a dangerous level.

As explained also in Chapter 5, the soundness of a country's financial system ultimately depends on its legal and regulatory institutions in the form of laws and regulations, as well as governmental agencies monitoring and enforcing the laws and regulations. The institutions of the US at the time evidently failed to stop its mortgage banks and investment banks taking excessive risks that brought the financial system of the country and even of the world to the brink of collapse. Economists have since identified at least three serious flaws in the system.[13] First, the derivatives industry, which repackaged high-risk mortgage loans and marketed them as low-risk securities to investors, were not regulated. Second, deregulation since the 1980s allowed investment banks to undertake functions similar to those of commercial banks but did not subject them to the risk management requirements for commercial banks (e.g., level of bank reserves and matching the terms of loans with those of deposits). Third, the same deregulation moves also significantly loosened the risk management requirements for commercial banks that issued most of the mortgage loans. In the presence of these holes and gaps in regulation, the real estate bubble injected a high-level risk into the asset portfolios of both homeowners and investors in mortgage-backed securities, including many of the largest financial companies in the world. As the US economy started to slow down in 2007, an increasing number of homeowners began to default and caused more and more banks to fail, eventually resulting in a near total loss of confidence in the financial system of the US and the world (since banks from many countries also invested heavily in US mortgage-backed securities). The global financial crisis and the Eurozone crisis in its aftermath also caused large amounts of capital to flow from the weaker countries seeking safety, creating turmoil in the foreign exchange markets also.

Recognizing the risks that the holes and gaps in the country's financial regulation pose to the stability of the national and world economy, the US has since enacted a series of reforms aimed at ensuring system stability, chief among them being the Dodd–Frank Wall Street Reform and Consumer Protection Act of 2010. Similar efforts in strengthening the financial system have also been made in Europe in the midst of the Eurozone crisis, which was partly due to the buildup and bursting of real estate bubbles in Ireland and Spain. Given that institutional reforms necessarily harm the interests of some powerful stakeholders and encounter fierce opposition from them, it remains to be seen whether the world has done enough to stop the next financial crisis before it happens.

Interim Summary

1. Both the Asian financial crisis and the global financial crisis provide illustrative cases showing how a financial crisis is simultaneously reflected in international foreign exchange markets and international capital markets.

2. The Asian financial crisis derived from political, financial, and managerial reasons. This crisis is a reminder that the growth of an emerging economy requires strong economic fundamentals, an efficient banking sector, transparent political institutions, counter-fluctuation capabilities, and clearly defined business–government relations.

3. The global financial crisis was also rooted in government policy missteps, deficiencies in the management systems of companies, and flaws in the legal and regulatory institutions of the countries involved. This crisis serves as a reminder that even the most developed countries need to be vigilant about potentially serious loopholes in their domestic institutions because a country regulatory system must keep up with the development of new business methods and practices.

Chapter Summary

1. The international monetary system is made up of the policies, institutions, regulations, and mechanisms that determine foreign exchange rates. Most countries today use the peg system, managed float system, target-zone system, or free-float system.

2. Each foreign exchange system has its merits and drawbacks. The floating exchange rate is less costly for the government or its central bank to adjust trade imbalances and can facilitate independence of trade policies. It may lead, however, to immense market fluctuations that hamper economic growth and cannot help the country balance trade for a long period.

3. In the long run, the purchasing power parity (PPP) tends to be a proper foundation to determine the foreign exchange rate. In the short run, the demand and supply in the foreign exchange market are crucial in determining changes in the floating rate.

4. The balance of payments summarizes a country's currency inflows and outflows and documents current account, capital account, and official reserves. Official reserves are made of gold, special drawing rights (SDRs), and foreign currencies. Many imports are actually "exported" by a nation's own companies investing abroad, making current account balance statistically less meaningful.

5. International financial markets consist of international foreign exchange markets and international capital markets. International capital markets in turn comprise money markets, bond markets, equity markets, and loan markets.

6. Foreign exchange markets perform three functions, including international payment, short-term supply of foreign currencies, and hedging against foreign exchange risks. These markets also offer opportunities for foreign exchange arbitrage.

7. International money markets are where foreign capital (such as Eurodollars) is financed or invested. Eurodollars are US dollar deposits in non-US banks. International loan markets deal with loans in any international currency provided by large commercial banks that must assess corporate credit or sovereign credit ranked by credit rating agencies.

8. International stock (or equity) markets are the places where company stocks are listed and traded on foreign stock exchanges. International bond markets are the places where corporate or government bonds are issued and traded in foreign countries. These markets not only provide financing for global operations but can also improve organizational recognition.

9. The Asian financial crisis demonstrates that international foreign exchange markets and capital markets can present risks destabilizing emerging economies that depend on international markets. This crisis also reveals the importance of transparent and efficient institutions (governments, banking sector, and legal systems) that govern financial markets.

Notes

1 See T. Agmon, R.G. Hawkins, and R.M. Levich, *The Future of the International Monetary System,* Lexington, MA: Lexington Books, 1984; R.N. Cooper, *The International Monetary System: Essays in World Economics,* Cambridge, MA: MIT Press, 1987.

2 E. Sohmen, *Flexible Exchange Rates: Theory and Controversy,* Chicago, IL: University of Chicago Press, 1969; I. Friedman, *Reshaping the Global Money System,* Lexington, MA: Lexington Books, 1987.

3 W.J. McKibben and J.D. Sachs, "Comparing the global performance of alternative exchange agreements," *Journal of International Money and Finance,* 7, 4, 1988, 387–410; J.R. Shafer and B.E. Loopesko, "Floating exchange rate after ten years," in *Brookings Papers on Economic Activity,* Washington, DC: Brookings Institution, 1983.

4 G. Dufey and I.H. Giddy, *The International Money Market,* 2nd edn, Englewood Cliffs, NJ: Prentice-Hall, 1994; V. Koromzay, J. Llewellyn, and S. Potter. "The rise and fall of the dollar: Some explanations, consequences, and lessons," *Economic Journal,* March 1987, 23–43.

5 R. I. McKinnon, "The rules of the game: International money in historical perspective," *Journal of Economic Literature,* March 1993, 1–44; E. Sohmen, *Flexible Exchange Rates: Theory and Controversy,* Chicago, IL: University of Chicago Press, 1969.

6 Dufey and Giddy, *The International Money Market.*

7 R.M. Kubarych, *Foreign Exchange Markets in the United States,* New York: Federal Reserve Bank of New York, 1983.

8 K.A. Chrystal, "A guide to foreign exchange markets," *Federal Reserve Bank of St. Louis Review,* March 1984, 5–18.

9 R.G.F. Coninx, *Foreign Exchange Dealer's Handbook,* Homewood, IL: Dow Jones-Irwin, 1986; I. Gregory and P. Moore, "Foreign exchange dealing," *Corporate Finance,* October 1986, 33–46.

10 M.G. Serapio and O. Shenkar, "Reflections on the Asian crisis," *Management International Review,* April 1999 (special issue), 3–10; *Far East Economic Review,* "Deep Impact: The Asian Crisis" (Special Report), July 16, 1998, 40–52.

11 The Economist, "Ten years on: How Asia shrugged off its economic crisis," *The Economist,* July 4, 2007.

12 International Monetary Fund, *World Economic Outlook,* Washington, DC, May 1998.

13 P. Krugman, *The Return of Depression Economics and the Crisis of 2008,* New York: W.W. Norton & Company, 2009; J.E. Stiglitz, M. Spence, D. Romer, and O.J. Blanchard, *In the Wake of the Crisis,* Cambridge, MA: MIT Press, 2012.

part 4

international business strategies

10 INTERNATIONAL ENTRY STRATEGIES   333

11 MNE ORGANIZATION STRUCTURE AND DESIGN   377

12 BUILDING AND MANAGING GLOBAL STRATEGIC
    ALLIANCES (GSAs)   405

13 MANAGING GLOBAL RESEARCH AND
    DEVELOPMENT (R&D)   433

chapter 10

international entry strategies

DIMENSIONS OF A MARKET ENTRY STRATEGY   335

INTERNATIONAL LOCATION SELECTION (*WHERE*)   336

TIMING OF ENTRY (*WHEN*)   347

ENTRY MODE SELECTION (*HOW*)   355

Do You Know?

1. What factors should managers take into account in choosing locations for FDI projects? Why has Rio de Janeiro in Brazil lured hundreds of large MNEs to invest there? How should location selection be linked to the firm's goals and experience? Why does Nike often locate its projects in underdeveloped areas, but Oracle does not?

2. How do MNEs benefit when they enter foreign markets as first movers? What challenges do early movers normally face? Why have some early movers such as Volkswagen and Siemens been quite successful in China, but other early movers there, such as Peugeot and Occidental Petroleum, have not?

3. What entry modes are available to companies interested in investing in another country? How do such entry modes vary in terms of expected risks and returns as well as required commitment? If you are concerned with organizational control over overseas operations, what entry modes would you elect?

OPENING CASE   DuPont's Entry Strategies into China

DuPont is one of the oldest and largest industrial corporations in the world. First entering China in 1984, DuPont has since invested over $300 million through various joint ventures and wholly owned subsidiaries. Some joint venture examples include partnerships with Shanghai Photomask Precision Company to produce photomasks, and with China Worldbest Development Corporation to manufacture Lycra spandex fiber. It has also formed joint ventures there with other foreign companies such as BASF Akitengesellschaft. DuPont's use of joint ventures was aimed at garnering greater loyalty by Chinese consumers. Joint ventures also allowed DuPont to overcome trade barriers and gain access to distribution channels. Meanwhile, the company set up wholly owned subsidiaries to produce those products that involve very sensitive technologies and require strong control over production and chemical patent protection.

DuPont was an early entrant to China's chemical and energy industries. As an early entrant, it was able to establish strong market power and create entry barriers for followers. It faced little competition because there were only a few companies in the country that participated in the same industry. DuPont also had the advantage of being the first company to make use of some of China's raw materials. It took advantage of these factors to build a strong foundation for itself while increasing its presence in China, gaining technological leadership, and establishing its brand name. Of course, the company also faced many operational risks as an early entrant. DuPont had to deal with high anti-imitation costs. In 1991, a local entrepreneur took one of DuPont's fiber formulas and started a rival firm to produce the same product. It was not until 1993 that new laws were introduced to supplement and strengthen China's patent regulations, extending patent protection from ten to 20 years and requiring patents to be registered in China.

DuPont chose China for its low labor costs, high demand, and abundant raw materials. It selected areas such as Shenzhen, Shanghai, and other cities in Guangdong province where the tax rates were lower. Guangdong, for example, is a coastal province offering tax rates of only 15 percent for qualifying foreign-invested enterprises. Shanghai was chosen because it is a major industrial and financial center.

Shanghai and other eastern coastal provinces such as Jiangsu, Shandong, and Zhejiang form the heart of China's chemical industry. A new chemical industrial zone was begun in 2001 on the outskirts of Shanghai at Caojing on Hangzhou Bay and continues to grow. In 1998, DuPont formed DuPont (China) Ltd. in Beijing to coordinate its entire operations in China.

The company's footprint in China grew substantially over the years, despite the divestiture of some of its Chinese subsidiaries (e.g., photomasks and Lycra spandex fiber) due to the restructuring of its global product portfolio. By 2013, DuPont had established over 50 wholly owned subsidiaries and joint ventures in China, with 7,500 employees and over $100 million in investment in a broad range of industries including chemicals, agriculture, food and nutrition, electronics, textiles, and automobiles.

Sources: DuPont company website, 2013; "Policies to attract foreign investment in Guangdong province," the People's Government of Zhanjiang City, 2012.

Dimensions of a Market Entry Strategy

It is helpful to apply the concept of value chain to the analysis of market entry strategies. The concept is rooted in the notion that every firm performs a collection of activities in order to deliver something of value—namely, a product or service—to its customers. The set of interconnected activities that a firm conducts can be conveniently represented in a **value chain** diagram.[1] The specifics of a value chain inevitably vary from industry to industry and often also vary from firm to firm within the same industry, reflecting the underlying economics of the firm's activities for the creation and delivery of its product or service.

Exhibit 10.1 presents a highly simplified value chain diagram for a firm that is possibly multi-national. The firm's **primary activities** include R&D, production, and marketing and sales. Each of these activities entails a set of resources or inputs. For the "production" link of the chain, for instance, the requisite inputs may include technology, plant and equipment, and labor. To ensure that these activities are carried out effectively and efficiently, the firm also needs to perform such **support activities** as planning, coordination, and human resource management that affect multiple or all of its primary activities. The value that the firm can deliver to its customers is measured by the amount its customers are willing to pay for its product or service. Each of its primary and support activities is intended to add to this value, but necessarily also entails a cost. The firm can increase its **profit margin** either by enhancing the **value** of its product or service, or by reducing the **costs** of its inputs. Expansion into international markets potentially affects both of the delivered value and the costs for creating and delivering the value.

A firm's international expansion necessarily involves placing some of its value-adding activities in a foreign location. The activities can be in the upstream of its value chain, such as R&D or sourcing of technology from a foreign supplier, or in the downstream, such as the sale of its product or service overseas. So, the first dimension of a market entry strategy is concerned with what value-adding activities to perform overseas. This *what* question cannot, however, be answered independently of the other critical questions concerning the **location** (*where*) of the expansion

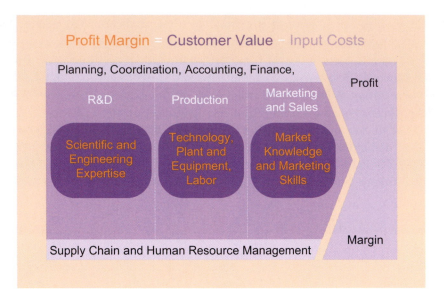

Exhibit 10.1 Value chain

destination, the **timing** (*when*) of the expansion, and the **mode** (*how*) for organizing the activities overseas. First, the effectiveness and efficiency of conducting a given activity can vary substantially from one location to another. Second, because of uncertainty and the need to learn about the conditions of any new foreign location, the timing and speed of expansion affect the dynamically evolving benefit and cost of the expansion into a given location or a given series of locations (e.g., a group of neighboring or otherwise related countries). Finally, the mode for organizing the firm's activities in a foreign location (e.g., a licensing agreement, a joint venture, or a wholly owned subsidiary) also influences the benefits and costs of conducting its activities in the location. We will examine factors that influence each of these dimensions in the rest of this chapter, but it is important to recognize that the optimal choice entails a simultaneous evaluation of all the dimensions due to their interconnectedness.

International Location Selection (*Where*)

The preceding case illustrates that several important decisions have to be made when entering a foreign market. **International entry strategies** concern where (location selection), when (timing of entry), and how (entry mode selection) international companies should enter and invest in a foreign territory during international expansion. These entry strategies are important because they determine an MNE's investment environment, operation treatment, resource commitment, and evolutionary path. In the opening case, DuPont views China as a strategic location not only in terms of being the primary offshore market but also by virtue of being the major manufacturing center of products marketed elsewhere. Even though it encountered tremendous uncertainty in the early 1980s, DuPont decided to enter this market as an early mover seeking market

336

leadership. The company's ambitious investments, however, were incremental. DuPont started with exports to China, followed by minority joint ventures, then majority joint ventures, and eventually wholly owned subsidiaries. This evolutionary entry path balances well its experience and capability with the risks and hazards it has faced in the past. This chapter details these issues, beginning with international location selection (e.g., Why China? And why Shanghai and Shenzhen within China?).

International location selection involves country selection *and* regional selection (e.g., state, province, or city) within the chosen country for an MNE's foreign direct investment project(s). The country selection determines the macro-environment for operations in a specific site. Siemens, for example, chose Brazil as an important platform for Latin America and the Caribbean nations. The company selected the city of Rio de Janeiro, rather than São Paulo, as its major production base, since Rio de Janeiro provides cheaper and more abundant resources (labor and supplies) and a superior infrastructure. Similarly, Motorola chose the city of Tianjin, instead of Beijing or Shanghai, as its major production base in China. This location strategy seems to have worked well, because the sales revenue generated by this base accounted for more than 10 percent of its worldwide revenue in 2002. After Google acquired Motorola Mobility in 2012, it divested Motorola's production unit in Tianjin to the Singapore-based global contract manufacturer Flextronics in the same year. To select an appropriate country and a region within that country, international managers should first appraise locational determinants that are likely to influence future operations and expected returns. These determinants, as well as the decision framework elaborated below, are generally applicable to both country selection and region (city or province) selection. The only distinction between them is that the breadth of locational determinants differs. Country selection should emphasize nationwide factors, whereas site selection should focus more on related factors that are specific to that region.

You may recall that we discussed country competitiveness in Chapter 5 and explained the relevance of country competitiveness to an MNE's location selection. The analysis of country competitiveness helps us to better understand a host country's national environment and is thus valuable to country selection. Nevertheless, location selection requires analyses and comparisons of specific factors (i.e., locational determinants) associated with the costs and revenues of investment in a specific site. For this purpose, we outline specific locational determinants managers need to consider when they calculate expected costs and payoffs from a potential foreign location.

Locational Determinants

Locational determinants can be categorized into the following groups: (1) cost/tax factors; (2) demand factors; (3) strategic factors; (4) regulatory/economic factors; and (5) sociopolitical factors. The importance of each of these factors to a specific firm depends on the firm's objectives and the business nature of the FDI project. For instance, high-tech FDI may depend more on strategic factors while labor-intensive projects may be more susceptible to cost/tax factors. Local market-focused investments may rely more on demand factors, whereas export market-focused investments may be impacted more by cost/tax conditions.

Cost and Tax Factors

1. *Transportation costs:* For country selection, MNEs should consider the costs incurred in transporting materials from a home (or foreign) country to a host country, or in transporting products from a host country to a home or international market. When an MNE's home country is the source of product components as well as the market for finished products, transportation costs associated with this two-way flow become even more important. For site selection, MNEs need to calculate the convenience and costs of the various transportation channels (air, sea, railway, and highway) from the candidate site to destinations of major local and foreign customers. When the Ford Motor Company entered the United Arab Emirates (UAE), it chose Dubai because of its convenience and low-cost connections to the rest of the country and the world.

2. *Wage rate:* Labor costs constitute a substantial proportion of total production costs. Foreign production is more likely to occur when production costs are lower abroad than at home. Labor costs sway investment location decisions, particularly for firms in labor-intensive industries. The decision by many MNEs to locate assembly plants in developing countries is heavily influenced by prevailing wages. Nike originally located its 13 footwear and 14 apparel factories along the Pearl River Delta in China because of the low wage rate of workers, relative to their productivity.

3. *Availability and costs of land:* Availability of suitable plant sites, the cost of land, space for expansion, and local government policy on renting or purchasing land have been recognized by international managers as critical factors in the early stages of project development and late stages of project operation. In some cases, this consideration may overwhelm other location factors, since it influences other costs such as transportation and construction. Mercedes-Benz selected Alabama in 1993 as its site for producing its sport-utility vehicles (SUVs) because the Alabama state government provided the company with 1,000 acres of land between Tuscaloosa and Birmingham.

4. *Construction costs:* This cost accounts for a substantial part of capital investment. Different sites vary in the cost of construction materials, labor, land, equipment rental, and quality of construction. Burger King had opened 1,640 restaurants in Europe by the end of 2001, 1,397 of which were franchise-owned operations. A major factor behind the franchise strategy is high construction costs in Europe.

5. *Costs of raw materials and resources:* MNEs are increasing the percentage of local outsourcing in total production. This localization reduces foreign exchange risks from devalued currencies and improves relationships with local governments and indigenous firms. Under these circumstances, the costs of local materials and resources needed in production will affect the firm's gross profit margin. IKEA, a leading furniture MNE based in Sweden, buys 90 percent of what it sells from closely monitored suppliers in many countries—mostly developing countries such as Poland and China. One of the major reasons the company chose these countries is the relatively low cost of raw materials.

6. *Financing costs:* The cost and availability of local capital are a major concern for MNEs because local financing provides much of the capital needed for mass production and operations. Financing by local banks and financial institutions also helps an MNE mitigate possible financial risks arising from fluctuations in foreign exchange rates and uncertain foreign exchange policies, as

well as political risk in a host country. Merck entered Brazil, sited specifically in São Paulo, Rio de Janeiro, Recife, Curitiba, and Campinas, because local banks are very supportive in financing Merck's investments or expansion.

7. *Tax rates:* Both statutory and effective tax rates influence a firm's profitability. **The statutory tax rate** determines the general level of the tax burden shouldered by firms. The **effective tax rate** on corporate income, which is the statutory corporate rate adjusted for all other taxes and subsidies affecting an MNE's taxable income, determines the company's net return from its revenues. Depending on the extent of these subsidies and other taxes, the statutory corporate tax rate may differ substantially from the effective corporate tax rate because the latter is adjusted to include tax-related incentives such as investment tax credits, tax breaks, and accelerated depreciation. MNEs need to assess both the statutory and the effective tax rate. Because regions within a diverse nation such as Brazil, China, and Indonesia may vary in terms of the statutory and/or effective rates, investors should compare these rates at both the country- and region-level. Since FDI projects are still subject to import or export tariffs when importing regulated materials or exporting licensed products, firms should also be aware of the level of these tariffs.

8. *Investment incentives:* Many countries, especially developing ones, are competing to attract FDI to support their domestic economies. In so doing, they often offer preferential incentives to foreign investors. Although these are country-specific, an array of investment incentives that attract FDI include the following (see also Chapter 3):

   (a) Tax breaks and/or reductions on corporate income taxes.

   (b) Financial assistance, such as preferential terms of financing, wage subsidies, investment grants, or low-interest loans.

   (c) Tariff concessions, including exemption from or reduction of duties on imports, or additional duties on imports of competing goods, or rebates of duties on imported inputs.

   (d) Business assistance, such as employee training, research and development support, land grants, site improvements, and site selection assistance.

   (e) Other incentives, such as infrastructure development and access, legal services, business consultation, and partner selection assistance.[2]

9. *Profit repatriation:* Repatriation restrictions have a negative impact on the net income or dividends remitted to foreign headquarters. Restrictions can involve a remittance tax on the cash repatriated to a home country or a ceiling on the cash amount. In other cases, investors must obtain approval from the central bank or foreign exchange administration department to repatriate dividends. These restrictions can become a deterrent to FDI. Today, profit repatriation restrictions have been gradually removed in many developing countries, so long as the required procedure (which can appear complex and cumbersome) is followed.

Demand Factors

1. *Market size and growth:* Although different MNEs may not emphasize the same level of marketing in a host country, it is rare for them not to consider local consumers. At the national level, the size and growth rate of markets signal market opportunities and potentials. Pfizer selected India to produce multi-vitamins targeting India's 300 million middle-class consumers.

In 1990, Toys "R" Us chose Japan, whose retail market expanded greatly in the 1980s as a result of the strong Japanese economy and increased consumer spending. At the subnational level, per capita consumption and the growth rate of consumption in respective regions (state, province, city) may be more accurate parameters for measuring market potential and growth. Average income growth among consumers in a target region is also an appropriate measure (see also Chapter 16).

2. *Presence of customers:* MNEs may find it desirable to locate their manufacturing sites in the area where they have longstanding customers. The closer operations are to major buyers, the better the cost efficiency and marketing effectiveness. Coca-Cola and PepsiCo both selected east coast provinces of China as project sites because the majority of their consumers are located there. Similarly, UPS (United Parcel Service) elected Cologne in Germany and Shanghai, Shenzen, and Hong Kong in greater China as its European and Asia-Pacific air hubs, respectively, because of the ease of reaching customers.

3. *Local competition:* The intensity of competition in a host country or specific region is important because it directly impacts a firm's market position and gross profit margin from local sales.[3] In general, MNEs locate sites in places where competition is relatively low unless they have sufficient advantages to ensure their competitive edge in the market. Competition may come from local rivals, as well as from other foreign rivals. When Coca-Cola made substantial new investments to strengthen its market position in east coast provinces of China in the early 1990s, PepsiCo began to expand to inland provinces in order to pioneer in this new territory.

Strategic Factors

1. *Investment infrastructure:* Today, MNEs attach increasing importance to infrastructure conditions. This is especially true for companies investing in knowledge or technology-intensive projects. Singapore attracted many of those MNEs mainly because of its ideal infrastructure. Major infrastructure variables include transportation (highways, ports, airports, and railroads), telecommunications, utilities, and governmental efficiency. The infrastructure also includes the availability of international seaports and import/export facilities, since most FDI projects have operational linkages with home and other international markets. When Hewlett-Packard (HP) entered Mexico, it did not choose Mexico City, but instead selected Ciudad Juarez, near the metropolitan area, which has excellent infrastructure conditions (access to roads and airports, strong support from local authorities, a superb export-processing environment, and the availability of an information-technology industry).

2. *Manufacturing concentration:* One of the major determinants of location selection is the strength of existing manufacturing activities. Cost savings can result from manufacturers locating in close proximity. A country or region with a strong concentration of manufacturing activity in certain industries or products is more likely to have an adequate labor pool and supply network supporting production or operations.[4] Just-in-time systems require a supplier base that is capable, reliable, and physically close. Otis opted for St. Petersburg as its primary manufacturing center in Russia because it has a well-established supply network for materials and components and has many skilled laborers and technicians for producing elevators and escalators.

3. *Industrial linkages:* The nature and quality of complementary industries and special services (distribution, consulting, auditing, banking, insurance, marketing services, etc.) are also important, as MNE operations interact actively with these sectors in a host country. Industrial linkages with these businesses affect the firm's ability to pursue value creation and addition. Mary Kay Cosmetics located its business center in Buenos Aires, which serves Argentina, Uruguay, and Chile, having considered the favorable industrial linkages in this city.

4. *Workforce productivity:* As a result of increasing technological permeation and process innovation, international production requires high workforce productivity and superior labor skills. The labor requirements of new systems and techniques are driving the need for a better educated direct-labor workforce. Just-in-time and total quality management systems place greater importance on the flexibility of workers and their ability to operate under growing autonomy. The increasing sophistication of product and process technologies has also increased skill requirements. The availability of a skilled managerial, marketing, and technical workforce is also crucial, because they are primary forces in gaining competitive advantages in the market.

5. *Inbound and outbound logistics:* Typical inbound (input) logistics include proximity to suppliers and sources of raw materials and inputs. Since MNEs have a tendency to rely more on local input sources, this type of logistics should be among the critical considerations for international managers. Outbound (market) logistics are based largely on proximity to major buyers and end consumers. This factor can heavily influence the effectiveness of customer responsiveness. When the firm pursues market penetration and product specialization strategies, the firm's profitability will be strongly associated with market logistics. A main reason why Procter & Gamble (P&G) chose Mexico City as its major production base for North America was the effective inbound and outbound logistics, which satisfy P&G's needs for production and marketing.

Regulatory Factors

1. *Industrial policies:* In many countries, industrial policies are used to control new entrants (both foreign and local firms), net profit margins, degree of competition, structural concentration, and social benefits. Typical industrial policies include antitrust rules, project approval and registration, categorization of industries and treatment differences among categories, and varying value-added tax among others (see also the last section of Chapter 4). In selecting a location, MNEs need to make sure that the target country or region allows foreign business entry and that industrial policies are reasonably favorable or at least not a hindrance. Industrial policies generally have a more direct impact on MNE operations than do macroeconomic policies of a host government.[5] Lucent Technologies moved into Brazil after the Brazilian government announced the "Real Plan" in 1994, which devalued its currency (*real*), privatized telecom services, and offered more favorable treatments to new entrants into the telecom infrastructure sector.

2. *FDI policies:* In determining a foreign location (country and region), MNEs need to learn how FDI policies there will impact their plans and payoffs. First, they should know what entry mode(s) are allowed. They might be allowed to enter into certain sites or industries only through certain

entry modes such as minority joint ventures. Second, a host government may require MNEs to locate projects in certain geographical regions to help boost regional economies. Projects in different locations may be taxed differently. Third, MNEs should check content localization requirements. A foreign company is often required to purchase and use local materials, parts, semi-products, or other supplies made by indigenous firms for the production of its final outputs. The required level of localization varies across countries or industries. Fourth, MNEs need to identify any geographical restrictions imposed on the breadth of the market. For example, prior to China's entry into the WTO, foreign banks were allowed to provide services only in the city in which they were located. Finally, MNEs must appraise foreign exchange control measures in a host country. These measures may hinder the free inflow and outflow of foreign capital and income.

3. *Availability of special economic zones:* One way many countries (especially in the developing world) attempt to attract FDI is through the establishment of special zones such as free trade zones (FTZs), special economic zones (SEZs), economic and technological development zones (ETDZs), high-tech development zones (HTDZs), open economic regions (OERs), bonded areas, and so on. In general, these zones provide preferential treatment in terms of taxation, import duties, land use, infrastructure access, and governmental assistance to MNEs. However, many of these zones are regulated regarding eligibility for preferential treatment. For instance, MNEs located in Chinese ETDZs must export 75 percent of output or bring in advanced technologies as verified by governmental authorities.

Sociopolitical Factors

1. *Political instability:* This factor reflects uncertainty over the continuation of present political and social conditions and government policies that are critical to the survival and profitability of a firm's operations in the host country. Changes in government policies may create problems related to repatriation of earnings, or, in extreme cases, expropriation of assets. Although international lobbying on foreign country policies has become pervasive, the magnitude of politically induced environmental uncertainty still overwhelms transaction-related risks affecting MNE operations.

2. *Cultural barriers:* Another trigger of uncertainty are differences in culture between the home and host countries. This factor determines a firm's receptivity and adaptability to the social context of a host country.[6] Language barriers are also an important consideration underlying location selection. Although every foreign business can recruit local people, communications with headquarters as well as between employees within the company are crucial to business success (see also Chapter 6).

3. *Local business practices:* Culture-specific business practices often constitute key forms of knowledge that MNEs must acquire. In fact, a prominent logic behind the formation of international cooperative ventures with developing country enterprises is to gain such country-specific knowledge. Superior technological and organizational skills cannot guarantee the success of international operations unless the firm is able to integrate country-specific knowledge with its firm-specific knowledge. The ability to integrate these two types of knowledge often determines the survival and growth of MNEs in foreign markets.

4. *Government efficiency and corruption:* International managers often perceive the "soft" infrastructure (e.g., regulatory environment and government efficiency) as having a greater and more enduring impact on firm operations than the "hard" infrastructure (e.g., transportation and communication). Efficient governments are more responsive to an MNE's requests or complaints, take shorter time periods for ratifying projects, and provide superior assistance and support in various matters. Governmental corruption implies not only low efficiency and excessive red tape, but also high costs of bribery in setting up governmental linkages in order to get project approval, infrastructure access, and acquisition of scarce resources (see Chapter 19).

5. *Attitudes toward foreign business:* Social and governmental attitudes toward foreign businesses often have visible or invisible influences on MNE operations and management. If the society and government of a host country are somewhat friendly to foreign business, MNEs will benefit from the congenial environment. This attitude has an enduring effect on both firm operations and the commitment of employees to the foreign firm. Burger King selected the Dominican Republic as its major site in the Caribbean (27 restaurants as of July 2012) because Dominicans (both government and the public) have a very positive view of the United States and American products. The country is now the Caribbean's largest democratic country and has a long-standing and close relationship with the United States (where many Dominicans legally immigrate).

6. *Community characteristics:* Site selection must include considerations of community environment aspects such as community size, educational facilities, housing facilities, police and fire protection, climate, suitability for expatriates and their families, facilities for children, the social environment for spouses, hotel accommodations, crime level, and other quality of life indicators. This environment is highly relevant because it affects costs, quality, and security of living for foreign expatriates and their families.

7. *Sustainable development and pollution control:* Environmental protection laws and regulations in the target location influence the cost of investments but may have differential effects on different companies. MNEs based in developed countries often already possess sophisticated pollution control technologies and thus may enjoy an advantage in meeting or exceeding local standards and winning goodwill with local groups advocating sustainable development. For instance, the adoption of stricter vehicle emission standards in some large Chinese cities under mounting public pressure against air pollution strengthened the advantage of MNE auto makers in the local market and boosted their confidence in making further investments in the country.[7] In the meantime, higher than normal environmental standards can also make it financially infeasible to invest in a country given the competition from firms based in other countries with less stringent standards. Rubbermaid entered Poland in 1995 and now views the country as its central low-cost site with access to Northern and Eastern Europe. A relatively low standard in pollution control (thus lower costs to comply with this standard) is one of the factors that attracted Rubbermaid to invest there.

Exhibit 10.2 summarizes the major locational determinants explained previously. Overall, site selection within a diverse country should be based on micro-context factors, whereas country selection should be made after a careful analysis of both micro-context and macro-context factors.

Micro-Context	Macro-Context
Cost/Tax Factors	*Regulatory Factors*
Transportation costs	Industrial policies
Wage rate	FDI policies
Land availability and costs	Availability of special zones
Construction costs	
Costs of raw materials and resources	*Sociopolitical Factors*
Financing costs	Political instability
Tax rates	Cultural barriers
Investment incentives	Local business practices
Profit repatriation	Government efficiency and corruption
	Attitudes toward foreign business
Demand Factors	Community characteristics
Market size and growth	Sustainable development
Customer presence	(e.g., pollution control
Local competition	and recycling requirements)
Strategic Factors	
Investment infrastructure	
Manufacturing concentration	
Industrial linkages	
Workforce productivity	
Inbound and outbound logistics	

Exhibit 10.2 Locational determinants

Country Box

Federal Express Shifts its Hub from Subic Bay to Guangzhou, China

In December 1992, the United States closed down its naval shipyard in Subic Bay, the Philippines, which was its largest overseas base. The departure of the military put Subic Bay in a deep economic slump and left 47,000 Filipinos unemployed. It also left an $8 billion facility unused, so the Philippine government decided to turn Subic Bay into a self-sustaining commercial investment center. It was immediately declared a free-trade zone area with unlimited duty-free imports and a hassle-free export system. In 1993, the management team from Federal Express went to Subic Bay to investigate the area for its central hub location. The government presented many investment incentives to FedEx, offering liberal air traffic rights, streamlined customs clearance procedures to accommodate the quick turnaround time of express carriers, and help in dealing with the bureaucracy. This all happened in a nation known for bureaucratic red tape and favoritism toward local companies. In September 1995, FedEx opened its Asian Pacific hub facility in Subic Bay at a cost of about $100 million. This strategic event enabled it to obtain 24-hour use of airport facilities and to employ the low-paid, well-educated, English-speaking laborers already located there. Hong Kong and Taipei did not have the 24-hour airport facilities critical to hub operations. Singapore was too far south, and Osaka of Japan was too far north. Federal Express's decision to open the regional hub in Subic Bay created an excellent strategic advantage for the company. The hub connected 13 major economic and financial centers in the region.

As China became the hub of the East Asian value chain for the final assembly of products in the 2000s, the flows of packages from and into the country, particularly the most important outsourcing region of Guangdong Province in southern China, drastically increased. The significantly altered pattern of international trade diminished the locational advantage of Subic Bay and compelled FedEx to reconfigure its own hub-and-spoke system of air transportation so that its transport routes would coincide with the flows of its packages. In 2009, FedEx closed the Subic Bay hub and moved its Asian Pacific hub to the Baiyun Airport in Guangzhou, southern China in an effort to provide better connectivity, improved services, and to realize greater cost efficiency. The new hub became the center of the company's intra-Asia network that provides next-day delivery services among 22 major cities in Asia and connects these cities to more than 220 countries and territories in the company's global system.

Sources: FedEx company website, 2009–2011; M. Emmanuel, "Baiyun the 'perfect home' for FedEx Asia's pacific hub," *Business Times*, September 28, 2009.

Decision Framework

The preceding section presented locational determinants that must be assessed in the course of choosing a location. These determinants constitute the core in the framework of a location decision-making process. Aside from this core, MNEs also need to take into account their strategic objectives, global integration, and market orientation.

Location and Strategic Objectives

If an MNE wishes to pursue market growth and a competitive position in a host country, demand factors and strategic factors appear to be its most critical considerations. Because these factors generally concern long-term investments and operations, macroeconomic and sociopolitical factors also have a moderate impact on location selection. If an MNE seeks short- or mid-term profitability, it should attach more value to cost and taxation factors. Infrastructure conditions and investment incentives may also play a role. The costs of production factors and operational expenses will determine the gross profit margin, whereas income tax rates will affect the net return. Remittance taxes or profit repatriation restrictions have a great impact on the level of dividends that the parent firm finally receives. If an MNE strives to diversify risks or operate in a stable environment, sociopolitical factors become fundamental to the decision. Because some macroeconomic factors such as exchange rate and the inflation rate are related to environmental uncertainty, they should also be included in the analytical framework. Finally, if an MNE intends to secure innovation, learning, and adaptation from international expansion, strategic factors often outweigh other groups of factors in affecting location choice. Nevertheless, industrial linkages, competition intensity, cultural distance, and attitudes toward foreign businesses may also influence the accomplishment of this goal.

345

Location and Global Integration

The location decision should be framed within the design of global integration. As the world economy becomes increasingly regionalized (see Chapter 8), MNEs may first decide which regional bloc they should enter. In this situation, location selection involves regional bloc selection, country selection, and site selection. In considering regional bloc selection, managers can review the preceding determinants at the integrated bloc level (e.g., EU vs. NAFTA) and find out how inter-country barriers that have been removed or lessened within the bloc reduce cost/tax burdens and change regulatory/economic environments (thus identifying new opportunities and new threats). Other groups of determinants such as demand, strategic, and sociopolitical factors are less affected by the formation of a regional bloc. Today, MNEs use host country sites to achieve global integration and/or regional integration. MNEs tend to locate labor-intensive processes in sites that are relatively well endowed with abundant labor or locate an R&D facility in an area where abundant technological capabilities exist. Linking activities across locations is fundamental to capturing international scale and scope. It is important for international managers to locate projects in such sites that provide an ideal environment for integrating operations with the rest of the MNE network. When Cisco entered France, it built distribution centers in Toulouse, which serve not only France, but also the Middle East. Today Cisco has a presence in over 165 countries, with their products distributed mostly through consolidated sites in respective world regions.[8]

Location and Market Orientation

Market orientation is concerned mainly with whether an MNE primarily targets a host country market, export market (home or other foreign markets), or both. Naturally, different market orientations vary in their relationship with locational determinants. Local market-oriented projects are highly sensitive to demand and strategic factors in the local environment. Some regulatory/economic factors are also relevant because they affect a firm's stability and the exposure of its operations to environmental turbulence. Certain sociopolitical variables, including cultural distance, government efficiency or corruption, and political stability, are likely to have a stronger effect on a local market orientation than on an export orientation. The latter, by contrast, relies more on cost/tax factors. Plants producing for an export market can be located with little regard for domestic demand. Therefore, cost/tax factors, together with strategic factors such as investment incentives, input logistics, labor productivity, and infrastructure, are prominent microcontextual determinants underlying this location strategy. For example, many US companies relocated their production facilities just south of the US–Mexico border after NAFTA took effect. These factories, called *maquiladoras,* assemble imported, duty-free components into finished goods, most of which are then re-exported to the United States. In addition to benefiting from lower labor costs, these companies enjoy reduced transportation costs, logistics convenience, and eliminated tariff burdens. By the early 2000s, approximately 4,000 maquiladoras with over 1.2 million employees operated along the border zone, accounting for nearly one-third of Mexico's industrial jobs and 45 percent of its total exports. After its entry into the WTO in 2001, however, China emerged as a major competitor to Mexico in low-end manufacturing, causing a significant decline in the number of maquiladoras and the number of workers in those factories. After a few years of rapid decline in employment and production at maquiladoras, also spurred by the global financial crisis of the late 2000s, steadily rising wage rates in China have once again made Mexico (and other low-cost labor countries like Bangladesh) an attractive production location. According to the Maquiladoras' Industry Association, their exports and foreign investment each grew by more than 50 percent between 2009 and 2012, to $196 billion and $7.4 billion, respectively.[9]

Finally, the dual-emphasis orientation may be influenced by all five group factors. In other words, the dual-emphasis orientation necessitates the most comprehensive scheme in the appraisal of locational determinants. Levi Strauss & Company's three manufacturing facilities in Mexico, located in Aguascalientes, Naucalpan, and Teziutlan, respectively, are ideal for this dual pursuit. All these facilities are close to Mexico City and physically close to California (the US headquarters). About half of the jeans made in these facilities are exported back to the United States while the other half targets local consumers (about 25 percent market share in Mexico).

Interim Summary

1. When selecting a foreign location, managers need to consider not only cost and tax factors but also market demand, investment infrastructure, regulatory and economic environments, and sociopolitical factors.
2. Managers should choose a foreign location that not only provides a favorable investment environment but also helps fulfill the firm's objectives underlying international entry.

Timing Of Entry (*When*)

Timing of entry involves three likely overlapping choices. The first is the immediacy of entry that is concerned with whether to enter a foreign market now or wait until a later time (e.g., after the resolution of some uncertainty). The second is a firm's relative position in the order of MNE entries into a foreign market (i.e., first mover, early follower, and late mover). The third is the speed of entry into a series of related foreign markets (e.g., a group of neighboring countries in some part of the world such as Europe or Latin America). There are two interrelated sets of factors affecting the timing decision: (1) the extent of uncertainty and potential for learning about a new foreign market; and (2) the trade-off between the risk of competitive preemption and the cost of pioneering.

Uncertainty and Potential for Learning

The conditions that determine the benefits and costs of entering a foreign market are almost always subject to uncertainty. These include the political and economic circumstances of the country, policies of the host government, receptiveness of the target customers, supplies and prices of production inputs, and capabilities and objectives of potential partners. It is possible, and indeed likely, that an MNE will gain new information about the various uncertain conditions over time. At some point in time, there may be sufficient new information for the MNE to consider the uncertainty about a particularly important issue to be resolved. For instance, after a prolonged debate, the government of the target country may decide to stop requiring foreign investors to export a significant percentage of their output, thus resolving the uncertainty that any MNE faces about the question. Similarly, after a period of trial sales via export, an MNE may find out with a high level of confidence that the foreign market for its product is large enough to justify the establishment of manufacturing plant.

An analytical framework that is very helpful to decision making under uncertainty, as discussed in Chapter 3, is the real option perspective. We will only outline here how uncertainty and potential for learning affect the timing decision based on this perspective, rather than giving a detailed explanation of the theory again. As explained in Chapter 3, we can distinguish between two types of uncertainty: *exogenous* uncertainty allows the decision maker to get new information by simply waiting (e.g., the result of a national election), while *endogenous* uncertainty cannot be resolved unless the decision maker invests a nontrivial amount of resources in information-gathering activities (e.g., initiating a period of trial sale in the target country via export).

Exogenous Uncertainty

In the face of high exogenous uncertainty (e.g., before a closely contested national election between two political parties with divergent economic policies), it pays for an MNE to withhold entry if the entry also entails substantial investment that is largely irreversible (i.e., the MNE will lose a significant part of the investment if it is forced to exit the market due to unfavorable government policies). This is because waiting allows the MNE to gather more information that helps reduce the uncertainty. Waiting is not always the best strategy under high uncertainty and high irreversibility, however. If the expected rate of return from the investment is sufficiently high, the optimal decision can still be immediate entry because the high rate of return means that the opportunity cost of waiting is also high. Furthermore, waiting will have little value if the opportunity to enter profitably is likely to be lost due to competitive preemption, as will be discussed in more detail below. So, a high risk of competitive preemption also favors immediate entry.

Endogenous Uncertainty

In the face of high endogenous uncertainty, early entry will help an MNE gather the needed information to resolve the uncertainty (e.g., about the local market's receptiveness to the firm's product), if it is feasible to enter the market on a small scale without committing a large amount of irreversible investment. Obviously, building a new manufacturing facility generally requires substantial investment that is likely to be partially irreversible, particularly if manufacturing in the industry is subject to large economies of scale. But if the MNE can first sell its product via export to the target market, such an entry can significantly reduce the risk of setting up a manufacturing plant later after getting more reliable information about the market's potential. Export, however, is sometimes infeasible if the MNE is in a service industry such as banking or retail. In such a case, the firm may still be able to test the foreign market by setting up only a small number of branches or stores before developing an extensive network of banks or stores. It should be noted that the threat of competitive preemption is also relevant under endogenous uncertainty. If there is a high chance that a competitor will enter the market on a large scale and become dominant, then the benefit from early entry on a small scale can be substantially reduced.

The same line of reasoning also applies to deciding the speed of entry into a series of related markets, such as a group of countries that are geographically proximate. If the countries are more distant culturally and institutionally, an MNE can gain from a slower pace of entry into the different markets because that gives the firm more time to learn about separate markets and adapt its practices to each. If the countries are highly similar and have a level of economic exchanges among them, not only does the value of waiting diminish but the risk of competitive preemption is also likely to be high. Then, a closely sequenced entry into the different markets at a fast pace is likely the optimal strategy.

Competitive Preemption and Pioneering Costs

Transnational investors are likely to have more preemptive investment opportunities in foreign markets than in their home markets. This is largely because of the different market and industry structures between home and host economies. By investing in a foreign market, a late mover in the home country could become an early entrant in the host country. It could enjoy more favorable business opportunities in sectors that are in early stages of the industry life cycle in the host country market, or in industries in which it has distinctive competitive advantages. Aside from noticing an opportunity, the decision on whether to be an early mover in a foreign market is broadly based upon an entrant's assessment of entry barriers erected by a host government and existing firms, relative to the factors promoting entry. Potential entrants weigh the expected benefits and costs of entry; entry occurs when the former outweigh the latter.

Early Mover Advantages

When entering a foreign market, pioneering MNEs (**first mover** or **early followers**) generally have advantages such as greater market power, more preemptive opportunities, and more strategic options over late entrants. These advantages might be ultimately reflected in higher economic returns compared with later movers. First, pioneering investors tend to outperform later entrants in acquiring *market power*. Early movers are able to invest strategically in facilities, distribution networks, product positioning, patentable technology, natural resources, and human and organizational expertise. If imitation of its product is expected to be expensive or involve a long time lag, a preemptive investment can be leveraged into significant long-run benefits for early movers. Moreover, market pioneers may benefit from the advantages of holding technical leadership, seizing scarce resources, and creating buyer switching costs.[10] Because of such switching costs, and because most customers are more loyal to an early mover's successful products and services, customer loyalty tends to be stronger for early mover products than for late mover products. This loyalty fortifies an early mover's market power and competitive position. Citibank and Bank of America were early movers into Latin America in both the prewar and postwar periods, relative to other foreign banks such as Barclays from Britain and the Bank of Nova Scotia from Canada. By 1929, for example, Citibank and Bank of America had branches or offices in Mexico City, Buenos Aires, Sâo Paulo, and Santiago. By the 1970s, these two US banks had branches or offices in almost every Latin American country. They have dominated these markets largely because of the market power they obtained from an early-entry position (loyal customers, close relations with local banks and governments, and established technological and service standards). This market power was further strengthened when they erected entry barriers against later movers in the form of acquiring local banks, partnering with Visa International, creating innovative banking approaches such as Internet banking and banking services via cable TV, and extending their network-type presence almost everywhere.

Second, early movers gain from *preemptive opportunities*. Early movers are able to preempt marketing, promotion, and distribution channels, while gaining product image, organizational reputation, and brand recognition. Toys "R" Us entered Japan in May 1990, right after MITI (the Japanese Ministry of International Trade and Industry) relaxed regulations and restrictions in the retail toy industry. By the end of 1996, it had opened 35 stores throughout Japan, with approximately $20 million annual sales per store, compared with $10 million per US store. The company's success involves, in part, the first mover opportunities it seized, such as preemptive marketing and promotion, as well as brand recognition and pioneer reputation. Similarly, Otis entered Russia as the first mover in the elevator industry and preempted the distribution channels previously built by the Russian government and used by local state-owned enterprises. It is incorrect to assume that foreign market opportunities are limitless, however. The window of opportunity may open only for a time and be available only to early movers.[11] For example, to pursue economic reform and political stability, China's State Council set up a ceiling on the number of FDI projects in the automobile industry. Today, Volkswagen remains one of the two dominant auto makers in China. Even though GM is sometimes ahead in total vehicle sales, nearly 40 percent of its sales are due to the low-margin Wuling minivans made at one of its joint ventures, whereas all Volkswagen's sales are in the higher-margin segments.

Third, early movers benefit from many *strategic options*. Pioneer investors often have more strategic options in selecting industries, locations, and market orientations (e.g., import substitution, local market-oriented, export market-oriented, infrastructure-oriented, etc.). In addition, early movers are often given priority access to natural resources, scarce materials, distribution channels, promotional arrangements, and infrastructure. As early movers into Poland, Matsushita and Philips were better able to access scarce or government-controlled resources such as local financing and state-instituted wholesale networks than later movers such as Toshiba and Samsung. Moreover, early investors have a superior option to select better local firms for equity/contractual joint ventures or for supply–purchase business relations. Charoen Pokphand (CP), one of the world's largest agro-industrial MNEs from Thailand, entered China in 1979 as the first mover into the Chinese agriculture sector. By 2012, CP's Chinese arm included more than 200 companies, employed more than 80,000 people and had annual sales exceeding 50 billion yuan ($8 billion).[12] Most of its projects are joint ventures with the best local firms in respective regions. Further, early movers enjoy low competition before late movers come in. The only competition comes from local firms (if any). Wal-Mart was among the first foreign superstores established in Korea, China, Costa Rica,

Argentina, Germany, Puerto Rico, and Brazil, to name a few. The only competition the company faced during early years was from some indigenous department stores in major metropolitan areas. When later movers are about to enter, early movers and local firms tend to establish alliances to drive out new entrants or maintain strong competitive power in the industry. Even when not forming alliances, early movers are still in a better position to deal with competition from local firms than late entrants. They can position their competitive advantage in businesses, industries, and markets where competition from local firms is weak or where they have better technological and organizational competencies.

Early Mover Disadvantages

Early movers, however, also suffer from some disadvantages compared to late entrants. Pioneer investors may be confronted with greater environmental uncertainty and operational risks. Environmental uncertainty generally comes from: (1) underdeveloped FDI laws and regulations in a host country; (2) the host government's lack of experience in dealing with MNEs; and (3) infant or embryonic stages of the industry or market in a host country. Operational risks originate from: (1) a shortage of qualified supply sources and other production inputs such as talented managers and R&D workforce; (2) under developed support services such as local financing, foreign exchange, arbitration, consulting, and marketing; (3) poor infrastructure in transportation, utilities, and communications; and (4) an unstable market structure in which market demand and supply are misaligned and local governments often interfere with MNE operations.

In contrast with early movers, **late investors** do not suffer, or suffer less, from the preceding uncertainties and risks.[13] When late movers arrive, the host-country environment is usually more stable, regulatory conditions are more favorable, and the market infrastructure is already developed. Relative to western MNEs, Korean MNEs (*chaebol*) are all late movers into China. They did not enter until 1994 when Hyundai, Samsung, LG, and Daewoo started their FDI in China, especially on the Shandong peninsula. In that year China significantly deepened economic reforms and liberalization, broadened the industries and geographical areas for MNE operations, and enacted various laws and regulations concerning inbound FDI. As late movers, Korean MNEs benefited greatly from these improved environments. Facing reduced uncertainty and a more stabilized environment, Korean *chaebol* were aggressive late movers who waited patiently until the best time but committed aggressively after entry to seize emerging opportunities. LG Group, for example, built 20 projects in China, amounting to $688 billion in the first two years after entering the country in 1994.

Early movers also tend to pay higher costs in learning and adapting to local environments and in countervailing imitation. Many early movers are compelled to invest more in building industrial infrastructure (e.g., supply bases and distribution networks) and technological or service standards. When Sharp and Hitachi entered China in the early 1980s to produce fax machines, they had to establish these standards and construct supply bases because the fax machine industry had not yet emerged in the country prior to their entry. It also cost early movers more in training local workers, technicians, and managers. Such human resources might be unavailable or lack skill before early FDI is undertaken. Late entrants, however, can benefit greatly from a pool of skilled laborers and favorable industrial infrastructure established by early entrants. In addition, early movers pay more to learn about the local environment (cultural, social, economic, legal, and political), unique business practices, social norms and customs, and consumer behavior. Conversely, later movers who use a wait-and-see strategy gain from lessons from early movers. In particular, they benefit from mimicking an early mover's business policies and strategies that have proved to be successful in a host country. For example, when the Franklin Templeton Group, a US financial service company, entered Brazil in 1998 as a late mover, it learned a great deal about viable strategies from early movers such as Citibank. As of December 2000, its mutual fund assets in Brazil reached $1.17 billion.

Finally, early movers may have to fight followers who imitate their strategies or innovations, counterfeit their products, or infringe on their industrial (e.g., trademark and brand) or intellectual property rights (e.g., patent, expertise, software). This cost is especially high when early movers invest in a country with underdeveloped and under-enforced legal systems in protecting these rights. Philip Morris entered Russia's tobacco market (Russians consume 300 billion cigarettes per year) in 1974 as a first mover. However, it has proved to be very costly for the company to protect its leading brands such as Marlboro and Parliament because about 30 percent of these brands sold on the street are counterfeits. When followers imitate a first mover's products or strategies, the latter needs to commit more to new innovations, new developments, and new strategies. When followers infringe on a first mover's property rights, the latter has to spend on litigation, investigation, lobbying, or arbitration. In addition to direct costs of anti-imitation, early movers have to pay higher switching and start-up costs. Later movers can piggyback on early investment if imitation is easy, thereby gaining profit without having to pay as much as innovators.

Because of the preceding uncertainties, risks, and costs, pioneer MNEs tend to select the joint venture mode for FDI entry. In the joint venture business, however, the objectives of local partners usually diverge from those of their foreign partners. The pursuit of self-interest rather than common goals, as well as lack of autonomy among local partners, can result in significant uncertainty for joint venture operations. This internal uncertainty is generally difficult for MNEs to control. Since late investors can usually choose to establish wholly owned subsidiaries, this uncertainty is less substantial than that faced by early movers.

Exhibit 10.3 summarizes the advantages and disadvantages of being an early mover. In general, the advantages of early movers are the disadvantages of late movers, and vice versa.

Decision Framework

Entry decisions must be based on rigorous cost-benefit analysis and then prudently timed. When assessing the advantages and disadvantages of the timing choice (i.e.., immediate entry vs. waiting, early vs. late mover, and fast-paced vs. slow-paced entry into a series of related markets), international managers need to consider the following factors in formulating timing strategy. These include: (1) the level and type of uncertainty the MNE faces; (2) the MNE's technological, organizational, and financial resources or capabilities; (3) the host-country environment in terms of infrastructure, industry structure, market demand, and governmental policies; and (4) potential competition from late foreign entrants as well as local entrants.

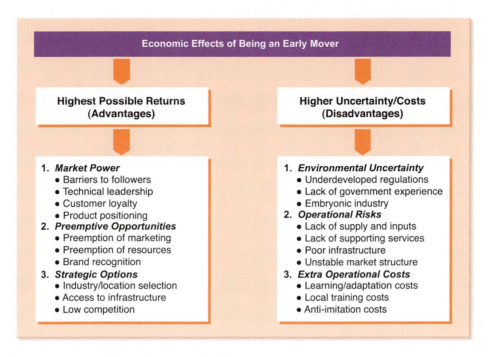

Exhibit 10.3 Advantages and disadvantages of early movers

Since the conditions that affect the benefits and costs of entry into a market are almost always subject to uncertainty, it is important to understand whether the predominant type of uncertainty is exogenous or endogenous. If the uncertainty is primarily exogenous (i.e., when new information is expected to arrive by itself, for instance, from the media), the international manager also needs to determine whether the entry entails substantial investment that is to a significant extent irreversible, what is the likely rate of return from the entry, and how high the risk of competitive preemption is. The combination of these factors helps determine the choice between immediate entry and delayed entry after further information gathering. If the uncertainty is primarily endogenous (i.e., new information can only be obtained via a nontrivial investment in some explorative activities), then the international manager needs to determine whether it is feasible to enter the market in an incremental manner with a small initial investment, and how high the risk of competitive preemption is. The combination of these factors helps determine whether early entry is advantageous to late entry, and whether a small initial footprint is superior to a large-scale entry from the beginning.

An MNE's resources and capabilities determine its ability to reduce early mover risks and seize preemptive investment opportunities. A pioneer entrant must wait for a feasible opportunity for investment, the appearance of which depends on the investor's foresight, skills, resources, and good fortune. Not every MNE is competent to be a pioneer mover. One prerequisite, for instance, is the firm's international experience and its ability to cultivate relationships with local authorities and handle environmental changes overseas. Motorola has been capable of being the first mover into many emerging markets due to its accumulated experience in a large number of developing countries, especially its experience in dealing with local governments and communities.

The real balance between costs and benefits, or between risks and returns for a timing decision, depends on actual dynamics and specific characteristics of the host-country environments. As explained in Chapter 5, the microeconomic business environment (industrial conditions and market situations) often impacts MNE activities more directly than the macroeconomic environment. The host-country conditions in infrastructure, technology, factor endowments, market demand, industry structure, and government policies are all likely to affect an MNE's timing of entry and its eventual success. Moreover, anticipated first mover opportunities may disappear, or unanticipated new opportunities may emerge, because of environmental changes in a host country. The transformation of national economies, market structures, and government policies is often so uncertain in foreign countries that pioneer MNEs may need to have second or even third backup plans. When Philip Morris (PM) entered Russia as the first mover, it built two projects: PM Izhora in Leningrad (now St. Petersburg) and PM Kuban in Krasnodar. The two projects were set in such a way that PM Kuban would switch from producing cigarettes to processing raw tobacco for PM Izhora if local suppliers were unable to supply processed tobacco and/or if the local market became more restricted.

The option of being a first mover is not entirely under the firm's control. Preemptive investment opportunities may be observed and reacted upon by local rivals as well as foreign competitors. The responses and actions of the firm's competitors need to be carefully examined. The MNE must study the strengths and weaknesses of potential rivals in areas such as technology, production, marketing, and capital. When an opportunity presents itself, the investor must decide whether it should enter the foreign territory as a first mover or early entrant, and then whether it has the capacity to build a sustainable advantage from its entry timing. If the answers are "Yes," the firm must then decide how to enter the host market and best exploit the opportunity, the critical issue being discussed next. Once a pioneering strategy is chosen, the investor must react faster than its rivals, commit to its own pioneering opportunities, and take measures to sustain its first mover advantages. If the investor chooses not to be an early mover, or if a rival has preempted this position, then the investor must decide whether, how, and when to follow.

Interim Summary

1. The combination of high exogenous uncertainty and high investment irreversibility tends to favor delayed entry, but a high anticipated rate of return from the entry or a high risk of competitive preemption favors immediate entry.
2. High endogenous uncertainty, on the other hand, tends to favor early entry if the MNE is able to enter on a small scale to gather information and reduce the uncertainty.
3. Compared to late entrants, early movers benefit from stronger market power, greater preemptive opportunities, and more strategic options, but suffer more from environmental uncertainty, operational risks, and extra operational costs.
4. Not every early mover can succeed abroad, nor should every firm be the first mover. The timing decision depends not only on the opportunity-risk balance but also on the firm's capabilities, the local environment, and new competition.

Entry Mode Selection (*How*)

Entry Mode Choices

As the Eclectic Paradigm (discussed in Chapter 3) suggests, the ability of an MNE to prosper in international markets generally rests in its possession of some superior production assets or resources such as technology, marketing expertise, or management know-how. In the meantime, the resources of the MNE can often be made even more productive if they are bundled with some local resources in the target country.[14] Such resource bundling may be accomplished in one of several ways. First, an exporter can benefit from contracting with a local distributor that runs a broad distribution network in the target country and possesses strong marketing expertise, especially country-specific expertise that the exporter may lack. Hill's Pet Nutrition, for instance, buys certain raw materials (e.g., wheat gluten) from China and also sells its pet food in the country via local distributors. Second, some companies find it more efficient to license their intellectual property to local firms rather than engaging in manufacturing and marketing activities in the target country themselves. Hallmark Cards, for instance, licenses its baby clothing designs to a number of Chinese companies for manufacturing and marketing in the local market. Third, even highly experienced manufacturing MNEs often find it beneficial to gain access to unique local know-how by acquiring or forming joint ventures with indigenous firms in the target country. As discussed in the opening case of this chapter, several of the companies that DuPont operates in China were initially established through acquisitions or joint ventures.

Entry modes refer to the different ways in which an MNE's activities are conducted in the target country, particularly what resources of the MNE are bundled with local resources, and how the local operations that utilize the combined resources are organized. There are three broad categories of entry modes: (1) *trade-centered* modes, whereby the MNE's local activities involve primarily the terminal sales of goods or services; (2) *transfer-centered* modes, whereby the MNE's local activities primarily involve the transfer of rights to use some productive assets or resources (e.g., equipment or technology) to a local entity for a specified period of time; and (3) *FDI-centered* modes, whereby the MNE holds full or partial ownership and control over a local entity that produces its goods or services. Along this sequence, the levels of resource commitment, organizational control, involved risks, and expected returns all tend to increase. Within each category, these levels differ somewhat between specific modes. Each mode has both advantages and disadvantages, and the balance between the advantages and disadvantages of a given mode varies with the nature of an MNE's activities in the target country. The choice of entry mode is, therefore, an important strategic decision that determines whether and how much an MNE can profit from its international expansion.

Trade-Centered Entry Modes

Trade-centered entry modes include exporting, subcontracting, and countertrade.

Exporting

It is natural for most firms to get their start in international expansion through **exporting**, in which the firm maintains its production facilities at home and sells its products abroad. Through exporting, the firm gains valuable expertise about operating internationally and specific knowledge concerning the individual countries in which it operates. Export offers the advantage of not requiring a very substantial presence in foreign countries. Generally, exporting is a type of international entry open to virtually any size or kind of firm, whereas other types of entry modes tend to demand greater resources and involve more risks. Over time, accumulated experience with exporting often prompts a firm to become more aggressive in exploiting new international exporting opportunities or to consider FDI in the country to which it previously exported. So, the low sunk cost of export often makes this mode a good one to start with when the firm perceives considerable uncertainty about the foreign market. In the meantime, high transport costs, high trade barriers, and lower labor rates in the target country can make export economically infeasible in the long run.

A firm can either export goods directly to foreign customers or buyers or through export intermediaries. **Export intermediaries** are third parties that specialize in facilitating imports and exports. These intermediaries may offer limited services such as handling only transportation, documentation, and customs claims, or they may perform more extensive services, including taking ownership of foreign-bound goods and/or assuming total responsibility for marketing and financing exports. Typical export intermediaries are export management companies. An **export management company** (EMC) is an intermediary that acts as its client's export department. Small firms may use an EMC to handle their foreign shipments, prepare export documents, and deal with customs offices, insurance companies, and/or commodity inspection agencies. EMCs are generally more knowledgeable about the legal, financial, and logistical details of exporting and importing, and thus free the exporter from having to develop such expertise in-house.

Managers involved in exporting must know the terms of sale (or terms of price). **Terms of sale** are conditions stipulating rights/responsibilities and costs/risks borne by exporter and importer. These terms have been harmonized and defined by the International Chamber of Commerce as standards, and thus are widely used in export transactions. Major terms of price include:

- *FOB* (Free on Board): A term of price in which the seller covers all costs and risks up to the point whereby the goods are delivered on board the ship in a designated shipment (export) port, and the buyer bears all costs and risks from that point on. This means that the buyer is responsible for the insurance and freight expenses in transporting goods from the shipment port to the destination port.
- *FAS* (Free Alongside Ship): A term of price in which the seller covers all costs and risks up to the side of the ship in a designated shipment (export) port. The buyer bears all costs and risks thereafter.
- *CIF* (Cost, Insurance, and Freight): A term of price in which the seller covers cost of the goods, insurance, and all transportation and miscellaneous charges to the named foreign port in the country of final destination.
- *C&F* (Cost and Freight): Similar to CIF, except that the buyer (rather than the seller) purchases and bears the cost of insurance.

Export managers should also be familiar with key documentation in exporting. The key documents frequently used include the letter of credit, the bill of lading, the bank draft, the commercial invoice, the insurance certificate, and the certificate of origin. **A letter of credit** (L/C) is a contract between an importer and a bank that transfers liability for paying the exporter from the importer to the importer's bank (for details, see the first section of Chapter 14). A **bill of lading** (B/L) is the document issued by a shipping company or its agent as evidence of a contract for shipping the merchandise and as a claim to ownership of the goods. In Chapter 14, we explain in detail how export managers deal with international payment, import and export financing, foreign exchange risk reduction, and collection of export accounts receivables. In fact, the provision of such banking (e.g., L/C issuance), shipping (e.g., ocean or air), and insurance (e.g., for goods in transport) services for international customers is a form of service trade that closely resembles the export of physical goods.

International Subcontracting

Subcontracting has been used extensively by MNEs seeking low labor costs in a host country. Generally, **subcontracting** is the process in which a foreign company provides a local manufacturer with raw materials, semi-finished products, sophisticated components, or technology for producing final goods that will be bought back by the foreign company. In most subcontracting businesses, local manufacturers are responsible only for processing or assembly in exchange for processing fees. In this situation, the local manufacturer does not own the property rights of materials or parts supplied by the foreign counterpart. Nike, for example, is still using subcontracting as its primary mode in China, Vietnam, Thailand, Indonesia, and Bangladesh. The company provides raw materials and technology, maintains proprietary rights over materials and products, controls production processes and product quality, and pays processing fees to local factories.

In the beginning of the twenty-first century, when falling trade barriers and increasing competition prompted large firms to cut costs, many MNEs producing sophisticated products began shrinking their manufacturing function by using the **original equipment manufacturing (OEM)** method. OEM is one specific form of international subcontracting, in which a foreign firm (i.e., original equipment manufacturer) supplies a local company with the technology and sophisticated components so that the latter can manufacture goods that the foreign firm will market under its own brand in international markets. Flextronics, a Singapore-based company, was during the 1990s a small contract assembler of circuit boards, but is now the world's third largest subcontractor in electronics, providing cost-efficient manufacturing services that free its OEM clients (e.g., Honeywell, GE, Pratt & Whitney, Compaq, Nortel) to concentrate on design, engineering, R&D, and global marketing. I-Berhad, a Malaysian subcontractor in PC assembly, has assembly plants in Shah Alam, Selangor, and Perak that provide subcontracting services (manufacturing and assembling) for many international brands such as Sanyo, Sharp, Toshiba, and Singer. China's Kelon served as GE's largest subcontractor for its household appliance products for many years, until it was acquired by Hisense in 2005 (now known as Hisense-Kelon). This subcontracting helped Kelon utilize its existing production capacity, benefit from technology transfer from GE, and learn managerial skills from the foreign firm, likely making it an even more attractive acquisition for Hisense. It also helped GE reduce production costs, rationalize its production process, and expedite large-volume productions. Today, other MNEs such as Ericsson, Siemens, Acer, HP, IBM, and Boeing are using OEM to cut costs while maintaining their competitive edge in the global marketplace.

Countertrade

Countertrade is a form of trade in which a seller and a buyer from different countries exchange merchandise with little or no cash or cash equivalents changing hands. Because of this nature, it is also viewed as a form of flexible financing or payment in international trade. Informed estimates suggest that countertrade accounts for about 20 percent of world trade.[15] Countertrade has evolved into a diverse set of activities that can be categorized as four distinct types of trading arrangements:

- Barter
- Counterpurchase
- Offset
- Buyback (or compensation)

Barter is the direct and simultaneous exchange of goods between two parties without a cash transaction. Barter trade occurs between individuals, between governments, between firms, or between a government and a firm. Barter may be the oldest form of trade, but it is certainly not history. For example, during Greece's recent debt crisis, marketplaces and organizations sprang up with individuals bartering goods or services such as English and computer lessons, baby-sitting, and plumbing repairs—anything they had in place of the euro, which was hard to come by.[16] Countries also still enter into barter agreements, as was the case with Iran in 2012, when it attempted to skirt sanctions by exchanging its oil for such goods as wheat, soybean meal, and consumer products from India and China.[17] Because firms using barter run the risk of having to accept goods that may be difficult to market or earn a satisfactory profit margin from, it is important for a party to ensure that trading-in products are heavily demanded in its own market.

A **counterpurchase** is a reciprocal buying agreement whereby one firm sells its products to another at one point in time and is compensated in the form of the other's products at some future time (e.g., Russia purchased construction machinery from Japan's Komatsu in return for Komatsu's agreement to buy Siberian timber). Counterpurchase is more flexible than barter in facilitating many transactions because the values of trade do not have to be equal, i.e., the dollar amount of goods exported need not be equal to the dollar amount of goods taken back. In this situation, two parties can either set up an escrow account or use cash to finally settle the differences. Unlike barter, which involves a single contract, a counterpurchase agreement usually involves three separate contracts—the sales contract, the purchase contract, and the protocol contract. The protocol contract serves as a protection contract, which explains what each party will do, and what each party should expect.

An **offset** is an agreement whereby one party agrees to purchase goods and services with a specified percentage of its proceeds from an original sale. Like counterpurchase, offset involves three contracts, including sales, protocol, and purchase. Unlike counterpurchase whereby exchanged products are normally unrelated, products taken back in an offset are often the outputs processed by this party in the original contract. For example, the Shanghai Aircraft Manufacturing Corp., China may buy jets from Boeing using its proceeds from manufacturing the tail sections of the jets for Boeing. Offset is particularly popular in sales of expensive military equipment or high-cost civilian infrastructure hardware. General Dynamics sold several hundred F-16 military jets to Belgium, Denmark, Norway, and the Netherlands by agreeing to allow those countries to offset the cost of the jets through co-production agreements whereby 40 percent of the value of the aircraft was produced in these countries.

Finally, **buyback** (or compensation arrangement) occurs when a firm provides a local company with inputs for manufacturing products (mostly capital equipment) to be sold in international markets, and agrees to take a certain percentage of the output produced by the local firm as partial payment. A buyback agreement involves two contracts: the sales contract and the purchase contract. In a buyback arrangement, the equipment supplier gets a cash portion in addition to the goods. For example, a steel producer might send its goods to a foreign company, which would use the steel to manufacture a product such as shelving. The steel producer would then buy back the shelves at a reduced price, in effect partially paying the manufacturer with the raw steel. Buybacks help developing country producers upgrade technologies and machinery and ensure after-sale service. Chinatex, a Shanghai-based clothing manufacturer, and Japan's Fukusuke Corp., arranged a buyback whereby the latter sold ten knitting machines and raw materials to the former in exchange for one million pairs of underwear to be produced on the knitting machines. Because the buyback links payment with output from the purchased goods, Chinatex benefited from Fukusuke's instructions on how to use the equipment and its excellent after-sale services. In a sense, offset and buyback are the reverse of each other. In an offset arrangement, a party in the host country makes part of the final product and purchases the final product using the proceeds earned from the manufacturing work as partial payment. In a buyback arrangement, a party from outside the host country sells manufacturing equipment or other production inputs to a local producer and purchases some of the output as payment for the provision of the equipment or production inputs.

Transfer–Centered Entry Modes

Transfer-centered entry modes are associated with the transfer of rights to use some productive assets or resources (e.g., equipment or technology) from a foreign entity to a local entity for a specified period of time in exchange for fee payments. They differ from trade-centered entry modes in that the focus of the transaction is the rights to use certain tangible or intangible assets within a specified period of time, rather than the terminal sales of certain goods (e.g., steel) or services (e.g., shipping). These modes are extensively employed in technology-related or intellectual/industrial property rights-related transactions. This category includes the following entry modes:

- International leasing
- International licensing
- International franchising
- Build-operate-transfer (BOT)

International Leasing

International leasing is an entry mode in which the foreign firm (lessor) leases out its new or used machinery or equipment to the local company (often in a developing country). International lease arises largely because developing country manufacturers (lessee) do not have financial capability or lack foreign currency to pay for the equipment. In many cases, the leased equipment sits idle, but is in good operational condition, thus having a market in developing countries. In this mode, the foreign lessor retains ownership of the property throughout the lease period during which the local user pays a leasing fee. The major advantages of this mode for MNEs include quick access to the target market, efficient use of superfluous or outmoded machinery and equipment, or accumulating experience in a foreign country. From the local firm's perspective, this mode helps reduce the cost of using foreign machinery and equipment, mitigates operational and investment risks, and increases its knowledge and experience with foreign technologies and facilities. For instance, about 50 percent of commercial aircrafts in use today are leased by airlines from such leasing companies as Boeing Capital Corp. and GE Capital.

International Licensing

International licensing is an entry mode in which a foreign licensor grants specified intangible property rights to the local licensee for a specified period of time in exchange for a royalty fee. Such property rights may include patents, trademarks, technology, managerial skills, and so on. They allow the licensee to produce and market a product similar to the one the licensor has already been producing in its home country without requiring the licensor to actually create a new operation abroad.

Generally, an MNE may use international licensing to: (1) obtain extra income from technical expertise and services, spread around the costs of company research and development programs, or maximize returns on research findings and accumulated expertise; (2) retain established markets that have been closed or threatened by trade restrictions, reach new markets not accessible by export from existing facilities, or expand into foreign markets quickly with minimum effort or risk; (3) augment limited domestic capacity and management resources for serving foreign markets, provide overseas sources of supply and services to important domestic customers, or develop market outlets for raw materials or components made by the domestic company; (4) build goodwill and acceptance for the company's other products or services, develop sources of raw materials or components for the company's other operations, or pave the way for future investment; or (5) discourage possible infringement, impairment, or loss of company patents or trademarks, or acquire reciprocal benefits from foreign expertise, research, and technical services.

As identified by the Internalization Theory (discussed in Chapter 3), technology licensing is subject to a number of drawbacks compared to FDI-centered modes. First, the negotiation of a licensing agreement can be difficult and may easily result in failure if the potential licensee perceives a high level of uncertainty about the efficacy of the technology and is concerned that the licensor tries to exaggerate the value of the technology. Second, if the technology is tacit in the sense that its transfer requires a substantial amount of person-to-person training and learning by doing, the licensor will have to exert considerable effort in training in order to have the knowledge fully transferred, even though the requisite effort cannot be fully specified in a contract and is difficult to enforce in the court of law. Under such conditions, the licensor may be tempted to shirk its transfer effort, causing the production operation of the licensee to be less efficient than otherwise. Both the perceived uncertainty about the value of the technology and the risk of an incomplete transfer can make a potential licensee reluctant to pay a high royalty fee, thus limiting the income that the owner can earn from its technology. Third, once the technology is largely transferred, the licensee may lose the incentive to continue paying the royalty and instead bargain for a reduction of the royalty rate by threatening to withdraw from the licensing agreement. A licensor often faces serious difficulties in enforcing its contractual rights in other countries due to differences in legal traditions and weaknesses in the host country's protection of contracts and intellectual property rights. Fourth, a licensee overseas can also become a competitor to the licensor. Even if the original licensing agreement stipulates the region within which the licensee is permitted to sell the licensed product, the licensee may still be able to market the product in third-country markets in competition with the licensor due to imperfections in the international protection of intellectual property rights. Fifth, it is often difficult for the licensor to maintain satisfactory control over the licensee's manufacturing and marketing operations. If the licensee finds it economically advantageous to produce and market a lower quality product in the local market, this can damage the licensor's trademark and reputation.

The above drawbacks can in general be avoided if the owner of the technology chooses an FDI-centered entry mode that enables it to have both ownership of and control over the local operations. In the meantime, because licensing requires only limited capital investment from the owner of the technology, it may the best mode to use in the initial entry in the face of high uncertainty about the local market if export is infeasible and if the licensor can limit the scope of the operation and technology transfer (e.g., only assembly and manufacture of some parts that do not involve many trade secrets).

International Franchising

International franchising is an entry mode in which the foreign franchisor grants specified intangible property rights (e.g., trademark or brand name) to the local franchisee, which must abide by strict and detailed rules as to how it does business. Compared to licensing, franchising involves longer commitments, offers greater control over overseas operations, and includes a broader package of rights and resources, which is why service MNEs such as KFC often elect franchising (whereas manufacturing firms often use licensing). Production equipment, managerial systems, operating procedures, access to advertising and promotional materials, loans, and financing may all be part of a franchise. The franchisee operates the business under the franchisor's proprietary rights and is contractually obligated to adhere to the procedures and methods of operation prescribed in the business system. The franchisor generally maintains the right to control the quality of products and services so that the franchisee cannot damage the company's image. In exchange for the franchise, the franchisor receives a royalty payment that amounts to a percentage of the franchisee's revenues. Sometimes the franchisor mandates that the franchisee must buy equipment or key ingredients used in the product. For example, Burger King and McDonald's require the franchisee to buy the company's cooking equipment, burger patties, and other products that bear the company name.

The merits and limitations of international franchising are similar to those of licensing. The main advantages include little political risk, low costs, and fast and easy avenues for leveraging assets such as a trademark or brand name. For example, McDonald's has been able to build a global presence quickly and at relatively low cost and risk by using franchises. Most of the drawbacks that afflict licensing arrangements are not as consequential in franchising arrangements for at least two reasons. First, unlike sophisticated manufacturing technologies that involve many tacit elements, the skills and operational routines that a franchisor needs to impart to its franchisees for effective and efficient operations are typically standardized and thus relatively easy to transfer. Second, the markets for most franchises are typically broader and deeper than the markets for new technologies. The presence of such a market makes it important for the franchisor to maintain its reputation with current and potential franchisees and thus motivates the franchisor to provide good training for its franchisees. Nevertheless, the franchisee may still damage the franchisor's image by not upholding its standards. Even if the franchisor is able to terminate the agreement, some franchisees still stay in business by slightly altering the franchisor's brand name or trademark and become competitors for essentially the same segment of customers.

Build-Operate-Transfer (BOT)

Build-operate-transfer (BOT) is a "turnkey" investment in which a foreign investor assumes responsibility for the design and construction of an entire operation, and, upon completion of the project, turns the project over to the purchaser and hands over management to local personnel whom it has trained. In return for completing the project, the investor receives periodic payments that are normally guaranteed. BOT is especially useful for very large-scale, long-term infrastructure projects such as power generation, airports, dams, expressways, chemical plants, and steel mills. Managing such complex projects requires special expertise. It is thus not surprising that most are administered by large construction firms such as Bechtel (United States), Hyundai (Korea), or Friedrich Krupp (Germany). Large companies sometimes form a consortium and bid jointly for a large BOT project. Airport International Group, a consortium of companies including the French Aéroports de Paris, the Greek J&P Avax, the Abu Dhabi Investment Company, and the EDGO group of Jordan, among others, was granted the contract to rehabilitate, expand, and operate the Queen Alia International Airport in Jordan in 2007. The consortium allows for a 25-year operation period, before it is turned back over to the country.[18]

Due in part to the difficulties of working out financing and equity arrangements, the BOT approach is often used in combination with other entry modes. Foreign businesses may set up BOT project firms by means of either equity or cooperative joint ventures with local partners. Because of their ability to provide foreign investors with returns in excess of their proportional contributions to the venture's total registered capital, contractual joint ventures have been the vehicles of choice for BOT infrastructure projects. For example, in 2001, Frankfurt Airport Corp., from Germany, was awarded a BOT contract by the Philippines government for the construction of the third passenger terminal at the Ninoy Aquino International Airport. It then formed a contractual joint venture, named Fraport, with the Philippines International Airport Transport Company, to construct this project.

FDI-Centered Entry Modes

In contrast to the preceding trade-centered and transfer-centered entry modes, **FDI-centered entry modes** involve *ownership* of property, assets, projects, and businesses invested in a host country. Accordingly, firms undertaking FDI also attain effective managerial *control* over their overseas operations and activities. FDI-centered entry modes are more complex than trade-centered modes, and involve higher risks and longer-term contributions than both trade- and transfer-centered choices. Compared with the latter, FDI-centered modes underline the firm's long-term strategic goals of international presence and necessitate continuous contribution and commitment to investments and operations abroad. In general, the ownership stake and effective control that an MNE has in its overseas operations make the firm more willing to transfer not only up-to-date technologies but also other knowledge-based assets to those operations, potentially contributing more to the economy of the host country. FDI-centered entry modes include:

- Operations Branch office
- Cooperative joint venture
- Equity joint venture
- Wholly owned subsidiary
- Umbrella holding company

The Branch Office

A **branch office** is a foreign entity in a host country in which it is not incorporated but exists as an extension of the parent and is legally constituted as a branch. Corporate law in many countries allows foreign companies to open branches that engage in production and operating activities. Unlike representative offices which by law are prohibited from engaging in direct, profit-making business activities (they serve instead as liaisons, establishing contacts with governments and handling market research and consulting activities), branch offices are entitled to run businesses within a specified scope or location. A foreign subsidiary can also open a branch office in another region of the host country to expand its operations there. Branch offices are particularly utilized by MNEs in service industries such as transnational banks, law firms, and accounting or consulting companies. For example, Standard Bank had 700 branches in South Africa in 2011, and was ranked the largest foreign bank in that country. It also had branch offices in 16 other sub-Saharan countries. Because of South Africa's traditionally strong financial infrastructure, and its long-established presence in the major financial centers of Africa, the bank is a match for foreign entrants in retail banking technology as well as wholesale payments, clearing, and custody. In most cases, branch offices may offer a relatively simple means for establishing or expanding a presence in a target country, but since they do not have legal-person status, the foreign parent company is liable if civil charges are brought against the branch. To shield the parent company from unlimited damage claims, foreign companies interested in establishing branch offices may designate an offshore subsidiary as the parent. For instance, the first McDonald's restaurant in Russia was launched by its Canadian subsidiary.

The Cooperative (or Contractual) Joint Venture

The **cooperative joint venture** (also known as contractual joint venture) is a collaborative agreement whereby profits and other responsibilities are assigned to each party according to a contract. These do not necessarily accord with each partner's percentage of the total investment. Each party cooperates as a separate legal entity and bears its own liabilities. Most cooperative joint ventures do not involve constructing and building a new legally and physically independent entity. As such, cooperative joint ventures normally take the form of a document (cooperative agreement), whereas equity joint ventures take the form of a new entity.

Many cooperative programs today involve joint activities without the creation of a new corporate entity. Instead, carefully defined rules govern the allocation of tasks, costs, and revenues. Joint exploration (e.g., offshore oil exploration consortia), research partnership, and co-production are typical forms of cooperative joint ventures. Others include joint marketing, long-term supply agreements, or technological training and assistance. Boeing entered China in the late 1970s through a co-production agreement with the Xian Aircraft Manufacturing Company which co-produced 737 vertical fins, horizontal stabilizers, and forward access doors; and another co-production agreement with the Shenyang Aircraft Manufacturing Company which co-produced 737 tail sections and 757 cargo doors. Chapter 12 details forms and features of various cooperative arrangements.

The Equity Joint Venture

The most common foreign entry for MNEs has been through equity joint ventures. An **equity joint venture** can be formed in either of two ways: (1) the establishment of a new entity (*de novo* joint venture) that is jointly owned and managed by two or more parent firms from different countries; and (2) an MNE's acquisition of a significant portion of the equity in an ongoing concern in the target country. To set up an equity joint venture, each partner contributes cash, facilities, equipment, materials, intellectual property rights, labor, or land-use rights. According to joint venture laws in most countries, a foreign investor's share must exceed a certain threshold of the total equity (25 percent in many nations). Generally, there is no upward limit in deregulated industries in most countries, whether developed or developing. However, in government controlled or institutionally restricted sectors, foreign investors are often confined with respect to equity arrangements.

Broadly, cooperative joint ventures and equity joint ventures are together called global strategic alliances (GSAs). The proliferation of such alliances among MNEs from different countries is transforming the global business environment. These alliances are gaining importance worldwide as global competition intensifies for access to markets, products, and technologies. Most large MNEs such as Siemens, Sony, GM, Daimler, and Toyota have built such alliances. In Japan alone, for example, Royal Dutch Shell has established more than 30 joint ventures. As a means of survival and growth, GSAs have become a fundamental element of many MNEs' key global business strategies. GSAs are explained in Chapter 12.

A joint venture allows the parent firms to share their resources and also gives each of them not only a stake in the outcome from the venture but also a measure of control over the venture's managerial decisions. The stake that each parent holds in the outcome provides it with some incentive to contribute its resources (e.g., technology or managerial expertise), and the control that each of them attains over at least a subset of the venture's managerial decisions may allow it to protect its core interests more effectively. In the meantime, since no parent firm bears the full outcome from a joint venture or holds full control over the venture's management, their incentives and their control rights are both to some extent compromised. In addition, a joint venture may also entail closer interactions among the personnel from the parent firms, possibly resulting in more unintended leakage of their proprietary knowledge to their partner(s). Potential goal conflicts and disagreements in decision making can also dissipate the value that can be created in a joint venture.

Since both the MNE and the indigenous firm can in principle acquire the other's complementary assets outright or contract for the services of those assets, one may wonder what conditions make joint ventures a superior mode when two firms see potential synergy or complementarity between their respective assets or resources. First, the purchase of a firm's complementary assets may be accomplished via an acquisition of either the entire firm or only a part of it, such as its R&D unit or distribution network. Because the target firm may be very large and highly diversified, another firm that wants to gain access to some of the firm's assets may find it difficult to manage the combined firm successfully or even to assess the value of the firm that also contains other unfamiliar assets. Even if one can clearly identify a specific part of the firm as containing the complementary assets, that part of the firm may be highly specialized to the rest of the firm, making it difficult to detach those assets and acquire them separately. For instance, the firm's R&D unit is often intricately linked to the firm's production operations and thus requires unified ownership and control to ensure effective and efficient coordination. Finally, as discussed earlier in this chapter, contracting with another firm for the service of its assets, such as in a licensing or franchising arrangement, can be subject to serious difficulties in contract negotiation and enforcement. Hence, a joint venture that gives its partners not only some incentive to contribute their assets, but also joint control over the decisions of their venture, is likely the optimal mode when neither party finds it economical to acquire the other's complementary assets or to contract with the other for the service of those assets.[19]

The Wholly Owned Subsidiary

The **wholly owned subsidiary** is an entry mode in which the investing firm owns 100 percent of the new entity in a host country. This new entity may be built from scratch by the investing firm (i.e., greenfield investment) or in acquiring a local business (i.e., cross-border acquisition). This mode offers foreign investors the highest level of ownership and managerial control. It allows international managers to make their own decisions without the burden of an uncooperative partner. Wholly owned subsidiaries also allow foreign investors to set up and protect their own processes and procedures, which leads to more careful strategic and operational oversight. During the 1990s, Japan's Kao Corporation established a large number of wholly owned manufacturing and marketing subsidiaries overseas. For example, it established a wholly owned subsidiary in Singapore for the following reasons:

- Coming out of a deeply rooted Japanese corporate culture, Kao's head office prefers tight control over its subsidiaries. Kao's preference for wholly owned operations clearly follows from this cultural bias.
- A wholly owned subsidiary gives a firm the tight control over operations in different countries that is necessary for global integration, thus leading to greater global value.
- A wholly owned subsidiary reduces the risk of losing control of a firm's technological expertise.
- A wholly owned mode better ensures that Kao's foreign operations will benefit from the detergent-producing skills that its domestic operation has possessed for decades.

Nevertheless, the establishment of a large, wholly owned project abroad, such as the Mercedez-Benz plant in Alabama, can be a complex, costly, and lengthy process. MNEs must choose between the importance of protecting core technology and manufacturing and marketing processes on the one hand, and the costs of establishing a new operation on the other. Many MNEs choose this alternative only after expanding into markets through other modes that have helped them accumulate host-country experience.

Wholly owned subsidiaries have traditionally been viewed by many host-country governments, particularly those of developing economies, as offering little in the way of technology transfer or other benefits to local economies. Recently, however, this entry mode has become more attractive to them. When domestic credit is tight, this mode provides host countries with a means of attracting foreign investment. Furthermore, more host governments now recognize that allowing MNEs to hold greater ownership and fuller control in their business are also likely to make them feel more at ease with investing in large-scale operations and transferring more proprietary expertise to local personnel, thus making more contributions to their economies. Nevertheless, governmental support for this mode still often trails far behind that of joint ventures in many countries.

Some notes of caution should be stated. First, even though a wholly owned subsidiary gives the MNE the most flexibility in managerial decision making, the MNE also has the least flexibility for switching to an alternative mode or withdrawing from the market in case the investment turns out to be unprofitable. This is because the FDI mode entails the highest level of resource commitment that is partly or even completely lost in a divestiture. Second, wholly owned subsidiaries must rely on indigenous agents to make liaisons on their behalf and help procure land, materials, and services. Third, wholly owned foreign subsidiaries may not be allowed to invest and operate in industries that are considered vital to the host-country economy. Fourth, since wholly owned subsidiaries operate without the control of local partners, investment approval authorities often hold them to higher standards on pollution control, technological level, capital contribution, foreign exchange administration, and the like. Finally, wholly owned subsidiaries are more vulnerable to criticism relating to cultural and economic sovereignty. Managers in wholly owned subsidiaries should recognize and address this concern. One way is to localize production, that is, to buy as many parts and components as possible from local suppliers, and to localize human resources (i.e., hire local managers).

The Umbrella Holding Company

The **umbrella holding company** is an investment company that unites the firm's existing investments such as branch offices, joint ventures, and wholly owned subsidiaries under one umbrella so as to combine sales, procurement, manufacturing, training, and maintenance within the host country. Many foreign companies are now seeking better integration of these functions for a broad range of products and services within a single important country (such as China and Brazil). Such coordination becomes necessary as each production division sets up its own foreign subunits separated from other divisions' foreign subunits in the same host country. DuPont faced this problem in China because some joint ventures there belong to, and are controlled only by, its pharmaceutical division, whereas others belong to its plastic or petroleum divisions. In 1989 it established DuPont China Ltd. as its holding company to unite and integrate existing investments originally undertaken by respective production divisions. The umbrella model is thus particularly useful for MNEs that are multidivisional, where each division enters and runs differently while the holding company coordinates them. The umbrella mode helps improve the cash flow and capital structure of various investments by acting as a clearing-house for intra-group financing. With a holding company in a host country, profits can be more easily transferred among different strategic business units (SBUs) and taken out of the country. It can also smooth the establishment of new investments. Like all legally independent subsidiaries, an umbrella company has legal person status in a host country. To establish an umbrella company, MNEs may need to comply with certain conditions set by the host-country government. In China, for example, the foreign investor must have established a minimum of ten subunits in the country and engaged in manufacturing or infrastructure construction to which it has contributed at least $30 million in registered capital.

A foreign investor may consider establishing an umbrella enterprise to achieve some or all of the following objectives: (1) investment in subsidiary projects; (2) facilitation of cash flow or foreign exchange balance for all local activities; (3) centralized purchase of production materials for subsidiary projects; (4) provision of product maintenance services and technical support; (5) training of subsidiary project personnel and end users of products; (6) coordination and consolidation of project management; and (7) marketing of subsidiary products.

Exhibit 10.4 highlights the implications of various entry modes in terms of risk, return, control, and commitment. These dimensions serve as base points for MNE managers considering various entry modes. Overall, risk, return, control, and commitment all increase along this sequence with the exception that BOT may involve even more commitment (especially capital and technology) and take even longer to build a new project than some FDI-centered entry modes such as branch offices and joint ventures.

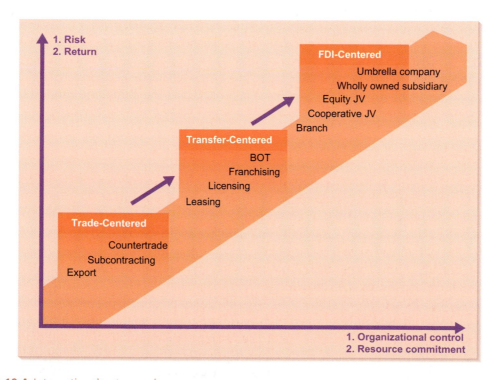

Exhibit 10.4 International entry modes

367

Decision Framework

To select an appropriate entry mode, MNEs should make sure they know all possible options for the entry into a target country before determining the best one. Once a foreign investor decides to pursue an FDI project, its choice of entry mode will depend on a wide range of considerations. Broadly, these can be classified into *country, industry, firm,* and *project* factors.

Country-Specific Factors

A number of host-country-specific factors have an impact on entry mode choice. First, *government FDI policies* may directly or indirectly influence entry mode selection. The laws in some countries mandate that foreign firms must choose joint ventures, as opposed to wholly owned subsidiaries, as an entry mode.[20] Second, *infrastructure conditions* affect the extent to which an MNE plans to commit distinctive resources to local operations, and the degree to which it perceives operational uncertainty and contextual unpredictability. These in turn influence the entry mode option. Third, *property right systems* and other legal frameworks in a host country appear to be increasingly important to entry mode selection. Without sufficient legal protection, an MNE's property rights such as trademarks, brand names, expertise, patents, and copyrights will be exposed to possible infringement and piracy by local firms. In such circumstances, the MNE may have to use a high-control entry mode such as a wholly owned subsidiary or dominant equity joint venture. Fourth, *host-country risks* including general political risks (e.g. instability of political system), ownership/control risks (e.g. price control, local content requirements), and transfer risks (e.g. currency inconvertibility, remittance control) may affect entry mode.[21] Licensing and joint ventures may be favored when country risk is high. Finally, *cultural distance* between home and host countries influences foreign entry decision and process. The greater the perceived distance between home and host countries, the more likely it is that the MNE will favor licensing/franchising or a joint venture over a wholly owned subsidiary.

Industry-Specific Factors

Several industry-specific factors are important considerations underlying entry mode selection. First, *entry barriers* into a target industry in the host country constitute a significant impediment to entry mode selection. Contractual or equity joint ventures may be an effective vehicle to bypass these barriers. Second, *industrial uncertainty and complexity* may lead MNEs to use low commitment entry modes that also permit effective control over certain critical decisions, such as representative or branch offices, licensing, franchising, loosely structured cooperative joint ventures with little resource commitment, or minority equity joint ventures. Finally, *availability and favorability of supply and distribution* in the industry will determine the rationalization of value chain linkages needed for an MNE's local operations and the vertical integration of other units within the MNE network. When an MNE relies more on local resource procurement and/or emphasizes the local market, industrial linkages with suppliers and distributors are more important to the MNE. Entry modes involving partners are superior when the MNE needs but lacks such linkages in the host country.

368

Firm-Specific Factors

Entry mode selection is contingent on several firm-specific traits as well. First, a firm's *resource possession* influences the firm's ability to explore market potential and earn a competitive edge in the global marketplace. A firm that lacks distinctive resources (technological, organizational, operational, and financial), but wishes to share in the risks associated with having them, is often compelled to enter the market through a joint venture where its resource commitment will be minimized.[22] Second, *the leakage risk of technologies* may affect entry mode. If this risk is high, a wholly owned subsidiary mode increases the firm's ability to use and protect these technologies. Third, a firm's *strategic goals* for international expansion are one of the foremost determinants underlying entry mode selection. When an MNE attempts to pursue local market expansion, high commitment choices such as cooperative or equity joint ventures, wholly owned subsidiaries, and umbrella companies are preferable because they enable the firm to have a deeper, more diverse involvement with the indigenous market, creating more opportunities to accumulate country-specific experience. If an MNE aims only to exploit factor endowment advantages, low commitment entry modes such as subcontracting, compensation trade, co-production, cooperative arrangement, and minority equity joint venture may be superior to other options because risks and costs are low. Finally, *international or host-country experience* influences entry mode selection. MNEs with little or no experience with international or host-country business may prefer low control/low resource commitment entry modes such as export, subcontracting, international leasing or franchising, or countertrade.[23] In contrast, MNEs with significant multinational experience prefer high control/ high resource commitment entry modes such as cooperative or equity joint ventures, wholly owned subsidiaries, and umbrella investment companies.

Project-Specific Factors

In the course of entry mode selection, MNEs also need to consider some attributes of the FDI project itself. First, firms may shy away from a wholly owned entry mode in favor of a joint venture when the *project size* is large. A large investment implies higher start-up, switching, and exit costs, thus involving higher financial and operational risks. Second, *project orientation* influences an MNE's resource dispersal and entry mode. MNEs investing in import-substitution projects may be inclined to establish partnerships with local government agencies or state-owned enterprises holding monopoly positions because this type of FDI project is vulnerable to host government control. If a project is local-market-oriented, the MNE may choose the cooperative or equity joint venture mode, because the local partner can provide distinctive supply and distribution channels, governmental networks, and culture-specific business knowledge and experience. If a project is technologically advanced, the firm may opt for a wholly owned subsidiary mode to protect its expertise, or a joint venture mode if it needs complementary technologies or knowledge from a partner firm. Finally, when a project is infrastructure-oriented, the MNE may apply the build-operate-transfer mode if it plans on having only a short-term run, or a majority joint venture mode if it has a long-term strategic plan and is willing to take risks. Finally, *the availability of proper local partners* for a particular project may affect an MNE's entry ability and choice. An MNE's ability to establish a joint venture or any other form of non-integrated entry mode depends upon the availability of capable, trustworthy partners. In the absence of acceptable local partners, the MNE may be forced to start a wholly owned subsidiary.

369

Greenfield Investment, Acquisition, and Merger

An MNE can set up a wholly owned subsidiary through either greenfield investment or international acquisition. A **greenfield investment** is an initial establishment of fully owned new facilities and operations undertaken by the company alone. An **international acquisition** is a cross-border transaction in which a foreign investor acquires an established local firm and makes the acquired local firm a subsidiary business within its global portfolio. International acquisition of a local firm or another foreign company with local ventures is the quickest way to expand one's investment in the target country. An acquisition is particularly useful for entering sectors formerly restricted to state-owned enterprises. Moreover, cash flow may be generated in a shorter time than in the case of greenfield investment, since the acquired firm, by definition, does not have to be built from scratch. Furthermore, acquisition deals may be more attractive than greenfield investment because acquisitions offer immediate access to a local acquiree's existing resources such as land, manufacturing facilities, distribution channels, supply networks, skilled labor, and customer base. Foreign investors generally target enterprises with strong market niches in sectors with potential for growth. MNEs interested in acquisition must evaluate various risks. Gaining government approval for the transfer of ownership and clearance of property titles is often a difficult hurdle. Foreign investors should be careful to obtain accurate information, particularly concerning existing liabilities, when buying into an indigenous entity. When the challenge of obtaining accurate information on the value of the acquisition target is more severe, an MNE will find it more difficult to ensure a profitable acquisition and is likely to find greenfield investment more attractive.[24]

An **international merger** shares the logic of equity joint ventures and is a cross-border transaction in which two firms from different countries agree to integrate their operations on a relatively co-equal basis because they have resources and capabilities that together may create a stronger competitive advantage in the global marketplace. An example is the 1998 merger between Daimler-Benz of Germany (Stuttgart) and Chrysler of the United States (Detroit), the largest international corporate marriage in history (though this, too, as in many mergers, eventually turned out to be an acquisition by the German firm). The two firms, however, might have overestimated the extent of synergy between them and eventually "divorced" in 2007. After Chrysler fell into bankruptcy and was taken over by the US government in the aftermath of the 2008 financial crisis, it merged with Fiat SpA of Italy, hoping to realize greater synergy with a new partner than with Daimler-Benz. Like joint ventures, cross-border mergers can generate many positive outcomes:

- Interpartner learning and resource sharing.
- Elevating economies of scale or scope.
- Reducing costs by eliminating expenditures for redundant resources.
- Capturing greater market share by providing more comprehensive offerings.
- Increasing revenue by cross-selling products to cross-border customers.

The major difference between *de novo* joint ventures and mergers is that the former involves formation of a third entity whose duration is often limited and specified in the contract, whereas the latter does not form any third party nor does it specify any duration. The parents of a *de novo* joint venture remain independent after forming a venture but a merger integrates the two firms into a single organization after the consummation of the merger. Also, mergers combine all of the partners' assets (though some may be spun off later), while a joint venture involves only some of those assets.

International mergers and acquisitions inevitably confront many challenges, especially during early operations. The fundamental challenges are often rooted in cross-national differences in culture, managerial styles, and corporate values (the Industry Box illustrates Unilever's experience in Brazil). To overcome these challenges, international managers should develop a new corporate mission, vision, and strategic objectives. It is also imperative to integrate communications and human resources. The new organization must develop mechanisms to identify the most appropriate organizational structures and management roles so as to enhance administrative efficiency and operational effectiveness.

Industry Box

Unilever's Acquisitions in Latin America

Unilever, the Anglo-Dutch conglomerate and one of the world's oldest MNEs, describes itself as a purveyor of products ranging from tea and ice-cream to shampoo and toothpaste. Unilever's acquisition of Kibon (Brazil) in 1997 marked another expansion of the company's already strong presence in Latin America. Its management of human resources illustrates the firm's ability to mix internationally savvy executives with the best local talent and practices. The company's approach is a mix of taking the best of the local culture and combining it with the firm's global intentions. Its success with Kibon stems from a deliberate but gradual integration process, particularly with regard to personnel changes. Rather than immediately imposing control from the top, Unilever's strategy centers on two important initial stages. It promoted dialogue with Kibon's staff during the initial period after the acquisition, then defined its priorities and assumed leadership. Management zeroed in on two priority areas: the ice-cream manufacturing process and R&D. Its preliminary studies of Kibon's best operations helped management make appropriate decisions about future layoffs and restructuring. Despite removing Kibon's entire board of directors, Unilever made a special effort to keep key personnel in priority areas, namely production and R&D. Once the groundwork was laid, Unilever did not hesitate to make changes. After carefully studying the acquired company, it quickly set out to forge a new identity and strategy and to rationalize production. Today, Kibon is only one of many of Unilever's successful ventures into South America, which, as of 2008, spanned 34 companies in 19 countries.

Source: Company website and press releases.

The Evolutionary Path

In many circumstances, international entry is not a one-step action but rather an evolutionary process involving a series of incremental decisions during which firms increase their commitment to the target market by shifting from low to high commitment entry modes.[25] Although some firms may bypass some steps or speed up the entire process, many MNEs follow the learning curve of gathering information and accumulating competence, knowledge, and confidence in the international entry process. They move sequentially from no international involvement to export, to overseas assembly or sales subsidiaries (subcontracting, branches, or franchising), to overseas production via contractual or equity joint ventures (also from minority to majority), and, ultimately, to overseas penetration and integration through wholly owned subsidiaries or umbrella companies.[26] Increasing levels of involvement in foreign markets relate to a firm's accumulation of experiential and local knowledge. While relevant knowledge and experience are acquired predominantly through actual presence and activities in a foreign market, joint ventures with local firms represent bridges between no equity involvement and equity involvement in a host country. In fact, many MNEs start an equity joint venture and a wholly owned subsidiary in sequence. This way, a foreign investor will obtain initial entry as part of an equity joint venture for a fixed period stipulated in the duration clause of the contract. Then, at the end of the stipulated term, it can take over the assets from the local partner and continue to run the operation as a wholly owned subsidiary. This is an attractive alternative if the added value of the local partner is significant, but limited to the early stages of the venture, or if the MNE needs a period of close interactions with the acquisition target to gather better accurate information on its true value. Some equity joint ventures have included this option in the termination clause of the joint venture contract.

Large and experienced MNEs may combine several entry modes at the same time. For instance, selecting between an equity joint venture and a wholly owned subsidiary is not necessarily an either–or decision. Sometimes a local partner has a strong distribution network or operates in a restricted sector that is attractive to a foreign investor. In such situations, foreign companies can, for instance, surround their wholly owned subsidiary production operation with equity joint ventures that supply resources, or market and sell their products in the host market. Siemens did exactly that in Brazil, where it owned four wholly owned manufacturing plants, surrounded by seven joint ventures with either local firms or other MNEs, such as Bosch GmbH or Philips, as supply bases, and had 13 sales and service branch offices throughout the nation as of the end of 2001.

Interim Summary

1. Entry modes available to international companies include trade-centered modes (exporting, subcontracting, and countertrade), transfer-centered modes (leasing, licensing, franchising, and BOT), and FDI-centered modes (branch, cooperative joint venture, equity joint venture, wholly owned subsidiary, and umbrella holding companies). The levels of involved risks, anticipated returns, resultant control, and required commitment generally increase along the preceding sequence.
2. International acquisition is a way to form a wholly owned subsidiary. Compared to greenfield investment, international acquisition generates some advantages such as quicker access, bypass of entry barriers, and utilization of an acquiree's existing resources.

372

Chapter Summary

1. International entry strategies concern where, when, and how firms should enter in their international expansion. Location selection concerns not only country selection but also project location within this country. Managers need to consider various locational determinants such as cost/tax factors, demand factors, strategic factors (e.g., investment infrastructure, manufacturing concentration, industrial linkage, workforce productivity, and inbound and outbound logistics), regulatory and economic factors, and sociopolitical factors.

2. The decision on location selection is also contingent on the firm's strategic objectives of expansion, required global integration between this location and the rest of the MNE network, and the project's market orientation (local market vs. export market). The firm may also take into account its familiarity with the location, geographical market coverage, competitors' location pattern, and regional block effects (e.g., European Union).

3. Each timing option, whether early mover or late entrant, has distinct advantages and disadvantages. Entry occurs when the firm anticipates gains to exceed risks or costs. Early movers benefit from: greater market power (barriers for followers, technological leadership, customer loyalty, and product positioning); greater preemptive opportunities in marketing, resources, and branding; and greater strategic options (site selection, infrastructure access, and low competition).

4. Early mover disadvantages are late mover advantages. Early movers tend to face greater uncertainty derived from variable regulations and rules and unstable industrial and market structures; greater operational risks as a result of less developed infrastructure, and a lack of supporting services and resources; and greater operational costs arising from adaptation, training, learning, and anti-imitation.

5. Firms can enter a target country through numerous entry modes, ranging from trade-centered modes (export, subcontracting, and countertrade), to transfer-centered modes (leasing, licensing, franchising, and BOT), to FDI-centered modes (branch, cooperative joint venture, equity joint venture, wholly owned subsidiary, and umbrella company). Levels of risk, control, and commitment vary significantly across categories and across entry modes within each category.

6. Most international companies, whether large or small, still actively participate in import and export businesses. Export intermediaries specialize in import and export management. Managers should familiarize themselves with key concepts such as terms of price (e.g., FAS, CIF, C&F, and FOB) and key documents (e.g., L/C and B/L) involved in import and export processes.

7. Original equipment manufacturing (OEM) is an increasingly popular mode used by many large MNEs looking for cheaper production overseas. Countertrade methods such as barter, counterpurchase, offset, and buyback offer more flexibility than conventional import and export since the former do not involve hard currency cash flows. Transfer-centered entry modes are widely used in technological, intellectual, or industrial property right transfers or transactions.

8. Joint venture and wholly owned subsidiary are the two major entry modes embedded in FDI. The joint venture enables the firm to share risks and costs with others, acquire new knowledge from others, bypass entry barriers in a host country, and capitalize on the partner's reputation, experience, networks, and marketing skills. The wholly owned entry mode provides the firm with stronger organizational control and knowledge protection.

Notes

1 M.E. Porter, *Competitive Advantage: Creating and Sustaining Superior Performance*, New York: Free Press, 1985.

2 J.H. Dunning, *Multinational Enterprises and the Global Economy*, Reading, MA: Addison-Wesley, 1993.

3 M.E. Porter, *Competition in Global Industries*, Boston, MA: Harvard Business School Press, 1986.

4 C.G. Culem, "The locational determinants of foreign direct investments among industrial countries," *European Economic Review*, 32, 4, 1988, 885–894; J. Friedman, D.A. Gerlowski, and J. Silberman, "What attracts foreign multinational corporations: Evidence from branch plant location in the United States," *Journal of Regional Science*, 32, 4, 1992, 403–418.

5 J.F. Hennart and Y.R. Park, "Location, governance, and strategic determinants of Japanese manufacturing investment in the United States," *Strategic Management Journal*, 15, 6, 1994, 419–436.

6 W. H. Davidson, "The location of foreign direct investment activity: Country characteristics and experience effects," *Journal of International Business Studies*, 11, 2, 1980, 9–22.

7 T. Han, "Tough new Beijing emission standard latest blow to domestic brands," *China Daily*, October 8, 2012; F. Li, "China biggest target for global automakers," *China Daily*, January 11, 2013.

8 Cisco Inclusion and Diversity pamphlet, Cisco Systems, Inc., 2012.

9 "Mexico's maquiladoras: Big mac attack," *The Economist*, October 26, 2013.

10 B. Mascarenhas, "Order of entry and performance in international markets," *Strategic Management Journal*, 13, 1992, 499–510; W. Mitchell, "Whether and when? Probability and timing of incumbents' entry into emerging industrial subfields," *Administrative Science Quarterly*, 34, 1989, 208–230.

11 Y. Luo, "Timing of investment and international expansion performance in China," *Journal of International Business Studies*, 29, 1988, 391–408.

12 S. Suwannakij and S. Vallikappen, "Cockfighting Thai billionaire makes top Chinese purchase," *Bloomberg*, December 11, 2012.

13 P.J. Buckley and M. Casson, "The optimal timing of a foreign direct investment," *The Economic Journal*, 91, 1981, 75–87.

14 J.-F. Hennart, "Down with MNE-centric theories! Market entry and expansion as the bundling of MNE and local assets," *Journal of International Business Studies*, 40, 9, 2009, 1432–1454.

15 D. West, "Countertrade," *Business Credit*, 103, 4, 2001, 64–67.

16 S. Poggioli, "Modern Greeks return to ancient system of barter," NPR, November 29, 2011.

17 I. Lakshmanan and P. Narayanan, "India and China skirt Iran sanctions with 'junk for oil'," *Bloomberg*, March 30, 2012.

18 "Queen Alia International Airport," Airport-technology.com, 2010.

19 J.-F. Hennart, "A transaction cost theory of equity joint ventures," *Strategic Management Journal*, 9, 4, 1988, 361–374; T. Chi, "Trading in strategic resources: Necessary conditions, transaction cost problems, and choice of exchange structure," *Strategic Management Journal*, 15, 4, 1994, 271–290.

20 B. Gomes-Casseres, "Firm ownership presences and host government restrictions: An integrated approach," *Journal of International Business Studies*, 21, 1, 1990, 1–21.

21 F.R. Root, *Entry Strategies for International Markets*, Washington, DC: Lexington Books, 1994.

22 S. Agarwal and S.N. Ramaswami, "Choice of foreign market entry mode: Impact of ownership, location, and internalization factors," *Journal of International Business Studies*, 23, 1, 1992, 1–27.

23 C.W.L. Hill, P. Hwang, and W.C. Kim, "An eclectic theory of the choice of international entry mode," *Strategic Management Journal*, 11, 1990, 117–128; J. Johanson and J.E. Vahlne, "The internationalization process of the firm: A model of knowledge development and increasing foreign market commitments," *Journal of International Business Studies*, 8, 1, 1977, 23–32.

24 S.-F. Chen, "A general TCE model of international business institutions: Market failure and reciprocity," *Journal of International Business Studies*, 41, 6, 2010, 935–959.

25 S.J. Chang, "International expansion strategy of Japanese firms: Capability building through sequential entry," *Academy of Management Journal*, 38, 1995, 383–407.

26 E. Anderson and H. Gatignon, "Modes of foreign entry: A transaction cost analysis and propositions," *Journal of International Business Studies*, 17, fall 1986, 1–26.

chapter 11

MNE organization structure and design

INTERNATIONAL STRATEGY AND ORGANIZATION DESIGN   378

MNE ORGANIZATIONAL STRUCTURES   383

INTEGRATING GLOBAL OPERATIONS   398

Do You Know?

1. Is the organizational design of the MNE a function of its strategy or vice versa?
2. Why does the MNE need to continuously monitor and adjust its structure?
3. Do you expect an MNE subsidiary in Mexico to be similar in strategic importance, knowledge flow, and authority to subsidiaries of the same MNE in the United Kingdom, Singapore, or China?
4. What types of organizational structure can an MNE choose from, and what are the selection criteria?
5. If you were an executive at Wal-Mart, how would you integrate the firm's global activities?

OPENING CASE   Procter & Gamble: Worldwide Structure

Founded in 1837, The Procter & Gamble Company (P&G) is one of the world's largest and most profitable consumer packaged-goods companies. The company has three times the number of billion-dollar brands of their closest competitor, with more than $10 billion in net earnings in 2012, when P&G's collection of 25 billion-dollar brands produced $84 billion in annual sales. P&G markets its products in over 180 countries around the world through six global hubs. Essential to their success is a corporate structure that is continuously monitored and updated to suit a changing environment and emerging business trends.

The P&G businesses are divided into two global business units (GBUs): (1) household care and (2) beauty and grooming. The two GBUs are responsible for overall brand strategy as well as for new product upgrades, innovations, and marketing plans. This leaves P&G's Market Development Organization to focus on marketing tactics at the local level. The GBUs are supported by a network of Global Business Services (GBS), which provide information technology and decision support. Corporate functions offer centralized problem solutions and various forms of aid to the company's subunits.

Facing a highly competitive market environment, P&G combines multiple tools for global integration to form an efficient and effective organization that successfully confronts global, regional, and local competitors. A three-dimension hierarchical matrix structure provides exposure to a multitude of challenges, from political and economic to technological, and facilitates strategic and operational monitoring, oversight, execution, and control that are mindful of a complex and rapidly changing global environment.

Source: Adapted from P&G 2013 Annual Report, website and press releases.

International Strategy and Organization Design

The objective of organization design is to provide, maintain, and develop the organizational structure that can serve as the best vehicle for achieving a company's strategic goals. The structure selected is aimed at providing a blueprint with which to translate the firm's vision and strategic objectives into a workable distribution and dissemination of rights, duties, and responsibilities to each of the various units and individual positions that make up the organizational apparatus. Although organizational structures are driven by strategy, they also drive it. In other words, the structure represents a constraint on the firm's mode of operations and in turn on its strategic thinking and strategy implementation. For instance, when Japan emerged as an economic power in the 1980s, it was noted that having a Japanese unit report to an Asian-Pacific regional division distracted corporate attention to this market; suggestions have hence been made to separate Japan from the regional division, with direct reporting to corporate headquarters as a way to elevate its strategic visibility.[1] Similar suggestions have been made vis-à-vis China in the new millennium.

Why is it important for MNEs to globally organize, structure, and coordinate geographically dispersed businesses? First, the complexity and rapid change of global business necessitate paying close attention to different sources of knowledge and expertise (e.g., intimate knowledge of a region, close understanding of a product line). Second, once an organization has been divided into separate divisions and units, each sub-unit becomes susceptible to its own interests, goals, and environmental demands that, if they go unchecked, can lead the unit to develop and pursue strategies that are consistent with its own interests, rather than those of the firm as a whole. To overcome these forces, the MNE seeks a structure that maximizes contributions to corporate performance while allowing sub-units the flexibility to adapt to their particular needs, be they a different local environment or a different product group. Third, in many industries, the MNE is no longer able to compete as a collection of independent subsidiaries. Heightened requirements for economies of scale and technological development have led many MNEs to integrate value chain activities dispersed across national subsidiaries. Integrating these activities means raising the level of interdependence among subsidiaries, requiring global coordination. Fourth, inter-unit sharing, learning, and resource flow necessitate extensive coordination, including the assignment of different mandates to various subsidiaries. For example, Geely Automobile Holdings, headquartered in Hangzhou, China, acquired Volvo cars from the Ford Motor Company in 2010. Under the new ownership, Volvo will add Chinese factories to its existing manufacturing plants in Sweden and Belgium, whereas research and development will be done in both China and Sweden. To execute such globally interdependent operations, firms must have organizing and integrating mechanisms in place. Fifth, financial management for global operations such as the use of transfer pricing (to reduce taxation) and the use of internal banking (for intra-corporate financing, foreign exchange hedging, and cash flow management) necessitates global coordination and integration. Finally, MNEs need to balance inconsistent product and regional demands, all the while maintaining group oversight, coordination, and control.

Global Integration and Local Responsiveness

Given increasing globalization, the dual imperatives of global integration (I) and local responsiveness (R) (also known as I-R balance) are more important than ever for the survival and growth of the MNE. **Global integration** refers to the coordination of activities across countries in an effort to build efficient operational networks and maximize the advantage of internalized synergies and similarities across locations. **Local responsiveness** concerns the attempt to respond to specific needs within each host country. Local responsiveness needs stem from the diversity of market conditions and social and political environments in the various countries in which the firm operates. Responsiveness is necessary to react to diversity in consumer tastes, distribution channels, advertising media, and government regulations and constraints. MNEs can choose to emphasize integration over responsiveness or vice versa, or they can compete on both dimensions, resulting in three basic responses: integrated, locally responsive, or multifocal. Firms that see the need to integrate as paramount use a strategy of global integration. Globally integrated businesses link activities across nations in an effort to lower overall costs, reduce taxes, and/or increase income. Locally responsive businesses are more tuned to local characteristics and requirements. Multifocal businesses attempt to respond simultaneously to pressures for integration and responsiveness.

The relative pressures of global integration and local responsiveness can be gauged at different levels, such as industry, division, or subsidiary. Levels of global integration and local responsiveness vary among MNEs and even across different divisions or subsidiaries within the same MNE. It is important that managers identify factors that determine these levels. In general, pressures to integrate globally derive from industrial and organizational forces that necessitate worldwide resource deployment. Strategic decisions are made to strengthen the collective organization so that activities are integrated across national boundaries. In contrast, local responsiveness pressures can be industry-based, and nation-based, and necessitate context-sensitive strategic decisions. Among market and industrial characteristics, the following features tend to trigger global integration: (1) similarity in customer needs, requiring relatively limited responsiveness; (2) having few but global major competitors; and (3) importance of scale economies. Features leading to higher local responsiveness include: (1) market structure diversity; (2) nation-specific distribution channels; (3) heterogeneous market demand and customer needs; and (4) strong requirements for product differentiation and customer responsiveness. Among sociopolitical characteristics, the following tend to boost local responsiveness: (a) a complex and volatile host environment; (b) opaque, cumbersome, and/or arbitrary government regulations; and (c) a strong and unique local business culture.

Among organizational characteristics, the level of global integration is likely to be higher if the firm: (1) engages in transfer pricing and tax minimization or wishes to realize transaction cost savings; (2) focuses on risk reduction or internalized financing; (3) emphasizes global vertical integration and global value chain control; (4) wishes to control key functions such as global branding, R&D, global distribution, and engineering; and (5) requires extensive sharing between corporate members in information, resources, and knowledge. In contrast, local responsiveness is likely to be higher if the firm: (1) targets local market expansion or building presence in highly uncertain markets; (2) aims to seize opportunities in international markets or develop a sustained competitive position in a host country; (3) seeks to acquire local firms' knowledge and experience; or (4) tries to improve organizational legitimacy through localization and adaptation.

MNE Strategy and Design

For the MNE, which operates in a highly complex, diverse, and rapidly changing environment, the organization design challenge is to configure a structure that works well in diverse locations but also brings units together in a coordinated fashion with a capability for rapid redeployment. Since organization design is a vehicle for strategy formulation and implementation, MNE strategy in organizing global operations is the key input in devising its structure. Three generic types of international strategy are used by MNEs. In a **multi-domestic strategy**, strategic and operational decisions are delegated to business units in each country. This permits customization but interferes with economies of scale and intra-organizational learning and sharing. In a **global strategy**, activities are standardized across national markets, allowing strategic and operational control. A global strategy leverages economies of scale and can quickly disseminate innovations across borders; however, it lacks in local responsiveness. Finally, a **transnational (or hybrid) strategy** seeks to achieve both global efficiency and local responsiveness. It requires shared vision and commitment through an integrated network, as well as diverse levels of integration between differing functions. For example, Honda has loose integration between its production and human resources departments, but tight integration between its engineering and R&D departments. Under transnational strategy, the roles and responsibilities of subsidiaries are varied to reflect differences in external environment, internal capabilities, and strategic role.

Subsidiary Roles and Imperatives

Subsidiary Autonomy

Subsidiary roles play a key part in balancing integration and local responsiveness. In an **autonomous role,** the subsidiary performs most activities of the value chain independently of headquarters, selling most of its output in the local market. In a **receptive role**, subsidiary functions are highly integrated with headquarters or with other business units, for example, exporting most of the subsidiary production to the parent company or other subsidiaries, while importing multiple products or components from them. In an **active role**, many activities are located locally, but carried out in close coordination with other subsidiaries. The autonomous role is typical of MNE subsidiaries employing a multidomestic strategy. The receptive role is common in MNE subsidiaries using global strategy. The active role is usually assigned to MNE subsidiaries that follow a transnational strategy, with strong mandate from headquarters and leeway for adaptation.[2] Among different subsidiaries of the same MNE, the level of autonomy may vary due to the different roles, or mandates, assigned to each. It is possible, for instance, that most subsidiaries in a firm using a global strategy are receptive, while a subsidiary serving as the center of excellence in design will be active or autonomous.

Subsidiary Knowledge Flow

Another way of looking at subsidiary role is in terms of knowledge flow across the MNE units.[3] The expertise transferred can be input (e.g., purchasing skills), throughput (e.g., product, process, and packaging design), or output (e.g., marketing knowledge, distribution expertise) oriented. MNE subsidiaries can be classified by the extent to which each (1) receives knowledge inflow from the rest of the corporation, and (2) provides knowledge outflow to the rest of the corporation. Four generic subsidiary roles emerge from the combination of these two elements: namely the **global innovator** (high outflow/low inflow); the **integrated player** (high outflow/high inflow); the **implementer** (low outflow/high inflow); and the **local innovator** (low outflow/low inflow). In the global innovator role, the subsidiary is the fountainhead of knowledge for other units. The integrated player role implies responsibility for creating knowledge that can be utilized by other subsidiaries;

the subsidiary exchanges knowledge with headquarters and with other subsidiaries on an ongoing basis. In the implementer role, the subsidiary hardly ever engages in knowledge creation and relies heavily on knowledge inflows from either the parent or peer subsidiaries. Finally, the local innovator role implies a subsidiary with almost complete local responsibility for the creation of relevant expertise; however, this knowledge is too idiosyncratic to be used outside its local market.

Subsidiary Importance and Competence

The strategic importance of the local environment and the capabilities of the foreign subsidiary are two key considerations in determining subsidiary roles.[4] The **strategic leader** role is played by a highly competent national subsidiary located in a strategically important market. The subsidiary serves as a partner to headquarters in developing and implementing strategy. **Contributor subsidiaries** operate in small or strategically less important markets, but have distinctive capabilities. **Implementer subsidiaries** operate in less strategically important markets, but are competent to maintain local operations. Their market potential is limited, as reflected in corporate resource commitment. The efficiency of an implementer is as important as the creativity of its strategic leaders because it provides the strategic leverage that affords MNEs their competitive advantage. Implementers create opportunities to capture economies of scale and scope that are crucial to global strategies. Finally, **black hole subsidiaries** operate in important markets where they barely make a dent, but their strong local presence is essential for maintaining global position.

In sub-units with lead roles, the head office ensures that strategies fit the overall goals and priorities of the MNE, while the headquarters' function is to provide strategic leadership by giving subsidiaries the resources and freedom needed for the innovative, entrepreneurial role they have been asked to play. If the unit is placed in a contributory role, the head office should redirect local resources to programs outside the unit's control. If a unit is in an implementer role, the head office needs to maintain tight control to capture the benefits of scale and learning. Finally, if a unit acts as a black hole, corporate management should develop resources and capabilities to make it more responsive to the local environment.

Interim Summary

1. MNEs need to organize, structure, and coordinate their global operations because each sub-unit may have its own interests, competing goals, and unique requirements. Need for economies of scale, technological advancement, and intra-corporate resource sharing impact the way by which MNE activities are organized.
2. The dual imperatives of global integration and local responsiveness are more critical than ever, requiring appropriate balance. Firms in different industries or environments and with different strategies or capabilities may have varying levels of integration and responsiveness.
3. Subsidiaries may differ in their strategic role, a result of their specific capabilities as well as corporate vision and strategy.

MNE Organizational Structures

The organization design decision can be summarized as a series of trade-offs concerning differentiation and integration and the proper balance between them. As noted, the need for differentiation is rooted in the diverse requirements and circumstances of different locales and business units. The need for integration comes from the managerial imperative to maintain overall coordination and control to ensure strategy implementation and to reap synergies via optimal resource deployment. In electing an optimal design, firms position themselves along the globalization-to-localization continuum and select from among different forms of differentiation and various mechanisms for coordination, integration, and control. In addition to their business environment, firm capabilities and resources are taken into account in making and implementing design choices.

The large MNE maintains multiple forms of differentiation. For example, it may utilize a product structure for manufacturing operations and a geographic design for sales and marketing. Below the primary lines of differentiation, other forms usually exist. For instance, when Procter & Gamble switched from a geographic to a product structure it retained geographical differentiation, albeit at a lower level. Typically in such changes, executives with specific international specialization (e.g., Central Europe) are retained either in staff capacity, providing advice to line personnel or report to products, or as divisional manager. The one exception to such prioritization is the matrix structure, where two or three bases of differentiation intersect to form a matrix of responsibilities.

As a company becomes more global, its structure changes to accommodate the higher volume and scope of business as well as the increasing diversity of its markets, production (or service provision) bases, and constituencies. A firm's phase of international evolution is, however, only one of the factors affecting its choice of organizational structure. Strategy, home and host country environments, projected market growth, the nature of business, and the human resources available to the firm are among the factors influencing the choice. Thus, it is not uncommon to observe different structures among firms otherwise similar in product and geographical spread. MNE management has considerable leeway in making design choices and it continuously monitors the suitability of the structure as its operations evolve and as its business environment, strategy, or capabilities change.

The National Subsidiary Structure

Until the early 1970s (earlier than that for European MNEs), many US MNEs used a national subsidiary structure. In this arrangement, also called a "mother-daughter" design, national subsidiaries reported directly to headquarters and were in a position to attract the firm's attention without having information filtered through an intermediary unit. This was the case, for instance, with the German subsidiaries of General Motors and Ford, respectively. Once a firm had expanded beyond a handful of subsidiaries, however, coordination and control in this structure became difficult. Each subsidiary developed its own way of conducting business, and corporate headquarters were hard pressed to guide them in line with overall corporate objectives. It also became increasingly clear that this structure did not permit an efficient and effective utilization of corporate resources, undermining the value of having a large global network.

383

The International Division Structure

The international division structure lets the firm's core structure focus on domestic business by placing all foreign operations into a semi-independent, separate division. The international division is in turn organized by function, product, or again by geography (e.g., country units within a region). In some firms, the international division was cast in a staff capacity; that is, it played an advisory role supporting mainline operations. The establishment of the international division was the result of the growing scope of international activities and a realization that foreign markets often offered the most promising growth opportunity. It also reflected a shortage of skills and capabilities: with few employees possessing knowledge and experience in international operations, it made sense to cluster them together to provide expertise where and when needed, rather than have them spread throughout the organization without a critical mass.

The international division format was used primarily by firms with a low ratio of foreign to domestic revenues and low foreign product diversity, and it was replaced when the proportion of international operations grew or when corporate vision had changed. For instance, Aetna ditched its international division structure in favor of a global product structure in 2000, when the company leadership came to believe in the importance of global markets. Still, the international division, or a variation thereof, can be found today. Wal-Mart initially assigned its Arkansas-based International Support Division such responsibilities as new store development, but later delegated this task to its foreign subsidiaries. Wal-Mart combined international and domestic buying to increase its bargaining power with suppliers. Japanese and Korean firms often maintain an international division devoted to marketing, sales, and distribution. The division maintains responsibility for new business development and sales in the firm's foreign outposts. However, other foreign activities (e.g., finance) report to functional counterparts in the home country. The international division structure is still common among developing country multinationals (DMNEs) in the early phases of internationalization, but these companies typically transition to other structures as their international capabilities grow.

The Global Functional Structure

Functional compartmentalization into research and development, marketing, production, human resources, and the like can be found in all organizations, including those differentiated primarily along product line, customers, or geography. However, in firms using function as a primary differentiation mode, functional divisions maintain responsibility for worldwide operations, with functional managers reporting directly to the senior-most office holders. This allows for centralized control and the accumulation of functional experience and expertise. Functional structures are usually adopted by MNEs with narrow, integrated product lines. GE is one example of a global functioning structure with its division of nine CEOs of various operations (Aviation, Energy management, Healthcare, etc.) all under the CEO and chairman of the company. In decades past, the global functional design was widely used in the automobile industry but, as firms grew internationally, it has been replaced by geographic and product line designs that place functional responsibilities at lower organizational levels.

The Global Geographic Structure

In a geographic structure, regional divisions or regional headquarters are responsible for all activities pertaining to all products or services rendered within an area. Corporate headquarters retain responsibility for worldwide planning and control, with coordination handled by central staff. Geographic divisions are based not only on political borders but also on cultural similarities, economic realities, business prospects, regional integration (e.g., the EU), and tax and logistic considerations. Regional units are in turn segmented into geographic (i.e., country units within a region), product, or functional sub-units. Regional and country managers can also operate in a staff capacity. In the early 1970s, geographic structures could be found in two-thirds of all MNEs, but their share was down to roughly one-third by the mid-1980s. Still, the share has stabilized in the twenty-first century with geographic elements making a comeback, though not necessarily in the form of a full-fledged geographic structure. Persistent cultural, social, and economic diversities continue to underpin the geographic structure, and many MNEs with other structures incorporate geographical elements in their organizational design. Martin Sorrell, CEO of advertising MNE WPP Group, explained why his company was reintroducing a geographic element:

> I think we're losing country focus, which is why we're creating country managers in Holland, Italy and China . . . Our clients are doing the same thing. If you don't have someone leading the business [locally], you don't get government contact, education contacts and political contacts.[5]

In addition to facilitating key contacts with local stakeholders, geographic structures enable rapid response to changing local tastes, regulatory regimes, and volatile rates of exchange and tariffs. The format is useful for a company that is marketing-oriented and requires substantial adaptation of its products or services to local markets. Firms that are relatively new to international markets or are in the midst of expansion into such markets will also benefit from that structure.[6] Whereas in the past, geographic structures were used mostly by firms with homogeneous, mature, and stable product lines, today such structures also appeal to firms with differentiated product lines, a changing technological environment, and those farther down the internationalization route.[7] In 2013, Toyota diluted its businesses into four components: one for the developed markets of North America, Europe, and Japan; the second for emerging markets (China and Latin America); the third for Lexus operations; and the fourth unit centered on the development and production of vehicle components (e.g., engines and transmissions). This structure consolidated operations and sped up the decision-making process between GBUs.[8]

Nestlé is a world leader in foods and beverages and is also engaged in the production and distribution of pharmaceuticals and cosmetics. The 130-year-old Swiss-based company obtains almost all of its revenues from foreign markets. Hailing from a small domestic market, Nestlé started its internationalization early on, opening a factory in Brazil in 1921. Its geographic structure reflects the vital importance of localization in its core food business, in which customer preference in taste, presentation, packaging, and the like vary across national boundaries, as does their emotional link to a given product. Nestlé deviates from geographic departmentalization when it comes to businesses

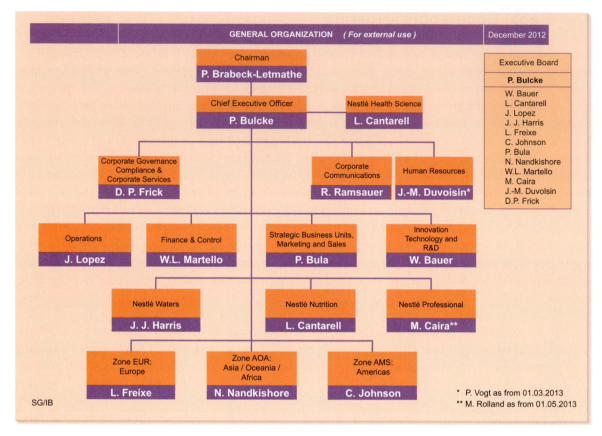

Exhibit 11.1 Nestlé's organizational chart
Source: Nestlé 2012, used with permission.

where product adaptation requirements are much smaller, such as pharmaceuticals or pet food. Nestlé also centralizes such functions as R&D, finance, purchasing, and back-office operations, where scale advantages are especially substantial, across all businesses (See Exhibit 11.1).

Underneath Nestlé's three main geographic regions of Europe, Asia/Oceana/Africa, and the Americas, are sub-regions. They encompass countries that are geographically contiguous, and, most importantly, share culture, language, and historical ties. Examples include Scandinavia (Sweden, Denmark, Norway, and Finland) and Iberia (Spain and Portugal) in the European region, or Canada and the United States in the Americas region. A large country, such as China, constitutes its own sub-region. The country manager directs all operations in his/her region in coordination with Nestlé's strategic business units under one executive. As in all geographic structures, however, the major operational responsibility rests with the country manager.

The geographic structure simplifies regional strategy and clearly defines accountability. Lines of authority are logical and provide direct channels for communication and evaluation

386

of individual performance. This structure also facilitates coordination of technical and functional capability across countries within a region. The structure facilitates consolidation of regional knowledge and expertise, with executives becoming highly familiar with the region under their jurisdiction. Regional divisions easily expand, if necessary, to accommodate new markets including acquisitions, a key advantage in today's business environment. From a career development perspective, geographic structures provide opportunities for broad management training, building a cadre of well-rounded senior executives. Many MNEs (e.g., Continental AG), now treat posting in certain regions as a requirement for promotions to senior positions. Muhtar Kent, Chairman and CEO of the Coca-Cola Company, outlines the importance of the regional experience:

> Ahmet, Steve and Irial are proven leaders with extensive international franchise, bottling operations and marketing experience. Ahmet is a strong international operator who has demonstrated success in leading our business in both emerging and developing markets. Steve has played a key role in leading our North America operations and ensuring a smooth and successful integration of CCE [Coca-Cola Enterprises]. Irial led the creation of BIG [Bottling Investment Group], and has been instrumental in driving executional excellence throughout our Company-owned bottling operations across four continents.[9]

The major disadvantages of the geographic structure are loss of global scale and coordination problems, especially in a context of diverse product lines and marketing characteristics. Product emphasis is weak, which interferes with the information flow between manufacturing and marketing. It is also difficult to transfer technology and ideas across regions, undermining leveraging of innovations. Systems and policies diverge and lose consistency, and there is costly duplication of functional and product investments and specialists. The result may be less than optimal deployment of resources and core competencies. Scale and synergy are reduced, although they can be maintained at the regional level (e.g., the Americas).

Generally speaking, a geographic structure makes sense when regional variations are substantial and important; that is, when those variations have the potential to alter the fundamental value proposition of the MNE or otherwise impact the way the company conducts its business. This is especially true when variations across product lines are relatively minor. For a manufacturing company, when the value-to-transport ratio is low, a geographic structure makes more sense. Similarly, a geographic design is more desirable when the firm needs to deliver service and support on-site, when it wants to be perceived as a local entity (e.g., due to nationalistic sentiments), and where geographical boundaries coincide with market segmentation.[10] In 2007, the Otis Elevator Company adopted a geographic structure. The corporation sells and services its products in more than 200 countries that differ in market characteristics, regulatory requirements, and the like. In 2012, Otis had six regional headquarters in four continents across the globe. In addition, 53,000 of its approximately 61,000 employees are located outside the United States and are subject to different labor laws and economic and technological conditions. [11]

Country Box

Internationalizing the Board of Directors

A crucial element linking ownership, governance, and organizational structure is the board of directors, which is the supreme decision-making organ for publicly traded corporations. The last decades saw a serious effort to internationalize the board of directors of companies, and in particular MNEs. The thinking was that a more internationally diverse board would be less ethnocentric in its strategic thinking and more tuned to developments in the global marketplace. Likewise, an internationally diverse board was expected to introduce different cultural perspectives and be more open to global staffing where executives hail from different parts of the world.

It can be assumed that differing types of firms require diverse styles of board internationalization. Research shows that both national and international directors with international experience have equal standing on the board, although hiring international directors may carry additional costs. In the Nordic region, research states that there is a high fraction of international board members in firms with a superior sales percentage abroad. In addition, there are more international directors in foreign firms, as well as more foreign ownership of firms whose shares are traded on foreign exchanges (Gregori et al., 22).

So far, however, change has been slow. Research conducted by Spencer Stuart shows that among the top 200 firms in the US in 2010, only 9 percent of members were from outside the US. Of this limited group, 19 percent came from the UK and 15 percent came from Canada, two countries that are in the same cultural cluster as the US, and hence less likely to produce much cultural diversity. Twelve percent came from India, where English is the primary business language, with 8 percent coming from Australia and France.

Sources: Spencer Stuart. Rep. no. 25: n.p., n.d., 2010; Spencer Stuart Board Index, Spencer Stuart, 2010. Web; Gregori, Aleksandra; Oxelheim, Lars; Randoy, Trond & Thomsen, Steen 2013. "On The Internationalization of Corporate Boards," Working Paper Series 951, Research Institute of Industrial Economics.

Combined Forms Using Geographic Areas

Some regional structures are run in line capacity as profit and loss centers, whereas others are operated in only staff capacity advising the line managers, with the regional headquarters providing vision and more informal coordination. Companies can also opt for mixed formats. In 2009, Mars adapted its global structure to leverage the growth of their biggest partners (BBDO, DDB, SapientNitro, and TBWA) and assigning them to different geographical locations. As of 2013, this was shown to be a successful avenue for handling the increasing interdependence between function, regional area, and product.[12]

Another mixed geographic structure is the Front-Back design that separates sales and service from R&D, manufacturing, and logistics. Such structures become more appealing when back-office operations are transferred to low-cost locations. Increasingly, however, such operations are outsourced to outside providers who contract with the MNE. ADP, a large outsourcing firm based in New Jersey, functions as human resource, payroll, tax, and benefits administration solutions from a single source hub for over 25,000 automotive dealerships internationally. Its mixed structure maintains internal cohesion while permitting firms to tap market opportunities, accommodate local regulatory environments, and coordinate and control multiple sources of diversity.

Region-Specific Factors in Establishing Geographic Structures

Effective drawing of regional boundaries minimizes duplication of functional and product efforts and facilitates intraregional and interregional coordination, allowing the MNE to maintain most of the advantages of a national subsidiary structure while pursuing a globally coordinated course. To achieve local responsiveness, regions are drawn to include countries that share political, economic, and logistic attributes while reflecting strategic considerations in terms of scale and product diffusion. In Chapter 6, we introduced the clustering of countries on the basis of employee attitudes, which can help in the drawing of regional boundaries in a geographic structure by incorporating cultural similarity and dissimilarity across regions. Visa facilitates electronic funds transfers through regional divisions. Visa Europe, a separate member-owned entity, operates in 36 countries across Europe, but its customers have access to Visa's global network, which spans over 200 countries worldwide, and which operates four main data centers across two continents. These centers are regionally specific, two in the United Kingdom, and two in the US.

A related decision in geographic structures is the location of the various regional headquarters. For instance, firms with an Asia-Pacific division can choose between Shanghai, Hong Kong, Singapore, Tokyo, Sydney, and Honolulu, among others, as locations for their regional headquarters. In making the decision, firms consider multiple factors, among them: proximity to major markets (e.g., Hong Kong is much closer to the Chinese Mainland than the other cities), cost and ease of doing business, communications, quality of life, and cultural barriers.[13] The success of Singapore shows the importance of infrastructure and human resources relative to geographic proximity. The island nation houses many MNE corporate and regional headquarters for companies such as Cloud Security Alliance, Panasonic, Castrol, and BP. Although Singapore is located in Southeast Asia, it attracts firms whose main operations extend from East Asia to North America.

The Global Product Structure

A firm embarks on a global strategy when it decides to locate manufacturing and other value-creation activities in the most appropriate global location to increase efficiency, quality, and innovation. In return for the gains obtained from such dispersion of activities, including learning, a company must cope with greater coordination and integration problems. It has to find a structure that can coordinate resource transfers between corporate headquarters and international units and among those units, while simultaneously providing the centralized oversight and control that global strategy requires.

In the global product format, product divisions are responsible for developing, producing, and/or marketing a product (or a line of products) worldwide. Structures may also be similarly organized along customer groups or market type. Product units are responsible for planning, design, production, and sales and hence must contain all functional resources, though they may occasionally pool resources across product lines, for instance, in the form of shared services. Product managers report to their corresponding divisions, which allows for integration of development, production, and marketing. MNEs that utilize product structures typically accommodate country-specific knowledge at the staff level, sometimes in an international division and sometimes within corporate headquarters. A product group headquarters, typically (but not always) located at central headquarters, coordinates the activities of both domestic and foreign operations within the product group. P&G recently moved the headquarters of their beauty and baby care business to Singapore to get close to the fast-growing Asian region. In addition, Unilever also moved some key executives from their corporate headquarters in London to their Singapore location.[14] Product group managers in the home country are responsible for organizing all aspects of value creation on a global basis.

The product group structure allows managers to decide how best to pursue a global strategy. In particular, executives must decide which value-creation activities, such as manufacturing or product design, should be performed in what country so as to leverage country-specific and firm-specific advantage. In recent years, MNEs have been moving manufacturing to low-cost countries like India or China, while establishing product design centers in Europe or the United States to take advantage of their respective capabilities, although this transition may be slowing down. While US and European MNEs often sought to accommodate such value chain dispersion within a global product structure, Japanese and South Korean MNEs tended to avoid this structure altogether, though some of them have introduced global product line elements. This should serve as a reminder that the home country of the MNE continues to exert important influence on major decisions, including organization design.

Generally speaking, the global product format is a response to the growing need to serve customers across borders as well as rapidly rising investment in product development that firms wish to spread across the largest possible number of markets and customers. As a result, this design is often found among diversified companies managing a portfolio of businesses in rapidly changing environments and in sectors where R&D expenditures are high and scale is especially important. Advances in communication technologies and decline in travel cost have made global product structures more attractive by making it possible to establish multinational teams consisting of staff stationed in disparate physical locations.

Types of Global Product Structure

The three basic types of product structures include the **related divisional format**, the **cluster format**, and the **unrelated holding company** format. In the related divisional format used in such firms as Interpublic (United States) and Sandvik (Sweden), product divisions report directly to headquarters. In the cluster format, used by AlliedSignal (United States) and Rhone-Poulenc (France; prior to its merger with Hoechst AG), a business reports to a cluster headquarters that is accountable to corporate headquarters for business results. In the unrelated holding company or conglomerate format, businesses are managed as investment centers, rather than profit centers, with wide reporting variations.[15]

In the past, Fiat, a diverse industrial enterprise that is Italy's largest private sector enterprise, was organized in a conglomerate-type structure. The company had divisions (operational sectors) reporting to a corporate head office that defined and oversaw group strategy and resource deployment. In 2010, the company took a step away from the conglomerate structure in order to allow the different departments to progress along their own paths.[16] US Airways Group, the holding company overseeing US Airways and merging with AMR, takes advantage of the holding company format. This structure makes it relatively easy to dispose of non-core assets while strengthening core assets.

Industry Box

"Ford 2000"

Effective from January 1, 1995, Ford Motor Company shifted from a geographic structure to a global product design. The company established five Vehicle Program Centers (VPCs): one for small front-wheel drive cars in Europe, split between Dunton, UK and Merkenich, Germany, and four in Dearborn, Michigan for large front-wheel drive cars, rear-wheel drive cars, personal-use trucks, and commercial trucks. Each VPC was assigned worldwide responsibility for the design, development, and engineering of the vehicles assigned to it. In changing its structure from geographic to product-based, Ford was hoping to avoid duplication and cut costs. As Alex Trotman, chairman and CEO at that time, suggested: "By integrating all our automotive processes and eliminating duplication of effort, we will use our creative and technical resources most effectively in our pursuit of total customer satisfaction . . . This new way of doing business . . . through simplification of engineering, supply, technical and other processes, will substantially reduce the cost of operating the automotive business."

While integrating North American and European product development processes, Ford decided to maintain separate Asian and Latin American operations for the time being. Apparently, these two markets were considered not only substantial in their future potential, but also sufficiently unique to merit the continuation of a geographical structure where country and regional adaptation are more easily obtained. Ford also maintained Jaguar and Aston Martin, its two acquisitions up until that time, as separate corporate entities, underlying the importance of maintaining their brand-name appeal.

"Ford 2000" encountered many challenges. Integration and coordination proved more difficult than expected and technical expertise was spread thinly across the five centers. British product developers had little understanding of the American consumer and found it difficult to come up with products that would appeal to that customer. For instance, they wondered why anyone would want a car with a red interior when that was long out of vogue in Europe. Similarly, the Ford Transit, a product sold mainly in the European market, was now under the responsibility of a vehicle center based in the United States. In 2002, Ford changed its structure, reintroducing geographical elements side-by-side with product line differentiation (e.g., the creation of the premium model group). Around 2008, it changed is structure again to the current design outlined in this chapter.

The main advantages of product-based structures are global vision and the ability to leverage resources across regions, encouraging strategic focus. Other advantages are simplicity, clear accountability, standardized product introduction, and enhanced speed and quality of decisions. New product lines are introduced on a self-contained basis, reducing interference from other operations. From a human resource perspective, product structures support the early testing of talented individuals and provide a focused career track. At the same time, this structure makes it difficult for different product groups to coordinate and exchange knowledge, and may be costly to maintain because its self-contained nature generates duplication and fragments organizational resources. Communications also tend to become difficult. For example, when Procter & Gamble shifted to a global product structure, establishing two global business units, it created a setting where Cincinnati-based employees report to a Venezuela-based manager. Employees complained about lack of communication with their bosses, having to hold videoconferences at inconvenient times.[17] Today, P&G have reworked their organizational structure so that marketing and development organizations are region-specific.

On the negative side, product designs are slow to adapt to local conditions. Firms can compensate for that deficiency by establishing a staff-level international division to handle business development, interact with key constituencies, and support line divisions. General Electric maintains an international division in Hong Kong headed by a vice-chairman to support its global growth and operations. The vice-chairman's roles also include a focus on high-growth marketplaces such as China, India, the Middle East, and Brazil, as well as search for potential alliance partners. The division places executives in more than 40 countries, although those are not full-fledged country managers but are rather growth leaders for the region. Still another solution to enhance the geographical sensitivity within a product structure is to establish a mixed product/geography format.

Samsung's organizational chart (Exhibit 11.2) shows a global product structure constructed around three main divisions (Consumer Electronics, IT & Mobile Communications, and Device Solutions), which are further parsed into smaller product line groups.

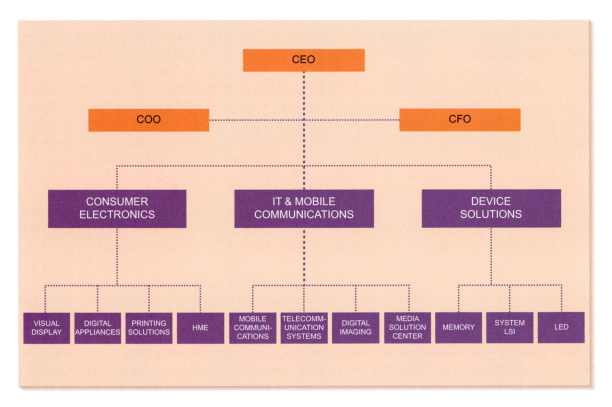

Exhibit 11.2 Samsung's organizational chart
Source: Samsung 2013, used with permission.

The Global Matrix Structure

The MNE structures described so far—the national subsidiary, international division, geographic, and product-based structures—have one thing in common: while they often use elements from other structures, priority is clearly assigned to the primary organizing element, be it the product in a product line structure, geography in the geographic structure, and so on. For example, regional managers will report to product managers in a product line structure. This provides clarity and unity of purpose, establishing an orderly "scalar chain" of duties and decision-making. Matrix designs are fundamentally different: they contain simultaneous, intersecting bases of differentiation and responsibility, though the process through which they function can differ. For instance, in some matrix structures, project or product teams "hire" and account for functional members from staff pools, whereas in other cases employees and other resources are assigned by a central authority. In either case, it is likely that some employees will simultaneously report to two or more supervisors. MNEs that use global matrix structures typically select a two-dimensional design that involves combinations of product and geography or product and function, though three-way structures are also prevalent.

Once thought of as the wave of the future, the matrix structure has lost some of its luster over the years; it has been criticized for its complexity and ambiguity.[18] The design is costly because it involves duplication of functions across units. Coordination difficulties undermine strategic focus and divert resources to coordination and integration tasks. Multiple, intersecting levels of authority slow decision-making, undermine accountability, and challenge performance evaluation, reducing the incentive for risk-taking. The operational complexity is especially manifested in an international context because of market and employee diversity.

Despite their complexity, many companies have developed the proficiency to run matrix structures effectively. These MNEs opt for the matrix design because it provides a way to simultaneously handle globalization and localization. The structure is designed "to help management cope with a highly complex, constantly changing global business environment by allowing the marshaling of diverse resources in multiple ways."[19] Among the advantages of the matrix structure are economies of scale and ease of transfer of technology to foreign operations and of new products to foreign markets, which, if properly handled, will lead to superior performance. The matrix can also be used as an interim structure for a firm shifting from one structure to another. For instance, Deutsche Bank adopted a matrix structure to ease its shift from a geographic to a global product design.

Several large European (e.g., Royal Dutch/Shell, Schlumberger) and US (Caterpillar, Cisco) MNEs that use the matrix structure successfully are highly diversified and have product lines that are based on similar technologies. Japanese, Chinese, and South Korean firms rarely use the matrix design, opting for functional structures combined with an international sales division. Successful matrix firms establish formal coordinating mechanisms, and while decisions are pushed down the line, corporate headquarters monitors, advises, and steers operational units. A common reporting system and intense effort at communications compensate for the matrix weaknesses. In addition, most matrix-structured MNEs are led by strong CEOs with solid international business experience who regard the matrix as a worthwhile investment whose return is a superior response to the complexity and diversity of global business. Most matrix MNEs also have a large cadre of executives who have spent most of their career in both foreign and domestic assignments with the same firm, facilitating coordination.

Opposite is the matrix structure of Caterpillar, a manufacturer of construction and mining equipment, diesel and natural gas engines, and diesel and electric locomotives. The structure (Exhibit 11.3) displays the three major differentiating themes, namely product, geography, and function. Note however that those elements are not uniformly present across the global organization, but are deployed almost on a "case-by-case" basis.

Another example of a matrix organization can be observed in Exhibit 11.4, which shows the structure of the Ford Motor Company in 2013. Since the company manufactures essentially one type of product (motor vehicle), the two axes of the matrix are function (left side of the matrix) and region. Similarly to the regional divisions found in many multinationals, the regions include the Americas (see Exhibit 11.5 for a detailed chart of this region), Europe, and Asia Pacifica, Africa and the rest of the world as a single region with tremendous differences but one where scale, at least until recently, did not justify creating a separate region (this is changing however with the rapid growth of Asian markets, especially China and India).

To prevent problems typical of matrix structures, Ford assigns clear responsibilities to the regions, which operate as profit and loss centers, and to the functions, which maintain professional and technical oversight. CEO Alan Mulally, who ran Boeing's commercial aircraft business before coming to Ford, notes that he rarely has to adjudicate disagreements and conflicts between the two axes of the matrix, though the structure requires intense interaction between and across functions and regions. As in other matrix organizations, Ford executives will often have two bosses, a functional and a regional head; their long-term career is more often tied to the professional side, where supervisors are more likely to be familiar with their area of specialization and with their career progression.

Interim Summary

1. As MNEs internationalize, they shift their structure from national subsidiary to international division and then to global designs.
2. MNEs select between a national subsidiary, international division, functional, geographic, global-product and matrix structures. Over the last decades, MNEs have gradually shifted away from geographic to global product structures. However, geography continues to play a key role in MNE structure and is seeing a partial comeback.
3. Two-dimension matrix structures in MNEs involve interfacing geographic/product or function/product combinations, while three-dimension structures are based on function/geographic/product differentiation. The matrix structure is the most complex to manage of all structural forms.

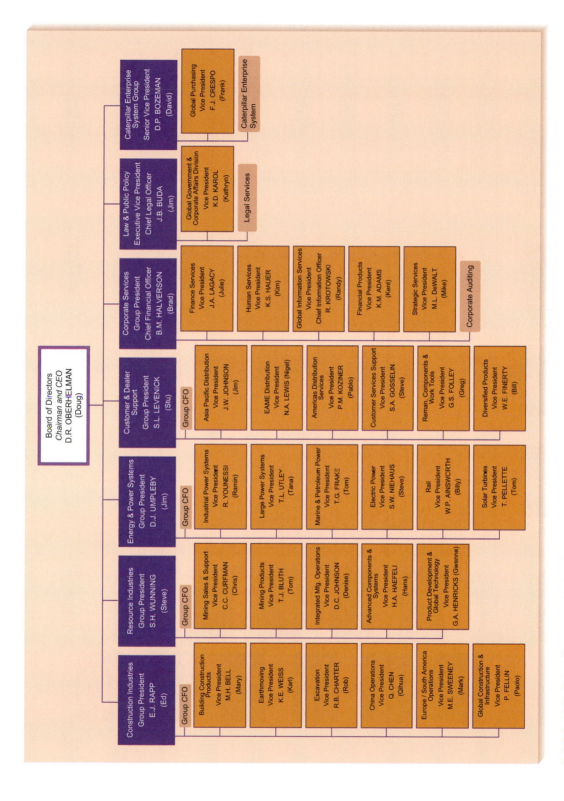

Exhibit 11.3 Caterpillar's organizational chart

Source: Reprinted Courtesy of Caterpillar Inc.

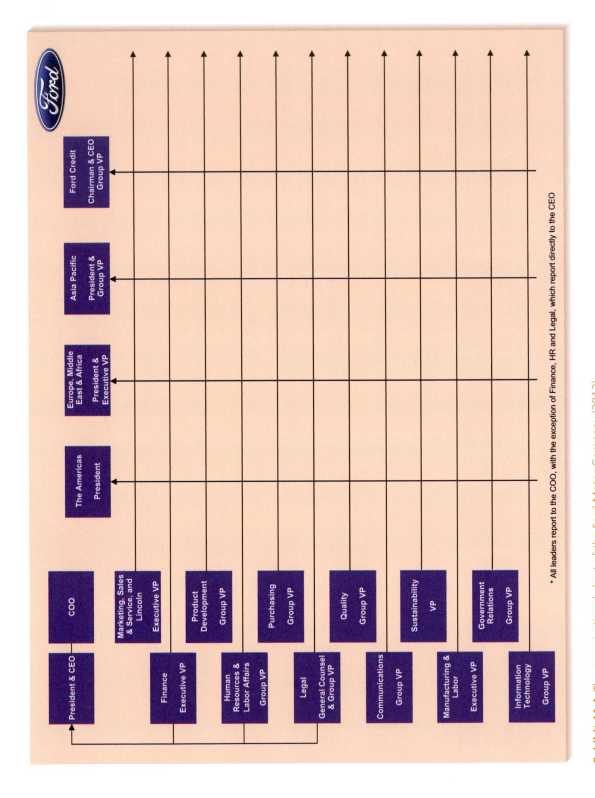

Exhibit 11.4 The organizational chart of the Ford Motor Company (2013)

Source: The Ford Motor company, 2013, used with permission.

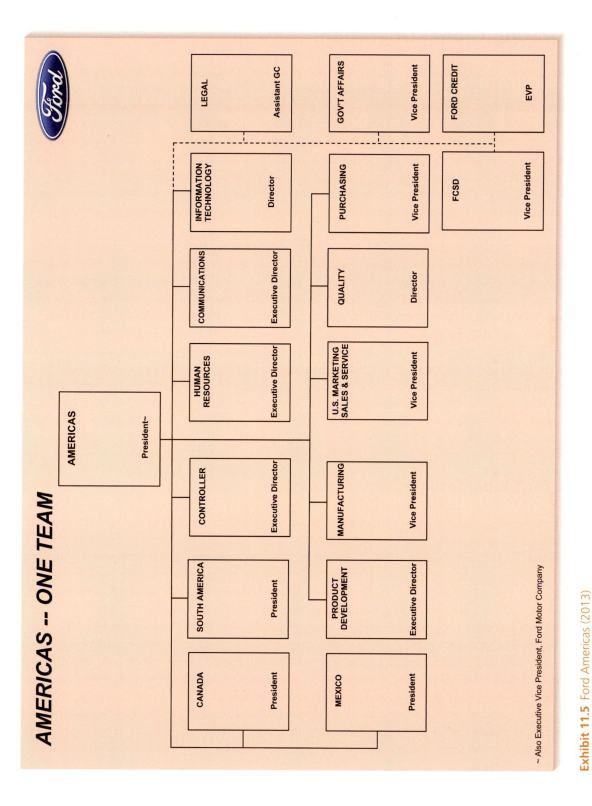

Exhibit 11.5 Ford Americas (2013)

Source: The Ford Motor company, 2013, used with permission.

Integrating Global Operations

The integration of sub-units in foreign countries in a large MNE relies on processes of control, coordination, and orientation. **Control** is the direct intervention in the operations of subsidiaries to ensure conformity with organizational goals. **Coordination** provides linkages between different task units across the organization, ensuring that they operate as parts of a whole rather than as separate organizations, preventing duplication, and maintaining unity of purpose. Coordination is associated with the integration of activities that are dispersed across subsidiaries, and is less direct, less costly, and has a longer time span than control. MNE headquarters are often unable to use centralized decision-making processes to maintain global control. Finally, **strategic orientation** is the indirect exercise of corporate direction, for instance, through the appointment of executives who share a strategic vision.

To control its subsidiaries, the MNE uses output (e.g., performance targets), bureaucratic (e.g., codified rules), and cultural mechanisms (e.g., the dissemination of corporate values). The diversity of countries, functions, and products challenges centralized control, making continuous monitoring necessary. Coordination helps the MNE deal with breadth (the number of units in the coordination network) and diversity (the number of functions coordinated). Formal coordination mechanisms include centralization, formalization, planning, output control, and behavioral control. Informal mechanisms include lateral relations (that is, horizontal linkages between units at the same or similar level), informal communication, and organizational culture. Coordination needs tend to be higher when international activities are more geographically dispersed. MNEs increasingly use strategic orientation in lieu of conventional controls to monitor the operation of foreign subsidiaries. Strategic orientation is less direct and less costly than control and coordination, but can have the most sustained effect.

Tools for Global Integration

Delegating decision-making to subsidiary managers abroad and/or product executives at headquarters without accompanying tools for integration will reduce the effectiveness and efficiency of international expansion. Major tools that can be used to maintain global integration include: (1) data and information system management; (2) managerial mechanisms and human resource management; (3) communication tools; (4) socialization practices; (5) expatriate selection and assignment; and (6) entry mode selection and sharing arrangements.

Data management tools can be used to control information systematically gathered by organizational members, the method by which such information is aggregated, analyzed, and interpreted, how and to whom it is circulated, and the way it is used in the decision-making and implementation process. Information systems must have a dual focus. Accounting and strategic data are aggregated for analytical purposes and to support integration (a portfolio of countries within a business) and responsiveness (a portfolio of businesses within a country). The flow of information can also be structured with sufficient asymmetry that individual managers will be encouraged to identify strongly with either responsive or integrative strategies, while others will develop more balanced perspectives.

Management tools can be used to set norms and standards of behavior as well as to establish sub-unit objectives that are consistent with a desired strategic direction. Such tools work both directly, through their actual impact on managers, and indirectly, through the precedents they set and the meanings they assign to specific situations and choices. Management tools also include conventional human resource management components such as career guidance, incentive systems, and management development. Less formal tools help develop norms, standards, and personal objectives. They assist in creating an internal advocacy process that reflects the conflicting needs for responsiveness and integration. Several managerial mechanisms can be used integrally: Planning processes can catalyze the process of strategic convergence and consensus building among executives whose initial perceptions and priorities differ. Management tools may create a climate in which executives are encouraged to interact and will be motivated to undertake and sustain successful lateral relationships. Rewards may be based more on participation and contribution than on individual results. Managerial development activities may emphasize a corporate-wide perspective and flexible attitudes. Career paths may create alternations between geographic and product-oriented responsibilities for individual managers so that they develop an empathy for both responsiveness and integration priorities.

Intensity of communication may be employed to balance integration-responsiveness relations. The communication intensity between a focal subsidiary and the rest of the MNE can be treated as a positive function of the frequency, informality, openness, and density of communications between the subsidiary, other units, and the head office. Frequent inter-unit communications facilitate the diffusion of innovations across subsidiaries. More intense communications create higher information-processing capacity, which is especially desirable when sub-units use differentiation strategies, rather than harvest or cost-leadership strategies. Effective adaptation to environmental uncertainty requires unstructured decision-making processes involving open communications. Overall, frequency, informality, openness, and density of communication between a focal subsidiary and the rest of the corporation should be higher for sub-units that play a greater part in global integration.

Corporate socialization of subsidiary managers can be an effective tool for global integration. **Corporate socialization** is the process by which subsidiary managers' values and norms are aligned with those of the parent corporation. Such socialization is a powerful mechanism for building identification with, and commitment to, the organization as a whole, as distinguished from the immediate sub-unit in which the manager is placed. Some of the key processes through which such socialization occurs are job rotation across foreign subsidiaries and management development programs involving participants from several sub-units. Global corporate socialization of a subsidiary's top management team should vary across subsidiary strategic roles. Socialization should be high for integrated players, medium for global innovators and implementers, and low for local innovators.

Dispatching expatriates to foreign subsidiaries and manipulating the ratio of expatriates in the top management team of subsidiaries are also important for maintaining global integration. Host-country nationals are generally more familiar with the local environment, develop stronger rapport with local managers, and have a stronger identification with, and commitment to, the local subsidiary than to the parent MNE. Cognitively, host-country nationals are likely to have a more comprehensive understanding of the local socio-cultural, political, and economic environment. In contrast, expatriate managers are likely to have a more comprehensive understanding of the MNE's overall global strategy. The local commitment of host-country nationals results from limited prospects for career progression outside the local subsidiary, though this may vary somewhat based on the subsidiary role, discussed earlier in this chapter. Expatriate managers tend to be more mobile, and so the ratio of expatriates as a percentage of the top management team should be higher for subsidiaries that play a bigger role in the MNE's global integration. We also know that MNEs hailing from high power-distance cultures tend to have a higher ratio of expatriates, so as to maintain higher control over subsidiaries.[20]

The entry mode selected also affects the MNE's ability to control local operations and integrate those businesses into its global network during subsequent operational stages. Other things being equal, the umbrella investment, wholly owned subsidiary, and dominant joint venture modes enable the MNE to exercise greater control and integration than a joint venture or other cooperative arrangements in which the MNE is a minority owner. Among other entry modes, the franchising and build-operate-transfer modes enable the MNE to better control foreign operations, as compared to licensing and leasing. MNEs should therefore align their entry mode selection with their needs for organizational control and global integration. In the case of joint ventures, the equity distribution between partners can make a substantial difference in control and integration. Majority equity ownership helps the MNE to not only protect its proprietary knowledge and control joint venture activities, but also to mitigate the partner firm's possible opportunism while strategically orienting the joint venture to be consistent with the MNE's global mission.

The Transition Challenge

Changing an organization design is never easy. First, the change requires many resources. For instance, for its transition to the "Ford 2000" structure, Ford assigned 27 senior executives to a transition team and embarked on a communications and training program for 1,700 senior and mid-level executives. The formal transition period lasted for eight months, although many of the changes and integration processes lingered for years. Second, during the transition, many companies suffer reduced performance as employees and outside constituencies (e.g., customers, suppliers) face ambiguities concerning assigned duties and responsibilities. Competitors will often take advantage of such vulnerability by going after the firm's customers during the vulnerable transition period.

The Corporate Headquarters

An essential component of organizational structure in MNEs is the corporate headquarters. While relatively small—a Conference Board report suggests that well-managed firms cap their headquarters staff at 2 percent of total head count—the board is a key player in MNE management. It is from its headquarters that the firm leverages and manages its resources, controls and coordinates its far-flung international operations, and balances scale and standardization with needs for local adaptation. The corporate headquarters provides overall leadership and strategic direction, and contributes to the development of company identity and vision. Even at ABB, where decisions are pushed down the line as much as possible, corporate headquarters monitors, advises, and "steers" operational units. In research and development, traditionally one of the most centralized functions, corporate headquarters sets a general direction while shifting more and more responsibilities, including product development, to centers in foreign locations (see also Chapter 13).

Corporate headquarters' employees can be found not only at headquarters, but also in divisional centers and in international locations where they provide added guidance to foreign subsidiaries and affiliates. Such guidance is especially important in the case of strategic alliances (e.g., joint ventures) that are an increasingly popular mode through which firms enter or defend their position in a foreign market.

Interim Summary

1. MNE headquarters integrate global operations through several mechanisms including output, bureaucratic mechanisms, and cultural mechanisms. Corporate culture and information systems also play an integration role.
2. Global integration tools are diverse (e.g., reporting system, communication intensity, and expatriate policy). To choose the right tools, MNEs must ensure that they possess the organizational infrastructure to implement them effectively.

Chapter Summary

1. Organizational design is driven by strategy, but it is also a driver of strategies. The basic strategies driving the MNE design are the multidomestic, the global, and the transnational.
2. The multidomestic strategy drives a decentralized system in which foreign subsidiaries are virtually independent. Under global strategy, international sub-units are under centralized control from corporate headquarters, with standardized products or services suitable for a variety of markets. Under transnational strategy, sub-units coordinate their activities with headquarters and with one another; they also share knowledge and resources.
3. A subsidiary's role can be: (a) autonomous, in which it enjoys a great deal of leeway; (b) receptive, in which it is closely integrated with headquarters; or (c) active, in which it coordinates with other subsidiaries. Subsidiary roles can also be classified by knowledge flow (global innovators, integrated players, implementers, and local innovators) and by subsidiary importance and competence (strategic leaders, contributors, implementers, and black holes).
4. MNE designs include the national subsidiary structure, the international division structure, the global functional structure, the global geographic structure, the global product structure, and the global matrix structure.
5. The main challenge of MNE design is to find the proper balance between differentiation and integration across functional, product, and regional lines. To do this properly, the MNE should devise effective mechanisms for global control, coordination, and integration, without hindering the subsidiaries in their roles.
6. Global integration tools include data management, information system, communication, entry mode, expatriate assignment, planning, human resource management, and socialization, among others. Information and culture-based control are becoming more important than rigid or bureaucratic control.

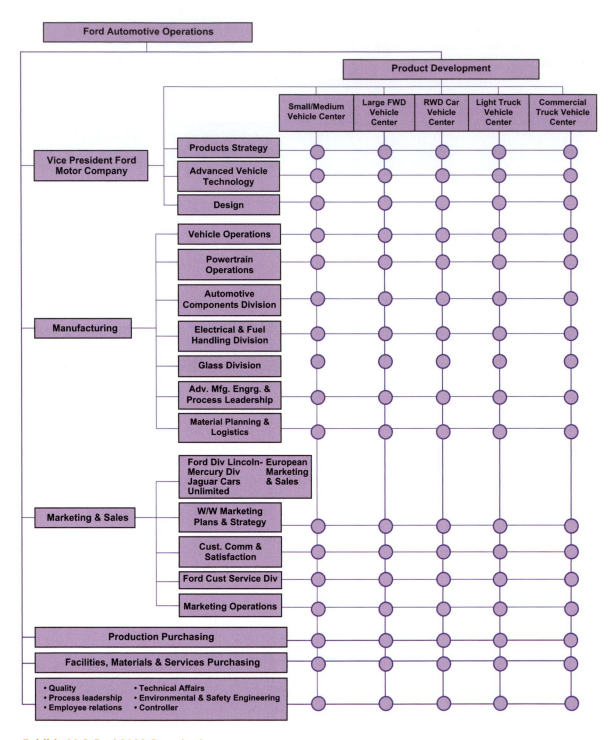

Exhibit 11.6 Ford 2000 Organization

Source: The Ford Motor Company, 1995, used with permission.

Notes

1   J.C. Abegglen and G. Stalk, Jr., *Kaisha: The Japanese Corporation*, New York: Basic Books, 1985.

2   J.C. Jarillo and J.I. Martinez, "Different roles for subsidiaries: The case of multinational corporations in Spain," *Strategic Management Journal*, 11, 7, 1990, 501–512.

3   A.K. Gupta and V. Govindarajan, "Knowledge flow and the structure of control within multinational corporations," *Academy of Management Review*, 16, 4, 1991, 768–792.

4   C.A. Bartlett and S. Ghoshal, *Managing Across Borders*, Boston, MA: Harvard Business School Press, 1989; C.K. Prahalad and Y. Doz, *The Multinational Mission: Balancing Local Demands and Global Vision*, New York: Free Press, 1987.

5   E. Hite and J.A. Trachtenberg, "One size doesn't fit all," *Wall Street Journal*, October 1, 2003, B1.

6   The Conference Board, "Organizing for global competitiveness: The business unit design," Report 1110-95-RR.

7   R.A. Daft, *Essentials of Organization Theory and Design*, New York: Thomson, 2000.

8   Yoshio Takahashi and Yoree Koh. "Toyota shakes up top rank." Editorial, *Wall Street Journal* [New York City], March 7, 2013, B3; *Wall Street Journal*, Web, March 7, 2013.

9   "The Coca-Cola Company announces new operating structure and senior leadership appointments," *The Coca-Cola Company*, n.p., July 30, 2012; Web, February 2013.

10 J.R. Galbraith, *Designing Organizations*, New York: Wiley, 1995.

11 "Otis 2012 Fact Sheet," *Fact Sheet*, Otis World Wide, 2012, Web, February 2013.

12 Mars, *Mars, Incorporated to Refine Global Creative Structure for Biggest Brands.Mars.com*, n.p., September 2009, Web, February 2013.

13 D. McClain and O. Shenkar, "Corporate downsizing, telecommunications and culture: Influence on Hawaii's competitiveness as a regional headquarters location," Report to the Department of Business, Economic Development and Tourism, State of Hawaii, 1995.

14 Jack Neff, "From Cincy to Singapore: Why P&G, others are moving key HQs," *Ad Age | Global*, n.p., June 11, 2012, Web, February 2013.

15 The Conference Board, "Organizing for global competitiveness: The product design," Report 1063-94-RR, 1994.

16 "Fiat to spin off industrial-vehicles business," *Wall Street Journal*, n.p., April 21, 2010, Web, February 2013.

17 E. Nelson, "Rallying the troops at P&G," *Wall Street Journal*, August 31, 2000, B1.

18 T.J. Peter and R.H. Waterman, *In Search of Excellence*, (reprint edition), New York City, NY: Harper-Collins, 2006.

19 The Conference Board, "Organizing for global competitiveness: The matrix design," Report #1088-94-RR, 1994.

20 D. Brock, O. Shenkar, A. Shoham and I.C. Siskocick, "National culture and expatriate deployment," *Journal of International Business Studies*, 39, 3, 2008, 1–18.

Acknowledgment: This chapter borrows from various Conference Board reports. We are grateful to the Conference Board for permission to use this material.

chapter 12

building and managing global strategic alliances (GSAs)

DEFINING GLOBAL STRATEGIC ALLIANCES   407

BUILDING GLOBAL STRATEGIC ALLIANCES   413

MANAGING GLOBAL STRATEGIC ALLIANCES   421

Do You Know?

1. Why have so many firms chosen global strategic alliances (GSAs) to expand globally, and why have many GSAs failed? What types of GSAs can firms choose? Can you distinguish between equity joint ventures and non-equity (cooperative) joint ventures? Do you think alliances between two competitors such as Toshiba and Philips are advisable?

2. How should firms select appropriate partners in another country? If you are planning to initiate an international joint venture, what criteria will underlie your partner selection, and how should you prepare for negotiating joint venture contracts?

3. How will you decide the ownership level in an equity joint venture? Is a majority status necessarily better than minority or a 50–50 status? If your company is the minority party, what measures could you take to have more control over the joint venture?

4. In what ways can inter-partner cooperation be nurtured to maximize joint payoff? How do you balance the tension between cooperation and control? If you are in charge of Xerox's alliance with Fuji in Japan, how do you safeguard your proprietary knowledge? If you want to exit from this alliance, how should it be done?

OPENING CASE Alliances between Infineon Technologies AG and Motorola, Inc.

Infineon Technologies AG of Germany and Motorola, Inc. of the US have developed a series of global strategic alliances (GSAs) despite the substantial changes in their respective corporate affiliations and business portfolios over the years.

Their most impactful GSA between the two companies was Semiconductor 300 in Germany. Infineon, a recognized market leader for the Chipcard IC, was at the time a subsidiary of Siemens AG, one of the world's largest and oldest electrical engineering and electronics companies based in Germany. Motorola was a leading provider of wireless communications, advanced electronics, two-way radios, and data communications. Given the strengths of each partner—Siemens's chip making and Motorola's semiconductor abilities—it is not surprising that these two companies joined forces to increase productivity and gain more advantages through the Semiconductor 300 GSA. This is not the first time the two have joined together for a project. In 1995, for example, Infineon and Motorola signed a memorandum of understanding to form a $1.5 billion GSA to establish a state-of-the-art eight-inch semiconductor plant in White Oak, Virginia. The successes in cooperative relationships between the two companies aided this new partnership. They were able to accelerate the decision-making process concerning issues such as ownership allocation and organizational form.

Semiconductor 300 was a 50–50 GSA (i.e., equal ownership). It sought to develop the next generation of 300-mm 12-inch wafers, an important innovation for the semiconductor industry, which constantly requires more powerful integrated circuits at lower prices. The GSA provided both companies with first mover advantages in the 300-mm memory chip technology arena. The Infineon and Motorola GSA also created a valuable resource synergy. While Infineon provided Motorola with world-class technology, service, and global reach, Motorola brought expertise in advanced logic products and leading-edge manufacturing equipment development. In addition, Infineon provided leadership in dynamic, random access memory, and logic products along with state-of-the-art 0.25-micron process technology. Teaming with Motorola, Infineon was able to expand its capacity to challenge the top five chip makers and expand its telecommunications portfolio.

Their collaboration continued and even expanded after Infineon was spun off from Siemens AG and Motorola spun off its semiconductor division, both in 1999. In 2002, the two partners formed a new company with Agere Systems (a spinoff from Lucent Technologies of the US) to develop digital signal processors (DSPs) that are widely used in communications systems, wireless phones, and consumer electronic products. In 2007, they again joined hands in the development of a new multi-mode single-chip frequency transceiver for 3G and 4G mobile phones. This long-term partnership has evidently helped both firms focus on what they each can do best and stay on the cutting edge of technology in their respective businesses.

Defining Global Strategic Alliances

Types of GSAs

As the preceding case illustrates, the global strategic alliance (GSA) has become a popular vehicle for MNEs to expand globally and improve their global competitive advantage. Through Semiconductor 300, Siemens and Motorola each gain more than they would by working individually. **Global strategic alliances** are cross-border partnerships between two or more firms from different countries with an attempt to pursue mutual interests through sharing their resources and capabilities. Broadly, there are two basic types of GSAs: *equity joint ventures* and *cooperative (or contractual) joint ventures*. The former involve equity contributions, the latter do not.

The equity joint venture (EJV) is a legal entity whose equity is jointly owned by two or more parent organizations that collectively invest financial as well as other resources to pursue certain objectives. It can be formed via either the establishment of a new legal entity (*de novo* joint venture) or one firm's partial acquisition of the equity in another firm with the original owner of the other firm (e.g., one or more owner-managers) retaining a nontrivial portion of the equity. In an international setting, these parent firms are from different countries. To set up an EJV, each partner contributes cash, facilities, equipment, materials, intellectual property rights, labor, or land-use rights. An EJV can be structured on a 50–50 ownership arrangement (e.g., the Prudential–Mitsui EJV in which Prudential Insurance and Mitsui Trust & Banking each have 50 percent ownership), or a majority-minority basis (e.g., the EJV between the US's Corning and Mexico's Vitro in which Corning assumes majority ownership, 51 percent, whereas Vitro owns 49 percent).

The **cooperative joint venture** (CJV) is a contractual agreement whereby profits and responsibilities are assigned to each party according to stipulations in a contract. Unlike an EJV, each partner that contributes assets to a CJV retains legal ownership and control rights to those assets, rather than turning them into the equity of a jointly owned venture. Although the two firms entering into a contractual partnership have the option of forming a limited liability entity with legal person status, most cooperative ventures involve joint activities without the creation of a new corporate entity. Non-equity cooperative ventures have freedom to structure their assets, organize their production processes, and manage their operations. This flexibility can be attractive for a foreign investor interested in property development, resource exploration, and other projects in which the foreign party incurs substantial up-front development costs. Further, this type of venture can be developed quickly to take advantage of short-term business opportunities, then dissolved when its tasks are completed.

CJVs include several sub-forms: *joint exploration, research and development consortia,* and *co-production,* all of which are typical forms of contractual partnerships. Others include *co-marketing, long-term supply agreements,* and *joint management.*

Joint exploration projects (e.g., Atlantic Richfield's offshore oil exploration consortia in Brazil, Ecuador, and Indonesia) are a special type of non-equity cooperative alliance whereby the exploration costs are borne by the foreign partner, with development costs later shared by a local entity. Although such explorations allow the foreign firm to manage specific projects, this type of alliance does not necessarily result in the establishment of new limited liability enterprises. By comparison, the costs of a **research and development consortium** (e.g., Microsoft's R&D consortium with Cambridge University, England) may be allocated according to an agreed-upon formula, but the revenue of each partner depends on what it does with the technology created. In **co-production or co-service** agreements, such as the Boeing 787 project involving Boeing, Japan Aircraft Development Corporation (itself a consortium of Mitsubishi, Kawasaki, and Fuji), and numerous other contracted firms, each partner is responsible for manufacturing a particular part of the product and, in the case of the 787, many firms also act as assemblers of intermediate parts before they are sent to Boeing's final assembly plant in Everett, Washington. Each partner's costs are therefore a function of its own efficiency in producing that part. Revenue is a function of prompt delivery by the intermediaries and successful sales of the 787 by the dominant partner, Boeing. In the co-service arrangement between Delta Air Lines and Air France, the focus is on aligning commercial policies and procedures, coordinating transatlantic operations, and combining frequent-flier programs. Although Delta and Air France each retain independent fleets, together they look for ways to improve operating efficiencies.

The **co-marketing arrangement** provides a platform in which each party can reach a larger pool of international consumers. For example, Praxair (US) and Merck KGA (Germany) established their global alliance in 1999 through which each uses the other's distribution channels to provide an offering combining Praxair's gases and Merck's wet chemicals to semiconductor customers. This co-marketing alliance gives both parties entry into the other's main markets. Praxair has a strong distribution infrastructure in North America, but is a minor player in Europe and Asia. Merck, in contrast, is strong in Europe and Asia, but absent from the US wet chemical market. In a typical **long-term supply agreement**, the manufacturing buyer provides the supplier with updated free information on products, markets, and technologies, which in turn helps ensure the input quality. IKEA, for example, offers such information to its dozens of foreign suppliers and also provides them with free periodic training. As a result, many of IKEA's foreign suppliers are committed to becoming its long-term exclusive suppliers. Finally, a **co-management arrangement** is a loosely structured alliance in which cross-national partners collaborate in training (technical or managerial), production management, information systems development, and value chain integration (e.g., integrating inbound logistics with production or integrating outbound logistics with marketing). Partnership provides a vehicle for firms to quickly and efficiently acquire skills that cannot be bought from a public market. Co-management arrangements occur because international companies often realize that they lack the managerial skills necessary for running foreign operations, while local companies often find that they can benefit from foreign counterparts' international experience and organizational skills. Therefore, foreign and local companies can benefit from complementary managerial expertise contributed through an alliance.

Rationales for Building GSAs

Although GSAs take several different forms, they share some common rationales. Firms team together seeking some synergy. **Synergy** means additional economic benefits (financial, operational, or technological) arising from cooperation between two parties that provide each other with complementary resources or capabilities. In practice, these synergies and related economic benefits can be the result of *risk reduction, knowledge acquisition, economies of scale and rationalization, competition mitigation, improved local acceptance,* and *market entry.*[1]

First, *a GSA allows a company to enter into activities that might be too costly and risky to pursue on its own.* If an investment project is too expensive or too risky for single firms to handle alone, they may join forces to share the risk. This is the case with oil exploration and commercial aircraft manufacturing where large, risky projects call for inter-firm collaboration. Having considered the fact that the design, development, and production of a new aircraft engine require more than ten years at a cost of close to $2 billion, General Electric (US) and Snecma (France) established CFM International, a 50–50 joint venture, to share the risks and costs involved in new aircraft engine development. Moreover, if the business environment in a host country is highly uncertain or unfriendly to foreign firms, a GSA with a local firm may allow an MNE to share political risks and defuse hostile local reactions. Finally, alliances can be used to cut the costs of leaving a business. Exiting an industry via an alliance also permits management to withdraw with the company's reputation intact. Minimizing exit costs is one of the considerations underlying Siemens' alliance with Toshiba and IBM to develop the 256-megabit dynamic random access memory chip.

Second, *a GSA allows a firm to acquire partner knowledge or resources to build competitive strength.* This knowledge acquisition may occur at significantly reduced costs—with capital investment much lower than if the firm either developed it alone or via an acquisition.[2] Access to a partner's technology enables a firm to enjoy the fruits of research and development while avoiding rapidly escalating R&D costs. Shell and ICI (Imperial Chemical Industries) share their complementary resources in producing rigid foam through a global alliance. ICI is highly regarded in the polyurethane market for its technical support and ability to bring new products to market, whereas Shell is a world leader in the technology for rigid polyether polyols.

Third, *a GSA allows a firm to enhance economies of scale or scope and to improve product rationalization.* By sharing financial resources that are otherwise not available to each individual partner, two smaller companies in an industry can form an alliance to achieve economies of scale similar to those that are enjoyed by their larger competitors. GSA partners may also cooperate to take advantage of pooled non-financial resources. The joint use of complementary resources, competencies, and skills possessed by different organizations can create synergistic effects, which none of the companies is able to achieve if acting alone. For example, Airbus aircrafts were manufactured under a consortium composed of France's Aerospatiale and Germany's Daimler-Benz Aerospace, British Aerospace, and Spain's Construcciones Aeronauticas up until 2001. Because most aerospace projects require huge capital outlays, pooling both technological and financial resources is a rational step. Today, Airbus retains its pan-European presence but is now a subsidiary of European Aeronautic Defense and Space Company, which was created via the series of mergers among the German, Spanish, and French constituents in the Airbus Consortium.

Fourth, *a GSA allows a firm to prevent or reduce competition (potential or existing) with a major rival.* Clark Equipment and Volvo formed an alliance to produce earth-moving equipment; alone, neither could generate enough volume in their traditional home markets (United States and Europe) to survive against such global industry leaders as Caterpillar and Komatsu. Meanwhile, a GSA may be used in a more aggressive strategy. Caterpillar Tractor linked up with Mitsubishi in Japan to put pressure on the profits and market share that their common competitor Komatsu enjoyed in its Japanese market (about 80 percent of Komatsu's global cash flow was generated from Japan). Thus, while the alliance proved quite beneficial to Caterpillar, since it removed Mitsubishi as a potential rival, it acted as a major thorn in Komatsu's side in the Japanese market it held so dear. In 2012, Caterpillar became sole owner of the allied venture, though Komatsu still retains a much higher share of the Japanese market.

GSAs can also be used to develop technological standards that help control the competition within an industry. For example, Sematech, a GSA among several electronic and semiconductor firms, facilitated the adoption of the UNIX standard operating system for workstation computer producers. Over a decade ago, IBM formed a strategic alliance with multiple other manufacturing, development, and technology firms focused on semiconductor research and development. The collaboration, known as Technology Development Alliance, has delivered multiple generations of advanced bulk processing technologies, and helped IBM retain its strong foothold in the industry.[3]

Fifth, *a GSA allows a firm to boost local acceptance as perceived by foreign consumers.* A foreign firm can piggyback on a local partner to gain access to the local market. With India and China emerging as two of the largest and fastest growing automotive markets in the world, GM knew it needed to expand its presence in the region. In 2002, GM formed a partnership with SAIC Motor and the Wuling Group in China to create SAIC-GM-Wuling Automobile Co. Ltd. Today, GM operates in China through ten different joint ventures, with the SAIC-GM-Wuling Automobile Co. contributing almost half of its Chinese sales and with sales in the Chinese market attributable for approximately 45 percent of GM's stock value.[4] Without fully understanding the consumer behavior, distribution network, and effective marketing strategies and practices in a specific country, a foreign wholly owned subsidiary has substantial potential for failure. The distinctive marketing and distribution practices in Japan encourage foreign companies to set up partnerships with Japanese companies as the most practical means of getting into the market. Similarly, many Japanese MNEs with little or no direct presence in Europe have moved aggressively to establish partnerships with their European counterparts.

Finally, *a GSA allows a firm to bypass entry barriers into a target foreign country.* Many governments, particularly in developing countries, pressure MNEs to conduct FDI in the form of equity joint ventures rather than wholly owned subsidiaries. To the foreign firm, an alliance with a local organization, either business or governmental, may be required in order to enter these countries. With Coca-Cola out, Pepsi entered India in the mid-1980s through a joint venture with the government-owned Punjab Agro Industrial Corporation (PAIC) and Voltas India Ltd. During that time, the Indian government imposed many restrictions on profit repatriation, technology transfer, and product distribution. Pepsi managed to overcome these obstacles through cooperation with local partners that contributed their market power, marketing channels, and strong ties with officials to the joint operations.

Challenges Facing GSAs

Not every firm should build GSAs to expand globally, nor is building GSAs necessarily a superior strategy to other investment choices under all circumstances. According to a survey by McKinsey & Company and Coopers & Lybrand, about 70 percent of GSAs fall short of expectations.[5] More complex than the single organization, GSAs involve multiple inter-organizational relationships (between the parent firms, between alliance managers and the foreign parent, between alliance managers and the local parent, and between alliance managers nominated by different parents). Each of these relationships can be extremely difficult to manage. GSAs represent an intercultural and inter-organizational linkage between two separate parent companies that join forces with different strategic interests and objectives. Inter-partner conflict may arise from sources such as cross-cultural differences, diverging strategic expectations, and incongruent organizational structures. These conflicts in turn can lead to instability and poor performance of the alliance.

The aforementioned complexity generates problems and risks for using GSAs. First, *loss of autonomy and control* often creates inter-partner conflicts and alliance instability. Each partner may want to control the alliance's operations, so coordination and governance costs are generally higher. Cross-cultural partners may disagree on long-term objectives, time horizons, operating styles, and expectations for the alliance.

Second, the *risk of possible leakage* of critical technologies may be high and often difficult to avoid. Committing distinctive resources is often necessary for gaining a competitive edge in a foreign market. This, however, may lead to leakage of valuable intellectual property (known as *appropriability hazard*). Because distinctive resources are relatively difficult to specify, contract, and monitor, hazards associated with limited protection of such rights are particularly high for these resources, especially in developing countries where intellectual property rights systems have not yet been fully established. In the absence of strong control over alliance

411

activities and self-protection mechanisms, local partners may disseminate the foreign investor's critical knowledge to third parties.

Third, inter-partner *differences in strategic goals* often lead to cumbersome decision-making processes, which may in turn cause strategic inflexibility. This may be compounded when the alliance managers do not share strategic directions and goals set by parent firms. In the absence of sufficient organizational control over alliance activities, GSAs may even be considered impediments to the flexibility of an MNE's global strategy. The MNE may need to maintain global integration of all parts of its network (outside the GSA) for strategic or financial purposes, but because of the inflexibility of the GSA, global optimization may not be possible for outsourcing, capital flows, tax reduction, transfer pricing, and rationalization of production.

Finally, local partners may *become global competitors* in the future, after developing skills and technology via the alliance. Japanese firms, for example, often plan ahead to increase the benefits they extract from a GSA, leaving the European or American partners in an inferior strategic position. In other words, they may look upon partnerships as a strategic competitive move, based on tactical expediency.[6] Reflecting on its GSA with NEC, one senior executive in Varian Associates (a US producer of advanced electronics including semiconductors) concluded that "all NEC had wanted to do was to suck out Varian's technology, not sell Varian's equipment."[7] More recently, there have been concerns that Chinese companies are gaining competitive advantages rapidly from their strategic alliance partners.[8] Any international business manager should be aware, however, that the risk of creating a competitor is present whenever a hi-tech firm works with a technologically less advanced partner, since unintentional leakage and intentional theft of industrial secrets have been on the rise ever since a Jesuit priest secretly copied the Chinese technology for making fine porcelain and took it back to Europe in the 1800s.[9] What is critical to the global success of hi-tech firms is to form a realistic assessment of the risk and develop an effective strategy for managing it. While the best approach for some firms may be to avoid involvement in GSAs, many high-tech MNEs are successful in managing the risk by tightly controlling the types of technologies being transferred and staying ahead of their partners through successive technological upgrades. Panasonic (formerly Matsushita), for instance, keeps its cutting-edge technologies (e.g., those for big-screen TVs) at home while employing Chinese engineers to design lower-end products (e.g., DVD players) at a much lower cost without compromising its competitive advantage.[10]

Because of the preceding drawbacks, international managers should make a strategic assessment about the necessity of building GSAs in the course of a feasibility study. This assessment emphasizes value creation and thus is more beneficial than conducting a cost-benefit analysis. This is especially true when the alliance is used to learn about a new environment and thereby to reduce the uncertainties present in a new territory. This calls for a strategic, rather than a financial, view to capture value creation. Along with the increasing competition and technological development, GSAs are increasingly engaging multiple sophisticated businesses, calling for distinctive resources from multiple partners. This makes value-creation analysis for building GSAs more important and more difficult at the same time. Following this assessment, managers need to plan carefully for partner selection, contract negotiations, and alliance structuring (see Exhibit 12.1).

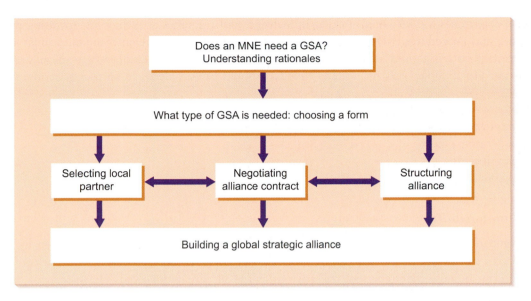

Exhibit 12.1 Key issues underlying building GSAs

Interim Summary

1. There are two basic types of GSAs: equity joint ventures and non-equity (cooperative or contractual) joint ventures. Cooperative joint ventures include joint exploration, R&D consortium, co-production, co-marketing, joint management, long-term supply agreement, and so forth. Major advantages of building GSAs include cost/risk sharing, knowledge acquisition, product rationalization, competition reduction, local acceptance, and market access.
2. Many GSAs have failed, owing to inability to overcome inherent challenges such as loss of control, knowledge leakage, goal incongruence, cultural clashes, differences in managerial philosophies, and emerging competition between partners.

Building Global Strategic Alliances

Selecting Local Partners

Partner selection is widely recognized as a vital factor in GSA success. All the benefits articulated in the preceding section may or may not be achieved depending on who has been selected as the partner. Benefits will accrue only through the retention of a partner that can provide the complementary skills, competencies, or capabilities that will assist the firm in accomplishing its strategic objectives.[11] Partner selection determines a GSA's mix of skills, knowledge, and resources as well as its operating policies, processes, and procedures.[12] During the process of GSA formation, foreign companies must identify what selection criteria should be employed as well as the relative importance of each criterion. Generally, as illustrated in Exhibit 12.2, five criteria (five Cs) should be considered in partner selection:

- Compatibility of goals
- Complementarity of resources
- Cooperative culture
- Commitment
- Capability

Goal Compatibility

Goal compatibility refers to the congruence of strategic goals set for an alliance between its parent firms. Goals for individual parents can be different, but goals set for the alliance must be compatible or congruent, because they represent collective gains for all parents involved. The success of the consortium between Boeing and three Japanese heavy industry companies to design and build the 767 is partially attributable to goal compatibility. Boeing sought foreign partners to ease its financial burden and operational risks, while the Japanese firms tried to expand their role in the aerospace industry. The Japanese are now significantly increasing their participation in the industry, providing an ever-increasing portion of production parts and assembly. Boeing has reduced the risks of development by adding more partners and by lowering the financial commitment required for production. When a GSA's collective goals set by different parents are incongruent, inter-partner conflicts are inevitable in the subsequent phase of operations. In this case, firms are more likely to use opportunistic rather than cooperative strategies during joint operations. For instance, foreign parents want joint ventures in China to target the local market, whereas Chinese parents may want these ventures to emphasize international markets or as a channel to acquire foreign technologies. This incongruence creates conflicts, as reflected in Peugeot's divorce from its local partner, Guangzhou Automotive Manufacturing Company.

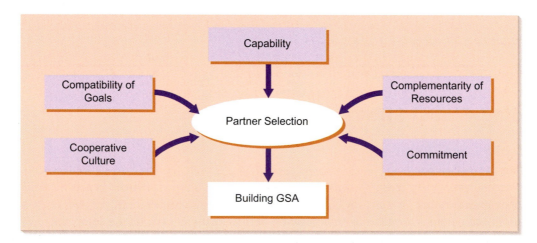

Exhibit 12.2 The five-Cs scheme of partner selection

To ensure goal compatibility, MNEs often partner with companies that have been cooperative in the past. For example, the GSA between Mitsubishi Electric and Westinghouse Corp. proceeded in an orderly fashion, partly because ties between the two companies date back to the 1920s. Previous relationships were also behind the partner selection process when LOF Glass and Nippon Sheet Glass (NSG) each spotted an opportunity in the nascent Korean auto industry. Similarly, NSG and Hankuk—which became the venture's local Korean partner—had technical and capital ties for 15 years. IBM and Siemens have also built on early ties to broaden and strengthen their alliance. Their cooperation dates back to a 1989 agreement to develop 16-megabit chips, and has continued to develop with various hardware platform collaborations and service agreements. Today, they are more united than ever, forming an alliance in 2009 which called for the integration of Siemens' Product Data Management environment with IBM's middleware, databases, and development tools to create a more valuable product for end users, via their increasingly extensive collaborations.[13]

Resource Complementarity

Resource complementarity is the extent to which one party's contributed resources are complementary to the other party's resources, resulting in synergies pursued by both. The greater the resource complementarity between foreign and local parents, the higher the new value added due to superior integration of complementary resources pooled by different parents. Resource complementarity also reduces governance and coordination costs and improves the learning curve.[14] For example, JVC was dependent on many different GSAs in its successful effort to make VHS (rather than Betamax) the industry standard for video. JVC stocked RCA with machines carrying the RCA label, set up licensing agreements with Japanese manufacturers, and formed alliances with Germany's Telefunken and Britain's Thorn-EMI Ferguson to help with manufacturing the video recorders. JVC's alliance with Thompson afforded it the knowledge necessary to succeed in the fragmented European market, while Thompson benefited from JVC's product technology and manufacturing prowess. As a result of these myriad GSAs, Sony conceded defeat in 1988, discontinued its production of Betamax, and began manufacturing VHS machines.

Complementary strengths were a major driving force behind the formation of Clark Equipment and Volvo's 50–50 GSA. The companies intended to operate and compete worldwide in the construction equipment business, but individually, neither partner had sufficient geographic presence and distribution capabilities to compete with the market leaders, Komatsu and Caterpillar. Volvo had roughly 70 percent of its sales in Europe and the Middle East, where Clark was very weak; Clark had 70 percent of its sales in North America, where Volvo had virtually no presence. Pooling their marketing resources resulted in a much broader geographic scope.

Cooperative Culture

Cooperative culture concerns the extent to which each party's corporate culture is compatible, thus leading to a more cooperative atmosphere during GSA operations. Normally, maintaining cooperation can become difficult for partners from different cultures. For instance, Americans tend to be individualistic; which is in sharp contrast to the Japanese emphasis on the group (see also Chapter 6). Such differences can be neutralized if both parties try to learn about each other's unique culture. Because both Toyota and GM were committed to learning about each other's corporate

415

culture, the mix of Toyota's team approach and GM's corporate focus on innovation contributed significantly to enhanced productivity at their California-based GSA-NUMMI (New United Motor Manufacturing Company).

A company must take a close look at compatibility in organizational and management practices with a potential partner. For instance, it should ask: Are both companies centralized or decentralized? If not, are managers from these two parties flexible and committed enough to overcome potential conflict? How compatible are customer service policies and philosophies? In order to mitigate the differences in managerial and marketing practices with local Chinese partners, Hewlett-Packard hired as middle managers local people well versed in Chinese business culture.

Commitment

Commitment concerns the extent to which each party will constantly and continuously contribute its resources and skills to joint operations and be dedicated to enhancing joint payoff. Without this commitment, complementary resources, compatible goals, and cooperative culture are no guarantee of a GSA's long-term success. A partner's commitment also affects ongoing trust building. Commitment counters opportunism and fosters cooperation. When GSAs face unexpected environmental changes, commitment serves as a stabilizing device offsetting environmental uncertainties. Commitment is therefore even more critical in a volatile environment. Daewoo and GM each blamed the other for the lackluster performance of the Pontiac LeMans in the United States. Daewoo accused GM of failing to market the LeMans aggressively, while GM maintained that the initial poor quality of the LeMans and the unreliable supplies soured dealers on the car. Lack of commitment ended this GSA in 1992.

Capability

In the context of GSAs, capability concerns three categories: *strategic* (including technology), *organizational,* and *financial.* **Strategic capabilities** of a partner firm generally include such areas as market power, marketing competence, technological skills, relationship building, industrial experience, and corporate image. A partner's market power often represents its industrial and business background, market position, and established marketing and distribution networks. Market power also enables the firm to mitigate some industry-wide restrictions on output, increase bargaining power, and offer economies-of-scale advantages. A local partner's market experience and accumulated industrial knowledge are of great value for the realization of MNE goals. A local partner's history and background in a host market often results in a good reputation or high credibility in the industry. Lengthy industrial/market experience signifies that the local firm has built an extensive marketing and distribution network.

Organizational capabilities include organizational skills, previous collaboration, learning ability, and foreign experience. In a GSA, people with different cultural backgrounds, career goals, and compensation systems begin working together with little advance preparation. This "people factor" can halt the GSA's progress, sometimes permanently. Organizational skills are reflected not only in the ability to blend cultures and management styles, but also in job design, recruitment and staffing, orientation and training, performance appraisal, compensation and benefits, career development, and labor–management relations. Among these, the ability to overcome cultural barriers, recruit qualified employees, and establish incentive structures is especially important. The international experience of partners is critical to the success of intercultural and cross-border venturing activities. International experience affects the organizational fit between partners in the early stages of joint venturing and the changes of fit over time as the alliance evolves.

Financial capabilities are reflected in risk management, exposure hedging, financing, and cash flow management. A partner's risk management ability affects a GSA's vulnerability to external hazards and internal stability. Risk reduction in the form of hedging and risk sharing largely determines a GSA's stability and pattern of growth. During the host-country operations, currency fluctuations can accentuate the volatility of earnings and cash flows. Such volatility can in turn distort management information systems and incentives, hinder access to capital markets, jeopardize the continuity of supplier and customer relationships, and even force the company into bankruptcy. In many foreign markets, MNEs are constrained in obtaining local financing resources. A local partner who maintains superior relationships with local financial institutions and knows how to secure local financing is an important asset to both the venture and the MNE. This ability determines optional composition of debt and equity that will minimize costs and risks. It also affects the GSA's profitability, liquidity, working capital structure, leverage, and cash positions, all of which influence a firm's financial position and structure.

Negotiating Alliance Contracts

Familiarity with general terms negotiated and specified in an alliance contract is important. Major terms stipulated in an equity joint venture agreement are summarized in Exhibit 12.3.

1.	Joint venture name and its legal nature (e.g., limited liability company or not)
2.	Scope and scale of production or operations
3.	Investment amount, unit of currency, and equity (ownership) distribution
4.	Forms of contribution (e.g., cash, technology, land, or equipment)
5.	Responsibilities of each party
6.	Technology or knowledge transfer
7.	Marketing issues (e.g., focusing on export market or local market)
8.	Composition of the board of directors (in EJVs)
9.	Nomination and responsibilities of high-level managers
10.	Joint venture project preparation and construction
11.	Labor management (e.g., various human resource issues)
12.	Accounting, finance, and tax issues (e.g., the currency unit of accounting)
13.	Alliance duration
14.	Disposal of assets after expiration
15.	Amendments, alterations, and discharge of the agreement
16.	Liabilities for breach of contract or agreement
17.	*Force majeure* (i.e., force or power that cannot be acted or fought against)
18.	Settlement of disputes (e.g., litigation or arbitration)
19.	Obligatoriness of the contract (e.g., when it will take effect) and miscellaneous issues

Exhibit 12.3 Major issues and terms during alliance contract negotiations

417

Negotiating tactics affect the bargaining process as well as outcomes. Assembling the negotiating team is a critical element in creating a workable alliance. Qualified negotiators must be able to effectively convey what their parents expect to achieve from the GSA, the plans for structuring and managing the alliance, the value of the contributions each partner brings to the table, and practical solutions to potential problem areas. Good negotiators are also aware of the culturally rooted negotiating styles of the parties. Negotiations about forming a GSA become much easier when the discussions involve negotiators experienced in dealing with diverse cultures.

MNEs often include alliance manager candidates in the negotiating teams. For example, in the alliance activities of ICL, Fujitsu, Westinghouse, Glaxo, Tanabe, Philips, Montedison, and Hercules, the companies usually bring their alliance executive candidates to the negotiating table. This kind of inclusion offers several benefits. First, it provides the executives with an opportunity to learn whether they are compatible with their potential partners. Second, it provides continuity; a GSA manager involved in structuring the deal will be aware of its objectives, its limitations, and the partner's strengths and weaknesses. Third, the expertise of the individuals who will manage the alliance can be valuable in structuring a workable contract. Finally, an alliance manager who takes part in creating the alliance is more likely to be committed to its success than one who has had the responsibility thrust upon him or her.

Another successful strategy for MNEs negotiating large, sophisticated alliance projects is to have two levels of negotiations. On one level, senior executives meet to define the general goals and form of cooperation. The negotiations concern broad strategy and whether the partners are committed to working together. At the second tier, operational managers or experts meet to work out the details of the alliance contract. Siemens, Toshiba, and IBM followed this strategy when they negotiated an R&D alliance to develop the 256-megabit DRAM chip. Senior executives at the three companies met and agreed on the principal objectives of the alliance contract. The three partners then organized a team to address many structural and managerial issues. Engineers and lower-level managers from each partner formed a single team to iron out the specifics of the development project and map out the work schedule and goals for the project.

Structuring Global Strategic Alliances

A critical decision underlying building GSAs, especially EJVs, is the ownership structure. The **ownership structure** is generally defined as the percentage of equity held by each parent. It is often interchangeably termed *equity ownership, sharing arrangement,* or *equity distribution.* This structure is particularly important for EJVs because the equity level determines the levels of control and profit sharing during the subsequent operations. Depending on contractual stipulations, the levels of control and profit sharing in non-equity cooperative alliances may or may not be the product of equity contribution. In the case of a two-party alliance (as earlier cases noted, alliances can have more than two partners), the joint venture is named a *majority-owned joint venture* when a foreign investor has a greater than 50 percent equity stake. It is a *minority-owned joint venture* if the investor owns less than a 50 percent equity stake. If ownership is equal to 50 percent, the joint venture is considered *co-owned* or *split-over.* Although there are other forms of joint ventures including those established between affiliated home-country-based firms, between unaffiliated home-country-based firms, or between home-country and third-country-based firms, joint ventures that are launched by home-country-based (foreign) and host-country-based (local) firms are the dominant form of joint venture partnership.

A majority equity holding means that the partner has more at stake in the alliance than the other partner(s). Normally, the equity position will be associated with an equivalent level of management control in the venture. In other words, control based upon equity ownership is often direct and effective. Nevertheless, the correlation between holding equity and managerial control is not always precise. It is possible for a partner to have a small equity holding but to exercise decisive control. This often occurs when a minority party maintains a greater bargaining power vis-à-vis the other party. For instance, because the other party depends on its resources, Burger King is able to control its joint venture operations in Moscow as a minority holder because the Russian partner relies on its expertise and experience in managing a large fast-food chain.

The ownership structure may end up equally split when both partners want to be majority equity holders. A 50–50 ownership split ensures that neither partner's interests will be compromised, other things being constant. A 50–50 split best captures the spirit of partnership and is particularly desirable in high-technology joint ventures as insurance that both partners will remain involved with technological development. In fact, equal ownership accounts for more than half of joint ventures in developed countries.[15] Split ownership can ensure equal commitment from each partner. Nevertheless, decision making must be based on consensus. This often means a prolonged decision process that can lead to deadlocks. The success of 50–50 equity ventures relies strongly on the synergy between partners over issues ranging from strategic analyses to daily management. It is important that partners speak a common language, have similar backgrounds, and share a set of short- and long-term objectives. By contrast, partners coming from diverse market environments, with different business backgrounds and conflicting goals, often have a harder time making a 50–50 venture a success.

In a minority position, the partner may transfer expertise to the local partner without sufficient returns. More importantly, the ability to control alliance operations is weakened. Generally, the number of votes in board meetings is in equal proportion to actual equity stake. Thus, key decisions made by the board might be more favorable to the majority party. Protecting proprietary resources contributed to the venture also becomes more difficult for the minority party. Nonetheless, the minority status involves lower levels of risks, resource commitment, start-up, or exit costs compared to a majority state.

Different MNEs attach varying importance to equity ownership level in joint ventures depending upon their strategic goals, global control requirements, resource dependence, firm experience, and alternatives for bargaining power, among others. A firm may not be interested in equity level because it has many other alternatives for gaining bargaining power and thus controlling joint venture activities. A firm lacking these alternatives, however, has to rely on equity arrangement for control purposes. Of course, high-equity ownership itself cannot ensure a party's satisfaction with joint venture performance. Venture performance depends more on successful management by both parties. This management, however, is challenging owing to inter-party differences in culture, language, philosophy, goals, and managerial style, as shown in Fujitsu's alliance in Spain (see Country Box).

Country Box

Spain

Fujitsu In Spain: Barriers to Alliance Management

Japan-based Fujitsu established a majority joint venture, SECOINSA (Sociedad Espanola de Communicationes e Infomatica, S.A.), partnering with the National Telephone Company of Spain and various Spanish banks. Fujitsu soon found that alliances are not a panacea. Communication proved to be difficult, and both firms had to rely on English as the common language, although it is the second language for both. The Japanese felt they could not disclose their true feelings in written English; they favored a more interpersonal and fluid rapport that adapted to issues as they arose. The Spanish managers, on their side, believed the Japanese were too business oriented and were hiding behind a barrage of company talk that prevented friendships or personal rapport. They also felt that the Japanese were not well rounded because their at-work and after-work personas merged into one. Spanish people favor a distinct separation between job and leisure. The Japanese rarely adapted to the ways of the Spanish, which made the Spanish believe that the Japanese looked down on local ways.

Disharmony also existed in management. Decision making at Fujitsu was through the *ringi-sho* system, in which an idea is documented and distributed to all relevant parties for approval. *Ringi-sho* is a conservative approach that could minimize risks but is time consuming. Further, the Spanish are inclined to assume that authority is earned through ability and merit, and that authority automatically leads to power, whereas the Japanese treat age as the determining factor in earning power and authority. Finally, Fujitsu wanted to maintain stringent control over its products and prevent imitation. It wanted all the components tested at its facilities in Japan, but because manufacturing was done in Spain, SECOINSA favored Spanish-made components. SECOINSA suggested that the work could be done in Europe if Fujitsu would supply the specifications, testing, and quality control methods. Fujitsu was willing to provide the needed information, but refused to reveal it to any outside parties and would not pass along any information in writing, thus making quality control difficult to ensure.

Source: A. Yan and Y. Luo, *International Joint Ventures: Theory and Practice*, Armonk, NY: M.E. Sharpe, 2001.

Interim Summary

1. Five criteria must be considered in partner selection (five Cs): compatibility of goals; complementarity of resources; cooperative culture; commitment; and capability. As the key criterion, capability should be assessed along strategic capabilities (e.g., market power, marketing competence, technological skills, corporate image), organizational capabilities (e.g., foreign experience, organizational skills, learning ability, and previous collaboration), and financial capabilities (e.g., risk management, exposure hedging, local financing, and cash management).

2. Many relatively standardized terms and clauses should be specified in joint venture contracts. Preparing for negotiations includes choosing a negotiating team, planning for multilevel negotiations, and knowing a partner's intention, strengths, and weaknesses.

3. Setting the ownership level in an equity joint venture is important because it infers, in part, control over the venture. Three strategic options are majority, minority, and equally split. If the minority party has strong bargaining power, it can still dominate the venture.

Managing Global Strategic Alliances

The management issues involved in global strategic alliances include managing inter-partner learning, exercising managerial control, accentuating cooperation and trust, and thinking ahead of exit (Exhibit 12.4).

Managing Inter-Partner Learning

In bringing together firms with different skills, knowledge bases, and organizational cultures, GSAs create unique learning opportunities for the partner firms.[16] By definition, alliances involve a sharing of resources. This access can be a powerful source of new knowledge that, in most cases, would not have been possible without the GSA. Learning opportunities are manifested in two areas: *operational* and *managerial. Operational knowledge* includes knowledge of technology, processes (including quality control), production, marketing skills, and operational expertise (e.g., relationship-building expertise). *Managerial knowledge* is comprised of organizational and managerial skills (e.g., leadership, human resource management, organizational structure, managerial efficiency, and employee participation); market (international and host country), industrial, and collaborative experience; and financial management (e.g., cost control,

Exhibit 12.4 Managing global strategic alliances

tax reduction, capital utilization, financing, risk reduction, resource deployment, and asset management).

To acquire partner knowledge, a firm needs to first identify what knowledge it needs and then extract and transfer this knowledge from its partner to its own organization. Germany's Bosch established "strategy meetings" focusing on what and how the firm can learn from its Japanese partners. Bosch sends trained German technicians and marketing managers to the Japanese joint ventures to help acquire partner skills and knowledge, including tips on how to improve customer satisfaction in Japan. The acquired knowledge is then shared by all members of the Bosch group who are trying to get access to Japanese clients. Similarly, when Chrysler joined forces with Mitsubishi Motors in 1986 to create Diamond Star Motors (DSM), its major objective was to gain firsthand knowledge of Japanese management and manufacturing principles. Chrysler deliberately ceded management control for daily operations to Mitsubishi to learn how that firm handled the complex engineering, functional, and operational tasks involved in launching and manufacturing a new range of mid-sized models.

Each party is expected to learn a certain amount about the other's capabilities. *Openness* is thus crucial to knowledge sharing or transfer between partners, because much of what the parties are trying to learn from each other or create together is difficult to communicate. This information is often embedded in a firm's practices and culture, and it can only be learned through working relationships that are not hampered by constraints. In order to enhance inter-partner trust, commitment from each party is necessary. However, to the party whose knowledge is very sensitive or constitutes its core competence (e.g., Coca-Cola's formula), knowledge protection becomes necessary. There are several ways to protect core knowledge from uncompensated leakage to partner firms.

First, *the design, development, manufacture, and service of a product manufactured (or a service rendered) by an alliance may be structured so as to protect the most sensitive technologies.* For example, in the GSA between GE and Snecma to build commercial aircraft engines, GE tried to reduce the risk of excess transfer by keeping certain sections of the production process secret. This modularization cut off the transfer of what GE felt was key competitive technology, while permitting Snecma access to final assembly. Similarly, in the GSA between Boeing and the Japanese to build the 767, Boeing walled off research, design, and marketing functions (considered more central to Boeing's competitive position), but allowed the Japanese to share production technology. Boeing also separated those technologies not required for 767 production.

Second, *contractual safeguards can be written into an alliance agreement.* For example, TRW has three strategic alliances with large Japanese auto component suppliers to produce seat belts, engine valves, and steering gears sold to Japanese-owned auto assembly plants in the United States. TRW has clauses in each of its GSA contracts that bar the Japanese companies from competing by introducing component parts. These protect TRW against the possibility that the Japanese companies may enter into alliances to gain access to TRW's home market and become its competitor.

Third, *both parties to a GSA can agree in advance to exchange specific skills and technologies that ensure equitable gain.* Cross-licensing agreements are one way of achieving this goal. For example, in the case of the alliance between Motorola and Toshiba, Motorola has licensed some of its microprocessor technology to Toshiba and in return Toshiba has licensed some of its memory chip technology to Motorola. An alliance relationship will be most stable and productive if both partners specialize in their respective areas of expertise without trying to gain the core competencies of the other. However, if it is infeasible to prevent at least one of them from acquiring the other's core competencies, a pattern of two-way exchanges between the partners is likely to yield greater stability and less conflict in the alliance than a pattern of one-way flow whereby only one of the partners acquires the core competencies of the other. When both become capable of doing what the other can do, they are more likely to continue the alliance as a vehicle for collaboration, since unconstrained price competition between two equally endowed rivals hurts the profitability of both. If only one of them learns the other's trade secrets while successfully walling off its own, that partner will likely lose the incentive to collaborate further.

Finally, *avoiding undue dependence on an alliance can help mitigate the leakage risk*. This is particularly important when an MNE establishes GSAs with competitors or uses its own core knowledge in alliances. GM limited its dependence on its Asian allies in its Saturn project in an attempt to independently replenish the knowledge critical to its business. When GSAs do involve core knowledge, managers must guard against shifts in the balance of power, maneuvering by other parties, and the taking of vital knowledge. Moreover, an MNE may reduce dependence on an alliance by creating several similar GSAs or by seeking to be the senior partner in each relationship. For instance, Toyota and Daewoo provided GM with different versions of high-quality, low-cost, small cars. Toyota exercises a dominant influence over its family of suppliers; it usually buys a large portion of their output, often helps finance them, and provides equipment and managerial advice.

Exercising Managerial Control

Parent control is the process through which a parent company ensures that an alliance is managed in a way that conforms to its own interest. The partners often have differing agendas for forming the alliance and their strategic objectives are not identical. In this case, the alliance's efforts and outcomes valued by one partner are not necessarily appreciated by the other. Therefore, for each partner, achieving hands-on control over the alliance's operation confers the right of participation in the alliance's decision making, through which it ensures its strategic goals will be vigorously pursued by the alliance management.[17]

Parent control is realized through equity control and managerial control. We explained earlier that the majority equity holder is generally able to maintain greater equity control over the GSA, and this equity control is often reflected in the voting power in board meetings. In routine management, however, it is managerial control rather than equity control that matters. **Managerial control** is the process in which a party influences alliance activities or decisions in a way that is consistent with its own interests through various managerial, administrative, or social tools. The really dominant party in alliance management is the one that dominates managerial control. As noted earlier, the minority equity holder may be able to exercise greater managerial control if it holds a stronger bargaining power over the majority counterpart.[18]

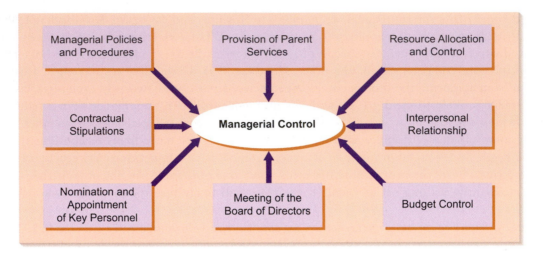

Exhibit 12.5 How to maintain managerial control over alliance activities

As Exhibit 12.5 shows, mechanisms of managerial control include the following:

1. *Nomination and appointment of key personnel:* Control requires knowledge of events and circumstances. Such knowledge is most readily available to the alliance's parents if it supplies key personnel to run or monitor operations or critical functions such as marketing, R&D, or corporate finance. The appointment of key staff as a control mechanism is especially important to parents that are geographically remote or occupy a minority position.

2. *Meetings of the board of directors:* Although a majority equity holder is in an advantageous position in terms of composition and representation on the board, a minority partner can manipulate the frequency of meetings and agenda coverage. In addition, a majority parent cannot consistently overrule or refuse to compromise with its partner without building ill-will and risking the long-term survival of the relationship. Further, minority parents can prevent the majority partner from implementing unilateral decisions by negotiating the inclusion in the alliance contract of veto rights over decisions important to their interests (e.g., dividend policy, new investment, transfer pricing, divestment, and selection of key managers). Finally, control at the board level is not simply a matter of votes. It also results from the ability to influence other board members on important issues. This is to a large extent a matter of bargaining power and negotiation skills.

3. *Managerial policies and procedures:* The behavior of executives in a GSA is influenced by various managerial policies and procedures devised by the owners. Since an alliance contract usually does not stipulate these policies and procedures, a minority partner can be more proactive by playing a larger part in formulating and adjusting such policies and procedures. Reward and report systems are particularly effective for the purpose of control. The former determines the incentive structure and performance evaluation, and the latter the information flow, dissemination, and accuracy.

4. *Budget control:* Five aspects of budget control can be implemented: (1) emphasis on the budget during performance evaluations, that is, using quantitative criteria in evaluating divisional manager performance; (2) participation in the budget process, that is, the partner's degree of involvement during budget development; (3) budget incentives, that is, linking pay and promotion prospects to meeting budget goals; (4) budget standard-setting difficulty, that is, the difficulty surrounding the setting of budget goals; and (5) budget controllability filters, that is, extenuating factors that are brought into the performance evaluation process. In general, minority partners can use all five budget control mechanisms to increase their overall or specific control over GSA operations and management.

5. *Provision of parent services:* In order to increase the likelihood that specific tasks in the alliance are performed in conformity with their expectations, parent firms may offer staff services and training, sometimes at no cost to the alliance. Such services can be provided irrespective of equity ownership level. Increased control accrues to parent firms in the following ways: (1) greater awareness of the parent to conditions within the GSA because of enhanced dialogue with the alliance employees; (2) increased loyalty from alliance employees who identify more with the parent and have assimilated its ethos; and (3) increased predictability of behavior in the GSA because its managers are more likely to use the guidelines within which they have been trained.

6. *Contract stipulations:* As one of the major mechanisms by which conflicts may be overcome and performance enhanced, contract stipulations serve to reduce managerial complexity in coordinating activities for collective goals; this is an institutionalized mechanism for mitigating opportunism and increasing forbearance. A minority partner can maintain greater control over subsequent GSA operations and management if terms and clauses in the contract are more favorable to that firm. Greater bargaining power and superior negotiation skills result in such favorable conditions. Various terms and conditions, RRB (responsibility-rights-benefits), managerial rules, and strategic goals are of particular relevance for the minority party that aims to increase control using this approach.

7. *Resource allocation and control:* While resource competence leads to bargaining power, resource allocation and utilization contribute to managerial control. In other words, allocation and control of key resources needed by the GSA are an effective mechanism for a minority party attempting to exert control over the GSA's business activities and management process. This control mechanism is often sustained because control of key resources makes both the GSA's success and the partner company's goal accomplishment dependent upon the firm. Local knowledge is the contribution most consistently associated with a minority share in the original GSA agreement.

8. *Interpersonal relationship:* An MNE can increase its control if it builds and maintains a trustworthy, enduring personal relationship with upper-level managers representing the partner firm. This approach has helped many MNEs, as minority parties, to successfully control their GSAs in developing countries. By arranging for managers from local firms to work at foreign headquarters, helping solve personal difficulties they face, or offering favors as needed, foreign companies are able to solidify relationships with local executives who will, in turn, remain loyal to the foreign company. This will eventually promote the foreign company's managerial effectiveness.

Heightening Cooperation

When a GSA is formed, alliance success will depend largely on inter-partner cooperation during subsequent operations and management. Cooperation, however, requires organizational commitments from both parties. Two important mechanisms nurturing cooperation include personal attachment and conflict reduction.

Personal Attachment

Governance mechanisms such as contractual stipulations and managerial control systems are insufficient for controlling opportunism and increasing cooperation. Ongoing business relationships often intermingle with social content, which generates strong expectations of trust. **Personal attachment** reflects socialization and personal relations between senior GSA managers from each party during their involvement in exchange activities. Personal attachment counters the pressure for dissolution, improves trust, and increases alliance duration and stability. Personal attachment is driven by interpersonal relationships as well as interpersonal learning of individual skills and knowledge. Personal attachment can be developed in the following ways.

First, *it is important that friendly personal contact is maintained between the leaders of the cooperating organizations*. This means planning for personal visits between partner chief executives at least once a year. Apart from the intrinsic merit such visits have in ironing out any differences between the partners and laying down broad plans for the future, they are very important in setting an example and establishing a climate of cooperation for the people working within the alliance.

Second, *careful consideration should be given to the length of appointment of key personnel to an alliance*. If this is short, say two years or under, the chances of achieving mutual bonding are reduced. Not only is there personal unfamiliarity to overcome, but, if a language has to be learned or improved, this clearly takes time as well. Personnel with longer-term appointments are also more likely to invest in establishing relationships within the alliance, for they see it as a more significant part of their overall career path. Western, and especially American, companies tend to assign people to alliances on contracts of four years maximum, whereas Japanese companies tend to appoint their people for up to eight years.

Third, *careful selection of people who are to work in an alliance will also improve the prospects for mutual bonding*. They should be selected not merely on the basis of technical competence, important though this is, but also on an assessment of their ability to maintain good relationships with people from other organizational and national cultures. Track records can reveal a lot in this respect. Some global companies have, for this reason, now created opportunities for successful alliance and expatriate managers to be able to remain in inter-organizational and international assignments without detriment to their long-term advancement within the home corporation.

Finally, *it is important for the alliance to encourage socializing between the partners' personnel*. Activities such as sports and social events as well as charitable and sponsorship activities in the local community can be helpful in overcoming social barriers. They help to bring about an acceptance of the alliance within its local community, and a strengthening of its external identity.

Reducing Conflicts

Most MNEs concede that conflict in GSAs is inevitable, given the rich diversity of capabilities, cultures, and constraints of each partner. There is likely to be a string of disputes over "hard" financial or technological issues and frictions of a "softer" cultural and interpersonal nature. In both cases, it is important to have mechanisms in place for resolving such conflicts from the very outset of the alliance's existence.

First, *it is important to understand and analyze the actions and/or positions of the partner firm from their perspective, rather than from one's own.* This helps one better appreciate the partner's position on issues and options available to that partner. This approach helped Fuji and Xerox overcome the common dividend dilemmas between the US and Japanese firms. US MNEs generally prefer high dividend payout due to pressure from Wall Street and institutional investors, whereas Japanese shareholders accept low payout in return for profits reinvested for growth. So, by understanding the constraints of both sides, each partner was more willing to opt for the middle ground: Fuji Xerox dividends generally hover around 30 percent of earnings.

Second, *having alliance executives jointly set milestones and principles helps mitigate possible conflicts.* Because many conflicts stem from unclear or misread signals between partners, it is important to jointly develop a set of operating principles for the alliance and establish effective communication systems. The communications system in Fuji Xerox includes a co-destiny task force, presidential summit meetings, functional meetings, resident directors meeting, and personnel exchanges. Such communications channels bridge the differences between Fuji and Xerox. Having regular meetings is an important step to jointly set principles for alliance operations. These meetings should establish the facts of any matters at issue and record the discussion and any solutions proposed. The records of such meetings provide a basis by which problems can be addressed at a higher level between the partners.

Third, *parent firms should steer the alliance clear of the goals and strategies of the parents.* Many executives view conflicts between an alliance and its parent organizations as a potential minefield. A GSA should steer clear of its parents' strategies, geographic expansion, and product lines. For example, many of the difficulties and tensions in the Rolls-Royce, Pratt & Whitney venture of forming International Aero Engines to manufacture V2500 engines stemmed from competitive conflicts with the parents. The V2500, a competitor to CFM International's own products, also competes directly with two Pratt & Whitney (P&W) engines—the JTAT 200 series and the P&W 2037, as well as Rolls-Royce's RB211 engine.

Fourth, *maintaining flexibility is crucial for avoiding conflicts.* It is important to have a formal specification of rules and guidelines that clarify important issues such as financial procedure and technology sharing for those working within the alliance. However, because market and environment conditions change, partners must be adaptable. Although a contract may legally bind partners together, an adherence to a rigid agreement may hamper adaptations. Cultivating a corporate culture that embraces adaptation is important.

Finally, *an understanding of human resource groups in alliances and their typical concerns is key to preventing or mitigating conflicts.* This understanding motivates alliance managers with different cultural backgrounds to be more committed to joint operations and more cooperative with their counterparts. Chapter 17 provides a detailed account of those issues.

Thinking Ahead of Exit

Because GSAs are not required to continue indefinitely, GSA divorce does not necessarily signal failure. It may mean in some cases that the business logic for the alliance no longer applies. Thus, the best scenario of alliance dissolution is that the *venture has already met its strategic goals set by both parties*. In particular, when each party aims to acquire knowledge from the other, this alliance does not have to maintain its longevity. For instance, Hercules and Montedison, two former competitors in polypropylene products, established an alliance and pooled together $900 million in assets to create Himont in November 1983. Each side enjoyed a competitive advantage in the industry that the other lacked and wanted. Through research and technological breakthroughs, Himont added new properties and applications for polypropylene and grew worldwide to include more than 3,000 employees, 38 manufacturing plants, and distribution capabilities in 100 countries. As a leader in the chemical industry with a return on equity of 38 percent, Himont earned at least $150 million per annum from new products. After successfully fulfilling its objectives (i.e., learning technologies), Hercules sold its equity stake in Himont to its partner.

In many other cases, nevertheless, GSAs are terminated owing to conflicts or failure to achieve alliance goals. *Differences in strategic or operational objectives often lead to divorce.* In several US–Japanese alliances producing auto parts, US partners often have a narrow focus—to gain access to the Japanese auto transplants in the United States. Their counterparts, however, have broader goals—to secure a foothold in the US market. Similarly, a former alliance between Corning and Ciba-Geigy of Switzerland derailed because of growing differences in the two partners' ambitions and operational objectives.

Differences in managerial styles can be a cause for termination. In the case of the Corning–Vitro alliance, the two partners had different ideas about how to define and provide "service" to customers. Corning was concerned about prompt service to retailers, such as Wal-Mart and Kmart. Vitro, having operated for years in a closed Mexican economy with little competition, was concerned only with product reliability.

Exit may also be attributed to differences in conflict resolution. In many alliances in China, for instance, the Chinese partners prefer not to pre-specify explicit conflict resolution terms, especially judiciary or arbitration resolutions, in an alliance contract. From their perspective, leaving these terms ambiguous may encourage inter-partner cooperation in the long term. When partnering with Western firms, however, this ambiguity can lead to alliance termination. For example, in 1994, Lehman Brothers sued Sinochem and Sinopec, the two giant state-owned Chinese firms, for failing to honor their obligations in swap transactions. This accusation, however, was rejected by the Chinese partners who argued that there was no explicit stipulation on these transactions in the agreement. As a result of this open confrontation, the partnership between Lehman Brothers and the two Chinese giants ended.

Other reasons underlying the end of GSAs include *inability to meet shifting targets* (e.g., DuPont and Philips terminated their alliance in optical media for this reason), *inability to meet financial requirements* (e.g., financial strains prompted Chrysler to sell its stake in Diamond Star Motors to Mitsubishi), *inability to predict partner competencies* (e.g., AT&T ended its partnership with Philips when it found that Philips NV's clout did not extend far beyond the Dutch market), and *inability to predict regulatory policies* (e.g., Rohm and Hass terminated its electronic chemical alliance with Tokyo Okha Kogyo to accommodate European regulatory concerns about possible overlaps with its pending acquisition of Morton International).

There are generally three forms of termination—*termination by acquisition* (equity transfer), *termination by dissolution,* and *termination by redefinition* of the alliance. In the first case, the alliance is terminated with one of the partners acquiring the stake of the other partner. Termination by acquisition could also take the form of one partner selling its equity stake in the alliance to another company (e.g., British Aerospace selling its equity stake in Rover to BMW), or both partners selling their shares to a third company. Most MNEs prefer reallocation of alliance ownership between existing parent firms. These changes in ownership and resource commitments are a function of both firms' evolving relationships to the venture. Termination by acquisition is most common in international equity alliances. For instance, New Japan Chemical recently agreed to buy out its partner Hercules' share in their alliance, Rika Hercules. After this acquisition, the two partners intend to maintain a friendly relationship including technological exchanges.

In lieu of termination, partners to a GSA may agree to redefine or restructure their original agreement. For example, Matsushita Electric Industries, Co. of Japan (now known as Panasonic) and Solbourne Computer, Inc. of Colorado entered into an ambitious partnership in 1987 to compete with Sun Microsystem's SPARC computers. When the venture failed, MEI and Solbourne agreed in 1992 to redraft their initial agreement into a more limited partnership arrangement. In this case, redefinition or restructuring of an old alliance may imply creation of a new alliance. In other words, the life cycle of the old alliance has ended while the life cycle of the new alliance has just begun.

To end this chapter, read what CEOs of Corning Incorporated and Emerson Electric say about their experience involving GSAs (see Industry Box).

Industry Box

Wisdom Gained from Experience in Building GSAs

James R. Houghton, chairman and CEO of Corning Incorporated, identified seven criteria that have helped Corning reach decisions to enter into alliances:

1. Start with a solid business opportunity.
2. Both partners should make comparable contributions to the new alliance.
3. The new alliance should have a well-defined scope and no major conflicts with either parent.
4. Trust is the most important ingredient of the alliance.
5. Management of each parent firm should have the vision and confidence to support the alliance.
6. An autonomous operating team should be formed.

7. Responsibility for alliances cannot be delegated. It must include the CEOs or board-level individuals from one or both partners who can make decisions.

Charles F. Knight, chairman and CEO of Emerson Electric, suggested five rules as pre-venture guidelines:

1. Do not go into business with a company in a turnaround situation.
2. Do not do business with a company that does not have good management.
3. Stick to core competencies.
4. Do a lot of due diligence work.
5. Involve the alliance management in every business plan and deal, and have them report annually to the board of directors.

And, finally, a word from the International Franchising Association to firms looking into forging strategic alliances:

> "Ask not what your strategic partner can do for you, but what you can do for the partnership?" [. . .] The most important point to keep in mind about a strategic alliance is that it will be mutually beneficial. If both parties are not benefitting from the partnership, it will languish over time, resulting in a damaged business relationship.

Source: The Conference Board, 1994, Making International Strategic Alliances Work, Report #1086–94-CH; J.F. Buckles, "Understanding the benefits and challenges of strategic alliances," *International Franchise Association,* 2011.

Interim Summary

1. A GSA is, among other things, a learning tool enabling the investing firms to acquire knowledge from foreign partners. Firms must identify what knowledge they seek and how complementary it is to existing knowledge. To protect sensitive technology from leakage, firms can use walling-off, contractual specification, and cross-licensing techniques.

2. Firms can execute non-equity-based control to influence GSAs. The tools of this control include appointment of key personnel, board meetings, managerial policies and procedures, budget control, provision of parent services, contract codification, resource control, and interpersonal relationship.

3. Cooperation can be facilitated by personal attachment between key managers from the parties. Firms should plan ahead for exit strategies with such options as termination by acquisition, termination by dissolution, and termination by redefining the alliance.

Chapter Summary

1. GSAs have become a pervasive vehicle for MNEs to further their globalization. Whether in the form of equity joint ventures or cooperative joint ventures, GSAs provide MNEs with possible gains such as access to foreign markets, learning from foreign firms, sharing start-up costs and project risks, reducing global competition, and improving local acceptance. Nonetheless, there exist many challenges in forming and managing GSAs.

2. GSAs cannot succeed in the absence of good partners. In selecting local partners, firms must seek a fit between a candidate's capabilities (strategic, organizational, and financial) and their own. Goal compatibility, resource complementarity, cooperative culture, and commitment are also important criteria underlying partner selection.

3. Many GSAs are unstable due to governance problems. Contract specifications and ownership arrangement are two critical *ex ante* mechanisms counteracting this problem. To what extent a joint venture contract should be specified and covered, and in what level the equity ownership should be sought, depend on the firm's strategic needs, bargaining power, and market uncertainty.

4. GSAs are like game fields in which both cooperation and control coexist. Firms exercise managerial control to direct GSAs to suit their needs. The minority equity holder can elevate its managerial control as long as it has bargaining power vis-à-vis the other party. Managerial control is achieved through both formal methods (e.g., appointing key personnel, managerial policies, budget control, and contract stipulation) and informal methods (e.g., interpersonal relations and setting board meeting agenda and locations).

5. Inter-partner learning is sometimes an overriding intention behind GSAs, especially those in developed countries. After acquiring a partner's knowledge, the firm must integrate it with its own knowledge base. No firm can build a sustained competitive advantage solely on the basis of acquired knowledge.

6. Joint payoffs from GSAs depend in part on trust building and ongoing cooperation. Continued commitment, parent support, mutual compromise and understanding, as well as satisfactory resolution of conflicts are necessary steps toward this end. Informal steps such as socialization (e.g., personal attachment between senior managers from different parties) also encourage cooperation.

7. GSAs are transitional, not permanent, in nature. Thus, firms should be prepared in advance with exit options and procedures. GSAs may be terminated as a result of achieving initial goals for all parties or failing to achieve these goals due to differences in managerial styles, conflict resolution, or strategic orientation. Equity transfer from one party to the other (or third party) is a common approach for termination.

Notes

1 A. Yan and Y. Luo, *International Joint Ventures: Theory and Practice*, Armonk, NY: M.E. Sharpe, 2000; F. J. Contractor and P. Lorange, *Cooperative Strategies in International Business*, Lexington, MA: Lexington Books, 1988; and Y.L. Doz and G. Hamel, *Alliance Advantage*, Boston, MA: Harvard Business School Press, 1998.

2 Y.L. Doz and G. Hamel, *Alliance Advantage: The Art of Creating Value through Partnering*. Boston, MA: Harvard Business School Press, 1998; J. Bleeke and D. Ernst, "The way to win in cross-border alliances," *Harvard Business Review*, 69, 6, 1991, 127–135.

3   IBM Website, "Semiconductor solutions: Collaborative innovation," 2013.

4   Trefis Team, "China can keep GM's growth in high gear," Forbes.com, August 6, 2013.

5   R.M. Kabterm, *When Giants Learn to Dance,* New York: Simon & Schuster, 1989; Y.L. Doz, "The evolution of cooperation in strategic alliances: Initial conditions or learning processes?," *Strategic Management Journal,* 17, summer 1996, 55–85.

6   R.B. Reich, "Japan Inc., USA," *The New Republic,* November 26, 1984, 19–23; F.J. Contractor and P. Lorange, "Competition vs. cooperation: A benefit/cost framework for choosing between fully-owned investment and cooperative relationships," *Management International Review,* Special Issue, 1988, 5–18; G. Hamel, "Competition for competence and interpartner learning within international strategic alliances," *Strategic Management Journal,* 12, summer Special Issue, 1994, 83–103.

7   S. Goldenberg, *International Joint Ventures in Action: How to Establish, Manage, and Profit from International Strategic Alliances,* London: Hutchinson Business Books, 1988; G. Hamel, Y.L. Doz and C.K. Prahalad, "Collaborate with your competitors and win," *Harvard Business Review,* January–February 1989, 133–139.

8   R. Kantner, "Trade secrets at risk overseas," *Dallas Business Journal,* December 28, 2012.

9   W. Rowe and T. Brook, *China's Last Empire: The Great Qing,* Cambridge, MA: The Belknap Press of Harvard University Press, 2000; E. Javers, *Broker, Trader, Lawyer, Spy: The Secret World of Corporate Espionage,* New York: Harper Business, 2010.

10 G. Parker, "Global firms take China to next level," *Wall Street Journal,* November 19, 2004.

11 G. Hamel, "Competition for competence and interpartner learning within international strategic alliances," *Strategic Management Journal,* 12, summer Special Issue, 1991, 83–103; K.R. Harrigan, *Managing for Joint Venture Success,* Lexington, MA: Lexington Books, 1986.

12 K.R. Harrigan, *Strategies for Joint Ventures,* Lexington, MA: D.C. Heath, 1985; J.P. Killing, *Strategies for Joint Venture Success,* New York: Praeger, 1983.

13 IBM Website, "Siemens PLM software," 2013.

14 P. Lorange and J. Roos, *Strategic Alliances: Formation, Implementation, and Evolution,* Cambridge, MA: Blackwell, 1992; B. Kogut, "Joint ventures: theoretical and empirical perspectives," *Strategic Management Journal,* 9, 4, 1988, 319–332; A.C. Inkpen, *The Management of International Joint Ventures: An Organizational Learning Perspective,* London: Routledge, 1995.

15 P.W. Beamish, "The characteristics of joint ventures in developed and developing countries," *Columbia Journal of World Business,* fall 1995, 13–19; P.W. Beamish, *Multinational Joint Ventures in Developing Countries,* New York: Routledge, 1988.

16 J.L. Badaracco, *The Knowledge Link: How Firms Compete through Strategic Alliances,* Boston, MA: Harvard Business School Press, 1991; G. Hamel, "Competition for competence and inter-partner learning within international strategic alliances," *Strategic Management Journal,* 12, 1991, 83–103; D. Lai, J.W. Slocum and R.A. Pitts, "Building cooperative advantage: Managing strategic alliances to promote organizational learning," *Journal of World Business,* 32, 3, 1997, 203–223.

17 J.M. Geringer and L. Hebert, "Control and performance of international joint ventures," *Journal of International Business Studies,* 20, 2, 1989, 235–254; A. Parkhe, "Strategic alliance structuring: A game theoretic and transaction cost examination of interfirm cooperation," *Academy of Management Journal,* 36, 1993, 794–829.

18 A. Yan and Y. Luo, *International Joint Ventures: Theory and Practice,* Armonk, NY: M.E. Sharpe, 2000; Y. Luo, *Entry and Cooperative Strategies in International Business Expansion,* Westport, CT: Quorum Books, 1999; S.H. Park, "Managing an inter-organizational network: A framework of the institutional mechanism for network control," *Organization Studies,* 17, 1996, 795–824.

chapter 13

managing global research and development (R&D)

WHY GLOBALIZE R&D?   435

DESIGNING AND STRUCTURING GLOBAL R&D   441

MANAGING AND OPERATING GLOBAL R&D   448

TECHNOLOGY TRANSFER ACROSS BORDERS   452

Do You Know?

1. Why do firms increasingly globalize R&D? What benefits and challenges can you outline for firms that locate and operate R&D laboratories in different countries?
2. What types of foreign R&D units are available for firms to choose from? If you work at Honeywell's corporate technology center in Minneapolis, what type do you think this center belongs to? If this center plans to build a new but specialized lab in Asia, what factors should you consider in opting for its location?
3. How should firms structure and integrate global R&D activities? Can you differentiate, for instance, between a polycentric decentralized structure model and a global central lab model? If you are a senior manager at Ericsson, which model may you recommend for the company?
4. How do managers of MNEs define autonomy of global R&D units, and what areas of human resource management are particularly important for managing global R&D?

OPENING CASE   Intel's R&D Network in Developing Countries

Intel has over 20,000 R&D employees located in more than 30 countries. Some of the facilities are owned by the parent firm while others are managed in collaboration with universities or through venture-capital investments in technology-intensive companies. Intel's R&D investments in developing countries, especially in China, India, and Russia, are growing faster than elsewhere. That expansion is motivated by the availability of an educated and skilled workforce with specific competencies in relevant areas. In these countries, Intel owns laboratories that conduct key research in a variety of fields; it has also signed a series of collaboration agreements with universities.

Intel China Research Center (ICRC) in Beijing was established in 1998 as the company's first research lab in the Asia-Oceania region. ICRC has conducted applied research in the areas of human computer interface, computer architecture, future workloads, and compilers and runtime. It currently has a staff of over 70 researchers, most of whom hold a PhD or MS from Chinese universities. Among the research innovations that have emerged from ICRC are Open Research Compiler, developed jointly with the Chinese Academy of Science; Audio Visual Speech Recognition, a system using computer vision to assist speech recognition; and Microphone Array and audio signal processing technology. A second Chinese R&D laboratory, Intel China Software Center (ICSC), is located in Shanghai and has over 500 employees, ranging from top engineering graduates from the best universities in China to technologists and marketing/business specialists recruited from around the world.

The Intel India Design Center in Bangalore employs more than 2,500 employees and is the company's biggest non-manufacturing center outside the US, focusing on the core areas of Intel's R&D. In comparison, the Nizhny Novgorod (Russia) software development center is home to 500 specialists and engineers developing software tools and applications for Intel.

Cooperation with universities abroad is an important aspect of Intel's global R&D strategy. The Intel Research Council, an internal group of technical experts, awards university research grants worldwide for projects in key areas. A final vector of Intel's global strategy is Intel Capital, Intel's strategic investment program. Its mission is to make and manage financially attractive investments that support Intel's strategic objectives. The overseas presence of Intel Capital grew from less than 5 percent of its total investments in 1998 to over 50 percent in 2011. In 2011, China alone accounted for 15 percent of its global investments, putting the country in second place behind only the US, with India in third place. Brazil, Russia, and Turkey are other key destinations of its investments.

Source: Abbreviated from The World Investment Report 2005, UNCTAD, and company websites.

Why Globalize R&D?

Like Intel, many MNEs are increasingly dedicating their important resources (financial, technological, and human) to global research and development (R&D) in search of sustained competitive advantages in the global marketplace. At the dawn of the twenty-first century, R&D has been fundamentally globalized, with core innovative capabilities remaining close to corporate headquarters in the home country. Many Western MNEs are extending their R&D activities not only in other developed countries but also in developing countries, especially emerging markets (e.g., IBM's R&D center in Beijing, China). At the same time, MNEs from newly industrialized nations such as Asia's mini-dragons (South Korea, Singapore, Taiwan, and Hong Kong) have begun to relocate many R&D activities abroad.

Globalizing R&D is a process of locating and operating R&D laboratories in different countries, under a system that is coordinated and integrated by the company's headquarters, in order to leverage the technical resources of each facility to further the company's overall technological capabilities and competitive advantage. For example, Exxon developed a synthetic base stock for formulating high-performance engine oils through the collaboration of process research laboratories in Canada and Louisiana, and a product development laboratory in the United Kingdom. While the two terms are often used interchangeably, *globalizing R&D* differs from *internationalizing R&D*. The former requires global integration of geographically dispersed R&D laboratories or centers, but the latter does not. From this standpoint, internationalizing R&D is an early stage of globalizing R&D, which evolves as a firm's international expansion grows larger and more complex in scale and scope. The R&D function serves as the key avenue for building and sustaining a company's global competitive advantage. MNEs with a well-designed strategy on globalizing R&D tend to achieve superior sales and profit performance.[1]

R&D intensity (i.e., total R&D expenditure relative to total sales during the same period) has been steadily increasing in many industries such as electronics, pharmaceuticals, chemicals, and medical equipment. For instance, the average R&D intensity relative to sales by global pharmaceutical MNEs was about 4.7 percent in 1977 but 18 percent in 2012. While American MNEs lead in innovation in many high-technology industries such as automobiles, computers, software, health care, and advanced materials, MNEs from Europe, Canada, Japan, and newly industrialized

435

countries such as Korea, Taiwan, and Israel also demonstrate high R&D level and inventive productivity. Some large MNEs each spend over $6 billion annually (see Exhibit 13.1). The main thrust of global firms has been to increase the patent output per unit of R&D spending and sharpen their global competitiveness.[2]

Managing global R&D receives greater attention by international business managers for these reasons: First, *technology is recognized as a major source of global competitive advantage*. International R&D expands and augments the overall R&D process of the firm. Second, *the nature of the technological innovation process has changed*. Technological innovations are often the result of the integration of technologies from different disciplines (an example is the convergence of electronic, telecommunication, and information technologies). As illustrated in Chapter 5, countries

2013 Rank	▲▼	2012 Rank	Company	Geography	Industry	R&D Spend ($Bn)*
1	▲	11	Volkswagen	Germany	Automotive	11.4
2	▲	6	Samsung	South Korea	Computing & Electronics	10.4
3	▶	3	Roche	Switzerland	Health	10.2
4	▲	8	Intel	United States	Computing & Electronics	10.1
5	▶	5	Microsoft	United States	Software & Internet	9.8
6	▼	1	Toyota	Japan	Automotive	9.8
7	▼	2	Novartis	Switzerland	Health	9.3
8	▼	7	Merck	United States	Health	8.2
9	▼	4	Pfizer	United States	Health	7.9
10	▲	12	Johnson & Johnson	United States	Health	7.7
11	▼	9	GM	United States	Automotive	7.4
12	▲	26	Google	United States	Software & Internet	6.8
13	▲	15	Honda	Japan	Automotive	6.8
14	▲	19	Daimler	Germany	Automotive	6.6
15	▼	13	Sanofi-Aventis	France	Health	6.3
16	▲	17	IBM	United States	Computing & Electronics	6.3
17	▼	16	GlaxoSmithKline	United Kingdom	Health	6.3
18	▼	10	Nokia	Finland	Computing & Electronics	6.1
19	▼	14	Panasonic	Japan	Computing & Electronics	6.1
20	▲	21	Sony	Japan	Computing & Electronics	5.7

* R&D spending data is based on the most recent full-year figures reported prior to July 1.

Exhibit 13.1 Top 20 R&D spenders in 2013

Source: Adapted and reprinted with permission from "The Global Innovation 1,000: Navigating the Digital Future" by Barry Jaruzelski, John Loehr, and Richard Holman from the Winter 2013 issue of *strategy+business* magazine, published by Booz & Company Inc. Copyright © 2013. All rights reserved. www.strategy-business.com.

differ in their competitive advantage, and the globalization of R&D enables firms to tap these various sources of strength. Third, *time is a critical competitive factor in a number of industries.* R&D activities are decentralized to accelerate the process of innovation and adaptation. Finally, *the growth of network and information exchange systems facilitates long-distance communication,* which lowers coordination costs associated with globalizing R&D activities.

Globalizing R&D is also a strategic response to changes in international markets. Along with a shortened product life cycle in many industries, foreign customers demand higher levels of technical service and customized products. Targeting and developing regional markets, such as the European Union, LAFTA (Latin American Free Trade Association), and CACM (Central American Common Market) may offer greater rewards for modifying products to meet market requirements. To gain access to cutting-edge technologies developed by foreign companies or improve the adaptability of their own innovations, MNEs send their own engineers and scientists to onsite laboratories. The globalization process is moving up the R&D value chain from technology support to product development and further to technology development. This indicates the increasingly important role assumed by foreign facilities in the creation of knowledge. Leading MNEs such as IBM, Philips, and Panasonic are expanding their networks worldwide. IBM, for instance, recently announced that it will open a new center of excellence in India which will focus on key technologies such as electronic commerce, cellular and mobile telephony, and distance learning.

Two distinctive patterns pertaining to globalizing R&D have emerged. First, while in the past the technology flow was unidirectional from the parent company to the affiliate abroad, *firms are now considering foreign R&D units as a critical source of knowledge and technology.* These units are assigned new tasks associated with the parent firm's global strategy. A part of these new tasks may involve deriving distinctive new product variants as part of a regional or world product mandate, or if a unique global product is envisaged, providing research input into its development. Second, *inter-organizational technology cooperation has become a widespread practice.* Such cooperation exists not only between the firms, but also between firms and academic institutions at home and abroad. Apart from cost and resource-sharing rationale, such cooperation is compelled by the increasing demand for skilled scientists and R&D personnel who are in short supply in the home countries. As rapid technological changes put increasing pressure on firms in advanced economies to accelerate innovation (e.g., US and Japan), competition among these firms for R&D talent drives up the costs of hiring scientists and engineers in their home countries. One strategy that many firms adopt is to let the best-trained R&D personnel in their home base concentrate on the most sophisticated work and farm out other work to R&D personnel in their foreign subsidiaries or affiliates, who often also cost less.[3]

Benefits and Challenges of Global R&D

The following benefits may be generated from globalizing R&D.

First, *globalizing R&D may provide a vehicle for access to, or extract benefits from, a target country's technical resources, scientific talent, or local expertise.* Israel, for instance, counts twice as many scientists (as a percentage of the population) as the United States, and is a very attractive country for companies that seek skilled engineers and researchers. MNEs such as IBM have established joint ventures or set up labs there, despite a fairly small local market for their products. MNEs may also receive benefits such as tax breaks and low interest financing offered by host governments (e.g., Indonesia, Malaysia, and Thailand) when they set up R&D centers overseas. The Country Box illustrates how India's rich pool of software engineers has lured many world-class MNEs to build global R&D centers there.

Second, globalizing R&D *may enhance a firm's global competitive advantage*. Building and maintaining a competitive position abroad necessitates localizing R&D in target countries, which improves proximity and responsiveness to local customers. Setting up research facilities in a host country signals long-term commitment to the local economy. For example, General Motors, among several world-class auto makers, was selected by the Chinese government to build mid-size cars in a joint venture with the Shanghai Automotive Industry Corporation because the US company offered to set up a technology institute in China. Today, GM's R&D center in Warren, Michigan coordinates and integrates the work being conducted at six Chinese universities and seven joint ventures. By locating R&D activity abroad, an MNE is able to improve its responsiveness to local needs both in terms of time and relevance. Hoffmann-LaRoche, the Swiss-based pharmaceutical company, established an R&D facility in Japan to become more aware of, and responsive to, consumption differences in Asia. Increased investments by MNEs in India, Brazil, Poland, and Mexico created a strong need for technical support and local adaptation abroad, which, in many cases, requires the presence of a permanent R&D group for expanded operations.

Finally, *globalizing R&D may enable the MNE to enjoy the benefits arising from international division of labor in R&D among multiple foreign countries or regions*. A well-coordinated MNE is able to allocate specific responsibilities to different yet integrated R&D subsidiaries depending upon their expertise, knowledge, and external resources. This multilateral cooperation enables the firm to obtain a more varied flow of new ideas, products, and processes, providing greater input into a firm's innovation process. This also creates a synergy earned from comparative advantages in R&D resources from each participating nation. Canon, for example, built technical centers in Shanghai (China), interactive systems in Surrey (United Kingdom), software systems in California (United States), imaging technology in Sydney (Australia), telecommunications in Rennes (France), and process development centers in Japan. This individually specialized, yet globally integrated, network nurtures synergy creation from global research and development.

Globalizing R&D is a complex process involving a series of challenges and difficulties. Globalizing R&D generally creates the following challenges.

First, *maintaining minimum efficient scale in foreign R&D operations is not always easy*. It may be difficult to staff the foreign labs with enough qualified people to achieve the minimum efficient scale. In addition, splitting up an MNE's most qualified people over numerous international R&D sites might dilute the critical mass at the home-based, centralized R&D facility. Further, government controls and political risks in a host country may increase the uncertainty of R&D operations. It may create a schism between an MNE's motivations and those of a local government. In certain developing countries where import restrictions exist, it may also be difficult to import the necessary research materials. Hiring local employees may also be subject to governmental control.

438

Second, *leakage of proprietary knowledge poses a serious threat when R&D is globalized*. This may arise because of the presence of a foreign joint venture partner, lax patent laws in the country, or perhaps the likelihood of foreign nationals being hired away by indigenous firms after they have acquired much of the MNE's expertise. McDonnell Douglas and Boeing faced such leakage risks when they partnered with Japanese firms on the F-15 Eagle fighter and the Boeing 767, respectively. Maintaining the confidentiality of technical information and knowledge is difficult and costly.

Finally, *globalizing R&D inevitably increases coordination and control costs*. An MNE may face coordination issues such as allocating research tasks among dispersed R&D centers, exchanging information among different R&D centers, and developing products that are responsive to market needs in different countries. The more decentralized and distant an MNE's R&D facilities, the more costly the coordination and control necessary for the arrangement to succeed. If R&D is done in just one country, there are fewer language and cultural barriers to surmount, as well as a shorter distance to be covered in order to hold face-to-face meetings. Lack of coordination and control can easily lead to costly duplication of effort since different facilities may not be fully aware of what others are doing. In addition, cultural and business differences between home and host countries may intensify the difficulty in running R&D activities overseas. For example, the relationship between engineers and managers is very different in the United States, Japan, and Europe. In the United States, managers traditionally hold less authority over engineers working under them than is the case in Japan and Europe. Problem solving also differs across countries. In Europe, it is customary to discuss problems and solutions before cost figures are considered, whereas Americans first wish to know whether a program is financially feasible.

Despite these challenges, we have witnessed increased globalization of R&D activities as MNEs become more internationalized. To most of them, overseas R&D activities have added net value to their growth in the global marketplace and created sustained competitive advantages over local and international competitors.[4] To obtain the advantages of global R&D while attenuating its disadvantages requires well-prepared design and structuring in the building phase and well-established systems of management, coordination, communication, and control in the operational phase. Managing global R&D activities is difficult and complex, requiring the consideration of multiple factors in formulating strategies and policies concerning R&D dispersion and control. These factors include not only the dynamics of external environments, such as market demands and governmental policies, but also the requirements of organizational development, such as the firm's strategic goals and internal rationales behind research and development. A firm's global R&D system should be structured to fulfill organizational needs while taking advantage of external opportunities. Internally, the R&D function faces an ongoing task of managing coordination and control across the company's international network of R&D laboratories. Externally, corporate R&D is increasingly called upon to create and manage technological cooperation with universities, research consortia, and even competitors in order to stay abreast of leading-edge developments. It is equally essential for the firm to manage such critical areas as communication and coordination, human resource management, technology transfer, and collaboration with local firms, among others. Without such management, the economic return of R&D dispersion cannot be ensured. We elaborate on these issues in the following section.

Interim Summary

1. An increasing number of MNEs have globalized R&D to take advantage of the expertise available in foreign markets, as well as to be responsive to the demands of those markets. Firms view foreign R&D units as a critical source of knowledge and an important vehicle for intra-MNE knowledge sharing and utilization.
2. Globalizing R&D involves challenges such as high costs, knowledge leakage, and coordination difficulty. Overcoming these challenges necessitates a well-designed global structure and a carefully planned organizational scheme.

Country Box

India

R&D Centers of Global Companies in India

Since 1997, a large number of global firms, especially those in the information technology (IT) industry, have started R&D centers in India to access research resources there, particularly a large pool of software engineers. Most global R&D centers are concentrated in Bangalore (e.g., IBM, Alcatel-Lucent, HP, Sony, Siemens, Telesoft, Philips, Texas Instruments, LG, Verifone, SAP, Huawei), with several others located in Hyderabad (e.g., Motorola, Bell Labs, Microsoft), Mumbai (e.g., Gateway, Informix, Shimadzu, E-gain), or Delhi (e.g., Oracle and Adobe). MNEs in Bangalore serve both as producers and consumers of software, turning the city into an international gateway for trained manpower. Bangalore has become the largest IT cluster in India, attributable to the presence of educational institutions, state support, venture capital, and an extensive network of technology developers and providers. Many prestigious research institutes such as the Indian Institute of Science, Jawaharlal Center for Advanced Scientific Research, National Aerospace Laboratory, Central Manufacturing Technology Institute, Aeronautical Research Center, and Central Power Research Institute are located in Bangalore.

The growth of Bangalore as an IT cluster was catalyzed by the founding of the first global R&D center by US firm Texas Instruments (TI). Originally founded in 1985, the center consists of 500 engineers specially trained in the design of circuits. In 1998 this center began to design digital signal processors (DSPs), the fastest growing sector of the global semiconductor market. It also designs chips, specifically Application Specific Integrated Circuits (ASICs). Fabrication is carried out in TI's US facility, with the designs being encrypted and transmitted from India through a dedicated satellite link. The establishment of the TI India R&D center was one of the reasons for Bangalore becoming a software hub, since TI gave R&D contracts to other firms such as Wipro and Sasken, thus acting as a catalyst for knowledge networking. Wipro is a leading Indian IT firm and a major exporter of software from India. Wipro has a R&D division consisting of 3,000 engineers working exclusively on telecom. The company's annual sales of engineering R&D services in 2012 were estimated to be $700 million.

The number of MNEs that have set up R&D centers in India continued to rise throughout the 2000s and early 2010s. In the 18 months prior to the release of a report by the research firm Zinnov in September 2013, 25 MNEs entered this segment of the India market, including Groupon, Unilever, Expedia, Panasonic, FireEye, Ricoh, Royal DSM, Ruckus Wireless, Abbott, and Sigma-Aldrich. By 2013, the number of R&D centers set up by MNEs reached 1,031, and the annual exports of engineering R&D services from India amounted to $16.3 billion.

Sources: J. Ribeiro, "Multinationals continue to expand India R&D centers," *IDG News Services*, July 22, 2010; S. John, "25 global companies set up R&D centers in India in last 18 months," *The Times of India*, September 21, 2013.

Designing and Structuring Global R&D

Types of Foreign R&D Units

Defining the type of a planned foreign R&D program is the first step in globalizing R&D. In relation to the role of foreign R&D units, R&D subsidiaries can be categorized into: (1) *corporate technology units*; (2) *specialized or regional technology units*; (3) *global technology units*; (4) *technology transfer units*; and (5) *indigenous technology units*.

A *corporate technology unit* is designed to generate basic, long-term technology of exploratory nature for use by the corporate parent. A *specialized technology unit* is set up to develop specialized technologies, products, or processes predefined by headquarters to serve either the global or regional market. A *global technology unit* is generally established for developing new products and processes for major world markets. A *technology transfer unit* focuses on facilitating the transfer of the corporate parent's technology to a subsidiary and providing local technical services. Finally, *an indigenous technology unit* is formed overseas to develop new products specifically for the local market.

Technology transfer units and indigenous technology units are both locally adapting laboratories. The major function of these two units is to help the production and marketing facilities in a host country make the most efficient use of the MNE's existing technology. They may also assist in the process of technology transfer by advising on necessary adaptation of the manufacturing technology. They may act as a technical service center by examining why a product may not fully satisfy a local market and by adapting it to better meet local needs. Exxon, CPC International, and Otis, for example, used this technique in the development of products for the European market. When indigenous technology units are designed to serve a key foreign market, they become locally integrated laboratories and involve some fundamental development activities. The particular host market (e.g., China) may be considerably large, diverse, and fast-growing and may necessitate a nationwide R&D head office to coordinate and integrate host-country R&D activities. IBM's R&D center in Beijing, or Xerox's R&D center in Shanghai, are each playing such a role.

Corporate technology units and global technology units are both globally interdependent laboratories. These two types of labs provide inputs into a centrally defined and coordinated R&D program, with no necessary connection with host-country production operations. Their major function focuses on research and development, rather than improvement and adaptation. They link mainly to corporate and divisional R&D, not local manufacturing. CPC International's R&D affiliates in Italy and Japan, and GE's John F. Welch Technology Center in Bangalore, India, are examples of successful corporate technology units. Major technology companies such as IBM and Microsoft have established several global technology units worldwide (each focusing on certain product-technology areas) developing products or processes that have universal applicability in all major foreign and domestic markets, furthering both the companies themselves and the industry as a whole.

Specialized technology units are globally controlled yet individually differentiated laboratories. Each of these specialized units is focused on specific technological areas defined by headquarters. Daimler AG (formerly Daimler-Benz), for example, has its corporate research center in Stuttgart, Germany. Its R&D center in Palo Alto, near Stanford University in Silicon Valley, focuses on applying the latest communication technologies in the company's vehicles. Its R&D center in Bangalore, India emphasizes the development of multimedia, telematics, and manufacturing solutions. In Shanghai, the auto maker's joint R&D center was established to focus on microelectronics and electronic packaging. These R&D activities are tightly coordinated with microelectronics research in Germany, and scientists are exchanged between China and Germany on a regular basis. Regional technology units are regionally integrated laboratories. In contrast to specialized units that focus on specific technological areas, regional units are responsible for their respective geographical areas. Both specialized and regional units are subject to the control and coordination of headquarters.

R&D unit designation may change over time as international expansion increases, the R&D subsidiary grows, or the MNE's strategy changes. The global R&D function may evolve in stages, along the degree of the MNE's internationalization. In the initial stage, firms may dedicate few technical resources overseas, and maintain domestically oriented management structures and a highly ethnocentric management group. As their commitment to overseas markets grows, companies build up technical capabilities abroad to respond to local market conditions, either by modifying the parent's products or by generating products for sale only in the local market. When the headquarters realizes that the overseas labs have achieved a level of technical competence beyond that of the rest of the company, it may switch its overseas laboratories' orientation from the host-country markets to the world market. The headquarters may assign new product development projects to overseas labs to take advantage of their specialized technical skills. In this situation, foreign R&D units benefit simultaneously from a wide variety of environmental conditions that stimulate new product development as well as from intra-company collaborations that create synergetic returns for the company as a whole.

Selecting R&D Location

Choosing a R&D location is an important and complex decision because external parameters such as market conditions, resource availability, and governmental policies vary across countries and even locations within a country. Once a laboratory is built, the costs of switching from one location to another are enormous. The location selection framework presented in Chapter 10 is generally applicable to the R&D site decision. Nevertheless, the following factors are specific in the location choice of overseas R&D.

First, *location selection depends on an R&D subsidiary's strategic role set by the parent company*. If the subsidiary is designed to serve a home market, managers should consider the availability of scientific knowledge and talent from foreign universities. For a subsidiary targeting the world market, location factors include accessibility to foreign scientific communities and availability of adequate infrastructure and universities.[5] When the subsidiary serves only as a technology transfer center, it should be located in countries where the company already has a substantial investment in marketing and/or manufacturing. R&D generally follows marketing and manufacturing in the globalization process. In cases where the labs are established to perform basic research or develop new products for the global market, they should be situated in places in which there is a concentration of advanced innovation and technology resources. This concentration is an important reason why MNEs tend to cluster their technology development centers into several hot spots, as illustrated in the examples in Exhibit 13.2.

Second, *host governmental policies may influence location decision*. Some of these policies include: government requirements to increase the local technological content of the firm's activities; work permit regulations for expatriate scientists, engineers, and managers; efficient patent laws; and tax subsidies to support the foreign firm's R&D activities. In the 1990s, many developing countries established high-tech development zones to attract MNEs' R&D investments. These zones offer a series of incentives to foreign companies such as tax exemption for a certain number of years, financing

Location	Technology	Major Companies
Austin, TX	Computers, Software	3M, Apple, HP, Dell, Google, Intel, university research centers
Baltimore, MD	Biotechnology	BioTechnical Institute of Maryland, Quest Diagnostics, BioPark at the University of Maryland
Boston, MA	Biotechnology, Computers, Pharmaceuticals, Software, Telecom	Massachusetts Biotechnology Council, MIT, over 150 bio technology firms, hundreds of tech start-ups
Denver, CO Metro Area	Aerospace, Biotechnology	Denver Technological Center, Ball Corp., IBM, Lockheed-Martin, Raytheon
Huntsville, AL	Aerospace, Defense Technology	Cummings Research Park, Marshall Space Flight Center, Redstone Arsenal, University of Alabama research programs
Raleigh-Durham Area, NC	Biotechnology, Computers, Pharmaceuticals, Telecom	Research Triangle Park, prestigious universities, over 170 global technology and research firms
Salt Lake City, UT	Chips, Software	Adobe, Electronic Arts, Oracle, Microsoft, University of Utah Research Park
San Francisco, CA Bay Area	Computers, Electronics, Nanotechnology, Software	HP, Intel, Apple, Oracle, Google, the Bay Area Nanotechnology Forum
Seattle, WA Metro Area	Aerospace, Communications, Software	Boeing, Microsoft, Amazon
Washington D.C Area	Biotechnology, Software, Telecom	Microsoft, LivingSocial, Lockheed-Martin, various universities and research institutes

Exhibit 13.2 US hot spots for technology development
Source: Compiled from Forbes.com and USA Today rankings, 2012–2013.

443

support from government-owned banks, reduction of land rent expenses, and priority in acquiring local resources. The government itself may also organize some high-profile research consortia soliciting foreign participation. In the United States, for example, the Microelectronics and Computer Technology Corporation, Semiconductor Research Corporation, and Semateck consortia focus on technologies in microelectronics and semiconductors. In Europe, broader consortia were fostered through the European Strategic Program for Research and Development in Information Technology (ESPRIT), Research Development in Advanced Communications Technology for Europe (RACE), and European Research Coordinating Agency (EUREKA), to name a few.

Third, *the local infrastructure and technological level of a foreign country are critical*. A threshold of technological capability must exist in the country to permit R&D to take place. Some MNEs may wish to start tapping into technology that is more advanced. For example, Germany is a world leader in such areas as chemistry, physics, metallurgy, and medicine, while the United Kingdom has traditionally spent heavily in chemicals and pharmaceuticals. The presence of research universities or local firms with advanced technology becomes important in these circumstances (see the Industry Box about Ford in Aachen).

Finally, *sociocultural factors may affect location selection*. MNEs have shown a preference for locating R&D facilities in nations with a similar culture and language,[6] which makes sense considering the difficulties associated with operating any business in a different cultural and social environment. It can be frustrating to operate in an environment where the most basic cultural, social, and business practices (which are taken for granted in one's home country) are quite different. Furthermore, the decision makers in headquarters should consider the attractiveness of the foreign country's lifestyle to the staff that will be assigned overseas. If the general consensus is that the location is undesirable, it may be difficult to find qualified people willing to work abroad. Because R&D largely depends on the creativity and efficiency of human resources, the working and living conditions overseas may determine the expatriates' incentives and commitments (see also Chapter 17).

Industry Box

Ford Locates its R&D Center in Aachen, Germany

Ford chose Aachen in Germany as its new European R&D location partly because of its proximity to one of the most industrialized regions in Europe. Aachen is centrally positioned in the heart of Europe, allowing for close cooperation with more than 40 universities in 16 different countries. Aachen is also home to one of the major prestigious technical universities in Europe (RWTH Aachen), enabling Ford to easily recruit highly qualified scientists and engineers. Technical cooperation with local universities and institutes facilitates the acquisition of new technologies and supports strategic technology monitoring. Aachen, which is located close to the Netherlands, Belgium, and France, serves as an ideal listening post for the notoriously diverse European tastes and expectations. Ford finds it easier to design and develop product variants or to monitor European Community politics from Aachen than from other locations. Today, Ford's Research Center in Aachen continues to play an important role for Ford's European subsidiary company, Ford of Europe AG, with about 200 researchers from 20 different countries working on sophisticated technologies to meet the growing demand for personal mobility, safety improvement, and emission control.

Structuring Global R&D Activities

In order to ensure global R&D success, MNEs must design an appropriate organizational structure governing R&D activities. Two critical factors should be considered in structuring global R&D operations: (1) *the level of authority an MNE plans to provide to its foreign R&D activities*; and (2) *the scope of geographical market to be covered*. Building on these two axes (autonomy level and market breadth), five models can be identified. They are: (1) *ethnocentric centralized*; (2) *polycentric decentralized*; (3) *specialized lab*; (4) *global central lab*; and (5) the *globally integrated network*. Exhibit 13.3 displays these five forms. You may note that these are choices about overall organizational structure governing an MNE's worldwide R&D, whereas the five types of global R&D units illustrated earlier are choices about a role played by a specific R&D laboratory within an MNE's global R&D network. A specific R&D lab is positioned within this network to help fulfill an MNE's overall goal in research and development. Each of these forms serves as an organizational framework in which different R&D units may be designed with different roles and types.

In the *ethnocentric centralized* R&D structure, all major R&D activities are concentrated in one home country. This structure contains a corporate technology unit at home, and may also include a few technology transfer units to distribute centralized R&D results to local operations. In this model, the core technologies are viewed as a national treasure in the home-country base, designing products that are subsequently manufactured in other locations and distributed worldwide. This structure ensures technology protection and enhances returns to scale in R&D. Its disadvantage is the lack of sensitivity to signals from foreign markets and insufficient consideration of local market demands. MNEs choose this structure only if they manufacture global, standardized products and do not consider differentiating between foreign markets. Nippon Steel of Japan, for example, has adopted this structure because its products are highly standardized in international

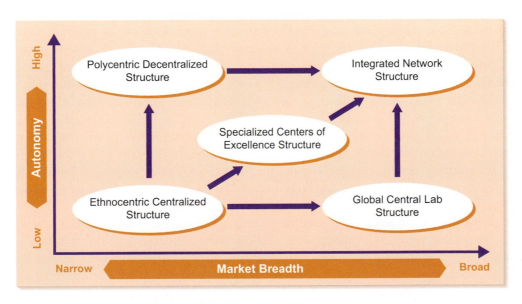

Exhibit 13.3 Organizational models for global R&D

445

markets. The company has four centralized R&D laboratories near Tokyo (about 1,000 researchers). This structure helps the company reduce costs considerably.

The *polycentric decentralized* R&D structure is characterized by a decentralized federation of R&D sites with no supervising corporate R&D center. This structure contains a number of indigenous technology units in major foreign markets. Foreign R&D laboratories are highly autonomous with little incentive to share information with other R&D units or central R&D. Overseas R&D laboratories emphasize product or process development in response to localization requests and local consumer demands. Royal Dutch/Shell, for example, used this structure during 1984–1997 to develop Carilon, a multiple-application polymer, in Shell's three decentralized R&D units, including Amsterdam R&D center, Westhollow Research center in Houston, and Belgium R&D laboratory. In this structure, efforts to preserve autonomy and national identity may impede cross-border coordination, and therefore lead to inefficiency on a corporate level and to duplication of R&D activities. The company may also lose its focus on a particular technology. Shell, therefore, restructured this R&D system in 1998 and authorized the Westhollow Research Center in Houston to lead in developing Carilon, with other centers focusing on commercialization. Today, Shell continues to assign its five major research centers differing areas of focus and encourages collaboration between centers, as well as between centers and other research networks, industrial associations, and customers.

In the *specialized laboratory* structure, foreign R&D units are assigned global mandates. The aim is to improve the global efficiency of the product development process, concentrating in a single location the resources relevant to development operations in a particular product category. This structure contains several specialized technology units in respective product areas. When there exists a leading market in terms of size and presence of customers, the MNE will assign the global responsibility for developing and manufacturing the product to the laboratories and plants in that country. This approach makes it possible to achieve economies of scale in R&D and to place the product development operations close to the company's key customers. For example, Alcatel-Lucent acquired Rockwell Company's R&D laboratory in the United States, the most sophisticated telecom market, and used it as the primary research base for its transmission systems. Because there are costs in transferring R&D to a manufacturing plant that is further away from the R&D center, global development laboratories are often selected on the basis of their proximity to the manufacturing plants. For instance, Ericsson specializes its R&D facilities on the basis of their historical background and major area of technical specialization, with R&D on silicon technology and chip design done in Australia, Italy, and Finland, and R&D on cloud computing done in its new facilities in Stockholm and Linköping, Sweden. Similarly, the organization of R&D at Siemens is based on worldwide centers of competence laboratories selected on the basis of their traditional scientific specialization and competence, and given worldwide responsibilities. Siemens' Italian subsidiary is a worldwide competence center for microwave radio systems and cellular telephones.

The *global central lab* structure is used to leverage a company's centralized technical resources to create new global products. Although it is also centralized, R&D under this structure covers a much broader market domain than R&D in the ethnocentric centralized model. In this structure, there may be more than one global technology unit to generate worldwide innovation. In this model, companies concentrate their technical resources in their country of origin. To make this structure work, it is important to create an effective market information network that provides a flow of information from the decentralized production or marketing units to the parent company. This enables the central development laboratories to generate products suitable for the global market and/or to adapt different product versions to individual markets. Nissan, for example, implemented this model in the early 1990s. In the development of the Primera automobile, targeted for the European market, Nissan formed a core project team in Western Europe. Back in Japan, this team was supported by some 100 engineers who had all experienced European culture during numerous visits.

The *globally integrated network* structure may be filled by a number of foreign R&D units with different roles and types, such as global technology unit, corporate technology unit, specialized technology unit, and indigenous technology unit. In this model, home R&D is no longer the center of control for all R&D activities, but rather one among many interdependent R&D units that are closely interconnected by means of flexible and varied coordination mechanisms. A central coordinating body exercises the necessary supervision to prevent duplication and to integrate the diverse contributions. Development processes whose results can be exploited across a number of markets involve resources from the different facilities whose work is coordinated according to a common plan. Each unit in the network specializes in a particular product, component, or technology area, and perhaps a set of core capabilities. At times, this unit takes over a lead role as a competence center, and is then responsible for the entire value generation process, not just for product-related R&D. Schindler Lifts, the world leader in escalators and second ranked in elevators, established its integrated R&D network in 1996. Its R&D is dispersed over several units in Switzerland, France, Spain, Sweden, and the United States. In order to avoid duplication and to realize synergy, its management has started to identify the core competencies in R&D. Each of the designated competence centers in the integrated R&D network assumes strategic roles for the entire company and is engaged in defining strategies and business development. Various MNEs, including Nestlé, Philips, and Bayer, moved from a polycentric decentralized organization toward an integrated R&D network.

Interim Summary

1. Foreign R&D units can be defined as one of the following types: corporate technology units, specialized or regional technology units, global technology units, technology transfer units, and indigenous technology units. To select an R&D location, managers must consider an intended role of the R&D unit, host government policies, and infrastructural, technological, and sociocultural conditions.

2. Structuring global R&D depends on the level of decentralization offered to foreign R&D activities and the scope of geographical market covered by foreign units. Five structuring models are: ethnocentric centralized model; polycentric decentralized model; specialized lab model; global central lab model; and globally integrated network model.

Managing and Operating Global R&D

The increasing dispersion of R&D laboratories in foreign markets forces MNEs to take a global view in managing their research operations through such areas as human resource management, autonomy specification, global planning, and communications improvement.

Human Resource Management

Chapter 17 discusses human resource management policies, many of which are applicable to managing human resources in global R&D. Nevertheless, R&D human resources should be managed in a way that fulfills the unique needs of global research and development. First, *selecting key personnel should be linked to the role or type of a foreign R&D unit*. If the laboratory belongs to an indigenous technology unit, for example, then well-qualified local talents should be considered for both R&D and management positions. If the lab is to accept technology from the parent company or belongs to a specialized or global technology unit, then qualified expatriates are preferable. Second, *personnel policies for foreign labs should be relatively standardized to the extent allowed by local laws and customs*. Promotions, titles, and reward and recognition programs should be as similar as possible. Because there should be frequent contact between home and overseas lab personnel, this uniformity of titles and managerial positions can help make foreign labs feel they are equal partners with the parent laboratories. Reward and recognition programs that are instituted at headquarters should be extended to include all the overseas laboratory personnel. Third, *maintaining some regular contacts and visits between foreign R&D units and the home lab center is useful*. This can take several forms: a visit to exchange information, an extended visit to work out a particularly difficult problem or to exploit a new discovery, or a regularly scheduled planning conference. 3M, for example, schedules regular conferences between US R&D and Japanese engineering groups. In addition, 3M's Japanese R&D subsidiary often sends its laboratory and production personnel to their counterpart labs and factories in the United States for up to six months of training on equipment similar to what is being built in Japan.

Autonomy Setting

In the context of this chapter, autonomy means an R&D unit's decision-making power concerning R&D activities. *The autonomy of a foreign R&D unit depends largely on the role it plays within the MNE network*. For example, managerial autonomy in a lab that serves as a specialized global competence center should be delegated greater power. In general, autonomy should be higher if the lab's technical resources are scarce, need to be located together in a center of excellence to attain critical mass, or should be put to use where they would create the most leverage for the company as a whole. When a foreign R&D unit serves as a technology transfer unit for the MNE network, its autonomy will be low and the decision-making authority will be centralized at headquarters. In this situation, the unit plays a role as effective adopter of new products and processes created by the parent company. If the unit functions as an indigenous, specialized technology laboratory, or global technology center, it requires a high level of autonomy and a low level of formalization (i.e., specifying the necessary behaviors in the form of rules, procedures, or programs). The subsidiaries require increased degrees of freedom and more resources dispensed by the parent companies. Some R&D subsidiaries of companies

448

such as Unilever, ITT, and Philips enjoy considerable strategic and operational autonomy, although headquarters exercises administrative control through the budgeting and financial reporting systems. These relatively autonomous subsidiaries were found to be generally more productive than other R&D units in these companies.[7] Recent research suggests that a combination of local autonomy and global connectedness via the MNE's network tends to result in greater R&D productivity.[8]

The autonomy of a foreign R&D unit is subordinating an MNE's strategic needs for global integration. There are positive associations between creation, adoption, and diffusion of innovations by a subsidiary and the extent to which the subsidiary is normatively integrated with the parent company and shares its overall strategy, goals, and values. Such integration is typically the result of a high degree of organizational socialization and is achieved through extensive travel and transfer of managers between the headquarters and the subsidiary, and through joint work in teams, task forces, and committees. Ericsson, Procter & Gamble (P&G), and NEC are convinced that these activities have helped them in developing a common context that significantly improves subsidiary contributions to the entire innovation processes.

Resource allocation is a crucial vehicle in balancing global integration and local autonomy for managing dispersed R&D units abroad. Generally, resources allocated to global technology units or specialized technology units may be those that focus on a core competency, strategic, and exploratory research, global market coverage, or significant investment areas. Resources likely to be duplicated in regional R&D centers are those that focus primarily on product development, as opposed to technology development. In addition to technological factors, considerations such as financial and geopolitical factors play a large role in determining proper allocation of resources. For example, Philips has set up an R&D facility in Palo Alto, California as a window on Silicon Valley for all of its divisions and business units. Finally, in aligning resources, it is important to consider the interface between human resources and physical resources in a new information technology environment. Networks connecting a company's facilities throughout the world enable researchers to work on one project from many locations. The major innovations that have been made in modeling and simulation technology allow more development and testing to be done in simulation, reducing the time and money spent on manufacturing prototypes or running tests on finished products.

Global Planning

The corporate R&D office has the important task of coordinating an increasingly dispersed global network of R&D laboratories. Global planning serves as a primary means of information exchange among decentralized R&D laboratories and projects. In the planning process, corporate headquarters outlines a strategic intent to globalize R&D and communicate it to foreign R&D units. Panasonic, for example, established a three-pillars blueprint, including:

■ Construction of a tri-pole R&D *network* between laboratories in North America and Europe and domestic research laboratories to establish advanced technological bases and create products for the global market.
■ Improved *efficiency* of R&D activities through expansion of collaborative relationships with international research institutions.
■ Increased *speed* of R&D globalization through effective communications and superior management across borders.

449

R&D planning activities can also contribute to learning throughout the MNE if they routinely solicit the participation of all scientists and technicians. The central R&D office can transform planning into an educational process. For example, Alcatel-Lucent holds biennial internal scientific conferences in which scientists exchange information with one another, and with strategic planning and business units. Planning activities can also facilitate global integration. Johnson & Johnson's Global Product Category Planning Groups provide a mechanism for incorporating foreign markets' product development priorities, which were often ignored in the past. Although budgeting is considered increasingly difficult because development cycles are five years long or more, global planning is easier owing to the ability to disseminate information and establish priorities.

Planning can help align the technological and business strategies of a company. Once the technology strategy is set, this alignment can be carried into specific project areas. A key aspect of R&D alignment on business objectives is cross-functional planning and execution. With the participation of marketing, manufacturing, and sales, R&D groups can optimize their process of project assessment, selection, and project portfolio balancing. Progress on R&D projects can also be evaluated more regularly and reported to multi-function teams. Nestlé's research center at Swiss headquarters sets budget and planning priorities through multi-functional strategic business units in close collaboration with operating businesses. After evaluating incoming development and product proposals through extensive information sharing, strategic business units (SBUs) set short- and medium-term priorities. Annual R&D work programs are updated and corrected on a rolling basis throughout the year.

It is usually impractical to combine product development, manufacturing, and R&D within the same organizational unit. This is particularly true in very large companies. Corporations such as IBM, General Foods, and Xerox have established committees or boards with coordination responsibility throughout the entire corporation. Membership in these committees is composed of representatives from business units, manufacturing, and R&D. AT&T has begun to experiment with having research managers at AT&T Labs report to both research management and product units. This new alignment is intended to improve the coupling between business and research. It is also designed to reduce the "time to market" between invention and product introduction.

Communication Improvement

Geographic distance poses a major challenge for communication across an international network of R&D labs. Cross-border communication breakdowns occur frequently, lowering R&D productivity. Moreover, the role of informal communication is especially important because much of the work can be accomplished only in teams. An effective communication system is needed not only within the R&D function but also between R&D and other functional activities such as marketing, manufacturing, and sales. To improve communication within a global R&D network, international managers need to be aware of the following issues.

Rules and Procedures

For overseas laboratories, careful reporting and documentation of research progress can help keep R&D personnel aware of research activity across the company. At Nestlé, progress reports are filed every six months and circulated to interested parties. In any given year, several hundred reports enter into the reporting system. Research progress reports supplement the communication flows related to the planning cycle, which can also serve an educational purpose.

Electronic Communication

Videoconferencing, facsimiles of visual and written material, electronic mail, and computer conferencing all offer greater possibilities for communication than a simple telephone call. They provide an essential infrastructure for accomplishing cross-border teamwork. However, they cannot replace the face-to-face informal communication that builds trust. Misunderstandings and excessively slow contact or feedback of information erode the climate of trust necessary for teamwork. Along with electronic means of communication, periodic meetings through direct, face-to-face contact are necessary.

Boundary Spanners

Headquarters R&D staff often perform the role of boundary spanners between the dispersed R&D laboratories. They travel frequently to each site location to share development elsewhere in the global R&D network and to discuss progress at the particular site. They may also divulge sensitive information across the network about developments with customers, joint venture partners, or suppliers. At Johnson & Johnson, the head office R&D group consists of "internal scouts" who are always on the lookout for opportunities to cross-fertilize research project ideas from one laboratory to another. At Nestlé, the corporate R&D staff visits foreign laboratories to optimize long-term research priorities, to develop personal contacts, and to identify potential key personnel.

Informal Network

Communication through informal networks is often an efficient means for teamwork. The central R&D group can stimulate informal networks, which may be created both inside and outside the company, locally or internationally.[9] An external local network consists of local suppliers, customers, and research institutions that provide the opportunity for learning from foreign environments. The central office R&D group can organize an external international network of academics who work on company projects. Private conferences bring these academics together to present their research and to exchange information. Locating and funding outside academic researchers can be supervised by the central office. Johnson & Johnson finances R&D projects in universities through a program called Focused Giving Program. The program funds $3 million of academic research in and outside of the United States, and gathers the recipients together once a year to deliver findings. An MNE's internal network can be activated most directly with international project teams. Project team members stay in their respective laboratories most of the time, and collaborate on projects using electronic means and personnel transfers.

Cultural Adaptation

Often, international R&D project teams must overcome cultural differences. Although many researchers can speak English, there is no assurance that the members of a multicultural R&D team understand one another. Research shows significant cross-cultural differences among R&D professionals on the dimensions of power (respect for hierarchy), risk avoidance, individualism, and masculinity/femininity (see also Chapter 6).[10] The Japanese believe that a manager who champions an innovation should work within the organizational rules, procedures, and hierarchy, whereas Americans do not hold this belief. Often, an effective means of reducing cultural differences is to socialize R&D professionals through a wide range of activities. International training seminars help create a shared corporate culture as well as a network of colleagues who can communicate on a much more informal basis. International assignments not only deepen the understanding of the individual transferred, but the host and home laboratories gain a much clearer picture of internal workings of other laboratories through this individual.

Interim Summary

1. Incentive systems such as recognition and reward should be as uniform as possible among different R&D units. Also, it is useful to maintain a regular program of exchange and visitation between global R&D units so as to foster unity and cooperation. Communication is important not only within an R&D unit and between R&D units but with other functional divisions such as marketing and sales as well.
2. Autonomy of foreign R&D units should be based on their strategic roles in overall corporate strategy and requirements for global integration. Having clear business and technology strategies within the company makes the integration of research much easier. Once the technology strategy is set, it can be carried into specific project areas, giving everyone a common frame of reference.

Technology Transfer Across Borders

A popular alternative to establishing foreign-based R&D labs or centers is to use technology transfers and collaborative agreements with foreign partners. This approach is especially attractive to those firms or projects that require large investments and involve high uncertainties. In Chapter 12 we illustrated a number of issues on how to build and manage global alliances. The discussion in this section focuses only on technology transfer.

International technology transfer is a process by which one firm's technology or knowledge is passed on to another firm in a different country for economic benefits. Through technology transfer, a firm can acquire needed technology or knowledge from a foreign provider. Frequently used methods of technology transfer include international licensing, non-equity or equity joint ventures, turnkey operations, and countertrade (see Chapter 10 which explains these modes). Generally, firms acquiring technology through international transfer seek increasing competitiveness, increasing profits by reducing development costs, enhancing technological positions in the market, or reducing prices while maintaining quality. If firms want to transfer their own technology to foreign companies, they need to consider such factors as protection of proprietary technology, competition, impact on a firm's existing market power, and earning of royalties from remote markets.

Technology transfer is a complex, ongoing activity, as demonstrated by the fact that many license relationships have been in effect for more than 50 years. Moreover, variations prevail across industry, company, or market lines. Even within an MNE network, policies and management of technology transfer differ according to subsidiaries, types of technologies, and stages of the technology life cycle. As such, it would be inappropriate for a firm to try to police it through uniform rules.

A frequent problem with technology transfer across borders is that much of the technological capability is not easily transferable from one partner to another. This is simply because the successful operationalization of many technologies depends to a great extent on the acquired experiences and expertise of critical personnel such as key scientists, engineers, equipment operators, suppliers, and such. The ways in which interdependent technologies are "fine-tuned" to work effectively within a complex system are often implicit or tacit in nature, relying on overall experiences, skills, and understandings that have been learned over time and internalized. Because of this, it is essential to check the absorptive capability of a transferee (e.g., a buyer of the technology). The **absorptive capability** concerns a firm's ability to acquire, assimilate, integrate, and exploit knowledge and skills that are transferred from others. This capability often depends on the level of the firm's related technology or skills already developed, the effectiveness of organizational learning systems, and the ability to combine a firm's own skills with newly acquired skills.

Effective technology transfer, especially via a joint venture, requires coordinating mechanisms linking two parties, which are often labeled bridges. There are three categories of bridges: procedural bridges, human bridges, and organizational bridges.[11] *Procedural bridges* involve the joint planning and joint staffing of activities, particularly around the time of the transfer of the technology. The emphasis in procedural bridges is on collaboration through joint planning, problem solving, and implementation. *Human bridges* rely on establishing direct interaction between individuals from different organizational areas, typically through the transfer and rotation of personnel. Such personal contact allows both responsibility and enthusiasm to be transferred from one person to another, and it establishes a common social and work-related context that should facilitate more learning and cooperative efforts. The success of the joint venture technology transfer project and continued collaboration between British GEC (General Electric Company) and the French Alcatel-Lucent is attributable to formal communication and informal social networks at the senior manager, project manager, and operational staff levels. *Organizational bridges* use dedicated transfer teams to establish more formal ties between organizational areas. These groups are created to build a more formal structure and common context for the effective transfer of experience. When British Celltech and American Cyanamid cooperated through joint venture-based technology transfer, for example, they faced many communication problems. Cyanamid is a vast, complex organization, and it took Celltech a number of years to understand where executive power lay, and with whom it had to negotiate to get decisions made. These problems were later solved by forming several transfer teams to build formal ties between project managers from the two parties.

Interim Summary

1. Cross-border technology transfer between different firms is an alternative to foreign R&D projects that involve large investments and/or high uncertainty. Licensing and joint ventures are especially common ways of achieving this transfer.
2. Effective technology transfer requires coordinating mechanisms linking two parties. These linkages include human bridges, procedural bridges, and organizational bridges.

Chapter Summary

1. Globalizing R&D is a process of distributing and operating R&D facilities in different countries under a coordinated system by headquarters. It is an important strategic response to changes in foreign market demands and global competition. Globalizing R&D provides access to other countries' technical or scientific resources or talents, strengthens competitive advantage and local adaptation, and facilitates inter-firm knowledge sharing.

2. Globalizing R&D is a complex process involving many challenges, including high costs and risks. Counteracting these challenges requires appropriate design, coordination, and management of various foreign R&D units. These units can be structured as corporate technology units, global technology units, specialized or regional technology units, technology transfer units, or indigenous technology units. Of these, the first two are more centralized and globally interdependent laboratories, whereas the last two are more decentralized and locally adapting units.

3. Carefully selecting location for foreign R&D units can lower the levels of risks, costs, and uncertainties. Location choice depends on an R&D unit's strategic role, foreign government policies, local infrastructure and technological level, and socio-cultural considerations.

4. The governance of global R&D often determines how much it contributes to global success. If an MNE adopts an ethnocentric structure, all major R&D activities will be concentrated in its home country. If it follows a polycentric structure, these activities will be scattered overseas with no supervising corporate R&D center. If it uses a specialized laboratory structure, each foreign R&D unit will be assigned global mandates. If it adopts a global central lab structure, major R&D activities are centralized in the home center, which serves a broad range of markets. Today, more MNEs follow a globally integrated network structure, which entails many interconnected foreign R&D units with different roles and types.

5. Personnel policies affect the productivity of foreign R&D units. These policies should be standardized to the extent allowed by local laws and customs. Unit members should be motivated to develop, share, and commercialize new knowledge. Parent firms should delegate sufficient autonomy to R&D units such that the latter can fulfill their goals effectively. Both formal and informal communication systems should be developed to spur inter-unit sharing of information, experience, and technology.

6. International technology transfer enables MNEs to acquire technology from foreign providers. This lowers research and development costs and expedites knowledge acquisition. Firms must develop absorptive capability and foster a learning environment for technology to be effectively transferred, exploited, and integrated with their own.

Notes

1   V. Chiesa, "Strategies for global R&D," *Research Technology Management*, 39, 5, 1996, 19–25.

2   B. Bowonder and S. Yadav, "R&D spending patterns of global firms," *Research Technology Management*, November–December 1999, 44–55; *The Changing Global Role of the Research and Development Function*, The Conference Board, 1995, 7.

3   A.Y. Lewin, S. Massini and C. Peeters, "Why are companies offshoring Innovation? The emerging global race for talent," *Journal of International Business Studies*, 40, 2009, 901–925; B. Dachs, F. Kampik, T. Scherngell, G. Zahradnik, D. Hanzl-Weiss, G. Hunya, N. Foster, S. Leitner, R. Stehrer and W. Urban, *Internationalization of Business Investments in R&D*, European Union, 2012.

4   M.E. Porter, "Competition in global industries: A conceptual framework." In *Competition in Global Industries*, M. E. Porter (ed.), pp. 15–60, Boston, MA: Harvard Business School Press, 1986; J.H. Dunning, "Multinational enterprises and the globalization of innovatory capacity." In *Technology Management and International Business: Internationalization of R&D and Technology*, O. Granstrand, L. Hakanson and S. Sjolander, (eds), pp. 19–51, Sussex, UK: John Wiley & Sons, 1992.

5   J.N. Behrman and W.A. Fischer, *Overseas R&D Activities of Transnational Companies*, Cambridge, MA: Oelgeschlager, Gunn & Hain, 1980; S.D. Julian and R.T. Keller, "Multinational R&D siting," *Columbia Journal of World Business*, fall 1991, 47–57.

6   S.D. Julian and R.T. Keller, "Multinational R&D siting, corporate strategies for success," *Columbia Journal of World Business*, 26, 2, 1991, 46–57; J. Howells, "The location and organization of research and development: New horizons," *Research Policy*, 19, 1990, 133–146.

7   A. De Meyer, "Management of an international network of industrial R&D laboratories." In *R&D Management Conference Proceedings*, "Managing R&D internationally," Manchester, UK: Manchester Business School, July 1992; R. Nobel and J. Birkinshaw, "Innovation in multinational corporations: Control and communication patterns in international R&D operations," *Strategic Management Journal*, 19, 1998, 479–496.

8   R. Mudambi, S.M. Mudambi, and P. Navarra, "Global innovation in MNCs: The effects of subsidiary self-determination and teamwork," *Journal of Product Innovation Management*, 24, 2007, 442–455; S. Athreye, G. Batsakis and S. Singh, "Subsidiary embeddedness is a strategic choice: Complementarity and the factors associated with different types of embeddedness," Working Paper, Danish Research Unit for Industrial Dynamics, 2013.

9   W. Kuemmerle, "Building effective R&D capabilities abroad," *Harvard Business Review*, March–April 1997, 61–70; R.D. Pearce, *The Internalization of Research and Development by Multinational Enterprises*, New York: St. Martin's Press, 1989.

10 S.A. Shane, "Cultural influences on national rates of innovation," *Journal of Business Venturing*, 8, 1993, 59–73; R.D. Pearce and S. Singh, *Globalizing Research and Development*, New York: St. Martin's Press, 1992.

11 R. Katz, E.S. Rebentisch and T.J. Allen, "A study of technology transfer in a multinational cooperative joint venture," *IEEE Transactions on Engineering Management*, 43, 1, 1996, 97–105.

part 5

functional international business areas

14 FINANCIAL MANAGEMENT FOR GLOBAL OPERATIONS   459

15 INTERNATIONAL ACCOUNTING FOR GLOBAL OPERATIONS   495

16 GLOBAL MARKETING AND SUPPLY CHAIN   523

17 GLOBAL HUMAN RESOURCE MANAGEMENT   563

chapter 14

---

financial management
for global operations

WHY LEARN FINANCIAL MANAGEMENT?   461

INTERNATIONAL TRADE FINANCE   462

FINANCING FOR GLOBAL BUSINESS   471

MANAGING FOREIGN EXCHANGE RISK AND EXPOSURE   476

WORKING CAPITAL MANAGEMENT   489

Do You Know?

1. In what ways does financial management influence the global success of MNEs? What are the major financial management issues that are especially important for global operations?
2. How do payment methods differ between domestic and international transactions? By what means are global payments most commonly conducted?
3. Where does financing for global business and export projects come from? If you are a manager of Siemens, which plans to list its stocks on the NASDAQ, what are the major stages and procedures you ought to know?
4. What steps do MNEs take to reduce risk from foreign exchange fluctuations? Can you distinguish between foreign exchange risk and foreign exchange exposure? If you work for GE, whose operations often involve foreign exchange risks, by what measures, internally or externally, can you reduce or eliminate such risks?

OPENING CASE   Minimizing Exposure in RTZ

RTZ, a $10 billion international mining company based in the United Kingdom, has revamped its foreign exchange policies following a radical review of the relationship between exchange risk management and shareholder value. After realizing that currency fluctuations can erode shareholder wealth, the company decided to abandon traditional short-term hedging strategies in favor of a dynamic, forward-looking focus on long-term results. Although RTZ's costs are largely denominated in the currencies of the countries where it operates, an analysis of its revenue structure showed that the US dollar, the Japanese yen, and the euro were the major currencies determining the price of its products. RTZ views its global net exposure as a portfolio of currency positions similar to a fund manager's treatment of a portfolio of equities. It tries to avoid excessive concentration of risk in any single currency. RTZ maintains a positive exposure in currencies that affect its revenues directly and a negative exposure in currencies in which it denominates its costs. When the firm needs liquidity, it borrows (usually long-term, to balance long-term exposure) in currencies where it has the greatest positive exposure, while holding surplus cash in currencies in which it has large negative exposure. In addition, some of RTZ's positive exposure offsets imports of commodities such as diesel fuel, which are denominated in major currencies. To facilitate implementation of this approach to foreign exchange risk management, corporate headquarters sets debt policies and handles most of the firm's borrowing operations. This centralized borrowing practice allows the corporate finance group and treasury to hedge the company's strategic exposure. Moreover, treasury controls the day-to-day management of the company's exposure. The finance director, a member of the executive committee, informs the CEO and other top executives about RTZ's exposure and actions taken to reduce risk.

460

Why Learn Financial Management?

International business decisions today can hardly be made without considering financial management issues. Thus, financial management should not be viewed as the domain of financial managers alone, but rather as required knowledge for all international business managers. For example, what does "exposure" mean? Is it true that foreign exchange risks involve only foreign currencies, and the domestic currency is risk free in international business? Why did RTZ centralize its foreign exchange risk/exposure management associated with worldwide business? If you are a marketing manager in an overseas subsidiary, how would you deal with headquarters' requirement for using currencies that may not be attractive to your clients? To answer these questions, we need to know the major functions of financial management for global operations.

Financial management is one of the major business functions. Financial management for global operations is, however, much more complex than its domestic equivalent because management must cope with different financial environments, markets, and systems. As the RTZ case shows, effective financial management for international business has become more significant as a result of greater risks and more opportunities. Financial management of MNEs' global operations occurs in an environment characterized by volatile foreign exchange rates, a variety of restrictions on capital flows, various levels of country risk, different tax systems, and a wide spectrum of institutional settings.

Increasing globalization of financial markets, the rise of global e-commerce, and heightened pressure for acting locally while thinking globally have fundamental implications for MNE corporate finance. In this environment, management's ability to seize opportunities and avoid unnecessary risk depends on its knowledge of the international environment and its financial management skills. Increasing global competition is causing senior financial managers such as *CFOs* (*Chief Financial Officers*) to review the cost structure, orientation, and strategic role of the finance function. Many are taking steps to reduce the cost of financial work, including automating the collection and processing of information, developing shared financial service facilities with higher transaction volumes, and improving automated systems. By emphasizing service over enforcement, they also initiate and motivate a role change from corporate policeman to business advocate and strategic partner. They often lead the global strategy process through their priority activities such as budgeting/planning, acquisition, or investment decisions.

As MNEs continue to expand globally, their assets are increasingly widely dispersed and specialized. Philips Electronics (Europe's largest electronics company), for example, has 120 production sites in 29 countries and sales and service outlets in approximately 100 countries, with the total number of employees worldwide exceeding 118,000. Although other companies may be less diversified, the trend toward a broader configuration of assets continues. As a result, headquarters management in many MNEs is obligated to shift from exercising centralized control toward managing a network of established foreign subsidiaries. Accordingly, formal financial coordination and control processes are now being supplemented by investment analysis, risk reduction, global mobilization of financial resources, and optimization of capital structure.

Knowledge of international financial management helps a global business in two important ways. First, it helps the financial manager decide how international events (e.g., changes in foreign exchange rates) will affect a firm and what steps can be taken to exploit positive developments

461

and insulate the firm from harmful ones. Second, it helps the manager anticipate events and make profitable decisions before the events occur. Today, it is difficult to think of any firm, international or domestic, that is not affected in some way by the international financial environment. A wide variety of firm decisions are tied to exchange rates and other developments in the global financial environment.

Financial management for global operations deals with the following major issues:

- International trade finance
- Financing global operations
- Managing foreign exchange risk and exposure
- Working capital management

Interim Summary

1. Modern international business is inextricably linked to financial management. For MNEs, financial management is much more complex than for other companies since they face multiple financial environments, systems, and markets.
2. Adequate international financial management helps an MNE maneuver past international events in the most beneficial way possible as well as to anticipate these events. This is important because many decisions are tied to exchange rates, which can have serious effects on the real income of a company.

International Trade Finance

International Trade Payment

The widely used payment methods in international trade include: (1) *cash in advance*; (2) *letter of credit (L/C)*; (3) *documentary collection*; and (4) *open account terms*. For an exporter, the risk of being unable to receive an importer's payments increases along this sequence.

Cash in Advance

Cash in advance affords the exporter the greatest protection because payment is received either before shipment or upon arrival of the goods. It is often used in a country where there is political instability or where the buyer's credit is shaky. Political crises or foreign exchange controls in the purchaser's country may cause payment delays or even prevent fund transfers, leading to a demand for cash in advance. In addition, in a circumstance where production of contracted products requires a vast amount of capital investment, prepayment is usually demanded, both to finance production and to reduce marketing risks.

Letter of Credit (L/C)

The majority of international trade uses letter of credit (L/C) as the payment method. The **letter of credit** is a letter addressed to the seller, written and signed by a bank acting on behalf of the buyer. In the letter, the bank promises it will honor drafts drawn on itself if the seller conforms to the specific conditions set forth in the L/C. These conditions usually conform to those stipulated in an export contract or sales agreement. If they are not in conformity, the exporter must comply with conditions specified in the L/C. Through an L/C, the bank substitutes its own commitment to pay for that of its customer (the importer). The letter of credit, therefore, becomes a financial contract between the issuing bank and a designated beneficiary that is separate from the commercial transaction.

The advantages of L/C for an exporter include:

- L/C *eliminates credit risk* if the bank that opens it is of good standing. It also reduces the risk that payment will be delayed or withheld due to exchange controls or other political acts.
- L/C *reduces uncertainty*. The exporter knows all the requirements for payment because they are clearly stipulated in the L/C.
- L/C can help *stabilize production*. The exporter that manufactures under contract a specialized piece of equipment runs the risk of contract cancellation before shipment. Opening a letter of credit will provide protection during the manufacturing phase.
- L/C *facilitates financing* because it ensures the exporter a ready buyer for its product.

While the L/C issuance often requires an importer to pre-deposit or have a savings account in the issuing bank (thus possibly forgoing interest earnings in another investment), the importer also gains some benefits from this method, including:

- Because payment is made only under compliance with the L/C's conditions, the importer is able to ascertain that the merchandise is actually shipped on, or before, a certain date by requiring an on-board bill of lading (B/L). An L/C also helps ensure that the quality and quantity of exporting merchandise conform to regulations described in the L/C.
- The bank bears responsibility for any oversight on checking the documents that are required in the L/C (a phenomenon known as *document discrepancies*). In commercial L/C transactions, banks deal in documents and not in goods. The importer can refuse to accept the bill of lading and decline to pay if it finds any, and even very minor, oversight in any of the requirement documents.
- Using L/C heightens the importer's bargaining power, and allows the importer to ask for a price reduction from the exporter.
- If prepayment is required, the importer should deposit its money with a bank, rather than with the seller, because it is then easier to recover the deposit if the seller is unable or unwilling to make a proper shipment.

Exhibit 14.1 shows the process of using an L/C in an export business from a Chinese trading company to a US importer. After a Chinese exporter in Shanghai has shipped the goods, it draws a draft against the issuing bank (Citibank) and presents it, along with the required documents, to its own bank, the Bank of China. The Bank of China, in turn, forwards the bank draft and attached

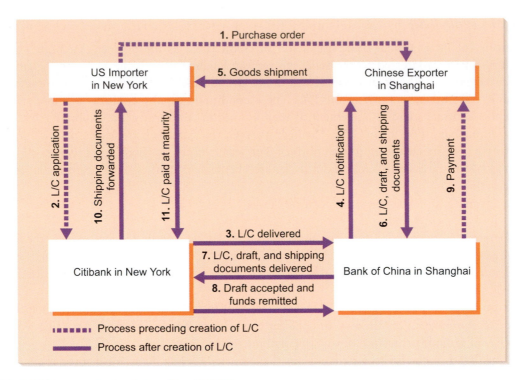

1. Purchase order

5. Goods shipment

US Importer in New York

Chinese Exporter in Shanghai

2. L/C application

10. Shipping documents forwarded

11. L/C paid at maturity

4. L/C notification

6. L/C, draft, and shipping documents

9. Payment

3. L/C delivered

Citibank in New York

7. L/C, draft, and shipping documents delivered

8. Draft accepted and funds remitted

Bank of China in Shanghai

┅┅┅┅ Process preceding creation of L/C

──── Process after creation of L/C

Exhibit 14.1 Process of using letter of credit (L/C)

documents to Citibank in New York. Citibank pays the draft upon receiving evidence that all conditions set forth in the L/C have been met.

Because there are several types of L/Cs, each export contract must specify which type should be used. Most L/Cs issued in connection with commercial transactions are **documentary**—that is, the exporter must submit, together with the draft, any necessary invoices and other documents such as the custom invoice, certificate of commodity inspection, packing list, and certificate of country of origin. L/Cs without the requirement for presentation of documents are called **clean L/Cs.** A clean L/C may be used for overseas bank guarantees, escrow arrangements, and security purchases. However, it is rarely used in import/export business.

The letter of credit can be revocable or irrevocable. A **revocable L/C** is a means of arranging payment, but it does not carry a guarantee. It can be revoked, without notice, at any time up to the time a draft is presented to the issuing bank. An **irrevocable L/C,** in contrast, cannot be revoked without the specific permission of all parties concerned, including the exporter. Most credits between unrelated parties are irrevocable.

A letter of credit can also be confirmed or unconfirmed. A **confirmed L/C** is issued by one bank and confirmed by another, obligating both banks to honor any drafts drawn in compliance. An **unconfirmed L/C** is the obligation of only the issuing bank. Naturally, an exporter will prefer an irrevocable letter of credit by the importer's bank with confirmation by another (domestic or foreign) bank. In this way, the exporter need look no further than a bank in its own country for compliance with terms of the letter of credit. For example, if the Bank of China had confirmed

FINANCIAL MANAGEMENT FOR GLOBAL OPERATIONS

the letter of credit issued by Citibank, and Citibank, for whatever reason, failed to honor its irrevocable L/C, a Chinese exporter could collect its accounts receivable from the Bank of China.

There are also special types of L/Cs that are used for specific purposes of an exporter. A **transferable L/C** is one under which the beneficiary has the right to instruct the paying bank to make the credit available to one or more secondary beneficiaries. No L/C is transferable unless specifically authorized in the letter of credit; moreover, it can be transferred only once. The stipulated documents are transferred along with the L/C. In effect, the exporter is the intermediary in a transferable credit, and usually has the credit transferred to one or more of its own suppliers. When the credit is transferred, the exporter is actually using the creditworthiness of the opening bank, thus avoiding having to borrow or use its own funds to buy the goods from its own suppliers.

A **back-to-back L/C** exists where the exporter, as beneficiary of the first L/C, offers its credit as security in order to finance the opening of a second credit in favor of the exporter's own supplier of the goods needed for shipment under the first or original credit from the advising bank. The bank that issues a back-to-back L/C not only assumes the exporter's risk but also the risk of the bank issuing the primary L/C. If the exporter is unable to produce documents or the documents contain discrepancies, the bank issuing the back-to-back L/C may be unable to obtain payment under the credit because the importer is not obligated to accept discrepant documents of the ultimate supplier under the back-to-back L/C. Thus, many banks are reluctant to issue this type of L/C.

A **revolving L/C** exists where the tenor (maturity) or amount of the L/C is automatically renewed pursuant to its terms and conditions. An L/C with a revolving maturity may be either cumulative or noncumulative. When cumulative, any amount not utilized during a given period may be applied or added to the subsequent period. If noncumulative, any unused amount is simply no longer available. If a revolving L/C is used, it must be explicitly stipulated in the export contract.

Documentary Collection

The **documentary collection** is a payment mechanism that allows exporters to retain ownership of the goods until they receive payment or are reasonably certain that they will receive it. In a documentary collection, the bank, acting as the exporter's agent, regulates the timing and sequence of the exchange of goods for value by holding the title documents until the importer either pays the draft—termed **documents against payment** (D/P)—or accepts the obligation to do so—termed **documents against acceptance** (D/A). The introduction of D/P and D/A is detailed in the "Uniform Rules for Collections" enacted by the International Chamber of Commerce (ICC).

The two principal control documents in a documentary collection are a *draft* and a *bill of lading (B/L)*. The *draft* is written by the drawer (exporter) to the drawee (importer) and requires payment of a fixed amount at a specific or determinable date to the payee (usually the exporter itself). A draft is a negotiable instrument that normally requires physical presentation as a condition for payment. A draft may be either a *sight draft* (i.e., payable upon presentation) or a *time draft* (i.e., payable at a determinable future date as specified in the draft). As introduced in Chapter 10, a *bill of lading* is the document of title (property rights of the shipped products), the document for shipment (usually ocean transportation), and the carrier's receipt for the goods being shipped. Exhibits 14.2 and 14.3 present a step-by-step procedural flow for D/P and D/A, respectively.

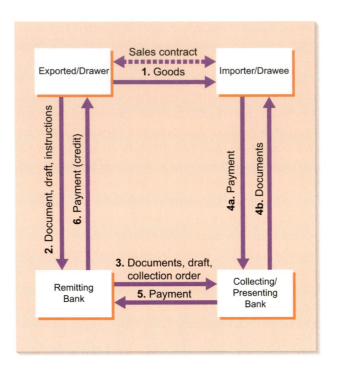

Exhibit 14.2 Documents against payment (D/P) flow

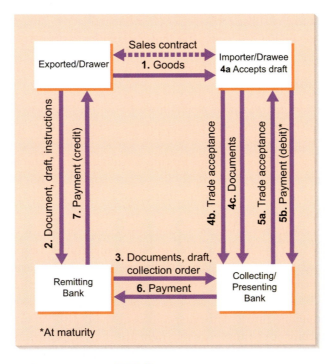

Exhibit 14.3 Documents against acceptance (D/A) flow

A sight draft is commonly used for D/P payment. Nevertheless, for export sales that take several months in ocean transportation, exporters and importers may agree to use D/P at 30, 60, 90, or 180 days, and the like. Bear in mind that sight drafts are not always paid exactly at presentation, nor are time drafts always paid at maturity. Firms can get bank statistics on the promptness of sight and time draft payments, by country, from bank publications such as Chase Manhattan's Collection Experience Bulletin.

In practice, D/A at sight is seldom used. D/A is usually accompanied with a time draft ranging from 30 days up to perhaps two years, which is why time draft-based collections are also viewed as an important commercial or corporate financing approach that is granted by the exporter to the importer. The flip side of this method is the high risk of receivable collection for the exporter. D/A is a riskier collection method than D/P because the importer can claim the title of goods under the "promise" of payment rather than actual payment. For this reason, most bad debts accumulated in international trade have been transactions that used D/A as terms of payment.

Open Account

Open account selling involves shipping goods first and billing the importer later. The credit terms are arranged between the importer and the exporter, but the exporter has little evidence of the importer's obligation to pay a certain amount at a certain date. Sales on open account, therefore, are made only to a foreign affiliate or to a customer with which the exporter has a long history of favorable business dealings. However, open account sales have greatly expanded because of the major increase in international trade, more accurate credit information about importers, and the greater familiarity with exporting in general. The benefits include greater flexibility (no specific payment dates are set) and lower costs, including fewer bank charges than with other methods of payment. As with shipping on consignment, the possibility of currency controls is an important factor because of the low priority in allocating foreign exchange normally accorded this type of transaction.

Means of Payment Remittance

Remittance can be made by several means. In documentary L/Cs or collections, the primary means of remittance is an airmail payment order in which an instruction is mailed from an importer's bank to an exporter's bank. These banks may also use *Telex/SWIFT (Society for Worldwide Information and Funds Transfer)* capabilities to settle the payment. For cash in advance or open account terms, the importers/buyers may use a company check, bank draft, or bank money order to remit the payment. A company check is also widely used for goods purchased on *cash with order (CWO)* or *cash on delivery (COD)*. Today, interbank email systems have been extensively applied in lieu of airmail payment orders between cross-border banks (especially between those in developed countries).

Export Financing

Export financing is important because many export projects require a large amount of start-up costs. External sources of export financing are twofold, including *private sources* and *governmental sources*. Of private sources, the institutions that provide trade financing include commercial banks, export finance companies, factoring houses, forfeit houses, international leasing companies, in-house finance companies, and private insurance companies. These sources offer different types of financing for exporters.

Private Sources

Bank Financing. Commercial bank financing for foreign trade business includes bank guarantees, bank line of credit, and buyer credit. A **bank guarantee** is a financial instrument that guarantees a specified sum of payment in the event of nonperformance by an exporter or by a foreign importer in the event of a payment default for goods purchased from a foreign supplier. Apart from regular bank guarantees, there are three other types of guarantees involved with commercial banks. These include: (1) the *loan guarantee,* which grants a loan conditional on security provided by the borrower; (2) a *distraint guarantee,* which helps a debtor recover control over its seized assets; and (3) a *bill of lading guarantee,* which ensures that the carrier will hand over the goods to the consignee when individual bills of lading are lost.

A **bank line of credit** is a sum of money allocated to an exporter by a bank or banks that the exporter can draw from in order to finance its export business. This could also be structured to finance an export transaction from the foreign customer's side. In effect, the bank line of credit allows the exporter to extend competitive credit terms to foreign customers. **Buyer credits** exist where one or more financial institutions in an exporter's country extend credit to a foreign customer of the exporter. Although most buyer credit financing is arranged to finance capital equipment purchases, other goods with payment terms of up to one year can be financed by buyer credits. Buyer credits are normally arranged under an export credit insurance program.

Export Factoring and Forfeiting

Export factoring is particularly suited for small and medium-sized exporters. This technique proceeds through factoring houses. **Factoring houses** not only provide financing, but can also perform credit investigations, guarantee commercial and political risks, assume collection responsibilities, and finance accounts receivable. In addition, these houses can perform such services as letters of credit, term loans, marketing assistance, and all other necessary services a small to medium-sized exporter cannot afford to handle. Often, a factoring house's service charges are quoted on a commission basis. Commissions can range anywhere between 1 to 3 percent of total transaction value.

Although factoring is a well-known export financing technique in the United States, forfaiting has been widely used for export financing in Europe. **Forfaiting,** a term derived from the French term *a forfeit,* is a transaction in which an exporter transfers responsibility of commercial and political risks for the collection of a trade-related debt to a forfaiter (often a financial institution), and in turn receives immediate cash after the deduction of its interest charge (the discount). The forfait market consists of a primary and secondary market. The primary market consists of banks and forfait houses that buy properly executed and documented debt obligations directly from exporters. The secondary market consists of trading these forfait debt obligations among themselves.

468

In general, a forfait financing transaction involves at least four parties to the transaction: an exporter, the forfaiter, the importer, and the importer's guarantor. The financial instruments in forfaiting are usually time drafts or bills of exchange and promissory notes. Forfaiting is used to finance the export of capital equipment where transactions are usually medium term (i.e., three to eight years) at fixed rate financing. The discount used by the forfaiter is based on its cost of funds plus a premium, which can range anywhere from 0.5 to 5 percent depending on the country of importation and level of risks involved.

Bankers Acceptance

The **bankers acceptance** (*BA*) is a time draft drawn on and accepted by banks. It is a two-armed instrument with one branch in financing and the other in investment. The bank first creates the BA by stamping "accepted" on the face of a draft presented by its customer (i.e., the drawer), then discounts the BA (i.e., it pays the drawer a sum less than the face value of the draft), followed by selling (rediscounting) the BA to an investor in the acceptance market. At maturity the bank settles the BA when it debits the drawer for the full amount of the BA and pays the full value to the investor who presents it. By definition, a bankers acceptance is a time draft (30, 60, 90, up to 180 days after sight or date) drawn on and accepted by a bank. The fee charged by the accepting bank varies depending on the maturity of the draft as well as the creditworthiness of the borrower. BA is mainly used for the export trade in raw materials, components, and general commodity financing. A deep secondary market for bankers acceptances combined with the lack of reserve requirements often enables the bank to obtain funding for eligible transactions at a cost significantly lower than alternative sources.

Corporate Guarantee

A **corporate guarantee** is where one company undertakes to pay if the principal debtor does not pay a matured debt obligation to a creditor. Typically in global business, creditors will ask the corporate or parent company to guarantee an obligation of one or more of its overseas subsidiaries or offshore affiliates that the creditor may consider not creditworthy for the export-related financing or credit limit. Because the parent company is often located outside of the exporting country, it is important to state in the financing contract by which country's law the guarantee will be governed.

Governmental Sources

Export-Import Bank Financing Many countries have put in place export-import financing programs that are similar in most respects to programs of the Export-Import Bank of the United States (Eximbank). Japan's Eximbank, for instance, is an independent governmental financial institution providing yen financing for exports, imports, and overseas investments. Exports are supported by parallel lending with these banks in the form of yen loans for major borrowing with medium- to long-term terms. South Korea Eximbank provides direct loans to both foreign and domestic firms. The loans are low-cost with medium- to long-term financing arranged in conjunction with larger commercial banks throughout the world. Their purpose is to encourage the export of capital goods and services, overseas investment, and major resource development. South Korea's Eximbank offers such services as direct lending to both suppliers and buyers, relending facilities to foreign financial institutions, and the issuance of guarantees and export insurance.

In the United States, the primary function of its Eximbank is to give US exporters the necessary financial backing to compete in other countries. Today this is done through a variety of different export financing and guarantee programs (e.g., direct loans, discount loans, guarantees, and export credit insurance) to meet specific needs. All are designed to be in direct support of US exports, whether the eventual recipient of the loans or guarantees are foreign or domestic firms. Generally, export-import banks do not compete with private sources of export financing. Their main purpose is to step in where private credit is not available in sufficiently large amounts at low rates or long terms, to allow home country exporters to compete in a foreign market.

Foreign Credit Insurance

Many industrialized and developing countries have set up foreign credit insurance or guarantee programs to assist their exporting companies. Even branches of foreign companies located in that country are often eligible for assistance. These programs are usually run by, and dependent on, the government. In the United States, such insurance programs are offered by both Eximbank and the Foreign Credit Insurance Association. In Canada, these services are provided by the Export Credits Insurance Corporation (ECIC). In Asia, Japan's International Trade Bureau (Export Insurance Section), Hong Kong's Export Credit Insurance Corporation, India's Export Credit & Guarantee Corporation Ltd., and Taiwan's Central Trust of China are all overseeing and offering these programs. In Latin America, similar programs can be found (e.g., in Compania Argentina de Seguros de Credito in Argentina and Instituto de Resseguros do Brasil in Brazil). Europe has an even longer history in providing export credit insurance. Les Assurances du Credit in Belgium, Export Credit Council in Denmark, Export Guarantee Board in Finland, Compagnie Francaise D'Assurance pour le Commerce Exterieur in France, Hermes Kreditversicherungs in Germany, and Instituto Nazionale delle Assicuranioni in Italy, for example, are all leading institutions offering foreign credit insurance and backed by their respective governments.

Because the services provided by these institutions are basically similar, let us use the case of the United Kingdom to illustrate the process and scope of these services. In the United Kingdom, commercial credit and political risks connected with exports can be insured with the Export Credits Guarantee Department (ECGD), a separate department of the British government. Even though ECGD is an arm of the British government, it is commercially independent. Risks covered by ECGD include commercial credit and political risk. More specifically, commercial credit risks include insolvency of the buyer, the buyer's failure to pay within six months of due date for goods already accepted, and the buyer's failure to accept goods that have been shipped (provided this nonacceptance was not caused by an action or noncompliance on the part of the exporter). Political risks covered by ECGD include government action that blocks payment to the exporter, cancellation of a valid import license in the buyer's country, war or any other cause of loss not within the control of the exporter or the buyer, or cancellation of an export license or imposition of new licensing restrictions. Generally, ECGD covers 95 percent of any loss resulting from political risk and 90 percent of the loss arising from most commercial risks.

Interim Summary

1. There are a number of accepted payment forms in international trade, including cash in advance, letter of credit (L/C), documentary collection (e.g., D/P and D/A), and open account terms. L/C is particularly desirable for the exporter because it eliminates credit risk, reduces uncertainty, and facilitates financing, whereas it ascertains the quality and quantity of a purchase for the importer.
2. Documentary collection is a riskier payment form than L/C for the exporter. In this system, a draft is delivered either upon receipt of goods or with a time-based maturity clause. The International Chamber of Commerce details uniform rules for documentary collection.
3. There are various means of acquiring bank financing. For smaller exporters, factoring, whereby a financing house fronts money for transactions on a commission basis, is a good choice. Capital may also be acquired from governmental sources which offer many of the same services as private banks, but are specifically intended to aid traders from their home country.

Financing for Global Business

Compared to financing for foreign trade activities, financing for MNEs' global productions, investments, and operations involves more choices but is more complex. Broadly, the sources of financing for global investments and operations include intercompany financing, equity financing, debt financing, and local currency financing (see Exhibit 14.4).

Intercompany Financing

Intercompany financing from the parent company or sister subsidiaries is a common means of financing for overseas subsidiaries or affiliates, which is done in the following ways:

- Allowing the subsidiary to keep a higher level of retained earnings.
- Obtaining financing from the parent company in the form of equity, loans, trade credit (e.g., longer maturity or extension for accounts payable), or borrowing with a parent guarantee.
- Arranging trade credit from other subsidiaries to this affiliate.

Parent loans are sometimes preferable to parent equity financing by MNEs, for several reasons. First, intercompany loan payments may be more readily remittable in the future than dividends. Second, loan interests reduce the tax burden. A subsidiary borrowing these loans will pay lower local corporate income tax after deducting interest expenses from the total taxable incomes. Third, the loan provided to the parent or a sister subsidiary and the loan received from the parent or another subsidiary are eliminated on consolidation. Cash has moved within the corporation without affecting the consolidated debt or equity accounts. Finally, short-term intercompany loans may be used to stabilize the subsidiary's working capital structure, and long-term intercompany loans

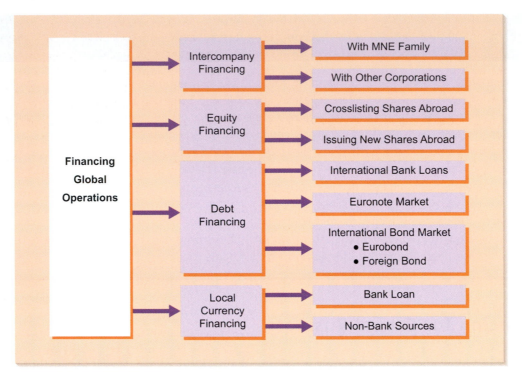

Exhibit 14.4 Sources of financing global operations

may be used to reduce its dependence on external banks. **Working capital** is the net position whereby a firm's current liability is subtracted from its current assets.

Equity Financing

Financing through equity markets can be realized in an MNE's home country, a foreign affiliate's host country, and/or a third country. An MNE's equity financing can take the form of either *crosslisting shares abroad* or *selling new shares* to *foreign investors*. Many US-based MNEs, for instance, have secured listing of their companies on foreign stock exchanges.

Cross listing an MNE's shares on foreign stock exchanges may provide many benefits:

- Improve the liquidity of existing shares by making it easier for foreign shareholders to trade in their home markets and currencies.
- Increase the share price by overcoming mis-pricing in a segmented, illiquid, home capital market.
- Increase the firm's visibility and political acceptance to its customers, suppliers, creditors, and host governments.
- Create a secondary market for shares that can be used to compensate local management and employees in foreign affiliates.[1]

472

Crosslisting is frequently accompanied by depositary receipts. In the United States, foreign shares are usually traded through **American depositary receipts** (or **ADRs**). These are negotiable certificates issued by a US bank in the United States to represent the underlying shares of stock, which are held in trust at a foreign custodian bank. ADRs are sold, registered, and transferred in the United States in the same manner as any share of stock. Because ADRs can be exchanged for the underlying foreign shares, or vice versa, arbitrage keeps foreign and US prices of any given share the same. To crosslist stocks abroad, an MNE must be committed to full disclosure of operating results and balance sheets. Today, the major liquid markets are London, New York (NYSE and NASDAQ), Tokyo, Frankfurt, and Paris. To decide where to crosslist, an MNE should consider its ownership expansion objectives, the size of the target stock market, the sophistication of market-making activities, and host governmental regulations.

An alternative to seeking international ownership through parent listings is the issuance of equity by local subsidiaries. Some countries require levels of minority or even majority ownership by local nationals. Firms typically have difficulty in achieving a broad-based ownership of their subsidiaries in the very thin capital markets of most developing countries. US MNEs, in particular, prefer the flexibility of operations that sole ownership affords. Firms that are technology-based are concerned with the loss of control over proprietary technology that taking on an equity partner or partners might portend. MNEs of other countries, however, sometimes want to take on local equity, especially in their US subsidiaries, thereby taking advantage of the remarkably broad and sophisticated US equity market. Exhibit 14.5 illustrates what foreign MNEs must know when selling stocks in the US, the largest capital market in the world.

Debt Financing

Chapter 9 introduced international capital markets, which are in fact the major source of an MNE's debt financing. Debt financing for global operations can be made through *international bank loans, the Euronote market,* and *the international bond market.* International bank loans are often sourced in the **Eurocurrency markets,** that is, in countries not using the denomination currency (e.g., a Japanese firm obtained yen loans from banks in the United States and Europe). As such, international

■ *Set up an ADR program.* With ADRs (American Depository Receipts), US depository banks maintain custody of deposited foreign securities at their overseas branches and issue receipts as proof of ownership. The receipt is transferable in the United States. Registration is made under either the Securities Act of 1933 or the Securities Exchange Act of 1934, or both.
■ *Listing.* Some MNEs permit their ADRs to be traded in the pink sheets, which list quotes for ADRs of nonlisted companies. Others are listed on NASDAQ or on an exchange from the outset. Firms listing on NYSE or NASDAQ face the same legal requirement. NYSE listings have two separate standards for domestic and foreign entities, with the latter facing more stringent requirements.
■ *Public offerings.* In a public offering, the foreign firm turns over its ordinary shares to its depository bank. The depository bank then issues ADRs, and it delivers them to the underwriters for resale and distribution.

Exhibit 14.5 Tapping Wall Street: three stages for non-US MNEs to be traded in the United States

bank loans are often called **Eurocredits.** Because of the large size of these loans, the lending banks usually form a syndicate in order to diversify their risk. The basic borrowing interest rate for Eurocurrency loans has long been tied to the *London Interbank Offered Rate (LIBOR),* which is the deposit rate applicable to interbank loans within London.

The **Euronote market** is the collective term used to describe short- to medium-term debt instruments sourced in the Eurocurrency markets. The Euronote is generally a less expensive source of short-term funds than syndicated loans, because the notes are placed directly with the investor public. Euronotes can be *underwritten* or *non-underwritten.* In an underwritten Euronote, there are normally one to three lead banks that organize a group of participating banks to take shares of the total commitment. The lead and participating banks stand ready to buy the borrower's notes in the event the notes could not be placed in the market at previously guaranteed rates. The non-underwritten Euronotes include *Euro-Commercial Paper (ECP)* and *Euro-Medium-Term Notes (EMTNs).* ECP is a short-term debt obligation of a corporation or bank. Maturity is typically one, three, and six months, while EMTNs' typical maturity ranges from as short as nine months to a maximum of ten years.

The international bond market comprises *Eurobonds* and *foreign bonds.* A **Eurobond** is underwritten by an international syndicate of banks and other securities firms, and is sold exclusively in countries other than the country in whose currency the issue is denominated (e.g., a bond issued by a Japanese firm residing in Tokyo, denominated in Japanese yen but sold to investors in Europe and the United States). Most Eurobonds use the straight fixed rate, with a fixed coupon, set maturity date, and full principal repayment upon final maturity. Recently, convertible Eurobonds have emerged. These bonds resemble the straight fixed-rate issue in practically all price and payment characteristics, with the added feature that they are convertible to stock prior to maturity at a specified price per share. A **foreign bond** is underwritten by a syndicate composed of members from a single country, sold principally within that country, and denominated in the currency of that country (a Japanese firm issued corporate bonds in US dollars and sold to US investors by US banks). Foreign bonds sold in the United States are also known as **Yankee bonds,** those sold in Japan as **Samurai bonds,** those sold in China as **Panda bonds,** and those sold in the United Kingdom as **Bulldog bonds.**

Local Currency Financing

The preceding description focused on corporate-level financing. Local currency financing in a host country opens an avenue for subsidiary financing. Access to various local financial markets in which an MNE operates can be advantageous in lowering the overall cost of capital and reducing financial risks. Thus, international managers should evaluate local financing choices as well as opportunities for investing the firm's surplus funds.

Financing in a host country generally includes two sources: *bank loans* and *nonbank sources.* *Bank loans* contain overdrafts, discounting, and loans. In countries other than the United States, banks tend to lend through overdrafts. An **overdraft** is a line of credit against which drafts (checks) can be drawn (written) up to a specified maximum amount. **Discounting** is a short-term financing technique by which a local bank discounts a firm's trade bills. These bills can often be rediscounted with the central bank. Discounting is particularly popular in Europe and Latin America because, according to the commercial laws in these countries (i.e., Code Napoleon in Europe), the claim of the bill holder is independent of the claim represented by the underlying transaction, which makes the bill easily negotiable. *Loans* can be term loans, line of credit, or revolving credit agreements. **Term loans** are straight loans that are made for a fixed period of time and repaid in a single lump sum. For frequent borrowers, term loans are relatively expensive, so they may instead seek a line of credit. A line of credit, which is usually good for one year with renewals renegotiated every year, allows the company to borrow up to a stated maximum amount from the bank. Similar to a line of credit, a revolving credit agreement permits the company to extend credit up to the stated maximum. The difference is that under this agreement the bank is legally committed to providing credit up to the specified maximum. The company has to pay interest on its outstanding borrowing plus a commitment fee on the unused portion of the credit line.

Nonbank sources of funds include commercial paper, factoring (see the preceding section), and local bond or equity markets, and parallel loans with a foreign company. Stanley Works, the $1.9 billion US manufacturer of hand and power tools, has seven joint ventures in Japan. Its local financing is made via listing on the Tokyo Exchange assisted by Nikko Securities Co. Goldman also assists Stanley to be listed in Hong Kong and Singapore where the company operates three manufacturing plants and several distribution centers. A **parallel loan** (also known as a *back-to-back loan*) involves an exchange of funds between firms in different countries, with the exchange reversed at a later date. For example, a US MNE's subsidiary in Brazil needs Brazilian reals while a Brazilian company's subsidiary in the United States needs dollars. The Brazilian firm can lend reals to the US-owned subsidiary in Brazil while it borrows an equivalent amount of dollars from the US parent firm in the United States.

Financing Decisions

Several considerations affect the financing decisions and choices for MNEs. These considerations include minimizing taxes, managing currency risk and political risk, and exploiting financial market distortions to raise money at below market rate.

Financing choices designed to minimize corporate taxes are often concerned with selecting the tax-minimizing currency, jurisdiction, and vehicle for issue and selecting the tax-minimizing mode of internal transfer of currency and/or profit. Many MNEs prefer parent loans, rather than parent investment, for funding subsidiaries because interest payments on debt are tax deductible, but dividends are not. Nevertheless, the debt/equity ratio of subsidiaries must be maintained within a reasonable limit. This is necessary to fulfill operating needs as well as local government requirements in certain countries.

In general, an MNE should seek financing in such a way that it balances the currency risks inherent in the operation. For instance, firms may reduce the risk of currency inconvertibility by appropriate inter-affiliate financing. Parent funds may be invested as debt rather than as equity. Back-to-back loans may be arranged, and as much local financing as possible may be sought. To reduce political risk, financing may be sought directly from the host and other governments, international development agencies, and overseas banks. When an MNE's offshore projects are financed by these government-based financial institutions, the firm may benefit from both financing and networking. Kennecott, for example, used this approach to finance its copper mine project in Chile.

Given the uncertainty in international financial markets, MNEs should ensure that their financing is not dependent on any one single source. Diversity of financing sources can help the MNE gain more from differences between capital markets across nations.[2] These differences are largely attributable to government credit and capital controls, which is why the cost of international borrowing is likely to be lower than that of domestic funding. Novo, a Danish MNE that produces industrial enzymes and pharmaceuticals, for example, has crosslisted in both the Copenhagen Stock Exchange and the NYSE and has used a multitude of other financing tools such as Eurobonds, Euronotes, local currency loans, and intercompany financing, among others. This strategy enables Novo to escape the shackles of its segmented national capital market and make the company more visible to foreign investors. Novo eventually reaped the full benefit of dramatic share price increase by selling a directed equity issue in the United States.

Interim Summary

1. MNEs have a broad range of choices in financing their global investment projects, including intercompany financing, equity financing, debt financing, and local currency financing. These choices are often more complex than export financing.
2. Equity financing involves either crosslisting shares on foreign exchanges or selling new shares to foreign investors. Many US MNEs finance their global operations through crosslisting their shares abroad. Three stages for non-US MNEs to be traded in Wall Street include: (a) setting up an ADR program; (b) listing; and (c) public offerings.
3. Debt financing is made through international bank loans, Euronote market, and international bond market. Subsidiaries can also obtain local currency financing through local banks or local bond or equity markets.

Managing Foreign Exchange Risk And Exposure

Foreign Exchange Risk and Exposure

Exchange risk is a critical issue in international business. Any company that operates in more than one nation or currency area or has cash flows across nations will face foreign exchange risk and foreign exchange exposure. Foreign exchange risk and exposure are two different concepts. **Foreign exchange risk** concerns the variance of the domestic-currency value of an asset, liability, or operating income that is attributable to unanticipated changes in exchange rates.[3] This definition implies that foreign exchange risk is not the unpredictability of foreign exchange rates themselves, but rather the uncertainty of values of a firm's assets, liabilities, or operating incomes owing to uncertainty in exchange rates. Therefore, volatility in exchange rates is responsible for exchange rate risk only if it translates into volatility in real values of assets, liabilities, or operating incomes. This makes foreign exchange risk dependent on foreign exchange exposure. A firm may not face foreign exchange risks unless it is "exposed" to foreign exchange fluctuations. For example, General Electric

(GE) and Hitachi both invest and operate in Mexico. Unlike Hitachi, which imports many parts for its production plants in Mexico, GE has built up its own supply base within Mexico. In this case, GE faces lower foreign exchange risks than Hitachi because GE is not exposed to fluctuations of the Mexican peso in the process of supply procurement.

Foreign exchange exposure refers to the sensitivity of changes in the real domestic-currency value of assets, liabilities, or operating incomes to unanticipated changes in exchange rates.[4] This implies that exposure involves the extent to which the home currency value of assets, liabilities, or incomes is changed by exchange rate variation. The "real" domestic currency value means the value that has been adjusted by the nation's inflation. Domestic currency-denominated assets (e.g., holdings of government bonds) can still be exposed to exchange rates if, for example, unanticipated depreciation of the country's currency causes its central bank to increase interest rates, thus lowering the market values of fixed-income securities.

Foreign exchange risk is a positive function of both foreign exchange exposure and the variance of unanticipated changes in exchange rates. Uncertainty of exchange rates does not mean foreign exchange risk for items that are not exposed. Similarly, exposure on its own does not mean foreign exchange risk if exchange rates are perfectly predicable. The levels of foreign exchange risk and exposure often differ between asset/liability items and operating income. Because current asset and current liability items, especially accounts receivables and payable, have fixed face value and are short-term oriented, they are extremely sensitive to the uncertainty of foreign exchange rates. Unlike these asset or liability items, operating incomes do not have fixed face values. Exposure of operating incomes depends not only on unexpected changes of exchange rates, but also on such factors as the elasticity of demand for imports or exports, the fraction of input prices that depend on exchange rates, and the flexibility of production to respond to market demand changes induced by exchange rate movements.

Transaction and Economic Exposures

Because foreign exchange risk is determined by foreign exchange exposure (along with the uncertainty of foreign exchange rates), managers must analyze and monitor foreign exchange exposure. MNEs encounter three types of foreign exchange exposure:

- Transaction exposure.
- Economic (or operating) exposure.
- Translation (or accounting) exposure (discussed in Chapter 15).

Transaction exposure is concerned with how changes in exchange rates affect the value, in home currency terms, of anticipated cash flows denominated in foreign currency relating to transactions already entered into. It arises when commitments in foreign currency are subject to settlements to exchange rate gains and losses due to changes in the currency rates. A change in exchange rates between the home or functional currency and the currency in which a transaction is denominated increases or decreases the expected amount of the functional or reporting currency cash flow on settlement of the transaction. For example, a US exporter expects to receive a payment of £200,000 in two months after it ships the products to the importer in London. With a current spot rate (£1 = $1.5), this export is worth $300,000. Two months later, however, the actual spot rate changes to £1 = $1.3, which reduces the actual dollar value to $260,000. This US exporter thus will suffer a $40,000 foreign exchange loss if it does not take steps to hedge its foreign exchange exposure and risk.

Transactions that give rise to foreign exchange exposure include:

- Purchasing or selling on credit goods and services whose prices are stated in foreign currencies (thus recorded as account payable or account receivables).
- Borrowing or depositing funds denominated in foreign currencies (reflected in foreign debt and credit).
- Transacting a foreign exchange contract.
- Various transactions denominated in foreign exchange.

Accordingly, transaction exposure can be a variety of foreign currency-denominated assets (export receivables or bank deposits), liabilities (account payable or loans), revenues (expected future sales), expenses (expected purchase of goods), or income (dividends).

Economic exposure, also called operating exposure, measures the change in the present value of the firm resulting from any change in the future operating cash flows caused by an unexpected change in exchange rates and macroeconomic factors. The change in value depends on the effect of the exchange rate change on future sales volume, prices, or costs. Unlike **translation exposure,** which refers to the potential for accounting-derived changes in owners' equity to occur because of the need to consolidate foreign currency financial statements, both transaction exposure and economic exposure exist because of unexpected changes in future cash flows. In contrast to transaction exposure, which is concerned with preexisting cash flows that will occur in the near future, economic exposure emphasizes expected future cash flows that are potentially impacted by unanticipated changes of exchange rates and macroeconomic conditions (e.g., unexpected changes in interest rates and inflation rates). Thus, economic exposure derives largely from economic analysis which requires integrated strategies in finance, marketing, outsourcing, and production.

An MNE's economic exposure is determined by several economic factors. First, it is influenced *by pricing flexibility* (i.e., a firm's ability to raise its foreign currency selling price sufficiently to preserve its home currency profit margin in the case of foreign currency depreciation).[5] This price flexibility depends mainly on price elasticity of demand, which is in turn determined by the level of competition in the market and the degree of product differentiation provided by the firm. For example, Motorola's subsidiaries in Indonesia and Thailand successfully maintained their US dollar gross profit margin for producing and selling cellular phones in these markets during the Asian financial crisis because of a local price increase, which was made possible by the high quality and superior innovation of their products.

Second, economic exposure is influenced *by production/outsourcing flexibility,* that is, the ability to shift production and outsourcing of inputs among different nations. MNEs with worldwide production systems can cope with currency changes by increasing production in a nation whose currency has undergone a real devaluation and decreasing production in a nation whose currency has revalued in real terms. For example, to cope with *endaka* (which means the strong Japanese yen period), many Japanese MNEs used the yen's strength to quickly and inexpensively set up integrated manufacturing bases in Asian countries with currencies pegged to the dollar. In addition, their earlier investments in the United States, Mexico, and Europe allowed them to play both sides of the yen–dollar swings, using cheaper dollar-denominated parts and materials to offset higher yen-related costs. For instance, 75 percent of the parts for the Toyota Camry built in Georgetown, Kentucky were from the United States, up from 60 percent when Toyota started manufacturing the car there in 1988. The Nissan Leaf electric car, built in Smyrna, Tennessee, had only 15 percent local content in its 2013 models, but the company plans to increase it to 45 percent in its 2014 models.[6] The planned capacity for having a high percentage of the Leaf's value added in the US, as well as in Japan, enables the company to hedge against exchange rate fluctuations between the dollar and the yen.

Finally, economic exposure is influenced *by an MNE's localization structure and export orientation.* Consider an MNE that makes and sells its products in a foreign country. A devaluation of the host-country currency will reduce the value of its revenues from local sales in terms of its home currency. The negative impact of the host-country currency devaluation will be lower if the MNE's localization of production inputs there is higher because the depreciation also lowers the subsidiary's production costs attributable to local inputs in terms of its home currency. In contrast, the higher the import content of production inputs, the less the production costs will decline. If the MNE instead uses its foreign subsidiary as an export platform, it will actually benefit from a host-country currency depreciation. Thus, in the face of a host-country currency devaluation, exporting products made of localized supplies is preferable to targeting a local market using local supplies. For risk minimization, targeting a local market using local supplies is normally better than targeting a local market but using imported supplies. It is important to realize, however, that a firm that makes and sells its products in its home country using only domestically sourced inputs is still exposed to foreign exchange risks because the devaluation or depreciation of a foreign country's currency enables its rivals from that country to price their products more competitively. Exhibit 14.6

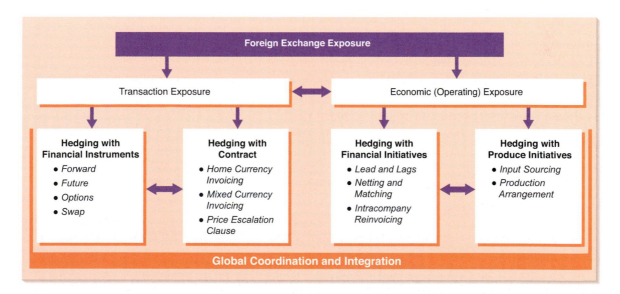

Exhibit 14.6 Framework of managing foreign exchange exposure

highlights major approaches that manage transaction exposure and economic exposure, respectively, which are further detailed below.

Managing Transaction Exposure

Hedging with Financial Instruments

Forward Market. Forward markets are available in most major currencies of the world. The period of forward contract coverage could extend to more than five years. Exhibit 14.7 shows how hedging via a forward contract works.

By the forward mechanism in this example, the UK exporter's accounts receivable is hedged, no matter what happens to the Canadian dollar/sterling spot and forward rates over the next two months. Once contracted, the forward is irrevocably fixed. In general, the expected cost of hedging is equal to the risk premium in the forward exchange rate plus forward transaction costs. The level of risk premium is reflected in the difference between the spot rate and the forward rate. The level of transaction cost is reflected in the spread on the particular forward rate. Since the forward rate is fixed in a completed forward contract, it is important for financial managers to accurately forecast currency appreciation or depreciation. The UK exporter mentioned earlier, for instance, sells the forward under the assumption that the Canadian dollar will depreciate or sterling will appreciate around the settlement date. If the realized spot rate actually moves in an opposite direction, this exporter will lose foreign exchange gains that it would otherwise have obtained.

Futures Market. Hedging via the futures market shares major principles with forward hedging. The difference is that in the forward market all the payment is made at the end, whereas with the

---

Contract data

Exporter	United Kingdom exporter
Importer	Canadian importer
Contract date	March 20, 2013
Expected payment date	May 20, 2013
Invoice amount	C$1 million

Exchange rate (C$/£) quotes on January 1, 2001

Spot rate	1.5527–1.5542
1 month forward/future	1.5534–1.5550
2 months forward/future	1.5542–1.5558
3 months forward/future	1.5544–1.5575

Mechanism of forward contract

March 20, 2013	UK exporter sells C$1 million 2-month forward at 1.5558 in the forward market (a bank handling foreign exchange transactions)
May 20, 2013	UK exporter receives C$1 million from Canadian importer, delivers C$1 million to the bank, and in return receives £642,738.37 at C$1.5558 per pound sterling.

Exhibit 14.7 Forward hedging example

futures market some of the payment is made through the margin account before the end. The balance of the margin account is adjusted on a daily basis reflecting the difference between the contract price and the price based on the spot market exchange rate of the day. In the preceding example, for example, the expected two-month future spot rate is 1.5558. If it turns out at the maturity date of the futures contracts that the actual spot rate is 1.4558, then the UK exporter will find it has contributed £44,149 to its margin/future account. It will, of course, receive £686,887 (C$1 million/1.4558) at the due date, rather than £642,738 that would have been received with a forward contract. However, after compensating for its contribution in the margin account, the UK exporter will be receiving £642,738, the same as if the Canadian dollar had been sold on the forward market. On the other hand, if the actual spot rate ends up at 1.6558, then the UK exporter will find it has gained £38,816 in its margin account. With this actual spot rate, it will receive £603,922. After adding its gains from the margin account, it will still receive £642,738. Thus we find that no matter what happens to the spot rate, the UK exporter still receives £642,738 from its C$1 million. In practice, the addition or subtraction to the margin account is done on a daily basis and is called *marking-to-market*. Because interest rates vary over time, it is unlikely that the amount in the margin account at the maturity of the futures contract will bring the eventual price of C$1 million to exactly £642,738. If interest rates are low when the margin account has a large amount in it, it is possible that slightly less than £642,738 is received. This is the marking-to-market risk of futures contracts.

Options Market. In the options market, a **call option** is to purchase a stated number of units of the underlying foreign currency at a specific price per unit during a specific period of time. Alternatively, a **put option** is to sell a stated number of units of the underlying foreign currency at a specific price per unit during a specific period of time. The *striking* (or *exercise*) *price* in this market refers to the price at which the option holder has the right to purchase or sell the price-underlying currency. A call whose strike price is above the current spot price of the underlying currency, or a put option whose strike price is below the current spot price of the underlying currency, is termed *out-of-the-money*. The reverse situation is called *in-the-money*. Although out-of-the-money options have no intrinsic value, in-the-money options have intrinsic value. Intrinsic value reflects the extent to which an option would currently be profitable to exercise. Similar to forward and futures markets, an option holder has to pay risk premium and transaction cost to the banks offering options service. Buying options, however, is more costly than using forwards and futures.

Consider the case in which Dow Corning has to pay £1 million in three months for materials imported from the United Kingdom, and thus needs to hedge this account payable. If Dow Corning buys call options on pounds at a strike price of $1.5/£1, the options will be exercised if the spot rate for the pound ends up above $1.50/£1, but will not be exercised if the spot rate for the pound is below $1.5/£1. This makes sense because it will cost Dow Corning less to buy the pounds at the actual spot rate when it is below $1.5/£1. In other words, a call option provides an *option* that will be exercised if the pound becomes more expensive to buy, or will not be exercised (using the actual spot rate instead) if the pound becomes cheaper. In a put option as in the example of the preceding UK exporter, which needs to hedge its accounts receivable amounting to C$1 million, the put option will be exercised if the actual spot rate ends up below C$1.5558/£1, or will not be exercised if the actual spot rate is above C$1.5558/£1, whatever generates more cash flow in pounds for the UK exporter.

Swaps. Swaps involve the exchange of interest or foreign currency exposures or a combination of both by two or more borrowers. It is a transformation of one stream of future cash flows into another stream of future cash flows with different features. An interest rate swap is an exchange between two parties of interest obligations (payments of interest) or receipts (investment income) in the same currency on an agreed amount of the principal for an agreed period of time. Currency swaps involve counterparty A exchanging fixed rate interest in one currency with counterparty B in return for fixed rate interest in another currency. Swaps can be used for different purposes such as investment, speculation, and hedging.

When a firm needs to hedge its accounts payable (as in the situation of Dow Corning, above), swaps hedging involves: (1) borrowing, if necessary, in home currency; (2) buying the foreign exchange on the spot market; (3) investing the foreign exchange; and (4) repaying the domestic currency debt. For example, Dow Corning can hedge its import of £1 million of denim fabric with payment due in three months by borrowing dollars, buying pounds spot with the dollars, and investing the pounds for three months in a pound-denominated security in London. If this is done, then in three months Dow Corning repays a known number of dollars of domestic debt, and pays accounts payable in pounds using its investment principal and earnings.

Hedging with Contract Invoicing and Clause

Home Currency Invoicing. Transaction exposure associated with international accounts receivables or payable can also be hedged via internal techniques. One of these techniques has to do with invoicing trade in their own (home) currency or a third-country currency whose value is stable and also acceptable to both parties. For example, if Dow Corning from the United States can negotiate the price of its imported denim fabrics in terms of US dollars, or the UK exporter can manage the export contract by invoicing at sterling, they need not face any foreign exchange transaction exposure on their imports or exports. In general, when business convention or the power that a firm holds in negotiating its purchases and sales results in agreement on prices in terms of the home currency, the firm that trades abroad will not face foreign exchange risk and exposure. This arrangement, of course, shifts the risk from the trader whose domestic currency is used in pricing to the other trader, who in turn may demand a higher (as an exporter) or lower (as an importer) price to compensate for taking the risk. In the end, an economically efficient choice of the pricing currency should reflect the relative abilities of the two parties to bear or hedge the risk. For instance, if a Mexican exporter of assembled electronics to the US happens to have some payments due around the same time for its purchases of equipment from US suppliers, the dollar receipts from its exports are hedged at least partially by its anticipated dollar payments.

Mixed-Currency Invoicing. It is not unusual for both parties in an import/export contract to prefer invoicing the transaction using their own home currencies. As a compromise, both parties may agree to denominate the contract partly in an importer's currency and partly in an exporter's currency. For example, Dow Corning's £1 million import contract may be invoiced as £500,000 and $750,000. If this were done and the exchange rate between dollars and pounds varied, Dow Corning's transaction exposure would involve only half of the funds payable—those that are payable in pounds. Similarly, the British exporter would face exposure on only the dollar component of its receivables. Additionally, international trading companies often use composite currency units such as the *Special Drawing Right* (or *SDR*) and the *European Currency Unit (ECU)* to denominate the export contract. Because these composite units are constructed by taking a weighted average of a number of major world currencies, their values are considerably more stable than that of any single currency. Because they offer some diversification benefits, the composite currency units will reduce transaction risk and exposure, though not completely.

Price Escalation Clause. If using currency invoicing is not realistic for the two parties of an export contract, both parties may consider including and specifying a special term in the contract, known as a *price escalation clause*. Under this special clause, both parties agree to adjust the sales price in full or in a certain proportion of fluctuations of the invoice currency. When the weak currency denominated in the contract depreciates 1 percent, for example, the contract price will automatically increase by 1 percent or another percentage agreed upon by both. This clause is often applied in export contracts denominated in an importer's currency that is highly volatile and will continue to depreciate in the global foreign exchange market. To reduce the transaction exposure, an exporter uses this clause to fully or partially transfer foreign exchange risk to an importer. Another technique similar to this clause is a risk-sharing arrangement between a buyer and a supplier for long-term collaborations. Both parties agree to adjust the price or share the foreign currency risk when the contracted currency fluctuates beyond a certain reasonable range. For example, Ford (United States) and Mazda (Japan) may agree that all purchases by Ford will be made in yen at the current exchange rate, as long as the spot rate on the date of invoice is between, say, ¥105/$1 and ¥125/$1. If the exchange rate remains within this range, Ford may agree to accept whatever transaction exposure exists. If, however, the rate falls beyond this limit, Mazda may agree to share the difference equally.

Managing Economic (Operating) Exposure

Financial Initiatives

Several financial initiatives such as using leads and lags, risk-sharing arrangement, and intracompany netting are extensively employed to minimize foreign exchange risk and exposure. Because transaction exposure and economic exposure are sometimes inseparable, these financial initiatives can also be used to lower transaction exposure in some circumstances. Nevertheless, they are designed mainly to manage operating exposure to protect the net present value of the firm resulting from any change in the future operating cash flows caused by exchange rate changes and macroeconomic factors.

Leads and Lags. By timing or retiming the transfer of funds, firms can reduce operating exposure. To lead is to pay early; to lag is to pay late. **Leads** exist when a firm holding a soft currency with debts denominated in a hard currency accelerates by using the soft currency to pay the hard currency debts before the soft currency drops in value. **Lags** exist when a firm holding a hard currency with debts denominated in a soft currency decelerates by paying those debts late. Leads and lags may also be used to reduce transaction exposure. An international trading company can collect soft foreign currency receivables early or collect hard foreign currency receivables later. For instance, if the UK exporter mentioned previously expects that the Canadian dollar will depreciate against the pound sterling, it may ask its Canadian importer to lead in paying its export sales.

Similarly, if Dow Corning in the preceding case predicts that the pound sterling will drop in value vis-à-vis the US dollar, it may decelerate paying its accounts payable to its UK importer. This practice should proceed within the permitted range by a host government. Italy, for example, has placed a 180-day limit on export and import lags on trade payments with non-EU countries.

Intracompany leads and lags within an MNE network are easier to implement than those between two independent companies. Under parent control and by sharing common goals, MNE subsidiaries can rely on this financial technique to improve their respective foreign exchange position and optimize local currency cash flow. On the other hand, headquarters treasury managers must ensure that the timing of the intracompany settlement is functional from a group perspective, rather than merely from a local one. They should also be aware that performance measurement may be affected if some subsidiaries are asked to lead and some to lag. The subsidiary that does the leading loses interest receivable and incurs interest charges on the funds led. To overcome this problem, evaluation of performance may be done on a pre-interest, pre-tax basis.

Netting and Matching. **Netting** is a practice by which subsidiaries or affiliates within an MNE network settle inter-subsidiary indebtedness for the net amount owed during the post-transaction period. Gross intra-MNE trade receivables and payables are netted out. This approach not only reduces transaction and fund transfer cost and provides an opportunity for subsidiaries to manipulate their financial position, but also helps foreign subsidiaries surpass the foreign exchange control barriers in respective countries. Netting occurs in either *bilateral* or *multilateral* form. *Bilateral netting* exists when two sister subsidiaries cancel out their receivables and payable and settle only the net payment. *Multilateral netting* involves three or more sister subsidiaries' inter-group debt and virtually necessitates the coordination of the headquarters treasury. For example, Pepsi's UK subsidiary buys $6 million worth of goods from the Swiss sister subsidiary, and the UK subsidiary sells $2 million worth of goods to the French sister subsidiary. During the same netting period, the Swiss subsidiary buys $2 million worth of goods from the French subsidiary. In this triangular case, the settlement of the inter-subsidiary debt within the three subsidiaries ends up involving a payment equivalent to $4 million from the UK subsidiary to the Swiss subsidiary.

For diversified MNEs, it is important to establish the netting center supervised by the headquarters treasury. Philips, for example, established what is called the Philips Multilateral Clearing System (PMC) in its headquarters to facilitate netting among affiliates (see Industry Box). Participating subsidiaries report all intra-MNE balances to the group treasury on an agreed date and the treasury subsequently advises all subsidiaries of amounts to be paid to and received from other subsidiaries on a specified date. Whether or not such netting operations function well largely depends on the effectiveness of information and communication systems and established discipline on the part of foreign subsidiaries.

Similar to netting, matching is often used for balancing accounts receivables and payable. However, it differs from netting in that matching may be used to match currency cash flows with firms outside the MNE network and occurs on the basis of the same foreign currency (netting may occur for different currencies). Specifically, **matching** is a mechanism whereby a company matches its foreign currency inflows with its foreign currency outflows in respect of the amount, timing, and currency unit. The prerequisite for a matching operation, either within or beyond the MNE network, is a two-way cash flow in the same foreign currency. For example, the US firm focusing on exports to Canada can acquire its debt capital in the Canadian dollar markets and use the relatively predictable Canadian dollar cash inflows from export sales to service the principal and interest payments on Canadian dollar debt. This US exporter has thus hedged an operational cash inflow by creating a financial cash outflow, and so does not have to actively manage the exposure with contractual financial instruments. This technique is effective in eliminating operating exposure when the exposed cash flow is relatively constant and predictable over time. In addition to acquiring Canadian debt, there are several other ways to create cash outflow in the same foreign currency stated in the firm's cash inflow. For instance, the US exporter could seek out potential suppliers in Canada as a substitute for raw materials or components previously procured from the United States. Another alternative is to pay foreign suppliers in a third country (e.g., Mexico or Venezuela) with Canadian dollars.

Intra-company Reinvoicing. This practice involves the establishment of a reinvoicing center within an MNE. The center is a separate corporate subsidiary that may be located in the MNE headquarters or in the country that is the center of financial intelligence for the MNE. Like the netting center, a reinvoicing center manages in one location all currency exposure from intracompany transactions. Thus, the reinvoicing center may be combined with, or migrated into, the netting center for some MNEs. The reinvoicing center often takes legal title of products but does not get involved in the physical movement of goods. In other words, it handles paperwork but has no inventory. For example, Acer's Korean subsidiary may ship goods directly to the Japanese sales affiliate. The invoice by the Korean subsidiary, which is denominated in Korean won, is passed on to Acer's reinvoicing center located in Singapore. The Singapore reinvoicing center takes legal title to the goods, then subsequently invoices the Japanese sales affiliate in Japanese yen. As a result, all operating subsidiaries deal only in their own currency, and all operating exposure lies with the reinvoicing center. In practice, such reinvoicing centers not only manage foreign exchange exposure for intracompany sales from one place but also oversee intracompany cash flows, including leads and lags. With a reinvoicing center, all subsidiaries settle intracompany accounts in their local currencies. The reinvoicing center need hedge only residual exposure for the entire MNE. Finally, in order to avoid some taxes such as interest withholding taxes or capital formation taxes, reinvoicing centers should avoid doing business with local suppliers or customers in the country of location. It is necessary for this special financial subsidiary to qualify for nonresident status, which helps the firm gain greater access to external foreign exchange markets and open bank accounts in foreign countries.

Production Initiatives

Input Outsourcing. A firm can mitigate its economic exposure through input outsourcing in the same currency as the one used in export sales. To mitigate the risk from *endaka* in the 1990s, Japanese auto makers protected themselves against the rising yen by purchasing a significant percentage of intermediate components from suppliers in Taiwan and South Korea. Because currencies of Taiwan and South Korea are closely linked to the US dollar, the yen-equivalent prices of the intermediate supplies tend to decline with the dollar, and thus lessen the impact of a falling dollar on the cost of Japanese cars sold in the United States. In using this approach, MNEs should consider flexibility in making substitutions among various sources of goods and services. Maxwell House, for example, can blend the same coffee whether using coffee beans from Brazil, the Ivory Coast, or other producers. The more outsourcing flexibility, the easier it is for the firm to reduce operating exposure through offsetting accounts receivables against accounts payable in the same currency. This strategy, of course, must be weighed against the extra costs and the requirements of product differentiation in different markets.

Production Arrangement. By production arrangement we mean that an MNE with worldwide production systems can adjust the quantity of its production in a specific location to respond to foreign exchange risk and exposure. An MNE may increase production in a nation whose currency has been devalued and decrease production in a country whose currency has been revalued. For example, with a well-developed portfolio of plants worldwide, Westinghouse Electric (United States) may ask its subsidiary in Spain to increase production of generators in response to a weakening peseta while arranging for another subsidiary in Canada to reduce generator production in response to a rising Canadian dollar. Similar examples can also be found at Ford and GM. These two

Industry Box

Netting in Philips

Philips, the Dutch lighting and electronics giant, uses what is known as the Philips Multilateral Clearing System (PMC) to facilitate cash movements cross-border among its affiliates. This system is managed by the Amsterdam-based bank, Mendes Cans. Inter-subsidiary cross-border payments are made monthly through the PMC. Units worldwide notify treasury in Eindhoven of expected payments beginning 20 days prior to settlement. The system then generates payment instructions automatically several days before settlement date. Although most major international banks provide competent multilateral netting systems, Mendes Cans has long enjoyed a reputation as an innovator and high-quality partner in this regard.

Philips uses an internal, worldwide information exchange system called IFIS for purchase orders, invoices, and other communications related to inter-subsidiary transactions. IFIS is in effect an internal EDI (Electronic Data Information) system. Externally, Philips uses EDI for purchase orders and invoices with just a few trade partners; ironically, related payments and collections are still processed with different systems. Having spent a large part of his time in centralizing and improving funding and foreign exchange management, Corporate Treasurer Jean-Pierre Lac is now focusing on improving Philips' cash management. He is particularly concerned with the company's disbursement and collection methods. About 6,000 people in the company spend their time cutting checks, cashing checks, and doing related activities. Today, Philips is shifting from checks to electronic payments wherever possible. How quickly it can move depends on each country's payments system. In the Netherlands, for example, Philips delivers all of its payment orders to banks by tape; Germany and the Scandinavian countries have similar systems.

companies have substantial leeway in reallocating various stages of production among their several plants in different countries, in line with relative production and transportation costs. Ford can shift production among the United States, Spain, Germany, the United Kingdom, Brazil, and Mexico. Obviously, this production initiative works better for MNEs whose products are standardized in the global market (see Chapter 16). Using the multiple production plants strategy to reduce currency risk must be weighed against the extra capital investment and operating costs. Standardized products benefit more from economies of scale and require fewer extra operating costs than specialized products.

Global Coordination of Exposure Management

Most of the techniques highlighted in Exhibit 14.6 cannot be instituted without headquarters coordination and guidance. Organizationally, an MNE's currency exposure should be coordinated and overseen by its netting and reinvoicing center which may or may not be located at headquarters. For MNEs without these centers, the treasurer's office at headquarters should play these roles. While most MNEs today are delegating more power in production and operations to overseas subsidiaries, they are using a centralized structure to manage currency exposure. Because of opportunities for offsetting exposures from different product divisions and/or different foreign subsidiaries, centralization of exposure management ensures offsetting and self-hedging, which in turn reduces transaction costs and hedging expenses.[7] Centralization also increases benefits from economies of scale in purchasing financial instruments for hedging. It further facilitates the integration of hedging with other important aspects of international financial management such as global mobilization of cash flow, working capital management, and financing for global operations.[8] Finally, centralization does not diminish the importance of having valuable insights and necessary feedback from local managers. Incorporating a local perspective into the decision framework for exposure management helps diffuse conflicts between subsidiaries and headquarters. In situations where hedging can only be available at a local level, the role of the treasury at headquarters should transform from centralization to assistance. The electronic systems available today can greatly assist the management of currency exposure in terms of both strategy formation and ongoing control. Financial EDI (electronic data information) systems have already been used by some MNEs such as Merck, SmithKline Beecham, Xerox, GE, and PepsiCo. EDI systems significantly improve the effectiveness of information flows within an MNE network. At the same time, EFT systems (electronic funds transfer) as applied by Philips, Siemens, and BMW have made cash flow shifts within an MNE network quicker and easier. The improved effectiveness of both information and cash flows in turn reduces the costs for exposure management and hastens the management process. Finally, global coordination should not rule out the importance of unique hedging techniques used in specific host countries. Local practices in exposure management may be more cost-effective. In Latin America, for example, many firms maintained a portion of excess cash in either gold- or dollar-related government bonds to hedge operating exposure during an inflationary period.

Interim Summary

1. MNEs with resources built up in foreign countries encounter transaction exposure, economic (operating) exposure, and translation (accounting) exposure. Transaction and operating exposures are caused by real changes in the value of a company's cash flows or assets, whereas accounting exposure is not caused by this real change but the use of differing exchange rates when financial statements in multiple currencies are consolidated.
2. There are a number of ways of handling risks related to transaction exposure. These include hedging with financial instruments (forward, futures, options, and swaps) and hedging with contract invoicing and special clauses. Managing operating exposure is achieved through financial initiatives (leads and lags, netting and matching, intracompany reinvoicing), and production initiatives (input outsourcing and product arrangement).

Country Box

India

India Faces Dilemma on Foreign Exchange Hedging

Growing trade deficits, high inflation, and declining economic growth caused the Indian rupee to depreciate from a high of 44 rupees per US dollar in July 2011 to a record low of 66 rupees per US dollar in September 2013. This significant depreciation was also accompanied by rising volatility, giving firms engaged in rupee-denominated foreign exchange transactions an added incentive to hedge those transactions. The declining trend, meanwhile, also induced speculators to bet against the rupee by selling rupees short in the futures market, which put a further downward pressure on the currency. This presents a dilemma to the Reserve Bank of India (RBI), the country's central bank. Trading in foreign exchange futures and other derivatives is a way for legitimate traders and investors in India to hedge against the rising currency risk, but the same financial instruments are also used by speculators to bet against the rupee, making the RBI's job of maintaining the stability of the currency more difficult. After considerable deliberation, the RBI decided in July 2013 to bar banks from buying and selling exchange-traded derivatives for their own accounts in order to support the value of the rupee. At the same time, the country's capital market regulators also made it more expensive for investors to trade in currency derivatives. These measures, aimed at curbing speculation, also raise the costs of foreign exchange hedging by legitimate traders and investors.

If the slide in the value of the rupee accelerates, the RBI may need to defend the currency on the foreign exchange market by selling large quantities of foreign exchanges in its reserve, such as the US dollar. At the time of a crisis, a country's central bank can quickly exhaust its foreign exchange reserves and lose completely its ability to maintain the stability of its currency. In order to increase its foreign exchange reserves, the RBI tried to encourage Indian banks to borrow abroad and help them set up deposit programs that are attractive to Indians living overseas. Since the money that the Indian banks borrow abroad has to be returned in foreign currencies, they face foreign exchange risks because the money the foreign depositors withdraw is likely to cost more in terms of the declining rupee. Under the RBI initiative, any Indian bank that collects deposits with maturities greater than three years can hedge against the currency risk through the RBI at the low rate of 3.5 percent per year, far below the market rate of 6.5 percent per year. This subsidized hedging program was expected to raise over $15 billion by November 2013, at a cost of $250 million for every $10 billion of foreign exchanges raised. The subsidy enabled many Indian banks to raise funds at low interest rates and reduced risks at the expense of the Indian government.

Sources: K. Vasant, "RBI to keep currency-trading curbs until rupee stabilizes," *Wall Street Journal*, August 3, 2013; S. Jain, "India's central bank program brings in billions," *Wall Street Journal*, October 24, 2013.

Working Capital Management

Quantitatively, working capital is equal to the amount of current assets minus the amount of current liabilities. In practice, working capital management concerns the efficiency enhancement of current assets such as cash, accounts receivable, and inventory. Because cash and accounts receivable are particularly vulnerable to the impact of currency fluctuations, potential exchange controls, and multiple tax jurisdictions, this section highlights the management of cash and accounts receivables.

Cash Management

Ideally, a global treasury would be a single finance company with the ability to disburse or collect all financial reserves worldwide instantaneously, and with the absolute minimum risk and transaction costs. In reality, however, there are many limits such as financial regulations, cash flow restrictions, and idiosyncratic tax structures in foreign territories in which operations take place. The global cash management system includes three elements: home-country cash management; host-country cash management; and cross-border cash management. Most MNEs centralize at home such activities as borrowing, global liquidity management, international banking relations, and foreign exchange exposure management. Meanwhile, local disbursement and collection, local banking relationships, payroll, or management of trade credit and purchasing are generally managed overseas.

MNE cash concentration, known as *pooling*, generally occurs in two stages. First, cash is collected and pooled in local currency and used for local expenses. If a company has several

489

subsidiaries in a single country, it is very efficient to use cash surpluses from one to fund the cash deficits of another. As introduced in Chapter 10, these activities are generally undertaken by the MNE's umbrella company, which plays a role as headquarters in the host country. Periodically, as net cash surpluses grow, unneeded funds are remitted. Siemens, for example, carefully manages national cash pools in each currency, using cash excesses from some units to fund the cash needs of others within the same host country. Treasury looks at balances and short-term cash projections for each national cash pool and decides how much to lend or draw out. Central borrowing is generally cheaper, but a special loan program or a high tax rate at the subsidiary level can sometimes make local borrowing more attractive. It is hence necessary to consider interest rates, tax rates, and the profitability of local operations when determining the most efficient funding route.

Another approach for global cash management is to build an efficient account structure, which also helps reduce banking fees and float. For example, Merck, a major US pharmaceutical producer, uses a network of accounts held within a single bank's global network to transfer funds between national pools and the Merck treasury center in London. The system works in this way: The global bank maintains branches in each country of Merck's operation. At each branch, there is now both a national pool account and a treasury center account, with the treasury center wielding authority over both accounts. If a French subsidiary has "long" French francs, it can place the funds with the treasury center in the form of a deposit (a loan to the treasury). This subsidiary first transfers those funds into the French national pool account with the global bank's Paris branch. Then the treasury center debits the national pool account and moves the funds into its own account at the Paris branch. By transferring funds in this way, the company can avoid lifting charges levied by many European banks for transfers from resident to non-resident accounts.

Today, many diversified large MNEs have found that their financial resources and needs are either too large or too sophisticated for the financial services available in many locations where they operate. In response, many have established *in-house banks* to manage not only currency exposure but also cash flows. Such an in-house bank is not a separate corporation; rather, it is a set of functions performed by the existing treasury department. Acting as an independent entity, the central treasury of the firm transacts with its various business units. The purpose of the in-house bank is to provide bank-like services to the various units of the firm. The in-house bank may be able to provide services not available in many country markets, and may do so at lower cost when available. In addition to providing financing benefits, in-house banks allow for more effective currency risk management. Foreign sub-units may sell their intra-MNE receivables to the in-house bank. The in-house bank is better equipped to deal with currency exposure and has a greater volume of international cash flow, allowing foreign sub-units as a whole to gain from more effective use of netting and matching. This approach frees the units of the firm from struggling to manage transaction exposures and allows them to focus on their primary business activities. Volvo Construction Equipment's treasury center in Brussels acts as an in-house bank that maintains a network of bank accounts for all intra-organizational transactions. This network of accounts is used primarily for inter-subsidiary payments, and subsidiaries are responsible for making third-party payments and collections through local banks.

Foreign Receivable Management

A firm's operating cash flow comes primarily from collecting its accounts receivables. Managing foreign receivables requires appropriate measures in three stages: pre-transaction stage; transaction stage; and post-transaction stage. In the *pre-transaction stage,* a firm must investigate the buyer or importer's corporate credibility and financial capability. This is particularly imperative when dealing with a new client from a foreign country. Many large international companies categorize foreign clients into several clusters such as superior customers, priority customers, normal customers, and risky customers. This categorization and related client information are then disseminated to sales managers and treasury managers. Such clustering is usually built upon a client's previous record, company size, corporate image, financial strengths, and targeted markets. An exporter can obtain this information from previous collaboration, bank reports, archival research, or credit investigation agents. In general, the selection of currency unit, terms of payment, and the length of credit are all contingent on a foreign buyer's creditability and repayment ability.

In a *transaction stage,* the exporting company needs to decide in what currency the transaction should be denominated and what the terms of payment (including the length of time draft) should be. Ideally, the exporting transaction should be denominated in a hard currency together with a letter of credit at sight. In practice, however, this is largely determined by the exporter's bargaining power vis-à-vis the importer. The hedging instruments, hedging clauses, and invoicing techniques introduced earlier are useful at this stage.

International firms must establish organizational systems for tracking, managing, and collecting foreign accounts receivables in a *post-transaction stage.* In these systems, managers in the accounting or treasury department should be able to track the collection record and coordinate with the international sales or marketing department (when D/P or D/A is used) or the bank (when L/C is used). They should also share the information concerning the foreign exchange gains or losses and uncollected due receivables with the sales or marketing managers so that the latter could better evaluate past transactions and better prepare future businesses. In many firms, collecting foreign accounts receivables is linked with the reward system for sales managers. The level of bonus, commission, or reward does not depend on the amount of sales, but rather on the actual revenues collected.

Interim Summary

1. Cash and accounts receivable are particularly vulnerable to currency fluctuations, exchange controls, and multiple tax jurisdictions. Many MNEs have established in-house banks to manage cash flows and accounts receivables.
2. Most MNEs centralize at home borrowing, global liquidity management, international banking relations, and foreign exchange exposure management while leaving the management of local cash disbursement and collection, local banking relations, payroll, and trade credit management to local managers.

Chapter Summary

1. Financial management for global operations occurs in an environment with foreign exchange risks, capital flow restrictions, country risks, and different tax systems. It deals with foreign trade finance, global financing, managing foreign exchange risk and exposure, and working capital management.

2. Payment for international transactions differs markedly from that for domestic transactions. To the exporter, bad debt risks ascend along cash in advance, letter of credit (L/C), documentary collection (D/P or D/A), and open account. Many uniform documents such as draft, bill of lading (B/L), and commercial invoice are needed in international payment.

3. Smaller international firms play an active part in international trade. To obtain export financing, they can use several channels, including private sources (commercial banks, factoring or forfait houses, and corporate guarantee) and government sources (export-import banks and foreign credit insurance).

4. FDI involves more yet complex financing choices, including intercompany financing, equity financing, debt financing, and local currency financing. Intercompany loans from parent or peer subsidiaries can also be used for the purpose of avoiding taxation or foreign exchange control. Crosslisting firm stocks on exchanges in different countries is a major financing source for large MNEs because it increases liquidity and visibility.

5. Eurocurrency markets are the major source of international bank loans (i.e., Eurocredits). Yankee bonds are foreign bonds sold in the United States, Panda bonds are foreign bonds sold in China, and Samurai bonds are foreign bonds sold in Japan. All financing decisions must consider currency risks, source diversity, taxation implications, and interest rates.

6. Foreign exchange risk and exposure are two related yet distinct concepts. The former concerns the variance of the home-currency value of an asset, liability, or income affected by unanticipated changes in exchange rates. The latter refers to the sensitivity of changes in the home-currency value of an asset, liability, or income to unanticipated changes in exchange rates. Risk is an increasing function of exposure and the variance of unanticipated changes in exchange rates.

7. MNEs encounter three types of foreign exchange exposure: transaction exposure, translation (accounting) exposure, and economic (operating) exposure. Transaction exposure can be hedged through financial instruments such as forward and options and production initiatives such as input sourcing.

8. Firms need to create a global management system for working capital, especially cash flow. Headquarters managers must clearly define what aspects of cash management are centralized and what should be decentralized. Meanwhile, they should formalize policies managing international account receivables.

Notes

1   See S. M. Saudagaran, "An empirical study of selected factors influencing the decision to list on foreign stock exchange," *Journal of International Business Studies*, spring 1988, 101–128; D. K. Eiteman, A. I. Stonehill and M. H. Moffett, *Multinational Business Finance*, New York: Addison-Wesley, 1998.

2   J. J. Choi, "Diversification, exchange risk, and corporate international investment," *Journal of International Business Studies*, spring 1989, 145–155; M. Adler and B. Dumas, "International portfolio choice and corporate finance: A synthesis," *Journal of Finance*, June 1983, 925–984.

3   See M.D. Levi, *International Finance*, New York: McGraw-Hill, 1996, p. 302.

4   See M. Adler and B. Dumas, "Exposure to currency risk: Definition and measurement," *Financial Management*, summer 1984, 41–50; C.R. Hekman, "Measuring foreign exchange exposure: A practical theory and its application," *Financial Analysts Journal*, September/October 1983, 59–65.

5   C.C.Y. Kwok, "Hedging foreign exchange exposures: Independent vs. integrative approaches," *Journal of International Business Studies*, summer 1987, 33–52; L. Oxelheim, "Managing foreign exchange exposure," *Journal of Applied Corporate Finance*, 3, 4, 1991, 73–82.

6   J. Voelcker, "US-made 2013 Nissan Leaf has only 15 percent local content; Here's why," *Green Car Reports*, September 30, 2013.

7   L. Oxelheim, *Managing in the Turbulent World Economy—Corporate Performance and Risk Exposure*, New York: Wiley, 1997; L.A. Soenen and J. Madura, "Foreign exchange management—A strategic approach," *Long Range Planning*, 24, 5, 1991, 119–124.

8   D.R. Lessard and S.B. Lightstore, "Volatile exchange rates can put operations at risk," *Harvard Business Review*, July/August 1986, 107–114; R.M. Stulz, "Rethinking risk management," *Journal of Applied Corporate Finance*, 9, 3, 1996, 8–24; W.R. Folks, Jr., "Decision analysis for exchange risk management," *Financial Management*, winter 1972, 101–112.

493

chapter 15

international accounting for global operations

COUNTRY DIFFERENCES IN ACCOUNTING   497

FOREIGN CURRENCY TRANSLATION   508

TRANSFER PRICING AND TAXATION STRATEGIES   514

TAX HAVENS, TREATIES, AND STRATEGIES   517

Do You Know?

1. What forces lead to different national accounting systems? How many accounting zones are there internationally and what are these zones based on? If you were a manager at Nokia, would you like to see international harmonization of such different systems? Why or why not?

2. Why is foreign currency translation so important yet difficult for MNEs? What are the major translation methods? Can US companies such as Honeywell choose a specific method they like or switch methods every year?

3. What are the main benefits of intra-MNE transfer pricing practices and how do taxation agencies ensure that these transactions are fair? If you are a manager in a large MNE such as 3M, what do you take into account in choosing a transfer pricing practice?

OPENING CASE Glaxo to Settle Tax Dispute with IRS for $3.4 Billion

Pharmaceutical giant GlaxoSmithKline plc will pay the US government $3.4 billion to settle a nearly two-decade-long dispute over how to tax dealings between the British company and its American subsidiary, in a case that underscores the Internal Revenue Service's resolve to confront corporate tax avoidance. The settlement, which the IRS said was the largest ever, covers taxes the agency said Glaxo owed for 1989 through 2005 because the company's American unit improperly overpaid its British parent for drugs, mainly the anti-ulcer blockbuster Zantac. It said those overpayments reduced the company's profit in the US, thus lowering its US tax bill.

Glaxo's decision to settle the dispute, which was headed for a trial in the US Tax Court in February, was particularly sweet for the IRS because it has a poor track record of winning disputes involving the accounting practice at stake in the Glaxo case. That practice, called "transfer pricing," is the art of attaching a monetary value to trademarks, patents, research, and other intangibles that one arm of a multinational company transfers to another. Transfer pricing determines how costs are distributed between the far-flung arms of a multinational company, and thus what profit is booked in what country. Higher costs cut into profit, lowering a company's tax bill, while lower costs do the opposite.

Disputes over transfer pricing tend to be among the biggest fights between the IRS and corporate taxpayers, and they are of growing importance since more than 60 percent of world trade occurs inside multinational companies. Every country wants to maximize the tax revenue on goods and services produced within its borders, and every company has an incentive to book profits where taxes are lowest. That has bred a slew of disputes between companies and tax authorities over the proper pricing.

Symantec Corp., a Cupertino, Calif. software maker, was in a $1 billion transfer-pricing Tax Court dispute with the IRS involving an Irish subsidiary of Veritas Software Corp., a company it acquired in 2005. The IRS argued that licensing fees paid by the subsidiary to Veritas in the US were too low and that Veritas credited the US business with too much of the cost of developing some technology. That wound up increasing the income of the subsidiary in Ireland—a lower-tax country—at the expense of income in the US, lowering the company's overall tax bill. Symantec sued the IRS in the US Tax Court and eventually won the case in 2010.

Source: Abbreviated from the *Wall Street Journal*, September 12, 2006, "Glaxo to settle tax dispute with IRS over US unit for $3.4 billion," A3. The update on the Symantec case is based on *Morningstar*, January 12, 2010, Symantec Corp. Q3 Earning Call Transcript.

Country Differences in Accounting

The GlaxoSmithKline case illustrates that MNEs should deal appropriately with accounting and tax issues that affect the firms' net incomes and cash flow. The aim of an *accounting system* is to identify, measure, and communicate economic information to allow informed judgments and decisions by users of the information. Today, the explosive expansion of cross-border transactions and the rapid growth of companies seeking capital in international markets have made international accounting issues a daily concern for international managers. **International accounting** involves accounting and taxation issues for companies that have internationalized their economic activities across countries in which accounting standards and practices vary. Four fundamental issues need to be understood by international business managers: (1) country differences in accounting and international harmonization; (2) foreign currency translation; (3) cross-border transfer pricing; and (4) tax havens, treaties, and strategies. We explain country differences in the next section.

Why Accounting Systems Differ Among Countries

To a large extent, accounting is a product of its external environment. It is shaped by, reflects, and reinforces characteristics peculiar to its national environment. No two countries have identical accounting systems. In a few cases—such as that of the United States and Canada, or the United Kingdom and Ireland—the differences are relatively few and minor. In other instances—for example, Germany and France, or China and India—the differences are much more fundamental.[1] In general, a country's accounting system is shaped by *institutions*, *societal culture*, and *external relations* with other countries. The institutions of the country, in particular how it organizes its economic, political, legal, taxation, and professional systems, are the central forces determining the development of the accounting system.

Institutions

Economic System. A country's economic system factors, such as the level of inflation, economic and industrial structures, and the complexity of business organizations, affect the accounting system. As inflation rates increase, the problems of historical cost accounting also increase. Developed countries rarely suffer severely from high inflation and thus tend to view inflation accounting with suspicion. Inflation continues to be a serious problem in countries such as Belarus, Ethiopia,

497

Venezuela, Iran, and Argentina. Obviously, when inflation is running at high levels, the historical cost of an asset quickly becomes irrelevant. Therefore, various forms of inflation accounting have been found in these countries. In Brazil, for example, a revised Corporation Law, introduced in 1976, regulated that official monthly price indices be employed to update the values of all assets, depreciation, cost of goods sold, and owner's equity.

Economic structure influences how such accounting issues as pensions, retained earnings, dividends, depreciation, and research and development (R&D) cost amortization are handled. For example, accounting for pensions is an important issue in the United States, which has a very complex and concrete pension standard. This reflects the particular institutional arrangements of the United States, where many companies oversee employee pension plans. In other regions such as Chile, Hong Kong, and Singapore, pensions are run by the state or through private arrangements, and accounting for pensions becomes less important. In some transitional economies such as China, Russia, and Hungary, accounting for owner's equity items such as initial capital, retained earnings, and dividends vary according to ownership form, i.e., state-owned, collectively owned, privately owned, and foreign-owned enterprises. Similarly, accounting for depreciation and R&D expense amortization differs across countries that have different levels of economic development. More advanced economies such as Japan and the United States tend to use a faster amortization schedule, reflecting a belief that intangible properties derived from R&D normally depreciate rapidly.

Industrial structure affects the consistency of accounting standards and practices among different industries. Whether or not a country stipulates industry-specific accounting principles depends on the relative importance of that industry to the economy. For example, in Vietnam, accounting standards governing the foreign trade sector differ significantly from those governing other sectors. Similarly, accounting for the oil and gas industry has been a crucial and contentious issue in the United States and subject to unique accounting rules and practices. In the United Kingdom, the standard on research and development was strongly influenced by the potential impact of alternative accounting methods on companies in the aerospace and other R&D-dependent industries.

The complexity of the business organizations that dominate an economy affects the complexity of the internal accounting information system and management accounting in general. For instance, if most companies in a country are small or family-owned, then there is little need for external, sophisticated reporting systems, and there should be relatively few accounting regulations. As a company increases in size and complexity, the demand for sophisticated management accounting systems heightens, with problems of control, performance evaluations, and decision making gaining center stage. Typically, when business organizations become more complex, firms will start to arrange themselves into groups, with subsidiaries, branches, joint ventures, or strategic alliances all gaining in importance. Accounting standards and practices must reflect these changes. For example, greater focus will be placed on the regulation of group financial statements and extra disclosure requirements.

Political System. The political system is a critical determinant of national accounting because the accounting system will reflect political philosophies and objectives. The most common system found in Western Europe, North America, Japan, and Australia, for instance, is the *liberal-democratic system.* A second important system is the *egalitarian-authoritarian political system* (e.g., North Korea and Cuba). In the egalitarian-authoritarian form, all production and operations are owned and controlled by governmental institutions. Accounting serves two roles in this circumstance: to help in centralized planning and to help in controlling the economy. Profit is essentially retained by the government instead of the firm. Therefore, "owner's equity" in state-owned enterprises actually reflects "state's equity" or "governmental equity." While dividend policy is important in Western countries, it is meaningless in central-planning systems.

Legal System. The legal system determines the extent to which company law governs the regulation of accounting. In countries such as France, Germany, and Argentina, in which *codified Roman law* dominates, accounting regulations and rules appear to be concrete and comprehensive. This contrasts with common law countries such as the United Kingdom and the United States whose judicial systems rely on precedents. As such, many split the accounting world into two groups based on the pervasiveness of the legal approach: *legalistic orientation* toward accounting (i.e., using codified Roman law) and *nonlegalistic orientation* (i.e., using common law). Laws in codified Roman law countries are a series of "*thou shalts*" (you shall) that stipulate the minimum standard of behavior expected. In most countries with a legalistic orientation, accounting principles are national laws and accounting practices are codified. Accounting rules tend to be prescriptive, detailed, and procedural. Because accounting standards and practices are set by legislators, whether or not they are adaptive and effective depends largely on the legislators' knowledge of accounting principles, practices, and implications.

By contrast, laws in countries with a nonlegalistic orientation are a series of "*thou shalt nots*" (you shall not) that establish the limits beyond which an activity or practice is unlawful. Within these boundaries, latitude and judgment are allowed and encouraged. Accounting practices in common law countries are in large part decided by accountants themselves. Thus they tend to be more flexible, innovative, and adaptive. Nevertheless, the legalistic approach may be used in a particular sector or a special circumstance in common law countries. For example, tax laws and the regulations enacted by the US Securities and Exchange Commission represent the legalistic approach to accounting. In addition, certain laws not directly related to accounting may have strong implications for accounting practices. For example, the major accounting effect of the *Foreign Corrupt Practices Act* in the United States is that US MNEs must establish a system of internal controls and an internal audit staff to ensure that bribes are not being offered (see Chapter 19).

Taxation System. The taxation system is an important factor in situations where accounting systems are strongly influenced by state objectives. In countries such as France and Germany, public accounting reports are used to determine tax liabilities. In the United States and the United Kingdom, published accounts are adjusted for tax purposes and submitted separately from the reports to shareholders. Overall, there are three types of tax systems that correspond to different financial reporting rules:

- Tax rules and financial reporting rules are kept entirely, or mostly, independent of each other (e.g., the United Kingdom and the United States).
- There is a common system, with many of the financial reporting rules also being used by the tax authorities (e.g., less developed British Commonwealth countries).
- There is a common system, with many of the tax rules also being used for financial reporting purposes (e.g., Austria and Western Europe).

Professional System. The accounting profession is influential because the way in which the profession is organized and society's attitude toward accountants affect their ability to control or audit companies and their reporting systems. The extent to which auditors are independent and hold power relative to the companies they audit influences the perceived value of financial statements. The accountant's role in formulating regulation also affects the national accounting system. Even though this role is largely contingent on the country's legal system, accounting regulations can be influenced by the professional who may act as an advisor to the government, provide input into the regulatory process, and issue standards or recommendations in areas where there are no legal regulations. The French professional organization of chartered accountants, Ordre des Experts Comptables (OEC), provides a good example of this approach.[2]

Societal Culture

Societal culture influences the accounting system. For example, the detailed accounting procedures instituted by the French government reflect France's statistical tradition. Australia's accounting requirements for public firms are generally permissive, reflecting the distrust of government power embedded in that country's individualistic, frontier culture. Cultural dimensions at the national level, initially identified by Hofstede,[3] which are particularly relevant to accounting development, are "uncertainty avoidance" and "individualism." As outlined in detail in Chapter 6, in a high uncertainty avoidance country, institutions will be organized in ways that minimize uncertainty. Rules and standards tend to be explicit, prescriptive, all-encompassing, and rigid. Individualism affects preferences for earnings measurement rules and disclosure practices, and influences the willingness to accept uniform accounting rules in preference to a more permissive system involving the use of professional discretion. Recent studies by accounting scholars suggest that countries with low uncertainty avoidance cultures (e.g., the United Kingdom, the United States, and Sweden) tend to have strong independent auditing professions that audit a firm's accounts to ensure they comply with *GAAP (Generally Accepted Accounting Principles)*.[4]

External Relations

External relations, economically and/or politically, with other countries influence accounting practices and regulations through colonialism or regionalization. Historically, colonies adopted or were forced to adopt the accounting system of the colonial power, even though it may not have been particularly appropriate at the colony's stage of development. Thus the accounting standards and practices in the British colonies were significantly influenced by British accounting, and the influence remains today in Hong Kong, Australia, New Zealand, India, and Jamaica. The same can be said for former French colonies, Spanish colonies, and others. Regionalization harmonizes national differences in accounting systems. For example, since the passage of NAFTA, the accounting systems in the United States, Canada, and Mexico have converged on a common set of norms. Similarly, the member nations of the European Union and the Central American Common Market (CACM) have expended great effort toward integrating their accounting systems.

As shown in Exhibit 15.1, the preceding forces, namely institutions, societal culture, and external relations, jointly affect or explain a country's accounting system, especially accounting objectives,

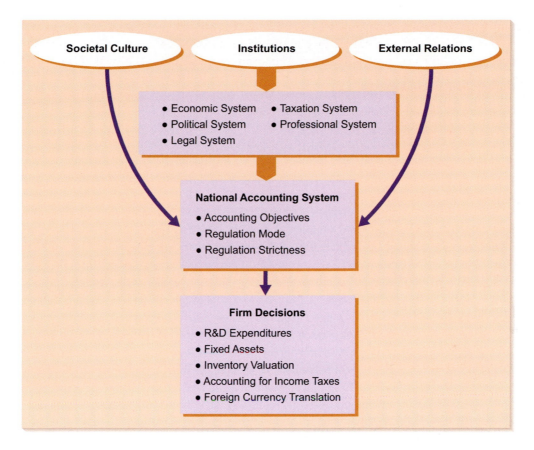

Exhibit 15.1 Forces shaping a country's accounting system

regulation mode, and regulation strictness. Accounting objectives refer to the extent they meet the needs of investors, creditors, the government, or other users. The mode of regulation concerns whether accounting rules and standards are regulated by government, the profession, or other groups. Finally, the strictness of regulation is the extent to which accounting rules and standards are strict and comprehensive. The Industry Box exhibits accounting diversity in Siemens as a company that does business in nearly 190 countries and has its shares traded on 11 stock exchanges in five different countries.

The characteristics of a national accounting system influence many company decisions, especially those concerning research and development (R&D) expenditure, fixed assets, inventory valuation, accounting for income taxes, and foreign currency translation. For example, Germany and the United States require immediate expense recognition for R&D expenditure under all circumstances, since they believe that there is a great deal of uncertainty as to whether the R&D will benefit future periods. Canada, France, the Netherlands, Switzerland, the United Kingdom, and *IAS (International Accounting Standards)*, however, allow this recognition only where the technical feasibility of a product or process has been established.[5]

Industry Box

Accounting Diversity in Siemens

Siemens AG, a German multinational engineering and electronics conglomerate headquartered in Munich and Berlin, is one of the largest industrial groups in the world. More than 80 percent of its sales occur outside Germany. Of its 370,000 employees, only 119,000 are located in Germany. Even though its home base is in the largest country in Europe, Siemens still finds the capital market in its home country to be too small for its appetite for capital, and it has its stocks listed in several different countries in order to gain access to the highly liquid international capital markets.

Currently, Siemens shares are traded on 11 stock exchanges in five different countries, including Germany, Italy, Switzerland, the United Kingdom, and the US. These include Frankfurt, Stuttgart, Munich, Hamburg/Hanover, Düsseldorf, Berlin/Bremen, Xetra, New York Stock Exchange, London Stock Exchange, Swiss Stock Exchange, and Italian Stock Exchange Milan. The company has 881 million shares in issue, with a market capitalization of £81,078 million on the LSEX, and 33.82 million ADRs traded on the NYSE. The London Stock Exchange requirements for listing demand that a company produce financial statements that are prepared and independently audited in accordance with standards appropriate for companies of international standing and repute. Any financial statements that comply with International Accounting Standards, UK, or US standards would automatically meet these requirements. In contrast, the SEC in the United States requires all foreign corporations to disclose, in their annual Form 20-F report, a US GAAP reconciliation of their reported net income and shareholders' equity. Siemens, along with many other corporations subject to these requirements, voluntarily reproduces some financial information in its annual report and accounts together with an explanation of the US GAAP differences.

National Accounting Zones

Although no two countries share identical accounting standards and practices, countries can be grouped into a few clusters based on critical similarities. This is possible because factors that shape a country's accounting system, as discussed earlier, can be similar to those facing another country. In light of dramatic changes in both external environment and accounting systems in many countries, especially emerging economies, we list five accounting zones. This is a modified list, building on a study by Mueller and his associates.[6] As highlighted in Exhibit 15.2, these five zones are:

1. British-American (or Anglo-Saxon)
2. Continental
3. South American
4. Transitional economy
5. Centrally planned economy

In *Anglo-Saxon nations*, accounting is oriented toward the decision needs of investors and creditors. Countries in the *Continental zone* include most of Continental Europe and Japan. Financial accounting is legalistic in its orientation, and practices tend to be highly conservative. Most countries

502

British-American Model

Australia	India	Panama
Bahamas	Indonesia	Papua New Guinea
Barbados	Ireland	Philippines
Benin	Israel	Puerto Rico
Bermuda	Jamaica	Singapore
Botswana	Kenya	South Africa
Canada	Liberia	Tanzania
Cayman Islands	Malawi	Trinidad & Tobago
Central America	Malaysia	Uganda
Colombia	Mexico	United Kingdom
Cyprus	Netherlands	United States
Dominican Republic	New Zealand	Venezuela
Fiji	Nigeria	Zambia
Ghana	Pakistan	Zimbabwe
Hong Kong		

Continental Model

Algeria	Germany	Norway
Angola	Greece	Portugal
Austria	Papua New Guinea	Senegal
Belgium	Italy	Sierra Leone
Burkina Faso	Ivory Coast	Spain
Cameroon	Japan	Sweden
Denmark	Luxembourg	Switzerland
Egypt	Mali	Togo
Finland	Morocco	Congo, Democratic Republic
France		

South American Model

Argentina	Chile	Paraguay
Bolivia	Ecuador	Peru
Brazil	Guyana	Uruguay

Transitional Economy Model

Armenia	Hungary	Russia
Azerbaijan	Kazakhstan	Serbia
Belarus	Kirgizia	Slovak Republic
Bosnia-Herzegovina	Latvia	Slovenia
Bulgaria	Lithuania	Tadzhikistan
Croatia	Moldavia	Turkmenistan
Czech Republic	Poland	Ukraine
Estonia	Romania	Uzbekistan
Georgia	China	

Centrally Planned Economy Model

Cuba	North Korea	Vietnam

Exhibit 15.2 Selected economies using the five major accounting models

in South America belong to the *South American zone*, with the exception of Brazil. A distinct feature in this zone is the persistent use of accounting adjustments for inflation. In the *transitional economy zone*, accounting standards vary according to ownership types. For collectively owned (e.g., township or village enterprises that are jointly owned by the local community, management, and workers) and privately owned enterprises, the accounting orientation moves toward a capitalist market, emphasizing information for investors, bankers, and taxation departments. State-owned enterprises (SOEs) that are no longer dominating their national economies operate under dual accounting systems. One provides information for managers accustomed to the former system oriented toward a command economy, which retains a heavy proportion of net profits earned by SOEs; the other employs a capitalist market orientation, trying to emulate the British-American accounting model. China is included in this zone because its SOEs no longer play a dominant role in shaping its growing economy. Chinese SOEs in many sectors have already adopted new accounting principles that are virtually similar to the GAAP in the United States. Finally, the accounting system in the *centrally planned economies*, in which central governments control production and resources of most enterprises, is characterized by high uniformity. Uniform accounting is necessary for tight central economic control. The primary users of financial statements are government planners. Assets are state-owned, and liabilities accrue through governmental arrangements via state banks. Initial or increased capital contribution was made and owned by the government. The overwhelming majority of net profits is either turned over to the state (often upper-level governmental authorities) or owned by the government. "Owner's equity" in a private sense does not exist.

International Accounting Harmonization

Having discussed national differences in accounting systems earlier, we can better appreciate the benefits that can be obtained from international harmonization and standardization. **Harmonization** is a process of increasing the compatibility of accounting practices by setting limits on how much they can vary. Harmonized standards minimize logical conflicts and improve the comparability of financial information from different countries.[7] The terms harmonization and standardization are often used interchangeably. Although highly related, these two concepts are not identical. **Standardization** means the imposition of a rigid and narrow set of rules and may even apply a single standard to all situations. Unlike harmonization, standardization does not necessarily accommodate national differences. As such, harmonization is a more appropriate term than standardization in the reconciliation of national differences in accounting standards. Accounting harmonization comprises three main components:

■ Harmonization of accounting standards that deal with measurement and disclosure.
■ Disclosures made by publicly traded companies in connection with securities offerings and stock exchange listings.
■ Auditing standards.

Not everyone agrees that national differences in accounting standards should be harmonized, however. Some argue that international standards setting was too simple a solution for a complex problem. They suspect that these standards could be adaptive enough to handle differences in social traditions, political systems, and economic environments among different countries. Along with the increasing integration of the world economy, however, the pressure for internationalizing and harmonizing accounting and auditing practices has been intensified. A growing body of evidence suggests that the need for international harmonization of accounting, disclosure, and auditing has been so widely accepted that the trend will accelerate. The globalized business community requires transparent, internationally comparable accounting practices consistent across borders. The two most notable developments that increase the necessity for harmonization are the evolution of MNEs and the development of international capital markets. For many MNEs, more than half of sales, profits, assets, or investments come from overseas operations. The heterogeneity of applicable accounting, auditing, and tax rules hampers an MNE's ability to prepare reliable financial information necessary for a careful analysis of various strategies. Meanwhile, the vast global capital market requires a common accounting language for the communication of financial information. In the absence of this common language, it is difficult to develop and maintain a truly efficient global capital market.

The major benefits of harmonization are threefold. First, comparable and transparent financial information helps enhance the reliability of foreign financial statements. It also helps in making informed decisions which, in turn, reduce risk for investors. Second, harmonized accounting reduces the costs of preparing financial statements and facilitates the task of investment analysts, investors, and other users in assessing business results. This saves on both the time and money currently spent consolidating divergent financial information. Third, many emerging and transitional economies regard uniform accounting as an efficient way of conforming to global norms. This is because they can avoid creating burdensome national standard-setting bodies of their own. For instance, China issued a core set of accounting standards in 2006 that are based on, and broadly comply with, international accounting standards (IAS).

International Accounting Standards

Harmonization proceeds through formulating and implementing international accounting standards. These standards have now been widely recognized and accepted in many countries throughout the world. For instance, a special television program was recently broadcast in Japan covering new accounting rules developed by the IAS Committee and their impact on corporate financial reporting in Japan. The key players in setting international accounting standards and in promoting international accounting harmonization include the following:

1. International Accounting Standards Board (IASB)
2. Commission of the European Union (CEU)
3. International Organization of Securities Commissions (IOSCO)
4. International Federation of Accountants (IFAC)
5. International Standards of Accounting and Reporting (ISAR), which is under the United Nations Conference on Trade and Development (UNCTAD)
6. Organization for Economic Cooperation and Development Working Group on Accounting Standards

IASB, the most dominant player in setting international accounting standards, was founded as the International Accounting Standards Committee (IASC) in 1973 by representatives of professional bodies in Australia, Canada, France, Germany, Japan, Mexico, the Netherlands, the United Kingdom, Ireland, and the United States. The organization was reconstituted in its current form in April 2001 with the responsibility of publishing and maintaining the International Financial Reporting Standards (IFRS), which incorporate the IAS initially developed by IASC and are followed by companies in over 100 countries around the world. When national and international standards differ, national standards usually take precedence. Companies that adopt more than one set of accounting standards must often issue one set of reports for each set of accounting standards they adopt. At the national level, some countries now use IFRS as the basis for national standards, whereas others use them as a benchmark against which to compare national practices. The standard-setting bodies in many developing countries are now using IFRS as the basis for national requirements although there are some who question the desirability of wholesale adoption without regard for differing economic circumstances. The Country Box offers an example in Australia.

An increasing number of MNEs report their accounting results by reference to IFRS. When the accounting standards in a home country conform with IFRS, accounting managers need not provide separate sets of financial statements; they just need to offer an explicit statement of conformity with IFRS as well as national standards. Groupe Saint Louis (a French MNE), for example, provides such a note attached to its consolidated financial statements:

The Saint Louis consolidated financial statements have been prepared in accordance with French accounting principles relating to consolidated accounts. The principles and methods used are also in conformity with the pronouncements of IFRS Committee.

When national and international standards differ, MNEs often include in the financial report a reconciliation showing the differences between national accounting practices and the requirements of IFRS. Profit before taxation and shareholders' equity are usually reported twice, with one based on IFRS and the other on the home country's standards. Some other companies provide full financial statements in conformity with IFRS, either as the main financial statements or in addition to the financial statements complying with national accounting practices. Nokia (Finland), for example, prepares the financial statements according to IFRS. At the same time, it provides a reconciliation between US GAAP and IFRS results.

Core standards as set forth by IFRS include the following categories:

- General, which involves disclosure of accounting policies, changes in accounting policies, and information disclosed in financial statements.
- Income statement, which deals with such issues as revenue recognition, construction contracts, production and purchase costs, depreciation, taxes, government grants, retirements benefits, research and development, interest, and hedging.
- Balance sheet, which covers various issues such as leases, inventories, deferred taxes, foreign currency, investments, joint ventures, business combinations, intangible assets, and goodwill.
- Other standards, which involve how to account for consolidated financial statements, subsidiaries in hyperinflationary economies, equity financing, earnings per share, discontinued operations, fundamental errors, and segment reporting.[8]

Interim Summary

1. Accounting practices in each nation are shaped by that country's institutions, culture, and external relations. Institutions include economic, political, legal, taxation, and professional systems. Legal systems divide accounting into two broad groups: the legalistic orientation based in countries with codified Roman law and the nonlegalistic orientation found in countries with common law systems.
2. Based on national accounting systems and practices, countries can generally be grouped into five accounting zones, including Anglo-Saxon, Continental, South American, transition economies, and centrally planned economies. Within each group, countries share not only similar accounting systems but also similar economic and organizational structures.

Country Box

Australia

Accounting in Australia

The Australian Accounting Standards Board (AASB), the main body governing accounting policies in Australia, issued the International Harmonization and Convergence Policy in 2002. The proposals reflect the AASB's statutory responsibility to participate in, and contribute to, the development of a single set of worldwide accounting standards. The AASB's objective is to pursue, through participation in the activities of the International Accounting Standards Committee (IASC) and the International Federation of Accountants' Public Sector Committee (PSC), the development of an internationally accepted single set of accounting standards that can be adopted in Australia for both domestic and worldwide use. In the short term, however, AASB aims to converge the Australian standards with those issued by IASC, but only where such standards are "in the best interests of both the private and public sectors in the Australian economy."

Since then, the AASB has worked closely with the IASC and PSC to remove incompatibilities between international standards and the corresponding Australian standards. For instance, AASB's ED#49 somewhat differs from IAS#38 in measuring, amortizing, and recognizing intangible assets (including R&D expenditure). When AASB harmonizes with IAS#38, it results in a value decrease of many existing intangible assets, fewer new intangibles being recognized as assets, and lower costs that can be recognized as expenses in developing intangible assets. IAS#38 imposes many more restrictions in recognizing internally generated intangibles such as goodwill, brand names, mastheads, and publishing titles than does AASB's ED#49. From 2002 to 2005, the AASB issued a number of standards that incorporate IASB standards and supersede the previous Australian standards for reporting periods beginning on or after January 1, 2005.

Source: Adapted from Jim Dixon, "Harmonization policy," *Accountancy*, October 1, 2001, 128, 1298, 1–2; Colin Parker and Daen Soukseun, "IAS 38: How tangible is the intangible standard," *Australian CPA*, December 1998, 68, 11, 32–33; AASB, *Pronouncements* at http://www.aasb.gov.au/Pronouncements.aspx, accessed November 25, 2013.

Foreign Currency Translation

Foreign currency translation is perhaps the most prominent accounting issue that directly and significantly affects the results revealed in MNEs' financial statements. MNEs, regardless of their home countries, cannot prepare consolidated financial statements unless their accounts and those of their subsidiaries are expressed in a single currency. For instance, one cannot add Chinese yuan (RMB) or Japanese yen to US dollars without a proper conversion of different currencies. Without foreign currency translation, MNE headquarters cannot appropriately plan, evaluate, integrate, and control overseas activities that should be coordinated within the network. The expanded scale of international investment activities also necessitates foreign currency translation. This occurs particularly when an MNE's subsidiary wishes to list its shares on a foreign stock exchange, contemplates a foreign acquisition or joint venture, or wants to communicate its operating results and financial position to its foreign stockholders.

   Translation is the process of restating accounting data recorded in one currency (e.g., the currency of a foreign subsidiary in Italy) into another currency (e.g., the currency of the parent company in the United States) for the purpose of aggregating data from different reporting entities. Translation differs from conversion; conversion refers to the physical exchange of one currency for another, whereas translation is simply a change in monetary expression, as when a balance sheet expressed in euro is restated to US dollar equivalents. No physical exchange occurs in the course of translation. Exhibit 15.3 outlines the definitions of other terms that are associated with foreign currency translation.

Conversion The exchange of one currency for another.

Current Rate The exchange rate in effect at the relevant financial statement date.

Discount When the forward exchange rate is below the current spot rate.

Exposed Net Asset Position The excess of assets that are measured or denominated in foreign currency and translated at the current rate over liabilities that are measured or denominated in foreign currency and translated at the current rate.

Foreign Currency Transactions Transactions (e.g., sales or purchases of goods or services or loans payable or receivable) whose terms are stated in a currency other than the entity's functional currency.

Foreign Currency Translation The process of expressing amounts denominated or measured in one currency in terms of another currency by use of the exchange rate between the two currencies.

Functional Currency The primary currency in which an entity conducts its operation and generates and expends cash. It is usually the currency of the country in which the entity is located and the currency in which the books of record are maintained.

Historical Rate The foreign exchange rate that prevailed when a foreign currency asset or liability was first acquired or incurred.

Local Currency Currency of a particular country; the reporting currency of a domestic or foreign operation.

Monetary Items Obligations to pay or rights to receive a fixed number of currency units in the future.

Reporting Currency The currency in which an enterprise prepares its financial statements.

Translation Adjustments Translation adjustments result from the process of translating financial statements from the entity's functional currency into the reporting currency.

Unit of Measure The currency in which assets, liabilities, revenue, and expense are measured.

Exhibit 15.3 Glossary of foreign currency translation terms

508

Countries are in different stages with respect to the financial statement consolidation requirement. Consolidation has long been a common practice in countries such as the Netherlands, the United Kingdom, and the United States, whereas it is a relatively recent phenomenon in many other European and Asian countries. For example, German MNEs have been required to present global consolidated financial statements since 1990. In Japan, consolidation is also quite recent with most companies not reporting full consolidated statements before the early 1980s. Today, consolidation has become much more widespread as a result of increasing globalization and heightened needs for information flow within and beyond the boundary of the MNE.

Commonly Used Translation Methods

There are four internationally accepted and commonly used translation approaches, which include:

- Current rate method
- Current/non-current method
- Monetary/non-monetary method
- Temporal method

The primary distinction among these methods is the classification of assets and liabilities that would be translated at either the current or historical rate. All four methods, which can be found today in various countries, produce considerably different foreign currency translation results. At present, the IFRS and the US GAAP both mandate use of the current rate method for translating the financial statements of a foreign entity.

1. **Current rate method.** A feature of this approach is that all assets and liabilities, both monetary and non-monetary, are translated at the current or closing rate. Foreign currency revenues and expenses are generally translated at exchange rates prevailing when these items are recognized (typically translated by an appropriately weighted average of current exchange rates for the period). All resulting exchange differences are classified as a separate component of equity of the reporting enterprise until disposal of the net investment in a foreign entity. The basis of this method is the "net investment concept," wherein the foreign subsidiary is viewed as a separate entity that the parent invested into, rather than being treated as part of the parent's operations. As an important consequence of this method, translating all foreign currency balances gives rise to translation gains and losses every time exchange rates change. Reflecting such exchange adjustments in current income could significantly distort reported measures of performance.

2. **Current/non-current method.** Current assets and liabilities are translated at the current rate, and non-current assets and liabilities at the applicable historical rates. Income statement items, with the exception of depreciation and amortization charges, are translated at average rates applicable to each month of operation or on the basis of weighted averages covering the entire period to be reported. A major weakness under this method is the treatment of inventory and long-term debt. As a current asset, inventory is translated at its current cost, which is a major departure from traditional GAAP. The translation of foreign-denominated long-term debt under this approach may be misleading to users, because it is translated at its historical value. For example, from the

perspective of a US reporting entity, if the dollar weakens internationally, it will take more dollars to repay this obligation, a fact that would not be apparent from the reporting entity's financial statements.

3. **Monetary/non-monetary method.** This method translates monetary assets and liabilities at the current rate. Non-monetary items such as fixed assets, long-term investments, and inventories are translated at historical rates. Income statement items are translated under procedures similar to those described for the use of the current/non-current approach. Under the US GAAP, if the foreign entity's local currency is the functional currency, it requires the current rate method. If the US dollar is the functional currency, US GAAP requires the re-measurement method which is essentially the same as the monetary/non-monetary framework. A limitation of this method is that not all items can be classified as monetary or non-monetary.

4. **Temporal method.** Monetary items such as cash, receivables, and payables are translated at the current rate. Non-monetary items are translated at the rates that preserve their original measurement bases. In other words, non-monetary assets carried on foreign currency statements at historical cost are translated at the historical rate. Non-monetary items carried abroad at current values are translated at the current rate. Revenue and expense items are translated at rates that prevailed when the underlying transactions occurred. The temporal method was the required method in the United States under Statement of Financial Accounting Standards (SFAS) #8 until it was superseded by SFAS #52, which requires the current rate method. The major points of the preceding four methods are summarized in Exhibit 15.4.

Items/Methods	Current	Current/Non-Current	Monetary/Non-Monetary	Temporal
Cash	CR	CR	CR	CR
Accounts receivable	CR	CR	CR	CR
Inventories				
Cost	CR	CR	HR	HR
Market	CR	CR	HR	CR
Investments				
Cost	CR	HR	HR	HR
Market	CR	HR	HR	CR
Fixed assets	CR	HR	HR	HR
Other assets	CR	HR	HR	HR
Accounts payable	CR	CR	CR	CR
Long-term debt	CR	HR	CR	CR
Common stock	HR	HR	HR	HR

CR = current rate; HR = historical rate.
* Example economies using the current method include Austria, Canada, France, Taiwan, Sweden, United States, and United Kingdom; Japan is an example using the current/non-current approach; Germany is an example using the monetary/non-monetary method; Before 1981, the United States used the temporal approach.

Exhibit 15.4 Foreign currency translation methods

All translations of foreign currencies will inevitably result in gains or losses associated with translation adjustment. The way in which such gains or losses are accounted for affects the operating results as perceived, particularly by the stockholders of a parent company. Approaches to accounting for translation adjustment include deferral, partial deferral, and no deferral. With a deferral approach, translation adjustments are excluded from the income statement and are instead accumulated separately as a part of equity in the consolidated balance sheet. Under the partial deferral approach, translation losses are recognized in a consolidated income statement as soon as they occur, whereas translation gains are recognized only as they are realized. A final method is to instantly recognize translation gains or losses in the income statement. Inclusion of such "paper" gains or losses in current income brings up a random element to earnings that could generate substantial earning gyrations whenever exchange rates fluctuate. Nevertheless, it is a widespread view that, if the reporting currency of the parent company is the unit of measure for the translated financial statements, immediate recognition of translation gains or losses in income is advisable. From a parent company point of view, translation gains or losses reflect changes in the domestic currency equity of the foreign investment and should be recognized.

Harmonization of Translation Methods

MNEs employing different translation approaches could produce divergent consolidated financial statements, which in turn hinders financial comparison and strategic decision making. For example, because most Continental EU countries have no standards, the practice is left up to the MNEs themselves. To harmonize the use of such methods, IAS #21 prepared by IASC (and later reissued by IASB) and SFAS #52 by the *Financial Accounting Standard Board (FASB)* are presently the two most important standards widely applied by international companies. Although they are basically compatible, IAS #21 differs from SFAS #52 in that the former advocates the current rate method in all circumstances (as explained earlier) whereas the latter emphasizes functional currency, which will determine an applicable translation method. Today, an increasing number of internationally listed MNEs are following IAS, and the world's stock exchanges are pressured to allow IAS in lieu of domestic standards for foreign company listings. While domestic MNEs in the United States are asked to follow SFAS #52, foreign MNEs in the United States are permitted to follow IAS #21.

The core premise of SFAS #52 centers on *functional currency*. SFAS #52 stipulates that the assets, liabilities, and operations of a foreign entity shall be measured using the functional currency of that entity. An entity's functional currency is the currency of the primary economic environment in which it operates; normally that is the environment in which an entity primarily generates and expends cash. For an entity with operations that are relatively self-contained and integrated within a particular country, the functional currency would generally be the currency of that country (e.g., RMB for a Shanghai subsidiary of a US parent). If a foreign entity keeps its accounts in a currency other than the functional currency (e.g., the German accounts of a US subsidiary whose functional currency is actually British pounds), its functional currency is the third-country currency (pounds). If a foreign subsidiary is merely an extension of a US parent company (e.g., Nike's assembly subsidiary in Thailand whose main function is to assemble shoes that will be exported to the United States), its functional currency is the US dollar.

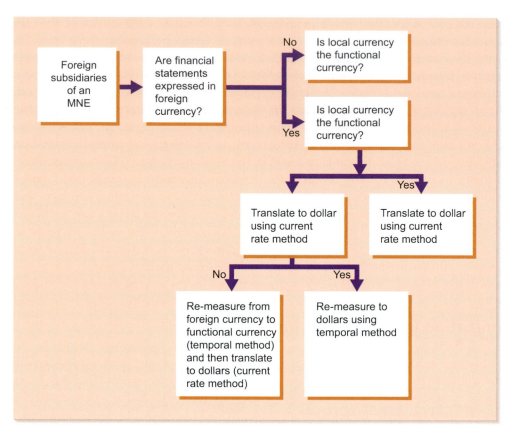

Exhibit 15.5 Process tree in foreign currency translation

According to SFAS #52, if a foreign entity's books of record are not maintained in its functional currency, re-measurement into the functional currency is required before translation into the reporting currency. If a foreign entity's functional currency is the reporting currency, re-measurement into the reporting currency obviates translation. The re-measurement process is intended to produce the same result as if the entity's books of record had been maintained in the functional currency. This means that an entity needs to maintain two sets of records, one in the local currency and one in the functional currency when these two are different. To help understand the preceding issues, see the process tree (Exhibit 15.5) on currency translation accrued in a foreign subsidiary of a US MNE.

International Accounting Information Systems

Consolidating financial statements is only one aspect of international financial reporting. As MNEs act more locally, accounting and financial reporting systems become increasingly critical. Global coordination has shifted from the previous rigid control mechanisms such as budget and bureaucratic control to information-based coordination, which is why international accounting information systems become fundamental. **International accounting information systems** (*IAIS*) involve accounting-related reporting systems, data management, and communication between various units of the same MNE. Financial controllers in MNE headquarters find themselves under increasing pressure to bring information to market more quickly, to deliver more extensive information than previously required, and to proactively manage business risk at a corporate level. Preparation of detailed MNE group information on a monthly basis is now the norm—with the result that headquarters' accountants and financial managers often spend most of their time preparing and monitoring information, rather than working with the output or reformulating accounting plans. Many MNEs have set up computerized accounting information systems with overseas affiliates to furnish the accounting information needed to plan, evaluate, and coordinate all business activities. Microsoft, with 54 financial groups charged with providing financial support to more than 85 global subsidiary operations, has struggled with these challenges. Its answer is the financial *digital nerve system,* an intranet-based environment that links all of the company's financial groups into a single, coherent system that provides its employees with real-time access to information and financial reports through the Internet. An effective IAIS provides an MNE with a competitive advantage arising from operational flexibility and transnational coordination in this increasingly competitive and complex global environment.

In general, MNEs tend to make internal reporting systems in their foreign subunits uniform. This allows easy comparison of corporations throughout the world and augments the consolidation process at the home office. This uniform reporting system, however, must be accommodated by the following considerations:

■ Different managerial styles of users may impose different standards on the design. European managers are more conservative decision makers than most US managers, which means European managers need more detailed accounting information to make decisions.

■ Intra-organizational interdependence in information flow, capital flow, resource flow, and product flow is a key factor determining design. The greater the interdependence, the more that intense communication and information exchange is indispensable.

■ Legislative and legal developments in both home and host countries may influence uniform reporting. For example, the Freedom of Information Act and the Fair Credit Reporting Act in the United States prohibits the improper use of personal data. European countries with data protection legislation do not allow name-linked data to be transmitted outside national boundaries.

Interim Summary

1. Translation is not the actual exchange of hard currency, but a re-expression in another currency (e.g., an MNE's home-country currency) for the purpose of consolidating financial statements.

2. The major translation approaches are: current rate method, in which all assets and liabilities are translated at the current rate; current/non-current method, by which current assets and liabilities are translated at the current rate and non-current assets and liabilities at the historical rates, income statements translated at average rates; monetary/non-monetary method, whereby monetary assets and liabilities are translated at the current rate, and non-monetary assets and liabilities at historical rates.

Transfer Pricing and Taxation Strategies

Why Transfer Pricing?

As one of the major international tax issues facing MNEs, **transfer pricing** refers to the pricing of goods and services transferred between members of an MNE network. These transfers are also termed intra-MNE transactions. The essence of transfer pricing is to earn economic benefits such as tax avoidance by manipulating the price of intra-MNE transactions. Transfer pricing can achieve the following benefits for the MNE:

1. *Tax and tariff reduction.* Tax minimization is the main driver behind transfer pricing policies. When tax rates are different in two countries, MNEs favor low transfer prices for goods and services bought by, and high transfer prices for goods and services sold by, an affiliate in a low-tax jurisdiction. Consider this example: Subsidiary A assembles shoes in China, whose corporate income tax is 33 percent, and needs to sell $10,000 worth of shoes to its sister subsidiary B in Japan, where the income tax is 55 percent. If these shoes were overpriced at $12,000, then it could lower subsidiary B's tax by $1,100 ($2,000@55 percent). Although subsidiary A had to pay $660 ($2,000@33 percent) more in taxes, the MNE network saved $440 ($1,100—660). Transfer pricing can also be used in a similar fashion to minimize import duties. The effect of tariffs could be reduced if the selling company underprices the goods it exports to the buying unit. For example, a product that normally sells for $100 has an import price of $120 because of a 20 percent tariff. If the invoice price were listed as $80 rather than $100, however, it would be imported for $96.

2. *Avoiding exchange controls.* Transfer pricing may be used to offset the volume effects of foreign exchange quotas. For example, if a government allocates a limited amount of foreign exchange for importing particular goods, a parent company may underprice products shipped to its subsidiary, thereby allowing a greater volume of imports. If an MNE wishes to move funds out of one country, it may consider charging higher prices on goods sold to its local affiliates. Similarly, an MNE may indirectly finance an affiliate by lowering the prices on goods sold to it.

3. *Increasing profits from joint ventures.* Transfer pricing enables the party to gain unilateral profit from controlling the joint venture's import and export activities. For example, some Hong Kong investors are not overly concerned with the reporting profits in their joint ventures in Mainland China. This is because they have already made noticeable returns from overpricing materials imported for the joint ventures and/or by underpricing joint venture outputs exported to headquarters. They normally control the material importation and products export for the ventures as specified in joint venture agreements.

Internally, the underlying problem of transfer pricing is possible conflict between the goals of subsidiaries and those of the parent when subsidiaries are evaluated as separate profit or investment centers. Overpricing outputs or underpricing inputs for subsidiaries in high-tax countries reduces their accounting-based profits. Therefore, MNEs should prepare corporate policies on internal transfer pricing and use different criteria to assess subsidiary performance when this practice has been used. Furthermore, if a transfer price is too high, tax authorities in the purchasing affiliate's country forgo income tax revenues. MNEs should check anti-taxation evasion measures adopted by related countries. This is explained below.

Transfer Pricing Techniques

From the tax authority perspective, intra-MNE transfer pricing must proceed following the arm's-length principle. The **arm's-length principle** in this context means that the transfer price struck between related companies should be the same as that negotiated between two independent entities acting in an open and unrestricted market. In the process of using transfer pricing, MNEs must become familiar with the methods used by taxation authorities in host and home countries to determine whether transfer pricing practices comply with the arm's-length principle. These methods delineate the legitimate range of transfer pricing that is allowed by tax authorities. Knowing these methods helps an MNE prepare appropriate transfer pricing policies. These methods are as follows:

- *Current open market prices:* Tax authorities generally view comparable open market prices as the most satisfactory method because it requires the fewest adjustments. If this method cannot be applied, they may compare the gross margin or operating profit the company earns from intercompany transactions with gross margins or operating profit earned in the open market. Differences between the terms of intercompany transactions and the terms of open-market transactions require adjustment before a true comparison can be made for taxation purposes.

- *Gross margin method:* This method relies on a certain range of gross margins achieved in comparable transactions between independent companies. The gross margin methods include: (1) the resale price method; and (2) the cost-plus method. The *resale price method* is used for transfers of goods to distributors, which sell them without further processing. The price paid for a final product by an independent party is used as a baseline, on which a suitable markup is deducted to allow for the seller's expenses and reasonable profit. The *cost-plus method* is used when one group company transfers items that need additional processing by the other group company before they can be sold to a final customer. Cost-plus simply marks up the cost of producing the transferred goods and services commensurate with functions performed by the transferring company. In this case the effective comparison is with the margin earned on similar transactions occurring at arm's-length. In effect, the procedure is the opposite of the resale price method.

- *Operating profit methods.* The difficulty of finding comparable transactions or gross margins often leads companies to use *operating profit methods* that include: (1) comparable profits method (CPM); (2) transactional net margin method (TNMM); and (3) profit split method (PSM). The *comparable profits method,* as its name suggests, simply compares the period percentage operating profit (e.g., return on sales or return on assets) in the controlled subsidiary with percentages in similar uncontrolled entities on a whole-company basis. The *transactional net margin* method is similar to CPM, but compares operating profit on transactions, rather than on a whole-company basis. Often, intragroup trading of goods and services is unique to a particular group. In this situation no external operating profit comparisons can exist so the *profit split method* may have to be used in this situation. Group companies simply reach an agreement on how profits from the final product will be shared between them, based on a considered assessment of the contribution made by each party to the transaction.

Transfer Pricing Regulations and Penalties

Concurrent with the increase in transfer pricing is an increase in scrutiny by cross-border tax authorities who want to ensure that their countries receive their fair shares of tax revenues. Tax authorities are acutely aware of the potential revenue losses associated with intracompany transfer pricing policies. For this purpose, tax authorities are requiring more reporting and documentation, carrying out more comprehensive audits, and introducing harsher penalty regimes. For example, the US Tax Court fined DHL for misstatement of income for the tax years 1990, 1991, and 1992 about the trademark royalty paid by its Hong Kong affiliate, DHL International. The IRS had sought more than $160 million in back taxes, plus penalties. DHL and the IRS varied widely on the value of the DHL trademark. DHL estimated the value as low as $20 million to $50 million. The IRS said the DHL trademark was worth as much as six times that amount when DHL sold its trademark to DHL International at what the tax agency said was not an "arm's-length" transaction.

The issue of *OECD Transfer Pricing Guidelines* (originally issued in 1995 and amended in 2009 and 2010) and the *US Section 482* are the two most important guidelines regulating transfer pricing practices. The *OECD Guidelines* provide information on the application of the arm's-length principle that the OECD hopes can be used by MNEs and tax authorities in all member countries. The OECD guidelines reject the use of splitting profits between jurisdictions on the basis of revenue and payroll. This latter method is considered to be against the arm's-length principles and is therefore considered an invalid transfer pricing method. *The US section 482 guidelines* are similar to the OECD model. The arm's-length standard is affirmed as the basis of the Section #482 regulations but requires that the best method be used. Taxpayers must demonstrate that their chosen method produces the most reliable arm's-length result. This means that MNEs will have to give full and documented consideration to all possible methods before settling on the most appropriate. Unlike the OECD model, the US rules accept the profit-based methods.

Both the OECD and US guidelines require the taxpayer to provide the supporting documentation for its transfer price on a timely basis, or suffer a non-deductible penalty of up to 40 percent in the United States and up to 100 percent in the United Kingdom, respectively. The strict US-initiated transfer pricing model (with accompanying documentation requirements, penalties, and enforcement) is spreading quickly to other nations around the globe and adding to the strain. Since 1997, new legislation and rulings have taken effect in many countries, including Australia, Brazil, Canada, Denmark, France, Korea, Mexico, and the United Kingdom. Most of these countries focus on the need to document adherence to the arm's-length standard, with the accompanying threat of large penalties for failure to do so.

To reduce the risk arising from transfer pricing/tax audit, many MNEs adopt an *advance pricing agreement (APA)* with the tax authorities of the countries in which an MNE generates taxable income. **An advance pricing agreement** is an agreement between the tax authority and the taxpayer on the transfer pricing methodology to be applied to any apportionment or location of income, deductions, credits, or allowances between two or more members within an organization. An APA allows an MNE to negotiate an understanding with one or more tax authorities that approves a transfer pricing methodology for a given term, resolving the uncertainty about its acceptability and reducing audit risk. An APA may be unilateral (least preferred by most tax authorities), bilateral,

516

or multilateral. Bilateral and multilateral agreements are more easily negotiated with tax authorities in countries that have existing tax treaties. The APA is also an alternative dispute resolution process that can reduce the number of transfer pricing cases requiring legal resolution, saving both time and money for the MNE and for the tax authority.

Interim Summary

1. Transfer pricing aims at gaining benefits through manipulation of prices of intra-MNE transactions on exchange controls, and increased profits from joint ventures. These benefits include tax and tariff reduction, foreign exchange control avoidance, and profit increase from joint ventures. Tax avoidance is the overriding intention behind this practice.
2. The legitimate range of transfer pricing allowed by tax authorities is determined by: (1) current open market prices; (2) gross margin method; or (3) operating profit methods.

Tax Havens, Treaties, and Strategies

Intra-MNE transfer pricing on tangible goods or intangible services is only one of the major vehicles to reduce worldwide taxation burdens for MNEs. Using tax havens and taking advantage of tax treaties between home and host countries have also served as important instruments for MNEs seeking tax reduction. Tax reduction or avoidance differs from tax evasion in that the latter is considered illegal, but the former is acceptable, aimed at keeping tax burdens to the minimum.

Tax Havens

High tax rates in many countries have forced MNEs to seek refuge in tax havens. **Tax havens** are geographical locations in which taxation is substantially lower than that in a home country. To avoid high taxation in a home country, an MNE may incorporate or register a company in a tax haven that may impose little or no corporate income taxes. For example, Bermuda has become a home to 75 percent of Fortune 100 companies, due to virtually zero income taxes (plus meetings and conventions in Bermuda are 100 percent US tax deductible for American corporations and associations). Because of low or no taxes on certain classes of income, thousands of so-called mailbox companies have sprung up in such exotic places as Liechtenstein, Vanuatu, and the Netherlands Antilles. Tax havens have the following categories:

■ Traditional tax havens with virtually no taxes whatsoever: the Bahamas, Bermuda, the Cayman Islands, Andorra, Bahrain, Campione, Monaco (except for French citizens), the Turks, Tonga, and Vanuatu.

- Tax havens that impose a relatively low rate: the British Virgin Islands, the Channel Islands, Gibraltar, Liechtenstein, Switzerland (except a few regions), Angola, the Netherlands Antilles, Kiribati and Tuvalu, Montserrat, Norfolk Island, the Solomon Islands, and several other small islands.
- Tax havens that tax income from domestic sources, but exempt all income from foreign sources, such as Hong Kong, Liberia, and Panama.
- Tax havens that allow special privileges, such as Brazil, Luxembourg, and the Netherlands.

To benefit from a tax haven, an MNE would ordinarily set up a subsidiary in the tax haven country through which different forms of income would pass. The goal is to shift income from high-tax to tax haven countries. For example, a US manufacturer could sell goods directly to a dealer in Japan and gather the profits in the United States, or it could sell the goods to its Bermuda subsidiary at cost and then sell the goods to the Japanese dealer, thus concentrating the profits in the Bermuda subsidiary. Specifically, MNEs can use tax havens through setting up holding companies, offshore banking, captive insurance companies, shipping companies, free-port manufacturing, or export and management companies. Most manufacturing MNEs seeking tax havens prefer the holding company mode. Companies can avoid tax in their home country by transferring assets to a holding company, over which they have control. The holding company then collects the income arising from the relevant assets (investments, loans, parent royalty, etc.). Ideal locations for such holding companies are countries that do not tax, or tax only lightly, the income in question. In the finance sector, a remarkable phenomenon is that the international banking industry has not remained in well-established finance centers such as London, New York, Tokyo, Zurich, and Luxembourg, but has moved offshore in search of more favorable climates for international banking operations (e.g., low tax, freedom from exchange controls, and freedom from withholding tax on interest). For example, the value of operations generated by US, Canadian, and European banks channeled through the Bahamas and Cayman Islands is still rising. Most banking institutions in the islands have highly reputable international connections. The majority are cubicle operations with neither offices nor staff of their own, but the amount of funds booked through these subsidiaries is phenomenal. For example, external assets of banks in the Bahamas amounted to $185 billion at the end of 1995. However, vigorous actions by the US government to curb tax evasion have raised concerns of many multinationals after a lawsuit against the Swiss Bank UBS and the subsequent settlement of the case. The settlement required UBS to hand over details of 4,450 accounts to the US tax authorities, which in turn could use the records to pursue suspected tax evaders.[9]

Tax Treaties

Where income earned and taxed in one country is remitted to investors in other countries, the income may be subject to multiple taxation. This is a particular, but not peculiar, problem to US investors, because the United States follows the worldwide concept of taxation. Two common approaches are used to avoid multiple taxation: *foreign tax credits* and *tax treaties*. The idea of the tax credit is that a company can reduce its tax liability by the amount of the credit. In determining the tax credit in the United States, for example, the predominant nature of the foreign tax must be that of an income tax as defined in the United States. With the spread of business worldwide, most nations in the world, both developed and developing, have signed numerous bilateral tax treaties. Accordingly, tax treaties have become the primary device for avoiding multiple taxation today.

The major purpose of international tax treaties is to eliminate international double taxation and to render mutual assistance in tax enforcement (e.g., preventing tax evasion) and in reducing barriers to trade and investment. Many countries avoid international double taxation by not taxing their taxpayers on foreign source income (e.g., China). To a large extent, the income tax treaties determine the amount of tax to be paid to the country where the income is produced and the amount to be paid to the taxpayer's country of residence. It does this by offering reduced rates of tax or complete exemptions from tax for certain specified items of income. For example, under US law, interest paid by a US company to a foreign recipient is subject to a 30 percent US withholding tax. Under the UK–US income tax treaty, this tax is eliminated. Each treaty may also differ from the others and results from negotiation between the two countries. In order to prevent a resident of a non-treaty country from using, for example, the UK treaty to invest in the United States, anti-conduit provisions were also included. If a Saudi Arabian investor were to lend money to a UK corporation that lent it to the US subsidiary, the anti-conduit provisions would treat the loan as coming directly from Saudi Arabia.

Other Tax Strategies for MNEs

1. *Setting up a holding company in a host country:* This technique for repatriating cash and reducing future taxes involves setting up a holding company in the same host country as a high-tax operating subsidiary. Funding is provided to that holding company to buy the shares of the operating company from the US parent, allowing direct future earnings to be repatriated without withholding taxes. The consolidation of the return of the holding company and the operating company allows not only deduction of the new interest, but also reduction of future foreign taxes. US law, through section 304 of the International Revenue Code, considers this for tax purposes as a dividend distribution, rather than a sale, because the ultimate ownership of the operating company has not changed. Foreign countries generally levied this as a sale by a foreign corporation, with no foreign tax on any capital gain.

2. *Establishing a holding company in an integrated region:* This approach involves a regional or other multicountry holding company. Given that intercompany dividends between European Union countries are tax free, a subsidiary in the country (e.g., the Netherlands) would borrow to buy shares of another subsidiary in another European country (e.g., Belgium). For this reason, MNEs need a holding company in a country that does not tax dividend income or capital gains and that has a low withholding rate on dividends back to the United States.

3. *Building a finance corporation:* In view of the tax incentives given to finance companies in some countries such as Belgium and Ireland, US MNEs may establish finance companies in these countries to manage group cash and currency exposure and to channel funds within Europe without bringing them back to the parent. For example, if an MNE has excess cash in Germany, it may want to finance a subsidiary in exchange for preferred shares in the finance company. The

German company reduces its cash, which may be particularly useful if it cannot pay dividends because of an insufficiency of earnings or reluctance to pay withholding tax.

4. *Locating projects in a low-tax region within a host country:* A large proportion of MNEs entering developing countries often invest their projects in special technological, investment, or trade zones which impose substantially lower tax rates or provide preferential tax terms. China provides an excellent example. MNE manufacturing projects located in Shenzhen, one of the five special economic zones in China, enjoy a reduced 15 percent rate on corporate income tax (as opposed to 33 percent in normal cases). They also receive an exemption of income tax for the first two years and a 50 percent reduction of income tax during the third to fifth years, starting from the first profit-making year. MNEs located in coastal cities such as Tianjin, Shanghai, Dalian, Qingdao, and Guangzhou are entitled to a 24 percent corporate income tax levied on general manufacturing projects and a 15 percent corporate income tax for those MNEs that are technologically intensive. Similarly, if projects are hosted in an Economic and Technological Development Zone (ETDZ) designated by the central government, MNEs will enjoy a 15 percent corporate income tax. If the project is more than ten years in duration, it enjoys a two-year exemption and a subsequent three-year 50 percent reduction of corporate income tax, and a 10 percent corporate income tax for MNEs with 70 percent of output exported, after a stipulated term.

In sum, there are several tax strategies used by MNEs in addition to transfer pricing or using tax havens and tax treaties. To deal with the complex international tax systems efficiently, MNEs set up holding companies or finance corporations in a foreign region (or country) or locate investment projects in special zones within a target foreign country. Because the taxation burden directly affects net profit that can be retained by the firm, these strategies add value to the firm's wealth and influence the firm's ability to reinvest overseas. Although the international taxation environment is much more complex than the domestic one, MNEs can benefit from opportunities arising from the differences in taxation rates and systems between countries. These benefits will not accrue unless MNEs have adopted realistic and viable strategies on taxation reduction.

Interim Summary

1. High tax rates in many countries often compel MNEs to incorporate or register a company in a tax haven. Bermuda is especially popular for American MNEs. Tax treaties and foreign tax credits are also used to avoid double taxation on the same income.
2. Other tax reduction strategies exist, dealing primarily with setting up holding companies to avoid taxation, creating finance firms in countries with tax incentives, and locating new projects in low-tax regions of host countries.

Chapter Summary

1. Accounting is fundamental to MNEs because their ultimate success needs to be reflected in accounting reports and because their key decisions are often made based on accounting information. Some accounting practices such as transfer pricing, accounting information systems, and cash flow management can add important value to an MNE.

2. When firms expand globally, they face different accounting systems in different nations. Such differences exist owing to different economic, political, legal, cultural, and taxation systems. These differences can affect a firm's decisions on R&D expenditure, fixed assets, inventory valuation, foreign currency translation, and accounting for income taxes.

3. MNEs will benefit from harmonizing accounting standards and practices between nations. The International Accounting Standards Committee (IASC) is the leading institution in setting international accounting standards. Increasing numbers of MNEs now report their accounting results by reference to IASC's standards.

4. Foreign currency translation can significantly affect the results in MNEs' consolidated financial statements. Widely accepted translation approaches include current rate method, current/non-current method, monetary/non-monetary method, and temporal method. IASC and the US GAAP now both mandate to use the current rate method. SFAS #52 details how this method is advanced.

5. Transfer pricing provides MNEs with several gains, especially reducing corporate income taxes in heavily taxed countries in which MNE subsidiaries are located. However, firms must conform to various restrictions and rules imposed by home- or host-country taxation authorities. Tax havens and treaties offer additional opportunities for tax avoidance.

Notes

1 See C. Roberts, P. Weetman, and P. Gordon, *International Financial Accounting*, London: Financial Times Management, 1998, pp. 8–9.

2 H.H.E. Fechner and A. Kolgore, "The influence of cultural factors on accounting practice," *International Journal of Accounting*, 29, 4, 1999, 265–277.

3 G. Hofstede, *Culture's Consequences: International Differences in Work-related Values*, Beverly Hills, CA: Sage, 1980. For details, refer to Chapter 6.

4 S.J. Gray, "Towards a theory of cultural influence on the development of accounting systems internationally," *Abacus*, 24, 1, 1988, 1–15, and S.B. Salter and F. Niswander, "Cultural influences on the development of accounting systems internationally," *Journal of International Business Studies*, 26, 1995, 379–397; R.J. Kirsch, "Towards a global reporting model: Culture and disclosure in selected capital markets," *Research in Accounting Regulation*, 8, 2004, 71–110.

5 For a detailed discussion on these accounting issues, see W.E. Becker and P. Brunner, "A summary of accounting principle differences around the world." In F.D.S. Choi (ed.), *International Accounting and Finance Handbook*, 3, 1997, pp. 1–33, New York: Wiley; and International Accounting Standards Committee, *International Accounting Standards 1996*, London, 1996.

6 See G.G. Mueller, H. Gernon, and G. Meek, *Accounting: An International Perspective*, New York: Business One Irwin, 1994.

7 F.D.S. Choi, C.A. Frost, and G.K. Meek, *International Accounting*, Upper Saddle River, NJ: Prentice-Hall, 1999.

8 For details, see B.J. Epstein and A.A. Mirza, *IAS 2000*, New York: Wiley, 2000.

9 C. Pryde, "UBS will hand over 4,450 account names in tax-case settlement," FRANCE 24, August 20, 2009.

chapter 16

global marketing and supply chain

THE INTERNATIONAL MARKETING CHALLENGE   525

GLOBALIZATION AND LOCALIZATION IN INTERNATIONAL MARKETS   528

THE GLOBAL SUPPLY CHAIN   544

Do You Know?

1. What determines the potential of a foreign market?
2. What adaptations, if any, are necessary for a product to sell in another country? For instance, if you were to sell a Ford Focus in Vietnam, what adjustments would you make in the car's appearance and technical specifications?
3. What influence does the country of origin of a manufacturer (or a service provider) have on the customer's decision to buy a product? Would you buy a Malaysian-made Proton car?
4. How do you make channel decisions in a foreign market? What should you do when your main channel (e.g., direct marketing) is deemed unlawful?
5. What transportation modes dominate international trade?
6. If you were a manager at Mattel, how would you prepare for a slowdown at California's ports?

OPENING CASE   Domino's Pizza

Founded in 1960 in Ypsilanti, Michigan, Domino's Pizza opened its first foreign store in 1983 in Winnipeg, Canada. It added Japan in 1984, the United Kingdom in 1985, and Mexico in 1989. Domino's successfully entered Hong Kong and Taiwan in 1984 and 1987, respectively, though it was not clear whether pizza would sell given the lack of milk-product tradition among Chinese, and it applied the lessons it had learned in those markets when entering the Chinese Mainland in 1994. In 2000, Domino's acquired a controlling stake in a Dutch Pizza company that operated 52 of its stores. International expansion continued in the new millennium, with international same-store sales registering uninterrupted growth from 2002 onward and the addition of international stores far outpacing the addition of domestic stores. On March 25, 2012, the company reported that it had 4,912 international stores—14 more than the number of its stores in the US.

Domino's has learned that country environments can vary substantially. The menu in the Chinese stores is adapted to local tastes, with shrimp, scallops, and squid added to the conventional toppings. The pepperoni pizza is called the American Pizza, and print advertising demonstrates how to eat pizza with your hands. While prices in China are slightly lower than in the United States, store sales volume is more than double the US average. Unlike in the United States, where home delivery is dominant, in China it accounts for only 10 to 15 percent of volume, with most orders placed in restaurants open from 9 am to 11 pm. However, competitive pressures from Pizza Hut and local outlets are pushing Domino's toward an expansion of home delivery in the Chinese market.

Master franchisees in each country are keys to Domino's marketing strategy. Many master franchisees and general managers are veterans of the US market; for example, Taiwan's general manager was a Domino's employee who spent many years in the United States. Master franchisees contribute to product adaptation, determine pricing, and devise national promotion and advertising. In Japan, the master franchisee came up with the idea of using a customized scooter for delivery in narrow alleys. The franchise concept has been developed in the United States before being extended overseas first in the form of overseas franchisees of US firms and subsequently also in the form of US franchisees of foreign businesses. The latter include, for instance, Bark Busters, a dog behavior control business headquartered in Australia, and Japan-based Kumon, a children supplemental education business started by Toru Kumon in Japan some 50 years ago, which now operates in 43 countries. Kumon of American has grown to become the largest foreign franchise in the United States.

Source: Domino's Pizza International, Inc. HEC case, 1998 and company updates to 2006; "Foreign franchise concepts find growth opportunities in the US market," *Wall Street Journal,* March 8, 2004, B8; L. Alfs, "International growth: Domino's Pizza's overseas store count surpasses US stores," *The Ann Arbor News,* May 1, 2012.

The International Marketing Challenge

International markets offer vast opportunities for firms with a product or a service potentially in demand abroad. As the Domino's case shows, even when the imported product deviates from local tastes and customs, it can penetrate a market. Novelty, cultural attractiveness, and appropriate marketing strategies can get a product through the door in some international markets. Some US products are even more successful abroad than at home. For example, US-based Kenny Rogers Roasters filed for bankruptcy in 1998 and was purchased the following year by Nathan's Famous; however, Kenny Rogers China, led by the former head of Kentucky Fried Chicken (KFC)'s operations there, continues to operate and expand in that country. Unfortunately, this is the exception, not the norm.

International markets are full of pitfalls and littered with failed attempts at foreign expansion. Dunkin' Donuts closed its China operations in 1999, as did Tex-Mex. Office Max closed its doors in Japan, four years after its initial entry. Gateway Computers divested its foreign operations altogether. Many otherwise successful brands do not sell well in foreign markets. For instance, Campbell's Soup did not do well in Brazil, and McDonald's failed to find a following in Barbados. When Home Depot entered the Chinese market, it had high hopes that the rapid growth of home ownership in the country would provide a large do-it-yourself (DIY) market for it to serve. After it set up its operations in the country, however, the company found out that home owners in China would rather hire others to renovate their houses and condominiums than do it themselves. Faced with slow sales and lack of profit, Home Depot closed its China operations in 2012. Initial success often proves elusive, evaporating when the novelty of the product wears off, or when pent-up demand slackens.[1] British wireless provider Vodafone retreated from Japan in 2006, having failed to find a following among Japanese consumers. For years, US and Japanese manufacturers attempted unsuccessfully to sell dishwashers in Japan; however, local housewives felt guilty not washing the dishes by hand, and they found the machine too bulky for their small kitchens and unwieldy when it came to Japanese staples such as sticky rice, raw eggs, and fermented soybeans. Manufacturers designed smaller dishwashers that are more energy efficient and more effective in cleaning sticky foods and eventually increased the possession rate from 7 percent in 2000 to 29 percent in 2012. However, this possession rate is still far lower than the US rate of 60 percent, and dishwashers remain the least used and most "disappointing" appliances in the Japanese house-hold, according to a nationwide survey.[2]

In addition to local adaptation, firms increasingly face the intense competition associated with globalization. Markets that in the past have been insular or relied on a single source of imports now have a bewildering array of offerings from multiple source countries. Indeed, the essence of international marketing, especially in more global industries, is that competition can come from anywhere on the globe. Being the country in which the product originated (e.g., a spaghetti noodle maker from Italy) can help, but it is no guarantee of success.

Success in international markets depends on meeting many challenges: accurate assessment of market potential; selection of the right product mix; and appropriate adjustments in distribution, pricing, packaging, and advertising. Cultural values and social mores, rules and regulations, economic conditions and political realities constitute the context within which international marketing takes place. The increasing diversity within many national environments (e.g., the growth of the Hispanic sector in the United States) represents an additional challenge, but also an opportunity: upstart Alo Vatan has become the third-largest provider of phone service for the large Turkish community in Germany by being tuned to the Turk's linguistic, cultural, religious, and social sensitivities.[3]

Assessing Market Potential

To assess the potential of a foreign market, firms seek to identify the aggregate demand for a product (or a service) and estimate the costs associated with product introduction and distribution, as well as with adapting the product to a new environment. Accessibility, profitability, and market size all play a role in deciding market priority. In and of itself, population size reveals little about short-term market potential. When China embarked on economic reforms in 1978, MNEs salivated at the prospect of "selling a toothbrush to every Chinese" in a country of well over a billion, only to discover that most Chinese had neither the desire, nor the money, to buy foreign products at that time. It has taken more than 20 years for China to become the substantial consumer market it is today, emerging as the world's largest market for cars, as well as for many other products.

Probably the single most important indicator of market potential is economic development and its correlate, disposable income.[4] Nominal income figures however say little about the consumers' ability to afford certain products and services. Thus, economists use purchasing power parity (PPP) to adjust nominal figures to the purchasing power of local consumers. Exhibit 16.1 plots the prices of the Big Mac in 56 countries around the world against the values of their GDP per capita. The straight orange line in the plot is the regression line, indicating a positive relationship between GDP per capita and Big Mac prices. Why does the same product made from essentially the same materials tend to sell at higher prices in wealthier countries? Since free trade tends to eliminate the price differentials in goods that are easily traded across countries, the reason lies in the costs of non-tradables, such as housing and services (including the services of restaurant workers), that tend to rise in price as the residents of a country have higher disposable incomes.[5]

In addition to income figures, per capita GDP figures are often used to gauge the potential in a given market. In Exhibit 16.2, the relationship between GDP levels and car ownership is shown for a variety of countries.

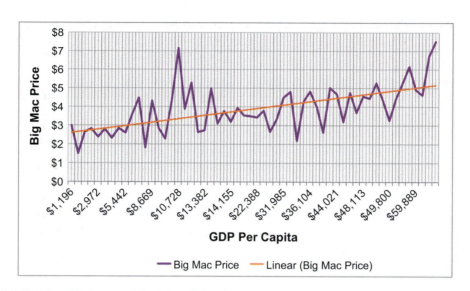

Exhibit 16.1 Relationship between the price of the Big Mac and GDP per capita in selected markets

Sources: The prices of the Big Mac are from *The Economist* (July 2013) and the data on GDP per capita are from the World Bank (2012).

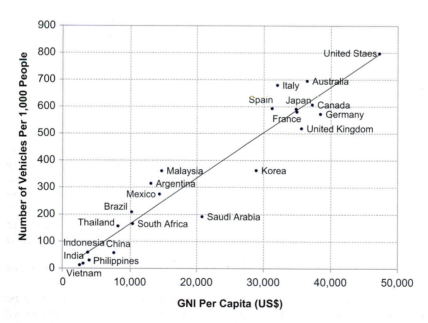

Exhibit 16.2 Relationship between vehicle ownership and GNI per capita

Source: World Bank, 2010.

While GDP and disposable income provide a preliminary measure of market potential, the actual opportunity will vary greatly based on local idiosyncrasies, way of life, and consumption patterns. For instance, research by the Boston Consulting group shows that, in some developing economies such as Colombia or the Philippines, Coca-Cola is a substitute for non-potable water. Other research shows that the French drink six times more wine than the British, whereas Germans consume six times the amount of beer as Italians,[6] and that Venezuelans, Mexicans, Russians, Turks, and South Africans (in that order) care most about their appearance.[7] Venezuelans also spend as much as 20 percent of their household income on personal care products, and hold the world record for deodorant use.[8] One-Hour Martinizing, a dry-cleaning franchise, decided to open its first foreign franchise in Ecuador after discovering that businessmen there changed their shirts as much as three times a day because of the hot, sticky weather.[9]

Demographics also play a role in estimating future market potential. For instance, Japan and many EU countries face low and even negative population growth and an aging population, whereas most Asian nations are forecast to grow and maintain relatively youthful populations (China is an exception due to the One Child policy). These forecasts spell, for example, strong market demand for toys in Indonesia and, at the same time, increased demand for health care products and services in the EU and Japan.

To explore those opportunities systematically, firms undertake international marketing research. The research is aimed at answering the following questions:[10] (a) What objectives should the firm pursue in the foreign market?; (b) What foreign market segments should the firm pursue?; (c) What are the best product, distribution, pricing, and promotion strategies for the foreign market?; (d) What should be the product–market–company mix in order to take advantage of foreign marketing opportunities?

Globalization and Localization in International Markets

As in other areas of international business, striking a balance between globalization and localization is a key challenge in international marketing. Lack of marketing globalization has proved to be detrimental to performance;[11] however, the same is true for indiscriminate standardization of marketing practices without attention to localization factors.[12] Here is how the globalization versus localization dilemma is described in a Conference Board report citing General Motors Europe:

Generally, the more closely defined the market segment, the less important are national stereotypes (Germans focus on ecology, Italians on performance). Across national markets, there is a trend toward greater similarity on product specifications, price, and packaging. On the other hand, cultural and national differences exist and require flexibility in communication with customers.

Globalization, in a marketing sense, is the standardization of products (or services), brands, marketing, advertising, and the supply chain across countries and regions. **Localization**, in contrast, is the adjustment of one or more of the above elements to be idiosyncratic characteristics of a given national market. Determining and fine-tuning the globalization–localization balance is a major challenge for the MNE. The challenge is approached and handled in different ways. Cees van der Hoven, CEO of Ahold NV, the number-three supermarket chain globally behind Wal-Mart and French Carrefour, summarizes his firm's strategy succinctly: "Everything the customer sees we localize, everything they don't see, we globalize." Carrefour, while preferring brand uniformity and substituting global brands for the local brands it acquires, also tailors its products to local markets.[13]

Globalization Forces

Once the most localized and decentralized business function, marketing is increasingly coordinated on a global basis. Regional blocks such as the EU and ASEAN accelerate the trend. For instance, Dell Computer utilizes a Pan-European office to take advantage of increasing standardization of European rules and requirements, as do Microsoft and other leading companies.

Global Brands

Behind the globalization trend is an assumption that despite local variations, many industrial and (to a lesser extent) consumer products can be standardized. "There are pipes all over the world and there are water leaks all over the world," says Richard Rennick, owner of American Leak Detection, whose franchises span more than 60 countries.[14] Kellogg designated Corn Flakes, Special K, Frosted Flakes, Fruit Loops, and Nutri-Grain bars as "global brands" because of their wide name recognition and global sales volume.[15] Avon launched its "Far Away" fragrance as a global product reflecting inputs from most of its foreign subsidiaries, retaining positioning, pricing, packaging, and advertising uniformity to the extent possible.[16]

Global products are products that enjoy worldwide recognition and are relatively unaltered in terms of brand and appearance when offered abroad. AC Nielsen, the marketing research firm, created a ranking of global brands. To be designated global, products had to be sold throughout the world under the same name with more than $1 billion in sales and more than 30 percent of those sales outside the home market.

Why Global Brands?

The primary motivation toward product and service globalization is to gain economies of scale. Selling an identical product using the same promotional message and distribution channels reduces cost and complexity. JC Penney closed its home-furnishing stores in Japan because so many products had to be made differently for the Japanese market that it became unprofitable to operate there.[17] Globalization permits firms to leverage experience accumulated in one market toward another, using communications technologies to facilitate coordination and integration. In addition, the allure of a "global" product can be an important selling point for some consumers.

Marketing Repercussions of a Global Approach

What does the current trend toward globalization mean to the marketing function? Here are some of the key ramifications:[18]

- Rapid rollout of new products across major markets, preempting competitors from introducing similar products.
- Product prioritization and targeting across markets, blocking local product offerings.
- Globally uniform branding and advertising to create a consistent message, reassure customers of global reach, and reduce cost and duplication. This improves the probability of entry into the increasingly crowded shelves of retailers that display only bestselling brands.
- Manufacturing relatively standardized products to scale economies.
- Transfer of marketing best practices across borders.

A Conference Board survey suggests that the greatest increase in globalization is set to occur in advertising, brand positioning, and package design. Further, such coordination seems to distinguish the successful from the less successful firms. Successful firms also coordinate product pricing across countries to some extent, but not necessarily new product development.[19]

A by-product of the increased globalization of the marketing function is the erosion in the authority of country managers (see Chapter 11 for a description of the country manager role). Today's country managers find themselves exercising lesser control over marketing budget, pricing, and other key marketing decisions. Although they usually maintain control over local brands and have some say in new product development, their influence over the marketing of global brands in their country of jurisdiction is on the wane. National brand managers, where they exist, report directly to a global marketing group rather than to the country manager.[20] An innovative design solution is AMP's global account group, which assigns marketing executives to work directly with key clients in the United States, Japan, and Europe.[21]

Localization Forces

As noted earlier, localization forces are pressures toward adjustment in product marketing or distribution to make it more appealing or to meet requirements particular to a foreign market. Following a spate of alleged product contamination and other problems in foreign markets, Coca-Cola executives noted that the firm's motto "think globally and act locally" needed to be changed to "think locally and act locally." Indeed, despite globalization, local conditions remain paramount. In the global music market, the share of recording by local artists has risen from 58 percent in 1991 to 68 percent in 2000.[22] US cable channels such as HBO acknowledge that they grossly underestimated the need for adjustment in Asian markets. Among other customization requirements, HBO has to satisfy Malaysian and Singaporean censors who demand that sensitive material be edited out.[23] Firms in other industries do not fare better. Metro Cash and Carry was "taken to the cleaners" when it tried to import its South African wholesale model to Israel.[24] Carrefour, the French supermarket giant, suffered huge losses in Japan where it never adjusted to the Japanese habit of purchasing small quantities of food each day.[25] Carrefour eventually pulled out of the

530

country. Similarly, Wal-Mart, the world's largest retailer, sold its South Korean stores to a Korean competitor who proceeded to remake them in Korean style. Wal-Mart also withdrew from Germany, where its store greeting, product mix, and store location model did not fare well.

Cross-national variations have a significant impact on sales and marketing. Differences in income levels create different consumer requirements. Diverse regulatory regimes put different constraints on product design, packaging, and promotion. Even in the EU, where logotype and trademarks are relatively standardized, promotion, pricing, and media mix are far from uniform.[26] For instance, regulations regarding vitamins in foodstuffs such as cereal force manufacturers to produce multiple versions of the same product, substantially increasing cost.[27] Social attitudes and public opinion also make a difference. Kellogg's Nutri-Grain, successful in the United States, did not do nearly as well in the United Kingdom, where health consciousness had not been raised at the time.[28] Opposition to genetically modified foods, muted in the United States, has been vocal in the EU and Canada, though many suggest that the limitation on the sales of such foods, where the US is the global leader, are a protectionist measure, a non-tariff trade barrier (see Chapter 2).

Culture also has a major influence on marketing. Cultures high on power distance and uncertainty avoidance place more emphasis on appearance as a way to reaffirm one's status and to reduce uncertainty regarding others' positions. Members of high power-distance cultures are more likely, for instance, to buy expensive watches, a status symbol. In cultures with high uncertainty avoidance, consumers buy more bottled water, but fewer used cars, because they want to minimize surprises. Jewelry purchase has been found to be more related to high masculinity scores than to purchasing power.[29] In high power-distance cultures, a sales pitch will be made in a formal manner and advertisements are likely to showcase a model "in control" of a situation,[30] whereas the pitch is likely to be personalized in individualistic countries.[31]

Cultural and social mores also shape the context in which a product is used. In Hong Kong, Taiwan, and mainland China, McDonald's restaurants serve as space for social activity for seniors in the late morning and for schoolchildren in the afternoon.[32] In this case, cultural rankings on collectivism are supplemented by physical realities: with residential space scarce, the restaurants provide an opportunity for social gatherings. This affects anything from restaurant design to hours of operations and product preference.

Product Adaptation

Faced with a foreign market with different characteristics, a firm may choose not to offer a product or a service in that market, offer the same product it offers in other markets, or adapt it to regional or country requirements. To make the decision, firms use "benefit/cost" and "user/need" models. **Benefit/cost models** assess the advantages and disadvantages of a product or distribution mode in a given market. **User/need models** test the needs of potential customers, including the circumstances in which the product or service are likely to be used. The analysis yields a decision to standardize or customize the product and/or its promotion and distribution.

Following disappointing sales in India, Ford decided to develop "an Indian car," the first designed and built for a developing market. While using the Ford Fiesta platform to lower development costs, the car shows little resemblance to the Fiesta. Extras were cut to make possible a price tag that would appeal to value-conscious consumers, and local content was beefed up to reduce costs and meet government requirements. Ford's designers and engineers drove many miles on India's roads with families of five, a key customer group, making the following adjustments to customer requirements:

Rear headroom was raised to make way for men in turbans, doors were adjusted to open wider than normal to avoid catching the flowing saris of women, air intake valves were fitted to avoid flooding during monsoon season, shock absorbers were toughened for pock-marked city streets, and air conditioning was revved up for summer heat.[33]

With the Indian market increasingly attractive, more companies make sure their product is adapted to local conditions. Nokia, for instance, sells in India cell phones with a dust-resistant touch pad, an anti-slip grip for humid conditions, and, of course, the ability to support Hindi.[34]

The Volkswagen Beetle (not the New Beetle), manufactured in Mexico, is not exported to the United States because compliance with US safety and emission standards would make it prohibitively expensive. Mitsubishi gave up building a "global car" and redesigned its cars sold in the United States to be "more American." Toyota and Nissan increased engine size and interior space in their US models and moved much of the design and development to the United States to be closer to the market. Honda credits its US market research with the addition of a third row of seats on its sports utility vehicle, something to which Japanese designers initially objected.[35] Coca-Cola, the quintessential global brand, tinkers with its formula to suit local taste. Its diet Coke is sold in France as Coke Light. Kraft Foods sweetens the flavors of Tang for sale in Latin America. In Israel, Pizza Hut features special toppings not offered elsewhere in the world, including imitation shrimp. In Egypt, Chili's offers a version of the Sohur (a special midnight buffet) during the month of Ramadan when Moslems fast from daylight to sunset.[36] *Time* magazine, whose first international edition dates back to 1942, publishes different editions for the US, Asian, and European markets, among others, as does the *Wall Street Journal*. In both cases, regional editions share some common material but use local content as appropriate. As in other cases, this customization has been greatly aided by technological advances that enable simultaneous printing in different locations.

While making adjustments to local tastes and customs, it is equally important for the MNE to leverage its name recognition and global reputation. McDonald's is the largest fast-food chain in the world, with more than 34,000 restaurants, more than half of these in 117 foreign countries, employing over 1.8 million people worldwide. With 56 percent of its operating profits coming from international sales, the firm's motto is "all business is local." As its then-head of international operations said, "We don't run Spain out of Portugal." McDonald's is selling Big Macs around the world, but in Seoul it also offers roast pork on a bun with garlicky soy sauce.[37] In selected Jerusalem outlets, Big Macs (minus the cheese) are kosher. In India, where cows are sacred, Veggie McNuggets are served. When the Indonesian rupee collapsed during the Asian financial crisis, rice was added to the menu as a substitute for expensive fries. While offering local variants, as shown in Exhibit 16.3,

Country	Adjustment
Switzerland	Veggie Mac, and ski-thru window in some restaurants
Singapore	Chicken rice, also reduced fat in foods, switched to vegetable oil in food preparation and in French fries
Saudi Arabia	Traditional first floor; family section on the second floor, all Muslim employees, non-pork menus including McArabia (a chicken grilled sandwich served on a flatbread)
India	Vegetable McNuggets and a mutton-based Maharaja Mac, to cater to Hindus who do not eat beef and Muslims who do not eat pork
China	McNuggets with chili garlic sauce, fried egg, and Chinese pancake for breakfast, delivery service to take advantage of low-cost migrant labor in cities
Portugal	Traditional bica (like espresso) served in porcelain instead of foam cups. Pasties de nata (Portuguese-style cakes) added to menus alongside traditional muffins and brownies
Paraguay	Use of computers and Internet in select restaurants, McMacos, McFiesta added to menus (lower price and smaller size)
Netherlands	McKroket (100 percent beef ragout with crispy layer around it, topped with fresh mustard and mayonnaise sauce)
Mexico	McNifica, McBurrito à la Mexicana
Japan	Teriyaki McBurger (sausage patty on a bun with teriyaki sauce)
Italy	Salads featuring Mediterranean flavors. Marinara (shrimp and salmon in fresh lettuce), Vegetariana (veggie), Mediteranea (cheese and olive), Fiordiriso (rice, tuna, ham, mushrooms)
Ireland	Shamrock shake (available during St. Patrick's Day celebrations)
Hong Kong	Curry potato pie; shake fries, red bean sundae
Germany	Translating quarter pounder to metric system is difficult, so they named it McRoyal and Hamburger Royal
Argentina	McCafe (a variety of coffees, pastries, desserts), McSwing (ice cream with various toppings)
Australia	McCafe with formal cutlery, special napkins, china cups, chocolate desserts, uniforms of black and gold
Chile	McPalta (made from avocados)

Exhibit 16.3 Product adjustments at McDonald's
Source: www.mcdonalds.com.

McDonald's makes full use of its scale and spread. It serves a global brand which customers can find in multiple locations.

The adaptation challenge extends to all marketing aspects. In Japan, manufacturers' relationships with suppliers and distributors often last for decades. Despite a growing proliferation of larger stores and retail chains, Japanese retail trade continues to be fragmented, dominated by small, family-owned merchants, with half of the retail establishments employing one or two people.[38] When Office Depot and OfficeMax launched their Japanese outlets as replicas of the firms' large, warehouse-type discount stores in the US, they soon discovered that the global efficiencies derived from this strategy were insufficient to compensate for high rents and for the reluctance to buy in an impersonal, warehouse-type store. The firms changed their strategies accordingly.[39] Still, a decade of Japanese economic stagnation has encouraged the entry of discount chains into the market, with many of those carrying imported merchandize, often from China.

Country Box

Kimchi Wars

Kimchi is a Korean national dish of fermented cabbage, which is also popular in Japan and a number of other East Asian countries. The dish received mixed reviews in foreign markets, with many customers complaining about strong taste and offending smell. A group of Korean food scientists was recently recruited by Doosan, South Korea's leading kimchi producer, to develop a version that would appeal to Americans and displace imports from Japan, which currently dominate international markets with a 70 percent share.

The South Korean team (known as "the kimchi doctors") faced a challenge similar to that of other international marketers: namely, how to develop a product that is attractive in a foreign market, yet retains the unique characteristics and allure of its country of origin, and how to differentiate its product from its major competitors. The team succeeded in developing kimchi with longer shelf life and a smell more appealing to Westerners. In the summer of 2001, Korean kimchi manufacturers won an important victory when the Codex Alimentarius, which sets international food standards accepted by the WTO, adopted a global standard for kimchi that corresponds to the Korean method of preparing the dish. Doosan also faces competition from other domestic manufacturers, among them a company previously allied with a kosher food manufacturer in New York that is now developing kimchi kraut for the European market and a kimchi-topped burger for McDonald's. Meanwhile, Pizza Hut has introduced a kimchi topping for its pizza that now accounts for 30 percent of its Korean sales.

This was not the end of the kimchi wars, however. In 2005, the South Korean authorities said they have found parasite eggs in kimchi imported from China and halted all kimchi imports from that country, which was about to pass the 100,000-ton mark (versus just 90 tons in 1999). Accusing the Koreans of protectionism, China promptly retaliated, stopping all kimchi imports from South Korea. Among those hurt by the move was Doosan, which established kimchi production in China in 2003. This kind of tit-for-tat kept recurring after both countries resumed imports from the other. In 2012, a Korean lawmaker accused China of selling contaminated kimchi to Korea, citing a study that found some Chinese brands to contain five times the level of lead than domestic brands. This caused a public uproar and forced the Korea Food and Drug Administration (KFDA) to conduct its own test. The KFDA concluded that the "Chinese-produced spicy pickled cabbage is safe to eat." Its findings, however, also contained some unwanted news for the champions of domestic kimchi makers: the domestic brands actually tested positive for lead more often than the Chinese brands. By the middle of 2013, it was estimated that about half of public eateries in Korea were using Chinese-made kimchi. In addition, because of rising imports from China, the share of Korean-made kimchi in its largest export market, Japan, fell by 19.2 percent the same year, the largest drop since 2007.

Source: Adapted from J. Solomon, "Stinking national dish seeks smell of success and a global market," *Wall Street Journal*, August 17, 2001, A1; T.I. Tsai, "Korea swallows its pride in Chinese kimchi war," *China Business*, November 22, 2005; T. Mock, "The kimchi war: China steps up assault on Korean 'kimchi sovereignty'," *HAPS*, July 24, 2013.

Country-of-Origin Effect

Country-of-origin effect is the influence of the country of manufacture's image upon the buying decision. The effect consists of these perceptual dimensions: innovativeness (i.e., the use of new technology and engineering advances); design (i.e., appearance, style, color, and variety); prestige (i.e., exclusivity), status, and brand name reputation; and workmanship, including reliability, durability, craftsmanship, and manufacturing quality.[40] There is strong evidence that country-of-origin influences buyers' perceptions, regardless of reality.[41] For instance, British firms are not associated in the consumer's mind with products and innovations they have actually created.[42]

Country-of-origin effect can change over time. In the 1960s, Japanese products had a reputation of shoddy quality, and it was decades before the country established a reputation for quality manufacturing. The same evolution occurred for products from South Korea and, more recently, for those made in China. Since products from developed nations tend to receive higher evaluation,[43] a country moving into the ranks of developed economies is also likely to enhance the reputation of its products. In the interim, firms from emerging economies often engage in reputation-enhancing activities. Giant Manufacturing, a Taiwanese bicycle maker, sponsors professional racing teams to build a reputation as a company staying on the leading edge of technology.[44]

Leveraging Positive Country Image

Country image varies across product categories.[45] German automotive firms take advantage of the country's reputation for advanced engineering, quality, and reliability. However, BMW, owner of the Rolls-Royce brand, assembles the car in England and touts its British origin because of the vehicle's association, in the consumer's mind, with British high class. Japanese automotive and electronics makers are known for the quality and reliability of their products and will often highlight the country of origin in their product promotion. Other countries may be noted for a single product, for example, Iranian carpets or Russian caviar. Here, a British publication laments the country's top ranking in merely one industry:

> *The United States is rated best for many key sectors, including retail, computers, and telecom; Germany is top for sectors such as engineering, cars, and beer; France for cosmetics, food, health care, spirits; Japan for consumer electronics and domestic appliances; Britain is rated top for just one commercial area: air travel.*[46]

A positive country image may lead to minimized customization that is not inherent to product use. The original appearance and packaging will be preserved to the extent permitted by law so as to highlight the product's national origin. An example is IKEA, the Swedish furniture retailer, which highlights its national origin to leverage the positive image of Scandinavian furniture as stylish, practical, well designed, and reasonably priced. At other times, the image may lead a company to customize a product so that it will remind the customer of a different locale; for instance, Anheuser-Busch has launched beers in the US that intentionally look like imports.[47]

Leveraging Nationalist Sentiments

Sometimes, the country of origin serves as a patriotic call-to-arms to buy domestic products or services. Many countries have seen campaigns where consumers are encouraged to "buy local" as a way of supporting local industry and employment. For example, a prospective car buyer may be reminded that, by buying a Chevrolet, he/she will prevent further deterioration of the US trade deficit with Japan, or that buying a Ford will keep jobs in the United States. To counterbalance the appeal of such calls, foreign car like Toyota and Honda who manufacture in the US take full-page advertisements touting the number of American jobs they create and their support of various community activities in the country.

Support of domestic products will sometimes deteriorate to vilification of foreign products. For example, Japanese farmers had placed ads in local newspapers accusing US orange growers of spreading "agent orange" on their fruit (Agent Orange was a chemical used by the US armed forces in Vietnam to retard vegetation growth and has no relation to the fruit). In India, angry protesters attacked Coke and Pepsi facilities after it had been alleged that their beverages contain pesticides (the companies retort that the water they use is safe and meets all international and local standards). Because of their visibility, companies such as Coca-Cola and McDonald's are often identified with their home country and hence are vulnerable to backlash related to its acts. When Serbian students demonstrated against US interests during NATO's military campaign, McDonald's and Coca-Cola topped the target list.[48] In the aftermath of the invasion of Iraq, McDonald's restaurants were targeted by terrorists in Turkey and Italy. Overall, the standing of US brands has suffered as a result of opposition to the Iraq war, but by 2006 their reputation appeared to have rebounded. Still, negative attitudes toward the United States have been leveraged in the launch of Mecca Cola, Arab Cola, and Muslim-Up to compete with the quintessential American brands in Arab countries, as well as in Europe, which has a substantial Muslim minority.

Some foreign firms attempt to disarm nationalist sentiment by emphasizing the local content in their product. **Local content** is the portion of a product (or service) that includes locally made and procured inputs. Airbus, in its ads in the United States, lists its many US suppliers. The aim is to "localize" the product, helping people feel that by buying the foreign product they are, in fact, supporting their countrymen. Finding a local angle is not always easy in an age when many products involve multiple nations and when the national flags of many countries are made abroad. Take, for example, the ad shown by German auto maker BMW during the Super Bowl in 2011 for its X3 model designed and manufactured in the United States. The firm touts that the plant produces every X3 in the world even at the height of the recession. Still others may downplay the foreign origin of the product, using brand names and packaging that embed local heritage. In Russia, "the beloved taste of real Russian butter" appears on the package of butter from New Zealand, while Zlato vegetable oil, featuring a Russian peasant family in its TV commercials, originates in Argentina. The phenomenon does not extend, however, to products not held in high esteem by local consumers.[49]

MNEs often point out that local firms do not necessarily suffer from their entry. Burger Ranch, an Israeli burger chain, continued to prosper following the entry of McDonald's and Burger King, which greatly increased the overall market. In Latvia, Kvas, a traditional fermented drink, initially disappeared from the market under pressure from Coca-Cola and PepsiCo. Then, using modern production and marketing techniques and boasting of its health benefits, Kvas recaptured one-third of the local market.[50] In Japan, locally based Askul successfully competed against Office Depot and OfficeMax with marketing that is better suited to the local environment.[51] With some creativity, a local player can even piggyback on the investment made by an MNE: A Russian detergent manufacturer took advantage of Procter & Gamble's campaign promoting its Ariel detergent over "ordinary powder" by introducing its "Ordinary Powder" brand. The local product, priced at about 15 percent of the import, managed to quickly capture a slice of the market. [52]

Branding

Branding is the process of creating and supporting positive perceptions associated with a product or service. In global markets, branding is especially complex given varying demand and environmental characteristics. Procter & Gamble entered China in 1988 with one product. Today, the company has dozens of brands and a multi-billion-dollar volume in profitable sales there. Here is how the former head of P&G's China operations views the principles that led P&G to create successful brands in China:

- Selecting the right (Chinese) name.
- In-depth understanding of the local market and willingness to make the necessary adaptations.
- Fine-tuning the right size/price/value formulation of offerings.
- Providing quality and reliability at a competitive price.
- Holistic marketing using a variety of channels.
- Turning trademarks into "trust-marks."
- Establishing leadership brands, changing social habits if necessary.
- Selecting the right allies and partners.

Exhibit 16.4 lists the top 100 global brands based on a report by Interbrand, and it also relates these brands to *Fortune*'s list of the top 50 most admired companies in the world. Interbrand's list focuses on a brand's financial performance. In its 2013 list, all but two of the top ten are US brands, while a decade earlier only one non-US brand made the list. Companies that enjoy overall prestige and reputation are in an especially advantageous position to leverage their branding power. The two rightmost columns of Exhibit 16.4 list the name and ranking of the firm that owns a given brand in Interbrand's list, if the firm appears in *Fortune*'s list of World's Most Admired Companies. *Fortune*'s ranking is developed via a survey of industry executives and stock analysts, and it is based entirely on their perceptions of a company's reputation. An inspection of the two rankings suggests that the top global brands tend be owned by companies that are perceived to have strong corporate reputations. *Fortune*'s list initially started with firms based in the US only and is still dominated by US firms, with only two companies (BMW and Toyota) from outside of the US among the top 30.

The global reach of some brands should not distract attention from the power of local brands. Ahold's CEO notes that discarding the Dutch company's Swedish brand ICA would be "ridiculous" since this brand ranks together with Volvo as one of the best-known brands in Sweden.[53]

Rank	Brand Name	Country	Sector	Brand Value (US$ million)	Name of Brand Owner if in *Fortune's* Most Admired List	Company Rank by *Fortune*
1	Apple	United States	Technology	98,316	Apple	1
2	Google	United States	Technology	93,291	Google	2
3	Coca-Cola	United States	Beverages	79,213	Coca-Cola*	4
4	IBM	United States	Business Services	78,808	IBM	6
5	Microsoft	United States	Technology	59,546	Microsoft	17
6	GE	United States	Diversified	46,947	General Electric	11
7	McDonald's	United States	Restaurants	41,992	McDonald's	12
8	Samsung	South Korea	Technology	39,610	Samsung Electronics	35
9	Intel	United States	Technology	37,257	Intel	42
10	Toyota	Japan	Automotive	35,346	Toyota Motor	29
11	Mercedes-Benz	Germany	Automotive	31,904		
12	BMW	Germany	Automotive	31,839	BMW	14
13	Cisco	United States	Technology	29,053	Cisco Systems	49
14	Disney	United States	Media	28,147	Walt Disney	9
15	HP	United States	Technology	25,843		
16	Gillette	United States	FMCG	25,105	Procter & Gamble*	15
17	Louis Vuitton	France	Luxury	24,893		
18	Oracle	United States	Technology	24,088		
19	Amazon	United States	Retail	23,620	Amazon.com	3
20	Honda	Japan	Automotive	18,490		
21	H&M	Sweden	Apparel	18,168		
22	Pepsi	United States	Beverages	17,892	PepsiCo	37
23	American Express	United States	Financial Services	17,646	American Express	13
24	Nike	United States	Sporting Goods	17,085	Nike	18
25	SAP	Germany	Technology	16,676		
26	IKEA	Sweden	Home Furnishings	13,818		
27	UPS	United States	Transportation	13,763	UPS	30
28	eBay	United States	Retail	13,162	eBay	47
29	Pampers	United States	FMCG	13,035	Procter & Gamble*	15
30	Kellogg	United States	FMCG	12,987		
31	Budweiser	United States	Alcohol	12,614		

Exhibit 16.4 Top global brands, listed by Interbrand's *Best Global Brands 2013*

Sources: Best Global Brands 2013 by Interbrand and World's Most Admired Companies 2013 by *Fortune*.

Notes: (1) Interbrand's Best Global Brands 2013 report is a look at the financial performance of a brand, role of the brand in the purchase decision process and the brand's strength. Go to www.bestglobalbrands.com for more information. (2) *Fortune*'s World's Most Admired Companies 2013 focuses on the corporate reputation of a company and is based on a survey of industry executives and stock analysts. For more details, go to money.cnn.com/magazines/fortune. (3) Because a company may own multiple brands, the same company in *Fortune*'s list may own more than one brand in Interbrand's list. An asterisk is placed to the right of the company's name in the fifth column with the heading "Name of Brand Owner if in *Fortune*'s Most Admired List" if it owns two or more brands in Interbrand's list.

32	HSBC	United Kingdom	Financial Services	12,183		
33	J.P. Morgan	United States	Financial Services	11,456	J.P. Morgan Chase	28
34	Volkswagen	Germany	Automotive	11,120	Volkswagen	33
35	Canon	Japan	Electronics	10,989		
36	Zara	Spain	Apparel	10,821		
37	Nescafé	Switzerland	Beverages	10,651	Nestlé*	32
38	Gucci	Italy	Luxury	10,151		
39	L'Oréal	France	FMCG	9,874		
40	Philips	Netherlands	Electronics	9,813		
41	Accenture	United States	Business Services	9,471	Accenture	44
42	Ford	United States	Automotive	9,181		
43	Hyundai	South Korea	Automotive	9,004		
44	Goldman Sachs	United States	Financial Services	8,536	Goldman Sachs Group	34
45	Siemens	Germany	Diversified	8,503		
46	Sony	Japan	Electronics	8,408		
47	Thomson Reuters	Canada	Media	8,103		
48	Citi	United States	Financial Services	7,973		
49	Danone	France	FMCG	7,968		
50	Colgate	United States	FMCG	7,833		
51	Audi	Germany	Automotive	7,767		
52	Facebook	United States	Technology	7,732	Facebook	48
53	Heinz	United States	FMCG	7,648	Berkshire Hathaway	8
54	Hermès	France	Luxury	7,616		
55	adidas	Germany	Sporting Goods	7,535		
56	Nestlé	Switzerland	FMCG	7,527	Nestlé*	32
57	Nokia	Finland	Electronics	7,444		
58	Caterpillar	United States	Diversified	7,125	Caterpillar	20
59	AXA	France	Financial Services	7,096		
60	Cartier	France	Luxury	6,897		
61	Dell	United States	Technology	6,845		
62	Xerox	United States	Business Services	6,779		
63	Allianz	Germany	Financial Services	6,710		
64	Porsche	Germany	Automotive	6,471		
65	Nissan	Japan	Automotive	6,203		
66	KFC	United States	Restaurants	6,192	Yum! Brands*	46
67	Nintendo	Japan	Electronics	6,086		
68	Panasonic	Japan	Electronics	5,821		
69	Sprite	United States	Beverages	5,811	Coca-Cola*	4
70	Discovery	United States	Media	5,756		
71	Morgan Stanley	United States	Financial Services	5,724		
72	Prada	Italy	Luxury	5,570		

Exhibit 16.4 (*Continued*)

Rank	Brand Name	Country	Sector	Brand Value (US$ million)	Name of Brand Owner if in *Fortune*'s Most Admired List	Company Rank by Fortune
73	Shell	Netherlands	Energy	5,535		
74	Visa	United States	Financial Services	5,465		
75	Tiffany & Co.	United States	Luxury	5,440		
76	3M	United States	Diversified	5,413	3M	21
77	Burberry	United Kingdom	Luxury	5,189		
78	MTV	United States	Media	4,980		
79	Adobe	United States	Technology	4,899		
80	John Deere	United States	Diversified	4,865	Deere	40
81	Johnson & Johnson	United States	FMCG	4,777	Johnson & Johnson	23
82	Johnnie Walker	United Kingdom	Alcohol	4,745		
83	Kia	South Korea	Automotive	4,708		
84	Santander	Spain	Financial Services	4,660	Procter & Gamble*	15
85	Duracell	United States	FMCG	4,645		
86	Jack Daniel's	United States	Alcohol	4,642		
87	Avon	United States	FMCG	4,610	Ralph Lauren	50
88	Ralph Lauren	United States	Apparel	4,584		
89	Chevrolet	United States	Automotive	4,578		
90	Kleenex	United States	FMCG	4,428	Starbucks	5
91	Starbucks	United States	Restaurants	4,399		
92	Heineken	Netherlands	Alcohol	4,331		
93	Corona	Mexico	Alcohol	4,276	Yum! Brands*	46
94	Pizza Hut	United States	Restaurants	4,269		
95	Smirnoff	United Kingdom	Alcohol	4,262		
96	Harley-Davidson	United States	Automotive	4,230		
97	MasterCard	United States	Financial Services	4,206		
98	Ferrari	Italy	Automotive	4,013		
99	Moët & Chandon	France	Alcohol	3,943		
100	Gap	United States	Apparel	3,920		

Exhibit 16.4 *(Continued)*

Channel Decisions

Channel decisions involve the length (the number of levels or intermediaries employed in the distribution process) and width (the number of firms in each level) of the channel used in linking manufacturers to consumers.[54] In business-to-business sales, channel decisions are often more important than brand name, advertising, and pricing.[55] A study of United Kingdom, Japanese, and German subsidiaries in the United States shows that they are more likely to localize channel decisions than product or pricing decisions. Localization is especially pronounced among UK affiliates, perhaps due to the assumption of cultural similarity.[56]

540

Intermediation

Many international sales are not made directly by companies but by export intermediaries. **Export intermediaries** are firms that mediate between firms, especially small and mid-size international enterprises (SMIEs), and their export markets, by providing logistics, documentation, and related services. While intermediaries play a central role for smaller firms, they are sometimes outsourced this function by large MNEs. When SED International, a leading international distributor of microcomputer and wireless communication products throughout the United States and Latin America, was designated a "Certified HP Top Value Reseller," it was given exclusive right to offer top-selling HP products in several international markets.[57] SED resells HP products, charging customers up to 5 percent over competitors in the direct distribution channel. Because of the amount of business it generates, HP prefers to deal with SED instead of handling multiple consumers.

Direct Marketing

Direct marketing involves selling directly to customers via individual agents who typically make a commission not only on their sales, but also on the sales of other agents they have recruited. The model was pioneered by cosmetic makers Avon and Mary Kay and was eventually adopted by manufacturers of other products. Amway has become the world's largest direct seller, with operations in many countries. Direct marketers face many problems abroad. The image of direct selling is quite low, especially in Asia. In China, the government initially ruled that direct sales constituted a "pyramid scheme" and banned such sales, though it has since retracted its position. In Japan, Avon found that its system of selling to random groups was ineffective, because people were reluctant to invite strangers into their home. However, once Avon tinkered with the system to rely on groups of friends and acquaintances, the operation prospered.

Niche Marketing

Niche marketing is narrowly directed toward a pre-defined segment of the market. In international markets, niche marketing may be directed not only to a product category (e.g., low end) but also to an ethnic or geographical segment. Big Boy in Thailand, Schlotzky's Delicatessen in Malaysia, Shakey's Pizza Restaurant in the Philippines, and Carl's Jr. in Mexico all target a specific niche in their target market.[58] Convencao, a small Brazilian soft-drink company, cut into the market share of industry giants Coke and Pepsi by offering lower priced soft drinks in its home market.[59] A niche play can also serve as a base for expansion. Timberland, known for its weather proofed boots, now exports casual wear to more than 50 (mostly developed) countries, including Italy.[60]

Pricing

Pricing is the decision and process of setting a price to a product or a service. In international markets, pricing is more complex due to varying cost structures (e.g., transportation costs, tariffs) and variable market positioning. An equally equipped car will sell for substantially different prices in different EU markets. A British buyer seeking to buy a car in Belgium will not only find the steering wheel on the wrong side, but could also face a reluctant dealer, deterred by exclusive

541

distribution agreements. The European Commission fined German auto maker Volkswagen for turning back German customers who sought to buy their cars from Italian dealers.

Price differentials facilitate market segmentation, allowing a firm to position its product differentially in different markets. Firms may hike prices where there is little competition and where consumer resistance to price increases is low. Or, they may price a brand higher so it can be positioned as "premium." Belgian brewer Interbrew markets its Stella beer in the United States under the slogan "reassuringly expensive."[61] Even if desirable, price consistency is not easy to achieve. For instance, some subsidiaries provide a higher level of service than others.[62] Prices are also influenced by host government decisions. The India government imposes a 100 percent tariff on all vehicle imports to protect its domestic auto industry, and a free trade agreement being negotiated with the EU to reduce the tariff on EU-made cars to 30 percent from 60 percent has encountered strong opposition from the Indian auto industry.[63] In the United States, pharmaceutical manufacturers have been lobbying to prevent cheaper medicine imports, mostly from Canada, arguing that cheaper drugs lower the incentives for domestic manufacturing and expose consumers to the risk of fakes. [64]

Predatory Pricing

Predatory pricing is the selling of goods below real cost so as to drive competitors out of the market (which enables the predator firms to eventually raise prices). Matsushita (now Panasonic) allegedly priced its TV sets below cost in the United States, subsidizing sales with its high margins in the Japanese market and driving US manufacturers out of business.[65] A complaint by Zenith was dismissed on the grounds that if Matsushita had priced its products below cost, it would have gone out of business in the 20 years the case took to resolve.[66] A similar complaint was filed by Republic Engineered Steels and Timken, which argued that Brazilian exporters were selling steel at 40 percent below their home-market price, or the cost of manufacturing the product in Brazil.[67] In recent years, Chinese products have become the subject of predatory pricing complaints in the United States (see also Chapter 2, description of "dumping"), though more recently China has started to initiate similar trade actions against foreign firms in its domestic markets.

Promotion

Globalization can yield substantial savings in product promotion. When United Distillers (now Diageo) bought control of its distributors, it consolidated more than 50 campaigns worldwide into one.[68] General Motors Europe uses a unified promotional approach to drive brand identity; however, it recognizes the need for adaptation in some markets. When it launched its Omega sedan, it created a single European campaign but held a separate campaign for Germany and Switzerland. Still, the savings must be assessed vis-à-vis existing local variations that may lower the effectiveness of global promotion.

Advertising

Like other marketing functions, if not more, advertising needs to be adjusted to local tastes, norms, and regulations if it is to be effective in international markets. When Lego used an advertising campaign in Japan that had been successful in the United States, it quickly flopped.[69] Like other firms, Lego discovered that moving advertising across borders is difficult linguistically, culturally, and socially.[70] Missteps are common. DHL Worldwide Express had to apologize for an ad that Indonesians felt likened then-President Suharto to a courier. Nike was criticized for an ad showing the Brazilian national team playing a soccer match against the devil, which viewers found blasphemous rather than humorous.[71] In another incident, Nike sold shoes with an imprint that reminded some Moslems of the Arabic scripture for "God." The perceived insult was especially severe because a shoe sole is considered by Moslems to be impure (e.g., it should not be shown to a counterpart to a conversation), and Nike had to pull 37,000 shoes off the shelves. Even savvy MNEs such as Coca-Cola, which announced that it would stay away from controversial topics such as religion, politics, and disease, encounter difficulty.[72] When a rumor spread in Egypt that the Coca-Cola logo contained the Arabic words for "no Mohammed, no Mecca," the firm countered with a decree from Egypt's Mufti, the country's top religious authority, that the logo did not defame Islam.[73] Some firms, in contrast, thrive on controversy: Benetton purposely includes religion, and subjects such as the death penalty and the AIDS epidemic, in its global advertising campaigns.

The temptation to standardize advertising is considerable. Standardization provides a coherent and consistent message and greatly reduces production cost by spreading it across multiple markets. McKinsey calculated that Gillette saved $20 million by creating a global campaign for its Sensor razor in 19 markets, out of a total advertising expense of $175 million.[74] Cable television and the Internet make a global campaign more feasible today than in the past. Coca-Cola, Benetton, and, more recently, Ford, have all launched global advertising campaigns. However, as the Conference Board notes, advertising uniformity depends on "the similarity of consumer buying motivations and of competitors' messages; the existence of specific government restrictions on content; and the availability of desired media channels."[75] In Canada, for example, infomercials can only be aired after midnight. Other countries prohibit the use of brand names during programs. Indeed, Coca-Cola abandoned its global ad campaign in 2002, although it maintained central "guidance, process, and strategy" for its advertising efforts.[76] However, in 2009 it initiated a new global ad campaign that it hopes will continue to build its brand with its new 2020 Vision.

As they globalize their marketing, firms increasingly seek advertising agencies with the global reach to provide a one-stop shop. Kellogg assigned responsibilities for three of its global brands to Leo Burnett and assigned two others to J. Walter Thompson. This is one reason for the consolidation of advertising agencies into global networks. Network members share the reach and brand recognition of the network while offering in-depth knowledge of the local market. At the same time, advertising agencies tap locations such as Canada and Mexico to lower their production cost of TV commercials, among other promotions.

Marketing Alliances

International strategic alliances are a major market entry venue. Such alliances, as well as mergers and acquisitions, allow a firm to quickly establish itself in a foreign market (see also Chapters 10 and 12). Leuven (Belgium)-based Interbrew grew through a series of acquisitions from a small family-owned brewery to the world's second-largest brewer and the owner of more than 200 brands.

543

Its typical strategy: retain the existing local brands while leveraging distribution channels to market high margin specialty brands.[77] Similar moves by Coca-Cola to acquire smaller rivals and link their distribution channels with its own have raised concerns among competition authorities in the EU and Mexico.[78] Marketing alliances are also established between large firms; for example, IBM and Dai Nippon Printing cooperate in database marketing. Swiss food giant Nestlé and French retailer Casino cooperate in marketing, logistics, and sales. The two share and analyze bar code information to learn how to enhance customer loyalty while reducing costs.[79]

Interim Summary

1. Market potential is a function of economic (e.g., disposable income), cultural, and social factors.
2. Globalization forces include the emergence of global brands, the prospect of cost savings and efficiencies, technological advances, and lower trade barriers. Localization forces include a variety of country-level factors that affect product appeal and adaptation requirements not only for the product itself but also for marketing channels, pricing, and promotion.
3. Country-of-origin exerts a substantial influence on consumer purchasing decisions.
4. Branding, channel decisions, and promotion all reflect the globalization–localization tension.

The Global Supply Chain

The term **global supply chain** covers both logistics and operations. It includes such activities as sourcing and outsourcing, procurement, order processing, manufacturing, warehousing, inventory control, servicing and warranty, custom clearing, wholesaling, and distribution. Supply chain management is a key component in a firm's global strategy, influencing major decisions such as plant and service location. A report published by the Conference Board states: "in today's world, it is supply chains that compete, not companies."[80] A survey of major US companies found that three-quarters of respondents believed that having an effective supply chain had a major impact on their company's ability to meet its strategic objectives. A reduced operating cost, improved sales and market share, and enhanced customer service have all been noted as being closely tied with supply chain effectiveness.[81] Not surprisingly, having an effective global supply chain can be a key competitive advantage.

In real terms, the cost of logistics has been falling for years,[82] though fluctuations (for example, the extra cost associated with the rise in oil prices and enhanced security since 9/11) are expected to continue. Inter-country variations remain substantial: whereas logistics represent roughly 8 percent of US GDP, the corresponding numbers are 11 percent for Europe, 13–14 percent for India, and 15–18 percent for China, but all these numbers have been going down for years.[83] The overall decline in logistics costs reflects increased efficiencies, for example, the incorporation of just-in-time production systems and the resulting decrease in inventory levels.[84] Stride Rite Corp., a retailer of athletic and casual footwear, cut the shipping time of shoes manufactured in Asia to its distribution center in Kentucky by one-third. The retailer cut 30 percent of its transportation cost and improved inventory turnaround time by 25 percent.[85]

Still, even e-commerce has so far failed to create a "seamless" supply chain. Among the 600 e-marketplaces seeking to match corporate buyers and suppliers in early 2000, "virtually none is capable of handling international logistics, credit verification and payment between companies in different countries." Issues such as international shipping costs, language, currency translation, customs documentation, and cross-border financial settlement are only beginning to be addressed.[86] Forrester Research found that most companies failed to calculate the total cost of shipping an international order, and many were losing money on shipments for failing to adjust pricing to reflect real costs (see also Chapter 18). Additionally,

> *Eighty-five percent of the companies noted that they could not fill overseas orders because of the complexity of shipping across borders. Of those that had problems shipping overseas, 75 percent cited their system's inability to register international addresses accurately or to price total delivery cost.*[87]

The Globalization of Supply Chains

This shift from domestic to global supply chains is driven by rapidly escalating capital costs and enhanced technologies, as well as by regional integration. To deliver a product or service effectively, firms increasingly consolidate production and distribution in a few strategic locations. The evolution of flexible manufacturing systems enables mass customization to meet customer demands at reasonable cost. Transport industry consolidation facilitates seamless transportation (e.g., Canada National Railways acquired Illinois Central in order to provide direct shipping between Canada, the United States, and Mexico). Developments in management information systems permit accurate tracking of variable customer demands and material flow. A logistics executive suggests the following:

> *In the past, for technical reasons, it was impossible to enter an order in one country, process it in another, and ship the goods from a third country. Now with the installation of a new client/server-based order management system, all this is possible.*[88]

Where integration has progressed, as in the EU, standardized regulations have been replacing national rules, enhancing the case for consolidation. French tire maker Michelin shifted from local plants manufacturing a variety of products to regional or global plants specializing in one type of product. The company now manufactures a given type of tire in just one or two European sites.[89] Nike consolidated its distribution operations in Belgium, and Energizer (the European arm of Eveready Battery) consolidated its 60 distribution systems into six. Becton Dickinson, a medical technology provider, developed a global supply chain as part of a broader shift from a decentralized geographical structure to a global design (see also Chapter 11). Other repercussions of supply chain globalization are extended supply and distribution chains, increased transportation from and to transportation centers, and more small-volume transactions.[90] These developments create opportunities for locals at the hub of logistics systems, especially if they manage to develop the requisite infrastructure.

The Challenge for SMIEs

SMIEs usually do not have the requisite economies to justify a specialized facility in a single location. One solution is **mutualization**: the sharing of logistics facilities by two or more partners.[91] SMIEs also form alliances with other firms, especially local companies. The local partner may already have a logistics component or a long-term logistics provider, which makes it difficult for the foreign firm to consolidate its supply chain locally. For instance, foreign investors in China found that their Chinese partner was not as helpful in resolving distribution obstacles as initially believed.[92] Sourcing logistics services from third parties is another solution for the SMIE that is also used by large firms such as Marks & Spencer and Phillips Semiconductors. In such alliances, the shipper takes the lead in strategy formulation while the provider leads day-to-day operations. There is a sole key provider (although some of those purchase services from subcontractors) with whom the manufacturer has a close working relationship.[93]

Global Sourcing

Global sourcing is the procurement of production or service inputs and components in international markets. Global sourcing provides the MNE with the opportunity to leverage its scale and competitive advantage in spotting procurement opportunities around the globe for use in its various divisions and locations. For example, because of its scale, Wal-Mart uses its huge volume to extract lower prices from suppliers; Ford uses component parts produced in its Chinese joint ventures in its Brazilian assembly plants. Toronto-based Canadian Tire sources in the United States and Asia, annually importing 8,000 and 4,000 container loads, respectively, from these locations.[94] Fashion house Donna Karan International sources more than half of its raw materials and finished products in Asia. MNEs also increasingly use **outsourcing**, or the buying of inputs outside their network. Firms may even outsource the logistics function itself.

Logistics Providers

While one-stop, international logistics provision remains an ultimate goal, national services are more likely to be replaced by regional providers. Texas Instruments Semiconductors Group contracts with a key logistics provider to manage forwarding and distribution in each region of the world.[95] TNT Logistics (now CEVA) distributes parts for Italian car maker Fiat throughout Europe, while Fritz Companies handles warehousing and distribution for General Motors' after-sale parts and accessories in Taiwan.[96] Consolidation among providers is also apparent, as in the merger between US-based AEI and Switzerland's Danzas. However, in other countries the number of logistics providers is actually increasing; for instance, the number of logistics service providers in Brazil has tripled in three years and is still growing.[97]

Customizing the Supply Chain

While the globalization of supply chain management proceeds, various factors require continuous attention to localization and customization. Three sets of factors underpin localization. The first is variation among national environments. The second is product customization that triggers logistics adjustments. The third is the existence of national borders that constrain the free flow of goods and services and hence limit global product flow. Manufacturing advances (e.g., the incorporation of suppliers' input at the product design phase) heighten dependencies and the logistics challenges that accompany the need to coordinate manufacturers and suppliers.

National Variation

World regions vary in size, terrain, and other characteristics that impact the supply chain. For example, the NAFTA land area is more than six times that of the EU, implying different logistics requirements and challenging the use of global "best practices." Skill level, quality of supplies, availability of process equipment and technologies, and the level of transportation and communications infrastructure vary substantially among regions. Asia, Africa, large parts of the Middle East, and Latin America suffer from poor infrastructure. Yet, although overall Asian infrastructure is relatively weak, Singapore has superb infrastructure in terms of both air and shipping. China has built remarkable infrastructure especially in its coastal region, while India's infrastructure remains weak (which of course spells opportunities for infrastructure developers).

"We have ordered a lot of bicycles with cool boxes," says Paul Wright, the general manager for Commercial Development at TNT Logistics Asia, who noted that in many Asian locations "neither the technology nor the regulatory environment support logistics integration."[98] Energizer maintains Central and Eastern European operations separately in an otherwise integrated European supply chain, reflecting the significant differences in development levels and the lack of integration with the EU. Even among developed nations, conditions often vary. For instance, in the United States it takes three weeks from the time of manufacturing for breakfast cereals to reach retailers' shelves, but it takes 11 weeks in France.[99] This may explain why domestic supply chains continue to dominate the transfer of goods. Furthermore, increased FDI in local production bases creates even more reliance on domestic supply chains.[100] Fragmented supply chains and a great number of intermediaries add to the problem.[101]

Product and Logistics Customization

Product customization challenges supply chain management characteristics because of its impact on modularity, packaging, transportation, tracking, shipping, and distribution. A "postponement" strategy, designed to delay customization to the latest possible value-adding phase, is not always feasible without compromising product variety.[102] Meritor, which used to provide a variety of automotive parts (mostly in North America), now manufactures only roofs, doors, and suspension systems, but provides them to car manufacturers across the globe from 28 facilities in 13 countries.[103] When McDonald's started operations in Russia, it consolidated all its processing operations in one large facility. This was a radical departure from McDonald's operations around the globe, but was necessary to overcome bottlenecks and supply disruptions.

Packaging

Standardization of packaging is appealing for logistics ease and because it promotes brand recognition. Coca-Cola uses similar color and logo (albeit in different alphabets or characters) to enhance its brand. Package standardization also produces savings in design and promotion costs.[104] Mattel reduced the number of packages it prints for a single product from 14 to three to save on cost. The firm is now able to ship toys from one market to another in mid-season.[105]

Some adaptations are necessary for logistics reasons, such as sturdier packaging to shield a product from outside elements in a harsh environment. Packaging size must often be adapted as well. Where space is scarce, as in the typical Japanese household, bulk packaging is less attractive to customers. Other adaptations are necessary to meet legal requirements. The 2003 German Packaging Regulation requires manufacturers to use environmentally friendly, recyclable packaging material where feasible.[106] A similar law went into effect in Japan in 1996.[107] Various laws also govern safety (e.g., use of nonflammable material) requirements. Other packaging adaptations are necessary for cultural or religious reasons. For example, Hogla-Kimberly, a joint venture between Kimberly Clark and an Israeli manufacturer, sells diapers to the religious sector in Israel in a specially designed, easy-to-prop-open packaging that meets religious requirements to avoid work on the Sabbath.

Labels in most countries must be printed in the local language (in Canada, labels must be printed in English and French), adding time and cost. The United States requires all food products to carry labels indicating their nutritional value. Most countries also require clear labeling of the country source of the product. In the United States, US content must be disclosed on cars, textile, wool, and fur products. Other producers need not specify US content, but must comply with Federal Trade Commission guidelines if they choose to do so. For instance, to merit a "Made in the USA" label, a product must be "all or virtually all" made in the United States with no, or "negligible," foreign content.[108]

Transportation Modes

Meeting customer demand in a timely and cost-effective fashion depends on effective transportation. Globalization has been one of the driving forces behind **intermodal transportation,** a term denoting the combination of ocean vessels (including short sea shipping), river transport, rail, road links, and air transport within a seamless supply chain. Intermodality poses many challenges, however. Comparing the price of alternative transportation modes is difficult because price is based on many product (e.g., weight, value, space) and non-product (e.g., port of shipment, custom administrative procedures) factors. Intermodality also requires modularity and standardization to permit the frequent transfer of goods from one mode to another.[109] Still, new technological developments, which facilitate the monitoring of goods as they pass through the supply chain, support intermodality. Additional obstacles to intermodality and seamless logistics lie at the legal and political level. For instance, Thai regulations require transport and warehousing to be handled by separate companies. In China, approval must be obtained from authorities in each province along the supply chain.[110]

Different transportation modes vary greatly by price and shipping time. For instance, sending a 40-foot container from Shanghai to New York via an all-water route would cost $3,500–3,900 and take 30–35 days to arrive. Sending the same goods via a ship to Los Angeles, and from there by truck to New York would cost $4,700–5,000, but the delivery time will be shortened to 20–25 days. Finally, sending the same goods by air will take only two–three days, but the cost will be $50,000.[111] And, depending on location, not all modes will be available.

Maritime Transportation

Maritime transportation serves well over 90 percent of international trade.[112] Of the 29 border crossing points between the United States and Mexico, nine ports handle most of US–Mexico trade.[113] Mexico-based Frigotux finished building a refrigerated terminal in the hope of diverting some of the 90 percent share of Mexican agricultural exports that is now handled by trucking, into marine shipping from Tuxpan to Philadelphia-Camden and Rotterdam (the Netherlands).[114] Historically global in use and regulation, impediments to the further globalization of maritime transport include the issuance of "flags of convenience," that is, the registering of ships in countries with less stringent regulations such as Liberia and Panama. Such registries not only provide for less stringent safety standards, but also confer labor and tax benefits; however, they do raise opposition in some of the countries where MNEs operate.

Port Facilities. Port facilities represent a crucial ingredient in the cost and convenience of maritime transport, which, among other reasons, explains the trend toward foreign investment in port facilities as a way to facilitate seamless transportation. For instance, many of the port facilities in Mexico and the United States are operated by foreign firms (you may recall the recent uproar in the United States when a company from the United Arab Emirates acquired a British company that was handling American port facilities).

Port facilities vary in quality. According to the Conference Board, the most competitive ports provide speed processing (cargo handling and administration), low cost, and superb intermodal links (road, rail, and air). Ports also vary according to their main function in the global supply system. There are four types of ports: (1) The maritime hub dedicated to transshipment from one ocean vessel to another or to a feeder vessel; (2) the gateway port, which is an interchange between the maritime hub and maritime and/or land transport; (3) the logistics-industrial port, which is an interchange between transport modes combined with logistics support; and (4) The trade port, where logistics activities are combined with other value-added international trade services.

Non-hub ports compete mostly by adopting niche strategies (e.g., specializing in a single product line to achieve expertise and economies of scale). For instance, the Port of Barcelona handles more than 700,000 cars a year.[115] One of the main challenges for ports as key links in the global supply chain has been to accommodate local distribution; for example, to integrate domestic and international shipping (now mostly separated) so as to accommodate situations such as when the final destination is closer to the port rather than to rail transportation.[116] Some ports try to take advantage of congestion in established ports, for instance, as a result of the surge in US–Asian trade. Prince Rupert, British Columbia plans to offer rapid logistics services despite its remote location and the fact that there is hardly any local demand for the shipped goods.[117]

Exhibit 16.5 ranks nations based on their water transport infrastructure (including internal waterways such as canals).

The Inland Port. "Port Columbus" in land-locked central Ohio is an "inland port." It utilizes 86 million square feet of warehousing and distribution facilities on the grounds of a former air force base located "within a 10-hour drive of over 50 percent of the United States and Canadian populations." The port has transportation arteries reaching to airports, highways (there are

Water transportation

Water transportation (harbors, canals, etc.) meets business requirements

#	Country	2013
1	Denmark	9.29
2	Netherlands	9.04
3	Hong Kong	9.00
4	Singapore	8.88
5	Finland	8.81
6	Germany	8.76
7	Iceland	8.74
8	Sweden	8.70
9	Norway	8.60
10	Canada	8.58
11	UAE	8.52
12	Taiwan	8.33
13	France	8.23
14	Belgium	8.20
15	USA	8.12
16	Latvia	8.07
17	Switzerland	8.04
18	Korea	7.85
19	United Kingdom	7.77
20	Estonia	7.69
21	Malaysia	7.58
22	Ireland	7.51
23	Japan	7.46
24	Spain	7.43
25	New Zealand	7.32
26	Portugal	7.11
27	China Mainland	7.06
28	Greece	7.05
29	Chile	6.99
30	Austria	6.98
31	Luxembourg	6.97
32	Australia	6.95
33	Lithuania	6.71
34	Romania	6.62
35	Slovenia	6.59
36	Qatar	6.49
37	Israel	6.26
38	Czech Republic	6.10
39	Thailand	5.98
40	Slovak Republic	5.82
41	South Africa	5.76
42	Mexico	5.75
43	Turkey	5.60
44	Jordan	5.47
45	Bulgaria	5.22
46	Italy	5.16
47	Croatia	5.06
48	Hungary	4.88
49	Russia	4.81
50	Argentina	4.73
51	Philippines	4.43
52	Kazakhstan	4.35
53	Indonesia	4.23
54	Peru	4.15
55	Colombia	3.96
56	Ukraine	3.90
57	India	3.81
58	Poland	2.30
59	Venezuela	2.30
60	Brazil	1.96

Exhibit 16.5 Ranking of countries by water transportation infrastructure

Source: World Competitiveness Yearbook, Copyright © 2013, IMD, Switzerland, www.imd.org/wcc.

130 trucking firms in the area), and to rail and coastal ports via agreements with the ports of New York/New Jersey, Virginia, and Los Angeles. Countries with vast, underdeveloped hinterlands, such as China, are interested in the inland port concept as a way of improving access to less developed regions which are located far from port facilities.

Trucking. Trucking plays an important role in international trade, particularly in Europe where distances are relatively short and economic integration expedites transportation time. Central European countries, such as Hungary and the Czech Republic, are major beneficiaries of the trend toward European integration, especially the flow of goods between Western and Eastern Europe, developing warehousing facilities and roads. Trucking is also a key means of transportation in other cross-border but geographically contiguous areas, such Texas/Mexico and Hong Kong/Shenzhen in southern China. Trucks also play an important role in the domestic distribution of products delivered internationally by ship, rail, or air; the use of containers has made such inter-modality substantially easier.

While the United States, Europe, and other, mostly developed countries have moved to standardize safety and other regulations pertaining to trucking, there remain substantial impediments to the globalization of truck transportation.[118] For example, there are different safety standards, a reason the United States gave at the time to justify its refusal to comply with NAFTA and let Mexican trucks cross into the United States. However, in 2011 the United States and Mexico struck a deal to allow Mexican trucks to cross into the United States again. Pressure from existing joint ventures between US and Mexican truck firms, as well as opposition from US organized labor, also played a role in the decision.[119] Traffic congestion is costly to trucking in terms of deteriorating service quality, delayed shipments, higher energy costs, and lower productivity of vehicles and workforce. The problem is especially pronounced in densely populated areas, such as Europe, and rapidly growing emerging economies, such as China and India. Developing countries have a higher proportion of unpaved roads than in the United States and other developed countries, imposing serious constraints on the domestic transportation of goods (see Exhibit 16.6).

Rail

A competitive time-to-cost ratio, as well as road and sky congestion, makes rail an attractive transportation mode domestically and internationally. For instance, about half of US grain exports to Mexico are transported by rail. One problem with rail transportation is variation in rail gauges, which means that goods need to be transferred from one system to another. In some countries, rail gauges even vary internally. This is the case, for instance, for Brazil and Argentina. Still, the two countries, together with Bolivia and Chile, have a substantial part of their system in standard, one-meter gauges, facilitating transport within MERCOSUR.[120]

Where rails are not contiguous, railways can still play an important role as part of intermodal transportation. The Baltic state of Estonia joined with five other Baltic states to form the 1520 Strategic Partnership to promote rail transport from Finland all the way to China. It believes that it can cut the current marine shipping time of 33 days to 17 to 24 days using intermodal containers, thus tapping into the huge trade volume between Asia and Europe.[121]

Exhibit 16.7 shows the density of rail networks, with Europe showing the highest density.

Roads

Density of the network, km roads/square km land area

			2011	
1	Belgium		5.08	1
2	Netherlands		5.00	1
3	Singapore		4.78	
4	Japan		3.18	
5	Hungary		2.10	
6	Slovenia		1.93	
7	Hong Kong		1.89	
8	France		1.87	1
9	Switzerland		1.73	1
10	Denmark		1.72	
10	United Kingdom		1.72	1
12	Czech Republic		1.66	
13	India		1.42	
14	Ireland		1.37	3
15	Spain		1.32	4
16	Austria		1.31	1
17	Estonia		1.29	1
18	Sweden		1.28	1
19	Lithuania		1.27	
20	Poland		1.23	1
21	Taiwan		1.14	
22	Luxembourg		1.11	
23	Latvia		1.07	1
24	Korea		1.05	1
25	Greece		0.89	1
26	Slovak Republic		0.88	
27	Israel		0.84	1
28	Qatar		0.79	
29	Philippines		0.71	
30	USA		0.67	1
31	Germany		0.65	
32	UAE		0.64	
33	Croatia		0.52	
34	Malaysia		0.48	
35	Turkey		0.47	1
36	China Mainland		0.43	
37	New Zealand		0.35	
38	Romania		0.34	1
39	Ukraine		0.28	1
40	Indonesia		0.25	2
41	Norway		0.24	
41	Portugal		0.24	1
43	Finland		0.23	1
44	Brazil		0.19	1
44	Mexico		0.19	1
46	Bulgaria		0.17	
46	Colombia		0.17	
48	Iceland		0.13	
48	Thailand		0.13	
50	Australia		0.11	
51	Canada		0.10	1
51	Chile		0.10	
51	Peru		0.10	1
54	Jordan		0.09	2
55	Russia		0.05	
56	Kazakhstan		0.03	
-	Argentina		-	
-	Italy		-	
-	Venezuela		-	
-	South Africa		-	

Exhibit 16.6 Ranking of countries by road density

Source: World Competitiveness Yearbook, Copyright © 2013, IMD, Switzerland, www.imd.org/wcc.

Railroads

Density of the network, km per square km

#	Country	2011	
1	Singapore	0.25	
2	Hong Kong	0.21	
3	Czech Republic	0.12	
4	Belgium	0.12	
5	Luxembourg	0.11	
6	Germany	0.09	
7	Switzerland	0.09	
8	Hungary	0.08	
9	Slovak Republic	0.07	
10	Netherlands	0.07	
11	United Kingdom	0.07	
12	Poland	0.06	
13	France	0.06	
14	Austria	0.06	
15	Slovenia	0.06	
16	Italy	0.06	
17	Japan	0.05	
18	Israel	0.05	
19	Denmark	0.05	
20	Croatia	0.05	
21	Taiwan	0.05	
22	Romania	0.05	
23	Korea	0.04	
24	Ukraine	0.04	
25	Bulgaria	0.04	
26	Spain	0.03	
27	Portugal	0.03	
28	Latvia	0.03	
29	Ireland	0.03	
30	Lithuania	0.03	
31	USA	0.02	
32	Sweden	0.02	
33	India	0.02	
34	Greece	0.02	
35	Finland	0.02	
36	Estonia	0.02	
37	South Africa	0.02	
38	New Zealand	0.01	
39	Mexico	0.01	
40	Norway	0.01	
41	Turkey	0.01	1
42	Argentina	0.01	
43	Thailand	0.01	
44	Chile	0.01	
45	China Mainland	0.01	
46	Malaysia	0.01	
47	Jordan	0.01	
48	Canada	0.01	
49	Kazakhstan	0.01	
50	Russia	0.00	
51	Brazil	0.00	
52	Philippines	0.00	1
53	Indonesia	0.00	
54	Peru	0.00	
55	Colombia	0.00	2
56	Venezuela	0.00	3
57	Australia	0.00	
58	Qatar	0.00	4
59	UAE	0.00	
60	Iceland	0.00	

Exhibit 16.7 Ranking of countries by railroad density

Source: World Competitiveness Yearbook, Copyright © 2013, IMD, Switzerland, www.imd.org/wcc.

Air Transport

Air transportation has grown rapidly in recent years. Expensive but generally more reliable, air shipments were initially confined to perishable or high-value items, but are increasingly in use. One impediment to the globalization of air transport is the stringent safety standards imposed by developed nations, especially the United States and the EU, vis-à-vis the relatively lax regimes common in many developing countries. The United States does not permit the landing of foreign aircraft that do not comply with certain safety standards, though US authorities have not always been effective in enforcing these standards.

Crossing National Borders

French tire maker Michelin calculates that 45.3 percent of its European sales come from import flows, meaning that almost half of the products it sells in one country are imported from another. For example, the vast majority of Michelin sales in the United Kingdom are imports.[122] It is difficult

Industry Box

Global Logistics at Wal-Mart

The largest retailer in the world, Arkansas-based Wal-Mart, started its international operations in 1991, when it opened in Mexico, where it is now the largest retailer. Today, Wal-Mart has more than 10,000 stores in 27 countries, including the United Kingdom, Argentina, Brazil, and China, which has been targeted for rapid expansion and where the company has agreed to accept union representation, something it has resisted in the United States and all its other foreign locations. In some locations (e.g., Germany and South Korea), the Wal-Mart business model did not work at all, leading the company to retreat from those markets in 2006.

Efficient, large-scale supply chain management has long been a Wal-Mart competitive advantage, which the firm sought to leverage in its foreign operations. Still, the firm faced the need to adjust to the different environments in which it operated. In Argentina, Wal-Mart expanded aisle size initially set to US standards to accommodate higher than expected customer traffic. As Joe Menzer, president and CEO of Wal-Mart International, suggested, "it wasn't such a good idea to stick to the domestic Wal-Mart blueprint in Argentina, or in some of the other international markets we've entered, for that matter." As 2000 drew to a close, Wal-Mart was fighting a bill introduced in the Buenos Aires legislature to limit hypermarkets' size to 20,000 square feet, one-tenth of Wal-Mart's Supercenters. In England, Wal-Mart had to adjust to ASDA's (its acquired chain) 65,000 square feet stores, roughly one-third of Wal-Mart's domestic average. The different store size and product composition required adjustments in store layout and display, as well as in transportation, warehousing, and distribution. Wal-Mart also replaced ASDA's information system with its own so as to benefit from worldwide sourcing, buying power, and distribution scale.

Source: Wal-Mart Annual Report, 2013; Y. Ono and N.N. Zimmerman, "Wal-Mart enters Japan with Seiyu stake," *Wall Street Journal*, March 15, 2002, B5; Company press releases and media reports, 2004–2013.

to establish a seamless supply chain spanning national borders, as customs inspection, processing, and other barriers associated with border crossing create unpredictable and costly delays.[123] In the aftermath of September 11, 2001, delays have increased, despite the revamping of import procedures to better handle the security of their supply chain, including the prescreening of certain shipments.[124] In 2012, a labor action in California's ports created a scare for Chinese exporters, as long delays caused higher fees before the busy Christmas season. [125]

The NAFTA agreement provides for non-tariff movement of goods across Canada, the United States, and Mexico, on the condition that the goods in question originate in one of the three countries. This requires substantial documentation to establish country-of-origin source. In addition, shortage of border-crossing points, bridges, rails, and docks undermine traffic expansion.[126] Paperwork, and the need to switch trailers have been identified as key reasons for delays in crossing the US borders with Mexico and Canada (delays have been worse on the Mexican border).[127] Most US–Mexico trade passes through border-crossing points between the two countries, mostly in Texas, but also in Arizona and California. One border crossing—Laredo—accounts for almost 40 percent of all exports from Mexico.[128] Yet, crossing Laredo can take upward of three hours as shipments are handled through an antiquated system.[129]

Every day, close to two billion-worth of goods cross the US–Canadian border, a number that has been increasing by 13 percent annually since 1994; 2,000 trucks pass through the Blaine border crossing between Washington and British Columbia daily. The cost associated with crossing the US–Canadian border is estimated at 5 to 10 percent of product cost. In an effort to reduce the cost, constituencies on both sides of the border have been pushing for increased integration, with some going as far as proposing the elimination of the border altogether.[130] Such calls have been largely silenced since 9/11 as concerns over the transfer of potential terrorists and their wares across the border have risen.

Exhibit 16.8 ranks countries on the extent to which the bureaucracy of customs hinders the efficient transit of goods. Finland, Singapore, and Hong Kong are ranked best with the smallest hindrance, whereas Argentina, Venezuela, and Indonesia close the list.

Interim Summary

1. Supply chains have undergone substantial globalization in recent years with firms consolidating sourcing and distribution; however, the trend has been more pronounced in some regions (e.g., the EU) than in others (e.g., Asia).
2. Customization remains an issue in product packaging and promotion, although here too there is an attempt to reduce the number of variants.
3. Transportation modes need to be considered in terms of their cost and efficacy, with special attention given to intermodal transportation.
4. Border-crossing has become more cumbersome in the aftermath of 9/11.

Customs' authorities

Customs' authorities do facilitate the efficient transit of goods

#	Country	2013
1	Sweden	8.60
2	Singapore	8.43
3	Ireland	8.24
4	UAE	8.18
5	Finland	8.04
6	New Zealand	8.03
7	Norway	7.96
8	Denmark	7.83
9	Hong Kong	7.67
10	Austria	7.66
11	Netherlands	7.48
12	Germany	7.46
13	United Kingdom	7.41
14	Australia	7.20
15	Switzerland	7.16
16	Belgium	7.06
17	Canada	7.02
18	USA	6.99
19	Chile	6.96
20	Estonia	6.95
21	Taiwan	6.82
22	Qatar	6.68
23	Luxembourg	6.66
24	Malaysia	6.63
25	Slovenia	6.50
26	Japan	6.49
27	Korea	6.47
28	France	6.46
29	Spain	6.23
30	Czech Republic	6.15
31	Israel	6.14
32	Portugal	6.10
33	Iceland	5.95
34	Hungary	5.88
35	Lithuania	5.83
36	Turkey	5.70
37	Italy	5.58
38	Latvia	5.48
39	Jordan	5.43
40	Romania	5.28
41	Mexico	5.27
42	South Africa	5.02
43	Colombia	5.01
44	Thailand	5.00
45	Greece	4.86
46	Slovak Republic	4.67
47	Kazakhstan	4.52
48	Peru	4.49
49	China Mainland	4.46
50	India	4.11
51	Croatia	3.80
52	Indonesia	3.77
53	Philippines	3.32
54	Bulgaria	3.27
55	Poland	2.55
56	Ukraine	2.50
57	Russia	2.44
58	Brazil	2.17
59	Argentina	1.81
60	Venezuela	1.63

Exhibit 16.8 Government efficiency—business legislation

Source: World Competitiveness Yearbook, Copyright © 2013, IMD, Switzerland, www.imd.org/wcc.

Chapter Summary

1. International markets are typically more difficult to enter than domestic markets, yet they represent tremendous potential for firms.

2. There are various ways to assess the potential of a foreign market. First and foremost is economic development and its correlate of disposable income; however, consumption patterns are determined by myriad other factors, including culture.

3. Companies standardize products and services, as well as the methods by which they are advertised, sold, distributed, and serviced, in an attempt to reduce costs and increase efficiencies. At the same time, there remain strong pressures to adapt products and services to the local environment in which they are offered.

4. Country of origin remains a powerful force in marketing and consumer behavior. It can lead consumers to purchase a product or a service (even if higher priced) from a country with a positive image and to avoid a product or a service from a country with a negative image.

5. Pricing pressures and economic integration push companies to consolidate their global supply chains from sourcing to delivery. Logistics providers respond by consolidating their own operations.

6. A trend toward "intermodal" transportation involves the simultaneous use of multiple transportation modes, namely rail, sea, and air.

Notes

1   J. Micklethwait, "Washed up?," *The Economist,* 338, 1996, S23–27.

2   Y. Ono, "Overcoming the stigma of dishwashers in Japan," *Wall Street Journal,* May 19, 2000, B1; P. Brasor and M. Tsubuku, "Automatic dishwashers: The square peg in the round hole of Japanese kitchens," *The Japan Times,* February 10, 2012; Euromonitor International, *Country Report: Dishwashers in Japan,* Euromonitor International, March 2013.

3   W. Boston and K. Richter, "Telecom firms battle to serve Germany's Turks," *Wall Street Journal,* November 6, 2000, B7B.

4   W.J. Keegan, *Global Marketing Management,* Englewood Cliffs, NJ: Prentice-Hall, 2001.

5   "Burgernomics beats reading the tea leaves," *The Economist,* April 29, 2000.

6   H. Riesenbeck and A. Freeling, "How global are global brands?," *European Business Report,* summer 1993, 13.

7   *The Economist,* September 2, 2000, p. 98, citing RoperASW.

8   *The Economist,* September 2, 2000, citing RoperASW.

9   "Franchises head overseas," CNNfn, September 11, 2000, 7.49 a.m. ET.

10 M.R. Czinkota and I.A. Ronkainen, *International Marketing,* Orlando, FL: Harcourt Brace, 1998.

11 *The Changing Global Role of the Marketing Function,* The Conference Board 1105-95-RR.

12 *The Changing Global Role of the Marketing Function,* The Conference Board 1105-95-RR; S. Samie and K. Roth, "The influence of global marketing standardization on performance," *Journal of Marketing,* April 1992, 1–17

13 S. Ellison, "Carrefour and Ahold find shoppers like to think local," *Wall Street Journal,* August 31, 2001.

14 "Franchises head overseas," CNNfn Internet edition, September 11, 2000, 7.49 a.m. ET.

15 A. Baar and A. McMains, "Kellogg realigns global brands," adweek com., May 29, 2000, 5.

16 "Launching a mass-market fragrance worldwide at Avon," The Conference Board 1105-95-RR, 15.

17 Y. Ono, "US superstores find Japanese are a hard sell," *Wall Street Journal*, February 14, 2000, B1.

18 *The Changing Global Role of the Marketing Function*, The Conference Board 1105-95-RR.

19 *The Changing Global Role of the Marketing Function*, The Conference Board 1105-95-RR.

20 *The Changing Global Role of the Marketing Function*, The Conference Board 1105-95-RR.

21 "Global accounts at AMP," The Conference Board 1105-95-RR p. 19.

22 Domestic recording artists boost share of market to 68 percent," *Wall Street Journal*, September 7, 2001, B6.

23 M. Flagg, "Asia proves unexpectedly tough terrain for HBO, Cinemax channels," *Wall Street Journal*, August 23, 2000, B1.

24 S. Bereger, "Expert: Metro Cash and Carry 'taken to the cleaners' in Israel," *The Jerusalem Post* (Digital Israel), September 14, 2001.

25 M. Tanikawa, "French supermarket struggles to fit it," *Wall Street Journal*, October 5, 2001.

26 J.N. Kapferer, "How global are global brands, ESOMAR seminar," cited in M. van Mesdag, "Culture-sensitive adaptation or global standardization—the duration of usage hypothesis," *International Marketing Review*, 17, 1, 1999, 74–84.

27 G.T. Sims, "Corn flakes clash shows the glitches in the European Union," *Wall Street Journal*, November 1, 2005, A1.

28 H. Riesenbeck, and A. Freeling, "How global are global brands?," *The McKinsey Quarterly*, 4, 1991, 3–18.

29 M. De Mooij, "Masculinity/femininity and consumer behavior," In G. Hofstede (ed.), *Masculinity and Femininity: The Taboo Dimension of National Cultures*, Thousand Oaks, CA: Sage, 1998, 55–73.

30 G.A. Fowler, "Marketers take heed: The Macho Chinese man is back," *Wall Street Journal*, December 18, 2002, B1.

31 K.F. Winsted, "Evaluating service encounters: A cross-cultural and cross-industry exploration," *Journal of Marketing Theory and Practice*, spring 1999, 106–123.

32 J.L. Watson, "China's Big Mac attack," *Foreign Affairs*, 79, 3, 2000, 130.

33 J.E. Hilsenrath, "Ford designs Ikon to suit Indian tastes," *Wall Street Journal*, August 8, 2000, A17, also cited in *Globe & Mail*, April 8, 2000.

34 "From top to bottom," *The Economist*, June 3, 2006, 17.

35 N. Shirouzu, "Tailoring world's cars to US tastes," *Wall Street Journal*, January 15, 2001, B1.

36 R. Martin, "Religion reshapes realities for US restaurants in Middle East," *Restaurant News*, February 16, 1998.

37 D. Barboza, "Market place: Pluralism under golden arches," *The New York Times*, 1999, C1.

38 Euromonitor, Retail Trade International, 2000 (11th ed).

39 Y. Ono, "US superstores find Japanese are a hard sell," *Wall Street Journal*, February 14, 2000, B1.

40 M.S. Roth, and J.B. Romeo, "Matching product category and country image perceptions: A framework for managing country-of-origin effects," *Journal of International Business Studies*, 3rd quarter, 1992, 477–497.

41 R.A. Peterson and A.J.P. Jolibert, "A meta-analysis of country-of-origin effect," *Journal of International Business Studies*, 4th quarter, 1995, 883–900.

42 C. Powell, "Why we really must fly the flag: Being cool isn't enough," *The Observer*, April 25, 1999, p. 4.

43 R. Daedeke, "Consumer attitudes towards products 'made in' developing countries," *Journal of Retailing*, summer 1973, 13–24.

44 J. Baum, "Riding high: A Taiwanese bicycle maker races to success in the West," *Far Eastern Economic Review*, May 7, 1998, 58–59.

45 M.S. Roth and J.B. Romeo, "Matching product category and country image perceptions: A framework for managing country-of-origin effects," *Journal of International Business Studies*, 3rd quarter, 1992, 477–497.

46 C. Powell, "Why we really must fly the flag," *The Observer*, April 25, 1999, 4, citing a BMP DDB survey.

47 C. Lawton, "Pushing foreign- and faux foreign-beer in the US," *Wall Street Journal*, June 27, 2003, B1.

48 J.L. Watson, "China's Big Mac attack," *Foreign Affairs*, 79, 3, 2000, 120.

49 G. Vchazan, "Foreign products get Russian makeovers," *Wall Street Journal*, January 16, 2001, A23.

50   B. Smith, "In Latvia, a traditional drink takes on Western production and Pepsi generation," *Wall Street Journal,* September 8, 2000, A17.

51   Y. Ono, "US superstores find Japanese are a hard sell," *Wall Street Journal,* February 14, 2000, B1.

52   "Spin Cycle," *The Economist,* August 14, 1999, 52.

53   S. Ellison, *Wall Street Journal,* August 31, 2001 A5.

54   M.R. Czinkota and I.A. Ronkainen, *International Marketing,* 5th edn, Orlando, FL: Harcourt Brace, 1998.

55   J. Kim and J.D. Daniels, "Marketing channel decisions of foreign manufacturing subsidiaries in the US: The case of metal and machinery industries," *Management International Review,* 31, 1991, 123–138.

56   J. Kim and J.D. Daniels, "Marketing channel decisions of foreign manufacturing subsidiaries in the US: The case of the metal and machinery industries," *Management International Review,* 31, 1991/2, 123–138.

57   "SED International, Inc. announces status as certified HP top value reseller," *Business Wire,* April 9, 1998.

58   R. Frank, "Big Boy's adventures in Thailand," *Wall Street Journal,* April 12, 2000.

59   G. Dyer, "Brazil's regional drink makers *slake* thirst for value," *Financial Times,* June 16, 1999, 5.

60   D. Summers, "Boots for global trip," *Financial Times,* October 12, 1995, 13.

61   "This Euro brew's for you," *Business Week,* July 24, 2000, 120–122.

62   T. Burt and D. Hargreaves, "Crackdown pledge as VW fine is upheld," *Financial Times,* July 7, 2000.

63   P. Doval, "Auto industry against inclusion in India-European Union free trade agreement," *The Times of India*, May 16, 2012.

64   L. McGinley, "Drug industry seeks to prevent importation of cheaper medicines," *Wall Street Journal,* July 19, 2000, A8.

65   C.W.L. Hill, *International Business: Competing in the Global Marketplace,* Boston, MA: McGraw-Hill, 1999.

66   R. Belderbos and P. Holmes, "An economic analysis of Matsushita revisited," *Antitrust Bulletin,* 40, 1995, 825–857.

67   "Trade barriers," *Journal of Commerce,* June 10, 1992, 5A.

68   H. Riesenbeck and A. Freeling, "How global are global brands?," *European Business Report,* summer 1993.

69   K. Kashani, "Beware the pitfalls of global marketing," *Harvard Business Review,* September/October 1989, 92–93.

70   J. Lafayette, "Marketing: Picking the right ad agency," *International Business,* 5, 1992, 106–110; D. Guthery and B.A. Lowe, "Translation problems in international marketing research," *The Journal of Language for International Business,* 4, 1992, 1–14.

71   L. Himelstein, "The swoosh heard round the world," *Business Week,* May 12, 1990, 76.

72   S. Donaton, "Not always Coca-Cola's policy threatens integrity of magazines," *Advertising Age,* 70, 1999, 36.

73   M. Gjalwash, "In Egypt, rumors of blasphemy swirl around Coca-Cola," *Online Athens,* July 25, 2000.

74   H. Riesenbeck and A. Freeling, "How global are global brands?," *European Business Report,* 7, summer 1993.

75   *The Changing Global Role of the Marketing Function,* The Conference Board, 1105-95-RR p. 14.

76   B. McKay, "Coke hunts for talent to re-establish its marketing might," *Wall Street Journal,* March 2002, B4.

77   "This Euro brew's for you," *Business Week,* July 24, 2000, 120–122.

78   "Unquenchable thirst," *Financial Times London,* April 30, 1999, 19.

79   *The Changing Global Role of the Marketing Function,* The Conference Board, 1105-95-RR.

80   *Meeting the Challenge of Global Logistics,* The Conference Board Europe Report #1207-98-CR.

81   Harris Interactive, Chicago '06 Longitudes Supply Chain Management Survey, April 2006.

82   P.P. Dornier, R. Ernst, M. Fender and P. Kouvelis, *Global Operations and Logistics,* New York: Wiley, 1998.

83   "The physical internet: a survey of logistics," *The Economist,* June 17, 2006, 8; N.S. Gupta, "India's logistic costs higher than BRIC nations," *The Times of India,* June 15, 2012; Xinhua News Agency, "Logistics costs remain high in China: Report," *China Daily,* February 8, 2013.

84   Prologis company information, 1999.

559

85   E. Chabrow, "Supply chains go global," *Informationweek.com,* April 3, 2000, 51.

86   "Exchanges fall short on global e-commerce," *Internetweek,* May 8, 2000, 1.

87   UNCTAD, Electronic commerce and development, 2000.

88   The Conference Board, 1105-95-RR.

89   P.P. Dornier, R. Ernst, M. Fender, and P. Kouvelis, *Global Operations and Logistics,* 62, New York: Wiley, 1998.

90   The Conference Board, 1105-95-RR.

91   P.P. Dornier, R. Ernst, M. Fender, and P. Kouvelis, *Global Operations and Logistics,* 180, New York: Wiley, 1998.

92   S.M. Shaw and J. Meier, "Second generation MNCs in China," *McKinsey Quarterly,* 4, 1993, 3–16.

93   S. Lal, P. Van Laarhoven, and G. Sharman, "Current research: Making logistics alliances work," *McKinsey Quarterly,* 3, 1995, 188–190.

94   The Conference Board, 1105-95-RR.

95   B. Radstaak and M.H. Ketelaar, *Worldwide Logistics,* Holland International Distribution Council, 1998.

96   Dornier et al., *Global Operations and Logistics.*

97   R. Morton, "Latin American business is looking up," *Transportation & Distribution,* October 2000, 52.

98   P. Wright "Logistics in Asia," The Conference Board, 1105-95-RR, 20.

99   "Nestlé on the win-win partnership with the retail trade," The Conference Board, 1105-95-RR.

100 The Conference Board, 1105-95-RR.

101 Dornier et al., *Global Operations and Logistics,* 226.

102 Dornier et al., *Global Operations and Logistics,* 120–121.

103 M. Yost, "Innovation lifts Meritor's profile in auto-parts business," *Wall Street Journal,* November 15, 1999, B4.

104 The Conference Board, 1105-95-RR, 14.

105 L. Bannon, "New playbook: Taking cues from GE, Mattel's CEO wants toy maker to grow up," *Wall Street Journal,* November 14, 2001, A1.

106 S. Livingstone and L. Sparks, "The new German packaging laws: Effects on firms exporting to Germany," *International Journal of Physical Distribution & Logistics Management,* 24, 1994, 15–25; "Trade Regulations and Standards in Germany," Globaltrad.net, March 13, 2011.

107 P.L. Grogan, "European influence," *BioCycle,* 38, 1997, 86.

108 US Department of Commerce, "Complying with the made in the USA standard."

109 The Conference Board, 1105-95-RR.

110 P. Wright, "Logistics in Asia," The Conference Board, 19.

111 N. King, "Panama Canal at crossroads," *Wall Street Journal,* January 7, 2004, B1.

112 S. Mankabady, *The International Maritime Organization,* London: Croom-Helm, 1984.

113 T. Drennan, "Where the action's at: The US–Mexican border," FAS on-line, US Department of Agriculture, 1999, 2.

114 D. McCosh, "A cool place for Mexican shippers," *Journal of Commerce,* April 28, 1999, 1; Farrar, Foss, "Mexico trade increases produce companies cluster for further growth," *Refrigerated Transporter,* August 1, 2000.

115 "The Port of Barcelona increased its container export levels by 12 percent during the first half of 2013 setting a new record," Catalan News Agency, August 2, 2013.

116 "Improving interchange management," *Intermodal Insights,* September 1999, 179.

117 D. Machlaba, "Tiny British Columbia port aims to be new venue for China trade," *Wall Street Journal. com,* August 8, 2006.

118 J. Braithwaite and P. Drahos, *Global Business Regulation,* New York: Cambridge University Press, 2000.

119 R. Gold, "Mexican trucks won't fill the US soon," *Wall Street Journal,* February 16, 2001, A2; H. Cooper and K. Chen, "US is told to let Mexican trucks enter," *Wall Street Journal,* February 7, 2001, A2.

560

120 W. Zinn, "Obstacles to supply chair efficiency in a trade block environment: Three cases in MERCOSUR," Working Paper, Fisher College of Business, The Ohio State University.

121 B. Smith, "Estonia mulls Beijing–Baltic rail link in bid to be gateway for Asian exports," *Wall Street Journal,* November 13, 2000, B19; "1520 partners debate co-operation," *Railway Gazette,* January 1, 2007.

122 Dornier, et al., *Global Operations and Logistics,* 63.

123 Dornier, et al., *Global Operations and Logistics.*

124 G.R. Simpson, "US to revise dealings with importers, reward those with enhanced security," *Wall Street Journal,* November 27, 2001, A24.

125 K. Wallis, "Exporters face delays and higher costs at US ports; Dock strike during peak shipping season before Christmas may see cargo being held up and shippers imposing extra fees," *South China Morning Post,* September 14, 2012.

126 A.W. Mathews, "On the borderline. Nafta reality check: Trucks, trains, ships face costly delays," *Wall Street Journal,* June 3, 1998, A1.

127 1991 Intermodal Association of North America (IANA) Intermodal Index.

128 T. Drennan, "Where the action's at: The US–Mexican border," FAS on-line, US Department of Agriculture, 1999; R. Guidi, "US–Mexico crossborder trade relationship improving," *KPBS,* January 14, 2011.

129 R. Gold, "Mexican trucks won't fill the US soon," *Wall Street Journal,* February 16, 2001, A2; H. Cooper and K. Chen, "US is told to let Mexican trucks enter," *Wall Street Journal,* February 7, 2001, A2; C.E. Wilson and E. Lee, "Whole nations waiting," *Site Selection,* July 2012.

130 B. Cameron, "Just blow it up," *National Post* (Canada), August 18, 2001, B3.

chapter 17

global human resource management

STRATEGIC IHRM	565
STAFFING THE MNE	567
THE EXPATRIATE WORKFORCE	573
HRM IN INTERNATIONAL AFFILIATES	586

Do You Know?

1. What are the staffing stages that an MNE goes through on its globalization route?
2. What are the reasons for assigning expatriates to MNE affiliates?
3. What are the elements of expatriate compensation?
4. How does human resource management differ between a WOS (wholly owned [foreign] subsidiary) and an IJV (international joint venture)?
5. Would you like to work for a foreign firm? Why or why not?

OPENING CASE   Managing Global Human Resources at HSBC

Founded in Asia in 1865 by a Scottish national, the Hong Kong and Shanghai Banking Corporation (HSBC) is one of the world's largest banks by assets and has more than 330,000 employees around the globe. Until two decades ago, the bank's top managerial ranks drew exclusively on an elite group of up to 800 international managers (IMs), all of them British men enjoying lucrative expatriate terms on their foreign postings. Today, the company, which has greatly expanded since, and which prides itself on its combination of local knowledge and global savvy, looks radically different. HSCB now has roughly 380 IMs, but these top executives hail from no less than 33 nationalities. The head of Asia Pacific operations, for instance, is of Indian origin. The same trend of human resource globalization can be observed in numerous other MNEs, from US-based Citibank to Swedish packaging firm Tetra Pack.

In addition to its IMs, HSBC also has in the range of 1,000–2,000 employees as "secondees," "contract executives," and short-term assignees (mostly technical staff) in international postings. Each of the three groups has its own compensation package, but generally speaking the terms of employment for members of those groups are not nearly as generous as those for the IMs. The bulk of HSBC's workforce (e.g., individuals working as bank tellers, data coders and the like) are local residents who work under so-called "local terms," that is, under similar (though usually competitive) terms to employees of local businesses in each of the countries where the bank operates, without any of the perks reserved for the other groups, such as housing and children's education.

Source: Adapted from HSBC company websites and "Traveling more lightly," *The Economist*, June 24, 2006, 27.

International human resource management (IHRM) is the procurement, allocation, utilization, motivation, and compensation of human resources in the international arena. IHRM is critical to the strategy and success of global operations. A Conference Board Survey identified "culture and people issues" as the biggest roadblocks to global success.[1] Research by Booz Allen Hamilton found that the problem of hiring quality personnel ranked as one of the main factors inhibiting expansion of US foreign investment in Japan. The Japanese, on their part, named conflict between expatriates and the local workforce as their main globalization concern.[2] Appointing people with significant experience in international operations is one way for companies to avoid those problems and improve integration and corporate performance worldwide.

The distinct features of IHRM are multiculturalism and geographic dispersion,[3] as well as the need to address issues such as international taxation, relocation, and foreign culture orientation. IHRM also generates more involvement in personal life (e.g., expatriate housing and educational assistance in the host country).[4] IHRM implies multiple constituencies, including a great variety of employee groups. The challenge for Johnson & Johnson, Bombardier, Teva, and other MNEs is to make proper adjustments in each of the markets in which they operate, yet maintain system-wide consistency and equity that will enable global deployment of talent in line with the firm's strategy.

From a career perspective, it is useful to note that international experience increasingly opens doors from initial entry and up to the CEO suite. HSBC is by no means the only MNE to instill global know-how and experience in its executives. Johnson & Johnson (J&J) seeks candidates with international experience (e.g., participation in a college exchange program) on the assumption that such individuals are better suited to the demands of a global business environment. J&J executives also go through Executive Development and Executive Conference programs which further develop their global mind-set.[5]

Strategic IHRM

Strategic international human resource management (SIHRM) is defined as "human resources, management issues, functions and policies and practices that result from the strategic activities of MNEs and that impact the international concerns and goals of these enterprises."[6] Compared to strategic human resource management in a domestic context, SIHRM is more complex because it concerns multiple environments and employee groups and because it must be aligned with the multi-faceted strategic considerations of the MNE. The SIHRM model has three possible orientations.

- The **adaptive** system imitates local HRM practices.
- The **exportive** system replicates the HRM system in the home country and other affiliates.
- The **integrative** system emphasizes global integration while permitting some local variations.

An optimal SIHRM is capable of balancing the different forces in the firm's environment, in particular the tension between local responsiveness and global integration.[7] The overall SIHRM strategy chosen by the parent—together with the affiliate's specific conditions (e.g., the cultural distance from the parent)—will determine the degree of similarity in SIHRM between the affiliate and headquarters. This, in conjunction with the criticality of the group, will determine the similarity of HRM practices for each employee group (see Exhibit 17.1).

Exhibit 17.2 shows the evolution in the firm's SIHRM system based on product life-cycle theory.[8] IHRM changes as firms go through the domestic, international, multinational, and global phases of internationalization. Exhibit 17.2 shows the phases and associated IHRM activities.[9]

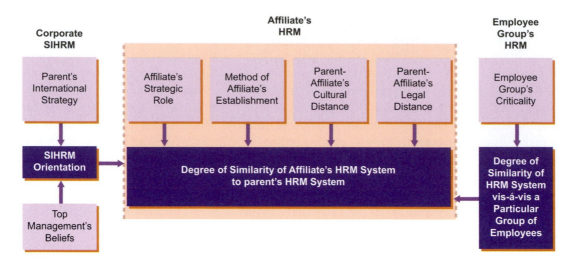

Exhibit 17.1 Model of strategic international human resource management (SIHRM)

Source: S. Taylor, S. Beechler, and N. Napier, "Toward an integrative model of strategic international human resource management," *Academy of Management Review*, 21, 4, 1996, 965.

Phase I Domestic: focus on home market and export
- Incidental brief visits to foreign agents/sales offices or short assignment on a project basis.
- Product and technical competence are the most important factors.
- Can scarcely speak of international HRM.

Phase II International: focus on local responsiveness and transfer of learning
- Managers are assigned to posts in foreign markets to provide general management, technical expertise, and financial control.
- In addition to technical competence, language skills, cross-cultural sensitivity, and adaptability are also important.
- Host-country nationals are frequently recruited for management positions in the areas of sales, marketing, and personnel.

Phase III Multinational: focus on global strategy, low cost, and price competition
- Selection focuses on recruiting the best managers for international positions, regardless of country of origin.
- Training and developing all members to share corporate values and norms.
- Management development, career counseling, and periodic transfers to different assignments.

Phase IV Global: focus on both local responsiveness and global integration
- The major issue is how to satisfy the requirements for global integration and national responsiveness.
- Large measure of cultural diversity.
- Offering promising managers the opportunity to grow and gain experience so that an environment for continuous learning will be created throughout the entire organization.

Exhibit 17.2 Phases of internationalization and IHRM

Source: Adapted from N.J. Adler, "Strategic human resource management: A global perspective." In R. Pieper (ed.), *Human Resource Management: An International Comparison*, Berlin: DeGruyter, 1990.

Interim Summary

1. As the MNE shifts from domestic to global strategy, the criteria by which it selects management, as well as its general HR policies, will change to reflect the new strategy.
2. In advanced phases of internationalization, growth opportunities for managers expand both vertically and geographically.

Staffing the MNE

The Globalization of Boards of Directors

A global survey conducted by the Conference Board found that the percentage of firms with non-national directors increased between 1995 and 1998 from 39 to 60 percent. The percentage of companies with three or more non-national directors increased from 11 to 23, with the majority of directors recruited in the last three years. By 1998, 10 percent of directors of surveyed firms were non-nationals, up from 6 percent three years earlier. Danone, which did not have any foreign directors in 2002, had three in 2013. Other firms are farther ahead. Take a look, for instance, at the following composition of Nestlé's board, where only six out of 14 board members are Swiss, and one of them is a Swiss-American (see Exhibit 17.3).

The Conference Board survey found that entering new markets and exposure to new demands from customers and investors are the primary internal drivers for seeking non-national board members. The initiative often comes from new managers wishing to expand international operations where the credibility and expertise of non-national directors makes a difference. Firms that initially took on non-nationals for "cosmetic" reasons learned to appreciate their added value over time. For Deutsche Telekom, the addition of France Telecom CEO Michel Bon to its supervisory board cemented the ties between the two firms, raised Deutsche Telekom's profile in the French market, and brought a new business perspective.

Selecting Global Board Members

Firms seeking to internationalize their boards typically begin by selecting someone with the same nationality, but an international perspective. In the next phase, firms look for individuals with in-depth cultural and business experience in a given part of the world. Even then, the majority of appointments are made from among employees with experience working or living in the home (headquarters) country. For example, US-based DuPont appointed to its board Percy Barnevik, then CEO of Swedish-Swiss concern ABB, and Goro Watanabe, an executive vice president of Japan's Mitsui. Both executives have had substantial experience in the US market.

Searches for non-national directors are difficult, resulting, on average, in nine to ten rejections for one acceptance. The extra time commitment (US and UK firms hold eight or nine annual board meetings, the average in continental Europe is four), difference in time zones, and lack of language and culture proficiency are barriers to the appointment of non-national directors, as is the board evaluation process. While Americans have had difficulty adjusting to a Japanese board that is seldom staffed by

Peter Brabeck-Letmathe *Austrian* • Chairman of the Board Of Directors, Nestlé • Chairman's and Corporate Governance Committee (Chairman) • Nomination Committee	Paul Bulcke *Belgian* • Chief Executive Officer, Nestlé S.A. • Member of the Board of Directors • Chairman's and Corporate Governance Committee	Andreas Koopmann *Swiss* • 1st Vice Chairman • Chairman's and Corporate Governance Committee • Compensation Committee • Nomination Committee (Chairman)	Rolf Hänggi *Swiss* • 2nd Vice Chairman • Chairman's and Corporate Governance Committee • Audit Committee (Chairman)	Daniel Borel *Swiss* • Compensation Committee (Chairman)
Jean-Pierre Meyers *Swiss* • Compensation Committee	Steven George Hoch *American/Swiss* • Nomination Committee	Naïna Lal Kidwai *Indian* • Audit Committee	Beat Hess *Swiss* • Audit Committee	Titia de Lange *Dutch* • Board of Directors
Jean-Pierre Roth *Swiss* • Compensation Committee	Ann M. Veneman *American* • Nomination Committee	Henri de Castries *French* • Audit Committee	Eva Cheng *Chinese* • Member of the Board of Directors	

Exhibit 17.3 Nestlé's Board of Directors 2013

Source: Nestlé website, 2013.

independent directors, Japanese directors serving on US boards find them "frighteningly open" in terms of the information flow between management and board. The Conference Board recommends accommodating non-nationals by reducing the number of annual meetings, rotating meeting locations, setting up orientation programs, and widening the definition of non-national director to include non-nationals living and working abroad who maintain strong ties with their home country.

Another obstacle to the appointment of non-national directors is representation. US institutional investors are concerned with having non-national directors in domestic firms as well as with having national directors in non-US firms. Since institutional investors have a fiduciary duty to protect shareholder interests, they must consider representation of shareholders in the decision to elect directors. This works well in the United States or the United Kingdom, but not in Continental Europe or Japan, where shareholders are only one of many constituencies represented by the board. Representation is more difficult when significant shareholders sit on the board, especially if they are family members, board members of companies with significant cross-shareholdings, board members of major suppliers, or labor or pension fund representatives. While US shareholders are relatively dispersed, shareholders with major control blocks are common in Europe, Latin America, and Asia.

Industry Box

Airline Pilots Go Global

With the entire US airline industry mired in recession since September 11, 2001, many US pilots who were furloughed and unable to find employment at home turned to foreign airlines from China and Vietnam, to Bolivia and Qatar. They followed in the footsteps of their British and Australian colleagues who, facing limited opportunities at home, for decades sought employment in other markets, from Singapore to Hong Kong. In Qatar, four out of five pilots are foreigners. The flow is likely to continue. Boeing estimate that China alone will need more than 35,000 new pilots in the next 20 years (1,786 a year), while the rest of Asia will require 56,500 new pilots during the same period. Most developing nations lack the training capacity to meet their pilot needs, and do not have enough ex-military pilots to fill the void, at least in the foreseeable future.

The global mobility of pilots has raised some safety concerns. For instance, having a captain who does not share a native language with a co-pilot and/or a traffic controller can lead to confusion, and language problems have been identified as contributing factors in a number of plane crashes, including that of an American Airlines plane in Colombia. Culture issues have also caused problems, for instance, in terms of the relationship between the captain and the co-pilot (as described in Chapter 6, co-pilots from high power-distance cultures often do not question the judgment of the captain). In 2011, the International Civil Aviation Organization, a UN agency, started a new service that helps member states to assess more accurately the speaking and listening ability in English of pilots and air traffic controllers. In the meantime, firms and entrepreneurs have also rushed to open flight training schools to address the pilot shortage. Despite the challenges of language communication and cultural adaptation, many US pilots still find jobs overseas more lucrative and more rewarding even today after the gradual recovery of the US air travel market.

Source: Adapted from S. Carey, B. Stanley, and J. Larkin, "With job scarce, US pilots sign on at foreign airlines," *Wall Street Journal*, May 5, 2006, A1; International Civil Aviation Organization, "ICAO promotes aviation safety by endorsing English language testing," Newsroom, October 13, 2011; CNN, "US pilots find high demand, high pay overseas," CCN Just In, June 4, 2012.

Country Box

Korean Companies Seek Global Talent

South Korean firms once employed almost exclusively Korean nationals as executives and engineers. No more. With the ranks of many Korean MNEs spread thin as they expand across the globe, and as global competition intensifies, these firms are increasingly looking for foreign nationals to fill the ranks not only in local affiliates, but also in their Korean home base. LG Electronics, Korea's leading home appliance maker, recently hosted a recruitment fair in Russia to attract Russian talent to its R&D center. "Discovering young talent from every corner of the globe is not a matter of choice," says the company, "it is now essential for survival." The Korean government now offers a special technology visa that allows qualified foreigners multiple entries over three years and makes it easier for them to work.

South Korean companies also attract foreign workers to their overseas subsidiaries where they are increasingly likely to conduct sophisticated, high-value work. For instance, 18 of Samsung's 24 R&D centers are situated outside Korea, including China, India, Israel, Russia, UK, and US.

Adapted from Samsung company websites and J.A. Song, "South Korean technology companies fill skill vacuum," *The Financial Times*, June 15, 2006, 22.

Staffing the MNE Ranks

Factors that affect MNE staffing (recruitment and selection) include firm strategy, organizational structure, and subsidiary-specific factors such as how long it has been in business, the production and marketing technologies employed, and host-country characteristics such as the level of development, political stability, regulation, and culture. The MNE can draw employees from the home country (parent-country nationals, or PCNs, who are by definition expatriates), from the country in which the overseas operation is located (host-country nationals, or HCNs), or from a third country that is neither a home country nor a host country (third-country nationals, or TCNs). For instance, Brazilian-born Carlos Gohsn is CEO of French car maker Renault and its Japanese affiliate Nissan.

Alternative philosophies of staffing abroad are ethnocentric, polycentric, regiocentric, and geocentric.[10] In **ethnocentric staffing**, PCNs are appointed to key positions regardless of the location of their assignment, as HSBC did until 20 years or so ago. Japanese companies tend to follow this mode more than European and US firms.[11] South Korean firms and most other DMNEs utilized ethnocentric (Samsung, for instance, not only had an all-Korean senior management team until 1999, but 90 percent of those people graduated from Seoul National University).[12] However, Korean firms are now rapidly increasing the ranks of non-Koreans as part of their globalization drive. LG Electronics is recruiting technological talent in Russia, among other regions, utilizing a new Korean government program providing foreign technology experts with a three-year work visa.[13] In China, recruitment of foreign executives is also on the rise. For instance, in 2006 Shanghai Automotive (SAIC) hired the former head of GM's China operations, and in 2013 Geely hired a senior German executive for its Volvo division. For many US firms, the greater the cultural distance to the host nation, the greater the proportion of US nationals in the subsidiary.[14]

In **polycentric staffing**, HCNs are hired to key positions in subsidiaries, but not at corporate headquarters. In **regiocentric staffing**, recruiting is conducted on a regional basis (e.g., Asian candidates are recruited for a position in Thailand). In **geocentric staffing**, managers are recruited worldwide based solely on their qualifications and regardless of their nationality. The value of this approach is not only in obtaining the best candidates, but also in introducing new perspectives into the company. Indeed, firms which considered themselves the most successful in globalization have had a significantly higher proportion of foreign citizens in senior management—20 to 25 percent versus 10 percent for other firms.[15] Nestlé and Johnson & Johnson are examples.

Most of the MNE workforce abroad consists of HCNs or, as they are sometimes called at the subsidiary level, "local employees." The reason is simple: HCNs are, in most instances, the most widely available and the easiest to employ, as they are normally (unless illegal immigrants) permitted to work and are likely to have local certification where needed (e.g., in the case of nurses, accountants, lawyers, and the like). HCNs also know more about the local environment and are generally cheaper to employ, especially in developing and emerging markets, though this is not necessarily the case for DMNEs investing in developing markets, say, the operations of Chinese appliance maker Haier in the United States.

You may recall from Chapter 3 on foreign direct investment that labor cost is an important consideration in location decisions especially for labor-intensive activities. Exhibit 17.4 provides comparative compensation costs for manufacturing workers in selected countries, showing considerable differences between countries. Such differentials explain, among other factors, why MNEs choose

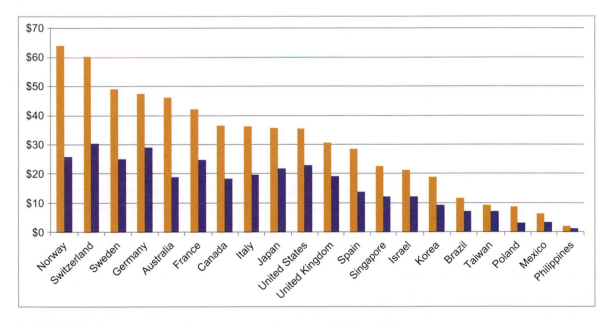

Exhibit 17.4 Hourly compensation costs in manufacturing, 1997 and 2011
Source: U.S. Bureau of Labor Statistics, 2012.

to invest in a particular location, though this will be especially pronounced for labor-intensive industries, such as garments and toys.

In 2010, majority foreign-owned firms employed 5.3 million workers in the US, accounting for 4.7 percent of the total private industry employment in the country. The role of foreign-owned firms is even more important in the manufacturing sector, with one in 12 US manufacturing workers being employed by a foreign-owned firm.[16] Honda alone employs more than 25,000 US employees in all 50 states. US firms, on their part, employ millions of people in foreign countries. The availability of qualified candidates is often a decisive factor in selecting a manufacturing or service location.[17] For years, foreign MNEs in Japan have found it difficult to hire qualified Japanese employees, although this situation is now changing. In some countries, hiring requires a government-controlled labor bureau that may assign employees to work for the MNE. In Singapore, which is high on the cultural dimensions of power distance and masculinity, it is legal to specify race, age, and sex requirements in job advertisements, which would violate American Equal Employment Opportunity law.

Once an employee is hired, the MNE needs to deal with communication and integration challenges. Sixty percent of Citigroup's workforce lack knowledge of English, a key obstacle to the firm's effort to leverage its global reach.[18] A formal career planning system, in which people are evaluated in terms of skills, abilities, and traits that will be tested, scored, and computerized, may appear to be impersonal in collective cultures. Individualistic societies use more cognitive testing because they emphasize performance, individual rights, and individual interests, whereas collective cultures emphasize loyalty and organizational compatibility that cannot be assessed via cognitive tests.[19] Personality profiles generated in the United States may be meaningless in Japan where assertiveness is not appreciated.

Finally, the MNE is expected to monitor employment conditions not only at home, but also in its subsidiaries and among its subcontractors. Wal-Mart has been accused of buying from vendors that use child labor in Bangladesh, whereas Nike recently admitted to worker abuse occurring in its Indonesian factories, ranging from verbal abuse to sexual coercion.[20] More recently, Apple has committed to rectify what it defined as minor variations from the labor code in its Chinese supplier, and it now conducts an extensive annual audit of its suppliers worldwide for compliance with both local laws and regulations and its own code of conduct. Even letting go of an errant supplier will no longer satisfy many of the NGOs (non-governmental organizations) that monitor worker treatment, as Disney found in early 2007 when a Hong Kong-based group protested its retreat from a mainland factory. In 2010, the company conducted 5,800 audits of the more than 25,000 facilities licensed to make its products in approximately 100 countries. To deal with unscrupulous suppliers that try to hide their violations (e.g., through bribery of external auditors), Disney has also set up an online system to collect reports on supplier violations of its labor and environmental standards.

Country-Specific Issues

As in other functional realms, the need for adjustment in corporate policies and practices is anchored in variations across labor markets. In transition economies like Vietnam and Romania, older employees who have grown accustomed to a central planning system often have difficulty adjusting to the higher productivity expected in an MNE. For younger, highly skilled employees, the problem is different. Despite having large workforces, skilled employees are often in short supply due to lack of educational infrastructure. In China, for example, one of the greatest problems facing MNEs is very high turnover, a problem that undermines investment in recruitment and training and stints growth prospects. To overcome the problem, Ford Motor Company offers retention incentives to its Chinese workers in the form of a housing loan that is forgiven after seven years of service and tuition reimbursement for those pursuing an MBA degree. China is also the only country in which Ford operates where individuals who have left the company can be rehired.

Interim Summary

1. Boards of directors increasingly include non-nationals as a way to deal with growing globalization and introduce new perspectives.
2. Ethnocentric, polycentric, regiocentric, and geocentric are the main staffing strategies of the MNE.
3. For reasons of local knowledge and cost, host-country nationals constitute the bulk of the MNE workforce abroad.

The Expatriate Workforce

Types and Distribution of Expatriates

Expatriate numbers are small relative to total MNE employment. Many MNEs (e.g., Ford and Johnson & Johnson) have attempted to reduce the number of their expatriates as a cost reduction measure, as well as to create career opportunities and tap the skills of local employees. Yet, with the growth of global operations and increased demand for their skills, expatriate numbers are growing. A 2006 Mercer survey found that 38 percent of the firms surveyed have increased the number of international transfers over the previous two years, while 47 percent maintained the same number. Forty-four percent reported an increase in international transfers between firm locations other than headquarters.[21]

There are different types of expatriates.[22] The **traditional expatriate**, typically an experienced executive, is selected for his/her managerial or technical skills for a period that usually lasts between one and five years. Some members of this group become **international cadres** who move from one foreign assignment to another, seldom returning to their home country, sometimes becoming **permanent expatriates** who stay in overseas assignments for extended periods of time, or even permanently. **Young, inexperienced expatriates** are sent for six months to five years, usually on local hire terms. **Temporaries** go on short assignments, up to one year. Organization Resource Counselors (ORC) reports that 77 percent of 500 MNEs it surveyed expect to increase temporary assignments.[23] Still another type is the **expatriate trainee**, who is placed abroad for training purposes as part of initiation into an MNE. For instance, Johnson & Johnson places new executive recruits in another country for an 18-month period.[24] A PricewaterhouseCoopers (PwC) survey of 270 European organizations employing 65,000 expatriates found a significant increase in "short-term, commuter, and virtual assignments" over the past two years. Short-term assignment increased by 54 percent whereas virtual assignments increased by 44 percent.

Two-thirds of the firms in the PwC survey employ virtual expatriates, up from 44 percent earlier. The **virtual expatriate** takes on foreign assignments without physically relocating. A frequent flier, the virtual expatriate uses videoconferencing and telecommunications to stay in touch. Examples include Ian Hunter, who manages the Middle East and Pakistan for London-based SmithKline Beecham, and Gerals Lukomsli, who manages Central Eastern Europe, the Middle East, and Africa for Motorola. Both manage from England. Rajiv Bhatia oversees hotels in Mexico and other countries from his New Jersey base for Cendant Corp., a franchisee for Howard Johnson and other US hotel chains. Arte Nathan, the senior human resource officer for Las Vegas-based Wynn Resorts, oversaw the recruitment of 5,000 employees for his company's new (2006) casino in Macau (a Special Administrative Region of China) mostly using electronic communications. Among the allures of the virtual expatriate are low cost, avoiding family adjustment, and not having to relocate.[25]

Using Expatriates: Pros and Cons

MNEs use expatriates "to get the business off the ground, put in the infrastructure, as well as to prepare a plan to eventually change the mix of expatriates versus nationals."[26] Still, expatriates continue to be necessary in many locations, and not only as a means to control operations and instill corporate culture. In many developing nations, locals are not yet ready to assume senior management positions. In addition to contributing essential knowledge and experience, expatriates serve as a mechanism of control and as a way to transmit corporate culture and goals.[27] By rotating expatriates, MNEs establish and maintain informal networks that are conducive to the sharing of knowledge and coordination among units. Expatriation creates a global perspective and is essential to knowledge and technology transfer. A senior Corning executive observed:

> *Five to ten years ago, companies were using expatriates largely for command and control or to transfer specific knowledge. Today, in an effective local organization we are looking for learning that the expatriates can use in their jobs as they move around the globe.*[28]

In addition to the high cost, reasons against using expatriates include the disincentive to the local workforce whose promotion is blocked and who would feel relatively deprived owing to their lower wage levels. Excessive use of expatriates can rob a company of the skills, insight, and initiative of local nationals. Another strike against expatriates is their high rate of failure, discussed in the next section.

Expatriate Failure

Expatriate failure can usually be observed in the case of a premature return to the home country (though the return can also be triggered by personal reasons) or when performance does not meet expectations and this cannot be attributed to objective business reasons (e.g., an economic downturn).

574

The expatriate failure rates reported by companies range widely, with some as low as 15 percent and others as high as 80 percent; it is also known that many expatriates who stay on the job perform inadequately.[29] Japan and China show the highest failure rates for US expatriates, probably a result of differences in culture and business environment.[30] Failure rates for European and Japanese expatriates are reportedly lower than for US expatriates.[31] The relative success of Japanese expatriates may be attributed to the country-specific training they receive for an entire year prior to their assignment; however, the gap may also reflect differences in evaluation methods. Unlike their US counterparts, Japanese expatriates are commonly evaluated on adjustment and host-country knowledge rather than on professional results. Also, because of culture (loss of "face") and other factors, Japanese firms are less likely to repatriate a low-performing expatriate.

The financial cost of expatriate failure is substantial, ranging from \$55,000 to \$150,000[32] and more in direct costs. The real cost of expatriate failure is considerably higher, however. It includes not only the cost of selection, training, preparation, and moving, but also the consequences of poor performance in lower revenues, lost business opportunities, and damage to the firm's reputation, which may undermine future ventures in the host country. Thus, it is important for companies to reduce the failure rate to the extent possible.

The reasons for expatriate failure include spouse's unhappiness (including dual-career issues which today involve almost three-quarters of expatriates), inability to adjust to an unfamiliar environment, personality or emotional immaturity, inability to cope with the responsibilities and stress posed by overseas work, and lack of technical competence.[33] Lack of motivation to work overseas, especially in a location to which the firm attaches little value, is also a problem.[34] More than 80 percent of firms surveyed by PwC had employees who refused overseas assignments due to dual-career and family concerns or the perceived career risk of being away from headquarters ("out of sight; out of mind"). Still, more than half of the firms surveyed reported an increase in the overall number of international assignments. More willing to relocate are executives who have relocated domestically, who find the host country culturally or otherwise appealing, and who see a match with their career plans. Spousal willingness to relocate also plays a major role. Older, better-educated spouses, often members of minority groups and with fewer children, are more likely to relocate.[35]

Despite the dramatic strides made by women up the corporate ladder, they remain underrepresented in the expatriate workforce. This is sometimes the result of an assumption that women will be ineffective in foreign cultures, especially those high on masculinity where women rarely occupy senior management positions (e.g., Japan, or Saudi Arabia, where women are kept away from management positions for religious reasons). The view that women will not be effective in high-masculinity locations is not empirically supported, as evidence suggests expatriate women are viewed first and foremost as foreigners; still, the perception persists.[36]

Expatriate Selection

Among the attributes MNEs are looking for in an expatriate are cultural empathy, adaptability and flexibility, language skills, education, leadership, maturity, and motivation.[37] Adler specifies these competencies: a global perspective, local responsiveness, synergistic learning (integrating learning from multiple cultures), transition and adaptation, cross-cultural interaction, collaboration, and foreign experiences. Especially important is the ability to exercise discretion in choosing when to be locally responsive and when to engage in global integration.[38]

Successful expatriates need three sets of skills. The first set are **personal skills** that facilitate mental and emotional well-being, for example, stress orientation, reinforcement, substitution, physical mobility, technical competence, dealing with alienation, isolation, and realistic expectation prior to departure. The second set are **people skills** such as relational abilities, willingness to communicate, non-verbal communication, respect for others, and empathy for others. The third set are **perception skills**, namely the cognitive process that helps executives understand the behavior of foreigners. This includes flexible attribution and breadth, as well as being open-minded and non-judgmental.[39] Extroversion and being culturally adventurous are important for expatriate success in culturally distant countries.

Expatriate Selection Instruments

A number of instruments assist in the selection of expatriates. The Prospector assesses the potential of aspiring international executives on 14 dimensions: (1) cultural sensitivity; (2) business knowledge; (3) courage; (4) motivational ability; (5) integrity; (6) insight; (7) commitment; (8) risk taking; (9) seeking feedback; (10) using feedback; (11) being culturally adventurous; (12) seeking learning opportunities; (13) open to criticism; and (14) having flexibility.[40] Another instrument is the Overseas Assignment Inventory (OAI), developed by Tucker International. This instrument uses these predictors of success on a foreign assignment: expectations; open-mindeness; respect for others' beliefs; trust in people; tolerance; locus of control; flexibility; patience; social adaptability; initiative; risk taking; sense of humor; and spouse communication.[41]

Role-based simulations have become especially popular in recent years as a selection tool. These simulations are either generic or country-specific, such as Motorola's China program. They have proved quite effective. Danone, the French food giant, was able to reduce the failure rate among its expatriates from 35 to 3 percent in the three years it has been using such evaluation and selection programs.[42]

Preparing for a Foreign Assignment

Expatriates entering a foreign country must adjust to new job responsibilities and to a new environment, including a different culture. The first adjustment phase is anticipatory and takes place before departure. In-country adjustment follows. Adjustment varies by individual factors (self-efficacy, relation, and perception skills), job-related factors (role clarity, role discretion, role novelty, and role conflict), organization culture (culture novelty, social support, and logistical help), organization socialization, and non-work factors such as culture novelty and family-spouse adjustment. Language fluency and previous assignments also influence adjustment.[43]

Adjusting to a new culture is an especially challenging task for expatriates. Five determinants of cross-cultural adjustment have been identified:[44] pre-departure cross-cultural training; previous overseas experience; multiple-candidate, multi-criteria selection; individual skills, including self-dimension skills (to maintain mental health, psychological well-being, self-efficacy, and effective stress management), relational skills (to interact with host nationals), and perceptual skills (to correctly perceive and evaluate the host environment); and non-work factors such as cultural distance and spouse and family adjustment. Matching expatriates' previous cross-cultural experiences with the target countries, and moving expatriates gradually from culturally similar countries to culturally distant countries, have also been found to mitigate cultural adjustment.[45] The U-Curve Theory suggests that individuals exposed to a new culture go through four stages of adjustment. In Stage 1, "honeymoon," they are fascinated by the new culture. In Stage 2, "culture shock," infatuation with the new culture is replaced by disillusionment and the frustration of having to cope with it on a daily basis. In Stage 3, "adjustment," individuals gradually adapt to the new culture and learn how to behave appropriately. In Stage 4, "mastery," individuals incrementally learn how to function smoothly in the new culture.[46]

Expatriate Training

Although such training has been proved to reduce expatriate failure,[47] only 30 percent of US firms conduct cross-cultural training, compared to 70 percent of European and Japanese firms. The reasons for the low US rate include a belief that cross-cultural training programs are ineffective, trainee dissatisfaction, a short span between selection and relocation, and a perception that the short-term nature of many overseas assignments does not warrant the expense of cross-cultural training.[48]

Training for an overseas assignment has two components.[49] The first is information-giving, consisting of: (a) practical information on living conditions in the destination country; (b) area studies (i.e., facts about the country's environment); and (c) cultural awareness information. There are no empirical studies that measure the effectiveness of practical information. Evidence suggests that areas studies training is generally useful, although it is not very helpful in terms of equipping expatriates with the skills necessary to work effectively in the destination culture. Similar evidence applies to cultural awareness programs. The second set of activities in cross-cultural training consists of experiential learning, which combines cognitive and behavioral techniques. The goal is to acquire intercultural effectiveness skills that include transition stress management, relationship building, cross-cultural communication, and negotiation techniques.[50] A number of studies suggest that such training is especially valuable.[51]

Effective cross-cultural training requires an integrated approach consisting of both general cultural orientation and specific cultural development. Content and sequencing of training content are critical for success. Yoshida and Brislin[52] list five cultural training guidelines. First, *identify*— become aware of which skills you need to function well in the target culture. Second, *understand*— know why, where, when, to whom, and how the behavior is appropriate. Third, use *cultural informants to understand specifics*—observe and consult people from the target culture to make sure you are using the behaviors in the proper context and are delivering them appropriately. Fourth, *practice*—it is only through practice that proficiency in a new skill is gained. Fifth, *deal with emotions*—trainees should anticipate strong emotional reactions to cultural differences, as well as to the new behaviors they will be using.

Harrison proposes a two-stage cultural orientation.[53] The first stage is designed to focus trainees' attention and prepare them for cross-cultural encounters in general. This stage consists of: (a) self-assessment of factors that may influence one's receptiveness to, and propensity for, effective cross-cultural assignments; and (b) cultural awareness of the general dimensions on which most cultures differ and the potential impact of these differences for expatriates. The second stage, specific cultural orientation, is designed to develop a trainee's ability to interact effectively within the specific culture to which he or she will be assigned. This stage also includes two phases: (1) knowledge acquisition (e.g., *retention*) of the language and customs in the specific culture, and (2) skills training (*reproduction*) in the application of appropriate behaviors in the specific culture.

Choosing a Training Method

Tung proposes a contingency framework for determining the nature and level of rigor of training based on the degree of interaction required in the overseas position and the cultural distance between the expatriate's native and new culture. If the expected interaction between expatriates and HCNS is low and the cultural distance is also low, training should focus on task-related rather than culture-related issues, and the level of rigor required is relatively low. If expected interaction and cultural distance are high, training should focus on the new culture and on cross-cultural skills development as well as on the new task, and the level of rigor should be moderate to high.[54]

Another training model is based on social learning theory and is focused on the degree of cognitive involvement by the trainee. The model distinguishes between processes-symbolic modeling, which is based on observation of modeled behavior, and participative modeling, which requires observation and participation in the modeled behaviors.[55] In addition to training methods, the model includes level of training rigor, the duration of training relative to the degree of interaction, and cultural novelty. For example, if the level of interaction and the cultural distance are low, the length of training should be less than a week and such methods as area or cultural briefings, films, and books are appropriate. If the individual is going overseas for a period of two to 12 months and is expected to have some interaction with host nationals, training should be more rigorous and last longer (one to four weeks), and role-play would be appropriate. If the individual is leaving for a novel culture and the expected interaction with host nationals is intense, training should be rigorous and last as long as two months. Sensitivity training and some field experiences would be appropriate.

Compensation

MNE compensation programs are geared to attract and retain qualified employees, facilitate transfer between HQ and affiliates, create consistency and equity in compensation, and maintain competitiveness.[56] Compensation systems derive from MNE international strategies (multi-domestic, international, global, and transnational) as well as its product and/or organizational life cycle. They also reflect the host-country laws, regulations, and cultural traditions. Research suggests that an appropriate compensation package should reduce expenses while enhancing commitment to the employer, job satisfaction, and willingness to relocate internationally.[57]

An effective compensation system starts with accurate performance appraisal. Challenges in conducting performance appraisal for expatriates include choosing the evaluator, difference in performance perceptions between home and host countries, communication difficulties with headquarters, inadequate recording of performance objectives, home (parent) country ethnocentrism, and indifference to the foreign experience of the expatriate. Other problems are difficulty in balancing local responsiveness and global integration, non-comparability of data from different subsidiaries/regions, and environmental variations across subsidiaries. Decisions need to be made regarding raters' location (home or host country) and their expatriate experience, and regarding the use of standard, customized, or hybrid evaluation forms.[58] Studies found that a balanced set of raters from host and home countries and more frequent appraisals relate positively to perceived accuracy of evaluation; however, most respondent firms did not follow these practices.[59] The use of a balanced set of raters from host and home country increased accuracy as did the use of host-country raters.

Cost and Elements of Expatriate Compensation

The cost of employing expatriates is high, up to three to five multiples of domestic salary for a local hire.[60] The cost can easily reach $350,000 and more for the first year and much more in high-cost locations such as Japan or Norway. Recent trends suggest an effort to reduce the costs of expatriate packages (rather than benefits) while retaining end-of-term bonus.[61]

Expatriate compensation comprises the following elements:

- **Salary**—Base pay plus incentives (merit, profit sharing, bonus plans), determined via job evaluation or competency-based plans. Incentives—in the form of cash or deferred payment—may be based on home-country plans, host-country plans, or both. Payment may be deferred until return if the home-country's tax rate is lower.
- **Housing**—Most MNEs pay allowances for housing or provide company-owned housing for expatriates. Housing allowance is provided to maintain expatriates' living standards at their home-country level.
- **Services allowance and premiums**—These are paid to compensate expatriates for differences in expenditures between the home and host country. Allowances are provided for higher cost of living in the host country, home leave (home-country visits), education (children's tuition, language classes), and relocation (moving, shipping, and storage, temporary living quarters). The balance sheet approach is the most widely used technique for equalizing the purchasing power of home- and host-country employees and to offset qualitative differences between locations.[62] The housing allowance is a function of the expected hardship in the host country and the job type, but it takes into account that the expatriate represents the employer in the host country. A hardship allowance is paid to compensate the expatriate for a variety of factors that make expatriate assignment difficult.

Exhibit 17.5 shows a hardship evaluation for an expatriate in Bangalore, India.

Tax equalization—Expatriates face two potential sources of income tax liability: home and host. Most countries tax resident citizens and noncitizen residents on their foreign incomes. The United States, however, taxes not only resident citizens and resident noncitizens, but also nonresident citizens on their foreign incomes (the only other country that has such a tax policy is Eritrea), although it exempts the first $95,100 (inflation adjusted) of foreign wages. In 2006, Congress effectively increased taxation on US expatriates by including housing benefits within the allotted

579

		Hardship Evaluation
Prepared for:	AIRINC	**Report Date:** March 2013
Location:	Bangalore, India	**Review Date:** November 2012

Total Points: 51
Percentage: 20%

	Maximum Points	Location Points
Category I: Assessment of Physical Threat		
Actual or potential violence in area	15	6
Hostility of local population	10	4
Prevalence of disease	15	10
Limited medical facilities and services	10	5
Total Category I	50	25
Category II: Assessment of Discomfort		
Difficult physical environment	10	7
Geographic isolation	10	6
Cultural or psychological isolation	10	4
Total Category II	30	17
Category III: Assessment of Inconvenience		
Shortcomings in educational system	5	2
Restricted availability or low quality of housing	5	3
Limited community and recreational facilities	5	2
Poor availability and quality of goods and services	5	2
Total Category III	20	9
Total Points	**100**	**51**

Exhibit 17.5 Hardship evaluation in international development
Source: ©2013 AIRINC Associates for International Research, Inc.

exemption. Depending on tax treaties and duration of stay, the host country may tax the expatriate as well, but the tax is credited on the US tax return. **Tax equalization** is an adjustment to expatriate pay to reflect tax rates in the home country.[63]

Exhibit 17.6 shows a sample of how foreign compensation is calculated. Note that the net foreign compensation is 60 percent more than the base salary. Exhibit 17.7 shows a sample of how the total cost of an overseas assignment is estimated.

Prepared for:	Sample Report		
Home Location:	United States	**Report Date:**	28 March 2013
Host Location:	Shanghai, China	**Effective Date:**	February 2013
Employee Name:	Sample	**Rate of Exchange (ROE):**	1 USD = 6.22 CNY
Family Size:	Differentials = 4 Taxes = 1		

All amounts are annual	CNY	ROE	USD
1 Base Salary			125,000
a. Home Location Hypothetical Tax			(34,355)
b. After-Tax Income			90,645
2 Additional Payments			
a. Hardship Premium (10% of Base Salary)			12,500
3 Housing and Utilities Costs			
a. Host Location (Variant: CLP)	594,393 /	6.22 =	95,562
b. Home Location			(19,836)
c. Housing and Utilities Differential			75,726
4 Goods and Services Costs			
a. Host Location (Variant: CLP)	511,876 /	6.22 =	82,295
b. Home Location			(60,378)
c. Goods and Services Differential			21,917
d. Goods and Services Index			136.3
5 Total Host Location Payments	1,106,269		
6 Net Foreign Compensation (1b) + (2a) + (3c) + (4c)			200,788

Notes:
Hypothetical Income Tax Detail (2013 US Federal Income Tax including Social Security):
Deduction: Homeowner
Federal Tax = USD (25,493)
Social Security = USD (8,862)
Total Hypothetical Income Tax = USD (34,355)

Goods and Services Costs Variant: CLP = Goods & Services Differentails (CLP)
Housing and Utilities Costs Variant: CLP = Rent Expenditures (CLP)

Host Location Housing & Utilities Detail:
Annual Host Rent Expenditure = CNY 534,232
Annual Host Utilities Expenditure = CNY 60,161

Exhibit 17.6 International compensation calculation
Source: ©2013 AIRINC Associates for International Research, Inc.

Assignment Cost Estimator

Prepared for:	AIRINC Non-Revenue
Home location:	Chicago, ILL, USA
Host location:	Singapore
Employee:	Sample
Employee title:	
Family size:	Differential=3, Tax=3
Base salary:	100,000 USD
Incentives:	15,000 USD
Social security paid in:	Host location
US filing status:	Joint

Policy:	Home-based Equalized
Effective date:	March 2013
Report currency rate:	1 USD = 1 USD
Exchange rate:	1 USD = 1.24 SGD
Assignment start:	28 March 2013
Assignment end:	28 March 2016
Duration:	3 Years, 1 Day
Report years:	Calendar
Annual compensation increase:	0%
Annual allowance increase:	0%

Executive summary: (in USD)

Category	2013	2014	2015	2016	2017
Salary and incentive compensation	87,900	115,000	115,000	27,600	0
Pre-assignment costs	82,300	0	0	0	0
Costs during assignment	168,000	220,000	220,000	52,900	0
Return costs	0	0	0	62,700	0
Tax costs	97,700	85,100	81,400	35,100	100
Assignment costs per year	435,900	420,100	416,400	178,300	100

Total assignment cost: **1,450,800**

Exhibit 17.7 Estimation of total assignment cost

Source: ©2013 AIRINC Associates for International Research, Inc.

Approaches to Expatriate Compensation

There are three basic approaches to expatriate compensation: home-based, host-based, and hybrid. All three approaches assume that the employee will remain vested in home-country social security, pensions, and other retirement programs. All three motivate employees to take the assignment, successfully complete it, and return without extraordinary loss or gain. A **home-country compensation system** links base expatriate salary to the salary structure of the home country. For instance, the salary of a US executive transferred to Sweden will be based on the United States level, rather than the Swedish one. In a **host country-based (localized) compensation system**, base salary for an expatriate is linked to the pay structure in the host country; however, supplemental compensation provisions are often linked to home-country salary structures. The combination produces an international compensation approach oriented toward the higher of host or home gross-salary level and the lowest of host-, home- or third-country taxes.[64] Elements related to home country will be gradually phased out from the fourth to the sixth years in the host country. A study by Watson Wyatt Worldwide found that, of the US-based foreign subsidiaries studied, 66 percent departed from their home-country compensation plans to offer US-style executive compensation plans.

Finally, a **hybrid compensation system** blends features from the home- and host-based approaches. The purpose is to create an international expatriate workforce that, while not hailing from a single location, is paid as if it were.[65] The simplest form of a hybrid system assumes that all expatriates, regardless of country of origin, belong to one nationality. Other derivatives of this system involve the application of identical cost-of-living allowances to all nationalities, uniform premiums, and uniform housing and other local allowances.

Exhibit 17.8 summarizes the features, advantages, and disadvantages of the three approaches.

Other expatriate compensation approaches include lump-sum/cafeteria and negotiation. The lump-sum or cafeteria approach offers expatriates more choices. Salary is set according to the home-country system, but instead of breaking compensation into its component parts, firms offer a total allowance package and each expatriate makes his or her own selection of pay and benefits. The logic is to avoid paying for items that expatriates do not need or value. The negotiation approach assumes that employer and employee find a mutually acceptable package and is most common in smaller firms with very few expatriates. This approach creates comparability and potentially inequity perceptions.

Culture and Compensation

Business performance improves when HRM practices are consistent with national culture (see also Chapter 6).[66] In masculine cultures, work units with more merit-based reward practices were found to perform better, while in feminine cultures, work units with fewer merit-based reward practices were higher performers. The propensity to use both seniority-based and skill-based compensation systems was positively correlated with uncertainty avoidance. Compensation practices based on individual performance were correlated with individualism. High masculinity was associated with less use of flexible benefits, workplace child-care programs, career-break schemes, and maternity-leave programs.[67] High collectivism was found to be negatively related to individual- and equity-based reward, and a merit-based promotion system.[68] However, there are occasions where collectivists compromise cultural traditions to help their organization survive.[69]

	Home-based	Host-based	Hybrid
Features	• Consistent treatment of expatriates of same nationality • Link with home-country structure/economy • Different pay levels for different nationalities • No relationship to local employee	• Equity with local nationals • All nationalities paid the same • Simple administration • Variation in "value" by localities • No link to home-country structure/economy	• All nationalities paid equitably • Some link to home-country structure/economy • No relationship to local employees
Applicable Conditions	• Temporary international assignment (2–5 years) • Expatriates will ultimately be repatriated to their country of origin • The number of different nationalities in any one host location is relatively low • International staff predominate in higher-level host location jobs	• International assignments are of indefinite duration • Expatriates tend to be assigned to high-pay countries and will ultimately be repatriated to their country of origin • The number of different nationalities in any one host location is relatively high • Host-country local staff predominate in higher-level host location jobs	
Advantages	• Expatriates neither gain nor lose financially • Facilitates mobility • Eases repatriation	• All employees operate on equivalent pay • System is easy to administer • All employees, including expatriates, are paid the same • Most suitable for international assignments of indefinite duration	• All expatriate nationalities are paid equitably • Assists transfers and development of an international management cadre
Disadvantages	• Expensive • No link to local pay structure • Expatriates of the same seniority from different origins will be paid differently • Administration can be complex	• Complicates reentry • Most applicable when salary and living standards improve, thereby becoming expensive • Unprotected fluctuations in the exchange rate put company and employee at additional risk • Certain host-country benefits are not applicable to expatriates • Difficult to transfer to lower-paying location	• Complicated administration • Sometimes difficult to communicate • No link to local pay structure

Exhibit 17.8 Expatriate compensation systems

Source: M.E. Schell and C.M. Solomon, *Capitalizing on the Global Workforce: A Strategic Guide to Expatriate Management*, New York: McGraw-Hill, 1997.

The following recommendations have been made vis-à-vis compensation in different cultures:[70]

■ In high power-distance cultures, MNEs should pursue hierarchical compensation for local managers, pay and benefits should be tied to position, and a large pay differential between echelons is desirable.

- In cultures with high individualism, performance-based pay and extrinsic rewards are important. In cultures with low individualism, group-based pay and compensation packages that reflect seniority and family needs are more acceptable.

- In cultures with high masculinity, MNEs should pursue a compensation strategy for local managers that recognizes and rewards competitiveness, aggressiveness, and dominance. In cultures with low masculinity, compensation should focus on social benefits, quality of work life, and equity.

- In cultures with high uncertainty avoidance, structured and consistent pay plans are preferred. Salary and benefits decisions should be centralized, with no variable pay plans or discretionary salary allocation. Where uncertainty avoidance is low, pay should be closely linked to performance.

- In high uncertainty-avoidance cultures, it is better to have centralized pension systems with multiple controls and safeguards.

- Low uncertainty-avoidance cultures are more open to defined contribution pensions with flexible plan implementation.

- Separate pension plans for different classes of employees are acceptable in high power-distance cultures.

- In masculine cultures with moderate to high uncertainty avoidance, policies designed to protect job security are more welcome.

- Employees from feminine cultures with moderate to high uncertainty avoidance prefer policies designed to protect income security.

- Employees from feminine cultures prefer family-friendly management practices, as well as other policies designed to maximize quality of work life.

- Employees in low individualistic and low power-distance cultures prefer flexible benefit programs.

- Health programs in low power-distance cultures should be uniform for all, while employee choice of health insurance providers works better in individualistic cultures.

Performance evaluation also varies across cultures. Management by Objectives (MBO), where subordinates and supervisors agree to measurable goals, tends to fail in high power-distance culture (e.g., in East Asia). Employees in such cultures also tend to shun "360 degrees" evaluation where subordinates participate in the evaluation of their superiors. In cultures with high uncertainty avoidance, it is hard to get subordinates to commit to risky goals. Cultural differences also affect the relative importance of different performance dimensions; for example, in collectivist cultures, group harmony and cohesiveness tend to be more important than performance.

Repatriation

The repatriation of expatriates represents an adjustment that is equally, if not more difficult, than the adjustment to the overseas assignment.[71] Some of the problems are mundane, from inability to borrow due to lack of credit history, to limitations to housing that got more expensive during one's absence; others are emotional, including, surprisingly, cultural adjustment. Returning expatriates do not expect their repatriation to be problematic because they are coming back to familiar turf. However, they do not take into account that their home environment has changed during their stay abroad and that they themselves have changed. Most returning employees are dissatisfied with the repatriation process. Most US firms do not provide a written guarantee of reassignment prior to departure, and most returnees do not know what their next assignment will be prior to repatriation. Even those with a suitable reassignment often feel that their employers fail to make effective use of their foreign experience. With the exception of housing assistance, most firms do not provide spouse career counseling or other forms of family repatriation assistance. It is therefore not surprising that a quarter of repatriated employees leave their firm within one year of repatriation,[72] and that many decline to undertake subsequent international assignments.

Interim Summary

1. MNEs use expatriate staff to get businesses off the ground, disseminate knowledge and corporate culture to the foreign subsidiary, develop their staff, and control and coordinate their subsidiaries.
2. Many expatriates have difficulty adjusting to a new country and to an unfamiliar business environment, and failure rates are high.
3. Adaptability and a non-judgmental stance toward other cultures help expatriates succeed in their mission.
4. Proper selection and training reduce expatriate failure rates.
5. Repatriation is a significant challenge which many firms have yet to address.

HRM in International Affiliates

Human resource issues and problems vary depending on the type of foreign affiliate involved. Although wholly owned subsidiaries (WOSs) employ up to three employee groups (PCNs, HCNs, and TCNs), international joint ventures (IJVs) employ multiple employee groups, as follows: (a) Foreign Parent(s) Expatriates (i.e., nationals of the country in which the headquarters of the foreign parent(s) is (are) located, assigned by that parent(s) to the affiliate); (b) Host Parent(s) Transferees (host-country nationals employed by the host parent(s) and transferred to the affiliate from the host-parent headquarters or one of its subsidiaries); (c) Host-Country Nationals (nationals of the host country, hired directly by the affiliate); (d) Third-Country Expatriates of the host parent(s) (third-country nationals who are neither nationals of the host country, nor of the foreign parent('s) country(ies) and assigned by the host parent(s) to work in the affiliate); (e) Third-Country Expatriates of the foreign parent(s) (third-country nationals assigned by the foreign parent(s) to work in the affiliate); (f) Third-Country Expatriates of the affiliate (third-country nationals recruited directly by the affiliate, who are neither nationals of the parent(s) country(ies) nor of the country in which the affiliate operates); (g) Foreign Headquarters Executives (i.e., policy makers at the headquarters of the foreign parent(s), who play a major role in the functioning of the affiliate at headquarters or are board members of the affiliate); (h) Host Headquarters Executives (i.e., policy makers at the headquarters of the host parent(s), who play a major role in the functioning of the affiliate at headquarters or are board members of the affiliate).

586

Human Resource Problems in Foreign Affiliates

The following human resource problems can be expected in WOSs and IJVs.[73]

- *Staffing Friction.* Parent companies prefer to appoint their own transferees or expatriates to key positions in the affiliate as a control measure. When the staffing policy is not contractually specified, friction often ensues. In many cases, friction also develops regarding the level of staffing, with the host parent looking at the IJV as a way of "unloading" extra staff. In both WOSs and IJVs, HCNs are often deprived of opportunities to staff the most senior positions.

- *Blocked Promotion.* In both types of affiliates, local employees can be frustrated by the lack of promotion opportunities if senior positions are reserved for "outsiders." This problem is especially serious in IJVs where the "outsiders" may not only be the foreign expatriates, but also transferees of the host parent. When such "outsiders" are abundant, local staff may be reluctant to join, stay, or contribute their best efforts to the affiliate.

- *Exile Syndrome and Reentry Difficulties.* Feeling "exiled" in an overseas assignment because of fear of interruption of one's career track back home occurs in both WOSs and IJVs. WOSs are more closely integrated, however, so an assignment to a subsidiary might be less disruptive. Assignees in an IJV, on the other hand, may be working with, or supervised by, employees of another company. They will not report directly to their parent headquarters, nor will their supervisors be in a position to assess their performance. Exile syndrome may be damaging to the foreign affiliate because it may lead employees to bypass their supervisors in the affiliate, report achievements rather than failures, and take a short-term perspective.

- *Split Loyalty.* Split loyalty is unique to IJVs. Employees recruited by the host or the foreign parent may remain loyal to that parent rather than shift their allegiance to the IJV. This happens especially where employees expect to return to the parent firm at the end of their assignment or when the IJV has a predetermined life span. The result is suspicion and low level of cooperation that prevents the venture from attaining its potential.

- *Compensation Gaps.* The problem of compensation gaps (e.g., HCNs receiving much lower pay than expatriates) occurs in both types of affiliates. For example, many US-based executives of foreign MNEs earn more than their superiors in Europe or Asia. IJVs suffer from an additional problem of relative deprivation however, where employees receive compensation packages that are not necessarily based on universal criteria, such as skills and experience, but on affiliation with a particular parent or the IJV itself. Each MNE has an established compensation policy, and in many cases, the differences are significant. Moreover, each employee group has a different perception about what is the most desirable package of benefits. The result is a feeling of deprivation and consequently reduced motivation and morale.

- *Blocked Communication.* Effective communication among parent firms and between a parent and an affiliate can be hampered by a combination of cultural differences and variations in organizational procedures and norms. Because of differences in parents' objectives, communications may be distorted or withheld by their respective employees. Such communication blockages represent an impediment to decision making. The problem is especially serious in IJVs with a 50/50 equity distribution.

- *Limited Delegation.* Many parent firms try to maintain control of their affiliate by limiting the scope of authority and decision-making power they delegate. This is especially true where parents have conflicting goals, where they depend on the affiliate for scarce and vital resources, and when they feel that the affiliate's staff is loyal to the other parent. Under these conditions, the affiliate's management finds it difficult to operate effectively, especially in a fast-changing environment.

■ *Screening of Information*. Many firms are hesitant to pass information and technology to an affiliate, especially an IJV whose partner might be a present or a future competitor. The result is self-defeating, with the other parent(s) limiting information as well. The venture is then unable to operate effectively.

■ *Unfamiliarity*. Expatriates who join a foreign affiliate are unfamiliar, in most cases, with the environment in which the venture operates. In IJVs, most employees are also unfamiliar with the unique structure of this organization and with its conflict-prone nature.

Research provides some suggestions for alleviating some of the human resource problems in foreign affiliates. Among the solutions are organization development and training, identifying and rewarding leadership, improving interpersonal and negotiation channels, and career planning that takes account of the overlapping yet diverse tracks among the member organizations. Still, relatively little is known about the training and preparation required for operating effectively in a specific foreign affiliate. At the same time, we are only beginning to consider the adjustments when moving, say, from a WOS to an IJV. Exhibit 17.9 provides a starting point.

Interim Summary

1. Wholly owned subsidiaries (WOSs) and international joint ventures (IJVs) share many human resource problems, though IJVS tend to be more problematic due to such problems as split loyalty
2. Firms should preempt and actively manage human resource problems in their international affiliates before they adversely affect performance.

Educational Focus	Wholly Owned Subsidiary	International Joint Venture
Cultural sensitivity/national	High	High
Cultural sensitivity/org. level	Low	High
Interpersonal skills	Low	High
Negotiation/bargaining skills	Med	High
Entrepreneurial skills	High	High
Leadership skills	High	High
Knowledge/global environment	High	High
Knowledge/regional	High	High
Knowledge/firm-specific	Med	Low
Knowledge/functional area	High	Med

Exhibit 17.9 Management education requirements in two types of foreign affiliates

Source: Adapted from E. Bailey and O. Shenkar, "Management education for international joint venture managers," *Leadership and Organization Development Journal* 14, 1993: 15–20.

Chapter Summary

1. Strategic international human resource management (SIHRM) determines the degree of similarity between the HRM practices of the parent company and those of its foreign affiliates. IHRM changes as the firm develops its international presence and capabilities.

2. Boards of directors are becoming more global, with a significant increase in the proportion of non-native members.

3. Although small in numbers, expatriate employees play a vital role in the operations of MNEs. Since expatriate failure rates are high, companies need to pay attention to their recruitment, selection, training, and compensation.

4. Approaches to expatriate compensation include home-based, host-based, and hybrid of both systems. Lump-sum/cafeteria and negotiation are additional approaches that offer more flexibility, but are difficult to administer.

5. Companies pay close attention to their local workforce and need to adapt practices to local environments within their overall strategic focus.

6. Significant correlations exist between cultural dimensions and human resource practices.

7. HRM problems in foreign affiliates vary by the type of affiliate (e.g., a wholly foreign-owned subsidiary versus an international joint venture), among other factors.

Notes

1   *How The CEOs Drive Global Growth*, Conference Board 1184-97RR.
2   *Wall Street Journal*, November 24, 1992, citing Towers Perrin.
3   N.J. Adler, "Cross-cultural management: Issues to be faced," *International Studies of Management and Organization*, 1983.
4   F. Acuff, *International and Domestic Human Resources Functions: Innovations in International Compensation*, New York: Organization Resources Counselors, 1984.
5   "Developing a global mindset at Johnson & Johnson—1998," IMD case #GM791, June 1, 1999.
6   S. Taylor, S. Beechler, and N. Napier, "Toward an integrative model of strategic international human resource management," *Academy of Management Review*, 21, 4, 1996, 959–985.
7   R. Schuller, P. Dowling, and H. DeCieri, "An integrative framework of strategic international human resource management," *International Journal of Human Resource Management*, 1, 1993, 717–764.
8   R.G. Vernon, "International investment and international trade in the product cycle," *Quarterly Journal of Economics*, 1996, 190–207.
9   N.J. Adler and F. Ghadar, "Strategic human resource management: A global perspective." In R. Pieper (ed.), *Human Resource Management: An International Comparison*, Berlin: DeGruyter, 1990.
10 H.V. Perlmutter, "The tortuous evolution of the multinational corporation," *Columbia Journal of World Business*, 4, 1969, 9–18.
11 R.L. Tung, "Selection and training procedures of US, European, and Japanese multinationals," *California Management Review*, 25, 1982, 57–71.
12 "Won Choi Hae, Korea's Samsung seeks a bit more worldliness," *Wall Street Journal*, March 22, 2002.
13 J.A. Song, "South Korean technology companies fill skills vacuum," *Financial Times*, June 15, 2006, 22.

14 N. Boyacigiller, "The role of expatriates in the management of interdependence, complexity and risk in multinational corporations," *Journal of International Business Studies,* third quarter, 1990, 357–381.

15 *How the CEOs Drive Global Growth*, Conference Board 1184–97-RR.

16 T. Anderson, "US affiliates of foreign companies," *Survey of Current Business*, US Bureau of Economic Analysis, August 2010; A. Linn, "Yes, we do still make things in America," *MSNBC*, March 15, 2010.

17 R. Kopp, "International human resource policies and practices in Japanese, European, and United States multinationals," *Human Resource Management,* 33, 1994, 581–599.

18 P. Beckett, "Citigroup's Menezes plays key game to lift growth via emerging markets," *Wall Street Journal,* February 21, 2001, C1.

19 N. Ramamoorthy and S.J. Carroll, "Individualism/collectivism orientations and reactions toward alternative human resource management practices," *Human Relations,* 51, 1998, 571–588.

20 "Nike admits worker abuse," CNNfn, February 22, 2001, 7.41a.m. ET.

21 "Traveling more lightly," *The Economist*, June 24, 2006, 77.

22 D.R. Briscoe, *International Human Resource Management,* Englewood Cliffs, NJ: Prentice-Hall, 1995.

23 Cited in *Wall Street Journal,* January 16, 2001, B12.

24 "Developing a global mindset at Johnson & Johnson—1998," IMD case #GM791, June 1, 1999.

25 J. Flynn, "E-mail, cellphones and frequent flier miles let 'virtual' expats work abroad but live at home," *Wall Street Journal,* October 25, 1999, A26; J. Millman, "Exporting management savvy," *Wall Street Journal,* October 24, 2000, B1; J.S. Lublin, "Global experience doesn't have to mean going to live overseas," *Wall Street Journal Online,* August 29, 2006.

26 *How The CEOs Drive Global Growth*, Conference Board 1184-97-RR.

27 M.S. Fenwick, H.L.D. DeCieri, and D.E. Welch, "Cultural and bureaucratic control in MNEs: The role of expatriate performance appraisal," *Management International Review,* 39, 1999, 107–124.

28 *How The CEOs Drive Global Growth*, The Conference Board, 1184–97-RR.

29 L. Copeland and L. Griggs, *Going International,* New York: Plume, 1985; D.R. Briscoe, *International Human Resource Management,* Englewood Cliffs, NJ: Prentice-Hall, 1995.

30 Marian Baird, "Eye opening research," *Australian Financial Review*, 86, September 12, 2008.

31 Windham International 1995 survey, cited in *The China Business Review,* May–June 1997, 30.

32 M.E. Mendenhall, E. Dunbar, and G.R. Oddou, "Expatriate selection, training and career pathing: A review and critique," *Human Resource Management,* 26, 1987, 331–345.

33 R.L. Tung, "Expatriate assignments: Enhancing success and minimizing failure," *Academy of Management Executive,* 1, 1987, 117–126.

34 M.E. Mendenhall and G.R. Oddou, "The overseas assignment: A practical look," *Business Horizons,* 31, 5, 1988, 78–84.

35 J.M. Brett and L.K. Stroh, "Willingness to relocate internationally," *Human Resource Management,* 34, 1995, 405–424.

36 N. Adler and D.N. Izraeli, "Women managers: Moving up and across borders." In *Global Perspectives of Human Resource Management,* Englewood Cliffs, NJ: Prentice-Hall, 1994, 165–193; O. Shenkar (ed.), *Business Week,* November 6, 2000, 14.

37 K.E. Baumgarten, "A profile for international managers and its implications for selection and training," Thesis, Faculty of Applied Educational Science, University of Twente, Enschede, the Netherlands, 1992.

38 N.J. Adler and S. Bartholomew, "Managing globally competent people," *Academy of Management Executive,* 6, 1992, 52–65.

39 M.E. Mendenhall and G.R. Oddou, "The overseas assignment: A practical look," *Business Horizons,* 31, 5, 1988, 78–84.

40 G.M. Spreitzer, M.W. McCall Jr. and J.D. Mahoney, "Early identification of international executive potential," *Journal of Applied Psychology,* 82, 1997, 6–29.

41 M.S. Schell and C.M. Solomon, *Capitalizing on the Global Workforce: A Strategic Guide to Expatriate Management,* Chicago, IL: Irwin Professional Publications, 1997.

42 D. Woodruff, "Distractions make global manager a difficult role," *Wall Street Journal,* November 21, 2000, B1.

43 J.S. Black, M. Mendenhall, and G. Oddou, "Toward a comprehensive model of international adjustment: An integration of multiple theoretical perspectives," *Academy of Management Review,* 16, 1991, 291–317.

44 M.E. Mendenhall and G.R. Oddou, "The overseas assignment: A practical look," *Business Horizons,* 31, 5, 1988, 78–84.

45 S. Ayree, Y.W. Char, and J. Chew, "An investigation of the willingness of managerial employees to accept an expatriate assignment," *Journal of Organizational Behavior,* 17, 1996, 267–283.

46 J.S. Black and M. Mendenhall, "The U-curve adjustment hypothesis revisited: A review and theoretical framework," *Journal of International Business Studies,* 22, 1991, 225–247.

47 R.L. Tung, "Expatriate assignments: Enhancing success and minimizing failure," *Academy of Management Executive,* 1, 1987, 117–126.

48 M.E. Mendenhall, E. Dunbar, and G.R. Oddou, "Expatriate selection, training and career pathing: A review and critique," *Human Resource Management,* 26, 1987, 331–345.

49 D.J. Kealey and D.R. Protheroe, "The cross-cultural training for expatriates: An assessment of the literature on the issue," *International Journal of Inter-cultural Relations,* 20, 1996, 141–165.

50 Kealey and Protheroe, "The cross-cultural training for expatriates: An assessment of the literature on the issue."

51 Kealey and Protheroe, "The cross-cultural training for expatriates: An assessment of the literature on the issue."

52 T. Yoshida and R.W. Brislin, "Intercultural skills and recommended behaviors: The psychological perspective for training program," In O. Shenkar (ed.), *Global Perspective of Human Resource Management,* Englewood Cliffs, NJ: Prentice-Hall, 1995, pp. 112–113.

53 J.K. Harrison, "Developing successful expatriate managers: A framework for the structural design and strategic alignment of cross-cultural training programs," *Human Resource Planning,* 17, 1992, 17–35.

54 R.L. Tung, "Expatriate assignments: Enhancing success and minimizing failure," *Academy of Management Executive,* 1, 1987, 117–126.

55 M.E. Mendenhall, E. Dunbar, and G.R. Oddou, "Expatriate selection, training and career pathing: A review and critique," *Human Resource Management,* 26, 1987, 331–345.

56 D.R. Briscoe, *International Human Resource Management,* Englewood Cliffs, NJ: Prentice-Hall, 1995.

57 H.B. Gregersen and L.K. Stroh, "Coming home to the Arctic cold: Antecedents to Finnish expatriate and spouse repatriation adjustment," *Personnel Psychology,* 50, 1997, 635–654; R.A. Guzzo, K.A. Noonan, and E. Elron, "Expatriate managers and the psychological contract," *Journal of Applied Psychology,* 79, 1994, 617–626.

58 H.B. Gregersen, J.S. Black, and J.M. Hite, "Expatriate performance appraisal: Principles, practices, and challenges." In J. Selmer (ed.), *Expatriate Management: New Ideas for International Business,* Westport, CT: Quorum Books, 1995.

59 H.B. Gregersen and J.M. Hite, "Expatriate performance appraisal in US multinational firms," *Journal of International Business Studies,* fourth quarter, 1996, 711–738.

60 The Conference Board 1148-96-RR.

61 C. Spielman and G.A. Tammaro, "Action items for expatriate planning in an economic downturn," *Workspan,* October 2009.

62 G.T. Milkovich and J.M. Newman, *Compensation,* Chicago, IL: Irwin/McGraw-Hill, 1999.

63 Milkovich and Newman, *Compensation.*

64 J.B. Anderson, "Compensating your overseas executives, Part 2: Europe in 1992," *Compensation and Benefits Review,* 1995.

65 M.S. Schell and C.M. Solomon, *Capitalizing on the Global Workforce: A Strategic Guide to Expatriate Management,* Chicago, IL: Irwin, 1997.

66 S. Schneider, "National vs. corporate culture: Implications for human resource management," *Human Resource Management,* 27, 231–246.

67 R.S. Schuller and N. Rogovsky, "Understanding compensation practice variations across firms: The impact of national culture," *Journal of International Business Studies,* 29, 1, 1998, 159–177.

591

68 N. Ramamoorthy and S.J. Carroll, "Individualism/collectivism orientations and reactions toward alternative human resource management practices," *Human Relations,* 51, 1998, 571–588.

69 C.C. Chen, "New trends in reward allocation preferences: A Sino–US comparison," *Academy of Management Journal,* 38, 1995, 408–424.

70 P.S. Hempel, "Designing multinational benefits programs: The role of national culture," *Journal of World Business,* 33, 1998, 277–294.

71 N.J. Adler, "Re-entry: Managing cross-cultural transitions," *Group & Organization Management,* 6, 1981, 341–356.

72 J.S. Black, H.B. Gregersen, and M.E. Mendenhall, "Toward a theoretical framework of repatriation adjustment," *Journal of International Business Studies,* 23, 1992, 737–760.

73 Based on O. Shenkar and Y. Zeira, "Human resource management in international joint ventures: Directions for research," *Academy of Management Review,* 12, 1987, 546–557.

part 6

emerging issues in international business

18 INTERNET AND GLOBAL E-COMMERCE   595

19 SOCIAL RESPONSIBILITY AND CORRUPTION IN THE
   GLOBAL MARKETPLACE   615

20 INTERNATIONAL ENTREPRENEURSHIP   639

chapter 18

internet and global e-commerce

INTERNET AND E-COMMERCE INFRASTRUCTURE   597

CROSS-BORDER E-COMMERCE   603

GLOBAL E-COMMERCE CHALLENGES   607

Do You Know?

1. When shopping online, do you know, or mind, in what country the seller is located?
2. Would having a website make your firm international? Why or why not?
3. Would global e-commerce remove barriers to trade, tariff, and non-tariff?
4. What are the prospects for global e-commerce in the years ahead? What are the opportunities and threats posed by e-commerce to the MNE and the SMIE?

OPENING CASE   eBay in China

The "e-commerce darling" of analysts and the world's leading electronic auctioneer, eBay has struggled in the lucrative and rapidly growing Chinese market. Having failed earlier in the lucrative Japanese market, which the company exited in 2002, eBay turned its attention to South Korea and China, especially the latter, which by 2006 had the second largest number of Internet users after the United States. Initially the market leader in China and South Korea, by 2006 eBay had slipped to second place in both countries. In China, the US-based company fell behind Alibaba's Taobao unit despite repeatedly cutting listing fees and offering listing waivers. In early 2006, after criticizing Alibaba on the grounds that "free is not a business model," eBay was forced to stop charging listing fees on its auction site altogether. Analysts note that the eBay China site was slow to adopt new applications and considered less friendly by users, though the company vigorously denied those claims.

In late 2006, as its market share plummeted to below 20 percent and Taobao's share soared to over 70 percent, eBay reached a cooperation agreement with Baidu, a leading Chinese Internet service company whose search engine dominates the market. The partnership was set up to target the model of multiple services utilized by market leader Alibaba. A number of analysts considered this a desperate move on the part of eBay to turn the tide around and regain a leadership position in the China market. This move, however, was insufficient to stem the hemorrhage. In the second quarter of 2007, as its market share was falling into the single digits, eBay turned its China operations into a joint venture with another Chinese company Tom Online, hoping that its new partner's extensive experience in China could reverse its fortunes in the strategically important market.

Source: M. Nangalindan, "China may be eBay's latest challenge as local rivals eat into market share," *Wall Street Journal*, October 12, 2006, C1; S. Lemon, "Baidu, eBay, expand partnership in China," *Infoworld*, November 9, 2006; S. So and J.C. Westland, *Red Wired: China's Internet Revolution*, London: Marshall Cavendish Business, 2010.

Internet And E-commerce Infrastructure

Internet Diffusion

Exhibit 18.1 shows the number of Internet users (in millions) and the Internet penetration rate (i.e., the percentage of people using the Internet) in each major region of the world. The blue bar represents the number of users in 2000, and the orange bar represents the number of users in 2012. The dramatic difference in height between the two bars for each region reveals rapid growth in the number of users around the world from 2000 to 2012, particularly in those regions with concentrations of developing countries. The exhibit also shows significant differences in Internet penetration rates among the world's regions, with the developed world—North America and Europe—showing a substantial lead over the developing world—Asia, the Middle East, Latin America and the Caribbean, and, in particular, Africa. This picture masks, however, substantial differences within a region; for instance, in Asia, South Korea has a very high usage rate while Vietnam has a very low rate. The number of

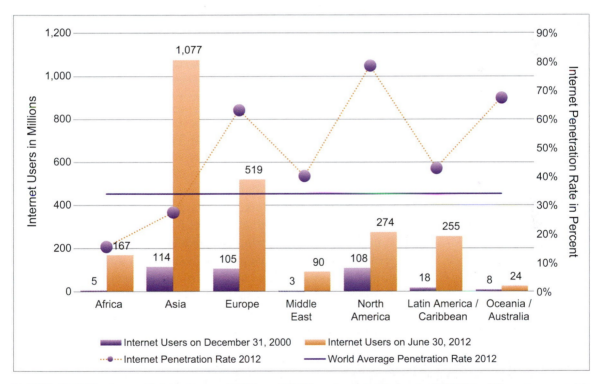

Exhibit 18.1 Numbers of Internet users (2000 and 2012) and penetration rates (2012) in different geographic regions of the world

Source: Internet World Stats—www.Internetworldststs.com. Copyright © 2001–2012, Miniwatts Marketing Group.

Notes: (1) Internet Usage and World Population Statistics are for June 30, 2012. (2) Demographic (population) numbers are based on data from the US Census Bureau and local census agencies. (3) Internet usage information comes from data published by Nielsen Online, by the International Telecommunications Union, by GfK, local ICT Regulators, and other reliable sources.

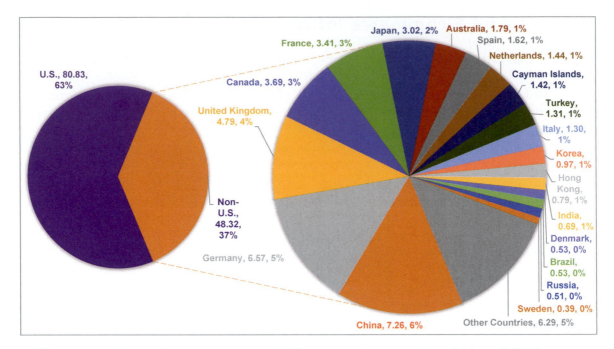

Exhibit 18.2 Distribution of domain names across different countries and regions of the world, 2013

Source: WebHosting.info, 2013.

Note: The first number after the name of each country or territory is the number of domains (in millions) hosted in that country or territory, and the second number is the country's or territory's share of the world total in percentage.

users is obviously not only a function of the penetration rate but also of population size, and is also changing fast. For instance, as noted in the opening case, China was already the second-largest Internet market by users in 2006; it soon surpassed the US to take the number one spot in 2008 and is forecasted to become the largest e-commerce market within the next few years. With a population size close to that of China, India is now the third-largest Internet market by users.

Another indicator of Internet penetration is the abundance of domain names hosted in a country. Exhibit 18.2 shows the distribution of domain names across different countries and territories of the world in 2013. The US, with over 80 million domain names, accounts for 63 percent of the world's total. The largest non-US domain name hosts are China, Germany, the United Kingdom, Canada, France, and Japan, as shown in the pie chart on the right side of the exhibit.

Country Box

The United States Lags Behind in High-Speed Internet Access

High-speed Internet access is not only about downloading music and movies, but rather is a major determinant of productivity growth, and a facilitator of e-commerce, among other contributions. Surprisingly to many, the United States, where the Internet was envisioned and launched, lags behind many other nations in high-speed Internet access. An OECD survey of its 30 member states ranked the US in 12th place among industrialized nations, with 16.8 broadband subscribers per 100 inhabitants. By comparison, Iceland had 26.7 subscribers per 100 residents, followed by South Korea, the Netherlands, Denmark, Switzerland, Finland, Norway, Canada, and Sweden, all with rates exceeding 20 subscribers per 100 inhabitants. In 2001, the United States ranked fourth in a similar survey. Further, the US is behind many industrialized nations in introducing next-generation Internet access, which runs through fiber-optic cable, rather than telephone lines or conventional cable.

The US government complains that the OECD survey is unfair because it does not take into account the large size of the country and its dispersed population, and notes that the United States still has more broadband subscribers than any other country in the world; however, countries such as Norway and Iceland have even lower population density. In many of the high-ranking countries, the government has taken an active role in building next-generation Internet access, something the US government has been reluctant to do. According to studies by IT consulting firms such as Akamai and Pando Networks, the US in 2011 was still well behind other developed countries in terms of access to high-speed Internet, ranging from 12th to 26th place, depending on how accessibility is measured.

Source: Adapted from Leila Abboud, "US lags behind in high-speed Internet access," *Wall Street Journal*, April 12, 2006, B2; Working Party on the Indicators for the Information Society, *ICT Access and Use by Households and Individuals*, OECD, 2006; K. MicNicholas, "The fastest Internet speeds in the world," *Forbes*, January 24, 2011; V. G. Kopytoff, "America: Land of the slow," *New York Times*, September 20, 2011.

E-Readiness

E-readiness refers to **the degree to which a country has developed the infrastructure necessary to facilitate electronic transactions** which are at the heart of e-commerce. This refers not only to technical infrastructure, but also to such factors as government regulations and the availability of skilled personnel. The Economist Intelligence Unit (EIU) ranks countries with regard to their digital economy (e-readiness) based on six criteria: connectivity and technology infrastructure (e.g., broadband penetration); business environment (e.g., regulation); social and cultural environment (e.g., education and innovation); legal environment (e.g., laws covering the Internet); government policy and vision (e.g., online public services); and consumer and business adoption (e.g., consumer Internet usage).

Exhibit 18.3 is a map of the world with 70 countries colored from dark orange (low) to dark blue (high) based on the EIU's digital economy ranking. The bar charts in the top middle and bottom left show, respectively, the top ten and bottom ten countries in the ranking. Note that four of the top ten nations are in Scandinavia and three are Anglo-Saxon (not counting Hong Kong and Singapore, both being former British colonies). The bottom group, as expected, is populated by developing nations in Asia and Africa, with a single European representative in the form of the Ukraine. In that case, as well as in the case of Iran, one suspects that low readiness is correlated not only with development level but also with a regime that for years has been bent on tight control of its population via control of information. The same may be true for Kazakhstan and Azerbaijan, which, like Ukraine, have been part of the Soviet Union.

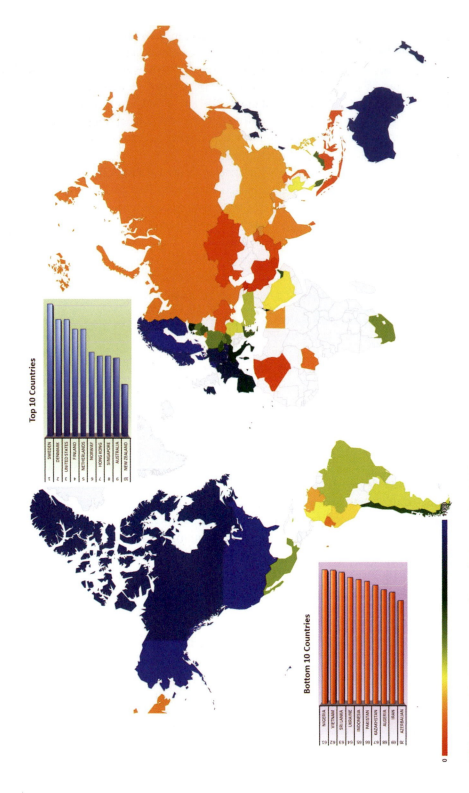

Top 10 Countries

1	SWEDEN
2	DENMARK
3	UNITED STATES
4	FINLAND
5	NETHERLANDS
6	NORWAY
7	HONG KONG
8	SINGAPORE
9	AUSTRALIA
10	NEW ZEALAND

Bottom 10 Countries

61	NIGERIA
62	VIETNAM
63	SRI LANKA
64	UKRAINE
65	INDONESIA
66	PAKISTAN
67	KAZAKHSTAN
68	ALGERIA
69	IRAN
70	AZERBAIJAN

Exhibit 18.3 Digital economy ranking of 70 countries, 2010

Source: Economist Intelligence Unit, 2010.

The level of development in a country's digital economy (or e-readiness) does not translate proportionally to the country's degree of attractiveness as an e-commerce market, which depends not only on infrastructure and consumer behavior, but also on market size and growth potential. Incorporating these additional factors, A.T. Kearney developed an index of online market attractiveness. The chart in Exhibit 18.4 shows the ranking of the most attractive online markets in the world according to its ranking. This important group of markets includes both highly developed economies (e.g., Japan, US, UK, Germany, and France) and large emerging economies that have achieved at least an upper-middle income level (e.g., China, South Korea, Brazil, Russia, and Turkey).

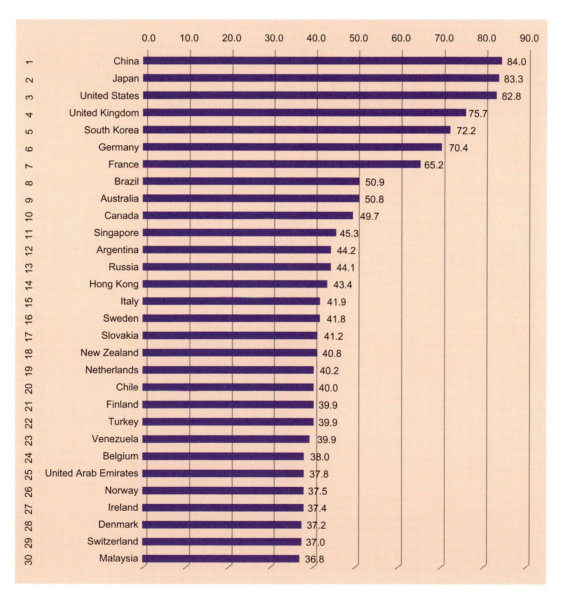

Exhibit 18.4 Online market attractiveness, 2013

Source: A.T. Kearney, 2013.

One aspect of e-readiness is a "wired" government. A government that is prepared to handle electronic communications helps to create more users who are tuned into Internet-provided information and who are comfortable with electronic transactions. An e-ready government also facilitates the working of firms, especially small and mid-size international enterprises (SMIEs), who engage in e-commerce and need to interact with the government for purposes of regulation and taxation, or to bid for government business. Exhibit 18.5 shows the top 25 countries in terms of their government e-readiness, an index consisting of site development, telecommunications infrastructure, and human capital. As in prior-year surveys, the top 25 group is dominated by highly developed

Rank 2012	Rank 2005	Country	Index Value	Online Service Component	Telecomm. Infrastructure Component	Human Capital Component
1	5	Republic of Korea	0.9283	1.0000	0.8356	0.9494
2	12	Netherlands	0.9125	0.9608	0.8342	0.9425
3	4	United Kingdom	0.8960	0.9739	0.8135	0.9007
4	2	Denmark	0.8889	0.8562	0.8615	0.9489
5	1	United States	0.8687	1.0000	0.6860	0.9202
6	23	France	0.8635	0.8758	0.7902	0.9244
7	3	Sweden	0.8599	0.8431	0.8225	0.9141
8	10	Norway	0.8593	0.8562	0.7870	0.9347
9	9	Finland	0.8505	0.8824	0.7225	0.9467
10	7	Singapore	0.8474	1.0000	0.6923	0.8500
11	8	Canada	0.8430	0.8889	0.7163	0.9238
12	6	Australia	0.8390	0.8627	0.6543	1.0000
13	13	New Zealand	0.8381	0.7843	0.7318	0.9982
14	N/A	Liechtenstein	0.8264	0.5882	1.0000	0.8910
15	17	Switzerland	0.8134	0.6732	0.8782	0.8888
16	24	Israel	0.8100	0.8497	0.6859	0.8945
17	11	Germany	0.8079	0.7516	0.7750	0.8971
18	14	Japan	0.8019	0.8627	0.6460	0.8969
19	28	Luxembourg	0.8014	0.6993	0.8644	0.8404
20	19	Estonia	0.7987	0.8235	0.6642	0.9085
21	16	Austria	0.7840	0.7451	0.6977	0.9091
22	15	Iceland	0.7835	0.5425	0.8772	0.9310
23	39	Spain	0.7770	0.7582	0.6318	0.9409
24	18	Belgium	0.7718	0.6471	0.7420	0.9264
25	26	Slovenia	0.7492	0.6667	0.6509	0.9300

Exhibit 18.5 E-government readiness index rankings (2005 and 2012, top 25 nations)
Source: United Nations, Global E-Government Readiness Report, 2012.

economies. It is interesting to note that some of the countries that have achieved high income levels recently (e.g., South Korea and Singapore) are ranked higher than many of those that have long been recognized as highly developed.

Interim Summary

1. Internet usage level, which is dramatically lower in poorer countries, is a crucial (though not the only) component of e-commerce readiness.
2. Government's e-readiness, one indicator of infrastructure for e-commerce activity, is much higher in developed nations.

Cross-Border E-commerce

Electronic commerce (E-commerce) is the conduct of transactions to buy, sell, distribute, or deliver goods and services over the Internet. E-commerce transactions are Business-to-Business (B2B), Business-to-Customer (B2C), or Customer-to-Customer (C2C). B2B, which currently drives much of the growth in global e-commerce, involves inter-firm transactions, including government procurement. B2C transactions are between firms and individuals purchasing goods or services over the Internet. Ordering a book online from a vendor is an example of a B2C transaction. C2C transactions involve individual transactions, for example, via online auction. All three types now occur globally as well as domestically. **Global e-commerce** is the conduct of electronic commerce, whether B2B, B2C, or C2C, across national boundaries (e.g., a US customer purchasing pharmaceuticals from a Canadian site), though, as we will see later in this chapter, the definition of borders is not always clear-cut in that environment (think, for instance, about the location of a server versus the location of a distribution center from which goods are sent to the final customer). Compared to the other types, B2B represents a considerably bigger share of the e-commerce pie.

While e-commerce activities still constitute a small portion of overall commercial activities, they are growing fast. For instance, according to the US Census Bureau, e-commerce sales represented 5.4 percent of overall retail sales in the country in late 2012, more than five times the percentage just a decade ago.

The Impact of E-commerce on International Business

Initially, the emergence of the Internet and e-commerce created initial expectations for exploding global electronic trade. The assumption was that "a firm marketing its products or services through the Internet is, by definition, a global firm because consumers worldwide can access it."[1] Others acknowledged that "the Internet won't magically ensure overseas success, but it can ease some of the pain of going global."[2] Today, we have developed a more balanced view, where the Internet

603

and e-commerce are making important inroads into global trade, but the progression is incremental and does not necessarily imply the demise of "bricks-and-mortar" retailers.

Even though "bricks-and-mortar" stores are still fighting vigorously for their share of the market, the rapid growth of the Internet and e-commerce around the world has altered the international strategies of companies in significant ways. First, the development of global electronic communication networks both within and between firms has enabled companies to achieve simultaneously the benefits of low production and storage costs via international outsourcing, precise order customization, and rapid delivery. For instance, global information technology (IT) product manufacturers, such as HP, Dell, and Lenovo, can send online orders to their plants overseas (often in southern China) instantly, assemble the products according to the exact specifications of the orders, and ship them by air overnight to their customers. Second, thanks to global e-commerce stores such as eBay, a new product launched in one country quickly becomes available to buyers in other countries where the company does not yet want the product to be available. This enables local imitators to introduce their own competing products to take up the market segment being targeted by the new product and reduce the size of the market available to the original developer. Apple, for instance, used to take months to launch a new version of the iPhone in all the major markets in an orchestrated sequence with adjustments in hardware (e.g., mobile frequency bands), software, and marketing strategy. The unauthorized resale of its new products without the corresponding warranty and service reduced the satisfaction of some customers and adversely affected its markets. In addition, this approach also resulted in widespread piracies of its new products and the emergence of unauthorized "Apple" stores selling imported iPhones in such major markets as China. To overcome these problems, Apple launched the iPhone 5c and 5s in all its major markets at essentially the same time.

Third, innovations spurred by the growth of the Internet have substantially altered the distribution of audio and visual products and the division of revenues from these products in the value chain. Digital sales have already surpassed or will soon surpass the sales of physical media products (e.g., CDs and DVDs) in most economies that have a highly developed technology infrastructure. The advent of peer-to-peer file sharing (e.g., BitTorrent) has made it even harder for media companies to control piracy in emerging markets where the piracy of CDs and DVDs was already rampant. Companies that take advantage of new online distribution technologies (e.g., Pandora and Spotify) have seen their markets grow exponentially, but their royalty structures are criticized as leaving too little for the creative artists. Finally, the measures that many countries have undertaken to make government services available online (i.e., e-government) have improved transparency and ease of market entry for foreign firms. These opportunities and pressures are likely to rise further as Internet access and e-commerce spread wider and grow deeper around the world.

Prospects for Large MNEs

For the larger MNE, the Internet and e-commerce create an opportunity for rapid global dissemination of products, but they also enable quicker imitation on the part of competitors. In theory, the Internet creates pressure toward price parity, posing a problem for the MNE with different distributors charging different prices in different markets. There is evidence, however, that e-commerce may actually encourage collusion. Sony and Phillips were faced with legal problems in Germany when trying to stop online sales of Primus Online, offering less expensive Sony and Phillips' products.[3]

In the previous section, we discussed the impact of the Internet and e-commerce on the outsourcing and distribution of physical products by large MNEs; the most significant impact, however, perhaps involves the provision of internal and external services at these companies. First, many MNEs have decided to outsource significant portions of their back-office services to companies in newly industrialized countries such as India and the Philippines, where semi-skilled labor is much less expensive. More often than not, an end-user who calls customer service in a developed economy such as the US will talk to someone overseas. Second, the increasing ease of using online audio and video conferencing allows companies to coordinate their international activities more effectively and more efficiently. For instance, via online video facilities, a company's R&D personnel located in different parts of the world can now collaborate in the design of a new product almost as if they were in the same place. Third, using Internet and mobile data communication technologies, logistics companies can nowadays track a shipment from overseas in real time and provide such information for their customers, who in turn can plan their production schedules accordingly. Finally, the ubiquitous use of corporate networks, and their connections to external networks, has also increased the risks of hacking and commercial espionage because the use of firewalls and tight security procedures cannot totally eliminate breaches resulting from human errors and misjudgments.

Industry Box

The Online Brokerage Industry Goes Global

In 2007, E-Trade Financial launched a pilot platform allowing US investors to buy, sell, and trade foreign stocks and currencies online. The service initially included six foreign markets (Canada, Germany, the United Kingdom, France, Japan, and Hong Kong) and eventually expanded to dozens of additional international markets. To customers, this meant not only faster execution but also lower fees. Instead of $100, they would pay only a $20 fee for an international trade.

E-Trade said the move was in response to customer demand. The company noted that a survey it conducted found that 67 percent of its customers were interested in direct trading on foreign exchanges. E-Trade predicted that its main competitors, such as Charles Schwab and TD Ameritrade, would soon mimic the move as global markets became increasingly important in individual portfolios. According to analysts, both competitors have paid less attention to international markets and will now have to play catch-up with E-Trade. In response to E-Trade's move, TD Ameritrade started allowing its customers to trade in foreign currencies directly in 2010. Charles Schwab moved more slowly and offered a new service in 2012, allowing its customers to invest directly in foreign stock markets using local currencies.

Source: Adapted from "E-Trade goes global," CNN Money.com, February 20, 2007; "E-Trade unveils global trading platform," The Associated Press/MSNBC.com, February 20, 2007; L. Bruno, "Schwab to let customers invest overseas in local currencies," *USA Today*, July 15, 2011.

Prospects for Small and Mid-size International Enterprises (SMIEs)

The reduction in barriers should, in theory, open doors to SMIEs, especially from developing countries that have been shut out of international trade and investment. It should lower transaction costs for such firms and improve their international competitiveness.[4] Many SMIEs have taken advantage of the new opportunities. Small Latin American start-ups became SMIEs almost overnight, opening local offices in Spain, Portugal, Mexico, Hispanic US, and Latin America.[5] To serve these SMIEs, a number of B2B e-commerce sites have sprung up in Latin America, including Mercatrade.com based in Panama, Mercantil.com based in Chile, Perfeto.com based in Guatemala, Brazilbiz.com.br based in Brazil, and Venexport.com based in Venezuela, although some SMIEs from the region find certain English sites to be more attractive due to their reputation and credibility to buyers.[6] Other SMIEs have piggybacked on intermediaries such as Amazon or L.L. Bean to reach international customers.

For physical goods however, barriers in the form of logistics challenges in dealing with multiple, dispersed customers remain significant for the smaller firm. There are indications that size and volume may matter even more in an e-commerce operation. The handling of a large and diverse number of customers may lie beyond the ability of many SMIEs that lack strategic and managerial capabilities. Alibaba.com, a Chinese B2B portal founded in 1999 to assist domestic SMIEs with export to international markets, has grown exponentially since its start and expanded into the C2C market via Taobao.com to compete with eBay China (see Opening Case of this chapter), into the B2C market via Tmall.com to compete with Amazon Marketplace, and into the online payment business via Alipay.com to compete with PayPal. By the end of 2012, it had become the largest e-commerce company in the world, reaching one trillion yuan (about $157 billion) in sales, compared to the annual sales of $50–60 billion by the next largest e-commerce company, Amazon.com.[7] OECD data show that, in most countries, Internet penetration is substantially lower in smaller businesses, putting them at a disadvantage in B2B applications as well.[8] A 2004 UNCTAD report notes that the SMIE's low brand visibility is a considerable negative in e-commerce where customers rely on brand names as a substitute for a retailer they do not know or see. This condition tends to accentuate the values of the services that intermediaries (such as Alibaba.com, which started as an SMIE itself) provide for SMIEs.

Prospects for Intermediaries

Although it was initially believed that the Internet would make intermediaries superfluous, the impact diverged. The number of intermediaries has indeed been reduced for digitalized products (e.g., software, music, movies, and certain educational and training programs) as well as services such as brokerage, retail, and auctions; however, intermediaries remained entrenched in other areas. Further, a new breed of value-adding intermediaries has emerged, no longer principally involved in the physical distribution of goods, but in the collection, collation, interpretation, and dissemination of vast amounts of information.[9] Akamai, for instance, provides technology platforms for clients to establish and maintain their e-commerce activities globally, with its services available in several of the common languages of the world. LinguaMetrics International, Inc., on the other hand, specializes in the translation of technical and commercial information into the target language for e-commerce purposes.

Other Impacts

E-commerce's impact extends to other realms. For example, it has made it more difficult to determine the origin of a product or a service, with concomitant implications for customs, tariffs, and taxation. This is because the server, the manufacturer, and the physical distributor may be located in different countries (see also section on taxation issues). E-commerce should also accelerate the mobility of people as a production factor. Jobs in back-office and customer service are likely to shift to lower-cost countries, especially where language is no obstacle (e.g., from the United States to Canada, Ireland, and India). For instance, Washington-based Talisma Corporation outsources customer service functions to Bangalore, India, where an abundance of highly educated workers can be found at a fraction of the US cost.[10]

Interim Summary

1. Cross-border e-commerce can alter the location decisions of MNEs.
2. Cross-border e-commerce has the capability to reduce, but not eliminate, friction in international business transactions.
3. Although e-commerce opens new opportunities for SMIEs, many lack the resources to capitalize on its promise.

Global E-commerce Challenges

Entering into global e-commerce is not easy. Dominant portals such as AOL found that penetrating Germany, the United Kingdom, and other European markets is difficult. In a departure from past patterns of MNE entry, AOL found that domestic competition on the part of European newcomers flared up almost immediately. As in other realms of international business, finding the right balance between globalization and localization has proven difficult. The next section illustrates how.

Standardization Forces

Many consumers from other nations reach into US sites. This is true for Canadians, who do much of their online shopping on US websites (although many resent buying from a US firm and seem to shift purchases to Canadian e-sellers where possible).[11] (Canadian sites, on their part, have been quite successful in selling pharmaceuticals to US citizens.) Latin Americans prefer to use US e-commerce sites over those developed in their own countries because of trust, convenience, and lower prices.[12] Yahoo found limited success with its Chinese e-commerce portal and shut it down based on an agreement with its partner Alibaba Group, now redirecting customers to Alibaba's Taobao.com site.[13]

Standardization at times is appealing. The position of English as a *lingua franca* has been considerably strengthened on the Internet, supported by the prevalence of English as a second language and by the dominance of US-hosted websites. However, as Exhibit 18.6 indicates, English may be the leading Internet language, but 70 percent of web pages are *not* in English. The Chinese language was used almost as widely as English in 2011 and is catching up fast. Exhibit 18.7 compares the numbers of Internet users in each of the ten most used languages on web pages in the world between 2000 and 2011 and also shows the penetration rates in these languages. Some languages (e.g., Chinese, Spanish, Portuguese, Arabic, and Russian) have exhibited rapid growth in Internet users, despite or perhaps because of their relatively low penetration rates. Other languages (e.g., Japanese, German, and Korean), while attaining high penetration rates, have exhibited limited growth.

Localization Challenges

As with other international business activities, the risks of neglecting customization are substantial. Many US firms underestimated the customization they would need to undertake in e-trading with foreign markets, whether tangible (tax, currencies, tariffs) or intangible (culture, buying habits).

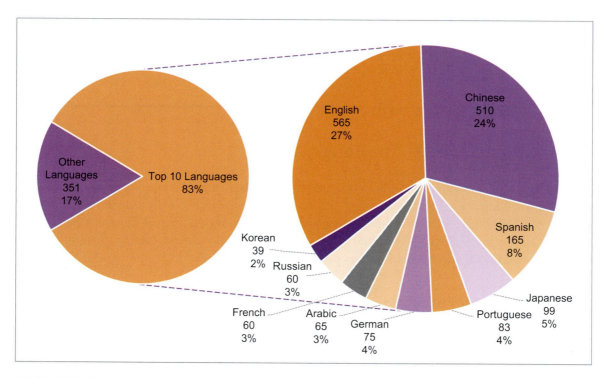

Exhibit 18.6 Top ten languages used on Internet web pages in the world (2011)

Source: Internet World Stats—www.Internetworldststs.com. Copyright © 2001–2012, Miniwatts Marketing Group

Notes: (1) The first number under the name of each language is the number of Internet users (in millions) speaking that language, and the second number is the language's share of the world's web pages in percentage. (2) Top Ten Languages Internet Stats were updated for May 31 2011. (3) The most recent Internet usage information comes from data published by Nielsen Online, International Telecommunications Union, GfK, and other reliable sources. (4) World population information comes from the U.S. Census Bureau.

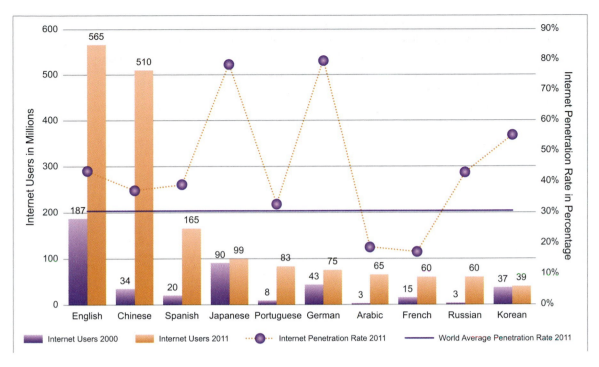

Exhibit 18.7 Top ten languages used on Internet web pages: Number of Internet users (2000 and 2011) and penetration rate (2011) in each language

Source: Internet World Stats—www.Internetworldststs.com. Copyright © 2001–2012, Miniwatts Marketing Group.

Notes: (1) Top Ten Languages Internet Stats were updated for May 31, 2011. (2) Internet Penetration is the ratio between the sum of Internet users speaking a language and the total population estimate that speaks that specific language. (3) The most recent Internet usage information comes from data published by Nielsen Online, International Telecommunications Union, GfK, and other reliable sources. (4) World population information comes from the U.S. Census Bureau.

Website Localization

Despite the promise of "instant globalization," MNEs engaged in e-commerce soon discover that the "liability of foreignness" persists. AOL has struggled behind local providers in the Latin American market, although it has failed to become the primary provider in the many Latin American markets it serves.[14] eBay had to withdraw from the potentially lucrative Japanese market, admitting such missteps as emphasizing collectibles, rather than new goods, in the belief that the Japanese market would mirror the development of the US site.[15] And, as the opening case showed, eBay lost ground in the South Korean and Chinese markets despite initial success and ended up withdrawing from the Chinese market.

Let's start with demographics. Even though women and men have approximately equal access to the Internet in the most developed countries such the US and Canada, there is still a considerable gender gap in the developing world, as shown in Exhibit 18.8. Meanwhile, women tend to spend a higher percentage of their online time on social activities than men, regardless of which region they are from, as Exhibit 18.9 indicates. This suggests that e-marketers can reach women more effectively via social media in countries where women have more limited access to the Internet.

	East Asia and Pacific	South Asia	Sub-Saharan Africa	Europe and Central Asia	Latin America and the Caribbean	Middle East and North Africa
Women's and girls' Internet access level	29%	8%	9%	35%	36%	18%
Men's and boys' Internet access level	37%	11%	16%	49%	40%	28%
Gender gap (weighted)	**20%**	**33%**	**43%**	**29%**	**10%**	**34%**
Global gender gap (144 developing countries)				23%		

Exhibit 18.8 The Internet gender gap in the developing world
Source: Intel Corporation, Women and the Web, © 2012.

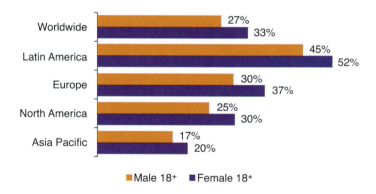

Exhibit 18.9 Share of time spent on social networking, email and instant messaging (% of total online time)
Source: comScore, Women on the Web, 2010.

In addition to demographic disparities, cultural "faux pas" are as common in e-commerce as in traditional trade. A British consulting firm used snapshots of colorful liquorish candy to symbolize "miscellaneous," which was widely recognized in England, but not in the United States, where a small yellow folder icon has been commonly used.[16] Auction house eBay posted prices in dollars on its British site. Language blunders are also common. "Getgift.com" may make sense in the United States, but its Swedish translation is "go get poison for goats." When US sites use American spellings for words such as *favorite, behavior, theater, liter,* and so on, some British consumers perceive these as misspellings.

Other variations also apply. For instance, European laws give Internet users more protection than do US laws.[17] The European laws are based on "safe harbor" principles requiring that a company seek explicit agreement before transferring personal data to another company. Also, under European law, a data subject must receive reasonable access to personal data to review and possibly correct it. Data collection is permitted when: (1) the subject has unambiguously given

610

consent; (2) the data are needed to complete a contract, such as billing; (3) the data are required by law or needed to protect the subject's vital interests; or (4) the data are needed for law-enforcement purposes. Under a tentative agreement negotiated by the US Department of Commerce, US firms can: (1) subject themselves to the data-protection authority in one of the EU nations; (2) show that they are subject to similar US privacy laws, such as those covering credit applications or videocassette rentals; (3) sign up with a self-regulatory organization, such as BBBOnline (Better Business Bureau), which provides an adequate level of privacy protection and is subject to oversight by the US Federal Trade Commission; or (4) agree to refer privacy disputes to a panel of European regulators.

A key response to localization pressures has been to establish local websites. It is here that Internet and e-commerce companies make a difference for MNEs: they need not establish physical premises in order to have local presence. Yahoo provides services in more than 45 languages and has localized versions of Yahoo! in 65 countries or regions. As far back as 1997, Sony had 13 country-specific sites; it now has as many as 45. UPS offers its services around the globe in multiple languages. Reebok has done the same after tracking its Web traffic.[18] A study found that firms with localized websites abroad were distinctly different from those that did not. Among other differences, those with localized websites had higher revenues, higher media visibility, wider global reach, and more alliances.[19]

Logistics

Logistics represents a key area where many companies have failed to make the necessary adjustments in terms of global e-commerce in general, or in terms of customizing the system to deal with the requirements in a given country. A Forrester study suggested:

> Eighty five percent of the companies noted that they could not fill overseas orders because of the complexity of shipping across borders. Of those that had problems shipping overseas, 75 percent cited their system's inability to register international addresses accurately (one European customer had his online order rejected because he could not fill the "state" section on the US order form[20]) or to price total delivery cost.[21]

Taxation Issues

In the international arena, the implications of e-commerce taxation are potentially ominous. While cross-border catalog sales existed for many years, they have not been substantial enough to generate a strong interest among governments. E-commerce has changed that.[22] In the EU, value-added taxes (VAT) ranging from 15 to 25 percent—representing a key portion of government revenues—are at risk. In itself, a website is not considered a fixed place of business that would trigger taxation, but it could be considered as such in conjunction with server location and other company operations in that country. However, Web and server locations as well as other components of e-commerce operations are increasingly difficult to pinpoint. Furthermore, e-commerce makes it increasingly easy for MNEs to shift their domicile to low-tax locations and to offshore tax havens as it becomes difficult, if not impossible, for other nations to claim physical presence of

611

the company in their territory. Problems such as transfer pricing become much more acute in this environment.

The Internet raises many other taxation issues. For instance, the traditional distinction between income and royalty taxation may be impossible to determine when a consumer downloads software from a vendor.[23] Individual income tax may be largely avoided in countries with a territorial tax base, whereas the few countries with a global taxation base, such as the United States, may find it increasingly difficult to enforce their tax legislation.

To the MNE as well as the SMIE, e-commerce taxation represents a significant challenge. In Chapter 15, we discussed the tax strategies employed by MNEs, including tax havens, tax treaties, and the creation of a holding or a finance corporation. Global e-commerce creates additional strategic opportunities, such as placing servers in low-tax jurisdictions. However, it also creates additional risks: for instance, most tax treaties do not refer to e-commerce activities, and they may be open to challenge.

Interim Summary

1. The localization challenge in global e-commerce entails customization of websites as well as of the supply chain and distribution network.
2. Country of origin is especially difficult to determine in global e-commerce transactions. Both MNEs and SMIEs have to deal with the challenges and opportunities posed by this reality in taxation as well as in other realms.

Chapter Summary

1. E-commerce could change some of the fundamental assumptions pertaining to trade and foreign investment, although it is too early to determine whether, for instance, it will "level the playing field" between the SMIE and the large MNE.
2. E-commerce is unlikely to terminate the role of global intermediaries but it is likely to shift their positioning toward knowledge analysis and dissemination. For instance, with their role as ticket issuers eliminated, travel agencies will need to focus on advice, niche, or wholesale activities.
3. As in other international business realms, international e-commerce requires a balance of globalization and localization. With foreign customers often logging into US sites, firms attempt to localize their websites in terms of language, culture, and currency units at the same time that they are adding multiple country sites.
4. Taxation is looming large as an obstacle to the promise of the free flow of goods and services on which e-commerce thrives. In the global arena, taxation could affect the competitiveness of US purveyors.
5. MNEs must take account of the repercussions of global e-commerce in such realms as competitive advantage, location, and taxation.

Notes

1 J.A. Quelch, and L.R. Klein, "The Internet and international marketing," *Sloan Management Review,* spring 1996, 60–75.
2 A. LaPlante, *Computerworld* online, October 1997.
3 N.E. Boudette, "Germany's Primus Online faces legal challenge," *Wall Street Journal,* January 6, 2000, A17.
4 "Building confidence: Electronic commerce and development," UNCTAD, 2000.
5 P. Druckerman, "Latin American Web concerns fight to stay in business," *Wall Street Journal,* October 9, 2000, A20.
6 T. Vuorinen, "Five top B2B marketplaces in Lain America," Newexportmarket.com, April 25, 2011.
7 J. Koetsier, "Alibaba reaches 1 trillion RMB ($157B) in sales to become biggest e-commerce company in the world," *VenterBeat,* December 3, 2012.
8 OECD, cited in *The Economist,* November 11, 2000.
9 J.A. Quelch and L.R. Klein, "The Internet and international marketing," *Sloan Management Review,* spring 1996, 60–75.
10 *Wall Street Journal,* November 21, 2000, A1.
11 R. Ricklefs, "US E-tailors expand efforts north of the border," *Wall Street Journal,* January 31, 2000, A21.
12 E. Rasmusson, "Targeting global E-customers," *Sales & Marketing Management,* 2000, 78.
13 Shu, Catherine. "Yahoo China shuts down its web portal," *TechCrunch,* September 1, 2013.
14 J. Karp, "AOL hangs tough in the dicey Latin market," *Wall Street Journal,* September 5, 2001, A22.
15 N. Wingfield, "E-Bay, admitting missteps, will close its site in Japan," *Wall Street Journal,* February 27, 2002. B4.
16 E.F. Sheridan and G.F. Simons, www.webofculture.com.
17 B. Mitchener and D. Wessel, "US in tentative pact protecting Europeans' privacy," *Wall Street Journal,* February 24, 2000 B11; "EU rejects US data privacy protection as inadequate," CCN online, July 7, 2000, 10.53 a.m. EDT.
18 S. Kalin, "The importance of being multiculturally correct," *Computerworld,* October 6, 1997.
19 S. Koth, V.R. Rindova, and F.T. Rothaermel, "Assets and actions: Firm specific factors in the internationalization of US Internet firms," *Journal of International Business Studies,* 32, 4, 2001, 769–791.
20 E. Rasmusson, "E-commerce around the world," *Sales & Marketing Management,* 1999, 94.
21 Forrester Research, "Mastering E-commerce logistics," 1999. Cited in *Building Confidence,* 50.
22 R. Dorenberg and L. Hinnekens, *Electronic Commerce and International Taxation,* The Hague: Kluwer Law International, 1999.
23 R. Dorenberg and L. Hinnekens, *Electronic Commerce and International Taxation.*

chapter 19

social responsibility and corruption in the global marketplace

CORPORATE SOCIAL RESPONSIBILITY IN INTERNATIONAL BUSINESS   617

CORRUPTION IN INTERNATIONAL BUSINESS   624

TYPES OF CORRUPT PRACTICES   628

Do You Know?

1. Why does the MNE face a greater array of social responsibility issues than a domestic firm?
2. What are the main elements of the MNE code of conduct?
3. What characteristics of a nation predispose it to corruption?
4. What are some of the drawbacks to corruption?
5. What are the most common corrupt practices in international business?
6. How would you react if the only way to close a deal would involve violating the MNE code of conduct?

OPENING CASE   Shell's Brent Spar Project

The Royal Dutch/Shell Group, known as Shell, grew out of an alliance between the Royal Dutch Petroleum Company of the Netherlands and the Shell Transport and Trading Company of the UK, in 1907. One of today's largest multinational oil companies, Shell invested heavily in the exploration and subsequent extraction of major oil and gas deposits in the North Sea, including at the Brent Field. Oil extracted from that field has been stored on the Brent Spar, a large floating oil platform. Unlike most other North Sea installations, the Brent Spar had most of its huge storage tanks under water. It weighed 14,500 tons, the equivalent of 2,000 double-decker buses. After 15 years of operation, the Spar was decommissioned in 1991, when a review of refurbishment costs showed that further use would not be economical.

After the Spar's decommission, in October 1991, Shell's subsidiary in the United Kingdom initiated a number of decommissioning studies to find out how to dispose of it. Due to its size, the platform could not be moved around easily and, except for the water to the North of Orkney, most of the North Sea was not deep enough to accommodate it. In a search for the Best Practicable Environmental Option (BPEO), Shell considered six options: (1) horizontal dismantling and onshore disposal; (2) vertical dismantling and onshore disposal; (3) infield disposal; (4) deepwater disposal; (5) refurbishment and reuse; and (6) continued maintenance. From these initial options, after a preliminary study, Shell chose to limit feasibility studies to the options of horizontal onshore dismantling and deepwater disposal. It eventually opted for the deepwater disposal option and submitted a request to the UK government which has endorsed it. However, Greenpeace, a non-governmental global environmental organization, opposed the deepwater disposal option which it saw as a dangerous precedent, given the 130 offshore spars still operating in the North Sea. The opposition prompted an outcry on the part of European political and various social groups, resulting in boycott campaigns and even the torching of Shell gas stations. Finally, on June 20, 1995, Shell reversed its decision to sink the Spar.

The Brent Spar experience and an outcry following the execution of a Nigerian environmentalist a few years earlier (which Shell has been criticized for not trying to stop) brought about soul searching in the company, which decided that it wanted to become a better global citizen. The Shell Report now provides full disclosure of social responsibility challenges, and the company uses a Social Impact Statement to assess the environmental impact of its decisions around the globe (see Industry Box). It also provides cheap heating and cooking oil in poor communities. Still, Shell continued to run into troubles. In 2004, it agreed to pay $150 million to US and UK regulators who alleged that the company has greatly over-stated its oil reserves. The debacle has led to corporate governance changes, among them the unification in 2005–2006 of its century-old dual-board structure.

Source: Excerpted from S.C. Zyglidopoulos. "The social and environmental responsibilities of multinationals: Evidence from the Brent Spar case," *Journal of Business Ethics*, 36, 1/2, 2002, 141–152; E. Becker, "At Shell, grades for citizenship," *The New York Times*, November 30, 2003, 2; Shell publications 2004–2006.

Corporate Social Responsibility in International Business

Corporate social responsibility encompasses the economic, legal, ethical and philanthropic, or discretionary expectations that society has of an organization at a given point of time. For the MNE, like other business firms, economic responsibilities are paramount, including, for instance, such principles as to how and where profit may be derived and disbursed. Such principles often vary from one country to another, as do the legal systems that govern company operation. For example, Chinese labor laws often are not enforced, and foreign investors discover that China's legal system resolves few disputes. Ethical responsibilities include activities and practices that are expected or prohibited by society, even though they may not be codified into law. Such responsibilities encompass norms, standards, and expectations that reflect what employees, consumers, shareholders, and the global community regard as fair, just, and consistent with the respect for, and protection of, stakeholders' moral rights.

The ethical category is where divergent views traceable to different cultures are likely to be most significant. Global business ethics are essentially about the reconciliation of home- and host-country ethical standards and the identification of norms that will satisfy both. The practice of moral relativism, wherein companies simply adapt to local norms, can create an untenable situation because many countries, especially those with emerging and developing economies, do not have articulated ethical standards that protect vulnerable stakeholders. Consider, for instance, the case of Google, which had encountered high pressure to comply with the Chinese government's demand to censor out politically sensitive terms, before it decided in March 2010 to redirect all search queries from Google.cn to Google.com.hk (Google Hong Kong), thereby bypassing Chinese regulators and allowing uncensored simplified Chinese search results. Moral universalism, a response or remedy to this deficiency, involves the identification of a particular set of ethical standards that has broad, international support, such as the UN Global Compact or the Global Reporting Initiatives.

Finally, philanthropic responsibilities reflect expectations that business will engage in social activities that are neither mandated by law nor generally expected of business in an ethical sense. Philanthropy today is more often than not strategic in nature, with businesses playing an active role

617

in global corporate citizenship. As in the case of law and ethics, philanthropic expectations vary widely by country, and savvy executives will carefully research expectations in each host country.

MNE Social Responsibilities

Generally speaking, the MNE bears greater social responsibility than its domestic counterparts. Globalization has increased calls for MNEs to use their resources to alleviate a wide variety of social problems. The pharmaceutical industry, for example, is asked to donate free drugs and vaccines to developing nations. MNEs engaged in manufacturing are encouraged to apply developed nations' laws and norms to issues such as child labor and environmental pollution in less developed countries, regardless of local laws and customs. Globalization has resulted in the proliferation of new laws and regulations that direct business activities to address diverse social problems. In recent years, MNEs such as Wal-Mart and Nike have come to recognize the importance of social responsibility at the global level. DMNEs such as India's Tata Group and Mittal Steel are showing similar concern, often displaying even higher sensitivities because of the paternalistic expectations in their home environment. For instance, in India, Tata channels some profit back to the community via major philanthropic trusts. Nearly 80 percent of the capital of the holding company, Tata Sons Limited, is held by these trusts, which helped establish leading institutions in the sciences, medicine, atomic energy, and performing arts.

An MNE's corporate social responsibility is typically focused on the relationships with several major stakeholders, namely host governments, the public (including non-governmental organizations, or NGOs), business partners, consumers, and employees. Getz suggested 15 areas of international standards for MNEs dealing with host governments, listed below:[1]

A. Economic and development policies

1. MNEs should consult with government authorities and national employers' and workers' organizations to assure that their investments conform to the economic and social development policies of their host countries.
2. MNEs should not adversely disturb the balance of payments or currency exchange rates of the countries in which they operate. They should try, in consultation with government officials, to resolve exchange rate difficulties when possible.
3. MNEs should cooperate with government policies regarding local equity participation.
4. MNEs should not dominate the capital markets of the countries in which they operate.
5. MNEs should provide necessary information to host government authorities so they can correctly assess taxes due.
6. MNEs should not engage in transfer pricing policies that modify the tax bases on which their entities are assessed.
7. MNEs should reinvest some profits in the countries in which they operate.

B. Laws and regulations

8. MNEs are subject to the laws, regulations, and jurisdictions of the countries in which they operate.
9. MNEs should respect the right of every country to exercise control over its natural resources and to regulate the activities of entities operating within its territory.

10. MNEs should use appropriate international dispute-settlement mechanisms, including arbitration, to resolve conflicts with the governments of the countries in which they operate.
11. MNEs should not request the intervention of their home governments in disputes with host governments.
12. MNEs should resolve disputes arising from expropriation by host governments under the domestic laws of the host countries.

C. Political involvement

13. MNEs should refrain from improper or illegal involvement in local political affairs.
14. MNEs should not pay bribes or render improper benefits to any public servant.
15. MNEs should not interfere in intergovernmental relations.

Environmental Responsibilities. MNEs operating in environmentally sensitive industries such as chemical, pharmaceutical, petroleum, mining, and natural resource exploration, to name a few, are expected to establish a viable sustainability program. Pollution, in its various forms, has been given a great deal of attention in recent years. While pollution in emerging economies such as China has become a key concern, so have the worries that industrialized nations will export their own environmental problems to developing markets. Basel Action Network (BAN), an environmental NGO, found out that many developing countries have become "a digital dump" for discarded computers. In Nigeria, more than 400,000 old computers and monitors arrive annually, and up to three-quarters of those are beyond repair and are simply dumped in informal rubbish dumps, creating an environmental hazard. Although the practice violates the Basel Convention on the Control of Trans Boundary Movements of Hazardous Waste, as well as other international agreements, the practice continues unabated.[2] In 2010, two foreign ships were arrested and detained for delivering toxic waste to Nigeria against the Basel Convention.[3]

The International Standards Organization (ISO) 14000 family of standards is the new European Union pollution guidelines initially established in 1996 and later updated to regulate global environment concerns (particularly ISO 14001, which sets out the core standard). This standard contains six components, each of which is relevant to MNEs: (1) environmental management systems; (2) environmental auditing; (3) performance evaluation; (4) environmental labeling; (5) life-cycle assessment; and (6) environmental product assessment. Here are some examples of what is required in a business environment governed by the ISO 14000 family of standards:

- Adopt management strategies that will enable firms to obtain certification in their industry.
- Reduce pollution and conserve resources as a means of meeting stringent environmental regulations.
- Shift from product changes to behavioral and manufacturing process changes, so as to manufacture products in a more environmentally sound manner.
- Reduce solid waste by incorporating recycling into the manufacturing process.

Baxter International, a manufacturer of pharmaceutical and biomedical products with production facilities in almost 30 countries, has a viable sustainability program in place. The external verification aspect of Baxter's program got its start in the mid-1990s in response to a stockholder group seeking assurance that environmental data presented to the public was accurate. Initially, Baxter only used its own staff to verify environmental data. External auditors were drawn into the verification process as a result of the stockholder group's concerns. Over time, the external report evolved to incorporate the reporting of health and safety data as well as environmental data. Currently, an external consultant, ERM Certification and Verification Services (ERM CVS), and Baxter have an arrangement by which they jointly verify select data at every facility audited. ERM CVS retains overall quality control of the process through verification protocols. Another firm that is taking sustainable development seriously is French telecommunications concern Alcatel (which merged with US-based Lucent in 2006). Alcatel's sustainable development strategy is based on strict published guidelines as well as social, environmental, and economic objectives defined by the company. Alcatel's sites around the world have benefited from an environmental management system, and through its "Digital Bridge" initiative, Alcatel technologies serve development in scores of countries. In 2003, the company joined the UN Global Compact, reinforced its corporate governance practices, updated its "Statement on Business Practices," and elaborated on its Social Charter, which emphasizes Alcatel's commitment to socially responsible practices.

Consumer Protection. Consumer protection is another important requirement in a global setting. MNEs are expected to respect the consumer protection laws and regulations of host countries and preserve the safety and health of consumers by disclosing appropriate information, applying proper labeling and using accurate advertising. Consumers also increasingly ask how "green" the company is before buying its products. Attributes such as corporate reputation, women, and minority employment and board membership, company participation in weapons production and use of nuclear power, product safety, employee safety and health, and environmental protection record, have become important dimensions of corporate social responsibility for the MNE.

Corporate Governance. Another vital area of social responsibility for the MNE is corporate governance, of which financial governance is one of the major responsibilities. Financial governance focuses on the structures and processes necessary for the pursuit of shareholder value. Key elements in this category are shareholder rights, protection of minority shareholders, and transparency and disclosure issues (e.g., disclosing the composition of the board, the number of independent directors, and special board committees). Here, too, variations across countries present a major challenge for the MNE. For instance, in Japan, female board membership is rarely heard of (only 3.8 percent), while in the United States women now represent about 31 percent of board members. A US MNE with a Japan subsidiary or a joint venture might therefore face a dilemma when considering appointing a woman to the board in that affiliate. According to a 2004 Conference Board survey, Japan is also the only industrialized country where boards of directors do not have a defined role in ethics.

Industry Box

Social Impact Assessment Steps at Shell

(1) Impact Identification through Integrated Impact Assessments

Experience has shown that the greatest business and societal benefit comes from effective identification and management of operational impacts during planning and design as well as through the operational life. We require that an integrated environmental, social, and health impact assessment is carried out prior to any new project or significant modification of an existing one. Conducting environmental, social, and health impact assessments provides a structured way of looking ahead at the potential positive and negative impacts that could arise throughout the project's life cycle. It is a tool to aid design and decision making.

2) Stakeholder Engagement Plans

Stakeholder engagement helps us build relationships with communities, governments, NGOs, and shareholders. It is also a critical mechanism for problem solving, improving business decisions, and achieving business objectives. Given this importance it is now a requirement for all businesses to establish and implement a Stakeholder Engagement Plan.

3) Social Performance Plans

Social Performance Plans have now been introduced as a requirement for all of Shell's businesses. Oil Products business has social performance plans in place at the 28 major facilities it operates near communities. Gas & Power will do the same in 2005 at the facilities it operates. The joint ventures where it does not have operational control are encouraged to develop social performance plans. Exploration & Production will put social performance plans in place in 2005 at operations where social impacts could be high. Plans have been in place since 2003 at our nine major Chemicals facilities, four of which surveyed community opinions in 2004 to measure social performance. These social performance plans guide our efforts to engage with stakeholders, reduce disruptive social impacts and generate benefits for the communities where we operate.

4) Social Performance Reviews

The tools that our businesses use to manage the impact of our operations include social performance reviews to identify key stakeholders and assess responses to our main social impacts. The first four major social performance reviews have been fundamental in helping the Shell Group develop guidance on how to better and more consistently manage the key social impacts of our operations. The social performance reviews also provide a way to help assure our performance in the social arena and bolster our continuous learning.

Global Guidelines and Mandates

There are many global guidelines by which MNEs measure their social responsibility. Many of those guidelines have been issued in the last decade by NGOs. The more prominent types of guidelines include the environment, supply chain management, hiring practices, community relations, internal management, information disclosure, and charitable donations. Some of the global benchmarks against which corporate performance on those issues is being measured include the United Nations Declaration of Human Rights, the International Labor Organization (ILO)'s labor standards, and several globally recognized voluntary standards, such as the Organization for Economic Co-operation and Development's guidelines for multinationals and the United Nations Global Compact, to name just a few.

Perhaps the most widely accepted reporting guideline is the Global Reporting Initiative (GRl), based in Amsterdam. Launched in 1997 and billed as a common framework for sustainable reporting, the GRI was developed by a group of organizations known for responsible business reporting.

Among them were representatives of the Association of Chartered Certified Accountants, the United Nations Environment Program, and the World Business Council for Sustainable Development. The GRI took the best practices in the area of human rights, labor relations, environmental management, and sustainable development, and crafted them into guidelines that enable any corporation to produce one comprehensive report.

Many global guidelines, such as the OECD Guidelines for Multinational Enterprises, are voluntary. These initiatives involve the issuance of codes of corporate conduct setting forth commitments in such areas as labor relations, environmental management, human rights, consumer protection, information disclosure, and corruption. The codes are often backed up by management systems that help firms fulfill their commitments in their day-to-day operations. More recent developments include guidelines on management, reporting and auditing standards and the emergence of supporting institutions (e.g., professional societies, consulting and auditing services). While the initiatives are often referred to as voluntary, MNEs are under increasing pressure to adopt them. Pressure stems from legal and regulatory institutions, employees, and public opinion.

A Culture of Social Responsibility

Levi Strauss & Co. illustrates the importance of corporate culture in improving an MNE's social responsibility. The company's core values—empathy, originality, integrity, and courage—underlie how the company competes in the global marketplace and how its executives, directors, and employees are expected to behave. These values guide its foundation's giving programs, the support it provides to communities where it has a business presence, and its employee community-involvement programs. In 1991, Levi became the first worldwide company to establish a comprehensive ethical code of conduct for manufacturing and finishing contractors working with the company. Over the period 2001–2004, the company has been ranked as one of "America's 50 Best Companies for Minorities" by *Fortune* magazine. Its philanthropy includes a focus on strengthening workers' rights and ultimately improving working and living conditions in communities where third-party contractors make Levi's products. The Levi Strauss Foundation provides innovative "sourcing" grants to local, regional, or global nonprofit organizations to support programs that:

- educate policy makers on the need to include human rights protections in trade agreements;
- increase local monitoring and enforcement of labor and health and safety laws;
- educate workers about their rights and increase their knowledge of financial literacy and health issues; and/or
- create positive partnerships between non profit organizations and contractors.

Exhibit 19.1 presents a brief analysis of Levi Strauss' guidelines for selecting business partners in global sourcing, which is part of the company's Global Sourcing and Operating Guidelines. The analysis examines in particular what issues are likely to arise in implementation and how these issues may have influenced the wording of each specific guideline.

Terms of Engagement for Selecting Partners	Analysis—Potential Issues in Implementation
• Full compliance with legal requirements and commitment to ethical standards compatible with those of Levi Strauss & Co.	o *Strict enforcement of legal compliance, but ethical commitment harder to ascertain and maintain*
• Commitment to environmental protection standards compatible with those of Levi Strauss & Co.	o *Adherence to environment protection often subject to significant uncertainty and costly to investigate*
• Favoring partners that involve the local community and try to improve community conditions	o *Difficult to make this a requirement given the cost pressures that apparel makers face today*
• Employment standards	
▪ Forbiddance of child labor and prison or forced labor	o *Strict adherence—violation typically resulting in severe public relations problems*
▪ Prohibition of disciplinary practices in the forms of physical or mental coercion	o *Likely an issue in developing countries with poor labor protection and high power distance*
▪ Requirement for safe and healthy working conditions and living conditions (if provided by the employer)	o *Such standards likely to vary from country to country depending on the level of economic development*
▪ Mandatory maximum working hours of sixty (60) and one day off in seven	o *Protects worker health, but may run counter to the desires of some workers wanting more pay*
▪ Payment of wages and benefits in compliance with local laws and prevailing local practices in the industry	o *Local laws and practices, again, likely to vary from country to country—difficult to establish universal or minimum standards*
▪ Permission of free association established by local laws or mutual agreement between the employer and worker organizations	o *Note the caveat regarding "local laws" and "mutual agreement," which may render free association infeasible in a locality*
▪ Favoring partners that employ workers based solely on their abilities, while recognizing local cultural differences	o *Recognizing the possibility that local culture may dictate certain forms of discrimination that the company finds very difficult to prevent*

Exhibit 19.1 An analysis of Levi Strauss & Co.'s Terms of Engagement with partners in global sourcing

Source: Levi Strauss & Co. Global Sourcing and Operating Guidelines.

Note: Levi Strauss & Co. Global Sourcing and Operating Guidelines includes two parts: (1) the Country Assessment Guidelines address large, external issues beyond the control of the company's individual business partners, and (2) the Business Partner Terms of Engagement deal with issues that are substantially controllable by individual business partners. The TOE is applicable to the selection of business partners in outsourcing. The analysis presented in the table is concerned with only the second part and examines particularly potential issues in implementation.

Auditing and Assessing MNE Social Responsibility

Many MNEs have implemented programs that help them respond to societal concerns about the economic, social, and environmental impacts of their activities. These programs assist them in managing compliance with legal or regulatory requirements and formulating responses to "soft" forms of social conduct, in which they commit to norms for appropriate conduct in a variety of areas of business ethics. Some MNEs have Chief Audit Executives who ensure that social responsibility is on the board's agenda and that the various codes and standards are upheld.

623

Even with the best of internal monitoring, however, MNEs sometimes turn to outside organizations to gauge and verify their social responsibility performance. There are four categories of organizations that provide external monitoring and verification services: (1) global accounting firms, such as KPMG and PricewaterhouseCoopers; (2) monitoring firms or NGOs focusing their efforts specifically on inspecting work sites for code of conduct violations; (3) forensic and investigation firms which typically use a network of professionals to investigate allegations of impropriety or perform due diligence assessments of potential or existing suppliers' ability to comply with codes; and (4) quality assurance or quality registrar or ISO certification firms. Building on the platform established by the International Standards Organization, an NGO established to promote the development of voluntary standards that govern quality and environmental impact, several quality registrars or quality certification firms have started performing workforce monitoring on codes of conduct and human rights issues.

Corruption in International Business

While social responsibility has been on the radar screen of MNEs for many years, corruption—perhaps the most blatant form of deviation from social responsibility laws and norms—is an issue seldom talked about. For instance, for almost three decades the United States was virtually the only country to criminalize bribe paying when doing business abroad. Other nations looked the other way, viewing bribe paying as a necessary, if unpleasant, part and cost of international business. Many nations treated corruption outside their national borders differently than at home, condoning the use of corrupt practices abroad while banning them at home. Some nations continue to do so today. Drawing the line at one's borders is increasingly tenuous, however. As *The Economist* noted, "companies have learned the hard way that they live in a CNN world, in which bad behavior in one country can be seized on by local campaigners and beamed on the evening news to customers back home."

Definition and Magnitude of Corruption

By nature, corruption defies a precise definition,[4] and definitions also vary from one country to another. However, most definitions of corruption view it as the illegitimate exchange of power for material remuneration mostly on the part of office holders who take advantage of their position to grant undeserving favors. Not all corruption violates the law. Some corrupt activities merely defy "accepted norms" or "customs."[5] In this chapter, we will use the following definition of **corruption**:

> *An exchange between two partners (the "demander" and the "supplier"), which (a) has an influence on the allocation of resources either immediately or in the future; and (b) involves the use or abuse of public or collective responsibility for private ends.*[6]

Understandably, corruption is difficult to measure. Most nations do not gauge corruption levels, and companies are reluctant to divulge information on corrupt activities that may put them in harm's way; they are also reluctant to jeopardize their government contacts or embarrass their home and/or host governments. Nevertheless, estimates of corrupt activities and their economic impact are available. *The Economist* puts the "shadow" or "underground" economy at $9 trillion.[7] Even in some developed economies (e.g., Italy and Belgium) underground economic activity represents a quarter of GDP[8], a figure comparable to that of the emerging economy of China.[9] World Bank figures from 2005 put the annual cost of corruption at $1.5 trillion, and the World Economic Forum estimates the global cost to be 5 percent of the world GDP, amounting to $2.6 trillion in 2008, with $1 trillion paid in bribes each year.[10]

Some industries are especially prone to corruption. The European Court of Auditors estimates that member states have wasted $1.2 billion on fraudulent infrastructure projects.[11] Between May 1994 and April 1998, 239 international contracts totaling $108 billion were influenced by bribes. About half of those contracts involved military procurement; the others involved aerospace, communications, infrastructure, energy, and transportation.[12] It is estimated that leading exporters, especially in the arms and construction industries, traditionally pay upward of 10 percent to a senior official to win a contract.[13] The US government cites a case in which a European aircraft maker offered agent commissions of 20 percent or more in an Asian market if its product was chosen.[14]

The Origins of Corruption

A number of conditions tend to increase the probability of corruption. First, developing economies are more prone to corruption, partly because of the lack of an adequate legal framework and weak enforcement; hybrid or transitional economies are susceptible because their institutions tend to lag behind the reality of fast economic and social change. A study by Shleifer and Vishny shows that, while Soviet officials extorted small bribes, officials in the transitional Russian system that followed extorted larger sums because they did not have to show concern for other bribe takers.[15] Additional factors supporting corruption, according to Transparency International (TI) data, include low public sector pay, immunity of public officials, secrecy in government, and media restrictions. Privatization, financial liberalization, and increase in FDI and trade also play a role.[16]

A second predictor of corruption is a high level and scope of government involvement in, and regulation of, economic activity, especially where public official pay is low and corruption is viewed as legitimate remuneration. Nigeria represents such an example, as do certain sectors in India and Vietnam, among other countries. A lack of transparency (e.g., public disclosure of financial information), more common in developing and hybrid economies but also evident in some developed economies (e.g., Italy), is also associated with higher corruption levels.

A third predictor of corruption is culture, which was found to correlate, for instance, with receptivity toward questionable accounting principles.[17] Uncertainty avoidance and masculinity (see Chapter 6) have been found to correlate with unethical decision making.[18] Husted formed a "cultural profile" of a corrupt country: high on uncertainty avoidance, masculinity, and power distance. Corruption is associated with high uncertainty avoidance because it is an uncertainty reduction mechanism. Masculinity creates corruption potential because it implies preference for material things. Power distance is associated with paternalism, a system where a superior grants favors to subordinates in return for loyalty, permitting arbitrary judgment and hence corruption.[19]

Drawbacks of Corruption

Ninety percent of the Asian executives surveyed by the *Far Eastern Economic Review* said that corruption slowed progress.[20] Corruption obstructs firm growth and development through the imposition of risk, the punishment suffered by violator firms, the damage to a firm's reputation, and the financial cost incurred in direct and indirect payments. According to the World Bank, the percentage of firms that see corruption as a problem for their operations and growth exceeds 40 percent in the Ukraine and 35 percent in Bulgaria.[21] From an economic perspective, corruption causes misallocation of capital, diverting resources from constructive activities such as innovation and technological development. It also produces incomplete, distorted, and undisclosed information, allowing one party to take advantage of another, which undermines cooperation and potential synergies between partners. The damage is especially pronounced in emerging economies, where internal funds often constitute the single most important source of capital, discouraging legitimate investment. As a headline describing the military coup in Pakistan read, "Pakistani stocks surge since military takeover amid hopes less corruption will lift economy."[22]

Corruption tends to undermine trade and FDI, depriving both the host countries and the investors of the benefits associated with trade and investment. One researcher calculated, for instance, that an increase in the level of corruption from the Singaporean (very low) to the Mexican level would be tantamount to an increase of more than 20 percent in the tax burden on foreign investment.[23] Further, the prospect of obtaining personal benefits may lead officials to oppose trade liberalization. Foreign investors, on their part, may be reluctant to invest in an economy known for its corrupt practices.[24] Cited about his company's exit from Bulgaria, a Unilever official said:

> *It was impossible for us to do business without getting involved in corruption. So we took the logical step and accepted the consequences. That meant packing our bags.*[25]

Corruption Rankings

Established in 1993 by a former World Bank official, Transparency International (TI) publishes the **Corruption Perception Index (CPI)**, a broad measure of corruption that is calculated from multiple survey responses. The 2013 report provides CPI scores for over 177 countries and territories studied. Exhibit 19.2 lists those with the lowest and highest levels of perceived corruption in the public sector, with their ranking and score. As expected, those with the best scores tend to be developed economies, while those with the worst scores tend to be developing economies. Still, the full rankings provide some interesting insights. For instance, among developed economies, Italy and Greece rank relatively low (69th and 80th, respectively), while among developing economies, Barbados and Uruguay rank near the top (15th and 19th, respectively). It is also interesting to note that all of the Scandinavian countries rank in the top ten with the lowest levels of perceived corruption, reinforcing the argument regarding the cultural correlates or corruption (please refer to Chapter 6, where these nations form a distinct Scandinavian culture cluster).

Lowest Perceived Corruption			Highest Perceived Corruption		
Rank	Country	Score	Rank	Country	Score
1	Denmark	91	157	Burundi	21
1	New Zealand	91	157	Myanmar	21
3	Finland	89	157	Zimbabwe	21
3	Sweden	89	160	Cambodia	20
5	Norway	86	160	Eritrea	20
5	Singapore	86	160	Venezuela	20
7	Switzerland	85	163	Chad	19
8	Netherlands	83	163	Equatorial Guinea	19
9	Australia	81	163	Guinea-Bissau	19
9	Canada	81	163	Haiti	19
11	Luxembourg	80	167	Yemen	18
12	Germany	78	168	Syria	17
12	Iceland	78	168	Turkmenistan	17
14	United Kingdom	76	168	Uzbekistan	17
15	Barbados	75	171	Iraq	16
15	Belgium	75	172	Libya	15
15	Hong Kong	75	173	South Sudan	14
18	Japan	74	174	Sudan	11
19	Uruguay	73	175	Afghanistan	8
19	United States	73	175	Korea (North)	8
21	Ireland	72	175	Somalia	8

Exhibit 19.2 Countries and territories with the lowest and highest perceived public sector corruption, 2013

Source: Data taken from © Transparency International, 2013. All rights reserved.

Note: The Corruption Perceptions Index measures the perceived level of public sector corruption in countries and territories around the world. The Index scores countries from 0 (highly corrupt) to 100 (highly clean).

As in other instances, it is useful to be aware of internal variations within countries. For instance, *The Economist* ranks Chechnya, Dagestan, and Primorsky as having the highest level of corruption in Russia. The Samara region has the lowest.[26]

Interim Summary

1. What constitutes corrupt business practices varies cross-nationally; still, anti-corruption norms are spreading.
2. In addition to misallocation of capital resources, corrupt countries create an artificial, usually ossified, economic atmosphere that makes firms less capable of competing in open, international markets.
3. The level of corruption varies cross-nationally with developing and transitional economies typically ranking high (that is, are more corrupt).

Types of Corrupt Practices

International business corruption takes many forms: a request from an exporter to pay a fee to "expedite" custom clearance, a "consultant fee" demanded from a foreign investor by government officials involved in project approval, a bid awarded to regulators and their proxies. Common forms of corruption in international business are listed below.

Smuggling

Smuggling is the illegal trade and transportation of goods devised to circumvent custom duties, quotas, and other constraints on the movement of goods (e.g., safety transportation requirements that may add to cost at destination). Smuggling diminishes national control over trade policies. It damages legitimate importers that find themselves in competition with same or similar products sold at a lower cost, as well as the manufacturer whose reputation is tarnished by the sale of inferior imitations and/or inability to serve products that are not under genuine warranty. Smuggling is especially likely to occur in economies sharing a contiguous border with substantial differences in the availability and cost of goods. A case in point: the Hong Kong border with southern China where local mainland authorities sometimes collude with the smugglers. In the past, this was a conduit for the smuggling of stolen cars into the mainland (easily detected, because the steering wheel is on the right-hand side). Nowadays, the flow consists more of counterfeit products into Hong Kong (since 1997, Hong Kong has been a Special Administrative Region of China, but it continues to be a separate entity for trade and customs purposes).

Cigarettes have been especially appealing to smugglers throughout the world due to high taxes and tariffs and the relative ease of transportation. The Canadian government alleged that cigarette makers have been exporting their Canada-made cigarettes to the United States only to have them smuggled back into Canada to avoid high taxes. The manufacturers, mostly affiliates of US firms, denied involvement but acknowledge the rampant smuggling of the product.[27] A recent study suggests that MNEs have not always been unwitting participants in the smuggling of cigarettes, but have often cooperated or at least did not initiate action against the phenomenon.[28] Cigarettes continued to top the list of goods seized by US custom authorities in 2004 and 2005.

Particularly appealing to smugglers are contraband goods such as drugs, liquor, and guns (where prohibited), because of the lack of competition from legitimate means of importation. Smuggling also occurs in products that seem difficult to ship and conceal, such as steel. Steel smuggling involves falsifying shipping documents to conceal the product source or its classification. The level of tariff on steel varies with both the source of the import and the type of steel. Given that there are about 100 nations exporting steel to the United States, and that there are almost 1,000 different types of steel, there is substantial incentive to smuggle the metal by altering the source or classification, because it is difficult for the US Customs Service to monitor it.[29]

The smuggling of illegal immigrants has become especially lucrative. Driven by hardship at home and the prospect of a better life elsewhere, individuals are often lured into paying exorbitant sums to organized gangs with the promise of entry into a developed country, most notably the United States and the EU. It is estimated that almost half a million illegal immigrants are smuggled into the EU annually, whereas 300,000 make their way into the United States.[30] A 2006 Congressional discussion suggests that the numbers are considerably higher.

Money Laundering

Money laundering involves concealing the source of ill-gotten funds by channeling them into legitimate business activities and bank deposits in other countries. Although not new, the phenomenon has been growing rapidly, partially because of a burgeoning drug trade and privatization in the former Soviet Union and other emerging economies. While it is impossible to accurately measure the extent of the problem, some estimates have put it as high as 5 percent of global GDP. The flow has been aided by electronic payment systems that made possible the transfer of huge sums of money at lightning speed. The chairman of the Bank of New York acknowledged that the bank's money-laundering lapse was the result of a "global payments system that put priority on speed rather than knowing whether the electronic money transfers are legal."[31] One way to launder money is through trade. This is done via the undervaluation of exports (e.g., a motor vehicle exported from the US to Jordan, for which the declared value was $377) or through overvaluation of exports (e.g., footballs imported into the US from Pakistan, for which the declared value was $142.50).[32] The events of September 11, 2001 have drawn much more attention to money laundering as a vehicle in international terrorism, triggering much closer scrutiny of the phenomenon which continues to this day.

Piracy and Counterfeiting

Counterfeiting and piracy account for 5 to 7 percent of world trade, or $200 to $300 billion in lost revenues.[33] Counterfeiting and piracy are not the same. **Piracy** means using illegal and unauthorized means to obtain goods, such as copying software. **Counterfeiting** goes a step beyond, attempting to pass the copied product as an original, such as producing and selling a fake Gucci bag or a Rolex watch. Both phenomena have been growing rapidly and represent a substantial threat to the original manufacturers. In piracy, the most significant threat is probably in intellectual property, such as computer software, music, and videos.

The growth in piracy of such goods is explained by industry growth and the globalization of intellectual property products. Technological advances make pirating easier: the price of disk production machinery declined precipitously in recent years, facilitating a cottage industry of pirated disks in China, Vietnam, and other countries. Counterfeit goods include not only videos and designer watches and handbags but, alarmingly, pharmaceuticals and aircraft spare parts. Counterfeit services can also be found in the form of unauthorized providers of automotive services, which put up the manufacturer's logo as a way to entice unsuspecting customers.

Both piracy and counterfeiting have greatly expanded in recent years, with violating products in pharmaceuticals, aircraft components, and automotive parts creating a serious threat to consumers. Both phenomena also discourage innovation by reducing the incentive for a company to invest in a new technology or product for fear they will not be able to capture the profit that comes from being a first entrant into the market. The violation of intellectual property rights, of which piracy

629

and counterfeiting are a prime example, is currently a major friction factor in the relationship between China and the United States.

Bribe Paying

Bribery, which often appears under such euphemisms as "fees," "commissions," "gratuities," and "sweeteners," is a perennial form of corruption in international business. Investigations by the Securities and Exchange Commission (SEC) during the 1970s found that more than 400 US companies made questionable payments totaling more than $300 million to foreign government officials, politicians, and political parties. Between mid-1994 and mid-1996, US firms lost 36 of 139 contracts, valued at $11 billion, to bribery.[34] Swiss authorities froze $100 million held by the government of Kazakhstan, allegedly used by American and European oil firms to bribe Kazakh officials in order to gain favorable exploration and use rights.[35] Among the companies discovering bribery in their overseas affiliates are Xerox, ABB, and IBM. Synchor, a US pharmaceutical company, saw its acquisition price lowered when the acquirer, Cardinal Health, discovered improper payments made by Syncor in Taiwan.

TI publishes a Bribe Payers Index (BPI) that ranks countries according to their propensity to bribe abroad (see Exhibit 19.3.) As in the case of the CPI, the developed economies are less likely to pay bribes in foreign markets than companies hailing from developing countries. Companies from the emerging economies of Russia, China, Mexico, and Indonesia are most likely to pay bribes when operating abroad.

China, with the second lowest score, is a good illustration of the costs, patterns, and underlying reasons for bribe paying. An internal report of the Chinese government estimated the state lost well over $50 billion in one decade from undervaluation of privatized assets by officials in return for payoffs. Hong Kong's Independent Commission against Corruption estimated that gifts and bribes add 3 to 5 percent to operating costs in China.[36] The same commission also found in a survey of 50 Hong Kong companies doing business on the Mainland that 35 admitted paying bribes, such as the purchase of "inspection certificates" necessary for the exportation of goods.[37] In recent years, the Chinese government has undertaken a number of campaigns against bribery, leading to the arrest of senior officials in 2005–2006 and again in 2012–2013, but the government acknowledges that the phenomenon remains widespread.

The Foreign Corrupt Practices Act (FCPA)

The origin of the **FCPA** can be traced to the 1970s, when press reports alleged US firms made questionable payments to foreign government officials. Payments were disbursed through hidden "slush funds" and financial records were often falsified to conceal them. The congressional investigations that ensued culminated in the enactment of the FCPA that was further amended in 1988. The FCPA criminalized the payment of bribes and other forms of special payment to foreign officials for the purpose of securing or retaining a deal (liability exists whether the deal has been consummated or not). It also required issuers of securities to meet accounting, record-keeping, and corporate control standards. Criminal and civil enforcement of the anti-bribery provisions with respect

Rank	Country/Territory	Score	Number of Observations	Standard Deviation	90% Confidence Interval	
					Lower Bound	Upper Bound
1	Netherlands	8.8	273	2.0	8.6	9.0
1	Switzerland	8.8	244	2.2	8.5	9.0
3	Belgium	8.7	221	2.0	8.5	9.0
4	Germany	8.6	576	2.2	8.5	8.8
4	Japan	8.6	319	2.4	8.4	8.9
6	Australia	8.5	168	2.2	8.2	8.8
6	Canada	8.5	209	2.3	8.2	8.8
8	Singapore	8.3	256	2.3	8.1	8.6
8	United Kingdom	8.3	414	2.5	8.1	8.5
10	United States	8.1	651	2.7	7.9	8.3
11	France	8.0	435	2.6	7.8	8.2
11	Spain	8.0	326	2.6	7.7	8.2
13	South Korea	7.9	152	2.8	7.5	8.2
14	Brazil	7.7	163	3.0	7.3	8.1
15	Hong Kong	7.6	208	2.9	7.3	7.9
15	Italy	7.6	397	2.8	7.4	7.8
15	Malaysia	7.6	148	2.9	7.2	8.0
15	South Africa	7.6	191	2.8	7.2	7.9
19	Taiwan	7.5	193	3.0	7.2	7.9
19	India	7.5	168	3.0	7.1	7.9
19	Turkey	7.5	139	2.7	7.2	7.9
22	Saudi Arabia	7.4	138	3.0	7.0	7.8
23	Argentina	7.3	115	3.0	6.8	7.7
23	United Arab Emirates	7.3	156	2.9	6.9	7.7
25	Indonesia	7.1	153	3.4	6.6	7.5
26	Mexico	7.0	121	3.2	6.6	7.5
27	China	6.5	608	3.5	6.3	6.7
28	Russia	6.1	172	3.6	5.7	6.6
	Average	**7.8**				

Exhibit 19.3 Bribe Payers Index

Source: ©Transparency International, 2011. All rights reserved.

Note: The 2011 Bribe Payers Index ranks the likelihood of companies from 28 leading economies to win business abroad by paying bribes. The Index scores countries from 0 (highest likelihood of companies from this country to engage in bribery when doing business abroad) to 10 (lowest likelihood of companies from this country to engage in bribery when doing business abroad).

to domestic concerns is the responsibility of the Justice Department. The Securities and Exchange Commission (SEC) is responsible for civil enforcement of the anti-bribery provisions with respect to issuers. In November 2012, the Criminal Division of the US Department of Justice and the Enforcement Division of the US Securities and Exchange Commission published the updated version of *A Resource Guide to the US Foreign Corrupt Practices Act*. The *Guide* addresses a wide variety of topics, including: who and what is covered by the FCPA's anti-bribery and accounting provisions; the definition of a "foreign official"; what constitute proper and improper gifts, travel and entertainment expenses; the nature of facilitating payments; how successor liability applies in the mergers and acquisitions context; the hallmarks of an effective corporate compliance program; and the different types of civil and criminal resolutions available in the FCPA context.

Under the FCPA, the term "officials of a foreign government" includes executives in state-owned firms, foreign political parties, or candidates for office. A payment may be "in kind," such as a gratuitous trip. "Facilitating payments" made within the context of routine government operation (e.g., obtaining permits, issuance of license, providing utilities) are permissible under the Act's 1988 amendment, but must be reported on the company's financial statement. Bona fide payments (e.g., for work-related travel) that are legal in the host country and are made for the purpose of product promotion or as part of contractual obligations are also allowed under the 1988 amendment.

Subject to the FCPA are not only US firms but also wholly owned US subsidiaries and other US entities controlled by foreign corporations, including their directors, employees, and agents. Actions taken abroad by US citizens, nationals, or residents are covered under the FCPA even if conducted for a foreign corporation. The FCPA also prohibits indirect foreign payments, which can be interpreted as covering the foreign subsidiaries of US corporations as well. However, it is not clear if the percentage of ownership in the subsidiary has a bearing on FCPA liability, and if an international joint venture between a US and a local company in a foreign country creates liability on the part of the local partner. This is an important question because firms often delegate functions with corruption potential (e.g., dealing with local government authorities) to their local partners. The FCPA also covers payment by intermediaries but requires proof that the US MNE knew about the practice. It also prohibits payments to a third party with the knowledge that the payment will end up in the hands of a foreign official.

Violations of the FCPA anti-bribery provisions can result in fines of up to $2 million to firms and up to $250,000, plus imprisonment for up to five years, for individuals. Both firms and individuals are also liable to a civil fine if they violate the anti-bribery provisions. In suits brought by the SEC, fines can reach as much as $500,000. Under federal criminal laws other than FCPA, individuals may be fined up to $250,000 or up to twice the amount of the gain or loss incurred. A firm or individual who violates the FCPA may also be barred from doing business with the US government. Other sanctions include ineligibility to receive export licenses and being barred from the securities business.

The Globalization of the Fight Against Corruption

Immediately following the passage of the FCPA, the United States tried to expand it to other nations. The efforts were initially unsuccessful, but since then many governments (e.g., Thailand, Zimbabwe, Poland, and China's Special Administrative Region, or SAR, of Hong Kong) have established independent commissions against corruption. In the NAFTA-created NADBank, the United States successfully won agreement from its NAFTA partner Mexico in 1996 to require companies to certify that they have not engaged in bribery of foreign or domestic officials in projects funded by the bank.

Companies must also have corporate policies that prohibit bribery and assert that they have not been convicted of bribery within five years of certification; otherwise they will be barred from future participation in a NADBank-funded or -guaranteed project.

In 1994, the United States sponsored the 1994 OECD Recommendation on Bribery in International Business Transactions that called on member states to take "concrete and meaningful steps" to deter, prevent, and combat bribery of foreign public officials. In 1999, the OECD adopted the Combating Bribery of Foreign Officials in International Business Act (CBFOIB). The Act is substantially modeled after the US FCPA. It makes the payment of bribes to elected or appointed foreign officials a criminal offense and abolishes its tax deductibility. The Act requires that sanctions against foreign corruption be comparable to those against public officials domestically. It also requires coordination in matters of jurisdiction, a key issue given the global nature of the phenomenon as well as coordination in legal matters (including extradition). Effective accounting and measures against money laundering are also set.

While 40 nations have signed the Convention (see also Exhibit 19.3), the results on the ground have been mixed. By 2012, according to Transparency International (TI), 18 signatory nations, about half of the total, "have achieved little or no enforcement." According to the OECD, there were only 50 prosecutions under the Convention from 1999 to 2006, but this figure rose dramatically to 708 in 2011. Austria, Australia, Canada, and Japan have each prosecuted only three or fewer cases.[38] While some governments have taken the results seriously (for instance, the UK announced in June 2006 the establishment of a special police task force to deal with the problem), it remains to be seen, according to TI, if overseas bribery will be treated "as a crime, not as a business strategy."[39] A recent study suggests that such anti-corruption laws need to be implemented and coordinated in multiple countries to become effective. Otherwise, investors in a country will have incentives to bypass them when competitors from other countries are not bound by similar legal constrains.[40] This study further shows that investors from countries that implemented the OECD Convention on Combating Bribery of Foreign Public Officials in International Business Transactions of 1997 reduced their investments in corrupt countries. Investors from the US, which were bound by the Foreign Corrupt Practices Act of 1977, also reduced investments in corrupt countries, but only after the OECD Anti-Bribery Convention was in place. Closer coordination among European and North American governments in recent years led to more rigorous enforcement of anti-corruption laws around the world and resulted in a number of well-known MNEs paying large fines. The UK firm BAE Systems, for instance, agreed to pay fines of $400 million in 2010 to both the US and UK governments for false accounting to cover bribes made to win contracts.[41]

International organizations have also been increasing their anti-corruption activities. Since 1996, the board of the World Bank required that all commissions paid to agents be disclosed, giving the board the right to audit contractors and suppliers, and strengthened provisions for cancellation of bribe-tainted contracts and for debarment of violators from contracting. Anti-bribery amendments have been added to the Bank's loan conditions and procurement rules, and standard bidding documents were approved. The amendments require disclosure of commissions and gratuities paid, or to be paid, to agents relating to their bids or to contract execution on World Bank-financed contracts. The Bank will reject proposals for a contract award or cancel the loan if the bidder or the borrower has engaged in fraud or corruption in the procurement or execution of the contract. Companies determined by the Bank to have engaged in corrupt or fraudulent practice will be blacklisted from participation in Bank-financed contracts, either indefinitely or for a stated period of time.

The International Monetary Fund has taken similar steps. The Council of Securities Regulators of the Americas (COSRA) adopted an anti-bribery resolution to ensure enforcement of and compliance with internal control and accurate books and records requirements. COSRA also agreed to facilitate closer cooperation among securities and banking regulators in investigations and in criminal prosecutions for bribery. In the WTO, the 1977 Government Procurement Agreement (GPA), while voluntary, assists in the anti-corruption drive although the signatories are predominantly industrialized countries, including the United States, Canada, EU member states, Israel, Japan, Norway, the Republic of Korea, and Switzerland.

Country Box

Drug Companies Face Bribery Probe on Payments to Officials of Foreign Emerging Markets

Federal investigators are looking at ways that drug makers could be paying bribes overseas to boost sales and speed approvals. Big companies, including Merck & Co., AstraZeneca PLC, Bristol-Myers Squibb Co., and GlaxoSmithKline PLC, have disclosed they are being investigated for possible violations of the FCPA. So far, none of the companies has been accused of wrongdoing. The Justice Department and the Securities and Exchange Commission requested that companies voluntarily report any violations of the FCPA. The investigation is targeting transactions in Brazil, China, Poland, Russia, and Saudi Arabia. Such requests from the government typically kick off internal investigations at companies, which generally comply with the requests in order to win leniency from the government if a violation is found.

Letters from the government identified four types of possible violations: bribing government-employed doctors to purchase drugs; paying company sales agents commissions that are passed along to government doctors; paying hospital committees to approve drug purchases; and paying regulators to win drug approvals. The pharmaceutical industry is particularly vulnerable because government plays a bigger role in administering medicine in many foreign countries than it does in the US, and drugs are highly regulated, which creates contact with public officials. Doctors and hospital administrators are often government employees overseas. Some of the alleged bribes could involve payments to doctors to influence drug trials. Justice Department officials have said publicly that drug companies could also face charges if they bribe government officials in the guise of payment for travel, meals, entertainment, or speaking fees. In China, GSK is currently in the midst of a scandal for using funds paid to travel agencies to bribe doctors and officials. The allegations state that the amount could be up to about 3 billion yuan ($489 million).

Sources: Adapted from Michael Rothfeld, "Drug firms face bribery probe—Justice Department, SEC seek information from companies on payments to overseas officials," *Wall Street Journal,* October 5, 2010; Ben Hirschler, "GSK replaces China chief amid corruption scandal," *Reuters,* July 25, 2013.

Interim Summary

1. Corruption in international business appears in many forms. Although bribery may be the first corrupt practice that comes to mind, it is by no means the only one. Smuggling, for instance, is a means of increasing profit margin even on legitimate goods by avoiding customs duties, tariffs, import quotas, and any other constraints on the movement of goods.

2. Violation of intellectual property rights, including piracy and counterfeiting of everything from luxury clothing to aircraft parts and pharmaceuticals, is becoming a critical problem, with countries such as China, Vietnam, and Russia the leading violators.

3. The FCPA, passed in the 1970s, made it illegal for US companies to bribe foreign officials. However, this fight against corruption did not become truly global and did not see ratification into international treaties until recently.

Chapter Summary

1. The MNE Code of Conduct defines the contours of social responsibility in international business in realms such as disclosure, employment, the environment, and corruption.

2. MNEs increasingly take a proactive view of social responsibility, establishing internal control systems as well as seeking the assistance of NGOs.

3. Corruption is correlated with the developing or emerging status of an economy, higher level and scope of government intervention, and certain cultural dimensions.

4. Corrupt practices in international business include smuggling, money laundering, piracy and counterfeiting, and bribe paying.

5. The Foreign Corrupt Practices Act (FCPA) penalizes US firms and individuals who engage in corrupt practices. The OECD Convention, if enforced, will level the playing field for US firms that until recently were the only ones to be legally deterred from corrupt practices by their home country.

Notes

1 K.A. Getz, "International codes of conduct: An analysis of ethical reasoning," *Journal of Business Ethics*, 9, 1990, 567–577.
2 J. Coomson, "The digital divide becomes a digital dump," *Ghanaian Chronicle*, February 8, 2006.
3 H. Buraimoh, "On toxic e-waste shipments to Nigeria," *Vanguard*, January 23, 2013.
4 A.J. Heidenheimer, M. Johnston and V.T. LeVine, *Political Corruption: A Handbook*, New Brunswick, NJ: Transaction Publishers, 1987.

5   R. Kahana, *Corruption in Israeli Society,* Jerusalem: Academon, 1984.

6   J. Macrae, 1982, 678, cited in B.W. Husted, "Wealth, culture and corruption," *Journal of International Business Studies,* 30, 2, 1999, 340.

7   "Black hole," *The Economist,* August 28, 1999, 59, citing a study by Friedrich Schneider.

8   "The termite hunter," *The Economist,* October 16, 1999, 72.

9   O. Shenkar, *The Chinese Century,* Wharton School Publishing, 2006.

10   World Economic Forum, *Clean Business Is Good Business—The Business Case Against Corruption,* July 17, 2008.

11   "Crime, corruption and multinational business," *International Business,* July 1995.

12   G.R. Simpson, "Bribes taint contract bids overseas often," *Wall Street Journal,* February 23, 1999, A3.

13   J. Mason, "Petty corruption set to move up agenda for multinationals," *Financial Times,* January 11, 2001, 13.

14   "US government report on transnational bribery," *National Export Strategy Report,* September 24, 1996.

15   A. Schleifer and R. Vishny, "Corruption," *Quarterly Journal of Economics,* autumn 1993.

16   Transparency International website, September 1999.

17   J.R. Cohen, L.W. Pant, and D.J. Sharp, "A methodological note on cross-cultural accounting ethics research," *International Journal of Accounting,* 31, 1, 1996, 55–66.

18   S.J. Vittell, S.L. Nwachukwo, and J.H. Barnes, "The effects of culture on ethical decision-making: An application of Hofstede's typology," *Journal of Business Ethics,* 12, 1993, 753–760.

19   B.W. Husted, "Wealth, culture and corruption," *Journal of International Business Studies,* 30, 2, 1999, 340. A similar argument is made in terms of the lax internal control of Japanese corporations as in the infamous Sumitomo fiasco where one trader caused billions of dollars in losses while his colleagues by and large covered up his activities. See, for instance, S. Wudunn, "Big new loss makes Japan look inward," *The New York Times,* June 17, 1996.

20   Asian Executive Poll, *The Far Eastern Economic Review,* July 1, 1999, 31.

21   World Bank, cited also in "Judge or be judged," *the Economist,* July 29, 2006, 68.

22   "Pakistani stocks surge since military takeover amid hopes less corruption will lift economy," *Wall Street Journal,* February 24, 2000.

23   "Who will listen to Mr. Clean?," *The Economist,* August 2, 1997, 52.

24   P. Mauro, "Corruption and growth," *Quarterly Journal of Economics,* 110, 3, 1995, 681–712.

25   G.P. Zachary, "Industrialized countries agree to adopt rules to curb bribery," *Wall Street Journal,* February 16, 1999, A18.

26   "Beyond the Kremlin's walls," *The Economist,* May 20, 2000, 65.

27   "Now exhale," *The Economist,* August 26, 2000, 19.

28   K. Gillespie, "Smuggling and the global firm," *Journal of International Management,* 9, 2003, 317–333.

29   R.G. Matthews, "Evasive maneuvers: Steel smugglers find many ways to enter lucrative US market," *Wall Street Journal,* November 1, 2001, A1.

30   WTO Statistics on Globalization, 2001.

31   E. Schmitt, "Chairman admits bank's 'lapse' in judgment in Russian laundering case," *The New York Times,* September 23, 1999 (Internet edition).

32   John Zdanowicz, cited in R. Block, "Policing trade to nab terrorists," *Wall Street Journal,* March 11–12, 2006, A4.

33   T. McGirk, "Chasing shadows," *Time* magazine, June 11, 2001.

34   US government, report on transnational bribery, Fourth Annual National Export Strategy Report, September 24, 1996.

35   J. Tagliabue, "Kazakhstan is suspected in 100 million of oil bribes," *The New York Times,* July 28, 2000, A5.

36   *Business Week,* December 6, 1993.

37   "Hong Kong business reveals the price of graft," *South China Morning Post,* July 25, 1993.

38 F. Heimann and G. Dell, *Exporting Corruption? Country Enforcement of the OECD Anti-Bribery Convention Progress Report 2012,* Transparency International, 2012.

39 H. Williamson and M. Peel, "Nations shamed over bribery," *Financial Times,* June 27, 2006, 4; Transparency International.

40 Alvaro Cuervo-Cazurra, "The effectiveness of laws against bribery abroad," *Journal of International Business Studies,* 39, 2008, 634–651.

41 D. Leigh, R. Evans, and M. Tran, "BAE pays fines of £285m over arms deal corruption claims," *Guardian,* February 5, 2010.

chapter 20

international
entrepreneurship

DEFINING INTERNATIONAL ENTREPRENEURSHIP   641

COMPARATIVE ENTREPRENEURSHIP   642

CROSS-BORDER ENTREPRENEURSHIP   652

Do You Know?

1. Have you ever considered starting your own firm?
2. If yes, have you considered a foreign country as a location, a market, or perhaps a funding source for your start-up business? What country, and why?
3. What are the features of global start-ups and how do they differ from those of established small businesses that have expanded internationally?
4. What makes a new international venture an attractive acquisition target for an MNE?
5. What countries are especially good at creating entrepreneurial firms and what does this say about their competitive advantage?

OPENING CASE Will Entrepreneurship Help Japan Regain its Lost Decades?

Japan has been plagued with an economic malaise for over two decades since the burst of its stock and real estate bubbles in 1991. Analysts have cited many factors that have held back the country's once roaring economy, including a rapidly aging population, high public debt, and low productivity of government-protected economic sectors (e.g., agriculture, chemicals, retail, and transport). One factor that may have contributed significantly to the slow recovery of the Japanese economy from its initial slowdown is the lack of opportunity-driven entrepreneurship.

The World Bank ranks Japan dead last among the members of the Organization for Economic Co-operation and Development (OECD) in terms of the average annual entry rate of new enterprises. According to the Global Entrepreneurship Monitor, 4.9 percent of US adults aged 18–64 are working actively to establish new businesses, while the figure in Japan is only 1.9 percent. Japan's venture capital industry is also small. A 2012 report by the government puts the total loans and investments in the industry at ¥124 billion ($1.55 billion), about one-nineteenth the amount in the US. The low level of entrepreneurship activities can be traced to both the country's regulatory system and its cultural heritage.

Entrepreneurs typically face myriad difficulties in starting a business in Japan. The World Bank ranks Japan 114 out of 185 countries in the world in the ease of starting a business. One particularly challenging task is to raise funds. Japanese banks typically require onerous loan guarantees when they lend money to entrepreneurs. For instance, Mr. Koki Uchiyama, a successful Internet entrepreneur, had to provide guarantees of ¥300 million—more than 50 times his annual income at the time—in order to get a loan of ¥300 million ($3.1 million) when he was starting his business. In addition, bankruptcy laws in Japan put the personal savings of entrepreneurs and their families at risk, due to the collateralization of their savings and the transfer of debt responsibilities to family members. Furthermore, the Japanese culture is high on collectivism and cherishes conformity and does not easily foster an atmosphere conducive to entrepreneurial activities that tend to break rules. Its educational system emphasizes academic performance as the only route to success, with almost all its high-achieving graduates going to large established corporations that typically practice some form of lifetime employment.

To rejuvenate its lethargic economy, Shinzo Abe became the first leader of the country to put the promotion of entrepreneurship high on his agenda after taking office as Prime Minister in 2012. He has created tax incentives for entrepreneurial activities, established special zones with simplified procedures for starting a new business, and initiated the process of changing rules for commercial banks to provide loans to business start-ups. These changes in the regulatory system can certainly be helpful. But will they also lead to changes in the attitudes of educated Japanese toward entrepreneurship and succeed in shifting the country to a faster path of growth?

Source: B. McLannahan, "Japan grapples with lack of entrepreneurs," *The Financial Times*, June 12, 2013; "Entrepreneurs in Japan: Time to get started," *The Economist*, August 31, 2013, 25.

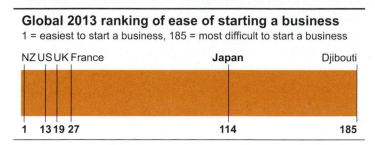

Global 2013 ranking of ease of starting a business
1 = easiest to start a business, 185 = most difficult to start a business

NZ US UK France   **Japan**   Djibouti

1   13 19 27   114   185

Exhibit 20.1 Japan's low rating on the ease of starting a business
Source: World Bank

Defining International Entrepreneurship

In recent years, interest in entrepreneurship has grown dramatically. Governments realized that entrepreneurial firms are a major source of economic growth, jobs, and competitive advantage, and have been trying to form an environment conducive to their formation and prosperity. Large, established firms came to view entrepreneurial firms as a source of innovation to be tapped. Individuals discovered that entrepreneurship was a way to fulfill one's dreams and realize opportunities unavailable from traditional employment. The rising interest in entrepreneurship occurred in tandem with an accelerated globalization of the business environment (see Chapter 1), heightening awareness of the entrepreneurial, funding, and marketing opportunities available beyond national borders.

International entrepreneurship is defined as "the discovery, enactment, evaluation and exploitation of opportunities—across national borders—to create future goods and services."[1] The study of international entrepreneurship consists of two thrusts, comparative and cross-border. Comparative entrepreneurship examines similarities and differences between countries on the level of entrepreneurial activity, the business environment (for example, the extent to which the regulatory environment is supportive of new business), or the motivations of would-be entrepreneurs. Cross-border entrepreneurship looks at entrepreneurial activities that leverage national differences in environment and resources, for instance, a US-based venture capital (VC) fund identifying promising start-ups in India, or an Irish high-tech start-up seeking an alliance with a Chinese company to produce its newly developed technology for sale in the US market.

Toward the conclusion of Chapter 4 on the MNE, we discussed the case of "born global" or "international new ventures," start-up firms that export their products or services to foreign markets even before they have sold a single product domestically. Oviatt and McDougall define the "born global" or "international new venture" (INV) as "a business organization that, from inception, seeks to derive significant competitive advantage from the use of resources and the sale of outputs in multiple countries."[2] Unlike other firms that typically undertake international expansion incrementally, the INV adopts an international mindset from day one. These firms are increasingly active on the international scene as exporters and foreign investors.

Comparative Entrepreneurship

Comparative entrepreneurship examines the variation in entrepreneurship rates and patterns across nations; it also looks at the underlying reasons for the variation. Exhibit 20.1, taken from the Global Entrepreneurship Monitor (GEM), shows the rates of entrepreneurial activities in different countries. The table groups countries into three categories based on the World Economic Forum's (WEF) Global Competitive Report. The WEF identifies three phases of economic development based on GDP per capita and the share of exports comprising primary goods. The first group of 11 countries are in the earliest stage of development, relying heavily on unskilled labor and natural resources in their economic activities. The second group of 30 countries have achieved a significant level of industrialization, relying increasingly on economies of scale and capital-intensive large businesses for further economic development through enhanced efficiency. The third group of 24 countries are in the advanced stage of development, relying primarily on innovation in knowledge-intensive high-technology manufacturing and service sectors for economic growth.

Nascent entrepreneurial activity, reflecting the level of new venture initiation, is led by Zambia, Nigeria, and Malawi; in contrast, Algeria, Tunisia, Italy, and Japan show very low rates. The percentage of new business owners, measured as the prevalence of new businesses that have paid salaries for more than three but less than 42 months, shows Uganda, Ghana, and Malawi at the top, with rates five to seven times higher than the US rate of 4 percent, while Russia, Tunisia, Belgium, Denmark, France, Germany, Ireland, Italy, Japan, Spain, and Sweden place at the bottom. Early stage entrepreneurial activity, which combines the former two measures, places Zambia at the top, followed by Ghana, Malawi, and Nigeria, while Russia, Italy, and Japan are at the bottom. The rate for established business owners, who have been in business for more than 42 months, is highest in Ghana, Uganda, and Thailand. Finally, countries with high rates of entrepreneurial activity also tend to be high in the rates of business discontinuation. Even though entrepreneurial activity rates are on average higher in less developed countries, there is still significant variation in these measured rates within each category of countries.

There are different reasons that individuals decide to pursue entrepreneurial activities. Many entrepreneurs are motivated by a perceived opportunity to improve their incomes, lifestyles (e.g., gaining independence), or levels of personal fulfillment and professional achievement (e.g., setting up an online store that has the potential for fundamentally changing the retail industry). However, many others decide to engage in entrepreneurship due to necessity, starting their own business for lack of suitable and rewarding employment. As can be seen in the two rightmost columns of Exhibit 20.2, entrepreneurial activities tend to be motivated less by *necessity* and more by *improvement* as a country develops further.

642

Exhibit 20.2

Country	Nascent Entrepreneurship Rate	New Business Ownership Rate	Early-stage Entrepreneurial Activity (TEA)	Established Business Ownership Rate	Discontinuation of Businesses	Necessity Driven (% of TEA)	Improvement Driven Opportunity (% of TEA)
FACTOR							
Algeria	2	7	9	3	7	30	47
Angola	15	19	32	9	26	24	38
Botswana	17	12	28	6	16	33	48
Egypt	3	5	8	4	5	34	23
Ethiopia	6	9	15	10	3	20	69
Ghana	15	23	37	38	16	28	51
Iran	4	6	11	10	5	42	36
Malawi	18	20	36	11	29	42	43
Nigeria	22	14	35	16	8	35	53
Pakistan	8	3	12	4	3	53	24
Palestine Territories	6	4	10	3	8	42	27
Uganda	10	28	36	31	26	46	42
Zambia	27	15	41	4	20	32	46
Average (unweighted)	12	13	24	11	13	35	42
EFFICIENCY							
Argentina	12	7	19	10	5	35	47
Barbados	10	7	17	12	3	12	63
Bosnia and Herzegovina	5	3	8	6	7	58	20
Brazil	4	11	15	15	5	30	59
Chile	15	8	23	8	5	17	69
China	5	7	13	12	4	37	39
Colombia	14	7	20	7	7	12	48
Costa Rica	10	5	15	3	3	20	48
Croatia	6	2	8	3	4	34	36
Ecuador	17	12	27	19	8	36	30
El Salvador	8	8	15	9	8	35	39
Estonia	9	5	14	7	4	18	49
Hungary	6	4	9	8	4	31	35
Latvia	9	5	13	8	3	25	46
Lithuania	3	4	7	8	2	25	51
Macedonia	4	3	7	7	4	52	29
Malaysia	3	4	7	7	2	13	61

Exhibit 20.2 Entrepreneurial activity across countries (2012), by phase of economic development

Source: Global Entrepreneurship Monitor 2012 Global Report.

Mexico	8	4	12	5	4	13	52
Namibia	11	7	18	3	12	37	37
Panama	7	3	9	2	2	19	57
Peru	15	6	20	5	7	23	53
Poland	5	5	9	6	4	41	30
Romania	6	4	9	4	4	24	38
Russia	3	2	4	2	1	36	31
South Africa	4	3	7	2	5	32	40
Thailand	9	11	19	30	3	17	67
Trinidad & Tobago	9	7	15	7	5	15	60
Tunisia	2	2	5	4	4	35	42
Turkey	7	5	12	9	5	31	55
Uruguay	10	5	15	5	5	18	40
Average (unweighted)	8	6	13	8	5	28	46
INNOVATION							
Austria	7	3	10	8	4	11	38
Belgium	3	2	5	5	2	18	62
Denmark	3	2	5	3	1	8	71
Finland	3	3	6	8	2	17	60
France	4	2	5	3	2	18	59
Germany	4	2	5	5	2	22	51
Greece	4	3	7	12	4	30	32
Ireland	4	2	6	8	2	28	41
Israel	3	3	7	4	4	19	46
Italy	2	2	4	3	2	16	22
Japan	2	2	4	6	1	21	66
Republic of Korea	3	4	7	10	3	35	46
Netherlands	4	6	10	9	2	8	66
Norway	4	3	7	6	1	7	70
Portugal	4	4	8	6	3	18	53
Singapore	8	4	12	3	4	15	54
Slovakia	7	4	10	6	5	36	43
Slovenia	3	3	5	6	2	7	64
Spain	3	2	6	9	2	26	33
Sweden	5	2	6	5	2	7	49
Switzerland	3	3	6	8	2	18	57
Taiwan	3	4	8	10	6	18	43
United Kingdom	5	4	9	6	2	18	43
United States	9	4	13	9	4	21	59
Average (unweighted)	4	3	7	7	3	18	51

Exhibit 20.2 (*Continued*)

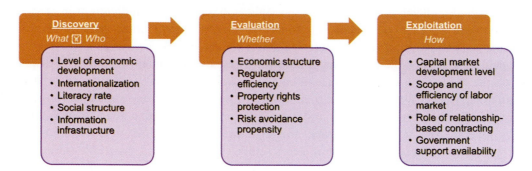

Exhibit 20.3 Key factors affecting how entrepreneurship processes differ across countries

Source: Adapted from Ted Baker, Eric Gedajlovic, and Michael Lubatkin, "A framework for comparing entrepreneurship processes across nations," *Journal of International Business Studies*, 36, 2005, 492–504.

There are good reasons for the substantial differences in entrepreneurial rates shown in Exhibit 20.2. Countries vary on the environmental characteristics that are considered conducive to entrepreneurial activity, in entrepreneurial motivation (for instance, whether individuals choose to become entrepreneurs as a means toward self-fulfillment or riches, or rather out of necessity because substitutes for upward mobility are scarce), and in their objectives (for example, whether they seek to grow a firm or head for a quick exit via an IPO and/or an acquisition).

Exhibit 20.3 provides a framework for understanding how entrepreneurship processes are likely to differ across countries. The first phase—discovery—is concerned with who recognizes what opportunities. The types of opportunities that exist in a country depend on the level of its economic development and openness to international trade and investment. What types of individuals would recognize these opportunities depends on the educational levels of the people in the various socio-economic groups, their expected roles in the society, and the dissemination of information about the opportunities. The second phase—evaluation—is where potential entrepreneurs assess a recognized opportunity and decide whether to take it. This phase is influenced by the employment opportunities of the evaluator, effectiveness and efficiency of the regulatory and property rights regimes, and risk-taking propensity of individuals in the culture. The final phase—exploitation—is where the entrepreneur gets funding from formal or informal sources (e.g., banks and venture capitalists vs. family and friends), hires employees on the labor market or from among relatives and acquaintances, sets up a sole-owned or jointly owned enterprise, and possibly receives support from government agencies. As shown in Exhibit 20.3, the country's economic institutions also exert marked influences on the entrepreneurship process in this phase.

Culture and Entrepreneurship

National culture is closely related to entrepreneurship levels and motivations.[3] Generally speaking, high individualism and low uncertainty avoidance encourage entrepreneurial activity, especially when opportunity-based. The relationship between culture and entrepreneurship is not a simple one, however. One study has found that while high individualism was associated with generating variety through innovation and new ventures, the leveraging of resources via internal or external ties required high collectivism.[4] It is hence possible to have levels of individualism that are "too high."[5] The venture creation decision was found to correlate with cultural dimensions in another study using a cognitive approach. Institutional features have also been found to correlate with entrepreneurial activities. In particular, normative aspects of the environment were found to be related to the inclination of individuals to engage in entrepreneurial activity, while the cognitive and regulatory aspects were related to their ability to raise funds from external investors.[6]

Three traits have been identified and related to entrepreneurial potential: internal locus of control, moderate risk-taking propensity, and high energy level.[7] Still, it is useful to remember that entrepreneurs share a lot in common across cultures: Baum found that the difference between Israeli entrepreneurs and non-entrepreneurs was greater than the difference between Israeli and US entrepreneurs.[8]

Funding New Ventures

One of the first challenges for the entrepreneur is raising money for the new venture. Most entrepreneurs use informal financing sources, such as that of family, friends, and sometimes strangers, and, of course, their own funds. Fewer solicit "classical" investment from professional venture capital firms which can invest in seed, start-up, early-stage, or expansion-stage firms.[9] Exhibit 20.4 shows classic venture capital (VC) investment as a percentage of GDP in various countries, with Israel, South Africa, and the US at the top (0.2 percent to 1.0 percent), while Serbia, Croatia, and Slovenia are at the bottom, with 0.01 percent or less. Remember that this is an overall rate across all types of ventures. When it comes to seed, start-up, and early-stage ventures, Israel by far leads the group of countries listed in Exhibit 20.3 (see also Industry Box).

Between 1991 and 2000, the amount of venture capital raised in the United States rose by a factor of 80, vis-à-vis a factor of 12 in Europe. European VC funds spend a higher proportion of their money on early-stage firms and are more likely to fund manufacturing ventures than their US counterparts. The growth in developed economies slowed down in the 2000s, particularly after the onset of the global economic downturn in 2008. In 2011, the annual VC investment reached $32.6 billion in the US and $6.1 billion in Europe. In emerging economies, however, VC investment has experience a boom since the mid-2000s. In China, for example, VC investment grew from $1.1 billion in 2005 to $5.9 billion in 2011, more than quintupling in six years. In the same time period, VC investment in India also grew five times from $0.3 billion to $1.5 billion. European VC firms tend to make proportionally smaller investments in more companies. While Europe shows a preference for early-stage investments, late-stage investments dominate the VC market in China.[10] In the US, institutional investment (e.g., investment funds) constitutes roughly two-thirds of VC investment versus about one-third in Europe.[11] There are also substantial differences in the reliance of venture capital firms on various information sources. US funds, like those in Hong Kong and Singapore, relied on accounting information culled from business plans, while those in India, for example, did not. Still, valuation methods did not vary much.[12] VC investments in a country also clearly respond to government policy changes. Investment in clean energy, for instance, rose in Europe and China as the governments of these countries adopted policies to encourage the development of such technology.[13]

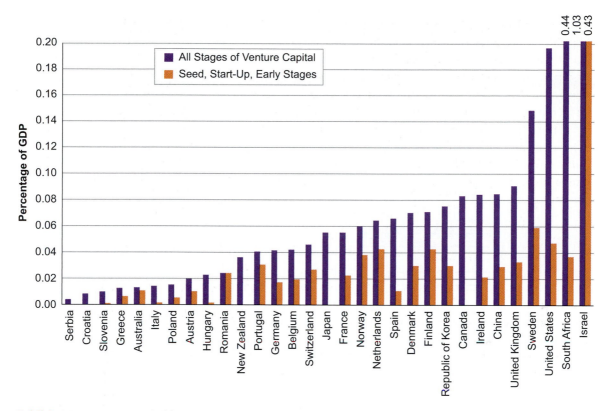

Exhibit 20.4 Venture capital investments as a percentage of GDP, by stage of the company
Source: Global Entrepreneurship Monitor 2009 Global Report.

When it comes to informal investment, the picture is quite different. Uganda, Guatemala, and Chile lead in the prevalence of informal investors with rates ranging from 10 percent to 19 percent, while China and Bosnia and Herzegovina lead in the prevalence of informal investment with the amount of informal capital accounting for over 10 percent of GDP. The United States is relatively high among advanced economies in the prevalence of both informal investors and informal investment (see Exhibits 20.5a and 20.5b). When a country's formal financial institutions are either underdeveloped or biased against medium and small enterprises (such as in the case of China), informal investment often fills the gaps. In the meantime, an overly regulated financial system can also leave little room for informal investment to function effectively.

There are additional factors that determine entrepreneurial level. For instance, being located within clusters of similar firms, suppliers, and customers makes it easier to establish new venture firms and make their success more probable.[14] Together with funding opportunities and a supportive culture, a regulatory environment that makes starting a new business trouble-free is of paramount importance to entrepreneurship. For instance, the minimum capital requirement to start a business in Syria prior to 2011 was over $60,000, more than 5,000 percent of the per capita income in the country, making

647

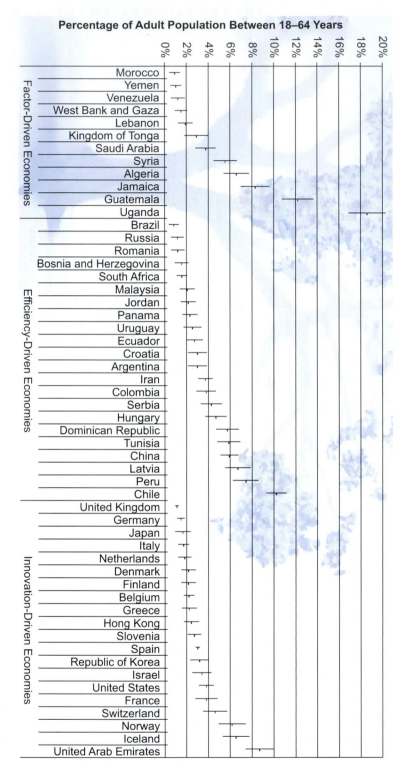

Exhibit 20.5a Prevalence rates of informal investors (2009), by phase of economic development, showing 95 percent confidence intervals

Source: Global Entrepreneurship Monitor 2009 Global Report.

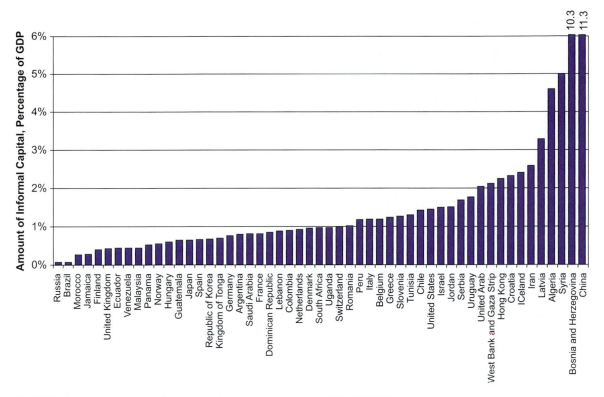

Exhibit 20.5b Amount of informal capital as a percentage of GDP (2009)
Source: Global Entrepreneurship Monitor 2009 Global Report.

it impossible for anyone but the wealthiest individuals to start a business. Similarly, in Suriname it takes nearly 700 days to complete business registration, versus just six days in the US and two days in Australia. Equatorial Guinea requires 21 different procedures to complete business registration, while Canada and New Zealand require only one.[15] Exhibit 20.6 summarizes the ease of starting a business based on the procedures, time, cost, and paid-up minimum capital for starting a business.

Interim Summary

1. International entrepreneurship covers the similarities and differences in entrepreneurial environments, capabilities, and motivations across countries.
2. Entrepreneurship tends to be higher in cultures high on individualism and low on uncertainty avoidance.
3. Funding opportunities and regulatory environment are among the main factors that determine the level of entrepreneurship.

Economy	Ease of Doing Business Rank	Starting a Business	Dealing with Construction Permits	Getting Electricity	Registering Property	Getting Credit	Protecting Investors	Paying Taxes	Trading Across Borders	Enforcing Contracts	Resolving Insolvency
Singapore	1	3	3	6	28	3	2	5	1	12	4
Hong Kong	2	5	1	5	89	3	3	4	2	9	19
New Zealand	3	1	12	45	2	3	1	23	21	18	12
US	4	20	34	13	25	3	6	64	22	11	17
Denmark	5	40	8	18	7	28	34	12	8	32	10
Malaysia	6	16	43	21	35	1	4	36	5	30	42
Korea, Rep.	7	34	18	2	75	13	52	25	3	2	15
Georgia	8	8	2	54	1	3	16	29	43	33	88
Norway	9	53	28	17	10	73	22	17	26	4	2
UK	10	28	27	74	68	1	10	14	16	56	7
Australia	11	4	10	34	40	3	68	44	46	14	18
Finland	12	55	36	22	26	42	68	21	9	8	3
Iceland	13	52	41	1	12	42	52	37	50	3	11
Sweden	14	61	24	9	38	42	34	41	6	25	20
Ireland	15	12	115	100	57	13	6	6	20	62	8
Taiwan	16	17	7	7	31	73	34	58	18	84	16
Lithuania	17	11	39	75	6	28	68	56	15	17	44
Thailand	18	91	14	12	29	73	12	70	24	22	58
Canada	19	2	116	145	55	28	4	8	45	58	9
Mauritius	20	19	123	48	65	42	12	13	12	54	61

Exhibit 20.6 Ease of starting a business

Source: World Bank, 2013.

Zimbabwe	170	150	170	157	93	109	128	142	167	118	156
Malawi	171	149	173	183	85	130	80	81	176	145	150
Timor-Leste	172	154	128	44	189	165	115	55	92	189	189
Mauritania	173	173	123	124	67	170	147	181	152	75	189
Benin	174	139	95	160	137	130	157	179	119	181	140
Guinea	175	146	155	91	140	159	178	186	136	134	145
Niger	176	159	164	123	80	130	157	162	178	143	154
Haiti	177	187	141	67	138	165	170	132	151	96	189
Senegal	178	110	165	182	174	130	170	182	80	167	122
Angola	179	178	65	170	132	130	80	155	169	187	189
Guinea-Bissau	180	159	119	188	170	130	138	153	125	148	189
Venezuela, RB	181	157	110	167	95	130	182	187	173	92	165
Myanmar	182	189	150	126	154	170	182	107	113	188	155
Congo, Dem. Rep.	183	185	90	142	133	159	147	176	171	177	167
Eritrea	184	188	189	95	184	186	115	150	170	67	189
Congo, Rep.	185	182	142	175	164	109	157	183	180	164	142
South Sudan	186	140	171	184	183	180	182	92	187	87	189
Libya	187	171	189	68	189	186	187	116	143	150	189
Central African Rep.	188	177	156	177	141	109	138	188	185	180	189
Chad	189	183	139	149	146	130	157	189	183	171	189

Exhibit 20.6 (*Continued*)

Cross-Border Entrepreneurship

Just as large MNEs leverage their access to multiple environments, each with its own comparative advantage, so can entrepreneurs leverage the resources, skills, and markets in various locations to tap broader opportunities and create synergies that would be impossible to create otherwise. Accelerated globalization permits the distribution of diverse activities across borders, say, the placement of financing in one location and sales and distribution in another. For instance, some European start-ups have chosen to do initial public offerings (IPOs) in the United States through American Depository Receipts (ADRs). This allowed them not only to raise funds but also to enhance their legitimacy in the United States and better penetrate that market. Such IPOs have also been found to increase the legitimacy of start-ups in their home countries.[16]

MNEs, for their part, not only increasingly realize that entrepreneurial capabilities and opportunities reside in their home country, but they are pursuing those opportunities. Since 1991, Intel has invested more than $10 billion in more than 1,250 firms in 54 countries. Of the $352 million the company invested in start-ups in 2012, 57 percent went to companies based outside North America, compared to a historical average of 37 percent.[17] The corporate venture arm of Motorola recently added an investment in BriefCam, a new quick-view video technology in Israel, to its portfolio.[18]

International new ventures (INVs) tend to internalize their activities to a much lesser extent than established MNEs, using alternatives such as strategic alliances. The INVs often take advantage of technological advances that permit knowledge mobility as leverage, but to do so they must internationalize from the very beginning. To achieve that, in turn, they need to have founders and managers that possess international experience and "think globally."[19]

In chapter 12, we have noted that such cooperative agreements are a good way to compensate for resource shortage, something that is typical of INVs. Yehezkel and her colleagues found that the number of Israeli medical technology start-ups that established alliances was three times greater than those who did not. Technology and R&D alliances were formed with both domestic and foreign partners at about the same ratio; however, the marketing alliances had a six-to-one ratio of foreign to local issues, not surprising for "born global" firms. Altogether, the companies that established alliances delivered lower return than those who did not, albeit at a lower risk level.[20]

Alliance formation was also found to be related to culture. One study found that firms from individualistic, uncertainty-tolerant cultures relied less on alliances in the technology area. Firms from high masculinity cultures tended to avoid technological alliances altogether.[21] Li and Atuahene-Gima found that start-ups in China, a relatively collectivistic culture, relied on alliances for both product development and political networking.[22]

Internationalizing the Born Global Enterprise

As discussed in Chapter 4, small firms are much more likely to engage in exports than undertake foreign direct investment, mostly because of their limited resources. The INV is no exception. Still, exports require a good understanding of a target market as well as recognition and acceptance in that market. European firms that did an IPO in the United States increased exports into the US market, especially when the listing was followed by a rising stock price.[23]

In a sense, entrepreneurial firms possess qualities that prepare them to face the vagaries of international markets. Being proactive (in other words, having a bias for action) and innovative, key features of the entrepreneurial firm, are important assets when it comes to international activities, especially those that go beyond a firm's current operations.[24] As is the case for large MNEs, US-based start-ups are less likely to reach into international markets because of the relatively large domestic market; they also benefit from ample financing and technological capabilities at home. Still, foreign markets are a draw for born global firms also in the United States. International experience of board members, larger firm size, and product, rather than cost, differentiation were found to be predictors of internationalization.[25] In particular, the international experience of the founders and managers was found to be a trigger of international expansion.[26] Such experience allows managers to identify entrepreneurial opportunities as well as have better knowledge about how to tap those opportunities. In contrast to large MNEs, international new ventures have not been found to be motivated by a desire to achieve economies of scale or cost reduction.[27]

INVs benefit from international expansion in a number of ways. By developing learning capabilities and tapping into various sources of innovation and different sets of comparative advantages, such ventures tend to extend their technological learning as well. A study by Hill, Zahra, and Hitt found that ventures with greater country diversity increased their technological capability, but only up to a point: those with the greatest diversity found their learning to go down, probably because of difficulty managing the learning process. Having high control modes, especially acquisitions, was also associated with better learning, as was having an environment with a culture similar to one's own.[28] This is not surprising. In general, knowledge of an international market was found to be an important determinant of international sales growth of entrepreneurial firms.[29]

Its advantages notwithstanding, internationalization also carries considerable risks for the entrepreneurial firm. Time, cost, and resource diversion are some of the main risks internationalization presents to new ventures.[30] Added risks appear when those firms enter risky and volatile markets. Some INVs are better able to handle those risks than others. For example, it has been found that innovative ventures with high growth objectives that served niche markets with low cost and focused product lines were able to generate more international revenues and enter riskier markets than other new venture firms.[31] For other firms, higher internationalization translated into a higher market share but not necessarily into superior return on investment.[32]

The INV that decides to export is still faced with entry-mode decisions (see Chapter 10) (e.g., the choice between direct exporting and the use of distributors). A study by Burgel and Murray found that 68 percent of the technology start-ups in their sample had international sales, selling 38 percent of their turnover in foreign markets; 33 percent sold more in international markets than domestically. A majority of those firms chose to export through distributors even when they had more international experience, though having managers with personal experience in international markets has led to direct exportation.[33]

Industry Box

Israeli Start-Ups in the Global Marketplace

Israel has seen dramatic growth in technological start-ups, which started to take off in the early 1990s. By the year 2000, the country already shared second place with the US (trailing Canada) in the prevalence of growth-oriented ventures; ranked second, following the US, in entrepreneurial motivation; and tied Canada for third place in the entrepreneurial capacity of its population.[34] Today, there are more Israeli firms on the NASDAQ than those of any other foreign (non-US) domicile, and dozens of Israeli companies are also listed on European and, more recently, Asian exchanges, sometimes in addition to their home bourse of Tel Aviv. Israel attracts more venture capital per person than any other nation in the world ($170 as compared to $75 in the US) and has the highest density of start-up companies in the world (one for every 1,844 people).[35] Start-up activity is concentrated in the high-technology sector, which accounts for the vast majority of Israel's industrial exports.

Well-equipped industrial parks provide the physical structure, as well as a supportive environment for high-tech entrepreneurial activity. Many of those parks provide incubators that accompany the entrepreneur from idea to market and provide a network of expert advice. Private parks, such as the Weizmann Biotechnology and Genetics Park in Nes Tziona,[36] provide infrastructure in specialized areas. Israel's more than 100 venture capital (VC) funds provide critical launch capital, as do many foreign MNEs. The Global Entrepreneurship Monitor shows classic venture capital investment in Israel at 1.03 percent of GDP, more than twice the US level. Many projects are also financed by the Chief Scientist office of the Ministry of Industry and Trade.

At the heart of Israel's success is its human resource pool, which boasts the highest ratio of engineers and scientists in the world. The pool has been augmented by immigrants from the former Soviet Union, 40 percent of whom hold academic degrees,[37] as well as by Israeli Silicon Valley veterans. Today, 24 percent of Israeli's workforce and 35 percent of the 25–64 age group hold university degrees, ranking the nation third in the world after the US and the Netherlands. Trade agreements with the US, the European Union, and EFTA have increased the exposure of Israelis to the outside world. Social norms now stress individualism, materialism, and independence. In tandem, entrepreneurship is increasingly accepted as a driving force in personal lives and in market development.

Chapter Summary

1. International entrepreneurship consists of both differences across countries on entrepreneurial levels and features and cross-national entrepreneurial activities.

2. Entrepreneurial levels are determined by economic development, cultural dispositions, and the regulatory environment, among other factors.

3. In a global/knowledge economy, entrepreneurial capabilities are increasingly a determinant of competitive advantage.

4. International new ventures display rapid internationalization often, but not always, across multiple national markets.

5. International entrepreneurship still has a long way to go, as entrepreneurs and executives are only beginning to tap the resources and opportunities available in other markets.

Notes

1 B.M. Oviatt and P.P. McDougall, "Defining international entrepreneurship and modeling the speed of internationalization," *Entrepreneurship Theory and Practice*, September 2005, 537–553.

2 B.M. Oviatt and P.P. McDougall, "Toward a theory of international new ventures," *Journal of International Business Studies*, 25, 1, 1994, 45–64.

3 R.K. Mitchell, B. Smith, K.W. Seawright, and E.A Morse, "Cross-cultural cognitions and the venture creation decision," *Academy of Management Journal*, 43, 5, 1994, 974–993.

4 J.H. Tiessen, "Individualism, collectivism, and entrepreneurship: A framework for international comparative research," *Journal of Business Venturing*, 12, 1997, 367–384.

5 M.H. Morris, D.L. Davis, and J.W. Allen, *Journal of International Business Studies*, 1st quarter, 1994, 67–89.

6 L.W. Busenitz, C. Gomez, and J.W. Spencer, "Country institutional profiles: Unlocking entrepreneurial phenomena," *Academy of Management Journal*, 43, 5, 2000, 994–1003.

7 A.S. Thomas and S.L. Mueller, "A case for comparative entrepreneurship: Assessing the relevance of culture," *Journal of International Business Studies*, 31, 2, 2000, 287–301.

8 J.R. Baum, J.D. Olian, M. Erez, E.R. Schnell, K.G. Smith, H.P. Sims, J.S. Scully, and K.A. Smith, "Nationality and work role interactions: A cultural contrast of Israeli and US entrepreneurs," *Journal of Business Venturing*, 8, 1993, 499–512.

9 Global Entrepreneurship Monitor, 2005, p. 49.

10 Ernst & Young Global Limited, *Global Venture Capital Insights and Tends Report 2011*.

11 L. Bottazzi and M. Da Rin, "Venture capital in Europe and the financing of innovative companies," *Economic Policy*, April 2002.

12 A. Lockett, M. Wright, H. Sapienza, and S. Pruthi, "Venture capital investors, valuation and information: A comparative study of the US, Hong Kong, India and Singapore," *Venture Capital*, 4, 2, 2002, 237–252.

13 Ernst & Young Global Limited, *Global Venture Capital Insights and Tends Report 2011*, 2011.

14 H. Matlay and J. Mitra, "Learning, innovation and globalization: The competitive advantage of collaborative entrepreneurship." In Leo-Paul Dana (ed.), *Handbook of International Entrepreneurship*, Cheltenham, UK: Edward Elgar, 2006.

15 The World Bank, *Doing Business in a More Transparent World*, The World Bank, 2012.

16 B.D. Cohen, "Internationalizing European IPOs in the United States." In L-P. Dana (ed.), *Handbook of International Entrepreneurship*, London: Edward Elgar, 2006.

17   Intel Capital, *Investing in Global Innovation, 2013*.

18   Motorola Solutions, "Motorola Solutions invests in BriefCam," *Business Wire*, March 13, 2013.

19   B.M. Oviatt and P.P. McDougall, "Toward a theory of international joint ventures," *Journal of International Business Studies*, 25, 1, 2014, 45–64.

20   O. Yeheskel, O. Shenkar, A. Feigenbaum, and E. Cohen, "Cooperative wealth creation: Strategic alliances in Israeli medical-technology ventures," *Academy of Management Executive*, 15, 1, 2001, 16–25.

21   H. Kevin Steensma, L. Marino, K. Mark Weaver, and P. H. Dickson, "The influence of national culture on the formation of technology alliances by entrepreneurial firms," *Academy of Management Journal*, 43, 5, 2000, 951–973.

22   H. Li and K. Atuahene-Gima, "Product innovation strategy and the performance of new technology ventures in China," *Academy of Management Journal*, 44, 5, 2001, 1123–1134.

23   B.D. Cohen, "Internationalizing European IPOs in the United States." In L-P. Dana (ed.), *Handbook of International Entrepreneurship*, Cheltenham, UK: Edward Elgar, 2006.

24   D. De Clercq, H.J. Sapienza, and H. Crijns, "The internationalization of small and medium-sized firms," *Small Business Economics*, 24, 2005, 408–119.

25   J.M. Bloodgood, H.J. Sapienza, and J.G. Almeida, "The internationalization of new high-potential US ventures: Antecedents and outcomes," *Entrepreneurship Theory and Practice*, summer 1996, 61–76.

26   P.P. McDougall, B.M. Oviatt, and R.C. Shrader, "A comparison of international and domestic new ventures," *Journal of International Entrepreneurship*, 1, 2003, 59–82.

27   C.G. Brush, *International Entrepreneurship*, New York: Garland Publishing, 1995.

28   S.A. Zahra, R.D. Ireland, and M.A. Hitt, "International expansion by new venture firms: International diversity, mode of market entry, technological learning, and performance," *Academy of Management Journal*, 43, 5, 2000, 925–950.

29   E. Autio, S. Erkko, H.J. Sapienza, and J.G. Almeida, "Effects of age at entry, knowledge intensity, and imitability on international growth," *Academy of Management Journal*, 43, 5, 2000, 909–924.

30   H.J. Sapienza, J. Harry , E. Autio, and S. Zahra, "Effects of internationalization on young firms' prospects for survival and growth," *Academy of Management Best Papers Proceedings*, 2003, G1–G7.

31   O. Shrader and P.P. McDougall, "How new ventures exploit trade-offs among international risk factors: Lessons for the accelerated internationalization of the 21st century," *Academy of Management Journal*, 43, 6, 2000, 1227–1247.

32   P. P. McDougall and B.M. Oviatt, "New venture internationalization, strategic change, and performance: A follow-up study," *Journal of Business Venturing*, 11, 1996, 23–40.

33   O. Burgel and G.C. Murray, "The international market entry choices of start-up companies in High Technology industries," *Journal of International Marketing*, 8, 2, 2000, 33–62.

34   M. Lerner and Y. Avrahami, *Global Entrepreneurship Monitor—1999 Israel Executive Report*.

35   "What next for the start-up nation? Israeli technology companies," *The Economist*, January 21, 2012, 69–70.

36   State of Israel Export Institute Report, Biotechnology in Israel, December 2000 1: 18.

37   State of Israel Investment Promotion Center Report, 2000.

Index

Page numbers in bold refer to figures/tables.

ABB 400, 567, 630
Abboud, L. 599
Abe, S. 641
Absolute advantage theory 24, 25, 40, 68; inability to explain 25
Absolute purchasing power parity (PPP) 306
Absorptive capability 453–54
Abu Dhabi Investment Company 362
Accounting 497–500, **501**, 505, 521n1, 521n2, 522n6; corruption and 190, 633; *see also* International accounting
Acer 131, **137**, 357, 485
Achievement cultures 206
Acquisitions 106–07, 365, 370; independent international agency oversight 327; international acquisitions 322 372; international lending 322; reorganization investment strategy 285; termination by acquisition 429
Actionable subsidies 63
Active/aggressive reciprocity 55
Active role 381
Adaptation 533; packaging and 548; product adaptation 531
Adler, N.J. 212, 216n8, 575, 589n3, 589n9, 590n36
Administrative barriers 65–66; dispute-resolution mechanisms and 66; foreign transport of goods and 66; import licensing procedures and 66; labeling practices and 66
Administrative barriers 65–66; *see also* Non-tariff barriers
Advertising 542
Aéroports de Paris 362
Aerospace equipment 64
Aerospatiale-Matra 136
Aetna 384
Affiliates 586–87; international human resource management and **566**, 586; *see also* Subsidiaries
Affinity 226

Africa 22, **43**, **99**, 226, 279, 646; banana trade and 22, 226; trade volume/growth 41
Agent Orange 65, 536
Aggressive reciprocity 55; *see* Active/aggressive reciprocity
Agricultural products 27, 41, 47, 279; banana wars and 22, 226; international market conditions and 266; merchandise trade 41, 53; Mexican imports **47**; production factor price equalization and 27
Airbus Industries 62
Aircraft Development Corporation 408
Air France 62, 242, 408
AIRINC Associates for International Research, Inc. **580–81**
Airline industry 11, 244, 569; Concorde crash 242; counterfeit parts and 629; foreign ownership of domestic airlines 244, 360; international route network expansion 345; joint venture, civilian jet engine production 75; landing rights regulation 67; multinational carriers 11; open skies agreement 50, 122; pilots, global mobility of 569; *see also* Airbus Industries; Boeing
Air transportation 554
Airport International Group 362
Akamai **110**, 599, 606
Alcan Aluminum 270
Alcatel-Lucent 450, 453
Alfano, A. 180
Alibaba 596, 606; Alipay.com 606; Taobao 606; Tmall.com 606
Alliance relationship 423; stability 423
Alliances 407–09, 543; international entrepreneurship and 652; marketing alliances 543; small/midsize enterprises and 230
Alliances 407–09, 543; *see also* Global strategic alliances (GSAs)
Allied Signal 390
Amazon 606; Amazon Marketplace 606
American Cyanamid 453

American depository receipts (ADRs) 652
American Enterprise Institute 227, **249**
America Online (AOL) 907, 909
Amgen Inc. 321
Amway 14, 235, 541
Andean Free Trade Area (Andean nations) 277
Anheuser-Busch 535
Animosity 221, 226
Anti-Bribery Convention 633, **637**
Antidumping laws 58–59; *see also* Dumping; Export controls
Anti-globalization activists 3
Antitrust legislation/enforcement 244–45
Apple 110 **122**, 604, 572
Appreciation in exchange value 292
Arab Spring 222, 234
Arab world 3
Arbitrage 317, 426, 473
Arbitration 242, 351; *see* Legal environment; Legal jurisdiction; Negotiation
Argentina 77, 298, 499, 551
Armaments 61, 64
Arm's-length principle 515–16
Ascriptive cultures 206
Asia **99**, 274–75, 324, 547, 597; computer/electronics industries 14; economic growth in 101, 274–75, 280; hierarchical culture, airline safety and 221, 569; production, relocation to 41, 131, 156, 547; trade volume/growth 41, 551; *see also* Asian financial crisis; China; Hong Kong; International monetary system; Japan; Korea; Regional-level cooperation among nations; South Korea
Asian financial crisis **296**, 324, 328–29; financial perspective on 325; managerial perspective 326; political/institutional perspective on 325; *see also* International capital markets; International monetary system
Asia-Pacific Economic Cooperation Forum (APEC) 274

Assembly plants overseas 75
Asset bubbles 164–167
Asset-seeking foreign direct investment (FDI) 76
Association of Chartered Certified Accountants 622
Association of Southeast Asian Nations (ASEAN) 269, 274; ASEAN+6 269, 274; free trade agreements 269–70, 276
AT&T **122**, 273, 428, 450
Atuahene-Gima, K. 656n22
Australia 265, 274, 507
Australian Accounting Standards Board (AASB) 507
Australia-New Zealand Closer Economic Relations Trade Agreement (CER) 268
Automotive industry 37, 91, 232, **436**, **538**; counterfeit parts and 629; design studios, foreign location of 92, 410; foreign direct investment/ multinational enterprises and 91; fuel-efficient cars and 56; global trade, income-preference similarity and 34; import surge protections 56; mergers and acquisition and 75, 370; motorcycles 173; political environment and 232, 389; sport-utility vehicle production 338; trucks, export controls and 64, 391; voluntary quotas and 60, 231
Autonomous role 381
Autonomy dimension 203, 205
Auto-stereotypes 212
Aviation 50, 245, 384, 569; see Airline industry
Avon 14, 89, 529
AXA insurance 4

Back-to-back letter of credit (L/C) 465
Back-to-back loans 475; see also Parallel loans
Backward vertical foreign direct investment 75
BAE Systems 633
Baiyun Airport 345
Baker, T. **645**
Balance of merchandise trade 53, 313
Balance of payments 311; capital account 313; current account 313; double-entry bookkeeping 311; implications 313; interpretation of 313; official reserves account 313; United States balance of payments 311, 313; United States trade deficits and 293–94, 313–14; see also International monetary system
Balance of trade 50
Baltic state 551
Banana wars 22
Bangladesh 49, **225**, 347, 357, 572
Bank of America **123**, 350, 349
Bank of the South 277
Banker's acceptance (BA) 469
Bank guarantee 468
Banking sector 26, 126, 328–29; lax regulation, global welfare and 67; multinational banks 315, 518; national competitiveness and 159
Bank of International Settlements (BIS) 314
Bank line of credit 468
Bank of Nova Scotia 350

Barbados 525, 626
Barclays 350
Bargaining power 136, 229
Barriers 57, 68; see Entry barriers; Non-tariff barriers; Quotas; Tariff barriers; Trade barriers
Barter 358
Basel Action Network (BAN) 619
BASF 273, 334
Baum, J. R. 655n8
Baxter International 619–20
Baxter medical equipment 65
Bayer 447
Bcom3 Group 124
Bear Stearns 327
Beechler **566**, 589n6
Benefit/cost model 531
Benetton 543
Benton & Bowles 124
Berkshire Hathaway **122**
Bermuda 517–18
Berne Convention for the Protection of Literary and Artistic Work 247
Best Global Brands 530, 537
Best practices 130, 530
Better Business Bureau Online (BBBOnline) 611
Bid 304
Bid-ask spread 304
Big Boy 541
Big Mac 526, *545*
Bilateral negotiations 8
Bill of lading (B/L) 357, 463, 492
Bimbo 80
BitTorrent 604
Black hole subsidiaries 382
Black markets 318
BMW 92, **121**, 535–37
Boards of Directors 388, 567
Body Shop 128
Boeing 64, 232, 408
Boeing Capital Corp. 360; exclusive supplier agreements and 63; foreign sales corporations and 64; joint ventures 364, 414; proprietary knowledge and 439; regulation of 243
Bolivia 220, **225**
Bolton, John. 214, 227
Bond, M. **216**
Bonded areas 342
Bonds 320, 474, 492; see International bond markets
Bootlegging 67
Borderless corporations 126
Born global firm 12, 147
Born international enterprises 34 147
Bottom-up management 89
Boycott 65
Branch office 363
Brand image 14, 77
Brand names 10, 259, 368; global brands 529, 537; see also Brand image; Branding; International marketing Branding
Branding 537
Brazil, xiii 59, 77, **225**, 285
Brent Spar project 616
Bretton Woods 263, 293–94, 297; Bretton Woods Agreement 293; Bretton Woods Institutions 263;

Bretton Woods system (1944–1973) 293, 297; post-Bretton Woods system (1973-present) 294, 297
Bribe Payers Index (BPI) 630, **631**
Bribery 630, 633
Brick-and-mortar retailers 604
Bridgestone 15, 246
Brislin, R. W. 577, 591n52
British Aerospace 410, 429
British Airways 102, 244
British-American (Anglo-Saxon) accounting zone 502
British Celltech 453
Brush, C. A. 144, 152n73, 656n27
Bubbles 164–65; asset market 164; markets for goods and services 164; see also Asset bubbles
Buffet, W. 194
Build-operate-transfer (BOT) investment 362
Bulldogs 474
Bundesbank 300
Burgel 653
Burger King 361, 536
Bush, G. W. 61
Business Environment Risk Intelligence (BERI) 156
Business etiquette 211; see Cultural/ business etiquette
Business-to-business (B2B) transactions 603
Business-to-consumer (B2C) transactions 603
Buy American Act 62, 65
Buyback 358–59, 373
Buyer credit 462, 468
Buy-local campaigns 65

Call centers 44
Call option 481
Cambodia 28, 134, 276, 301
Campbell Soup 285, 525
Canada 66, 193, **202**, 238, 270, 543; call centers in 3, 79, 193; Canadian dollar 302–03, 485; French Canadians 193; Manufacturers Life Insurance and 239–40; regional-level politics 237; small international enterprise exports to 145; United States trade and 270
Canada-United States Free Trade Agreement (CUFTA) 268
Canadian-American Commercial Arbitration Commission 242
Canadian Tire 546
Capability building 88, 159–60; financial capabilities 416–17; global strategic alliances and 130, 418; organizational capabilities 416; strategic capabilities 416
Capability deployment 88, 129
Capability exploitation 88
Capital 29, 142, 264, 329, 502; management skills, mobility of 89, 255; national wealth accumulation and 24; private capital 56, 264; production function 27; small/midsize international enterprises and 139; venture capital funds 646; working capital management 489; see also Foreign direct investment (FDI); International capital markets

Capital accounts 311, 313
Capital flow 171, 310, 319, 328; efficient international capital markets 311, 505; global capital flow 9; interest rate parity and 308; international business and 142, 497; sustainable pattern 165, 171; *see also* Cash flow
Capital-intensive exports 23
Caracas, Venezuela 277
Cardinal Health 630
Carey, S. 569
Caribbean 24; absolute advantage theory 24; banana trade and 24; *see also* Caribbean Community and Common Market (CARICOM); Regional-level cooperation among nations
Caribbean Community and Common Market (CARICOM) 255, 277
Carl's Jr. 541
Cash on delivery (COD) remittance 467
Cash flow 370, 478, 487, 491; cash flow management skills 89; foreign currencies, selection of 478, 485; *see also* Capital flow; Financial management/global operations
Cash management 489–90
Cash with order (CWO) remittance 467
Caterpillar 394, 410, 415
Caves, R. 15, 18n8
Cemex **131**, 270
Cendant Corp. 547
Centers of excellence 89, 129
Central African Economic and Customs Union (UDEAC) 279
Central American Common Market (CACM) 255, 268, 277, 437, 500
Central America-United States Free Trade Agreement (CAFTA) 268
Central banks 10, 315
Central and Eastern Europe/Middle East/Africa (CEMEA) 574
Central-planning systems 499
Centrally planned economy accounting zone 502, 504
CFA franc zone 291
Channel decisions 540, 544; direct marketing 541; intermediation 541; niche marketing 541; predatory pricing and 542; pricing process 541
Charles Schwab 605
Charoen Pokphand (CP) 131, 134, 350
Chavez, H. 220
Checkpoint firm 12
Chemical industries 409
Chevron 80, **120, 122**
Child labor 270, 572, 618
Chile 102, 277, 647
China, xiii, 134–14, 50, **131**, 133, **202, 225**, 276, 334, 646; advertising laws 245; alliances with local firms/multinationals and 230, 546, 652; automotive industry and 37; bogus blue-eyed venture in 134; bribery and 630; conglomerate foreign direct investment and 75; copy-machine industry 172; direct marketing and 541; dumping complaints and 59; DuPont entry strategies 334; eBay in 596; entry into the WTO 63; environmental degradation and 226;

exchange rate policies 50; expatriate failure rate and 575; familiarity theory and 98, 106; foreign exchange reserves and 299, 313; foreign investment in 80; furniture exports 59; garment exports and 60, 63; high-tech development zones 342; ideology, operational modes/practices and 211; imports from 60, 534; infant industry argument and 30, 55–56; intellectual property violations and 67; investment requirements of 230; Israeli airborne aircraft-warning systems and 227; kimchi wars 534; labor laws in 617; market economy in 59; Ministry of Commerce 3; multinational enterprises 118; personal relations, business ties and 173; predatory pricing and 542; production, relocation to 80; regional-level politics and 237; religion, business practices and 194; rule by man/not by law in 239; safety of exports and 67; Sinostone 13; small international enterprise exports to 140–41; Special Administrative Regions 106; staff turnover, retention incentives and 573; steel production and 60; tax rates and 339, 520; trade volume/growth 41; United States trade and 46; United States trade reciprocity and 54; World Trade Organization membership 63
China International Trust and Investment Corporation (CITIC) 320
Chinese Cultural Connection 202
Chinese Values Survey (CVS) 202
Chiquita Brands International 22
Chrysler 232, 244
Ciba-Geigy 173, 428
Cigarette advertising 245
Cigarette smuggling 628
Cisco 64, 346, 374n8, 393
Citibank 97, 317, 349, 352, 465
CITIC Group 120, **122**, 131, 320
Citigroup 73, 97, **122**, 572
Civil law 239
Clark Equipment 410, 415
Clause 260, 483
Clean float 301
Clean letter of credit (L/C) 464
Clearing House Interbank Payments System (CHIPS) 316
Cluster format 390
Clustering of cultures 207
Clusters of similar firms 647
Coalition building 231
Coca-Cola Company 2–3, 12, 245, 543
Cochabamba, Bolivia 277
Code Napoleon 474
Colgate 129, 539
Collective bargaining 425
Collectivism dimension. 197, **200**; *see* Individualism/collectivism (I/C) dimensions
Colombia 24, 79, 277, 280; absolute advantage theory 24; foreign direct investment 79
Co-management arrangement 409
Co-marketing arrangement 408
Combating Bribery of Foreign Officials in International Business Act (CBFOIB) 633

Commercial banks 319, 322, 468
Commercial Development at TNT Logistics Asia 547
Commercial espionage 605
Commercialization process 169
Commercial services 40, 44, 46
Commission of the European Union (CEU) 505
Commitment 416, 323–24
Commodities 9, 25, 27, 256; commodity prices 9, 282; comparative advantage in 25; import of 460; primary commodities 23, 34; streamlined flow of 9; *see also* Commodity cartel; Commodity-level cooperation among nations
Commodity cartel 281
Commodity-level cooperation among nations 281; commodity cartels and 281; Intergovernmental Council of Copper Exporting Countries 283; International Bauxite Association 283; International Cocoa Agreement 284; International Coffee Agreement 284; International Natural Rubber Agreement 284; International Sugar Agreement 284.; International Tin Agreement 284; Multifiber Arrangement 60; Organization of Petroleum Exporting Countries 282; Wheat Trade Convention 284; *see also* International economic integration/institutions
Common goals 484
Common law system 239
Common market 255
Communication services 44, 163
Communications technology 444
Communitarianism 205
Community characteristics 343–44
Company clusters 10
Comparable profits method 515
Comparative advantage theory 25; sources of advantage 26; *see also* International/foreign trade
Comparative production cost 26
Compensation 578; *see also* buyback; expatriate workforce; host country-based/localized compensation system; salaries
Competition 340, 351, 454; core competencies and 78; domestic rivalry/government policies and 173, 182, 341; early movers and 78; fair competition 126; foreign direct investment and 341; horizontal foreign direct investment and 85, 111; host country competitive advantages 78; internalization and 85; international business and 73, 140, 235; international trade, real-life imperfect competition and 35; knowledge, service economy and 9, 340; laws on competition 244; liability of foreignness and 75; local competition, location selection and 340; mitigation, alliances and 409; multinational enterprises, competitive advantage of 125; organizational learning and 78; relationship

building and 78; surge in imports, emergency import protections and 63; technology gaps and 30; *see also* National competitiveness
Competitive power 95
Computer industry 137, 285, 410
Conagra Foods 58
Confirmed letter of credit (L/C) 464
Conflict reduction 426
Confucian dynamism 201
Conglomerate foreign direct investment 75
Conglomerates 75, 133; diversification in 133; unrelated holding companies 390; *see also* Conglomerate foreign direct investment
Consortia for projects 408
Construcciones Aeronauticas 410
Construction costs 338
Consumers 163, 540, 536, 618; customer responsiveness and 15, 173, 341; globalization effects and 280; location selection and 340; protections for 620
Consumption 33, 39, 50; balanced growth 165–66; imbalances between consumption and savings 167
Continental accounting zone 502
Continental AG 387
Continental Airlines 63, 122, 242
Contraband goods 628
Contract invoicing 482
Contractual alliances 75, 407
Contractual joint venture 363; *see* Cooperative/contractual joint venture
Contributor subsidiaries 382, 401
Control 64, 398, 425
Controlling instruments 41
Convencao 541
Convention on the Control of Trans-boundary Movements of Hazardous Waste 619
Convergence hypothesis 214
Conversion 508; *see also* Foreign currency translation
Cooperative/contractual joint venture 408
Cooperative culture 414–15; *see also* Global-level cooperation among nations
Coopetition 227
Coordination 398, 439, 487
Co-production/co-service agreement 408
Copyrights 10, 143, 368
Core competencies 78
Core knowledge 422-23
Corning Incorporated 429
Corporate citizenship behaviors 210, 399; *see also* Corporate socialization; Corporate social responsibility
Corporate Credit Service 323
Corporate culture 210, 215; classifications of 209, 215; demographic features and 211; ethnicity and 210; ideology and 211; industry types and 210; national norm and 210; profession, cultural affiliation and 210; *see also* Corporate citizenship behaviors; Corporate social responsibility; Cultural environment
Corporate guarantee 469
Corporate headquarters 400

Corporate socialization 399
Corporate social responsibility 617; audit/assessment of 623; consumer protection and 620; corporate governance and 620; culture of social responsibility 622; developing country multinational enterprises and 125; economic/development policies and 618; environmental responsibilities and 619; ethical behavior and 246; global guidelines/mandates for 621; green companies 616; laws/regulations and 618; multinational enterprises 640; philanthropic responsibilities and 617; political involvement and 619; Royal Dutch Shell case 616; social impact assessment and 620; verification services and 620; *see also* Corruption
Corporate technology units 441
Corruption 67, 624; bribery 630; collusion, e-commerce and corruption 622; communications technology and 141; cost of 625; cultural receptivity toward 342; definition/magnitude of 624; developing economies and 67, 224, 626; drawbacks of 626; Foreign Corrupt Practices Act and 630; global fight against 632; government involvement/regulation and 343; money laundering 629; Motorola case 407; nation rankings in 626; origins of 625; piracy/counterfeiting 629; slush funds 630; smuggling 628; transitional economies and 625; types of corrupt practices 628; *see also* Corporate social responsibility
Corruption Perception Index (CPI) 626
Co-service agreement 408 *see* Co-production/ co-service agreement
Cosmetic industry 535, 541
Cost-benefit analysis 352
Cost and freight (C&F) pricing 356
Cost/insurance/freight (CIF) pricing 356
Cost-leadership strategies 77, 399
Costs 335, 337–38, **344**; construction costs 338, **344**; financing costs 338, **344**; investment incentives 339; land costs 338, **344**; locational determinants and 337, **344**; profit repatriation 339, **344**; raw materials/ resources 338, **344**; tax rates 339, **344**; transportation costs 338, **344**; wage rate 338, **344**; *see also* International location selection
Council of Securities Regulators of the Americas (COSRA) 634
Counterfeiting 629, 635
Counterfeit products 352, 628–29
Counterpurchase 358
Countertrade 358
Countervailing duties 55, 63, 261
Country competitiveness 159, **161**, 171, 179, 185; *see* National competitiveness
Country-of-origin effect 535; nationalist sentiments and 536; positive country image, leveraging of 535; *see also* Global e-commerce; International marketing

Country-specific factors 86, 368; entry mode choice 368; international human resource management 564; *see also* Country-of-origin effect; International marketing
CPC International 441
Craig, C. S. 137, 151n37
Crawling peg system 298, *302*
Creditor panic 299
Credit rating agencies 323, 329
Credit Suisse First Boston Corp. 234
Cross-border acquisitions 75, 370
Cross-border mergers 75, 370
Cross-cultural training 576–77; *see* Expatriate workforce
Cross-national enterprise 139, 645; *see* Developing/emerging nation multinational enterprise (DNMEs); Globalization; Global operations; International business; Multinational enterprises (MNEs); Small/midsize international enterprises (SMIEs)
Cross rate 305
Cuba 65, 222, 226, 297
Cultural barriers 342, **344**; *see also* Cultural distance; Cultural environment
Cultural/business etiquette 211
Cultural chauvinism 188
Cultural distance 207, 209, 578
Cultural environment 209, 444, 451, 577; achievement vs. acscriptive cultures and 206; communitarianism vs. individualism and 205; convergence vs. divergence hypotheses and 214; corporate culture and 210; cultural barriers 342; cultural/business etiquette and 211; cultural distance and 207; cultural industries and 210; cultural/national boundaries, overlap of 209–210; culture clustering concept 207; culture, features of 189; demographic variables and 211; diffuse vs. specific cultures and 206; embeddedness vs. autonomy dimensions and 203; ethnicity and 210; face concept and 209; Globes classification framework and 205; hierarchy vs. egalitarianism dimensions and 204; high-context vs. low-context cultures and 206; Hofstede's dimensions of culture 197; ideology and 211; individualism/ collectivism dimensions and 200; industry type and 210; international business and 189; language and 191; liability of foreignness and 189; lingua franca and 193; long-term orientation dimension and 201; masculinity/ femininity dimensions and **201**; mastery vs. harmony dimensions and 204; motivation patterns and 135; neutral vs. emotional cultures 205; noncultural environmental variables and 190; nonverbal language and 193; power distance dimension and 197; race 190; religion and 194; research and development process and 91, 454; Ronen/Shenkar clustering classification and 207, **208**; Schwartz's

dimensions of culture 203; social clusters 209; stereotyping practices and 212; time, culturally-influenced attitudes toward 206; Trompenaars/ Hampden-Turner classification system 205; uncertainty avoidance dimension 197; universalism vs. particularism 205; *see also* Environmental dynamics; Expatriate workforce; Legal environment; Political environment
Cultural imperialism 193
Cultural industries 54
Culture 189; globally unified compensation systems 578; international business 189; international trade activities 40, 274; residual variable of 190; *see also* Cultural environment; Culture clustering
Culture clustering 207
Currency crisis 9
Currency translation 508–09; *see also* Foreign currency translation
Currency valuation 291; decline in 291; fluctuations in 291; hard/strong currency 292; soft/weak currency 292; *see also* Foreign currency translation
Current account 313
Current/noncurrent method of accounting 509
Current open market prices 515
Current rate 508; *see* Exchange rate systems; Foreign exchange rates
Current rate method of accounting 509
Customers 335, 491; *see* Consumers; Customer-to-customer (C2C) transactions
Customer-to-customer (C2C) transactions 603
Customized products 173, 437
Customs bureaucracy 555
Customs union 255
Cyprus 139, 273, 300
Czech Republic 6, 170, 205, 271, 551

Daewoo Motor 194
Daimler AG **122**, 322, 442
Daimler Benz 126, 322, 370, 442
DaimlerChrysler 75, 244, 320
Damon's restaurants 75
Danone 117, 567, 576
Dassault Aviation 136
Databases 10, 415
Data management tools 398, 401
Dealogic 321
de Blij, H. J. 194
Debt financing 473
de Cordoba, J. 221
Deep niche strategies 147
Defensive market motives 14
Del Monte Produce 22
Delphi 3
Delta Airlines 122, **124**
Demand 29; demand bias, capital-intensive goods 29; internal demand, manufactured goods 34; location selection 34; market demand 34; per capita income 34; *see also* Supply-demand conditions
De Mooij, M. 201, 558n29
Democratic Party (PD) Italy 180

Democratic Republic of Congo 161, 223
Denmark 178, **199**, 205, 386
Dentsu 124
Dependency model 227
Depreciation 292
Derivatives 68, 583
Deutsche Bank 4, 102, **123**, 393
Deutsche marks (DM) 300
Deutsche Telekom **121**, 567
Devaluation 291, 303
Developed nations 8, 59, 122, 131, 140; developing-country imports and 59–60; foreign direct investment and 9, 16, 265; intellectual property rights and 259, 261; internal demand for goods and 34; international trade in manufactures and 34, 39; job loss, domestic wage and 8; preference similarity and 34; services, investment in 231; underground economic activities and 625
Developing/emerging economies 8, 59, 131, 502, 535; communications services, exportation of 44; digital dumps and 619; foreign direct investment and 72, 149, 626; globalization scores and 6; infant industry argument and 30, 55–56; intellectual property rights and 240, 629; least developed countries 8; non-tariff barriers and 57, 59; production facilities, relocation to 11, 619; quotas, production levels and 60; surge in imports, standard of remedies and 63; sustainable development and 78; world merchandise trade and **41**, 46; *see also* Developed nations; Developing/emerging nation multinational enterprises (DNMEs)
Developing/emerging nation multinational enterprises (DNMEs) xiii, 131; bargaining power of 136; conglomerated foreign direct investment and 131; developing economies, obstacles to multinationals and 134; diversified industry composition and 133; features of 135; generic drug production and 136; global markets, advantages in 138; governance of 136; home government support of 134, 230; industry domain in 136; internationalization patterns and 135; largest developing-country multinationals 131; other developing markets, focus on 136; raw materials and 134; strategic activity of 136–37; strategic flexibility and 135; third parties, reliance on 136; *see also* Globalization; Multinational enterprises (MNEs); Small/midsize international enterprises (SMIEs)
Development zones 342, 443
DHL International 516
Diamond framework of national advantage 172, 174
Diffuse cultures 197, 206
Digital Bridge initiative 620
Digital divide 635
Digital dumps 635

Dimensions of culture 197; *see* Cultural environment; Hofstede's dimensions of culture
Direct investment. 73, 313; *see* Foreign direct investment (PD!)
Direct marketing 541; China and 541; international marketing and 541; operational risk and 235; pyramid schemes and 541
Direct quote 304
DirecTV 321
Dirty float 301
Discount 508
Discounting 474
Discrimination 260
Disney 572
Disneyland Europe 75
Disposable income 526, 557
Dispute Settlement Body (DSB) 261
Distribution availability/favorability 368
Distribution channels 15, 544; channel decisions 540; distribution laws 334; foreign direct investment for 77, 411; home market distribution network 89, 129, 410; Mexican truck transport of goods 66
Diversification 76, 127, 136, 322; Asian financial crisis and 324, 328; diversified industries, international lending and 149–50, 322; horizontal foreign direct investment and 74; multinational enterprises and 127, 369; ownership risk and 235
Diversity of business systems 17
Divestment 235, 424
Dixit, A. 35, 69n16
Documentary collection 465
Documentary letter of credit (L/C) 464
Documents against acceptance (D/A) 465, **466**
Documents against payment (DIP) 465, **466**
Doha Development Agenda (DDA) 259
Dole Foods 22
Dollar crisis 294
Domestic business 11–12, 15; foreign direct investment, impact of 18, 265; international business and 642, 652
Domino's Pizza 524
Donna Karan International 546
Double-entry bookkeeping 311
Douglas, S. P. 151n37
Dow Chemical 8
Dow Corning 481–82
Downstream integration 14, 254
Doz, Y. 94, 113n14, 249n39, 431n2, 432n5
Draft 465
Dual-emphasis market orientation 347
Dumping 58
Dunkin' Donuts 525
DuPont 334–37
Duty-free treatment 62
Dynamic capabilities 88
Dynamic environmental conditions 12, 90
Dynamic-random-access memory (DRAM) chip 407, 409

Early mover/follower advantages 349, **353**
Early-mover/follower disadvantages 351, 353
Earnings repatriation 78, 342

East African Economic Community (EAEC) 297
Eastern Europe 131, 138, 343, 574
East India Company 119
eBay 596, 606, 609–10
E-business 603
E-commerce 603; B2B 603; B2C 603; C2C 603; e-readiness 599; Internet, e-commerce infrastructure 597; see also Global e-commerce
E-readiness 599
E-Trade Financial 605
Eclectic paradigm 86
Economic aid packages 226
Economic Community of West African States (ECOWAS) 279
Economic Cooperation Market (ECO) 268
Economic development 157, 226, 624; negative outcomes 226
Economic development zones 276, 342
Economic exposure 478
Economic freedom 233
Economic integration 255–56, 257, 269; see also Global integration; International economic integration/institutions
Economic motives 13–14; motivation patterns 135; special economic zones 342
Economic soundness 164
Economic stability 164, 166, 300; economies of location 15; economies of scale 15; economies of scope15; economic integration and 255; global strategic alliances and 346; global strategy and 346; monopolistic advantages and 83, 85
Economist Intelligence Unit (EIU) 599
Ecuador 220, 282, 408
EDGO group 362
Education 167, 170; see Education services; Expatriate trainee; Knowledge; Public education spending
Effective tax rate 339
Efficiency-seeking foreign direct investment (FDI) 76, 101
Egalitarianism dimension 204
E-government readiness 602
Egypt 78, 116, 536, 543
EJV see Equity joint venture (EJV)
Elberton Granite Association 13
Electronic funds transfer (EFT) 389, 487
Electronics industry 157, 285, 406; clusters 173; digital dumps and 619; export controls and 64; hard disk drive industry 156; non-tariff barriers and 57, 59; semiconductor/software industry 406, 544
Embargo 65
Embeddedness dimension 203
Embraer 134, 137–38
EMC 110, 356; see Export management company (EMC)
Emerging-market MNE; see Developing/emerging economies; Developing/emerging nation multinational enterprises (DNMEs); Multinational enterprises (MNEs)
Emerging nations 6, 131, 261; see Developing/emerging nation; multinational enterprises (DNMEs)

Emerson Electric 429–30
Emotional cultures 206, 585
Employment 573; see Expatriate workforce; Labor market; Workforce
EMS 294, 300; see European Monetary System (EMS)
Engineering-oriented industries 173
Engineers 179
Entrepreneurial behavior 190
Entrepreneurial skills 86
Entrepreneurs, xiii, 645–46; see also International entrepreneurship
Entry barriers, xiii, 334, 368
Entry decision framework 352, 368; cost-benefit analysis and 352; global integration and 345; market orientation and 345; strategic objectives and 345; timing of decisions 352; see also International entry strategies
Entry mode 355
Entry mode selection 355; country-specific factors 368; decision framework for 368; entry mode choices 355; export activities 355–56; FDI-centered 362, 367; firm-specific factors 369; foreign direct investment, related entry modes 357; global integration and 345; industry-specific factors 368; international subcontracting 357; project-specific factors 369; trade-centered 355, 367; trade-centered entry modes 355, 359, 367; transfer-centered entry modes 359, 262, 367; see also International entry strategies
Entry strategies 335; see International entry strategies
Environmental dynamics 12; firm-level influence on competitiveness and 177, 181; investment environment 108; service multinationals, growth conditions for 122
Environmental dynamics 12; see also Cultural environment; Legal environment; Political environment; Sociopolitical factors
Environmental issues 617, 619–20; corporate social responsibility and 617, 620; distribution laws 242, 245; environmental protection laws 343, 620; environmental standards 183, 572, 619; globalization and 8–9, 618; lax regulation and 67
Environmental protection laws 343, 620
E.On. 120, 244
Equal Employment Opportunity law 572
Equant NV 244
Equity distribution 418, 587
Equity financing 472
Equity joint venture (EJV) 364, 407
Equity markets 321; see also International stock/equity markets
Equity ownership 418–19
Equity transfer 429, 431
Erez, M. 655n8
Ericsson 357, 446, 449
ERM Certification and Verification Services (ERM CVS) 620
Escape clauses 260

Estonia 105, 273, 300, 551
Ethical behavior 246
Ethier, W. 35, 69n16
Ethnicity 210
Ethnocentric beliefs 212
Ethnocentric centralized research and development 445–46
Ethnocentric staffing 570, 573
Euro 317–18
Euro zone see Eurozone
Eurobond market 320, 474
Eurocredits 474, 492, 510
Eurocurrency markets 319, 473
Eurodollars 320
Euronote market 472, 474
Europe 271, 444, 551, 646; direct marketing and 14, 530; trade volume/growth 41, 551; see also Eastern Europe; European Union; Regional-level cooperation among nations
European Aeronautic Defense and Space Company 410
European Central Bank (ECB) 300
European Commission 272
European Community (EC) 271
European Court of Auditors 272
European Court of Justice 272
European currency unit (ECU) 267
European Economic Community (EEC) 271, 300
European Economic and Monetary Union (EMU) 300
European Free Trade Association (EFTA) 269
European Monetary System (EMS) 294, 300
European Research Coordinating Agency (EUREKA) 444
European Strategic Program for Development in Information Technology (ESPRIT) 444
European Union (EU) 271; accounting system integration and 398; automotive products and 37; banana quotas/tariffs 22; economic integration, sequential nature of 237, 256, 269, 271; euro and 271; European Monetary System and 271, 300; foreign sales corporations and 64; global research and development and 245, 435; import surge quotas, garment imports and 63; open skies agreement and 50, 122; pollution guidelines 619; production subsidies and 62; regional integration agreements 267, 280; regional-level politics and 237; rule-of-origin laws 80; United States trade and 22, 44; see also Regional-level cooperation among nations
Eurozone 281, 291–92, 309, 313, 315
Eurozone financial crisis 263, 328
Evolutionary entry path 371
Evolutionary perspective 90
Exchange rate systems 297, 302; central exchange rate and 298; composite baskets of currencies and 298; crawling peg system 298, 302; euro and 298, 300; European Central Bank and 300; European Monetary System

and 300; excess volatility and 301; fixed rate system 297, **302**; Hong Kong, fixed peg system and 299; independent/clean float system 301, **302**; managed/dirty float system 301, **302**; special drawing rights and 291; target-zone arrangement 300; *see also* Foreign exchange rates; International monetary system

Executive agreements 246

Exile syndrome 587

Eximbank 469–70

Expatriate trainee 573

Expatriate workforce 573; advantages/disadvantages of 584; calculation of compensation 578–79, 583; compensation gaps 587; compensation systems for 578–79; expatriate failure and 574; hardship evaluation 579; housing allowance 579; income tax liability of 579; international managers 574; national culture, compensation levels and 578–79; performance appraisals 578; preparation for foreign assignment 576; repatriation of 585; selection criteria/instruments 576; service allowance/premiums for 579; skill set requirements for 585; training components 577; types/distribution of 573; u-curve theory of adjustment and 577; unfamiliar environments 575; virtual expatriates 574; women in 575

Experience curve 56

Experience transferability 189

Experiential knowledge 90

Expertise 67, 355, 360, 421

Export activities 36–37, 40, 514

Export controls 64; balance of trade 23, 65; dumping/antidumping 58; embargoes 65; government policy 23; national security issues 57; *see also* Exports; Import controls; Non-tariff barriers; Tariff barriers

Export Credits Guarantee Department (ECGD) 470

Export Credits Insurance Corporation (ECIC) 470

Export financing 467, 470; *see* Financial management; global operations

Export intermediaries 541

Export management company (EMC) 356

Export-import bank financing 469–70

Exporters 45, 145, 468, **480**

Exports **33**, 45, 48, 313, 469; innovation, imitation lag and 30, 349; Leontief paradox and 28–29; major exporters 45; national security issues and 57; product life-cycle model and 31, **32**; production factor price equalization 27; production factor quality and 27; small/midsize international enterprises 139; United States trade partners 46; *see also* Export controls; Foreign direct investment(FDI)

Externalities 35

Extraction industries 126

Extraterritorial Income 64

Exclusion 64

ExxonMobil 103, **120, 122**

Factor endowments 26

Factoring houses 468, 492

Factor-intensity reversal 29

Factors of production 26; *see* Production factors

Fair competition 126

Familiarity theory 91, 98, 209

Fashion industry 173, 380, 415

FCN 246; *see* Treaties of friendship/commerce/navigation (FCN)

Federal Express 344

Food and Drug Administration (FDA) 134, 243

Federal Reserve Bank 316, 327; *see* US Federal Reserve Bank

Femininity 197, 201; *see* Masculinity/femininity (M/F) dimensions; Women

Fiat 390, 546

Finance corporations 519

Financial Accounting Standards Board (FASB) 511

Financial arbitrage 95

Financial assets 74; foreign portfolio investment and 74; portfolio theory and 74

Financial capabilities 129, 417, 420

Financial crisis 324; Asian Financial Crisis 324; Global Financial Crisis **296**, 327–28; Eurozone crisis **297**, 328; Eurozone financial crisis 328

Financial EDI systems 487

Financial management/global operations 461–62; banker's acceptance and 469; bank financing and 468; bank line of credit and 468; bank loans **472**, 474; buyer credit and 468; cash in advance and 462; contract invoicing/clause hedging 482; corporate guarantee and 469; debt financing **472**, 473, 476; depository receipts and 473; documentary collection 462, 465; economic exposure 478, **479**; equity financing **472**, 476; export factoring/forfaiting and 467; export financing 467; exposure management, global coordination of financial management 461–62; financial initiatives 483; financing decisions 475; foreign exchange exposure 476–77, **479**; foreign exchange risk 476; forward market hedging 480; futures market hedging 480; global business financing 471; government sources of financing 469; hedging techniques 480; input outsourcing 485; intercompany financing 471; international trade finance 462; international trade payment methods 462; intra-company reinvoicing 485; leads/lags and 483; letter of credit and 463; local currency financing 471; netting/matching and 484; nonbank sources of funds 474–75; open account selling 467; options market hedging 481; payment remittance options 467; private sources of financing 468; production arrangement 486; production initiatives 485; RTZ case 460; Swaps 482; transaction exposure 477, **479**; translation exposure 477; working

capital management 489; *see also* International accounting

Financial markets **314**, 321, 324; *see* Global financial markets; International capital markets; International financial markets; International foreign exchange markets

Financial panic 299

Financial regulatory system 166

Financial risk 74

Financial services 50, 259, 322

Financing costs 338

Finland 178, 231, 386

Firestone 15, 246

Firm-level factors in competitiveness 176–77

Firm-specific advantages 83, 135

Firm-specific factors 369

Firm-specific traits 369

Firms 140, 144, 177; core competencies and 78; dynamic capabilities and 88; indigenous firms 355, 439; international firms 140, 314, 491; internationally leaning firms 117; international vs. domestic business and 144, 230; organizational learning, growth from 78

First mover 349, 354

Fixed/managed exchange rate system 291; *see also* Exchange rate systems; Floating/flexible exchange rate system

Flexibility 94–95, 135; *see* Floating flexible exchange rate system; Strategic flexibility

Flextronics 357

Floating/flexible exchange rate system 291, 302; advantages/disadvantages of 302; independent float system 301–02; managed float system 301–02; target-zone arrangement floating 300; *see also* Exchange rate systems; Fixed/managed exchange rate system

Flow of foreign direct investment (FDI) 74

Food and Agriculture Organization (FAO) **266**

Footwear products 173, 338

Ford Motor Company 37, 91, **121, 396**; Ford 2000 391, **402**; foreign research and development unit of 92, 232, 379; global advertising 542; matrix structure of 394; retention incentives 573

Foreign affiliates 73, 96; wages in 8; *see also* Affiliates; Foreign direct investment (FDI); Subsidiaries

Foreign assignments 576; *see* Expatriate workforce

Foreign bond 320, 474

Foreign Corrupt Practices Act (FCPA) 630

Foreign credit insurance 470

Foreign Credit Insurance Association 470

Foreign currency transactions **508**

Foreign currency translation **508**; conversion and **508**; current/noncurrent method 509, 513; current rate method 509 513; glossary of terms **508**; harmonization of translation methods 511; methods of 509–11; monetary/nonmonetary

663

method 509–10, 513; *see also* International accounting
Foreign direct investment (FDI) 73, 111; automotive industry and 91–92; capital contributions and 362; concentration of manufacturing 340; conglomerate foreign direct investment 75; core competencies and 78; current theories on 82; decision criteria for 109; destination country 79–80; domestic enterprises and 80; dynamic capability perspective and 88; efficiency-seeking foreign direct investment 76; employment effect 79; entry mode and 75; evolutionary perspective of 90; familiarity theory and 91; financing of 470, 476, 321; flow of 74; foreign portfolio investment and 74; global competition for 83, 111, 235; greenfield investments/mergers and acquisitions and 75; high-tech investment and 109; horizontal foreign direct investment 74, 76; host country, impact on 80; Host Economy Transnationality Index and 103; inflows of 74, 101; integration-responsiveness perspective and 94; internalization theory and 84; investment approaches in 75, 87; investment environment and 108; Japan case and 72; liability of foreignness and 75; liberalization of markets and 108, 228; location advantages and 77; location selection, policies and 337; market-seeking foreign direct investment 76; monopolistic advantage theory and 83, 85; multinational enterprises, benefits to 84–86; multinational enterprises, foreign direct investment flows and 86; new perspectives on 88; organizational learning, growth from 78; origin country 79; outflows of 74, **102**; ownership advantages, increasing return from 77; ownership/location/internalization framework and 86; patterns worldwide of 95; product life-cycle theory and 82; rationalized foreign direct investment 285; relationship building and 411, 417; resource-seeking foreign direct investment attempts and 76; service facilities and 73, 105; small-package investment 146; special economic zones and 72, 105; spillover from 80–81; stock of 74; strategic asset-seeking foreign direct investment 76; strategic flexibility and 72; strategic logic of 76; structural discrepancies, improved performance and 77; transnationality, individual nation economic performance and 103; types of 74; uncertain environments and 93; vertical foreign direct investment 75–76; *see also* Foreign direct investment-related entry modes; Multinational enterprises (MNEs)
FDI-centered entry modes 362; branch offices 363; cooperative/contractual joint venture 363; equity joint venture 363–64; global strategic alliances and 364; umbrella holding company 363, 366; wholly owned subsidiaries 363, 365; *see also* Entry mode selection; International entry strategies
Foreign exchange 291; crisis in Mexico 290; demand/supply, distortion of 297; *see also* Exchange rate systems; Foreign exchange rates; International foreign exchange markets; International monetary system
Foreign exchange arbitrage 317, 319
Foreign exchange exposure 477
Foreign exchange hedging systems 40, 316
Foreign exchange markets 314; *see* International foreign exchange markets
Foreign exchange rate quotations 303; bids/offers 304; cross rate 305; direct/indirect quotes 304; spot rate/forward rate 304; *see also* Foreign currency translation; Foreign exchange rates; forward discount; forward premium; International foreign exchange markets
Foreign exchange rates 291, **309**; absolute purchasing power parity and 306; changes in exchange rates 291; determination of 303; forecasting foreign exchange rates 310; foreign exchange black markets and 318; foreign exchange forecasting, multinational enterprises and 310; gold standard and 305; interest rate parity principle and 305, 307; international Fisher effect and 308; nominal 291; overshooting 308; purchasing power parity principle and real 306; types of exchange rates 291; volatility 303; *see also* Exchange rate systems; Foreign currency translation; Foreign exchange; Foreign exchange rate quotations; International foreign exchange markets; International monetary system
Foreign exchange reserves 23, 299, 302, 313
Foreign exchange risk 476
Foreign exchange transactions 314
Foreign invested enterprises (FIEs) 80, 125, 334
Foreign portfolio investment (FPI) 74; financial assets and 74; physical assets and 74; portfolio theory and 74
Foreign receivables management 491
Foreign sales corporations (FSCs) 64, 68
Foreign subsidiaries 73, 366, 399
Foreign trade 53, 471; *see* International/foreign trade
Forfaiting 468–69
Fortune 537
Forward-forward swap 317
Forward market hedging 480
Forward rate 304–05
Forward transactions 316
Four Tigers countries 190
Foxconn 137
France 62, **120**, **225**, 238, 242, 501, 601
France Telecom 244
Franchising 361–62; *see also* International franchising
Frankfurt Airport Corp. 362
Franklin Templeton Group 352
Free alongside ship (FAS) pricing 356
Free on board (FOB) pricing 356
Free trade 54, 57; buy-local campaigns and 65; emergency import protection 63; factor price equalization and 27; lowest common denominator argument and 8, 54; opposition to 53–54; regional integration agreements 267; service industries and 54, 67; skilled vs. unskilled workers and 53; sovereignty argument and 54; trade adjustment assistance and 54; trade reciprocity and 54–55; zones of 342; *see also* North American Free Trade Agreement (NAFTA)
Free trade area 255
Free Trade Area of the Americas (FTAA) 255
Freeport-McMoran Copper & Gold 238
Fuji Heavy Industries 65
Fujita, M. 151n57, n64, 152n71, n76, n77, n81, n86
Fujitsu 420
Furniture industry 79, 173
Futures market hedging 480, 488

G20 261
Gannon, J.J. 200, 226n20
Garment industry 63
Gateway Computers 73
GATT *see* General Agreement on Tariffs and Trade (GATT)
Gedajilovic, E. **645**
Geely *see* Geely Automobile
Geely Automobile 4, 201, 379, 570
General Agreement on Tariffs and Trade (GATT) 57, 258
General Electric (GE) 64, 75, 102, 120, **122**, 125, 392, 409, 496; GE Capital 175, 360; John F. Welch Technology Center 442
General Electric Company (GEC) **120**, 453
General Foods 450
General Motors (GM) 92, 194, 131; SAIC-GM-Wuling Automobile Co. Ltd. 410
Generalized System of Preferences (GSP) 62, 260
Generally Accepted Accounting Principles (GAAP) 500
Generic drug production 134
Geneva Phonograph Convention 247
Geocentric staffing 571
Georgia Pacific Paper 107
German Bank 292
Germany **120**, **225**, 244, 406, 444, 502; advertising laws 245, 620; apprenticeship programs 177; build-operate-transfer project 362; Packaging Regulation 548
Getz, K. A. 636, 653n1
Ghosn, C. 188
Gillette 543
Glass-Steagall Act 320
GlaxoSmithKline PLC 496, 634
Global brands 529, **538–40**
Global business units (GBUs) 378, 392
Global central laboratory 446, 454
Global Competitiveness Index 170, 183
Global e-commerce 603; brick-and-mortar retailers and 604; challenges

to 607–612; e-readiness and 599; e-trade and 603; human resource mobility and 607; intermediaries and 606; international business, e-commerce and 603; Internet diffusion and 597; large multinational enterprises and 604; liability of foreignness and 609; localization challenges and 608; logistics challenges 611; origin of product/service and 604; physical goods, logistics challenges of 606; small/midsize multinational enterprises and 606; standardization forces and 607; taxation issues and 611; transactions in 545, 612; website localization and 609; *see also* E-commerce; Internet
Global economic integration 255
Global Entrepreneurship Monitor 642
Global Financial Crisis 327–28
Global financial markets 314; *see also* International capital markets; International foreign exchange market
Global firms 119, 440, 653; operations location, economic considerations 11, 122; *see also* Multinational enterprises (MNEs)
Global functional structure 384
Global geographic structure 385; disadvantages of 387; factors in 389; mixed geographic structure and 388; Nestlé case 385; regional headquarters, role of 385, 389; regional strategy/accountability and 389; region-specific factors in 389; *see also* Global operations; Multinational enterprises (MNEs)
Global human resource management 564, **566**; *see* International human resource management (IHRM)
Global industry 237, 410
Global innovators 399, 401
Global integration 94; strategic international human resource management and tools for 565; *see also* Global operations
Global leadership 173
Global marketing 530; *see* International marketing
Global matrix structure 393
Global operations 398, 461–62; Citigroup case 73; control and 398; coordination and 398; corporate headquarters, role of 400; corporate socialization and 399; global functional structure 384; global geographic structure 385; global integration, local responsiveness and 379; global matrix structure 393; global product structure 389; global strategy 380–81; integrated global operations 398; integration tools 378, 398; international division structure 384; international strategy/organizational design 378; multidomestic strategy 381, 401; multinational enterprise organizational structures 383; multinational enterprise strategy/design 380; national subsidiary

structure 383; strategic orientation and 398; subsidiary roles/imperatives 381; transition challenge and 400; transnational/hybrid strategy 381; *see also* Financial management/global operations; Global research and development; International accounting; International human resource management (IHRM); International marketing
Global products 529
Global product structure 389; cluster format 390; global product design 392; related divisional format 390; types of 390; unrelated holding company format 390; *see also* Global operations
Global Reporting Initiative (GRI) 621
Global research and development 435; absorptive capability and 453; autonomy setting in 448; benefits of 437; boundary spanners and 451; challenges of 438; communication networks, improvement in 450; competitive advantage of 438; coordination/control costs and 439; corporate technology units 441; cultural adaptation and 451; division of labor and 438; ethnocentric centralized structure of 445; foreign units for 437; global central laboratory structure of 445–46; globally integrated network structure of 445, 447; global planning and 449; global technology units 441; high-tech development zones and 442; human resource management and 448; India case 440; indigenous technology units 441; informal communication networks and 451; information exchange systems and 452; Intel case 434; interorganizational technology cooperation and 437; location, selection of 442; management of 436; minimum efficient scale and 438; organizational model for 445; polycentric decentralized structure of 445–46; proprietary knowledge and 439; rationale for globalization 459; research and development intensity and 435; specialized laboratory structure of 445–46; specialized technology units 441; technological/business strategies alignment 450; technological innovation process and 436; technology transfer process and 452–53; technology transfer units 441; time factor, competitive advantage and 438; transfer coordination mechanisms 447
Global sourcing 546
Global start-ups xiii, 148; *see also* International entrepreneurship
Global strategic alliances (GSAs) 407; building global strategic alliances 413; challenges to 411; co-management arrangement 409; co-marketing arrangement 408; commitment and 416; competition mitigation 409; conflict reduction and 427; contract negotiations 425; cooperation strategies 426; cooperative culture and 415; cooperative joint ventures 407–08;

co-production/co-service agreements 408; core knowledge, uncompensated leakage and 423; economies of scale/rationalization and 409; equity joint ventures 407; exit/termination strategies and 428; goal compatibility 414; interpartner learning, management of 421; joint exploration projects 408; knowledge/resource acquisition, competitive strength and 409; leakage risk 411; local acceptance, improvement in 410; long-term supply agreement 408; majority/minority-owned joint ventures 418; management of 421; managerial control, exercise of 423–24; market entry barriers and 409, 411; ownership structure and 418; parent control 423; partner selection criteria 414; personal attachment and 426; rationales for 409; redefinition/restructuring agreements 429; research and development consortium 408; resource complementarity and 415; risk/cost reduction and409; split-over joint venture 418; structuring global strategic alliances 418; synergy and 409; types of 407
Global strategy 381
Global supply chain 544; crossing national borders and 554; customization of supply chains 546; customs bureaucracy and 555; globalization of supply chains 545; global sourcing 546; logistics customization 547; logistics providers 546; national variations and 547; packaging/labels and 547; postponement strategy and 547; product customization 547; small/midsize enterprises and 546; *see also* International marketing; Transportation modes
Global warming 67
Global welfare 67
Global-level cooperation among nations **257**; General Agreement on Tariffs and Trade 57, 258; International Monetary Fund 257, 263; Organization For Economic Cooperation and Development 265; specialized international economic organizations 266; United Nations Conference on Trade and Development 266; World Bank Group 264; World Trade Organization 258; *see also* International economic integration/institutions
Globalization, xiii 3–5, 528; anti-globalization 3, 54; beneficiaries of 6; capability building and 88; career prospects and 10; Coca-Cola Company case and 2; definition of 3; developing/emerging economies and 6, 9, 11; diversity of business systems and 17, 393; domestic business and 11; environmental issues and 617, 619–20; global capital flow, vulnerable nations and 9; Globalization Index rankings 7; global thinking/local action and 461; government decisions 8, 147;

bilateral agreements and 8, 280; impact of 8; infrastructure for 9; international business and 10; multinational enterprises and 11; opposition to 9; promises/threats of 9; regionalization and 279, 281; service sector and 4; supply chains and 545; transnationalization index and 11; wealthy nations and 9; world merchandise trade, share of developing countries 8; *see also* Foreign direct investment (FDI); Global research and development; International business; International/ foreign trade; International marketing
Globalization Index 5–6
Globalization infrastructure 9
Globalization of markets 5, 461
Globalization of operations 398, 461–62; *see also* Global operations
Globalizing research and development (R&D) 435
Globally integrated network structure 445, 447, 454
GLOBE classification framework 205, 209
Goal compatibility 414
Goldman Sachs 322
Gold reserves 264, 292
Gold standard 305
Goods 34, 306, 358; balance of trade, United States and 23, 53, 311, 313; capital-intensive goods, demand bias and 29; international business and 10; international/foreign trade and 53, 170; locally produced goods, prices of 303; physical goods, e-commerce and 606; *see also* Products; Services
Google 110, 617; Google.cn 617; Google. com.hk 617
Gorky Automobile Plant (GAZ) 262
Government bodies 10
Government efficiency **236**, 343
Government liaison executives 222
Government policies 182, 227, 341; antitrust policies 341; boycotts and 65; employment opportunity expansion 642; export controls and 64; foreign direct investment and 341; global research and development and 435, 442; industrial policies 182, 341; infrastructure improvements 339; multinational enterprises and 565; national competitiveness and 159, 179; policy consensus 231; regulatory function and 429; sustained investment goals and 183; *see also* Legal environment; Political environment
Government Procurement Agreement (GPA) 634
Government sources of export financing 492
Grace T.H.W. Group 237
Graham, J. L. 212, 217n46
Great Britain *see* United Kingdom **120**, 200, 202
Great China Circle 276
Great Depression 292
Greece **199**, **255**, 273, 358, 626; financial crisis 321
Greenfield investment 75, 106

Greenspan, A. 327
Gross domestic product (GDP) 310
Gross margin method 515
Gross national product (GNP) 310
Group of Seven (G7) 294–95
Growth opportunities, xiii 567; escape clauses, infant industries and 260; globalization and 528, 567
Growth Triangles 276
Guangzhou 344
Guidelines for Multinational Enterprises 622
Gulf Cooperation Council (GCC) 279

Hacking 587
Haier 80
Hall, T. 216n29
Hallmark Cards 355
Hamad, K. 214
Hampden-Turner, C. 189, 215, 217n35
Hard disk drive industry 156
Hard/strong currency 292
Harmonization 504–05, 511; benefits of 511; foreign currency translation and 508, 511; international accounting harmonization 504; standardization and 504; *see also* International accounting; International economic integration/institutions
Harmonized Tariff Schedule 57
Harmony dimension 200, 205
Harrison, J. K. 577, 591n53
Hazardous waste 619
Headquarters 117, 401, 586
Health care products 82, 116, 528
Health care services 96, 122, 163, 528
Heartland By-Products 58
Heckscher, Eli 26, 69n4
Heckscher-Ohlin theorem 26, 34, 40; Stolper-Samuelson theorem 27
Heinz 58, **539**
Helpman, B. 35, 69n16
Hetero-stereotypes 212
Hewlett Packard 340, 416
Hierarchy dimension 204–05
High-context cultures 206
High-level human skills 29–30
High-tech development zones 342, 443
Hill's Pet Nutrition 355
Hisense 357
Hitachi 319
Hitt, M. A. 653, 656n28
Hoffmann-La Roche 438
Hofstede, G. 189, **203**, 500, 521n3
Hofstede's dimensions of culture 197, **204**; criticism of 202; individualism/ collectivism 200; long-term orientation 201, **202**; masculinity/ femininity 201; power distance 197; uncertainty avoidance 197, **199**; *see also* Cultural environment
Holden 4
Holding companies 518–19
Home country compensation system 583
Home country experience/reputation 89, 129
Home currency invoicing 482
Home Depot 102, 525
Homogeneity assumption 10
Honda 92, 210, 381, 572

Honeywell 245, 357
Hon Hai Precision Industries 120
Hong Kong, xiii 62, 75, **199**, 276, 299; conglomerate foreign direct investment and 75; corrupt practices 628, 630; familiarity theory and 98, 106; fixed peg system and 299; garment exports and 62; gateway to China 226; multinational enterprise in 10, 119; regional-level politics 238; smuggling and 628
Hong Kong Monetary Authority (HKMA) 291, 299
Hong Kong and Shanghai Banking Corporation (HSBC) 564
Hoppe, M. H. 216n24, 202
Horizontal foreign direct investment 74
Host country 73; competitive advantages 77, 159; domestic enterprises and 80; employment benefits and 79; entry mode selection and 368–69; foreign direct investment, impact of 74; global research and development location and 379, 442; greenfield investment/ mergers and acquisitions and 106; holding companies in 366, 519; host country nationals 586; host country risk 342, 369; knowledge transfer limits, intermediate technology and 84; low-tax regions in 520; regulatory/ industrial environments and 78; *see also* Multinational enterprises (MNEs); Political environment
Host country-based/localized compensation system 583; foreign affiliates 73, 96; *see also* Expatriate workforce; Salaries
Host country nationals (HCNs) 79, 390, 570, 586
Host Economy Transnationality Index 103
Howse, R. 55, 67, 70n28n35
Hufbauer, G. 66, 69n11
Human capital 602
Human resource management 448, 565; global research and development 439, 449; mobility of human resources 444; *see also* International human resource management (IHRM)
Human rights issues 621–22, 624
Human skills 29; dynamic capability perspective 88; technology gaps 30; *see also* Human capital
Hume, David 23, 69n1
Hungary 116, 170, 271
Huntington, S. P. 190, 207, 215n3, 217n30
Hussein, Saddam 234
Hutchison Whampoa 120, **122**, 131
Hybrid compensation system 583
Hybrid strategy 381; *see also* Hybrid compensation system; Transnational/ hybrid strategy
Hymer, Stephen H. 83, 112n6
Hyundai 92, 238, 326

I-Berhad 357
I-R balance 379
IBM 88, 91, 450, 535
Idea exchange 173
Ikea 535
Illegal immigrants 571, 628

Image marketing 173
IMD *see* International Institute for Management Development (IMD)
Imitation lag 30; product life-cycle model 31, **32**, 82; *see also* Imitators
Imitators 33, 67
Immigration controls 67
Imperfect competition 35
Imperial Chemical Industries (Id) 409
Implementer 381–82
Import controls 465, 514; balance of trade and 50, 311; boycotts 65; licensing procedures for 67; steel industry and 60–61; *see also* Export controls; Imports
Importers 45–46, **480**
Imports 33, 45, 60, 313, 339; commodities and 9, 45, 256; Leontief paradox and 28; major importers 37, 45–46; pre-shipment inspections and 67; price equalization and 27; surge in imports 63; United States trade partners 361; *see also* Import controls; Importers; Quotas; Tariff barriers
In-house banks 490
Income 34, 167, 579; *see also* Expatriate workforce; Labor market; Salaries
Income-preference similarity theory 34
Increasing returns 35–37
Independent Commission Against Corruption 630
Independent float system 301
India, xiii 89, **255**, 488, 617; back-office operations 89; corporate social responsibility 617; dumping complaints and 59; global research and development and 434; high-tech operations and 89; production 89, 411; relocation to 579; software development and 434; trade volume/growth 41; unrelated diversification and 235
Indigenous firms 355, 439
Indigenous technology units 441
Indirect quote 304
Individual mobility 67
Individual-level factors in competitiveness 178
Individualism 500, 585
Individualism/collectivism (I/C) dimensions 200, 202
Indonesia **225**, 240
Industrial complexity development 498
Industrial development 182, 435; *see also* Newly industrialized economies
Industrial organization 83
Industrial policies 341
Industrial pollution 3
Industry-specific factors 368
Infant industry 55; Protection 55–56; harmful effects (of protection) 56; expiration (of protection) 56; institutional weaknesses 56
Infant industry argument 30, 55
Infineon Technologies AG 406–07
Inflation 164, 311; Inflation accounting 497–98; United States dollar devaluation 293
Inflow of foreign direct investment (WI) 74
Influence tactics 231

Informal capital 647, **649**
Informal Investors 647
Information 505, 513, 577, 588; communications technology, knowledge-intensive operations and 23; information flows 487; knowledge transfer, centers of excellence and 89; new information 92–94, 348, 353; *see also* Knowledge
Information communication technology (ICT) 444
Information networks 10
Information services 44, 122
Information systems 512
Information technology industry 144, 169
Infrastructure 163; transport networks 163; communications networks 163; education and training system 163; health care system 163; public utility networks 163
Infrastructure variables 340
Initial public offerings (IPOs) 652
Innovation 176, 179, 436, 449; engineers/designers, competitive edge and 179; foreign direct investment and 176; global innovator role 381; imitation lag and of 30; imitation of 30; intellectual property rights and 10, 629; local innovator role 381; national competitiveness and 159, 179; process innovations 436, 449; product innovation 82, 449; product life-cycle model and 31, **32**, 82; rivalries, business practices and 173; technological innovation process 167, 169, 436
Input outsourcing 485
Institute of International Economics 18n6, 53
Institute of Manufacturing Technology (IMF) 157, 440
Institute of Microelectronics (IME) 157
Institutional reforms 180, 274, 328
Institutional system 161
Institutions 161; administrative system 162; market-oriented system 162; protection of contractual and consumer rights 162; quality 162; *see also* International economic integration/institutions
Insurance services 44
Integrated player 381
Integration of production 84
Integration-responsiveness (I-R) perspective 94
Integrative systems 398
Intel 91, 109, **110**, 434, 652
Intel Capital 435
Intel China Research Center (1CRC) 434
Intel India Design Center 434
Intellectual property exports 50
Intellectual property rights 143, 247
Inter-American Commercial Arbitration Commission 242
Interbrand 537
Intercompany financing 471, **472**
Interdependence 18, 513; *see* Globalization
Interest groups 224–25, 231
Interest rate parity (IRP) principle 307

Interest rates 12, 290, 320
Intergovernmental Council of Copper Exporting Countries (CIPEC) 283
Intermediation 541
Intermodal transportation 548
Internalization theory 84–86; *see also* Ownership/location/internalization (OLI) framework
International accounting 497; accounting systems, cross-national diversity in 497; economic system diversity 497; external relations diversity 500; finance corporations and 520; foreign currency translation methods 509; GlaxoSmithKline case 496; harmonization/standardization 504; holding companies in host countries and 519; holding companies in integrated regions and 519; industrial structure, accounting standards and 498; inflation accounting 497; internal accounting information system and 498, 513; international accounting information systems 512; international accounting standards 505; legal system diversity 499; national accounting zones 502; pension accounting 498; political system diversity 498; professional system diversity 499; societal culture diversity 500; taxation system diversity 499; tax havens 497, 517; tax strategies for multinationals 517, 519; tax treaties 518; transfer pricing/taxation strategies 514; transitional economies 502; Volvo case 490; *see also* Financial management
International accounting information systems (IAJS) 512
International accounting standards 505
International Accounting Standards Board (IASB) 505
International Accounting Standards Committee (IASC) 505
International acquisitions 322, 371
International Bank for Reconstruction and Development (IBRD) 264
International Bauxite Association (IBA) 283
International bond markets **314**, 320, 474; Bulldog bonds 474; Eurobonds 474; foreign bonds 474; Panda bonds 474; Samurai bonds 474; Yankee bonds 474
International business, xiii, 10; definition of 10; diversity in business systems and 17; domestic business and 11; e-commerce, impact of 17; economic motives and 14; economies of scale and 15, 83; environmental dynamics of 12; factor endowments and 26; foreign sales corporations and 64; globalization and 18, 528; global/local forces, simultaneous existence of 10; globally unified compensation system and 578; homogeneity assumption and 10; interdependence among nations and 11; international firms and 11; international new ventures/global startups and 12; international trade/investment

and 11; international transactions and 11; market motives and 14; motivations for 14; operational nature of 12; strategic motives and 14; suitcase companies and 12; transnationalization index 11; *see also* Cultural environment; Foreign direct investment(FDI); Globalization; International/foreign trade; Multinational enterprises (MNEs); National competitiveness

International capital markets 314, 319; Asian financial crisis 324, 328; credit rating agencies and 323; international bond markets **314**, 320, 329; international loan markets **314**, 322, 329; international money markets **314**, 319, 329; international stock/equity markets **314**, 321; leveraged buy-outs and 322; *see also* International foreign exchange markets; International monetary system

International capital movements 9; efficient capital markets9; *see also* International capital markets

International Chamber of Commerce 356, 465

International Civil Aviation Organization 569

International Cocoa Agreement (ICCA) 284

International Coffee Agreement (ICA) 284

International Court of Arbitration 242

International Court of Justice in the Hague 242

International Development Association (IDA) 264

International division structure 384

International economic integration/ institutions 255–56; Andean Free Trade Area 277; Asia-Pacific Economic Cooperation Forum 274; Association of Southeast Asian Nations 274; Caribbean Community and Common Market 277; Central African Economic and Customs Union 279; Central American Common Market 277; commodity-level cooperation and 281; common market and 255; customs union and 255; distributional gains 256; East African Economic Community 279; Economic Community of West African States 279; economic integration, forms of 255; economic outcomes of integration 256; economic union and 256; efficiency gains 256; escape clauses and 260; European Union 271; free trade area and 255; globalization vs. regionalization and 297; global-level cooperation and 257; Gulf Cooperation Council 279; Intergovernmental Council of Copper Exporting Countries 283; International Bauxite Association 283; International Cocoa Agreement 284; International Coffee Agreement 284; International Monetary Fund 263; International Natural Rubber Agreement 284; International Sugar Agreement 284; International Tin Agreement 284; Latin American Free Trade Association 255, 277; Latin American Integration Association 277; most-favored-nation treatment and 260; Multifiber Arrangement 60; multilateral cooperation and 256; multinational enterprises, strategic responses of 298; national treatment and 260; North American Free Trade Agreement 255, 269–70; Organization for Economic Cooperation and Development 261; Organization of Petroleum Exporting Countries 282; pan-European communication and 254, 529; political union and 256; postwar regional integration and 267–69; Preferential Trade Areas 260, 342; regional integration agreements 280; regional-level cooperation 267; sequential economic integration *112;* South Asian Association for Regional Cooperation 276; Southern Common Market Treaty 255, 277; specialized international economic organizations 278; trade creation 280; trade diversion 280; 3M, European market integration 254; United Nations Conference on Trade and Development 284; Wheat Trade Convention 284; World Bank 9, 112n3; World Trade Organization 258

International entrepreneurship, xiii, 641; alliance formation and 652; born global firms 642; born global firms, internationalization of 652; comparative entrepreneurship and 642; cross-border entrepreneurship and 652; cultural factors and 645; ease of venture initiation 642; international new ventures 652; Israeli case 654; Japanese in Hawaii case 640; motivation for 641; national context and 645; national rates of entrepreneurial activities 642; opportunity-to-necessity ratio and 642; venture capital funds and 641

International entry strategies 336, 373; cost-benefit analysis and 352; early-mover advantages 349; early-mover disadvantages 351; entry mode choices 355; entry mode decision framework 352, 368; entry mode selection 355; evolutionary entry path 371; greenfield investment, international acquisitions/mergers and 370; international location selection 336–37; location 335; locational determinants and 337; location decision framework 368; mode 336; timing of entry 336, 347; timing of entry 336 347

International equity market 321; *see* International stock/equity markets

International experience 129, 417, 565

International Federation of Accountants (IFAC) 505

International Finance Corporation (IFC) 264

International financial markets **314**

International Financial Reporting Standards (IFRS) 506

International firms 11

International Fisher effect 308

International foreign exchange markets **314**; black market 318; Bretton Woods system and 293, 297; computer-based communications systems and 315; efficiency in 316; floating exchange rate system 361; foreign exchange arbitrage 317; foreign exchange black markets 318; foreign exchange markets 314; foreign exchange rate quotations 303; foreign exchange transaction 314; government intervention 181–82; markets participants/functions 315; parallel market 318; transaction forms 316; twenty-four hour market 315; *see also* Exchange rate systems; Foreign exchange rates; International capital markets; International foreign exchange transactions; International monetary system

International foreign exchange transactions 314; Clearing House Interbank Payments System and 316; forward-forward swap 317; spot-forward swap 317; spot transactions 316; swap transactions 317; *see also* International foreign exchange markets; International monetary system

International/foreign trade 23; absolute advantage theory and 24; banana wars and 22; comparative advantage theory and 25; economies of scale and 15; export structures and 39; externalities and 35; future theoretical developments 39; Heckscher-Ohlin theorem and 26; human skills/technology-based views and 29; income-preference similarity theory and 34; inter-industry vs. intra-industry trade, drivers of 35; laissez-faire doctrine and 24; Leontief paradox and 28; market demand and 34, 39; mercantilist doctrine and 23; new trade theory and 35; opportunity cost and 25; product life-cycle model and 31, **32**; social-cultural matrix and 26; specialization in production and 25; terms of trade and 39; theory assessment and 37; *see also* Free trade; International/foreign trade patterns; Trade barriers

International/foreign trade patterns 23, 40; balance of trade and 23, 50; factor endowments and 26; free trade, opposition to 53–54; Heckscher-Ohlin theorem and 26; income-preference similarity theory and 34; Leontief paradox and 28; major exporters/importers 45–46; new trade theory and 35; reciprocity/retaliation and 54; regional integration agreements 267, 269, 281; service trade and 44, 54–55; trade statistics, harmonized classification system and 45; trade volume/growth 40–41;

United States trade partners 46–47;
see also International/foreign trade;
Trade barriers
International franchising 359, 361;
Drawbacks 361
International human resource management
(IHRM) 564; affiliates and 586–87;
boards of directors, globalization
of 567; communication/integration
challenges and 587; compensation
gaps and 587; country-specific issues in
572; delegation of authority/decision-
making power and 587; ethnocentric
staffing and 570; exile syndrome/
reentry difficulties and 587; friction
in staffing policy and 587; geocentric
staffing and 571; global deployment
of talent and 565; global integration/
local responsiveness and 379, 565,
579; host country nationals and 586;
HSBC case 564; information screening
and 588; international joint ventures,
employee groups in 632; labor cost
571; phases of 565; polycentric
staffing and 571; problems in foreign
affiliates 587; promotion blocking and
587; rank/file staffing 570; regiocentric
staffing and 571; split loyalties
and 587; strategic international
human resource management 565;
unfamiliar environments and 588;
see also Expatriate workforce; Global
operations
International Institute for Management
Development (IMD) 156, 167,
168, 177, 183, **184, 236, 241**, 550,
552–53, 556
International investment 11, 88, 90
International joint ventures (IJVs) 632
International Labor Organization (ILO)
266, 621
International leasing 359
International licensing 359–60
International loan markets 322, 329
International location selection 336–37;
cost/tax factors 337–38; demand
factors 337, 339; Federal Express,
Philippine location and 344; global
research and development and
346; locational determinants 337;
location decision framework 345;
regulatory/economic factors 337,
341; sociopolitical factors 337, 342;
strategic factors 337, 340; *see also*
International entry strategies
International managers (IMs) 412
International marketing 525; advertising
542; alliance forming and 543;
branding and 537; challenges to
525–26; country-of-origin effect
and 535; cross-national variations
and 531; cultural influences 531;
cultural/social mores and 531;
distribution channel decisions
540; Domino's Pizza case *524–25;*
economic development, disposable
income and 545; globalization
forces 529; localization forces 530; market
function, globalization and 528,
530; market potential, assessment

of 526; nationalist sentiments and
536; positive country image and 535;
promotion activities 542; *see also*
Global supply chain
International mergers 370
International Monetary Fund (IMF) 9,
263; anti-corruption activities 633;
Asian financial crisis and 324, 328–29;
Bretton Woods Institutions and 263;
Eurozone financial crisis 328; foreign
exchange reserves and 264; functions/
structures of 346, 384, 396; multilateral
surveillance and 263; national fiscal/
monetary policies, coordination of
256, 263; private capital, development
and 264; quota changes 263; special
drawing right and 264
International monetary system 291–92;
Asian financial crisis and 324,
328–29; balance of payments 311;
Bretton Woods system (1944–1973)
293; changes in exchange rates
and 291; crawling peg system 298;
dollar, devaluation of 291; European
Central Bank and 300; European
Monetary System and 256, 296;
exchange rate systems 264, 297,
329; fixed-rate system 297;
floating/flexible exchange rate system
297; foreign currencies, selection
of 291, 319; foreign exchange rates
and 291; foreign exchange rates,
determination of 303; gold standard
period (1876–1914) 292; Group of
Seven and 294; history of 291–92;
independent float system 301; interest
rate parity principle 305, 307;
international capital markets 314,
319; international financial markets
314; international Fisher effect and
308; international foreign exchange
markets 314; interwar years/World
War 11(1914–1944) 292; Louvre
Accords and 294; managed/dirty float
system 301; Mexico, foreign exchange
crisis in 290; multinational enterprises
and 306–07; oil crisis of 1973 and
294; post-Bretton Woods system
(1973–present) 294; purchasing power
parity principle and 305–06; special
drawing rights and 291; target-zone
arrangement 300; *see also* International
capital markets; International foreign
exchange markets
International money markets **314**, 319, 329
International Natural Rubber Agreement
(INRA) 284
International new ventures *(INVs)* 652,
655
International Organization of Securities
Commissions (IOSCO) 505
International Organization for
Standardization (ISO) **266**
International Standards of Accounting
and Reporting (ISAR) 505
International Standards Organization
(ISO) 619, 624
International stock/equity markets 321;
see also International capital markets;
International monetary system

International subcontracting 357
International Sugar Agreement (ISA) 284
International technology transfer 452
International Telephone & Telegraph
(ITT) 449
International Tin Agreement (ITA) 284
International trade 23, 40, 68; *see*
International/foreign trade;
International/foreign trade patterns
International Trade Organization (ITO)
258
International trade theories 23; *see*
international/foreign trade
International transactions 11
Internationalization **161**, 170; developing
nation multinationals and 8, 384;
national competitiveness and 159,
179; size issues and 209; small/
midsize international enterprises 118
Internationally committed company 117
Internationally leaning firms 117
Internet 175, 597, 603; convergence
hypothesis and 214; diffusion of 597;
domain name **598**; e-commerce and
597; gender, access levels and 163;
gender gap 609; penetration rate **597**;
see also Global c-commerce
Interpublic 390
Interwar years 297
Intra-company reinvoicing 485
Intra-firm trade 40, 68
Investment 93, 313, 367
balanced growth 165, 171; build-operate-
transfer investment 362; defensive
export substituting investment
strategy 284; environment for 72,
230; infrastructure variables and 340;
international transactions and 311,
319, 492; multilateral investment
agreements 284, 284; offensive export
substituting investment strategy
285; portfolio investment 74, 313;
portfolio theory and 74; production
factor quality and 27; rationalized
foreign direct investment strategy
285; reorganization investment
strategy 285; return on investment,
delay in 201; safe haven investment
locations 235; sustained investment
goals 183; *see also* Foreign direct
investment (FDI)
Investment approaches 75, 87
Investment incentives 339
Invoicing 482, 491
Inward Foreign Direct Investment
Performance Index **100**, 105
Inward Foreign Direct Investment
Potential Index 105
iPhone 34, 604
iPod 4, 228
Iran 64–65, 105, **282**
Iraq 65, **282**, 298
Iraq-United States War 536
Ireland 23, 89, **225**, 321; back-office
operations and 89; financial crisis
321; government policy consensus
and 23; high skill level in 11; small
international enterprise exports to 11
Ireland, D. 656
Irreversibility 93, 354

Irrevocable letter credit (L/C) 464
Islam 194, 214
Israel 110, 227, 654; airborne aircraft-warning systems 227; embargoes/boycotts against 65; entrepreneurial activities in 646; export controls and 64; foreign direct investment and 110; foreign direct production and 11, 134; high skill levels in 110; high-tech operations and 89; software security firm 12
Israel-Lebanon conflict 227
Issuer Credit Ratings (ICR) 323
Italy 80, **120**, 139, **225**, 483, 625

Jaguar 107, 391
Japan 6, 33, 37, 48–49, 56, 60, 72–73, 145, 159, 172, 176–77, 231, 240, 244, 246, 284, 350, 379, 411, 420, 485, 505, 525, 533, 548, 572, 575, 609, 620, 640–41; antitrust legislation 244; automotive exports 11, 37, 38, 39; culture, role of 190, 197–98, 206; direct marketing and 541; entrepreneurship and 640; expatriate failure rate and 575; firm-level standards and 176; foreign direct investment and 72, 73, 91, 92, 99–100; horizontal foreign direct investment and 74; infant industry argument and 56; Liberal Democratic Party of 58; patent laws 246; product liability enforcement 246; rice tariffs and 58; steel production and 60; uncertainty avoidance and 197, **199**; United States trade and 46–50, 51–52; US-made Hondas and 62; worker's loyalty in 178
Jardine Matheson 132
Jelinek, M. 212
Jewelry industries 173
Job loss 9, 79
Johnson & Johnson 116, 450, 451, 565, 574
Joint exploration project 408
Joint ventures **144**, 344, 355, 362; control 364, 365; cooperative 363, 364; de novo 364, 370; equity 364; incentive 364, 365
Jordan 226, 362
J&P Avax 362
JPMorgan Chase 122
Judiciary systems 239
Just-in-time (JIT) system 88, 340, 341

Kao Corporation 365
Kazakhstan 630
Kearney, A. T. 601
Keesing, D. B. 30
Kelley, L 190
Kenny Rogers China 525
Kent, M. 387
Kentucky Fried Chicken (KFC) 525
Kimberly Clark 548
Kimchi wars 536
Knowledge: alliances, external knowledge acquisition and 130; centers of excellence and 129; communications technology, knowledge-intensive operations and 123; core knowledge, uncompensated leakage and 422; education, knowledge-based economies and 179; evolutionary perspective and 90–91; foreign direct investment and 74, 83–85; high-knowledge functions 92; internationalization process and 90; knowledge creation/dissemination 179; knowledge transfer, multinational enterprises and 85, 89, 125; learning capability and 129–30; local business practices 342; managerial knowledge 421; market knowledge, experiential nature of 90; monopolistic advantages and 83; operational knowledge 421; proprietary knowledge 77, 84–85; proprietary knowledge, research and development and 439; small-midsize international enterprises and 142; subsidiary knowledge flow 381–82
Knowledge intensive exports 9–10
Kodak 128
KOF Swiss Economic Institute 5
Kogut, B. 94–95, 207
Komatsu 358, 410
Korea 56, 106, 139, 191, 193, 202, 222, 231, 294, 326, 485, 570; buy local campaigns in 65; chaebol 351; Chinese market economy and 609; English study and 194; infant industry argument and 56; kimchi wars 534; multinational enterprises in 135, 137, 390
Kosovo crisis 227
KPMG 624
Kraft Foods 532
Krugman, P. 35
Krupp 362
Kuwait 206, 279, 282

Labeling practices 66, 548, 620
Labor costs 143, 326, 338, 357
Labor-intensive exports 22, 37, 59, 145
Labor-intensive industry 79
Labor market: banana exports 22; child labor 270; competitively priced labor 11, 134; division of labor 438; globally unified compensation system and 10; high value-added jobs, home country and 125; inter-country differences in costs 14; international business and 10; job loss, globalization and 9, 79; labor migration 30, 49; multinational enterprises and 11, 125; semi-skilled labor 47; skilled labor 29–30, 33; unskilled labor 9, 33, 642; see also Expatriate workforce; International human resource management (IHRM); Workforce
Lags 483–85, 598
Laissez-faire doctrine 24
Lancaster, K. 69n6
Land Rover 107
Language 191–94; language barriers 342; lingua franca and 193–94; multilingualism 194; non-verbal 193, 576
Laos 279

Late investor 351–52
Latin America 101, 269, 277; banana quotas/tariffs and 22; banking industry, foreign domination of 226, 350; regime change in 220, 234; trade volume/growth 255; United States trade and 50, 80; see also Regional-level cooperation among nations
Latin American Free Trade Area (LAFTA) 277
Latin American Integration Association (LAIA) 277
Latvia 300
Laurent, A. 210
Law-making treaties 246
Leads 483
Leakage risk of technologies 369
Learning capability 129
Learning effect see Experience curve
Leasing see International leasing
Least developed countries (LDCs) status 8
Legal environment 239–47; antitrust legislation/enforcement 244–45; civil law 239; common law 239; competition laws 244–45; conflict resolution mechanisms 428; corporate law, branch offices and 363; environmental protection laws 343; equal employment opportunity law 572; executive agreements 246; fair administration of justice **241**; institutional context and 239; intellectual property rights and 84–85, 143, 247, 361; international treaties 247; law-making treaty 246; legal jurisdiction 242; marketing/distribution laws 245; multinationals, legal issues of 243; patent laws 246; product liability laws 245–46; property rights systems 411; rule of origin 244; separation of powers 239; theocratic law 239; treaties of friendship/commerce/and navigation 246; treaty agreements 246–47; see also Cultural environment; Environmental dynamics; Political environment
Legal jurisdiction 242–43; alien-tort precedents 243; international jurisdiction 242–43; jurisdictional levels and 242; national jurisdiction 243; regional jurisdiction 243; see also Legal environment
Legitimacy 228, 652
Lehman Brothers 428
Lenovo 14
Leontief paradox 28–30, 39, 49
Leontief, Wassily 28
Lesotho 60
Letta, Enrico 180
Letter of credit (L/C) 463–65; back-to-back letter of credit 465; clean letter of credit 464; confirmed letter of credit 464; documentary letter of credit 464; irrevocable letter of credit 464; revocable letter of credit 464; revolving letter of credit 465; transferable letter of credit 465; unconfirmed letter of credit 464
Leveraged buy-outs (LBOs) 322

Levi Strauss 245, 622–23
Levi Strauss Foundation 622
Lewis, D. 119
LG Electronics 570
Li, H. 135
Liability of foreignness 75, 189, 226, 609
Liability laws 245–46
Libya 222, 234, 279
License fees 45, 50
Licensing: cross-licensing agreements 422; difficulties 83–84; drawbacks 360–61; foreign markets and 91; host-country risk levels and 368; international licensing 360–61
Linder, Steffan B. 34
Linder's income-preference similarity theory 34, 39
Lingua franca 193–94, 607
LinguaMetrics International, Inc. 606
Lion Air of Indonesia 231
Lippo 136
Lithuania 503
Living standards 179, 259
L.L. Bean 606
Loan market see International loan markets
Local business practices 342
Local content 244, 532, 536
Local currency 474–76
Local firms: foreign direct investment and 80; global players and 350–51; multinationals, learning opportunities and 125, 368, 372
Local infrastructure for research 444
Local innovator 381, 399
Localized compensation see Host country-based/localized compensation system
Local responsiveness 94, 379–81
Location advantages 77
Location-specific variables 86; locational determinants 337; see also Global research and development; International entry strategies; International location selection
Logistics providers 546
London Interbank Offer Rate (LIBOR) 320
Long position 317
Long-term orientation (LTO) dimension 201–02
Long-term supply agreement 408
Louvre Accords 294
Low-context cultures 206
Lowest common denominator argument 54
Low-tax regions 520
Lucent Technologies 75, 341
Luxury consumer goods 34

Maastricht Treaty 271
Macroeconomic stability 167
Macroeconomic strength 168
Madrid Trademark Convention 247
Malaysia 137, 146, 239, 274, 276, 294
Malta 271, 273, 300
Managed exchange rate see Fixed/managed exchange rate system; Managed float system
Managed float system 301
Management by Objectives (MBO) 585
Management tools 398, 399
Managerial control 423, 424

Managerial skills 128–29, 409, 421, 653; Asian financial crisis and 326–27; convergence of management 173; hierarchical management practices 173, 211; knowledge transfer, centers of excellence and 89, 144; manager-employee relationships 206, 411, 425; multinational enterprises and 622; national competitiveness and 584–85; strategic flexibility and 94–95
Manufacturers life insurance 239, 240
Manufactures 34
Manufacturing concentration 340
Maquiladoras 346, 347
Maritime transportation 349
Market failure: Asian financial crisis and 324; structural market failure 87; transactional market failure 87
Market motives 14; defensive motives 14; dual-emphasis orientation 347; location decision, market orientation and 346; location selection and 346; offensive motives 14
Market orientation 346
Market power 143, 349, 350, 416
Market share 60, 63, 76, 135, 173, 284, 370, 544, 596
Marketing 523–43; alliances for 543; core competency and 449; cross-border marketing, globalization and 525–26; foreign direct investment for 76; image marketing 173; laws for 534–35; niche marketing 541; see also International marketing; Marketing
Marketing skills 335, 421
Markets: demand conditions 172; domestic markets, globalization levels and 5; life-cycle stages in 77, 528; market breadth 445; market demand 159, 172, 182; market knowledge, experiential nature of 90; see also international marketing; Marketing
Market-seeking foreign direct investment (FDI) 76
Mary Kay Cosmetics 14, 341, 541
Masculinity/femininity (M/F) dimensions 201
Mastery dimension 204
Matching mechanism 484
Mattel 547–48
Matthews, R.G. 636
Maxwell House 486
Mazda 92, 483
McClelland, D. C. 200, 211
McDonald's 88, 127, 214, 228, 361, 532, 533, 536, 547
McDonnell Douglas Corporation 64
McDougall, P.P. 642
Mecca Cola 12, 536
Media services 122, 126, 223, 231, 543, 604
Mental maps 212
Mercantilism 23–24; logical holes 24
Mercedes-Benz 338
Mercenary armies 23
Merchandise trade see World merchandise trade
Merck 339, 408, 490
Mergers 106–07, 370–71; independent international agency oversight 245;

international mergers 370–71; see also Global strategic alliances (GSAs)
Merrill Lynch 128, 166
Mexico 9, 32, 50, 346–47, 549; alliances with local firms/multinationals and; automotive products and 37; dumping complaints and 59; economic liberalization in 77; foreign exchange crisis in 290–91, 318–19; garment exports and 60, 79; multinational enterprises in 92, 145; North American Free Trade Agreement and 269–71, 555; production, relocation to 14, 33, 79; production technology and 169; truck transport of goods and 551; United States trade and 46–47, 279; see also International monetary system
Microelectronics and Computer Technology Corporation 444
Microsoft 91, 408, 513
Middle East 279, 283, 315, 597; see also Regional-level cooperation among nations
Midsize firms see Small/midsize international enterprises (SMIEs)
Milkovich, G.T. 591n62, 591n63
Mineral extraction See also Extraction industries
Minimum efficient scale 438
Mining see Extraction industries
Ministry of International Trade and Industry (MITI) 350
Mitsubishi 410, 422, 532
Mixed-currency invoicing 482
MNE organizational structures 383; international division structure 384; global functional structure 384; global geographic structure 385; global matrix structure 393; global product structure 389; national subsidiary structure 383
MNE Strategy 380; global strategy 381; multi-domestic 381
Mobility restrictions 67
Mobutu Sese Seko 223
Monetary items 508, 510
Monetary/nonmonetary method of accounting 509–10
Monetary unions 291
Money laundering 629
Money markets see International money markets
Monopolistic advantage 83, 84, 86, 87, 97, 101, 109
Moody's 323
Moore, K. 119, 150n5
Morales, Evo 220, 221
Moral hazard 85
Mortgage-backed securities 328
Mortgage banks 327, 328
Most-favored-nation (MFN) treatment 260
Mother-daughter design 383
Motorola 78, 110, 125, 130, 337, 353, 406, 407, 422, 423, 478, 652
Multidomestic firms 117
Multidomestic strategy 381, 401
Multifiber Agreement (MFA) 60
Multifocal strategy 94

Multilateral Investment Guarantee Agency (MIGA) 264
Multilateral trade agreements 258, 267
Multinational enterprises (MNEs) 77, 115–48, 383–85, 622; alliances, external knowledge acquisition and 130; automotive industry and 91; borderless corporations, myth/reality of 126; born international enterprises 147; born national enterprises 174; capability deployment and 88; communications technology and 123; competitive advantage of 127–28; competitive advantage, technology gap and 128; core competencies and 135; cost-leadership strategies and 77; defensive export-substituting investment strategy 284; diversification, strength of 74, 127–28; dynamic capability perspective and 88; economic transformation and 122; efficiency-seeking foreign direct investment and 76; familiarity theory and 91; firm capabilities and 128; foreign direct investment and 75, 76, 85, 87, 89, 97–98, 102, 117–18, 131, 136, 146, 284, 341–42, 352, 363; foreign exchange forecasting and 310; global functional structure 384; globalization and liberalization of regulatory systems 122; global resources of 10; historic foundation for 119; horizontal foreign direct investment and 74; host countries, foreign direct investment impacts on 222; image of 125–26; integration-responsiveness perspective and 94–95; international division structure 384; international expansion of 85; largest multinationals 120; learning capability and 129; liabilities of foreignness and 129; local firms, learning opportunities and 78; location advantages, efficiency from 77; managerial skills and 128–29; nationally-independent subsidiaries and 85; national subsidiary structure 383; offensive export-substituting investment strategy 285; organizational learning, growth from 78; organizational structures 383–85; ownership advantages, increasing return from 77–78; pluralistic goals of 76; public eye perception of 125–26; rationalized foreign direct investment strategy 285; relationship building and 416; reorganization investment strategy 285; service multinationals, growth of 122; sovereignty threats of 125; strategic capabilities and 128; strategic flexibility and 94–95; strategy/design of 136–37, 141; structural discrepancies, improved performance and 127–28; Transnationality Index, degree of internationalization and 118; vertical foreign direct investment and 74–75; See also Developing/emerging nation multinational enterprises (DNMEs); Foreign direct

investment (FDI); Global operations; International business; International human resource management (IHRM); National competitiveness; Small/midsize international enterprises (SMIEs); transnational/hybrid 381
Multi-sourcing strategy 176, 185
Murdoch, Rupert 244
Murphy, A.B. 194
Murray, G.C. 653
Musical instruments 173
Muslim 194, 214, 536
Mutualization 546
Myanmar 146, 222, 276

NADBank 632, 633
NAFTA see North American Free Trade Agreement (NAFTA)
Namiki N. 147
Napier, N. **566**, 589n6
NASDAQ 473
Nathan's Famous 525
National competitiveness 40, 157–84; banking system solvency and 470; basic infrastructure, development levels of **550**; cluster industries 207; commercialization process and 169; comparative advantages of nations and 157; competitiveness scoreboard **184**; currency valuation and 295; definition of 157–58; demand conditions and 172; diamond paradigm of national advantage 174; e-commerce and 175–76; economic soundness and 164; education services and 179; engineers/designers and 179; factor conditions and 172; firm-level determinants of 160; global operations location and 159; global strategy and 159–60; government policies and 179; hard currency reserves and 311; hard disk drive industry case 156–57; individual-level determinants of 178; industry-level determinants of 181; industry selection and 159; innovation/capability building and 159; internationalization and 170; international trade/investment and 169; investment levels and 170; managerial skills and 128–29, 178; multinational enterprises, effects on 159–60; national protectionism levels and 170; nation-level determinants of 171; openness of the economy and 170; performance of economic sectors and 167; politicians/government policies and 179; productivity and 158; real income/consumption per capita and 166; related/supporting industries and 172–73; rivalry, business practices and 173; science/education/innovation and 167; surge in imports, emergency protections and 63; sustained advantages and 380; worker productivity and 178; see also Multinational enterprises (MNEs)
National economies: boycotts and 65; free trade and 24, 53–54, 255;

growth of, foreign trade and 80; production factors and 26–27; structures of 176, 179; see also National competitiveness
National Grid 107
National Highway Traffic Safety Administration 246
National Institutes of Health 169
Nationalization 78, 220–22, 229
National protectionism 170
National Science and Technology Board (NSTB) 156
National security issues 50, 61, 64, 244
National subsidiary structure 383, 389, 401
National Telephone Company of Spain 420
National treatment 260
National wealth 23, 157, 178, 181
Nationalist sentiments 230, 536
Natural resources see Raw materials
NEC 412, 449
Need see User/need model
Negotiation: alliance contract negotiation 412, **413**, 417–18, 421, 424–25, 428; bilateral negotiations 8; expatriate compensation 583; Free Trade Area of the Americas (FTAA) 270–71; price of proprietary knowledge 84–84, 360; Regional Comprehensive Economic Partnership (RCEP) 274; Russia 262; tariff/non-tariff barrier reduction 59, 258; Trans-Pacific Partnership (TPP) 276; skills 193, **588**; WTO/GATT 58, 255, 258–59, 261–62
Neo-mercantilism 23, 227
Nepal 105, 205, 206, 276
Nestlé 4, 58, 117, 129; board of directors 567, **568**; geocentric staffing and 177, 571; global geographic structure of 385, **386**; polycentric decentralized research organization and 449–51
Net investment concept 509
Netherlands 79, 98, 165, 179, 205, 210, 501, 506, 509, 518
Netting practice 483–90
Neutral cultures 205
News Corporation 244
New trade theory 35–40, 49; beggar-thy-neighbor policy 36; concerns 36; constant returns to scale 35; externality 35; government trade interventions 36; increasing returns to scale 35
New York Stock Exchange (NYSE) 321–22, 473, 476
New Zealand 139
Newly industrialized economies 178
Newman, J. M. 591n62, 591n63
Niche marketing 173, 541
Nigeria 80, 102, 191, 202, 205, 240, 619, 625, 642
Nigerian National Petroleum Corporation (NNPC) 80
Nike 159, 357, 511, 543, 545, 572
Ninoy Aquino International Airport 362
Nissan 4, 15, 92, 188, 284, 447, 532
Nissan Leaf 479
Nokia 11, 506, 532
Nominal exchange rate 291
Nomura 214
Nonactionable subsidies 63

Noncurrent method of accounting *see* Current/ noncurrent method of accounting
Nongovernmental Organizations (NGOs) 65, 238, 572, 618, 621
Nonmonetary method *see* Monetary/ nonmonetary method of accounting
Non-tariff barriers 59–67; administrative barriers 65–66; boycotts 65; buy local campaigns and 65; corruption and 67; embargoes 65; foreign sales corporations and 64; labeling practices and 66; service trade, barriers to 67; surge in imports, emergency protection and 63; technical standards and 66–67; *see also* Tariff barriers; Trade barriers
Norman, V. 35, 69n16
North America 41, 146, 269–70, 597; computer/electronics industries 14; trade volume/growth 46–50; *See also* Canada; Regional-level cooperation among nations; United States
North American Free Trade Agreement (NAFTA) 28, 47, 92, 255, 269–70, 274, 279, 285, 500, 547, 551, 555, 632
North Korea 222, 297
Northern Marianas 228
Norway 105, 244, 245, 579, 599

OAI *see* Overseas Assignment Inventory (OAI)
Occidental Petroleum 78
OECD Transfer Pricing Guidelines 516
OEM *see* Original equipment manufacturing (OEM)
Offensive export-substituting investment 285
Offensive market motives 14
Offers 108, 229, 260, 265, 315, 409, 465, 470, 532, 573, 611
Office Depot 533, 537
Office Max 525, 533, 537
Official reserves account 331, 333
Offset 358–59
Offshore extractive investments 75
Ohlin, B. 26
Oil crisis of 1973, 294
OLI framework *see* Ownership/location/ internalization (OLI) framework
Online brokerage 605
Opel 4
Open account selling 467
Open economic regions 342
Open Skies agreements 50, 67, 122
Openness 40, 72, 105, 108, 123, 137, 170, 182, 269, 645
Operating profit methods 515
Operational capabilities 89
Operational flexibility 86, 94, 513
Operational nature 12
Operational risk 91, 235, 334, 351, 369
Opportunity cost 25–26
Opportunity-driven entrepreneurship 640
Optics industry 173
Optimal tariff theory 55
Options market 481
Organizational capabilities 90, 128–29, 416
Organizational learning 78, 86
Organizational skills 77–78, 342, 416

Organizational systems 86, 491; hierarchical organization 173, 204, 378, 584; political institutional context and 226–27; upgrading of 164, 174; *See also* Cultural environment; Global operations; International economic integration/ institution negative effects of foreign direct investment on
Organization for Economic Cooperation and Development (OECD) 140, 265–66, 516, 598–99, 622, 633, 640
Organization for European Economic Cooperation (OEEC) 265
Organization of Petroleum Exporting Countries (OPEC) 282–83, 294
Organization Resource Counselors (ORC) 573
Original equipment manufacturing (OEM) method 357
Otis Elevator 82, 387
Outflow of foreign direct investment (FDI) 74, 97
Outsourcing 478, 485–86, 546, 604; southern China 345, 604
Outward Foreign Direct Investment Performance Index 104
Overconfidence 165
Overdrafts 474
Overseas assembly plants 372
Overseas Assignment Inventory (OAI) 576
Oviatt, B. M. 148, 642
Owner's equity 498–99
Ownership advantages 77–78, 135
Ownership/location/internalization (OLI) framework 86
Ownership risk 235
Ownership-specific advantages 83, 87
Ownership structure 418–19

Pacific countries: banana trade and 22; *see also* Asia-Pacific Economic Cooperation Forum (APEC)
Packaging 547–48
Pakistan 202, 276, 626
Pan-European communication 254
Panama 105, 518, 549
Panasonic 412, 449, 542
Pando Networks 599
Pandora 604
Panic 299
Parallel loans 475
Parallel markets 318
Parent control 423, 484
Paris Convention for the Protection of Industrial Property 247
Paris Convention for the Protection of Intellectual Property 247
Particularism 205
Partner selection *see* Global strategic alliances (GSAs)
Par value rate 298
Passive reciprocity 55
Patents 139, 169, 246–47, 334
Paternalism 625
Pedroni, F. 180
Peer-to-peer file sharing 604
Pegged exchange rate system 291
Pemberton, John 2
Pension accounting 313

People of Liberty Party (PDL) Italy 180
People skills 576
PepsiCo Inc. 77, 127, 340
Per capita income 34, 167
Perception skills 576
Permanent expatriates 573
Personal attachment 426
Peru 166, 277
Petrobras 220
Petroleum industry: backward vertical foreign direct investment and 75; environmental responsibilities 617; negative effects of foreign direct investment on 80; *see also* Organization of Petroleum Exporting Countries (OPEC)
Peugeot-Citroen 14
Pfizer 339
Pharmaceutical industry 634
Philanthropic responsibilities 617
Philip Morris 352, 354
Philippines 146, 274, 276, 605
Philips 285, 428, 449, 484, 486
Philips Multilateral Clearing System (PMC) 484, 486
Phnom Penh, Cambodia 274
Physical assets 74
Pickering, Thomas 232
Pictet & Cie 148
Pieper, R. **566**, 589n9
Piggybacking strategy 146
Pioneering Costs 349
Piracy 629
Pizza Hut 532
Poland 180
Political behavior 221
Political engagement 5
Ownership advantages 77, 135
Political environment 221–29; affinity/ animosity between nations and 226–27; Asian financial crisis and 263–64; bargaining power, multinationals-host governments 235; coalition building/influence tactics and 231–32; coopetition and 227–28; economic aid packages 226; economic freedom and 233; geopolitical considerations and 227; government liaison executives and 222; home government, multinational enterprises and 230–31; host government investment support 230; host government, multinational enterprises and 228; host government objectives 229; institutional context and 226; intellectual property 227; legitimacy and 228; liability of foreignness and 75; micro-region political processes and 238; multinationals, political objectives in host countries and 228; nationalization of natural resources 222; nature of international business activity and 222; political behavior and 221; political processes and 221; political risk and 221; preferential trade agreements and 227
Regional-level politics and 237; *see also* Cultural environment; Environmental dynamics; Legal environment
Political instability 342

Political relations 227; multipolar/ multicivilizational nature of 227; national competitiveness and 228–30; *see also* Legal environment; Political environment

Political risk 233–35; management strategies for 237; measurement of 234; operational risk 235; ownership risk 235; political instability **236**; risk opportunity 235; terrorism 234; transfer risk 235; types of 235

Political stability/instability 161, 234

Political System 222–26; authoritarian 223–24; authoritarian regimes 224; authoritarianism 223; democratic 223; democracy 223; Democracy Index **225**; flawed democracies 224; full democracies 224; hybrid regimes 224; representative democracy 223; totalitarian 223–24; quality of governance 224

Political union 256

Pollution *see* Industrial pollution

Polycentric decentralized research and development 445–46

Polycentric staffing 571

Porter, M.E. 69n13, 172, **174**, 186n10, 374n1, 455n4

Portfolio investment 74

Portfolio theory 74

Portugal 25; financial crisis 297

Power distance (PD) 197

Prahalad, C.K. 94

Pratt & Whitney 427

Pre-shipment inspection 67

Predatory pricing 542

Preemption 93, 348–49

Preemptive opportunities 349–50

Preference similarity 34

Preferential trade agreement (PTA) 227

Price escalation clause 483

Price-fixing agreements 53

Prices: comparative advantage and 26; competitiveness of 32, 423; consumers, globalization effects and 4; fair prices, dumping and 58–59; gold reserves and 23; international marketing and 526; price-fixing agreements 53; production factor prices 26; supply-demand conditions and 26

PricewaterhouseCoopers (PWC) 140, 574, 624

Pricing process 515

Primary commodities 34

Primary products 34

Private enterprise 175

Private sources of export financing 470

Privatization 78, 625

Procter & Gamble 76, 82, 127, 383, 537

Product origin 244, 526; blurred national identity and 4; production facilities, relocation of 11, 73, 346; rule of origin and 244; service sector and 642; *see also* Products; Quotas; Tariff barriers; Trade barriers

Product liability laws 245–46

Product life-cycle 31, 82–83, 86–87, **566**

Production arrangement 486

Production factors 26; advanced factors 30; comparative production cost 26; factor endowments 34, 37; factor-intensity reversal and 29; Heckscher-Ohlin theorem and 26; human skills 29; institutional factors 31; international integration of production 84; national competitiveness and 156, 159, 182–83; prices of 27; production inputs 24, 359, 479; quality of 26, 126; specialization in production 256; technology gaps 29; traditional factors 31; wage differentials 50

Production function 27

Production movement 95

Production subsidies 62

Productivity of labor 180

Products: contraband goods 628; counterfeit products 628; customized products 173, 437; growth-product stage 32; manufactures 34; mature-product stage 32; national economic structures and 176; new-product stage and 32; primary products/ natural resource products 34; product knowledge, monopolistic advantages and 83; product life-cycle model and 31; quality of products 146, 361; responsiveness/product adaptation 531–32; *see also* Export controls; Exports; Global product structure; Import controls; Imports

Professional services 122

Professional skills 30

Profit: borderless corporations and 126–27; branch offices and 363; developing vs. developed markets and 135–37; foreign crude oil producers and 220; monopoly profits 128; optimal tariff theory and 55; owner's equity vs. state's equity 516–17; transfer pricing and 514

Profit repatriation 339

Prohibited subsidies 63

Project-specific factors 369

Property rights systems 411

Proprietary knowledge 77, 84–85; unintended leakage 439

The Prospector instrument 576

Protectionism 170

Public education spending 6

Purchasing power parity (PPP) principle 305–06, 526

Put option 481

Pyramid schemes 451

Quaker Oats 285

Quality-based deployment of resources 88

Quality control system 176

Quantity-based deployment of resources 88

Quito, E. 277

Quotas 60; banana exports and 22; differences (from a tariff) 62; Multifiber Arrangement and 60; rule of origin and 62; similarities (to a tariff) 62; surge in imports, emergency protections and 63–64; voluntary quotas 63; *see also* Tariff barriers; Trade barriers

Rail transportation 551

Rate of return 74, 93, 348

Rationalization 410

Rationalized foreign direct investment strategy 285

Raw materials 334–35, 341, 485; costs of 338; developing nations exporters 355; exploration industries 408; Intergovernmental Council of Copper Exporting Countries 234; International Bauxite Association 283; international business and 357, 485; location determinant of **344**; national wealth accumulation and 23; natural gas resource 220; Organization of Petroleum Exporting Countries 294; *see also* Resources

Reagan, President Ronald 60, 294

Real estate bubbles *see* Asset bubbles

Real exchange rate 291

Real-life imperfect competition 35

Real Option 92–94

Real option perspective *see* Real option theory

Real option theory 92

Recipient country *see* Host country

Recommendation on Bribery in International Business Transactions 633

Red tape 162

Regiocentric staffing 571

Regional Comprehensive Economic Partnership (RCEP) 269, 274

Regional-level cooperation among nations 267–81; Andean Free Trade Area 277; Asia-Pacific Economic Cooperation Forum 274; Association of Southeast Asian Nations 274; Caribbean Community and Common Market 277; Central African Economic and Customs Union 279; Central American Common Market 277; East African Economic Community 279; Economic Community of West African States 279; effects of 280; European Union 271; Growth Triangles 276; Gulf Cooperation Council 279; Latin American Free Trade Association 277; Latin American Integration Association 277; multinational enterprises, responses of 284–85; North American Free Trade Agreement 269; postwar regional integration 267; Preferential Trade Area 279; regional integration agreements 279; regionalization vs. globalization and 279; Southern Common Market Treaty 277; subnational-level trade liberalization 275; subregional economic zones 275–76; *see also* International economic integration/institutions

Regions 10, 105, 386–87, 547, 597; disenfranchised regions, subsidies and 63; foreign direct investment flows/performance and 105; *see also* Regional-level cooperation among nations

Regulatory environment 341–42, 647; floating/flexible exchange rates and 302; foreign direct investment policies 341; industrial policies 341; location selection and 342
Reinvoicing 485
Related divisional format 390
Relational structures 89
Relationship building 416, 577
Relative purchasing power parity (PPP) 305–06, 526
Religion 194, 195–96; cultural religions 194; global religions 194
Renault 188
Reorganization investment strategy 285
Repatriation of earnings 342
Repatriation of workers 585–86
Repsol 220
Reputation 77; corporate 537–38; damage to 575, 626, 628; transferability of 89
Research and development (R&D) activities: globalization of 435, 437–38; limitations on 418; offshore research centers 82; See also Global research and development
Research and development (R&D) consortium 408
Research and development (R&D) intensity 435
Research and development (R&D) management 448–49
Research Development in Advanced Communications Technology for Europe (RACE) 444
Reserve Bank of India (RBI) 488
Re-shoring 28
Resource complementarity 415
Resources: allocation, research and development activities and 73; competitively priced resources 11; costs of 283, 338; efficient global allocation of 86; locational determinant of 337–38; misallocation of 297, 626; possession of, entry mode selection and 368; quantity-based/quality-based deployment of resources 88; transferability of resources 88–89; see also Raw materials
Resource-seeking foreign direct investment (FDI) 76
Responsiveness see Integration-responsiveness (I-R) perspective; Local responsiveness
Retirement fund investment 4
Retraining funds 54
Return on investment (ROI) 201, 653
Revaluation 291
Revocable letter of credit (L/C) 464
Revolving letter of credit (L/C) 465
Rhombic Corp. 126
Rhone-Poulenc 390
Ricardo, David 25
Risk 12, 136, 326–28, 353, 356, 367, 369, 409, 461, 463, 470, 475–77, 482–83, 653; coproduction, minimized risk and 483; corruption and 626; entrepreneurs and 178; financial risk 74, 338–39, 417; foreign investment and 74–75; guaranteed rate of return and 74;

host-country risk 368; technology leakage risk 411; volatile exchange rates and 291; see also Political risk
Rivalries 173
RMB/yuan **296–297**, 299, 508
Robots 125
Rogue states 65
Role-based simulations 576
Rolls-Royce 64, 427
Romania 205
Ronen, S. 207
Royal Dutch Shell 364
Royalties 220, 452
RTZ 460–61
Rubbermaid 85, 343
Rugman, A. 94
Rule of law 162, 224
Rule by man/not by law 239
Rule-of-origin laws 244
Rupee 488–89
Russia 108, 164, 229, 352, 358, 536, 570, 627, 642; WTO entry 262

Saab 3
Safe haven investment locations 235
Saipan 228, 243
Salaries: compensation gaps, foreign affiliates and 587; developing nations 50; disposable income 526; expatriate compensation systems **584**; foreign affiliates and 587; globalization and 7, 578; globally unified compensation systems 10; luxury consumer goods and 33–34; wage differentials 50, **198**; wage rate, location selection and 338; see also Expatriate workforce; Labor market; Workforce
Sales on open account 467
Sales outlets overseas 75
Samsung 137, 138, **392**, 570
Samuelson, P. 27
Sanctions 64
Sandoz 173
Sandvik 390
Sano, Y. 212
Saudi Arabia 231, 283, 519
Scandinavian model see Uppsala/Scandinavian model
Schindler Lifts 447
Schlotzky's Delicatessen 541
Schlumberger 393
Schneider, S. 210
Schwartz, S.H. 203–05, 209
Scientific knowledge 172, 285, 442
Sea shipping see Maritime transportation
Seattle Ministerial Conference 265
Secrets of the trade 361, 423
Securities and Exchange Commission (SEC) 499, 630–31
Self-interest, pursuit of 352
Sematech 410
Semiconductor Research Corporation 444
SeraNova 107
Serbia 536, 646
Service facilities 73, 461
Service multinational enterprises 122–23
Services 44, 122; balance of trade, United States and 50; fair/transparent transactions of 9; international

business and 4; international/foreign trade and 40–42; knowledge, competitive advantage and 172; multilateral agreements and 9; national competitiveness and 159; service trade 44; service trade, barriers to 67; see also Goods
Shadow economy 625
Shadow price 310
Shakey's Pizza Restaurant 541
Shanghai Automotive Industry Corporation (SAIC) 232, 438; SAIC-GM-Wuling Automobile Co. Ltd. 410
Shared coding schemes 89
Sharia Law 214
Sharing arrangement 483
Shell see Royal Dutch Shell
Shenkar, O. 207, 209
Shenyang Aircraft Manufacturing Company 364
Shipper's Export Declarations 45
Shleifer, A. 625
Short position 317
Siemens 273, 285, 406–07, 415, 446, 502
Sight draft 465, 467
Silicon Valley 173
Silverline Technologies 107
Singapore 105, 131, 156–57, 276, 340, 389, 547, 572; government policy consensus and 231; hard disk drive industry and 159; worker diligence and 178
Singh, H. 207
Sinostone 13
Skills see Human skills; Workforce
Sleeman Brewing 147
Slovakia 105, 273, 300
Slovenia 108, 109, 231, 273, 300, 646
Slowdowns 9, 96, 110
Slush funds 630
Small Business Administration (SBA) 139, 143
Small/midsize international enterprises (SMIEs) 118, 139–48, 606; advantages in internationalization for 143; capital, access to 142; definitions of 139; developed markets, emphasis on 146; exporter profile of 145; foreign direct investment by 146–47; globalization, selective approach to 147; intellectual property violations, vulnerability to 143; internationalization motivation and 143; internationalization, obstacles to 143; internationalization, size and 147; investment banking and 147; knowledge, deficits in 142; market power, lack of 143; mutualization and 546; patterns in internationalization and 144; piggybacking strategy and 146; scale, transaction constraints and 142; strategic activity of 147; see also Developing/emerging nation multinational enterprises (DNMEs); Multinational enterprises (MNEs)
Smith, Adam 24, 55
Smithsonian Agreement 293
Smoot-Hawley Act of 1930, 57
Smuggling 628

Snecma 75, 422
Social-cultural matrix 26
Social learning theory 578
Social obligations 201
Social Performance Plans 621
Social responsibility *see* Corporate social responsibility
Society for Worldwide International Financial Telecommunications (SWIFT) 315
Sociocultural factors in research and development 444
Sociopolitical factors: community characteristics 343; cultural barriers 342; foreign business, attitudes toward 343; government efficiency/corruption 343; language barriers 342; local business practices 342; local responsiveness and 379–80; market orientation and 346; political instability 342; pollution control 343
Sociopolitical factors 337, 342–47; *see also* International location selection
Software development 50, 285, 434, 440, 629
Software maintenance 107
Soft/weak currency 292
Song, J.A. 570
Sony 89, 415, 604, 611
Soros, George 294
Sourcing *see* Global sourcing; Global supply chain
South American accounting zone 503–04
South American Community of Nations (CSN) 277
South Asian Association for Regional Cooperation (SAARC) 276
South Korea 118, 135, 138, 223, 231, 326, 390, 534, 570
Southeast Asia 37, 274
Southern Common Market Treaty (MERCOSUR) 255, 277
Sovereignty argument 54
Sovereignty at bay model 227
Sovereign Credit Ratings 323
Soviet Union 229, 599, 629
Soybean production 525
Spain 206, 420; financial crisis 263, 273
Special Administrative Regions 106, 233, 628, 632
Special drawing rights (SDRs) 298, 313
Special economic zones 342
Specialization in production 25, 37
Specialized laboratory structure 446
Specialized technology units 442, 446, 449
Specific cultures 206
Spot-forward swap 317
Spotify 604
Spot rate 304–05, 308, 480–81
Spot transactions 316
Stakeholder Engagement Plan 621
Standard & Poor's **323**
Standard Bank 363
Standardization: environmental standards 183; global e-commerce and 607; international accounting and 505; *see also* Living standards
Stanley Works 475
Staples 79
Starbuck's Coffee 129

Start-ups *see* Global start-ups
State-owned enterprises (SOEs) 504
Statement of Financial Accounting Standards (SFAS) 510
Statutory tax 339
Steel industry 60–61
Steel smuggling 628
Stereotypes 212–13
St. Lucia 22
Stock of foreign direct investment (FDI)
Stock markets *see* International capital markets; International monetary system
Stolper, Wolfgang 27
Strategic asset-seeking foreign direct investment (FDI) 74
Strategic capabilities 128, 416
Strategic flexibility 94–95; early movers, strategic options and 94, 349–50, 353; open account sales and 467; rivalries, business practices and 342; *See also* Global research and development
Strategic goals 363, 369, 412, 414
Strategic international human resource management (SIHRM) 565, **566**
Strategic leadership 382
Strategic motives 14, 340–41; inbound/outbound logistics 178, 341; industrial linkages 341; investment infrastructure 340; location decision, strategic objectives and 345; location selection and 336–37; manufacturing concentration 340; workforce productivity 341; *see also* Global operations; Global strategic alliances (GSAs)
Strategic options 340
Strategic orientation 398
Strong currency *see* Hard/strong currency
Structural discrepancies 77
Structural market failure 87
Subaru 65
Subcontracting 357, 369
Subsidiaries: black hole subsidiaries 382; contributor subsidiaries 382; foreign subsidiaries 384; implementer subsidiaries 382; integration-responsiveness perspective and 94; internalization theory and 85; mother-daughter design 383; nationally-independent subsidiaries and 85; national subsidiary structure 383; subsidiary autonomy 381; subsidiary importance/competence 382; subsidiary knowledge flow 381; transferability of resources/knowledge and 89; wholly foreign-owned subsidiaries 75; wholly owned subsidiaries 586; *see also* Global operations; Global research and development
Subsidies 62–63; actionable subsidies 63; countervailing duties and 63; differences (from a tariff or quota) 62; intra-firm trade and 39; non-actionable subsidies 63; prohibited subsidies 63; similarities (to a tariff or quota) 62
Sudan 228, 279
Suitcase companies 12
Sumitomo 123

Sunk cost 93
Supply availability/favorability 368
Supply chains *see* Global supply chain
Supply-demand conditions 26, 172, 182
Supporting industries 172
Surge in imports 61, 63
Sustainable development 343, 620
Svenska Cellulosa 107
Swap 482
Swap transaction 317; Sweden 158, 300, 379, 537; SWIFT *see* Society for Worldwide International Financial Telecommunications (SWIFT)
Switzerland 148, 167, 518
Symantec Corp. 496–97
Synchor 630
Synergy 409, 438
Syria 226, 234, 647

Taiwan 106, 131, 135, 137, 160, 190, 211, 276, 285
Talisma Corporation 607
Target-zone arrangement 300–01
Tariff barriers 57–59; absolute advantage theory and 24–25; ad valorem setting of 57; circumventing 58, 108; customs union and 255; duty-free treatment, Generalized System of Preferences and 62; Harmonized Tariff Schedule and 57; infant industry argument for 55; optimal tariff theory and 55; punitive tariffs 58; rule of origin and 62; sanctions and 64; tariffs 55, 57–58; *see also* General Agreement on Tariffs and Trade (GATT); Non-tariff barriers; Quotas; Trade barriers
Tata Group 618
Tata Motors 4
Tax avoidance 95, 514
Tax havens 517–18
Taxation: effective tax rate 339; expatriate workforce and 579–80; global e-commerce and 607; international accounting and 505; international bond markets and 320; locational determinant of 338–39; statutory tax 339; taxation system 166, 499; tax evasion 166; tax havens and 517–18; tax treaties 518–19; transfer pricing practices and 515–16; *see also* US tax system
Taylor, S. **566**, 589n6
TD Ameritrade 605
Technical capabilities 442
Technical standards 66
Technological connectivity 599
Technological development zones 342
Technological innovation process 436
Technological leadership 334
Technology gaps 30; developing nations, mediated technology and 30; e-business race and 175; product life-cycle model and 31; *see also* Global research and development
Technology transfer process 441, 443, 445, 448, 452–53
Technology transfer units 441, 445
Temporal method of accounting 510
Term loans 475

676

Terms of price 356
Terms of sale 356
Terms of trade 39
Terrorism 234
Tesco 245
Teva 134, 138
Texaco 80
Tex-Mex 525
Thailand 274, 276, 280, 325
Theocratic law 239
Thinking globally/acting locally 94
Thomson-CSF 136
3M 254, 448
360 degree evaluation 585
Timberland 541
Time as competitive factor 437
Time draft 467, 469
Time horizons in cultures 206, 411
Timing of entry 347–52; decision
    framework for 352; delayed 353;
    early-mover advantages 349–51;
    early-mover disadvantages 351;
    immediacy 347; immediate 348;
    late investors 351; preemptive
    opportunities and 349; relative
    position 347; speed 347; waiting 348;
    see also International entry strategies
Tom Online 596
Top-down management 89
Toshiba 130, 423
Total Entrepreneurial Activity (TEA) **642**
Toyota 198, 385, 423; design studios of
    92; foreign direct investment and 102;
    just-in-time system of 129; quality
    control system of 88
Toys "R" Us 340, 350
Trade: balance of trade 50; banana
    22–23; human skills/technology-based
    view of 29–30, 39; increasing returns
    and 35; international transactions
    and 11, 311; intra-firm trade 36,
    39; manufactured goods 31, 47;
    multilateral trade agreements 258;
    regional integration agreements 269,
    279–80; rule of origin and 62, 244;
    sustainable pattern 165; terms of
    trade 39; winners and losers 27–28;
    see also Free trade; International/
    foreign trade; International/foreign
    trade patterns; Trade barriers
Trade barriers 57–67; automobile industry
    and 59; corruption and 67; General
    Agreement on Tariffs and Trade and
    57; infant industries and 55–56;
    non-tariff barriers 59; optimal tariff
    theory and 55; production subsidies
    and 62; quotas 60; regionalization-
    globalization, complementarity
    between 281; rule of origin and 62;
    service trade and 67; steel industry
    and 60–61; tariff barriers 57; see also
    Export controls; Import controls
Trade-centered entry modes 355–59;
    barter 358; counterpurchase 358;
    countertrade 358; export activities
    355–57; international subcontracting
    357; offest agreement 358; original
    equipment manufacturing method and
    357; see also Entry mode selection;
    International entry strategies

Trade-Related Intellectual Property
    Agreement (TRIP) 261
Trade secrets 128, 423
Trade theories see International/foreign
    trade
Trademarks 143, 259, 360
Training for overseas see Expatriate
    trainee; Expatriate workforce
Transactional market failure 86–87
Transactional net margin method 515
Transaction cost 84–85, 142, 304, 480,
    606; coordination breakdowns 85
Transaction exposure 477–78, 480, 482–83
Transactions see International foreign
    exchange transactions; Transaction
    cost; Transaction exposure
Transfer-centered entry modes 359–62;
    build-operate-transfer investment
    362; international franchising
    361–62; international leasing 359–60;
    international licensing 360–61; royalty
    fees and 360; see also Entry mode
    selection; International entry strategies
Transfer pricing 496, 514–16
advance pricing agreement and 516;
    arm's-length principle and 516;
    comparable profits method and
    515; current open market prices
    and 515; documentation of 516;
    exchange controls, avoidance of 514;
    gross margin method and 515; joint
    ventures, increased profits from 514;
    operating profit methods and 515;
    regulations/penalties 516; tax/tariff
    reduction and 514; techniques of 515;
    transactional net margin method 515;
    See also International accounting
Transferable letter of credit (L/C) 465
Transfer risk 235
Transferability of resources 88–89
Transitional economy accounting zone 502
Translation see Foreign currency
    translation; Translation exposure
Translation exposure 478
Transnational firms 117
Transnational/hybrid strategy 381
Transnationality index (TNI) 103, **104**,
    118
Trans-Pacific Partnership (TPP) 276
Trans-Pacific Strategic Economic
    Partnership (TPSEP) 276
Transparency 259, 281
Transparency International (TI) 625–26
Transportation costs 338
Transportation modes 548; air transport
    554; intermodal transportation 551;
    maritime transportation 549; railroad
    transport 551–52; trucking 551
Transportation services 44
Travel services 44
Treaties of friendship/commerce/
    navigation (FCN) 246
Treaty agreements 246–47
Treaty on European Union 271
Trebilcock, M.J. 55, 67
Triad countries (Europe/Japan/United
    States) 98
Trompenaars, F. 189, 205–06, 214
Trompenaars/Hampden-Turner
    classification system 205–06

Truck transportation 551
Tung, R.L. 578
Tunisia 279, 642
Turkey 125, 226
Turnkey investment 362
Twenty-four hour market 315
2020 Project Report 4

UBS 4, 518
Uchiyama, K. 640
U-curve theory of adjustment 577
Umbrella holding company 366
Uncertainty 12, 342, 347–48; cultural
    barriers and 342; diversification
    in multinationals and 39, 74,
    127, 235; early movers and 130,
    350–52; endogenous uncertainty
    348; exogenous uncertainty 348;
    host country environments and 78,
    342; industrial uncertainty 368;
    international business operations and
    159; managerial decision, emerging
    conditions and 94, 364; national
    economies, global capital flow and 9
Uncertainty avoidance (UA) 197, **199**,
    200, 500, 585, 625
Unconfirmed letter of credit (L/C) 464
UNCTAD see United Nations Conference
    on Trade and Development
    (UNCTAD)
Underground economy 625
Unemployment benefits 54
Unilever 371
Union membership 53
Union of South American Nations
    (UNASUR) 277
United Airlines 124
United Arab Emirates 338
United Kingdom 34, 98, 109, 207, 444,
    470, 499, 516
United Nations Conference on Trade and
    Development (UNCTAD) 22, 103,
    105, 108, 117–18, 120, 122, 142–43,
    147, 150n4, 266–67, 505, 606
United Nations Convention on Contracts
    for the International Sale of Goods 243
United Nations Convention on the
    Recognition and Enforcement of
    Foreign Arbitration Awards 243
United Nations Declaration of Human
    Rights 621
United Nations Environment Program
    (UNEP) 622
United Nations Global Compact 621
United Nations Security Council 5
United States 5, 30, 45, 62, 473,
    499, 518–19, 524–25, 535–36,
    548–49, 652; absolute advantage
    theory and 24; anti-American
    sentiment 12; antitrust legislation
    244–45; automotive industry and
    4, 37, 91–92, 232, 532; balance
    of payments 65, 293, 294, **312**;
    balance of trade and 50; banana
    trade and 22; bond market in
    321; dollar crisis 294; embargoes/
    boycotts and 65; export structures
    and 23–25, 27; farm subsidies
    and 259; free trade, opposition to
    54, 64; garment imports into 60;

government policy consensus and 231; import surge quotas and 63, 270; inflation, dollar devaluation and 293; intellectual property rights and 143, 270; Internet diffusion gaps in 598; Leontief paradox and 28; multinational enterprises in 91–92, 511; open skies agreements and 50; product liability enforcement 246; product life-cycle model and 82–83; quotas and 60, 62–63; research and development focus and 437, 451, 498; service multinationals, growth in 123; skilled labor in 29, 30; steel industry and 60–61, 628; tariff setting and 48, 49, 58; trade partners of 46–47; trade statistics and **47**; trade volume/growth 40; wages in 50, 109; *see also* Free trade; International monetary system; US tax system; *specific US headings*
United Technologies Corp. 82
Universal Copyright Convention 247
Universalism 205, 617
Unrelated holding company format 390
Uppsala/Scandinavian model 90
Upstream integration 15, 254
US Customs Service 628
US Federal Aviation Administration (FAA) 243
US Federal Reserve Bank 292, 327
US Federal Trade Commission (FTC) 244, 548, 611
US Foreign Trade Anti-Trust Improvement Act 53
US International Trade Commission 59, 61
US National Intelligence Council 4
US National Research Council 66
US tax system: corporate tax, foreign-source income and 64; Extraterritorial Income Exclusion and 64; foreign sales corporations and 64
US Treasury 50, 64
User/need model 531

Value-added taxes (VAT) 611
Value chain 335–6
Value-chain activities 335; primary 335; support 335
Value-creation activities 78, 389
Venezuela 79, 220–23, 229, 234, 277
Venture capital (VC) 646, 654
Verbeke, A. 94
Verification services 620
Vernon, Raymond 31–32, 82
Vertical foreign direct investment (FDI) 74–75
Vertical integration 14, 75, 255, 368
ViaVoice 128
Videoconferencing 451, 574
Vietnam 170, 227, 274, 276; foreign direct investment and 12, 146; production, relocation to 11, 14, 572; rule by man/not by law in 162, 239; textile exports 48

Virtual expatriate 574
Visa International 350
Vishny, R. 625
Visteon 3
Vodafone 525
Voice-recognition systems 88, 128
Volkswagen 3, 350
Voluntary export restraints 56
Voluntary quotas 63
Volvo 107, 159, 201, 379, 410, 415

Wages *see* Salaries
Wake-up-call effect 325
Wal-Mart 96, 350–51, 384, 531, 554
Walt Disney Company 75
Wanli Stone Group 13
Weak currency *see* Soft/weak currency
Wealth accumulation 24
Wealthy nations 8
Weizmann Biotechnology and Genetics Park 654
Welfare: global welfare 67; national welfare 79
Westhollow Research Center 446
Westinghouse 415, 486
Wheat Trade Convention (WTC) 284
Whirlpool 285
Wholly foreign-owned subsidiaries 75
Wholly owned subsidiaries (WOSs) 586
Women: expatriate workers 575; Internet access and 609–10
Workforce 79, 573; child labor 270; displaced workers 79; dynamic capability perspective and 88–89; educated workforces 6; flexibility in 341; foreign affiliates, wage levels and 587; foreign direct investment and 79; labor cost 145, 326, 338; production function and 27; productivity of 158; retraining funds 54; skill of 89; unemployment benefits 54; workforce-related capabilities, transferability of 89; *see also* Expatriate workforce; International human resource management (IHRM); Labor market
Working capital 489; cash management 489–90; foreign receivables management 491
World Bank 224, 257, 264–65; anti-corruption activities and 633; Bretton Woods Institutions and 263; corruption, cost of 625; corruption rankings 626, **627**; development strategy of 265; functions/structures of 264–65; High Level Working Group on Coherence and 265; private sector growth and 265
World Bank Group 264
Worldbest Development Corporation 334
World Business Council for Sustainable Development 622
World Competitiveness Scoreboard **184**
World Economic Forum (WEF) 167, 183, 642

World Financial Crisis *see* Global financial crisis
World Health Organization (WHO) 266
World Intellectual Property Organization (WIPO) 266
World merchandise trade 8
World's Most Admired Companies 537–38
World Tourism Organization (WTO) 266
World Trade Organization (WTO) 8, 258; anti-corruption activities 634; background/structure of 258–59; banana quotas/tariffs 22; Chinese membership in 63; conflict resolution role and 8; customs unions/free trade areas and 260; developing nations, unfair treatment of 261; dispute-settlement system 261; Doha Development Agenda and 259; dumping remedies and 261; emerging issues, forum for 261; escape clauses and 260; foreign sales corporations and 64; functions/measures of 260–61; Generalized System of Preferences and 62, 260; government investment support and 230; import licensing procedures and 67; international standards and 67; mergers/acquisition oversight and 245; most-favored-nation treatment and 260; national treatment and 260; protections/trade barriers and 170; regional integration, global trading systems and 280–81; rules of origin agreement 62; safeguards to economies and 260; subsidies and 63; surge in imports and 63; tariff negotiations 258; *see also* General Agreement on Tariffs and Trade (GATT)
World War I 292
World War II 292, 293
World Wide Web (WWW) *see* Internet
Wright, P. 547
Wuling 350; SAIC-GM-Wuling Automobile Co. Ltd. 410

Xerox 79, 172, 313, 406, 427, 487
Xi'an Aircraft Manufacturing Company 364

Yahoo! 611
Yam, J. 299
Yamaha 177
Yankee bonds 474
Yeheskel, O. 656n20
Yoshida, T. 577
Yuan *see* RMB/yuan
Yugoslavia 223
Yugosphere 223

Zahra, S. A. 653
Zakak, A. 176
Zaire 223
Zenith 542
Zero-sum game 24
Zone currencies 301